FIFTH EDITION

JAVA™

Illuminated

An Active Learning Approach

Julie Anderson
Rollins College

Hervé Franceschi
Loyola University Maryland

JONES & BARTLETT
LEARNING

World Headquarters
Jones & Bartlett Learning
5 Wall Street
Burlington, MA 01803
978-443-5000
info@jblearning.com
www.jblearning.com

Jones & Bartlett Learning books and products are available through most bookstores and online booksellers. To contact Jones & Bartlett Learning directly, call 800-832-0034, fax 978-443-8000, or visit our website, www.jblearning.com.

23993-5

Production Credits
Director of Product Management: Matthew Kane
Product Manager: Laura Pagluica
Product Assistant: Rebecca Feeney
Production Manager: Carolyn Pershouse
Production Manager: Dan Stone
VP, Manufacturing and Inventory Control: Therese Connell
Media Development Editor: Shannon Sheehan
Rights & Media Specialist: Thais Miller
Cover & Title Page Design: Kristin E. Parker
Cover Image (Title Page, Part Opener, Chapter Opener): © itsskin/Getty Images
Printing and Binding: LSC Communications
Cover Printing: LSC Communications

Library of Congress Cataloging-in-Publication Data
Names: Anderson, Julie, 1947- author. | Franceschi, Herve, author.
Title: Java illuminated : an active learning approach / Julie Anderson, Herve Franceschi.
Description: Fifth edition. | Burlington, MA : Jones & Bartlett Learning, [2019] | Includes index.
Identifiers: LCCN 2017058434 | ISBN 9781284140996
Subjects: LCSH: Java (Computer program language)
Classification: LCC QA76.73.J3 A533 2019 | DDC 005.13/3--dc23
LC record available at https://lccn.loc.gov/2017058434

6048

Printed in the United States of America
22 21 20 19 18   10 9 8 7 6 5 4 3

Dedications

To the memory of my parents, Glenn and Rosemary Austin, my first teachers. – *Julie Anderson*

A ma mère, trop tôt disparue, et à mon père. – *Hervé Franceschi*

Contents

Preface

Purpose of This Text and Its Audience

Java Illuminated, Fifth Edition, covers all of the material required for the successful completion of an introductory course in Java. While the focus is on the material required for the Computer Science I (CS1) and Computer Science II (CS2) curricula, students enrolled in Information Systems, Information Technology, or self-directed study courses will find the text useful as well. It has been written to provide introductory computer science students with a comprehensive overview of the fundamentals of programming using Java as the teaching language. In addition, the text presents other topics of interest, including graphical user interfaces (GUI), data structures, file input and output, and graphical applications.

Throughout the text, we take an "active learning" approach to presenting the material. Instead of merely presenting the concepts to students in a one-sided, rote manner, we ask them to take an active role in their understanding of the concepts through the use of numerous interactive examples, exercises, and projects.

Coverage and Approach

Our approach is to teach object-oriented programming in a progressive manner. We start in Chapter 1 by presenting an overview of object-oriented programming. In Chapter 3, we delve a little deeper into the concepts of classes and objects and introduce the student to many of the useful classes in the Java Class Library. Our emphasis at this point is on using classes; we teach the student how to read APIs in order to determine how to instantiate objects and call methods of the classes. In Chapter 7, we move on to designing user-defined classes, and in Chapter 10, we present inheritance, polymorphism, and interfaces. Throughout the text, we present concepts in an object-oriented context.

Our philosophy is to emphasize good software engineering practices by focusing on designing and writing correct, maintainable programs. As such, we discuss pseudo-code, testing techniques, design trade-offs, and other software engineering tips.

We teach the student basic programming techniques, such as accumulation, counting, calculating an average, finding maximum and minimum values, using flag and toggle variables, and basic searching and sorting algorithms. In doing so, we emphasize the patterns inherent in programming. Concepts are taught first, followed by fully implemented examples with source code. We promote Java standards, conventions, and methodologies.

What's New in *Java Illuminated*

In this edition, we have incorporated the latest features of Java in Java 8 and Java 9: the jshell sandbox, *Streams*, functional interfaces and lambda expressions, the use of *default* methods in interfaces, JavaFX graphics, using *FXML* in JavaFX applications, tying a JavaFX GUI component to data in a Collection, JavaFX animations, and the *StackWalker* class. We have converted all graphics examples and graphical Programming Activities to JavaFX.

Throughout the book, we updated, improved, and replaced examples.

In Chapter 1, we added instructions for making a JAR file.

In Chapter 2, we use the Java 9 jshell sandbox to demonstrate the definition of variables, assigning of values to variables, and the results of performing arithmetic calculations.

In Chapter 3, we augmented the existing example on *Strings* with more explanations *of String* methods, and added another example with illustrations to demonstrate Strings Processing techniques. In both examples, we emphasize sending arguments to methods and receiving return values.

We converted Chapter 4 to JavaFX. To make it easier for the students to write JavaFX applications, we provide a utility class that encapsulates the overhead code to create a window. As a result, the students can concentrate on calling methods of the *GraphicsContext* class. We provide an online version of the Swing version of Chapter 4 from the fourth edition for those instructors who prefer the Swing graphics system.

In Chapter 7, we modified mutator methods to change instance variable values only if the parameter value is valid. Otherwise, the instance variable value is unchanged and we no longer output an error message. After we introduce the implicit reference, *this*, we implement the standard Java coding style of defining parameters with the same name as the instance variable. Further, we allow mutator methods to be chained by returning a reference to the object being modified. We have also moved the material on creating packages to an online supplement.

In Chapter 10, we converted the polymorphism example to JavaFX. We revised our existing interface example to use a default method and added an example demonstrating polymorphism with interfaces.

In Chapter 11, we added sections showing how to read file data into a *Stream*, and then filter and process that *Stream* using lambda expressions. We also added an example that reads and parses JSON data from a remote location on the Internet.

We converted Chapter 12 from Swing to JavaFX (the Swing version of Chapter 12 from the Fourth Edition is now available online). We added how to define a View using *FXML*, as well as programmatically, how to process touches, how to tie a GUI component to a *Collection* so that it is automatically updated as the data changes using *ObservableLists*, how to play sounds, and how to perform animations using JavaFX. We explain how to write event handlers using lambda expressions.

In Chapter 13, we use the *StackWalker* class to illustrate the state of the stack as recursive calls are made.

Learning Features

Recognizing today's students' growing interest in visualization, we distribute techniques for producing graphical output throughout the book, starting in Chapter 4 with graphical applications. An example using either animation or graphical output is included in most chapters. Instructors who are not interested in incorporating graphics into their curriculum can simply skip these sections. In addition, some of our examples are small games, which we find motivational for students.

In each chapter, we include one or two Programming Activities, which are designed to provide visual feedback to the students so that they can assess the correctness of their code. In most Programming Activities, we provide a framework, usually with a graphical user interface, to which the student adds code to complete the application. The student should be able to finish the Programming Activity in about 15 to 20 minutes; thus, these activities can be used in the classroom to reinforce the topics just presented. Each Programming Activity also includes several discussion questions that test the student's understanding of the concepts the activity illustrates. The Programming Activities are also appropriate for a closed or open laboratory environment. In short, this text can be used in a traditional lecture environment, a computer-equipped classroom, or a lab environment.

In addition, we supplement each chapter with a browser-based module that animates sample code, visually illustrating concepts such as the assignment of variable values, evaluation of conditions, and flow of control.

We also provide the instructor and students with an extensive variety of end-of-chapter material: multiple-choice questions, examples that ask the student to predict the output of prewritten code or to fill in missing code, debugging activities, short exercises, programming projects, technical writing assignments, one or more learning-to-learn exercises called Look It Up, and a higher-difficulty group project.

Chapter-by-Chapter Overview

The chapters are logically organized from simple to more difficult topics, while incorporating object orientation as needed, taking into account the specifics of the Java language. Here is a brief summary of the topics covered in each chapter:

Chapter 1: Introduction to Programming and the Java Language

We introduce the student to the concept of programming, first covering computer hardware and operating systems, and following with a brief evolution of programming languages, including an introduction to object-oriented programming. We explain programming basics and pseudocode as a program design technique. The student writes, compiles, and debugs their first program using an integrated development environment.

Chapter 2: Programming Building Blocks—Java Basics

In this chapter, we concentrate on working with variables and constants of primitive data types and composing arithmetic expressions. We illustrate the differences between integer and floating-point calculations and introduce operator precedence. We introduce jshell, the programming sandbox now available with Java 9. We use a combination of jshell sessions and complete programs to demonstrate the concepts at hand.

Chapter 3: Object-Oriented Programming, Part 1: Using Classes

Chapter 3 introduces classes from the user, or client, standpoint and discusses the benefits of encapsulation and code reuse. The student learns how to instantiate objects and call methods. We also demonstrate useful Java classes for console input and output, formatting output, performing mathematical calculations, generating random numbers, and using methods of the Wrapper classes. We use methods of the *String* class to visually illustrate the passing of arguments and receiving of and use of return values.

Chapter 4: Introduction to Graphical Applications

Chapter 4 presents several methods of the JavaFX *GraphicsContext* class that can be used to create graphical output by drawing shapes, text, and sprites. The windowing graphics coordinate system is explained and using color is also explored. We demonstrate these graphics methods in JavaFX applications. Instructors wishing to postpone or skip graphics coverage altogether can use as little or as much of this chapter as they desire.

Chapter 5: Flow of Control, Part 1: Selection

Various forms of the *if*, *if/else*, and *if/else if* statements are presented, along with the appropriate situations in which to use each form. We also demonstrate nested *if/else* statements and testing techniques. We begin our coverage of scope by introducing block scope. Later chapters build upon this foundation. As part of our object-oriented programming coverage, we teach the importance of comparing objects using the *equals* method. This chapter also covers the conditional operator and the *switch* statement.

Chapter 6: Flow of Control, Part 2: Looping

This is probably the most important chapter in the book. We have found that looping and repetition are the most difficult basic programming concepts for the average student to grasp. We try to ease the student's understanding of looping techniques by presenting patterns to follow in coding basic algorithms: accumulation, counting, calculating an average, and finding minimum and maximum values. Looping is further explored as a tool for validation of input values. We also introduce toggle variables and flag variables as tools to facilitate writing loops. We continue our coverage of scope by illustrating the scope of variables declared within the *while* loop body and *for* loop header. We concentrate on using the *while* loop *for* event-controlled and sentinel-controlled repetition and the *for* loop for count-controlled looping. A large section focuses on constructing loop conditions, which is often a challenging task for the student. Sections are also provided on testing techniques for loops. In this chapter, we also introduce reading data from a text file using the *Scanner* class.

Chapter 7: Object-Oriented Programming, Part 2: User-Defined Classes

In this chapter, we teach the student to write classes, as well as client applications that instantiate objects and call methods of the class. We present class design techniques and standard patterns for writing constructors, mutators and accessors, and the *toString*, *equals*, and other user-defined methods. We further explain scope in the context of class members and method parameters. We also explain how to write classes with *static* methods and *static* data. Additionally, we illustrate how to write methods so that the method calls can be chained. *Enum* is also covered as a user-defined class type. Finally, we teach the student how to use Javadoc.

Chapter 8: Single-Dimensional Arrays

This chapter begins with the declaration, instantiation, and initialization of single-dimensional arrays. From there, the student learns to perform the basic programming techniques (accumulation, counting, calculating an average, and finding maximum and minimum values) on array elements. We also cover arrays as instance variables of a class, and demonstrate maintaining encapsulation while accepting arrays as method parameters and returning arrays from methods. We demonstrate how to represent an array as a bar chart. Basic searching and sorting algorithms are also presented, including sequential and binary searches and Selection and Insertion sorts.

Chapter 9: Multidimensional Arrays and the *ArrayList* Class

We focus in this chapter on two-dimensional array processing, including techniques for processing the elements in the entire array, or the elements in a specific column or row. We also demonstrate the extra processing needed to handle arrays with rows of different lengths. Creating a bar chart of the data in the array is also demonstrated. In addition, we extrapolate the concepts from two-dimensional arrays to discuss multidimensional arrays.

We present the *ArrayList* class as an expandable array and demonstrate using classes with generic types, the enhanced *for* loop, and autoboxing and unboxing.

Chapter 10: Object-Oriented Programming, Part 3: Inheritance, Polymorphism, and Interfaces

Continuing our object-oriented programming coverage, we discuss the important concepts and benefits of inheritance and the design of class hierarchies, including abstract classes. We cover inherited members of a class, constructing objects of a subclass, adding specialization to a subclass, overriding inherited methods, and calling methods of the superclass. We discuss the trade-offs of declaring members as *protected* versus *private*. We demonstrate polymorphism with a graphical example. We introduce the student to interfaces, emphasizing code reuse as the motivation for defining interfaces. We explain *default* methods and how we can use them in new versions of a program so that our old code does not break as we add new features. We also demonstrate polymorphism using interfaces. Interfaces are used extensively in Graphical User Interfaces (See Chapter 12.) We introduce UML diagrams to help students visualize the inheritance hierarchy of the examples.

Chapter 11: Exceptions and Input/Output Operations

Recognizing that building robust applications requires error handling, we present exception handling as a tool for validating user input and recovering from errors at run time. We demonstrate handling predefined exceptions and writing user-defined exceptions.

With this knowledge, the student is ready to perform file input and output operations. We demonstrate reading and writing *Strings* and primitive data types to text files, and reading and writing objects directly to files. The *Scanner* class is used to read and parse input from text files and *Strings*. We demonstrate how to read and place file contents into a *Stream* and how to filter and process that *Stream*. We use lambda expressions when processing the *Stream*. We demonstrate how to read data from a remote file located on the Internet, including parsing JSON data and converting that data into a *Stream* for filtering and processing.

Chapter 12: Graphical User Interfaces Using JavaFX

This chapter introduces the student to event-driven programming and writing event handlers for text fields, buttons, radio buttons, checkboxes, combo boxes, sliders, and mouse and touch activities. We also demonstrate panels and several layout managers for organizing GUI components, as well as how to nest components. In our examples, we illustrate how to separate the graphical user interface code from the underlying data and program logic using the Model-View-Controller architecture. We demonstrate how to use *FXML* to define a View, and we also show how we can define a View programmatically. Showing bar charts and pie charts, we demonstrate how we can use Collections with JavaFX components so that the GUI is automatically updated when its model (a Collection) is changed. We explain how to write lambda expressions and use them throughout the chapter. We demonstrate how we can use the various animation classes of JavaFX to animate a sprite, including performing sequential and parallel animations.

Chapter 13: Recursion

Recursion is presented as a design technique, reducing the size of a problem until an easy-to-solve problem is reached. We demonstrate recursive methods with one base case and with multiple base cases, and with and without return values. Specific examples provided include computing the factorial of a number, finding the greatest common divisor, performing a binary search, determining if a phrase is a palindrome, calculating combinations, and solving the Towers of Hanoi problem. We use the *StackWalker* class to demonstrate how values are pushed onto and popped off the stack as recursive calls are executed. The benefits and trade-offs of recursion versus iteration are also discussed.

Chapter 14: An Introduction to Data Structures

In this chapter, we cover data structures by exploring the concepts and implementations of various types of linked lists, stacks, and queues. We demonstrate many types and uses of linked lists: a singly linked list, a linked list as a stack, a linked list as a queue, a doubly linked list, a sorted linked list, and a recursively defined linked list. Arrays as stacks and circular arrays as queues are also covered in detail.

We begin with a list of primitive types (*int*) and progress to a list consisting of objects of a user-defined *Player* class. Then we cover defining a class using generic types to demonstrate how a list can be defined to hold generic objects.

Chapter 15: Running Time Analysis

We explain how to evaluate the performance of an algorithm in this chapter. We explain the Big-Oh notation and orders of magnitude. Students learn various methods for deriving performance estimates: counting statements in loops, iterative, handwaving, and proof by induction analyses for recursive methods. We demonstrate how the coding of an algorithm influences its running time. Worst-case, best-case, and average-case performances are explained and illustrated.

Pedagogy

Concepts are always taught first, followed by complete, executable examples illustrating these concepts. Most examples demonstrate real-life applications so that the student can understand the need for the concept at hand. The example code is colored to better illustrate the syntax of the code and to reflect the use of colors in today's IDE tools, as shown in this example from Chapter 3:

```
 1 /*  A demonstration of reading from the keyboard using Scanner
 2      Anderson, Franceschi
 3 */
 4
 5 import java.util.Scanner;
 6
 7 public class DataInput
 8 {
 9   public static void main( String [ ] args )
10   {
11       Scanner scan = new Scanner( System.in );
12
13       System.out.print( "Enter your first name > " );
14       String firstName = scan.next( );
15       System.out.println( "Your name is " + firstName );
16
17       System.out.print( "\nEnter your age as an integer > " );
18       int age = scan.nextInt( );
19       System.out.println( "Your age is " + age );
20
21       System.out.print( "\nEnter your GPA > " );
22       float gpa = scan.nextFloat( );
23       System.out.println( "Your GPA is " + gpa );
24   }
25 }
```

EXAMPLE 3.10   Reading from the Keyboard Using *Scanner*

Note that in this example and throughout the text, we place the opening curly brace of a block on a line of its own. We have found this placement easier for a student new to Java to understand where a block begins and ends.

Figures and tables are used to illustrate or summarize the concept at hand, such as these from Chapters 6 and 7:

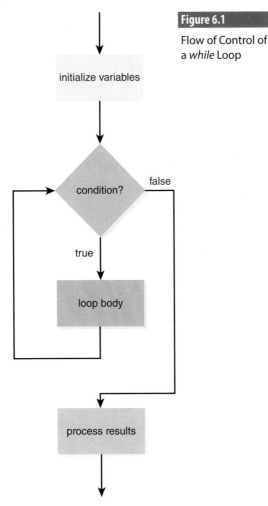

Figure 6.1

Flow of Control of a *while* Loop

TABLE 7.1	ACCESS MODIFIERS
Access Modifier	**Class or member can be referenced by ...**
public	methods of the same class, as well as methods of other classes
private	methods of the same class only
protected	methods in the same class, as well as methods of subclasses and methods in classes in the same package
no modifier (package access)	methods in the same package or same folder only

In each chapter, we emphasize good design concepts using "Software Engineering Tips," such as the one to the left from Chapter 7.

We also provide "Common Error Traps," such as the one to the left from Chapter 5, to alert students against common syntax and logic errors.

In each chapter, "active learning" Programming Activities reinforce concepts with enjoyable, hands-on projects that provide visual feedback to the students. These activities can be done in lab-type classrooms or can be assigned as projects. A header for a Programming Activity looks like this:

6.9   Programming Activity 1: Using *while* Loops

In this activity, you will work with a sentinel-controlled *while* loop, performing this activity:

> Write a *while* loop to process the contents of a grocery cart and calculate the total price of the items. It is important to understand that, in this example, we do not know how many items are in the cart.

Because technology is ever-changing, students need to be able to learn new concepts and find relevant classes on their own. To promote the development of this important skill of "learning-to-learn," we include one or more "Look It Up" questions in the end-of-chapter exercises. These questions require the student to perform some research to acquire the knowledge necessary to answer the question and write the required code.

Within the online resources, for each chapter, we provide a movie that illustrates the execution of code implementing the concepts taught in the chapter. Each movie animates a brief code sample, one line at a time, and is controlled by the user via a

CODE IN ACTION

To see two step-by-step illustrations of *do/while* loops, look for this chapter's movie within the online resources. Click on the link to start the movie.

"Next Step" button. These modules can be beneficial for students who learn best with visual aids, graphs, illustrations, and at their own pace outside the classroom. The modules are announced in each chapter using a special icon as in the sample above.

Graphics Coverage

Graphics are distributed throughout the book and are used to engage the student and reinforce the chapter concepts. The graphics coordinate system, methods for drawing shapes and text, and color concepts are presented with simple JavaFX applications in Chapter 4. At least one graphical example is presented in subsequent chapters using JavaFX. In Chapter 5, a *switch* statement is used to draw dots on a die; in Chapter 6, a loop is used to draw a bull's eye target. Classes for displayable objects are presented in Chapter 7; drawing a bar chart of array data is illustrated in Chapters 8 and 9; polymorphism is demonstrated using a Tortoise and Hare Race in Chapter 10; GUIs, dynamic charts, and JavaFX animations are covered in Chapter 12. The two figures that follow illustrate graphical examples from Chapters 7 and 8.

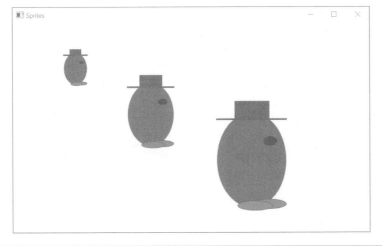

Figure 7.11

The *SpriteClient* Window

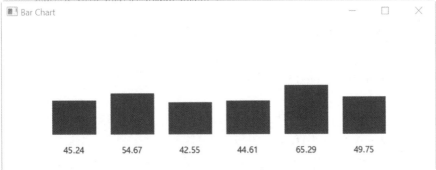

Figure 8.15

The *cellBills* Array as a Bar Chart

End-of-Chapter Exercises and Problems

A large collection of exercises and problems is proposed at the end of each chapter. Short exercises cover programming from a variety of angles: multiple choice concept questions, reading and understanding code segments, filling in some code, correcting errors, and interpreting compiler error messages to diagnose application bugs. Many programming projects are proposed with an emphasis on writing *classes*, not just a *program*. A more challenging group project is proposed in each chapter, allowing students to work as a group and develop communication skills, in accordance with recommendations from accreditation organizations and potential employers in the computer industry. Small, essay-type questions are also proposed to enable students to acquire proficiency in technical writing and communication.

Web Materials Accompanying This Book

Available on the Jones & Bartlett Learning website (www.jblearning.com):

- Programming Activity framework code
- Full example code from each chapter
- Browser-based modules with visual step-by-step demonstrations of code execution
- Swing versions of Chapters 4 and 12.
- A supplement on creating packages

Appendices

The appendices include the following:

- Java reserved words and keywords
- Operator precedence
- Unicode character set
- Representing negative numbers
- Representing floating-point numbers
- Answers to selected exercises

Instructor Resources

These materials are available to instructors on the Jones & Bartlett Learning website (go.jblearning.com/Java5e), and include

- Programming activity solution code (for instructors only)
- Answers to many end-of-chapter exercises
- Lecture slides in PowerPoint format for each chapter
- Test banks for each chapter

Contacting the Authors

We have checked and rechecked the many technical details in this text. Despite our best efforts, however, we realize that some errors may have been missed. If you discover a technical error in the text, please contact us at JulieAustinAnderson@gmail.com or hjfranceschi@loyola.edu. We will post any corrections on the text's website: go.jblearning.com/Java5e.

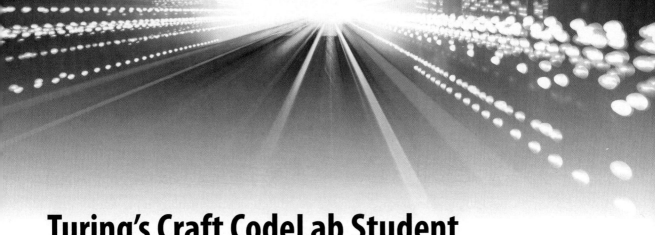

Turing's Craft CodeLab Student Registration Instructions

CodeLab is the web-based interactive programming exercise service that accompanies this text. It is designed to reduce attrition and raise the overall level of the class. Since 2002, CodeLab has analyzed over twenty-two million exercise submissions from more than 75,000 students.

CodeLab has over 300 short exercises, each focused on a particular programming idea or language construct. The student types in code and the system immediately judges its correctness, offering hints when the submission is incorrect. Through this process, the student gains mastery over the semantics, syntax, and common usage of the language elements.

For the Students

CodeLab offers a tree-based table of content navigation system augmented by prev/next buttons that permit sequential traversal. Exercises are organized within a hierarchy of topics that match the textbook's organization and can be reconfigured as needed by the instructor. The student interface offers three tabs for each exercise: a work-area tab containing the instructions of the exercise and a text area for typing in a submission; a results tab that indicates the correctness of the student's submission and provides an analysis of the submission code in the event of an error; a solutions tab which, by default, is invisible but may be made available at the discretion of the instructor. The solutions tab contains one or more solutions to the exercise; the results tabs contains one or more of the following: correctness indicator, ad hoc hints, marked-up submission indicating possible errors, compiler messages, table of passed and failed test cases. In addition, the usual online amenities of preferences, account management, documentation, and customer support options are provided.

A unique student access code can be found at the beginning of this textbook. Length of student access is 52 weeks for this version of the textbook.

Students can also purchase the access code online at jblearning.turingscraft.com.

For the Instructors

CodeLab provides the preceding student interface and in addition provides

- a **Course Manager** that permits the instructor to rearrange, rename, and/or omit topics and exercises. It also allows instructors to assign deadlines, specify dates when solutions can be seen by students, dates past which student work will not be "counted," and dates prior to which the exercises will be invisible to students.

- a **Grading Roster** that presents a graphical spreadsheet view of student work, where each row corresponds to a student and each column to an exercise. It is also possible to mail and/or download rosters in CSV format.

- an **Exercise Creation Tool** that permits faculty to create their own exercises.

Custom CodeLab

CodeLab is customized to this textbook as follows:

1. The organization of the CodeLab matches the organization of the textbook.

2. For each chapter that covers an appropriate standard introductory programming topic, the CodeLab offers approximately 50 CodeLab exercises, taken from either the standard set of existing CodeLab exercises or added to fill in any gaps in coverage.

3. Each chapter in the CodeLab implements 5 exercises taken from this text, and, if necessary, the exercises are modified to meet CodeLab requirements.

Demonstration Site for CodeLab

A Jones & Bartlett Learning demonstration site is available online at

jblearning.turingscraft.com

Visitors to this site will be directed to a landing page that provides an overview of the product. By clicking on the selected Jones & Bartlett Learning textbook cover, you will be led to more detailed product description pages. In the detailed product description pages there are further descriptions, examples of or links to examples of specific examples of custom CodeLab tie-ins with this textbook, and a link to a fully functional demo version of the Custom CodeLab. The latter offers full functionality and contains all of the exercise content of the particular Custom CodeLab. To make use of this link, instructors will need a unique Section Creation access code provided by their Jones & Bartlett Learning Computer Science Account Specialist at 1-800-832-0034, or online at www.jblearning.com.

Using this CodeLab Section Creation Code permits instructors to use the online tool to create their own unique CodeLab sections based on the Custom CodeLab. This permits instructors to have instructor accounts that enable access to the Course Manager, roster, and exercise creation tools described above.

Additonally Turing's Craft provides online documentation and support for both prospective adopters and actual faculty users of this text. In creating sections for classroom adopting, instructors will receive CodeLab Section Access Codes that should be provided to their students—enabling their students to associate their accounts (i.e., join their instructor's CodeLab section).

System Requirements: CodeLab runs on recent versions of most browsers (e.g. Internet Explorer, Firefox, Safari) on Windows and MacOS and on many versions of Linux. CodeLab does require the installation of the latest Flash Reader, available from www.adobe.com. (Most systems come with Flash pre-installed.) More details about CodeLab browser compatibility can be found at:

www.turingscraft.com/browsers.html

Acknowledgments

We would like to acknowledge the contributions of many partners, colleagues, and family members to this book.

First and foremost, we would like to thank our publisher, Jones & Bartlett Learning, especially Laura Pagluica, Product Manager; Daniel Stone, Production Manager; and Rebecca Sweeney and Mary Menzemer, Product Assistants. We also want to thank the compositor, codeMantra; the proofreader, Eileen Worthley; and Kristin Parker, who designed the cover.

Second, we extend our thanks to the reviewers: Zareh Gorjian, Pasadena City College; Lee Nicholson, Alpharetta High School; Jody Paul, Metropolitan State University of Denver; Steven Kreutzer, Bloomfield College; Larry Henderson, Wenatchee Valley College; Fred D'Angelo, Pima Community College; Waleed Farag, Indiana University of Pennsylvania; Jason Smith, University of Texas, Dallas; Valerie Chau, Palomar College; Jeanann Boyce, Montgomery College; Kevin Brunner, Graceland University; Patrick Plunkett, Wheeling Jesuit University; Russel Bruhn, University of Arkansas, Little Rock; Burdett E. Wilson, Macon Area Career and Technical Education Center; Jonathan Sprague, College of Lake County; Giuseppe Turini, Kettering University; Nary Subramanian, University of Texas, Tyler; Jeffrey Kimball, Southwest Baptist University; Zhiling Lan, Illinois Institute of Technology; Peter L. Stanchev, Kettering University; Jacquelyne Lewis, North Carolina Wesleyan College; Vicky Hardin, Jefferson Community & Technical College; Jesse Kidd, Motlow State Community College; Mark Meysenburg, Doane College; Derrf Seitz, Georgia Military College; Ellen Spertus, Mills College; Scott Reed, College of Lake County; Peter Johnson, South Central College; and Sungbum Hong, Jackson State University. We have taken your thoughtful comments to heart and we think the book is better for them.

Julie Anderson would also like to acknowledge the pedagogical insight of Richard Rasala and Viera Proulx of Northeastern University. Thanks also to Jon Dornback, Garth Gerstein, and our former colleagues Pat Smit and the late Earl Gottsman.

I am extremely grateful for the help extended by many family members: my father, Glenn Austin, sons Brian and Jon Anderson, daughter-in-law Silvia Eckert, grandson, Ben Anderson (for his sound effects), sister Kathleen Austin, and mother-in-law Virginia Anderson. And of course, much gratitude goes to my loving husband, Tom, for his support and encouragement.

—Julie Anderson

I also recognize the support of my family. In particular, my brother, Paul, provided feedback on our sample chapter and the movies, and my wife, Kristin, gave her support and provided advice.

—Hervé Franceschi

CHAPTER 1
Introduction to Programming and the Java Language

CHAPTER CONTENTS

Introduction

Computer applications touch almost every aspect of our lives. They run automated teller machines, the grocery store's checkout register, the appointment calendar at your doctor's office, airport kiosks for flight check-in, a restaurant's meal-ordering system, and online auctions, just to name a few applications. On your personal computer, you may run a word processor, virus detection software, a spreadsheet, computer games, and an image processing system.

Someone, usually a team of programmers, wrote those applications. If you're reading this text, you're probably curious about what's involved in writing applications, and you would like to write a few yourself. Perhaps you have an idea for the world's next great application or computer game.

In this text, we'll cover the basics of writing applications. Specifically, we'll use the Java programming language. Keep in mind, however, that becoming a good programmer requires more than mastering the rules, or **syntax**, of a programming language. You also must master basic programming techniques. These are established methods for performing common programming operations, such as calculating a total, finding an average, or arranging a group of items in order.

You also must master good software engineering principles so that you design code that is readable, easily maintained, and reusable. By readable, we mean that someone else should be able to read your program and figure out what it does and how it does it. Writing readable code is especially important for programmers who want to advance in their careers, because it allows someone else to take over the maintenance of your program while you move on to bigger and better responsibilities. Ease of maintenance is also an important aspect of programming, because the specifications for any program are continually changing. How many programs can you name that have had only one version? Not many. Well-designed code allows you and others to incorporate prewritten and pretested modules into your program, thus reducing the time to develop a program and yielding code that is more robust and has fewer bugs. One useful feature of the Java programming language is the large supply of prewritten code that you are free to use in your programs.

Programming is an exciting activity. It's very satisfying to decompose a complex task into computer instructions and watch your program come alive. It can be frustrating, however, when your program either doesn't run at all or produces the wrong output.

Writing correct programs is critical. Someone's life or life savings may depend on the correctness of your program. Reusing code helps in developing correct programs, but you must also master effective testing techniques to verify that the output of your program is correct.

In this text, we'll concentrate not only on the syntax of the Java language, but also on basic programming techniques, good software engineering principles, and effective testing techniques.

Before you can write programs, however, it's important to understand the platform on which your program will run. A platform refers to the computer hardware and the operating system. Your program will use the hardware for inputting data, for performing calculations, and for outputting results. The operating system will start your program running and will provide your program with essential resources, such as memory, and services, such as reading and writing files.

1.1 Basic Computer Concepts

1.1.1 Hardware

As shown in Figure 1.1, a computer typically includes the following components:

- a CPU, or central processing unit, which executes the instructions of a program
- a memory unit, which holds the instructions and data of a program while it is executing
- a hard disk, used to store programs and data so that they can be loaded into memory and accessed by the CPU
- a keyboard used for input of data
- a monitor, used to display output from a program
- an Ethernet port and wireless networking transceiver for connecting to the Internet or a Local Area Network (LAN)
- other components (not shown) such as a graphics card and a DVD drive

For example, if you were to go to a computer store in search of the latest personal computer, you might be shown a computer with this set of specifications:

- a 3.4-GHz Intel Core i3-3240 processor
- a touch screen
- 3 MB of cache memory
- 8 GB of RAM (Random Access Memory)
- a 1 TB (Terabyte) hard disk

Figure 1.1

A Typical Design
of a Personal
Computer

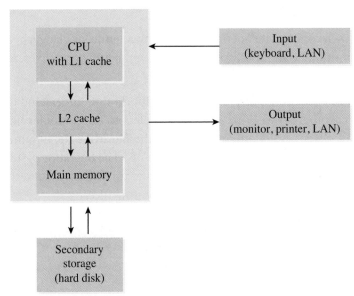

In these specifications, the Intel Core i3-3240 is the CPU. Other processors used as CPUs in personal computers and servers include the AMD Athlon, the Oracle SPARC, and the IBM POWER processor.

CPUs consist of an Arithmetic Logic Unit (ALU) [also called an Integer Unit (IU)], which performs basic integer arithmetic and logical operations; a Floating Point Unit (FPU), which performs floating-point arithmetic; a set of hardware registers for holding data and memory addresses; and other supporting hardware, including a control unit to sequence the instructions. Each CPU comes with its own set of instructions, which are the operations that it can perform. The instructions typically perform arithmetic and logic operations, move data from one location to another, and change the flow of the program (that is, determine which instruction is to be executed next).

A program consists of many instructions. The first step in executing a program is loading it into memory. Each instruction in the program is executed using a **Fetch-Decode-Execute Cycle**. The **Program Counter** keeps track of the next instruction to be fetched. The CPU fetches the next instruction from memory and places it into the **Instruction Register**. The instruction is decoded (is the instruction a move, load, store, etc.?). Then, the instruction is executed. This Fetch-Decode-Execute Cycle repeats until the program ends.

The speed of a CPU is related to its clock cycle, typically rated in GHz (gigahertz); at the time of this edition, a high-end CPU speed would be rated at 3.4 GHz. The clock speed, measured in clock cycles per second, determines how fast a processor can perform operations such as fetching, decoding, and executing instructions. A CPU rated at 2.5 GHz executes 2.5 billion clock cycles a second. Current RISC processors feature pipelining, which allows the CPU to process several instructions at once, so that while one instruction is executing, the processor can decode the next instruction and fetch the next instruction after that. This greatly improves performance of applications.

Memory or storage devices, such as L2 cache, memory, or hard disks, are typically rated in terms of their capacity, expressed in bytes. A **byte** is eight binary digits, or **bits**. A single bit's value is 0 or 1. Depending on the type of memory or storage device, the capacity will be stated in kilobytes, megabytes, gigabytes, or even terabytes. The sizes of these units are shown in Table 1.1.

For the CPU to execute at its rated speed, however, instructions and data must be available to the CPU at that speed as well. Instructions and data come directly from the L1 cache, which is memory directly located on the CPU chip. Since the L1 cache is located on the CPU chip, it runs at the same speed as the CPU. However, the L1 cache, which can be several Mbytes, is typically much smaller than main memory, and eventually the CPU will need to process more instructions and data than can be held in the L1 cache at one time.

At that point, the CPU typically brings data from what is called the L2 cache, which is located on separate memory chips connected to the CPU. A typical speed for the L2 cache would be a few nanoseconds (billionths of a second) access time, and this will considerably slow down the rate at which the CPU can execute instructions. L2 cache size today is typically 3 to 8 Mbytes, and again, the CPU will eventually need more space for instructions and data than the L2 cache can hold at one time.

At that point, the CPU will bring data and instructions from main memory, also located outside, but connected to, the CPU chip. This will slow down the CPU even more, because main memory typically has an access time of about 20 to 50 nanoseconds. Main memory, though, is significantly larger in size than the L1 and L2 caches, typically anywhere between 3 and 8 Gbytes. When the CPU runs out of space again, it will have to get its data from the hard disk, which is typically 1 Tbyte or more, but with an access time in the milliseconds (thousandths of a second) range.

TABLE 1.1   Memory Units and Their Sizes

Memory Unit	Size
KB, or Kbytes, or kilobytes	About 1,000 bytes (exactly 2^{10} or 1,024 bytes)
MB, or Mbytes, or megabytes	About 1 million bytes (exactly 2^{20} or 1,048,576 bytes)
GB, or Gbytes, or gigabytes	About 1 billion bytes (exactly 2^{30} or 1,073,741,824 bytes)
TB, or Tbytes, or terabytes	About 1 trillion bytes (exactly 2^{40} or 1.09951×10^{12} bytes)

As you can see from these numbers, a considerable amount of speed is lost when the CPU goes from main memory to disk, which is why having sufficient memory is very important for the overall performance of applications.

Another factor that should be taken into consideration is cost per kilobyte. Typically the cost per kilobyte decreases significantly stepping down from L1 cache to hard disk, so high performance is often traded for low price.

Main memory (also called RAM) uses DRAM, or Dynamic Random Access Memory technology, which maintains data only when power is applied to the memory and needs to be refreshed regularly in order to retain data. The L1 and L2 caches use SRAM, or Static Random Access Memory technology, which also needs power but does not need to be refreshed in order to retain data. Memory capacities are typically stated in powers of 2. For instance, 256 Kbytes of memory is 2^{18} bytes, or 262,144 bytes.

Memory chips contain cells, each cell containing a bit, which can store either a 0 or a 1. Cells can be accessed individually or as a group of typically 4, 8, or 16 cells. For instance, a 32-Kbit RAM chip organized as $8K \times 4$ is composed of exactly 2^{13}, or 8,192 units, each unit containing four cells. This RAM chip will have four data output pins (or lines) and 13 access pins (or lines), enabling access to all 8,192 units because each access pin can have a value of 0 or 1. Table 1.2 compares the features of various memory types.

1.1.2   Operating Systems

An operating system (OS) is a software program that

- controls the peripheral devices (for instance, it manages the file system)
- supports multitasking, by scheduling multiple programs or tasks to execute during the same interval
- allocates memory to each program, so that there is no conflict among the memory of any programs running at the same time
- prevents the user from damaging the system. For instance, it prevents user programs from overwriting the operating system or another program's memory

The operating system loads, or **boots**, when the computer system is turned on and is intended to run as long as the computer is running.

Examples of operating systems are macOS, Microsoft Windows, Linux, and iOS and Android for mobile devices.

TABLE 1.2 A Comparison of Memory Types

Device	Location	Type	Speed	Capacity (MB)	Cost/KB
L1 cache	On-chip	SRAM	Very fast	Very small	Very high
L2 cache	Off-chip	SRAM	Fast	Small	High
Memory	Off-chip	DRAM	Moderate	Moderate	Moderate
Hard disk	Separate	Disk media	Slow	Large	Small

1.1.3 Application Software

Application software consists of the programs written to perform specific tasks. These programs are run by the operating system, or as is typically said, they are run "on top of" the operating system. Examples of applications are word processors, such as Microsoft Word or Apache OpenOffice; spreadsheets, such as Microsoft Excel; database management systems, such as Oracle or Microsoft SQL Server; Internet browsers, such as Mozilla Firefox, Google Chrome, or Microsoft Edge; and most of the programs you will write during your study of Computer Science.

1.1.4 Computer Networks and the Internet

Computer Networks

Computer networks connect two or more computers. A common network used by many corporations and universities is a LAN, or Local Area Network. A typical LAN connects several computers that are geographically close to one another, often in the same building, and allows them to share resources, such as a printer, a database, or a file system. In a LAN, most user computers are called **clients**, and one or more computers act as **servers**. The server controls access to resources on the network and can supply services to the clients, such as answering database requests, storing and serving files, or managing email. The computers on the network can exchange data through physical cables or through a wireless network.

The Internet

The Internet is a network of networks, connecting millions of computers around the world. The Internet evolved from ARPANET, a 1969 U.S. military research project whose goal was to design a method for computers to communicate. Most computers on the Internet are clients, typically requesting resources, such as webpages, through an Internet browser. These resources are provided by web servers, which store webpages and respond to these requests.

Every machine on the Internet has a unique ID called its IP address (IP stands for Internet Protocol). Special computers called **routers** find a path through the Internet from one computer to another using these IP addresses. A computer can have a static IP address, which is dedicated to that machine, or a dynamic IP address, which is assigned to the computer when it connects to the Internet. An IP address is made up of four octets, whose values in decimal notation are between 0 and 255. For instance, 58.203.151.103 could represent such an IP address. In binary notation, this IP address is 111010.11001011.10010111.1100111. Later in this chapter, we will learn how to convert a decimal number, such as 103, to its binary equivalent, 1100111.

Most people are familiar with URL (Uniform Resource Locator) addresses that look like *http://www.oracle.com/technetwork/java/index.html*. A URL is actually an Internet domain name as well as the path on that domain to a specific web page. In this URL, the domain name is *www.oracle.com*. The page requested is *index.html*, which is located in the *java* folder under the *technetwork* folder.

Domain name resolution servers, which implement the Domain Name System (DNS), convert domain names to IP addresses, so that Internet users don't need to know the IP addresses of websites they want to visit. The World Wide Web Consortium (W3C), an international group developing standards for Internet access, prefers the term Uniform Resource Identifier (URI) rather than URL, because URI covers future Internet addressing schemes.

Skill Practice
with these end-of-chapter questions

1.7.1   Multiple Choice Exercises

Questions 1, 2, 3, 4

1.7.3   General Questions

Questions 21, 22, 23

1.7.4   Technical Writing

Questions 31, 32, 33

1.2   Practice Activity: Displaying System Configuration

We have explored hardware and operating systems in general. Now, let's discover some information about the hardware and operating system on your computer. Depending on whether you're using a Windows operating system or a Mac OS operating system, choose the appropriate directions that follow to display the operating system's name, the CPU type, and how much memory the computer has.

1.2.1   Displaying Windows Configuration Information

To display system configuration information on a computer running Windows 10, run *msinfo32.exe* from the command line. From the *Start* menu, type *cmd* to start the Command Prompt program and then type *msinfo32* into the Command Prompt window. You will get a display similar to the one in Figure 1.2, although the information displayed varies, depending on your hardware and the version of Windows you are running.

Item	Value
OS Name	Microsoft Windows 10 Enterprise
Version	10.0.14393 Build 14393
Other OS Description	Not Available
OS Manufacturer	Microsoft Corporation
System Name	PC07WK39
System Manufacturer	LENOVO
System Model	20FAS3QE00
System Type	x64-based PC
System SKU	LENOVO_MT_20FA_BU_Think_FM_ThinkPad T460s
Processor	Intel(R) Core(TM) i7-6600U CPU @ 2.60GHz, 2808 Mhz, 2 Core(s), 4 Logical Processor(s)
BIOS Version/Date	LENOVO N1CET47W (1.15), 8/8/2016
SMBIOS Version	2.8
Embedded Controller Version	1.09
BIOS Mode	Legacy
BaseBoard Manufacturer	LENOVO
BaseBoard Model	Not Available
BaseBoard Name	Base Board
Platform Role	Mobile
Secure Boot State	Unsupported
PCR7 Configuration	Binding Not Possible
Windows Directory	C:\windows
System Directory	C:\windows\system32
Boot Device	\Device\HarddiskVolume1
Locale	United States
Hardware Abstraction Layer	Version = "10.0.14393.206"
User Name	UNIVERSITY\USER
Time Zone	Eastern Daylight Time
Installed Physical Memory (RAM)	12.0 GB
Total Physical Memory	11.4 GB
Available Physical Memory	8.41 GB
Total Virtual Memory	13.8 GB
Available Virtual Memory	10.2 GB
Page File Space	2.38 GB
Page File	C:\pagefile.sys
Device Guard Virtualization based security	Not enabled
Hyper-V - VM Monitor Mode Extensions	Yes
Hyper-V - Second Level Address Translation Extensions	Yes
Hyper-V - Virtualization Enabled in Firmware	Yes
Hyper-V - Data Execution Protection	Yes

Figure 1.2

Windows System Information

Screen shots reprinted with permission from Microsoft.

Figure 1.3

Mac Operating System Information

As you can see in Figure 1.2, this computer is running Intel™ Core™ i7-6600U CPU processor running at 2.6 GHz, and the computer has 12 Gbytes of memory, 8.41 Gbytes of which is not being used at the time of the display.

1.2.2   Displaying Mac OS Configuration Information

To display system information on a Mac OS computer, click on the apple icon on the top left of the screen and select "About This Mac." You will see something similar to the display in Figure 1.3, which displays the version of the MAC OS operating system that is running on the computer.

As you can see, this iMac is running macOS High Sierra version 10.13.1. The processor is an Intel Core i5 running at 3.2 GHz and the iMac has 16 Gbytes of memory. Your information may be different from that shown in the figure, depending on your hardware and operating system version.

DISCUSSION QUESTIONS

1. Compare the system information on several computers. Is it the same or different from computer to computer? Explain why the information is the same or different.

2. In the sample display for Windows 10, the computer has 12 Gbytes of memory, but only 8.41 Gbytes of memory is available. Why do you think some memory is not available?

3. Compare your computer to the ones on the previous pages shown here. Which do you think would have better performance? Explain your answer.

1.3   Data Representation

1.3.1   Binary Numbers

As mentioned earlier, a CPU understands only binary numbers, whose digits consist of either 0 or 1. All data is stored in a computer's memory as binary digits. A bit holds one binary digit. A byte holds eight binary digits.

Binary numbers are expressed in the base 2 system, because there are only 2 values in that system, 0 and 1. By contrast, most people are used to the decimal, or base 10, system, which uses the values 0 through 9.

There are other number systems, such as the octal, or base 8, system, which uses the digits from 0 to 7, and the hexadecimal, or base 16, system, which uses the digits 0 to 9 and the letters A to F.

As we know it in the decimal system, the number 359 is composed of the following three digits:

> 3, representing the hundreds, or 10^2
>
> 5, representing the tens, or 10^1
>
> 9, representing the ones, or 10^0

Therefore, we can write 359 as

$$359 = 3*10^2 + 5*10^1 + 9*10^0$$

Thus, the decimal number 359 is written as a linear combination of powers of 10 with coefficients from the base 10 alphabet, that is, the digits from 0 to 9. Similarly, the binary number 11011 is written as a linear combination of powers of 2 with coefficients from the base 2 alphabet, that is, the digits 0 and 1.

For example, the binary number 11011 can be written as

$$11011 = 1*2^4 + 1*2^3 + 0*2^2 + 1*2^1 + 1*2^0$$

Table 1.3 lists the binary equivalents for the decimal numbers 0 through 8, while Table 1.4 lists the decimal equivalents of the first 15 powers of 2.

Note that in Table 1.3, as we count in increments of 1, the last digit alternates between 0 and 1. In fact, we can see that for even numbers, the last digit is always 0 and for odd numbers, the last digit is always 1.

Because computers store numbers as binary, and people recognize numbers as decimal values, conversion between the decimal and binary number systems often takes place inside a computer.

TABLE 1.3   Binary Equivalents of Decimal Numbers 0 Through 8

Decimal	Binary
0	0000
1	0001
2	0010
3	0011
4	0100
5	0101
6	0110
7	0111
8	1000

TABLE 1.4   Powers of 2 and Their Decimal Equivalents

2^{14}	2^{13}	2^{12}	2^{11}	2^{10}	2^9	2^8	2^7	2^6	2^5	2^4	2^3	2^2	2^1	2^0
16,384	8,192	4,096	2,048	1,024	512	256	128	64	32	16	8	4	2	1

Let's try a few conversions. To convert a binary number to a decimal number, multiply each digit in the binary number by $2^{\text{position}-1}$, counting the rightmost position as position 1 and moving left through the binary number. Then add the products together.

Using this method, let's calculate the equivalent of the binary number 11010 in our decimal system.

```
11010 = 1*2⁴ + 1*2³ + 0*2² + 1*2¹ + 0*2⁰
      = 16 + 8 + 0 + 2 + 0
      = 26
```

Now let's examine how to convert a decimal number to a binary number. Let's convert the decimal number 359 into its binary number equivalent. As we can see from the way we rewrote 11011, a binary number can be written as a sum of powers of 2 with coefficients 0 and 1.

The strategy to decompose a decimal number into a sum of powers of 2 is simple: first find the largest power of 2 that is smaller than or equal to the decimal number, subtract that number from the decimal number, then do the same with the remainder, and so on, until you reach 0.

The largest power of 2 that is smaller than 359 is 256, or 2^8 (the next larger power of 2 would be 512, which is larger than 359). Subtracting 256 from 359 gives us 103 ($359 - 256 = 103$), so we now have

```
359 = 2⁸*1 + 103
```

Now we apply the same procedure to 103. The largest power of 2 that is smaller than 103 is 64, or 2^6. That means that there is no factor for 2^7, so that digit's value is 0. Subtracting 64 from 103 gives us 39.

Now we have

```
359 = 2⁸*1 + 2⁷*0 + 2⁶*1 + 39
```

Repeating the procedure for 39, we find that the largest power of 2 smaller than 39 is 32 or 2^5. Subtracting 32 from 39 gives us 7.

So we now have

```
359 = 2⁸*1 + 2⁷*0 + 2⁶*1 + 2⁵*1 + 7
```

Repeating the procedure for 7, the largest power of 2 smaller than 7 is 2^2, or 4. That means that there are no factors for 2^4 or 2^3, so the value for each of those digits is 0. Subtracting 4 from 7 gives us 3, so we have

```
359 = 2⁸*1 + 2⁷*0 + 2⁶*1 + 2⁵*1 + 2⁴*0 + 2³*0 + 2²*1 + 3
```

Repeating the procedure for 3, the largest power of 2 smaller than 3 is 2, or 2^1, and we have:

```
359 = 2⁸*1 + 2⁷*0 + 2⁶*1 + 2⁵*1 + 2⁴*0 + 2³*0 + 2²*1 + 2¹*1 + 1
```

1 is a power of 2; it is 2^0, so we finally have

```
359 = 2⁸*1 + 2⁷*0 + 2⁶*1 + 2⁵*1 + 2⁴*0 + 2³*0 + 2²*1 + 2¹*1 + 2⁰*1
```

Removing the power of 2 multipliers, 359 can be represented in the binary system as

```
359 = 2⁸*1 + 2⁷*0 + 2⁶*1 + 2⁵*1 + 2⁴*0 + 2³*0 + 2²*1 + 2¹*1 + 2⁰*1
    =   1     0      1      1      0      0      1      1      1
```

or

```
1 0110 0111
```

CODE IN ACTION

To see a step-by-step demonstration of converting between decimal and binary numbers, look for the movie within the online resources. Click on the link to start the movie.

In a computer program, we will use both positive and negative numbers. Appendix D explains how negative numbers, such as −34, are represented in the binary system. In a computer program, we also use floating-point numbers, such as 3.75. Appendix E explains how floating-point numbers are represented using the binary system.

1.3.2   Using Hexadecimal Numbers to Represent Binary Numbers

As you can see, binary numbers can become rather long. With only two possible values, 0 and 1, it takes 16 binary digits to represent the decimal value +32,768. For that reason, the hexadecimal, or base 16, system is often used as a shorthand representation of binary numbers. The hexadecimal system uses 16 digits: 0 to 9 and A to F. The letters A to F represent the values 10, 11, 12, 13, 14, and 15.

The maximum value that can be represented in four binary digits is $2^4 - 1$, or 15. The maximum value of a hexadecimal digit is also 15, which is represented by the letter F. So you can reduce the size of a binary number by using hexadecimal digits to represent each group of four binary digits.

Table 1.5 displays the hexadecimal digits along with their binary equivalents.

To represent the following binary number in hexadecimal, you simply substitute the appropriate hex digit for each set of four binary digits.

```
0001 1010 1111 1001 1011 0011 1011 1110
 1    A    F    9    B    3    B    E
```

Here's an interesting sequence of hexadecimal numbers. The first 32 bits of every Java applet are:

```
1100 1010 1111 1110 1011 1010 1011 1110
```

Translated into hexadecimal, that binary number becomes:

```
CAFE BABE
```

TABLE 1.5   Hexadecimal Digits and Equivalent Binary Values

Hex Digit	Binary Value	Hex Digit	Binary Value
0	0000	8	1000
1	0001	9	1001
2	0010	A	1010
3	0011	B	1011
4	0100	C	1100
5	0101	D	1101
6	0110	E	1110
7	0111	F	1111

1.3.3   Representing Characters with the Unicode Character Set

Java represents characters using the Unicode Worldwide Character Standard, or simply Unicode. Each Unicode character is represented as 16 bits, or two bytes. This means that the Unicode character set can encode 65,536 characters.

The Unicode character set was developed by the Unicode Consortium, which consists of computer manufacturers, software vendors, the governments of several nations, and others. The consortium's goal was to support an international character set, including the printable characters on the standard QWERTY keyboard, as well as international characters such as é or λ.

Many programming languages store characters using the ASCII (American Standard Code for Information Interchange) character set, which uses 7 bits to encode each character, and thus, can represent only 128 characters. For compatibility with the ASCII character set, the first 128 characters in the Unicode character set are the same as the ASCII character set.

Table 1.6 shows a few examples of Unicode characters and their decimal equivalents.

For more information on the Unicode character set, see Appendix C or visit the Unicode Consortium's website at *http://www.Unicode.org*.

TABLE 1.6   Selected Unicode Characters and Their Decimal Equivalents

Unicode Character	Decimal Value	Hex Value
NUL, the null character (a nonprintable character)	0	0000
*	42	002A
1	49	0031
2	50	0032
A	65	0041
B	66	0042
a	97	0061
b	98	0062
}	125	007D
delete (a nonprintable character)	127	007F

Skill Practice
with these end-of-chapter questions

1.7.1   Multiple Choice Exercises

Questions 5, 6, 7, 8

1.7.2   Converting Numbers

Questions 15, 16, 17, 18, 19, 20

1.7.3   General Questions

Questions 24, 25, 26

1.4   Programming Languages

1.4.1   High- and Low-Level Languages

Programming languages can be categorized into three types:

- machine language
- assembly language
- high-level language

In the early days of computing, programmers often used machine language or assembly language. Machine language uses binary codes, or strings of 0s and 1s, to execute the instruction set of the CPU and to refer to memory addresses. This method of programming is extremely challenging and time consuming. Also, the code written in machine language is not portable to other computer architectures because each CPU has its own set of instructions. Machine language's early popularity can be attributed largely to the fact that programmers had no other choices. However, programmers rarely use machine language today.

Assembly languages are one step above machine language, using symbolic names for memory addresses and mnemonics for processor instructions—for example: *BEQ* (branch if equal), *SW* (store), or *LW* (load). An Assembler program converts the code to machine language before it is executed. Like machine language, assembly languages are also CPU-dependent and are not portable among computers with different processors (for instance, between Intel and SPARC). Assembly language is easier to write than machine language but still requires a significant effort and, thus, is usually used only when the program requires features, such as direct hardware access, that are not supported by a high-level language.

High-level languages, such as Java, C++, Swift, PHP, and Python, are closer to the English language than they are to machine language, making them a lot easier to use for software development and more portable among CPU architectures. For this reason, programmers have embraced high-level languages for more and more applications.

Characteristics of high-level languages, such as Java, are

- The languages are highly symbolic. Programmers write instructions using keywords and special characters and use symbolic names for data.

- The languages are somewhat portable (some more portable than others) among different CPUs.

- Some high-level programming languages, such as C++, Java, and Python, can be used for general-purpose applications, and some high-level programming languages can be used for specialized applications, such as Swift for iPhone development and PHP for Internet applications.

High-level languages are compiled, interpreted, or a combination of both. A program written in a compiled language, such as C++, is converted by a compiler into machine code, then the machine code is executed.

By contrast, a program written using an interpreted language, such as Perl, is read and converted to machine code, line by line, at execution time. Typically, a program written in an interpreted language will run more slowly than its equivalent written in a compiled language.

Java uses a combination of a compiler and an interpreter. A Java program is first compiled into processor-independent **byte codes**, then the byte code file is interpreted at run time by software called the **Java Virtual Machine (JVM)**.

1.4.2 An Introduction to Object-Oriented Programming

Initial high-level languages, such as Fortran or C, were procedural. Typically, programmers wrote task-specific code in separate procedures, or functions, and invoked these procedures from other sections of the program in order to perform various tasks. The program's data was generally shared among the procedures.

In the mid-1970s, the first object-oriented programming language, Smalltalk, was introduced, enabling programmers to write code with a different approach. Whereas procedures or functions dealt mainly with basic data types such as integers, real numbers, or single characters, Smalltalk provided the programmer with a new tool: classes and objects of those classes.

A class enables the programmer to encapsulate data and the functions to manipulate that data into one package. A class essentially defines a template, or model, from which objects are created. Creating an object is called **instantiation**. Thus, objects are created—instantiated—according to the design of the class.

A class could represent something in real life, such as a person. The class could have various attributes such as, in the example of a "person" class, a first name, a last name, and an age. The class would also provide code, called **methods**, that allow the creator of the object to set and retrieve the values of the attributes.

One big advantage to object-oriented programming is that well-written classes can be reused in new programs, thereby reducing future development time.

Smalltalk was somewhat successful, but had a major deficiency: its syntax was unlike any syntax already known by most programmers. Most programmers who knew the procedural C programming language were attracted by the object-oriented features of Smalltalk but were reluctant to use it because its syntax was so different from C's syntax. C++ added object-oriented features to C, but also added complexity.

Meanwhile, the Internet was growing by leaps and bounds and gaining popularity daily. Web developers used HTML to develop webpages and soon felt the need to incorporate programming features not only on the server side, but also directly on the client side. Fortunately, Java appeared on the scene.

1.4.3 The Java Language

On May 23, 1995, Sun Microsystems introduced Java, originally named Oak, as a free, object-oriented language targeted at embedded applications for consumer devices. A Java Virtual Machine was incorporated immediately into the Netscape Navigator Internet browser, and as the Internet grew, small Java programs, known as applets, began to appear on webpages in increasing numbers. Java syntax is basically identical (with some minor exceptions) to that of C++, and soon programmers all over the world started to realize the benefits of using Java. Those benefits include

- syntax identical to that of C++, except that Java eliminates some of C++'s more complex features
- object orientation
- Internet-related features, such as servlets, which are run by the web server
- an extensive library of classes that can be reused readily, including classes for providing a Graphical User Interface and Java Database Connectivity (JDBC) for communicating with a database
- portability among every platform that supports a Java Virtual Machine
- built-in networking
- open source availability of the Java Development Kit

As we mentioned earlier, a Java program is first compiled into processor-independent byte codes, then the byte codes are interpreted at run time by the Java Virtual Machine (JVM). As its name implies, the JVM simulates a virtual processor with its own instruction set, registers, and instruction pointer. Thus, to run a Java program, we only need a JVM. Fortunately, JVMs are available on every major computing platform.

Because Java programs are interpreted at run time, they typically run more slowly than their C++ counterparts. However, many platforms provide Java compilers that convert source code directly to machine code. This results in greater execution speed, but with an accompanying loss of portability. Just-in-Time (JIT) compilers are also available. These JITs compile code at run time so that subsequent execution of the same code runs much faster.

Java programs can be written as servlets, Android apps, or applications.

Java servlets are invoked by the web server and run on the server, without being downloaded to the client. Typically, servlets dynamically generate web content by reading and writing to a database using JDBC (Java Database Connectivity).

The Android Open Source project has chosen Java to be the language for developing apps for Android devices, such as cell phones, tablets, and smart TVs.

Java applications run standalone on a client computer. In this text, we will write Java applications.

Oracle Corporation, which acquired Sun Microsystems in January 2010, provides a valuable Java website (*www.oracle.com/technetwork/java*), which has information on using the prewritten classes, a tutorial on Java, and many more resources for the Java programmer. We will refer you to that site often in this text.

1.5   An Introduction to Programming

1.5.1   Programming Basics

In many ways, programming is like solving a puzzle. We have a task to perform and we know the operations that a computer can perform (input, calculations, comparisons, rearranging of items, and output). As programmers, our job is to decompose a task into individual, ordered steps of inputting, calculating, comparing, rearranging, and outputting.

For example, suppose our task is to find the sum of two numbers. First, our program needs to read (input) the numbers into the computer. Next, our program needs to add the two numbers together (calculate). Finally, our program needs to write (output) the sum.

Notice that this program consists of steps, called **instructions**, which are performed in order ("First," "Next," "Finally"). Performing operations in order, one after another, is called **sequential processing**.

The order in which instructions are executed by the computer is critical in programming. You can't calculate the sum of two numbers before you have read the two numbers, and you can't output a sum before you have calculated it. Programming, therefore, requires the programmer to specify the ordering of instructions, which is called the **flow of control** of the program. There are four different ways that the flow of control can progress through a program: sequential execution, method call, selection, and looping. We've just seen sequential execution, and we'll discuss the other types of flow of control in the next section.

Because getting the flow of control correct is essential to getting a program to produce correct output, programmers use a tool called **pseudocode** (pronounced *sue dough code*) to help them design the flow of control before writing the code.

1.5.2   Program Design with Pseudocode

Pseudocode, from *pseudo*, which means "appearing like," is a method for expressing a program's order of instructions in the English language, rather than a programming language. In this way, the programmer can concentrate on designing a program without also being bogged down in the syntax of the particular programming language.

The pseudocode for calculating the sum of two numbers would look like Example 1.1.

```
read first number
read second number
set total to (first number + second number)
output total
```

EXAMPLE 1.1   Pseudocode for Summing Two Numbers

Fortunately, the rules for writing pseudocode are not rigid. Essentially, you can use any wording that works for you.

Let's look at another example. Suppose our program needs to calculate the square root of a number. The instructions for calculating a square root are rather complex; fortunately, Java provides prewritten code that computes the square root of a number. The prewritten code is called a **method**, and our program can execute that code by **calling the method**. As part of the method call, we tell the method which number's square root we want to calculate. This is called **passing an argument to the method**. When the method finishes executing its instructions, control is passed back to our program just after the method call and our program can use the square root of the number calculated by the method. This is called **returning a value**. Another way of looking at method calls is to consider what happens when we're reading a book and find a word we don't understand. We mark our place in the book and look up the word in a dictionary. When we're finished looking up the word, we go back to our place in the book and continue reading.

Example 1.2 shows the pseudocode for calculating the square root of an integer.

```
read a number
call the square root method, passing the number and receiving the square root
output the square root of the number
```

EXAMPLE 1.2   Using a Method Call to Calculate a Square Root

The order of operations is still input, calculate, and output, but we're calling a method to perform the calculation for us.

Now suppose our task is to determine whether a number is positive or negative. First, our program should input the number into the computer. Next, we need to determine whether the number is positive or negative. We know that numbers greater than or equal to 0 are positive and numbers less than 0 are negative, so our program should compare the number to 0. Finally, our program should write a message indicating whether the number is positive or negative.

Like Examples 1.1 and 1.2, the operations are input, calculate, and output, in that order. However, depending on whether the number is positive or negative, our program should write a different message. If the number is greater than or equal to 0, the program should write a message that the number is positive, but if the number is less than 0, the program should write a message that the number is negative. Code used to handle this situation is called **selection**; the program selects which code to execute based on the value of the data.

The pseudocode for this program could be written as that shown in Example 1.3.

```
read a number
if the number is greater than or equal to 0
  write "Number is positive."
else
  write "Number is negative."
```

EXAMPLE 1.3   Using Selection

Notice the indentation for the code that will be selected based on the comparison of the number with 0. Programmers use indentation to make it easier to see the flow of control of the program.

Now let's get a little more complicated. Suppose our program needs to find the sum of a group of numbers. This is called **accumulating**. To accomplish this, we can take the same approach as if we were adding a group of numbers using a calculator. We start with a total of 0 and add each number, one at a time, to the running total. When we have no more numbers to add, the running total is the total of all the numbers.

Translating this into pseudocode, we get the code shown in Example 1.4.

```
set total to 0
read a number
while there was a number to read, repeat next two instructions
  add number to total
  read the next number
write total
```

EXAMPLE 1.4   Accumulating a Total

The indented code will be repeated for each number read until there are no more numbers. This repeated execution of the same code is called **looping**, or **iteration**, and is used extensively in programming whenever the same processing needs to be performed on each item in a set.

Accumulating a total and determining whether a number is positive or negative are just two of many commonly performed operations. In programming, we will often perform tasks for which there are standard methods of processing, called **algorithms**. For example, the algorithm for accumulation is to set a total to 0, use looping to add each item to the total, then output the total. More generally, we can think of an algorithm as a strategy to solve a problem. Earlier in the chapter, we used an algorithm to convert a decimal number to its binary representation.

Other common programming tasks are counting items, calculating an average, sorting items into order, and finding the minimum and maximum values. In this text, we will learn the standard algorithms for performing these common operations. Once we learn these algorithms, our programming job will become easier. When we recognize that a program requires any of these tasks, we can simply plug in the appropriate algorithm with some minor modifications.

Programming, in large part, is simply reducing a complex task to a set of subtasks that can be implemented by combining standard algorithms that use sequential processing, method calls, selection, and looping.

The most difficult part of programming, however, is recognizing which algorithms to apply to the problem at hand. This requires analytical skills and the ability to see patterns. Throughout this text, we will point out common patterns wherever possible.

SOFTWARE ENGINEERING TIP
Looking for patterns will help you determine the appropriate algorithms for your programs.

1.5.3 Developing a Java Application

Writing a Java application consists of several steps: writing the code, compiling the code, and executing the application. Java source code is stored in a text file with the extension *.java*. Compiling the code creates one or more *.class* files, which contain processor-independent byte codes. The Java Virtual Machine (JVM) translates the byte codes into machine-level instructions for the processor on which the Java application is running. Thus, if a Java application is running on an Intel i7 processor, the JVM translates the byte codes into the i7's instruction set.

Oracle provides a Java SE Development Toolkit (JDK) on its website (*www.oracle.com/technetwork/java*), which is downloadable free of charge. The JDK contains a compiler, JVM, and jshell, which is a tool for immediate execution of Java code. In addition, the JDK contains a broad range of prewritten Java classes that programmers can use in their Java applications.

If you are downloading and installing Java yourself, be sure to follow the directions on the Oracle website, including the directions for setting the path for *javac*, the Java compiler. You need to set the path correctly so that you can run the Java compiler from any folder on your computer.

To develop an application using the JDK, write the source code using any text editor, such as Notepad on Windows, TextEdit on Macs, or the vi editor on Linux. To compile the code, invoke the compiler from the command line:

```
javac ClassName.java
```

where *ClassName.java* is the name of the source file.

If our program, written in the file *ClassName.java*, compiles correctly, a new file, *ClassName.class*, will be created in our current directory.

To run the application, we invoke the JVM from the command line:

```
java ClassName
```

Typically, programmers use an Integrated Development Environment (IDE) to develop applications rather than invoking the compiler and JVM from the command line. An IDE consists of a program editor, a compiler, and a run-time environment, integrated via a Graphical User Interface. The advantage to using an IDE is that errors in the Java code that are found by the compiler or the JVM can be linked directly to the program editor at the line in the source file that caused the error. Additionally, the Graphical User Interface enables the programmer to switch among the editor, compiler, and execution of the program without launching separate applications.

Some of the many available IDEs include Eclipse from the Eclipse Foundation, Inc.; JGRASP, developed at Auburn University; NetBeans, downloadable from Oracle; and TextPad from Helios Software Solutions. Some IDEs are freely available, while others require a software license fee.

Skill Practice
with these end-of-chapter questions

1.7.1   Multiple Choice Exercises

Questions 9, 10, 11, 12, 13, 14

1.7.3   General Questions

Questions 27, 28, 29, 30

1.7.4   Technical Writing

Question 34

1.5.4   Programming Activity 1: Writing a First Java Application

Let's create our first Java program. This program prints the message, "Programming is not a spectator sport!"

Start by launching your IDE and open a new editor window. This is where you will write the code for the program.

Before you type any code, however, let's name the document. You do this by saving the document as *FirstProgram.java*. Be sure to capitalize the F and the P and keep the other letters lowercase. Java is case-sensitive, so Java considers *firstprogram.java* or even *Firstprogram.java* to be a different name. Also, note that there is no space between *First* and *Program*.

Keeping case sensitivity in mind, type in the program shown in Example 1.5.

```
1 // First program in Java
2 // Anderson, Franceschi
3
4 public class FirstProgram
5 {
6   public static void main( String [ ] args )
7   {
8     System.out.println( "Programming is not a spectator sport!" );
9
10    System.exit( 0 );
11  }
12 }
```

EXAMPLE 1.5   A First Program in Java

At this point, we ask that you just type the program as you see it here, except for the line numbers, which are not part of the program. Line numbers are displayed in this example to allow easy reference to a particular line in the code. We'll explain a little about the program now; additional details will become clear as the semester progresses.

The first two lines, which start with two forward slashes, are comments. They will not be compiled or executed; they are simply information for the programmer and are used to increase the readability of the program.

Line 4 defines the class name as *FirstProgram*. Notice that the class name must be spelled exactly the same way—including capitalization—as the file name, *FirstProgram.java*.

The curly braces in lines 5 and 12 mark the beginning and ending of the *FirstProgram* class, and the curly braces in lines 7 and 11 mark the beginning and ending of the *main* method. Every Java application must define a class and a *main* method. Execution of a Java application always begins with the code inside *main*. So when this application begins, it will execute line 8, which writes the message "*Programming*

COMMON ERROR TRAP
Java is case-sensitive. The class name and the file name must match exactly, including capitalization.

is not a spectator sport!" to the system console. Next, it executes line 10, *System.exit(0)*, which exits the program. Including this line is optional; if you omit this line, the application will still exit normally.

As you type the program, notice that your IDE automatically colors your text to help you distinguish comments, *String* literals (*"Programming is not a spectator sport!"*), Java class names (*String, System*), and keywords (*public, class, static*), which are reserved for specific uses in Java. Curly braces, brackets, and parentheses, which have syntactical meaning in Java, are usually displayed in color as well. Your IDE may use different colors than those shown in Example 1.5.

When you have completed typing the code in Example 1.5, compile it. If everything is typed correctly, the compiler will create a *FirstProgram.class* file, which contains the byte codes for the program.

If you received any compiler errors, check that you have entered the code exactly as it is written in Example 1.5. We give you tips on finding and fixing the errors in the next section.

If you got a clean compile with no errors, congratulations! You're ready to execute the application. This will invoke the JVM and pass it the *First Program.class* file created by the compiler. If all is well, you will see the message, *Programming is not a spectator sport!*, displayed on the Java console, which is the text window that opens automatically. Figure 1.4 shows the correct output of the program.

Figure 1.4

Output from Example 1.5

```
Programming is not a spectator sport!
```

Debugging Techniques

If the compiler found syntax errors in the code, these are called **compiler errors**, not because the compiler caused them, but because the compiler found them. When the compiler detects errors in the code, it writes diagnostic information about the errors.

For example, try typing *println* with a capital P (as *Println*), and recompiling. The compiler displays the following message:

```
FirstProgram.java:8: error: cannot find symbol
    System.out.Println( "Programming is not a spectator sport!" );
                ^
  symbol: method Println(String)
  location: variable out of type PrintStream
1 error
```

The first line identifies the file name that contains the Java source code, as well as the line number in the source code where the error occurred. In this case, the error occurred on line 8. The second line displays line 8 from the source code with a caret (^) pointing to *Println* as being the cause of the error. The symbol and location information in the third and fourth lines indicate that the *Println* method is unknown. Remember that Java is case-sensitive, so *println* and *Println* are considered to be different. As you gain experience with Java, these error messages will become more meaningful to you. With most IDEs, double-clicking on the first line in the error message transfers you to the source code window with your cursor positioned on line 8 so you can correct the error.

Many times, the compiler will find more than one error in the source code. When that happens, don't panic. Often, a single problem, such as a missing semicolon or curly brace, can cause multiple compiler errors.

For example, after correcting the preceding error, try deleting the left curly brace in line 7, then recompiling. The compiler reports four errors:

```
FirstProgram.java:6: error: ';' expected
        public static void main( String [ ] args )
                                                  ^
FirstProgram.java:10: error: <identifier> expected
        System.exit( 0 );
                ^
FirstProgram.java:10: error: illegal start of type
        System.exit( 0 );
                  ^
FirstProgram.java:12: error: class, interface or enum expected
}
^
4 errors
```

As you can see, the compiler messages do not always report the problem exactly. When you receive a compiler message, looking at the surrounding lines will often help you find the error. Depending on your IDE, you might see messages other than those shown here because some IDEs attempt to interpret the error messages from the compiler to provide more relevant information on the errors.

It is sometimes easier to fix one error at a time and recompile after each fix, because the first fix might eliminate many of the reported errors.

When all the compiler errors are corrected, you're ready to execute the program.

It is possible to get a clean bill of health from the compiler, yet the program still won't run. To demonstrate this, try eliminating the brackets in line 6 after the word

SOFTWARE ENGINEERING TIP

Because one syntax error can cause multiple compiler errors, correct only the obvious errors and recompile after each correction.

String. If you then compile the program, no errors are reported. But when you try to run the program, you get a **run-time error**.

Instead of *Programming is not a spectator sport!*, the following message is displayed on the Java console:

```
Error: Main method not found in class FirstProgram, please define the main
method as:
   public static void main(String[] args)
or a JavaFX application class must extend javafx.application.Application
```

This means that the *main* method header (line 6) was not typed correctly.

Thus, we've seen that two types of errors can occur while you are developing a Java program: compiler errors, which are usually caused by language syntax errors or misspellings, and run-time errors, which are often caused by problems using the prewritten classes. Run-time errors can also be caused by exceptions that the JVM detects as it is running, such as an attempt to divide by zero.

Testing Techniques

Once your program compiles cleanly and executes without run-time errors, you may be tempted to conclude that your job is finished. Far from it—you must also verify the results, or output, of the program.

In the sample program, it's difficult to get incorrect results—other than misspelling the message or omitting the spaces between the words. But any nontrivial program should be tested thoroughly before declaring it production ready.

To test a program, consider all the possible inputs and the corresponding correct outputs. It often isn't feasible to test every possible input, so programmers usually test **boundary conditions**, which are the values that sit on the boundaries of producing different output for a program.

For example, to test the code that determines whether an integer is negative or nonnegative, you would feed the program −1 and 0. These are the boundaries of negative and nonnegative integers. In other words, the boundary between negative and nonnegative integers is between −1 and 0.

When a program does not produce the correct output, we say the program contains **logic errors**. By testing your program thoroughly, you can discover and correct most logic errors. Table 1.7 shows types of program errors and their usual causes.

We'll talk more about testing techniques throughout the text.

TABLE 1.7   Types of Program Errors and Their Causes

Type of Error	Usual Causes
Compiler errors	Incorrect language syntax or misspellings
Run-time errors	Incorrect use of classes
Logic errors	Incorrect program design or incorrect implementation of the design

? DISCUSSION QUESTIONS

1. In the Debugging Techniques section, we saw that making one typo could generate several compiler errors. Why do you think that happens?

2. Explain why testing boundary conditions is an efficient way to verify a program's correctness.

3. Did any errors occur while you were developing the first application? If so, explain whether they were compiler or run-time errors and what you did to fix them.

1.5.5 Making a JAR File

After we finish writing, compiling, and testing our application, we may want to distribute it. Java programs are typically distributed as **JARs**, which stands for Java ARchive. The JAR format allows the compression and aggregation of multiple files into one. The *.jar* extension is, by default, associated with the Java Virtual Machine. Thus, a user can double-click on a JAR file and launch its corresponding application directly. Most IDEs include a tool to easily create a JAR file. But you can also create a JAR file from the command line. The general syntax to create a JAR file is:

```
jar cf jarfile inputfile(s)
```

- The *c* and *f* characters are options. The *c* option means that we want to create a JAR file. The *f* option means that we want to send the output to a file.

- *jarfile* is the name of the JAR file that we want to create; it can be a different name from the name of our Java file(s).

- inputfile(s) is a space-separated list of files that we want to include in the JAR file. It typically includes the .class files and may include folders or files containing resources used in our application, such as images or sounds.

We can create a JAR file named *Greeting.jar* from our *FirstProgram* application by typing the following at the command line:

```
jar cf Greeting.jar FirstProgram.class
```

Note that the input file is the *.class* file, not the *.java* file. Figure 1.5 shows the contents of the folder after executing the command above.

The file *Greeting.jar* is created in the current folder, as shown in Figure 1.5.

If our application includes several Java files, we can use the wildcard character * to include all the corresponding *.class* files. The following creates a JAR file for all the *.class* files located in the current folder:

```
jar cf Greetings.jar *.class
```

Figure 1.5

The Folder After the JAR File Is Created

FirstProgram.class
CLASS File
487 bytes

FirstProgram
jGRASP Java file
247 bytes

Greeting
Executable Jar File
795 bytes

CHAPTER REVIEW

- Basic components of a computer include the CPU, memory, a hard disk, keyboard, and monitor.

- Each type of CPU has its own set of instructions for performing arithmetic and logical operations, moving data, and changing the order of execution of instructions.

- An operating system controls peripheral devices, supports multitasking, allocates memory to programs, and prevents the user from damaging the system.

- Computer networks link two or more computers so that they can share resources, such as files or printers.

- The Internet connects millions of computers around the world. Web servers deliver webpages to clients running Internet browsers.

- Binary numbers are composed of bits. Each bit has the value 0 or 1. A byte holds eight binary digits.

- To convert a binary number to a decimal number, multiply each digit in the binary number by $2^{position-1}$, counting the rightmost position as position 1 and moving left through the number. Then add the products together.

- To convert a decimal number into a binary number, first find the largest power of 2 that is smaller than or equal to the decimal number, subtract that number from the decimal number, then do the same with the remainder, and so on, until the decimal number reaches 0.

- Hexadecimal digits can be used to represent groups of four bits.

- The Unicode character set, which Java uses, can encode up to 65,536 characters using 16 bits per character.

- Machine language and assembly language are early forms of programming languages that require the programmer to write to the CPU's instruction set. Because this low-level programming is time consuming and difficult, and the programs are not portable to other CPU architectures, machine language and assembly language are rarely used.

- High-level languages are highly symbolic and somewhat portable. They can be compiled, interpreted, or as in the case of Java, converted to byte codes, which are interpreted at run time by the Java Virtual Machine.

- A good program is readable, easily maintainable, and reusable.

- Object-oriented programming uses classes to encapsulate data and the functions needed to manipulate that data. Objects are instantiated according to the class design. An advantage to object-oriented programming is the ability to reuse classes.

- Programs use a combination of sequential processing, method calls, selection, and iteration to control the order of execution of instructions. Performing operations in order, one after another, is called sequential processing. Temporarily executing other code, then returning, is called a method call. Selecting which code to execute based on the value of data is called selection. Repeating the same code on each item in a group of values is called iteration, or looping.

- Pseudocode allows a programmer to design a program without worrying about the syntax of the language.

- In programming, we often perform tasks for which there are standard methods of processing, called algorithms. For example, accumulating is a common programming operation that finds the sum of a group of numbers.

- Programming, in large part, is reducing a complex task to a set of subtasks that can be implemented by combining standard algorithms that use sequential processing, selection, and looping.

- Java source code is stored in a text file with an extension of *.java*. Compiling the code produces one or more *.class* files.

- An Integrated Development Environment (IDE) consists of a program editor, a compiler, and a run-time environment, integrated via a Graphical User Interface.

- Compiler errors are detected by the compiler and are usually caused by incorrect Java syntax or misspellings. Run-time errors are detected by the Java Virtual Machine and are usually caused by exceptions or incorrect use of classes. Logic errors occur during program execution and are caused by incorrect program design.

1.7   Exercises, Problems, and Projects

1.7.1   Multiple Choice Exercises

1. Which one of these is not an operating system?

    ❏ Linux

    ❏ Java

    ❏ Windows

    ❏ Android

2. Which one of these is not an application?

    ❏ Word

    ❏ Firefox

    ❏ Linux

    ❏ Excel

3. How many bits are in three bytes?

    ❏ 3

    ❏ 8

    ❏ 24

    ❏ 0

4. In a network, the computers providing services to the other computers are called

    ❏ clients.

    ❏ servers.

    ❏ laptops.

5. A binary number ending with a 0

    ❏ is even.

    ❏ is odd.

    ❏ cannot tell.

6. A binary number ending with a 1

   ❑ is even.

   ❑ is odd.

   ❑ cannot tell.

7. A binary number ending with two 0s

   ❑ is a multiple of 4.

   ❑ is not a multiple of 4.

   ❑ cannot tell.

8. Using four bits, the largest positive binary number we can represent is 1111.

   ❑ true

   ❑ false

9. Which one of these is not a programming language?

   ❑ C++

   ❑ Java

   ❑ Windows

   ❑ Fortran

10. Which one of these is not an object-oriented programming language?

    ❑ C

    ❑ Java

    ❑ C++

    ❑ Smalltalk

11. What is the file extension for a Java source code file?

    ❑ .java

    ❑ .exe

    ❑ .class

12. What is the file extension of a compiled Java program?

    ❑ .java

    ❑ .exe

    ❑ .class

13. In order to compile a program named *Hello.java*, what do you type at the command line?

  ❑ java Hello

  ❑ java Hello.java

  ❑ javac Hello

  ❑ javac Hello.java

14. You have successfully compiled *Hello.java* into *Hello.class*. What do you type at the command line in order to run the application?

  ❑ java Hello.class

  ❑ java Hello

  ❑ javac Hello

  ❑ javac Hello.class

1.7.2 Converting Numbers

15. Convert the decimal number 67 into binary.

16. Convert the decimal number 1,564 into binary.

17. Convert the binary number 0001 0101 into decimal.

18. Convert the binary number 1101 0101 0101 into decimal.

19. Convert the binary number 0001 0101 into hexadecimal.

20. Convert the hexadecimal number D8F into binary.

1.7.3 General Questions

21. A RAM chip is organized as × 8 memory, i.e., each unit contains 8 bits, or a byte. There are 7 address pins on the chip. How many bytes does that memory chip contain?

22. If a CPU is rated at 2.5 GHz, how many clock cycles per second are performed?

23. If a CPU's clock cycles 2.6 billion times per second, what is the rating of the CPU in MHz?

24. Suppose we are using binary encoding to represent colors. For example, a black-and-white color system has only two colors and therefore needs only 1 bit to encode the color system as follows:

Bit   Color

0   black

1   white

With 2 bits, we can encode four colors as follows:

Bit pattern   Color

00   black

01   red

10   blue

11   white

With 5 bits, how many colors can we encode?

With n bits (n being a positive integer), how many colors can we encode? (Express your answer as a function of n.)

25. In HTML, a color can be coded in the following hexadecimal notation: *#rrggbb*, where

rr represents the amount of red in the color

gg represents the amount of green in the color

bb represents the amount of blue in the color

rr, *gg*, and *bb* vary between 00 and FF in hexadecimal notation, i.e., 0 and 255 in decimal equivalent notation. Give the decimal values of the red, green, and blue values in the color #33AB12.

26. RGB is a color system representing colors: R stands for red, G for green, and B for blue. A color can be coded as *rgb* where *r* is a number between 0 and 255 representing how much red there is in the color, *g* is a number between 0 and 255 representing how much green there is in the color, and *b* is a number between 0 and 255 representing how much blue there is in the color. The color gray is created by using the same value for *r*, *g*, and *b*. How many shades of gray are there?

27. List three benefits of the Java programming language.

28. What is the name of the Java compiler?

29. Write the pseudocode for a program that finds the product of two numbers.

30. Write the pseudocode for a program that finds the sums of the numbers input that are greater than or equal to 10 and the numbers input that are less than 10.

1.7.4   Technical Writing

31. List the benefits of having a Local Area Network versus standalone computer systems.

32. For one day, keep a diary of the computer applications that you use. Also note any features of the applications that you think should be improved or any features you'd like to see added.

33. You are looking at two computers with the following specifications, everything else being equal:

    PC # 1   PC # 2

    3.4-GHz CPU   3.3-GHz CPU

    16 MB L2 cache   16 MB L2 cache

    1 GB RAM   4 GB RAM

    1 TB hard drive   1 TB hard drive

    $399 $399

    Which PC would you buy? Explain the reasoning behind your selection.

34. Go to Oracle's Java site (*www.oracle.com/technetwork/java*). Explain what resources are available there for someone who wants to learn Java.

1.7.5 Group Project (for a group of 1, 2, or 3 students)

35. In the octal system (base 8), numbers are represented using digits from 0 to 7; a 0 is placed in front of the octal number to indicate that the octal system is being used. For instance, here are some examples of the equivalent of some octal numbers in the decimal system:

Octal	Decimal
000	0
001	1
007	7
010	8
011	9

In the hexadecimal system, numbers are represented using digits from 0 to 9 and letters A to F; 0x is placed in front of the hexadecimal number to indicate that the hexadecimal system is being used. For instance, here are some examples of the decimal equivalents of some hexadecimal numbers:

Hexadecimal	Decimal
0x0	0
0x1	1
0x9	9
0xA	10
0xB	11
0xF	15
0x10	16
0x11	17
0x1C	28

1. Convert 0xC3E (in hexadecimal notation) into an octal number.

2. Convert 0377 (in octal notation) into a hexadecimal number.

3. Discuss how, in general, you would convert a hexadecimal number into an octal number and an octal number into a hexadecimal number.

CHAPTER 2
Programming Building Blocks—Java Basics

CHAPTER CONTENTS

Introduction

If we boil it down to the basics, a program has two elements: instructions and data. The instructions tell the CPU what to do with the data. Typically, a program's structure will consist of the following operations:

1. Input the data.

2. Perform some processing on the data.

3. Output the results.

The data used by a program can come from a variety of sources. The user can enter data from the keyboard, for example, when we type a new document into a word processor. The program can read the data from a file, for example, when we load an existing document into the word processor. Or the program can generate the data randomly, for example, when a computer card game deals hands. Finally, some data is already known; for example, the number of hours in a day is 24, the number of days in December is 31, and the value of pi is 3.14159. This type of data is constant. The Java language provides a syntax for describing a program's data using keywords, symbolic names, and data types.

Although the data may be different in each execution of the program, the instructions stay the same. In a word processor, the words (data) are different from document to document, but the operation (instructions) of the word processor remains the same. When a line becomes full, for example, the word processor automatically wraps to the next line. It doesn't matter which words are on the line, only that the line is full. When we select a word and change the font to bold, it doesn't matter which word we select; it will become bold. Thus, a program's instructions (its algorithm) must be written to correctly handle any data it may receive.

We will write our programs by translating our algorithms into the basic operations that the computer can perform: input and output of data and various operations related to processing data, such as arithmetic calculations, comparisons of data and subsequent changes to the flow of control, and movement of data from one location in memory to another.

In this chapter, we'll look at basic Java syntax for defining the data to be used in the program, performing calculations on that data, and outputting program results to the screen.

2.1   Java Application Structure

Every Java program consists of at least one class. It is impossible to write a Java program that doesn't use classes. Classes describe a logical entity that has data as well as methods (the instructions) to manipulate that data. An object is a physical instantiation of the class that contains specific data. In Example 2.1 we provide a shell that contains the basic format of a Java application with a class name of *ShellApplication*. Our source code will use this format, changing the class name as appropriate.

```
1  /* An application shell
2     Anderson, Franceschi
3  */
4  public class ShellApplication
5  {
6    public static void main( String [ ] args ) // required
7    {
8       // write your code here
9    }
10 }
```

EXAMPLE 2.1   A Shell for a Java Application

In Example 2.1, the numbers to the left of each line are not part of the program code; they are included here for our convenience. IDEs typically allow us to display line numbers.

From application to application, the name of the class, *ShellApplication*, will change, because we will want to name our class something meaningful that reflects its function. Each Java source code file must have the same name as the class name with a *.java* extension. In this case, the source file must be *ShellApplication.java*. Whatever name we select for a class must comply with the Java syntax for identifiers.

Java **identifiers** are symbolic names that we assign to classes, methods, and data. Identifiers must start with a **Java letter** and may contain any combination of letters and digits, but no spaces. A Java letter is any character in the range *a–z* or *A–Z*, the underscore (_), or the dollar sign ($), as well as many Unicode characters that are used as letters in other languages. Digits are any character between 0 and 9. The length of an identifier is essentially unlimited. Identifier names are case sensitive, so *Number1* and *number1* are considered to be different identifiers.

In addition, none of Java's **reserved words** can be used as identifiers. These reserved words, which are listed in Appendix A, consist of keywords used in Java instructions, as well as three special data values: *true*, *false*, and *null*. As of Java 9, the single underscore (_) is a reserved word and cannot be used as an identifier. Given that Java identifiers are case sensitive, note that it is legal to use *True* or *TRUE* as identifiers, but *true* is not a legal variable name. Table 2.1 lists the rules for creating Java identifiers.

The shell code in Example 2.1 uses four identifiers: *ShellApplication*, *main*, *String*, and *args*. The remainder of Example 2.1 consists of comments, Java keywords, and required punctuation.

SOFTWARE
ENGINEERING
TIP
Liberal use of
white space
makes your
program more
readable.
It is good
programming
style to surround
identifiers,
operands, and
operators with
spaces and
to skip lines
between logical
sections of the
program.

The basic building block of a Java program is the **statement**. A statement is terminated with a semicolon and can span several lines.

Any amount of **white space** is permitted between identifiers, Java keywords, operands, operators, and literals. White space characters are the space, tab, newline, carriage return, and a few other rarely used characters. Liberal use of white space makes our program more readable. It is good programming style to surround identifiers, operands, and operators with spaces and to skip lines between logical sections of the program.

A **block**, which consists of 0, 1, or more statements, starts with a left curly brace ({) and ends with a right curly brace (}). Blocks are required for class and method definitions and can be used anywhere else in the program that a statement is legal. Example 2.1 has two blocks: the class definition (lines 5 through 10) and the *main* method definition (lines 7 through 9). As we can see, nesting blocks within blocks is perfectly legal. The *main* block is nested completely within the class definition block.

SOFTWARE
ENGINEERING
TIP
Include a block
comment at the
beginning of
each source file
that identifies
the author of
the program and
briefly describes
the function of
the program.

Comments document the operation of the program and are notes to ourselves and to other programmers who read our code. Comments are not compiled and can be coded in two ways. **Block comments** can span several lines; they begin with a forward slash-asterisk (/*) and end with an asterisk-forward slash (*/). Everything between the /* and the */ is ignored by the compiler. Note that there are no spaces between the asterisk and forward slash. Lines 1–3 in Example 2.1 are block comments and illustrate the good software engineering practice of providing at the beginning of our source code a few comments that identify ourselves as the author and briefly describe what the program does.

The second way to include comments in our code is to precede the comment with two forward slashes (//). There are no spaces between the forward slashes. The compiler ignores everything from the two forward slashes to the end of the line. In Example 2.1, the compiler ignores all of line 8, but only the part of line 6 after the two forward slashes.

TABLE 2.1   Rules for Creating Identifiers

Java Identifiers
▪ Must start with a Java letter (*A–Z, a–z, _, $*, or many Unicode characters)
▪ Can contain an almost unlimited number of letters and/or digits (0–9)
▪ Cannot contain spaces
▪ Are case sensitive
▪ Cannot be a Java reserved word

Let's look at an example to get a sense of what a simple program looks like and to get a feel for how a program operates. Example 2.2 calculates the area of a circle.

```java
1 /* Calculate the area of a circle
2    Anderson, Franceschi
3 */
4
5 public class AreaOfCircle
6 {
7   public static void main( String [ ] args )
8   {
9      // define the data we know
10     final double PI = 3.14159;
11
12     // define other data we will use
13     double radius = 3.5;
14
15     // perform the calculation and store the result
16     double area = PI * radius * radius;
17
18     // output the result
19     System.out.println( "The area of the circle is " + area );
20   }
21 }
```

EXAMPLE 2.2   Calculating the Area of a Circle

Figure 2.1a shows the output when the program is run with a radius of 3.5. To calculate the area of a circle with a different radius, replace the value 3.5 in line 13 with the new radius value. For example, to calculate the area of a circle with a radius of 20, change line 13 to

```java
double radius = 20;
```

Then recompile the program and run it again. Figure 2.1b shows the output for a radius of 20.

```
The area of the circle is 38.4844775
```

Figure 2.1a

Output from Example 2.2 with a Radius of 3.5

```
The area of the circle is 1256.636
```

Figure 2.1b

Output from Example 2.2 with a Radius of 20

We can see that Example 2.2 has the basic elements that we saw in the *ShellApplication* (Example 2.1). We have added some statements in lines 9 through 19 that do the work of the program. First, we identify the data we will need. To calculate the area of a circle, we use the formula (πr^2). We know the value of π (3.14159), so we store that value in a memory location we name PI (line 10). We also need places in memory to hold the radius and the area. In line 13 we name the radius and, we give the radius a value; here we have chosen 3.5, but our program will need to work with any value for the radius.

Now we're ready to calculate the area. We want this program to output correct results with any radius, so we need to write the algorithm of the program using the formula for calculating a circle's area given above. Java provides arithmetic operators for performing calculations. We use Java's multiplication operator (*) in line 16 to multiply PI times the radius times the radius and store the result into the memory location we named *area*. Now we're ready to output the result. On line 19, we write a message that includes the *area* value we calculated.

With Java 9, we have another option to running Java code. If we just want to try out some Java code without writing a complete application, we can use the **jshell** utility. The jshell utility is an REPL (Read, Evaluate, Print, Loop) tool that allows us to type small amounts of code, called snippets, and see the immediate result without compiling. Some IDEs (Integrated Development Environments) already provide an interactive utility like jshell. For example, jGRASP (*jgrasp.org*) provides an Interactions tool. We will use jshell to illustrate many concepts in this chapter. You will find jshell in the *bin* folder where the Java JDK is stored. If you have already updated your classpath environment variable for javac and java, then it is automatically set for jshell because these three programs are in the same folder. Consult your operating system instructions for details about setting the classpath.

To use jshell, open a command line application and launch jshell. To try out some code, simply type it at the prompt. To see a complete list of jshell commands, type */help*. As you will see, jshell commands start with a forward slash (/). To exit jshell, type */exit*.

2.2 Data Types, Variables, and Constants

In Example 2.2, we used as data the value of PI and the radius, and we calculated the area of the circle. For each of these values, we assigned a name. We also used the Java keyword *double,* which defines the **data type** of the data. The keyword *double* means that the value will be a floating-point number.

Java allows us to refer to the data in a program by defining **variables**, which are named locations in memory where we can store values. A variable can store one data value at a time, but that value might change as the program executes, and it might change from one execution of the program to the next. The real advantage of using variables is that we can name a variable, assign it a value, and subsequently refer to the name of the variable in an expression rather than hard coding the specific value.

When we use a named variable, we need to tell the compiler which kind of data we will store in the variable. We do this by giving a data type for each variable.

Java supports eight primitive data types: *byte, short, int, long, float, double, char,* and *boolean*. They are called primitive data types because they are part of the core Java language.

The data type we specify for a variable tells the compiler how much memory to allocate and the format in which to store the data. For example, if we specify that a data item is an *int*, then the compiler will allocate four bytes of memory and store its value as a 32-bit signed binary number. If, however, we specify that a data item is a *double* (a double-precision floating-point number), then the compiler will allocate 8 bytes of memory and store its value as a double-precision IEEE 754 floating-point number.

Once we declare a data type for a data item, the compiler will monitor our use of that data item. If we attempt to perform operations that are not allowed for that type or are not compatible with that type, the compiler will generate an error. Because the Java compiler monitors the operations on each data item, Java is called a **strongly typed language**.

Take care in selecting identifiers for your programs. The identifiers should be meaningful and should reflect the data that will be stored in a variable, the concept encapsulated by a class, or the function of a method. For example, the identifier *age* clearly indicates that the variable will hold the age of a person. When we select meaningful variable names, the logic of our program is more easily understood, and we are less likely to introduce errors. Sometimes, it may be necessary to create a long identifier in order to clearly indicate its use, for example, *numberOfStudentsWhoPassedCS1*. Although the length of identifiers is essentially unlimited, avoid creating extremely long identifiers because they are more cumbersome to use. Also, the longer the identifier, the more likely we are to make typos when entering the identifier into our program. Finally, although it is legal to use identifiers, such as *TRUE*, which differ from Java keywords only in case, it isn't a good idea because they easily can be confused with Java keywords, making the program logic less clear.

SOFTWARE ENGINEERING TIP

When selecting identifiers, choose meaningful names that reflect the use of the identifier in the program; this will make your code self-documented. Use as many characters as necessary to make the identifier clear, but avoid extremely long identifiers. Also, for clarity in your program logic, avoid identifiers that resemble Java keywords.

2.2.1 Declaring Variables

Every variable must be given a name and a data type before it can be used. This is called **declaring a variable**.

The syntax for declaring a variable is:

```
dataType identifier; // this declares one variable
```

or

```
dataType identifier1, identifier2, ...; // this declares multiple
                                        // variables of the same
                                        // data type
```

Note that a comma follows each identifier in the list except the last identifier, which is followed by a semicolon.

SOFTWARE ENGINEERING TIP

Begin variable names with a lowercase letter. If the variable name consists of more than one word, begin each word after the first with a capital letter. Avoid underscores in variable names, and do not begin a variable name with a dollar sign.

By convention, the identifiers for variable names should start with a lowercase letter. If the variable name consists of more than one word, then each word after the first should begin with a capital letter. For example, these identifiers are conventional Java variable names: *number1*, *highScore*, *booksToRead*, *ageInYears*, and *xAxis*. Underscores conventionally are not used in variable names; they are reserved for the identifiers of constants, as we shall discuss later in the chapter. Similarly, do not use dollar signs to begin variable names. The dollar sign is reserved for the first letter of programmatically generated variable names—that is, variable names generated by software, not people. Although this may sound arbitrary now, the value of following these conventions will become clearer as we gain more experience in Java and our programs become more complex.

2.2.2 Integer Data Types

An integer data type is one that evaluates to a positive or negative whole number. Java provides four integer data types: *int*, *short*, *long*, and *byte*.

The *int*, *short*, *long*, and *byte* types differ in the number of bytes of memory allocated to store each type and, therefore, the maximum and minimum values that can be stored in a variable of that type. All of Java's integer types are signed, meaning that they can be positive or negative; the high-order, or leftmost, bit is reserved for the sign.

Table 2.2 summarizes the integer data types, their sizes in memory, and their maximum and minimum values.

In most applications, the *int* type will be sufficient for our needs, since it can store positive and negative numbers into the 2 billion range. The *short* and *byte* data types typically are used only when memory space is critical, and the *long* data type is needed only for data values larger than 2 billion.

Let's look at some examples of integer variable declarations. Note that the variable names clearly indicate the data that the variables will hold.

```
int testGrade;
int numPlayers, highScore, diceRoll;
short xCoordinate, yCoordinate;
long cityPopulation;
byte ageInYears;
```

2.2.3 Floating-Point Data Types

Floating-point data types store numbers with fractional parts. Java supports two floating-point data types: the single-precision *float* and the double-precision *double*.

The two types differ in the amount of memory allocated and the size and precision of the number that can be represented. The single-precision type (*float*) is stored in 32 bits, while the double-precision type (*double*) is stored in 64 bits. *Floats* and *doubles* can be positive or negative.

Table 2.3 summarizes Java's floating-point data types, their sizes in memory, and their maximum and minimum positive nonzero values.

Because of its greater precision, the *double* data type is usually preferred over the *float* data type. However, for calculations not requiring such precision, *floats* are often used because they require less memory.

Although integers can be stored as *doubles* or *floats*, it isn't advisable to do so because floating-point numbers require more processing time for calculations.

Let's look at a few examples of floating-point variable declarations:

```
float salesTax;
double interestRate;
double paycheck, sumSalaries;
```

REFERENCE POINT

Floating-point numbers are stored using the IEEE 754 standard, which is discussed in Appendix E.

TABLE 2.2 Integer Data Types

Integer Data Type	Size in Bytes	Minimum Value	Maximum Value
byte	1	−128	127
short	2	−32,768	32,767
int	4	−2,147,483,648	2,147,483,647
long	8	−9,223,372,036,854,775,808	9,223,372,036,854,775,807

TABLE 2.3   **Floating-Point Data Types**

Floating-Point Data Type	Size in Bytes	Minimum Positive Nonzero Value	Maximum Value
float	4	1.4E-45	3.4028235E38
double	8	4.9E-324	1.7976931348623157E308

2.2.4   Character Data Type

REFERENCE POINT
The encoding of ASCII and Unicode characters is discussed in Appendix C.

The *char* data type stores one Unicode character. Because Unicode characters are encoded as unsigned numbers using 16 bits, a *char* variable is stored in two bytes of memory.

Table 2.4 shows the size of the *char* data type, as well as the minimum and maximum values. The maximum value is the unsigned hexadecimal number *FFFF*, which is reserved as a special code for "not a character."

Obviously, since the *char* data type can store only a single character, such as a *K*, a *char* variable is not useful for storing names, titles, or other text data. For text data, Java provides a *String* class, which we'll discuss later in this chapter.

Here are a few declarations of *char* variables:

```
char finalGrade;
char middleInitial;
char newline, tab, doubleQuotes;
```

TABLE 2.4   **The Character Data Type**

Character Data Type	Size in Bytes	Minimum Value	Maximum Value
char	2	The character encoded as *0000*, the *null* character	The value *FFFF*, which is a special code for "not a character"

2.2.5   Boolean Data Type

The *boolean* data type can store only two values, which are expressed using the Java reserved words *true* and *false*, as shown in Table 2.5.

Booleans are typically used for decision making and for controlling the order of execution of a program.

TABLE 2.5   The *boolean* Data Type

boolean Data Type	Possible Values
boolean	*true*
	false

Here are examples of declarations of *boolean* variables:

```
boolean isEmpty;
boolean passed, failed;
```

2.2.6   The Assignment Operator, Initial Values, and Literals

When we declare a variable, we can also assign an initial value for the data. To do that, we use the **assignment operator** (=) with the following syntax:

```
dataType variableName = initialValue;
```

This statement is read as "*variableName* **gets** *initialValue*".

or

```
dataType variable1 = initialValue1, variable2 = initialValue2;
```

Notice that assignment is right to left. The initial value is assigned to the variable.

One way to specify the initial value is by using a **literal value**. In the following statement, the value *100* is an *int* literal value, which is assigned to the variable *testGrade*.

```
int testGrade = 100;
```

Table 2.6 summarizes the legal characters in literals for all primitive data types.

Notice in Table 2.6 under the literal format for *char*, that \n and \t can be used to format output. We'll discuss these and other escape sequences in the next section of this chapter.

Example 2.3 shows a jshell session where we declare variables and assign a value using a literal. We then execute the jshell */vars* command to see our variables and their values.

Another way to specify an initial value for a variable is to assign the variable the value of another variable, using this syntax:

```
dataType variable2 = variable1;
```

COMMON ERROR TRAP
Although Unicode characters occupy two bytes in memory, they still represent a single character. Therefore, a literal value must also represent only one character.

Two things need to be true for this assignment to work:

- *variable1* needs to be declared and assigned a value before this statement appears in the source code.

- *variable1* and *variable2* need to be compatible data types; in other words, the precision of *variable1* must be lower than or equal to that of *variable2*.

TABLE 2.6   Literal Formats for Java Data Types

Data Type	Literal Format
int, short, byte	Optional initial sign (+ or −) followed by digits 0–9 in any combination. A literal in this format is an *int* literal; however, an *int* literal may be assigned to a *byte* or *short* variable if the literal is a legal value for the assigned data type. An integer literal that begins with a 0 digit is considered to be an octal number (base 8) and the remaining digits must be 0–7. An integer literal that begins with 0x is considered to be a hexadecimal number (base 16) and the remaining digits must be 0–9 or A–F.
long	Optional initial sign (+ or −) followed by digits 0–9 in any combination, terminated with an *L* or *l*. It's preferable to use the capital *L*, because the lowercase *l* can be confused with the number *1*. An integer literal that begins with a 0 digit is considered to be an octal number (base 8) and the remaining digits must be 0–7. An integer literal that begins with 0x is considered to be a hexadecimal number (base 16) and the remaining digits must be 0–9 or A–F.
float	Optional initial sign (+ or −) followed by a floating-point number in fixed or scientific format, terminated by an *F* or *f*.
double	Optional initial sign (+ or −) followed by a floating-point number in fixed or scientific format.
char	- Any printable character enclosed in single quotes. - A decimal value from 0 to 65,535. - '\unnnn' where nnnn are hexadecimal digits. - '\m', where \m is an escape sequence. For example, '\n' represents a newline, and '\t' represents a tab character.
boolean	*true* or *false*

```
jshell> int testGrade = 100;
testGrade ==> 100

jshell> long cityPopulation = 425612340L;
cityPopulation ==> 425612340

jshell> byte numberOfPets = 2;
numberOfFPetS ==> 2

jshell> short ageInYears = 19;
ageInYears ==> 19

jshell> float salesTax = .05F;
salesTax ==> 0.05

jshell> double interestRate = 0.0425;
interestRate ==> 0.0425

jshell> double avogadroNumber = +6.022E23;
avogadroNumber ==> 6.022E23

jshell> char finalGrade = 'A';
finalGrade ==> 'A'

jshell> boolean isEmpty = true;
isEmpty ==> true

jshell> /vars
|    int testGrade = 100
|    long cityPopulation = 425612340
|    byte numberOfPets = 2
|    short ageInYears = 19
|    float salesTax = 0.05
|    double interestRate = 0.0425
|    double avogadroNumber = 6.022E23
|    char finalGrade = 'A'
|    boolean isEmpty = true

jshell>
```

EXAMPLE 2.3   Declaring and Initializing Variables

For example, in these statements:

```
jshell> boolean isPassingGrade = true;
isPassingGrade ==> true

jshell> boolean isPromoted = isPassingGrade;
isPromoted ==> true
```

isPassingGrade is given an initial value of *true*. Then *isPromoted* is assigned the value already given to *isPassingGrade*. Thus, *isPromoted* is also assigned the initial value *true*. If *isPassingGrade* were assigned the initial value *false*, then *isPromoted* would also be assigned the initial value *false*.

And in these statements,

```
jshell> float salesTax = .05f;
sales Tax ==> 0.05

jshell> double taxRate = salesTax;
taxRate ==> 0.05000000074505806
```

the initial value of .05 is assigned to *salesTax* and then to *taxRate*. It's legal to assign a *float* value to a *double*, because all values that can be stored as *floats* are also valid *double* values. Note that after assigning the *float* value to the *double,* that *taxRate* has some extraneous digits. This is due to rounding errors when converting the *float* value to a *double*. Essentially, the two values are equivalent.

However, assigning a *double* value to a *float* variable is *not* valid:

```
jshell> double taxRate = .05;
taxRate ==> 0.05

jshell> float salesTax = taxRate;
|  Error:
|  incompatible types: possible lossy conversion from double to float
|  float salesTax = taxRate;
                    ^    ^
                    _  _ _
```

Even though .05 is a valid *float* value, the compiler will generate a "possible lossy conversion" error similar to the error shown in jshell above.

Similarly, we can assign a lower-precision integer value to a higher-precision integer variable.

Table 2.7 summarizes compatible data types; a variable or literal of any type in the right column can be assigned to a variable of the data type in the left column.

Variables need to be declared before they can be used in our program, but be careful to declare each variable only once; that is, specify the data type of the variable only the first time that variable is used in the program. If we attempt to declare a variable that has already been declared, as in the following statements:

```
double twoCents;
double twoCents = 2; // incorrect, second declaration of twoCents
```

TABLE 2.7 Valid Data Types for Assignment

Data Type	Compatible Data Types
byte	byte
short	byte, short
int	byte, short, int, char
long	byte, short, int, char, long
float	byte, short, int, char, long, float
double	byte, short, int, char, long, float, double
boolean	boolean
char	char

we will receive a compiler error similar to the following:

```
twoCents is already defined
```

Similarly, once we have declared a variable, we cannot change its data type. Thus, these statements:

```
double cashInHand;
int cashInHand; // incorrect, data type cannot be changed
```

will generate a compiler error similar to the following:

```
cashInHand is already defined
```

COMMON ERROR TRAP
Declare each variable only once, the first time the variable is used. After the variable has been declared, its data type cannot be changed.

CODE IN ACTION

Within the online resources, you will find a movie showing a step-by-step illustration of declaring variables and assigning initial values. Click on this chapter's link to start the movie.

© Hemera Technologies/
Photos.com/Thinkstock

2.2.7 *String* Literals and Escape Sequences

In addition to literals for all the primitive data types, Java also supports *String* literals. *String* literals are objects of Java's *String* class.

A *String* **literal** is a sequence of characters enclosed by double quotes. One set of quotes "opens" the *String* literal and the second set of quotes "closes" the literal. For example, these are all *String* literals:

```
"Hello"
"Hello world"
"The value of x is "
```

We used *String* literals in output statements in Example 2.2 to label the data that we printed:

```
System.out.println( "The area of the circle is " + area );
```

The + operator is the *String* **concatenation operator**. Among other uses, the concatenation operator allows us to print the values of variables along with *String* literals. As we can see from the output of Example 2.2, the characters in the *String* literal are output exactly as typed, whereas the variable *area* is replaced by its current value.

String literals cannot extend over more than one line. If the compiler finds a newline character in the middle of a *String* literal, it will generate a compiler error. For example, the following statement is not valid:

SOFTWARE ENGINEERING TIP
Add a space to the end of a *String* literal before concatenating a value for more readable output.

```
System.out.println( "Never pass a water fountain
                without taking a drink." );
```

In fact, that statement will generate errors:

```
jshell> System.out.println( "Never pass a water fountain
|  Error:
|  unclosed string literal
|  System.out.println( "Never pass a water fountain
|                      ^
```

COMMON ERROR TRAP
All open quotes for a *String* literal should be matched with a set of closing quotes, and the closing quotes must appear before the line ends.

If we have a long *String* to print, break it into several strings and use the concatenation operator. This statement is a correction of the previous invalid statement:

```
jshell> System.out.println( "Never pass a water fountain"
   ...>                      + "without taking a drink." );
Never pass a water fountain without taking a drink.
```

Another common programming error is omitting the closing quotes. Be sure that all open quotes have matching closing quotes on the same line.

Now that we know that quotes open and close *String* literals, how can we define a literal that includes quotes? This statement, which has quotes inside a *String* literal

```
System.out.println( "She said, "Java is fun"."); // illegal quotes
                                                 // within literal
```

generates this error:

```
jshell> System.out.println( "She said, "Java is fun"." );
|  Error:
|  ')' expected
|  System.out.println( "She said, "Java is fun"." );
|                             ^
```

And since *String* literals can't extend over two lines, how can we create a *String* literal that includes a newline character? Java solves both problems by providing a set of escape sequences that can be used to include a special character within *String* and *char* literals. The escape sequences \n, \t, \b, \r, and \f are nonprintable characters. Table 2.8 lists the Java escape sequences.

Using the \" escape character, we can now output embedded quotes as:

```
jshell> System.out.println( "She said, \"Java is fun\"." );
She said, "Java is fun".
```

We can force part of the output to the next line by inserting a \n escape character, as in:

```
jshell> System.out.println( "One potato\nTwo potatoes" );
One potato
Two potatoes
```

TABLE 2.8   Java Escape Sequences

Character	Escape Sequence
newline	\n
tab	\t
double quotes	\"
single quote	\'
backslash	\\
backspace	\b
carriage return	\r
form feed	\f

We will find that the \n escape character is useful for skipping lines in output.

Finally, we can format output by inserting \t where we want a tab, as in:

```
jshell> System.out.println( "\tTabs can make the output easier to read." );
        Tabs can make the output easier to read.
```

2.2.8   Constants

Sometimes we know the value of a data item, and we know that its value will not (and should not) change during program execution, nor is it likely to change from one execution of the program to another. In this case, it is a good software engineering practice to define that data item as a **constant**.

Defining constants uses the same syntax as declaring variables, except that the data type is preceded by the keyword *final*.

```
final dataType CONSTANT_IDENTIFIER = assignedValue;
```

Assigning a value is optional when the constant is defined, but we must assign a value before the constant is used in the program. Also, once the constant has been assigned a value, its value cannot be changed (reassigned) later in the program. Any attempt by our program to change the value of a constant will generate the following compiler error:

```
cannot assign a value to final variable
```

Think of this as a service of the compiler in preventing our program from unintentionally corrupting its data.

By convention, *CONSTANT_IDENTIFIER* consists of all capital letters, and embedded words are separated by an underscore. This makes constants stand out in the code and easily identified as constants. Also, constants are usually defined at the top of a program where their values can be seen easily.

Example 2.4 shows how to use constants in a program.

```
1 /* Constants Class
2    Anderson, Franceschi
3 */
4
5 public class Constants
6 {
7     public static void main( String [ ] args )
8     {
9             final char ZORRO = 'Z';
```

```
10              final double PI = 3.14159;
11              final int DAYS_IN_LEAP_YEAR = 366, DAYS_IN_NON_LEAP_YEAR = 365;
12
13              System.out.println( "The value of constant ZORRO is " + ZORRO );
14              System.out.println( "The value of constant PI is " + PI );
15              System.out.println( "The number of days in a leap year is "
16                                      + DAYS_IN_LEAP_YEAR );
17              System.out.println( "The number of days in a non-leap year is "
18                                      + DAYS_IN_NON_LEAP_YEAR );
19
20              // PI = 3.14;
21              // The statement above would generate a compiler error
22              // You cannot change the value of a constant
23      }
24 }
```

EXAMPLE 2.4   Using Constants

SOFTWARE ENGINEERING TIP
Use all capital letters for a constant's identifier; separate words with an underscore (_). Declare constants at the top of the program so their value can be seen easily.

Lines 9, 10, and 11 define four constants. On line 11, note that both *DAYS_IN_LEAP_YEAR* and *DAYS_IN_NON_LEAP_YEAR* are constants. We don't need to repeat the keyword final to define two (or more) constants of the same data types. Lines 13 to 18 output the values of the four constants. If line 20 were not commented out, it would generate a compiler error because once a constant is assigned a value, its value cannot be changed. Figure 2.2 shows the output of Example 2.4.

Constants can make our code more readable: PI is more meaningful than 3.14159 when used inside an arithmetic expression. Another advantage of using constants is to keep programmers from making logic errors: Let's say we set a constant to a particular value and it is used at various places throughout the code (for instance, a constant representing a tax rate); we then discover that the value of that constant needs to be changed. All we have to do is make the change in one place, most likely at the beginning of the code. If we had to change the value at many places throughout the code, that could very well result in logic errors or typos.

SOFTWARE ENGINEERING TIP
Declare as a constant any data that should not change during program execution. The compiler will then flag any attempts by your program to change the value of the constant, thus preventing any unintentional corruption of the data.

```
The value of constant ZORRO is Z
The value of constant PI is 3.14159
The number of days in a leap year is 366
The number of days in a non-leap year is 365
```

Figure 2.2

Output of Example 2.4

Skill Practice
with these end-of-chapter questions

2.6.1	Multiple Choice	
	Questions 1, 2	
2.6.2	Reading and Understanding Code	
	Questions 4, 5, 6	
2.6.3	Fill In the Code	
	Questions 23, 24, 25, 26	
2.6.4	Identifying Errors in Code	
	Questions 33, 34, 38, 39	
2.6.5	Debugging Area	
	Questions 40, 41	
2.6.6	Write a Short Program	
	Question 46	
2.6.8	Technical Writing	
	Question 52	

2.3   Expressions and Arithmetic Operators

2.3.1   The Assignment Operator and Expressions

In a previous section, we mentioned using the assignment operator to assign initial values to variables and constants. Now let's look at the assignment operator in more detail.

The syntax for the assignment operator is:

```
target = expression;
```

An expression consists of operators and operands that evaluate to a single value. The value of the expression is then assigned to *target* (*target* gets *expression*), which must be a variable or a constant having a data type compatible with the value of the expression.

If *target* is a variable, the value of the expression replaces any previous value the variable was holding. For example, let's look at these instructions:

```
jshell> int numberOfPlayers = 10;
numberOfPlayers ==> 10

jshell> numberOfPlayers = 8;
numberOfPlayers ==> 8

jshell> /vars
|    int numberOfPlayers = 8
```

The first instruction declares an *int* named *numberOfPlayers*. This allocates four bytes in memory to a variable named *numberOfPlayers* and stores the value 10 in that variable. Then, the second statement changes the value stored in the variable *numberOfPlayers* to 8. The previous value, 10, is discarded. Note that we do not repeat "*int*." As mentioned earlier, we declare the data type only the first time we use a variable.

An expression can be a single variable name or a literal of any type, in which case, the value of the expression is simply the value of the variable or the literal. For example, in these statements,

```
jshell>  int legalAge = 18;
legalAge  ==> 18

jshell> int voterAge = legalAge;
voterAge ==> 18
```

the literal 18 is an expression. Its value is 18, which is assigned to the variable *legalAge*. Then, in the second statement, *legalAge* is an expression, whose value is 18. Thus, the value 18 is assigned to *voterAge*. So after these statements have been executed, both *legalAge* and *voterAge* will have the value 18.

One restriction, however, is that an assignment expression cannot include another variable unless that variable has been defined previously. The statement defining the *length* variable that follows is **invalid**, because it refers to *width*, which is not defined until the next line.

```
int length = width * 2; // invalid, width is not yet defined
int width = 30;
```

The compiler will flag the statement defining *length* as an error with a message similar to the one in the jshell session below

```
jshell> int length = width * 2;
|  Error:
|  cannot find symbol
|    symbol: variable width
|  int length = width * 2;
|
|                ^---^
```

TABLE 2.9   Arithmetic Operators

Operator	Operation
+	addition
−	subtraction
*	multiplication
/	division
%	modulus (remainder after division)

because *width* has not yet been defined.

An expression can be quite complex, consisting of multiple variables, constants, literals, and operators. Before we can look at examples of more complex expressions, however, we need to discuss the **arithmetic operators**.

2.3.2   Arithmetic Operators

Java's arithmetic operators are used for performing calculations on numeric data. Some of these operators are shown in Table 2.9.

All these operators take two operands; thus, they are called **binary operators**. Each operand is an expression.

In Example 2.5, we make a variety of calculations to demonstrate the addition, subtraction, multiplication, and division arithmetic operators. We will discuss integer division and the modulus operator later in the chapter. The output from this program is shown in Figure 2.3.

```
 1 /* Arithmetic Operators
 2    Anderson, Franceschi
 3 */
 4
 5 public class ArithmeticOperators
 6 {
 7   public static void main( String [ ] args )
 8   {
 9     // calculate the cost of lunch
10     double salad = 5.95;
11     double water = .89;
12     System.out.println( "The cost of lunch is $"
13                       + ( salad + water ) );
14
```

```
15       // calculate your age as of a certain year
16       int targetYear = 2025;
17       int birthYear = 2005;
18       System.out.println( "Your age in " + targetYear + " is "
19                             + ( targetYear - birthYear ) );
20
21       // calculate the total calories of apples
22       int caloriesPerApple = 127;
23       int numberOfApples = 3;
24       System.out.println( "The calories in " + numberOfApples
25                             + " apples is " +
26                             + ( caloriesPerApple * numberOfApples ) );
27
28       // calculate miles per gallon
29       double miles = 426.8;
30       double gallons = 15.2;
31       double mileage = miles / gallons;
32       System.out.println( "The mileage is "
33                             + mileage + " miles per gallon." );
34   }
35 }
```

EXAMPLE 2.5   Using Arithmetic Operators

Example 2.5 demonstrates a number of small operations. To calculate a total price
(lines 12 and 13), we add the individual prices. To calculate an age (lines 18 and 19),
we subtract the birth year from the target year. To calculate the number of calories
in multiple apples (lines 24–26), we multiply the number of calories in one apple by
the number of apples. We calculate miles per gallon by dividing the number of miles
driven by the number of gallons of gas used (line 31). Note that we can either store the
result in another variable, as we did in line 31, and subsequently output the result (lines
32–33), or we can output the result of the calculation directly by writing the expression
in the *System.out.println* statement, as we did in the other calculations in this example.

SOFTWARE
ENGINEERING
TIP
For readable
code, insert a
space between
operators and
operands.

SOFTWARE
ENGINEERING
TIP
Developing and
testing your
code in steps
makes it easier
to find and fix
errors.

2.3.3   Operator Precedence

The statements in Example 2.5 perform simple calculations, but what if we want
to make more complex calculations using several operations, such as calculating
how much money we have in coins? Let's say we have two quarters, three dimes,

```
The cost of lunch is $6.84
Your age in 2025 is 20
The calories in 3 apples is 381
The mileage is 28.078947368421055 miles per gallon.
```

Figure 2.3

Output from
Example 2.5

and two nickels. To calculate the value of these coins in pennies, we might use this expression:

```
int pennies = 2 * 25 + 3 * 10 + 2 * 5;
```

In which order should the computer do the calculation? If the value of the expression were calculated left to right, then the result would be

```
= 2 * 25 + 3 * 10 + 2 * 5
=    50   + 3 * 10 + 2 * 5
=         53   * 10 + 2 * 5
=              530   + 2 * 5
=                    532 * 5
=                        2660
```

Clearly, 2,660 pennies is not the right answer. To calculate the correct number of pennies, the multiplications should be performed first, then the additions. This, in fact, is the order in which Java will calculate the preceding expression.

The Java compiler follows a set of rules called **operator precedence** to determine the order in which the operations should be performed.

Table 2.10 provides the order of precedence of the operators we've discussed so far. The operators in the first row—parentheses—are evaluated first, then the operators in the second row (*, /, %) are evaluated, and so on with the operators in each row. When two or more operators on the same level appear in the same expression, the order of evaluation is left to right, except for the assignment operator, which is evaluated right to left.

As we introduce more operators, we'll add them to the Order of Precedence chart. The complete chart is provided in Appendix B.

Using Table 2.10 as a guide, let's recalculate the number of pennies:

TABLE 2.10   Operator Precedence

Operator Hierarchy	Order of Same-Statement Evaluation	Operation
()	left to right	parentheses for explicit grouping
*, /, %	left to right	multiplication, division, modulus
+, −	left to right	addition, subtraction
=	right to left	assignment

```
int pennies = 2 * 25 +  3 * 10 + 2 * 5;
            =   50   +    30   +   10
            = 90
```

As we can see, *90* is the correct number of pennies in two quarters, three dimes, and two nickels.

We also could have used parentheses to clearly display the order of calculation. For example,

```
int pennies = ( 2 * 25 ) + ( 3 * 10 ) + ( 2 * 5 );
            =      50    +     30    +     10
            =      90
```

The result is the same, 90 pennies as shown below:

```
jshell> int pennies = 2 * 25 + 3 * 10 + 2 * 5;
pennies ==> 90

jshell> pennies = ( 2 * 25 ) + ( 3 * 10 ) + ( 2 * 5 );
pennies ==> 90
```

It sometimes helps to use parentheses to clarify the order of calculations, but parentheses are essential when our desired order of evaluation is different from the rules of operator precedence. For example, to calculate the value of this formula:

$$\frac{x}{2+y}$$

we could write this code:

```
double result = x / 2 + y;
```

This would generate incorrect results because, according to the rules of precedence, *x/2* would be calculated first, then *y* would be added to the result of that division. In algebraic terms, the preceding statement is equivalent to:

$$\frac{x}{2} + y$$

To code the original formula correctly, we need to use parentheses to force the addition to occur before the division:

```
double result = x / ( 2 + y );
```

2.3.4 Programming Activity 1: Converting Inches to Centimeters

Now that we know how to define variables and constants and make calculations, let's put this all together by writing a program that converts inches into the equivalent centimeters.

Locate the *MetricLength.java* source file found in this chapter's Programming Activity 1 folder in the supplied code files. Copy the file to your computer.

Open the *MetricLength.java* source file. You'll notice that the class already contains some source code. Your job is to fill in the blanks.

When we write a program, we begin by considering these questions:

1. What data values does the program require?

    a. What data values do we know?

    b. What data values will change from one execution of the program to the next?

2. What processing (algorithm) do we need to implement?

3. What is the output?

The comments in the source file will guide you through the answers to these questions, and by doing so, you will complete the program. Search for five asterisks in a row (*****). This will position you to the places in the source code where you will add your code. The *MetricLength.java* source code is shown in Example 2.6. Sample output for a value of 5.2 inches is shown in Figure 2.4.

Figure 2.4

Sample Output for Programming Activity 1

```
5.2 inches are equivalent to 13.208 centimeters.
```

```
 1 /* MetricLength - converts inches to centimeters
 2    Anderson, Franceschi
 3 */
 4
 5 public class MetricLength
 6 {
 7   public static void main( String [ ] args )
 8   {
 9
10     /***** 1. What data values do we know?
11         We know that there are 2.54 centimeters in an inch.
12         Declare a double constant named CM_PER_INCH.
13         Assign CM_PER_INCH the value 2.54.
14     */
15
16
17     /***** 2. What other data does the program require?
18         For this program, we require the number of inches.
19         Declare a double variable named inches.
20         Assign any desired value to this variable.
```

```
21      */
22
23
24      /***** 3. Calculation: convert inches to centimeters
25         Declare a double variable named centimeters.
26         Multiply inches by CM_PER_INCH
27         and store the result in centimeters.
28      */
29
30
31      /***** 4. Output
32         Write one or two statements that output
33         the original inches and the equivalent centimeters.
34         Try to match the sample output in Figure 2.4
35      */
36
37
38
39  }
40 }
```

EXAMPLE 2.6 Converting Inches to Centimeters

? DISCUSSION QUESTIONS

1. **How do you know that your program results are correct?**

2. **If you change the inches data value, does your program still produce correct results?**

2.3.5 Integer Division and Modulus

Division of a floating-point number by another floating-point number will result in a floating-point number; that is, a number with a fractional part. This is like the result you would receive using a calculator. For example, 12.6 / 2.4 will yield 5.25.

Division with two integer operands, however, is performed in the Arithmetic Logic Unit (ALU), which can calculate only an integer result. Any fractional part is truncated; no rounding is performed. The remainder after division is available, however, as an integer, by taking the modulus (%) of the two integer operands. Thus, in Java, the integer division (/) operator will calculate the quotient of the division, whereas the modulus (%) operator will calculate the remainder of the division.

In Example 2.7, we have 113 pennies and we want to convert those pennies into quarters. We can find the number of quarters by dividing 113 by 25. The *int* variable *pennies* is assigned the value 113 at line 10. At line 12, the variable *quarters* is assigned the result of the integer division of *pennies* by the constant *PENNIES_PER_QUARTER*. Since the quotient of the division of 113 by 25 is 4, *quarters* will be assigned 4. At line 16, we use the modulus operator to assign to the variable *penniesLeftOver* the remainder of the division of *pennies* by *PENNIES_PER_QUARTER*. Since the remainder of the division of 113 by 25 is 13, 13 will be assigned to *penniesLeftOver*. Notice that integer division and modulus are independent calculations. We can perform a division without also calculating the modulus, and we can calculate the modulus without performing the division.

```
 1 /* DivisionAndModulus Class
 2     Anderson, Franceschi
 3 */
 4
 5 public class DivisionAndModulus
 6 {
 7   public static void main( String [ ] args )
 8   {
 9     final int PENNIES_PER_QUARTER = 25;
10     int pennies = 113;
11
12     int quarters = pennies / PENNIES_PER_QUARTER;
13     System.out.println( "There are " + quarters + " quarters in "
14             + pennies + " pennies" );
15
16     int penniesLeftOver = pennies % PENNIES_PER_QUARTER;
17     System.out.println( "There are " + penniesLeftOver
18             + " pennies left over" );
19
20     final double MONTHS_PER_YEAR = 12;
21     double annualSalary = 50000.0;
22
23     double monthlySalary = annualSalary / MONTHS_PER_YEAR;
24     System.out.println( "The monthly salary is " + monthlySalary );
25   }
26 }
```

EXAMPLE 2.7   How Integer Division and Modulus Work

At line 23, we divide a *double* by a *double;* therefore, a floating-point division will be performed by the floating-point unit (FPU), and the floating-point result will be assigned to the variable *monthlySalary*. Figure 2.5 shows the output of the program.

Figure 2.5

Output of
Example 2.7

```
There are 4 quarters in 113 pennies
There are 13 pennies left over
The monthly salary is 4166.666666666667
```

The modulus is a useful operator. As we will see later in this text, it can be used to determine whether a number is even or odd, to control the number of data items that are written per line, to determine if one number is a factor of another, and for many other uses.

CODE IN ACTION

To see arithmetic operators used in a program, look for this chapter's movie within the online resources. Click on this chapter's link to start the movie.

Skill Practice
with these end-of-chapter questions

2.6.2	Reading and Understanding Code
	Questions 7, 8, 9, 10, 11, 12, 13
2.6.3	Fill In the Code
	Questions 27, 29, 32
2.6.4	Identifying Errors in Code
	Question 35
2.6.6	Write a Short Program
	Question 44

2.3.6 Division by Zero

As we might expect, Java does not allow integer division by 0. If we include this statement in our program,

```
int result = 4 / 0;
```

the code will compile without errors, but at run time, when this statement is executed, the JVM will generate an exception and print an error message on the Java console:

```
Exception in thread "main" java.lang.ArithmeticException: / by zero
```

In most cases, this stops the program. After we discuss selection techniques, we will be able to avoid dividing by zero by first testing whether the divisor is zero before performing the division.

In contrast, floating-point division by zero does not generate an exception. If the dividend is not zero, the answer is *Infinity*. If both the dividend and divisor are zero, the answer is *NaN*, which stands for "Not a Number."

Example 2.8 illustrates the three cases of dividing by zero. As we can see on the output shown in Figure 2.6, line 16 never executes. We can see from the last line in the figure:

```
at DivisionByZero.main(DivisionByZero.java.15)
```

that an exception is generated at line 15 and the program halts execution. Line 16 was not executed.

```
 1 /* DivisionByZero Class
 2    Anderson, Franceschi
 3 */
 4
 5 public class DivisionByZero
 6 {
 7   public static void main( String [ ] args )
 8   {
 9     double result1 = 4.3 / 0.0;
10     System.out.println( "The value of result1 is " + result1 );
11
12     double result2 = 0.0 / 0.0;
13     System.out.println( "The value of result2 is " + result2 );
14
15     int result3 = 4 / 0;
16     System.out.println( "The value of result3 is " + result3 );
17   }
18 }
```

EXAMPLE 2.8   **Results of Division by Zero**

Although floating-point division by zero doesn't bring our program to a halt, it doesn't provide useful results either. It's a good practice to avoid dividing by zero in the first place.

2.3.7   Mixed-Type Arithmetic and Type Casting

So far, we've used a single data type in the expressions we've evaluated. But life isn't always like that. Calculations often involve data of different primitive types.

Figure 2.6

Output of
Example 2.8

```
The value of result1 is Infinity
The value of result2 is NaN
Exception in thread "main" java.lang.ArithmeticException: / by zero
        at DivisionByZero.main(DivisionByZero.java:15)
```

When calculations of mixed types are performed, lower-precision operands are converted, or **promoted**, to the type of the operand that has the higher precision.

The promotions are performed using the *first* of these rules that fits the situation:

1. If either operand is a *double*, the other operand is converted to a *double*.
2. If either operand is a *float*, the other operand is converted to a *float*.
3. If either operand is a *long*, the other operand is converted to a *long*.
4. If either operand is an *int*, the other operand is promoted to an *int*.
5. If neither operand is a *double*, *float*, *long*, or an *int*, both operands are promoted to *int*.

Table 2.11 summarizes these rules of promotion.

This arithmetic promotion of operands is called **implicit type casting** because the compiler performs the promotions automatically, without our specifying that the conversions should be made. Note that the data type of any promoted variable is not permanently changed; its type remains the same after the calculation has been performed.

Table 2.11 shows many rules, but essentially, any arithmetic expression involving integers and floating-point numbers will evaluate to a floating-point number.

The code snippet below illustrates the rules of promotion. We calculate the area of a circle using a radius that is an *int* and 3.14159, which is a *double*. Our first calculation is to square the radius. Because *radius* is an *int*, the result is also an *int*. Then we multiply *radiusSquared* by 3.14159, a *double*. At this point, the *radiusSquared* value is promoted to a *double* and the resulting area is a *double*. Note that when we list our variables that *radiusSquared* is still an *int*.

TABLE 2.11 Rules of Operand Promotion

Data Type of One Operand	Data Type of Other Operand	Promotion of Other Operand	Data Type of Result
double	*char, byte, short, int, long, float*	*double*	*double*
float	*char, byte, short, int, long*	*float*	*float*
long	*char, byte, short, int*	*long*	*long*
int	*char, byte, short*	*int*	*int*
short	*char, byte*	Both operands are promoted to *int*	*int*
byte	*char*	Both operands are promoted to *int*	*int*

```
jshell> int radius = 4;
radius ==> 4

jshell> int radiusSquared = radius * radius;
radiusSquared ==> 16

jshell> double area = 3.14159 * radiusSquared;
area ==> 50.26544

jshell> /vars
|    int radius = 4
|    int radiusSquared = 16
|    double area = 50.26544
```

Sometimes, it's useful to instruct the compiler specifically to convert the type of a variable. In this case, we use **explicit type casting**, which uses this syntax:

```
(dataType) ( expression )
```

The expression will be converted, or type cast, to the data type specified. The parentheses around *expression* are needed only when the expression consists of a calculation that we want to be performed before the type casting.

Type casting is useful in calculating an average. The snippet below shows how to calculate an average test grade. The test scores are 94, 86, 88, and 97, making the combined total score 365. We expect the average to be 91.25.

Our first attempt to calculate the average results in the wrong answer. Because *totalScores* and *count* are both integers, integer division is performed. This truncates any remainder, as shown by the value of the temporary variable $3 (91). When we then assign the integer result to the *double average*, the integer value is promoted to a *double*. The result, 91.0, appears to be accurate to one decimal place, but it is, in fact, incorrect.

```
jshell> int totalScores = 94 + 86 + 88 + 97;
totalScores ==> 365

jshell> int count= 4;
count ==> 4

jshell> totalScores / count
$3 ==> 91

jshell> double average = totalScores / count;
average ==> 91. 0
```

In our second attempt, we explicitly type cast the division to a double. But we are too late. The integer division is performed first (which we've seen is 91), then the result of the integer division is type cast to a double. Again, we receive the same incorrect and misleading result, 91.0.

```
jshell> ( double ) ( totalScores / count )
i7 ==> 91.0

jshell> average = ( double ) ( totalScores / count );
average ==> 91.0
```

In our third attempt, we calculate the correct answer by type casting the *totalScores* variable to a *double*, then dividing. The result is that floating-point division is performed and we get the correct answer, 91.25. It doesn't matter whether we type cast *totalScores* or *count* to a *double* before performing the division. Casting either to a *double* forces floating-point division.

```
jshell> ( double ) ( totalScores ) / count
$9 ==> 91.25

jshell> average = ( double ) ( totalScores ) / count;
average ==> 91.25
```

CODE IN ACTION

To see the calculation of an average using mixed data types, look for this chapter's movie within the online resources. Click on this chapter's link to start the movie.

© Hemera Technologies/ Photos.com/Thinkstock

2.3.8   Shortcut Operators

A common operation in programming is adding 1 to a number (**incrementing**) or subtracting 1 from a number (**decrementing**). For example, if we want to count how many data items the user enters, every time we read another data item, we could add 1 to a count variable.

Because incrementing or decrementing a value is so common in programming, Java provides shortcut operators to do this: ++ and --. (Note that there are no spaces between the two plus and minus signs.) The statement

```
count++;
```

adds 1 to the value of *count*, and the statement

```
count--;
```

subtracts 1 from the value of *count*. Thus,

```
count++;
```

is equivalent to

```
count = count + 1;
```

and

```
count--;
```

is equivalent to

```
count = count - 1;
```

Both of these operators have **prefix** and **postfix** versions. The prefix versions precede the variable name (++a or --a) whereas the postfix versions follow the variable name (a++ or a--). Both increment or decrement the variable. If they are used as a single, atomic statement (as in the preceding statements), there is no difference between the two versions. So

```
a++;
```

is functionally equivalent to

```
++a;
```

and

```
a--;
```

is functionally equivalent to

```
--a;
```

However, if they are used inside a more complex expression, then they differ as follows. The prefix versions increment or decrement the variable first, then the new value of the variable is used in evaluating the expression. The postfix versions increment or decrement the variable after the old value of the variable is used in the expression.

Example 2.9 illustrates this difference.

```
 1 /* ShortcutOperators Class
 2    Anderson, Franceschi
 3 */
 4
 5 public class ShortcutOperators
 6 {
 7   public static void main( String [ ] args )
 8   {
 9       int a = 6;
10       int b = 2;
11
12       System.out.println( "At the beginning, a is " + a );
13       System.out.println( "Increment a with prefix notation: " + ++a );
14       System.out.println( "In the end, a is " + a );
15
16       System.out.println( "\nAt the beginning, b is " + b );
17       System.out.println( "Increment b with postfix notation: " + b++ );
18       System.out.println( "In the end, b is " + b );
19   }
20 }
```

EXAMPLE 2.9 Prefix and Postfix Increment Operators

Lines 9 and 10 declare and initialize two *int* variables, *a* and *b*, to 6 and 2, respectively. In order to illustrate the effect of both the prefix and postfix increment operators, we output their original values at lines 12 and 16. At line 13, we use the prefix increment operator to increment *a* inside an output statement; *a* is incremented before the output statement is executed, resulting in the output statement using the value 7 for *a*. At line 17, we use the postfix increment operator to increment *b* inside an output statement; *b* is incremented after the output statement is executed, resulting in the output statement using the value 2 for *b*. Lines 14 and 18 simply output the values of *a* and *b* after the prefix and postfix operators were used at lines 13 and 17. Figure 2.7 shows the output of this example.

Another set of shortcut operators simplify common calculations that change a single value. For example, the statement

```
a = a + 2; // add 2 to a
```

can be simplified as

```
a += 2; // add 2 to a
```

The value added to the target variable can be a variable name or a larger expression.

The shortcut addition operator (+=) is a single operator; there are no spaces between the + and the =. Also, be careful not to reverse the order of the operators. For example, in the following statement, the operators are reversed, so the compiler interprets the statement as "assign positive 2 to a."

```
a =+ 2 ; // Incorrect! Assigns positive 2 to a
```

COMMON ERROR TRAP
No spaces are allowed between the arithmetic operator (+) and the equal sign. Note also that the sequence is +=, not =+.

Java provides shortcut operators for each of the basic arithmetic operations: addition, subtraction, multiplication, division, and modulus. These operators are especially useful in performing repetitive calculations and in converting values from one scale to another. For example, to convert feet to inches, we multiply the number of feet by 12. So we can use the *= shortcut operator:

```
int length = 3; // length in feet
length *= 12; // length converted to inches
```

Converting from one scale to another is a common operation in programming. For example, earlier in the chapter we converted quarters, dimes, and nickels to pennies.

```
At the beginning, a is 6
Increment a with prefix notation: 7
In the end, a is 7

At the beginning, b is 2
Increment b with postfix notation: 2
In the end, b is 3
```

Figure 2.7

Output of Example 2.9

We might also need to convert hours to seconds, feet to meters, or Fahrenheit temperatures to Celsius.

Example 2.10 demonstrates each of the shortcut arithmetic operators. The output is shown in Figure 2.8.

```java
1 /* Shortcut Arithmetic Operators
2    Anderson, Franceschi
3 */
4
5 public class ShortcutArithmeticOperators
6 {
7   public static void main( String [ ] args )
8   {
9      int a = 5;
10     System.out.println( "a is " + a );
11
12     a += 10;     // a = a + 10;
13     System.out.println( "\nAfter a += 10; a is " + a );
14
15     a -= 3;      // a = a - 3;
16     System.out.println( "\nAfter a -= 3; a is " + a );
17
18     a *= 2;      // a = a * 2;
19     System.out.println( "\nAfter a *= 2; a is " + a );
20
21     a /= 6;      // a = a / 6;
22     System.out.println( "\nAfter a /= 6; a is " + a );
23
24     a %= 3;      // a = a % 3;
25     System.out.println( "\nAfter a %= 3; a is " + a );
26   }
27 }
```

EXAMPLE 2.10   Shortcut Arithmetic Operators

Figure 2.8

Output of
Example 2.10

```
a is 5

After a += 10; a is 15

After a -= 3; a is 12

After a *= 2; a is 24

After a /= 6; a is 4

After a %= 3; a is 1
```

Table 2.12 summarizes the shortcut operators, and Table 2.13 shows where the shortcut operators fit into the order of operator precedence.

TABLE 2.12   Shortcut Operators

Shortcut Operator	Example	Equivalent Statement
++	a++; or ++a;	a = a + 1;
−−	a−−; or −−a;	a = a − 1;
+=	a += 3;	a = a + 3;
−=	a −=10;	a = a − 10;
*=	a *= 4;	a = a * 4;
/=	a /= 7;	a = a / 7;
%=	a %= 10;	a = a % 10;

TABLE 2.13   Order of Operator Precedence

Operator Hierarchy	Order of Same-Statement Evaluation	Operation
( )	left to right	parentheses for explicit grouping
++, −−	**right to left**	**shortcut postincrement**
++, −−	**right to left**	**shortcut preincrement**
*, /, %	left to right	multiplication, division, modulus
+, −	left to right	addition or *String* concatenation, subtraction
=, +=, −=, *=, /=, %=	right to left	assignment operator and **shortcut assignment operators**

Skill Practice
with these end-of-chapter questions

2.6.1   Multiple Choice Exercises

Question 3

2.6.2   Reading and Understanding Code

Questions 14, 15, 16, 17, 18, 19, 20, 21, 22

2.4   Programming Activity 2: Temperature Conversion

For this Programming Activity, you will write a program to convert a temperature in Fahrenheit to Celsius. The conversion formula is the following:

$$T_c = 5 / 9 \, (T_f - 32)$$

where T_c is the temperature in Celsius and T_f is the temperature in Fahrenheit, and 32 is the freezing point of water.

Locate the *TemperatureConversion.java* source file found in this chapter's Programming Activity 2 folder in the supplied code files. Copy the file to your computer. The source code is shown in Example 2.11.

```
1  /* Temperature Conversion
2     Anderson, Franceschi
3  */
4
5  public class TemperatureConversion
6  {
7    public static void main( String [ ] args )
8    {
9        //***** 1. declare any constants here
10
11
12        //***** 2. declare the temperature in Fahrenheit as an int
13
```

```
14
15        //***** 3. calculate equivalent Celsius temperature
16
17
18        //***** 4. output the temperature in Celsius
19
20
21        //***** 5. convert Celsius temperature back to Fahrenheit
22
23
24        //***** 6. output Fahrenheit temperature to check correctness
25
26
27    }
28 }
```

EXAMPLE 2.11   *TemperatureConversion.java*

Open the *TemperatureConversion.java* source file. You'll notice that the class already contains a class name and the *main* method. Your job is to fill in the blanks.

To verify that your code produces the correct output, add code to convert your calculated Celsius temperature back to Fahrenheit and compare that value to the original Fahrenheit temperature. The formula for converting Celsius to Fahrenheit is:

$T_f = 9 / 5 * T_c + 32$

Before writing this program, you need to design a plan of attack. Ask yourself:

- What data do I need to define?
- What calculations should I make?
- What is the output of the program?
- How do I select data values so they will provide good test data for my code?

Choose any input value for the Fahrenheit temperature. After you write the program, try changing the original temperature value, recompiling and rerunning the program to verify that the temperature conversion works for multiple input values.

? DISCUSSION QUESTIONS

1.   How did you change the expression 5 / 9 so that the value was not 0?

2.   What constant(s) did you define?

3.   What data type did you use for the Celsius temperature? Why?

CHAPTER REVIEW

2.5 Chapter Summary

- Java programs consist of at least one class.

- Identifiers are symbolic names for classes, methods, and data. Identifiers should start with a letter and may contain any combination of letters and digits, but no spaces. The length of an identifier is essentially unlimited. Identifier names are case sensitive.

- Java's reserved words cannot be used as identifiers.

- The basic building block of a Java program is the statement. A statement is terminated with a semicolon and can span several lines.

- Any amount of white space is permitted between identifiers, Java keywords, operands, operators, and literals. White space characters are the space, tab, newline, and carriage return.

- A block, which consists of 0, 1, or more statements, starts with a left curly brace and ends with a right curly brace. Blocks can be used anywhere in the program that a statement is legal.

- Comments are ignored by the compiler. Block comments are delineated by /* and */. Line comments start with // and continue to the end of the line.

- Java supports eight primitive data types: *double, float, long, int, short, byte, char,* and *boolean.*

- The jshell utility, part of the JDK, is a tool that allows us to type code and see the immediate result without compiling.

- Variables must be declared before they are used. Declaring a variable is specifying the data item's identifier and data type. The syntax for declaring a variable is: `dataType identifier1, identifier2, . . .;`

- Begin variable names with a lowercase letter. If the variable name consists of more than one word, begin each word after the first with a capital letter. Do not put spaces between words.

- An integer data type is one that evaluates to a positive or negative whole number. Java recognizes four integer data types: *int, short, long,* and *byte.*

- Floating-point data types store numbers with fractional parts. Java supports two floating-point data types: the single-precision type *float,* and the double-precision type *double.*

- The *char* data type stores one Unicode character. Because Unicode characters are encoded as unsigned numbers using 16 bits, a *char* variable is stored in two bytes of memory.

- The *boolean* data type can store only two values, which are expressed using the Java reserved words *true* and *false.*

- The assignment operator (=) is used to give a value to a variable.

- To assign an initial value to a variable, use this syntax when declaring the variable:

  `dataType variable1 = initialValue1;`

- Literals can be used to assign initial values or to reassign the value of a variable.

- Constants are data items whose value, once assigned, cannot be changed. Data items that we know should not change throughout the execution of a program should be declared as a constant, using this syntax:

  `final dataType CONSTANT_IDENTIFIER = initialValue;`

- Constant identifiers, by convention, are composed of all capital letters with underscores separating words.

- An expression consists of operators and operands that evaluate to a single value.

- The value of an expression can be assigned to a variable or constant, which must be a data type compatible with the value of the expression and cannot be a constant that has been assigned a value already.

- Java provides binary operators for addition, subtraction, multiplication, division, and modulus.

- Calculation of the value of expressions follows the rules of operator precedence.

- Integer division truncates any fractional part of the quotient.

- When an arithmetic operator is invoked with operands that are of different primitive types, the compiler temporarily converts, or promotes, one or both of the operands.

- An expression or a variable can be temporarily cast to a different data type using this syntax:

  `(dataType) ( expression )`

- Shortcut operators ++ and -- simplify incrementing or decrementing a value by 1. The prefix versions precede the variable name and increment or decrement the variable, then use its new value in evaluation of the expression. The postfix versions follow the variable name and increment or decrement the variable after using the old value in the expression.

- Java provides shortcut operators for each of the basic arithmetic operations: addition, subtraction, multiplication, division, and modulus.

2.6   Exercises, Problems, and Projects

2.6.1   Multiple Choice Exercises

1. What is the valid way to declare an integer variable named *a*? (Check all that apply.)

   ❑ `int a;`

   ❑ `a int ;`

   ❑ `integer a;`

2. Which of the following identifiers are valid?

   ❑ `a`

   ❑ `sales`

   ❑ `sales&profit`

   ❑ `int`

   ❑ `inter`

   ❑ `doubleSales`

   ❑ `TAX_RATE`

   ❑ `1stLetterChar`

   ❑ `char`

3. Given three declared and initialized *int* variables *a*, *b*, and *c*, which of the following statements are valid?

   ❑ `a = b;`

   ❑ `a = 67;`

   ❑ `b = 8.7;`

   ❑ `a + b = 8;`

   ❑ `a * b = 12;`

☐ c = a - b;

☐ c = a / 2.3;

☐ boolean t = a;

☐ a /= 4;

☐ a += c;

2.6.2   Reading and Understanding Code

4. What is the output of this code sequence?

```
double a = 12.5;
System.out.println( a );
```

5. What is the output of this code sequence?

```
int a = 6;
System.out.println( a );
```

6. What is the output of this code sequence?

```
float a = 13f;
System.out.println( a );
```

7. What is the output of this code sequence?

```
double a = 13 / 5;
System.out.println( a );
```

8. What is the output of this code sequence?

```
int a = 13 / 5;
System.out.println( a );
```

9. What is the output of this code sequence?

```
int a = 13 % 5;
System.out.println( a );
```

10. What is the output of this code sequence?

```
int a = 12 / 6 * 2;
System.out.println( a );
```

11. What is the output of this code sequence?

```
int a = 12 / ( 6 * 2 );
System.out.println( a ) ;
```

12. What is the output of this code sequence?

```
int a = 4 + 6 / 2;
System.out.println( a );
```

13. What is the output of this code sequence?

```java
int a = ( 4 + 6 ) / 2;
System.out.println( a );
```

14. What is the output of this code sequence?

```java
double a = 12.0 / 5;
System.out.println( a );
```

15. What is the output of this code sequence?

```java
int a = (int) 12.0 / 5;
System.out.println( a );
```

16. What is the output of this code sequence?

```java
double a = (double) ( 12 ) / 5;
System.out.println( a );
```

17. What is the output of this code sequence?

```java
double a = (double) ( 12 / 5 );
System.out.println( a );
```

18. What is the output of this code sequence?

```java
int a = 5;
a++;
System.out.println( a );
```

19. What is the output of this code sequence?

```java
int a = 5;
System.out.println( a-- );
```

20. What is the output of this code sequence?

```java
int a = 5;
System.out.println( --a );
```

21. What is the output of this code sequence?

```java
int a = 5;
a += 2;
System.out.println( a );
```

22. What is the output of this code sequence?

```java
int a = 5;
a /= 6;
System.out.println( a );
```

2.6.3   Fill In the Code

23. Write the code to declare a *float* variable named *a* and assign *a* the value 34.2.

```java
// your code goes here
```

24. Write the code to assign the value 10 to an *int* variable named *a*.

```
int a;
// your code goes here
```

25. Write the code to declare a *boolean* variable named *a* and assign *a* the value *false*.

```
// your code goes here
```

26. Write the code to declare a *char* variable named *a* and assign *a* the character B.

```
// your code goes here
```

27. Write the code to calculate the total of three *int* variables *a*, *b*, and *c* and print the result.

```
int a = 3;
int b = 5;
int c = 8;

// your code goes here
```

28. Write the code to calculate the average of two *int* variables *a* and *b* and print the result. The average should be printed as a floating-point number.

```
int a = 3;
int b = 5;

// your code goes here
```

29. Write the code to calculate and print the remainder of the division of two *int* variables with the values 10 and 3 (the value printed will be 1).

```
int a = 10;
int b = 3;

// your code goes here
```

30. This code increases the value of a variable *a* by 1, using the shortcut increment operator.

```
int a = 7;

// your code goes here
```

31. This code multiplies the value of a variable *a* by 3, using a shortcut operator.

```
int a = 7;

// your code goes here
```

32. Assume that we have already declared and initialized two *int* variables, *a* and *b*. Convert the following sentences to legal Java expressions and statements.

❑ b gets a plus 3 minus 7

❑ b gets a times 4

❑ a gets b times b

❑ a gets b times 3 times 5

❑ b gets the quotient of the division of a by 2

❑ b gets the remainder of the division of a by 3

2.6.4   Identifying Errors in Code

33. Where is the error in this code sequence?

```
int a = 3.3;
```

34. Where is the error in this code sequence?

```
double a = 45.2;
float b = a;
```

35. Where is the error in this code sequence?

```
int a = 7.5 % 3;
```

36. What would happen when this code sequence is compiled and executed?

```
int a = 5 / 0;
```

37. Where is the error in this code sequence?

```
int a = 5;
a - = 4;
```

38. Is there an error in this code sequence? Explain.

```
char c = 67;
```

39. Is there an error in this code sequence? Explain.

```
boolean a = 1;
```

2.6.5   Debugging Area—Using Messages from the Java Compiler and Java JVM

40. You coded the following on line 8 of class *Test.java*:

```
int a = 26.4;
```

When you compile, you get the following message:

```
Test.java:8 error: incompatible types: possible lossy conversion from double
to int
   int a = 26.4;
        ^
1 error
```

Explain what the problem is and how to fix it.

41. You coded the following on line 8 of class *Test.java*:

```
int a = 3
```

When you compile, you get the following message:

```
Test.java:8 error: ';' expected
int a = 3
         ^
```

Explain what the problem is and how to fix it.

42. You coded the following in class *Test.java*:

```
int a = 32;
int b = 10;
double c = a / b;
System.out.println( "The value of c is " + c );
```

The code compiles properly and runs, but the result is not what you expected.
The output is

```
The value of c is 3.0
```

You expected the value of c to be 3.2. Explain what the problem is and how to
fix it.

43. You coded the following in class *Test.java*:

```
int a = 5;
a =+ 3;
System.out.println( "The value of a is " + a );
```

The code compiles properly and runs, but the result is not what you expected.
The output is

```
The value of a is 3
```

You expected the value of a to be 8. Explain what the problem is and how to fix it.

2.6.6   Write a Short Program

44. Write a program that calculates and outputs the square of each integer from
1 to 9.

45. Write a program that calculates and outputs the average of integers 1, 7, 9, and
34.

46. Write a program that outputs the following:

```
****
```

2.6.7 Programming Projects

47. Write a program that prints the letter X composed of asterisks (*). Your output should look like this:

```
*    *

 *  *

  *

 *  *

*    *
```

48. Write a program that converts 10, 50, and 100 kilograms to pounds (1 lb = 0.454 kg).

49. Write a program that converts 2, 5, and 10 inches to millimeters (1 inch = 25.4 mm).

50. Write a program to compute and output the circumference of a circle having a radius of 3.2 inches.

51. Write a program that outputs this *String*:

$a^3 + b^3 = c^3$

2.6.8 Technical Writing

52. Some programmers like to write code that is as compact as possible, for instance, using the increment (or decrement) operator in the middle of another statement. Typically, these programmers use very few comments in their programs. Discuss whether this is a good idea, keeping in mind that a program "lives" through a certain period of time.

53. Compare the following data types for integer numbers: *int, short*, and *long*. Discuss their representation in binary, how much space they take in memory, and the purpose of having these data types available to programmers.

CHAPTER 3
Object-Oriented Programming, Part 1: Using Classes

CHAPTER CONTENTS

Introduction

Writing computer programs that use classes and objects is called **object-oriented programming**, or **OOP**. Every Java program consists of at least one class.

In this chapter, we'll introduce object-oriented programming as a way to use classes that have already been written. Classes provide services to the program. These services might include writing a message to the program's user, popping up a dialog box, performing some mathematical calculations, formatting numbers, drawing shapes in a window, or many other basic tasks that add a more professional look to even simple programs. The program that uses a class is called the **client** of the class. Thus, in this chapter we will be writing client programs.

One benefit of using a prewritten class is that we don't need to write the code ourselves; it has already been written and tested for us. This means that we can write our client programs more quickly. In other words, we shorten the development time of the program. Using prewritten and pretested classes provides other benefits as well, including more reliable programs with fewer errors.

In this chapter, we'll explore how using prewritten classes can add functionality to our programs.

3.1   Class Basics and Benefits

In Java, classes are composed of data and operations—or functions—that operate on the data. Objects of a class are created using the class as a template, or guide. Think of the class as a generic description, and an object as a specific item of that class. Or you can think of a class as a cookie cutter; the objects of that class are the cookies made with the cookie cutter. For example, a *Student* class might have the following data: name, year, and grade point average. All students have these three data items. We can create an object of the *Student* class by specifying an identifier for the object (for example, *student1*) along with a name, year, and grade point average for a particular student (for example, *Maria Gonzales, Sophomore, 3.5*). The identifier of the object is called the **object reference**. Creating an object of a class is called **instantiating an object**, and the object is called an **instance of the class**. Many objects can be instantiated from one class. There can be many instances of the *Student* class, that is, many *Student* objects can be instantiated from the *Student* class. For example, we could create a second object of the *Student* class, *student2*, with its data as *Mike Smith, Junior, 3.0*.

The data associated with an object of a class are called **instance variables**, or **fields**, and can be variables and constants of any primitive data type (*byte, short, int, long, float, double, char*, and *boolean*), or they can be objects of a class.

The operations for a class, called **methods**, set the values of the data, retrieve the current values of the data, and perform other class-related functions on the data. For example, the *Student* class would provide methods to set the values of the name, year, and grade point average; retrieve the current values of the name, year, and grade point average; and perhaps promote a student to the next year. Invoking a method on an object is called **calling the method**. With a few exceptions, only the methods of a class can directly access or change the instance variables of an object. Programs using the class, such as clients, must call the methods to set or retrieve the values of the instance variables. Together, the fields and methods of a class are called its **members**.

In essence, a class is a new data type, which is created by combining items of Java primitive data types and objects of classes. Just as the primitive data types can be manipulated using arithmetic operators (+, −, *, /, and %), an object can be manipulated by calling the methods of its class.

The data of a class is typically declared to be *private*. In this case, only the methods of the class can change the data of an object, and thus the methods provide a protective layer around the data. In other words, the class **encapsulates** the data, and the methods of the class provide the only interface to set or change the data values from outside the class. The benefit from this encapsulation is that the class methods ensure that only valid values are assigned to an object. For example, a method to set a student's grade point average would accept values only between 0.0 and 4.0.

Let's look at another example of a class. The *SimpleDate* class, written by the authors of this text, has the instance variables *month, day,* and *year*. An object of this class, *independenceDay*, could be instantiated with data values of *7, 4,* and *1776*. Another object of the *SimpleDate* class, *moonWalking*, might be instantiated with the values *7, 20, 1969*. Methods of the *SimpleDate* class ensure that only valid values are set for the month, day, and year. For example, the methods would not allow us to set a date with a value of January 32. Other methods of the class increment the date to the next day and provide the date in *mm/dd/yyyy* format.

Notice that the class names we used, *Student* and *SimpleDate*, begin with a capital letter, and the object names, *student1, independenceDay,* and *moonWalking*, start with a lowercase letter. By convention, class names start with a capital letter. Object names, instance variables, and method names conventionally start with a lowercase letter. Internal words start with a capital letter in class names, object names, variables, and methods.

There are many benefits to using classes in a program. Some of the most important benefits include reusability (not only in the current program but also in other programs), encapsulation, and reliability.

SOFTWARE ENGINEERING TIP

By convention, class names in Java start with a capital letter. Method names, instance variables, and object names start with a lowercase letter. In all of these names, embedded words begin with a capital letter.

A well-written class can be reused in many programs. For example, a *SimpleDate* class could be used in a calendar program, an appointment-scheduling program, an online shopping program, and many more applications that rely on dates. Reusing code is much faster than writing and testing new code. As an added bonus, reusing a tested and debugged class in another program makes the program more reliable.

Further, encapsulation of a class's data and methods helps to isolate operations on the data. This makes it easier to track the source of a bug. For example, when a bug is discovered in an object of the *Student class*, then we know to look for the problem in the methods of the *Student class*, because no other code in our program can directly change the data in a *Student object*.

We do not need to know the implementation details of a class in order to use it in our program. Does the *SimpleDate* class store the date in memory as three integers, *month*, *day*, and *year*? Or is the date stored as the number of milliseconds since 1980? The beauty of object orientation is that we don't need to know the implementation of the class; all we need to know is the class **application programming interface (API)**, that is, how to instantiate objects and how to call the methods of the class.

3.2   Creating Objects Using Constructors

A class describes a generic template for creating, or instantiating, objects. In fact, an object must be instantiated before it can be used. To understand how to instantiate an object of a class and how to call methods of the class, we must know the API of a class, which the creators of the class make public. Table 3.1 shows the API of the *SimpleDate* class, written by the authors of this text.

Instantiating an object consists of defining an object reference—which will hold the address of the object in memory—and calling a special method of the class called a **constructor**, which has the same name as the class. The job of the constructor is to assign initial values to the data of the class.

Example 3.1 illustrates how to instantiate objects of the *SimpleDate* class. Note that we store the *SimpleDate.java* file in the same folder as *Constructors.java*.

```
1 /* A Demonstration of Using Constructors
2    Anderson, Franceschi
3 */
4
5 public class Constructors
6 {
7   public static void main( String [ ] args )
8   {
9     SimpleDate independenceDay;
```

```
10      independenceDay = new SimpleDate( 7, 4, 1776 );
11
12      SimpleDate nextCentury = new SimpleDate( 1, 1, 2101 );
13
14      SimpleDate defaultDate = new SimpleDate( );
15   }
16 }
```

EXAMPLE 3.1   Demonstrating Constructors

TABLE 3.1   The *SimpleDate* Class API

SimpleDate Class Constructor Summary		
SimpleDate( )		
creates a *SimpleDate* object with initial default values of 1, 1, 2000.		
SimpleDate(int mm, int dd, int yy)		
creates a *SimpleDate* object with the initial values of *mm*, *dd*, and *yy*.		
SimpleDate Class Method Summary		
Return value	**Method name and argument list**	
int	getMonth( )	
	returns the value of *month*	
int	getDay( )	
	returns the value of *day*	
int	getYear( )	
	returns the value of *year*	
void	setMonth(int mm)	
	sets the *month* to *mm*; if *mm* is invalid, does not change the value of *month*	
void	setDay(int dd)	
	sets the *day* to *dd*; if *dd* is invalid, does not change the value of *day*	
void	setYear(int yy)	
	sets the *year* to *yy*	
void	nextDay( )	
	increments the date to the next day	
String	toString( )	
	returns the value of the date in the form: *month/day/year*	

Declaring an object reference is very much like declaring a variable of a primitive type; we specify the data type and an identifier. For example, to declare an integer variable named *number1*, we provide the data type (*int*) and the identifier (*number1*), as follows:

```
int number1;
```

One notable difference in declaring an object reference is that its data type is the class name, not a primitive data type. Here is the syntax for declaring an object reference:

```
ClassName objectReference1, objectReference2, ...;
```

In Example 3.1, lines 9, 12, and 14 declare object references for a *SimpleDate* object. *SimpleDate*, the class name, is the data type, and *independenceDay*, *nextCentury*, and *defaultDate* are the object references.

Object references can refer to **any** object of its class. For example, *SimpleDate* object references can point to any *SimpleDate* object, but a *SimpleDate* object reference cannot point to objects of other classes, such as a *Student* object.

Once an object reference has been declared, we instantiate the object using the following syntax:

```
objectReference = new ClassName( argument list );
```

This calls a constructor of the class to initialize the data. The **argument list** consists of a comma-separated list of initial data values to assign to the object. Classes often provide multiple constructors with different argument lists. Depending on which constructor we call, we can accept default values for the data or specify initial values for the data. When we instantiate an object, our argument list—that is, the number of arguments and their data types—must match one of the constructors' argument lists.

As shown in Table 3.1, the *SimpleDate* class has two constructors. Note that the API of a constructor does not have a return value; nevertheless, constructors implicitly return an object reference to the newly instantiated object. The first constructor, *SimpleDate( )*, is called the **default constructor**, because its **argument list is empty**. This constructor assigns default values to all data in the object. Thus, in line 14 of Example 3.1, which uses the default constructor, the data for the *defaultDate* object is set to the default values for the *SimpleDate* class, which are *1, 1*, and *2000*.

We see from Table 3.1 that the second constructor for the *SimpleDate* class, *SimpleDate(int mm, int dd, int yy)*, takes three arguments, all of which should evaluate to integer values. The first argument is the value for the month, the second argument is the value for the day, and the third argument is the value for the year.

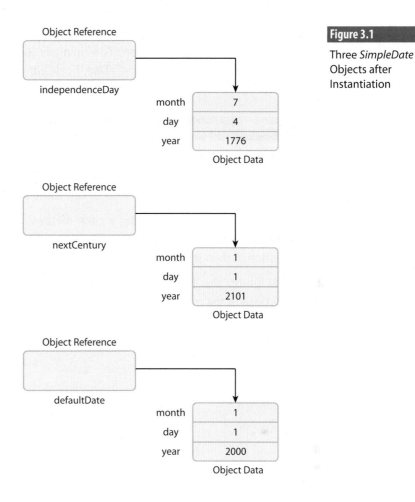

Figure 3.1

Three *SimpleDate* Objects after Instantiation

Lines 10 and 12 of Example 3.1 instantiate *SimpleDate* objects using the second constructor. In line 10, the argument list tells the constructor to give the value *7* to the month, *4* to the day, and *1776* to the year. In line 12, the argument list tells the constructor to give the value *1* to the month, *1* to the day, and *2101* to the year. Note that no data types are given when calling the constructors, only the initial values for the data. The data types of the arguments are specified in the API so that the client of the class knows what data types the constructor is expecting for its arguments.

Lines 12 and 14 also illustrate that we can combine the declaration of the object reference and instantiation of the object in a single statement.

When an object is instantiated, the JVM allocates memory to the new object. The object reference is assigned an address that the JVM uses to find that object in memory. Figure 3.1 shows the three objects instantiated in Example 3.1.

It's important to understand that an object reference and the object data are different: The object reference represents a memory location. Notice in Figure 3.1 that the object references, *independenceDay*, *nextCentury*, and *defaultDate*, point to the locations of the object data.

3.3   Calling Methods

Once an object is instantiated, we can use the object by calling its methods. As we mentioned earlier, the authors of classes publish their API so that their clients know what methods are available and how to call those methods.

Figure 3.2 illustrates how calling a class method alters the flow of control in our program. When this program starts running, the JVM executes instruction 1, then instruction 2, then it encounters a method call.

At that point, the JVM **transfers control to the method** and starts executing instructions in the method. When the method finishes executing, the JVM transfers control back to the program immediately after the point the method was called and continues executing instructions in the program.

Figure 3.2

Flow of Control of a Method Call

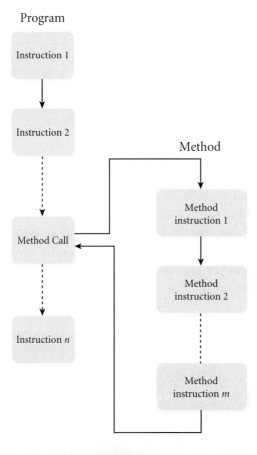

A class API consists of the class method names, their return values, and their argument lists. The argument list for a method indicates the order and number of arguments to send to the method, along with the data type of each argument. Each item in the argument list consists of a data type and a name. The arguments sent to the method can be literals, constants, variables, or any expression that evaluates to the data type specified in the API of the method. For example, the API in Table 3.1 shows that the *setMonth, setDay,* and *setYear* methods all take one argument, which must evaluate to an integer value.

A method may or may not return a value, as indicated by a data type, class type, or the keyword **void** in front of the method name. If the method returns a value, then the data type or class type of its **return value** will precede the method's name. For instance, in Table 3.1, the *getDay, getMonth,* and *getYear* methods each return an integer value. The call to a **value-returning method** can be used in an expression. When the method finishes executing, its return value will replace the method call in the expression. If the keyword *void* precedes the method name, the method does not return a value. Because methods with a *void* return type have no value, they cannot be used in an expression; instead, a method call to a method with a *void* return type is a complete statement. In Table 3.1, the *setMonth, setDay, setYear,* and *nextDay* methods do not return a value.

Another keyword we will see preceding the method call in an API is *public*. This keyword means that any client of the class can call this method. If the keyword *private* precedes the method name, only other methods of that class can call that method. Although we will not formally include the *public* keyword in the API, all the methods we discuss in this chapter are *public*.

To call a method for an object of a class, we use **dot notation**, as follows:

```
objectReference.methodName( arg1, arg2, arg3, ... )
```

The object reference is followed immediately by a **dot** (a period), which is followed immediately by the method name. (Later in the chapter, when we call *static* methods, we will substitute the class name for the object reference.) The arguments for the method are enclosed in parentheses.

Let's look again at the methods of the *SimpleDate* class. The first three methods in the *SimpleDate* class API, *getMonth, getDay,* and *getYear,* take an empty argument list and return an *int*; thus, those methods have a return value of type *int*. We can call these methods in any expression in our program where we could use an *int*. The value of the first method, *getMonth( )*, is the value of the month in the object. Similarly, the value of *getDay( )* is the value of the day in the object, and the value of *getYear( )* is the value of the year. These "get" methods are formally called **accessor methods** or **getters**; they enable clients to access the value of the instance variables of an object.

The next three methods in the *SimpleDate* class API, *setMonth, setDay,* and *setYear,* take one argument of type *int* and do not return a value, which is indicated by the keyword *void*. These methods are called in standalone statements. The first method, *setMonth(int mm)*, changes the value of the month in the object to the value of the method's argument, *mm*. Similarly, *setDay(int dd)* changes the value of the day in the object, and *setYear(int yy)* changes the value of the year in the object to the value of the method's argument. These "set" methods are formally called **mutator methods** or **setters**; they enable a client to change the value of the instance variables of an object. If, however, we send an argument to the *setDay* or *setMonth* method that is invalid, such as a day value of 0 or a month value of 13, the methods will not change the value of the instance variables. Thus, the methods ensure that the data of an object is always valid. In addition, the *nextDay* method, which takes no arguments and does not return a value, increments the date to the day following its current value. Thus, if the month, day, and year were 5, 31, and 2020, calling the *nextDay* method would change the month to 6 and the day to 1.

COMMON ERROR TRAP
When calling a method that takes no arguments, remember to include the empty parentheses after the method's name. The parentheses are required even if there are no arguments.

Example 3.2 illustrates how to use some of the methods of the *SimpleDate* class. Line 10 calls the *getMonth* method for the *independenceDay* object. When line 10 is executed, control transfers to the *getMonth* method. When the *getMonth* method finishes executing, the value it returns (7) replaces the method call in the statement. The statement then effectively becomes:

```
int independenceMonth = 7;
```

In lines 15–16, we print the value of the day in the *nextCentury* object. Again, control transfers to the *getDay* method, then its return value (1) replaces the method call. So the statement effectively becomes:

```
System.out.println( "The day for nextCentury is "
                    + 1 );
```

COMMON ERROR TRAP
When calling a method, include only values or expressions in your argument list. Including data types in your argument list will cause a compiler error.

Line 18 calls the *setDay* method, which is used to change the value of the day for an object. The *setDay* method takes one *int* argument and has a *void* return value. Line 18 is a complete statement, because the method call to a method with a *void* return value cannot be used in an expression. The method changes the value of the day in the *nextCentury* object, which we illustrate in lines 19–20 by printing the new value as shown in Figure 3.3. Then, on line 22, we instantiate another object, *programmersDay,* with a month, day, and year of 9, 12, 2009, which we demonstrate by printing the values returned by calls to the *getMonth, getDay,* and *getYear* methods. International Programmers Day is the 100th (base 16) day of the year, with the first Programmers Day in 2009. However, since 2009 was not a leap year, the 100th day is actually 9, 13, 2009. So on line 28, we call the *nextDay* method, which has a *void* return value, to increment the date to the next day, and then we print the new values of the *programmersDay* object.

```
1  /* A demonstration of calling methods
2     Anderson, Franceschi
3  */
4
5  public class Methods
6  {
7    public static void main( String [ ] args )
8    {
9      SimpleDate independenceDay = new SimpleDate( 7, 4, 1776 );
10     int independenceMonth = independenceDay.getMonth( );
11     System.out.println( "Independence day is in month "
12                            + independenceMonth );
13
14     SimpleDate nextCentury = new SimpleDate( 1, 1, 2101 );
15     System.out.println( "The day for nextCentury is "
16                            + nextCentury.getDay( ) );
17
18     nextCentury.setDay( 2 );
19     System.out.println( "The revised day for nextCentury is "
20                            + nextCentury.getDay( ) );
21
22     SimpleDate programmersDay = new SimpleDate( 9, 12, 2009 );
23     System.out.println( "The first Programmers Day was "
24                            + programmersDay.getMonth( ) + '/'
25                            + programmersDay.getDay( ) + '/'
26                            + programmersDay.getYear( ) );
27
28     programmersDay.nextDay( );
29     System.out.println( "The actual date for Programmers Day is "
30                            + programmersDay.getMonth( ) + '/'
31                            + programmersDay.getDay( ) + '/'
32                            + programmersDay.getYear( ) );
33   }
34 }
```

EXAMPLE 3.2   Calling Methods

```
Independence day is in month 7
The day for nextCentury is 1
The revised day for nextCentury is 2
The first Programmers Day was 9/12/2009
The actual date for Programmers Day is 9/13/2009
```

Figure 3.3

Output of
Example 3.2

For now, we'll postpone discussion of the last method in the class API, *toString*, except to say that its function is to convert the object data to text suitable for printing.

3.4   Using Object References

As we have mentioned, an object reference points to the data of an object. The object reference and the object data are distinct entities. An object can have more than one object reference pointing to it, or an object can have no object references pointing to it.

In Example 3.3, we declare two *SimpleDate* object references, *d1* and *d2*, and we instantiate their objects at lines 9 and 14. Lines 10–12 and 15–18 output the respective data member values of *d1* and *d2*. Then, line 20 uses the assignment operator to copy the object reference *d1* to the object reference *d2*. Note that only the value of the object reference is copied, not the object data. After line 20, both object references have the same value and therefore point to the location of the same object, as shown in Figure 3.4. The second object, with values (9, 28, 2021), no longer has an

Figure 3.4

Two Object
References
Pointing to the
Same Object

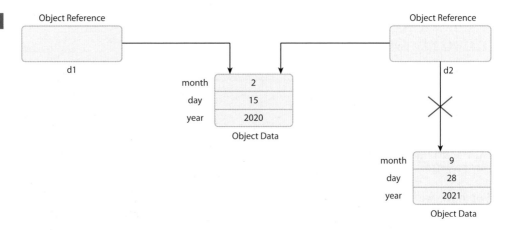

object reference pointing to it and is now marked for **garbage collection**. The **garbage collector**, which is part of the JVM, releases the memory allocated to objects that no longer have an object reference pointing to them. Lines 22–24 and 25–27 output the respective instance variable values of *d1* and *d2* again. These are now identical, as shown in Figure 3.5.

```
1 /* A demonstration of object reference assignment
2    Anderson, Franceschi
3 */
4
5 public class ObjectReferenceAssignment
6 {
7   public static void main( String [ ] args )
8   {
9      SimpleDate d1 = new SimpleDate( 2, 15, 2020 );
10     System.out.println( "d1 is " + d1.getMonth( )
11                        + "/" + d1.getDay( )
12                        + "/" + d1.getYear( ) );
13
14     SimpleDate d2 = new SimpleDate( 9, 28, 2021 );
15     System.out.println( "d2 is "
16                        + d2.getMonth( )
17                        + "/" + d2.getDay( )
18                        + "/" + d2.getYear( ) );
19
20     d2 = d1;
21     System.out.println( "\nAfter assigning d1 to d2:" );
22     System.out.println( "d1 is " + d1.getMonth( )
23                        + "/" + d1.getDay( )
24                        + "/" + d1.getYear( ) );
25     System.out.println( "d2 is " + d2.getMonth( )
26                        + "/" + d2.getDay( )
27                        + "/" + d2.getYear( ) );
28  }
29 }
```

EXAMPLE 3.3 **Demonstrating Object Reference Assignments**

```
d1 is 2/15/2020
d2 is 9/28/2021

After assigning d1 to d2:
d1 is 2/15/2020
d2 is 2/15/2020
```

Figure 3.5

Output of
Example 3.3

When an object reference is first declared, but has not yet been assigned to an object, its value is a special literal value, **null**.

If we attempt to call a method using an object reference whose value is *null*, Java generates either a compiler error or a run-time error called an **exception**. The exception is a *NullPointerException* and results in a series of messages printed on the Java console indicating where in the program the *null* object reference was used. Line 10 of Example 3.4 will generate a compiler error, as shown in Figure 3.6, because *aDate* has not been instantiated.

```java
1  /* A demonstration of trying to use a null object reference
2       Anderson, Franceschi
3  */
4
5  public class NullReference
6  {
7    public static void main( String [ ] args )
8    {
9      SimpleDate aDate;
10     aDate.setMonth( 5 );
11   }
12 }
```

EXAMPLE 3.4   Attempting to Use a *null* Object Reference

COMMON ERROR TRAP
Using a *null* object reference to call a method will generate either a compiler error or a *NullPointerException* at run time. Be sure to instantiate an object before attempting to use the object reference.

Java does not provide support for explicitly deleting an object. One way to indicate to the garbage collector that our program is finished with an object is to set its object reference to *null*. Obviously, once an object reference has the value *null*, it can no longer be used to call methods.

Example 3.5 shows a *NullPointerException* being generated at run time. Line 9 instantiates the *independenceDay* object, and lines 10–11 print the month. Line 13 assigns *null* to the object reference, and lines 15–16 attempt to print the month again. As Figure 3.7 shows, a *NullPointerException* is generated. Notice that the console message indicates the name of the application class (*NullReference2*), the method *main*, and the line number *16*, where the exception occurred. The JVM often prints additional lines in the message, depending on where in our program the error occurred.

Figure 3.8 shows the *independenceDay* object reference and object data after setting the object reference to *null*.

Figure 3.6

Compiler Error from Example 3.4

```
NullReference.java:10: error: variable aDate might not have been initialized
    aDate.setMonth( 5 );
    ^
1 error
```

```
1 /* A demonstration of trying to use a null object reference
2    Anderson, Franceschi
3 */
4
5 public class NullReference2
6 {
7   public static void main( String [ ] args )
8   {
9     SimpleDate independenceDay = new SimpleDate( 7, 4, 1776 );
10    System.out.println( "The month of independenceDay is "
11                        + independenceDay.getMonth( ) );
12
13    independenceDay = null; // set object reference to null
14    // attempt to use object reference
15    System.out.println( "The month of independenceDay is "
16                        + independenceDay.getMonth( ) );
17  }
18 }
```

EXAMPLE 3.5   Another Attempt to Use a *null* Object Reference

```
The month of independenceDay is 7
Exception in thread "main" java.lang.NullPointerException
   at NullReference2.main(NullReference2.java:16)
```

Figure 3.7

Output of
Example 3.5

Object Reference

null

independenceDay

Object Data

month	7
day	4
year	1776

Figure 3.8

The
independenceDay
Object Reference
Set to *null*

3.5   Programming Activity 1: Calling Methods

Let's put this all together with a sample program that uses a *SimpleDate* object. In this Programming Activity, you'll use a program that displays the values of the object data as you instantiate the object and call the methods of the class.

Copy all the files in this chapter's Programming Activity 1 folder in the supplied code files to a folder on your computer. Note that all files should be in the same folder.

Open the *DateDrawing.java* source file. You'll notice that the class already contains some source code. Your job is to fill in the blanks. Search for five asterisks in a row

(*****). This will position you to the places in the source code where you will add your code. This section of code is shown in Figure 3.9.

Notice that line 22 is a declaration of a *SimpleDate* object reference, *dateObj*.

```
private SimpleDate dateObj; // SimpleDate object reference
```

You will use this object reference for instantiating an object and for calling the methods of the *SimpleDate* class.

In the source file, you will see nine commented lines that instruct you to instantiate the object or call a method. You will also notice that there are nine lines that look like this:

```
// animate( n );
```

where n is a number between 1 and 9.

Figure 3.9

Partial Listing of
DateDrawing.java

```
37    public void workWithDates( )
38    {
39      /***** Add your code here *****/
40      /***** 1. Instantiate dateObj using an empty argument list  */
41
42      //animate( 1 );
43
44      /***** 2. Set the month to the month you were born */
45
46      //animate( 2 );
47
48      /***** 3. Set the day to the day of the month you were born */
49
50      //animate( 3 );
51
52      /***** 4. Set the year to the year you were born */
53
54      //animate( 4 );
55
56      /***** 5. Call the nextDay method */
57
58      //animate( 5 );
59
60      /***** 6. Set the day to 32, an illegal value */
61
62      //animate( 6 );
63
64      /***** 7. Set the month to 13, an illegal value */
65
```

```
66      //animate( 7 );
67
68      /***** 8. Assign the value null to dateObj */
69
70      //animate( 8 );
71
72      /***** 9. Attempt to set the month to 1 */
73
74      //animate( 9 );
75
76    }
```

These lines are calls to an *animate* method in this class that displays the object reference and the object data after you have executed your code. The *n* value refers to an action your code just performed. The *animate* method will display a message, as well as the object data. Note that when you call a method in the same class, you don't use an object reference and dot notation.

To complete the Programming Activity, write the requested code on the line between the numbered instruction and the *animate* method call. Then **uncomment** (remove the two slashes from) the *animate* method call.

For example, after you've written the code for the first instruction, lines 40 through 42 should look as follows.

```
/* 1. Instantiate dateObj using an empty argument list */
dateObj = new SimpleDate( );
animate(1);
```

Compile *DateDrawing.java* and run *DateApplication* and you will see a window that looks like the one in Figure 3.10.

As you can see, the *dateObj* reference points to the *SimpleDate* object, and the *month*, *day*, and *year* instance variables have been assigned default values.

Write the code for the remaining instructions, compiling and running the program after completing each task. The program will display the changes you make to the object data.

? DISCUSSION QUESTIONS

1. After instructions 6 and 7 have executed, why are the day and month values not changed?

2. At the end of the execution of the program, a *NullPointerException* is generated. Which statement in the program causes this error? Explain why.

Figure 3.10

Programming
Activity 1 Output

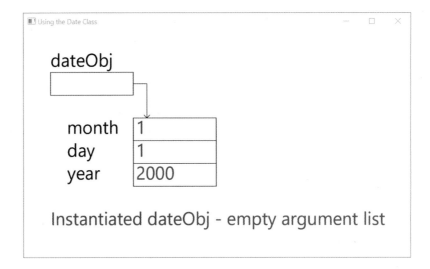

Instantiated dateObj - empty argument list

3.6 The Java Class Library

Java provides more than 2,000 predefined classes that we can use to add functionality to our program. In this chapter, we'll discuss a few commonly used Java classes:

- *String*, which provides a data type for character sequences along with methods for searching and manipulating strings

- *Random*, which generates random numbers

- *Scanner*, which provides methods for reading input from the keyboard

- *System* and *PrintStream*, which provide data members and methods for printing data on the Java console

- *DecimalFormat* and *NumberFormat*, which allow us to format numbers for output

- *Math*, which provides methods for performing mathematical operations

- Object wrappers, which provide an object equivalent to primitive data types so they can be used in our program as if they were objects

The Java classes are arranged in **packages**, grouped according to functionality.

Table 3.2 describes some of the Java packages that we will cover in this text. We can find more details on these classes on Oracle's Java website: *www.oracle.com/technetwork/java*.

Many of the commonly used classes, such as *String* and *Math*, reside in the *java.lang* package. Any class in the *java.lang* package is automatically available to our program.

TABLE 3.2   Commonly Used Java Packages

Package	Categories of Classes
java.lang	Basic functionality common to many programs, such as the *String* class, *Math* class, and object wrappers for the primitive data types
java.text	Classes for formatting numeric output
java.util	The *Scanner* class, the *Random* class, and other miscellaneous classes
java.io	Classes for reading from and writing to files

To use a class from the Java Class Library that is not in the *java.lang* package, we need to tell the compiler in which package the class resides; in other words, we need to tell the compiler where to find the class. To do this, we include an **import** statement in our program. The *import* statement is inserted at the top of the program after our introductory comments, but before the *class* statement that begins the program.

For example, if we want to use the *DecimalFormat* class to format a floating-point number for output, we would import the *DecimalFormat* class from the *java.text* package as follows:

```
import java.text.DecimalFormat;
```

If we're using more than one class from a package, we can import all those classes we use by replacing the class name with an asterisk, as in the following example:

```
import java.text.*;
```

3.7   The *String* Class

As we've discussed, Java provides the *char* primitive data type, which stores one character. Almost every program, however, needs a data type that stores more than one character. Programs need to process names, addresses, or labels of many kinds. For example, many programs involve a login procedure where the user has to enter a user ID and a password. The program reads the user ID and password, compares them to values stored in a database, and allows the user to continue only if the user ID and password match the database values.

To handle this type of data, Java provides a *String* class. Because the *String* class is part of the *java.lang* package, it is automatically available to any Java program and we do not need to use the *import* statement. The *String* class provides several constructors, as well as a number of methods to manipulate, search, and compare

String objects. In addition, the Java language provides two concatenation operators to combine *String* objects with variables, literals, or other *String* objects.

Let's look at two of the *String* class constructors shown in Table 3.3. Example 3.6 shows how to use these two constructors in a program.

```java
1  /* Demonstrating String methods
2     Anderson, Franceschi
3  */
4  public class StringDemo
5  {
6    public static void main( String [ ] args )
7    {
8      String s1 = new String( "OOP in Java " );
9      System.out.println( "s1 is: " + s1 );
10     String s2 = "is not that difficult. ";
11     System.out.println( "s2 is: " + s2 );
12
13     String s3 = s1 + s2; // new String is s1, followed by s2
14     System.out.println( "s1 + s2 is: " + s3 );
15
16     System.out.println( "s1 is still: " + s1 ); // s1 is unchanged
17     System.out.println( "s2 is still: " + s2 ); // s2 is unchanged
18
19     String empty = new String( );
20     System.out.println( "\nThe length of the empty String is "
21                         + empty.length( ) );
22
23     String greeting = "Hello"; // instantiate greeting
24     int len = greeting.length( );  // len will be assigned 5
25     System.out.println( "\nThe length of " + greeting + " is " + len );
26
27     String greetingUpper = greeting.toUpperCase( );
28     System.out.println( greeting + " converted to upper case is "
29                         + greetingUpper );
30     System.out.println( greeting + " converted to lowercase is "
31                         + greeting.toLowerCase( ) );
32
33     char firstChar = greeting.charAt( 0 );
34     char lastChar = greeting.charAt( greeting.length( ) - 1 );
35     System.out.println( "\nThe first and last characters of "
36                         + greeting + " are " + firstChar
37                         + " and " + lastChar );
38
39     int indexOfE = greeting.indexOf( 'e' );
```

```
40        System.out.println( "\nThe index of e is " + indexOfE );
41        System out.println( "The index of l is "
42                                + greeting.indexOf( 'l' ) );
43        System.out.println( "The index of lo is "
44                                + greeting.indexOf( "lo" ) );
45        System.out.println( "The index of h is "
46                                + greeting.indexOf( 'h' ) );
47
48        System.out.println( "\nThe middle three characters of Hello are "
49                                + greeting.substring( 1, 4 ) );
50        System.out.println( "All characters of Hello except the first are "
51                                + greeting.substring( 1 ) );
52    }
53 }
```

EXAMPLE 3.6   **Demonstrating *String* Methods**

When this program runs, it will produce the output shown in Figure 3.11.

The first constructor

`String( String str )`

allocates a *String* object and sets its value to the sequence of characters in the argument *str*, which can be a *String* object or a *String* literal. Line 8 instantiates the *String* *s1* and sets its value to "OOP in Java".

The second constructor

`String( )`

creates an empty *String*—in other words, a *String* containing no characters. We can add characters to the *String* later. This constructor will come in handy in programs where we build up our output, piece by piece. Line 19 uses the second constructor to instantiate an empty *String* named *empty*.

TABLE 3.3   ***String* Class Constructors**

String Class Constructor Summary
`String( String str )`
allocates a *String* object with the value of *str*, which can be a *String* object or a *String* literal
`String( )`
allocates an empty *String* object

Figure 3.11

Output from
Example 3.6

```
s1 is: OOP in Java
s2 is: is not that difficult.
s1 + s2 is: OOP in Java is not that difficult.
s1 is still: OOP in Java
s2 is still: is not that difficult.

The length of the empty String is 0

The length of Hello is 5
Hello converted to upper case is HELLO
Hello converted to lowercase is hello

The first and last characters of Hello are H and o

The index of e is 1
The index of l is 2
The index of lo is 3
The index of h is -1

The middle three characters of Hello are ell
All characters of Hello except the first are ello
```

Additionally, because *Strings* are used so frequently in programs, Java provides special support for instantiating *String* objects without explicitly using the *new* operator. We can simply assign a *String* literal to a *String* object reference. For example, at line 10, we assign a *String* literal to the *s2 String* reference.

Java also provides special support for appending a *String* to the end of another *String* through the **concatenation operator** (+) and the **shortcut version of the concatenation operator** (+=). This concept is illustrated in Example 3.6. Lines 8–11 declare, instantiate, and print two *String* objects, *s1* and *s2*. Line 13 concatenates *s1* and *s2*, and the resulting *String* is assigned to the *s3 String* reference, which is printed at line 14. Finally, we output *s1* and *s2* again at lines 16 and 17 to illustrate that their values have not changed.

Note that the *String* concatenation operator is the same character as the addition arithmetic operator. In some cases, we need to make clear to the compiler which operator we want to use. For example, this statement uses both the *String* concatenation operator and the addition arithmetic operator:

```
System.out.println( "The sum of 1 and 2 is " + ( 1 + 2 ) );
```

Notice that we put *1 + 2* inside parentheses to let the compiler know that we want to add two *ints* using the addition arithmetic operator (+). The addition will be performed first because of the higher operator precedence of parentheses. Then it will become clear to the compiler that the other + operator is intended to be a *String* concatenation operator because its operands are a *String* and an *int*.

Example 3.6 also demonstrates some useful methods of the *String* class, which are summarized in Table 3.4.

TABLE 3.4 *String* Methods

String Class Method Summary	
Return value	**Method name and argument list**
int	length( )
	returns the length of the *String*
String	toUpperCase( )
	returns a copy of the *String* with all letters in uppercase
String	toLowerCase( )
	returns a copy of the *String* with all letters in lowercase
char	charAt(int index)
	returns the character at the position specified by *index*
int	indexOf(String searchString)
	returns the index of the beginning of the first occurrence of *searchString* or −1 if *searchString* is not found
int	indexOf(char searchChar)
	returns the index of the first occurrence of *searchChar* in the *String* or −1 if *searchChar* is not found
String	substring(int startIndex, int endIndex)
	returns a substring of the *String* object beginning at the character at index *startIndex* and ending at the character at index *endIndex* − 1
String	substring(int startIndex)
	returns a substring of the *String* object beginning at the character at index *startIndex* and continuing to the end of the *String*

The *length* Method

The *length* method returns the number of characters in a *String*, including any spaces and punctuation. Sometimes, the number of characters in a user ID is limited, for example, to eight, and this method is useful to ensure that the length of the ID does not exceed the limit.

The *length* method is called using a *String* object reference and the dot operator. As we can see in Table 3.4, the *length* method does not take any arguments and returns an *int*, which contains the number of characters in the *String*. We can output the return value or we can store the return value in an *int* variable. In Example 3.6, at line 21, we call the *length* method inside the output statement. The return value replaces the method call, so the result is that we output the number of characters—in this case 0, as seen in Figure 3.11. At line 24, we store the return value from the *length* method in the variable *len*. This allows us to refer to that value in the next line to output the number of characters in the *String greeting*.

The *toUpperCase* and *toLowerCase* Methods

The *toUpperCase* method returns a copy of the *String* with all the letters in uppercase, while the *toLowerCase* method returns a copy of the *String* with all the letters in lowercase. Digits and special characters are unchanged.

Both methods do not take any arguments. If we want to convert the original *String* to upper- or lowercase, we need to assign the return value to the original *String*. Optionally, we can assign the converted *String* to another *String* object or output the return value directly.

At line 27 in Example 3.6, we call the *toUpperCase* method on *greeting* and store the returned capitalized *String* into a new *String greetingUpper*. We then output *greetingUpper* at lines 28–29. The *String greeting* is unchanged.

We call the *toLowerCase* method at lines 30–31 in an output statement and print the return value directly. Again, the *String greeting* is unchanged.

Before discussing the remaining methods in Table 3.4, we need to introduce the concept of **indexes**. Each character in a *String* is assigned an index representing its position within the *String*. The index of the first character is always 0. The index of the second character is always 1, and so on. It stands to reason, then, that the index of the last character is always the length of the *String* – 1.

Shown below is the *String greeting* and the indexes of its characters. As we can see, the index of the first letter, *H*, is 0, and the index of the last letter, *o*, is 4, which is one less than the length of the *String* (5).

character	H	e	l	l	o
index	0	1	2	3	4

Several of the *String* methods use these indexes to identify which characters within the *String* to process.

The *charAt* Method

The *charAt* method returns the character at a specified index in a *String*.

One of the uses of this method is for extracting just the first character of a *String*, which might be advantageous when prompting the user for an answer to a question.

For example, we might ask users if they want to play a game again. They can answer "y," "yes," or "you bet!" Our only concern is whether the first character is a *y*, so we could use this method to store just the first character of their answer into a *char* variable. Assuming the user's answer was previously read and stored into a *String* variable named *answerString*, we could use the following statement to extract the first character of *answerString*:

```
char answerChar = answerString.charAt( 0 );
```

Later in this text, when we talk about selection, we will be able to test whether *answerChar* is a 'y'.

As shown in Table 3.4, the *charAt* method takes one argument, an *int*, which is the index of the character within the *String* to extract. The method returns that character as a *char*. In Example 3.6, at line 33, we call the *charAt* method with an argument of 0 to extract the first character in *greeting* and store the return value in the *char* variable, *firstChar*. At line 34, we extract the last character in *greeting* by calling the *charAt* method with the argument *greeting.length( ) – 1* and store the return value in the *char* variable, *lastChar*. Although in this case we could have sent an argument of *4* and gotten the same result, sending an argument of *length( ) -1* to the *charAt* method will extract the last character of any *String*. We then output both characters (lines 35–37). Note that we assume that *greeting* has at least one character; otherwise, the expression *greeting.length( ) –1* is equal to *-1*, an invalid index.

The *indexOf* Methods

The *indexOf* methods are useful for searching a *String* for a specific character or *String*. Table 3.4 shows two versions of this method, one that accepts a single *char* as the argument and one that accepts a *String* as an argument. In either case, the methods return as an *int* the index of the first occurrence of the *char* or the first occurrence of the first character of the *String*. If the character or *String* is not found, the *indexOf* methods return –1.

In Example 3.6, we use the *indexOf* method to search the *String greeting* for various characters. First, at line 39, we search *greeting* for the character '*e*' and store the returned index in *indexOfE*. When we output that index at line 40, we see in Figure 3.11 that '*e*' was found at index 1. At lines 41–42, we search *greeting* for the letter '*l*' and output the returned index. Notice that *greeting* has two letter *l*s, but the *indexOf* method returns only the index of the first occurrence, which is 2. Then at lines 43–44, we search *greeting* for the *String* "*lo*", which the *indexOf* method finds beginning at index 3. Finally, at lines 45–46, we search *greeting* for the lowercase letter '*h*', which is not in our *String*. We see when outputting the return value that the method returned –1, indicating that the *indexOf* method did not find a lowercase *h* in *greeting*.

The *substring* Methods

The *substring* methods are useful for creating a new *String* from characters in an existing *String*. The *substring* method returns a group of characters, or **substring**, from a *String*. The original *String* is unchanged. Table 3.4 shows two versions of the *substring* method. The first version takes two *int* arguments. The first argument is the index at which to start extracting the characters, and the second argument is the index of the first character not to extract. Thus, the *endIndex* argument is one position past the last character to extract. We know this sounds a little awkward, but setting up the arguments this way actually makes the method easier to use, as we will demonstrate.

In Example 3.6, we create and output a new *String* containing the middle three characters of *greeting* (lines 48–49). The first argument specifies that the new *String* should start with the character at index 1, which is an '*e*', and the *String* should include all succeeding characters up to but not including the character at index 4. The result is a *String* containing "*ell*".

The second version of the *substring* method is convenient for extracting all characters in a *String* from one position to the end of the *String*. This version of *substring* takes only one *int* argument, which is the index at which to start collecting characters. The returned *String* will consist of all characters starting at *startIndex* and continuing to the end of the *String*. We call this version at lines 50–51, where we extract and output all characters in *greeting* except the first.

String Processing

With the popularity of large search engines and Big Data, the ability to find, extract, and reformat information in a *String* of characters is becoming an important part of computer science. We call this **string processing**. For example, using the *String* methods we have just discussed, we can write an application to extract and format a first and last name from a *String*. Assume we know that a *String* contains a name in this format:

`<lastname>, <firstname>`

that is, with the last name first, followed by a comma and a space, then the first name.

Our job is to produce a *String* in this format:

`<Firstname> <Lastname>`

with a space separating the first and last names and with the first character of each name capitalized and all other letters in lowercase.

Example 3.7 shows the code to accomplish this, and its output is shown in Figure 3.12. In this example, we have hard-coded the name in the *String invertedName* (line 8) to be: "lincoln, abraham" but the code we write needs to work for any name in this format.

Let's look at the characters and indexes of this *String*. (Again, this is just one example. We are writing code to work with any name in this format.)

character	l	i	n	c	o	l	n	,		a	b	r	a	h	a	m
index	0	1	2	3	4	5	6	7	8	9	10	11	12	13	14	15

Let's begin by extracting the last name. We know the last name starts at the beginning of the *String* and ends at the character before the comma, so we need to find the comma. As we have seen, the *indexOf* method allows us to search for the location of a character. At line 10, we call the *indexOf* method, sending it a comma as the search argument, and storing the return value in the *int* variable, *indexOfComma*. We output the *indexOfComma* at lines 11–12 to verify that we have indeed found the comma at index 7.

character	l	i	n	c	o	l	n	,		a	b	r	a	h	a	m
index	0	1	2	3	4	5	6	7	8	9	10	11	12	13	14	15

indexOfComma

We then use the *substring* method to extract all the characters from the first character up to, **but not including**, the location of the comma. Our two arguments, then, are 0 as the start index, and *indexOfComma* as the end index. At line 16, we output the extracted last name.

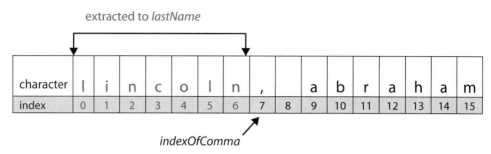

Next, we want to extract the first name. Looking at our inverted name above, we see that the first name starts at the character after the space (index 9 in this case) and continues to the end of the *String*. We could either search for the space, or we could specify the starting index for the first name as an offset from the location of the comma that we have already found. Let's do the latter.

Because we want to extract all characters starting two positions after the comma until the end of the *String*, we can use the version of the *substring* method that accepts one argument. At line 19, we call the *substring* method with the argument *indexOfComma + 2*. This will extract all characters from index 9 to the end of *invertedName*. We output the returned *String*, *firstName*, at line 20.

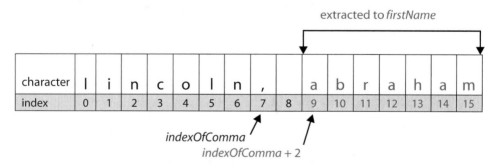

We have now isolated the first and last names in their own *Strings*.

We have one more task to perform: formatting the capitalization of the names. As mentioned, we want to capitalize the first character of each name and make the rest of the characters lowercase. We can do this by dividing each name into two *Strings*: one *String* that will contain just the first character, and the second *String* that will contain the remaining characters. At line 23, we extract just the first character of the first name using the *substring* method with the start index being 0 and the end index being 1. We then capitalize the first letter by calling the *toUpperCase* method on that *String* and storing the return value back into *first-NameStart* (line 24). We again call the *substring* method to extract the remaining characters of the first name (line 25), starting at index 1 and continuing to the end of the *String* and convert that *String* to lowercase by calling the *toLowerCase* method *(line 26)*, storing the result back into the *firstNameRemainder String*. We can now combine those two *Strings* into a formatted first name using the *String* concatenation operator (line 27).

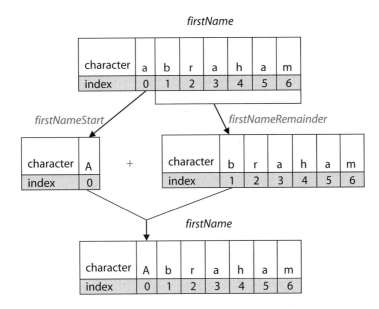

At lines 29–33, we perform the corresponding operations on the last name.

At this point, the formatting of the name is complete and we concatenate the first name, a space, and the last name to form the full name (line 35), which we output at lines 36–37.

```
1 /* Demonstrating String Processing
2    Anderson, Franceschi
3 */
4 public class StringProcessing
5 {
6   public static void main( String [ ] args )
7   {
8     String invertedName = "lincoln, abraham";
9
```

COMMON ERROR TRAP
Specifying a negative start index or a start index past the last character of the *String* will generate a *StringIndexOutOfBoundsException*. Specifying a negative end index or an end index greater than the length of the *String* will also generate a *StringIndexOutOfBoundsException*.

```
10      int comma = invertedName.indexOf( ',' ); // find the comma
11      System.out.println( "\nThe index of ',' in \""
12                           + invertedName + "\" is " + comma );
13
14      // last name: extract all characters before the comma
15      String lastName = invertedName.substring( 0, comma );
16      System.out.println( "The last name is " + lastName );
17
18      // first name: extract all characters after the space
19      String firstName = invertedName.substring( comma + 2 );
20      System.out.println( "The first name is " + firstName );
21
22      // convert the first letter of each name to uppercase
23      String firstNameStart = firstName.substring( 0, 1 );
24      firstNameStart = firstNameStart.toUpperCase( );
25      String firstNameRemainder = firstName.substring( 1 );
26      firstNameRemainder = firstNameRemainder.toLowerCase( );
27      firstName = firstNameStart + firstNameRemainder;
28
29      String lastNameStart = lastName.substring( 0, 1 );
30      lastNameStart = lastNameStart.toUpperCase( );
31      String lastNameRemainder = lastName.substring( 1 );
32      lastNameRemainder = lastNameRemainder.toLowerCase( );
33      lastName = lastNameStart + lastNameRemainder;
34
35      String fullName = firstName + " " + lastName;
36      System.out.println( "\nThe formatted full name is "
37                           + fullName );
38   }
39 }
```

EXAMPLE 3.7   *StringProcessing.java*

Try running this example with your name and with a mixture of upper- and lower-case letters to verify that it does indeed work with other names.

When we are calculating indexes and the number of characters to extract, we need to be careful not to specify an index that is not in the *String*, because that will generate a run-time error, *StringIndexOutOfBoundsException*.

REFERENCE POINT
You can read more about the *String* class on Oracle's Java website *www.oracle.com/technetwork/java.*

Figure 3.12

The Output of Example 3.7

```
The index of ',' in "lincoln, abraham" is 7
The last name is lincoln
The first name is abraham

The formatted full name is Abraham Lincoln
```

3.8 Formatting Output with the *DecimalFormat* Class

In a computer program, numbers represent a real-life entity, for instance, a price or a winning percentage. Floating-point numbers, however, are calculated to many decimal places and, as a result of some computations, can end up with more significant digits than our programs need. For example, the price of an item after a discount could look like 3.466666666666666, when all we really want to display is $3.47; that is, a leading dollar sign and two significant digits after the decimal point. The *DecimalFormat* class allows us to specify the number of digits to display after the decimal point and to add dollar signs, commas, and percentage signs (%) to our output.

The *DecimalFormat* class is part of the *java.text* package, so to use the *DecimalFormat* class, we include the following *import* statement in our program:

```
import java.text.DecimalFormat;
```

We can instantiate a *DecimalFormat* object using a simple constructor that takes a *String* object as an argument. This *String* object represents how we want our formatted number to look when it's printed. The API for that constructor is shown in Table 3.5.

The pattern that we use to instantiate the *DecimalFormat* object consists of special characters and symbols and creates a "picture" of how we want the number to look when printed. Some of the more commonly used symbols and their meanings are listed in Table 3.6.

TABLE 3.5 A *DecimalFormat* Constructor and the *format* Method

DecimalFormat Class Constructor	
DecimalFormat(String pattern)	
instantiates a *DecimalFormat* object with the output pattern specified in the argument	
The *format* Method	
Return value	**Method name and argument list**
String	format(double number)
	returns a *String* representation of *number* formatted according to the *DecimalFormat* object used to call the method

TABLE 3.6   *Special Characters for DecimalFormat Patterns*

Common Pattern Symbols for a *DecimalFormat* object	
Symbol	**Meaning**
0	Required digit. Do not suppress leading or terminating 0s in this position.
#	Optional digit. Do not include a leading or terminating digit that is 0.
.	Decimal point.
,	Comma separator.
$	Dollar sign.
%	Multiply by 100 and append a percentage sign.

```java
1  /* Demonstrating the DecimalFormat class
2     Anderson, Franceschi
3  */
4
5  // import the DecimalFormat class from the java.text package
6  import java.text.DecimalFormat;
7
8  public class DemoDecimalFormat
9  {
10   public static void main( String [ ] args )
11   {
12     // first, instantiate a DecimalFormat object specifying a
13     // pattern for currency
14     DecimalFormat pricePattern = new DecimalFormat( "$0.00" );
15
16     double price1 = 78.66666666;
17     double price2 = 34.5;
18     double price3 = .3333333;
19     int price4 = 3;
20     double price5 = 100.23;
21
22     // then print the values using the pattern
23     System.out.println( "The first price is: "
24                 + pricePattern.format( price1 ) );
25     System.out.println( "\nThe second price is: "
26                 + pricePattern.format( price2 ) );
27     System.out.println( "\nThe third price is: "
28                 + pricePattern.format( price3 ) );
```

```
29       System.out.println( "\nThe fourth price is: "
30                       + pricePattern.format( price4 ) );
31       System.out.println( "\nThe fifth price is: "
32                       + pricePattern.format( price5 ) );
33
34       // instantiate another new DecimalFormat object
35       // for printing percentages
36       DecimalFormat percentPattern = new DecimalFormat( "0.0#%" );
37
38       double average1 = .98;
39       System.out.println( "\nThe first average is: "
40                       + percentPattern.format( average1 ) );
41       double average2 = .98748;
42       System.out.println( "\nThe second average is: "
43                       + percentPattern.format( average2 ) );
44
45       // now instantiate another new DecimalFormat object
46       // for printing time as two digits
47       DecimalFormat timePattern = new DecimalFormat( "00" );
48
49       int hours = 5, minutes = 12, seconds = 0;
50       System.out.println( "\nThe time is "
51                       + timePattern.format( hours ) + ":"
52                       + timePattern.format( minutes ) + ":"
53                       + timePattern.format( seconds ) );
54
55       // now instantiate another DecimalFormat object
56       // for printing numbers in the millions.
57       DecimalFormat bigNumber = new DecimalFormat( "#,###" );
58
59       int millions = 1234567;
60       System.out.println( "\nmillions is "
61                       + bigNumber.format( millions ) );
62   }
63 }
```

EXAMPLE 3.8   Demonstrating the *DecimalFormat* Class

Once we have instantiated a *DecimalFormat* object, we format a number by passing it as an argument to the *format* method, shown in Table 3.5. Example 3.8 demonstrates the use of the *DecimalFormat* patterns and calling the *format* method. The output for this program is shown in Figure 3.13.

In Example 3.8, line 14 instantiates the *DecimalFormat* object, *pricePattern*, which will be used to print prices. In the pattern

```
"$0.00"
```

Figure 3.13

Output from
Example 3.8

```
The first price is: $78.67
The second price is: $34.50
The third price is: $0.33
The forth price is: $3.00
The fifth price is: $100.23
The first average is: 98.0%
The second average is: 98.75%
The time is 05:12:00
millions is 1,234,567
```

the first character of this pattern is the dollar sign ($), which we want to precede the price. The 0 specifies that there should be at least one digit to the left of the decimal point. If there is no value to the left of the decimal point, then insert a zero. The two 0s that follow the decimal point specify that exactly two digits should be to the right of the decimal point; that is, if more than two digits are to the right of the decimal point, round to two digits; if the last digit is a 0, include the zero, and if there is no fractional part to the number, include two zeroes. Using this pattern, we see that in lines 23–24, *price1* is printed to two decimal places. In lines 25–26, *price2* is printed with a zero in the second decimal place.

COMMON ERROR TRAP
When using a % symbol to *format* a percentage, do not multiply the value by 100. The *format* method will do that for you.

In lines 29–30, we print *price4*, which is an integer. The *format* method API calls for a *double* as the argument; however, because all numeric data types can be promoted to a *double*, any numeric data type can be sent as an argument. The result is that two zeroes are added to the right of the decimal point.

Finally, we use the *pricePattern* pattern to print *price5* in lines 31–32, which needs no rounding or padding of extra digits.

Next, line 36 instantiates a *DecimalFormat* object, *percentPattern*, for formatting percentages to one or two decimal places ("0.0#%"). Lines 38–40 and 41–43 define the variables *average1* and *average2* then print them using the *format* method in an output statement. Notice that we do not multiply the averages by 100 before we format the percentage. A % in the pattern signals to the *format* method that it should multiply the value by 100 before converting the number to a *String*.

REFERENCE POINT
You can read more about the *DecimalFormat* class on Oracle's Java website: *www.oracle.com/ technetwork/ java.*

Line 47 defines another pattern, "00", which is useful for printing the time with colons between the hour, minutes, and seconds. When the time is printed on lines 50–53, the hours, minutes, and seconds are padded with a leading zero, if necessary.

Line 57 defines our last pattern, "#,###", which can be used to insert commas into integer values in the thousands and above. Lines 60–61 print the variable *millions* with commas separating the millions and thousands digits. Notice that the pattern is extrapolated for a number that has more digits than the pattern.

3.9 Generating Random Numbers with the *Random* Class

Random numbers come in handy for many operations in a program, such as rolling dice, dealing cards, timing the appearance of a nemesis in a game, or other simulations of seemingly random events.

There's one problem in using random numbers in programs, however: Computers are **deterministic**. In essence, this means that given a specific input to a specific set of instructions, a computer will always produce the same output. The challenge, then, is generating random numbers while using a deterministic system. Many talented computer scientists have worked on this problem, and some innovative and complex solutions have been proposed.

The *Random* class, which is in the *java.util* package, uses a mathematical formula to generate a sequence of numbers. The constructor generates a **seed** value, which determines where in that sequence the set of *random* numbers will begin. As such, the *Random* class generates numbers that appear to be, but are not truly, random. These numbers are called **pseudorandom** numbers, and they work just fine for our purposes.

Table 3.7 shows a constructor for the *Random* class and a method for retrieving a random integer. The default constructor creates a random number generator using a seed value. Once the random number generator is created, we can ask for a random number by calling the *nextInt* method. Other methods, *nextDouble*, *nextBoolean*, *nextByte*, and *nextLong*, which are not shown in Table 3.7, return a random *double*, *boolean*, *byte*, or *long* value, respectively.

TABLE 3.7   A *Random* Class Constructor and the *nextInt* Method

Random Class Constructor	
`Random( )`	
creates a random number generator with a seed generated using the system time	
The *nextInt* Method	
Return value	**Method name and argument list**
`int`	`nextInt( int number )`
	returns a random integer ranging from 0 up to, but not including, *number* in uniform distribution

To demonstrate how to use the random number generator, let's take rolling a die as an example. To simulate the roll of a six-sided die, we need to simulate random occurrences of the numbers 1 through 6. If we call the *nextInt* method with an argument of 6, it will return an integer between 0 and 5. To get randomly distributed numbers from 1 to 6, we can simply add 1 to the value returned by the *nextInt* method. Thus, if we have instantiated a *Random* object named *random*, we can generate random numbers from 1 to 6 by calling the *nextInt* method in this way:

```java
int die = random.nextInt( 6 ) + 1;
```

In general, assuming than n is smaller than m, if we want to generate random numbers from n to m, we should call the *nextInt* method with the number of possible random values $(m - n + 1)$, and then add the first value of our sequence (n) to the returned value. Thus, this statement generates a random number between 10 and 100 inclusive:

```java
int randomNumber = random.nextInt( 100 - 10 + 1 ) + 10;
```

Line 18 of Example 3.9 generates a random number between 20 and 200 inclusive.

```java
 1 /*A demonstration of the Random class
 2   Anderson, Franceschi
 3 */
 4 import java.util.Random;
 5
 6 public class RandomNumbers
 7 {
 8   public static void main( String [ ] args )
 9   {
10     Random random = new Random( );
11
12     // simulate the roll of a die
13     int die = random.nextInt( 6 ) + 1;
14     System.out.println( "\nThe die roll is " + die );
15
16     // generate a random number between 20 and 200
17     int start = 20, end = 200;
18     int number = random.nextInt( end - start + 1 ) + start;
19     System.out.println( "\nThe random number between " + start
20                         + " and " + end + " is " + number );
21   }
22 }
```

EXAMPLE 3.9   A Demonstration of the *Random* Class

REFERENCE POINT
You can read more about the *Random* class on Oracle's Java website: *www. oracle.com/ technetwork/ java.*

When the *RandomNumbers* program executes, it will produce output similar to Figure 3.14. The output will vary from one execution of the program to the next because different random numbers will be generated.

```
The die roll is 2

The random number between 20 and 200 is 117
```

Figure 3.14

Output from
Example 3.9

3.10   Input from the Console Using the *Scanner* Class

As our programs become more complex, we will need to allow the users of our programs to input data. User input can be read into our program in several ways:

- from the keyboard
- from a file
- through a Graphical User Interface (GUI)

The Java Class Library provides classes for all types of data input. In this chapter, we will concentrate on inputting data from the keyboard.

The *Scanner* class provides methods for reading *byte, short, int, long, float, double, boolean,* and *String* data types from the keyboard. These methods are shown in Table 3.8.

The *Scanner* class is defined in the *java.util* package, so we need to include the following *import* statement:

```
import java.util.Scanner;
```

In order to use the *Scanner* class, we must first instantiate a *Scanner* object and associate it with a data source. We will use the *System.in* input stream, which by default is tied to the keyboard. Thus, our data source for input will be *System.in*. The following statement will instantiate a *Scanner* object named *scan* and associate the keyboard as its data source.

```
Scanner scan = new Scanner( System.in );
```

Once the *Scanner* object has been instantiated, we can use it to call any of the *next. . .* methods to input data from the keyboard. The specific *next. . .* method we call depends on the type of input we want from the user. Each of the *next. . .* methods returns a value from the input stream, that is, the value the user types into the keyboard. We need to assign the return value from the *next. . .* methods to a variable to complete the data input. Obviously, the data type of our variable must match or be compatible with the data type of the value returned by the *next. . .* method.

The *next. . .* methods just perform input. They do not tell the user what data to enter. Before calling any of the *next* methods, therefore, we need to prompt the user for the input we want. We can print a prompt using *System.out.print*, which is similar to using *System.out.println*, except that the cursor remains after the printed text rather than advancing to the next line.

TABLE 3.8   **Selected Methods of the *Scanner* Class**

A *Scanner* Class Constructor
`Scanner( InputStream dataSource )`   creates a *Scanner* object that will read from the *InputStream dataSource*. To read from the keyboard, we will use the predefined *InputStream System.in*.

Selected Methods of the *Scanner* Class	
Return value	**Method name and argument list**
`byte`	`nextByte( )` returns the next input as a *byte*
`short`	`nextShort( )` returns the next input as a *short*
`int`	`nextInt( )` returns the next input as an *int*
`long`	`nextLong( )` returns the next input as a *long*
`float`	`nextFloat( )` returns the next input as a *float*
`double`	`nextDouble( )` returns the next input as a *double*
`boolean`	`nextBoolean( )` returns the next input as a *boolean*
`String`	`next( )` returns the next token in the input line as a *String*
`String`	`nextLine( )` returns the unread characters of the input line as a *String*

When writing a prompt for user input, we should keep several things in mind. First, our prompt should be specific. If we want the user to enter his or her full name, then our prompt should say just that:

```
Please enter your first and last names.
```

If the input should fall within a range of values, then we should tell the user which values will be valid, for example:

```
Please enter an integer between 0 and 10.
```

We should also keep in mind that users are typically not programmers. It's important to phrase a prompt using language the user understands. Many times, programmers write a prompt from their point of view, as in this bad prompt:

```
Please enter a String:
```

Users don't know, and don't care, about *Strings* or any other data types, for that matter.
Users want to know only what they need to enter to get the program to do its job.

When our prompts are clear and specific, the user makes fewer errors and therefore
feels more comfortable using our program.

Line 13 of Example 3.10 prompts the user to enter his or her first name. Line 14 captures the user input and assigns the word entered by the user to the *String* variable
firstName, which is printed in line 15. Similarly, line 17 prompts for the user's age,
line 18 captures the integer entered by the user and assigns it to the *int* variable *age*,
and line 19 outputs the value of *age*. Reading other primitive data types follows the
same pattern. Line 21 prompts for the user's grade point average (a *float* value). Line
22 captures the number entered by the user and assigns it to the *float* variable *gpa*,
and line 23 outputs the value of *gpa*.

> **SOFTWARE ENGINEERING TIP**
>
> Provide the user with clear prompts for input. Prompts should be phrased using words the user understands and should describe the data requested and any restrictions on input values.

```java
 1 /* A demonstration of reading from the keyboard using Scanner
 2    Anderson, Franceschi
 3 */
 4
 5 import java.util.Scanner;
 6
 7 public class DataInput
 8 {
 9   public static void main( String [ ] args )
10   {
11     Scanner scan = new Scanner( System.in );
12
13     System.out.print( "Enter your first name > " );
14     String firstName = scan.next( );
15     System.out.println( "Your name is " + firstName );
16
17     System.out.print( "\nEnter your age as an integer > " );
18     int age = scan.nextInt( );
19     System.out.println( "Your age is " + age );
20
21     System.out.print( "\nEnter your GPA > " );
22     float gpa = scan.nextFloat( );
23     System.out.println( "Your GPA is " + gpa );
24   }
25 }
```

EXAMPLE 3.10   Reading from the Keyboard Using *Scanner*

SOFTWARE ENGINEERING TIP

End your prompts with some indication that input is expected, and include a trailing space for better readability.

When this program executes, the prompt is printed on the console and the cursor remains at the end of the prompt. Figure 3.15 shows the output when these statements are executed and the user enters Syed, presses *Enter*, enters 21, presses *Enter*, and enters 3.875, and presses *Enter* again.

The methods *nextByte, nextShort, nextLong, nextDouble*, and *nextBoolean* can be used with the same pattern as *next, nextInt*, and *nextFloat*.

Note that we end our prompt with a space, an angle bracket, and another space. The angle bracket indicates that we are waiting for input, and the spaces separate the prompt from the input. Without the trailing space, the user's input would immediately follow the prompt, which is more difficult to read, as we show in Figure 3.16.

As you review Table 3.8, you may notice that the *Scanner* class does not provide a method for reading a single character. To do this, we can use the *next* method, which returns a *String*, then extract the first character from the *String* using the *charAt(0)* method call, as shown in Example 3.11. Line 14 inputs a *String* from the user and assigns it to the *String* variable *initialS*, then line 15 assigns the first character of *initialS* to the *char* variable *initial*; *initial* is then printed at line 16 as shown in Figure 3.17.

Figure 3.15

Data Input with Example 3.10

```
Enter your first name > Syed
Your name is Syed

Enter your age as an integer > 21
Your age is 21

Enter your GPA > 3.875
Your GPA is 3.875
```

Figure 3.16

Prompt and Input Running Together

```
Enter your age as an integer >21
```

```
1  /* A demonstration of how to get character input using Scanner
2     Anderson, Franceschi
3  */
4
5  import java.util.Scanner;
6
7  public class CharacterInput
8  {
9    public static void main( String [ ] args )
10   {
11      Scanner scan = new Scanner( System.in );
12
13      System.out.print( "Enter your middle initial > " );
14      String initialS = scan.next( );
```

```
15        char initial = initialS.charAt( 0 );
16        System.out.println( "Your middle initial is " + initial );
17    }
18 }
```

EXAMPLE 3.11   Using *Scanner* for Character Input

A *Scanner* object divides its input into sequences of characters called **tokens**, using **delimiters**. The default delimiters are the standard **white space** characters, which among others include the space, tab, and *newline* characters. The complete set of Java white space characters is shown in Table 3.9.

By default, when a *Scanner* object tokenizes the input, it skips leading white space, then builds a token composed of all subsequent characters until it encounters another delimiter. Thus, if we have this code,

```
System.out.print( "Enter your age as an integer > " );
int age = scan.nextInt( );
```

and the user types, for example, three spaces and a tab, *21*, and a newline:

```
<space><space><space><tab>21<newline>
```

then the *Scanner* object skips the three spaces and the tab, starts building a token with the character *2*, then adds the character *1* to the token, and stops building the token when it encounters the *newline* character. Thus, *21* is the resulting token, which the *nextInt* method returns and which is then assigned to the *age* variable.

```
Enter your middle initial > A
Your middle initial is A
```

Figure 3.17

Output of
Example 3.11

TABLE 3.9   Java White Space Characters

Character	Unicode equivalents
space	\u00A0, \u2007, \u202F
tab	\u0009, \u000B
line feed	\u000A
form feed	\u000C
carriage return	\u000D
file, group, unit, and record separators	\u001C, \u001D, \u001E, \u001F

An input line can contain more than one token. For example, if we prompt the user for his or her name and age, and the user enters the following line, then presses *Enter*:

```
<tab>Jon<space>Olsen,<space>21<space>
```

then, the leading white space is skipped and the *Scanner* object creates three tokens:

- *Jon*
- *Olsen,*
- *21*

Note that commas are not white space, so the comma is actually part of the second token. To input these three tokens, our program would use two calls to the *next* method to retrieve the two *String* tokens and a call to *nextInt* to retrieve the age.

To capture a complete line of input from the user, we use the method *nextLine*. Unlike other *Scanner* methods, the *nextLine* method returns a *String* containing any leading and trailing white space, except for the *newline* character, which is the *nextLine* method's only delimiter. Example 3.12 shows how *nextLine* can be used in a program. Figure 3.18 shows a sample run of the program with the user entering data.

REFERENCE POINT
You can read more about the *Scanner* class on Oracle's Java website: *www .oracle.com/ technetwork/ java.*

If the user's input (that is, the next token) is not compatible with the data type of the *next. . .* method call, then an *InputMismatchException* is generated and the program stops. Figure 3.19 demonstrates Example 3.10 when the program calls the *nextInt* method and the user enters a letter, rather than an integer. It is possible to avoid this exception, and we show how when we discuss looping.

```
 1 /* A demonstration of using Scanner's nextLine method
 2    Anderson, Franceschi
 3 */
 4
 5 import java.util.Scanner;
 6
 7 public class InputALine
 8 {
 9   public static void main( String [ ] args )
10   {
11     Scanner scan = new Scanner( System.in );
12
13     System.out.print( "Enter a sentence > " );
14     String sentence = scan.nextLine( );
15     System.out.println( "You said: \"" + sentence + "\"" );
16   }
17 }
```

EXAMPLE 3.12   **Using the *nextLine* Method**

```
Enter a sentence > Scanner is useful.
You said: "Scanner is useful."
```

Figure 3.18

Output of
Example 3.12

```
Enter your first name > Sarah
Your name is Sarah

Enter your age as an integer > a
Exception in thread "main" java.util.InputMismatchException
    at java.base/java.util.Scanner.throwFor(Unknown Source)
    at java.base/java.util.Scanner.next(Unknown Source)
    at java.base/java.util.Scanner.nextInt(Unknown Source)
    at java.base/java.util.Scanner.nextInt(Unknown Source)
    at DataInput.main(DataInput.java:18)
```

Figure 3.19

An Exception
When Input Is
Not the Expected
Data Type

If the user doesn't type anything when prompted, or if the user types some characters but doesn't press *Enter*, the program will simply wait until the user does press *Enter*.

Skill Practice
with these end-of-chapter questions

3.18.1   Multiple Choice Exercises

Questions 1, 11

3.18.2   Reading and Understanding Code

Questions 14, 15, 16

3.18.3   Fill In the Code

Questions 24, 25, 26, 27

3.18.4   Identifying Errors in Code

Questions 36, 37, 38, 39, 43

3.18.5   Debugging Area

Questions 45, 49

3.18.6   Write a Short Program

Questions 50, 51, 52, 55, 56

3.11 Calling *Static* Methods and Using *Static* Class Variables

Classes can also define ***static* methods**, which can be called without instantiating an object. These are also called **class methods**. The API of these methods has the keyword *static* before the return type:

```
static dataType methodName( arg1, arg2, . . . )
```

One reason a class may define *static* methods is to provide some quick, one-time functionality without requiring the client to instantiate an object. For example, as part of a larger calculation, we might want to calculate the square root of a number. Creating an object just to calculate a square root is a waste of memory and processor time. Fortunately, the *Math* class provides a *static* method that finds the square root of a number.

Class, or *static*, methods are invoked using the class name, rather than an object reference, as in the following syntax:

```
ClassName.staticMethodName( argumentList );
```

For example, in this statement:

```
absValue = Math.abs( someNumber );
```

the class name is *Math*, and the *static* method is *abs*, which returns the absolute value of the argument (*someNumber*). We use the class name rather than an object reference, because *static* methods can be called without instantiating an object. Later in this chapter, we will explore some *static* methods of the *Math* class in greater detail.

Because *static* methods can be called without an object being instantiated, *static* methods cannot access the instance variables of the class (because instance variables are object data and exist only after an object has been instantiated). *Static* methods can access ***static* data**, however, and classes often declare *static* data to be used with *static* methods. *Static* data belong to the class, rather than to a particular object, or instance, of the class.

A common use of *static* class variables is to define constants for commonly used values or for parameters for the *static* class methods. For example, the *Math* class defines two *static* constants to facilitate the use of pi and the natural logarithm, e.

Like *static* methods, *static* constants are also accessed using the class name and dot operator, as in this syntax:

```
ClassName.staticConstant
```

Thus, the *static* constant representing the value of pi can be accessed this way:

```
Math.PI
```

At first, this may appear to go against our earlier discussion of encapsulation and the restrictions on clients directly accessing object data. Remember we said that the client needed to use accessor methods (getters) and mutator methods (setters) to access object data. The reasoning behind encapsulation is to protect the object data from corruption by the client. However, in this case, the *static* data is constant, so the client is unable to change it. For the client, directly accessing the class constant is easier and faster than calling a method.

3.12   Using *System.in* and *System.out*

In order to print program output to the screen, we have been using statements like

```
System.out.println( "The value of b is " + b );
```

and

```
System.out.print( "Enter your first name > " );
```

And to instantiate a *Scanner* object, we used this statement:

```
Scanner scan = new Scanner( System.in );
```

It is now time to look at these statements in depth and understand them completely.

System is an existing Java class in the *java.lang* package. One of its fields is a *static* constant, *out*, which represents the Java console by default. Another of its fields is a *static* constant, *in*, which represents the keyboard by default. Because *in* and *out* are *static*, we refer to them using the class name, *System*, and the dot notation:

```
System.out
System.in
```

Table 3.10 shows these *static* constants as well as the *static exit* method, which can be used to terminate a program. Calling *exit* at the end of a program is optional. After the last instruction is executed, the program will end in any case. However, the *exit* method of the *System* class can be useful if we want to stop execution at a place other than the usual end of the program.

System.out is an object of the *PrintStream* class, which is also an existing Java class; it can be found in the *java.io* package. The *out* object refers to the **standard output device**, which by default is the Java console.

The methods *print* and *println* belong to the *PrintStream* class and take arguments of any primitive type, a *String*, or an object reference. The only difference between *print* and *println* is that *println* will also print a *newline* character after it writes the output. Table 3.11 shows some methods of the *PrintStream* class, which can be used with *System.out*.

Example 3.13 demonstrates various ways to use the *print* and *println* methods:

TABLE 3.10   *Static* Constants of the *System* Class and the *exit* Method

Constant	Value
in	*static* constant that represents the standard input stream, by default the keyboard
out	*static* constant that represents the standard output stream, by default the Java console
A Useful *System* Method	
Return value	**Method name and argument list**
void	exit(int exitStatus)
	static method that terminates the Java Virtual Machine. A value of 0 for *exitStatus* indicates a normal termination. Any other values indicate an abnormal termination and are used to signal that the program ended because an error occurred.

TABLE 3.11   *PrintStream* Methods for Use with *System.out*

Useful *PrintStream* Methods	
Return value	**Method name and argument list**
void	print(argument)
	prints *argument* to the standard output device. The argument can be any primitive data type, a *String* object, or another object reference.
void	println(argument)
	prints *argument* to the standard output device, then prints a *newline* character. The argument can be any primitive data type, a *String*, or another object reference.
void	println( )
	prints a *newline* character. This method is useful for skipping a line in the program's output.

```
1 /* Testing the print and println methods
2    Anderson, Franceschi
3 */
4
5 public class PrintDemo
```

```
6  {
7    public static void main( String [ ] args )
8    {
9      System.out.println( "Combine the arguments using concatenation" );
10     System.out.println( "A double: " + 23.7 + ", and an int: " + 78 );
11
12     System.out.print( "\nJava is case sensitive: " );
13     System.out.println( 'a' + " is different from " + 'A' );
14
15     System.out.println( "\nCreate a variable and print its value" );
16     String s = new String( "The grade is" );
17     double grade = 3.81;
18     System.out.println( s + " " + grade );
19
20     System.out.println( ); // skip a line
21     SimpleDate d = new SimpleDate( 4, 5, 2020 );
22     System.out.println( "Explicitly calling toString, d is "
23                          + d.toString( ) );
24     System.out.println( "Implicitly calling toString, d is " + d );
25
26     System.exit( 0 ); // optional
27   }
28 }
```

EXAMPLE 3.13   Demonstrating the *print* and *println* Methods

Lines 10 and 13 show how *print* or *println* can be used with various data types such as *double, int*, and *char*. Variables and expressions can also be used instead of literals, as shown in line 18, where two *Strings* and the *double* variable *grade* are output.

We can also print objects. All classes have a *toString* method, which converts the object data to a *String* for printing. The *toString* method is called automatically whenever an object is used as a *String*. Notice that our *SimpleDate* class, introduced earlier in the chapter, had a *toString* method that returned the object data as a *String* in the format *mm/dd/yyyy*.

The *toString* method's API is

```
String toString( )
```

After the *SimpleDate* object reference *d* is instantiated at line 21, it is printed at lines 22–23 and again at line 24. At lines 22–23, the method *toString* is called explicitly; at line 24, it is called automatically. The output of Example 3.13 is shown in Figure 3.20. Finally, we terminate the program by calling the *exit* method of the *System* class.

REFERENCE POINT
You can read more about the *System* and *PrintStream* classes on Oracle's Java website: *www. oracle.com/ technetwork/ java.*

Figure 3.20

The Output from
Example 3.13

```
Combine the arguments using concatenation
A double: 23.7, and an int: 78

Java is case sensitive: a is different from A

Create a variable and print its value
The grade is 3.81

Explicitly calling toString, d is 4/5/2020
Implicitly calling toString, d is 4/5/2020
```

3.13 The *Math* Class

The *Math* class is also part of the *java.lang* package. As such, it is automatically available to any Java program; we do not need to use the *import* statement. The *Math* class provides two *static* constants (*E* and *PI*), as well as a number of *static* methods that save the programmer from writing some complex mathematical code.

The two constants, *E* and *PI*, are both *doubles* and represent, respectively, *e* (the base of the natural logarithm, i.e., log e = 1) and **pi**, the ratio of the circumference of a circle to its diameter. Approximate values of *e* and *pi*, as we know them, are 2.78 and 3.14, respectively. These constants are shown in Table 3.12.

Because *E* and *PI* are *static* data members of the *Math* class, they are referenced using the name of the *Math* class and the dot notation as follows:

```
Math.E
Math.PI
```

Useful methods of the *Math* class are shown in Table 3.13. All the methods of the *Math* class are *static*; so they are called using the class name, *Math*, and the dot notation as follows:

```
Math.abs( -5 )
```

Example 3.14 demonstrates how the *Math* constants and the *abs* method can be used in a Java program. In lines 9 and 10, we print the values of *e* and *pi* using the *static* constants of the *Math* class. Then in lines 12 and 15, we call the *abs* method, which returns the absolute value of its argument.

TABLE 3.12   *Static* Constants of the *Math* Class

Constant	Value
E	*e*, the base of the natural logarithm
PI	*pi*, the ratio of the circumference of a circle to its diameter

We then print the results in lines 13 and 16. The output of Example 3.14 is shown in Figure 3.21.

TABLE 3.13   Useful Methods of the *Math* Class

Math Class Method Summary	
Return value	**Method name and argument list**
dataTypeOfArg	abs(arg)
	static method that returns the absolute value of the argument *arg*, which can be a *double, float, int,* or *long*.
double	log(double arg)
	static method that returns the natural logarithm (in base *e*) of its argument, *arg*. For example, log(1) returns 0 and log(*Math.E)* returns 1.
dataTypeOfArgs	min(argA, argB)
	static method that returns the smaller of the two arguments. The arguments can be *doubles, floats, ints,* or *longs*.
dataTypeOfArgs	max(argA, argB)
	static method that returns the larger of the two arguments. The arguments can be *doubles, floats, ints,* or *longs*.
double	pow(double base, double exp)
	static method that returns the value of *base* raised to the *exp* power.
long	round(double arg)
	static method that returns the closest integer to its argument, *arg*.
double	sqrt(double arg)
	static method that returns the positive square root of *arg*.

```
1 /* A demonstration of the Math class methods and constants
2    Anderson, Franceschi
3 */
4
5 public class MathConstants
6 {
7   public static void main( String [ ] args )
8   {
9     System.out.println( "The value of e is " + Math.E );
10    System.out.println( "The value of pi is " + Math.PI );
11
```

```
12      double d1 = Math.abs( 6.7 ); // d1 will be assigned 6.7
13      System.out.println( "\nThe absolute value of 6.7 is " + d1 );
14
15      double d2 = Math.abs( -6.7 ); // d2 will be assigned 6.7
16      System.out.println( "\nThe absolute value of -6.7 is " + d2 );
17   }
18 }
```

EXAMPLE 3.14   *Math* **Class Constants and the** *abs* **Method**

The operation and usefulness of most *Math* class methods are obvious. But several methods—*pow*, *round*, and *min/max*—require a little explanation.

Figure 3.21

Output from Example 3.14

```
The value of e is 2.718281828459045
The value of pi is 3.141592653589793

The absolute value of 6.7 is 6.7

The absolute value of -6.7 is 6.7
```

The *pow* Method

Example 3.15 demonstrates how some of these *Math* methods can be used in a Java program.

```
1 /* A demonstration of some Math class methods
2    Anderson, Franceschi
3 */
4
5 public class MathMethods
6 {
7   public static void main( String [ ] args )
8   {
9     double d2 = Math.log( 5 );
10    System.out.println( "\nThe log of 5 is " + d2 );
11
12    double d4 = Math.sqrt( 9 );
13    System.out.println( "\nThe square root of 9 is " + d4 );
14
15    double fourCubed = Math.pow( 4, 3 );
16    System.out.println( "\n4 to the power 3 is " + fourCubed );
17
18    double bigNumber = Math.pow( 43.5, 3.4 );
19    System.out.println( "\n43.5 to the power 3.4 is " + bigNumber );
20  }
21 }
```

EXAMPLE 3.15   **A Demonstration of Some** *Math* **Class Methods**

```
The log of 5 is 1.6094379124341003

The square root of 9 is 3.0

4 to the power 3 is 64.0

43.5 to the power 3.4 is 372274.65827529586
```

Figure 3.22

Output from
Example 3.15

The *Math* class provides the *pow* method for raising a number to a power. The *pow* method takes two arguments; the first is the base and the second is the exponent.

Although the argument list for the *pow* method specifies that the base and the exponent are both *doubles*, we can, in fact, send arguments of any numeric type to the *pow* method because all numeric types can be promoted to a *double*. No matter what type the arguments are, however, the return value is always a *double*. Thus, when line 15 calls the *pow* method with two integer arguments, the value of *fourCubed* will be 64.0. If we prefer that the return value be 64, we can cast the return value to an *int*.

Line 18 shows how to use the *pow* method with arguments of type *double*. The output of Example 3.15 is shown in Figure 3.22.

The *round* Method

The *round* method converts a *double* to its nearest integer using these rules:

- Any fractional part .0 to .4 is rounded down.
- Any fractional part .5 and above is rounded up.

Lines 9–13 in Example 3.16 use the *round* method with various numbers. Figure 3.23 shows the output.

```
 1 /* A demonstration of the Math round method
 2    Anderson, Franceschi
 3 */
 4
 5 public class MathRounding
 6 {
 7   public static void main( String [ ] args )
 8   {
 9     System.out.println( "23.4 rounded is " + Math.round( 23.4 ) );
10     System.out.println( "23.49 rounded is " + Math.round( 23.49 ) );
11     System.out.println( "23.5 rounded is " + Math.round( 23.5 ) );
12     System.out.println( "23.51 rounded is " + Math.round( 23.51 ) );
13     System.out.println( "23.6 rounded is " + Math.round( 23.6 ) );
14   }
15 }
```

EXAMPLE 3.16   A Demonstration of the *Math round* Method

Figure 3.23

Output from
Example 3.16

```
23.4 rounded is 23

23.49 rounded is 23

23.5 rounded is 24

23.51 rounded is 24

23.6 rounded is 24
```

The *min* and *max* Methods

The *min* and *max* methods return the smaller or larger of their two arguments, respectively. Example 3.17 demonstrates how the *min* and *max* methods can be used in a Java program. Figure 3.24 shows the output. Thus, the statement on line 9 of Example 3.17 will assign 2 to the *int* variable *smaller*. At line 12, a similar statement using the *max* method will assign 8 to the *int* variable *larger*.

```java
1  /* A demonstration of min and max Math class methods
2       Anderson, Franceschi
3  */
4
5  public class MathMinMaxMethods
6  {
7    public static void main( String [ ] args )
8    {
9      int smaller = Math.min( 8, 2 );
10     System.out.println( "The smaller of 8 and 2 is " + smaller );
11
12     int larger = Math.max( 8, 2 );
13     System.out.println( "The larger of 8 and 2 is " + larger );
14
15     int a = 8, b = 5, c = 12;
16     int tempSmaller = Math.min( a, b ); // find smaller of a & b
17     int smallest = Math.min( tempSmaller, c ); // compare result to c
18     System.out.println( "The smallest of " + a + ", " + b + ", and "
19                           + c + " is " + smallest );
20   }
21 }
```

EXAMPLE 3.17   **A Demonstration of the *min* and *max* Methods**

REFERENCE POINT
You can read more about the *Math* class on Oracle's Java website: *www. oracle .com/ technetwork/ java.*

The *min* method can also be used to compute the smallest of three variables. After declaring and initializing the three variables (*a*, *b*, and *c*) at line 15, we assign to a temporary variable named *tempSmaller* the smaller of the first two variables, *a* and *b*, at line 16. Then, at line 17, we compute the smaller of *tempSmaller* and the third variable, *c*, and assign that value to the variable *smallest*, which is output at lines 18 and 19.

The pattern for finding the largest of three numbers is similar, and we leave that as an exercise at the end of the chapter.

```
The smaller of 8 and 2 is 2
The larger of 8 and 2 is 8
The smallest of 8, 5, and 12 is 5
```

Figure 3.24

Output from Example 3.17

Skill Practice
with these end-of-chapter questions

3.18.1 Multiple Choice Exercises

Questions 6, 7, 8, 13

3.18.2 Reading and Understanding Code

Questions 17, 18, 19, 20, 21, 22, 23

3.18.3 Fill In the Code

Questions 28, 29, 30, 31, 32, 34

3.18.4 Identifying Errors in Code

Questions 40, 41, 42

3.18.5 Debugging Area

Questions 46, 47, 48

3.18.6 Write a Short Program

Questions 53, 54

CODE IN ACTION

To see a step-by-step illustration of how to instantiate an object and call both instance and *static* methods, look for this chapter's movie within the online resources.
Click on the link to start the movie.

3.14 Formatting Output with the *NumberFormat* Class

Like the *DecimalFormat* class, the *NumberFormat* class can also be used to format numbers for output. The *NumberFormat* class, however, provides specialized *static* methods for creating objects specifically for formatting currency and percentages.

The *NumberFormat* class is part of the *java.text* package, so we need to include the following *import* statement at the top of our program.

```
import java.text.NumberFormat;
```

The *static* methods of the *NumberFormat* class to format currency and percentages are shown in Table 3.14.

As we can see from the first two method headers, their return type is a *NumberFormat* object. These *static* methods, called **factory methods**, are used instead of constructors to create objects. Thus, instead of using the *new* keyword and a constructor, we will call one of these methods to create our formatting object.

The *getCurrencyInstance* method returns a formatting object that reflects the local currency. In the United States, that format is a leading dollar sign and is two digits to the right of the decimal place. The *getPercentInstance* method returns a formatting object for printing a fraction as a percentage by multiplying the fraction by 100, rounding to the nearest whole percent, and adding a percent sign (%).

We then use the *format* method from the *NumberFormat* class to display a value either as money or a percentage. The *format* method takes one argument, a *double,* which is the variable or value that we want to print; it returns the formatted version of the value as a *String* object, which we can then print.

TABLE 3.14   Useful Methods of the *NumberFormat* Class

NumberFormat Method Summary	
Return value	**Method name and argument list**
NumberFormat	getCurrencyInstance( )
	static method that creates a format object for money
NumberFormat	getPercentInstance( )
	static method that creates a format object for percentages
String	format(double number)
	returns a *String* representation of *number* formatted as a currency or percentage, depending on the object used to call the method

Example 3.18 is a complete program illustrating how to use these three methods.

```java
1 /* Demonstration of currency and percentage formatting
2    using the NumberFormat class.
3    Anderson, Franceschi
4 */
5
6 // we need to import the NumberFormat class from java.text
7 import java.text.NumberFormat;
8
9 public class DemoNumberFormat
10 {
11   public static void main( String [ ] args )
12   {
13     double winningPercentage = .675;
14     double price = 78.9;
15
16     // get a NumberFormat object for printing a percentage
17     NumberFormat percentFormat = NumberFormat.getPercentInstance( );
18
19     // call format method using the NumberFormat object
20     System.out.print( "The winning percentage is " );
21     System.out.println( percentFormat.format( winningPercentage ) );
22
23     // get a NumberFormat object for printing currency
24     NumberFormat priceFormat = NumberFormat.getCurrencyInstance( );
25
26     // call format method using the NumberFormat object
27     System.out.println( "\nThe price is: "
28                         + priceFormat.format( price ) );
29   }
30 }
```

EXAMPLE 3.18   Demonstrating the *NumberFormat* Class

The output of this program is shown in Figure 3.25. As with *DecimalFormat*, the *NumberFormat format* method multiples the fraction to be formatted by 100. Note that the winning percentage is formatted as a rounded whole number. If we wanted to print the fraction .675 as 67.5%, we would need to use a *DecimalFormat* object.

```
The winning percentage is 68%
The price is: $78.90
```

Figure 3.25

Output from Example 3.18

3.15   The *Integer, Double, Character,* and Other Wrapper Classes

Most programs use a combination of primitive data types and objects. Some class methods, however, will accept only objects as arguments, so we need some way to convert a primitive data type into an object. Conversely, there are times when we need to convert an object into a primitive data type. For example, let's say we have a GUI where we ask users to type their age into a text box or a dialog box. We expect the age to be an *int* value; however, text boxes and dialog boxes return their values as *Strings*. To perform any calculations on an age in our program, we will need to convert the value of that *String* object into an *int*.

For these situations, Java provides **wrapper classes**. A wrapper class "wraps" the value of a primitive type, such as *double* or *int*, into an object. These wrapper classes define an instance variable of that primitive data type, and also provide useful constants and methods for converting between the objects and the primitive data types. Table 3.15 lists the wrapper classes for each primitive data type.

All these classes are part of the *java.lang* package. So, the *import* statement is not needed in order to use wrapper classes in a program.

Java provides special support for converting between a primitive numeric type and its wrapper class. For example, we can simply assign an *int* variable to an *Integer* object reference. Java will automatically provide the conversion for us. This conversion is called **autoboxing**. In Example 3.19, the conversion is illustrated in lines 9 and 10. The *int* variable, *intPrimitive*, and the *Integer* object, *integerObject*, are output at lines 12 and 13 and have the same value (42). The output is shown in Figure 3.26.

TABLE 3.15   Wrapper Classes for Primitive Data Types

Primitive Data Type	Wrapper Class
double	Double
float	Float
long	Long
int	Integer
short	Short
byte	Byte
char	Character
boolean	Boolean

Similarly, when an *Integer* object is used as an *int*, Java also provides this conversion, which is called **unboxing**. Thus, when we use an *Integer* object in an arithmetic expression, the *int* value is automatically used. Line 15 of Example 3.19 uses the *Integer* object *integerObject* in an arithmetic expression, adding the *Integer* object to the *int* variable *intPrimitive*. As shown in Figure 3.26, the result is the same as if both operands were *int* variables.

Similar operations are possible using other numeric primitives and their associated wrapper classes.

In addition to automatic conversions between primitive types and wrapper objects, the *Integer* and *Double* classes provide methods, shown in Table 3.16, that allow us to convert *Strings* to numbers.

The *parseInt, parseDouble,* and *valueOf* methods are *static* and are called using the *Integer* or *Double* class name and the dot notation. The *parse* methods convert a *String* to a primitive type, and the *valueOf* methods convert a *String* to a wrapper object. For example, line 18 of Example 3.19 converts the *String* "76" to the *int* value 76. Line 19 converts the *String* "76" to an equivalent *Integer* object.

```
1  /* A demonstration of the Wrapper classes and methods
2     Anderson, Franceschi
3  */
4
5  public class DemoWrapper
6  {
7    public static void main( String [ ] args )
8    {
9      int intPrimitive = 42;
10     Integer integerObject = intPrimitive;
11
12     System.out.println( "The int is " + intPrimitive );
13     System.out.println( "The Integer object is " + integerObject );
14
15     int sum = intPrimitive + integerObject;
16     System.out.println( "Their sum is " + sum );
17
18     int i1 = Integer.parseInt( "76" );     // convert "76" to an int
19     Integer i2 = Integer.valueOf( "76" ); // convert "76" to Integer
20     System.out.println( "\nThe value of i1 is " + i1 );
21     System.out.println( "The value of i2 is " + i2 );
22
23     double d1 = Double.parseDouble( "58.32" );
24     Double d2 = Double.valueOf( "58.32" );
25     System.out.println( "\nThe value of d1 is " + d1 );
```

```
26      System.out.println( "The value of d2 is " + d2 );
27    }
28 }
```

EXAMPLE 3.19   A Demonstration of the Wrapper Classes

REFERENCE POINT
You can read more about the wrapper classes on Oracle's Java website: *www .oracle.com /technetwork /java.*

Similarly, line 23 converts the *String* "58.32" to a *double*, and line 24 converts the same *String* to an equivalent *Double* object.

Because a *char* is a primitive type, we can't call methods on a *char* variable. By wrapping a *char* variable into an object, however, the *Character* class provides some helpful methods for dealing with *chars*. Often, we may want to determine whether a character is a digit or a letter. For example, if we are checking whether a password is secure, we may want to determine whether the password has at least one digit, or we may want to change the case of a *char* variable. Table 3.17 shows some useful

TABLE 3.16   Methods of the *Integer* and *Double* Wrapper Classes

Useful Methods of the *Integer* Wrapper Class	
Return value	**Method name and argument list**
int	parseInt(String s)
	static method that converts the *String s* to an *int* and returns that value
Integer	valueOf(String s)
	static method that converts the *String s* to an *Integer* object and returns that object
Useful Methods of the *Double* Wrapper Class	
Return value	**Method name and argument list**
double	parseDouble(String s)
	static method that converts the *String s* to a *double* and returns that value
Double	valueOf(String s)
	static method that converts the *String s* to a *Double* object and returns that object

Figure 3.26

Output from Example 3.19

```
The int is 42
The Integer object is 42
Their sum is 84

The value of i1 is 76
The value of i2 is 76

The value of d1 is 58.32
The value of d2 is 58.32
```

TABLE 3.17   Useful Methods of the *Character* Wrapper Class

Useful *static* Methods of the *Character* Wrapper Class	
Return value	**Method name and argument list**
boolean	isDigit(char c)
	returns true if *c* is a character from '0' to '9' or a digit in other languages; false, otherwise
boolean	isLetter(char c)
	returns true if *c* is a letter; false, otherwise
boolean	isLowerCase(char c)
	returns true if *c* is a lowercase letter; false, otherwise
boolean	isUpperCase(char c)
	returns true if *c* is an uppercase letter; false, otherwise
char	toLowerCase(char c)
	returns the lowercase version of *c* if *c* is a letter; otherwise it returns *c* unchanged
char	toUpperCase(char c)
	returns the uppercase version of *c* if *c* is a letter; otherwise it returns *c* unchanged

methods of the *Character* class. All these methods are *static*, so we call them using the *Character* class name instead of an object reference. The first four methods test whether a *char* is a digit, a letter, lowercase, or uppercase. For each of these methods, we send the *char* variable as an argument and the method returns *true* or *false*. The next two methods, *toLowerCase* and *toUpperCase*, convert the *char* argument to lower- or uppercase if the *char* is a letter. We send the *char* variable to the method, and it returns a copy of the *char* variable after converting its case, if possible.

Example 3.20 demonstrates the use of these methods.

Lines 12–14 prompt the user for a character to test or convert. Remember that *Scanner* does not have a *nextChar* method, so we need to use the *next* method to read a *String* and then extract the first character of the inputted *String* using the *charAt* method.

Lines 16–17 output the decimal Unicode value of the *char* variable by type casting it to an *int*.

At lines 19–20, we test whether the *char* is a digit by calling the *isDigit* method and output the returned value of *true* or *false*. Similarly, at lines 22–23, we test whether the *char* is a letter by calling the *isLetter* method and output the returned value of *true* or *false*.

At lines 24–27, we test whether the *char* is an uppercase or lowercase letter, again outputting the return value of *true* or *false*.

Finally, at lines 29–32, we attempt to convert the *char* to an uppercase letter and then to a lowercase letter. If *c* is not a letter, or if it is already an uppercase or lowercase letter, the methods return the value unchanged.

```java
1 /*  Character Methods
2      Anderson, Franceschi
3 */
4 import java.util.Scanner;
5
6 public class CharacterMethods
7 {
8   public static void main( String [ ] args )
9   {
10     Scanner scan = new Scanner( System.in );
11
12     System.out.print( "Enter a character > " );
13     String input = scan.next( );
14     char c = input.charAt( 0 );
15
16     System.out.println( "The Unicode decimal value of " + c + " is: "
17                                   + ( int ) c );
18
19     System.out.println(  "\n" + c + " is a digit: "
20                                   + Character.isDigit( c ) );
21
22     System.out.println(  "\n" + c + " is a letter: "
23                                   + Character.isLetter( c ) );
24     System.out.println(  c + " is uppercase: "
25                                   + Character.isUpperCase( c ) );
26     System.out.println(  c + " is lowercase: "
27                                   + Character.isLowerCase( c ) );
28
29     System.out.println(  "\n" + c + " in uppercase is: "
30                                   + Character.toUpperCase( c ) );
31     System.out.println(  c + " in lowercase is: "
32                                   + Character.toLowerCase( c ) );
33   }
34 }
```

EXAMPLE 3.20   Character Methods

Figure 3.27 shows the output of the program when the user enters *d*.

```
Enter a character > d
The Unicode decimal value of d is: 100

d is a digit: false

d is a letter: true
d is uppercase: false
d is lowercase: true

d in uppercase is: D
d in lowercase is: d
```

Figure 3.27

Output from
Example 3.20

Skill Practice
with these end-of-chapter questions

3.18.1   Multiple Choice Exercises

Question 12

3.18.3   Fill In the Code

Question 33

3.18.4   Identifying Errors in Code

Question 35

3.18.5   Debugging Area

Question 44

3.18.8   Technical Writing

Questions 71, 72

3.16   Programming Activity 2: Using Predefined Classes

In this Programming Activity, you will write a short program using some of the classes and methods discussed in this chapter. Your program will perform the following operations:

1. a. Prompt the user for his or her first name

    b. Print a message saying hello to the user

    c. Tell the user how many characters are in his or her name

2. a. Ask the user for the year of his or her birth

b. Calculate and print the age the user will be this year

c. Declare a constant for average life expectancy; set its value to 78.94

d. Print a message that tells the user the percentage of his or her expected life lived so far formatted to one decimal place

3. a. Generate a random number between 1 and 20

b. Output a message telling the user that the program is thinking of a number between 1 and 20 and ask for a guess

c. Output a message telling the user the number and how far away from the number the user's guess was

To complete this Programming Activity, copy the contents of this chapter's Programming Activity 2 folder in the supplied code accompanying this text. Open the *PracticeMethods.java* file and look for four sets of five asterisks (*****), where you will find instructions to write *import* statements and items 1, 2, and 3 for completing the Programming Activity.

Example 3.21 shows the *PracticeMethods.java* file, and Figure 3.28 shows the output from a sample run after you have completed the Programming Activity. Your output might vary from that shown because we use 2020 as the current year for calculating age and because item 3 generates a random number.

```
1 /* Chapter 3 Programming Activity 2
2     Calling class methods
3     Anderson, Franceschi
4 */
5
6 // ***** 1. add your import statements here
7
8 public class PracticeMethods
9 {
10   public static void main( String [ ] args )
11   {
12     //*****
13     // 2.  a. Create a Scanner object to read from the keyboard.
14     //     b. Prompt the user for their first name.
15     //     c. Print a message that says hello to the user.
16     //     d. Print a message that says how many letters
17     //                 are in the user's name.
18     // Your code goes here
19
20
21     //*****
```

```
22    // 3.  a. Skip a line, then prompt the user for the year
23    //           they were born.
24    //       b. Declare a constant for the current year.
25    //       c. Calculate and print the age the user will be this year.
26    //       d. Declare a constant for average life expectancy,
27    //             set its value to 78.94.
28    //       e. Calculate and print the percentage
29    //             of the user's expected life they've lived.
30    //          Use the DecimalFormat class to format the percentage
31    //             to one decimal place.
32    // Your code goes here
33
34
35    //*****
36    // 4.  a. Generate a secret random integer between 1 and 20
37    //       b. Skip a line, then ask the user for a guess.
38    //       c. Print a message telling the user the secret number
39    //          and how far from the number the user's guess was
40    //          (hint: use Math.abs).
41    // Your code goes here
42
43  }
44 }
```

EXAMPLE 3.21   *PracticeMethods.java*

```
Enter your first name > Esmerelda
Hello, Esmerelda
Your name has 9 letters.

In what year were you born? 2002
This year, you will be 18 years old.
So far, you have lived 22.9% of your expected life span.

I'm thinking of a number between 1 and 20
What is your guess? 15
The secret number was 2
Your guess was 13 away.
```

Figure 3.28

Console Output from a Sample Run of Programming Activity 2

?   DISCUSSION QUESTIONS

1. **Which methods of the *Scanner* class did you choose for reading the user's name and birth year? Explain your decisions.**

2. **How would you change your code to generate a random number between 10 and 20?**

CHAPTER REVIEW

3.17　Chapter Summary

- Object-oriented programming entails writing programs that use classes and objects. Using prewritten classes shortens development time and creates more reliable programs. Programs that use prewritten classes are called clients of the class.

- Benefits of object-oriented programming include encapsulation, reusability, and reliability.

- Classes consist of data, plus instructions that operate on that data. Objects of a class are created using the class as a template. Creating an object is called instantiating an object, and the object is an instance of the class. The *new* keyword is used to instantiate an object.

- The object reference is the variable name for an object and points to the data of the object.

- The data of a class are called fields and consist of instance variables and *static* variables. The instructions of the class are called methods. Methods of a class get or set the values of the data or provide other services of the class.

- The name of a method, along with its argument list and return value, is called the Application Programming Interface (API) of that method. Methods that are declared to be *public* can be called by any client of the class.

- By convention, class names in Java start with a capital letter. Method names, instance variables, and object names start with a lowercase letter. In all these names, embedded words begin with a capital letter.

- When our program makes a method call, control transfers to the instructions in the method until the method finishes executing. Then control is transferred back to our program.

- Instance methods are called using the object reference and the dot notation.

- A constructor is called when an object is instantiated. A constructor has the same name as the class and its job is to initialize the object's data. Classes can have multiple constructors.

- A method's data type is called the method's return type. If the data type is anything other than the keyword *void*, the method returns a value to the program. When a value-returning method finishes executing, its return value replaces the method call in the expression.

- Accessor methods, also called getters, allow clients to retrieve the current value of object data. Mutator methods, also called setters, allow clients to change the value of object data.

- When an object reference is first declared, its value is *null*. Attempting to use a *null* object reference to call a method generates an error.

- The garbage collector runs occasionally and deletes objects that have no object references pointing to them.

- Java packages are groups of classes arranged according to functionality. Classes in the *java.lang* packages are automatically available to Java programs. Other classes need to be imported.

- The *String* class can be used to create objects consisting of a sequence of characters. *String* constructors accept *String* literals, *String* objects, or no argument, which creates an empty *String*. The *length* method returns the number of characters in the *String* object. The *toUpperCase* and *toLowerCase* methods return a *String* in upper or lower case. The *charAt* method extracts a character from a *String*, while the *substring* method extracts a *String* from a *String*. The *indexOf* method searches a *String* for a character or substring.

- The *DecimalFormat* class, in the *java.text* package, provides methods to format numeric output. For example, we can specify the number of digits to display after the decimal point or add dollar signs and percentage signs (%).

- The *Random* class, in the *java.util* package, provides methods to generate random numbers.

- The *Scanner* class, in the *java.util* package, provides methods for reading input from the keyboard. Methods are provided for reading primitive data types and *Strings*.

- When prompting the user for input, phrase the prompt in language the user understands. Describe the data requested and any restrictions on valid input values.

- *Static* methods, also called class methods, can be called without instantiating an object. *Static* methods can access only the *static* data of a class.

- *Static* methods are called using the class name and the dot notation.

- *System.out.println* prints primitive data types or a *String* to the Java console and adds a *newline* character. *System.out.println* with no argument skips a line. *System.out.print* prints the same data types to the Java console, but does not add a *newline*. Classes provide a *toString* method to convert objects to a *String* in order to be printed.

- The *Math* class provides *static* constants *PI* and *E* and *static* methods to perform common mathematical calculations, such as finding the maximum or minimum of two numbers, rounding values, and raising a number to a power.

- The *NumberFormat* class, in the *java.text* package, provides *static* methods for creating objects to format numeric output as currency or a percentage.

- Wrapper classes provide an object interface for a primitive data type. The *Integer* and *Double* wrapper classes provide *static* methods for converting between *ints* and *doubles* and *Strings*.

- The *Character* wrapper class provides methods for testing whether a character is a digit or a letter, and for converting letters to upper- or lowercase.

3.18   Exercises, Problems, and Projects

3.18.1   Multiple Choice Exercises

1. If you want to use an existing class from the Java Class Library in your program, what keyword should you use?

    ❑ use

    ❑ import

    ❑ export

    ❑ include

2. A constructor has the same name as the class name.

    ❑ true

    ❑ false

3. A given class can have more than one constructor.

    ❑ true

    ❑ false

4. What is the keyword used to instantiate an object in Java?

    ❑ make

    ❑ construct

    ❑ new

    ❑ static

5. In a given class named *Quiz*, there can be only one method with the name *Quiz*.

   ❏ true

   ❏ false

6. A *static* method is

   ❏ a class method.

   ❏ an instance method.

7. In the *Quiz* class, the *foo* method has the following API:

   ```
   public static double foo( float f )
   ```

   What can you say about *foo?*

   ❏ It is an instance method.

   ❏ It is a class field.

   ❏ It is a class method.

   ❏ It is an instance variable.

8. In the *Quiz* class, the *foo* method has the following API:

   ```
   public static void foo( )
   ```

   How would you call that method?

   ❏ `Quiz.foo( );`

   ❏ `Quiz.foo( 8 );`

   ❏ `Quiz( foo( ) );`

9. In the *Quiz* class, the *foo* method has the following API:

   ```
   public double foo( int i, String s, char c )
   ```

   How many arguments does *foo* take?

   ❏ 0

   ❏ 1

   ❏ 2

   ❏ 3

10. In the *Quiz* class, the *foo* method has the following API:

```
public double foo( int i, String s, char c )
```

What is the return type of method *foo*?

- ❑ double
- ❑ int
- ❑ char
- ❑ String

11. *String* is a primitive data type in Java.

- ❑ true
- ❑ false

12. Which one of the following is not an existing wrapper class?

- ❑ Integer
- ❑ Char
- ❑ Float
- ❑ Double

13. What is the proper way of accessing the constant *E* of the *Math* class?

- ❑ Math.E( );
- ❑ Math.E;
- ❑ E;
- ❑ Math(E);

3.18.2 Reading and Understanding Code

14. What is the output of this code sequence?

```
String s = new String( "HI" );
System.out.println( s );
```

15. What is the output of this code sequence?

```
String s = "A" + "BC" + "DEF" + "GHIJ";
System.out.println( s );
```

16. What is the output of this code sequence?

```
String s = "Hello";
s = s.toLowerCase( );
System.out.println( s );
```

17. What is the output of this code sequence?

```
int a = Math.min( 5, 8 );
System.out.println( a );
```

18. What is the output of this code sequence?

```
System.out.println( Math.sqrt( 4.0 ) );
```

19. What is the output of this code sequence? (You will need to actually compile this code and run it in order to have the correct output.)

```
System.out.println( Math.PI );
```

20. What is the output of this code sequence?

```
double f = 5.7;
long i = Math.round( f );
System.out.println( i );
```

21. What is the output of this code sequence?

```
System.out.print( Math.round( 3.5 ) );
```

22. What is the output of this code sequence?

```
int i = Math.abs( -8 );
System.out.println( i );
```

23. What is the output of this code sequence?

```
double d = Math.pow( 2, 3 );
System.out.println( d );
```

3.18.3   Fill In the Code

24. This code concatenates the three *Strings* "Intro ", "to", " Programming" and outputs the resulting *String*. (Your output should be *Intro to Programming*.)

```
String s1 = "Intro ";
String s2 = "to";
String s3 = " Programming";
// your code goes here
```

25. This code prints the number of characters in the *String* "Hello World".

```
String s = "Hello World";
// your code goes here
```

26. This code prompts the user for a *String*, then prints the *String* and the number of characters in it.

```
// your code goes here
```

27. This code uses only a single line *System.out.println. . .* statement in order to print
"Welcome to Java Illuminated"
on one line using the following variables and the *String* concatenation operator:

```
String s1 = "Welcome ";
String s2 = "to ";
String s3 = "Java ";
String s4 = "Illuminated";
// your code goes here
```

28. This code uses exactly four *System.out.print* statements in order to print
"Welcome to Java Illuminated"
on the same output line.

```
// your code goes here
```

29. This code assigns the maximum of the values 3 and 5 to the *int* variable *max*
and outputs the result.

```
int max;
// your code goes here
```

30. This code calculates the square root of 5 and outputs the result.

```
double d = 5.0;
// your code goes here
```

31. This code asks the user for two integer values, then calculates the minimum of
the two values and prints it.

```
// your code goes here
```

32. This code asks the user for three integer values, then calculates the maximum
of the three values and prints it.

```
// your code goes here
```

33. This code prompts the user for a single character and prints "true" if the character is a letter and "false" if it is not a letter.

```
// your code goes here
```

34. This code asks the user for a *double*, then prints the square of that number
using the *pow* method of the *Math* class.

```
// your code goes here
```

3.18.4   Identifying Errors in Code

35. Where is the error in this statement?

```
import text.NumberFormat;
```

36. Where is the error in this statement?

```
import java.util.DecimalFormat;
```

37. Where is the error in this code sequence?

```
String s = "Hello World";
system.out.println( s );
```

38. Where is the error in this code sequence?

```
String s = String( "Hello" );
System.out.println( s );
```

39. Where is the error in this code sequence?

```
String s1 = "Hello";
String s2 = "ello";
String s = s1 - s2;
```

40. Where is the error in this code sequence?

```
short s = Math.round( 3.2 );
System.out.println( s );
```

41. Where is the error in this code sequence?

```
int a = Math.pow( 3, 4 );
System.out.println( a );
```

42. Where is the error in this code sequence?

```
double pi = Math( PI );
System.out.println( pi );
```

43. Where is the error in this code sequence?

```
String s = 'H';
System.out.println( "s is " + s );
```

3.18.5   Debugging Area—Using Messages from the Java Compiler and Java JVM

44. You coded the following program in the file *Test.java:*

```
public class Test
{
  public static void main( String [ ] args )
  {
    int a = 6;
    NumberFormat nf = NumberFormat.getCurrencyInstance( );
  }
}
```

When you compile, you get the following message:

```
Test.java: 6: error: cannot find symbol
  NumberFormat nf = NumberFormat.getCurrencyInstance( );
  ^

  symbol : class NumberFormat
  location: class Test
```

```
Test.java: 6: error: cannot find symbol
  NumberFormat nf = NumberFormat.getCurrencyInstance( );
                    ^
  symbol : variable NumberFormat
  location: class Test
2 errors
```

Explain what the problem is and how to fix it.

45. You coded the following on lines 10–12 of class *Test.java:*

```
String s;                       // line 10
int l = s.length( );            // line 11
System.out.println( "length is " + l );       // line 12
```

When you compile, you get the following message:

```
Test.java:11: error: variable s might not have been initialized.
int l = s.length( );          // line 11
        ^
1 error
```

Explain what the problem is and how to fix it.

46. You coded the following on lines 10 and 11 of class *Test.java:*

```
double d = math.sqrt( 6 );          // line 10
System.out.println( "d = " + d );   // line 11
```

When you compile, you get the following message:

```
Test.java: 10: error: cannot find symbol
double d = math.sqrt( 6 ); // line 10
           ^
symbol : variable math
location: class Test
1 error
```

Explain what the problem is and how to fix it.

47. You coded the following on lines 10 and 11 of class *Test.java:*

```
double d = Math.PI( );              // line 10
System.out.println ( "d = " + d ); // line 11
```

When you compile, you get the following message:

```
Test.java:10: error: cannot find symbol
  double d = Math.PI( );    // line 10
                  ^
symbol : method PI( )
location: class Math
1 error
```

Explain what the problem is and how to fix it.

48. You coded the following on lines 10 and 11 of class *Test.java:*

```
double d = Math.e;                    // line 10
System.out.println( "d = " + d ); // line 11
```

When you compile, you get the following message:

```
Test.java:10: error: cannot find symbol
        double d = Math.e;                    // line 10
                       ^
symbol : variable e
location: class Math
1 error
```

Explain what the problem is and how to fix it.

49. You imported the *DecimalFormat* class and coded the following in the class *Test.java:*

```
double grade = .895;
DecimalFormat percent =
   new DecimalFormat( "#.0%" );

System.out.println( "Your grade is " + grade );
```

The code compiles properly and runs, but the result is not what you expected. You expect this output:

```
Your grade is 89.5%
```

But instead, the output is

```
Your grade is 0.895
```

Explain what the problem is and how to fix it.

3.18.6   Write a Short Program

50. Write a program that reads two words representing passwords from the keyboard and outputs the number of characters in the smaller of the two. For example, if the two words are *open* and *sesame*, then the output should be *4*, the length of the shorter word, *open*.

51. Write a program that prompts the user for a domain name. Your program should then concatenate that name with *www.* and *.com* in order to form an Internet domain name and output the result. For instance, if the name entered by the user is *yahoo*, then the output will be *www.yahoo.com*.

52. Write a program that reads a word from the keyboard. Your program should output the word in uppercase letters only, output that word in lowercase letters only, and then, at the end, output the original word.

53. Write a program that generates two random numbers between 0 and 100 and prints the smaller of the two numbers.

54. Write a program that takes a *double* as an input, then computes and outputs the cube of that number using the *pow* method of the *Math* class.

55. Write a program that reads a file name from the keyboard. You should expect that the file name has one . (dot) character in it, separating the file name from the file extension. Retrieve the file extension and output it. For instance, if the user inputs *index.html*, you should output *html*; if the user inputs *MyClass.java*, you should output *java*.

56. Write a program that reads a full name (first name and last name) from the keyboard as a single line; you should expect the first name and the last name to be separated by a space. Retrieve and output the first and last names.

3.18.7   Programming Projects

57. Write a program that reads three integer values from the keyboard representing, respectively, a number of quarters, dimes, and nickels. Convert the total coin amount to dollars and output the result with a dollar notation.

58. Write a program that reads from the keyboard the radius of a circle. Calculate and output the area and the circumference of that circle. You can use the following formulas:

area = $\pi * r^2$
circumference = $2 * \pi * r$

59. Write a program that generates five random integers between 60 and 100 and calculates the smallest of the five numbers.

60. Write a program that generates three random integers between 0 and 50, calculates the average, and prints the result to one decimal place.

61. Write a program that reads two integers from the keyboard: one representing the number of shots taken by a basketball player, the other representing the number of shots made by the same player. Calculate the shooting percentage and output it with the percent notation.

62. Write a program that reads three *double* numbers from the keyboard representing, respectively, the three coefficients a, b, and c of a quadratic equation. Solve the equation using the following formulas:

$x1$ = (− b + square root (b^2 − 4 ac)) / (2a)
$x2$ = (− b − square root (b^2 − 4 ac)) / (2a)

Run your program on the following sample values:
$a = 1.0, b = 3.0, c = 2.0$
$a = 0.5, b = 0.5, c = 0.125$
$a = 1.0, b = 3.0, c = 10.0$

Discuss the results for each program run, in particular what happens in the last case.

63. Write a program that reads two numbers from the keyboard representing, respectively, an investment and an interest rate (you will expect the user to enter a number such as .065 for the interest rate, representing a 6.5% interest rate). Your program should calculate and output (in $ notation) the future value of the investment in 5, 10, and 20 years using the following formula:

future value = investment * (1 + interest rate)^{year}

We will assume that the interest rate is an annual rate and is compounded annually.

64. Write a program that reads from the keyboard the (x,y) coordinates for two points in the plane. You can assume that all numbers are integers. Using the *Point* class from the Java Class Library (you may need to look it up on the Web), instantiate two *Point* objects with your input data, then output the data for both *Point* objects.

65. Write a program that reads an email address. Assuming that the email address contains one at sign (@), extract and print the username and the domain name of the email address.

66. Write a program that reads a telephone number from the keyboard as a *String* of 10 digits. You should output that same telephone number formatted as (nnn) nnn-nnnn.

67. Write a program that reads a sentence from the keyboard. The sentence has been encrypted so that the message consists of only the first five characters with even-numbered indexes. All other characters should be discarded. Decrypt the sentence and output the result. For example, if the user inputs "Hiejlzl3ow", your output should be *Hello*.

68. Write a program that reads a commercial website URL from the keyboard; you should expect that the URL starts with *www.* and ends with *.com*. Retrieve the name of the site and output it. For instance, if the user inputs *www.yahoo.com*, you should output *yahoo*.

3.18.8   Technical Writing

69. At this point, we have written and debugged many examples of code. When you compile a Java program with the Java compiler, you get a list of all the errors in your code. Do you like the Java compiler? Do the error messages it displays when your code does not compile help you determine what's wrong? How?

70. Computers, computer languages, and application programs existed before object-oriented programming. However, OOP has become an industry standard. Discuss the advantages of using OOP compared to using only basic data types in a program.

71. Explain and discuss a situation where you would use the method *parseInt* of the class *Integer*.

72. In addition to the basic data types (*int, float, char, boolean,…*), Java provides many prewritten classes, such as *Math*, *NumberFormat*, and *DecimalFormat*. Why is this an advantage? How does this impact the way a programmer approaches a programming problem in general?

3.18.9   Group Project (for a group of 1, 2, or 3 students)

73. Write a program that calculates a monthly mortgage payment; we will assume that the interest rate is compounded monthly.

   You will need to do the following:

   ❑ Prompt the user for a *double* representing the annual interest rate. For example, 3.5% would be entered as .035.

   ❑ Prompt the user for the number of years the mortgage will be held (typical input here is 10, 15, or 30).

   ❑ Prompt the user for a number representing the mortgage amount borrowed from the bank.

   ❑ Calculate the monthly payment using the following formulas:

   ▪ Monthly payment = $(mIR * M) / (1 - (1 / (1 + mIR)^{(12*nOY)}))$, where:

   ▪ mIR = monthly interest rate = annual interest rate / 12

   ▪ nOY = number of years

   ▪ M = mortgage amount

❑ Output a summary of the mortgage problem, as follows:

- the annual interest rate in percent notation

- the mortgage amount in dollars

- the monthly payment in dollars, with only two significant digits after the decimal point

- the total payment over the years, with only two significant digits after the decimal point

- the overpayment, i.e., the difference between the total payment over the years and the mortgage amount, with only two significant digits after the decimal point

- the overpayment as a percentage (in percent notation) of the mortgage amount

CHAPTER 4
Introduction to Graphical Applications

Introduction

Graphical output is an integral part of many programs today. One compelling reason for using graphics in a program is the ability to present data in a format that is easy to comprehend. For example, our application could output average monthly temperatures as text, as shown in Figure 4.1.

Or we could produce the bar chart shown in Figure 4.2.

The bar chart presents the same information as the text output, but it adds a visual component that makes it easier to compare the monthly temperatures—for example, to find the highest or lowest temperature or to spot temperature trends throughout the year. The colors also add information, with the low temperatures

Figure 4.1

Outputting Monthly Temperatures as Text

Jan	31
Feb	24
Mar	45
Apr	60
May	69
Jun	80
Jul	88
Aug	87
Sep	75
Oct	65
Nov	43
Dec	23

Figure 4.2

Bar Chart of Monthly Temperatures

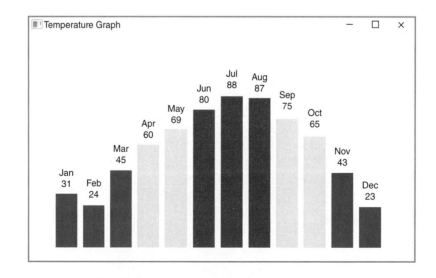

shown in blue, the moderate temperatures in yellow, and the high temperatures in red.

In this chapter, we use JavaFX to write programs that produce graphical output.

4.1 JavaFX Application Structure

Over the years, Java has provided several incarnations of graphics systems. The first was Abstract Window Toolkit (AWT), which was subsequently replaced by Swing. Java's current system for building graphics applications is JavaFX. JavaFX makes it possible to create rich user interfaces with animations and special effects. In this chapter, we concentrate on JavaFX's features for creating graphical output for applications.

All the classes we need to build a JavaFX application are downloaded with the Java SE SDK. Oracle provides tutorial information on JavaFX at *http://docs.oracle.com/javafx/2/get_started/jfxpub-get_started.htm* and documentation for all the JavaFX classes is included with the Java version 9 documentation.

JavaFX uses a mixed performance/art metaphor. We start with a stage (a window) to which we add one or more scenes. To produce graphical output, we add a canvas to our scene, and we draw shapes and text on the canvas. When our application begins, the window opens and displays whatever we have drawn on the canvas.

REFERENCE POINT
For a tutorial on JavaFX, visit Oracle's website at http://docs.oracle.com/javafx/2/get_started/jfxpub-get_started.htm

We, the authors, are providing two classes to get you started. First, we provide a utility program, *JIGraphicsUtility.java*, to manage some of the common code needed to set up a JavaFX application. Second, we provide *ShellGraphicsApplication.java*, which provides a framework for adding your custom drawing code. The *JIGraphicsUtility.java* class, shown in Example 4.1, has one *static* method, *setUpGraphics*, which is designed to be called from our graphics application to set up our window title and size. We show the *JIGraphicsUtility* class here for completeness, but we do not need to make any modifications to this file. All we need to do is include this file in the same folder as our graphics application and call the *setUpGraphics* method from our application. The *setUpGraphics* method has the API shown in Table 4.1.

TABLE 4.1 The *static setUpGraphics* Method

Return value	Method name and argument list
GraphicsContext	setUpGraphics(Stage stage, String title, int width, int height)
	initializes a scene on the *stage*, sets the title of the window to *title*, and adds a canvas with the *width* and *height* specified; returns a *GraphicsContext* object

In our graphics application, we use the *GraphicsContext* object returned from the *setUpGraphics* method to call methods that draw shapes and text on the window.

```
 1 /* JIGraphicsUtility
 2    Utility class for building JavaFX graphics applications
 3    Anderson, Franceschi
 4 */
 5
 6 import javafx.scene.Group;
 7 import javafx.scene.canvas.Canvas;
 8 import javafx.scene.canvas.GraphicsContext;
 9 import javafx.scene.Scene;
10 import javafx.stage.Stage;
11
12 public class JIGraphicsUtility
13 {
14     public static GraphicsContext setUpGraphics( Stage stage,
15                           String title, int height, int width )
16     {
17         stage.setTitle( title );
18         Canvas canvas = new Canvas( height, width );
19         GraphicsContext gc = canvas.getGraphicsContext2D( );
20         Group root = new Group( canvas );
21         stage.setScene( new Scene( root ) );
22         stage.show( );
23         return gc;
24     }
25 }
```

EXAMPLE 4.1   *JIGraphicsUtility* **Class**

Example 4.2 shows the *ShellGraphicsApplication* class. This class provides skeleton code for an application. We create a new application by modifying this code.

```
 1 /* A Shell for creating graphics applications
 2    Anderson, Franceschi
 3 */
 4
 5 import javafx.application.Application;
 6 import javafx.scene.canvas.GraphicsContext;
 7 import javafx.stage.Stage;
 8
 9 public class ShellGraphicsApplication extends Application
10 {
11     @Override
12     public void start( Stage stage )
13     {
```

```
14          // set up window title and size
15          GraphicsContext gc = JIGraphicsUtility.setUpGraphics(
16                  stage, "Shell Graphics Application", 700, 400 );
17
18          // your drawing code goes here
19      }
20
21      public static void main( String [ ] args )
22      {
23          launch( args );
24      }
25 }
```

EXAMPLE 4.2   *ShellGraphicsApplication.java*

Lines 5–7 import the minimum classes needed for a JavaFX application. Notice that all the package names begin with *javafx*.

We define our application name in line 9. Here the name is *ShellGraphicsApplication*. For each new application we write, we will change this name to reflect the application's purpose. The phrase "*extends Application*" means that we inherit basic functionality and methods from the JavaFX *Application* class.

One of the methods we inherit is the *start* method, which the JavaFX platform calls automatically when the application begins. It receives one parameter, *stage*, which represents the application's window. We need to write our own version of the *start* method (lines 11–19), however, in which we put our method calls to draw shapes and text on the window. We use the *@Override* annotation in line 11 to indicate that our *start* method replaces the *start* method in the *Application* class.

Our first order of business is to call the *setUpGraphics* method (lines 14–16). Because *setUpGraphics* is a *static* method, we call it using the *JIGraphicsUtility* class name. Here we send as arguments the stage representing our window; a title for the window; and a size for the window, in this case a width of 700 pixels and a height of 400 pixels. For our applications, we can change the title to something appropriate and alter the window size as needed.

Line 18 indicates where we add code to create our graphics.

In lines 21–24 we define the *main* method. Its only job is to launch the JavaFX application by calling the *launch* method of the *Application* class, passing through any arguments that were sent to the *main* method. Because this code will be the same for every application, we place *main* at the end of the program.

Thus, to run a JavaFX graphics application, we alter the *ShellGraphicsApplication* *.java* class to add our custom graphics code, and we put the *JIGraphicsUtility.java* class and our custom class in the same folder. We then compile both classes and execute our custom class.

4.2 The Graphics Coordinate System and Color

JavaFX's *GraphicsContext* class, in the *javafx.scene.canvas* package, provides methods to draw figures such as rectangles, circles, and lines; to set the colors for drawing; and to write text in a window.

To draw on the window, we specify the location where we want to put our shapes and the color we want the shapes to have.

A window is composed of pixels, which can be thought of as colored dots. A window with a width of 700 pixels and a height of 400 pixels has a total of 28,000 (700 * 400) pixels. Each pixel has a location expressed using an (x, y) coordinate system. The x coordinate specifies the horizontal position, beginning at 0 on the left side of the window and increasing as you move to the right. The y coordinate specifies the vertical position, starting at 0 at the top of the window and increasing as you move down. Thus, for a window that is 700 pixels wide and 400 pixels high, the coordinate (0, 0) corresponds to the upper-left corner; (699, 0) is the upper-right corner; (0, 399) is the lower-left corner; and (699, 399) is the lower-right corner. Figure 4.3 shows a window with a few sample pixels and their (x, y) coordinates.

Each pixel also has a color. When a window opens, all pixels are set to the **background color**, which by default is white. Any drawing we perform is done in the **foreground colors**, which are the **stroke color** and the **fill color**. Most of the drawing methods have a stroke and a fill version, where the stroke version draws an

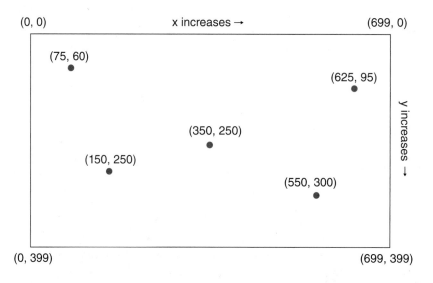

Figure 4.3

The *GraphicsContext* Coordinate System

outlined shape in the current stroke color and the fill version draws a solid shape in the current fill color. By default, both the stroke color and fill color are black, but we can set either to any color we prefer. The values set for the colors remain in effect until we set either the stroke color or the fill color to another color. For example, if we set the stroke color to blue and the fill color to red, then draw an outlined rectangle and a line, as well as a solid oval, the rectangle and line will be drawn in blue and the oval will be drawn in red. Then if we set the fill color to yellow and draw a solid rectangle, that rectangle will be drawn in yellow.

To set the foreground colors, we call the *setFill* or *setStroke* methods of the *Graphics-Context* class as shown in Table 4.2. These methods take as an argument, a *Paint* object. Because objects of the *Color* class are also *Paint* objects, we can send *Color* objects as arguments to the *setFill* and *setStroke* methods.

The *Color* class, which is in the *javafx.scene.paint* package, defines colors using the RGB (red, green, blue) system. Any RGB color is composed of red, green, and blue components. Each component's value can range from 0 to 255 (00 to FF in hexadecimal); the higher the value, the higher the concentration of that component in the color. For example, a color with red = 255, green = 0, and blue = 0 is pure red, and a color with red = 0, green = 0, and blue = 255 is pure blue.

The color white is (255, 255, 255): its red, green, and blue components have the maximum value. Black is (0, 0, 0): its red, green, and blue components have the minimum value. Gray consists of equal amounts of each component. The higher the value of the components, the lighter the color of gray. This makes sense because the closer a color gets to white, the lighter that color will be. Similarly, the closer the gray value gets to 0, the darker the color of gray, because the color is approaching black.

For convenience in setting stroke and fill colors, the *Color* class provides approximately 150 *static Color* constants. Table 4.3 lists some *Color* constants for common colors and their corresponding red, green, and blue components in hexadecimal. For a complete list of *Color* constants, see the documentation for the *Color* class in the Java Class Library.

TABLE 4.2   Methods of the *GraphicsContext* Class to Set the Foreground Colors

Return value	Method name and argument list
void	`setStroke( Paint color )`
	sets the current outline color to *color*
void	`setFill( Paint color )`
	sets the current fill color to *color*

Each color constant is a predefined *Color* object, so you can simply assign the constant to your *Color* object reference. *Color* constants can be used wherever a *Color* or *Paint* object is expected. For example, assuming that *gc* is a *GraphicsContext* reference, this statement sets the current stroke color to orange:

```
gc.setStroke( Color.ORANGE );
```

If none of these 150 predefined colors meets our needs, we can create a custom color using any of the 16.7 million possible combinations of the component values. The *Color* class has a number of methods for creating colors, but for our purposes we'll need only the *static* factory method shown in Table 4.4.

TABLE 4.3   Selected *Color* Constants and Their Red, Green, and Blue Components

Color Constant	Red	Green	Blue
Color.BLACK	00	00	00
Color.BLUE	00	00	FF
Color.CYAN	00	FF	FF
Color.DARKGRAY	A9	A9	A9
Color.GRAY	80	80	80
Color.GREEN	00	FF	00
Color.LIGHTGRAY	D3	D3	D3
Color.MAGENTA	FF	00	FF
Color.ORANGE	FF	A5	00
Color.PINK	FF	C0	CB
Color.RED	FF	00	00
Color.WHITE	FF	FF	FF
Color.YELLOW	FF	FF	00

TABLE 4.4   A *Color* Class *static* Factory Method

Return value	Method name and argument list
Color	rgb(int rr, int gg, int bb)
	creates a *Color* object with an *rr* red component, *gg* green component, and *bb* blue component

Skill Practice
with these end-of-chapter questions

4.7.1   Multiple Choice Exercises

Questions 1, 2, 3, 4, 5, 10

4.7.3   Fill In the Code

Question 16

4.7.4   Identifying Errors in Code

Questions 23, 24, 25, 26, 27

4.7.5   Debugging Area

Questions 29, 30

4.7.8   Technical Writing

Question 38

4.3   Drawing Shapes and Text

Now we're ready to create some graphics. Let's start with drawing lines.

Table 4.5 shows some useful methods of the *GraphicsContext* class for drawing shapes and displaying text in a window.

As you can see, all these methods have a *void* return type, so they do not return a value. Method calls to these methods should be stand-alone statements.

The pattern for the method names is simple. The *draw* methods render the outline of the figure, while the *fill* methods render solid figures. The *clearRect* method draws a rectangle in the background color, which effectively erases anything drawn within that rectangle.

Figure 4.4 shows the relationship among the method arguments and the figures drawn.

TABLE 4.5   Drawing Methods of the *GraphicsContext* Class

Return value	Method name and argument list
void	`strokeLine( double xStart, double yStart,` `                double xEnd, double yEnd )`
	draws a line starting at (*xStart, yStart*) and ending at (*xEnd, yEnd*)

(continued)

TABLE 4.5   Drawing Methods of the *GraphicsContext* Class (*continued*)

Return value	Method name and argument list
void	`strokeRect( double x, double y, double width,` `                    double height )`
	draws the outline of a rectangle with its top-left corner at (*x, y*), with the specified *width* and *height* in pixels
void	`fillRect( double x, double y, double width,` `                double height )`
	draws a solid rectangle with its top-left corner at (*x, y*), with the specified *width* and *height* in pixels
void	`clearRect( double x, double y, double width,` `                double height )`
	draws a solid rectangle in the current background color with its top-left corner at (*x, y*), with the specified *width* and *height* in pixels
void	`strokeOval( double x, double y, double width,` `                    double height )`
	draws the outline of an oval inside an invisible bounding rectangle with the specified *width* and *height* in pixels; the top-left corner of the bounding rectangle is (*x, y*)
void	`fillOval( double x, double y, double width,` `                double height )`
	draws a solid oval inside an invisible bounding rectangle with the specified *width* and *height* in pixels; the top-left corner of the bounding rectangle is (*x, y*)
void	`strokeText( String s, double x, double y )`
	displays the *String s* with the (*x, y*) coordinate indicating the lower-left corner of the first character; the text is drawn in the current stroke color and line width
void	`fillText( String s, double x, double y )`
	displays the *String s* with the (*x, y*) coordinate indicating the lower-left corner of the first character; the text is drawn in the current fill color
void	`setLineWidth( double width )`
	sets the current stroke line width to *width* pixels
void	`setFont( Font f )`
	sets the font to *f* for displaying text

strokeLine(*x*Start, *y*Start, *x*End, *y*End)

Figure 4.4

The Arguments
for Drawing Lines,
Rectangles, Ovals,
and Text

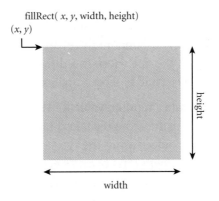

fillRect(*x*, *y*, width, height)

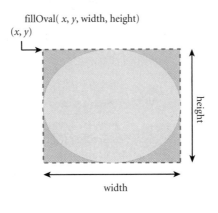

fillOval(*x*, *y*, width, height)

fillText(string, *x*, *y*)

Example 4.3 shows a graphics application that draws some lines, and Figure 4.5 shows the output from this application. For this application, we have modified *Shell-GraphicsUtility.java*, renamed it to *DrawingLines.java*, and placed our application and *JIGraphicsUtility.java* in the same folder.

Lines 5–8 import the JavaFX classes we use in this application, including the *Color* class. We also import the *Random* class from the standard Java Class Library on line 10.

In the call to the *setUpGraphics* method (lines 19–21), we specify the window title to be "Drawing Lines" and set the size of the window to be 700 by 400 pixels.

On lines 23–24, we draw a line by calling the *strokeLine* method, sending as arguments the start and end coordinates of the line. The line is horizontal because the *y* values for the start and end coordinates are the same. The line's color is the default stroke color, black.

Next we draw a vertical red line (lines 26–29). We first set the stroke color to red, using the predefined *Color* constant, *Color.RED*. We make the line 5 pixels wide by calling the *setLineWidth* method with an argument of 5. This line width will stay in effect until we set the line width to a different value. The line is vertical because the *x* values for the start and end coordinates are the same.

Finally, we generate a random value for the stroke color (lines 31–37) by generating random values for the red, green, and blue components, then we use those values to create a *Color* object using the *rgb* factory method. We send FF to the *nextInt* method of the *Random* class because each red, green, and blue component's value can range from 00 to FF in hexadecimal. Note that preceding an integer literal value with 0x indicates that the value is hexadecimal. Line 39 draws a diagonal line in this random color from the top-left corner of the window to the bottom-right corner, using the width and height of the window defined in lines 17 and 18.

```
 1 /* Drawing Lines
 2    Anderson, Franceschi
 3 */
 4
 5 import javafx.application.Application;
 6 import javafx.scene.canvas.GraphicsContext;
 7 import javafx.scene.paint.Color;
 8 import javafx.stage.Stage;
 9
10 import java.util.Random;
11
12 public class DrawingLines extends Application
13 {
14     @Override
15     public void start( Stage stage )
16     {
17         final int WIDTH = 700;
18         final int HEIGHT = 400;
19         // set up window title and size
20         GraphicsContext gc = JIGraphicsUtility.setUpGraphics(
21                 stage, "Drawing Lines", WIDTH, HEIGHT );
22
23         // draw a vertical black line
24         gc.strokeLine( 100, 125, 100, 300 );
25
26         // draw a horizontal red line
```

```
27        gc.setStroke( Color.RED );
28        gc.setLineWidth( 5 ); // widen the line
29        gc.strokeLine( 300, 75, 550, 75 );
30
31        // draw a diagonal line in a random color
32        Random rand =  new Random( );
33        int red = rand.nextInt( 0xFF );
34        int green = rand.nextInt( 0xFF );
35        int blue = rand.nextInt( 0xFF );
36        Color randomColor = Color.rgb( red, green, blue );
37        gc.setStroke( randomColor );
38
39        gc.strokeLine( 0, 0, WIDTH − 1, HEIGHT − 1 );
40    }
41
42    public static void main( String [ ] args )
43    {
44        launch( args );
45    }
46 }
```

EXAMPLE 4.3   *DrawingLines.java*

Example 4.4 shows how to use the *GraphicsContext* methods for drawing shapes, and Figure 4.6 shows the output of this application. To draw a rectangle, we call the *strokeRect* or *fillRect* methods with the (*x*, *y*) coordinate of the upper-left corner, as well as the width in pixels and the height in pixels. As you might expect, to draw a square, we specify equal values for the width and height. Line 23 draws an outlined rectangle with an upper-left corner at the coordinate (100, 50) and is 80 pixels wide and 200 pixels high; line 24 draws a solid square with

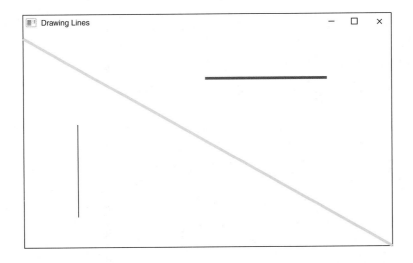

Figure 4.5

Output from
DrawingLines.java

an upper-left corner at the coordinate (275, 75) with sides that are 160 pixels in length.

Drawing an oval or a circle is a little more complex. As you can see in Figure 4.4, we need to imagine a rectangle bounding all sides of the oval or circle. Then the (x, y) coordinate we specify in the *strokeOval* or *fillOval* method is the location of the upper-left corner of the bounding rectangle. Accordingly, the width and height are the width and height of the bounding rectangle. Line 27 in Example 4.4 draws a filled oval whose upper-left corner is at coordinate (100, 50) and is 80 pixels wide and 200 pixels high. These are the same arguments we sent to the *strokeRect* method in line 23; thus, that rectangle at line 23 is the bounding rectangle for this oval, and we see that the filled oval is drawn exactly inside that rectangle. Line 28 draws an outlined oval 200 pixels wide and 80 pixels high, the same dimensions as the oval drawn at line 27 but rotated 90 degrees.

We draw a circle by calling the *strokeOval* or *fillOval* methods, specifying equal values for the width and height. Sometimes it seems more natural to identify circles by giving a center point and a radius. In this case, we can convert the center point and radius into the arguments for the *strokeOval* or *fillOval* methods as done in lines 32–35.

```
1  /* Drawing Shapes
2      Anderson, Franceschi
3  */
4
5  import javafx.application.Application;
6  import javafx.scene.canvas.GraphicsContext;
7  import javafx.scene.paint.Color;
8  import javafx.stage.Stage;
9
10 public class DrawingShapes extends Application
11 {
12     @Override
13     public void start( Stage stage )
14     {
15         // set up window title and size
16         GraphicsContext gc = JIGraphicsUtility.setUpGraphics(
17                 stage, "Drawing Shapes", 700, 400 );
18         // specify colors
19         gc.setFill( Color.CYAN );
20         gc.setStroke( Color.ORANGE );
21
22         // draw rectangles
23         gc.strokeRect( 100, 50, 80, 200 );  // outlined rectangle
```

```
24          gc.fillRect( 275, 75, 160, 160 );   // solid square
25
26          // draw ovals
27          gc.fillOval( 100, 50, 80, 200 );    // oval inside rectangle
28          gc.strokeOval( 100, 275, 200, 80 ); // outlined oval
29
30          // draw circle using center point and radius
31          gc.setFill( Color.MEDIUMSEAGREEN );
32          int centerX = 550, centerY = 275;
33          int radius = 75;
34          gc.fillOval( centerX - radius, centerY - radius,
35                      radius * 2, radius * 2 );
36      }
37
38      public static void main( String [ ] args )
39      {
40          launch( args );
41      }
42 }
```

EXAMPLE 4.4   *DrawingShapes.java*

Example 4.5 shows how to use display text using the *fillText* method. The coordinate we specify is the lower-left corner of the first character in the *String*. The first call to *fillText* (line 23) displays our message in the default font. As you can see in Figure 4.7, the default text size is quite small. To display a message in a larger font, we can use the *setFont* method of the *GraphicsContext* class as shown in Table 4.5. First, however, we need to create a *Font* (line 25) using the *Font* constructor shown

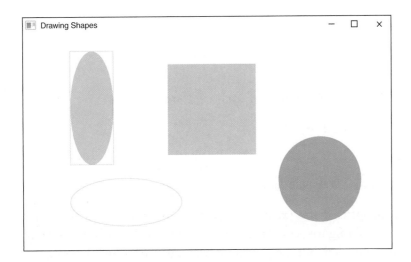

Figure 4.6

Output from *DrawingShapes .java*

in Table 4.6. Its only argument is a requested point size for the font; in this case, we request a font size of 28. We then set the font in line 26. Line 29 redisplays the message in the larger font with a call to *strokeText* so that the text is outlined.

```
1  /* Drawing Text
2     Anderson, Franceschi
3  */
4
5  import javafx.application.Application;
6  import javafx.scene.canvas.GraphicsContext;
7  import javafx.scene.paint.Color;
8  import javafx.scene.text.Font;
9  import javafx.stage.Stage;
10
11 public class DrawingText extends Application
12 {
13     @Override
14     public void start( Stage stage )
15     {
16         // set up window title and size
17         GraphicsContext gc = JIGraphicsUtility.setUpGraphics(
18                 stage, "Drawing Text", 700, 400 );
19
20         String message = "Programming is not a spectator sport!";
21         gc.setFill( Color.RED );
22
23         gc.fillText( message, 100, 100 );
24
25         Font largeFont = new Font( 28 );
26         gc.setFont( largeFont );
27         gc.setStroke( Color.RED );
28
29         gc.strokeText( message, 100, 250 );
30     }
31
32     public static void main( String [ ] args )
33     {
34         launch( args );
35     }
36 }
```

EXAMPLE 4.5   *DrawingText.java*

COMMON ERROR TRAP
If you want the whole drawing to be visible, be careful to ensure that all parts of your shape are enclosed within the bounds of the window.

What happens if the (*x*, *y*) coordinate you specify for a figure isn't inside the window? If a figure's coordinates are outside the bounds of the window, no error will be generated, but the portion of the figure outside the window bounds won't be visible.

Figure 4.7

Output from
DrawingText.java

TABLE 4.6   A *Font* Class Constructor

Font Constructor
`Font( double size )`
creates a *Font* object with a height of *size* in the default typeface

---

CODE IN ACTION

Within the online resources, you will find a movie illustrating step-by-step how to use the *GraphicsContext* drawing methods. Click on the link to start the movie.

Putting all this together, we can now write an application that draws a sprite, which is a graphics object that can be positioned and drawn as a unit. Example 4.6 shows the code to do that, and Figure 4.8 shows our sprite.

```
1 /* Drawing a Sprite
2    Anderson, Franceschi
3 */
4
5 import javafx.application.Application;
6 import javafx.scene.canvas.Canvas;
7 import javafx.scene.canvas.GraphicsContext;
8 import javafx.scene.paint.Color;
9 import javafx.stage.Stage;
```

```
10
11 public class DrawingASprite extends Application
12 {
13     @Override
14     public void start( Stage stage )
15     {
16         // set up window title and size
17         GraphicsContext gc = JIGraphicsUtility.setUpGraphics(
18                 stage, "Drawing a Sprite", 700, 400 );
19
20         // drawing the sprite
21         int sX = 275;
22         int sY = 100;
23         gc.setFill( Color.CORAL ); // body
24         gc.fillOval( sX, sY + 20, 120, 160 );
25         gc.setFill( Color.DARKGOLDENROD ); // hat
26         gc.fillRect( sX + 30, sY, 60, 30 );
27         gc.setStroke( Color.DARKGOLDENROD ); // hat brim
28         gc.setLineWidth( 3 );
29         gc.strokeLine( sX, sY + 30, sX + 120, sY + 30 );
30         gc.setFill( Color.CHOCOLATE ); // eye
31         gc.fillOval( sX + 80, sY + 60, 24, 16 );
32         gc.setFill( Color.DARKSALMON ); // feet
33         gc.setLineWidth( 1 );
34         gc.fillOval( sX + 64, sY + 166, 60, 16 );
35         gc.strokeOval( sX + 64, sY + 166, 60, 16 );
36         gc.fillOval( sX + 36, sY + 170, 60, 16 );
37         gc.strokeOval( sX + 36, sY + 170, 60, 16 );
38     }
39
40     public static void main( String [ ] args )
41     {
42         launch( args );
43     }
44 }
```

EXAMPLE 4.6   *DrawingASprite.java*

To draw our sprite, we use ovals for the body, eye, and feet, and we use a rectangle and line for the hat. We use various line widths to draw the hat brim, and we outline ovals to help define the feet.

It's important to realize that the rendering of the shapes occurs in the order in which the *stroke* or *fill* methods are executed. Any new shape that occupies the same space as a previously drawn shape will overwrite the previously drawn shape. In this drawing, we intentionally draw the eye and hat after drawing the body; and for the feet, we draw the filled ovals first, then outline the feet using stroked ovals.

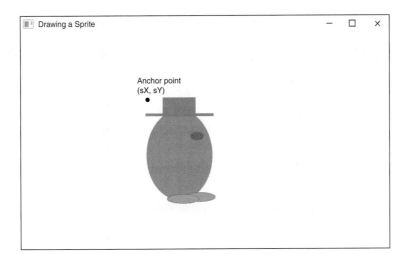

Figure 4.8

Output from *DrawingASprite .java* with the *Anchor Point Indicated*

In lines 21–22, we declare and initialize two variables, *sX* and *sY*. These define an **anchor point** for drawing the sprite. As indicated in Figure 4.8, the anchor point is the top-left point of the sprite's bounding rectangle. When we send *x* and *y* arguments to the *fillRect, strokeLine, fillOval,* and *strokeOval* methods, we specify those values relative to this starting (*sX, sY*) coordinate, or anchor point. By specifying these values relative to the anchor point—for example, *sX* + 60—we are using **offsets**. By using offsets, we can easily change the position of the sprite on the window by simply changing the values of *sX* and *sY*. We don't need to change any of the arguments sent to the *GraphicsContext* methods. To demonstrate this, try changing the values of *sX* and *sY* and rerunning the application.

SOFTWARE ENGINEERING TIP
When drawing a figure using graphics, specify coordinates as offsets from a starting (*x, y*) coordinate.

4.4 Drawing Custom Shapes

To draw custom shapes we create a path, which consists of a series of coordinates between which the JavaFX platform should draw lines. Our resulting shape can be displayed either outlined or filled. Only one path can be defined at a time. Table 4.7 shows the methods we use to create and display a path.

In Example 4.7, we illustrate drawing paths by creating an outlined triangle and a filled hexagon.

To draw our outlined triangle, we start by defining our anchor point coordinates (lines 21–22), which is the top point of the triangle. Then we call the *beginPath* method (line 23) to create an empty path. Next, we call the *moveTo* method (line 24) to set the origin of our drawing at the top point of the triangle, which is our anchor point. Of course, we could begin at any of the triangle's three points. We

TABLE 4.7   Path Drawing Methods of the *GraphicsContext* Class

Return value	Method name and argument list
void	beginPath( )
	sets the drawing path to empty
void	moveTo(double x, double y)
	moves to the (*x*, *y*) location without adding a line to the path
void	lineTo(double x, double y)
	adds a line to the current path from the previous location to (*x*, *y*)
void	closePath( )
	closes the path by adding a line from the previous location to the first location of the path
void	stroke( )
	draws the path using the current stroke color
void	fill( )
	draws the path using the current fill color

COMMON ERROR TRAP
Forgetting to close the path could result in an incomplete shape.

call the *lineTo* method (lines 25–26) twice to specify one line from the origin to the lower-left point and a second line from that location to the lower-right point.

We call the *closePath* method (line 27) to finish the shape; this method adds a line from our current position to the origin. Optionally, we could complete the shape by writing a third *lineTo* method call that creates a line from the lower-right point to the origin. In either case, once the path is fully defined, we draw the triangle by setting the stroke color and calling the *stroke* method (lines 29–31).

Drawing the hexagon is similar. We define coordinates for an anchor point (the leftmost point of the hexagon), begin a new path, move to our anchor point, define five lines of the hexagon using *lineTo* method calls, and close the path to finish the shape (lines 35–44). We display the filled hexagon by setting the fill color and calling the *fill* method (lines 46–49).

The resulting figures are shown in Figure 4.9.

```
1  /* Drawing Shapes Using Paths
2     Anderson, Franceschi
3  */
4
5  import javafx.application.Application;
6  import javafx.scene.canvas.GraphicsContext;
7  import javafx.scene.paint.Color;
8  import javafx.stage.Stage;
```

```
 9
10 public class DrawingPaths extends Application
11 {
12     @Override
13     public void start( Stage stage )
14     {
15         // set up window title and size
16         GraphicsContext gc = JIGraphicsUtility.setUpGraphics(
17                     stage, "Using Paths", 700, 400 );
18
19         // drawing a triangle
20         // 1. create the path
21         int startX = 175;
22         int startY = 120;
23         gc.beginPath( );
24         gc.moveTo( startX, startY );
25         gc.lineTo( startX - 50, startY + 175 );
26         gc.lineTo( startX + 50, startY + 175 );
27         gc.closePath( );
28
29         // 2 draw the path
30         gc.setStroke( Color.CRIMSON );
31         gc.stroke( );
32
33         // draw a hexagon
34         // 1. create the path
35         startX = 350;
36         startY = 200;
37         gc.beginPath( );
38         gc.moveTo( startX, startY );
39         gc.lineTo( startX + 50, startY - 100 );
40         gc.lineTo( startX + 175, startY - 100 );
41         gc.lineTo( startX + 225, startY );
42         gc.lineTo( startX + 175, startY + 100 );
43         gc.lineTo( startX + 50, startY + 100 );
44         gc.closePath( );
45
46         // 2. draw the path
47         gc.setFill( Color.CORNFLOWERBLUE );
48         gc.fill( );
49     }
50
51     public static void main( String [ ] args )
52     {
53         launch( args );
54     }
55 }
```

EXAMPLE 4.7   *DrawingPaths.java*

Figure 4.9

Output from
DrawingPaths
.java

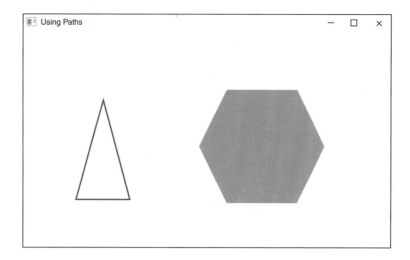

Skill Practice
with these end-of-chapter questions

4.5 Programming Activity 1: Writing an Application with Graphics

In this programming activity, you will create an application that uses graphics to draw a picture of your own design. The objective of this programming activity is to gain experience with the window coordinate system, the *stroke* and *fill* graphics methods, and using colors.

1. Start with the *ShellGraphicsApplication* class, change the name of the class to represent the figure you will draw, and add an *import* statement for the *Color* class. Remember to include the *JIGraphicsUtility.java* file in the same folder.

2. Create a drawing of your own design. It's helpful to sketch the drawing on graph paper first, then translate the drawing into the coordinates of the application window. Your drawing should define an anchor point, and include at least two each of rectangles, ovals, and lines, plus a path. Your drawing should also use at least three colors, one of which is a custom color.

3. Label your drawing using the *fillText* method.

Be creative and have fun with your drawing!

? DISCUSSION QUESTIONS

1. If you define the starting (*x, y*) coordinate of the drawing as (800, 400), you might not be able to see the drawing. Explain why.

2. What is the advantage to drawing a figure using a starting (*x, y*) coordinate as an anchor point?

CHAPTER REVIEW

4.6 Chapter Summary

- Graphical applications, which extend the JavaFX *Application* class, open a window and allow us to create graphical output.

- JavaFX applications use a performance/art metaphor with a stage corresponding to the window and a scene on which we can place a canvas.

- We put the code to draw shapes and text in the *start* method, which is called automatically when the application begins.

- The *GraphicsContext* class provides methods to draw on a canvas. Methods are provided for drawing figures, such as rectangles, ovals, custom shapes, and lines; to set the colors for drawing; and to display text in a window.

- An (x, y) coordinate system is used to specify locations in the window. Each coordinate corresponds to a pixel (or picture element). The x value specifies the horizontal position, beginning at 0 on the left-hand side of the window and increasing as you move right across the window. The y value specifies the vertical position, starting at 0 at the top of the window and increasing as you move down the window.

- All drawing on a graphics window is done in the current stroke or fill foreground color, which are changed using the *setStroke* and *setFill* methods, respectively. The stroke color is used for lines and outlined shapes; the fill color is used for drawing solid shapes. Either the stroke or fill color can be used for text.

- Objects of the *Color* class can be used to set the current stroke or fill color. The *Color* class provides *static* constants for convenience in using colors.

- Custom *Color* objects can be instantiated by using the *rgb* factory method and specifying the red, green, and blue components of the color.

- When displaying text, we can set the size of the text by instantiating a *Font* object and calling the *setFont* method of the *GraphicsContext* class.

- A custom shape can be drawn using a path. We start by creating a new path and moving to our origin. We then define points to which lines should be drawn. When finished, we close the path, then either fill the path as a solid figure or stroke the path as an outlined figure.

- A sprite is a graphics object composed of shapes that is intended to move as a unit. When drawing a sprite, define a starting (x, y) coordinate as an anchor point and specify all x and y values for the drawing methods as offsets from the starting coordinate.

4.7 Exercises, Problems, and Projects

4.7.1 Multiple Choice Exercises

1. What package does the *GraphicsContext* class belong to?
   - ❑ *javafx.scene.paint*
   - ❑ *javafx.scene.canvas*
   - ❑ *javafx.stage*
   - ❑ *javafx.application*

2. If a window is 400 by 800 pixels, how many pixels does the window contain?
   - ❑ 1,200 pixels
   - ❑ 32,000 pixels
   - ❑ 320,000 pixels

3. A JavaFX graphical application opens a window.
   - ❑ true
   - ❑ false

4. In JavaFX graphical applications, the *start* method is called automatically; the programmer does not code the method call.
   - ❑ true
   - ❑ false

5. Look at the following code:
   ```
   Color c = Color.BLUE;
   ```
   What is *BLUE?*
   - ❑ a *static* constant of the class *Color*
   - ❑ an instance variable of the class *Color*
   - ❑ a *static* method of the class *Color*
   - ❑ an instance method of the class *Color*

6. What can be stated about the line drawn by the following code?

```
gc.strokeLine( 100, 200, 300, 200 );
```

❑ The line is vertical.

❑ The line is horizontal.

❑ The line is diagonal.

❑ None of the above.

7. What do the arguments 10, 20 represent in the following statement?

```
gc.strokeRect( 10, 20, 100, 200 );
```

❑ the (x, y) coordinate of the upper-left corner of the rectangle we are drawing

❑ the width and height of the rectangle we are drawing

❑ the (x, y) coordinate of the center of the rectangle we are drawing

❑ the (x, y) coordinate of the lower-right corner of the rectangle we are drawing

8. What do the arguments 100, 200 represent in the following statement?

```
gc.strokeRect( 10, 20, 100, 200 );
```

❑ the (x, y) coordinate of the upper-left corner of the rectangle we are drawing

❑ the width and height of the rectangle we are drawing

❑ the height and width of the rectangle we are drawing

❑ the (x, y) coordinate of the lower-right corner of the rectangle we are drawing

9. How many arguments does the *fillOval* method take?

❑ 0

❑ 2

❑ 4

❑ 5

10. In RGB format, a gray color can be coded as *A A A,* where the first *A* represents the amount of red in the color, the second *A* the amount of green, and the third *A* the amount of blue. *A* can vary from 0 to 255, including both 0 and 255; how many possible gray colors can we have?

❑ 1

❑ 2

❑ 255

❑ 256

❑ 257

4.7.2   Reading and Understanding Code

In questions 11 through 15, assume that *gc* is a *GraphicsContext* reference.

11. In what color will the rectangle be drawn?

```
gc.setFill( Color.BLUE );
gc.fillRect( 10, 20, 100, 200 );
```

12. What is the length of the line being drawn?

```
gc.strokeLine( 50, 20, 50, 350 );
```

13. What is the width of the rectangle being drawn?

```
gc.fillRect( 10, 20, 250, 350 );
```

14. What is the (x, y) coordinate of the upper-right corner of the rectangle being drawn?

```
gc.fillRect( 10, 20, 250, 350 );
```

15. What is the (x, y) coordinate of the lower-right corner of the rectangle being drawn?

```
gc.strokeRect( 10, 20, 250, 350 );
```

4.7.3   Fill In the Code

16. This code sets the current fill color to red and the current stroke color to green.

```
// assume you have a GraphicsContext object named gc
// your code goes here
```

17. This code draws the *String* "Fill In the Code" with the lower-left corner of the first character (the *F*) being at the coordinate (100, 250).

```
// assume you have a GraphicsContext object named gc
// your code goes here
```

18. This code draws a filled rectangle with a width of 100 pixels and a height of 300 pixels, starting at the coordinate (50, 30).

```
// assume you have a GraphicsContext object called gc
// your code goes here
```

19. This code draws a filled rectangle starting at (50, 30) for its upper-left corner with a lower-right corner at (100, 300).

```
// assume you have a GraphicsContext object called gc
// your code goes here
```

20. This code draws a circle of radius 100 with its center located at (200, 200).

```
// assume you have a GraphicsContext object called gc
// your code goes here
```

4.7.4   Identifying Errors in Code

In questions 21 through 25, assume that *gc* is a *GraphicsContext* reference.

21. Where is the logic error in this code sequence that attempts to draw a solid blue rectangle?

```
gc.setStroke( Color.BLUE );
gc.fillRect( 10, 20, 100, 200 );
```

22. Where is the error in this code sequence?

```
gc.fillText( 'Find the bug', 100, 200 );
```

23. Where is the error in this code sequence?

```
gc.setFill( GREEN );
```

24. Where is the error in this code sequence?

```
gc.setColor( Color.RED );
```

25. Where is the error in this code sequence?

```
gc.color = Color.RED;
```

26. Where is the error in this statement?

```
import java.GraphicsContext;
```

27. Where is the error in this statement?

```
import java.stage.Stage;
```

4.7.5   Debugging Area—Using Messages from the Java Compiler and Java JVM

28. You coded the following program in the file *MyDrawingApp.java*.

```
import javafx.application.Application;
import javafx.scene.canvas.GraphicsContext;
import javafx.stage.Stage;
public class MyDrawingApp extends Application
{
    @Override
```

```
public void start( Stage stage )
{
    GraphicsContext gc = JIGraphicsUtility.setUpGraphics(
                stage, "Tester", 700, 400 );
    gc.strokeRect( 725, 200, 50, 50 );
}

public static void main( String [ ] args )
{
    launch( args );
}
}
```

You get no compiler errors, but when you run the program, the rectangle doesn't appear. Explain what the problem is and how to fix it.

29. You imported the *Color* class and coded the following on line 10 of the class *MyApplication.java*:

```
Color c = Color.rgb( 1.4, 234, 23 );    // line 10
```

When you compile, you get the following message:

```
MyApplication.java:10: error: incompatible types: possible lossy conversion
from double to int
Color c = Color.rgb( 1.4, 234, 23 );    // line 10
                     ^

1 error
```

Explain what the problem is and how to fix it.

30. You coded the following on line 10 of the class *MyApplication.java*:

```
Color c = Color.Blue;    // line 10
```

When you compile, you get the following message:

```
MyAppliction.java:10: error: cannot find symbol
    Color c = Color.Blue;    // line 10
                    ^
symbol : variable Blue
location : class Color
1 error
```

Explain what the problem is and how to fix it.

4.7.6   Write a Short Program

31. Write an application that displays the five Olympic rings.

32. Write an application that displays a tic-tac-toe board. Include a few Xs and Os.

33. Write an application that displays a rhombus (i.e., a parallelogram with equal sides). Your rhombus should not be a square.

4.7.7 Programming Projects

34. Write an application that displays two eyes. An eye can be drawn using an oval, a filled circle, and lines. On the window, write a word or two about these eyes.

35. Write an application that displays the following coins: a quarter, a dime, and a nickel. These three coins should be drawn as basic circles (of different diameters) with the currency value displayed inside the coin (for example, "25¢"). (Hint: Use the Unicode currency symbols chart to find the encoding for a cent sign.)

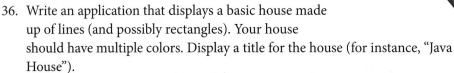

36. Write an application that displays a basic house made up of lines (and possibly rectangles). Your house should have multiple colors. Display a title for the house (for instance, "Java House").

37. Write an application that displays four concentric circles. Each circle should have a lighter shade of the same color. (Hint: Look up the *brighter* method in the *Color* class.)

4.7.8 Technical Writing

38. Explain some advantages to displaying data visually as charts. Also, explain the role that color can play in communicating data values.

39. If the *strokeRect* method did not exist, but you still had the *strokeLine* method available, explain how you would be able to draw a rectangle.

4.7.9 Group Project (for a group of 1, 2, or 3 students)

40. Write an application that displays the following:

    ❑ a drawing of two or three chessboard pieces as sprites; use a path for at least part of the drawing

    ❑ a description of one of the chessboard pieces (for instance, a rook) and its main legal moves

    In order to make the description visually appealing, use several colors and several fonts.

CHAPTER 5
Flow of Control, Part 1: Selection

CHAPTER CONTENTS

Introduction

The order of a program's instructions, called the **flow of control** of the program, is critical to producing correct results. There are essentially four types of flow of control: sequential execution, method calls, selection, and looping. Most programs use a combination of all types of flow of control.

With sequential execution in an application, the JVM executes each instruction in order. Whenever one of the instructions includes a method call, control transfers to the method, where its instructions are executed. When the method completes, we resume execution of the original instructions in order.

Sometimes, however, we don't want to execute every instruction. Some instructions should be executed only for certain input values, but not for others. For example, we may want to count only the odd numbers or perform only the operation that the user selects from a menu. For these applications, we need a way to determine at run time the input values we have and, therefore, which instructions we should execute.

In this chapter, we'll discuss **selection**, which gives us a way to test for certain conditions and to select the instructions to execute based on the results of the test. To perform selection, Java provides a number of alternatives: *if, if/else, if/else if,* the conditional operator (?:), and *switch*.

5.1   Forming Conditions

Often in a program, we need to compare variables or objects. For instance, to determine whether someone can shop online, we want to know if the person's age is at least 18. Or, if we are adding students to the honor roll, we want to add only those students with averages of 90 or better. Similarly, if we are sending warnings to students, we want to send those warnings only to students whose averages are below 60.

Java provides equality, relational, and logical operators to evaluate and test whether an expression is true or false. It also provides selection statements to transfer control to a different part of the program depending on the result of that test.

5.1.1   Equality Operators

A common operation is to compare two variables or values of the same data type to determine if their values are equal. For example, we need to compare the user's input to a 'y' to determine whether he or she wants to play a game again. Or if we want to print a list of students who will continue next year, we need to eliminate the students who are graduating seniors.

To compare values of primitive data types, Java provides the **equality operators** shown in Table 5.1. Both are binary operators, meaning that they take two operands. The operands may be expressions that evaluate to a primitive numeric or *boolean* type or an object reference. The result of an expression composed of a relational operator and its two operands is a *boolean* value, that is, *true* or *false*.

For instance, if an *int* variable *age* holds the value 32, then

the expression (`age == 32`) will evaluate to *true*, and

the expression (`age != 32`) will evaluate to *false*.

The following expression can be used to eliminate seniors by testing whether the value of the *int* variable *yearInCollege* is not equal to 4:

```
yearInCollege != 4
```

The following expression can be used in a game program to determine whether the user wants to play again:

```
playAgain == 'y'
```

Assuming the user's input is stored in the *char* variable *playAgain*, then if the user typed 'y', the expression evaluates to *true*; with any other input value, the expression evaluates to *false*.

A common error is to use the assignment operator instead of the equality operator. For example:

```
playAgain = 'y'
```

actually **assigns** the value *y* to the variable *playAgain*.

Although the equality operators can be used to compare object references, these operators cannot be used to compare object data. We discuss the comparison of objects later in the chapter.

COMMON ERROR TRAP
Do not confuse the equality operator == (double equal signs) with the assignment operator = (one equal sign).

TABLE 5.1 Equality Operators

Equality Operator	Type	Meaning
==	binary	is equal to
!=	binary	is not equal to

5.1.2 Relational Operators

To compare values of primitive numeric types, Java provides the **relational operators** shown in Table 5.2. These operators are binary, meaning that they take two operands, each of which is an expression that evaluates to a primitive numeric type. The relational operators cannot be used with *boolean* expressions or with object references.

Again, if an *int* variable *age* holds the value 32, then

the expression (`age < 32`) will evaluate to *false,*

the expression (`age <= 32`) will evaluate to *true,*

the expression (`age > 32`) will evaluate to *false,* and

the expression (`age >= 32`) will evaluate to *true.*

This expression tests whether an *int* variable *testScore* is at least 90:

```
testScore >= 90
```

This code tests whether that test score is less than 60:

```
testScore < 60
```

TABLE 5.2   Relational Operators

Relational Operator	Type	Meaning
<	binary	is less than
<=	binary	is less than or equal to
>	binary	is greater than
>=	binary	is greater than or equal to

5.1.3 Logical Operators

A common operation in a program is to test whether a combination of conditions is true or false. For these operations, Java provides the **logical operators** !, &&, and ||, which correspond to the Boolean logic operators NOT, AND, and OR. These operators, which are shown in Table 5.3, take *boolean* expressions as operands. A *boolean* expression can be a combination of variables, operators, and method calls that result in a *boolean* value.

The NOT operator (!) takes one *boolean* expression as an operand and inverts the value of that operand. If the operand is *true,* the result will be *false*; and if the operand is *false,* the result will be *true.*

The AND operator (&&) takes two *boolean* expressions as operands; if both operands are *true,* then the result will be *true*; otherwise, the result will be *false.*

TABLE 5.3   Logical Operators

Logical Operator	Type	Meaning
!	unary	NOT
&&	binary	AND
||	binary	OR

TABLE 5.4   Truth Table for Logical Operators

Operands		Operations		
a	b	!a	a && b	a || b
true	true	false	true	true
true	false	false	false	true
false	true	true	false	true
false	false	true	false	false

The OR operator (||) also takes two *boolean* expressions as operands. If both operands are *false*, then the result will be *false*; otherwise, it will be *true*. The OR operator consists of two vertical bars with no intervening space. On the PC keyboard, the vertical bar is the shifted character above the *Enter* key.

The truth table for these logical operators is shown in Table 5.4.

The order of precedence of the relational and logical operators is shown in Table 5.5, along with the arithmetic operators. Note that the Unary NOT operator (!) has the

REFERENCE POINT
The complete Operator Precedence Chart is provided in Appendix B.

TABLE 5.5   Operator Precedence

Operator Hierarchy	Order of Same-Statement Evaluation	Operation
( )	left to right	parentheses for explicit grouping
++, --	right to left	shortcut postincrement/postdecrement
++, --, !	right to left	shortcut preincrement/predecrement, logical unary NOT
*, /, %	left to right	multiplication, division, modulus
+, -	left to right	addition or *String* concatenation, subtraction

(Continued)

TABLE 5.5   Operator Precedence (*Continued*)

Operator Hierarchy	Order of Same-Statement Evaluation	Operation
<, <=, >, >=	left to right	relational operators: less than, less than or equal to, greater than, greater than or equal to
==, !=	left to right	equality operators: equal to and not equal to
&&	left to right	logical AND
||	left to right	logical OR
=, +=, -=, *=, /=, %=	right to left	Assignment operator and shortcut assignment operators

highest precedence of the relational and logical operators, followed by the relational operators, then the equality operators, then AND (&&), then OR (||).

Example 5.1 shows these operators at work.

```
1 /* Using Logical Operators
2    Anderson, Franceschi
3 */
4
5 public class LogicalOperators
6 {
7  public static void main( String [ ] args )
8  {
9    int age = 75;
10   boolean test;
11
12   test = ( age > 18 && age < 65 );
13   System.out.println( age + " > 18 && " + age + " < 65 is " + test );
14
15   // short circuitry with AND
16   test = ( age < 65 && age > 18 );
17   System.out.println( age + " < 65 && " + age + " > 18 is " + test );
18
19   // short circuitry with OR
20   test = ( age > 65 || age < 18 );
21   System.out.println( age + " > 65 || " + age + " < 18 is " + test );
22
23   // AND has higher precedence than OR
24   test = ( age > 65 || age < 18  && false );
25   System.out.println( age + " > 65 || " + age
```

```
26                         + " < 18 && false is " + test );
27
28    // use of parentheses to force order of execution
29    test = ( ( age > 65 || age < 18 )  && false );
30    System.out.println( "( " + age + " > 65 || " + age
31                        + " < 18 ) && false is " + test );
32  }
33 }
```

EXAMPLE 5.1   How Logical Operators Work

Line 12 evaluates whether the variable *age* is greater than 18 and less than 65 and assigns the result to the *boolean* variable *test*. Since line 9 set the value of *age* to 75, the first operand (*age > 18*) evaluates to *true*. The second operand (*age < 65*) evaluates to *false*; finally,

```
true && false
```

evaluates to *false*, and *false* is assigned to *test*, which is printed at line 13. Line 16 evaluates the same expression as in line 12, but in reverse order. Now the first operand (*age < 65*) evaluates to *false*, and therefore, since the operator is the logical AND, the overall expression evaluates to *false*, independently of the value of the second operand. Because (*false &&* something) always evaluates to *false*, the second operand (*age > 18*) will never be evaluated by the JVM. This is called **short-circuit evaluation**.

Line 20 shows an example of short-circuit evaluation for the logical OR operator. The first operand (*age > 65*) evaluates to *true*, resulting in the overall expression evaluating to *true*, independently of the value of the second operand. Because (*true ||* something) always evaluates to *true*, the second operand will never be evaluated by the JVM.

As shown in Table 5.5, the logical AND operator has higher precedence than the logical OR operator. Thus, the expression in line 24 is not evaluated from left to right; rather, the second part of the expression (*age < 18 && false*) is evaluated first, which evaluates to *false*. Then (*age > 65 || false*) evaluates to *true*, which is assigned to *test*, and then output at lines 25–26. If we want to evaluate the expression from left to right, we have to use parentheses to force this, as in line 29. Then, (*age > 65 || age < 18*) is evaluated first and evaluates to *true*; (*true && false*) is evaluated next and evaluates to *false*.

Figure 5.1 shows the output of Example 5.1.

Suppose we have three *ints: x, y,* and *z,* and we want to test if *x* is less than both *y* and *z*. A common error is to express the condition this way:

Figure 5.1

Output from
Example 5.1

```
75 > 18 && 75 < 65 is false
75 < 65 && 75 > 18 is false
75 > 65 || 75 < 18 is true
75 > 65 || 75 < 18 && false is true
( 75 > 65 || 75 < 18 ) && false is false
```

```
x < y && z // incorrect comparison of x to y and z
```

**COMMON ERROR
TRAP**
Be sure that
both operands
of the logical
AND and logical
OR operators
are *boolean*
expressions.
Expressions such
as x < y && z,
with *x*, *y*, and *z*
being numeric
types, are illegal.
Instead, use the
expression
x < y && x < z

Because *z* is not a *boolean* variable, this statement will generate a compiler error. Both operands of the logical AND and logical OR operators must evaluate to a *boolean* expression. The correct expression is the following:

```
x < y && x < z
```

There are often several ways to express the same condition using the Java logical operators. For instance, suppose we have two boolean variables called *flag1* and *flag2*, and we want to test if at least one of them is *false*.

In plain English, we would translate it as *flag1 is false* OR *flag2 is false*.

Table 5.6 provides several equivalent expressions for the preceding test.

Although all the expressions in Table 5.6 are equivalent, the first expression, which is the simplest translation of the condition to test, is the easiest to understand and would be the best selection for readability.

DeMorgan's Laws

Thanks to the work of the British mathematician Augustus DeMorgan, we have a set of rules to help develop expressions that are equivalent. DeMorgan, who is known for his work in Boolean algebra and set theory, developed what are known as DeMorgan's Laws. They are the following:

1. NOT(A AND B) = (NOT A) OR (NOT B)

2. NOT(A OR B) = (NOT A) AND (NOT B)

TABLE 5.6   Examples of Equivalent Expressions

Equivalent Expressions	English Meaning
(flag1 == false) || (flag2 == false)	*flag1* is false OR *flag2* is false
!flag1 || !flag2	*!flag1* is true OR *!flag2* is true
! (flag1 && flag2)	not both *flag1* and *flag2* are true

In Java, therefore, using the first law, we see that

!(a && b) is equivalent to !a || !b

Using the second law, we see that

!(a || b) is equivalent to !a && !b

These laws are illustrated in the extended truth table shown in Table 5.7.

Thus, to use DeMorgan's Laws, we change the AND operator to OR and change the OR operator to AND, and apply the NOT operator (!) to each operand of a logical operator. When the operands are expressions using relational or equality operators, the negated expressions are shown in Table 5.8.

For instance, suppose we have an *int* variable named *age*, representing the age of a person, and we want to assess whether *age* is less than or equal to 18 or greater than or equal to 65.

Table 5.9 provides several equivalent expressions for the preceding test.

Again, although all the expressions in Table 5.9 are equivalent, the first expression, which is the simplest translation of the condition to test, is the easiest to read.

TABLE 5.7   Truth Table for DeMorgan's Laws

a	b	!a	!b	a && b	a || b	!(a && b)	!a || !b	!(a || b)	!a && !b
true	true	false	false	true	true	false	false	false	false
true	false	false	true	false	true	true	true	false	false
false	true	true	false	false	true	true	true	false	false
false	false	true	true	false	false	true	true	true	true

TABLE 5.8   The Logical NOT Operator Applied to Relational and Equality Operators

Expression	!(Expression)
a == b	a != b
a != b	a == b
a < b	a >= b
a >= b	a < b
a > b	a <= b
a <= b	a > b

TABLE 5.9   More Examples of Equivalent Expressions

Equivalent Expressions	English Meaning
(age <= 18 || age >= 65)	*age* is less than or equal to 18 or *age* is greater than or equal to 65
!(age > 18 && age < 65)	*age* is not between 18 and 65
!(age > 18) || !(age < 65)	*age* is not greater than 18 or *age* is not less than 65

Skill Practice
with these end-of-chapter questions

5.14.1   Multiple Choice Exercises

Questions 1, 2, 3, 4, 5, 6, 7

5.14.2   Reading and Understanding Code

Questions 10, 11

5.14.4   Identifying Errors in Code

Questions 31, 32

5.2   Simple Selection with *if*

The simple selection pattern is appropriate when our program needs to perform an operation for one set of data, but not for all other data. For this situation, we use a simple *if* statement, which has this pattern:

```
if ( condition )
{
  true block
}
next statement
```

The true block can contain one or more statements and is executed only if the condition evaluates to *true*. After the true block executes, the instruction following the *if* statement is executed. If the condition is *false*, the true block is skipped and execution picks up at the next instruction after the *if* statement. If the true block contains only one statement, the curly braces are optional. Figure 5.2 illustrates the flow of control of a simple *if* statement.

In Example 5.2, we first prompt the user to enter a grade at lines 12–13. Then we prompt the user for any extra credit points at lines 15–16. At line 18, we test whether the extra credit points are greater than 0. If so, we add the extra credit points to the test grade at line 19. Then, no matter what the extra credit was, lines 21–22 are executed, which print the final grade. Figures 5.3 and 5.4 show two runs of the program, one with extra credit greater than 0, and one with no extra credit.

Figure 5.2

Flow of Control of a Simple *if* Statement

```java
1 /* Using if to calculate a final test grade
2    Anderson, Franceschi
3 */
4 import java.util.Scanner;
5
6 public class TestGrade
7 {
8   public static void main( String [ ] args )
9   {
10    Scanner scan = new Scanner( System.in );
11
12    System.out.print( "Enter your test grade > " );
13    int grade = scan.nextInt( );
14
15    System.out.print( "Enter your extra credit > " );
16    int extraCredit = scan.nextInt( );
17
18    if ( extraCredit > 0 )
19        grade += extraCredit;
20
21    System.out.println( "Your final test grade is "
22                  + grade );
23  }
24 }
```

EXAMPLE 5.2   Working with *if* Statements

```
Enter your test grade > 85
Enter your extra credit > 10
Your final test grade is 95
```

Figure 5.3

Output of Example 5.2 with 10 Extra Credit Points

```
Enter your test grade > 85
Enter your extra credit > 0
Your final test grade is 85
```

Figure 5.4

Output of Example 5.2 with No Extra Credit

Notice the indentation of the true block (line 19). Indenting clarifies the structure of the program. It's easy to see that we add the extra credit to the test grade only if the condition is true. Notice also that we skipped a line after the end of the *if* statement; this further separates the true block from the instruction that follows the *if* statement, making it easier to see the flow of control.

Many software engineers believe it's a good practice to include the curly braces even if only one statement is included in the true block, because it increases clarity and ease of maintenance. The curly braces increase clarity because they highlight the section of code to be executed when the condition is *true*. Program maintenance is easier because if the program requirements change and we need to add a second statement to the true block, the curly braces are already in place.

Note that there is no semicolon after the condition. If we place a semicolon after the condition, as in this **incorrect** statement,

```
if ( grade >= 60 ); // incorrect to place semicolon here
      System.out.println( "You passed" );
```

the compiler will not generate an error. Instead, it will consider the semicolon to indicate that the true block of the *if* statement is empty, because a semicolon by itself indicates a statement that does nothing. In this case, the compiler concludes that there is no instruction to execute when the condition is *true*. As a result, when the program runs, the statement

```
System.out.println( "You passed" );
```

is treated as though it follows the *if* statement, and therefore, the message "You passed" will be printed regardless of the value of *grade*.

5.3   Selection Using *if/else*

The second form of an *if* statement is appropriate when the data falls into two mutually exclusive categories and different instructions should be executed for each category. For these situations, we use an *if/else* statement, which has the following pattern:

```
if ( condition )
{
   true block
}
else
{
   false block
}
next statement
```

If the condition evaluates to *true*, the true block is executed and the false block is skipped. If the condition evaluates to *false*, the true block is skipped and the *false* block is executed. In either situation, the statement following the *if* statement is executed next. Figure 5.5 illustrates the flow of control of an *if/else* statement.

If the true or false block contains only one statement, the curly braces are optional for that block.

Again, notice the indentation of the true and false blocks and that the *else* and curly braces line up under the *if*. This coding style makes it easy to see which statements belong to the true block and which belong to the false block. If the indentation is incorrect, a reader of our program may misunderstand which statements will be executed. In any event, the compiler ignores the indentation; the indentation is designed only to make it easier for humans to understand the logic of the code.

In Example 5.3, we test a grade to determine whether it is a passing grade (>= 60) or a failing grade (any other value). This is a case where the data is mutually exclusive: either the grade is a passing grade or it is not. We want to print a different message depending on the grade. After prompting the user for a numeric grade, we declare a *String* to hold the appropriate message (line 16), which will be determined in our *if/else* statement. If the *if* condition, (grade >= 60), is true, then we assign "You passed" to *message*. If the condition is false, we assign "You failed" to *message*. On line 22,

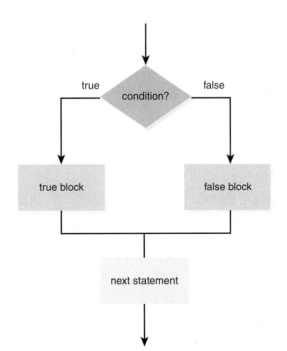

Flow of Control of an *if/else* Statement

after the *if/else* statement completes, we print whatever *String* we have assigned to *message*. Figures 5.6 and 5.7 show two runs of the program, first with a grade greater than or equal to 60, and then with a grade less than 60.

```
1 /* Using if/else
2    Anderson, Franceschi
3 */
4
5 import java.util.Scanner;
6
7 public class PassingGrade
8 {
9  public static void main( String [ ] args )
10  {
11     Scanner scan = new Scanner( System.in );
12
13     System.out.print( "Enter a grade > " );
14     int grade = scan.nextInt( );
15
16     String message;
17     if ( grade >= 60 )
18      message = "You passed";
19     else
20      message = "You failed";
21
22     System.out.println( message );
23  }
24 }
```

EXAMPLE 5.3   Working with *if/else* Statements

Note that we could have used two sequential *if* statements, as in:

```
if ( grade >= 60 )
   message = "You passed";

if ( grade < 60 )
   message = "You failed";
```

However, if the first condition, (grade >= 60), is false, the second condition, (grade < 60), must be true. So an *if/else* simplifies our processing and avoids unnecessarily testing two conditions when only one of the conditions can be true.

Figure 5.6

Output from
Example 5.3 with
grade >= 60

```
Enter a grade > 60
You passed
```

```
Enter a grade > 59
You failed
```

Figure 5.7

Output from
Example 5.3 with
grade < 60

Block Scope

The **scope** of a variable is the region within a program where the variable can be **referenced**, or used. When we declare a variable, its scope extends from the point at which it is declared until the end of the block in which we declared it. A method, such as *main*, is a block. Thus, in Example 5.3, the scope of the object reference *scan* extends from line 11 through the end of *main*. Thus, we can legally reference *scan* on line 14. Similarly, the scope of *grade* extends from its declaration (line 14) through the end of *main*, and we can legally reference it on line 17 in the *if* condition. Finally, the scope of the *String message* extends from line 16 through the end of *main*, and thus we can legally reference *message* on lines 18, 20, and 22.

The true blocks and false blocks for *if* statements are also blocks. Thus, if instead of declaring the *String message* on line 16, we declare it inside the true block of the *if* statement as in the following,

```
if ( grade >= 60 )
{
   String message = "You passed";
}
else
   message = "You failed";

System.out.println( message );
```

then the scope of *message* extends from its declaration only until the end of the true block. In this case, the compiler will generate "cannot find symbol" error messages for the references to *message* inside the false block and for the *System.out.println* statement after the *if* statement because *message* is out of scope outside of the true block.

CODE IN ACTION

Within the online resources, you will find a movie illustrating step-by-step how to use an *if/else* statement. Click on this chapter's link to start the movie.

Skill Practice
with these end-of-chapter questions

5.4   Selection Using *if/else if*

The last form of an *if* statement is appropriate when the data falls into more than two mutually exclusive categories and the appropriate instructions to execute are different for each category. For this situation, Java provides the *if/else if* statement.

The *if/else if* statement follows this pattern:

```
if ( condition 1 )
{
     true block for condition 1
}
else if ( condition 2 )
{
     true block for condition 2
}
. . .
else if ( condition n )
{
     true block for condition n
}
```

```
else
{
      false block for all conditions being false
}
next statement
```

The flow of control for this form of the *if* statement is shown in Figure 5.8.

There can be any number of conditions in an *if/else if* statement. As we can see, once a condition evaluates to *true* for any value, control moves to the true block for that condition, then skips the remainder of the conditions, continuing execution at any statement that follows the *if/else if* statement. The final false block (along with the final *else*) is optional and is executed only when none of the conditions evaluates to *true*. Note that if the final *else* is used, then the condition it covers is not coded. The *else* stands alone on the line.

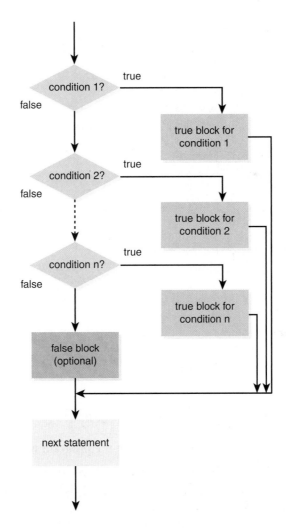

Figure 5.8

Flow of Control of an *if/else if* Statement

We can use the *if/else if* statement to determine a student's letter grade based on his or her numeric grade. Example 5.4 demonstrates a Java application that prompts a student for a test grade and translates that grade into a letter grade.

```java
1  /* A program to translate a numeric grade into a letter grade
2     Anderson, Franceschi
3  */
4
5  import java.util.Scanner;
6
7  public class LetterGrade
8  {
9    public static void main( String [ ] args )
10   {
11     Scanner scan = new Scanner( System.in );
12
13     char letterGrade;
14
15     System.out.print( "Enter your test grade: " );
16     int grade = scan.nextInt( );
17
18     if ( grade >= 90 )
19         letterGrade = 'A';
20
21     else if ( grade >= 80 )
22         letterGrade = 'B';
23
24     else if ( grade >= 70 )
25         letterGrade = 'C';
26
27     else if ( grade >= 60 )
28         letterGrade = 'D';
29
30     else  // grade fits none of the conditions
31         letterGrade = 'F';
32
33     System.out.println( "Your test grade of " + grade
34                     + " is a letter grade of " + letterGrade );
35   }
36 }
```

COMMON ERROR TRAP
In an *if/else* or *if/else/if* statement, do not specify a condition for the final *else*.

EXAMPLE 5.4   A Demonstration of *if/else if*

Figure 5.9 shows the output from the program when a student enters a grade of 83.

Notice that each condition is a simple relational expression. Even though we assign a *B* letter grade when the numeric grade is between 80 and 89, the condition for a *B* letter grade (line 21) is simply:

```
Enter your test grade: 83
Your test grade of 83 is a letter grade of B
```

Figure 5.9

Output from
Example 5.4

```
if ( grade >= 80 )
```

We don't need to write the condition as

```
if ( grade >= 80 && grade < 90 )
```

because by the time the condition is tested at line 21, all numeric grades greater than or equal to 90 have been eliminated by the test condition at line 18. Any grade greater than or equal to 90 causes the condition at line 18, (grade >= 90), to evaluate to *true*. For those grades, the flow of control is to assign an *A* to *letter-Grade* at line 19, then skip the remainder of the conditions, continuing execution at the statement following the *if/else if* statement, which is line 33 in this example. Thus, if the condition at line 21 is evaluated, we know that the *grade* must be less than 90. Note that in line 30, the final *else* covers the only other possibility: that the grade is less than 60. We do not code that condition; rather we include only the *else*.

CODE IN ACTION

Within the online resources, you will find a movie illustrating step-by-step how to use an *if/else if* statement. Click on this chapter's link to start the movie.

Skill Practice
with these end-of-chapter questions

5.14.1   Multiple Choice Exercises

Question 8

5.14.2   Reading and Understanding Code

Question 15

5.14.4   Identifying Errors in Code

Questions 36, 37, 38

5.5   Sequential and Nested *if/else* Statements

When we need the results of one *if* statement's processing before we can evaluate the next condition, we can write multiple *if* statements either sequentially or nested within other *if* statements.

5.5.1   Sequential *if/else* Statements

Finding the Minimum or Maximum Values

To illustrate sequential *if* statements, let's look at the problem of finding the smallest of three numbers.

We can use multiple, sequential *if* statements. First we find the smaller of the first two numbers, then we find the smaller of that result and the third number. The pseudocode for this application is:

```
read number1
read number2
read number3

if number1 is less than number2
   smallest is number1
else
   smallest is number2
if number3 is less than smallest
   smallest is number3
```

Translating the pseudocode into Java, we get the application in Example 5.5, which prompts the user for three integers and outputs the smallest of the three numbers. In this application, we use two sequential *if* statements. The first *if* statement (lines 23–26) uses an *if/else* statement to find the smaller of the first two integers and stores that value into the variable *smallest*. Then, the second *if* statement (lines 28–29) compares the third integer to the value stored in *smallest*. In the second *if* statement, we don't use an *else* clause, because we need to change the value in *smallest* only if the condition is *true*, that is, if the third number is less than *smallest*. Otherwise, the smallest value is already stored in *smallest*.

```
1   /* Find the smallest of three integers
2      Anderson, Franceschi
3   */
4
5   import java.util.Scanner;
6
7   public class FindSmallest
```

```
8   {
9     public static void main( String [ ] args )
10    {
11        int smallest;
12        int num1, num2, num3;
13
14        Scanner scan = new Scanner( System.in );
15
16        System.out.print( "Enter the first integer: " );
17        num1 = scan.nextInt( );
18        System.out.print( "Enter the second integer: " );
19        num2 = scan.nextInt( );
20        System.out.print( "Enter the third integer: " );
21        num3 = scan.nextInt( );
22
23        if ( num1 < num2 )
24            smallest = num1;
25        else
26            smallest = num2;
27
28        if ( num3 < smallest )
29            smallest = num3;
30
31        System.out.println( "The smallest is " + smallest );
32    }
33 }
```

EXAMPLE 5.5   An Application with Sequential *if* Statements

When the program in Example 5.5 is run using 6, 7, and 5 for the three integers, the output is as shown in Figure 5.10.

One more point. The code only checks that one number is less than another. What happens if two or more of the numbers are equal? The code still works! We only need to find the smallest value; we don't care which of the variables holds that smallest value.

5.5.2   Nested *if/else* Statements

If statements can be written as part of the true or false block of another *if* statement. These are called nested *if* statements. Typically, we nest *if* statements when more information is required beyond the results of the first *if* statement.

```
Enter the first integer: 6
Enter the second integer: 7
Enter the third integer: 5
The smallest is 5
```

Figure 5.10

Output from Example 5.5

One difficulty that arises with nested *if* statements is specifying which *else* clause pairs with which *if* statement, especially if some *if* statements have *else* clauses and others do not. The compiler matches any *else* clause with the most previous *if* statement that doesn't already have an *else* clause. If this matching is not what we want, we can use curly braces to specify the desired *if/else* pairing.

In this code, we have one *if* statement nested within another *if* statement.

```java
if ( x == 2 )
        if ( y == x )
           System.out.println( "x and y equal 2" );
        else
           System.out.println( "x equals 2, but y does not" );
```

Without curly braces, the entire second *if* statement comprises the true block of the first condition (x == 2), and the *else* is paired with the second condition (y == x), because this is the most previous *if* condition that doesn't have an *else*.

However, we can force the *else* clause to be paired with the first condition by using curly braces, as follows:

```java
if ( x == 2 )
{
   if ( y == x )
      System.out.println( "x and y equal 2" );
}
else
   System.out.println( "x does not equal 2" );
```

With the curly braces added, the *if* condition (y == x), along with its true block, becomes the complete true block for the condition (x == 2), and the *else* clause now belongs to the first *if* condition (x == 2).

Why can't we just alter the indentation to indicate our meaning? Remember that indentation increases the readability of the code for humans. The compiler ignores indentation and instead follows Java's syntactic rules.

COMMON ERROR TRAP
Be sure that all *else* clauses match an *if* condition. Writing *else* clauses that don't match *if* conditions will generate an `'else' without 'if'` compiler error.

Dangling else

A common error is writing *else* clauses that don't match any *if* conditions. This is called a **dangling else**. For example, the following code, which includes three *else* clauses and only two *if* conditions, will generate this compiler error:

```
'else' without 'if'
```

```java
if ( x == 2 )

   if ( y == x )
```

```
        System.out.println( "x and y equal 2" );

    else // matches y==x
        System.out.println( "y does not equal 2" );

else // matches x==2
    System.out.println( "x does not equal 2" );

else // no matching if!
    System.out.println( "x and y are not equal" );
```

For a more complex and real-world example of nested *if* statements, let's generate a random number between 1 and 10. After we generate the random number, we'll prompt the user for a guess. First we'll verify that the guess is between 1 and 10. If it isn't, we'll print an error message. Otherwise, we'll check whether the user has guessed the number. If so, we'll print a congratulatory message. If the user has not guessed the number, we'll display the number, then determine whether the guess was close. We'll define "close" as within three numbers. We'll print a message informing the user whether the guess was close, then we'll wish the user better luck next time. The pseudocode for this program looks like this:

```
generate a secret random number between 1 and 10
prompt the user for a guess

if guess is not between 1 and 10
    print message
else
  if guess equals the secret number
    print congratulations
  else
    print the secret number
    if guess is not within 3 numbers
      print "You missed it by a mile!"
    else
      print "You were close."
    print "Better luck next time."
```

This pseudocode uses three *if* statements; the first determines if the guess is within the requested range of numbers. If it isn't, we print a message. Otherwise, a nested *if* statement tests whether the user has guessed the secret number. If so, we print a congratulatory message. If not, we print the secret number, and our last nested *if* statement determines whether the guess was not within 3 numbers of the secret number. If not, we print "You missed it by a mile!"; otherwise, we print "You were close." In either case, we print "Better luck next time."

Example 5.6 is the result of translating this pseudocode into a Java application.

```
1    /* Guess a number between 1 and 10
2       Anderson, Franceschi
3    */
4
5    import java.util.Random;
6    import java.util.Scanner;
7
8    public class GuessANumber
9    {
10     public static void main( String [ ] args )
11     {
12       Random random = new Random( );
13       int secretNumber = random.nextInt( 10 ) + 1;
14
15       Scanner scan = new Scanner( System.in );
16
17       System.out.print( "I'm thinking of a number"
18                   + " between 1 and 10. What is your guess? " );
19       int guess = scan.nextInt( );
20
21       if ( guess < 1 || guess > 10 )
22       {
23          System.out.println( "Well, if you're not going to try,"
24                                   + " I'm not playing." );
25       }
26       else
27       {
28         if ( guess == secretNumber )
29              System.out.println( "Hoorah. You win!" );
30         else
31         {
32              System.out.println( "The number was " + secretNumber );
33
34              if ( Math.abs( guess - secretNumber ) > 3 )
35                  System.out.println( "You missed it by a mile!" );
36              else
37                  System.out.println( "You were close." );
38
39              System.out.println( "Better luck next time." );
40         }
41       }
42     }
43  }
```

EXAMPLE 5.6   Nested *if* statements

Figure 5.11

Output from the
GuessANumber
Program in
Example 5.6

```
I'm thinking of a number between 1 and 10. What is your guess? 2
The number was 10
You missed it by a mile!
Better luck next time.
```

On line 34, we used the *abs* method of the *Math* class to determine whether the guess was within three integers of the secret number. By taking the absolute value of the difference between the guess and the secret number, we don't need to worry about which number is higher than the other; we will always receive a positive difference from the *abs* method.

Figure 5.11 shows the output of a sample run of this program.

5.6   Testing Techniques for *if/else* Statements

When an application uses *if/else* statements, the application's flow of control depends on the user's input or other data values. For one input value, the application may execute the true block, while for another input value, the application may execute the false block. Obviously, running an application only once is no guarantee that the program is correct, because if the true block was executed, then the false block was not executed, and therefore, was not tested. Similarly, if the false block was executed, then the true block was not executed, and therefore was not tested.

To test an application for correctness, we could attempt to test all execution paths. To do this, we devise a **test plan** that includes running the application with different data values designed to execute all the statements in the application.

For example, an application that determines whether an integer is positive or negative might have this code:

```
System.out.print( "Enter an integer > " );
int x = scan.nextInt( );
if  ( x > 0 )
   System.out.println( x + " is positive" );
else
   System.out.println( x + " is negative" );
```

We could test this code by running the application twice, the first time entering the value 1, and the second time entering the value −1. We see that the results for those two values are correct: 1 is positive and −1 is negative. We have executed all the statements successfully, but can we say for certain that the program is correct? What if we entered the value 0, which is considered neither a positive nor a negative integer? As written, our program determines that 0 is negative, which is incorrect.

We see, then, that testing the true and false blocks is not sufficient; we need to test the condition of the *if/else* statement as well. There are three possibilities: *x* is less than 0, *x* is equal to 0, or *x* is greater than 0. To test the condition, we should run the application with input values that meet these three criteria. So we should run the application one more time with the input value of 0. This will show us that the program is incorrect, because our code identifies 0 as a negative number.

To correct the program, we should add another condition (x < 0) so we can separate 0 from the negative numbers. The code would then become:

```
System.out.print( "Enter an integer > " );
int x = scan.nextInt( );
if ( x > 0 )
    System.out.println( x + " is positive" );
else if ( x < 0 )
    System.out.println( x + " is negative" );
else
    System.out.println( "The integer is 0" );
```

Now if we retest the program with input values −1, 1, and 0, we get correct results for each of these values.

Notice that the test values we chose are −1, 0, and 1. We call these values the *boundary values* because they are the first possible values to cause the conditions (x > 0, and x < 0, and the implicit x == 0 condition) to evaluate to true. If we had incorrectly coded the first condition as x > 1 and we chose, for example, 2, to test our code, our test value of 2 would make the code appear to be correct. However, the code would not work correctly for the value 1. For this reason, we recommend using boundary values to test the execution paths in a program.

Another testing method is to treat the program like a black box, that is, as if the program's inner workings are unknown and unknowable to us. We devise our test plan based solely on the specifications of the program and develop input values that test the program logically. Thus, if our specifications are that we should determine whether an integer is positive or negative, we deduce that we should run the program with inputs that are a negative number, a positive number, and the special case, 0.

Both testing methods work together to ensure that a program is correct.

SOFTWARE ENGINEERING TIP

When testing your program, develop input values that test the boundary values for all execution paths and confirm that the logic implements the program specifications.

5.7   Programming Activity 1: Working with *if/else*

In this activity, you will write an *if/else* selection statement to decide how a golfer's score compares to par.

Copy to a folder on your computer all the files from the source code provided with this text for this chapter's Programming Activity 1.

Open the *SelectionPractice1Controller.java* source file. You will add your code to the *workWithIfElse* method. Part of the method has been coded for you. Search for ***** in the source file.

You should be positioned at the code shown in Example 5.7.

```java
public void workWithIfElse( int score )
{
    String result = "???";
    // ***** Student code starts here
    // If score is greater than 72, assign "over par" to result
    // If score is equal to 72, assign "par" to result
    // If score is less than 72, assign "below par" to result



    //
    // Student code ends here
    //

    animate( score, result );
}
```

EXAMPLE 5.7   The Student Code Portion of Programming Activity 1

Where indicated in the code, you should write an *if/else* statement to perform the following function:

- In the method header of the method *workWithIfElse*, you see (int score). The *int* variable *score* represents a golf score. This variable will be an input from the user; the text box that allows the user to enter the score has already been coded for you and stores the user's input in the variable *score*, which is available to your code as a parameter of the *workWith-IfElse* method. Do not declare the variable *score* inside the method; just use it.

- We want to know if the golf score is "over par," "par," or "below par." Par is 72.

- Inside the *if/else* statement, you need to assign a value to the *String* variable named *result*, as follows:

    If *score* is higher than 72, then assign "over par" to *result*; if score is exactly 72, assign "par" to *result*; and if score is lower than 72, assign "below par" to *result*.

- You do not need to write the code to call the method *animate*; that part of the code has already been written for you.

Figure 5.12

The Beginning of
the Application

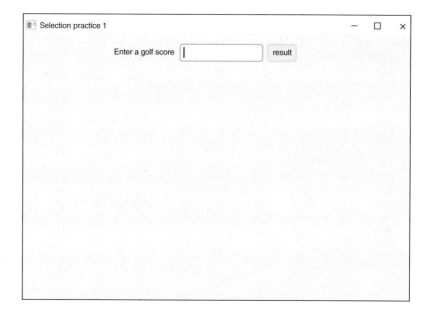

Animation: The application window will display the correct path of the *if/else* statement (in green), which may or may not be the same as your path, depending on how you coded the *if/else* statement. The animation will also assess your result, that is, the value of the variable *result*, and give you feedback on the correctness of your result.

To test your code, compile *SelectionPractice1Controller.java* and run *SelectionPractice1Application* and enter an integer in the text box. Try the following input values for *score*: 71, 72, and 73. Be sure your code produces the correct result for all input values.

When the program begins, you will see a graphics window with the text box of Figure 5.12, prompting you for an integer value.

Figure 5.13 demonstrates the correct code path when the input value is 73 and assesses that the student's code is correct.

Figure 5.14 again demonstrates the correct code path when the input value is 73, but in this case, the student's code is incorrect.

DISCUSSION QUESTIONS **?**

1. **How many conditions did you use in the complete *if/else* statement?**

2. **Your code should be correct if the application gets correct results for the input values 71, 72, and 73. Explain why.**

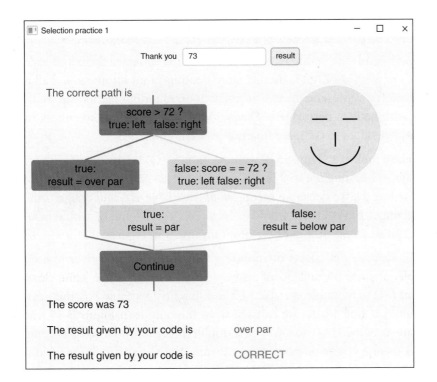

Figure 5.13

A Correct *if/else* Statement

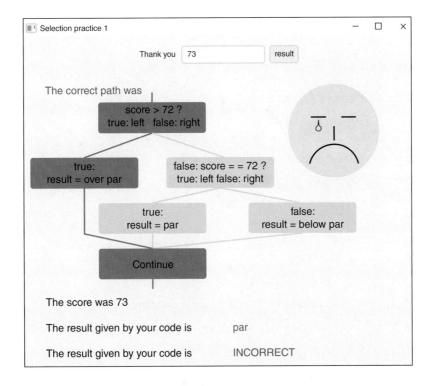

Figure 5.14

An Incorrect *if/else* Statement

5.8 Comparing Floating-Point Numbers

Java's *floats* and *doubles* are stored using IEEE 754 standard format. Because a finite number of bits (32 or 64) is used to store floating-point numbers, not all real-world values can be represented. As a result, minor rounding errors can be introduced when arithmetic is performed. That said, it is not advisable to simply rely on the equality operators to compare floating-point numbers.

REFERENCE POINT

Binary representation of floating-point numbers is discussed in an appendix.

Let's take a look at Example 5.8, which computes 11 * .1 two ways. First, at line 11, we assign .0 to a *double* variable, *d1*, and at lines 12–22 we add .1 to *d1* eleven times. Then, at line 24, we declare a second *double* variable, *d2*, and assign it the result of multiplying .1 times 11. We would expect, then, that *d1* and *d2* would have the same value. Not so, as the output of the program shows in Figure 5.15.

We can also see the effects of rounding when comparing a *float* to a *double*. For example, at lines 35 and 36 of Example 5.8, we assign the same floating-point number (PI) to a double variable *piD* and to a float variable *piF*, then compare the two values at line 40. As we can see from the output in Figure 5.15, they do not compare as equal. The reason is that double-precision floating-point numbers are able to store a larger number of significant digits than single-precision floating-point numbers.

```
 1 /* Using equality operators on floating-point numbers
 2     Anderson, Franceschi
 3 */
 4
 5 public class EqualityFloatingPoint
 6 {
 7   public static void main( String [ ] args )
 8   {
 9     // Part 1: Compute 11 * .1 two ways
10
11     double d1 = .0; // add .1 to 0 eleven times
12     d1 += .1;  // 1
13     d1 += .1;  // 2
14     d1 += .1;  // 3
15     d1 += .1;  // 4
16     d1 += .1;  // 5
17     d1 += .1;  // 6
18     d1 += .1;  // 7
19     d1 += .1;  // 8
20     d1 += .1;  // 9
21     d1 += .1;  // 10
22     d1 += .1;  // 11
```

```
23
24    double d2 = .1 * 11; // compute 11 * .1
25
26    System.out.println( "d1 = " + d1 );
27    System.out.println( "d2 = " + d2 );
28    if ( d1 == d2 )
29        System.out.println( "d1 and d2 are equal" );
30    else
31        System.out.println( "d1 and d2 are not equal" );
32
33    // Part 2: Compare float and double with same value
34
35    float  piF = 3.141592653589793f;
36    double piD = 3.141592653589793;
37
38    System.out.println( "\npiF = " + piF );
39    System.out.println( "pid = " + piD );
40    if ( piF == piD )
41        System.out.println( "piF and piD are equal" );
42    else
43        System.out.println( "piF and piD are not equal" );
44  }
45 }
```

EXAMPLE 5.8   Using the Equality Operator to Compare Floating-Point Numbers

Instead of using the equality operator to compare floating-point numbers, it's better to compare the absolute value of the difference to a small value, called a *threshold*. The value of the threshold should be the difference we can tolerate and still consider the numbers equal. Let's redo Example 5.8. Instead of using the equality operator, we'll use the *Math.abs* method to compute a difference between the two numbers and compare the difference to a threshold value. We'll set the threshold at .0001, meaning that if the numbers differ by less than .0001, we'll consider them equal. The results of this approach are shown in Example 5.9 and the output is given in Figure 5.16.

```
d1 = 1.0999999999999999
d2 = 1.1
d1 and d2 are not equal

piF = 3.1415927
pid = 3.141592653589793
piF and piD are not equal
```

Figure 5.15

Output from
Example 5.8

```
1 /* Using a threshold to compare floating-point numbers
2    Anderson, Franceschi
3 */
4
5 public class ComparingFloatingPoint
6 {
7  public static void main( String [ ] args )
8  {
9    final double THRESHOLD = .0001;
10
11   // Part 1: Compute 11 * .1 two ways
12   double d1 = .0; // add .1 to 0 eleven times
13   d1 += .1;  // 1
14   d1 += .1;  // 2
15   d1 += .1;  // 3
16   d1 += .1;  // 4
17   d1 += .1;  // 5
18   d1 += .1;  // 6
19   d1 += .1;  // 7
20   d1 += .1;  // 8
21   d1 += .1;  // 9
22   d1 += .1;  // 10
23   d1 += .1;  // 11
24
25   double d2 = .1 * 11; // compute 11 * .1
26
27   System.out.println( "d1 = " + d1 );
28   System.out.println( "d2 = " + d2 );
29   if ( Math.abs( d1 - d2 ) < THRESHOLD )
30       System.out.println( "d1 and d2 are considered equal" );
31   else
32       System.out.println( "d1 and d2 are not equal" );
33
34   // Part 2: Compare float and double with same value
35   float  piF = 3.141592653589793f;
36   double piD = 3.141592653589793;
37
38   System.out.println( "\npiF = " + piF );
39   System.out.println( "piD = " + piD );
40   if ( Math.abs( piF - piD ) < THRESHOLD )
41       System.out.println( "piF and piD are considered equal" );
42   else
43       System.out.println( "piF and piD are not equal" );
44 }
45 }
```

EXAMPLE 5.9   Comparing Floating-Point Numbers Using a Threshold

```
d1 = 1.0999999999999999
d2 = 1.1
d1 and d2 are considered equal

piF = 3.1415927
pid = 3.141592653589793
piF and piD are considered equal
```

Figure 5.16

Output of
Example 5.9

TABLE 5.10   The *BigDecimal* Class API

BigDecimal Class Constructor Summary		
`BigDecimal( String ddd )`		
creates a *BigDecimal* object equivalent to the decimal number expressed as a *String*		

BigDecimal Class Method Summary		
Return value	**Method name and argument list**	
`BigDecimal`	`add( BigDecimal num )`	
	returns a *BigDecimal* object equal to the current *BigDecimal* object plus *num*	
`BigDecimal`	`subtract( BigDecimal num )`	
	returns a *BigDecimal* object equal to the current *BigDecimal* object minus *num*	
`BigDecimal`	`multiply( BigDecimal num )`	
	returns a *BigDecimal* object equal to the current *BigDecimal* object times *num*	
`BigDecimal`	`divide( BigDecimal num )`	
	returns a *BigDecimal* object equal to the current *BigDecimal* object divided by *num*	
`int`	`compareTo( BigDecimal num )`	
	returns 0 if the current *BigDecimal* object is equal to *num*; −1 if the current *BigDecimal* object is less than *num*; and 1 if the current *BigDecimal* object is greater than *num*	

When we need exact precision in calculations with decimal numbers, we can use the *BigDecimal* class in the Java Class Library. The *BigDecimal* class, which is in the *java.math* package, provides methods that perform addition, subtraction, multiplication, and division of *BigDecimal* objects so that the results are exact, without the rounding errors caused by floating-point operations. Table 5.10 shows a constructor of the *BigDecimal* class and several useful methods for performing calculations and comparing *BigDecimal* objects.

In Example 5.10, we perform the same calculations as in Example 5.9, but we use *Big-Decimal* objects instead of *doubles*. On lines 11 and 12, we instantiate two *BigDecimal*

REFERENCE POINT
You can read more about the *BigDecimal* class on Oracle's Java website www .oracle.com /technetwork /java.

Figure 5.17

Output of
Example 5.10

```
d1 = 1.1
d2 = 1.1
d1 and d2 are equal
```

objects: *d1* will hold the sum and is initialized to 0.0; *pointOne* is assigned the value 0.1 and will be repeatedly added to *d1*. Then on lines 16–26, we call the *add* method to add 0.1 to *d1* 11 times. We instantiate two more *BigDecimal* objects on lines 29 and 30, then call the *multiply* method to multiply 0.1 * 11. On line 35, we compare the resulting *BigDecimal* objects by calling the *compareTo* method, and find that the two results are in fact equal. The output of Example 5.10 is shown in Figure 5.17.

```
1  /* Using BigDecimal to compute precise decimal numbers
2      Anderson, Franceschi
3  */
4
5  import java.math.BigDecimal;
6
7  public class UsingBigDecimal
8  {
9   public static void main( String [ ] args )
10  {
11     BigDecimal d1 = new BigDecimal( "0.0" );
12     BigDecimal pointOne = new BigDecimal( "0.1" );
13
14     // Compute 11 * .1 two ways
15     // add .1 to d1 eleven times
16     d1 = d1.add( pointOne ); // 1
17     d1 = d1.add( pointOne ); // 2
18     d1 = d1.add( pointOne ); // 3
19     d1 = d1.add( pointOne ); // 4
20     d1 = d1.add( pointOne ); // 5
21     d1 = d1.add( pointOne ); // 6
22     d1 = d1.add( pointOne ); // 7
23     d1 = d1.add( pointOne ); // 8
24     d1 = d1.add( pointOne ); // 9
25     d1 = d1.add( pointOne ); // 10
26     d1 = d1.add( pointOne ); // 11
27
28     // multiply .1 * 11
29     BigDecimal d2 = new BigDecimal( "0.1" );
30     BigDecimal eleven = new BigDecimal( "11" );
31     d2 = d2.multiply( eleven );
32
33     System.out.println( "d1 = " + d1 );
34     System.out.println( "d2 = " + d2 );
```

```
35    if ( d1.compareTo( d2 ) == 0 )
36        System.out.println( "d1 and d2 are equal" );
37    else
38        System.out.println( "d1 and d2 are not equal" );
39  }
40 }
```

EXAMPLE 5.10   Comparing Floating-Point Numbers Using *BigDecimal*

5.9   Comparing Objects

5.9.1   The *equals* Method

Often, we want to compare whether two objects are equal; typically, we will say that two objects are equal if they have the same data. If we use the equality operator (==) to compare object references, however, we are comparing the value of the object references. In other words, we are comparing whether the object references point to the same object, that is, the same memory location. To compare object data, we need to use the *equals* method, which all classes inherit from the *Object* class. Many classes provide a custom version of the *equals* method. The API of the *equals* method is the following:

```
public boolean equals( Object ob )
```

Typically, the *equals* method returns *true* if the data in the parameter object matches the data in the object for which the method was called.

The program in Example 5.11 creates the *SimpleDate* object references and objects shown in Figure 5.18. The program compares the object references using the

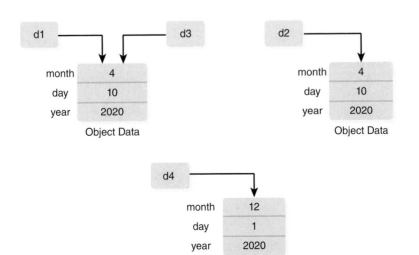

Figure 5.18

SimpleDate Objects and References

equality operator and then compares the object data using the *equals* method. The output from this program is shown in Figure 5.19.

```
 1 /*  Comparing object references and data
 2      Anderson, Franceschi
 3 */
 4
 5 public class ComparingObjects
 6 {
 7   public static void main( String [ ] args )
 8   {
 9     // instantiate two SimpleDate objects with identical data
10     SimpleDate d1 = new SimpleDate( 4, 10, 2020 );
11     SimpleDate d2 = new SimpleDate( 4, 10, 2020 );
12
13     // assign object reference d1 to d3
14     SimpleDate d3 = d1;  // d3 now points to d1
15
16     // instantiate another object with different data
17     SimpleDate d4 = new SimpleDate( 12, 1, 2020 );
18
19     // compare references using the equality operator
20     if ( d1 == d2 )
21        System.out.println( "d1 and d2 are equal\n" );
22     else
23        System.out.println( "d1 and d2 are not equal\n" );
24
25     if ( d1 == d3 )
26        System.out.println( "d1 and d3 are equal\n" );
27     else
28        System.out.println( "d1 and d3 are not equal\n" );
29
30     // compare object data using the equals method
31     if ( d1.equals( d2 ) )
32        System.out.println( "d1 data and d2 data are equal\n" );
33     else
34        System.out.println( "d1 data and d2 data are not equal\n" );
35
36     if ( ! d1.equals( d4 ) )
37        System.out.println( "d1 data and d4 data are not equal" );
38     else
39        System.out.println( "d1 data and d4 data are equal" );
40   }
41 }
```

EXAMPLE 5.11   Comparing Object Data

```
d1 and d2 are not equal
d1 and d3 are equal
d1 data and d2 data are equal
d1 data and d4 data are not equal
```

Figure 5.19

Output from
Example 5.11

Lines 10 and 11 instantiate two *SimpleDate* objects with the same data. Line 14 sets the *d3* object reference to point to the *d1* object. Line 17 instantiates the *d4* object with different data.

In line 20, when we compare *d1* and *d2* using the equality operator, the result is *false*, because the object references *d1* and *d2* point to two different objects. However, when we compare *d1* and *d3* (line 25), the result is *true*, because *d1* and *d3* point to the same object. Thus, object references are equal only when they point to the same object.

COMMON ERROR TRAP
Do not use the equality operators to compare object data; instead, use the *equals* method.

We get different results using the *equals* method. When line 31 compares *d1* and *d2* using the *equals* method, the result is *true*, because *d1* and *d2* have identical data. As we would expect, *d1* and *d4* are not equal (line 36) because the objects have different data. Line 36 demonstrates that we can test for inequality by using the NOT operator (!) to negate the return value from the *equals* method.

5.9.2 *String* Comparison Methods

Because *Strings* are objects, we can also compare *Strings* using the *equals* method. In addition, the *String* class provides two other methods, *equalsIgnoreCase* and *compareTo*, for comparing the values of *Strings*. These methods, along with the *equals* method are summarized in Table 5.11.

The *equalsIgnoreCase* method is similar to the *equals* method, except that it is insensitive to case. Thus, the *equalsIgnoreCase* method returns *true* if the two *String* objects have the same sequence of characters, regardless of capitalization. For example, the *equalsIgnoreCase* method considers *ABC*, *AbC*, and *abc* to be equal.

The *compareTo* method returns an integer value, rather than a *boolean* value. The *compareTo* method's return value represents whether the *String* object is less than, equal to, or greater than the *String* argument passed to the *compareTo* method. The *compareTo* method uses lexicographic order—the Unicode collating sequence—to compare the *Strings*. Using the Unicode collating sequence means that a character with a lower Unicode numeric value is considered less than a character with a higher Unicode numeric value. Thus, an *a* is lower than a *b*; an *A* is lower than a *B*; and *0* is lower than *1*.

REFERENCE POINT
The first 128 Unicode values are given in Appendix C.

TABLE 5.11   Comparison Methods of the *String* Class

String Methods for Comparing *String* Values	
Return value	**Method name and argument list**
boolean	equals(String str)
	compares the value of two *Strings*. Returns *true* if the *Strings* are equal; *false* otherwise.
boolean	equalsIgnoreCase(String str)
	compares the value of two *Strings*, treating upper and lowercase characters as equal. Returns *true* if the *Strings* are equal; *false* otherwise.
int	compareTo(String str)
	compares the value of the two *Strings* in lexicographic order. If the *String* object is less than the *String* argument, *str*, a negative integer is returned. If the *String* object is greater than the *String* argument, a positive number is returned; if the two *Strings* are equal, 0 is returned.

The *compareTo* method scans the two *Strings* from left to right. If it finds different characters in the same position in the two *Strings*, it immediately returns an integer value representing the difference between the Unicode values of those characters. For example, the distance between *a* and *c* is −2; the distance between *K* and *F* is 5.

If the *Strings* differ in length, but the characters they have in common are identical, then the *compareTo* method returns the difference in the length of the *Strings*.

In most cases, however, the exact return value is not important; it is sufficient to know whether the *String* object is less than, greater than, or equal to the *String* argument. In other words, all that we usually need to know is whether the return value is positive, negative, or 0.

Example 5.12 demonstrates how these methods can be used in a Java application to compare *Strings*. The output of the program is shown in Figure 5.20.

```
1 /* Demonstration of the String comparison methods
2    Anderson, Franceschi
3 */
4
5 public class ComparingStrings
6 {
7   public static void main( String [ ] args )
```

```
8   {
9     String title1 = "Green Pastures";
10    String title2 = "Green Pastures II";
11    String title3 = "green pastures";
12
13    System.out.print( "Using equals: " );
14    if ( title1.equals( title3 ) )
15      System.out.println( title1 + " equals " + title3 );
16    else
17      System.out.println( title1 + " is not equal to " + title3 );
18
19    System.out.print( "Using equalsIgnoreCase: " );
20    if ( title1.equalsIgnoreCase( title3 ) )
21      System.out.println( title1 + " equals " + title3 );
22    else
23      System.out.println( title1 + " is not equal to " + title3 );
24
25    System.out.print( "Using compareTo: " );
26    if ( title1.compareTo( title3 ) > 0 )
27      System.out.println( title1 + " is greater than " + title3 );
28    else if ( title1.compareTo ( title3 ) < 0 )
29      System.out.println( title1 + " is less than " + title3 );
30    else
31      System.out.println( title1 + " is equal to " + title3 );
32
33    System.out.print( "Using compareTo: " );
34    if ( title1.compareTo( title2 ) > 0 )
35      System.out.println( title1 + " is greater than " + title2 );
36    else if ( title1.compareTo( title2 ) < 0 )
37      System.out.println( title1 + " is less than " + title2 );
38    else
39      System.out.println( title1 + " is equal to " + title2 );
40  }
41 }
```

EXAMPLE 5.12   Comparing Strings

In Example 5.12, we define three similar *Strings*: *title1 (Green Pastures), title2 (Green Pastures II)*, and *title3 (green pastures)*. When we compare *title1, Green Pastures, to title3, green pastures*, using the *equals* method (line 14), the result is *false*, because

```
Using equals: Green Pastures is not equal to green pastures
Using equalsIgnoreCase: Green Pastures equals green pastures
Using compareTo: Green Pastures is less than green pastures
Using compareTo: Green Pastures is less than Green Pastures II
```

Figure 5.20

Output from
Example 5.12

the *Strings* do not match in case. When we perform the same comparison using the *equalsIgnoreCase* method (line 20), however, the result is *true*, because except for capitalization, these two *Strings* are identical in character sequence and length.

Using the *compareTo* method (line 34), *Green Pastures* evaluates to less than *Green Pastures II*. Although all the characters of the first *String* are found in the second *String* in the same order, the first *String* has fewer characters than the second *String*. The reason that *Green Pastures* evaluates to less than *green pastures* (line 26) is not so obvious—until we look at the Unicode character chart. The capital letters have lower numeric values than the lowercase letters, so a capital *G* is less than a lowercase *g*.

5.10   The Conditional Operator (?:)

The conditional operator (?:), while not a statement in itself, can be used in expressions. It evaluates a condition and contributes one of two values to the expression based on the value of the condition. The conditional operator is especially useful for handling invalid input and for outputting similar messages. The syntax of the conditional operator is shown here:

```
( condition ? expression1 : expression2 )
```

The value of an expression containing a conditional operator is determined by evaluating the condition, which is any expression that evaluates to *true* or *false*. If the condition evaluates to *true, expression1* becomes the value of the expression; if the condition evaluates to *false, expression2* becomes the value of the expression.

When assigning the result of that expression to a variable, the statement:

```
variable = ( condition ? expression1 : expression2 );
```

is equivalent to

```
if ( condition )
      variable = expression1;
else
      variable = expression2;
```

Some programmers like to use the conditional operator because it enables them to write compact code; other programmers feel that an *if/else* sequence is more readable.

Suppose we want to determine whether a number is even or odd. We know that if we divide a number by 2 and the remainder is 0, the number is even. If the remainder is 1, the number is odd. We could do this using the following *if/else* statement:

```
if ( number % 2 == 0 )
   System.out.println( number + " is even." );
else
   System.out.println( number + " is odd." );
```

Notice that the only difference in the output is the last word.

Example 5.13 shows how we can perform the same processing using the conditional operator.

```
 1 /* Using the conditional operator
 2    Anderson, Franceschi
 3 */
 4
 5 import java.util.Scanner;
 6
 7 public class OddOrEven
 8 {
 9  public static void main( String [ ] args )
10  {
11    Scanner scan = new Scanner( System.in );
12
13    System.out.print( "Enter an integer > " );
14    int number = scan.nextInt( );
15
16    String outcome = ( number % 2 == 0 ? "even." : "odd." );
17
18    System.out.println( number + " is " + outcome );
19
20  }
21 }
```

EXAMPLE 5.13   Using the Conditional Operator

In lines 13 and 14, we ask the user to input an integer. In line 16, we use the conditional operator to determine whether the integer is even or odd, assigning the result to the *String outcome*. Then in line 18, we print the number, the word " is " and then the value of *outcome*. Figure 5.21 shows the output from Example 5.13 when the user enters an even number, and Figure 5.22 shows the output when the user enters an odd number.

```
Enter an integer > 12
12 is even.
```

Figure 5.21
Output of Example 5.13 When the Input Is Even

```
Enter an integer > 13
13 is odd.
```

Figure 5.22
Output of Example 5.13 When the Input Is Odd

TABLE 5.12   Operator Precedence

Operation Hierarchy	Order of Same- Statement Evaluation	Operation
()	left to right	parentheses for explicit grouping
++, --	right to left	shortcut postincrement
++, --, !	right to left	shortcut preincrement, logical unary NOT
*, /, %	left to right	multiplication, division, modulus
+, -	left to right	addition or *String* concatenation, subtraction
<, <=, >, >=	left to right	relational operators: less than, less than or equal to, greater than, greater than or equal to
==, !=	left to right	equality operators: equal to and not equal to
&&	left to right	logical AND
||	left to right	logical OR
?:	left to right	conditional operator
=, +=, -=, *=, /=, %=	right to left	assignment operator and shortcut assignment operators

Table 5.12, Operator Precedence, shows that the conditional operator is low in precedence, being just above the assignment operators.

5.11   The *switch* Statement

The *switch* statement can be used instead of an *if/else if* statement for selection when the condition consists of comparing the value of an expression to constant integers (*byte*, *short*, or *int*), characters (*char*), or *Strings*. The syntax of the *switch* statement is the following:

```
switch ( expression )
{
    case constant1:
          statement1;

          . . .

          break; // optional
    case constant2:
          statement1;

          . . .
```

```
      break; // optional
  . . .
  default:  // optional
      statement1;

      . . .

}
```

The expression is first evaluated, then its value is compared to the *case* constants in order. When a match is found, the statements under that *case* constant are executed in sequence. The execution of statements continues until either a *break* statement is encountered or the end of the *switch* block is reached. If other *case* statements are encountered before a *break* statement, then their statements are also executed. This allows us to execute the same code for multiple values of the expression.

As we can see in the preceding syntax, the *break* statements are optional. Their job is to terminate execution of the *switch* statement. The *default* label and its statements, which are also optional, are executed when the value of the expression does not match any of the *case* constants. The statements under a *case* constant are also optional, so multiple *case* constants can be written in sequence if identical operations will be performed for those values. We'll use this feature in our examples of the *switch* statement.

Let's look at how a *switch* statement can be used to implement a simple calculator. We first prompt the user for two numbers on which they want to perform a calculation, and then the operation they want to perform. We let them enter either the words ADD, SUBTRACT, MULTIPLY, or DIVIDE, or the symbol for the operation (+, -, *, or /). We can use a *switch* statement to determine the selected operation and *case* constants for each possible operation. Example 5.14 shows the code for our simple calculator.

```
 1 /* A simple calculator
 2    Anderson, Franceschi
 3 */
 4
 5 import java.text.DecimalFormat;
 6 import java.util.Scanner;
 7
 8 public class Calculator
 9 {
10   public static void main( String [ ] args )
11   {
12     double fp1, fp2;
13     String operation;
```

```
14
15      Scanner scan = new Scanner( System.in );
16
17      // set up the output format of the result
18      DecimalFormat twoDecimals = new DecimalFormat( "#,###,###.##" );
19
20      // print a welcome message
21      System.out.println( "Welcome to the Calculator" );
22
23      // read the two operands
24      System.out.print( "Enter the first operand: " );
25      fp1 = scan.nextDouble( );
26      System.out.print( "Enter the second operand: " );
27      fp2 = scan.nextDouble( );
28
29      //  print a menu, then prompt for the operation
30      System.out.println( "\nOperations are: "
31                          + "\n\t ADD or + for addition"
32                          + "\n\t SUBTRACT or - for subtraction"
33                          + "\n\t MULTIPLY or * for multiplication"
34                          + "\n\t DIVIDE or / for division" );
35      System.out.print( "Enter your selection: " );
36      operation = scan.next( );
37      operation = operation.toUpperCase( );
38
39      //perform the operation and print the result
40      switch ( operation )
41      {
42       case "ADD":
43       case "+":
44          System.out.println( "The sum is "
45                  + twoDecimals.format( fp1 + fp2 ) );
46          break;
47       case "SUBTRACT":
48       case "-":
49         System.out.println( "The difference is "
50                  + twoDecimals.format( fp1 - fp2 ) );
51          break;
52       case "MULTIPLY":
53       case "*":
54         System.out.println( "The product is "
55                  + twoDecimals.format( fp1 * fp2 ) );
56          break;
57       case "DIVIDE":
58       case "/":
59          if ( fp2 == 0.0 )
```

```
60              System.out.println( "Dividing by 0 is not allowed" );
61          else
62              System.out.println( "The quotient is "
63                        + twoDecimals.format( fp1 / fp2 ) );
64          break;
65      default:
66          System.out.println( operation + " is not valid." );
67      }
68  }
69 }
```

EXAMPLE 5.14   A Simple Calculator

We declared the two numbers on which to perform the operation as *doubles* (line 12) and prompt the user using the *nextDouble* method of the *Scanner* class (lines 23–27). Because a *double* variable can hold any numeric value equal to or lower in precision than a *double*, using *doubles* for our calculator allows the user to enter either *ints* or *doubles*. Conversely, if we used *int* variables and the *nextInt* method of the *Scanner* class, the user would be restricted to entering integers only.

When the calculator begins, we set up a *DecimalFormat* object for outputting the result to a maximum of two decimal places (line 18).

We print a menu to let the user know what options are available, using the newline (\n) and tab (\t) escape characters to format the menu message (lines 29–35). To read the user's selection (lines 36–37), we use the *next* method of the *Scanner* class, which returns a *String*. We convert the input to uppercase using the *toUpperCase* method of the *String* class. This allows the user to enter the desired operation in any combination of uppercase or lowercase letters.

We are now ready to determine which operation the user has chosen, by using a *switch* statement with the user's input as the *switch expression*. We determine which operation the user has selected by providing two *case* statements for each possible operation. We can use uppercase words as the *case* constants, because we have converted the input to uppercase. We handle the situation where the user has entered a mathematical symbol instead of a word by adding a second *case* constant to each operation. For example, if the user enters ADD (in any combination of uppercase and lowercase letters) or a plus sign (+), the input will match one of our *case* constants on lines 42 and 43. We will then execute the addition and output the result on lines 44 and 45. When we encounter the *break* statement on line 46, the execution of the *switch* statement ends. The *break* statement is important. If we had omitted the *break* statement, execution would have continued onto lines 49 and 50, and we would have performed the subtraction as well.

Figure 5.23

The Calculator
Performing
Multiplication

```
Welcome to the Calculator
Enter the first operand: 23.4
Enter the second operand: 3

Operations are:
   ADD or + for addition
   SUBTRACT or - for subtraction
   MULTIPLY or * for multiplication
   DIVIDE or / for division
Enter your selection: multiply
The product is 70.2
```

Figure 5.24

The Calculator
with an Invalid
Entry for the
Operation

```
Welcome to the Calculator
Enter the first operand: 52
Enter the second operand: 34.5

Operations are:
   ADD or + for addition
   SUBTRACT or - for subtraction
   MULTIPLY or * for multiplication
   DIVIDE or / for division
Enter your selection: f
f is not valid
```

Then the *break* statement on line 51 would have ended the execution of the *switch* statement.

What if the user doesn't enter any of the valid words or mathematical symbols? This is where the *default* case comes in handy, allowing us to write an error message to the user (lines 65–66).

Figure 5.23 shows the output from Example 5.14 when the user selects multiplication, and Figure 5.24 shows the output when the user enters an unsupported operation.

One more note on the calculator: We need to check whether the divisor is 0 before performing division (line 59). Although we discussed earlier in the chapter that we should compare floating-point numbers by comparing the difference between the two numbers with a threshold value, in this case, we care only if the second operand is exactly 0, so we can safely compare its value to 0.0. If the second operand is 0.0, we print an error message; otherwise, we perform the division.

Let's look at an example that performs a *switch* on an integer. We'll create a graphical application that simulates rolling a die and drawing the die corresponding to the roll. Example 5.15 shows the code to do this.

```java
 1 /* Rolling and drawing a die
 2    Anderson, Franceschi
 3 */
 4
 5 import javafx.application.Application;
 6 import javafx.scene.canvas.GraphicsContext;
 7 import javafx.scene.paint.Color;
 8 import javafx.scene.text.Font;
 9 import javafx.stage.Stage;
10
11 import java.util.Random;
12
13 public class RollDie extends Application
14 {
15     @Override
16     public void start( Stage stage )
17     {
18         // set up window title and size
19         GraphicsContext gc = JIGraphicsUtility.setUpGraphics(
20                 stage, "Roll a Die", 700, 400 );
21
22         final int START_X = 300, START_Y = 150, ROLL_Y = 125;
23         final int DIE_SIZE = 120, DOT_SIZE = 20;
24         final int DOT_1 = DOT_SIZE / 2,
25                   DOT_2 = DIE_SIZE / 2 - DOT_SIZE / 2,
26                   DOT_3 = DIE_SIZE - DOT_SIZE / 2 - DOT_SIZE;
27         Font largeFont = new Font( 20 );
28         gc.setFont( largeFont );
29
30         // roll the die
31         Random rand = new Random( );
32         int roll = rand.nextInt( 6 ) + 1;
33
34         // draw a pink die
35         gc.setFill( Color.PINK );
36         gc.fillRect( START_X, START_Y, DIE_SIZE, DIE_SIZE );
37
38         // set dot color
39         gc.setFill( Color.BLACK );
40
41         switch ( roll )
42         {
```

```
43              case 5: // draw upper right and lower left dots
44                gc.fillOval( START_X + DOT_3, START_Y + DOT_1,
45                            DOT_SIZE, DOT_SIZE );
46                gc.fillOval( START_X + DOT_1, START_Y + DOT_3,
47                            DOT_SIZE, DOT_SIZE );
48              case 3: // draw upper left and lower right dots
49                gc.fillOval( START_X + DOT_1, START_Y + DOT_1,
50                            DOT_SIZE, DOT_SIZE );
51                gc.fillOval( START_X + DOT_3, START_Y + DOT_3,
52                            DOT_SIZE, DOT_SIZE );
53              case 1: // draw center dot
54                gc.fillOval( START_X + DOT_2, START_Y + DOT_2,
55                            DOT_SIZE, DOT_SIZE );
56              break; // stop executing the switch
57
58              case 6: // draw middle left and right dots
59                gc.fillOval( START_X + DOT_1, START_Y + DOT_2,
60                            DOT_SIZE, DOT_SIZE );
61                gc.fillOval( START_X + DOT_3, START_Y + DOT_2,
62                            DOT_SIZE, DOT_SIZE );
63              case 4: // draw upper right and lower left dots
64                gc.fillOval( START_X + DOT_3, START_Y + DOT_1,
65                            DOT_SIZE, DOT_SIZE );
66                gc.fillOval( START_X + DOT_1, START_Y + DOT_3,
67                            DOT_SIZE, DOT_SIZE );
68              case 2: // draw upper left and lower right dots
69                gc.fillOval( START_X + DOT_1, START_Y + DOT_1,
70                            DOT_SIZE, DOT_SIZE );
71                gc.fillOval( START_X + DOT_3, START_Y + DOT_3,
72                            DOT_SIZE, DOT_SIZE );
73              break; // stop executing the switch
74
75          } // end switch
76
77          // display the roll number
78          gc.fillText( "The roll is " + roll, START_X, ROLL_Y );
79
80      }
81
82      public static void main( String [ ] args )
83      {
84          launch( args );
85      }
86 }
```

EXAMPLE 5.15   Rolling and Drawing a Die

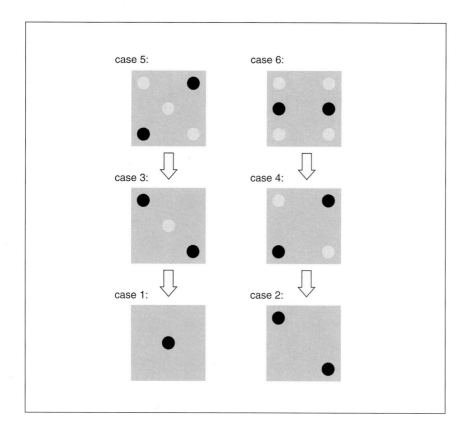

Figure 5.25

Each *case* Statement Draws Only the Dots That Are Common in the Succeeding *cases*.

In Example 5.15, we generate a random number between 1 and 6 to simulate the roll of a die (lines 30–32). We define constant values that we will use to draw the die, position the dots, and display the roll (lines 22–26). Then, we set the font to 20 points for displaying the die roll (lines 27–28). We draw the die itself as a pink square (lines 34–36). We set the color to black for drawing the dots (line 39) and we use a *switch* statement on *roll* (lines 41–75) to determine which dots we should draw. Finally, we display the roll (lines 77–78) to verify that we are drawing the correct roll.

If we look at a die, we see that many of the rolls cause one or more of the same dots to be drawn. One advantage to the *switch* statement is that once a match is found between the *switch* variable and a *case* constant, all following statements are executed until a *break* is encountered.

Using this feature, we can combine the processing for rolls 5, 3, and 1. As shown in Figure 5.25, for *case* 5, we simply draw the upper right and lower left dots

© Hemera Technologies/
Photos.com/Thinkstock

Figure 5.26

Sample Output
from Example 5.15

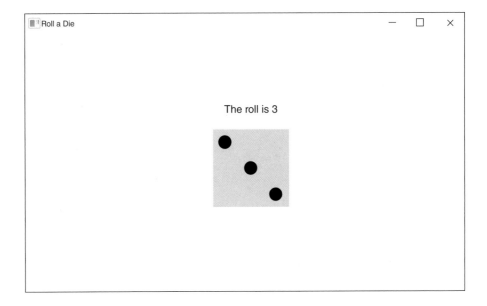

(lines 30–34), then fall through to *case* 3, where we draw the upper left and lower right dots (lines 35–39), then fall through to *case* 1, where we draw the center dot (lines 40–42). At this point, we code the *break* (line 43) to stop processing of the *switch* statement. Similarly, we combine the processing for rolls 6, 4, and 2.

Note that we don't need a *default* case because the random generator will only generate values from 1 to 6, and we have provided *case* statements to handle each of those values. The output from one roll of the die is shown in Figure 5.26.

CODE IN ACTION

To see a step-by-step illustration of using a *switch* statement, look for the movie within the online resources. Click on this chapter's link to start the movie.

Skill Practice
with these end-of-chapter questions

5.12   Programming Activity 2: Using the *switch* Statement

In this activity, you will write a *switch* statement that selects a path depending on an input value. The framework will animate your code so that you can watch the path that the code takes in the *switch* block.

Copy to a folder on your computer all the files in this chapter's Programming Activity 2 folder in the supplied code accompanying this book.

Search for five stars (*****) in the *SelectionPractice2Controller.java* source code to find where to add your code. The five stars are above the method *workWithSwitch* (the method header has already been coded for you).

You should be positioned at the code shown in Example 5.16.

```java
// ***** 1 student writes this method
public void workWithSwitch( int value )
{
 //
 // Student code starts here
 //


 //
 // Student code ends here
```

```
//


}
// end of workWithSwitch
```

EXAMPLE 5.16   The Student Code Portion of Programming Activity 2

Where indicated in the code, write a *switch* statement, as follows:

- In the method header of the method *workWithSwitch*, you see (int value). The *int* variable *value* represents the input from the user; the text box that allows the user to input the score has already been coded for you. This variable, *value*, is the value entered by the user and should be used as the condition for the *switch* statement; it is available to your code as a parameter of the *workWithSwitch* method. Do not declare the variable *value* inside the method; just use it.

- Write *case* statements for the following integer constants: *0, 1, 2, 3, 4*, as well as a *default* statement.

- Within each *case* statement, you should do two things:

  - Print a message to the screen indicating which value was input. The message for the *default* case should indicate that the input value is not one of the valid values.
  - Call the *animate* method. The API for the *animate* method is

    ```
    void animate( int caseConstant, int value )
    ```

    The first argument is the *case* constant; the second argument is the input variable, *value*. For instance, for the statement case 2:, your *animate* method call is

    ```
    animate( 2, value );
    ```

    For the default case, the method call should be

    ```
    animate( -1, value );
    ```

To test your code, compile the *SelectionPractice2Controller.java* file and run the *SelectionPractice2Application* application. When the program begins, you will see an empty graphics window with a text box as shown in Figure 5.27.

To execute your *switch* statement, enter an integer in the text box and press the "Test" button. Depending on how you coded the *case* statements, the *break* statements, and the input value, the window will display (in green) the path of execution of your code. For example, Figure 5.28 demonstrates the code path when the input value is 3. If the path is not what you expected, you will need to correct your code.

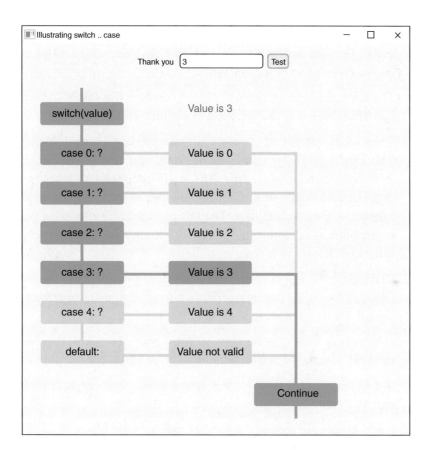

Figure 5.27

The Input Box of the Application

Figure 5.28

A Sample Run of the Application

To test your code, enter each integer from 0 to 4, plus some other integer value into the text box, pressing the "Test" button each time. To exit the application, close the window.

DISCUSSION QUESTIONS

1. **Explain the purpose of the *default* case in a *switch* statement.**

2. **Explain what happens when you omit a *break* statement in a *case* statement.**

CHAPTER REVIEW

5.13   Chapter Summary

- Java provides equality, relational, and logical operators to evaluate a condition, and selection statements to choose which instructions to execute based on whether a condition evaluates to *true* or *false*.

- The equality operators (`==`, `!=`) are used to test whether two operands are equal. The operands are expressions that evaluate to a primitive numeric or *boolean* type or an object reference.

- The relational operators (`<`, `<=`, `>`, `>=`) compare the values of two operands that are expressions that evaluate to a primitive numeric type.

- The logical operators (`!`, `&&`, and `||`) take *boolean* expressions as operands. The logical NOT (`!`) takes one operand, and inverts its value, changing *true* to *false* and *false* to *true*. The AND operator (`&&`) takes two *boolean* expressions as operands; if both operands are *true*, then the result is *true*; otherwise, the result is *false*. The OR operator (`||`) also takes two *boolean* expressions as operands. If both operands are *false*, then the result is *false*; otherwise, the result is *true*.

- The logical NOT operator (`!`) has the highest precedence of these operators, followed by the relational operators, then the equality operators, then the logical AND (`&&`), then the logical OR(`||`).

- DeMorgan's Laws can be used to form equivalent logical expressions to improve readability of the code.

- The *if* statement is used to perform certain operations for one set of data and to do nothing for all other data.

- Curly braces are required when the true or false block of an *if* statement consists of more than one statement.

- The *if/else* statement is used to perform certain operations for one set of data and other operations for all other data.

- The *if/else if* statement is appropriate when the data falls into more than two mutually exclusive categories and the appropriate instructions to execute are different for each category.

- *if/else* statements can be coded sequentially and can be nested inside other *if/else* statements.

- When *if* statements are nested, the compiler matches any *else* clause with the most previous *if* condition that doesn't already have an *else* clause.

- Because rounding errors can be introduced in floating-point calculations, do not use the equality operators to compare two floating-point numbers. Instead, compare the absolute value of the difference between the numbers to some threshold value.

- When we need exact precision in calculations with decimal numbers, you can use the *BigDecimal* class in the Java Class Library.

- Using the equality operator on object references compares the values of the references, not the object data. Two object references will be equal only if they point to the same object.

- Use the *equals* method to determine whether the data in two objects are equal.

- In addition to the *equals* method, two *Strings* can also be compared using the *equalsIgnoreCase* method and the *compareTo* method of the *String* class.

- The conditional operator (?:) is used in expressions where one of two values should be used depending on the evaluation of a condition. The conditional operator is useful for validating input and for outputting similar messages.

- The *switch* statement evaluates an integer or character expression or a *String*, then compares the expression's value to *case* constants. When a match is found, it executes the statements until either a *break* statement or the end of the *switch* block is encountered.

5.14 Exercises, Problems, and Projects

5.14.1 Multiple Choice Exercises

1. Given the following code declaring and initializing two *int* variables *a* and *b* with respective values 3 and 5, indicate whether the value of each expression is *true* or *false*.

```
int a = 3;
int b = 5;
```

Expression	true	false
❑ a < b	_____	_____
❑ a != b	_____	_____

❏ `a == 4`   _____   _____

❏ `( b - a ) <= 1`   _____   _____

❏ `Math.abs( a - b ) >= 2`   _____   _____

❏ `( b % 2 == 1 )`   _____   _____

❏ `b <= 5`   _____   _____

2. Given the following code declaring and initializing three *boolean* variables *a*, *b*, and *c*, with respective values *true*, *true*, and *false*, indicate whether the value of each expression is *true* or *false*.

```
boolean a = true;
boolean b = true;
boolean c = false;
```

Expression	true	false
❏ `!a`	_____	_____
❏ `a && b`	_____	_____
❏ `a && c`	_____	_____
❏ `a || c`	_____	_____
❏ `!( a || b )`	_____	_____
❏ `!a || b`	_____	_____
❏ `!( !( a && c ) )`	_____	_____
❏ `a && !( b || c )`	_____	_____

3. Given two *boolean* variables *a* and *b*, are the following expressions equivalent?

❏ `!( !a )`

❏ `a`

4. Given two *boolean* variables *a* and *b*, are the following expressions equivalent?

❏ `!( a && b )`

❏ `!a || !b`

5. Given two *boolean* variables *a* and *b*, are the following expressions equivalent?

❏ `!( !a && !b )`

❏ `a && b`

6. Given two *boolean* variables *a* and *b*, are the following expressions equivalent?

   ❏ `!( !a && !b )`

   ❏ `a || b`

7. Given the following code declaring and initializing two *int* variables *a* and *b* with respective values 3 and 5, indicate whether the operand (`b < 10`) will be evaluated.

```
int a = 3;
int b = 5;
```

Expression	yes	no
❏ `a < b || b < 10`	____	____
❏ `a != b && b < 10`	____	____
❏ `a == 4 || b < 10`	____	____
❏ `a > b && b < 10`	____	____

8. Mark all the valid Java selection keywords.

   ❏ `if`

   ❏ `else if`

   ❏ `else`

   ❏ `elsif`

9. How do we compare the value of two *String* objects in Java? (Mark all that apply.)

   ❏ using the = operator

   ❏ using the == operator

   ❏ using the *equals* method

5.14.2 Reading and Understanding Code

10. What is the output of this code sequence?

```
boolean a = true;
System.out.println( a );
```

11. What is the output of this code sequence?

```
boolean a = ( true && false );
System.out.println( a );
```

12. What is the output of this code sequence?

```
if ( ( true || false ) && ( false || true ) )
    System.out.println( "Inside true block" );
System.out.println( "End of sequence" );
```

13. What is the output of this code sequence?

```
if ( 27 % 3 == 0 )
    System.out.println( "27 is divisible by 3" );
else
    System.out.println( "27 is not divisible by 3" );
System.out.println( "End of sequence" );
```

14. What is the output of this code sequence?

```
String s = "Hello";
if ( s.equals( "hello" ) )
    System.out.println( "String is hello" );
else
    System.out.println( "String is not hello" );
System.out.println( "End of sequence" );
```

15. What is the output of this code sequence?

```
int grade = 77;
if ( grade >= 90 )
    System.out.println( "A" );
else if ( grade >= 80 )
    System.out.println( "B" );
else if ( grade >= 70 )
    System.out.println( "C" );
else
    System.out.println( "D or lower" );
System.out.println( "Done" );
```

16. What is the output of this code sequence?

```
int a = 65;
boolean b = false;

if ( a >= 70 )
{
    System.out.println( "Hello 1" );
    if ( b == true )
        System.out.println( "Hello 2" );
}
else
{
    System.out.println( "Hello 3" );
    if ( b == false )
```

```
            System.out.println( "Hello 4" );
    }
    System.out.println( "Done" );
```

17. What is the output of this code sequence?

```
int season = 3;
switch ( season )
{
    case 1:
        System.out.println( "Season is Winter" );
        break;
    case 2:
        System.out.println( "Season is Spring" );
        break;
    case 3:
        System.out.println( "Season is Summer" );
        break;
    case 4:
        System.out.println( "Season is Fall" );
        break;
    default:
        System.out.println( "Invalid season" );
}
```

18. What is the output of this code sequence?

```
char c = 'e';
switch ( c )
{
    case 'H':
        System.out.println( "letter 1" );
        break;
    case 'e':
        System.out.println( "letter 2" );
        break;
    case 'l':
        System.out.println( "letters 3 and 4" );
        break;
    case 'o':
        System.out.println( "letter 5" );
        break;
    default:
        System.out.println( "letter is not in Hello" );
}
```

19. What is the output of this code sequence?

```
int n = 3;
switch ( n )
```

```
        {
          case 1:
            System.out.println( "Number 1" );
          case 2:
            System.out.println( "Number 2" );
          case 3:
            System.out.println( "Number 3" );
          case 4:
            System.out.println( "Number 4" );
          default:
            System.out.println( "Other number" );
        }
```

5.14.3   Fill In the Code

For Exercises 20 through 30, assume that a *boolean* variable named *a* has been declared and assigned the value *true* or *false*. You should also assume that two *int* variables named *b* and *c* have been declared and assigned some integer values.

20. If *a* is *true*, increment *b* by 1.

```
// your code goes here
```

21. If *a* is *true*, increment *b* by 2; if *a* is *false*, decrement *b* by 1.

```
// your code goes here
```

22. If *a* is *true*, change *a* to *false*; if *a* is *false*, change *a* to *true*.

```
// your code goes here
```

23. If *b* is equal to *c*, then assign *true* to *a*.

```
// your code goes here
```

24. If *b* is less than *c*, increment *b* by 1; otherwise, leave *b* unchanged.

```
// your code goes here
```

25. If *b* is a multiple of *c*, set *a* to *true*; otherwise, set *a* to *false*.

```
// your code goes here
```

26. If *c* is not equal to 0, assign to *b* the value of *b* divided by *c*.

```
// your code goes here
```

27. If the product *b* times *c* is greater than or equal to 100, then invert *a* (if *a* is *true*, *a* becomes *false*; if *a* is *false*, *a* becomes *true*); otherwise, assign *true* to *a*.

```
// your code goes here
```

28. If *a* is *true* and *b* is greater than 10, increment *c* by 1.

```
// your code goes here
```

29. If both *b* and *c* are less than 10, then assign *true* to *a*; otherwise, assign *false* to *a*.

```
// your code goes here
```

30. If *b* or *c* is greater than 5, then assign *true* to *a*; otherwise, assign *false* to *a*.

```
// your code goes here
```

5.14.4 Identifying Errors in Code

For Exercises 31 through 38, assume that two *boolean* variables named *b1* and *b2* have been declared and assigned the value *true* or *false* earlier in the program. You should also assume that two *int* variables named *a1* and *a2* have been declared and assigned some integer values earlier in the program.

31. Where is the error in this code sequence?

```
b1 = a1 && a2;
```

32. Where is the error in this expression?

```
( b2 == b1 ) AND ( a1 <= a2 )
```

33. Where is the logical error in this code sequence?

```
if ( a1 == 4 );
    System.out.println( "a1 equals 4" );
```

34. Where is the error in this code sequence?

```
boolean b1 = true;
if b1

    System.out.println( "b1 is true" );
```

35. Where is the error in this code sequence?

```
if { b2 == true }
    System.out.println( "b2 is true" );
```

36. Where is the error in this code sequence?

```
if ( b1 == true )
    System.out.println( "b1 is true" );
else
    System.out.println( "b1 is false" );
else if ( a1 < 100 )
    System.out.println( "a1 is <= 100" );
```

37. Is there an error in this code sequence? Explain.

```java
if ( b2 == b1 )
      System.out.println( "b2 and b1 have the same value" );
else if ( a1 == a2 )
      System.out.println( "a1 and a2 have the same value" );
else
      System.out.println( "All variables are different" );
```

38. Is there an error in this code sequence? Explain.

```java
if ( b2 )
      System.out.println( "b2 is true" );
else if ( a1 <= 10 || a2 > 50 )
{
      System.out.print( "a1 <= 10 or " );
      System.out.println( "a2 > 50" );
}
else
      System.out.println( "none of the above" );
```

5.14.5   Debugging Area—Using Messages from the Java Compiler and Java JVM

39. You coded the following in class *Test.java:*

```java
boolean b = true;
if ( b )
      System.out.println( "Inside true block" );
      System.out.println( "b was true" );
else          // line 12
      System.out.println( "Inside false block" );
```

At compile time, you get the following error:

```
Test.java:12: error: 'else' without 'if'
else      // line 12
^
1 error
```

Explain what the problem is and how to fix it.

40. You coded the following in the class *Test.java:*

```java
int a = 32;
if ( a = 31 )      // line 9
      System.out.println( "The value of a is 31" );
else
      System.out.println( "The value of a is not 31" );
```

At compile time, you get the following error:

```
Test.java:9: error: incompatible types
if ( a = 31 )     // line 9
        ^
1 error
```

Explain what the problem is and how to fix it.

41. You coded the following in the class *Test.java*:

```
boolean b = true;
if ( b )
{
        System.out.println( "Inside true block" );
        System.out.println( "b was true" );
else          // line 13
        System.out.println( "Inside false block" );
}
System.out.println( "Done" );
```

At compile time, you get the following error:

```
Test.java:13: error: 'else' without 'if'.
else          // line 13
^
1 error
```

Explain what the problem is and how to fix it.

5.14.6   Write a Short Program

42. Write a program that takes two *ints* as input from the keyboard, representing the number of hits and the number of at-bats for a batter. Then calculate the batter's hitting percentage and check if the hitting percentage is above .300. If it is, output that the player is eligible for the All Stars Game; otherwise, output that the player is not eligible.

43. Write a program that reads a *char* as an input from the keyboard and outputs whether it is a valid character to start an identifier. (Hint: look for a method in the *Character* class.)

44. Write a program that calculates the area of the following figures:

   ❑ a square of side 0.666666667

   ❑ a rectangle of sides 1/9 and 4

   Test the two calculated areas for equality; discuss your result.

45. Write a program that reads a sentence from the keyboard. Depending on the last character of the sentence, print a message identifying the sentence as declarative (ends with a period), interrogative (ends with a question mark), exclamatory (ends with an exclamation point), or other.

46. An email address contains the @ character. Write a program that takes a word from the keyboard and outputs whether it is an email address based on the presence of the @ character. Do not worry about what else is in the word.

47. Write a program that takes two words as input from the keyboard, representing a password and the same password again. (Often, websites ask users to type their password twice when they register to make sure there was no typo the first time around.) Your program should do the following:

   ❑ if both passwords match, then output "You are now registered as a new user"

   ❑ otherwise, output "Sorry, there is a typo in your password"

48. Write a program that takes a word as input from the keyboard, representing a user ID. (Often, websites place constraints on user IDs.) Your program should do the following:

   ❑ if the user ID contains between 6 and 10 characters inclusive, then output "Welcome, barbara" (assuming *barbara* is the user ID entered)

   ❑ otherwise, output "Sorry, user ID invalid"

5.14.7   Programming Projects

49. Write a program that reads a web address (for instance, *www.yahoo.com*) from the keyboard and outputs whether this web address is for a government, a university, a business, an organization, or another entity.

   ❑ If the web address ends with *gov*, it is a government web address.

   ❑ If the web address ends with *edu*, it is a university web address.

   ❑ If the web address ends with *com*, it is a business web address.

   ❑ If the web address ends with *org*, it is an organization web address.

   ❑ Otherwise, it is a web address for another entity.

50. Write a program that reads a temperature as a whole number from the keyboard and outputs a "probable" season (winter, spring, summer, or fall) depending on the temperature.

    ❑ If the temperature is greater than or equal to 90, it is probably summer.

    ❑ If the temperature is greater than or equal to 70 and less than 90, it is probably spring.

    ❑ If the temperature is greater than or equal to 50 and less than 70, it is probably fall.

    ❑ If the temperature is less than 50, it is probably winter.

    ❑ If the temperature is greater than 110 or less than −5, then you should output that the temperature entered is outside the valid range.

51. Write a program that takes a *String* as input from the keyboard, representing a year. Your program should do the following:

    ❑ If the year entered has two characters, convert it to an *int*, add 2000 to it, and output it.

    ❑ If the year entered has four characters, just convert it to an *int* and output it.

    ❑ If the year entered has neither two nor four characters, output that the year is not valid.

52. Write a program that takes two words as input from the keyboard, representing a user ID and a password. Your program should do the following:

    ❑ If the user ID and the password match "admin" and "open," respectively, then output "Welcome."

    ❑ If the user ID matches "admin" and the password does not match "open," output "Wrong password."

    ❑ If the password matches "open" and the user ID does not match "admin," output "Wrong user ID."

    ❑ Otherwise, output "Sorry, wrong ID and password."

5.14.8 Technical Writing

53. When comparing two *doubles* or *floats* for equality, programmers calculate the difference between the two numbers and check if that difference is sufficiently small. Explain why and give a real-life example.

54. Look at the following code segment:

```
int b = 44;
if ( b = 23 )
      System.out.println( "Inside true block" );
```

In Java, this code will generate the following compiler error:

```
Test.java:9: error: incompatible types
if ( b = 23 )
       ^
required: boolean
found: int
1 error
```

In the C++ programming language, the equivalent code will compile and run and will give you the following output:

```
Inside true block
```

Discuss whether Java handles this situation better than C++ and why.

5.14.9 Group Project (for a group of 1, 2, or 3 students)

55. We want to build a simple "English language" calculator that does the following:

❑ takes three inputs from the keyboard, two of them single digits (0 to 9)

❑ takes a *char* from the keyboard, representing one of five operations from the keyboard: + (addition), – (subtraction), * (multiplication), / (division), and ^ (exponentiation)

❑ outputs the description of the operation in plain English, as well as the numeric result

For instance, if the two numbers are 5 and 3, and the operation is *, then the output should be

```
five multiplied by three is 15
```

Note that the result is given as a number, not a word.

If the two numbers are 2 and 9, and the operation is –, then the output should be

```
two minus nine is -7
```

If the two numbers are 5 and 2, and the operation is ^, then the output should be

```
five to the power two is 25
```

Hint: to perform the exponentiation, use the *pow* method of the *Math* class.

If the two numbers are 5 and 0, and the operation is /, then the output should be

`Division by zero is not allowed`

Here the operation will not be performed.

If the two numbers are 25 and 3, and the operation is +, then the output should be

`Invalid number`

because 25 has two digits.

As for the operators, they should be translated into English as follows:

+   plus

−   minus

*   multiplied by

/   divided by

^   to the power

You should use the *switch … case* selection statement to translate the input values into words.

You need to consider these special situations:

- ❏ For division, there is a special constraint: you cannot divide by 0, and you should therefore test whether the second number is 0. If it is 0, then you should output a message saying that you are not allowed to divide by 0.

- ❏ The "operator" is not one of the preceding five operators; in that case, output a message saying that the operator is not a valid one.

- ❏ One or two of the numbers is not a valid digit; again, you should output a message to that effect.

- ❏ Hint: You can deal with these special situations in the *default* statement of the *switch* block and possibly use some *boolean* variables to keep track of this information, as you may need it later in your program.

CHAPTER 6
Flow of Control, Part 2: Looping

CHAPTER CONTENTS

Introduction

Have you ever watched the cashier at the grocery store? Let's call the cashier Jane. Jane's job is to determine the total cost of a grocery purchase. To begin, Jane starts with a total cost of $0.00. She then reaches for the first item and scans it to record its price, which is added to the total. Then she reaches for the second item, scans that item to record its price, which is added to the total, and so on. Jane continues scanning each item, one at a time, until there are no more items to scan. Usually, the end of an order is signaled by a divider bar lying across the conveyor belt. When Jane sees the divider bar, she knows she is finished. At that point, she tells us the total cost of the order, collects the money, and gives us a receipt.

So we see that Jane's job consists of performing some preliminary work, processing each item one at a time, and reporting the result at the end.

In computing, we often perform tasks that follow this same pattern:

1: initialize values

2: process items one at a time

3: report results

The flow of control that programmers use to complete jobs with this pattern is called **looping**, or **repetition**.

6.1   Event-Controlled Loops Using *while*

If we attempt to write pseudocode for the grocery store cashier, we may start with something like this:

```
set total to $0.00
reach for first item
if item is not the divider bar
    add price to total
reach for next item
if item is not the divider bar
    add price to total
reach for next item
if item is not the divider bar
    add price to total
… (finally)
reach for next item
item is the divider bar,
    tell the customer the total price
```

We can see a pattern here. We start with an order total of $0.00. Then we repeat a set of operations for each item. We reach for the item and check whether it's the divider bar. If the item is not the divider bar, we add the item's price to the order total. We reach for the next item and check whether it's the divider bar, and so on. When we reach for the item and find that it is the divider bar, we know there are no more items to process, so the total we have at that time is the total for the whole order. In other words, we don't know the number of items that will be placed on the conveyor belt. We just process the order, item by item, until we see the divider bar, which we do not process.

In Java, the *while* loop is designed for repeating a set of instructions for each input value when we don't know at the beginning how many input values there will be. We simply process each input value, one at a time, until a signal—an event—tells us that there is no more input. This is called **event-controlled looping**. In the cashier's case, the signal for the end of input was the divider bar. In other tasks, the signal for the end of the input may be a special value that the user enters, called a **sentinel value**, or it may be that we've reached the end of an input file.

6.2 General Form for *while* Loops

The while loop has this syntax:

```
// initialize variables
while ( condition )
{
    // process data; loop body
}
// process the results
```

The condition is a *boolean* expression, that is, any expression that evaluates to *true* or *false*. When the *while* loop statement is encountered, the condition is evaluated; if the value is *true*, the statements in the **loop body** are executed. The condition is then reevaluated and, if *true*, the loop body is executed again. This repetition continues until the loop condition evaluates to *false*, at which time, the loop body is skipped and execution continues at the instruction following the loop body.

The curly braces are needed only if the loop body has more than one statement— that is, if more than one statement should be executed if the condition evaluates to *true*.

The scope of any variable defined within the *while* loop body extends from its declaration to the end of the *while* loop. Thus, any variable that is declared within a *while* loop body has block scope and cannot be referenced after the *while* loop ends.

The flow of control of a *while* loop is shown in Figure 6.1.

Each execution of the loop body is called an **iteration** of the loop. Thus, if the loop body executes five times before the condition evaluates to *false*, we say there were five iterations of the *while* loop.

What happens if the loop condition is *false* the first time it is evaluated? Because the loop condition is evaluated before executing the *while* loop body, and the loop body is executed only if the condition is *true*, it is possible that the *while* loop body is never executed. In that case, there would be **zero iterations** of the loop.

Using a *while* loop construct, the pseudocode for the cashier would look like this:

Figure 6.1

Flow of Control of a *while* Loop

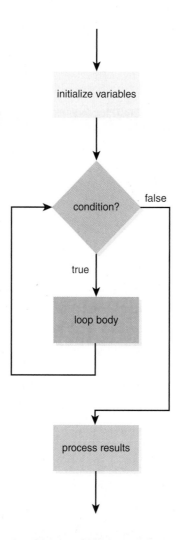

```
set total to $0.00
reach for first item
while item is not the divider bar
{
    add price to total
    reach for next item
}
// if we get here, the item is the divider bar
output the total price
```

It is also possible to construct a *while* loop whose condition *never* evaluates to *false*. That results in an **endless loop**, also known as an **infinite loop**. Because the condition always evaluates to *true*, the loop body is executed repeatedly, without end. One symptom of an endless loop is that the program doesn't terminate; it appears to "hang." However, if the program writes some output in the loop body, we will see that output spewing out on the Java console. Normally, the only recourse is for the user to abort the program.

The way to ensure that the condition will eventually evaluate to *false* is to include code, called a **loop update statement**, within the loop body that appropriately changes the variable that is being tested by the loop condition. If, for example, the loop condition tests for reading a specific value, the loop update statement should read the next input value.

One common logic error that causes an endless loop is putting a semicolon after the condition, as in the following:

```
while ( condition ); // semicolon causes endless loop if condition is true
```

A semicolon immediately following the condition indicates an empty loop body. Although some advanced programming techniques call for the use of an empty loop body, we will not be using those techniques in this chapter.

6.3   Event-Controlled Looping

The *while* loop is used when we don't know how many times the loop will execute; that is, when the loop begins, we don't know how many iterations of the loop will be required. We rely on a signal, or **event**, to tell us that we have processed all the data. For example, when the cashier begins checking out an order, she doesn't (necessarily) know how many items are in the grocery cart; she only knows to stop when she sees the divider bar on the conveyor belt. We call this an event-controlled loop because we continue processing data until an event occurs, which signals the end of the data.

When we're prompting the user to enter data from the console, and we don't know at the beginning of the loop how much data the user has to be processed, we can define

COMMON ERROR TRAP
Avoid putting a semicolon after the condition of a *while* loop. Doing so creates an empty loop body and could result in an endless loop.

a special input value, called the sentinel value. The sentinel value can vary from task to task and is typically a value that is outside the normal range of data for that task.

Sometimes the data our program needs are in a text file. For example, a file could store a company's monthly sales for the last five years. We may want to calculate average monthly sales or perform other statistical computations on that data. In this case, we need to read our data from the file, instead of asking the user to enter the data from the keyboard. Typically, we use a file when a large amount of data is involved because it would be impractical for a user to enter the data manually.

Reading from a file is also an event-controlled loop because we don't know at the beginning of the program how much data is in the file. Thus, we need some way to determine when we have finished processing all the data in the file. Java enables us to test if we have reached the end of the file. Thus, for input from a file, sensing the end-of-file indication is the event that signals that there is no more data to read.

6.3.1   Reading Data from the User

Let's look at the general form for using a *while* loop to process data entered from the user.

```
initialize variables
read the first data item // priming read
while data item is not the sentinel value
{
    process the data

    read the next data item // update read
}
report the results
```

After performing any initialization, we attempt to read the first item. We call this the **priming read** because, like priming a pump, we use that value to feed the condition of the *while* loop for the first iteration. If the first item is not the sentinel value, we process it. Processing may consist of calculating a total, counting the number of data items, comparing the data to previously read values, or any number of operations. Then we read the next data item. This is called the **update read** because we update the data item in preparation for feeding its value into the condition of the *while* loop for the next iteration. This processing, followed by an update read, continues until we do read the sentinel value, at which time we do not execute the *while* loop body. Instead, we skip to the first instruction following the *while* loop. Note that the sentinel value is not meant to be processed. Like the divider bar for the cashier, it is simply a signal to stop processing.

We illustrate this pattern in Example 6.1, which prompts the user for integers and echoes to the console whatever the user enters. We chose the sentinel value to be −1; that is, when the user enters a −1, we stop processing.

```java
1 /*  Working with a sentinel value
2      Anderson, Franceschi
3 */
4 import java.util.Scanner;
5
6 public class EchoUserInput
7 {
8    public static void main( String [ ] args )
9    {
10        final int SENTINEL = -1;
11        int number;
12
13        Scanner scan = new Scanner( System.in );
14
15        // priming read
16        System.out.print( "Enter an integer, or -1 to stop > " );
17        number = scan.nextInt( );
18
19        while ( number != SENTINEL )
20        {
21            // processing
22            System.out.println( number );
23
24            // update read
25            System.out.print( "Enter an integer, or -1 to stop > " );
26            number = scan.nextInt( );
27        }
28
29        System.out.println( "Sentinel value detected. Goodbye" );
30    }
31 }
```

EXAMPLE 6.1   Echoing Input from the User

Figure 6.2 shows the output from this program when the user enters 23, 47, 100, and −1.

On line 10, we declare the sentinel value, −1, as a constant because the value of the sentinel will not change during the execution of the program, and it lets us clearly

Figure 6.2

Output from
Example 6.1,
Using a Sentinel
Value

```
Enter an integer, or -1 to stop > 23

23

Enter an integer, or -1 to stop > 47

47

Enter an integer, or -1 to stop > 100

100

Enter an integer, or -1 to stop > -1

Sentinel value detected. Goodbye
```

state via the *while* loop condition (line 19) that we want to execute the loop body only if the input is not the sentinel value.

Then on lines 16–17, we perform the priming read. The *while* loop condition on line 19 checks for the sentinel value. If the user enters the sentinel value first, we skip the *while* loop altogether and execute line 29, which prints a message that the sentinel value was entered, and we exit the program. If the user enters a number other than the sentinel value, we execute the body of the *while* loop (lines 21–26). In the *while* loop, we simply echo the user's input to the console, then perform the update read. Control then skips to the *while* loop condition, where the value the user entered in the update read is compared to the sentinel value. If this entry is the sentinel value, the loop is skipped; otherwise, the body of the loop is executed: The value is echoed, then a new value is read. This same processing continues until the user does enter the sentinel value. Note that the sentinel value (–1) is not echoed to the output.

COMMON ERROR TRAP
Omitting the update read may result in an endless loop.

A common error in constructing *while* loops is forgetting the update read. Without the update read, the *while* loop continually processes the same data item, leading to an endless loop.

Another common error is omitting the priming read and, instead, reading data inside the *while* loop before the processing, as in the following pseudocode:

```
initialize variables
while data item is not the sentinel value
{
    read the next data
    process the data
}
report the results
```

This structure has several problems. The first time we evaluate the *while* loop condition, we haven't read any data, so the result of that evaluation is unpredictable. Second, when we do read the sentinel value, we will process it, leading to incorrect results.

COMMON ERROR TRAP
Omitting the priming read leads to incorrect results.

6.3.2 Reading Data from a Text File

The *Scanner* class enables us to read data easily from a text file. Java also provides a whole set of classes in the *java.io* package to enable programmers to perform user input and output with a file.

For the *Scanner* class, the general form for reading data from a text file is a little different from reading the data from the user. First, instead of reading a value and checking whether it is the sentinel value, we check whether there is more data in the file, then read a value. Second, we don't need to print a prompt because the user doesn't enter the data; we just read the next value from the file. With the *Scanner* class, the pseudocode for reading from a text file is shown here:

```
initialize variables
while we have not reached end of file
{
    read the next data item
    process the data
}
report the results
```

Scanner class methods, including a constructor for reading from a text file, are shown in Table 6.1. Another class we will use is the *File* class, which associates a file name with a file. The constructor for the *File* class is shown in Table 6.2.

The constructor shown in Table 6.1 can be used to associate a *Scanner* object with a file. The *Scanner* object will tokenize the contents of the file and return the tokens as we call the next methods. The *hasNext* method in the *Scanner* class returns *true* if the input has another token, and *false* otherwise. Thus, when the *hasNext* method returns *false*, we know we have reached the end of the file.

Example 6.2 reads integers from a file named *input.txt* and echoes the integers to the console. The contents of *input.txt* are shown in Figure 6.3 and the output from the program is shown in Figure 6.4.

On line 14 of Example 6.2, we use the constructor of the *File* class to convert the file name, *input.txt*, to a platform-independent file name. Because we are specifying the simple file name, the JVM will look for the file in the same folder as our source file. If the file is located in another folder, we need to specify the path as well as

23
47
100

Figure 6.3

Contents of *input. txt*

TABLE 6.1 Selected Methods of the *Scanner* Class

Selected Methods of the *Scanner* Class	
Constructor	
`Scanner( File file )`	
creates a *Scanner* object and associates it with a file	
Return value	**Method name and argument list**
`boolean`	`hasNext( )`
	returns *true* if there is another token in the input stream; *false*, otherwise
`byte`	`nextByte( )`
	returns the next input as a *byte*
`short`	`nextShort( )`
	returns the next input as a *short*
`int`	`nextInt( )`
	returns the next input as an *int*
`long`	`nextLong( )`
	returns the next input as a *long*
`float`	`nextFloat( )`
	returns the next input as a *float*
`double`	`nextDouble( )`
	returns the next input as a *double*
`boolean`	`nextBoolean( )`
	returns the next input as a *boolean*
`String`	`next( )`
	returns the next token in the input line as a *String*

TABLE 6.2 *File* Class Constructor

A Constructor for the *File* Class
`File( String pathname )`
constructs a *File* object with the *pathname* file name so that the file name is platform independent

the file name. For example, if the file were located on a flash drive in a Windows system, we would pass the *String* "*e:\\input.txt*" to the constructor. Notice that we need to use an escape sequence of two backslashes in order to specify the pathname, *e:\input.txt*.

The *File* class belongs to the *java.io* package, so we include an *import* statement for that class in line 5.

In line 15, we construct a *Scanner* object associated with the *inputFile* object. If the file is not found, the constructor generates a *FileNotFoundException*. It is also possible that an *IOException* may be generated if we encounter problems reading the file. Java requires us to acknowledge that these exceptions may be generated. One way to do that is to include the phrase *throws IOException* in the header for *main* (line 10). We also import the *IOException* class on line 6.

On line 17, the first time our *while* loop condition is evaluated, we check whether there is any data in the file. If the file is empty, the *hasNext* method will return *false*, and we will skip execution of the loop body, continuing at line 25, where we print a message and exit the program.

The body of the *while* loop (lines 19–22) calls the *nextInt* method to read the next integer in the file and echoes that integer to the console. We then reevaluate the *while* loop condition (line 17) to determine if more data is in the file. When no more integers remain to be read, the *hasNext* method returns *false*, and we skip to line 25, where we print a message and exit the program.

Notice that we do not use a priming read because the *hasNext* method essentially peeks ahead into the file to see if there is more data. If the *hasNext* method returns *true*, we know that there is another integer to read, so we perform the read in the first line of the *while* loop body (line 20).

REFERENCE POINT
You can read more about the *Scanner* class on Oracle's Java website: www.oracle.com/technetwork/java.

```
1 /* Reading a Text File
2    Anderson, Franceschi
3 */
4 import java.util.Scanner;
5 import java.io.File;
6 import java.io.IOException;
7
8 public class EchoFileData
9 {
10    public static void main( String [ ] args ) throws IOException
11    {
12       int number;
13
14       File inputFile = new File( "input.txt" );
```

```
15          Scanner file = new Scanner( inputFile );
16
17          while ( file.hasNext( ) )
18          {
19              // read next integer
20              number = file.nextInt( );
21              // process the value read
22              System.out.println( number );
23          }
24
25          System.out.println( "End of file detected. Goodbye" );
26      }
27 }
```

EXAMPLE 6.2   Echoing Input from a File

Figure 6.4

Output from
Example 6.2,
Reading from a
File

```
23

47

100

End of file detected. Goodbye
```

6.4   Looping Techniques

The *while* loop is an important tool for performing many common programming operations on a set of input values. For example, the *while* loop can be used to calculate the sum of values, count the number of values, find the average value, find the minimum and maximum values, and perform other operations.

6.4.1   Accumulation

Let's look at a common programming operation for which a *while* loop is useful: calculating the sum of a set of values. To do this, we will build a simple calculator that performs one function: addition. We will prompt the user for numbers one at a time. We'll make the sentinel value a 0; that is, when the user wants to stop, the user will enter a 0. At that point, we will print the total.

The calculator can be developed using an event-controlled *while* loop and a standard computing technique: **accumulation**. In the accumulation operation, we initialize a *total* variable to 0. Each time we input a new value, we add that value to the *total*. When we reach the end of the input, the current value of *total* is the total for all the input.

Here is the pseudocode for the addition calculator:

```
set total to 0
read a number // priming read
while the number is not the sentinel value
{
    add the number to total
    read the next number // update read
}
output the total
```

Notice that this operation is almost identical to the grocery cashier's job in that we perform a priming read before the *while* loop. Inside the *while* loop, we process each number one at a time—adding each number to the total, then we read the next value, until we see the sentinel value, which is the signal to stop.

Example 6.3 provides the code for the addition calculator, and Figure 6.5 shows the output for a sample execution of the calculator.

```
 1 /*  Addition Calculator
 2      Anderson, Franceschi
 3 */
 4
 5 import java.util.Scanner;
 6
 7 public class Calculator
 8 {
 9    public static void main( String [ ] args )
10    {
11        final int SENTINEL = 0;
12        int number;
13        int total = 0;
14
15        Scanner scan = new Scanner( System.in );
16
17        System.out.println( "Welcome to the addition calculator.\n" );
18
19        System.out.print( "Enter the first number"
20                              + " or 0 for the total > " );
21        number = scan.nextInt( );
22
23        while ( number != SENTINEL )
24        {
25            total += number;
26
```

```
27              System.out.print( "Enter the next number"
28                          + " or 0 for the total > " );
29          number = scan.nextInt( );
30      }
31
32      System.out.println( "The total is " + total );
33  }
34 }
```

EXAMPLE 6.3   An Addition Calculator

Output from a
Sample Run of
the Addition
Calculator

```
Welcome to the addition calculator.

Enter the first number or 0 for the total > 34
Enter the next number or 0 for the total > -10
Enter the next number or 0 for the total > 2
Enter the next number or 0 for the total > 5
Enter the next number or 0 for the total > 8
Enter the next number or 0 for the total > 0
The total is 39
```

COMMON ERROR TRAP
Forgetting
to initialize
the total to 0
will produce
incorrect results.

SOFTWARE ENGINEERING TIP
Indent the body
of a *while* loop to
clearly illustrate
the logic of the
program.

COMMON ERROR TRAP
Choosing the
wrong sentinel
value may result
in logic errors.

Line 13 declares and initializes the *total* to 0. This is an important step because the loop body will add each input value to the total. If the total is not set to 0 before the first input, we will get incorrect results. Furthermore, if *total* is declared but not initialized, our program will not compile.

Lines 19–21 read the first input value (the priming read). The *while* loop begins at line 23, and its condition checks for the sentinel value. The first time the *while* loop is encountered, this condition will check the value of the input from the priming read.

The loop body processes the input (line 25), which consists of adding the input value to the *total*. The final step in the loop body (lines 27–29) is to read the next input (the update read).

When the end of the loop body is reached, control is transferred back to line 23, where the loop condition is again tested with the input value read on line 29. If the condition is *true*, that is, if the input just read is not the sentinel value, then the loop body is reexecuted and the condition is retested, continuing until the input is the sentinel value, which causes the condition to evaluate to *false*. At that time, the loop body is skipped and line 32 is executed, which reports the results by printing the *total*.

Notice that the body of the *while* loop is indented and that the opening and closing curly braces are aligned in the same column as the *w* in the *while*. This style lets us easily see which statements belong to the *while* loop body.

It is important to choose the sentinel value carefully. Obviously, the sentinel value cannot be a value that the user might want to be processed. In the addition calculator, we want to allow the user to enter positive or negative integers. We chose 0 as the sentinel value for two reasons. First, adding 0 to a total has no effect, so it is unlikely that the user will want to enter that value to be processed. Second, to the user, it is logical to enter a 0 to signal that there are no more integers to be added.

CODE IN ACTION

To see a step-by-step illustration of a *while* loop with a sentinel value, look for the movie within the online resources. Click on the link to start the movie.

6.4.2 Counting Items

Counting is used when we need to know how many items are input or how many input values fit some criterion, for example, how many items are positive numbers or how many items are odd numbers. Counting is similar to accumulation in that we start with a count of 0 and increment (add 1 to) the count every time we read a value that meets the criterion. When there are no more values to read, the count variable contains the number of items that meet our criterion.

For example, let's count the number of students who passed a test. The pseudocode for this operation is as follows:

```
set countPassed to 0
read a test score
while the test score is not the sentinel value
{
   if the test score >= 60
   {
      add 1 to countPassed
   }
   read the next test score
}
output countPassed
```

The application in Example 6.4 counts the number of students that passed a test. We also calculate the percentage of the class that passed the test. To do this, we maintain a second count: the number of scores entered. This value will be incremented each time we read a score, whereas the *countPassed* value will be incremented only if the score is greater than or equal to 60. The sentinel value is −1. A sample run of this program is shown in Figure 6.6.

```java
1 /* Counting passing test scores
2     Anderson, Franceschi
3 */
4
5 import java.util.Scanner;
6 import java.text.DecimalFormat;
7
8 public class CountTestScores
9 {
10    public static void main( String [ ] args )
11    {
12      int countPassed = 0;
13      int countScores = 0;
14      int score;
15      final int SENTINEL = -1;
16
17      Scanner scan = new Scanner( System.in );
18
19      System.out.println( "This program counts "
20                   + "the number of passing test scores." );
21      System.out.println( "Enter a -1 to stop." );
22
23      System.out.print( "Enter the first score > " );
24      score = scan.nextInt( );
25
26      while ( score != SENTINEL )
27      {
28        if ( score >= 60 )
29        {
30              countPassed++;
31        }
32
33        countScores++;
34
35        System.out.print( "Enter the next score > " );
36        score = scan.nextInt( );
37      }
38
39      System.out.println( "You entered " + countScores + " scores" );
40      System.out.println( "The number of passing test scores is "
41                   + countPassed );
42      if ( countScores != 0 )
```

```
43      {
44          DecimalFormat percent = new DecimalFormat( "0.0%" );
45        System.out.println(
46          percent.format( (double) ( countPassed ) / countScores )
47          + " of the class passed the test" );
48      }
49   }
50 }
```

EXAMPLE 6.4   Counting Passing Test Scores

```
This program counts the number of passing test scores.
Enter a -1 to stop.
Enter the first score > 98
Enter the next score > 75
Enter the next score > 60
Enter the next score > 59
Enter the next score > 45
Enter the next score > 88
Enter the next score > 94
Enter the next score > 96
Enter the next score > 56
Enter the next score > 77
Enter the next score > 82
Enter the next score > 89
Enter the next score > 100
Enter the next score > 78
Enter the next score > 55
Enter the next score > -1
You entered 15 scores
The number of passing test scores is 11
73.3% of the class passed the test
```

Figure 6.6

Counting Passing
Test Scores

Lines 12 and 13 declare the variables *countPassed* and *countScores* and initialize both to 0. Initializing these values to 0 is critical; otherwise, we will get the wrong results or a compiler error. We initialize these values to 0 because at that point, we have not yet processed any test scores.

Our *while* loop framework follows the familiar pattern. We perform the priming read for the first input (lines 23–24); our *while* loop condition checks for the sentinel value (line 26); and the last statements of the *while* loop (lines 35–36) read the next value.

In the processing portion of the *while* loop, line 28 checks if the score just read is a passing score, and if so, line 30 adds 1 to *countPassed*. For each score entered, regardless of whether the student passed, we increment *countScores* (line 33).

COMMON ERROR TRAP
Forgetting to initialize the count variables will produce a compiler error.

When the sentinel value is entered, the *while* loop condition evaluates to *false* and control skips to line 39, where we output the number of scores entered and the number of passing scores. So that we avoid dividing by 0, note that line 42 checks whether no scores were entered. Note also that in line 46 we type cast *countPassed* to a *double* to force floating-point division, rather than integer division, so that the fractional part of the quotient will be maintained.

6.4.3 Calculating an Average

Calculating an average is a combination of accumulation and counting. We use accumulation to calculate the total and we use counting to count the number of items to average.

Here's the pseudocode for calculating an average:

```
set total to 0
set count to 0
read a number
while the number is not the sentinel value
{
    add the number to total
    add 1 to the count

    read the next number
}
set the average to total / count
output the average
```

Thus, to calculate an average test score for the class, we need to calculate the total of all the test scores, then divide by the number of students who took the test.

```
average = total / count;
```

It's important to remember that if we declare *total* and *count* as integers, then the *average* will be calculated using integer division, which truncates the remainder. To get a floating-point average, we need to type cast one of the variables (either *total* or *count*) to a *double* or a *float* to force the division to be performed as floating-point.

```
double average = (double) ( total ) / count;
```

Although the parentheses around *total* are not required because *total* is a single value, we include them here to emphasize that we are type casting only *total* to a *double* before the division is performed.

The application in Example 6.5 calculates an average test score for a class of students. The output is shown in Figure 6.7.

```
1 /* Calculate the average test score
2    Anderson, Franceschi
3 */
4
5 import java.util.Scanner;
6 import java.text.DecimalFormat;
7
8 public class AverageTestScore
9 {
10   public static void main( String [ ] args )
11   {
12     int count = 0;
13     int total = 0;
14     final int SENTINEL = -1;
15     int score;
16
17     Scanner scan = new Scanner( System.in );
18
19     System.out.println( "To calculate a class average," );
20     System.out.println( "enter each test score." );
21     System.out.println( "When you are finished, enter a -1" );
22
23     System.out.print( "Enter the first test score > " );
24     score = scan.nextInt( );
25
26     while ( score != SENTINEL )
27     {
28       total += score;   // add score to total
29       count++;          // add 1 to count of test scores
30
31       System.out.print( "Enter the next test score > " );
32       score = scan.nextInt( );
33     }
34
35     if ( count != 0 )
36     {
37         DecimalFormat oneDecimalPlace = new DecimalFormat( "0.0" );
38         System.out.println( "\nThe class average is "
39           + oneDecimalPlace.format( (double) ( total ) / count ) );
40     }
41     else
42         System.out.println( "\nNo grades were entered" );
44   }
45 }
```

EXAMPLE 6.5   Calculating an Average Test Score

Calculating the
Average Test
Score

```
To calculate a class average,
enter each test score.
When you are finished, enter a -1
Enter the first test score > 88
Enter the next test score > 78
Enter the next test score > 96
Enter the next test score > 75
Enter the next test score > 99
Enter the next test score > 56
Enter the next test score > 78
Enter the next test score > 84
Enter the next test score > 93
Enter the next test score > 79
Enter the next test score > 90
Enter the next test score > 85
Enter the next test score > 79
Enter the next test score > 92
Enter the next test score > 99
Enter the next test score > 94
Enter the next test score > -1

The class average is 85.3
```

In Example 6.5, lines 12 and 13 declare both *count* and *total* variables as *ints* and initialize each to 0. Again, our *while* loop structure follows the same pattern. Lines 23–24 read the first input value; the *while* loop condition (line 26) checks for the sentinel value; and the last statements in the *while* loop (lines 31–32) read the next score. For the processing portion of the *while* loop, we add the score to the total and increment the count of scores (lines 28–29). When the sentinel value is entered, we stop executing the *while* loop and skip to line 35.

COMMON ERROR TRAP
Forgetting to check whether the denominator is 0 before performing division is a logic error.

In line 35, we avoid dividing by 0 by checking whether *count* is 0 (that is, if no scores were entered) before performing the division. If *count* is 0, we simply print a message saying that no grades were entered. If *count* is not 0, we calculate and print the average. We first instantiate a *DecimalFormat* object (line 37) so that we can output the average to one decimal place. Remember that we need to type cast the total to a *double* (lines 38–39) to force floating-point division, rather than integer division.

6.4.4 Finding Maximum or Minimum Values

In previous examples, we calculated a total for a group of numbers by keeping a running total. We started with a total of 0, then added each new input value to the running total. Similarly, we counted the number of input items by keeping a running count. We started with a count of 0 and incremented the count each time we read a new value. We can apply that same logic to calculating a maximum or minimum. For example, to find the maximum of a group of values, we can keep a "running," or current, maximum. We start by assuming that the first value we read is the maximum. In fact, it is the largest value we have seen so far. Then as we read each new value, we compare it to our current maximum. If the new value is greater, we make the new value our current maximum. When we come to the end of the input values, the current maximum is the maximum for all the input values.

Finding the minimum value, of course, uses the same approach, except that we replace the current minimum only if the new value is less than the current minimum.

Here's the pseudocode for finding a maximum value in a file:

```
read a first number and make it the maximum
while there is another number to read
{
    read the next number
    if number > maximum
    {
        set maximum to number
    }
}
output the maximum
```

Example 6.6 shows the code to find a maximum test grade in a file. As shown in Figure 6.8, the grades are stored as integers, one per line, in the file *grades.txt*. When this program runs, its output is shown in Figure 6.9.

```
1  /* Find the maximum test grade
2      Anderson, Franceschi
3  */
4
5  import java.util.Scanner;
6  import java.io.*;
7
8  public class FindMaximumGrade
9  {
10     public static void main( String [ ] args ) throws IOException
11     {
12         int maxGrade;
13         int grade;
```

88
78
96
75
99
56
78
84
93
79
90
85
79
90
85
79
92
99
94

Figure 6.8

The Contents of *grades.txt*

```
14
15          Scanner file = new Scanner( new File( "grades.txt" ) );
16
17          System.out.println( "This program finds the maximum grade "
18                                        + "for a class" );
19
20          if ( ! file.hasNext( ) )
21          {
22              System.out.println( "No test grades are in the file" );
23          }
24          else
25          {
26             maxGrade = file.nextInt( ); // make first grade the max
27
28             while ( file.hasNext( ) )
29             {
30                grade = file.nextInt( ); // read next grade
31
32                if ( grade > maxGrade )
33                   maxGrade = grade; // save as current max
34             }
35
36             System.out.println( "The maximum grade is " + maxGrade );
37          }
38     }
39 }
```

EXAMPLE 6.6   Finding the Maximum Value

Figure 6.9

Finding the
Maximum Value

```
This program finds the maximum grade for a class
The maximum grade is 99
```

In line 20, we call the *hasNext* method to test whether the file is empty. If so, we print a message (line 22) and the program ends. If, however, the file is not empty, we read the first value and automatically make it our maximum by storing the grade in *maxGrade* (line 26). In line 28, our *while* loop condition tests whether we have reached the end of the file. If not, we execute the body of the *while* loop (lines 30–33). We read the next grade and check whether that grade is greater than the current maximum. If so, we assign that grade to *maxGrade*; otherwise, we leave *maxGrade* unchanged. Then control is transferred to line 28 to retest the *while* loop condition.

When we do reach the end of the file, the *while* loop condition becomes *false*; control is transferred to line 36, and we output *maxGrade* as the maximum value.

A common error is to initialize the maximum or minimum to an arbitrary value, such as 0 or 100. This will not work for all conditions, however. For example, let's say we are finding the maximum number and we initialize the maximum to 0. If the user enters all negative numbers, then when the end of data is encountered, the maximum will still be 0, which is clearly an error. The same principle is true when finding a minimum value. If we initialize the minimum to 0, and the user enters all positive numbers greater than 0, then at the end of our loop, our minimum value will still be 0, which is also incorrect.

COMMON ERROR TRAP
Initializing a maximum or a minimum to an arbitrary value, such as 0 or 100, is a logic error and could result in incorrect results.

Skill Practice
with these end-of-chapter questions

6.14.1 Multiple Choice Exercises

Question 1

6.14.2 Reading and Understanding Code

Questions 5, 6, 7, 8, 20

6.14.3 Fill In the Code

Questions 21, 22, 23, 24, 25, 26

6.14.4 Identifying Errors in Code

Questions 30, 31

6.14.5 Debugging Area

Question 37

6.14.6 Write a Short Program

Questions 44, 45

6.14.8 Technical Writing

Questions 70, 71

6.5   Type-Safe Input Using *Scanner*

One problem with reading input using *Scanner* is that if the next token does not match the data type we expect, an *InputMismatchException* is generated, which stops execution of the program. This could be caused by a simple typo on the user's part; for example, the user may type a letter or other nonnumeric character when our program prompts for an integer. To illustrate this problem, Example 6.7 shows a small program that prompts the user for an integer and calls the *nextInt* method of the *Scanner* class to read the integer, and Figure 6.10 shows the *InputMismatchException* generated when the user enters an *a* instead of an integer. Notice that the program ends when the exception is generated; we never execute line 15, which would echo the age to the console.

```
 1 /* Reading an integer from the user
 2    Anderson, Franceschi
 3 */
 4 import java.util.Scanner;
 5
 6 public class ReadInteger
 7 {
 8    public static void main( String [ ] args )
 9    {
10         Scanner scan = new Scanner( System.in );
11
12         System.out.print( "Enter your age as an integer > " );
13         int age = scan.nextInt( );
14
15         System.out.println( "Your age is " + age );
16    }
17 }
```

EXAMPLE 6.7   Reading an Integer

Figure 6.10

Input Failure

```
Enter your age as an integer > a
Exception in thread "main" java.util.InputMismatchException
    at java.base/java.util.Scanner.throwFor(Unknown Source)
    at java.base/java.util.Scanner.next(Unknown Source)
    at java.base/java.util.Scanner.nextInt(Unknown Source)
    at java.base/java.util.Scanner.nextInt(Unknown Source)
    at ReadInteger.main(ReadInteger.java:13)
```

We can make our program more robust by checking, before we read, that the next token matches our expected input. The *Scanner* class provides *hasNext* methods for doing this, which are shown in Table 6.3. The *hasNext* methods return *true* if the next token can be read as the data type requested. For example, if we expect an integer, we can test whether the user has typed characters that can be interpreted as an integer by calling the *hasNextInt* method. If that method returns *true*, it is safe to read the value using the *nextInt* method. If the next token is not what we need, that is, if the *hasNextInt* method returns *false*, then reading that value as an

TABLE 6.3 *Scanner* **Methods for Testing Tokens**

Selected Input Stream Testing Methods of the *Scanner* Class	
Return value	**Method name and argument list**
boolean	hasNext( )
	returns *true* if there is another token in the input stream; *false*, otherwise
boolean	hasNextByte( )
	returns *true* if the token in the input stream can be read as a *byte*; *false*, otherwise
boolean	hasNextShort( )
	returns *true* if the token in the input stream can be read as a *short*; *false*, otherwise
boolean	hasNextInt( )
	returns *true* if the token in the input stream can be read as an *int*; *false*, otherwise
boolean	hasNextLong( )
	returns *true* if the token in the input stream can be read as a *long*; *false*, otherwise
boolean	hasNextFloat( )
	returns *true* if the token in the input stream can be read as a *float*; *false*, otherwise
boolean	hasNextDouble( )
	returns *true* if the token in the input stream can be read as a *double*; *false*, otherwise
boolean	hasNextBoolean( )
	returns *true* if the token in the input stream can be read as a *boolean*; *false*, otherwise
String	nextLine( )
	returns the remainder of the input line as a *String*

int will generate the *InputMismatchException*. In that case, we need to notify the user that the value typed is not valid and reprompt for new input. But first we need to clear the invalid input. We can flush the invalid input by calling the *nextLine* method of the *Scanner* class, which returns any remaining tokens on the input line as a *String*. Then we just ignore that *String*. Example 6.8 shows a revised version of Example 6.7 that is type-safe, meaning we guarantee we have an integer to read before reading it.

On line 14 of Example 6.8, we prompt for the integer. Then on line 15, the *while* loop condition checks whether the user has, indeed, typed an integer value. If not, we ignore whatever the user did type by calling the *nextLine* method (line 17). On line 18, we reprompt the user. The *while* loop continues executing until the user does enter an integer and the *hasNextInt* method returns *true*. At that point, we execute line 20, which reads the integer into the *age* variable. Note that we need to use a *while* loop rather than an *if* statement because an *if* statement will test only the first invalid input value. Using a *while* loop allows us to keep prompting the user as many times as needed until a valid value is entered. Figure 6.11 shows the output of this program when the user enters data other than integers, then finally enters an integer.

```
1   /* Type-Safe Input Using Scanner
2      Anderson, Franceschi
3   */
4
5   import java.util.Scanner;
6
7   public class TypeSafeReadInteger
8   {
9      public static void main( String [ ] args )
10     {
11        Scanner scan = new Scanner( System.in );
12        String garbage;
13
14        System.out.print( "Enter your age as an integer > " );
15        while ( ! scan.hasNextInt( ) )
16        {
17            garbage = scan.nextLine( );
18            System.out.print( "\nPlease enter an integer > " );
19        }
20        int age = scan.nextInt( );
21        System.out.println( "Your age is " + age );
22     }
23  }
```

EXAMPLE 6.8   Type-Safe Input

```
Enter your age as an integer > asd

Please enter an integer > 12wg

Please enter an integer > 12.4

Please enter an integer > 23

Your age is 23
```

Figure 6.11

Reprompting
Until the User
Enters an Integer

6.6   Constructing Loop Conditions

Constructing the correct loop condition may seem a little counterintuitive. The loop executes as long as the loop condition evaluates to *true*. Thus, if we want our loop to terminate when we read the sentinel value, then the loop condition should check that the input value is *not* the sentinel value. In other words, the loop continuation condition is the inverse of the loop termination condition. For a simple sentinel-controlled loop, the condition normally follows this pattern:

```
while ( inputValue != sentinel )
```

In fact, we can see that the loop conditions in many of the examples in this chapter use this form of *while* loop condition.

For some applications, there may be multiple sentinel values. For example, suppose we provide a menu for a user with each menu option being a single character. The user can repeatedly select options from the menu, with the sentinel value being *S* for stop. To allow case-insensitive input, we want to recognize the sentinel value as either *S* or *s*. To do this, we need a compound loop condition, that is, a loop condition that uses a logical AND (&&) or logical OR (||) operator.

Our first inclination might be to form the condition this way, which is **incorrect:**

```
while ( option != 'S' || option != 's' ) // INCORRECT
```

With this condition, the loop will execute forever. Regardless of what the user enters, the loop condition will be *true*. If the user types S, the first expression (option != 'S') is *false*, but the second expression (option != 's') is *true*. Thus, the loop condition evaluates to true and the *while* loop body is executed. Similarly, if the user types *s*, the first expression (option != 'S') is *true*, so the loop condition evaluates to *true* and the *while* loop body is executed.

An easy method for constructing a correct *while* loop condition consists of three steps:

1. Define the loop termination condition; that is, define the condition that will make the loop stop executing.

2. Create the loop continuation condition—the condition that will keep the loop executing—by applying the logical NOT operator (!) to the loop termination condition.

3. Simplify the loop continuation condition by applying DeMorgan's Laws, where possible.

   DeMorgan's Laws are the following:

   NOT(A AND B) = (NOT A) OR (NOT B)

   and

   NOT(A OR B) = (NOT A) AND (NOT B)

Let's use these three steps to construct the correct loop condition for the menu program.

1. Define the loop termination condition:

   The loop will stop executing when the user enters an *S* or the user enters an *s*. Translating that into Java, we get

   ```
   ( option == 'S' || option == 's' )
   ```

2. Create the loop continuation condition by applying the ! operator:

   ```
   ! ( option == 'S' || option == 's' )
   ```

3. Simplify by applying DeMorgan's Laws:

   To apply DeMorgan's Laws, we change the == equality operators to != and change the logical OR operator (||) to the logical AND operator (&&), producing an equivalent, but simpler expression:

   ```
   ( option != 'S' && option != 's' )
   ```

We now have our loop condition.

To illustrate, let's write an application that calculates the cost of an order at Bonnie's Burgers. We provide a menu with prices, and the user selects items from the menu one at a time until the user enters *S* or *s* to stop. This is an accumulation operation because we are accumulating the cost of the user's order. Example 6.9 shows the code for this application, and Figure 6.12 shows the output of a sample run.

```
1 /* Order from a menu
2    Anderson, Franceschi
3 */
4
5 import java.util.Scanner;
6 import java.text.DecimalFormat;
7
```

```
 8  public class BonniesBurgers
 9  {
10      public static void main( String [ ] args )
11      {
12          String menu = "\tC Cheeseburger: $7.49";
13                 menu += "\n\tH Hot dog: $6.99";
14                 menu += "\n\tL Lemonade: $2.50";
15                 menu += "\n\tT Iced tea: $2.75";
16
17
18          char option;
19          double orderCost = 0;
20
21          DecimalFormat money = new DecimalFormat( "$#.00" );
22          Scanner scan = new Scanner( System.in );
23
24          System.out.println( "Welcome to Bonnie's Burgers. "
25                             + "Select from our menu: " );
26
27          System.out.println( menu ); // print the menu
28          System.out.print( "Order an item, "
29                             + "or \"S\" to stop > " );
30          option = scan.next( ).charAt( 0 );
31
32          while ( option != 'S' && option != 's' )
33          {
34            switch ( option )
35            {
36              case 'c':
37              case 'C':
38                  System.out.print( "Cheeseburger ordered. " );
39                  orderCost += 7.49;
40                  break;
41              case 'h':
42              case 'H':
43                  System.out.print( "Hot dog ordered. " );
44                  orderCost += 6.99;
45                  break;
46              case 'l':
47              case 'L':
48                  System.out.print( "Lemonade ordered. " );
49                  orderCost += 2.50;
50                  break;
51              case 't':
52              case 'T':
53                  System.out.print( "Iced tea ordered. " );
54                  orderCost += 2.75;
```

```
55                    break;
56                 default:
57                    System.out.println( "Unrecognized menu item." );
58              }
59
60           System.out.println( "Subtotal: "
61                                     + money.format( orderCost ) );
62
63           System.out.print( "\nOrder another item, "
64                                 + "or \"S\" to stop > " );
65           option = scan.next( ).charAt( 0 );
66        }
67
68        System.out.println( "\nTotal order cost is "
69                                     + money.format( orderCost ) );
70    }
71 }
```

EXAMPLE 6.9   A Compound Loop Condition

Figure 6.12

Ordering from a
Menu

```
Welcome to Bonnie's Burgers. Select from our menu:

         C Cheeseburger: $7.49

         H Hot dog: $6.99

         L Lemonade: $2.50

         T Iced tea: $2.75

Order an item, or "S" to stop > h

Hot dog ordered. Subtotal: $6.99

Order another item, or "S" to stop > T

Iced tea ordered. Subtotal: $9.74

Order another item, or "S" to stop > s

Total order cost is $9.74
```

We use the compound condition in the *while* loop (line 32). Then within the *while* loop, we use a *switch* statement (lines 34–58) to determine which menu item the user has chosen. We handle case-insensitive input by including *case* constants for both the lowercase and uppercase versions of each letter option. After the *switch* statement, we include the update read (lines 63–65) to input the user's next item.

Note that we don't provide *case* statements for the sentinel values. Instead, we use the *while* loop condition to detect when the user enters the sentinel values.

6.7   Testing Techniques for *while* Loops

It's a good feeling when our code compiles without errors. Getting a clean compile, however, is only part of the job for the programmer. The other part of the job is verifying that the code is correct; that is, that the program produces accurate results.

It usually isn't feasible to test a program with all possible input values, but we can get a reasonable level of confidence in the accuracy of the program by concentrating our testing in three areas:

1. Does the program produce correct results with a set of known inputs?

2. Does the program produce correct results if the sentinel value is the first and only input?

3. Does the program deal appropriately with invalid input?

Let's take a look at these three areas in more detail:

1. Does the program produce correct results with known input?

To test the program with known input, we select valid input values and determine what the results should be by performing the program's operation either by hand or by using a calculator. For example, to test whether a total or average is computed correctly, enter some values and compare the program's output to a total or average we calculate by entering those same values into a calculator.

It's especially important to select input values that represent boundary conditions, that is, values that are the lowest or highest expected values. For example, to test a program that determines whether a person is old enough to vote in a presidential election (that is, the person is 18 or older), we should select test values of 17, 18, and 19. These values are the boundary conditions for `age >= 18`; the test values are one integer less, the same value, and one integer greater than the legal voting age. We then run the program with the three input values and verify that the program correctly identifies 17 as an illegal voting age and 18 and 19 as legal voting ages.

2. Does the program produce correct results if the sentinel value is the first and only input?

In our *while* loops, when we find the sentinel value, the flow of control skips the *while* loop body and picks up at the statement following the *while* loop. When the sentinel value is the first input value, our *while* loop body does not execute at all. We simply skip to the statement following the *while* loop. In cases like this, the highly respected computer scientist Donald Knuth recommends that we "do exactly nothing, gracefully."

In many programs that calculate a total or an average for the input values, when no value is input, our program should either report the total or average as 0 or output a message that no values were entered. It's important to write our program so that it tolerates the only input being the sentinel value; therefore, we need to test our programs by entering the sentinel value first.

Let's revisit the earlier examples in this chapter to see how they handle the case when only the sentinel value is entered.

In the addition calculator (Example 6.3), we set the total to 0 before the *while* loop and simply report the value of total after the *while* loop. So we get the correct result (0) with only the sentinel value.

SOFTWARE ENGINEERING TIP
Expect that the user might enter the sentinel value first. The program needs to handle this special case.

In Example 6.4 where we count the percentage of passing test scores, we handle the sole sentinel value by performing some additional checking after the *while* loop. If only the sentinel value is entered, the count will be 0. We check for this case and if we find a count of 0, we skip reporting the percentage so that we avoid dividing by 0. We use similar code in Example 6.5, where we calculate the average test score. If we detect a count of 0, we also skip the calculation of the average to avoid dividing by 0 and simply report the class average as 0.

   3. Does the program deal appropriately with invalid input?

If the program expects a range of values or certain discrete values, then it should notify the user when the input doesn't fit the expected values.

In Example 6.9, we implemented a menu for ordering food items. The user could enter *c, h, l, or t* (or the corresponding capital letters) representing their desired options. If the user entered a letter other than those expected values, we used the *default* clause of the *switch* statement to issue an error message, "*Unrecognized menu item.*"

In the next section, we explain how to validate that user input is within a range of values using a *do/while* loop.

6.8 Event-Controlled Loops Using *do/while*

Another form of loop that is especially useful for validating user input is the *do/while* loop. In the *do/while* loop, the loop condition is tested at the end of the loop (instead of at the beginning, as in the *while* loop). Thus the body of the *do/while* loop is executed at least once.

The syntax of the *do/while* loop is the following:

```
// initialize variables
do
{
```

```
  // body of loop
} while ( condition );
// process the results
```

Figure 6.13 shows the flow of control of a *do/while* loop.

To use the *do/while* loop to validate user input, we insert the prompt for the input inside the body of the loop, then use the loop condition to test the value of the input. Like the *while* loop, the body of the loop will be reexecuted if the condition is *true*. Thus, we need to form the condition so that it's *true* when the user enters invalid values. Be aware that because of scope, any variable that will be referenced in the *while* condition must be defined before the *do/while* loop begins.

Example 6.10 implements a *do/while* loop (lines 14–18) that prompts the user for an integer between 1 and 10. Figure 6.14 shows the output of the program. If the user enters a number outside the valid range, we reprompt the user until the input is between 1 and 10. Thus, the condition for the *do/while* loop (line 18) checks

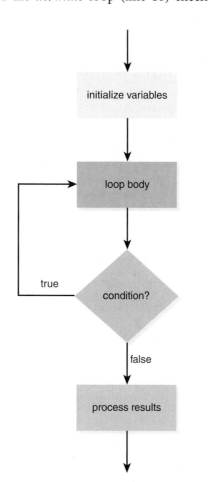

Figure 6.13

The Flow of Control of a *do/while* Statement

whether the number is less than 1 or greater than 10. Note also that because we will be referencing *number* in the *while* condition, we must define *number* before the *do/while* loop begins (line 11).

```
 1 /* Validate input is between 1 and 10
 2    Anderson, Franceschi
 3 */
 4
 5 import java.util.Scanner;
 6
 7 public class ValidateInput
 8 {
 9   public static void main( String [ ] args )
10   {
11     int number; // input value
12     Scanner scan = new Scanner( System.in );
13
14     do
15     {
16       System.out.print( "Enter a number between 1 and 10 > " );
17       number = scan.nextInt( );
18     } while ( number < 1 || number > 10 );
19
20     System.out.println( "Thank you!" );
21   }
22 }
```

EXAMPLE 6.10   Validating User Input

Figure 6.14

Validating Input

```
Enter a number between 1 and 10 > 20

Enter a number between 1 and 10 > −1

Enter a number between 1 and 10 > 0

Enter a number between 1 and 10 > 11

Enter a number between 1 and 10 > 5

Thank you!
```

For validating input, we may be tempted to use an *if* statement rather than a *do/while* loop. For example, to perform the same validation as Example 6.10 we may try this **incorrect** code:

```
System.out.print( "Enter a number between 1 and 10 > " );
number = scan.nextInt( );
```

```
if ( number < 1 || number > 10 ) // INCORRECT!
{
    System.out.print( "Enter a number between 1 and 10 > " );
    number = scan.nextInt( );
}
```

The problem with this approach is that the *if* statement will reprompt the user only once. If the user enters an invalid value a second time, the program will not catch it. A *do/while* loop, however, will continue to reprompt the user as many times as needed until the user enters a valid value.

COMMON ERROR TRAP
Do not use an *if* statement to validate input because it will catch invalid values entered the first time only. Use a *do/while* loop to reprompt the user until the user enters a valid value.

Skill Practice
with these end-of-chapter questions

CODE IN ACTION

To see two step-by-step illustrations of *do/while* loops, look for the movie within the online resources. Click on the link to start the movie.

6.9   Programming Activity 1: Using *while* Loops

In this activity, you will work with a sentinel-controlled *while* loop, performing this activity:

> Write a *while* loop to process the contents of a grocery cart and calculate the total price of the items. It is important to understand that, in this example, we do not know how many items are in the cart.

The framework will animate your code and display the current subtotal so that you can check the correctness of your code. The window will display the various *Item* objects moving down a conveyor belt toward a grocery bag. It will also display the unit price of the item and your current subtotal, as well as the correct subtotal.

For example, Figure 6.15 demonstrates the animation: We are currently scanning the first item, a milk carton, with a unit price of $2.00; thus, the correct subtotal is $2.00.

As the animation will show, *Item* objects could be milk, cereal, orange juice, or the divider bar. The number of *Item* objects in the cart is determined randomly; as you watch the animation, sometimes you will find that there are two items in the cart, sometimes six, sometimes three, sometimes only the divider bar, and so forth. Scanning the divider bar signals the end of the items in the cart.

Task Instructions

Copy the files in this chapter's Programming Activity 1 folder in the source code provided with this text to a folder on your computer. Searching for five stars

Figure 6.15

Animation of the *Cashier* Application

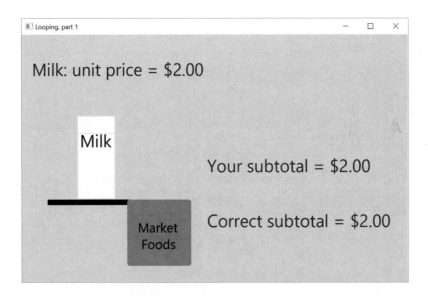

(*****) in the *CashierDrawing.java* source code will show you where to add your code. You will add your code inside the *checkout* method of the *CashierDrawing* class (the method header for the *checkout* method has already been coded for you). Example 6.11 shows a fragment of the *CashierDrawing* class, where you will add your code:

```java
public void checkout( )
{
 /* ***** Student writes the body of this method ***** */
 //
 //  Using a while loop, calculate the total price
 //  of the groceries.
 //
 // The getNext method (in this CashierDrawing class) returns the
 // next item on the conveyor belt, which is an Item object
 // (we do not know which item and we do not know how many items
 // are in the cart - this is randomly generated).
 // getNext does not take any arguments. Its API is:
 //       Item getNext( )
 //
 // Right after you update the current subtotal,
 // you should call the animate method.
 // The animate method takes one argument: a double,
 // which is your current subtotal.
 // For example, if the name of your variable representing
 // the current subtotal is total, your call to the animate
 // method should be:
 //    animate( total );
 //
 // The instance method getPrice of the Item class
 // returns the price of the Item object.
 // The method getPrice does not take any arguments.
 // Its API is:
 //         double getPrice( )
 //
 // The cart is empty when the getNext method returns
 // the divider Item.
 // You detect the divider Item because its price
 // is -0.99. So an Item with a price of -0.99
 // is the sentinel value for the loop.
 //
 // After you scan the divider, print the total to the console.

 // End of student code
}
```

EXAMPLE 6.11   The *checkout* Method in *CashierDrawing.java*

- You can access items in the cart by calling the *getNext* method of the *CashierDrawing* class, which has the following API:

```
Item getNext( )
```

The *getNext* method returns an *Item* object, which represents an *Item* in the cart. As you can see, the *getNext* method does not take any arguments. Since we call the method *getNext* from inside the *CashierDrawing* class, we call the method without an object reference. For example, a call to *getNext* could look like the following:

```
Item newItem;
newItem = getNext( );
```

The *getNext* method is already written and contains code to randomly generate *Items*. It is written in such a way that the first *Item* object on the conveyor belt may or may not be the divider. (If the first *Item* is the divider, the cart is empty.)

- After you get a new *Item*, you can "scan" the item to get its price by calling the *getPrice* method of the *Item* class. The *getPrice* method has this API:

```
double getPrice( )
```

Thus, you would get an item, then get its price using code like the following:

```
Item newItem;
double price;

newItem = getNext( );
price = newItem.getPrice( );
```

- After adding the price of an item to your subtotal, call the *animate* method of the *CashierDrawing* class. This method will display both your subtotal and the correct subtotal so that you can verify that your code is correct.

The animate method has the following API:

```
void animate( double subtotal )
```

Thus, if your variable representing the current total is *total*, you would call the animate method using the following code:

```
animate( total );
```

- You want to exit the loop when the next *Item* is the divider. You will know that the *Item* is the divider because its price will be –0.99 (negative 0.99); thus, scanning an *Item* whose price is –0.99 should be your condition to exit the *while* loop.

- When your loop ends, verify that your total matches the correct subtotal displayed.

- To test your code, compile *CashierDrawing.java* and run the application from the *CashierApplication* class.

Troubleshooting

If your method implementation does not animate or animates incorrectly, check these items:

- Verify that you have correctly coded the priming read.
- Verify that you have correctly coded the condition for exiting the loop.
- Verify that you have correctly coded the body of the loop.

? DISCUSSION QUESTIONS

1. **What is the sentinel value of your *while* loop?**

2. **Explain the purpose of the priming read.**

6.10 Count-Controlled Loops Using *for*

Before the loop begins, if we know the number of times the loop body should execute, we can use a **count-controlled loop**. The *for* loop is designed for count-controlled loops, that is, when the number of iterations is determined before the loop begins.

6.10.1 Basic Structure of *for* Loops

The *for* loop has this syntax:

```
for ( initialization; loop condition; loop update )
{
      // loop body
}
```

Notice that the initialization, loop condition, and loop update in the *for* loop header are separated by semicolons (not commas). Notice also that there is no semicolon after the closing parenthesis in the *for* loop header. A semicolon here would indicate an empty *for* loop body. Although some advanced programs might correctly write a *for* loop with an empty loop body, the programs we write in this text will have at least one statement in the *for* loop body.

The scope of any variable declared within the *for* loop header or body extends from the point of declaration to the end of the *for* loop body.

The flow of control of the *for* loop is shown in Figure 6.16. When the *for* loop is encountered, the initialization statement is executed. Then the loop condition is evaluated. If the condition is true, the loop body is executed, then the loop update statement is executed, and the loop condition is reevaluated. Again, if the condition

COMMON ERROR TRAP
Be sure to use semicolons, rather than commas, to separate the statements in a *for* loop header.

COMMON ERROR TRAP
Adding a semicolon after the closing parenthesis in the *for* loop header indicates an empty loop body and will likely cause a logic error.

Figure 6.16

Flow of Control of the *for* Loop

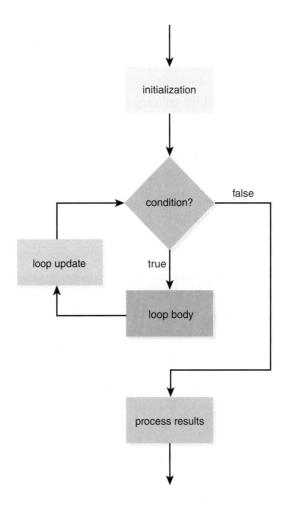

is true, the loop body is executed, followed by the loop update, then the reevaluation of the condition, and so on, until the condition is false.

The *for* loop is equivalent to the following *while* loop:

```
// initialization
while ( loop condition )
{
    // loop body
    // loop update
}
```

As we can see, *while* loops can be used for either event-driven or count-controlled loops. A *for* loop is especially useful for count-controlled loops, however. Because all the loop control is contained in the *for* loop header, we can easily see what condition will stop the loop and how the condition will be updated after each iteration.

6.10.2   Constructing _for_ Loops

Typically, we use a **loop control variable** in a _for_ loop; that control variable is usually used for counting. We set its initial value in the initialization statement, increment or decrement its value in the loop update statement, and check its value in the loop condition.

For example, if we want to find the sum of five integers, we know the loop body should execute five times—once for each integer. We set our loop control variable to 1 in the initialization statement, increment the loop control variable by 1 in the loop update statement, and check if its value is less than or equal to 5 in the loop condition. The pseudocode for this program is the following:

```
set total to 0
for i = 1 to 5 by 1
{
    read integer
    add integer to total
}
print the total
```

With a _for_ loop, we do not need to perform a priming read because the condition for exiting the loop is controlled by a counter, not by an input value.

Example 6.12 shows the _for_ loop for calculating the sum of five integers.

```
 1 /* Find the total of 5 numbers
 2     Anderson, Franceschi
 3 */
 4
 5 import java.util.Scanner;
 6
 7 public class Sum5Numbers
 8 {
 9   public static void main( String [ ] args )
10   {
11     int total = 0;    // stores the sum of the 5 numbers
12     int number;       // stores the current input
13
14     Scanner scan = new Scanner( System.in );
15
16     for ( int i = 1; i <= 5; i++ )
17     {
18       System.out.print( "Enter an integer > " );
19       number = scan.nextInt( );
20
```

```
21        total += number;  // add input to total
22      }
23
24      // process results by printing the total
25      System.out.println( "The total is " + total );
26   }
27 }
```

EXAMPLE 6.12   Finding the Sum of Five Numbers

In this example, which is a standard accumulation operation, the *for* loop initialization statement declares *i*, which will be our loop control variable. We start *i* at 1, and after each execution of the loop body, we increment *i* by 1 in the loop update statement. The loop condition checks if the value of *i* is less than or equal to 5; when *i* reaches 6, we have executed the loop body five times. Figure 6.17 shows the execution of this *for* loop.

Note that because we declare our loop counter variable *i* in the *for* loop header, we cannot reference *i* after the *for* loop ends. Thus, this code would generate a compiler error, because *i* is out of scope on line 24:

```
16      for ( int i = 1; i <= 5; i++ )
17      {
18        System.out.print( "Enter an integer > " );
19        number = scan.nextInt( );
20
21        total += number;  // add input to total
22      }
23
24      System.out.println( "The total for the " + ( i - 1 )
25                                  + " numbers is " + total ); // i is out of scope
```

Defining a new variable using the same name as a variable already in scope is invalid and generates a compiler error. However, a variable name can be reused when a previously defined variable with the same name is no longer in scope. In the code above, the scope of the variable *i* defined in line 16 is limited to the *for* loop on

Figure 6.17

Finding the Sum
of Five Integers

```
Enter an integer > 12

Enter an integer > 10

Enter an integer > 5

Enter an integer > 7

Enter an integer > 3

The total is 37
```

lines 16–22. We cannot define another variable named *i* in that *for* loop; however, as shown below, we could reuse the name *i* in a subsequent *for* loop (lines 24–29), because the first *i* is no longer in scope. In fact, programmers often reuse the variable name *i* for the counter variable in their *for* loops.

```
16      for ( int i = 1; i <= 5; i++ )
17      {
18        System.out.print( "Enter an integer > " );
19        number = scan.nextInt( );
20
21        total += number; // add input to total
22      }
23
24      for ( int i = 1; i <= 10; i++ )
25      {
26        System.out.print( "Enter integer " + i + " > " );
27        number = scan.nextInt( );
28      }
```

If we do want to refer to the loop variable after the loop ends, we can define the variable before the *for* loop, as shown in the following code:

```
15      int i;
16      for ( i = 1; i <= 5; i++ )
17      {
18        System.out.print( "Enter an integer > " );
19        number = scan.nextInt( );
20
21        total += number; // add input to total
22      }
23
24      System.out.println( "The total for " + ( i - 1 ) // i is 6
25                            + " numbers is " + total );
```

We can also increment the loop control variable by values other than 1. Example 6.13 shows a *for* loop that increments the control variable by 2 to print the even numbers from 0 to 20.

The pseudocode for this program is the following:

```
set output to an empty String
for i = 0 to 20 by 2
{
    append i and a space to the output String
}
print the output String
```

We start with an empty *String* variable, *toPrint*, and with each iteration of the loop we append the next even number and a space. When the loop completes, we output *toPrint*, which prints all numbers on one line, as shown in Figure 6.18

```
1 /* Print the even numbers from zero to twenty
2    Anderson, Franceschi
3 */
4
5 public class PrintEven
6 {
7   public static void main( String [ ] args )
8   {
9     String toPrint = ""; // initialize output String
10
11    for ( int i = 0; i <= 20; i += 2 )
12    {
13       toPrint += i + " "; // append current number and a space
14    }
15
16    System.out.println( toPrint ); // print results
17  }
18 }
```

EXAMPLE 6.13   Printing Even Numbers

Figure 6.18

Printing Even
Numbers from
0 to 20

```
0 2 4 6 8 10 12 14 16 18 20
```

In this example, we initialize the loop control variable to 0, then increment *i* by 2 in the loop update statement (i += 2) to skip the odd numbers. Notice that we used the value of the loop control variable *i* inside the loop, illustrating that the loop control variable can perform double duty such as being the counter and the data.

The loop control variable also can be used in our prompt to the user. For example, in Example 6.12 we could have prompted the user for each integer using this statement:

```
System.out.print( "Enter integer " + i + " > " );
```

Then the user's prompt would look like that shown in Figure 6.19.

```
Enter integer 1 > 23

Enter integer 2 > 12

Enter integer 3 > 10

Enter integer 4 > 11

Enter integer 5 > 15

The total is 71
```

Figure 6.19

Adding the Loop
Control Variable
to the Prompt

CODE IN ACTION

To see a step-by-step illustration of a *for* loop, look for the movie within the online resources. Click on the link to start the movie.

A *for* loop can be especially useful for processing a *String* character by character. We define the loop control variable so that it corresponds to the index of each character in the *String*. We initialize the loop control variable to 0 (the index of the first character in a *String*), increment the loop control variable by 1 in the loop update, and set the condition of the *for* loop to be that the loop control variable is less than the length of the *String*. In each iteration of the loop, we process one character of the *String* by extracting the character at the loop control variable using the *charAt* method of the *String* class.

Example 6.14 demonstrates this technique. In this example, we prompt the user for a sentence and count the number of tokens in the sentence. A token is defined as a sequence of non-white space characters delimited by one or more white space characters; that is, spaces or tabs.

To count the tokens, we look at each character in the sentence, one at a time. If a character is not a white space character, then it is part of a token. When we find a white space character, however, it is a signal that the token is complete. At that time, we increment our token count.

Tokens may be separated by more than one white space character, however, so we need to detect when we find multiple consecutive white space characters and ignore all but the first white space character. To do this, we define a *boolean* variable, called a **flag**. We set the flag to true when we see a white space character and to false when we see a non-white space character. If we find a white space character when the flag is false, it must be the first white space character. If the flag is set to true, however, we have found an extra white space character, which we should ignore.

The pseudocode for this example is

```
read a sentence
remove leading and trailing white space
if sentence is empty
      print message no tokens found
else
    set countTokens = 1
   initialize flag variable to false to indicate that the current character is not
   white space
   for i = 0 to (sentence length -1) by 1
   {
       get character at position i in sentence
       if ( character is a space or tab )
           if flag variable is false
               we have found the end of a token, so increment countTokens
               set flag variable to true to indicate that current character is
               white space
       else
           set flag variable to false to indicate that current character is not
           white space
   }
   print the number of tokens found
```

Example 6.14 shows our code. We prompt the user for a sentence using *Scanner*'s *nextLine* method, which reads all characters on the line including leading and trailing white space. We want to remove those extraneous white space characters, so we call the *trim* method of the *String* class (line 14), shown in Table 6.4, which will remove any leading and trailing white space for us.

It is possible that the user pressed the enter key without entering any characters (or only white space characters). In that case, the trimmed sentence will be empty. We check for an empty *String* on line 16, and if true, we output a message and do nothing more.

If, however, the user has entered some characters, we initialize our flag variable, *inWhiteSpace,* to *false* (line 22), because we have indeed not processed any characters and thus have not found white space.

TABLE 6.4   The *trim* Method of the *String* Class

The *trim* Method of the *String* Class	
Return value	**Method name and argument list**
String	trim( )
	returns a *String* with leading and trailing white space characters removed

We detect tokens by finding the white space following the token, but when we finish processing the sentence, the last character will not be white space because we trimmed the sentence. Thus we will have one more token than the number of times we found white space. To account for that last token, we initialize our *tokenCount* variable to 1 (line 23).

Now we are ready for our *for* loop (lines 25–41), which processes each character in the sentence looking for white space and counting tokens. As mentioned, the loop control variable, *i*, corresponds to the index of the current character being processed. We initialize *i* to 0, the first index of the *String*; increment *i* by 1 in the loop update; and check that *i* is less than *sentence.length( )* in the loop condition (line 25). We extract the character at *i* using the *charAt* method (line 27).

In line 28, we check whether the current character is a space or a tab. If so, we have detected white space. If the flag is not set to *true* (line 30), then this is the first white space character in a possible sequence of white space characters, and we count the token, then set the flag to *true* so that we ignore any succeeding white space characters (lines 32–33). If the current character is not white space, we set the flag to *false* to indicate that we are inside a token (line 38).

When the loop ends, we print a message with the token count (lines 42–43). Figure 6.20 shows the output when the user enters a sentence with six tokens separated by spaces and a tab character.

```
 1 /* Count tokens in a sentence
 2 *  Anderson, Franceschi
 3 */
 4
 5 import java.util.Scanner;
 6 public class CountTokens
 7 {
 8   public static void main( String [ ] args )
 9   {
10       Scanner scan = new Scanner( System.in );
11
12       System.out.println( "Enter a sentence:" );
13       String sentence = scan.nextLine( );
14       sentence = sentence.trim( ); // remove leading/trailing white space
15
16       if ( sentence.length( ) == 0 )
17       {
18           System.out.println( "The sentence is empty." );
19       }
20       else
21       {
22               boolean inWhiteSpace = false;
```

```
23            int countTokens = 1;
24
25            for ( int i = 0; i < sentence.length( ); i++ )
26            {
27               char c = sentence.charAt( i );
28               if ( c == ' ' || c == '\t' )
29               {
30                  if ( ! inWhiteSpace )
31                  {
32                      countTokens++;
33                      inWhiteSpace = true;
34                  }
35               }
36               else // not a white space character
37               {
38                  inWhiteSpace = false;
39               }
40
41            }
42            System.out.println( "The sentence contains " + countTokens
43                          + ( countTokens == 1 ? " token." : " tokens." ) );
44       }
45   }
46 }
```

EXAMPLE 6.14   Counting Tokens

We can also decrement the loop control variable. Example 6.15 shows an application that reads a sentence entered by the user and prints the sentence backward.

The pseudocode for this program is the following:

```
set backwards to an empty String
read a sentence

for i = ( length of sentence – 1 ) to 0 by –1
{
   get character at position i in sentence
   append character to backwards
}
print backwards
```

Figure 6.20

Output from
Example 6.14

```
Enter a sentence:

Programming is not a spectator     sport!

The sentence contains 6 tokens.
```

To print a sentence backward, we treat the sentence, a *String*, like a stream of characters; each iteration of the loop extracts and processes one character from the *String*, using the *charAt* method of the *String* class. Line 12 declares a *String*, *backwards* (initialized as an empty *String*), to hold the reverse of the user's sentence. Lines 14–15 prompt the user for a sentence. Lines 17 through 20 make up the *for* loop, whose purpose is to copy the original sentence into the *String backwards* with its characters in reverse order. We do this by starting the copying at the last character in the *original String* and moving backward one character at a time until we have copied the first character. Thus, we initialize our loop variable to the position of the last character in *original* (original.length( ) − 1) and extract one character at a time, appending it to *backwards*. The loop update statement (i−−) moves the loop variable backward by one position, and our loop condition (i >= 0) checks whether we have reached the beginning of the *String original*. Figure 6.21 shows the execution of the program with the user entering the sentence, "*Programming is not a spectator sport!*"

```java
1  /* Print a sentence backwards
2     Anderson, Franceschi
3  */
4  import java.util.Scanner;
5
6  public class Backwards
7  {
8    public static void main( String [ ] args )
9    {
10     Scanner scan = new Scanner( System.in );
11
12     String backwards = "";
13
14     System.out.println( "Enter a sentence:" );
15     String original = scan.nextLine( );
16
17     for ( int i = original.length( ) - 1; i >= 0; i-- )
18     {
19         backwards += original.charAt( i );
20     }
21
22     System.out.println( "The sentence backwards is: \n" + backwards );
23   }
24 }
```

EXAMPLE 6.15   Printing a Sentence Backwards

Figure 6.21

Printing a
Sentence
Backward

```
Enter a sentence:
Programming is not a spectator sport!
The sentence backwards is:
!trops rotatceps a ton si gnimmargorP
```

We can display some interesting graphics using *for* loops. The graphical application in Example 6.16 draws the bull's-eye target shown in Figure 6.22. To make the bull's-eye target, we draw 12 concentric circles (circles that have the same center point), beginning with the largest circle and successively drawing a smaller circle on top of the circles already drawn. Thus, the bull's-eye target circles have the same center point, but different diameters. The pseudocode for this program is

```
for diameter = 300 to 25 by -25
{
    draw the circle with current diameter
    if color is black
        set color to red
    else
        set color to black
}
```

Translating the pseudocode into Java, we get the code shown in Example 6.16.

```
 1 /* Bull's-eye Target
 2    Anderson, Franceschi
 3 */
 4
 5 import javafx.application.Application;
 6 import javafx.scene.canvas.Canvas;
 7 import javafx.scene.canvas.GraphicsContext;
 8 import javafx.scene.paint.Color;
 9 import javafx.stage.Stage;
10
11 public class BullsEye extends Application
12 {
13
14     @Override
15     public void start( Stage stage )
16     {
17         // set up window title and size
18         GraphicsContext gc = JIGraphicsUtility.setUpGraphics(
19                 stage, "Bull's Eye", 700, 400 );
20
21         // center of the bull's eye
22         final int CENTER_X = 350, CENTER_Y = 200;
```

```
23
24          // start and end diameter, amount to decrease diameter
25          final int START_DIAMETER = 300, END_DIAMETER = 25,
26                  DECREMENT = 25;
27
28          // color of first circle
29          Color toggleColor = Color.BLACK;
30          gc.setFill( toggleColor );
31
32          for ( int diameter = START_DIAMETER; diameter >= END_DIAMETER;
33                  diameter -= DECREMENT )
34          {
35            // draw circle with current diameter value
36            gc.fillOval( CENTER_X - diameter / 2, CENTER_Y - diameter / 2,
37                      diameter, diameter );
38            // switch color
39            if ( toggleColor.equals( Color.BLACK ) )
40                  toggleColor = Color.RED;
41            else
42                  toggleColor = Color.BLACK;
43
44            gc.setFill( toggleColor );
45
46          }
47      }
48
49      public static void main( String [ ] args )
50      {
51          launch( args );
52      }
53 }
```

EXAMPLE 6.16   Drawing a Bull's Eye

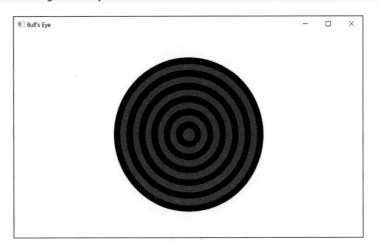

Figure 6.22

Drawing a Bull's-Eye

Our *for* loop initialization statement in lines 32–33 sets up the diameter of the largest circle as 300 pixels and the loop update statement decreases the diameter of each circle by 25 pixels. The smallest circle we want to draw should have a diameter of 25 pixels, so we set the loop condition to check that the diameter is greater than or equal to 25. We need to start with the largest circle rather than the smallest circle so that new circles we draw don't hide the previously drawn circles.

Drawing the bull's-eye target circles illustrates two common programming techniques: conversion between units and a toggle variable.

We need to convert between units because the *fillOval* method of the *GraphicsContext* class takes as its arguments the upper-left (*x, y*) coordinate and the width and height of the circle's bounding rectangle. However, all our circles have the same center point, but not the same upper-left *x* and *y* coordinates. Given the diameter and the center point of the circle, however, we can calculate the (*x, y*) coordinate of the upper-left corner. Figure 6.23 shows how we make the conversion.

The difference between the center point and the upper-left corner of the bounding rectangle is the radius of the circle, which is half of the diameter (`diameter / 2`). So, the upper-left *x* value is the *x* value of the center point minus half the diameter (`centerX - diameter / 2`). Similarly, the upper-left *y* value is the *y* value of the center point minus half the diameter (`centerY - diameter / 2`).

Figure 6.23

Drawing a Bull's-Eye

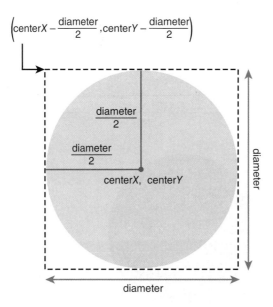

Thus, we draw each circle using the following statement:

```
gc.fillOval ( centerX - diameter / 2,
              centerY - diameter / 2,
              diameter, diameter );
```

To alternate between red and black circles, we use a **toggle variable**, which is a variable whose value alternates between two values. We use a *Color* object for our toggle variable, *toggleColor*, and initialize it to *Color.BLACK*. After drawing each circle, we switch the color (lines 38–42). If the current color is black, we set it to red; otherwise, the color must be red, so we set the color to black.

SOFTWARE ENGINEERING TIP
Use a toggle variable when you need to alternate between two values.

6.10.3 Testing Techniques for *for* Loops

One of the most important tests for *for* loops is that the starting and ending values of the loop variable are set correctly. For example, to execute a *for* loop five times, we could set the initial value of the loop variable to 0 and use the condition ($i < 5$), or

Skill Practice
with these end-of-chapter questions

we could set the initial value of the loop variable to 1 and use the condition (i <= 5). Either of these *for* loop headers will cause the loop to execute five times.

```
for ( int i = 0; i < 5; i++ ) // executes 5 times
```

or

```
for ( int i = 1; i <= 5; i++ ) // executes 5 times
```

However, the following *for* loop header is incorrect; the loop will execute only four times.

```
for ( int i = 1; i < 5; i++ ) // INCORRECT! executes only 4 times
```

Thus, to test the *for* loop in Example 6.12 that prompts for five integers, we need to verify that the program outputs exactly five prompts. To test that we are prompting the user five times, we can enter the integers 1, 2, 3, 4, and 5 at the prompts. Another option, shown in Figure 6.24, is to append a number to the prompt, which does double duty. Besides keeping the user informed of the number of integers entered so far, it also helps to verify that we have the correct number of prompts.

Like *while* loops, the body of a *for* loop may not be executed at all. If the loop condition is *false* the first time it is tested, the body of the *for* loop is skipped. Thus, when testing, we want to simulate input that would cause the loop condition to be *false* when the *for* loop statement is first encountered. For example, in the *Backwards* class in Example 6.15, we need to test the *for* loop with an empty sentence. In other words, when the prompt appears to enter a sentence, we simply press the Enter key. If we try this, we will find that the application still works, as Figure 6.25 shows.

Figure 6.24

Counting Five Prompts

```
Enter integer 1 > 23

Enter integer 2 > 12

Enter integer 3 > 10

Enter integer 4 > 11

Enter integer 5 > 15

The total is 71
```

Figure 6.25

The *Backwards* Class with an Empty Sentence

```
Enter a sentence:

The sentence backwards is
```

The program works correctly with an empty sentence because the *for* loop initialization statement is

```
int i = original.length( ) - 1;
```

Because the length of an empty *String* is 0, this statement sets *i* to –1. The loop condition (`i >= 0`) is immediately *false*, so the loop body is never executed. The flow of control skips to the statement following the loop,

```
System.out.println( "The sentence backwards is: \n" + backwards );
```

which prints an empty *String*. Although it would be more user friendly to check whether the sentence is empty and print a message to that effect, the program does indeed "do exactly nothing, gracefully."

6.11   Nested Loops

Loops can be nested inside other loops; that is, the body of one loop can contain another loop. For example, a *while* loop can be nested inside another *while loop* or a *for* loop can be nested inside another *for* loop. In fact, the nested loops do not need to be the same loop type; that is, a *for* loop can be nested inside a *while* loop, and a *while* loop can be nested inside a *for* loop.

Nested loops may be useful if we are performing multiple operations, each of which has its own count or sentinel value. Going back to Jane, our grocery cashier, her workday can be modeled using nested loops. In Programming Activity 1, we wrote the code for our cashier to calculate the total cost of the contents of one customer's grocery cart. But cashiers check out multiple customers, one after another. While the line of people in front of the cashier is not empty, she will help the next customer. For each customer, she will set the total order to $0.00 and start scanning items and add the prices to the total. While the current customer still has items in the cart, Jane will scan the next item. When Jane finishes processing a customer's cart, she will check to see if there is a customer waiting in line. If there is one, she will set the total to $0.00 and start scanning the next customer's items.

Thus, the cashier's job can be described using a *while* loop nested inside another *while* loop. The pseudocode for these nested loops is shown here:

```
look for a customer
while there is a customer in line
{
  set total to $0.00
  reach for first item
  while item is not the divider bar
  {
```

```
          add price to total
          reach for next item
   }
   // if we get here, the item is the divider bar
   output the total price

   look for another customer
}
```

The important point to understand with nested loops is that the inner (or nested) loop executes completely (executes all its iterations) for each single iteration of the outer loop.

Let's look at a simple example that uses nested *for* loops. Suppose we want to print five rows of numbers as shown here:

```
1
1 2
1 2 3
1 2 3 4
1 2 3 4 5
```

We can see a pattern here. In the first line, we print one number; in the second line, we print two numbers, and so on. In other words, the quantity of numbers we print and the line number are the same. The pseudocode for this pattern is the following:

```
for line = 1 to 5 by 1
{
    for number = 1 to line by 1
    {
      print number and a space
    }
    print a new line
}
```

Translating this pseudocode into nested *for* loops, we get the code shown in Example 6.17.

```
1 /*  Printing numbers using nested for loops
2      Anderson, Franceschi
3 */
4
5 public class NestedForLoops
6 {
7   public static void main( String [ ] args )
```

```
 8   {
 9       // outer for loop prints 5 lines
10       for ( int line = 1; line <= 5; line++ )
11       {
12         // inner for loop prints one line
13         for ( int number = 1; number <= line; number++ )
14         {
15           // print the number and a space
16           System.out.print( number + " " );
17         }
18
19         System.out.println( ); // print a newline
20       }
21   }
22 }
```

EXAMPLE 6.17   Nested *for* Loops

Notice that the inner *for* loop (lines 12–17) uses the value of *line*, which is set by the outer *for* loop (lines 9–20). Thus, for the first iteration of the outer loop, *line* equals 1, so the inner loop executes once, printing the number 1 and a space. Then we print a newline character because line 19 is part of the outer *for* loop. The outer loop then sets the value of *line* to 2, and the inner loop starts again at 1 and executes two times (until *number* equals the line number in the outer loop). Then we again print a newline. This operation continues until the *line* exceeds 5, when the outer loop terminates. The output from Example 6.17 is shown in Figure 6.26.

Note that we needed to use different names for our *for* loop control variables. The loop control variable *line* is in scope from lines 10 to 20, which includes the inner *for* loop.

Let's look at another example of a nested loop. We'll let the user enter positive integers, with a 0 being the sentinel value. For each number, we'll find all its factors; that is, we will find all the integers that are evenly divisible into the number, except 1 and the number itself.

If a number is evenly divisible by another, the remainder after division will be 0. The modulus operator (%) will be useful here, because it calculates the remainder after

```
1

1 2

1 2 3

1 2 3 4

1 2 3 4 5
```

Figure 6.26

Output from Example 6.17

integer division. Thus, to find all the factors of a number, we can test all integers from 1 up to the number to see if the remainder after division is 0. But let's think about whether that's a good approach. The number 1 will be a factor for every number, because every number is evenly divisible by 1. So we can test integers beginning at 2. Then, because 2 is the smallest factor, there's no need to test integers higher than *number* / 2. Thus, our range of integers to test will be from 2 to *number* / 2.

For this example, we'll use a *for* loop nested inside a *while* loop. The pseudocode for this example is

```
read first number // priming read
while number is not 0
{
    print "The factors for number are "
    for factor = 2 to ( number / 2 ) by 1
    {
      if number % factor is 0
          print factor and a space
    }
    print a new line

    read next number // update read
}
```

But what happens if we don't find any factors for a number? In that case, the number is a prime number. We can detect this condition by using a *boolean* flag variable. We set the flag to *false* before starting the *for* loop that checks for factors. Inside the *for* loop, we set the flag to *true* when we find a factor. In other words, we signal (or flag) the fact that we found a factor. Then, after the *for* loop terminates, we check the value of the flag. If it is still *false*, we did not find any factors and the number is prime. Our pseudocode for this program now becomes

```
read first number // priming read
while number is not 0
{
    print "The factors for number are "
    set flag to false
    for factor = 2 to ( number / 2 ) by 1
    {
        if number % factor is 0
        {
            print factor and a space
```

```
          set flag to true
        }
    }
  if flag is false
      print "number is prime"

  print a new line

  read next number // update read
}
```

Since we want to read positive numbers only, the lines "read first number" and "read next number" in the preceding pseudocode will actually be more complex than a simple statement. Indeed, we will prompt the user to enter a positive number until the user does so. In order to do that, we will use a *do/while* loop to validate the input from the user. Therefore, inside the *while* loop, we nest not only a *for* loop, but also a *do/while* loop. In the interest of keeping the pseudocode simple, we did not show that *do/while* loop. However, it is included in the code in Example 6.18 at lines 17–23 and 45–51.

Translating this pseudocode into Java, we get the code shown in Example 6.18; the output of a sample run of the program is shown in Figure 6.27.

```
1  /* Factors of integers
2      with checks for primes
3      Anderson, Franceschi
4  */
5  import java.util.Scanner;
6
7  public class Factors
8  {
9    public static void main( String [ ] args )
10   {
11     int number; // positive integer entered by user
12     final int SENTINEL = 0;
13     boolean factorsFound; // flag signals whether factors are found
14
15     Scanner scan = new Scanner( System.in );
16
17     // priming read
18     do
19     {
20       System.out.print( "Enter a positive integer "
21                           + "or 0 to exit > " );
22       number = scan.nextInt( );
```

```
23      } while ( number < 0 );
24
25      while ( number != SENTINEL )
26      {
27        System.out.print( "Factors of " + number + ": " );
28        factorsFound = false; // reset flag to no factors
29
30        for ( int factor = 2; factor <= number / 2; factor++ )
31        {
32          if ( number % factor == 0 )
33          {
34              System.out.print( factor + " " );
35              factorsFound = true;
36          }
37        } // end of for loop
38
39        if ( ! factorsFound )
40            System.out.print( "none, " + number + " is prime" );
41
42        System.out.println( ); // print a newline
43        System.out.println( ); // skip a line
44
45        // read next number
46        do
47        {
48            System.out.print( "Enter a positive integer "
49                                + "or 0 to exit > " );
50            number = scan.nextInt( );
51        } while ( number < 0 );
52      } // end of while loop
53  }
54 }
```

EXAMPLE 6.18   Finding Factors

Figure 6.27

Output of Finding
Factors

```
Enter a positive integer or 0 to exit > 100
Factors of 100: 2 4 5 10 20 25 50

Enter a positive integer or 0 to exit > 25
Factors of 25: 5

Enter a positive integer or 0 to exit > 21
Factors of 21: 3 7

Enter a positive integer or 0 to exit > 13
Factors of 13: none, 13 is prime

Enter a positive integer or 0 to exit > 0
```

6.12   Programming Activity 2: Using *for* Loops

In this activity, you will write a *for* loop:

For this Programming Activity, you will again calculate the total cost of the items in a grocery cart. This time, however, you will write the program for the Express Lane. In this lane, the customer is allowed up to 10 items. The user will be asked for the number of items in the grocery cart. Your job is to write a *for* loop to calculate the total cost of the items in the cart.

Like Programming Activity 1, the framework will animate your *for* loop, displaying the items in the cart moving down a conveyor belt toward a cashier station (a grocery bag). It will also display the unit price of the item, the correct subtotal, and your current subtotal. By comparing the correct subtotal to your subtotal, you will be able to check whether your code is calculating the correct value.

Figure 6.28 demonstrates the animation. The cart contains five items. The third item, a carton of milk, is being scanned at a unit price of $2.00, bringing the correct subtotal for the cart to $9.00.

Instructions

Copy the files in this chapter's Programming Activity 2 folder in the source code provided with this text to a folder on your computer. Searching for five stars (*****) in the *CashierDrawing.java* code will show you where to add your code. You will add your code inside the *checkout* method of the *CashierDrawing* class (the method header for the *checkout* method has already been coded for you). Example 6.19 shows a fragment of the *CashierDrawing* class, where you will add your code:

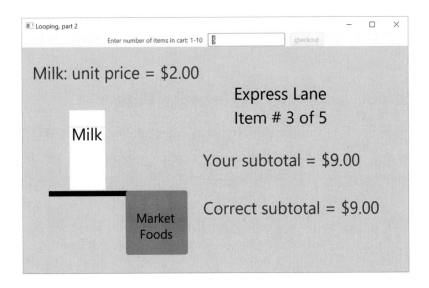

Figure 6.28

Sample Animation

```java
public void checkout( int numberOfItems )
{
    /* ***** Student writes the body of this method ***** */
    //
    //  The parameter of this method, numberOfItems,
    //  represents the number of items in the cart. The
    //  user will be prompted for this number.
    //
    //  Using a for loop, calculate the total price
    //  of the groceries in the cart.
    //
    //  The getNext method (in this CashierDrawing class) returns the next
    //   item in the cart, which is an Item object (we do not
    //   know which item will be returned; this is randomly generated).
    //   getNext does not take any arguments. Its API is
    //       Item getNext( )
    //
    // As the last statement of the body of your for loop,
    // you should call the animate method.
    // The animate method takes one argument a double,
    // which is your current subtotal.
    // For example, if the name of your variable representing
    // the current subtotal is total, your call to the animate
    // method should be:
    //     animate( total );
    //
    // The getPrice method of the Item class
    // returns the price of the Item object as a double.
    // The getPrice method does not take any arguments. Its API is
    // double getPrice( )
    //
    //  End of student code
    //
    //
}
```

EXAMPLE 6.19   The *checkout* Method in the *CashierDrawing* Class

To write the body of your *for* loop, you can use the following methods:

- You can access items in the cart using the *getNext* method of the *CashierDrawing* class, which has the following API:

  ```java
  Item getNext( )
  ```

  The *getNext* method returns an *Item* object, which represents an *Item* in the cart. As you can see, the *getNext* method does not take any arguments.

Since we call the method *getNext* from inside the *CashierDrawing* class, we can simply call the method without an object reference. For example, a call to *getNext* could look like the following:

```
Item newItem;
newItem = getNext( );
```

■ After you get a new *Item*, you can "scan" the item to get its price by calling the *getPrice* method of the *Item* class. The *getPrice* method has this API:

```
double getPrice( )
```

Thus, you would get the next item, then get its price using code like the following:

```
Item newItem;
double price;
newItem = getNext( );
price = newItem.getPrice( );
```

When you have finished writing the code for the *checkout* method, compile *CashierDrawing.java* and run the application from the *CashierApplication* class. When the application finishes executing, verify that your code is correct by:

■ checking that your subtotal matches the correct subtotal displayed

■ checking that you have processed all the items in the cart by verifying that the current item number matches the total number of items. For example, if the cart has five items, check that the message in the top right of the screen displays: `Item # 5 of 5`.

Troubleshooting

If your method implementation does not animate or animates incorrectly, check these items:

■ Verify that you have correctly coded the header of your *for* loop.

■ Verify that you have correctly coded the body of the loop.

? DISCUSSION QUESTIONS

1. **Explain why a *for* loop is appropriate for this activity.**

2. **Explain how you set up your *for* loop; that is, what initialization statement did you use, what was your condition, and what was the loop update statement?**

CHAPTER REVIEW

6.13 Chapter Summary

- Looping repeats a set of operations for each input item while a condition is *true*.

- The *while* loop is especially useful for event-controlled looping. The *while* loop executes a set of operations in the loop body as long as the loop condition is *true*. Each execution of the loop body is an iteration of the loop.

- If the loop condition evaluates to *false* the first time it is evaluated, the body of the *while* loop is never executed.

- If the loop condition never evaluates to *false*, the result is an infinite loop.

- In event-controlled looping, processing of items continues until the end of input is signaled either by a sentinel value or by reaching the end of the file.

- A sentinel value is a special input value that signals the end of the items to be processed. With a sentinel value, we perform a priming read before the *while* loop. The body of the loop processes the input, then performs an update read of the next data item.

- When reading data from an input file, we can test whether we have reached the end of the file by calling a *hasNext* method of the *Scanner* class.

- In the accumulation programming technique, we initialize a total variable to 0 before starting the loop. In the loop body, we add each input value to the total. When the loop completes, the current total is the total for all processed input values.

- In the counting programming technique, we initialize a count variable to 0 before starting the loop. In the loop body, we increment the count variable for each input value that meets our criteria. When the loop completes, the count variable contains the number of items that met our criteria.

- To find an average, we combine accumulation and counting. We add input values to the total and increment the count. When the loop completes, we calculate the average by dividing the total by the count. Before computing the average, however, we should verify that the divisor (that is, the count) is not 0.

- To find the maximum or minimum values in a set of input, we assign the first input to a running maximum or minimum. In the loop body, we compare each input value to our running maximum or minimum. If the input value is less than the running minimum, we assign the input value to the running minimum. Similarly, if the input value is greater than the running maximum, we assign the input value to the running maximum. When the loop completes, the running value is the maximum or minimum value of all the input values.

- To avoid generating exceptions when the user types characters other than the data type expected, use the *hasNext* methods of the *Scanner* class.

- To construct a loop condition, construct the inverse of the loop termination condition.

- When testing a program that contains a loop, test that the program produces correct results by inputting values and comparing the results with manual calculations. Also test that the results are correct if the loop body never executes. Finally, test the results with input that is invalid.

- The *do/while* loop checks the loop condition after executing the loop body. Thus, the body of a *do/while* loop always executes at least once. This type of loop is useful for validating input.

- The *for* loop is useful for count-controlled loops, that is, loops for which the number of iterations is known when the loop begins.

- When the *for* loop is encountered, the initialization statement is executed. Then the loop condition is evaluated. If the condition is *true*, the loop body is executed. The loop update statement is then executed and the loop condition is reevaluated. Again, if the condition is *true*, the loop body is executed, followed by the loop update, then the reevaluation of the condition, and so on, until the condition evaluates to *false*.

- Typically, we use a loop control variable in a *for* loop. We set its initial value in the initialization statement, increment or decrement its value in the loop update statement, and check its value in the loop condition.

- The loop update statement can increment or decrement the loop variable by any value.

- In a *for* loop, it is important to test that the starting and ending values of the loop variable are correct. Also test with input for which the *for* loop body does not execute at all.

6.14 Exercises, Problems, and Projects

6.14.1 Multiple Choice Exercises

1 How do you discover that you have an infinite loop in your code?

❑ The code does not compile.

❏ The code compiles and runs but gives the wrong result.

❏ The code runs forever.

❏ The code compiles, but there is a run-time error.

2 If you want to execute a loop body at least once, what type of loop would you use?

❏ *for* loop

❏ *while* loop

❏ *do/while* loop

❏ none of the above

3 What best describes a *for* loop?

❏ It is a count-controlled loop.

❏ It is an event-controlled loop.

❏ It is a sentinel-controlled loop.

4 You can simulate a *for* loop with a *while* loop.

❏ true

❏ false

6.14.2   Reading and Understanding Code

5. What is the output of this code sequence? (The user successively enters 3, 5, and –1.)

```
System.out.print( "Enter an int > " );
int i = scan.nextInt( );
while ( i != -1 )
{
    System.out.println( "Hello" );

    System.out.print( "Enter an int > " );
    i = scan.nextInt( );
}
```

6. What is the output of this code sequence? (The user successively enters 3, 5, and –1.)

```
int i = 0;
while ( i != -1 )
{
```

```
        System.out.println( "Hello" );
        System.out.print( "Enter an int > " );
        i = scan.nextInt( );
    }
```

7. What is the output of this code sequence? (The user successively enters 3, 5, and –1.)

```
System.out.print( "Enter an int > " );
int i = scan.nextInt( );
while ( i != -1 )
{
    System.out.print( "Enter an int > " );
    i = scan.nextInt( );

    System.out.println( "Hello" );
}
```

8. What are the values of i and *sum* after this code sequence is executed?

```
int sum = 0;
int i = 17;
while ( i % 10 != 0 )
{
    sum += i;
    i++;
}
```

9. What are the values of i and *product* after this code sequence is executed?

```
int i = 6;
int product = 1;
do
{
    product *= i;
    i++;
} while ( i < 9 );
```

10. What are the values of i and *product* after this code sequence is executed?

```
int i = 6;
int product = 1;
do
{
    product *= i;
    i++;
} while ( product < 9 );
```

11. What is the output of this code sequence?

```
for ( int i = 0; i < 3; i++ )
    System.out.println( "Hello" );
System.out.println( "Done" );
```

12. What is the output of this code sequence?

```
for ( int i = 0; i <= 2; i++ )
    System.out.println( "Hello" );
System.out.println( "Done" );
```

13. What is the value of *i* after this code sequence is executed?

```
int i = 0;
for ( i = 0; i <= 2; i++ )
    System.out.println( "Hello" );
```

14. What is the value of *i* after this code sequence is executed?

```
int i = 0;
for ( i = 0; i < 2034; i++ )
    System.out.println( "Hello" );
```

15. What are the values of *i* and *sum* after this code sequence is executed?

```
int i = 0;
int sum = 0;
for ( i = 0; i < 5; i++ )
{
  sum += i;
}
```

16. What are the values of *i* and *sum* after this code sequence is executed?

```
int i = 0;
int sum = 0;
for ( i = 0; i < 40; i++ )
{
    if ( i % 10 == 0 )
        sum += i;
}
```

17. What is the value of *sum* after this code sequence is executed?

```
int sum = 0;
for ( int i = 1; i < 10; i++ )
{
    i++;
    sum += i;
}
```

18. What is the value of *sum* after this code sequence is executed?

```
int sum = 0;
for ( int i = 10; i > 5; i-- )
{
    sum += i;
}
```

19. What is printed when this code sequence is executed?

```
for ( int i = 0; i < 5; i++ )
{
    System.out.println( Math.max( i, 3 ) );
}
```

20. What are the values of *i* and *sum* after this code sequence is executed?

```
int i = 0;
int sum = 0;
while ( i != 7 )
{
    sum += i;
    i++;
}
```

6.14.3   Fill In the Code

21. This *while* loop generates random integers between 3 and 7 until a 5 is generated and prints all the random integers, excluding 5.

```
Random random = new Random( );
int i = random.nextInt( 5 ) + 3;
```

22. This *while* loop takes an integer input from the user, then prompts for additional integers and prints all integers that are greater than or equal to the original input until the user enters 20, which is not printed.

```
System.out.print( "Enter a starting integer > " );
int start = scan.nextInt( );
// your code goes here
```

23. This *while* loop takes integer values as input from the user and finds the sum of those integers until the user types in the value –1 (which is not added).

```
System.out.print( "Enter an integer value, "
                  + "enter -1 to stop > " );
int value = scan.nextInt( );
// your code goes here
```

24. This loop calculates the sum of the first four positive multiples of 7 using a *while* loop (the sum will be equal to $7 + 14 + 21 + 28 = 70$).

```
int sum = 0;
int countMultiplesOf7 = 0;
int count = 1;
// your code goes here
```

25. This loop takes words as input from the user and concatenates them until the user types in the word "end" (which is not concatenated). The code then outputs the concatenated *String*.

```
String sentence = "";
String word;
// your code goes here

while ( ! word.equals( "end" ) )
{
   //  and your code goes here

}
System.out.println( "The sentence is " + sentence );
```

26. This loop reads integers from a file (already associated with the *Scanner* object reference *file*) and computes the sum. We don't know how many integers are in the file.

```
int sum = 0;
// your code goes here
```

27. Here is a *while* loop; write the equivalent *for* loop.

```
int i = 0;
while ( i < 5 )
{
    System.out.println( "Hi there" );
    i++;
}

// your code goes here
```

28. This loop reads integers from the user until the user enters either 0 or 100. Then it prints the sum of the numbers entered (excluding the 0 or 100).

```
// your code goes here
```

29. This loop calculates the sum of the integers from 1 to 5 using a *for* loop.

```
int sum = 0;
// your code goes here
```

6.14.4   Identifying Errors in Code

30. Where is the problem with this code sequence (although this code sequence does compile)?

```
int i = 0;
while ( i < 3 )
    System.out.println( "Hello" );
```

31. Where is the error in this code sequence that is supposed to read and echo integers until the user enters –1?

```
int num;
while ( num != -1 )
{
    System.out.print( "Enter an integer > " );
    num = scan.nextInt( );
    System.out.println( num );
}
```

32. The following code sequence intends to print *Hello* three times; however, it prints *Hello* only once. Where is the problem in this code sequence?

```
for ( int i = 0; i < 3; i++ );
    System.out.println( "Hello" );
```

33. Where is the error in this code sequence, which is intended to print *Hello* 10 times?

```
for ( int i = 10; i > 0; i++ )
    System.out.println( "Hello" );
```

34. Where is the problem with this code sequence? The code is intended to generate random numbers between 1 and 10 until the number is either a 7 or a 5.

```
Random random = new Random( );
int number = 1 + random.nextInt( 10 );
while ( number != 5 || number != 7 )
{
    number = 1 + random.nextInt( 10 );
}
System.out.println( "The number is " + number );
```

35. Where is the error with this code sequence?

```
int sum = 0;
for ( int i = 1; i < 6; i++ )
    sum += i;

System.out.println( "The value of i is " + i );
```

6.14.5   Debugging Area—Using Messages from the Java Compiler and Java JVM

36. You coded the following in the class *Test.java*:

```
int i = 0;
int sum = 0;
do
{
    sum += i;
    i++;
} while ( i < 3 ) // line 11
```

At compile time, you get the following error:

```
Test.java:11: error: ';' expected
while( i < 3 ) // line 11
     ^

1 error
```

Explain what the problem is and how to fix it.

37. You coded the following in the class *Test.java*:

```
int i = 0;
while ( i < 3 )
{
   System.out.println( "Hello" );
   i--;
}
```

The code compiles but never terminates.
Explain what the problem is and how to fix it.

38. You coded the following in the class *Test.java*:

```
for ( int i = 0; i++; i < 3 ) // line 5
   System.out.println( "Hello" );
```

At compile time, you get the following error:

```
Test.java:5: error: not a statement
for ( int i = 0; i++; i < 3 ) // line 5
                      ^

1 error
```

Explain what the problem is and how to fix it.

39. You coded the following in the class *Test.java*:

```
for ( int i = 1; i < 3; i++ ) // line 5
   System.out.println( "Hello" );
```

The code compiles and runs, but prints *Hello* only twice, whereas we expected to print *Hello* three times.

Explain what the problem is and how to fix it.

40. You coded the following in the class *Test.java*:

```
int product = 1;
for ( int i = 1, i < 5, i++ ) // line 8
    product *= i;
System.out.println( "Product is " + product );        // line 10
```

At compile time, you get the following errors:

```
Test.java:8: error: ';' expected
    for ( int i = 1, i < 5, i++ ) // line 8
                   ^

Test.java:8: error: illegal start of type
    for ( int i = 1, i < 5, i++ )          // line 8
                   ^

2 errors
```

Explain what the problem is and how to fix it.

41. You coded the following in the class *Test.java*:

```
for ( int i = 0; i < 3; i++ )
    System.out.println( "Hello" );
System.out.println( "i = " + i ); // line 8
```

At compile time, you get the following error:

```
Test.java:8: error: cannot find symbol
        System.out.println( "i = " + i ); // line 8
                                     ^

symbol : variable i
location: class Test
1 error
```

Explain what the problem is and how to fix it.

42. You coded the following in the class *Test.java*:

```
int i = 0;
for ( int i = 0; i < 3; i++ ) // line 6
    System.out.println( "Hello" );
```

At compile time, you get the following error:

```
Test.java:6: error: variable i is already defined in main( String[] )
    for( int i = 0; i < 3; i++ )        // line 6
             ^
```

```
1 error
```

Explain what the problem is and how to fix it.

6.14.6   Write a Short Program

43. Write a program that prompts the user for a value greater than 10 as an input (you should loop until the user enters a valid value) and finds the square root of that number and the square root of the result, and continues to find the square root of the result until you reach a number that is smaller than 1.01. The program should output how many times the square root operation was performed.

44. Write a program that expects a word containing the @ character as an input. If the word does not contain an @ character, then your program should keep prompting the user for a word. When the user types in a word containing an @ character, the program should simply print the word and terminate.

45. Write a program that reads *double* values from a file named *input.txt* and outputs the average.

46. Write a program that uses a *for* loop to output the sum of all the integers between 10 and 20, inclusive, that is, $10 + 11 + 12 + \ldots + 19 + 20$.

47. Write a program that uses a *for* loop to output the product of all the integers between 3 and 7, inclusive, that is, $3 * 4 * 5 * 6 * 7$.

48. Write a program that uses a *for* loop to count how many multiples of 7 are between 33 and 97, inclusive.

49. Write a program that reads a value (say *n*) from the user and outputs *Hello World n* times. Verify that the user has entered an integer. If the input is 3, the output will be *Hello World* printed three times.

50. Write a program that takes a word as an input from the keyboard and outputs each character in the word, separated by a space.

51. Write a program that takes a value as an input from the keyboard and outputs the factorial of that number; the factorial of an integer *n* is

    $n * (n - 1) * (n - 2) * \ldots * 3 * 2 * 1$. For instance, the factorial of 4 is

    $4 * 3 * 2 * 1$, or 24.

52. Using a loop, write a program that takes 10 integer values from the keyboard and outputs the minimum value of all the values entered.

53. Alter Example 6.14 that counts the tokens in a sentence so that it prints each token and counts the number of tokens.

6.14.7   Programming Projects

54. Write a program that inputs a word representing a binary number (0s and 1s). First, your program should verify that it is indeed a binary number, that is, the number contains only 0s and 1s. If that is not the case, your program should print a message that the number is not a valid binary number. Then, your program should count how many 1s are in that word and output the count.

55. Perform the same operations as Question 54, with the following modification: If the word does not represent a valid binary number, the program should keep prompting the user for a new word until a word representing a valid binary number is input by the user.

56. Write a program that inputs a word representing a binary number (0s and 1s). First, your program should check that it is indeed a binary number, that is, the number contains only 0s and 1s. If that is not the case, your program should output that the number is not a valid binary number. If that word contains exactly two 1s, your program should output that that word is "accepted," otherwise that it is "rejected."

57. Perform the same operations as Question 56, with the following modification: If the word does not represent a valid binary number, the program should keep prompting the user for a new word until a word representing a valid binary number is input by the user.

58. Write a program that inputs a word representing a binary number (0s and 1s). First, your program should check that it is indeed a binary number, that is, that it contains only 0s and 1s. If that is not the case, your program should output that the number is not a valid binary number. If that word contains at least three consecutive 1s, your program should output that that word is "accepted," otherwise that it is "rejected."

59. Write a program that inputs 7 double values from a file *dja. txt* that represent the Dow Jones Average for 7 days. Your program should output the lowest value for those 7 days and the number of the day on which the lowest value occurred. For this program, instead of setting the initial minimum value to the first value in the file, use the maximum value for a *double*. The Java Class Library provides this value as a constant in the *Double* wrapper class. Be sure to handle the case of the file being empty.

60. Write a program that takes website names as keyboard input until the user types the word *stop* and counts how many of the website names are commercial website names (i.e., end with *.com*), then outputs that count.

61. Using a loop, write a program that takes 10 values representing exam grades (between 0 and 100) from the keyboard and outputs the minimum value, maximum value, and average value of all the values entered. Your program should not accept values less than 0 or greater than 100.

62. Write a program that takes an email address as an input from the keyboard and, using a loop, steps through every character looking for an @ sign. If the email address has exactly one @ character, then print a message that the email address is valid; otherwise, print a message that it is invalid.

63. Write a program that takes a user ID as an input from the keyboard and steps through every character, counting how many digits are in the user ID; if there are exactly two digits, output that the user ID is valid, otherwise that it is invalid.

64. Write a program that takes an integer value as an input and converts that value to its binary representation; for instance, if the user inputs 17, then the output will be 10001.

65. Write a program that takes a word representing a binary number (0s and 1s) as an input and converts it to its decimal representation; for instance, if the user inputs 101, then the output will be 5; you can assume that the *String* is guaranteed to contain only 0s and 1s.

66. Write a program that simulates an XOR operation. The input should be a word representing a binary number (0s and 1s). Your program should XOR all the digits from left to right and output the results as "True" or "False." In an XOR operation, *a* XOR *b* is true if *a* or *b* is *true* but not both; otherwise, it is *false*. In this program, we will consider the character "1" to represent true and a "0" to represent false. For instance, if the input is 1011, then the output will be 1 (1 XOR 0 is 1, then 1 XOR 1 is 0, then 0 XOR 1 is 1, which causes the output to be "True"). You can assume that the input word is guaranteed to contain only 0s and 1s.

67. Write a program that takes a sentence as an input and checks whether that sentence is a palindrome. A palindrome is a word, phrase, or sentence that is symmetrical; that is, it is spelled the same forward and backward. Examples are "otto," "mom," and "Able was I ere I saw Elba." Your program should be case insensitive; that is, "Otto" should also be counted as a palindrome.

68. Write a program that takes an HTML-like sequence as an input and checks whether that sequence has the same number of opening brackets (<) and closing brackets (>).

6.14.8   Technical Writing

69. In programming, a programmer can make syntax errors that lead to a compiler error; these errors can then be corrected. Other errors can lead to a runtime error; these errors can also be corrected. Logic errors, however, can lead to an incorrect result or no result at all. Discuss examples of logic errors that can be made when coding loops and the consequences of these logic errors.

70. Discuss how you would detect whether you have an infinite loop in your code.

6.14.9   Group Project (for a group of 1, 2, or 3 students)

71. Often on a webpage, the user is asked to supply personal information, such as a telephone number. Your program should take an input from the keyboard representing a telephone number. We will consider that the input is a valid telephone number if it contains exactly 10 digits and any number of dash (-) and whitespace characters. Keep prompting the user for a telephone number until the user gives you a valid one. Once you have a valid telephone number, you should assume that the digits (only the digits, not the hyphen[s] nor the white space) in the telephone number may have been encrypted by shifting each number by a constant value. For instance, if the shift is 2, a 0 becomes a 2, a 1 becomes a 3, a 2 becomes a 4, ..., an 8 becomes a 0, and a 9 becomes a 1. However, we know that the user is from New York where the decrypted area code (after the shift is applied), represented by the first three digits of the input, is 212. Your program needs to decrypt the telephone number and output the decrypted telephone number with the format 212-xxx-xxxx, as well as the shift value of the encryption. If there was an error in the input and the area code cannot be decrypted to 212, you should output that information.

CHAPTER 7
Object-Oriented Programming, Part 2: User-Defined Classes

CHAPTER CONTENTS

Introduction

When you see the title of this chapter, you might say, "Finally, we get to write our own classes." Actually, we've been writing classes all along. All Java source code belongs to a class. The classes we've been writing are application classes. Now it's time to write some service classes—classes that encapsulate data and methods for use by applications or service classes. These are called **user-defined classes** because we, rather than the Java authors, create them.

First, let's take a moment to examine why we want to create user-defined classes.

We have written a lot of programs using Java's primitive data types (*boolean, char, int, double,* etc.), but the real world requires manipulation of more complex data than just individual *booleans* or *ints*. For example, if you are the programmer for an online bookstore, you will need to manipulate data associated with books. Books typically have an ISBN, a title, an author, a price, an in-stock quantity, and perhaps other pieces of data. We can create a *Book* class so that each object will hold the data for one book. For example, the ISBN, the title, and the author can be represented by *Strings*, the price by a *double*, and the in-stock quantity by an *int*. If we create this *Book* class, our program will be able to store and manipulate all the data of a book as a whole. This is one of the concepts of object-oriented programming.

By incorporating into the class the methods that work with the book data, we also are able to hide the details involved with handling that data. An application can simply call the methods as needed. Thus, creating your own classes can simplify your program.

Finally, a well-written class can be reused in other programs. Thus, user-defined classes speed up development.

7.1   Defining a Class

Classes encapsulate the data and functionality for a person, place, or thing, or more generally, an object. For example, a class might be defined to represent a student, a college, or a course.

To define a class, we use the following syntax:

```
accessModifier class ClassName
{
    // class definition goes here
}
```

SOFTWARE ENGINEERING TIP
Use a noun for the class name, and start the class name with a capital letter.

This syntax should look familiar as the first line in our programs. You may also notice that the class names in the Java Class Library are nouns and start with a capital letter: *Scanner, String, Math*, for example. The Java developers encourage programmers to use these conventions to name their user-defined classes.

Inside the curly braces we define the data of the class, called its **fields**, and the methods. An important function performed by the class methods is maintaining the values of the class data for the **client programs**, which are the users of the class, in that the clients create objects and call the methods of the class. Our programs have been clients of many Java classes, such as *String, DecimalFormat*, and *Math*. The fields and methods of a class are called the **members** of the class.

For each class and for each member of a class, we need to provide an **access modifier** that specifies where the class or member can be used (see Table 7.1). The possible access modifiers are *public, private*, and *protected*, or no modifier at all, which results in package access. The *public* access modifier allows the class or member to be used, or **referenced**, by methods of the same or other classes. The *private* access modifier specifies that the class or member can be referenced only by methods of the same class. Package access specifies that the class or member can be accessed by methods in classes that are in the same package or in the same folder. Later in the chapter, we will learn how to create our own package.

TABLE 7.1   Access Modifiers

Access Modifier	Class or Member can Be Referenced by ...
public	methods of the same class, as well as methods of other classes
private	methods of the same class only
protected	methods in the same class, as well as methods of subclasses and methods in classes in the same package
no modifier (package access)	methods in the same package or same folder only

Typically, the *accessModifier* for a class will be *public*, and we know that a *public* class must be stored in a file named *ClassName.java* where *ClassName* is the name of the class.

Let's start to define a class that represents an automobile, which we can use to calculate miles per gallon. We'll name the class *Auto*, and we'll use the *public* access modifier so that any application can use this class. The class header will look like the following:

```
public class Auto
{
}
```

When we write a class, we will make known the *public* method names and their APIs so that a client program will know how to instantiate objects and call the methods of the class. We will not publish the implementation (or code) of the class, however. In other words, we will publish the APIs of the methods, but not the method bodies. This is called **data hiding**. A client program can use the class without knowing how the class is implemented, and we, as class authors, can change the implementation of the methods as long as we don't change the interface, or APIs.

7.2   Defining Instance Variables

The instance variables of a class hold the data for each object of that class. Thus, we also say that the instance variables represent the properties of the object. Each object, or instance of a class, gets its own copy of the instance variables, each of which can be given a value appropriate to that object. The values of the instance variables, therefore, can represent the state of the object.

Instance variables are defined using the following syntax:

```
accessModifier dataType identifierList;
```

The *private* modifier is typically used for the nonconstant instance variables of the class. This permits only methods of the same class to set or change the values of the instance variables. In this way, we achieve encapsulation; the class provides a protective shell around the data.

The data type of an instance variable can be any of Java's primitive types or a class type.

The *identifierList* consists of one or more names for instance variables of the same data type and can optionally assign initial values to the instance variables. If more than one instance variable name is given, a comma is used as a separator. By convention, identifier names for instance variables are nouns and begin with a lowercase letter; internal words begin with a capital letter. Each instance variable and class variable must be given a name that is unique to the class. It is legal to use the same names for instance variables in different classes, but within a class, the same name cannot be used for more than one instance variable or class variable. Thus, we say that the fields of a class have **class scope**.

Optionally, you can declare an instance variable to be a constant (*final*).

The following statements are examples of instance variable definitions:

```
private String name = "";    // an empty String
private final int PERFECT_SCORE = 100, PASSING_SCORE = 60;
private int startX, startY, width, height;
```

What criteria should you use to select the instance variables of the class? The answer is to select the data that all objects will have in common. For example, for a *Student* class, you might select the student name, grade point average, and projected graduation date. For a *Calculator* class, you might select two operands, an operator, and a result.

Thus, for our *Auto* class, we will define instance variables to hold the model of the automobile, the number of miles the auto has been driven, and the gallons of gas used. As a result, our *Auto* class definition now becomes the following:

```java
public class Auto
{
    private String model;
    private int milesDriven;
    private double gallonsOfGas;
}
```

7.3 Writing Class Methods

We declared the instance variables of the *Auto* class as *private* so that only the methods of the *Auto* class will be able to access or change the values of the instance variables directly. Clients of the *Auto* class will need to use the methods of the class to access or change any of the instance variables. We will therefore need to write some methods.

Methods have this syntax:

```java
accessModifier returnType methodName( parameter list ) // method header
{
    // method body
}
```

where *parameter list* is a comma-separated list of data types and variable names.

The method header syntax should be familiar because we've seen the API for many class methods. One difference is just a matter of semantics. The method caller sends **arguments**, or **actual parameters**, to the method; the method refers to these arguments as its **formal parameters**.

Because methods provide a function for the class, typically method names are verbs. Like instance variables, the method name should begin with a lowercase letter, with internal words beginning with a capital letter.

SOFTWARE ENGINEERING TIP
Use nouns for identifier names for instance variables. Begin the identifier with a lowercase letter and capitalize internal words.

SOFTWARE ENGINEERING TIP
Define instance variables for the data that all objects will have in common.

SOFTWARE ENGINEERING TIP
Use verbs for method names. Begin the method name with a lowercase letter and begin internal words with a capital letter.

The access modifier for methods that provide services to the client will be *public*. Methods that provide services only to other methods of the class are typically declared to be *private*.

The return type of a method is the data type of the value that the method returns to the caller. The return type can be any of Java's primitive data types, any class type, or *void*. Methods with a return type of *void* do not return a value to the caller.

The body of each method, which consists of the code that performs the method's function, is written between the beginning and ending curly braces. Unlike *if* statements and loops, however, these curly braces are not optional; the curly braces are required, regardless of the number of statements in the method body.

Several compiler errors can result from forgetting one or both of the curly braces. You might receive either of these messages:

```
illegal start of expression
```

or

```
';' expected
```

In the method body, a method can declare variables, call other methods, and use any of the program structures we've discussed: *if/else* statements, *while* loops, *for* loops, *switch* statements, and *do/while* loops.

All objects of a class share one copy of the class methods.

We have actually written methods already. For example, we've written the method *main*. Its definition looks like this:

```
public static void main( String [ ] args )
{
    // application code
}
```

We know that the *static* keyword means that the Java Virtual Machine (JVM) can call *main* to start the application running without first instantiating an object. The return type is *void* because *main* does not return a value. The parameter list expects one argument, a *String* array.

We have not previously written a value-returning method. A value-returning method sends back its results to the caller using a *return* statement in the method body. The syntax for the *return* statement is

```
return expression;
```

As you would expect, the data type of the expression must match the return type of the method. Recall that a value-returning method is called from an expression, and when the method completes its operation, its return value replaces the method call in the expression.

If the data type of the method is *void*, as in *main*, we have a choice of using the *return* statement without an expression, as in this statement:

```
return;
```

or omitting the *return* statement altogether. Given that control automatically returns to the caller when the end of the method is reached, most programmers omit the *return* statement in *void* methods. Optionally, a *return* statement can be used if needed to exit a method before reaching the end of the method's code.

7.4 Writing Constructors

A constructor is a special method that is called when an object is instantiated using the *new* keyword. A class can have several constructors. The job of the class constructors is to initialize the fields of the new object.

The syntax for a constructor follows:

```
accessModifier ClassName( parameter list )
{
    // constructor body
}
```

Notice that a constructor has the same name as the class and has no return type—not even *void*.

It's important to use the *public* access modifier for the constructors so that applications can instantiate objects of the class.

The constructor can either assign default values to the instance variables or the constructor can accept initial values from the client through parameters.

Providing a constructor for a class is optional. If you don't write a constructor, the compiler provides a **default constructor**, which is a constructor that takes no arguments. This default constructor assigns default initial values to all instance variables; this is called **autoinitialization**. Numeric variables are given the value of 0, characters are given the Unicode null character, *boolean* variables are given the value *false*, and object references are given the value *null*. Table 7.2 shows the values the default constructor assigns to instance variables.

SOFTWARE ENGINEERING TIP
Define constructors to be *public* so that clients can instantiate objects of the class.

TABLE 7.2   Default Initial Values of Instance Variables

Data Type	Initial Value
byte	0
short	0
int	0
long	0
float	0.0
double	0.0
char	null character ('\u0000')
boolean	*false*
object reference	*null*

If we do provide a constructor, any instance variables our constructor does not initialize will still be given the predefined default value. Also, if we do provide a constructor, the compiler no longer generates a default constructor for us.

Example 7.1 shows Version 1 of our *Auto* class with two constructors.

```
1  /* Auto class, Version 1
2      Anderson, Franceschi
3  */
4
5  public class Auto
6  {
7      // instance variables
8      private String model;          //  model of auto
9      private int milesDriven;       //  number of miles driven
10     private double gallonsOfGas;   //  number of gallons of gas
11
12     // Default constructor:
13     //   initializes model to "unknown";
14     //   milesDriven is autoinitialized to 0
15     //         and gallonsOfGas to 0.0
16     public Auto( )
17     {
18        model = "unknown";
19     }
```

```
20
21     // Overloaded constructor:
22     // allows client to set beginning values for
23     //   model, milesDriven, and gallonsOfGas.
24     public Auto( String startModel,
25                  int startMilesDriven,
26                  double startGallonsOfGas )
27     {
28        model = startModel;
29
30        // validate startMilesDriven parameter
31        if ( startMilesDriven >= 0 )
32            milesDriven = startMilesDriven;
33
34        // validate startGallonsOfGas parameter
35        if ( startGallonsOfGas >= 0.0 )
36            gallonsOfGas = startGallonsOfGas;
37     }
38 }
```

EXAMPLE 7.1   The *Auto* Class, Version 1

Our default constructor (lines 12–19) does not set values for the *milesDriven* and *gallonsOfGas* instance variables. Because *ints* and *doubles* are autoinitialized to 0 and 0.0, respectively, we just accept those default values.

However, it is necessary for our constructor to set the *model* instance variable to a valid *String* value. Because *Strings* are object references, they are autoinitialized to *null*. Any attempt to call a method using the *model* instance variable with a *null* value would generate a *NullPointerException*.

As mentioned earlier, we can provide multiple constructors for a class. We provide a second constructor (lines 21–37) that lets the client set initial values for all the instance variables. Because the class is the caretaker of its fields, it is the class's responsibility to ensure that the data for each object is valid. Thus, when the constructor sets initial values for the instance variables, it should first check whether its parameters are, indeed, valid values. What constitutes a valid value for any instance variable depends in part on the data type of the variable and in part on the class and is a design decision. For our *Auto* class, we have decided that *milesDriven* and *gallonsOfGas* cannot be negative. If the constructor finds that the *startMilesDriven* or *startGallonsOfGas* parameters are negative, it lets the instance variables be assigned default values of 0 and 0.0, respectively. Some methods in the Java Class Library generate an exception when a parameter value is invalid; others substitute a default value for the invalid parameter. Again, how your classes handle invalid argument values is a design decision.

When we provide multiple constructors, we are **overloading** a method. To overload a method, we provide a method with the same name but with a different number of parameters, or with the same number of parameters but with at least one parameter having a different data type. The name of the method, along with the number, data types, and order of its parameters, is called the method's **signature**. Thus, to overload a method, the new method must have a different signature. Notice that the return type is not part of the signature.

When a client calls a method that is overloaded, Java determines which version of the method to execute by looking at the number, data types, and order of the arguments in the method call. Example 7.2 shows a client program that instantiates three *Auto* objects.

```
 1  /* Auto Client, Version 1
 2      Anderson, Franceschi
 3  */
 4
 5  public class AutoClient
 6  {
 7    public static void main( String [ ] args )
 8    {
 9       System.out.println( "Instantiate sedan" );
10       Auto sedan = new Auto( );
11
12       System.out.println( "\nInstantiate suv" );
13       Auto suv = new Auto( "Trailblazer", 7000, 437.5 );
14
15       System.out.println( "\nInstantiate mini" );
16       // attempt to set invalid value for gallons of gas
17       Auto mini = new Auto( "Mini Cooper", 200, -1.0 );
18    }
19  }
```

EXAMPLE 7.2   The *Auto* Client, Version 1

SOFTWARE
ENGINEERING
TIP
Provide, at
the minimum,
a default
constructor and
a constructor
that accepts
initial values
for all instance
variables.

Line 10 causes the default constructor to be called because no arguments are passed to the constructor. Line 13 causes the overloaded constructor to be called because it passes three arguments to the constructor. If the client attempted to instantiate a new object with a number of parameters other than 0 or 3, the compiler would generate an error because there is no constructor that matches those arguments. In general, the arguments sent to an overloaded method must match the formal parameters of some version of that method.

The number of constructors we provide is a design decision and depends on the class. Providing multiple constructors gives the client a choice of ways to create an object. It is good practice to provide, at minimum, a default constructor. The reason for this will become clear as we explore classes in more depth. It is also good practice to provide another constructor that accepts values for all the instance variables.

On line 17, we instantiate an *Auto* object with an invalid argument for gallons of gas. The object is still created, but the value of its *gallonsOfGas* instance variable is autoinitialized to 0.0. The output of Example 7.2 is shown in Figure 7.1.

Beware of this common error: declaring a *void* return type for a constructor. Remember that constructors have no return type at all. For example, the following invalid constructor definition declares a return type of *void*:

```
// Error! void return value specified
public void Auto( String model,
                  int startMilesDriven,
                  double startGallonsOfGas )
{
    // body of constructor
}
```

This is a difficult error to find. The class file will compile without an error because the compiler doesn't recognize this method as a constructor. Instead, the client program will get a compiler error when it attempts to instantiate an *Auto* object. For example, this statement in a client program

```
Auto gm = new Auto( "Prius", 350, 15.5 );
```

```
Instantiate sedan

Instantiate suv

Instantiate mini
```

Figure 7.1

Output from *Auto* Client, Version 1

would generate this compiler error:

```
AutoClient.java:13: error: constructor Auto in class Auto cannot be applied to given
types;
        Auto gm = new Auto( "Prius", 350, 15.5 );
                  ^
  required: no arguments
  found: String,int,double
  reason: actual and formal argument lists differ in length
1 error
```

COMMON ERROR TRAP
Specifying a return value for a constructor will cause a compiler error in the client program when the client attempts to instantiate an object of that class.

Notice that both constructors access the instance variables directly. Remember that instance variables have class scope, which means that they can be accessed anywhere in the class. Thus, any method of the class can access any of the instance variables directly. In our *Auto* class, any method can access the instance variables *model, milesDriven,* and *gallonsOfGas.*

Methods have class scope as well. Any method can call any of the methods in the class, regardless of whether the methods have been declared *private, public,* or *protected.*

In addition to accessing the instance variables, a method can also access its own parameters. When a method begins executing, its parameters have been declared and have been given the values of the arguments sent by the caller of the method.

The parameters have **local scope** in that a method can access its parameters directly. We call this local scope because the parameters can be accessed only in that method; that is, a method can access its own parameters, but attempting to access another method's parameters generates a compiler error.

Similarly, the method can define variables to be used within the method. These variables also have local scope and are accessible from the point of definition until the end of the method or the end of the block in which the variable was defined, whichever comes first.

Table 7.3 summarizes the rules of scope.

Attempting to use an identifier that is not in scope will generate the following compiler error:

```
cannot find symbol
```

When the client in Example 7.2 runs, it instantiates three objects, but there is nothing more our application can do with them. To allow our client to manipulate the *Auto* objects further, we need to provide more methods.

TABLE 7.3   Rules of Scope

A method in a class can access
• the instance variables of its class
• any parameters sent to the method
• any variable the method declares within its body from the point of declaration until the end of the method or until the end of the block in which the variable was declared, whichever comes first
• any methods in the class

Skill Practice
with these end-of-chapter questions

7.18.1   Multiple Choice Exercises

Questions 1, 2, 3, 4, 5, 6, 7

7.18.3   Fill In the Code

Questions 28, 30, 31

7.18.5   Debugging Area

Questions 47, 48, 49

7.18.8   Technical Writing

Question 77

7.5   Writing Accessor Methods

Because clients cannot directly access *private* instance variables of a class, classes usually provide *public* accessor methods for the instance variables. These methods have a simple, almost trivial, standard form:

```
public returnType getInstanceVariable( )
{
    return instanceVariable;
}
```

The standard name of the method is *get*, followed by the instance variable's name with an initial capital letter. Because the method names usually start with "get," accessor methods are often called **getters**. The method takes no arguments and simply returns the current value of the instance variable. Thus, the return type is the same data type as the instance variable.

You can see this simple pattern in the accessor methods for Version 2 of our *Auto* class, shown in Example 7.3 (lines 39–58).

```
 1 /* Auto class, Version 2
 2    Anderson, Franceschi
 3 */
 4
 5 public class Auto
 6 {
 7     // instance variables
 8     private String model;         //  model of auto
 9     private int milesDriven;      //  number of miles driven
10     private double gallonsOfGas;  //  number of gallons of gas
11
12     // Default constructor:
13     //  initializes model to "unknown";
14     //  milesDriven is autoinitialized to 0
15     //         and gallonsOfGas to 0.0
16     public Auto( )
17     {
18        model = "unknown";
19     }
20
21     // Overloaded constructor:
22     // allows client to set beginning values for
23     //    model, milesDriven, and gallonsOfGas.
24     public Auto( String startModel,
25                  int startMilesDriven,
26                  double startGallonsOfGas )
27     {
28        model = startModel;
29
30        // validate startMilesDriven parameter
31        if ( startMilesDriven >= 0 )
32           milesDriven = startMilesDriven;
33
34        // validate startGallonsOfGas parameter
35        if ( startGallonsOfGas >= 0.0 )
36           gallonsOfGas = startGallonsOfGas;
37     }
```

```
38
39     // Accessor method:
40     // returns current value of model
41     public String getModel( )
42     {
43        return model;
44     }
45
46     // Accessor method:
47     // returns current value of milesDriven
48     public int getMilesDriven( )
49     {
50        return milesDriven;
51     }
52
53     // Accessor method:
54     //  returns current value of gallonsOfGas
55     public double getGallonsOfGas( )
56     {
57        return gallonsOfGas;
58     }
59 }
```

EXAMPLE 7.3   *Auto* **Class, Version 2**

In the client code in Example 7.4, we've added a few statements to call the accessor methods for the two *Auto* objects we've instantiated. Then we print the values, as shown in Figure 7.2.

```
1 /* Auto Client, Version 2
2     Anderson, Franceschi
3 */
4
5 public class AutoClient
6 {
7     public static void main( String [ ] args )
8     {
9         Auto sedan = new Auto( );
10        String sedanModel = sedan.getModel( );
11        int sedanMiles = sedan.getMilesDriven( );
12        double sedanGallons = sedan.getGallonsOfGas( );
13        System.out.println( "sedan: model is " + sedanModel
14                  + "\n miles driven is " + sedanMiles
15                  + "\n gallons of gas is " + sedanGallons );
16
17        Auto suv = new Auto( "Trailblazer", 7000, 437.5 );
18        String suvModel = suv.getModel( );
```

```
19              int suvMiles = suv.getMilesDriven( );
20              double suvGallons = suv.getGallonsOfGas( );
21              System.out.println( "suv: model is " + suvModel
22                          + "\n miles driven is " + suvMiles
23                          + "\n gallons of gas is " + suvGallons );
24      }
25 }
```

EXAMPLE 7.4   *Auto* Client, Version 2

Figure 7.2

Output from *Auto*
Client, Version 2

```
sedan: model is unknown
 miles driven is 0
 gallons of gas is 0.0
suv: model is Trailblazer
 miles driven is 7000
 gallons of gas is 437.5
```

**SOFTWARE
ENGINEERING
TIP**

Provide *public*
accessor
methods for any
instance variable
for which the
client should be
able to retrieve
the value.
Each accessor
method returns
the current
value of the
corresponding
instance
variable.

Because the *sedan* object was instantiated by calling the default constructor, its model is *unknown* and the miles driven and gallons of gas are set to default values. On the other hand, the *suv* object data reflects the values sent to the overloaded constructor when the *suv* object was instantiated.

Thus, Version 2 of our *Auto* class lets our clients instantiate objects and get the values of the instance variables. But we still need to give the client a way to change the instance variables. In order to do this, we provide mutator methods.

7.6   Writing Mutator Methods

As we have discussed, we declare the instance variables as *private* to encapsulate the data of the class. We allow only the class methods to directly set the values of the instance variables. Thus, it is customary to provide a *public* **mutator** method for any instance variable that the client will be able to change. Because the method names usually start with "set," mutator methods are often called **setters**.

The general form of a mutator method is the following:

**SOFTWARE
ENGINEERING
TIP**

Provide a
mutator method
for any instance
variable that you
want to allow
the client to
change.

```
public void setInstanceVariable( dataType newValue )
{
    // validate newValue, then assign to the instance variable
}
```

We declare mutator methods as *public* so that client programs can use the methods to change the values of the instance variables. We do not return a value, so we declare the return type as *void*. By convention, the name of each mutator method starts with the lowercase word *set* followed by the instance variable name with an initial capital letter. For obvious reasons, the data type of the method's parameter should match the data type of the instance variable being set.

Whenever possible, the body of your mutator method should validate the parameter value passed by the client. If the parameter value is valid, the mutator assigns that value to the instance variable.

Example 7.5 shows Version 3 of our *Auto* class.

```
1  /* Auto class, Version 3
2      Anderson, Franceschi
3  */
4
5  public class Auto
6  {
7      // instance variables
8      private String model;          //  model of auto
9      private int milesDriven;       //  number of miles driven
10     private double gallonsOfGas;   //  number of gallons of gas
11
12     // Default constructor:
13     //  initializes model to "unknown";
14     //  milesDriven is autoinitialized to 0
15     //         and gallonsOfGas to 0.0
16     public Auto( )
17     {
18        model = "unknown";
19     }
20
21     // Overloaded constructor:
22     // allows client to set beginning values for
23     //   model, milesDriven, and gallonsOfGas.
24     public Auto( String startModel,
25                  int startMilesDriven,
26                  double startGallonsOfGas )
27     {
28        model = startModel;
29        setMilesDriven( startMilesDriven );
30        setGallonsOfGas( startGallonsOfGas );
31     }
32
33     // Accessor method:
34     // returns current value of model
35     public String getModel( )
36     {
37        return model;
```

```
38        }
39
40        // Accessor method:
41        // returns current value of milesDriven
42        public int getMilesDriven( )
43        {
44          return milesDriven;
45        }
46
47        // Accessor method:
48        //  returns current value of gallonsOfGas
49        public double getGallonsOfGas( )
50        {
51          return gallonsOfGas;
52        }
53
54        // Mutator method:
55        // allows client to set model
56        public void setModel( String newModel )
57        {
58          model = newModel;
59        }
60
61        // Mutator method:
62        // allows client to set value of milesDriven;
63        // if new value is not less than 0
64        public void setMilesDriven( int newMilesDriven )
65        {
66          if ( newMilesDriven >= 0 )
67            milesDriven = newMilesDriven;
68        }
69
70        // Mutator method:
71        // allows client to set value of gallonsOfGas;
72        // if new value is not less than 0.0
73        public void setGallonsOfGas( double newGallonsOfGas )
74        {
75          if ( newGallonsOfGas >= 0.0 )
76            gallonsOfGas = newGallonsOfGas;
77        }
78 }
```

EXAMPLE 7.5   *Auto* **Class, Version 3**

The mutator methods for the *milesDriven* (lines 61–68) and *gallonsOfGas* (lines 70–77) instance variables validate that the parameter value is greater than or equal

to 0. If the parameter value is less than 0, the methods do not change the value
of the instance variable. In previous versions of our *Auto* class, the constructor
performed the same validation. Now that the mutator methods perform this validation, the constructor can call the mutator methods (lines 29–30) passing its
parameters through to the mutator methods. In this way, we eliminate duplicate
code; the validation of each parameter's value is performed in one place. If later we
decide to impose other restrictions on any instance variable's value, we will need to
change the code in only one place. In this way, a client cannot set invalid values for
milesDriven or *gallonsOfGas*, either when the object is instantiated or by calling a
mutator method.

```
1 /* Auto Client, Version 3
2    Anderson, Franceschi
3 */
4
5 public class AutoClient
6 {
7   public static void main( String [ ] args )
8   {
9      Auto suv = new Auto( "Trailblazer", 7000, 437.5 );
10
11     // print initial values of instance variables
12     System.out.println( "suv: model is " + suv.getModel( )
13            + "\n miles driven is " + suv.getMilesDriven( )
14            + "\n gallons of gas is " + suv.getGallonsOfGas( ) );
15
16     // call mutator method for each instance variable
17     suv.setModel( "Sportage" );
18     suv.setMilesDriven( 200 );
19     suv.setGallonsOfGas( 10.5 );
20
21     // print new values of instance variables
22     System.out.println( "\nsuv: model is " + suv.getModel( )
23            + "\n miles driven is " + suv.getMilesDriven( )
24            + "\n gallons of gas is " + suv.getGallonsOfGas( ) );
25
26     // attempt to set invalid value for milesDriven
27     suv.setMilesDriven( -1 );
28     // print current values of instance variables
29     System.out.println( "\nsuv: model is " + suv.getModel( )
30            + "\n miles driven is " + suv.getMilesDriven( )
31            + "\n gallons of gas is " + suv.getGallonsOfGas( ) );
32   }
33 }
```

EXAMPLE 7.6   *Auto* **Client, Version 3**

SOFTWARE ENGINEERING TIP

Write the validation code for instance variables in mutator methods and have the constructor call the mutator methods to set initial values.

In Example 7.6, our client instantiates one *Auto* object, *suv* (line 9), and prints the values of its instance variables (lines 11–14). Then we call each mutator method, setting new values for each instance variable (lines 16–19). We again print the values of the instance variables (lines 21–24) to show that the values have been changed. Then, in line 27, we attempt to set an invalid value for *milesDriven*. As Figure 7.3 shows, the mutator method does not change the value, which we verify by again printing the values of the instance variables (lines 28–31).

When a method begins executing, the parameters have been defined and have been assigned the values sent by the client. When the client calls the *setModel* method at line 17, the *newModel* parameter has the value *Sportage* when the method starts executing.

A common error in writing mutator methods is using the instance variable name for the parameter name. When a method parameter has the same name as an instance variable, the parameter hides the instance variable. In other words, the parameter has **name precedence**, so any reference to that name refers to the parameter, not to the instance variable.

For example, the intention in this incorrectly coded method is to set a new value for the *model* instance variable:

```java
// Incorrect!  parameter hides instance variable
public void setModel( String model )
{
    model = model;
}
```

Because the parameter, *model*, has the same identifier as the *model* instance variable, the result of this method is to assign the value of the parameter to the parameter! This is called a ***No-op***, which stands for "No operation," because the statement

Figure 7.3

Output from *Auto* Client, Version 3

```
suv: model is Trailblazer
  miles driven is 7000
  gallons of gas is 437.5

suv: model is Sportage
  miles driven is 200
  gallons of gas is 10.5

suv: model is Sportage
  miles driven is 200
  gallons of gas is 10.5
```

has no effect. To avoid this logic error, we can choose a different name for the parameter. To avoid name conflicts, we name each parameter using the pattern *newInstanceVariable*.

A similar common error is to declare a local variable with the same name as the instance variable, as shown in the following incorrectly coded method:

```
// Incorrect! declared local variable hides instance variable
public void setModel( String newModel )
{
      String model; // declared variable hides instance variable
      model = newModel;
}
```

Any variable that a method declares is a local variable because its scope is local to the method. Thus, the declared variable, *model*, is a local variable to the *setModel* method.

With the preceding code, the *model* local variable hides the instance variable with the same name, so the method assigns the parameter value to the local variable, not to the instance variable. The result is that the value of the *model* instance variable is unchanged.

The instance variable, *model*, is defined already in the class. Thus, the method should simply assign the parameter value to the instance variable without attempting to declare the instance variable (again) in the method.

Finally, another common error is declaring the parameter, as shown below:

```
// Incorrect! Declaring the parameter; parameters are declared already
public void setModel( String newModel )
{
      String newModel; // local variable has same name as parameter
      model = newModel;
}
```

This code generates this compiler error:

```
variable newModel is already defined in method setModel(String)
```

COMMON ERROR TRAP
Be aware that a method parameter or local variable that has the same name as an instance variable hides the instance variable.

COMMON ERROR TRAP
Do not declare the parameters of a method inside the method body. When the method begins executing, the parameters exist and have been assigned the values set by the client in the method call.

7.7 Writing Data Manipulation Methods

Now we finally get down to the business of the class. Usually you will define a class not only to encapsulate the data, but also to provide some service. Thus, you would provide one or more methods that perform the functionality of the class. These methods might calculate a value based on the instance variables and/or parameters, or manipulate the instance variables in some way. The API of these methods depends on the function being performed. If a method merely manipulates the instance variables, it requires no parameters because instance variables are accessible from any method and, therefore, are in scope.

For example, in our *Auto* class, part of the functionality of our class is to calculate miles per gallon and the gas cost, so we provide the *milesPerGallon* and *moneySpentOnGas* methods in our *Auto* class, Version 4, shown in Example 7.7.

```
1   /* Auto class, Version 4
2      Anderson, Franceschi
3   */
4
5   public class Auto
6   {
7       // instance variables
8       private String model;        //  model of auto
9       private int milesDriven;     //  number of miles driven
10      private double gallonsOfGas; //  number of gallons of gas
11
12      // Default constructor:
13      //  initializes model to "unknown";
14      //  milesDriven is autoinitialized to 0
15      //          and gallonsOfGas to 0.0
16      public Auto( )
17      {
18         model = "unknown";
19      }
20
21      // Overloaded constructor:
22      // allows client to set beginning values for
23      //   model, milesDriven, and gallonsOfGas.
24      public Auto( String startModel,
25                   int startMilesDriven,
26                   double startGallonsOfGas )
27      {
28         model = startModel;
29         setMilesDriven( startMilesDriven );
30         setGallonsOfGas( startGallonsOfGas );
31      }
32
33      // Accessor method:
34      // returns current value of model
35      public String getModel( )
36      {
37         return model;
38      }
39
```

```
40      // Accessor method:
41      // returns current value of milesDriven
42      public int getMilesDriven( )
43      {
44         return milesDriven;
45      }
46
47      // Accessor method:
48      // returns current value of gallonsOfGas
49      public double getGallonsOfGas( )
50      {
51         return gallonsOfGas;
52      }
53
54      // Mutator method:
55      // allows client to set model
56      public void setModel( String newModel )
57      {
58         model = newModel;
59      }
60
61      // Mutator method:
62      // allows client to set value of milesDriven;
63      // if new value is not less than 0
64      public void setMilesDriven( int newMilesDriven )
65      {
66        if ( newMilesDriven >= 0 )
67           milesDriven = newMilesDriven;
68      }
69
70      // Mutator method:
71      // allows client to set value of gallonsOfGas;
72      // if new value is not less than 0.0
73      public void setGallonsOfGas( double newGallonsOfGas )
74      {
75        if ( newGallonsOfGas >= 0.0 )
76           gallonsOfGas = newGallonsOfGas;
77      }
78
79      // Calculates miles per gallon.
80      //  if no gallons of gas have been used, returns 0.0;
81      //  otherwise, returns miles per gallon
82      //        as milesDriven / gallonsOfGas
83      public double milesPerGallon( )
84      {
85        if ( gallonsOfGas >= 0.0001 )
```

```
86                return milesDriven / gallonsOfGas;
87          else
88                return 0.0;
89       }
90
91       // Calculates money spent on gas.
92       //   returns price per gallon times gallons of gas
93       public double moneySpentOnGas( double pricePerGallon )
94       {
95          return pricePerGallon * gallonsOfGas;
96       }
97   }
```

EXAMPLE 7.7   *Auto* Class, Version 4

Our class now provides the method to calculate mileage and estimate gas cost for an *Auto* object. The *milesPerGallon* method (lines 79–89) needs no parameters since it accesses only instance variables of the class, which are in scope. As you can see from the code, we guard against dividing by 0 by checking the value of *gallonsOfGas* before using it as the divisor. If *gallonsOfGas* is not equal to zero, we divide *miles-Driven* by *gallonsOfGas* and return the result as a *double*. Otherwise, we return 0.0.

The *moneySpentOnGas* method (lines 91–96) accepts one parameter that represents the average price of a gallon of gas. It returns the amount of money spent on gas, calculated by multiplying that parameter by the *gallonsOfGas* instance variable.

Notice that we do not format the returned values from *milesPerGallon* or *moneySpentOnGas*. Returning a *double* allows the client to use those values in further calculations. If the client wants to display the values to the user, the client can format the values at that time.

Example 7.8 shows a client program that instantiates an *Auto* object, calls the *milesPerGallon* and *moneySpentOnGas* methods, and prints their return value, as shown in Figure 7.4.

```
1 /* Auto Client, Version 4
2    Anderson, Franceschi
3 */
4
5 import java.text.DecimalFormat;
6 import java.text.NumberFormat;
7
8 public class AutoClient
9 {
10    public static void main( String [ ] args )
```

```
11   {
12     Auto suv = new Auto( "Trailblazer", 7000, 437.5 );
13
14     double mileage = suv.milesPerGallon( );
15     DecimalFormat mpgFormat = new DecimalFormat( "0.0" );
16     System.out.println( "Mileage for suv is "
17                             + mpgFormat.format( mileage ) );
18
19     double gasCost = suv.moneySpentOnGas( 2.79 );
20     NumberFormat money = NumberFormat.getCurrencyInstance( );
21     System.out.println( "Gas cost for suv is "
22                             + money.format( gasCost ) );
23   }
24 }
```

EXAMPLE 7.8 *Auto* **Client, Version 4**

```
Mileage for suv is 16.0
Gas cost for suv is $1,220.62
```

Figure 7.4

Output from *Auto* Client, Version 4

Skill Practice
with these end-of-chapter questions

7.18.1   Multiple Choice Exercises

Questions 8, 9, 10, 11, 12, 13

7.18.2   Reading and Understanding Code

Questions 17, 18, 19, 20, 24, 26

7.18.3   Fill In the Code

Questions 32, 33, 36, 37

7.18.4   Identifying Errors in Code

Questions 38, 39, 43, 45

7.18.5   Debugging Area

Question 52

7.8   Programming Activity 1: Writing a Class Definition, Part 1

In this programming activity, you will write the methods for an *Airport* class. Then you will run a prewritten client program that instantiates several *Airport* objects, calls the methods that you have written, and displays the values of the objects' data.

The *Airport* class has two instance variables: the airport code and the number of gates.

In this chapter's Programming Activity 1 folder in the supplied code files, you will find multiple files. Copy these files to a folder on your computer. Note that all files should be in the same folder.

Load the *Airport.java* source file; you'll notice that the class already contains some source code. The method names and APIs are described in comments. Your job is to define the instance variables and write the methods. It is important that you define the method headers exactly as described, including method name, return value, and parameters, because our *AirportDrawing* class will call each method to test it. Search for five asterisks in a row (*****). This will position you at the seven places in the class definition where you will add your code. The *Airport.java* code is shown here in Example 7.9.

```
 1 /* Airport class
 2    Anderson, Franceschi
 3 */
 4
 5 public class Airport
 6 {
 7    // 1. ***** Define the instance variables  *****
 8    //  airportCode is a String
 9    //  gates is an integer
10
11
12
13    // 2. ***** Write this method *****
14    // Default constructor:
15    // method name: Airport
16    // return value:  none
17    // parameters: none
18    // function: sets the airportCode to an empty String
19
20
21
22    // 3. ***** Write this method *****
23    // Overloaded constructor:
24    // method name: Airport
```

```
25    // return value: none
26    // parameters:  a String startAirportCode and an int startGates
27    // function:
28    //       calls the setAirportCode method,
29    //       passing startAirportCode parameter;
30    //       calls the setGates method, passing startGates parameter
31
32
33
34
35    // 4. ***** Write this method *****
36    // Accessor method for the airportCode instance variable
37    // method name: getAirportCode
38    // return value: String
39    // parameters: none
40    // function: returns airportCode
41
42
43
44    // 5. ***** Write this method *****
45    // Accessor method for the gates instance variable
46    // method name: getGates
47    // return value: int
48    // parameters: none
49    // function: returns gates
50
51
52
53    // 6. ***** Write this method *****
54    // Mutator method for the airportCode instance variable
55    // method name: setAirportCode
56    // return value: void
57    // parameters: String newAirportCode
58    // function: assigns airportCode the value of the
59    //        newAirportCode parameter
60
61
62
63    // 7. ***** Write this method *****
64    // Mutator method for the gates instance variable
65    // method name: setGates
66    // return value:  void
67    // parameters: int newGates
68    // function: validates the newGates parameter.
69    //   if newGates is greater than or equal to 0,
70    //       sets gates to newGates;
71    //       otherwise, does not change the value of gates
```

```
72
73
74
75   }  // end of Airport class definition
```

EXAMPLE 7.9   *Airport.java*

When you finish writing the methods for the *Airport* class, compile the source file. When *Airport.java* compiles without errors, load the *AirportPractice1Application.java* file. This source file contains *main*, so you will execute the application from this file. When the application begins, you should see the window shown in Figure 7.5.

As you can see, the *AirportDrawing* has declared two *Airport* object references, *airport1* and *airport2*. The references are *null* because no *Airport* objects have been instantiated.

The client application will instantiate the *Airport* objects and call the methods you have written for the *Airport* class. As the application does its work, it displays a status message at the bottom of the window that indicates which method it has called. It also displays the current values of both *Airport* objects. You can check your work by comparing the values in the objects with the status message. Figure 7.6 shows the *AirportPractice1Application* application when it has finished instantiating *Airport* objects and calling *Airport* methods.

Figure 7.5

Programming
Activity 1
Opening Window

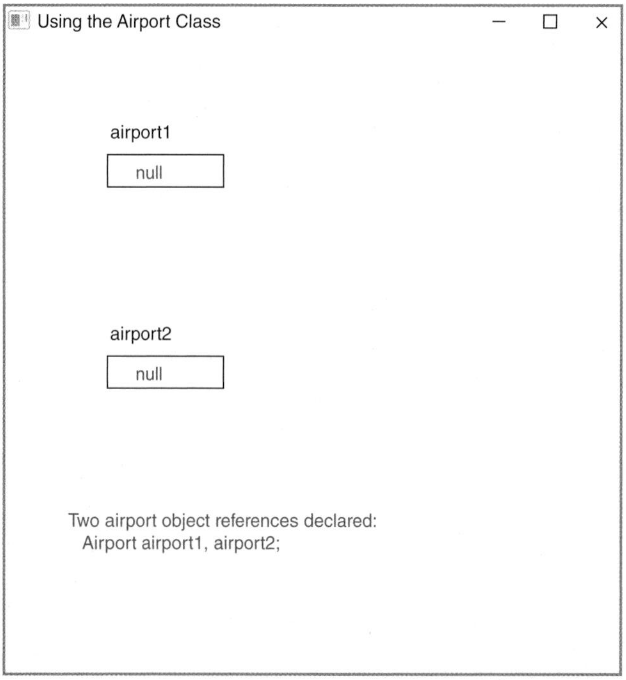

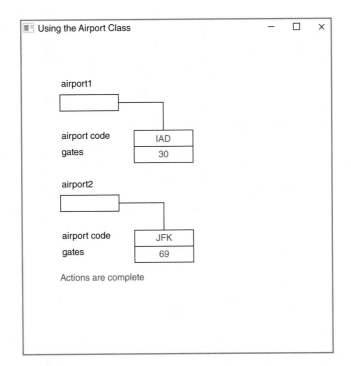

Figure 7.6

AirportPractice1-Application When Complete

1. **Why does the default constructor need to set a value for the airport code?**

2. **Explain the importance of using standard naming conventions for accessor and mutator methods.**

7.9   The Object Reference *this*

When an object is instantiated, a copy of each of the instance variables is created. However, all objects of a class share one copy of the methods. How, then, does a method know for which object the method was called? In other words, how does a method know which object's data it should get, set, or use to calculate a value? The answer is the special object reference named ***this***.

When a method begins executing, the JVM sets the object reference, *this*, to refer to the object for which the method has been called. That object reference is called the **implicit parameter**. When a method references an instance variable, it will access the instance variable that belongs to the object that the implicit parameter references. In other words, by default, any instance variable referred to by a method is considered to be *this.instanceVariable*.

Preceding an instance variable name with *this* is optional; when just the instance variable name is used (without any object reference), *this* is assumed. Consequently, we usually omit the *this* reference and use just the instance variable name.

However, in methods where you need to avoid ambiguity in variable names, you can precede an instance variable name with *this*. That approach comes in handy as a way to avoid one of the common errors we discussed earlier in the chapter: A parameter of a mutator method with the same name as the instance variable hides the instance variable. We can eliminate this problem by using the *this* reference with the instance variable, which effectively uncovers the instance variable name.

For example, some programmers would code the *setModel* mutator as follows:

```
public void setModel( String model )
{
   this.model = model;
}
```

Here we give the parameter, *model*, the same name as the instance variable it represents. Then in the assignment statement, we use the *this* reference to distinguish the instance variable from the parameter. Now it is clear that the parameter value, *model*, should be assigned to the instance variable, *this.model*.

Furthermore, some programmers, particularly in the Android community, would code the *setModel* mutator so that it returns a reference to *this Auto*, as follows:

```
public Auto setModel( String model )
{
   this.model = model;
   return this;
}
```

The benefit of returning *this* is that we can chain method calls. For example, assuming the *setMilesDriven* and *setGallonsOfGas* mutators also return *this* and *sporty* is an *Auto* object, we could chain method calls as follows:

```
sporty.setGallonsOfGas( 3.4 ).setMilesDriven( 67 );
```

Since the . (dot) operator associates left to right, the above statement is equivalent to:

```
( sporty.setGallonsOfGas( 3.4 ) ).setMilesDriven( 67 );
```

Since the *setGallonsOfGas* method returns *this*—that is, the object reference that called it—it returns *sporty* in the above statement. Thus, the expression `sporty.setGallonsOfGas( 3.4 )` evaluates to *sporty*, which in turns calls the method *setMilesDriven* with argument *67*, as shown below:

```
( sporty ).setMilesDriven( 67 );
```

Example 7.10 shows Version 5 of our *Auto* class. The three mutators (lines 54–60, 62–70, and 72–80) all use and return the *this* reference.

```
1   /* Auto class, Version 5
2      Anderson, Franceschi
3   */
4
5   public class Auto
6   {
7       // instance variables
8       private String model;         //  model of auto
9       private int milesDriven;      //  number of miles driven
10      private double gallonsOfGas;  //  number of gallons of gas
11
12      // Default constructor:
13      //   initializes model to "unknown";
14      //   milesDriven is autoinitialized to 0
15      //        and gallonsOfGas to 0.0
16      public Auto( )
17      {
18          model = "unknown";
19      }
20
21      // Overloaded constructor:
22      // allows client to set beginning values for
23      //    model, milesDriven, and gallonsOfGas.
24      public Auto( String startModel,
25                   int startMilesDriven,
26                   double startGallonsOfGas )
27      {
28          model = startModel;
29          setMilesDriven( startMilesDriven );
30          setGallonsOfGas( startGallonsOfGas );
31      }
32
33      // Accessor method:
34      // returns current value of model
35      public String getModel( )
36      {
37          return model;
38      }
39
40      // Accessor method:
41      // returns current value of milesDriven
42      public int getMilesDriven( )
43      {
44          return milesDriven;
```

```
45      }
46
47      // Accessor method:
48      // returns current value of gallonsOfGas
49      public double getGallonsOfGas( )
50      {
51         return gallonsOfGas;
52      }
53
54      // Mutator method:
55      // allows client to set model
56      public Auto setModel( String model )
57      {
58         this.model = model;
59         return this;
60      }
61
62      // Mutator method:
63      // allows client to set value of milesDriven;
64      // if new value is not less than 0
65      public Auto setMilesDriven( int milesDriven )
66      {
67        if ( milesDriven >= 0 )
68           this.milesDriven = milesDriven;
69        return this;
70      }
71
72      // Mutator method:
73      // allows client to set value of gallonsOfGas;
74      // if new value is not less than 0.0
75      public Auto setGallonsOfGas( double gallonsOfGas )
76      {
77        if ( gallonsOfGas >= 0.0 )
78           this.gallonsOfGas = gallonsOfGas;
79        return this;
80      }
81
82      // Calculates miles per gallon.
83      //  if no gallons of gas have been used, returns 0.0;
84      //  otherwise, returns miles per gallon
85      //        as milesDriven / gallonsOfGas
86      public double milesPerGallon( )
87      {
88        if ( gallonsOfGas >= 0.0001 )
```

```
89              return milesDriven / gallonsOfGas;
90          else
91              return 0.0;
92      }
93
94      // Calculates money spent on gas.
95      //   returns price per gallon times gallons of gas
96      public double moneySpentOnGas( double pricePerGallon )
97      {
98        return pricePerGallon * gallonsOfGas;
99      }
100  }
```

EXAMPLE 7.10   *Auto* Class, Version 5

At line 10 of Example 7.11, we demonstrate how we can chain calls to methods that return the *this* reference. Figure 7.7 shows the output of the program.

```
1 /* Auto Client, Version 5
2    Anderson, Franceschi
3 */
4
5 public class AutoClient
6 {
7    public static void main( String [ ] args )
8    {
9      Auto sporty = new Auto( "Spyder", 0, 0.0 );
10     sporty.setGallonsOfGas( 3.4 ).setMilesDriven( 67 );
11
12     int sportyMiles = sporty.getMilesDriven( );
13     double sportyGallons = sporty.getGallonsOfGas( );
14
15     System.out.println( "Miles driven is " + sportyMiles
16              + "\nGallons of gas is " + sportyGallons );
17   }
18 }
```

EXAMPLE 7.11   *Auto* Client, Version 5

```
Miles driven is 67
Gallons of gas is 3.4
```

Figure 7.7

Output from *Auto* Client, Version 5

7.10   The *toString* and *equals* Methods

In addition to constructors, mutator methods, and accessor methods, a well-designed class usually implements the *toString* and *equals* methods.

The *toString* method is called automatically when an object reference is used as a *String*. For example, the *toString* method for an object is called when the object reference is used with, or as, a parameter to *System.out.println*. The function of the *toString* method is to return a printable representation of the object data.

The *equals* method is designed to compare two objects for equality; that is, it typically returns *true* if the corresponding instance variables in both objects are equal in value. The *equals* method takes an *Object* reference parameter that is expected to be an *Auto* reference and returns *true* if the values of its fields are equal to the values of the fields of this *Auto* object, *false* otherwise.

All classes inherit a version of the *toString* and the *equals* methods from the *Object* class, but these versions do not provide the functionality we described earlier. Thus, it is good practice to provide new versions of these methods. To do that, we use the same header as the methods in the *Object* class but provide a new method body. This is called **overriding a method.**

The APIs of the *toString* and *equals* methods are the following:

```
public String toString( )
public boolean equals( Object o )
```

Example 7.12 shows the code added in Version 6 of the *Auto* class with implementations of the *toString* method (lines 103–112) and the *equals* method (lines 114–132). When overriding a method, a good programming practice is add the *@Override* annotation before the method header (lines 104 and 116). It tells the compiler that the method that follows is overriding a method inherited from another class. And in turn, the compiler warns us if our method header does not in fact override the inherited method.

```
1 /* Auto class, Version 6
2    Anderson, Franceschi
3 */
4
5 import java.text.DecimalFormat;
6
7 public class Auto
8 {
9
```

```
         ...
103     // toString: returns a String of instance variable values
104     @Override
105     public String toString( )
106     {
107         DecimalFormat gallonsFormat = new DecimalFormat( "#0.00" );
108         return "Model: " + model
109                 + "; miles driven: " + milesDriven
110                 + "; gallons of gas: "
111                 + gallonsFormat.format( gallonsOfGas );
112     }
113
114     // equals: returns true if fields of parameter object
115     //          are equal to fields in this object
116     @Override
117     public boolean equals( Object o )
118     {
119         if ( ! ( o instanceof Auto ) )
120             return false;
121         else
122         {
123             Auto objAuto = ( Auto ) o;
124             if ( model.equals( objAuto.model )
125                     && milesDriven == objAuto.milesDriven
126                     && Math.abs( gallonsOfGas - objAuto.gallonsOfGas )
127                                             < 0.0001 )
128                     return true;
129             else
130                     return false;
131         }
132     }
133 }
```

EXAMPLE 7.12   *Auto* Class, Version 5

In the *toString* method (lines 103–111), we begin by instantiating a *DecimalFormat* object for formatting the gallons of gas as a floating-point number with one decimal place. Note that *gallonsFormat* is a local variable for the *toString* method; that is, only the *toString* method can use the *gallonsFormat* object. To use the *DecimalFormat* class, we import the class on line 5. We then build the *String* to return by concatenating labels for each instance variable with the values of the instance variables. The *toString* method can be used in a client class containing the *main* method, for instance, to print *Auto* objects using a single statement instead of calling all the class accessor methods.

To implement our *equals* method (lines 113–130), we first need to check that the parameter's type is *Auto*. The **instanceof** binary operator, whose left operand is an object reference and right operand is a class, evaluates to *true* if the object reference can be cast to an instance of the class (for example, if it is an object reference of that class) and *false* otherwise (Table 7.4.). We use the *instanceof* operator at line 117 to determine if the parameter *o* can be cast to an *Auto* object reference (most likely, when sent by a client, *o* will be an *Auto* reference). If it cannot, we return *false*; otherwise, we can proceed with comparing *o*'s fields and this *Auto* object's fields. Before performing the comparison, we must cast the *Object* reference *o* to an *Auto* (line 121). Otherwise, there would be a compiler error when trying to access the instance variable *model* with the *Object o*, because *model* is an instance variable of class *Auto* and not of class *Object*.

TABLE 7.4　The *instanceof* Operator

Operator	Syntax	Operation
instanceof	*objectReference* instanceof *ClassName*	evaluates to *true* if *objectReference* is of *ClassName* type; *false* otherwise

We compare each instance variable in the parameter object, *objAuto*, with the same instance variable in this object. We return *true* if the corresponding instance variables in each object have the same values; otherwise, we return *false*.

Notice that line 122 calls the *equals* method of the *String* class to compare the values of *model* in the objects because *model* is a *String* object reference. Notice also that because instance variables are in scope for methods, our *equals* method is able to directly access the instance variables of both this object and the *Auto* object, *objAuto*.

Example 7.13 puts Version 6 of the *Auto* class to work. We instantiate two objects that differ only in the model. On line 10, we explicitly call *toString* to print the fields of the *sporty* object. On line 14, we implicitly call the *toString* method; *toString* is called automatically because the *compact* object is the argument sent to the *println* method. On lines 16–19, we compare the two objects using the *equals* method and print the results. The output is shown in Figure 7.8.

```
1  /* Auto Client, version 6
2     Anderson, Franceschi
3  */
4
5  public class AutoClient
```

```
 6  {
 7    public static void main( String [ ] args )
 8    {
 9       Auto sporty = new Auto( "Spyder", 0, 0.0 );
10       System.out.println( sporty.toString( ) );
11
12       Auto compact = new Auto( "Accent", 0, 0.0 );
13       System.out.println( );
14       System.out.println( compact );
15
16       if ( compact.equals( sporty ) )
17         System.out.println( "\nsporty and compact are equal" );
18       else
19         System.out.println( "\nsporty and compact are not equal" );
20    }
21  }
```

EXAMPLE 7.13   *Auto* Client, Version 6

Notice that the *toString* method returns a *String*. It does not output the data itself using *System.out.println*. By returning the object values as a *String*, the class is more reusable. The client can choose how best to handle the returned values. If the client is a text application, it may indeed print the values using *System.out.println*. But if the client has a graphics window, it may want to display the data in a text box or by using the JavaFX *fillText* method. Notice also that the *equals* method does not output a message stating whether the two objects are equal. Instead, the *equals* method returns *true* or *false* so that the client can test the return value and change its behavior depending on whether the objects are equal or not equal. For similar reasons, the accessors return the values of the instance variables rather than outputting those values.

As a general software engineering principle, class methods should communicate only with the client. The client, in turn, communicates with the user. In particular, the class methods should not output anything; the decision on what to output should be left to the client of the class. Thus, the client accepts requests from the

SOFTWARE ENGINEERING TIP

The class methods should communicate directly with the client, and the client should handle the communications with the user.

```
Model: Spyder; miles driven: 0; gallons of gas: 0.00

Model: Accent; miles driven: 0; gallons of gas: 0.00

sporty and compact are not equal
```

Figure 7.8

Output from Example 7.13

© Hemera Technologies/
Photos.com/Thinkstock

Figure 7.9

Communication
Flow among the
User, Client, and
Class

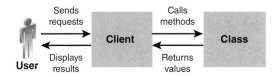

user, calls the class methods and receives the returned values from the class, and then communicates those results to the user, as appropriate. Figure 7.9 illustrates this design principle.

CODE IN ACTION

Within the online resources, you will find a movie with step-by-step illustrations on how to define a class. Click on the link to start the movie.

7.11 *Static* Class Members

As we have mentioned, a separate set of instance variables is created for each object that is instantiated. In addition to instance variables, classes can define **class variables**, which are created only once, when the JVM initializes the class. Thus, class variables exist before any objects are instantiated, and each class has only one copy of its class variables.

You can designate a class variable by using the keyword *static* in its definition. Also, *static* variables that are constants are usually declared to be *public* because they typically are provided to make it easier to use the class. For example, the *PI* and *E* *static* constants in the *Math* class are provided so that our applications do not need to define those commonly used values. The *Color* class provides *public static* color constants, such as *RED,* for convenience when using common colors. Also, the maximum and minimum values for data types are made available as the *MAX_VALUE* and *MIN_VALUE public static* constants of the *Integer, Double,* and *Character* wrapper classes.

If, however, you define a *static* variable for your class that is not a constant, it is best to define it as *private* and provide accessor and mutator methods, as appropriate, for client access to the *static* variable.

We finish our *Auto* class, with Version 7, partially shown in Example 7.14, by defining a *private static* variable to count the number of objects that have been instantiated during the application. We call this class variable *countAutos* and initialize it to 0 (line 14). Because a constructor is called whenever an object is instantiated, we can update the count by incrementing the value of *countAutos* in the class constructors (lines 24 and 37).

When you define a *static* variable for your class, its accessor and mutator methods must be defined as **static methods**, also called **class methods**. To do this, insert the keyword *static* in the method headers after the access modifier. We provide a *static* accessor method for the client to get the count of *Auto* objects (lines 61–66). We do not provide a mutator method, however, because clients of the class should not be able to update the value of *countAutos*. The constructors update the count automatically.

Methods that are defined to be *static* are subject to the following important restrictions, which are summarized in Table 7.5:

- *static* methods can reference only *static* variables.
- *static* methods can call only *static* methods.
- *static* methods cannot use the object reference *this*.

Again, it makes sense that *static* methods cannot access instance variables because *static* methods are associated with the class, not with any object. Further, a *static* method can be called before any objects are instantiated, so there will be no instance variables to access. Attempting to access an instance variable *xxx* from a *static* method will generate this compiler error:

```
non-static variable xxx cannot be referenced from a static context
```

TABLE 7.5   Access Restrictions for *static* and Non-*static* Methods

	static Method	Non-*static* Method
Access instance variables?	no	yes
Access *static* class variables?	yes	yes
Call *static* class methods?	yes	yes
Call *non-static* instance methods?	no	yes
Use the reference *this*?	no	yes

Notice that the *getCountAutos* method (lines 61–66) is declared to be *static* and references only the *static countAutos* variable.

A non-*static*, or **instance**, method, on the other hand, can reference both class variables and instance variables, as well as class methods and instance methods.

```java
1  /* Auto class, Version 7
2     Anderson, Franceschi
3  */
4
5  import java.text.DecimalFormat;
6
7  public class Auto
8  {
9      // instance variables
10     private String model;          //  model of auto
11     private int milesDriven;       //  number of miles driven
12     private double gallonsOfGas;   //  number of gallons of gas
13
14     private static int countAutos = 0;  // static class variable
15
16     // Constructors:
17     //   initializes model to "unknown";
18     //   milesDriven is autoinitialized to 0
19     //       and gallonsOfGas to 0.0;
20     // increments countAutos
21     public Auto( )
22     {
23        model = "unknown";
24        countAutos++;    // increment static count of Auto objects
25     }
26
27     // allows client to set beginning values for
28     // model, milesDriven, and gallonsOfGas;
29     // increments countAutos
30     public Auto( String startModel,
31                  int startMilesDriven,
32                  double startGallonsOfGas )
33     {
34        model = startModel;
35        setMilesDriven( startMilesDriven );
36        setGallonsOfGas( startGallonsOfGas );
37        countAutos++;    // increment static count of Auto objects
38     }
```

```
         . . .
61       // Accessor method:
62       // returns countAutos
63       public static int getCountAutos( )
64       {
65         return countAutos;
66       }
         . . .
145    }
```

EXAMPLE 7.14 *Auto* Class, Version 7

Example 7.15 shows Version 7 of our *AutoClient* class. At line 11 we call the *getCountAutos* method before instantiating any objects, then in line 17 we call the *getCountAutos* method again after instantiating one object. As Figure 7.10 shows, the *getCountAutos* method first returns 0, then 1. Notice that in both calls to the *static* method, we use the dot operator with the class name rather than an object reference.

```
1  /* Auto Client, Version 7
2     Anderson, Franceschi
3  */
4
5  public class AutoClient
6  {
7    public static void main( String [ ] args )
8    {
9      System.out.println( "Before instantiating an Auto object:"
10                         + "\nthe count of Auto objects is "
11                         + Auto.getCountAutos( ) );
12
13     Auto sporty = new Auto( "Spyder", 0, 0.0 );
14
15     System.out.println( "\nAfter instantiating an Auto object:"
16                         + "\nthe count of Auto objects is "
17                         + Auto.getCountAutos( ) );
18   }
19 }
```

EXAMPLE 7.15 *Auto* Client, Version 6

Well, there it is. We've finished defining our *Auto* class. Although it's a large class, we were able to build the *Auto* class incrementally using stepwise refinement.

Figure 7.10

Output from
Example 7.15

```
Before instantiating an Auto object:
the count of Auto objects is 0

After instantiating an Auto object:
the count of Auto objects is 1
```

7.12 Graphical Objects

Now that we know how to design our own classes, we can separate a graphical object from an application. For example, we can define a sprite in its own *Sprite* class and write a client application that will instantiate and draw *Sprite* objects. This will allow us to encapsulate the sprite's data and the code for drawing the sprite within the *Sprite* class. It also promotes reuse of the *Sprite* class by other programmers who might want to create *Sprite* objects for different applications.

The *Sprite* class is shown in Example 7.16. We start by defining the instance variables. We need the starting (x, y) coordinate to draw the sprite, so we define two *int* instance variables to hold those values (lines 9–10). The *sX* variable is the leftmost point of the drawing (the upper-left corner of the rectangle enclosing the body), and *sY* represents the topmost point (the top of the sprite's hat).

In addition, we added one more instance variable, *scale* (line 11), to allow the client to draw sprites of different sizes. For example, a scaling factor of 1.0 will draw the sprite at full size, 0.5 will draw the sprite at half size, and 2.0 will draw a double-sized sprite.

We provide a default constructor (lines 13–19) that autoinitializes *sX* and *sY* to 0 and sets *scale* to 1. Our overloaded constructor (lines 21–29) accepts values for the three instance variables and passes those values to the appropriate mutator methods.

We provide one mutator method to change both *x* and *y* values (lines 31–40), as well as another mutator to change the scaling factor (lines 42–49).

We provide a method, *draw* (lines 51–79), that draws the sprite on a canvas. Because the sprite is drawn using methods of the *GraphicsContext* class, the application client needs to pass its *GraphicsContext* object as an argument to the *draw* method. In the *draw* method, we draw the sprite, multiplying any length measurement by the scaling factor.

We do not provide accessor methods, a *toString* method, or an *equals* method for the *Sprite* class. For a graphical object, these methods are less useful, given that the major purpose of graphical objects is to be drawn.

```
1  /* Sprite class
2     Anderson, Franceschi
3  */
4  import javafx.scene.canvas.*;
5  import javafx.scene.paint.*;
6
7  public class Sprite
8  {
9      private int sX;
10     private int sY;
11     private double scale;
12
13     /** default constructor
14      *  sX = sY = 0; scale is set to 1
15      */
16     public Sprite( )
17     {
18        scale = 1;
19     }
20
21     /* overloaded constructor
22        accepts values for starting x and y coordinates
23        and scale
24      */
25     public Sprite( int sX, int sY, double scale )
26     {
27        setCoordinates( sX, sY );
28        setScale( scale );
29     }
30
31     /* setCoordinates
32      * accepts new values for starting x and y;
33      * returns a reference to this object
34      */
35     public Sprite setCoordinates( int sX, int sY )
36     {
37        this.sX = sX;
38        this.sY = sY;
39        return this;
40     }
```

```
41
42    /* mutator for scale
43     * returns a reference to this object
44     */
45    public Sprite setScale( double scale )
46    {
47       this.scale = ( scale > 0 ? scale : this.scale );
48       return this;
49    }
50
51    /* draw method
52     *  draws Sprite at current sX and sY
53     *  multiplying lengths by scale
54     *  accepts GraphicsContext for canvas
55     */
56    public void draw( GraphicsContext gc )
57    {
58       gc.setFill( Color.CORAL ); // body
59       gc.fillOval( sX, sY + 15 * scale, 90 * scale, 120 * scale );
60       gc.setFill( Color.DARKGOLDENROD ); // hat
61       gc.fillRect( sX + 23 * scale, sY, 45 * scale, 22 * scale );
62       gc.setStroke( Color.DARKGOLDENROD ); // hat brim
63       gc.setLineWidth( 3 );
64       gc.strokeLine( sX, sY + 23 * scale,
65                          sX + 90 * scale, sY + 23 * scale );
66       gc.setFill( Color.CHOCOLATE ); // eye
67       gc.fillOval( sX + 60 * scale, sY + 45 * scale,
68                     18 * scale, 12 * scale );
69       gc.setFill( Color.DARKSALMON ); // feet
70       gc.setLineWidth( 1 );
71       gc.fillOval( sX + 45 * scale, sY + 125 * scale,
72                     45 * scale, 12 * scale );
73       gc.strokeOval( sX + 45 * scale, sY + 125 * scale,
74                      45 * scale, 12 * scale );
75       gc.fillOval( sX + 27 * scale, sY + 127 * scale,
76                     45 * scale, 12 * scale );
77       gc.strokeOval( sX + 27 * scale, sY + 127 * scale,
78                      45 * scale, 12 * scale );
79    }
80 }
```

EXAMPLE 7.16   The *Sprite* Class

Now we can create the client application, *SpriteClient.java*, which is shown in Example 7.17. An advantage to separating the *Sprite* class from the *SpriteClient* class is that we can now easily draw two or more sprites with different sizes in different locations. The *SpriteClient* class defines three *Sprite* references as instance variables (line 11). We instantiate these *Sprite* objects with different starting coordinates and scales (lines 18–20). We call the *draw* method for each *Sprite* object (lines 22–24), passing to the *draw* method the *GraphicsContext* object reference *gc* that was returned by the *JIGraphicsUtility*'s *setUpGraphics* method (lines 16–17). The application window is shown in Figure 7.11.

```
1 /* A client for the Sprite class
2    Anderson, Franceschi
3 */
4
5 import javafx.application.Application;
6 import javafx.scene.canvas.GraphicsContext;
7 import javafx.stage.Stage;
8
9 public class SpriteClient extends Application
10 {
11     private Sprite s1, s2, s3;
12
13     @Override
14     public void start( Stage stage )
15     {
16         GraphicsContext gc = JIGraphicsUtility.setUpGraphics(
17                 stage, "Sprites", 700, 400 );
18         s1 = new Sprite( 100, 50, .5 );
19         s2 = new Sprite( 225, 100, 1 );
20         s3 = new Sprite( ).setCoordinates( 400, 150 ).setScale( 1.5 );
21
22         s1.draw( gc );
23         s2.draw( gc );
24         s3.draw( gc );
25     }
26
27     public static void main( String [ ] args )
28     {
29         launch( args );
30     }
31 }
```

EXAMPLE 7.17 The *SpriteClient* Class

Figure 7.11

The *SpriteClient*
Window

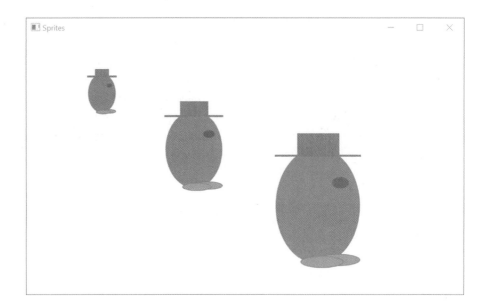

7.13   Enumeration Types

Enumeration types are designed to increase the readability of programs. The enumeration type *enum* is a special kind of class declaration. It allows us to define a set of named constant objects that can be used instead of numbers in a program.

Enum types are useful for managing ordered sets where each member of the set has a name. Examples are the days of the week, months of the year, and playing cards. To represent these sets in a program, we often use numbers, such as 1 through 7 for days of the week or 1 through 12 for months of the year. The problem is that to input or output these values, we need to convert between our internal numeric representation (for example, 1–7) and the words that users recognize (Sunday, Monday, Tuesday, etc.). The *enum* type allows us to instantiate a constant object for each value in a set. The set of objects will be ordered so that we can refer to the objects by name, without the need for using numbers.

The *enum* functionality is built into *java.lang*, so we can define *enum* types without using an *import* statement.

The syntax for creating a set of *enum* objects is

```
enum EnumName { obj1, obj2, . . . };
where obj1, obj2, etc. are names for the constant objects.
```

For example, the following statement defines an *enum* type to represent the days of the week:

```
enum Days { Sun, Mon, Tue, Wed, Thur, Fri, Sat };
```

When that statement is executed, an object is instantiated for each name in the list. Each name in the list, therefore, is a reference to an object of the *enum* type *Days*.

Note that the values in the initialization list are object references (*Sun*), not *String* literals ("*Sun*").

Each object has an instance variable that holds a numeric value, which is determined by its position in the list of *enum* objects. By default, the first object has the value 0, the second object has the value 1, and so on. Because the objects are an ordered set, for example, the object *Thur* is higher in value than *Wed*. We can use the *enum* objects, however, without relying on the specific value of each object.

The *enum* objects are instantiated as constant objects, meaning that their values cannot be changed.

To refer to any of the constant objects in an *enum* type, we use the following dot syntax:

```
enumType.enumObject
```

Thus, to refer to the *Wed* object in our *Days enum* type, we use this syntax:

```
Days.Wed
```

Once we have defined an *enum* type, we can declare an object reference of that type. For example, the following statement defines a *Days* object reference *d*:

```
Days d;
```

Like any other object reference, the value of *d* will be *null* initially. To assign a value to the reference *d*—for example, *Thur*—we use the following statement:

```
d = Days.Thur;
```

Table 7.6 lists some useful methods that can be called with *enum* objects, and Example 7.18 demonstrates the use of these methods.

TABLE 7.6   Useful Methods for *enum* Objects

Useful Methods for *enum* Objects	
Return type	**Method name and argument list**
int	compareTo(Enum eObj)
	compares two *enum* objects and returns a negative number if *this* object is less than the argument, a positive number if *this* object is greater than the argument, and 0 if the two objects are the same

(continued)

TABLE 7.6   Useful Methods for *enum* Objects (*continued*)

Useful Methods for *enum* Objects	
Return type	**Method name and argument list**
boolean	equals(Object eObj)
	returns *true* if this object is equal to the argument *eObj*; returns *false* otherwise
int	ordinal( )
	returns the numeric value of the *enum* object; by default, the value of the first object in the list is 0, the value of the second object is 1, and so on
String	toString( )
	returns the name of the *enum* constant
enum	valueOf(String enumName)
	static method that returns the *enum* object whose name is the same as the *String* argument *enumName*

```
1  /* Demonstration of enum
2     Anderson, Franceschi
3  */
4
5  public class EnumDemo
6  {
7    public enum Days { Sun, Mon, Tue, Wed, Thur, Fri, Sat };
8
9    public static void main( String [ ] args )
10   {
11     Days d1, d2;  // declare two Days object references
12
13     d1 = Days.Wed;
14     d2 = Days.Fri;
15
16     System.out.println( "Comparing objects using equals" );
17     if ( d1.equals( d2 ) )
18       System.out.println( d1 + " equals " + d2 );
19     else
20       System.out.println( d1 + " does not equal " + d2 );
21
22     System.out.println( "\nComparing objects using compareTo" );
23     if ( d1.compareTo( d2 ) > 0 )
```

```
24            System.out.println( d1 + " is greater than " + d2 );
25         else if ( d1.compareTo( d2 ) < 0 )
26            System.out.println( d1 + " is less than " + d2 );
27         else
28            System.out.println( d1 + " is equal to " + d2 );
29
30         System.out.println( "\nGetting the  ordinal value" );
31         System.out.println( "The value of " + d1 + " is "
32                                 + d1.ordinal( ) );
33
34         System.out.println( "\nConverting a String to an object" );
35         Days day = Days.valueOf( "Mon" );
36         System.out.println( "The value of day is " + day );
37   }
38 }
```

EXAMPLE 7.18   A Demonstration of *enum* Methods

Line 7 defines the *enum* type *Days*; this instantiates the seven constant objects representing the days of the week. On line 11, we declare two object references of the *Days enum* type. Then on lines 13 and 14, we assign *d1* a reference to the *Wed* object, and we assign *d2* a reference to the *Fri* object.

Line 17 compares *d1* and *d2* using the *equals* method. Because *Wed* and *Fri* are different objects, the *equals* method returns *false*. Lines 18 and 20 implicitly call the *toString* method, which prints the name of the objects.

Lines 23 and 25 call the *compareTo* method, which returns a negative number, indicating that *Wed* is lower in value than *Fri*.

We then retrieve the value of the *d1* object by calling the *ordinal* method (lines 31–32), which returns 3 because *Wed* is the fourth object in the *enum* list.

Finally, line 35 converts from a *String* to an *enum* object using the *valueOf* method. Notice that the *valueOf* method is *static*, so we call it using our *enum* type, *Days*.

If the *String* passed to the *valueOf* method is not a name in our set of defined *enum* objects, the *valueOf* method generates an *IllegalArgumentException*.

The output from Example 7.18 is shown in Figure 7.12.

We can use *enum* objects in *switch* statements to make the *case* constants more meaningful, which in turn makes the code more readable. Example 7.19 uses our *Days enum* class to display the daily specials offered in the cafeteria.

Figure 7.12

Output from
Example 7.18

```
Comparing objects using equals
Wed does not equal Fri

Comparing objects using compareTo
Wed is less than Fri

Getting the ordinal value
The value of Wed is 3

Converting a String to an object
The value of day is Mon
```

```java
 1  /** Specials of the Day
 2      Anderson, Franceschi
 3  */
 4
 5  import java.util.Scanner;
 6
 7  public class DailySpecials
 8  {
 9    public enum Days { Sun, Mon, Tue, Wed, Thur, Fri, Sat };
10
11    public static void main( String [ ] args )
12    {
13      Scanner scan = new Scanner( System.in );
14
15      System.out.print( "Enter a day\n"
16                          + "(Sun, Mon, Tue, Wed, Thur, Fri, Sat) > " );
17      String inputDay = scan.next( );
18      Days day = Days.valueOf( inputDay );
19
20      switch ( day )
21      {
22        case Mon:
23            System.out.println( "The special for "
24                                  + day + " is barbeque chicken." );
25            break;
26
27        case Tue:
28            System.out.println( "The special for "
29                                  + day + " is tacos" );
30            break;
31
32        case Wed:
```

```
33                  System.out.println( "The special for "
34                                    + day + " is chef's salad" );
35              break;
36
37          case Thur:
38                  System.out.println( "The special for "
39                                    + day + " is a cheeseburger" );
40              break;
41
42          case Fri:
43                  System.out.println( "The special for "
44                                    + day + " is fish fillet" );
45              break;
46
47          default: // if day is Sat or Sun
48                  System.out.println( "Sorry, we're closed on "
49                                    + day );
50      }
51   }
52 }
```

EXAMPLE 7.19   *DailySpecials* Class

Figure 7.13 shows the output from Example 7.19 when the user enters *Fri*.

In the *DailySpecials* program, we prompt the user for a day (lines 15–17), then read the *String* entered by the user and attempt to convert it to an *enum* object by calling the *valueOf* method at line 18.

Once we have a valid *enum* value, we can use it as a *switch* variable (line 20).

Notice that we use each *enum* object name in a *case* label without qualifying it with the *Days* type. Including the *enum* type in a *switch* statement generates the following compiler error:

```
an enum switch case label must be the unqualified name of an enumeration constant
```

Notice also that if the user enters a *String* that does not match one of the seven valid day values, the call to the *valueOf* method at line 18 will cause an *IllegalArgument-Exception* to occur at run time.

```
Enter a day
(Sun, Mon, Tue, Wed, Thur, Fri, Sat) > Fri
The special for Fri is fish fillet
```

Figure 7.13

Output from *DailySpecials*

Skill Practice
with these end-of-chapter questions

7.18.1   Multiple Choice Exercises

       Questions 14, 15, 16

7.18.2   Reading and Understanding Code

       Questions 21, 22, 23, 25, 27

7.18.3   Fill In the Code

       Questions 29, 34, 35

7.18.4   Identifying Errors in Code

       Questions 40, 41, 42, 44, 46

7.18.5   Debugging Area

       Questions 50, 51, 53, 54

7.18.6   Write a Short Program

       Questions 55, 56, 57, 58, 59, 60, 61, 62, 63, 64

7.18.8   Technical Writing

       Question 76

7.14   Programming Activity 2: Writing a Class Definition, Part 2

In this programming activity, you will complete the definition of the *Airport* class. Then you will run a prewritten client program that instantiates several *Airport* objects, calls the methods that you have written, and displays the values of the objects' data.

Copy into a folder on your computer all the files from this chapter's Programming Activity 2 folder in the supplied code files. Note that all files should be in the same folder.

Load the *Airport.java* source file; you'll notice that the class already contains the class definition from Programming Activity 1. Your job is to complete the class definition by adding a *static* class variable (and its supporting code) and writing the *toString* and *equals* methods. It is important to define the *static* class variable and the methods exactly as described in the comments, because the *AirportDrawing* class will call each method to test its implementation. Searching for five asterisks in a row (*****) will position you at the six places in the class definition where you will add your code. The *Airport.java* code is shown here in Example 7.20:

```
1  /* Airport class
2       Anderson, Franceschi
3  */
4
5  public class Airport
6  {
7
8      // instance variables
9      private String airportCode;
10     private int gates;
11
12     // 1. ***** Add a static class variable *****
13     //   countAirports is an int
14     //   assign an initial value of 0
15
16
17     // 2. ***** Modify this method *****
18     // Default constructor:
19     // method name: Airport
20     // return value:  none
21     // parameters: none
22     // function: sets the airportCode to an empty String
23     //     ***** add 1 to countAirports class variable
24     public Airport( )
25     {
26         airportCode = "";
27
28     }
29
30     // 3. ***** Modify this method *****
31     // Overloaded constructor:
32     // method name: Airport
```

```
33    // return value: none
34    // parameters:  a String airport code and an int startGates
35    // function: assigns airportCode the value of the
36    //      startAirportCode parameter;
37    //      calls the setGates method,
38    //      passing the startGates parameter
39    //    ***** add 1 to countAirports class variable
40    public Airport( String startAirportCode, int startGates )
41    {
42       airportCode = startAirportCode;
43       setGates( startGates );
44
45    }
46
47    // Accessor method for the airportCode instance variable
48    // method name: getAirportCode
49    // return value: String
50    // parameters: none
51    // function: returns airportCode
52    public String getAirportCode( )
53    {
54       return airportCode;
55    }
56
57    // Accessor method for the gates instance variable
58    // method name: getGates
59    // return value: int
60    // parameters: none
61    // function: returns gates
62    public int getGates( )
63    {
64       return gates;
65    }
66
67    // 4. ***** Write this method *****
68    // Accessor method for the countAirports class variable
69    // method name: getCountAirports
70    // return value: int
71    // parameters: none
72    // function: returns countAirports
73
74
75
76
77    // Mutator method for the airportCode instance variable
78    // method name: setAirportCode
```

```
79   // return value:  Airport
80   // parameters: String airportCode
81   // function: assigns airportCode the value of the
82   //                    airportCode parameter
83   public Airport setAirportCode( String airportCode )
84   {
85      this.airportCode = airportCode;
86      return this;
87   }
88
89   // Mutator method for the gates instance variable
90   // method name: setGates
91   // return value:  Airport
92   // parameters: int gates
93   // function: validates the gates parameter.
94   //   if gates is greater than 0, sets gates to gates;
95   //   otherwise, does not change value of gates
96   public Airport setGates( int gates )
97   {
98      if ( gates  >=  0 )
99         this.gates = gates;
100       return this;
101   }
102
103  // 5. ***** Write this method *****
104  // method name:  toString
105  // return value: String
106  // parameters: none
107  // function:  returns a String that contains the airportCode
108  //    and gates
109
110
111
112
113
114
115  // 6. ***** Write this method *****
116  // method name: equals
117  // return value: boolean
118  // parameter:  Airport object
119  // function:  returns true if airportCode
120  //     and gates in this object
121  //     are equal to those in the parameter object;
122  //     returns false otherwise
123
124
```

```
125
126
127
128
129
130  }  // end of Airport class definition
```

EXAMPLE 7.20   The *Airport.java* File

When you finish modifying the *Airport* class, compile the source file. When *Airport. java* compiles without any errors, load and compile the *AirportPractice2Application. java* file. This source file contains *main*, so you will execute the application from this file. When the application begins, you should see the window shown in Figure 7.14.

As you can see, the client class has declared two *Airport* object references, *airport1* and *airport2*. The references are *null* because no *Airport* objects have been instantiated. Note also that the value of the *countAirports* class variable is displayed.

The client class will call methods of the *Airport* class to instantiate the two *Airport* objects, call the *toString* and *equals* methods, and get the value of the *static* class variable, *countAirports*. As the application does its work, it displays a status message at the bottom of the window indicating which method has been called, and it also displays the current state of the *Airport* objects. You can check your work by comparing the state of the objects with the status message.

Figure 7.14

*AirportPractice2-
Application*
Opening Window

1. Explain why the *countAirports* class variable has a value of 0 before any *Airport* objects have been instantiated.

2. How does a client call the *getCountAirports* method?

3. Explain why when directly comparing the object references *airport1* and *airport2* using the following *if* statement:

    ```
    if ( airport1 == airport2 )
    ```

    the condition evaluates to *false*?

7.15 Creating Packages

As we have mentioned, one of the advantages of a well-written class is that it can be reused. Ideally, as you write programs, you will look for functionality that is common to many programs. It is a good practice to encapsulate this functionality into a class so that you can reuse that code in future programs. Java provides the concept of a package for easily reusing classes.

A **package** is a collection of related classes that can be imported into programs. We have imported classes from multiple Java packages: *java.util*, *java.text*, and others. We can also create our own packages, which allows us to reuse a class without needing to physically store that class in the same folder as our other source files. Instead, we create the package and *import* the class from that package into our source file. For instructions on how to create a package, please see our additional resources online.

7.16 Generating Web-Style Documentation with Javadoc

In most corporations and organizations, programmers share code and frequently use classes developed by another programmer. If the class is well designed and well documented, it will be easy for others to use that class. After all, that is essentially what we have been doing by using existing Java classes. It has been easy to understand what functions these existing classes perform, what they encapsulate, how the constructors work, what the methods do, and how to use the classes. The reason that these classes are easy to understand and use is not only that they are well designed and written, but also that the available documentation, particularly on Oracle's Java website, is clear, easy to understand, complete, and represents these classes well.

We, too, will learn how to produce HTML-based documentation similar to the documentation available on Oracle's Java website.

There is a tool called **Javadoc**, provided in the Java Development Kit (JDK), to do just that. Javadoc is an executable program (actually *javadoc.exe*) located in the *bin* folder. It is invoked much the same way as the *javac* compiler, except that instead of creating *.class* files, it creates *.html* files that document the class.

For instance, to generate documentation for our *Auto* class, we would type the following at the command line:

```
javadoc Auto.java
```

If we want to generate documentation for all the source files in the directory, we would type:

```
javadoc *.java
```

Your IDE may provide easy access to Javadoc through its menus.

Table 7.7 shows the files generated for the *Auto* class.

TABLE 7.7   HTML Files Generated by Javadoc

File Name	Short Description
Auto.html	*Auto* class documentation (without frames)
allclasses-frame.html	List of the classes with links (with frames)
allclasses-noframe.html	List of the classes with links (without frames)
constant-values.html	Constants of the class with links
index.html	*Auto* class documentation (with frames)
package-frame.html	Frame for this package
package-list	List of packages
package-summary.html	Class hierarchy
script	Javascript file
stylesheet.css	Style sheet

REFERENCE POINT
The full documentation for using Javadoc can be found at www .oracle.com/ technetwork/ java.

If you double-click on *index.html*, you will open a webpage with the same look as the ones on Oracle's Java website.

We will review a few basic Javadoc features here. Full documentation on Javadoc is available on Oracle's website.

To write comments that will be included in the Javadoc documentation, we use a special form of block comment ahead of any class, field, constructor, or method. The syntax for including Javadoc comments follows.

```
/**
Javadoc comment here
*/
```

As we already know, the syntax for a Java block comment is

```
/*
Java block comment here
*/
```

A Javadoc comment is just a special Java block comment. The *javac* compiler will simply ignore it, but the Javadoc executable will look for it and generate the appropriate documentation. Javadoc discards all white space characters and the * at the beginning of each line until a character other than white space or * is encountered. The industry convention is to start every line of a Javadoc comment with an *. Therefore, we recommend the following syntax:

```
/**
*   A Javadoc comment here
*   A second Javadoc comment here
*   . . . .
*/
```

**SOFTWARE
ENGINEERING
TIP**
When coding a documentation block, use an * at the beginning of each line to indicate that this is a documentation comment.

Class documentation comprises two parts:

- A description section
- A tag section

Javadoc recognizes two types of tags: block tags and inline tags. We will discuss block tags only.

Block tags start with the character @. Table 7.8 lists two block tags, *@param* and *@return*, along with an explanation of each.

TABLE 7.8   Selected Javadoc Tags

Tag	Most Common Syntax	Explanation
@param	@param variableName description	Adds a parameter to the parameter section
@return	@return text	Adds a description for the return type

In the description section and inside the tag section, the text should be written in HTML; therefore, HTML tags such as
 (break) or <strong> (bold) can be used. The tag <br> inserts a new line; the tag <strong> will change the text style to bold until the end tag </strong> is encountered. Starting with Java 9, Javadoc supports HTML5.

Example 7.21 shows a simplified version of our *Auto* class incorporating some documentation comments:

```
1 /**  Simplified Auto Class with Javadoc comments
2       Anderson, Franceschi
3 */
4
5 public class SimplifiedAuto
6 {
7   private String model;
8   private int milesDriven;
9   private double gallonsOfGas;
10
11  /**
12  * Default constructor:<br>
13  * initializes model to "unknown"<br>
14  * milesDriven are autoinitialized to 0, and gallonsOfGas to 0.0
15  */
16  public SimplifiedAuto( )
17  {
18      model = "unknown";
19  }
20
21  /**
22  * Mutator method:<br>
23  * Allows client to set value of milesDriven<br>
24  * <strong>setMilesDriven</strong> does not change the value
25  * of <strong>milesDriven</strong> if newMilesDriven has negative value
26  * @param milesDriven the new number of miles driven
27  * @return a reference to this object
28  */
29  public Auto setMilesDriven( int milesDriven )
30  {
31      if ( milesDriven > 0 )
32          this.milesDriven = newMilesDriven;
33      return this;
34  }
35
36  /**
37  * Accessor method for milesDriven:<br>
38  * @return an int, the value of milesDriven
39  */
40  public int getMilesDriven( )
41  {
42      return milesDriven;
43  }
44 }
```

EXAMPLE 7.21   The *SimplifiedAuto* Class

SOFTWARE ENGINEERING TIP

When you write a class, add a few documentation comments and generate the web-style documentation. Show the webpages to friends or colleagues and ask them if they fully understand what the class encapsulates and what it is about. Ask them a few questions about the constructor and the methods. This is a good way to check if your class is well designed and ready for reuse.

Figure 7.15 shows part of the generated *index.html* file, and Figure 7.16 shows the generated documentation for the *setMilesDriven* and *getMilesDriven* methods.

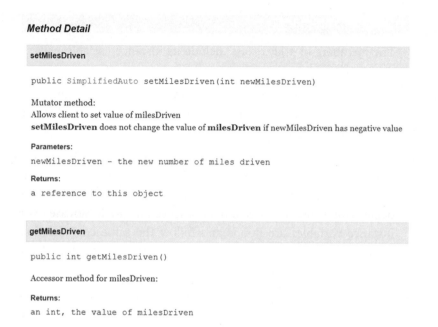

Method Detail

setMilesDriven

```
public SimplifiedAuto setMilesDriven(int newMilesDriven)
```

Mutator method:
Allows client to set value of milesDriven
setMilesDriven does not change the value of **milesDriven** if newMilesDriven has negative value

Parameters:
```
newMilesDriven - the new number of miles driven
```

Returns:
```
a reference to this object
```

getMilesDriven

```
public int getMilesDriven()
```

Accessor method for milesDriven:

Returns:
```
an int, the value of milesDriven
```

Figure 7.15

SimplifiedAuto
Class Web-Style
Documentation

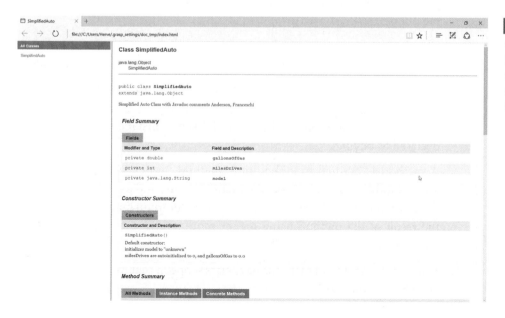

Figure 7.16

Web-Style
Documentation
for the Mutator
and Accessor
Methods

CHAPTER REVIEW

7.17 Chapter Summary

- The members of a Java class include its instance variables, class variables, and methods.

- One copy of each instance variable is created for every object instantiated from the class. One copy of each class variable and method is shared by all objects of the class.

- By convention, class names are nouns and begin with a capital letter; all internal words begin with a capital letter, and other letters are lowercase. Method names are verbs and begin with a lowercase letter; internal words begin with a capital letter, and all other letters are lowercase. Nonconstant instance variables are nouns and follow the same capitalization rules as methods. Constant fields have all capital letters with internal words separated by an underscore.

- The *public* access modifier allows the class or member to be accessed by other classes. The *private* access modifier specifies that the class or member can be accessed only by other members of the same class. Package access allows other classes in the same package or folder to access the class or class members.

- Classes, constructors, *final* class variables, and class methods typically are declared as *public*, and instance variables typically are declared as *private*.

- Instance variables reflect the properties that all objects will have in common. Instance variables are defined by specifying an access modifier, data type, identifier, and, optionally, an initial value. Instance variables can be declared to be *final*.

- A method is defined by providing a method header, which specifies the access modifier, a return type, the method name, and a parameter list. The method body is enclosed in curly braces. Value-returning methods return the result of the method using one or more *return* statements. A method with a *void* return type does not return a value.

- Instance variables and methods have class scope in that they can be accessed anywhere in the class.

- A method can reference the instance variables of its class, the parameters sent to the method, and local variables declared by the method, and it can call other methods of its class.

- A method can be overloaded by defining another method with the same name but a different signature; that is, with a different number of parameters or with parameters of different data types.

- Constructors are responsible for initializing the instance variables of the class.

- If we don't provide a constructor, the compiler provides a default constructor, which is a constructor that takes no arguments. This default constructor assigns default initial values to all the instance variables. Numeric variables are given the value of 0, characters are given the value of the Unicode null character, *boolean* variables are given the value of *false*, and object references are given the value of *null*. Local variables declared in methods are not given initial values automatically.

- Accessor methods are named *getIV*, where *IV* is an instance variable name; the return data type is the same as the instance variable, and the body of the method simply returns the value of the instance variable.

- Mutator methods are named *setIV*, where *IV* is an instance variable name; the return data type is *void* or a reference to *this* object, and the method takes one argument, which is the same data type as the instance variable and contains the new value for the instance variable. The body of the method should validate the new value and, if the new value is valid, assign the new value to the instance variable.

- When a method begins executing, the JVM sets the object reference *this* to refer to the object for which the method has been called.

- The *toString* method is called automatically when an object reference is used as a *String*, and its job is to provide a printable representation of the object data.

- The *equals* method compares two objects for equality; that is, it should return *true* only if the corresponding instance variables in both objects are equal in value, and *false* otherwise.

- *Static* class variables are created when the class is initialized. Thus, class variables exist before any objects are instantiated, and each class has only one copy of the class variables. *Static* variables that are constants are usually declared to be *public* because they typically are provided to allow the client to set preferences for the operations of a class.

- *Static* class methods can reference only *static* variables, can call only *static* methods, and cannot use the object reference *this*.

- A non-*static*, or instance, method can reference both class and instance variables, as well as class and instance methods, and the reference *this*.

- A graphical object usually has instance variables for the starting (*x*, *y*) coordinate. It also provides a *draw* method that takes a *GraphicsContext* object as a parameter and includes the code to draw the graphical object.

- Enumeration types can be defined to give meaning to ordered sets that are represented in a program by numbers. For each name in an *enum* type initialization list, a constant object is created with an instance variable having a sequential numeric value. References can be defined of the *enum* type. Objects of the *enum* type can be compared, printed, and requested to return their numeric value.

- Javadoc, which is part of the JDK, generates documentation for classes. To use Javadoc, you enclose a description of each class, method, and field in a block comment beginning with /** and ending with */. In addition, you can describe each parameter using the *@param* tag and return value using the *@return* tag.

7.18   Exercises, Problems, and Projects

7.18.1   Multiple Choice Exercises

1. What can you say about the name of a class?

   ❏ It must start with an uppercase letter.

   ❏ The convention is to start with an uppercase letter.

2. What can you say about the name of constructors?

   ❏ They must be the same name as the class name.

   ❏ They can be any name, just like other methods.

3. What is a constructor's return type?

   ❏ *void*

   ❏ *Object*

   ❏ The class name

   ❏ A constructor does not have a return type.

4. It is legal to have more than one constructor in a given class.

   ❏ true

   ❏ false

5. In a class, if a field is *private*,

   ❏ it can be accessed directly from any class.

   ❏ it can be accessed directly only from inside its class.

6. In a typical class, what is the general recommendation for access modifiers?

   ❏ Instance variables are *private* and methods are *private*.

   ❏ Instance variables are *private* and methods are *public*.

   ❏ Instance variables are *public* and methods are *private*.

   ❏ Instance variables are *public* and methods are *public*.

7. In a class, fields

   ❏ can only be basic data types.

   ❏ can only be basic data types or existing Java types (from existing classes).

   ❏ can be basic data types, existing Java types, or user-defined types (from user-defined classes).

8. Accessors and mutators are

   ❏ instance variables of a class.

   ❏ used to access and modify field variables of a class from outside the class.

   ❏ constructor methods.

9. Accessor methods typically take

   ❏ no parameter.

   ❏ one parameter, of the same type as the corresponding field.

10. Mutator methods typically take

    ❏ no parameter.

    ❏ one parameter, of the same type as the corresponding field.

11. Accessor methods typically

    ❏ are *void* methods.

    ❏ return the same type as the corresponding field.

12. To enable method chaining, mutator methods

   ❑ return a reference to *this* object.

   ❑ return the same type as the corresponding field.

13. When coding a method that performs calculations on fields of that class,

   ❑ these fields must be passed as parameters to the method.

   ❑ these fields do not need to be passed as parameters to the methods because the class methods have direct access to them.

14. What is the keyword used for declaring a constant?

   ❑ *static*

   ❑ *final*

   ❑ *constant*

15. What is the keyword used for declaring a class variable or method?

   ❑ *static*

   ❑ *final*

   ❑ *class*

16. What can you say about *enum*?

   ❑ It is part of the package *java.lang*.

   ❑ It can be used for self-documentation, improving the readability of your code.

   ❑ An *enum* object is a constant object.

   ❑ All of the above.

7.18.2   Reading and Understanding Code

For Questions 17 and 18, consider that inside the class *Sky*, we have already coded the following:

```java
public class Sky
{
    private Color color;
    public Sky( Color c )
    {
        color = c;
    }
}
```

17. Consider the following method header:

```
public Color getColor( )
```

Is this method a constructor, mutator, or accessor?

18. Consider the following method header:

```
public void setColor( Color c )
```

Is this method a constructor, mutator, or accessor?

For Questions 19 through 24, consider that the class *Airplane* has two methods with the following method headers; we also have a default constructor already coded.

```
public static double foo1( String s )
public String foo2( char c )
```

19. What is the return type of method *foo1*?

20. What is the return type of method *foo2*?

21. Is method *foo1* a class or instance method? Explain.

22. Is method *foo2* a class or instance method? Explain.

23. Write a line or two of code to call method *foo1* from a client class.

24. Write a line or two of code to call method *foo2* from a client class. Assume we have instantiated an object named *a1*.

25. Inside method *main*, we see code like

```
Airplane.foo3( 34.6 );
```

From this, reconstruct the header of method *foo3* (which belongs to the class *Airplane*); make appropriate assumptions if necessary.

26. Inside method *main*, we see code like

```
Airplane a = new Airplane( );
int n = a.foo4( "Hello" );
```

From this, reconstruct the header of method *foo4* (which belongs to class *Airplane*).

27. If you have defined the following *enum* constants

```
enum Seasons { Winter, Spring, Summer, Fall };
```

what is the output of the following code sequence?

```
System.out.println( Seasons.Spring.ordinal( ) );
```

7.18.3   Fill In the Code

28. Declare two instance variables: *grade*, which is an integer, and *letterGrade*, which is a *char*.

```
// declare grade here
// declare letterGrade here
```

29. Declare a class field for a federal tax rate, a constant, with value .07.

```
// declare federal tax rate constant; value is 0.07
```

For Questions 30 through 37, we will assume that class *TelevisionChannel* has three fields: *name*, a *String*; *number*, an integer; and *cable*, a *boolean*, which represents whether the channel is a cable channel.

30. Code a default constructor for that class: initialize the fields to an empty string, 0, and *false*, respectively.

```
// your default constructor code goes here
```

31. Code a constructor for that class that takes three parameters.

```
// your constructor code goes here
```

32. Code the three accessors for that class.

```
// your code goes here
```

33. Code the three mutators for that class.

```
// your code goes here
```

34. Code the *toString* method.

```
// your code goes here
```

35. Code the *equals* method.

```
// your code goes here
```

36. Code a method returning the number of digits in the channel number. For instance, if the channel number is 21, the method returns 2; if the channel number is 412, the method returns 3.

```
// your code goes here
```

37. Code a method returning the word *cable* if the current object represents a cable channel and returning the word *network* if the current object does not represent a cable channel.

```
// your code goes here
```

7.18.4 Identifying Errors in Code

For Questions 38 through 45, consider that inside the class *Gift*, we have already coded the following:

```java
public class Gift
{
    private String description;
    private double price;
    private String occasion;
    private boolean taxable;

    public static final double TAX_RATE = 0.05;

    public Gift( String d, double p, String o, boolean t )
    {
        description = d;
        price = p;
        occasion = o;
        taxable = t;
    }
    public void setPrice( double p )
    {
        price = p;
    }
    public void setTaxable( boolean t )
    {
        taxable = t;
    }
}
```

38. We are coding the following inside the class *Gift*; where is the error?

```java
public void getPrice( )
{
    return price;
}
```

39. We are coding the following inside the class *Gift*; where is the error?

```java
public void setOccasion( String occasion )
{
    occasion = occasion;
}
```

40. We are coding the following inside the class *Gift*; where is the error?

```
public String toString( )
{
  System.out.println( "description = " + description );
  System.out.println( "price = " + price );
  System.out.println( "occasion = " + occasion );
  System.out.println( "taxable = " + taxable );
}
```

41. We are coding the following inside the class *Gift*; where is the error?

```
public boolean equals( Object g )
{
  return ( this == g );
}
```

42. We are coding the following inside the class *Gift*; where is the error?

```
public void setTaxRate( double newTaxRate )
{
    TAX_RATE = newTaxRate;

}
```

43. We are coding the following inside the class *Gift*; where is the error?

```
public double calcTax( TAX_RATE )
{
  return ( TAX_RATE * price );
}
```

44. We are coding the following in the *main* method inside the class *GiftClient*; where is the error?

```
Gift g = new Gift( "radio", 59.99, "Birthday", false );
Gift.setPrice( 99.99 );
```

45. We are coding the following in the *main* method inside the class *GiftClient*; where is the error?

```
Gift g = new Gift( "radio", 59.99, "Birthday", false );
g.setTaxable( ) = true;
```

46. Where are the errors in the following statement?

```
enum Months = { "January", "February", "March" };
```

7.18.5   Debugging Area—Using Messages from the Java Compiler and Java JVM

For Questions 47 and 48, consider the following class *Grade*:

```java
public class Grade
{
    private char letterGrade;

    public Grade( char lg )
    {
        letterGrade = lg;
    }
    public char getLetterGrade( )
    {
        return   letterGrade;
    }
    public void setLetterGrade( char lg )
    {
        letterGrade = lg;
    }
}
```

47. In the *main* method of the class *GradeClient*, you have coded

```java
Grade g = new Grade( 'B' );
g.letterGrade = 'A';            // line 10
```

When you compile, you get the following message:

```
GradeClient.java:10: error: letterGrade has private access in Grade
g.letterGrade = 'A';            // line 10
  ^

1 error
```

Explain what the problem is and how to fix it.

48. In the *main* method of the class *GradeClient*, you have coded

```java
Grade g = new Grade( "A" );    // line 10
```

When you compile, you get the following message:

```
GradeClient.java:10: error: incompatible types: String cannot be converted to
char
Grade g = new Grade ( "A" ); // line 10
                      ^

Note: Some messages have been simplified; recompile with -Xdiags:verbose to get
full output
1 error
```

Explain what the problem is and how to fix it.

49. You coded the following definition for the class *Grade*:

```java
public class Grade
{
    private char letterGrade;
    public char Grade( char startLetter )
    {
        letterGrade = startLetter;
    } // line 8
}
```

When you compile, you get the following message:

```
Grade.java:8: error: missing return statement
  } // line 8
  ^
1 error
```

Explain what the problem is and how to fix it.

50. You coded the following definition for the class *Grade*:

```java
public class Grade
{
  private char letterGrade;

  public Grade( char lg )
  {
    letterGrade = lg;
  }

  public String toString( )      // line 10
  {                              // line 11
      return letterGrade;        // line 12
  }                              // line 13
}
```

When you compile, you get the following message:

```
Grade.java:12: error: incompatible types: char cannot be converted to String
return letterGrade; // line 12
        ^
1 error
```

Explain what the problem is and how to fix it.

51. You coded the following definition for the *Grade* class:

```
public class Grade
{
  private char letterGrade;

  public Grade( char lg )
  {
    letterGrade = lg;
  }

  public String toString( )    // line 10
  {                            // line 11
    return lg;                 // line 12
  }                            // line 13
}
```

When you compile, you get the following message:

```
Grade.java:12: error: cannot find symbol
 return lg; // line 12
        ^
   symbol   : variable lg
   location: class Grade
1 error
```

Explain what the problem is and how to fix it.

52. You coded the following definition for the *Grade* class:

```
public class Grade
{
  private int numberGrade;
  public Grade( int numberGrade )
  {
    numberGrade = numberGrade;
  }
  public int getGrade( )
  {
    return numberGrade;
  }
}
```

In the *main* method of the *GradeClient* class, you have coded:

```
Grade g1 = new Grade( 95 );
System.out.println( g1.getGrade( ) );
```

The code compiles properly and runs, but the result is not what you expected. The client's output is 0, not 95.

Explain what the problem is and how to fix it.

53. You have defined the following *enum* constants:

```
enum Seasons { Winter, Spring, Summer, Fall };
```

In the *main* method of the class *Test*, you have coded:

```
Seasons s = Seasons.Spring;
if ( s.equals( Winter ) )    // line 10
      System.out.println( "It is cold" );
else
      System.out.println( "The weather is fine" );
```

When you compile, you get the following message:

```
Test.java:10: error: cannot find symbol
  if ( s.equals( Winter ) )  // line 10
                 ^
    symbol   : variable Winter
    location: class Test
1 error
```

Explain what the problem is and how to fix it.

54. You have defined the following *enum* constants:

```
enum Seasons { Winter, Spring, Summer, Fall };
```

In the *main* method of the class Test, you have coded

```
Seasons.Fall = Autumn;  // line 10
```

When you compile, you get the following message:

```
Test.java:10: error: cannot assign a value to final variable Fall
  Seasons.Fall = Autumn;  // line 10
          ^
Test.java:10: cannot find symbol
  Seasons.Fall = Autumn;  // line 10
                 ^
    symbol   : variable Autumn
    location: class Test
2 errors
```

Explain what the problem is and how to fix it.

7.18.6   Write a Short Program

55. Write a class encapsulating the concept of a team (for example, "Orioles"), assuming a team has only one attribute: the team name. Include a constructor, the accessor and mutator, and methods *toString* and *equals*. Write a client class to test all the methods in your class.

56. Write a class encapsulating the concept of a television set, assuming a television set has the following attributes: a brand and a price. Include a constructor, the accessors and mutators, and methods *toString* and *equals*. Write a client class to test all the methods in your class.

57. Write a class encapsulating the concept of a course grade, assuming a course grade has the following attributes: a course name and a letter grade. Include a constructor, the accessors and mutators, and methods *toString* and *equals*. Write a client class to test all the methods in your class.

58. Write a class encapsulating the concept of a course, assuming a course has the following attributes: a code (for instance, CS1), a description, and a number of credits (for instance, 3). Include a constructor, the accessors and mutators, and methods *toString* and *equals*. Write a client class to test all the methods in your class.

59. Write a class encapsulating the concept of a student, assuming a student has the following attributes: a name, a Social Security number, and a GPA (for instance, 3.5). Include a constructor, the accessors and mutators, and methods *toString* and *equals*. Write a client class to test all the methods in your class.

60. Write a class encapsulating the concept of website statistics, assuming website statistics have the following attributes: number of visitors and type of site (commercial, government, etc.). Include a constructor, the accessors and mutators, and methods *toString* and *equals*. Write a client class to test all the methods in your class.

61. Write a class encapsulating the concept of a corporate name (for example, "IBM"), assuming a corporate name has only one attribute: the corporate name itself. Include a constructor, the accessors and mutators, and methods *toString* and *equals*. Also include a method returning a potential domain name by adding *www.* at the beginning and *.com* at the end of the corporate name (for instance, if the corporate name is IBM, that method should return *www .ibm.com*). Write a client class to test all the methods in your class.

62. Write a class encapsulating the concept of a file, assuming a file has only a single attribute: the name of the file. Include a constructor, the accessors and mutators, and methods *toString* and *equals*. Also, code a method returning the

extension of the file; that is, the letters after the last dot in the file (for instance, if the file name is *Test.java*, then the method should return *java*); if there is no dot in the file name, then the method should return "*unknown extension.*" Write a client class to test all the methods in your class.

63. Writing *System.out.println* every time we want to output a message is annoying. Write a class that enables us to write *S.pln("Hello world")* instead. Test your class in a client.

64. Write a class that enables us to write code like:

```
int number = Utility.getInt( "Enter an int", '>' );
```

to replace something like:

```
System.out.println( "Enter an int > " );
Scanner scan = new Scanner( System.in );
int number = scan.nextInt( );
```

Test your class in a client.

7.18.7 Programming Projects

65. Write a class encapsulating the concept of the weather forecast, assuming that it has the following attributes: the temperature and the sky conditions, which could be sunny, snowy, cloudy, or rainy. Include a constructor, the accessors and mutators, and methods *toString* and *equals*. Temperature, in Fahrenheit, should be between –50 and +150; the default value is 70, if needed. The default sky condition is sunny. Include a method that converts Fahrenheit to Celsius. Celsius temperature = (Fahrenheit temperature – 32) * 5 / 9. Also include a method that checks whether the weather attributes are consistent (there are two cases where they are not consistent: when the temperature is above 32 and it is snowy, and when the temperature is below 32 and it is rainy). Write a client class to test all the methods in your class.

66. Write a class encapsulating the concept of a domain name, assuming a domain name has a single attribute: the domain name itself (for instance, *www.yahoo .com*). Include a constructor, the accessors and mutators, and methods *toString* and *equals*. Also include the following methods: one returning whether the domain name starts with *www*; another returning the extension of the domain name (i.e., the letters after the last dot, for instance *com*, *gov*, or *edu*; if there is no dot in the domain name, then you should return "*unknown*"); and another returning the name itself (which will be the characters between *www* and the extension; for instance, *yahoo* if the domain is *www.yahoo.com*—if there are

fewer than two dots in the domain name, then your method should return "*unknown*"). Write a client class to test all the methods in your class.

67. Write a class encapsulating the concept of an HTML page, assuming an HTML statement has only a single attribute: the HTML code for the page. Include a constructor, the accessors and mutators, and methods *toString* and *equals*. Include the following methods: one checking that there is a > character following each < character, one counting how many images are on the page (i.e., the number of *img* tags), and one counting how many links are on the page (i.e., the number of times we have "*a href*"). Write a client class to test all the methods in your class.

68. Write a class encapsulating the concept of coins, assuming that coins have the following attributes: a number of quarters, a number of dimes, a number of nickels, and a number of pennies. Include a constructor, the accessors and mutators, and methods *toString* and *equals*. Also code the following methods: one returning the total amount of money in dollar notation with two significant digits after the decimal point, and others returning the money in quarters (for instance, 0.75 if there are three quarters), in dimes, in nickels, and in pennies. Write a client class to test all the methods in your class.

69. Write a class encapsulating the concept of a user-defined *double*, assuming a user-defined *double* has only a single attribute: a *double*. Include a constructor, the accessor and mutator, and methods *toString* and *equals*. Add a method, taking one parameter specifying how many significant digits we want to have, and returning a *double* representing the original *double* truncated so that it includes the specified number of significant digits after the decimal point (for instance, if the original *double* is 6.9872 and the argument of the method is 2, this method will return 6.98). Write a client class to test all the methods in your class.

70. Write a class encapsulating the concept of a circle, assuming a circle has the following attributes: a *Point* representing the center of the circle, and an integer, the radius of the circle. Include a constructor, the accessors and mutators, and methods *toString* and *equals*. Also include methods returning the perimeter ($2 * \pi * radius$) and area ($\pi * radius^2$) of the circle. Write a client class to test all the methods in your class.

71. Write a class encapsulating the concept of a rational number, assuming a rational number has the following attributes: an integer representing the numerator of the rational number, and another integer representing the denominator of the rational number. Include a constructor, the accessors and mutators, and methods *toString* and *equals*. You should not allow the denominator to be

equal to 0; you should give it the default value 1 in case the corresponding argument of the constructor or a method is 0. Also include methods performing multiplication of a rational number by another and addition of a rational number to another, returning the resulting rational number in both cases. Write a client class to test all the methods in your class.

72. Write a class encapsulating the concept of an investment, assuming the investment has the following attributes: the amount of the investment and the interest rate at which the investment will be compounded. Include a constructor, the accessors and mutators, and methods *toString* and *equals*. Also include a method returning the future value of the investment depending on how many years we hold it before selling it, which can be calculated using the following formula:

```
future value = investment ( 1 + interest rate )^numberOfYears
```

We will assume that the interest rate is compounded annually. Write a client class to test all the methods in your class.

73. Write a class encapsulating the concept of a telephone number, assuming a telephone number has only a single attribute: a *String* representing the telephone number. Include a constructor, the accessor and mutator, and methods *toString* and *equals*. Also include methods returning the area code (the first three digits/characters of the phone number; if there are fewer than three characters in the phone number or if the first three characters are not digits, then this method should return "*unknown area code*"). Write a client class to test all the methods in your class. Look up the *getClass* method in the *Object* class and the *getName* method in the *Class* class and use them in your client.

74. Write a class that encapsulates the concept of a tennis match score (best of 3 sets). It has the following instance variables: two *ints* for the score in the first set, two *ints* for the score in the second set, two *ints* for the score in the third set, and two *Strings* for the score in the current game. You do not need to keep track of who is serving. Your score should comply with basic tennis rules (a game score

for a given player is either LOVE, 15, 30, 40, or AD). A set must be won by 2 (there is no tie breaker in this format). Write the following methods: a default constructor, *toString*, a method to update the score (when a player wins a point), and a method to check if the game is over. The method that updates the score takes one parameter, a *boolean*; if it is *true*, the first player won the point, if it is *false*, the second player won the point. Furthermore, if the game is over, the score should not be changed. The method that checks if the game is over returns *0* if the game is not over, *1* if the first player won, and *2* if the second player won. Write a client that enables the user to play.

75. Write a class that encapsulates an icon for your favorite TV channel or Internet website. Your icon should be made of a minimum of three colors and three shapes. It should be scalable by specifying the value of one instance variable, and the client should be able to change the colors easily. Your class should include a constructor, a draw method, and mutators to enable the user to change the scale, to change the colors in the icon, and to change the top-left coordinates of the icon.

7.18.8   Technical Writing

76. An advantage of object-oriented programming is code reuse, not just by the programmer who wrote the class, but by other programmers. Describe the importance of proper documentation and how you would document a class so that other programmers can use it easily.

77. Java has a number of naming conventions for classes, methods, and field variables. Is this important? Why is it good to respect these conventions?

7.18.9   Group Project (for a group of 1, 2, or 3 students)

78. Write a program that solves a quadratic equation in all cases, including when both roots are complex numbers. For this, you need to set up the following classes:

   Complex, which encapsulates a complex number

   ComplexPair, which encapsulates a pair of complex numbers

   Quadratic, which encapsulates a quadratic equation

   SolveEquation, which contains the *main* method

Along with the usual constructors, accessors, and mutators, you will need to code additional methods:

In the *Complex* class, a method that determines whether a complex object is real

In the *ComplexPair* class, a method that determines whether both complex numbers are identical

In the *Quadratic* class, a method to solve the quadratic equation and return a *ComplexPair* object

Additionally, you need to include code in the *main* method to solve several examples of quadratic equations input from the keyboard. Your output should make comments as to what type of roots we get (double real root, distinct real roots, distinct complex roots). You should check that your code works in all four basic cases:

❑ The quadratic equation is actually a linear equation.

❑ Both roots are complex.

❑ There is a double real root.

❑ There are two distinct real roots.

CHAPTER 8
Single-Dimensional Arrays

CHAPTER CONTENTS

Introduction

Up to this point, we have been working with individual, or scalar, variables; that is, each variable has held one value at a time. To process a group of variables of the same type—for example, counting the number of odd integers entered by the user—we used a *while* loop or a *for* loop.

Thus, to find the average high temperature for the last year, we would use a *for* loop:

```java
double dailyTemp;
double total = 0.0;
for ( int i = 1; i <= 365; i++ )
{
   System.out.print( "Enter a temperature" );
   dailyTemp = scan.nextDouble( );
   total += dailyTemp;
}
double average = total / 365;
```

We defined one variable, *dailyTemp*, to hold the data. We read each temperature into our *dailyTemp* variable, added the temperature to our total, then read the next value into the *dailyTemp* variable, added that temperature to the total, and so on, until we finished reading and processing all the temperatures. Each time we read a new temperature, it overwrote the previous temperature, so that at the end of the loop, we had access to the last temperature only.

But suppose we want to perform multiple operations on those temperatures. Perhaps we want to find the highest or lowest temperature or find the median. Or suppose we don't know what operations we will perform, or in what order, until the user chooses them from a menu. In those cases, one scalar variable, *dailyTemp*, won't work; we want to store all the temperatures in memory at the same time. An array allows us to do just that without declaring 365 variables individually.

An **array** is a sequence of variables of the same data type. The data type could be any Java primitive data type, such as *int, float, double, byte, boolean, char, short,* or *long,* or it could be a class. Each variable in the array, called an **element**, is accessed using the array name and a subscript, called an **index**, which refers to the element's position in the array.

Arrays are useful for many applications: for example, calculating statistics on a group of data values or processing data stored in tables, such as matrices or game boards.

8.1 Declaring and Instantiating Arrays

In Java, arrays are implemented as objects, so creating an array takes two steps:

1. Declaring the object reference for the array.

2. Instantiating the array.

In arrays of primitive types, each element in the array contains a value of that type. For example, in an array of *doubles*, each element contains a *double* value. In arrays of objects, each element is an object reference, which stores the location of an object.

8.1.1 Declaring Arrays

To declare an array, we specify the name of the array and the data type, as we would for any other variable. Adding an empty set of brackets ([ ]) indicates that the variable is an array.

Here is the syntax for declaring an array:

```
datatype [ ] arrayName;
```

For example, the following statement creates a reference to an array that will hold daily high temperatures:

```
double [ ] dailyTemps; // each element is a double
```

The brackets can be placed before or after the array name. So the following syntax is also valid:

```
datatype arrayName [ ];
```

Thus, we could have declared the preceding array using the following statement:

```
double dailyTemps [ ];
```

Although Java code can be written using either syntax, we prefer the first format with the brackets right after the data type, because it's easier to read as "a *double* array."

To declare an array to hold the titles of all tracks on a CD, we might declare it this way:

```
String [ ] cdTracks; // each element is a String object reference
```

Similarly, this statement declares an array to hold the answers to a true/false test:

```
boolean [ ] answers; // each element is a boolean value
```

Assuming we have written an *Auto* class, this statement declares an array to hold *Auto* objects:

```
Auto [ ] cars; // each element is an Auto object reference
```

We can declare multiple arrays of the same data type in one statement by inserting a comma after each array name, using this syntax:

```
datatype [ ] arrayName1, arrayName2;
```

For example, the following statement will declare three integer arrays to hold quiz scores for current courses:

```
int [ ] cs101, bio201, hist102; // all elements are int values
```

COMMON ERROR TRAP
Putting the size of the array inside the brackets in the array declaration will generate a compiler error.

Note that an array declaration does not specify how many elements the arrays will have. The declaration simply specifies an object reference for the array and the data type of the elements. Thus, **declaring an array does not allocate memory for the array**.

8.1.2 Instantiating Arrays

As we mentioned earlier, Java arrays are objects, so to allocate memory for an array, we need to instantiate the array using the *new* keyword. Here is the syntax for instantiating an array:

```
arrayName = new datatype [size];
       where size is an expression that evaluates to an integer and
       specifies the number of elements in the array.
```

The following statements will instantiate the arrays declared earlier:

```
dailyTemps = new double [365]; // dailyTemps has 365 elements

cdTracks = new String [15];    // cdTracks has 15 elements

int numberOfQuestions = 30;
answers = new boolean [numberOfQuestions]; // answers has 30 elements

cars = new Auto [3];           // cars has 3 elements

cs101 = new int [5];           // cs101 has 5 elements

bio201 = new int [4];          // bio201 has 4 elements

hist102 = new int [6];         // hist102 has 6 elements
```

When an array is instantiated, the elements are given initial values automatically.

TABLE 8.1   Default Initial Values of Array Elements

Element Data Type	Initial Value
double	0.0
float	0.0
int, long, short, byte	0
char	null character ('\u0000')
boolean	*false*
object reference	*null*

Numeric elements are set to 0, *boolean* elements are set to *false, char* elements are set to the Unicode null character, and object references are set to *null*, as shown in Table 8.1.

Thus, all the elements in the *dailyTemps* array are given an initial value of 0.0; the elements in the *cs101, bio201*, and *hist102* arrays are given an initial value of 0; the elements of the *answers* array are given an initial value of *false*; and the elements of the *cdTracks* and *cars* arrays are given an initial value of *null*.

8.1.3   Combining the Declaration and Instantiation of Arrays

Arrays also can be instantiated when they are declared. To combine the declaration and instantiation of an array, we use this syntax:

```
datatype [ ] arrayName = new datatype [size];
```

```
    where size is an expression that evaluates to an integer and
    specifies the number of elements in the array.
```

Thus, this statement:

```
double [ ] dailyTemps = new double [365];
```

is equivalent to:

```
double [ ] dailyTemps;
dailyTemps = new double [365];
```

Similarly, this statement:

```
String [ ] cdTracks = new String [15];
```

is equivalent to:

```
String [ ] cdTracks;
cdTracks = new String [15];
```

8.1.4   Assigning Initial Values to Arrays

Java also allows us to instantiate an array by assigning initial values when the array is declared. To do this, we specify the initial values using a comma-separated list within curly braces:

```
datatype [ ] arrayName = { value0, value1, value2, ... };

    where valueN is an expression that evaluates to the data type
    of the array and is the value to assign to the element at index N.
```

COMMON ERROR TRAP
An initialization list can be given only when the array is declared. Attempting to assign values to an array using an initialization list after the array is instantiated will generate a compiler error.

Note that we do not use the *new* keyword and we do not specify a size for the array. The number of elements in the array is determined by the number of values in the initialization list.

For example, this statement declares and instantiates an array of odd numbers:

```
int nine = 9;
int [ ] oddNumbers = { 1, 3, 5, 7, nine, nine + 2, 13, 15, 17, 19 };
```

Because 10 values are given in the initialization list, this array has 10 elements. Notice that the values can be an expression, for example, *nine* and *nine + 2*.

COMMON ERROR TRAP
The *new* keyword is not used when an array is instantiated using an initialization list. No size is given; the number of values in the list specifies the size of the array.

Similarly, we can declare and instantiate an array of objects by providing objects in the list, as shown next. The *cars* array of *Auto* objects has three elements.

```
Auto sportsCar = new Auto( "Ferrari", 0, 0.0 );
Auto [ ] cars = { new Auto( "BMW", 100, 15.0 ), sportsCar, new Auto( ) };
```

8.2   Accessing Array Elements

Elements of an array are accessed using this syntax:

```
arrayName[exp]

    where exp is an expression that evaluates to an integer.
```

Exp is the element's position, or **index**, within the array. The index of the first element in the array is always 0; the index of the last element is always 1 less than the number of elements.

TABLE 8.2   Accessing Array Elements

Element	Syntax
Element 0	`arrayName[0]`
Element *i*	`arrayName[i]`
Last element	`arrayName[arrayName.length - 1]`

Arrays have a read-only, integer instance variable, **length**, which holds the number of elements in the array. To access the number of elements in an array named *arrayName*, use this syntax:

```
arrayName.length
```

Thus, to access the last element of an array, use this syntax:

```
arrayName[arrayName.length - 1]
```

Note that regardless of the data type of the elements in an array, the *length* of an array is always an integer, because *length* represents the number of elements in the array.

Table 8.2 summarizes the syntax for accessing elements of an array.

For example, suppose we want to analyze our monthly cell phone bills for the past six months. We want to calculate the average bill, the total payments for the six months, and the lowest and highest bills. We can use an array of *doubles* with six elements, as shown in Example 8.1.

COMMON ERROR TRAP
Note that for an array, *length*—with no parentheses—is an instance variable, whereas for *Strings*, *length( )*—with parentheses—is a method. Note also that the instance variable is named *length*, rather than *size*.

```
 1 /* Array of Cell Phone Bills
 2    Anderson, Franceschi
 3 */
 4
 5 public class CellBills
 6 {
 7   public static void main( String [ ] args )
 8   {
 9     // declare and instantiate the array
10     double [ ] cellBills = new double [6];
11
12     // assign values to array elements
13     cellBills[0] = 45.24;
14     cellBills[1] = 54.67;
15     cellBills[2] = 42.55;
16     cellBills[3] = 44.61;
```

```
17      cellBills[4] = 65.29;
18      cellBills[5] = 49.75;
19
20      System.out.println( "The first monthly cell bill is "
21                              + cellBills[0] );
22      System.out.println( "The last monthly cell bill is "
23                              + cellBills[cellBills.length - 1] );
24   }
25 }
```

EXAMPLE 8.1   The *cellBills* Array

In lines 9–10, we declare and instantiate the *cellBills* array. Because the elements of *cellBills* are *doubles*, instantiating the array also initializes each element to 0.0 and sets the value of *cellBills.length* to 6. Thus, Figure 8.1 represents the *cellBills* array after line 10 is executed.

Lines 12–18 store values into each element of the array. The element at index *i* of the array is *cellBills[i]*. Remember that the first element of an array is always at index 0. Thus, the last element is *cellBills[5]*, or equivalently, *cellBills[cellBills. length – 1]*. Figure 8.2 shows how the *cellBills* array looks after lines 13–18 are executed.

Lines 20–21 print the value of the first element, and lines 22–23 print the value of the last element. The output of Example 8.1 is shown in Figure 8.3.

Array indexes *must* be between 0 and *arrayName.length* – *1*. Attempting to access an element of an array using an index less than 0 or greater than *array-Name.length* – *1* will compile without errors, but will generate an *ArrayIndex-OutOfBoundsException* at run time. By default, this exception halts execution of the program.

Figure 8.1

The *cellBills* Array
After Instantiation

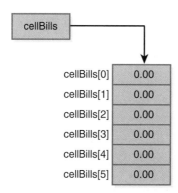

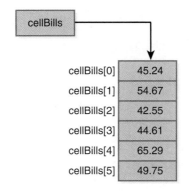

Figure 8.2

The *cellBills* Array After Assigning Values

```
The first monthly cell bill is 45.24

The last monthly cell bill is 49.75
```

Figure 8.3

Output of Example 8.1

For example, all the following expressions are invalid:

```
// invalid indexes for the cellBills array!!
cellBills[-1]                   // the lowest valid index is 0
cellBills[cellBills.length]     // the highest valid index is
                                // cellBills.length - 1
cellBills[150]                  // the highest valid index is 5
```

COMMON ERROR TRAP
Attempting to access an element of an array using an index less than 0 or an index greater than *arrayName. length – 1* will generate an *ArrayIndex-OutOfBounds-Exception* at run time.

Instantiating an array with a class data type involves two steps:

1. Instantiate the array.
2. Instantiate the objects.

Remember that the elements of an array with a class data type are object references. When the array is instantiated, all elements are set to *null*. Thus, the second step needs to be instantiating each object and assigning its reference to an array element.

Example 8.2 illustrates how to work with an array of objects. In this example, we use an *Auto* class whose API is shown in Table 8.3.

```
1 /* Working with an Array of Objects
2    Anderson, Franceschi
3 */
4
```

TABLE 8.3   The *Auto* Class API

Auto Class Constructor Summary
`Auto( )`
creates an *Auto* object with initial default values of "unknown," 0, and 0.0.
`Auto( String model, int milesDriven, double gallonsOfGas )`
creates an *Auto* object with the initial values of *model, milesDriven,* and *gallonsOfGas*

Auto Class Method Summary	
Return value	**Method name and argument list**
`String`	`getModel( )`
	returns the value of *model*
`int`	`getMilesDriven( )`
	returns the value of *milesDriven*
`double`	`getGallonsOfGas( )`
	returns the value of *gallonsOfGas*
`Auto`	`setModel( String model )`
	mutator for *model*
`Auto`	`setMilesDriven( int milesDriven )`
	mutator for *milesDriven*
`Auto`	`setGallonsOfGas( double gallonsOfGas )`
	mutator for *gallonsOfGas*
`double`	`milesPerGallon( )`
	returns the gas mileage for this *Auto* object
`String`	`toString( )`
	returns a *String* representation of this object
`boolean`	`equals( Object obj )`
	compares this *Auto* object to another object

```
5 public class AutoArray
6 {
7   public static void main( String [ ] args )
8   {
9     // 1. instantiate cars array
```

```
10      Auto [ ] cars = new Auto [3];
11
12      // 2. instantiate Auto objects
13      Auto sportsCar = new Auto( "Ferrari", 100, 15.0 );
14      cars[0] = sportsCar;      // assign sportsCar to element 0
15      cars[1] = new Auto( );    // default Auto object
16      // cars[2] has not been instantiated and is null
17
18      // call Auto methods
19      System.out.println( "cars[0] is a " + cars[0].getModel( ) );
20
21      Auto myCar = cars[1];
22      System.out.println( "myCar has used " + myCar.getGallonsOfGas( )
23                          + " gallons of gas" );
24
25      // attempt to call method when Auto object is not instantiated
26      System.out.println( "cars[2] is a " + cars[2].getModel( ) );
27    }
28 }
```

EXAMPLE 8.2   Working with an Array of Objects

At lines 9–10, we declare and instantiate *cars*, an array of three *Auto* objects. At this point, each element has the value of *null*. Thus, our second step is to instantiate objects of the *Auto* class and assign their references to the array elements.

At lines 13–14, we instantiate the *Auto* object *sportsCar* and assign the *sportsCar* reference to element 0. At line 15, we instantiate a default *Auto* object and assign its reference to element 1. We do not instantiate an object for element 2, which remains *null*.

We then call methods of the *Auto* class. Because the array elements are object references, to call a method for an object in an array, we use the array name and index, along with the dot notation. This is illustrated in line 19, where we print the model of element 0 by calling the *getModel* method. In lines 21–23, we assign element 1 to the *Auto* reference *myCar*, then call the *getGallonsOfGas* method using the *myCar* reference.

Finally, line 26 attempts to retrieve the model of element 2; however, because *cars[2]* is *null*, a *NullPointerException* is generated. Figure 8.4 shows the output of this program.

COMMON ERROR TRAP

With an array of objects, be sure that an array element points to an instantiated object before attempting to use that element to call a method of the class. Otherwise, a *NullPointer-Exception* will be generated.

Figure 8.4

Output of
Example 8.2

```
cars[0] is a Ferrari
myCar has used 0.0 gallons of gas
Exception in thread "main" java.lang.NullPointerException
        at AutoArray.main(AutoArray.java:26)
```

Skill Practice
with these end-of-chapter questions

8.11.1   Multiple Choice Exercises

Questions 1, 2, 3, 4, 5, 7, 8

8.11.2   Reading and Understanding Code

Questions 13, 14, 15

8.11.4   Identifying Errors in Code

Questions 36, 37, 38, 40, 42, 44

8.11.5   Debugging Area

Question 45

8.11.8   Technical Writing

Questions 73, 75

8.3   Aggregate Array Operations

Once the array is declared and instantiated, it would be convenient if we could just use the array name to perform operations on the whole array, such as printing the array, copying the array to another array, inputting values to the array, and so on. Unfortunately, Java does not support these aggregate operations on arrays.

For example, attempting to print the array using the array name will *not* print all the elements of the array. Instead, this statement:

```
System.out.println( cellBills ); // incorrect attempt to print array!
```

calls the *toString* method of the *Array* class, which simply prints the name of the object's class and the hash code of the array name, for example, [D@310d42.

8.3.1   Printing Array Elements

To print all elements of an array, we need to use a loop that prints each element individually. A *for* loop is custom made for processing all elements of an array in order. In fact, the following *for* loop header is a standard way to process all array elements with the loop control variable representing each index in the array:

```
for ( int i = 0; i < arrayName.length; i++ )
```

Note that the initialization statement:

```
int i = 0;
```

sets *i* to the index of the first element of the array.

The loop update

```
i++
```

increments *i* to the next index so that we process each element in order.

The loop condition:

```
i < arrayName.length
```

continues execution of the loop as long as the index is less than the *length* of the array.

Note that we use the *less than* operator (<) in the condition. Using the *less than or equal to* operator (<=) would cause us to attempt to reference an element with an index of *arrayName.length*, which is beyond the end of the array.

Inside the *for* loop, we refer to the current element being processed as

```
arrayName[i]
```

Example 8.3, whose output is shown in Figure 8.5, demonstrates how to print each element in an array.

```
 1 /* Printing Array Elements
 2    Anderson, Franceschi
 3 */
 4
 5 public class PrintingArrayElements
 6 {
 7   public static void main( String [ ] args )
 8   {
 9     double [ ] cellBills = new double [6];
10     cellBills[0] = 45.24;
11     cellBills[1] = 54.67;
12     cellBills[2] = 42.55;
```

COMMON ERROR TRAP

In a *for* loop, using the condition:

```
i <=
arrayName.
length
```

will generate an *ArrayIndex-OutOfBounds-Exception* because the index of the last element of an array is *arrayName. length – 1*.

```
13     cellBills[3] = 44.61;
14     cellBills[4] = 65.29;
15     cellBills[5] = 49.75;
16
17     System.out.println( "Element\tValue" );
18     for ( int i = 0; i < cellBills.length; i++ )
19     {
20       System.out.println( i + "\t" + cellBills[i] );
21     }
22   }
23 }
```

EXAMPLE 8.3   Printing All Elements of an Array

Figure 8.5

Output of
Example 8.3

```
Element   Value

0         45.24

1         54.67

2         42.55

3         44.61

4         65.29

5         49.75
```

In lines 9–15, we instantiate the *cellBills* array and assign values to its six elements. In line 18, we use the standard *for* loop header. Inside the *for* loop (line 20), we print each element's index and value.

8.3.2   Reading Data into an Array

Similarly, we can use the standard *for* loop to input data into an array. In Example 8.4, we use a *for* loop to prompt the user for each monthly cell phone bill and to assign the input value to the appropriate array elements.

```
1 /* Reading data into an array
2    Anderson, Franceschi
3 */
```

```
 4
 5 import java.util.Scanner;
 6
 7 public class ReadingDataIntoAnArray
 8 {
 9   public static void main( String [ ] args )
10   {
11     Scanner scan = new Scanner( System.in );
12
13     double [ ] cellBills = new double[6];
14     for ( int i = 0; i < cellBills.length; i++ )
15     {
16       System.out.print( "Enter bill amount for month "
17                         + ( i + 1 ) + "\t" );
18       cellBills[i] = scan.nextDouble( ); // read current bill
19     }
20   }
21 }
```

EXAMPLE 8.4   **Reading Data from the Keyboard into an Array**

At lines 14–19, our *for* loop prompts the user for a value for each element in the *cell-Bills* array. Note that our prompt uses the expression $(i + 1)$ for the month number. Although array indexes start at 0, people start counting at 1. If we used the array index in the prompt, we would ask the user for the bills for months 0 to 5. By adding 1 to the array index, we are able to prompt the user for months 1 through 6, which are the month numbers that the user expects.

SOFTWARE
ENGINEERING
TIP
Prompt for data
in terms the user
understands.

The output of Example 8.4 is shown in Figure 8.6.

```
Enter bill amount for month 1    63.33

Enter bill amount for month 2    54.27

Enter bill amount for month 3    71.19

Enter bill amount for month 4    59.03

Enter bill amount for month 5    62.65

Enter bill amount for month 6    65.08
```

Figure 8.6

Reading Data into
an Array

8.3.3 Summing the Elements of an Array

To sum the elements of the array, we again use the standard *for* loop, as shown in Example 8.5.

```
1 /* Summing Array Elements
2    Anderson, Franceschi
3 */
4
5 import java.text.NumberFormat;
6
7 public class SummingArrayElements
8 {
9   public static void main( String [ ] args )
10  {
11    double [ ] cellBills = new double [6];
12    cellBills[0] = 45.24;
13    cellBills[1] = 54.67;
14    cellBills[2] = 42.55;
15    cellBills[3] = 44.61;
16    cellBills[4] = 65.29;
17    cellBills[5] = 49.75;
18
19    double totalBills = 0.0; // initialize total
20    for ( int i = 0; i < cellBills.length; i++ )
21    {
22      totalBills += cellBills[i];
23    }
24
25    NumberFormat priceFormat = NumberFormat.getCurrencyInstance( );
26    System.out.println( "Total for the bills: "
27                        + priceFormat.format( totalBills ) );
28  }
29 }
```

EXAMPLE 8.5   Summing the Elements of an Array

We fill the *cellBills* array with values at lines 12–17. We declare the *double* variable *totalBills* and initialize it to 0.0 at line 19. The *for* loop, at lines 20–23, adds each element of the array to *totalBills*. We use the *NumberFormat* class to format the value of *totalBills* as currency for output (lines 25–27). The output of Example 8.5 is shown in Figure 8.7.

```
Total for the bills: $302.11
```

Figure 8.7

Calculating
the Total of All
Elements

8.3.4   Finding Maximum or Minimum Values

Suppose we want to find the month that has the lowest bill. That would require finding a minimum value in the array and noting its index. Similarly, to find a month with the highest bill, we would need to find a maximum value in the array and note its index.

To find a maximum or minimum value in an array, we use a variation of the standard *for* loop. Example 8.6 finds the highest array value and its array index for our *cellBills* array of monthly cell bills.

```java
 1 /* Finding the maximum array value
 2    Anderson, Franceschi
 3 */
 4
 5 import java.text.NumberFormat;
 6
 7 public class MaxArrayValue
 8 {
 9  public static void main( String [ ] args )
10  {
11     double [ ] cellBills = new double [6];
12     cellBills[0] = 45.24;
13     cellBills[1] = 54.67;
14     cellBills[2] = 42.55;
15     cellBills[3] = 44.61;
16     cellBills[4] = 65.29;
17     cellBills[5] = 49.75;
18
19     int maxIndex = 0; // initialize to index of first element
20     for ( int i = 1; i < cellBills.length; i++ )
21     {
22      if ( cellBills[i] > cellBills[maxIndex] )
23        maxIndex = i; // save index of maximum value
24     }
25
26     NumberFormat priceFormat = NumberFormat.getCurrencyInstance( );
27     System.out.println ( "The highest bill, "
```

```
28                         + priceFormat.format( cellBills[maxIndex] )
29                         + ", was found at index " + maxIndex );
30  }
31 }
```

EXAMPLE 8.6   Finding a Maximum Value in an Array

We start by assuming that the first element is a maximum value. So we initialize an integer variable, *maxIndex*, to 0, at line 19. Then, at lines 20–24, starting at element 1, we step through the array, comparing the value of each element with the element at *maxIndex*. Whenever we find a value higher than the current maximum, we assign its index to *maxIndex* (line 23). When the *for* loop completes, *maxIndex* holds the index of the array element with a highest value. We then print both that index and the corresponding array value at lines 26–29. The output is shown in Figure 8.8.

What happens if the array has only one value? Will we still get the correct result? The answer is yes, because the single element will be at index 0. We start by assigning 0 to *maxIndex*. Then the *for* loop body will not execute because the condition will evaluate to *false*. So *maxIndex* will not be changed and remains set to 0.

What happens if more than one element holds the highest value? We find the index of the first element only, because our condition requires that the element value must be greater than the current maximum to change *maxIndex*.

8.3.5   Copying Arrays

Suppose we create a second array to hold a copy of our cell phone bills, as shown in the following statement:

```
double [ ] billsBackup = new double [6];
```

At this point, all elements of the *billsBackup* array are initialized automatically to 0.0. Figure 8.9 shows the current state of the *cellBills* and *billsBackup* arrays.

Then, if we want to copy the elements of the *cellBills* array to the corresponding elements of the *billsBackup* array, we might be tempted to use the assignment operator:

```
billsBackup = cellBills; // incorrect attempt to copy array elements!
```

Figure 8.8

Output of
Example 8.6

```
The highest bill, $65.29, was found at index 4
```

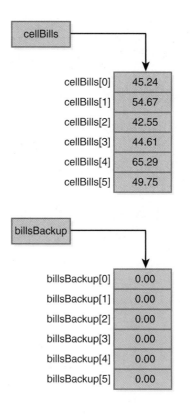

Figure 8.9

The *cellBills* and *billsBackup* Arrays

This won't work. Because arrays are objects, the assignment operator copies the *cellBills* object reference to the *billsBackup* object reference. Both *cellBills* and *billsBackup* now point to the same object. The array data was not copied. In fact, we just lost the original *billsBackup* array. With no object reference pointing to it, the array is a candidate for garbage collection, as shown in Figure 8.10.

If we were to assign a new value to an element in the *billsBackup* array, we would in fact change the element in the *cellBills* array, because they are now the same array.

This statement:

```
billsBackup[4] = 38.00;
```

has the effect shown in Figure 8.11.

Figure 8.10

Assigning *cellBills* to *billsBackup*

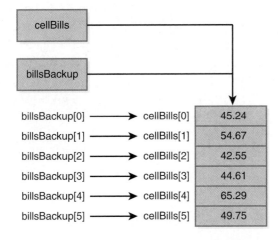

Figure 8.11

Altering *billsBackup* Alters *cellBills* Array

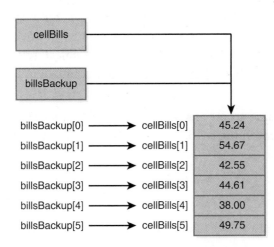

Example 8.7 shows how to copy the elements in one array to another array.

```
1 /* Copying Array Elements to Another Array
2    Anderson, Franceschi
3 */
4
5 public class CopyingArrayElements
6 {
7  public static void main( String [ ] args )
8  {
9     double [ ] cellBills = { 45.24, 54.67, 42.55, 44.61, 65.29, 49.75 };
10
11    double billsBackup [ ] = new double [cellBills.length];
12    for ( int i = 0; i < cellBills.length; i++ )
13    {
14      billsBackup[i] = cellBills[i]; // copy each element
15    }
16
17    billsBackup[4] = 38.00; // change value in billsBackup
18
19    System.out.println( "cellBills\nElement\tValue " );
20    for ( int i = 0; i < cellBills.length; i++ )
21    {
22      System.out.println ( i + "\t" + cellBills[i] );
23    }
24
25    System.out.println( "\nbillsBackup\nElement\tValue " );
26    for ( int i = 0; i < billsBackup.length; i++ )
27    {
28      System.out.println ( i + "\t" + billsBackup[i] );
29    }
30  }
31 }
```

EXAMPLE 8.7 Copying Array Elements into Another Array

At line 9, we instantiate the array *cellBills* using an initialization list. At line 11, we declare and instantiate the array *billsBackup* to have the same size as the original array *cellBills*. At lines 12–15, we use a standard *for* loop to copy one element at a time from the *cellBills* array to the corresponding element in the *billsBackup* array.

Now the *billsBackup* array and the *cellBills* array are separate arrays with their own copies of the element values, as shown in Figure 8.12. Changing an element in one array will have no effect on the value of the corresponding element in the other array.

Figure 8.12

Arrays After
Copying Each
Element

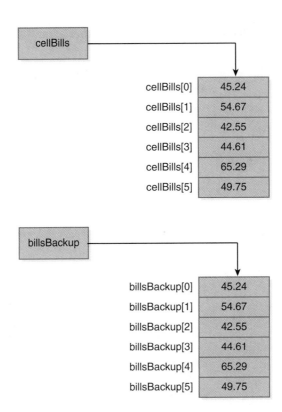

We illustrate this by assigning a new value to an element in the array *bills-Backup* (line 17). Finally, we use two *for* loops to print the contents of both arrays. As Figure 8.13 shows, the value for element 4 is changed only in the array *billsBackup*.

Be aware, however, that when we copy an array whose elements are objects, even using the *for* loop structure, we are copying object references. The result is that the corresponding elements of each array will point to the same object. If an object's data in one array is changed, that change will be reflected in the other array as well.

8.3.6 Changing the Size of an Array

Arrays are assigned a length when they are instantiated, and the *length* of an array becomes a constant value. But what if we want to change the number of elements in an array after it has been instantiated?

```
cellBills
Element  Value
0        45.24
1        54.67
2        42.55
3        44.61
4        65.29
5        49.75


billsBackup
Element  Value
0        45.24
1        54.67
2        42.55
3        44.61
4        38.0
5        49.75
```

Figure 8.13

Output of
Example 8.7

For example, our *cellBills* array contains six elements, holding six months' worth of cell phone bills. If we decide to collect a year's worth of cell phone bills, we would need an array with 12 elements. We could instantiate a new version of the *cellBills* array with 12 elements, using this statement:

```
cellBills = new double [12];
```

That statement instantiates a new array of *doubles* all initialized to 0.0. But what happened to the original array of six elements? Since the *cellBills* reference now refers to the new, 12-element array, the 6-element array has no object reference pointing to it, so there is no way we can access the array's values. That is not the result we intended!

To expand the size of an array while maintaining the values of the original array, we can use the following technique:

1. Instantiate an array with the new size, giving the new array a temporary reference.
2. Copy the elements from the original array to the new array.
3. Point the original array reference to the new array.
4. Assign a *null* value to the temporary array reference.

Thus, instead of immediately pointing *cellBills* to the new array, we should instantiate a 12-element array using a temporary array name, copy the six elements from the *cellBills* array into the 12-element array, assign the *cellBills* reference to the new array, and assign *null* to the temporary array reference. The following code will do that:

```
double [ ] temp = new double [12]; //instantiate new array

// copy all elements from cellBills to temp
for ( int i = 0; i < cellBills.length; i++ )
{
      temp[i] = cellBills[i]; // copy each element
}
cellBills = temp; // assign temp to cellBills
temp = null;      // temp no longer points to cellBills
```

The last statement sets *temp* to *null* so that we don't have two references to the *cellBills* array.

8.3.7   Comparing Arrays for Equality

To compare whether two arrays are equal, first determine if they are equal in length, and then use a *for* loop to compare the corresponding elements in each array. That is, compare element 0 in the first array to element 0 in the second array; compare element 1 in the first array to element 1 in the second array; and so on. If all elements in the first array are equal to the corresponding elements in the second array, then the arrays are equal. Example 8.8 compares two arrays of *doubles*, a primitive data type.

```
 1 /* Comparing Arrays of primitive data types
 2    Anderson, Franceschi
 3 */
 4
 5 public class ComparingArrays
 6 {
 7  public static void main( String [ ] args )
 8  {
 9   double [ ] cellBills1 = { 45.24, 54.67, 42.55, 44.61, 65.29, 49.75 };
10   double [ ] cellBills2 = { 45.24, 54.67, 41.99, 44.61, 65.29, 49.75 };
11
12   boolean isEqual = true;
```

```
13   if ( cellBills1.length != cellBills2.length )
14   {
15     isEqual = false; // arrays are not the same size
16   }
17   else
18   {
19     for ( int i = 0; i < cellBills1.length && isEqual; i++ )
20     {
21       if ( Math.abs( cellBills1[i] - cellBills2[i] ) > 0.001 )
22       {
23           isEqual = false; // elements are not equal
24       }
25     }
26   }
27
28   if ( isEqual )
29     System.out.println( "cellBills1 and cellBills2 are equal" );
30   else
31     System.out.println( "cellBills1 and cellBills2 are not equal" );
32 }
33 }
```

EXAMPLE 8.8   Comparing Arrays of Primitive Data Types

Before we begin the *for* loop, we declare at line 12 a *boolean* variable, *isEqual*, and set it to *true*. In this way, we assume the arrays are equal. Then, our first step is to compare whether the two arrays have the same length (line 13). If they are not the same size, the arrays cannot be equal, so we set *isEqual* to *false* and execution skips to line 28. If the two arrays are the same size, we use a *for* loop at lines 19–25 to test whether the corresponding elements in each array are equal. Note that we have added a second test to the *for* loop condition (*isEqual*). If any corresponding elements are not equal, we set *isEqual* to *false* at line 23. This will cause the condition of the *for* loop to evaluate to *false*, and we exit the *for* loop. Thus, when the *for* loop finishes executing, if any corresponding elements did not match, *isEqual* will be *false*. If both arrays are the same size and all corresponding elements are equal, we never change the value of *isEqual*, so it remains *true*. The output from this example is shown in Figure 8.14.

```
cellBills1 and cellBills2 are not equal
```

Figure 8.14

Output of
Example 8.8

Naturally, if the elements of the arrays are *ints, booleans,* or *chars,* we would use the equality operator (!=) at line 21 as in:

```
if ( intArray1[i] != intArray2[i] )
```

assuming the two arrays we are comparing have names *intArray1* and *intArray2.*

If the elements of the arrays are objects, our *for* loop should call the *equals* method of the objects' class. Thus, to compare two arrays of *Auto* objects, named *cars1* and *cars2,* we would use the following code instead of the condition at line 21:

```
if ( ! cars1[i].equals( cars2[i] ) )
```

COMMON ERROR TRAP
Because arrays are objects, attempting to compare two arrays using the equality operator (==) will compare whether the two array references point to the same array in memory, not whether the data in the two arrays are equal. Calling the *equals* method inherited from the *Object* class yields similar results.

A pitfall to avoid is attempting to test whether two arrays are equal using the equality operator (==). This code:

```
if ( cellBills == billsBackup )
```

will not compare the data of the two arrays. It will compare whether the *cellBills* and *billsBackup* object references are equal; that is, whether they point to the same array.

Similarly, the *equals* method inherited from *Object* also returns the wrong results.

This code:

```
if ( cellBills.equals( billsBackup ) )
```

will return *true* only if both object references point to the same array.

8.3.8   Displaying Array Data as a Bar Chart

One way to display array data is graphically, by drawing a bar chart. For example, the bar chart in Figure 8.15 displays the data in the *cellBills* array.

Each bar is simply a rectangle. Example 8.9 shows the code to generate Figure 8.15.

```
1 /* A bar chart application
2    Anderson, Franceschi
3 */
4
5 import javafx.application.Application;
6 import javafx.stage.Stage;
7 import javafx.scene.canvas.GraphicsContext;
8 import javafx.scene.paint.Color;
9
```

```
10 public class BarChartApplication extends Application
11 {
12   final int LEFT_MARGIN = 35;          // starting x coordinate
13   final int BASE_Y_BAR  = 150;         // bottom of the bars
14   final int BASE_Y_VALUE = 175;        // bottom of the values
15   final int BAR_WIDTH = 30;            // width of each bar
16   final int SPACE_BETWEEN_BARS = 10;   // pixels between bars
17
18   private double [ ] cellBills
19     = { 45.24, 54.67, 42.55, 44.61, 65.29, 49.75 };
20   private String [ ] months
21      = { "March", "April", "May", "June", "July", "August" };
22
23   @Override
24   public void start( Stage stage )
25   {
26     // set up window title and size
27     GraphicsContext gc = JIGraphicsUtility.setUpGraphics(
28                 stage, "Bar Chart", 600, 200 );
29
30     gc.setFill( Color.BLUE );          // bars will be blue
31     int xStart = LEFT_MARGIN;          // x value for first bar
32
33     for ( int i = 0; i < cellBills.length; i++ )
34     {
35       gc.fillRect( xStart, BASE_Y_BAR - cellBills[i],
36                 BAR_WIDTH, cellBills[i] );
37
38       gc.fillText( Double.toString( cellBills[i] ),
39                 xStart, BASE_Y_VALUE );
40
41       // move to starting x value for next bar
42       xStart += BAR_WIDTH + SPACE_BETWEEN_BARS;
43     }
44   }
45
46   public static void main( String [ ] args )
47   {
48     launch( args );
49   }
50 }
```

EXAMPLE 8.9   Displaying Array Values as a Bar Chart

Figure 8.15

The *cellBills* Array
as a Bar Chart

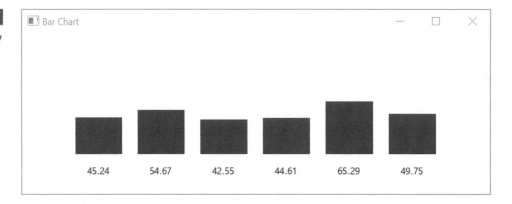

To create the bar chart, we use our standard *for* loop at lines 31–41 in the *start* method and call the *fillRect* method of the *GraphicsContext* class to draw a rectangle for each element (lines 33–34). We use the *fillText* method at lines 36–37 to display the value of each element.

The *fillRect* method takes four arguments: the upper-left *x* value, the upper-left *y* value, the rectangle's width, and the rectangle's height.

We can determine the argument values for the *fillRect* method for each element using the following approach, as illustrated in Figure 8.16:

- Width: The width of the bar is a constant value. For our bar chart, we chose a width of 30 pixels; the constant *BAR_WIDTH* stores that value (line 15).

- Height: The height for each bar is the value of the array element being charted. Thus, in the *fillRect* method call (lines 35–36), we represent the height of a bar as:

  `cellBills[i]`

- Upper-left *y* value: Similarly, the upper-left *y* value will be the height of the bar subtracted from the base *y* value for all the bars; the base *y* value for all the bars is the constant *BASE_Y_BAR* defined in line 13. We subtract the value of the element from the base of the bar because *y* values increase from the top of the window to the bottom. Thus, in our *fillRect* method call, we represent the upper-left *y* value of a bar as:

  `BASE_Y_BAR - cellBills[i]`

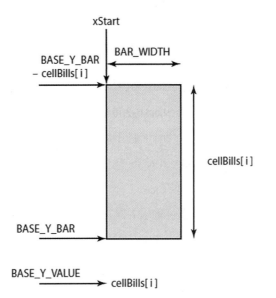

Figure 8.16

Arguments for
Drawing Each Bar

- Upper-left x value: We'll start the first bar at the left side of the window, plus a left margin value, represented by the constant *LEFT_MARGIN* (line 12). After we draw each bar, our *for* loop needs to move the starting x value to the position of the next bar. To do this, at line 42, we increment the starting x value by the width of the bar, *BAR_WIDTH* (defined on line 15), plus the space between bars, *SPACE_BETWEEN_BARS* (defined on line 16).

The arguments to the *fillText* method of the *GraphicsContext* class are the *String* to display and the base x and y values. At line 36, we convert the *cellBills* element to a *String* using the *toString* method of the *Double* wrapper class. The base x value is the same as the starting x value for the element's bar, and the base y coordinate, *BASE_Y_VALUE*, is the base position for printing the array values (defined on line 14).

CODE IN ACTION

Within the online resources, you will find a movie with step-by-step illustrations of working with arrays. Click on the link for this chapter to start the movie.

Skill Practice

with these end-of-chapter questions

8.4   Programming Activity 1: Working with Arrays

In this activity, you will work with a 15-element integer array. Specifically, you will write the code to perform the following operations:

1. fill the array with random numbers between 30 and 99

2. print the array

3. set every array element to a specified value

4. count the number of elements with a specified value

5. find the minimum value in the array

The framework for this Programming Activity will animate your algorithm so that you can check the accuracy of your code. For example, Figure 8.17 shows the application counting the elements having the value 73.

At this point, the application has found the value 73 in element 0 and is comparing the value 73 with the value 69 in element 4.

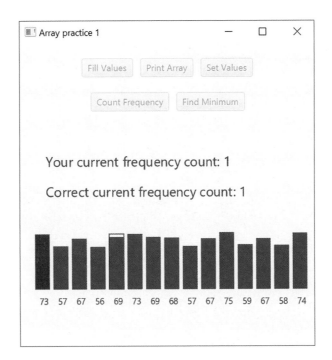

Figure 8.17

Animation of the
Programming
Activity

Instructions

In this chapter's Programming Activity 1 folder in the supplied code files, you will find the source files needed to complete this activity. Copy all the files to a folder on your computer. Note that all files should be in the same folder.

Open the *ArrayPractice1Controller.java* source file. Searching for five asterisks (*****) in the source code will position you at the sample method and the four other locations where you will add your code. We have provided the sample code for task number 1, which you can use as a model for completing the other tasks. In every task, you will fill in the code for a method that will manipulate an existing array of 15 integers. You should not instantiate the array; we have done that for you. Example 8.10 shows the section of the *ArrayPractice1Controller* source code where you will add your code.

Note that for the *countFrequency* and *findMinimum* methods, we provide a dummy *return* statement (*return 0;*) We do this so that the source code will compile. In this way, you can write and test each method separately, using stepwise refinement. When you are ready to write the *countFrequency* and *findMinimum* methods, just replace the dummy *return* statements with the appropriate *return* statement for that method.

```
// ***** 1. The first method has been coded as an example
/**   Fills the array with random numbers between 50 and 80.
 *    The instance variable arr is the integer array
 *    to be filled with values
 */
```

```java
public void fillValues( )
{
    Random rand = new Random( );
    for ( int i = 0; i < arr.length; i++ )
    {
        arr[i] = rand.nextInt( 31 ) + 50;
        animate( i, arr[i] ); // needed to create visual feedback
    }
}
// end of fillValues method

// ***** 2. student writes this method
/** Prints the array to the console with elements separated
 *      by a space
 *    The instance variable arr is the integer array to be printed
 */
public void printArray( )
{
 // Note: to animate the algorithm, put this method call as the
 // last statement in your for loop:
 //                    animate( i, arr[i] );
 //      where i is the index of the current array element
 // Write your code here:


} // end of printArray method

// ***** 3. student writes this method
/** Sets all the elements in the array to parameter value
 *    The instance variable arr is the integer array to be processed
 *    @param value the value to which to set the array elements
 */
public void setValues( int value )
{
 // Note: to animate the algorithm, put this method call as the
 // last statement in your for loop
 //            animate( i arr[i] );
 //      where i is the index of the current array element
 // Write your code here:


} // end of setValues method

// ***** 4. student writes this method
/** Counts number of elements equal to parameter value
 *    The instance variable arr is the integer array to be processed
 *      @param value the value to count
 *      @return the number of elements equal to value
```

```java
*/
public int countFrequency( int value )
{
// Note: to animate the algorithm, put this method call as the
// last statement in your for loop
//          animate( i, count );
//        where i is the index of the current array element
//                  count is the variable holding the frequency
// Write your code here:


    return 0; // replace this line with your return statement

} // end of countFrequency method

// ***** 5. student writes this method
/** Finds and returns the minimum value in arr
*    The instance variable arr is the integer array to be processed
*      @return the minimum value found in arr
*/
public int findMinimum( )
{
// Note: to animate the algorithm, put this method call as the
// last statement in your for loop
//          animate( i, minimum );
//        where i is the index of the current array element
//                  minimum is the variable holding the minimum
// Write your code here:


    return 0; // replace this line with your return statement

} // end of findMinimum method

// End of student code
```

EXAMPLE 8.10   Location of Student Code in *ArrayPractice1Controller*

Our framework will animate your algorithm so that you can watch your code work. For this to happen, be sure that your *for* loop calls the *animate* method. The arguments that you send to *animate* will differ depending on the task you are coding. Detailed instructions for each task are included in the code.

To test your code, compile *ArrayPractice1Controller.java* and run the *ArrayPractice1-Application* source code. Figure 8.18 shows the graphics window when the program begins. Because the values of the array are randomly generated, the values will be different each time the program runs. To test any method, click the appropriate button.

The Graphics
Window When
the Application
Begins

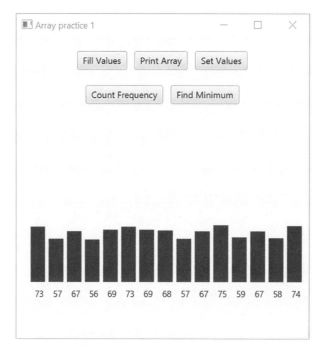

Troubleshooting

If your method implementation does not animate, follow these tips:

- Verify that the last statement in your *for* loop is a call to the *animate* method and that you passed the appropriate arguments to the *animate* method.

- Verify that your *for* loop has curly braces. For example, the *animate* method call is outside the body of this *for* loop:

```
for ( int i = 0; i< arr.length; i++ )
    System.out.println ( arr [i] );
    animate( i ); // this statement is outside the for loop
```

Remember that without curly braces, the *for* loop body consists of only the first statement following the *for* loop header. Enclosing both statements within curly braces will make the *animate* method call part of the *for* loop body.

```
for ( int i = 0; i < arr.length; i++ )
{
    System.out.println ( arr [i] );
    animate( i );
}
```

- Verify that you did not instantiate a new array. Perform all operations on the instance variable array named *arr*.

1. **Could you use the following *for* loop header in every method? Explain why or why not.**

    ```
    for ( int i = 0; i < arr.length; i++ )
    ```

2. **How would you modify the *findMinimum* method to return the index of the minimum value?**

8.5 Using Arrays in Classes

8.5.1 Using Arrays in User-Defined Classes

An array can be used inside a user-defined class just like any other variable. In particular,

-   an array can be an instance variable.

-   an array can be a parameter to a method.

-   a method can return an array.

-   an array can be a local variable inside a method.

To define a method that takes an array as a parameter, use this syntax:

```
accessModifier returnType methodName( dataType [ ] arrayName )
```

The syntax for a method header that returns an array is

```
accessModifier dataType [ ] methodName( parameterList )
```

To pass an array as an argument to a method, just use the array name without brackets as the argument value:

```
methodName( arrayName )
```

In Example 8.11, we define a class named *CellPhone* that illustrates the use of arrays in a class.

```
 1 /** CellPhone class
 2  *    Anderson, Franceschi
 3  */
 4
 5 import java.text.DecimalFormat;
 6
 7 public class CellPhone
 8 {
 9   public final int MONTHS = 6; // default number of months
```

COMMON ERROR TRAP
If we think of the brackets as being part of the data type of the array, then it's easy to remember that the brackets are included in the method header—where the data types of parameters are given—but that brackets are not included in method calls, where the data itself is given.

```
10   private String phoneNumber;
11   private double [ ] cellBills;
12
13   /** Default constructor
14    *    creates cellBills with MONTHS elements
15    */
16   public CellPhone( )
17   {
18      phoneNumber = "";
19      cellBills = new double [MONTHS];
20   }
21
22   /** Constructor
23    *   @param phoneNumber cell phone number
24    *   @param cellBills array of monthly bills
25    */
26   public CellPhone( String phoneNumber, double [ ] cellBills )
27   {
28     this.phoneNumber = phoneNumber;
29
30     // instantiate array with same length as parameter
31     this.cellBills = new double [cellBills.length];
32
33     // copy parameter array to cellBills array
34     for ( int i = 0; i < cellBills.length; i++ )
35     {
36       this.cellBills[i] = cellBills[i];
37     }
38   }
39
40   /** Accessor for the phone number
41    *    @return the phone number
42    */
43   public String getPhoneNumber( )
44   {
45     return phoneNumber;
46   }
47
48   /** Accessor for the cell phone bills
49    *    @return copy of cellBills array
50    */
51   public double [ ] getCellBills( )
52   {
53     double [ ] temp = new double [cellBills.length];
54     for ( int i = 0; i < cellBills.length; i ++ )
55     {
```

```
56        temp[i] = cellBills[i];
57      }
58      return temp;
59   }
60
61   /** Calculates total of all cell phone bills
62    *    @return total of all elements in cellBills array
63    */
64   public double calcTotalBills( )
65   {
66      double total = 0.0; // initialize total to 0.0
67
68      for ( int i = 0; i < cellBills.length; i++ )
69      {
70        total += cellBills[i]; // add current element to total
71      }
72      return total;
73   }
74
75   /** Finds a maximum bill
76    * @return largest value in cellBills array
77    */
78   public double findMaximumBill( )
79   {
80      double max = cellBills[0]; // assume first element is max
81
82      for ( int i = 1; i < cellBills.length; i++ )
83      {
84        if ( cellBills[i] > max )
85          max = cellBills[i]; // save new maximum
86      }
87      return max;
88   }
89
90   /** Returns printable version of CellPhone object
91    *    @return phone number plus each month's bill
92    */
93   @Override
94   public String toString( )
95   {
96      String returnValue = phoneNumber + "\n";
97      DecimalFormat money = new DecimalFormat( "$##0.00" );
98      for ( int i = 0; i < cellBills.length; i++ )
99      {
100         returnValue += money.format( cellBills[i] ) + "\t";
101      }
```

```
102     returnValue += "\n";
103
104     return returnValue;
105   }
106
107   /**  Compares two CellPhone objects for equality
108    *    @param c CellPhone object
109    *    @return true if objects are equal; false, otherwise
110    */
111   @Override
112   public boolean equals( Object c )
113   {
114     if ( !( c instanceof CellPhone ) )
115         return false;
116     else
117     {
118         CellPhone objCP = ( CellPhone ) c;
119         if ( !( phoneNumber.equals( objCP.phoneNumber ) ) )
120           return false;
121
122         if ( cellBills.length != objCP.cellBills.length )
123           return false; // arrays are not the same length
124
125         for ( int i = 0; i < cellBills.length; i++ )
126         {
127             if ( cellBills[i] != objCP.cellBills[i] )
128               return false;
129         }
130         return true;
131     }
132   }
133 }
```

EXAMPLE 8.11　　The *CellPhone* Class

Our *CellPhone* class defines three instance variables in lines 9–11: the phone number (a *String* named *phoneNumber*), monthly bills (an array of *doubles* named *cellBills*), and a constant named *MONTHS*, whose value, 6, represents the number of monthly cell bills, and therefore the length of the *cellBills* array if a *CellPhone* object is instantiated using the default constructor. Note that since *MONTHS* is a constant, we made it *public*.

When our class has instance variables that are arrays, we need to take a little extra care to ensure that encapsulation is not violated.

Let's start with initialization of the array. The overloaded constructor of the *Cell-Phone* class, whose method header is at line 26, includes an array parameter. With parameters of primitive types, the constructor can simply assign the value of the parameter to the instance variable. As we have seen, however, the name of an array is an object reference, which contains the location of the array in memory. If the constructor merely assigns the array parameter, *cellBills*, to our array instance variable, *cellBills*, as in the following code:

```
this.cellBills = cellBills; // incorrect! Client still has reference!
```

then the parameter *cellBills* and the instance variable *cellBills* would point to the same array. That means that the client still has a reference to the array, and the client can change the array values without going through the mutator methods of the class. For example, if the client executes this statement:

```
bills[2] = 75.00;
```

then *cellBills[2]* also gets the value 75.00, because they are the same array. This is clearly a violation of encapsulation, which means that a client should be able to change the *private* fields of a class only by calling the mutator methods of the class.

To avoid this problem, our constructor instantiates a new *cellBills* array that is the same size as the array passed as a parameter, and then copies the elements of the parameter array into the new *cellBills* array (lines 30–37).

There are similar considerations in implementing the accessor method of an array instance variable. With instance variables of primitive types, the accessor methods simply return the value of the instance variable. Our accessor for *cellBills* (lines 48–59) has an array as a return value. If we return the *cellBills* reference, however, we run into the same problem with encapsulation; that is, if our accessor for the *cellBills* instance variable uses this statement:

```
return cellBills; // incorrect! Client has reference to instance variable
```

we give the client a reference to the *cellBills* array, and the client can directly change the values of the array without calling the mutator methods of the class. Just as the constructor instantiated a new array and copied the parameter array's value to the new array, the accessor method should instantiate a new array, copy the *cellBills* array to it, and return a reference to the new array. Thus, at line 53, we declare and instantiate a local array variable named *temp*. At lines 54–57, we copy the contents of *cellBills* into *temp*, and return *temp* at line 58.

SOFTWARE ENGINEERING TIP

Sharing array references with the client violates encapsulation. To return an array from a method, copy the elements of the instance variable array to a temporary array and return a reference to the temporary array. Similarly, to accept an array as a parameter to a method, instantiate a new array and copy the elements of the parameter array to the new array.

We also provide a method *calcTotalBills* (lines 61–73) that calculates the total of the monthly bills using the accumulation technique discussed earlier in the chapter and a *findMaximumBill* method (lines 75–88), which finds a maximum value in the *cellBills* array, also using techniques discussed earlier in the chapter.

Our *toString* method (lines 90–105) builds up a *String* named *returnValue* by first including *phoneNumber*, then formatting each bill using a *DecimalFormat* pattern for money and concatenating that value, plus a tab, to *returnValue*.

The *equals* method (lines 107–132) compares the phone number and each element of the *cellBills* array in the object with the phone number and corresponding element in the *cellBills* array in the parameter object.

We can test our *CellPhone* class with the client class shown in Example 8.12. The output is shown in Figure 8.19.

```
 1 /**   Client to exercise the CellPhone class
 2 *     Anderson, Franceschi
 3 */
 4
 5 import java.text.DecimalFormat;
 6
 7 public class CellPhoneClient
 8 {
 9    public static void main( String [ ] args )
10    {
11      double [ ] bills = new double[3]; // array of cell phone bills
12      bills[0] = 24.60; // assign values
13      bills[1] = 48.75;
14      bills[2] = 62.50;
15
16      // instantiate CellPhone object using default constructor
17      CellPhone c1 = new CellPhone( );
18
19      // instantiate two identical CellPhone objects
20      CellPhone c2 = new CellPhone( "555-555-5555", bills );
21      CellPhone c3 = new CellPhone( "555-555-5555", bills );
22
23      // print data from c1 and c2
24      System.out.println( "c1 = " + c1.toString( ) );
25      System.out.println( "c2 = " + c2.toString( ) );
26
27      // find and print maximum bill
28      DecimalFormat money = new DecimalFormat( "$##0.00" );
```

```
29        System.out.println( "\nThe highest bill is "
30                         + money.format( c2.findMaximumBill( ) ) );
31
32        // find and print total of all bills
33        System.out.println( "\nThe total of all bills is "
34                         + money.format( c2.calcTotalBills( ) ) );
35
36        System.out.println( ); // print blank line
37        // call equals method
38        if ( c2.equals( c3 ) )
39            System.out.println( "c2 and c3 are equal" );
40        else
41            System.out.println( "c2 and c3 are not equal" );
42
43        // test encapsulation
44        // set new value in original array
45        bills[2] = 100.00;
46        // print c2 to show value in object not changed
47        System.out.println( "\nafter client changes original array\n"
48                           + "c2 = " + c2.toString( ) );
49
50        // test encapsulation further
51        // get array of cell bills and store in new array
52        double [ ] billsCopy = c2.getCellBills( );
53
54        billsCopy[1] = 50.00; // change value of one element
55        // print c2 to show value in object not changed
56        System.out.println( "\nafter client changes returned array\n"
57                           + "c2 = " + c2.toString( ) );
58    }
59 }
```

EXAMPLE 8.12   The *CellPhoneClient* Class

In the *CellPhoneClient*, we instantiate three *CellPhone* objects. We instantiate *c1* using the default constructor (line 17), giving it an empty phone number and six months of bills initialized to 0.00, as shown in line 24, when we use the *toString* method to print *c1*'s data. We set up a *bills* array with three values (lines 11–14) and pass *bills* to the overloaded constructor (lines 20–21) to instantiate *c2* and *c3* with identical data. We then use *toString* to print *c2*'s data (line 25).

We then call the *findMaximumBill* method and print its return value (lines 27–30). Next, we call the *calcTotalBills* method and print its return value (lines 32–34).

```
c1 =
$0.00 $0.00 $0.00 $0.00 $0.00 $0.00


c2 = 555–555–5555
$24.60 $48.75 $62.50


The highest bill is $62.50


The total of all bills is $135.85


c2 and c3 are equal


after client changes original array
c2 = 555–555–5555
$24.60 $48.75 $62.50


after client changes returned array
c2 = 555–555–5555
$24.60 $48.75 $62.50
```

A call to the *equals* method to compare *c2* and *c3* (lines 37–41) returns a value of *true*, because the two objects have the same data.

Finally, we test encapsulation two ways. First, we change a value in the *bills* array, then print *c2* again to verify that its data has not changed (lines 43–48). Second, we call the accessor method for the *cellBills* array and change a value in the array returned from the method call. We again print *c2* to verify that its data is unchanged (lines 50–57). Testing the *CellPhone* class with such an example is helpful in checking that we have correctly implemented the class.

8.5.2 Retrieving Command Line Arguments

The syntax of an array parameter for a method might look familiar to you. We've seen it repeatedly in Java applications in the header for the *main* method:

```
public static void main( String [ ] args )
```

As we can see, *main* receives a *String* array as a parameter. That array of *Strings* holds the arguments, if any, that the user sends to the program from the command line. An argument might be the name of a file for the program to read or some configuration parameters that specify preferences in how the application should perform its function.

The sample program in Example 8.13 demonstrates how to retrieve the parameters sent to a Java application. Because *args* is a *String* array, we can use the *length* field to get the number of parameters (lines 8–9), and we use our standard *for* loop format (lines 10–13) to retrieve and print each parameter, as shown in Figure 8.20.

```
1  /** Print Command Line arguments
2   *    Anderson, Franceschi
3   */
4  public class CommandLineArguments
5  {
6    public static void main( String [ ] args )
7    {
8      System.out.println( "The number of parameters is "
9                             + args.length );
10     for ( int i = 0; i < args.length; i ++ )
11     {
12         System.out.println( "args[" + i + "]: " + args[i] );
13     }
14   }
15 }
```

EXAMPLE 8.13   Retrieving Command Line Arguments

Figure 8.20 shows the output produced when we invoke the program as

```
java CommandLineArguments input.txt output.txt
```

```
The number of parameters is 2

args[0]: input.txt

args[1]: output.txt
```

Figure 8.20

Output from
Example 8.13

Skill Practice

with these end-of-chapter questions

8.6   Searching and Sorting Arrays

Arrays are great instruments for storing a large number of related values. As seen earlier in this chapter, we can use arrays to store daily temperatures, CD titles, telephone bills, quiz grades, and other sets of related values. Once the data is stored in an array, we will want to manipulate that data. A very common operation is searching an array for a specific value.

8.6.1   Sequential Search of an Unsorted Array

Let's assume we manage a movie theater. We give each customer a frequent moviegoer card with a unique member ID. We have decided to pick four member IDs at random and give those members a free gift the next time they visit the theater. So we set up a *MovieWinners* class with two array instance variables:

- An array of *ints* that holds the member IDs of the winners
- An array of *Strings* that holds the corresponding prizes

Note that both arrays have four elements and that there is a one-to-one correspondence between the two arrays. Winner #1 will receive prize #1, winner #2 will receive prize #2, and so on. This programming technique is called using **parallel arrays**.

We fill the *winners* array with member IDs chosen randomly. We fill the *prizes* array with *Strings* representing prize descriptions. When a member buys a movie ticket, we look through the *winners* array for the member's ID. If the member's ID is in the *winners* array, we use its index to retrieve the corresponding prize from the *prizes* array that the member won. If the member ID is not found in the array, we know the member is not a winner.

The *MovieWinners* class is shown in Example 8.14.

```java
 1 /** Winners of Free Movies and Other Prizes
 2 *    Anderson, Franceschi
 3 */
 4
 5 import java.util.Random;
 6
 7 public class MovieWinners
 8 {
 9    public final int MEMBERS = 5000;
10    // array to hold winning member numbers chosen at random
11    private int [ ] winners;
12    // parallel array that holds prizes
13    private String [ ] prizes = { "2 free movie tickets!",
14                                  "1 free movie ticket!"
15                                  "free popcorn!",
16                                  "free box of candy!" };
17    /** Default constructor instantiates winners array
18    * and randomly generates winning member IDs
19    */
20    public MovieWinners( )
21    {
22      winners = new int [prizes.length];
23      fillWinners( ); // generate winner member IDs
24    }
25
26    /** Utility method generates winner member IDs
27    *      and stores them in the winners array
28    */
29    private void fillWinners( )
30    {
31      Random rand = new Random( );
32      for ( int i = 0; i < winners.length; i++ )
33      {
34        winners[i] = rand.nextInt( MEMBERS ) + 1;
35      }
36    }
37
38    /** Calls indexOfWinner with the member number
39    *    then translates return value into the prize won
```

```
40    *    @param memberNumber value to find
41    *    @return prize
42    */
43    public String getPrize( int memberNumber )
44    {
45      int prizeIndex = indexOfWinner( memberNumber );
46      if ( prizeIndex == -1 )
47          return "Sorry, member is not a winner.";
48      else
49          return "You win " + prizes[prizeIndex];
50    }
51
52    /** Performs sequential search of winners array
53     *    @param key member ID to find in winners array
54     *    @return index of key if found, -1 if not found
55     */
56    private int indexOfWinner( int key )
57    {
58      for ( int i = 0; i < winners.length; i++ )
59      {
60          if ( winners[i] == key )
61              return i;
62      }
63      return -1;
64    }
65
66    /** Returns printable version of MovieWinners object
67     *    @return winning numbers separated by a tab
68     */
69    @Override
70    public String toString( )
71    {
72      String returnValue = "";
73      for ( int i = 0; i < winners.length; i++ )
74      {
75        returnValue += winners[i] + "\t";
76      }
77      return returnValue;
78    }
79 }
```

EXAMPLE 8.14   The *MovieWinners* Class

The constructor randomly generates values to fill the array by calling the utility method, *fillWinners* (lines 26–36). In the interest of keeping things simple, we have coded the *fillWinners* method in such a way that it does not necessarily generate different numbers; however, the likelihood of two winning numbers being equal is very small. We declare the *fillWinners* method as *private* because it is designed to be called only by the methods of this class.

Our *indexOfWinner* method (lines 52–64) performs a **Sequential Search**, which compares the member ID to each element in the array one by one. The *indexOfWinner* method accepts a parameter, *key*, which is the member ID to search for in the array. If *key* is found, *indexOfWinner* returns the index of that array element. If *key* is not found, that is, if none of the elements in the array matches the value of *key*, *indexOfWinner* returns −1. Since −1 is not a valid array index, it's a good value to use to indicate that the search was unsuccessful.

Notice that if the current array element matches the *key*, the *indexOfWinner* method returns immediately to the caller (line 61); that is, the method stops executing. The return value is the index of the element that matched the *key*. If, however, the method finishes executing all iterations of the *for* loop, then the method has looked at every element in the array without finding a match. In that case, the method returns −1 (line 63), indicating that the *key* was not found.

Our *getPrize* method (lines 38–50) calls *indexOfWinner* to check if its *member-Number* parameter is a winning number; if it is, it uses the array index returned by *indexOfWinner* to return the corresponding element in the array *prizes* (line 49).

Example 8.15 shows a client application that uses our *MovieWinners* class.

```
1 /** Client for the MovieWinners class
2      Anderson, Franceschi
3 */
4 import java.util.Scanner;
5
6 public class MovieWinnersClient
7 {
8   public static void main( String [ ] args )
9   {
10     // instantiate the winningIDs array
11     MovieWinners winningIDs = new MovieWinners( );
12
13     // prompt for the member ID
14     Scanner scan = new Scanner( System.in );
15     System.out.print( "Enter the member's ID "
16                          + "or 0 to stop > " );
```

```
17        int searchID = scan.nextInt( );
18
19        while ( searchID != 0 )
20        {
21           // determine whether member is a winner
22           System.out.println( winningIDs.getPrize( searchID ) );
23
24           System.out.print( "\nEnter the next member's ID "
25                                        + "or 0 to stop > " );
26           searchID = scan.nextInt( );
27        }
28
29        System.out.println( "\nThe winners were "
30                                        + winningIDs.toString( ) );
31     }
32 }
```

SOFTWARE
ENGINEERING
TIP
When you write
a class that uses
corresponding
lists of items
with different
data types,
consider using
parallel arrays.

EXAMPLE 8.15   Client Application for the *MovieWinners* Class

We instantiate a *MovieWinners* object reference named *winningIDs* (lines 10–11). We then prompt for a member ID (lines 15–17) and call the *getPrize* method (line 22) in order to output any prize that may have been won by the current member. Figure 8.21 shows a possible output of running the *MovieWinnersClient* application.

Figure 8.21

Output of
Example 8.15

```
Enter the member's ID or 0 to stop > 1234
Sorry, member is not a winner.

Enter the next member's ID or 0 to stop > 3980
You win free popcorn!

Enter the next member's ID or 0 to stop > 0

The winners were 619 4510 3980 4004
```

8.6.2   Selection Sort

The member IDs in the preceding *winners* array were in random order, so when a member was not a winner, our *findWinners* method needed to look at every element in the array before discovering that the ID we were looking for was not in the array. This is not efficient, since most members are not winners. The larger the array, the more inefficient a sequential search becomes. We could simplify the search by arranging the elements in numeric order, which is called **sorting the array**. Once the array is sorted, we can use various algorithms to speed up a search. Later in this chapter, we discuss how to search a sorted array.

In this chapter, we present two basic sorting algorithms, **Selection Sort** and **Insertion Sort**.

Selection Sort derives its name from the algorithm used to sort the array. We select a largest element in the array and place it at the end of the array. Then we select a next-largest element and put it in the next-to-last position in the array. To do this, we consider the unsorted portion of the array as a **subarray**. We repeatedly select a largest value in the current subarray and move it to the end of the subarray, then consider a new subarray by eliminating the elements that are in their sorted locations, until the subarray has only one element. At that time, the array is sorted.

In more formal terms, we can state the Selection Sort algorithm, presented here in pseudocode, in this way:

```
To sort an array with n elements in ascending order:
1. Consider m elements as a subarray with m = n elements.
2. Find the index of a largest value in this subarray.
3. Swap the values of the element with the largest value and the element in the
   last position in the subarray.
4. Consider a new subarray of m = m − 1 elements by eliminating the last element in
   the previous subarray.
5. Repeat steps 2 through 4 until m = 1.
```

For example, let's walk through a Selection Sort on the following array. At the beginning, the entire array is the subarray (shown here with shading).

We begin by considering the entire array as an unsorted subarray. We find that the largest element is 26 at index 1.

Next we move element 1 to the last element by swapping the values of the elements at indexes 1 and 3.

The value 26 is now in the right place, and we consider elements 0 through 2 as the unsorted subarray.

	Unsorted subarray			Sorted element
Value	**17**	2	5	26
Index	0	1	2	3

The largest element in the new subarray is 17 at index 0. So we move element 0 to the last index of the subarray (index 2) by swapping the elements at indexes 0 and 2.

The value 17 is now in the right place, and we consider elements 0 and 1 as the new unsorted subarray.

	Unsorted subarray		Sorted elements	
Value	**5**	2	17	26
Index	0	1	2	3

The largest element in the new subarray is 5 at index 0. We move element 0 to the last index of the subarray (index 1) by swapping the elements at indexes 0 and 1.

The value 5 is now in the right place, and we consider element 0 as the new subarray. But because there is only one element in the subarray, the subarray is sorted. Thus the whole array is sorted, and our job is done.

	Unsorted subarray		Sorted elements	
Value	2	5	17	26
Index	0	1	2	3

A critical operation in a Selection Sort is swapping two array elements. Before going further, let's examine the algorithm for swapping two array elements.

To swap two values, we need to define a temporary variable that is of the same data type as the values being swapped. This variable will temporarily hold the value of one of the elements, so that we don't lose the value during the swap.

The algorithm, presented here in pseudocode, involves three steps:

```
To swap elements a and b:
1.  Assign the value of element a to the temporary variable.
2.  Assign the value of element b to element a.
3.  Assign the value in the temporary variable to element b.
```

For instance, if an *array* named *array* has *int* elements, and we want to swap the element at index 3 with the element at index 6, we will use the following code:

```
int temp = array[3];      // line 1
array[3] = array[6];      // line 2
array[6] = temp;          // line 3
```

The order of these operations is critical; changing the order might result in loss of data and erroneous data stored in the array.

The following illustrates line by line what happens during the swap:

Before line 1 is executed, our array looks like this:

Value	23	45	7	33	78	90	82	80	90	66
Index	0	1	2	3	4	5	6	7	8	9

Line 1 assigns the value of element 3 to *temp*. After line 1 is executed, the value of *temp* is 33. The array is unchanged.

Value	23	45	7	33	78	90	82	80	90	66		33
Index	0	1	2	3	4	5	6	7	8	9		temp

Line 2 assigns the value of element 6 (82) to element 3. After line 2 is executed, both element 6 and element 3 have the same value. But that's OK, because we saved the value of element 3 in *temp*.

Value	23	45	7	82	78	90	82	80	90	66		33
Index	0	1	2	3	4	5	6	7	8	9		temp

Line 3 assigns the value we saved in *temp* to element 6. After line 3 is executed, the values of elements 3 and 6 have been successfully swapped.

COMMON ERROR TRAP
When swapping elements, be sure to save a value before replacing it with another value to avoid losing data.

Value	23	45	7	82	78	90	33	80	90	66		33
Index	0	1	2	3	4	5	6	7	8	9		temp

Example 8.16 shows the *Sorter* class, which provides a *static selectionSort* method for an integer array.

```
1  /* Sort Utility Class
2   * Anderson, Franceschi
3   */
4
5  public class Sorter
6  {
7    /** Uses Selection Sort to sort
8     *      an integer array in ascending order
9     *    @param array the array to sort
10    */
11   public static void selectionSort( int [ ] array )
12   {
13     int temp; // temporary location for swap
14     int max; // index of maximum value in subarray
15
16     for ( int i = 0; i < array.length - 1; i++ )
17     {
18       find index of largest value in subarray
19       max = indexOfLargestElement( array, array.length - i );
20
21       // swap array[max] and array[array.length - i - 1]
22       temp = array[max];
23       array[max] = array[array.length - i - 1];
24       array[array.length - i - 1] = temp;
25     }
26   }
27
28   /** Finds index of largest element
29    *    @param    size the size of the subarray
30    *    @param    array the array to search
31    *    @return   the index of the largest element in the subarray
32    */
33   private static int indexOfLargestElement( int [ ] array, int size )
34   {
35     int index = 0;
36     for ( int i = 1; i < size; i++ )
37     {
```

```
38        if ( array[i] > array[index] )
39            index = i;
40      }
41    return index;
42  }
43 }
```

EXAMPLE 8.16   The *Sorter* Class

Part of the Selection Sort algorithm is finding the index of the largest element in a subarray, so we implement the Selection Sort with two methods. At lines 7–26 is the *selectionSort* method, which implements the Selection Sort algorithm. To perform its work, the *selectionSort* method calls the utility method, *indexOfLargestElement* (lines 28–42), which returns the index of the largest element in a subarray. This method uses the algorithm discussed earlier in the chapter for finding a maximum value in an array. We declare this method *private* because its only function is to provide a service to the *selectionSort* method. The *indexOfLargestElement* method must also be declared as *static* because the *selectionSort* method is *static*, and thus can call only *static* methods.

In Example 8.17, the client code instantiates an integer array and prints the array before and after the Selection Sort is performed. Because *selectionSort* is a *static* method, we call it using the *Sorter* class name. The output of a sample run is shown in Figure 8.22.

```
1 /** Client for Selection Sort
2 *     Anderson, Franceschi
3 */
4 import java.util.Random;
5
6 public class SelectionSortClient
7 {
8   public static void main( String [ ] args )
9   {
10     // instantiate an array and fill with random values
11     int [ ] numbers = new int [6];
12     Random rand = new Random( );
13     for ( int i = 0; i < numbers.length; i++ )
14     {
15       numbers[i] = rand.nextInt( 5000 ) + 1;
16     }
17
18     System.out.println( "Before Selection Sort, the array is" );
19     for ( int i = 0; i < numbers.length; i++ )
```

```
20          System.out.print( numbers[i] + "\t" );
21      System.out.println( );
22
23      Sorter.selectionSort( numbers ); // sort the array
24
25      System.out.println( "\nAfter Selection Sort, the array is" );
26      for ( int i = 0; i < numbers.length; i++ )
27          System.out.print( numbers[i] + "\t" );
28      System.out.println( );
29  }
30 }
```

EXAMPLE 8.17   Using Selection Sort

Figure 8.22

Using Selection
Sort

```
Before Selection Sort, the array is
3394    279    1181    2471    3660    221


After Selection Sort, the array is
221     279    1181    2471    3394    3660
```

8.6.3   Insertion Sort

Like Selection Sort, Insertion Sort derives its name from the algorithm used to sort the array. The basic approach to an Insertion Sort is to sort elements much like a card player arranges the cards in sorted order in his or her hand. The player inserts cards one at a time in such a way that the cards on the left side of his or her hand are sorted at all times; the cards on the right side of his or her hand have

Figure 8.23a

The next card to
insert is a 4

not yet been inserted into the sorted part of the hand. As Figure 8.23a shows, the three yellow cards on the left (3, 5, and 9) are already arranged in sorted order, and the white cards on the right (4, 2, and 8) have yet to be inserted into their correct location. Note that the "sorted" yellow cards on the left side are not necessarily in their final position yet. We will now insert the 4. We first compare it to the 9; since 4 is smaller than 9, we shift the 9 to the right (Figure 8.23b). We then compare the 4 to the 5; since 4 is smaller than 5, we shift the 5 to the right (Figure 8.23c). We then compare the 4 to the 3; since 4 is larger than 3, the 3 stays in place and we insert the 4 in the empty slot (Figure 8.23d). We are now ready to insert the next card, the 2.

Figure 8.23b

9 is shifted to the right

Figure 8.23c

5 is shifted to the right

Figure 8.23d

4 is inserted

To sort an array of n elements in ascending order, Insertion Sort implements a double loop:

- The outer loop executes $n - 1$ times and iterates through the array elements from indexes 1 through $n - 1$. If the variable i represents the counter of the outer loop, the array can be thought of as made of three parts:

  - a sorted subarray (although the elements may not be in their final position yet) from index 0 to $i - 1$,

  - the array element (at index i) that we are currently inserting, and

  - a subarray (from index $i + 1$ to $n - 1$) of elements that have not yet been inserted.

- At each iteration of the outer loop, we insert the current array element at its proper place within the sorted subarray. The inner loop compares the current array element to the elements of the sorted array from right to left and shifts these elements to the right until it finds the proper insert location.

- After all elements have been inserted, the array is sorted.

The pseudocode for the Insertion Sort is

```
for i = 1 to last array index by 1
    j = i
    temp = element at index i
    while ( j != 0 and value of element at index j − 1 > temp)
        shift element at index j − 1 to the right
        decrement j by 1
    assign value stored in temp to element at index j
```

For example, let's walk through an Insertion Sort on the following array. At the beginning, the unsorted array is

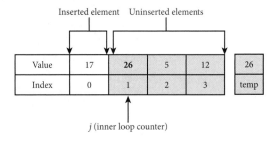

The first element of the array, 17, is automatically in the correct position when we consider the subarray as consisting of that element only. The value of the

outer loop counter (*i*) is 1, and we will now insert the second array element, 26, into the left subarray. First, we save the value of the element to be inserted by storing it in *temp*. We need to save the value because it is possible that we will shift other values, in which case we would overwrite that element. The value of the inner loop counter (*j*) is set to the value of the outer loop counter (*i*), i.e., 1. We compare elements 26 (index *j* = 1) and 17 (index *j* – 1 = 0). Since 26 is larger than 17, we exit the inner loop (and therefore we do not shift 17 to the right). We then assign the value of the current element, 26, stored in *temp*, to the element at index *j* = 1; in this case, there is no change to the array. The value 26 has been inserted.

The outer loop counter (*i*) is incremented, and its value is 2. We will now insert the third array element, 5, into the left subarray (at this point comprised of the two inserted elements, 17 and 26).

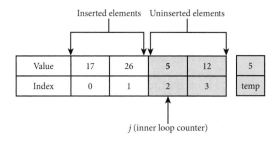

The value of the inner loop counter (*j*) is set to the value of the outer loop counter (*i*), i.e., 2. We compare the current element, 5, stored in *temp*, and 26 (index *j* – 1 = 1). Since 5 is smaller than 26, we shift 26 to the right and decrement *j* by 1; *j* now has the value 1.

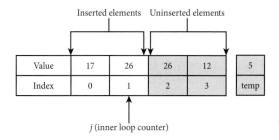

We then compare the current element, 5, stored in *temp*, and 17 (index *j* – 1 = 0). Since 5 is smaller than 17, we shift 17 to the right and decrement *j* by 1; *j* now has the value 0.

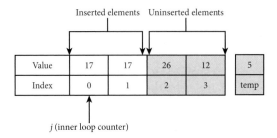

Since j is 0, we exit the inner loop and assign the value of the current element, 5, stored in *temp,* to the array element at index $j = 0$. The value 5 has now been inserted.

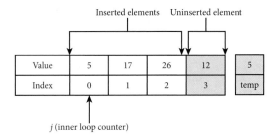

The outer loop counter (i) is incremented, and its value is 3. We will now insert the fourth array element, 12, into the left subarray (at this point comprising the three inserted elements, 5, 17, and 26).

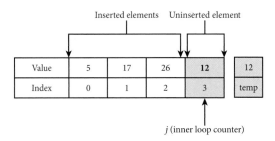

The value of the inner loop counter (j) is set to the value of the outer loop counter (i), i.e., 3. We compare the current element, 12, stored in *temp,* and 26 (index $j - 1 = 2$). Since 12 is smaller than 26, we shift 26 to the right and decrement j by 1; j now has the value 2.

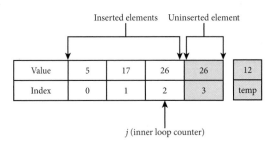

We then compare the current element, 12, stored in *temp,* and 17 (index $j - 1 = 1$). Since 12 is smaller than 17, we shift 17 to the right and decrement *j* by 1; *j* now has the value 1.

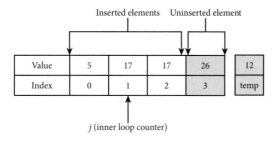

We then compare the current element, 12, stored in *temp,* and 5 (index $j - 1 = 0$). Since 12 is not smaller than 5, we exit the inner loop; we then assign the value of the current element, stored in *temp,* to the element at index $j = 1$; the value 12 has been inserted.

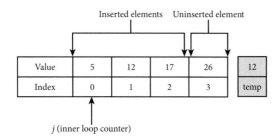

The outer loop counter (*i*) is incremented, and its value is 4, which causes the outer loop to terminate. All the elements have been inserted; the array is now sorted.

Example 8.18 shows our *Sorter* class with the Insertion Sort algorithm implemented in lines 43–63.

```
1 /* Sort Utility Class
2    Anderson, Franceschi
3 */
4
5 public class Sorter
6 {
7    /** Performs a Selection Sort on
8     *     an integer array
9     *     @param the array to sort
10    */
11   public static void selectionSort( int [ ] array )
12   {
13       int temp; // temporary location for swap
```

COMMON ERROR TRAP

When looping through an array, be careful not to access an element outside the bounds of the array. Your code will compile, but will generate an *ArrayIndexOut-OfBounds-Exception* at run time.

```
14      int max; // index of maximum value in subarray
15
16      for ( int i = 0; i < array.length - 1; i++ )
17      {
18        // find index of largest value in subarray
19        max = indexOfLargestElement( array, array.length - i );
20
21        // swap array[max] and array[array.length - i - 1]
22        temp = array[max];
23        array[max] = array[array.length - i - 1];
24        array[array.length - i - 1] = temp;
25      }
26    }
27
28    /**  Finds index of largest element
29     *     @param     size the size of the subarray
30     *     @return     the index of the largest element in the subarray
31     */
32    private static int indexOfLargestElement( int [ ] array, int size )
33    {
34      int index = 0;
35      for ( int i = 1; i < size; i++ )
36      {
37          if ( array[i] > array[index] )
38              index = i;
39      }
40      return index;
41    }
42
43    /**  Performs an Insertion Sort on an integer array
44     *    @param array array to sort
45     */
46    public static void insertionSort( int [ ] array )
47    {
48      int j, temp;
49
50      for ( int i = 1; i < array.length; i++ )
51      {
52        j = i;
53        temp = array[i];
54
55        while ( j != 0 && array[j - 1] > temp )
56        {
57           array[j] = array[j - 1];
58           j--;
```

```
59          }
60
61          array[j] = temp;
62      }
63  }
64 }
```

EXAMPLE 8.18   *Sorter* **Class with Insertion Sort**

Example 8.19 shows a client program that instantiates an integer array, fills it with random values, and then prints the array before and after performing the Insertion Sort. Figure 8.24. shows a sample run, using the Insertion Sort algorithm to sort an array of integers.

```
1 /** Client for Insertion Sort
2 *    Anderson, Franceschi
3 */
4 import java.util.Random;
5
6 public class InsertionSortClient
7 {
8   public static void main( String [ ] args )
9   {
10    // instantiate an array and fill with random values
11    int [ ] numbers = new int [6];
12    Random rand = new Random( );
13    for ( int i = 0; i < numbers.length; i++ )
14    {
15      numbers[i] = rand.nextInt( 5000 ) + 1;
16    }
17
18    System.out.println( "Before Insertion Sort, the array is" );
19    for ( int i = 0; i < numbers.length; i++ )
20      System.out.print( numbers[i] + "\t" );
21    System.out.println( );
22
23    Sorter.insertionSort( numbers ); // sort the array
24
25    System.out.println( "\nAfter Insertion Sort, the array is" );
26    for ( int i = 0; i < numbers.length; i++ )
27        System.out.print( numbers[i] + "\t" );
28    System.out.println( );
29  }
30 }
```

EXAMPLE 8.19   Using Insertion Sort

Figure 8.24

Using Insertion
Sort

```
Before Insertion Sort, the array is

2856    2384    3979    3088    1176    284


After Insertion Sort, the array is

284     1176    2384    2856    3088    3979
```

8.6.4 Sorting Arrays of Objects

We saw earlier in the chapter that data items to be sorted can be primitive data types, such as integers or *doubles*. But they can also be objects. With an array of objects, it is important to understand that we need to sort the objects themselves, not the array elements, which are merely the object references, or memory locations of the objects.

Arrays of objects are sorted using a sort key, which is one or more of the instance variables of the objects. For instance, if we have email objects, they can be sorted by date received, by author, by subject, and so on. It is important to note that when we sort objects, the integrity of the objects must be respected; for instance, when we sort a collection of email objects by sender, we sort a collection of email objects, not a collection of senders.

Thus, to perform the Insertion Sort on the *cars* array of *Auto* objects, we need to decide which field (or fields) of the *Auto* object determines the order of the objects. If we say that the *model* is the sort field, then the comparison statement would compare the models in two objects, that is, two *Strings*. The *compareTo* method of the *String* class compares the values of two *Strings*. It returns a positive number if the *String* for which the method is invoked is greater than the *String* passed as an argument.

To sort the *cars* array using an Insertion Sort, we would need to make several revisions to the *InsertionSort* method. First, the data type of the array must be declared as an *Auto* in the parameter list. Second, *temp* needs to be defined as an *Auto* reference, and finally, we need to substitute the *compareTo* method in the condition that compares array elements.

The revised Insertion Sort code becomes:

```
/* * Insertion sorts an array of Autos
 *      @param arr an array of Autos
 */
```

```
public static void insertionSort( Auto [ ] arr )
{
  Auto temp;
  int j;

  for ( int i = 1; i < arr.length; i++ )
  {
      j = i;
      temp = arr[i];

      while ( j != 0 && ( temp.getModel( ) ).compareTo(
             arr[j - 1].getModel( ) ) < 0 )
      {
          arr[j] = arr[j - 1];
          j--;
      } // end while loop

      arr[j] = temp;

  } // end for loop
}   // end InsertionSort method
```

8.6.5   Sequential Search of a Sorted Array

Earlier in the chapter, the *MovieWinners* class sequentially searched an array. The algorithm assumed the elements were not in order. If we sort the array, a Sequential Search can be implemented more efficiently for the case when the search key is not present in the array. Instead of searching the entire array before discovering that the search key is not in the array, we can stop as soon as we pass the location where that element would be if it were in the array. In other words, if the array is sorted in ascending order, we can recognize an unsuccessful search when we find an element in the array that is greater than the search key. Because the array is sorted in ascending order, all the elements after that array element are larger than that element, and therefore are also larger than the search key.

To implement this algorithm, we can add another test to the *for* loop condition, so that we exit the loop as soon as we find an element that is greater than the search key. The improved algorithm shown next could be used to replace the *indexOf-Winner* method shown in Example 8.14 for Sequential Search of a sorted *winners* array:

```
public int indexOfWinner( int key )
{
  for ( int i = 0; i < winners.length && winners[i] <= key; i++ )
```

```
    {
      if ( winners[i] == key )
      return i;
    }

    return -1; // end of array reached without finding key
               // or an element larger than the key was found
    }
```

In fact, if the array is sorted, it can be searched even more efficiently using an algorithm called Binary Search, which we explain in the next section.

8.6.6   Binary Search of a Sorted Array

If you've played the "Guess a Number" game, you probably have used the concept of a **Binary Search.** In this game, someone asks you to guess a secret number between 1 and 100. For each number you guess, they tell you whether the secret number is larger or smaller than your guess. A good strategy is to guess the number in the middle, which in this example is 50. Whether the secret number is larger or smaller than 50, you will have eliminated half of the possible values. If the secret number is greater than 50, then you know your next guess should be 75 (halfway between 50 and 100). If the secret number is less than 50, your next guess should be 25 (halfway between 1 and 50). If you continue eliminating half the possible numbers with each guess, you will quickly guess the secret number. This approach works because we are "searching" a sorted set of numbers (1 to 100).

Similarly, a Binary Search of a sorted array works by eliminating half the remaining elements with each comparison. First, we look at the middle element of the array. If the value of that element is the search key, we return its index. If, however, the value of the middle element is greater than the search key, then the search key cannot be found in elements with array indexes higher than that element. Therefore, we will search the left half of the array only. Similarly, if the value of the middle element is lower than the search key, then the search key cannot be found in elements with array indexes lower than the middle element. Therefore, we will search in the right half of the array only. As we keep searching, the subarray we search keeps shrinking in size. In fact, the size of the subarray we search is cut in half at every iteration.

If the search key is not in the array, the subarray we search will eventually become empty. At that point, we know that we will not find our search key, and we return −1.

Example 8.20 shows our Binary Search algorithm.

```
1  /** Binary Search
2   *   Anderson, Franceschi
3   */
4
5   import java.util.Scanner;
6
7   public class BinarySearcher
8   {
9     public static void main( String [ ] args )
10    {
11      // define an array sorted in ascending order
12      int [ ] numbers = { 3, 6, 7, 8, 12, 15, 22, 36, 45,
13                          48, 51, 53, 64, 69, 72, 89, 95 };
14
15      Scanner scan = new Scanner( System.in );
16      System.out.print( "Enter a value to search for > " );
17      int key = scan.nextInt( );
18
19      int index = binarySearch( numbers, key );
20      if ( index != -1 )
21          System.out.println( key + " found at index " + index );
22      else
23          System.out.println( key + " not found" );
24    }
25
26    public static int binarySearch( int [ ] arr, int key )
27    {
28      int start = 0;
29      int end = arr.length - 1;
30      int middle;
31
32      while ( end >= start )
33      {
34        middle = ( start + end ) / 2; // element in middle of array
35
36        if ( arr[middle] == key )
37        {
38            return middle; // key found at middle
39        }
40        else if ( arr[middle] > key )
```

```
41        {
42            end = middle - 1; // search left side of array
43        }
44        else
45        {
46            start = middle + 1; // search right side of array
47        }
48     }
49     return -1;
50  }
51 }
```

EXAMPLE 8.20   Binary Search of a Sorted Array

We start by declaring and initializing an integer array with 17 sorted elements (lines 12–13). We then prompt the user for a search key and call the *binarySearch* method (lines 16–19).

The *binarySearch* method is coded at lines 26–50. The local variables *start* and *end* store the first and last index of the subarray to search. Because we begin by searching the entire array, we initialize these to the indexes of the first and last element of the array that was passed as a parameter. The local variable *middle,* declared at line 30, will store the index of the middle element in the subarray to search.

The search is performed in a *while* loop (lines 32–48), whose condition determines whether the subarray is empty. If the subarray is not empty, we calculate the value for *middle* by adding the indexes of the first and last elements and dividing by 2 (line 34). Next we test whether the value at the *middle* index is equal to the key. If so, we have found the key and we return its index, which is *middle* (lines 36–39). If not, we test whether the value in the middle of the subarray is greater than the key. If so, if the key is in the array, it will be found in the left half of the array. Thus, we reduce the subarray to the elements with indexes less than *middle* (lines 40–43) and greater than or equal to *start.* If the value in the middle of the subarray is less than the key, then if the key is in the array, it will be found in the right half of the array. Thus, we reduce the subarray to the elements with indexes greater than *middle* (lines 44–47) and smaller than or equal to *end.*

When the *while* loop continues, we continue making our comparisons and either returning the index of the search key or reducing the size of the subarray. If the search key is not in the array, the subarray eventually becomes empty, and we exit the *while* loop and return –1 (line 49). Figure 8.25 shows the output when the search key is found.

```
Enter a value to search for > 64

64 found at index 12
```

Figure 8.25

Output from
Example 8.20

Let's run through the Binary Search algorithm on the key 7 to illustrate how the algorithm works when the key is found in the array. Here is the array *numbers:*

Value	3	6	7	8	12	15	22	36	45	48	51	53	64	69	72	89	95
Index	0	1	2	3	4	5	6	7	8	9	10	11	12	13	14	15	16

When the *binarySearch* method is called, it sets *start* to 0 and *end to arr.length − 1,* which is 16. Thus, the value of *middle* is 8.

The element at index 8 (45) is greater than 7, so we set *end* to 7 (*middle − 1*), and we will now search the left subarray, highlighted next. The value of middle is now 3 ((0 + 7) / 2).

Value	3	6	7	8	12	15	22	36	45	48	51	53	64	69	72	89	95
Index	0	1	2	3	4	5	6	7	8	9	10	11	12	13	14	15	16

The element at index 3 (8) is greater than 7, so we set *end* to 2 (*middle − 1*) and keep searching in the left subarray, highlighted next. The value of *middle* is now 1 ((0 + 2) / 2).

Value	3	6	7	8	12	15	22	36	45	48	51	53	64	69	72	89	95
Index	0	1	2	3	4	5	6	7	8	9	10	11	12	13	14	15	16

The element at index 1 (6) is smaller than 7, so we set *start* to 2 (*middle + 1*) and search in the right subarray, highlighted next. The value of *middle* is now 2 ((2 + 2) / 2).

Value	3	6	7	8	12	15	22	36	45	48	51	53	64	69	72	89	95
Index	0	1	2	3	4	5	6	7	8	9	10	11	12	13	14	15	16

The element at index 2 (7) is equal to 7. We have found the value and return its index, 2.

Let's now run the preceding example on the key 34 to illustrate how the algorithm works when the key is not found in the array.

Here is the array *numbers* again:

Value	3	6	7	8	12	15	22	36	45	48	51	53	64	69	72	89	95
Index	0	1	2	3	4	5	6	7	8	9	10	11	12	13	14	15	16

Again, when the *binarySearch* method is called, it sets *start* to 0 and *end* to *arr.length* – 1, which is 16. Thus, *middle* is assigned the value 8 for the first comparison.

The element at index 8 (45) is greater than 34, so we set *end* to 7 (*middle* – 1), and keep searching in the left subarray. The value of *middle* becomes 3 for the next comparison.

Value	3	6	7	8	12	15	22	36	45	48	51	53	64	69	72	89	95
Index	0	1	2	3	4	5	6	7	8	9	10	11	12	13	14	15	16

The element at index 3 (8) is smaller than 34, so we search in the right subarray highlighted below. The value of *middle* is now 5.

Value	3	6	7	8	12	15	22	36	45	48	51	53	64	69	72	89	95
Index	0	1	2	3	4	5	6	7	8	9	10	11	12	13	14	15	16

The element at index 5 (15) is smaller than 34, so we search in the right subarray. The value of *middle* is now 6.

Value	3	6	7	8	12	15	22	36	45	48	51	53	64	69	72	89	95
Index	0	1	2	3	4	5	6	7	8	9	10	11	12	13	14	15	16

The element at index 6 (22) is smaller than 34, so we search in the right subarray. The value of *middle* is now 7.

Value	3	6	7	8	12	15	22	36	45	48	51	53	64	69	72	89	95
Index	0	1	2	3	4	5	6	7	8	9	10	11	12	13	14	15	16

At this point, *start, end,* and *middle* all have the value 7. The element at index 7 (36) is larger than 34, so we assign *end* the value *middle* – 1, which is 6. This makes *end* less than *start* and consequently makes the while loop condition evaluate to *false*. We have not found 34, so we return –1.

8.7 Programming Activity 2: Searching and Sorting Arrays

In this activity, you will work again with a 15-element integer array, performing these activities:

1. Write a method to perform a Sequential Search of an array.

2. Write a method to implement the Bubble Sort algorithm to sort an array.

The basic approach to a Bubble Sort is to make multiple passes through the array. In each pass, we compare adjacent elements. If any two adjacent elements are out of order, we put them in order by swapping their values.

To sort an array of n elements in ascending order, Bubble Sort implements a double loop:

- The outer loop executes $n - 1$ times.

- For each iteration of the outer loop, the inner loop steps through all the unsorted elements of the array and does the following:

  - Compares the current element with the next element in the array.

  - If the next element is smaller, it swaps the two elements.

At this point, $n - 1$ elements have been moved to their correct positions. That leaves only the element at index 0, which is therefore automatically at the correct position within the array. The array is now sorted.

As the outer loop counter goes from 0 to $n - 2$, it iterates $n - 1$ times.

Outer loop counter	Indexes of element(s) at the sorted position
0	$n-1$
1	$n-2, n-1$
2	$n-3, n-2, n-1$
...	...
$n-3$	$2, 3, 4, \ldots, n-3, n-2, n-1$
$n-2$	$1, 2, 3, 4, \ldots, n-3, n-2, n-1$

The pseudocode for the Bubble Sort is

```
for i = 0 to last array index − 1 by 1
  for j = 0 to ( last array index − i −1 ) by 1
    if (2 consecutive elements are in the wrong order)
      swap them
```

For example, let's walk through a Bubble Sort on the following array. At the beginning, the unsorted array is

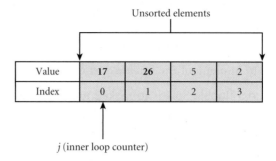

The value of the outer loop counter (i) is 0, and the value of the inner loop counter (j) is also 0. We compare elements 17 (index $j = 0$) and 26 (index $j + 1 = 1$). Since 17 is smaller than 26, we do not swap them.

The inner loop counter (j) is incremented, and its value is now 1.

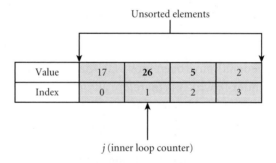

We compare elements 26 (index $j = 1$) and 5 (index $j + 1 = 2$). Since 26 is larger than 5, we swap them. The inner loop counter (j) is incremented, and its value is now 2.

We compare elements 26 (index $j = 2$) and 2 (index $j + 1 = 3$). Since 26 is larger than 2, we swap them.

The inner loop counter (j) is incremented, and its value is now 3; therefore, we exit the inner loop. (We have reached the end of the unsorted subarray, which at this point is the whole array.) At the end of one execution of the inner loop, the value 26 has "bubbled up" to its correct position within the array.

We now go back to the outer loop, and the outer loop counter (i) is incremented; its value is now 1. We reenter the inner loop, and the value of the inner loop counter (j) is reinitialized to 0.

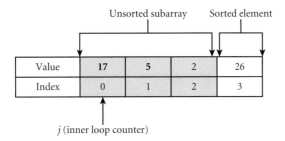

We compare elements 17 (index $j = 0$) and 5 (index $j + 1 = 1$). Since 17 is larger than 5, we swap them. The inner loop counter (j) is incremented, and its value is now 1.

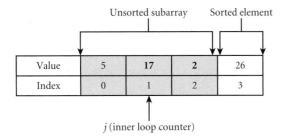

We compare elements 17 (index $j = 1$) and 2 (index $j + 1 = 2$). Since 17 is larger than 2, we swap them.

The inner loop counter (j) is incremented, and its value is now 2; therefore, we exit the inner loop. (We have reached the end of the unsorted subarray.) At this point, the element 17 has "bubbled up" to its correct position within the array.

We go back to the outer loop, and the outer loop counter (i) is incremented; its value is now 2, and this will be the last iteration of the outer loop. We reenter the inner loop, and the value of the inner loop counter (j) is reinitialized to 0.

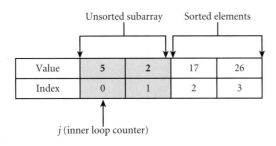

We compare elements 5 (index $j = 0$) and 2 (index $j + 1 = 1$). Since 2 is smaller than 5, we swap them.

The inner loop counter (j) is incremented, and its value is now 1; therefore, we exit the inner loop. (We have reached the end of the unsorted subarray.) At this point, the element 5 has "bubbled up" to its correct position within the array.

We go back to the outer loop, and the outer loop counter (i) is incremented; its value is now 3, and therefore, we exit the outer loop. For the four elements in the array, we executed the outer loop three times.

Automatically sorted   Sorted elements

Value	2	5	17	26
Index	0	1	2	3

The array is now sorted.

The framework for this Programming Activity will animate your algorithm so that you can watch your algorithm work and check the accuracy of your code. For example, Figure 8.26 demonstrates the Bubble Sort at work. At this point, the program has completed four passes through the array and just finished comparing the values of elements 3 and 4.

Instructions

In this chapter's Programming Activity 2 folder in the supplied code files, you will find the source files needed to complete this activity. Copy all the files to a folder on your computer. Note that all files should be in the same folder.

Open the *ArrayPractice2Controller.java* source file. Searching for five asterisks (*****) in the source code will position you at the two locations where you will add your code. Your first task is to complete the *sequentialSearch* method, which searches the *arr* array, an instance variable of the *ArrayPractice2Controller* class. The array *arr* has already been instantiated for you and filled with random values. The second task is to complete the *bubbleSort* method. Example 8.21 shows the section of the *ArrayPractice2Controller* source code where you will add your code. Note that in each method, you are asked to call the *animate* method so that your method code can be animated as it works. Note also that for the *sequentialSearch* method, we provide a dummy *return* statement (*return 0;*). We do this so that the source code will compile. In this way, you can write and test each method separately, using stepwise refinement. When you are ready to write the *sequentialSearch*

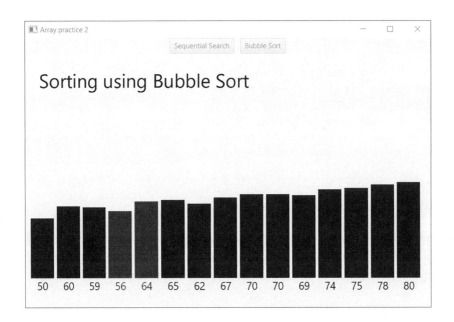

Figure 8.26

The Bubble Sort at Work

method, just replace the dummy *return* statement with the appropriate *return* statement for that method.

```
// 1. ***** student writes this method
/**  Searches for key in integer array named arr
//     arr is an instance variable of the class and has been
//     instantiated and filled with random values.
// @param key value to search for
// @return if key is found, the index of the first element
//     in array whose value is key; if key is not found,
//     the method returns -1
*/
public int sequentialSearch( int key )
{
// Note:  To animate the algorithm, put this method call as the
// first statement in your for loop
//  animate( i );
//         where i is the index of the current array element


   return 0; // replace this statement with your return statement

} // end of sequentialSearch
// 2. *****  student writes this method
/**  Sorts arr in ascending order using the bubble sort algorithm
```

```
*/
public void bubbleSort( )
{
// Note: To animate the algorithm, put this method call as the
// last statement in your innermost for loop
//   animate( i, j );
//          where i is the value of the outer loop counter
//          and j is the value of the inner loop counter,
//          or the index of the current array element

} // end of bubbleSort
```

EXAMPLE 8.21   Student Section of *ArrayPractice2Controller*

When you have finished writing your code, compile *ArrayPractice2Controller*.java and run *ArrayPractice2Application*. Figure 8.27 shows the graphics window when the application begins. To test any method, click on the appropriate button.

Troubleshooting

If your method implementation does not animate, consider these tips:

- Verify that your *for* loop calls the *animate* method as instructed in the method comments.

- Verify that you did not instantiate a new array. Perform all operations on the instance variable array named *arr*.

Figure 8.27

Opening Window of *ArrayPractice2-Application*

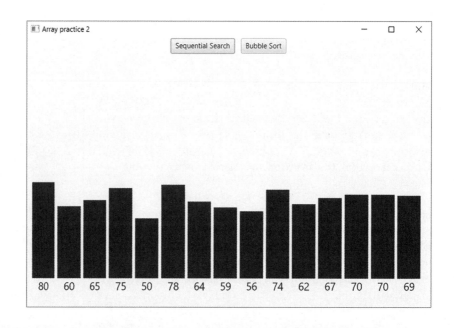

1. **The sequential search finds only the first occurrence of the parameter *key*. How would you modify the *sequentialSearch* method to count the occurrences of *key*?**

2. **It is possible that the array might be completely sorted before all the passes have been completed. How would you modify your code so that you exit the *bubbleSort* method as soon as possible?**

8.8 Using Arrays as Counters

In some circumstances, it is useful to use an array of integers as an ordered group of accumulators, or counters. For example, suppose we are analyzing a survey that has four possible answers, 0 through 3. We want to count how many people selected each answer. We could set up four counters and use an *if/else* statement to increment the appropriate counter. The pseudocode would be:

```
read first survey
while ( not end of surveys )
{
 if answer is 0
   increment counter0
 else if answer is 1
   increment counter1
 else if answer is 2
   increment counter2
 else if answer is 3
   increment counter3
 read next survey
}
```

That would work if we have only a few possible answers, but what if we had 100 or more answers? We would end up writing a very long *if/else* statement.

Instead, we could set up an array of counters and let the counter for answer 0 be *array[0]*, the counter for answer 1 be *array[1],* and so on. This approach—using an array of counters—is simpler to code and saves processing time.

As another example, suppose we want to throw a die 500 times and count the number of times each outcome occurs; that is, we want to count the number of ones, twos, threes, fours, fives, and sixes that are rolled. To do this, we set up a simple *Die* class shown in Example 8.22, with a method for rolling a value. Then we set up the client class, *DieCount,* shown in Example 8.23, that has an array with six integer elements; each element will hold the number of times a particular roll occurs.

```java
1 /** Die class
2 *    Anderson, Franceschi
3 */
4 import java.util.Random;
5
6 public class Die
7 {
8     public final int SIDES = 6;
9     private Random rand;
10
11    /** default constructor
12     * instantiates the Random object
13     */
14    public Die( )
15    {
16        rand = new Random( );
17    }
18
19    /** rolls the die
20     * @return the value of the roll
21     */
22    public int roll( )
23    {
24        return rand.nextInt( SIDES ) + 1;
25    }
26 }
```

EXAMPLE 8.22   The *Die* Class

```java
1 /** DieCount Class
2 *    Anderson, Franceschi
3 */
4
5 public class DieCount
6 {
7   public static void main( String [ ] args )
8   {
9      final int FACES = 6, NUMBER_OF_ROLLS = 500;
10
11     // instantiate the counter array
12     // which sets initial values to 0
13     int [ ] rollCount = new int [FACES];
14
15     // instantiate the Die
```

```
16        Die d1 = new Die( );
17
18        // roll the die 500 times
19        for ( int i = 1; i <= NUMBER_OF_ROLLS; i++ )
20        {
21            int myRoll = d1.roll( );
22            rollCount[myRoll - 1]++; // increment the counter for roll
23        }
24
25        // print count for each roll
26        System.out.println( "Roll\tCount" );
27        for ( int i = 0; i < rollCount.length; i++ )
28        {
29            System.out.println( ( i + 1 ) + "\t" + rollCount[i] );
30        }
31    }
32 }
```

EXAMPLE 8.23   The *DieCount* Class

In the *Die* class constructor, we instantiate the *Random* object *rand,* which will be used by the *roll* method (lines 19–25), which in turn generates a random number between 1 and 6 to simulate the roll of a die.

In the *DieCount* class, we instantiate our array of six counters, *rollCount,* on line 13, which autoinitializes each element to 0—exactly what we want for counters.

To count the number of times each roll occurs, we use a *for* loop that iterates 500 times, with each iteration calling the *roll* method of the *Die* class. We then need to count each roll. That's where our array of counters, *rollCount,* comes in.

Since the *rollCount* array has six elements, the index of the first element is 0, and the index of the last element is 5. We will use *rollCount[0]* to hold the number of times we rolled a 1, *rollCount[1]* to hold the number of times we rolled a 2, and continue that way until we use *rollCount[5]* to hold the number of times we rolled a 6. Thus, to get the index of the appropriate counter, we need to decrement the roll by 1. So our statement to increment the count for a roll (line 22) becomes

```
rollCount[myRoll - 1]++;
```

After rolling the die 500 times and counting each roll, we print the total times each roll occurred (lines 25–30). Note that we increment the loop variable to convert between our counter index and the roll number. The output from a sample run of this program is shown in Figure 8.28. Because the program generates the rolls randomly, your output may be slightly different.

Figure 8.28

Output from
DieCount

Roll	Count
1	81
2	82
3	89
4	78
5	87
6	83

Our algorithm is not ideal, however. We need to subtract 1 from the index in order to increment the counter, and we need to add 1 to the index to print the outcome.

A better approach would be to create the array with seven elements. Then we can use elements 1 through 6 as the counters for the rolls 1 through 6. The index and the roll number will be the same. What happens to element 0? Nothing. We just ignore it.

The revised *DieCount2* class is shown in Example 8.24.

```
 1 /** DieCount2 Class
 2 *    Anderson, Franceschi
 3 */
 4
 5 public class DieCount2
 6 {
 7   public static void main( String [ ] args )
 8   {
 9     final int FACES = 7, NUMBER_OF_ROLLS = 500;
10
11     // instantiate the counter array
12     // which sets initial values to 0
13     int [ ] rollCount = new int [FACES];
14
15     // instantiate the Die
16     Die d1 = new Die( );
17
18     // roll the die 500 times
19     for ( int i = 1; i <= NUMBER_OF_ROLLS; i++ )
20     {
21       int myRoll = d1.roll( );
22       rollCount[myRoll]++; // increment the counter for roll
23     }
24
25     // print count for each roll
26     System.out.println( "Roll\tCount" );
```

```
27        for ( int i = 1; i < rollCount.length; i++ )
28        {
29          System.out.println( i + "\t" + rollCount[i] );
30        }
31    }
32 }
```

EXAMPLE 8.24   The *DieCount2* Class

Notice the changes to the code in this example. First, we set *FACES* to 7 (line 9), so we will instantiate an array with seven elements. Then we can use the roll of the die as the index into the counter array to increment the appropriate count (line 22). One last change is that when we loop through the *rollCount* array to print the counters, we initialize our loop counter to 1 (line 27), since we are not using element 0 as a counter and we simply use *i* as the roll number.

It's true that we're allocating an extra integer (four bytes of memory) that is never used, but we're eliminating 500 subtract operations and 6 addition operations! The program is more efficient, easier to write, and easier to read.

Skill Practice
with these end-of-chapter questions

8.11.1   Multiple Choice Exercises

Question 12

8.11.4   Identifying Errors in Code

Question 44

8.11.6   Write a Short Program

Question 57

8.11.8   Technical Writing

Question 74

8.9   Methods Accepting a Variable Number of Arguments

Sometimes, the number of arguments to be sent to a method cannot be determined until run time. For example, we may have a method that validates inputs for other methods. The number of inputs may vary from one method call to the next.

In these cases, we can use a feature in the Java language named **varargs**. We specify in the method header that the method will accept a variable number of arguments by typing three dots immediately after the data type of the last parameter.

The syntax is the following:

```
accessModifier returnType methodName( (0 to many parameters,)
                                    dataType... lastParameter )
```

Note that there is no space between the data type and the three dots.

A parameter that a method specifies using the *varargs* syntax must be the last parameter listed in the method header.

When the method starts executing, the *varargs* parameters are available to the method as if the client had passed the arguments as an array. Thus, the method treats the parameter as an array.

When calling a method that accepts a variable number of arguments, we can pass a single argument, several arguments, an array of arguments, or we can pass no arguments.

Example 8.25 shows a *Seller* class with a method that accepts a variable number of arguments, and Example 8.26 shows a client program that calls the method. In this example, we are updating the average rating a seller receives on an auction website. Each seller could have a different number of new ratings, so we specify the new ratings as a variable number of arguments.

```
 1 /** Seller class
 2 *    Anderson, Franceschi
 3 */
 4 import java.text.DecimalFormat;
 5
 6 public class Seller
 7 {
 8   private String sellerName;
 9   private double rating;
10   private int numberOfRatings;
11   private static final DecimalFormat ONE_PLACE
12                        = new DecimalFormat( "0.0" );
13
14   /** constructor
15     * @param sellerName seller name
16   */
17   public Seller( String sellerName )
18   {
19     this.sellerName = sellerName;
```

```
20   }
21
22   /** calcRating method
23     * @param newRatings 0 to many new ratings
24     * updates rating and numberOfRatings instance variables
25   */
26   public void calcRating( int... newRatings )
27   {
28     if ( newRatings != null && newRatings.length > 0 )
29     {
30       int totalNewRatings = 0;
31       for ( int i = 0; i < newRatings.length; i++ )
32         totalNewRatings += newRatings[i];
33
34       rating = ( ( rating * numberOfRatings ) + totalNewRatings )
35               / ( newRatings.length + numberOfRatings );
36       numberOfRatings += newRatings.length;
37     }
38     // else, no new ratings, so no change to instance variables
39   }
40
41   /** toString method
42     * @return the seller name
43     * and rating (formatted to 1 decimal place)
44   */
45   @Override
46   public String toString( )
47   {
48     return sellerName + ": rating " + ONE_PLACE.format( rating );
49   }
50 }
```

EXAMPLE 8.25   The *Seller* Class

In the *Seller* class, we define three instance variables representing the seller name, the current average rating, and the number of ratings the seller has received (lines 8–10). We also define a *static* constant *ONE_PLACE* that the *toString* method (lines 41–49) uses to format the average rating.

The *calcRating* method (lines 22–39) accepts one *varargs* parameter, *newRatings*. Note that if the method accepted other parameters, the *newRatings* parameter would need to be listed last. When the method starts executing, the arguments sent to the method by the caller have been assembled into an *int* array with the parameter's name, *newRatings*. Thus, *newRatings.length* will hold the number of arguments actually sent to the method. In the *calcRating* method we first check that the array reference is not *null* and that the array is not empty (line 28). We then use a *for* loop to calculate the total of the new ratings (lines 30–32). Finally, we calculate the new average rating and update the instance variables *rating* and *numberOfRatings*. If the *varargs* parameter is *null* or the array is empty, we do nothing.

In the client program, *SellerRatings*, we instantiate a *Seller* object (line 9), then successively call the *calcRating* method with one argument, two arguments, an array, and no arguments. After each method call, we output the new rating by implicitly calling the *toString* method in the *Seller* class (lines 11–22). Figure 8.29 shows the output from Example 8.25.

```
1 /** SellerRatings - client for Seller
2  *   Anderson, Franceschi
3  */
4
5 public class SellerRatings
6 {
7    public static void main( String [ ] args )
8    {
9      Seller seller = new Seller( "Mary" );
10
11       seller.calcRating( 4 ); // one value
12       System.out.println( seller );
13
14       seller.calcRating( 5, 5 ); // two values
15       System.out.println( seller );
16
17       int [ ] arrayOfRatings = { 4, 4, 5 };
18       seller.calcRating( arrayOfRatings ); // array
19       System.out.println( seller );
20
21       seller.calcRating( ); // no values
22       System.out.println( seller );
23    }
24 }
```

EXAMPLE 8.26   The *SellerRatings* Class

Figure 8.29

Output from
the *SellerRatings*
Application

```
Mary: rating 4.0

Mary: rating 4.7

Mary: rating 4.5

Mary: rating 4.5
```

CHAPTER REVIEW

8.10   Chapter Summary

- An array is a sequence of variables of the same data type. The data type can be any Java primitive data type, such as *int, float, double, byte, short, long, boolean, or char,* or it can be a class.

- Each element in the array is accessed using the array name and an index, which refers to the element's position in the array.

- Arrays are implemented as objects. Creating an array consists of declaring an object reference for the array and instantiating the array. The size of the array is given when the array is instantiated.

- In arrays of primitive types, each element of the array contains a value of that type. In arrays of objects, each element is an object reference.

- When an array is instantiated, the elements are given initial values automatically, depending on the data type. Numeric types are set to 0; *boolean* types are set to *false; char* types are set to the Unicode null character; and object references are set to *null.*

- Instantiating an array of object references involves two steps: instantiating the array and instantiating the objects.

- Arrays can be instantiated when they are declared by assigning initial values in a comma-separated list within curly braces. The number of values in the initialization list determines the number of elements in the array.

- Array elements are accessed using the array name and an index. The first element's index is 0 and the last element's index is the size of the array −1.

- Arrays have an integer instance variable, *length,* which holds the number of elements in the array.

- Attempting to access an element of an array using an index less than 0 or greater than *arrayName.length* − 1 will generate an *ArrayIndexOutOf-BoundsException* at run time.

- Aggregate array operations, such as printing and copying arrays, are not supported *for* arrays. Using a *for* loop, we can process each array element individually.

- To change the size of an array, instantiate an array of the desired size with a temporary name, copy the appropriate elements from the original array to the new array, and assign the new array reference to the original array. Assign *null* to the temporary array name.

- Arrays can be passed as arguments to methods and can also be the return type of methods.

- When an array is an instance variable of a class, the constructor should instantiate a new array and copy the elements of the parameter array into the new array.

- A Sequential Search determines whether a particular value, the search key, is in an array by comparing the search key to each element in the array.

- A Selection Sort arranges elements in the array in order by value by reducing the array into successively smaller subarrays and placing the largest element in each subarray into the last position of the subarray.

- An Insertion Sort arranges elements of an array much like a card player arranges cards in sorted order in his or her hand. The elements are inserted one at a time in ascending order into the left side of the array.

- To sort an array of objects, we can use the class method provided to compare objects' values.

- A sorted array can be searched more efficiently using a Binary Search, which successively reduces the number of elements to search by half.

- Arrays of integers can be used as an ordered group of counters.

- Methods can accept a variable number of parameters using the *varargs* … syntax.

8.11   Exercises, Problems, and Projects

8.11.1   Multiple Choice Exercises

1. What are the valid ways to declare an integer array named *a*? (Check all that apply.)

     ❏   `int [ ] a;`

     ❏   `int a[ ];`

     ❏   `array int a;`

     ❏   `int array a;`

2. What is the index of the first element of an array?

   ❑ −1

   ❑ 0

   ❑ 1

3. An array *a* has 30 elements; what is the index of its last element?

   ❑ 29

   ❑ 30

   ❑ 31

4. What is the default value of the elements in an array of *ints* after declaration and instantiation of the array?

   ❑ 0

   ❑ *null*

   ❑ undefined

5. How do you access the element of array *a* located at index 6?

   ❑ `a{6}`

   ❑ `a( 6 )`

   ❑ `a[6]`

6. Which of the following assertions is true?

   ❑ An array cannot be sized dynamically.

   ❑ An array can be sized dynamically, but cannot be resized without instantiating it again.

   ❑ An array can be sized dynamically and can also be resized without instantiating it again.

7. How do you retrieve the number of elements in an array *a*?

   ❑ `a.length( )`

   ❑ `a.length`

   ❑ `a.size( )`

   ❑ `a.size`

8. All the elements of an array must be of the same data type.

   ❑ true

   ❑ false

9. Array aggregate assignment is possible in Java.

   ❏ true

   ❏ false

10. Aggregate comparison of arrays is possible in Java.

    ❏ true

    ❏ false

11. An array can be returned by a method.

    ❏ true

    ❏ false

12. A Sequential Search on a sorted array can be written more efficiently than a Sequential Search on an unsorted array.

    ❏ true

    ❏ false

8.11.2 Reading and Understanding Code

13. What is the output of this code sequence?

```
double [ ] a = { 12.5, 48.3, 65.0 };
System.out.println( a[1] );
```

14. What is the output of this code sequence?

```
int [ ] a = new int [6];
System.out.println( a[4] );
```

15. What is the output of this code sequence?

```
double [ ] a = { 12.5, 48.3, 65.0 };
System.out.println( a.length );
```

16. What is the output of this code sequence?

```
int [ ] a = { 12, 48, 65 };

for ( int i = 0; i < a.length; i++ )
    System.out.println( a[i] );
```

17. What is the output of this code sequence?

```
int [ ] a = { 12, 48, 65 };
```

```
for ( int i = 0; i < a.length; i++ )
    System.out.println( "a[" + i + "] = " + a[i] );
```

18. What is the output of this code sequence?

```
int s = 0;
int [ ] a = { 12, 48, 65 };

for ( int i = 0; i < a.length; i++ )
    s += a[i];
System.out.println( "s = " + s );
```

19. What is the output of this code sequence?

```
int [ ] a = new int[10];

for ( int i = 0; i < a.length; i++ )
    a[i] = i + 10;

System.out.println( a[4] );
```

20. What is the output of this code sequence?

```
double [ ] a = { 12.3, 99.6, 48.2, 65.8 };
double temp = a[0];

for ( int i = 1; i < a.length; i++ )
{
    if ( a[i] > temp )
        temp = a[i];
}

System.out.println( temp );
```

21. What is the output of this code sequence?

```
int [ ] a = { 12, 48, 65, 23 };
int temp = a[1];
a[1] = a[3];
a[3] = temp;

for ( int i = 0; i < a.length; i++ )
    System.out.print( a[i] + " " );
```

22. What does this method do?

```
public int foo( int [ ] a )
{
    int temp = 0;
```

```
    for ( int i = 0; i < a.length; i++ )
    {
        if ( a[i] == 5 )
            temp++;
    }
    return temp;
}
```

23. What does this method do?

```
public int foo( int [ ] a )
{
    for ( int i = 0; i < a.length; i++ )
    {
        if ( a[i] == 10 )
            return i;
    }
    return -1;
}
```

24. What does this method do?

```
public boolean foo( int [ ] a )
{
    for ( int i = 0; i < a.length; i++ )
    {
        if ( a[i] < 0 )
            return false;
    }
    return true;
}
```

25. What does this method do?

```
public String [ ] foo( String [ ] a )
{
    String [ ] temp = new String[a.length];
    for ( int i = 0; i < a.length; i++ )
    {
        temp[i] = a[i].toLowerCase( );
    }
    return temp;
}
```

26. What does this method do?

```
public boolean [ ] foo( String [ ] a )
{
    boolean [ ] temp = new boolean[a.length];
```

```
    for ( int i = 0; i < a.length; i++ )
    {
            if (a[i].indexOf( "@" ) != -1 )
                    temp[i] = true;
            else
                    temp[i] = false;
    }
    return temp;
}
```

8.11.3   Fill In the Code

27. This code assigns the value 10 to all the elements of an array *a*.

```
int [ ] a = new int[25];
for ( int i = 0; i < a.length; i++ )
{
        // your code goes here
}
```

28. This code prints all the elements of array *a* that have a value greater than 20.

```
double [ ] a = { 45.2, 13.1, 12.8, 87.4, 99.0, 100.1, 43.8, 2.4 };

for ( int i = 0; i < a.length; i++ )
{
        // your code goes here
}
```

29. This code prints the average of the elements of array *a*.

```
int [ ] a = { 45, 13, 12, 87, 99, 100, 43, 2 };

double average = 0.0;
for ( int i = 0; i < a.length; i++ )
{
        // your code goes here
}
// ... and your code continues here
```

30. This code calculates and prints the dot product of two arrays ($\Sigma\ a[i] * b[i]$).

```
int [ ] a = { 3, 7, 9 };
int [ ] b = { 2, 9, 4 };
int dotProduct = 0;

for ( int i = 0; i < a.length; i++ )
```

```
{
        // your code goes here
}
```

31. This code prints the following three lines:

```
a[0] = 3
a[1] = 6
a[2] = 10

int [ ] a = { 3, 6, 10 };
for ( int i = 0; i < a.length; i++ )
{
        // your code goes here
}
```

32. This method returns *true* if an element in an array of *Strings* passed as a parameter contains the substring *IBM*; otherwise, it returns *false*.

```
public boolean foo( String [ ] a )
{
        // your code goes here
}
```

33. This method returns the number of elements in an array passed as a parameter that are multiples of 7.

```
public int foo( int [ ] a )
{
        // your code goes here
}
```

34. This method returns true if the first two elements of the array passed as a parameter have the same value; otherwise, it returns *false*.

```
public boolean foo( String [ ] a )
{
        // your code goes here
}
```

35. This method takes an array of *ints* as a parameter and returns an array of *booleans*. For each element in the parameter array whose value is 0, the corresponding element of the array returned will be assigned *false*; otherwise, the element will be assigned *true*.

```
public boolean [ ] foo( int [ ] a )
{
        // your code goes here
}
```

8.11.4 Identifying Errors in Code

36. Where is the error in this code sequence?

```
double [ ] a = { 3.3, 26.0, 48.4 };
a[4] = 2.5;
```

37. Where is the error in this code sequence?

```
double [ ] a = { 3.3, 26.0, 48.4 };
System.out.println( a[-1] );
```

38. Where is the error in this code sequence?

```
double [ ] a = { 3.3, 26.0, 48.4 };
System.out.println( a{1} );
```

39. Where is the error in this code sequence?

```
double [ ] a = { 3.3, 26.0, 48.4 };
for ( int i = 0; i <= a.length; i++ )
 System.out.println( a[i] );
```

40. Where is the error in this code sequence?

```
double a[3] = { 3.3, 26.0, 48.4 };
```

41. Where is the error (although this code will compile and run) in this code sequence?

```
int a[ ] = { 3, 26, 48, 5 };
int b[ ] = { 3, 26, 48, 5 };

if ( a != b )
     System.out.println( "Array elements are NOT identical" );
```

42. Where is the error in this code sequence?

```
int [ ] a = { 3, 26, 48, 5 };
a.length = 10;
```

43. Where is the logic error in this code sequence?

```
int [ ] a = { 3, 26, 48, 5 };
System.out.println( "The array elements are " + a );
```

44. Where is the error in this code sequence?

```
Integer i1 = 10;
Integer i2 = 15;
Double d1 = 3.4;
String s = new String( "Hello" );
Integer [ ] a = { i1, i2, d1, s };
```

8.11.5 Debugging Area—Using Messages from the Java Compiler and Java JVM

45. You coded the following on line 26 of the class *Test.java*:

```
int a[6] = { 2, 7, 8, 9, 11, 16 }; // line 26
```

When you compile, you get the following messages:

```
Test.java:26: error: ']' expected
        int a[6] = { 2, 7, 8, 9, 11, 16}; // line 26
            ^
Test.java:26: error: not a statement
        int a[6] = { 2, 7, 8, 9, 11, 16}; // line 26
                 ^
Test.java:26: error: ';' expected
        int a[6] = { 2, 7, 8, 9, 11, 16}; // line 26
                  ^
3 errors
```

Explain what the problem is and how to fix it.

46. You coded the following on lines 26, 27, and 28 of the class *Test.java*:

```
int [ ] a = { 2, 7, 8, 9, 11, 16 }; // line 26 of class Test.java
for ( int i = 0; i <= a.length; i++ ) // line 27 of class Test.java
    System.out.println( a[i] ); // line 28 of class Test.java
```

The code compiles properly, but when you run, you get the following output:

```
2
7
8
9
11
16
Exception in thread "main" java.lang.ArrayIndexOutOfBoundsException: 6
at Test.main(Test46.java:28)
```

Explain what the problem is and how to fix it.

47. You coded the following in the class *Test.java*:

```
int [ ] a = { 1, 2, 3 };
int [ ] b = { 1, 2, 3 };
if ( a == b )
    System.out.println( "Arrays are equal" );
else
    System.out.println( "Arrays are NOT equal" );
```

The code compiles properly and runs, but the result is not what you expected; the output is

```
Arrays are NOT equal
```

Explain what the problem is and how to fix it.

48. You coded the following in the class *Test.java*:

```
int [ ] a = { 1, 2, 3 };
System.out.println( a );
```

The code compiles properly and runs, but the result is not what you expected; instead of 1 2 3, the output is similar to the following:

```
[I@f0326267
```

Explain what the problem is and how to fix it.

8.11.6   Write a Short Program

49. Write a value-returning method that returns the number of elements in an integer array.

50. Write a value-returning method that returns the product of all the elements in an integer array.

51. Write a *void* method that sets to 0 all the elements of an integer array.

52. Write a *void* method that multiplies by 2 all the elements of an array of *floats*.

53. Write a method that returns the percentage of elements greater than or equal to 90 in an array of *ints*.

54. Write a method that returns the difference between the largest and smallest elements in an array of *doubles*.

55. Write a method that returns the sum of all the elements of an array of *ints* that have an odd index.

56. Write a method that returns the percentage of the number of elements that have the value *true* in an array of *booleans*.

57. Write a method that returns *true* if an array of *Strings* contains the *String* "Hello"; *false* otherwise.

58. Write a method that prints all the elements of an array of *chars* in reverse order.

59. Write a method that returns an array composed of all the elements in an array of *chars* in reverse order.

60. Write an array-returning method that takes a *String* as a parameter and returns the corresponding array of *chars*.

61. Code an array-returning method that takes an array of *ints* as a parameter and returns an array of *booleans*, assigning *true* for any element of the parameter array greater than or equal to 100; and *false* otherwise.

8.11.7   Programming Projects

62. Write a class encapsulating the concept of statistics for a baseball team, which has the following attributes: a number of players, a list of number of hits for each player, a list of number of at-bats for each player.

    Write the following methods:

    ❑ A constuctor with two equal-length arrays as parameters, the number of hits per player, and the number of at-bats per player.

    ❑ Accessors, mutators, *toString*, and *equals* methods.

    ❑ Generate and return an array of batting averages based on the attributes given.

    ❑ Calculate and return the total number of hits for the team.

    ❑ Calculate and return the number of players with a batting average greater than .300.

    ❑ A method returning an array holding the number of hits, sorted in ascending order.

    Write a client class to test all the methods in your class.

63. Write a class encapsulating the concept of student grades on a test, assuming student grades are composed of a list of integers between 0 and 100.

    Write the following methods:

    ❑ A constructor with just one parameter, the number of students; all grades can be randomly generated

    ❑ Accessor, mutator, *toString*, and *equals* methods

    ❑ A method returning an array of the grades sorted in ascending order

    ❑ A method returning the highest grade

    ❑ A method returning the average grade

    ❑ A method returning the median grade (*Hint:* The median grade will be located in the middle of the sorted array of grades.)

❑ A method returning the mode (the grade that occurs most often) (*Hint:* Create an array of counters; count how many times each grade occurs; then pick the maximum in the array of counters; the array index is the mode.)

Write a client class to test all the methods in your class.

64. Write a class encapsulating the concept of daily temperatures for a week.

Write the following methods:

❑ A constructor accepting an array of seven temperatures as a parameter

❑ Accessor, mutator, *toString*, and *equals* methods

❑ A method returning how many temperatures were below freezing

❑ A method returning an array of temperatures above 100 degrees

❑ A method returning the largest change in temperature between any two consecutive days

❑ A method returning an array of daily temperatures, sorted in descending order

Write a client class to test all the methods in your class.

65. Write a class encapsulating the concept of a tic-tac-toe game as follows:

Two players will be playing, player 1 and player 2.

The board is represented by an array of 9 integer elements: elements at indexes 0, 1, and 2 represent the first row; elements at indexes 3, 4, and 5 represent the second row; elements at indexes 6, 7, and 8 represent the third row.

The value 0 in the array indicates that this space is available; the value 1 indicates the space is occupied by player 1; and the value 2 indicates that this space is occupied by player 2.

In the *main* method of your client class, your program will simulate a tic-tac-toe game from the command line, doing the following:

❑ Create a *TicTacToe* object and instantiate it.

❑ In a loop, prompt for plays, as *ints*, from the user. At each iteration of the loop, you will need to call methods of the *TicTacToe* class to update the *TicTacToe* object. You need to keep track of who is playing (player 1 or 2), enforce the rules, check if either player has won the game. It is clear that if anyone has won the game, it is the last player who played.

❑ If a player wins, you will need to exit the loop and present the result of the game. If the game ends in a tie, you should output that result.

In your *TicTacToe* class, you will need to code the following methods:

❑ A default constructor instantiating the array representing the board.

❑ A method that allows a player to make a move; it takes two arguments: the player number and the position played on the board.

❑ A method checking if a play is legal.

❑ A method checking if a player has won the game; you can break up that method into several methods if you like (for instance, check if a player has won the game by claiming an entire horizontal row).

❑ A method that checks whether the game is a tie (if no player has won and all squares have been played, the game is tied).

❑ A method that displays the results of the game ("Player 1 won," "Player 2 won," or "Tie game").

Write a client class, where the *main* method is located, to test all the methods in your class and enable the user to play.

66. When a new user logs in for the first time on a website, the user has to submit personal information, such as user_id, password, name, email address, telephone number, and so forth. Typically, there are two fields for passwords, requiring the user to enter the password twice, to ensure that the user did not make a typo in the first password field.

Write a class encapsulating the concept of processing a form with the following elements:

User_id

Password

Reenter password

Email address

Name

Street address

City

State

Zip

Telephone

In your class, write the following methods:

- ❑ A constructor with one parameter, a sequence of 10 words in an array of *Strings*, your only instance variable.

- ❑ Accessor, mutator, *toString*, and *equals* methods.

- ❑ A method checking that no *Strings* in the array are empty. (All fields are mandatory.) If at least one is empty, it returns *false*; otherwise, it returns *true*.

- ❑ A method returning the number of characters in the user_id.

- ❑ A method checking if the two *Strings* representing the passwords (representing the password typed in twice) are identical. If they are, it returns *true*; if not, it returns *false*.

- ❑ A method checking if the *String* representing the email address actually "looks like" an email address; to simplify, we can assume that an email address contains one and only one @ character and contains one or more periods after the @ character. If it does "look like" an email address, then the method returns *true*; otherwise, it returns *false*.

- ❑ A method checking if the *String* representing the state has exactly two characters. If it does, it returns *true*; otherwise, it returns *false*.

Write a client class to test all the methods in your class.

67. We want to write a program that performs some syntax checking on HTML code; for simplicity reasons, we will assume that the HTML code is syntactically correct if the number of < characters in any word is the same as the number of > characters in that word. We will also assume that the syntax is correct if the first word is *<html>* and the last word is *</html>*.

Write a class encapsulating that concept, including the following methods:

- ❑ A constructor with one parameter, an array of the words in the HTML sentence, your only instance variable. Your constructor should then get user input from the console for that same number of words and store them in an array of *Strings*, your only data member.

- ❑ Accessor, mutator, *toString*, and *equals* methods.

- ❑ A method returning how many words are in the array.

- ❑ A method returning *true* if the first word is *<html>* and the last word is *</html>*; false otherwise.

❑ A method checking if each array element contains the same number of < characters as > characters. If that is the case, the method returns *true*; otherwise, it returns *false*. For this, we suggest the following method to help you:

    ❑ Write an *int*-returning method that takes a *String* and a *char* as parameters and returns how many times that *char* appears in the *String*; you can convert the *String* to an array of *chars* and loop through it, or use another strategy of your choice.

❑ A method counting and returning the number of *img* tags overall.

Write a client class to test all the methods in your class.

68. Write a class encapsulating the concept of converting integer grades to letter grades (A, B, C, D, or F), assuming grades are composed of a list of integers between 0 and 100.

Write the following methods:

❑ A constructor with just one parameter, the number of students; all grades can be randomly generated.

❑ Accessor, mutator, *toString*, and *equals* methods.

❑ A method returning an array of *chars* corresponding to the integer grades (90 or above should be converted to A, 80 or above to B, 70 or above to C, 60 or above to D, and 59 or less to F).

❑ A method returning the number of A's.

❑ A method returning an array of *ints* counting how many A's, B's, C's, D's, and F's were received.

Write a client class to test all the methods in your class.

69. Write a class that includes a method that converts two parallel arrays of *Strings* to a *Hashtable* (look up the *Hashtable* class in the Java Class Library) such that the keys of the *Hashtable* are the elements of the first array and its corresponding values are the elements of the second array. Test your method with a client program.

70. Write a class encapsulating the concept of a team of baseball players, assuming a baseball player has the following attributes: a name, a position, and a batting percentage. In addition to that class, you will need to design and code a *Player* class to encapsulate the concept of a baseball player.

    In your class encapsulating the team, you should write the following methods:

    ❑ A constructor taking an array of *Player* objects as its only parameter and assigning that array to the array data member of the class, its only instance variable. In your client class, when you test all your methods, you can hard-code nine baseball *Player* objects.

    ❑ Accessor, mutator, *toString*, and *equals* methods.

    ❑ A method checking that all positions are different, returning *true* if they are, *false* if they are not.

    ❑ A method returning the batting percentage of the team.

    ❑ A method checking that we have a pitcher (that is, the name of the position) on the team. If we do not have any, it returns *false*; otherwise, it returns *true*.

    ❑ A method returning the array of *Player* objects sorted in ascending order using the batting percentage as the sorting key.

    ❑ A method checking if a certain person (a parameter of the method) is on the team, based on the name of that person. If the person is on the team, the method returns *true*; otherwise, it returns *false*.

    ❑ A method returning an array of *Player* objects, sorted in ascending order based on batting percentages.

    Write a client class to test all the methods in your class.

71. Write a class encapsulating a similar concept to the one used in the die counting problem of Section 8.8. Here, we want to roll two dice; the total of the numbers rolled will be between 2 and 12. We want to keep track of how many times each possible total was rolled.

    Write the following methods:

    ❑ A constructor with no parameter; it randomly generates two numbers between 1 and 6, representing the dice.

    ❑ Accessor, mutator, *toString*, and *equals* methods.

    ❑ A method returning the total of the two dice.

    ❑ A method checking if the two dice have identical values. If they do, it returns *true*; otherwise, it returns *false*.

The number of times we roll the dice should be an input from the user at the command line (not inside the program). Your program should output the total for each possible roll (from 2 to 12), as well as the number of times the two dice had identical values.

Write a client class to test all the methods in your class.

72. Write a graphical application that creates two *Die* objects and rolls the two dice 5,000 times. Display the results showing the frequency of each possible total in a bar chart. Pick a scale that is appropriate for the maximum height of your bar chart.

8.11.8   Technical Writing

73. What do you think are advantages and disadvantages of arrays?

74. Write the pseudocode to perform a Selection Sort on an array of *Auto* objects based on the instance variable *model*.

75. When you try to use an array index that is out of bounds, your code will compile, but you will generate a run-time exception. Discuss whether this is an advantage or a disadvantage, and why.

76. When instantiating an array, you can assign the number of elements in the array dynamically, using a variable (as opposed to using a constant). Discuss a situation where that would be useful.

8.11.9   Group Project (for a group of 1, 2, or 3 students)

77. Security is an important feature of information systems. Often, text is encrypted before being sent, and then decrypted upon receipt. We want to build a class (or several classes) encapsulating the concept of encryption. You will need to test that class with a client program where the *main* method is located.

For this project, encrypting consists of translating each character into another character. For instance, if we consider the English alphabet, including characters *a* through *z*, each character is randomly encrypted into another, which could be the same character. (If you like, you can design your program so that no character is encrypted into itself.) To represent this concept, we can have an array of characters for the original alphabet, and another array of characters for the encrypted alphabet. For example, we could have

Original alphabet	Encrypted alphabet
a	u
b	p
c	h
d	a
e	s
f	x
g	z
h	b
i	j
. . .	. . .

To encrypt a word, each letter in the word is replaced by the corresponding letter in the encryted alphabet. For example, the word *caged* would be encrypted into *huzsa*. To decrypt a word, the letters in the encrypted word are replaced by the corresponding letter in the original alphabet. For example, the encrypted word *xssa* would be decrypted as *feed*.

If we have 26 different characters in the original alphabet, then we will have 26 different characters in the encrypted alphabet. Furthermore, the encrypted alphabet should be randomly generated.

In your *main* method, you should prompt the user for a sentence. Your program should encrypt the sentence, output the encrypted sentence, then decrypt it, and output the decrypted sentence, which should be identical to the original sentence that was input by the user.

For extra credit, use an array to keep track of the number of occurrences of each character. Convert these occurrences to percentages, and then use these percentages to attempt to decrypt a large, encrypted message.

CHAPTER 9
Multidimensional Arrays and the *ArrayList* Class

CHAPTER CONTENTS

Introduction

Arrays can be useful when we have a lot of data to store in memory. If we write a program to perform statistics on last year's temperatures, it is convenient to set up an array of *doubles* of size 365 to store the daily temperature data.

But what if in addition to analyzing daily temperatures, we want to analyze temperatures by the week, or by a particular day of the week? For instance, if we sail on weekends, we could want to know how many times the temperature was above 65 degrees on Saturdays and Sundays. If we are considering investing in air conditioning at home, we might be interested in knowing how many weeks had temperatures above 90 degrees. If we are avid skiers, we could be interested in the number of weeks with temperatures lower than 32 degrees.

In this situation, we would want to organize our data along two dimensions: weeks and days of the week. If we were to visualize the data as a table, we could imagine a table made up of 52 rows, each row representing a week. Each row would have seven columns, representing the days of the week. This table is shown in Figure 9.1.

Figure 9.1

Temperature Data for the Previous 52 Weeks

	Sunday	Monday	Tuesday	Wednesday	Thursday	Friday	Saturday
Week 1	35	28.6	29.3	38	43.1	45.6	49
Week 2	51.9	37.9	34.1	37.1	39	40.5	43.2
...							
...							
...							
...							
...							
Week 51	56.2	51.9	45.3	48.7	42.9	35.5	38.2
Week 52	33.2	27.1	24.9	29.8	37.7	39.9	38.8

Or we could imagine a table of seven rows, each row representing a day of the week, and 52 columns, each column representing a week of the year. In either case, we can represent the rows and columns of our temperature table using a two-dimensional array. More generally, **multidimensional** arrays allow us to represent data organized along *n* dimensions with a single array.

9.1 Declaring and Instantiating Multidimensional Arrays

Just like single-dimensional arrays, multidimensional arrays are implemented as objects, so creating a multidimensional array takes the same two steps as creating a single-dimensional array:

1. declaring the object reference for the array
2. instantiating the array

In arrays with elements of primitive types, each element of the array contains a value of that type. For example, in an array of *doubles*, each element contains a *double* value. In arrays with a class data type, each element is an object reference, which points to the location of an object of that class.

9.1.1 Declaring Multidimensional Arrays

To declare a multidimensional array, we use the same syntax as for a single-dimensional array, except that we include an empty set of brackets for each dimension.

Here is the syntax for declaring a two-dimensional array:

```
datatype [ ][ ] arrayName;
```

Here is the syntax for declaring a three-dimensional array:

```
datatype [ ][ ][ ] arrayName;
```

In order to keep things simple, we will concentrate on two-dimensional arrays at this point. We will discuss three- and four-dimensional arrays later in the chapter.

The following statement declares an array that we can use to hold the daily high temperatures for the last 52 weeks:

```
double [ ][ ] dailyTemps;
```

The brackets can be placed before or after the array name. So the following syntax for declaring a two-dimensional array is also valid:

```
datatype arrayName [ ][ ];
```

We prefer to put the brackets right after the data type, because it's easier to read.

To store quiz grades for students, we could declare a two-dimensional array, where each row will store the quiz grades for a particular student and each column will store the grades for a particular quiz:

```
char [ ][ ] quizzes; // each element is a char
```

The syntax is the same whether we declare arrays with basic data types or class types.

Imagine that we are interested in keeping track of a fleet of cars within a multinational corporation. The corporation operates in various countries, and in each of these countries, some employees have a company car. For this situation, we can declare a two-dimensional array where the first dimension will represent the country and the second dimension will represent the employee. Assuming we have an *Auto* class, the following statement declares this two-dimensional array to hold *Auto* objects:

```
Auto [ ][ ] cars;
```

We can also declare multiple multidimensional arrays of the same data type in one statement by inserting a comma after each array name, using this syntax:

```
datatype [ ][ ] arrayName1, arrayName2;
```

For example, the following statement will declare two integer arrays to hold the number of stolen bases for two baseball players for each game in their career:

```
int [ ][ ] brian, jon;
```

The first dimension represents the games (per season), and the second dimension represents the season.

COMMON ERROR TRAP

Specifying the size of any of the dimensions of a multidimensional array in the declaration will generate a compiler error.

Notice that when we declare a multidimensional array, we do not specify how many elements the array will have. Declaring a multidimensional array does not allocate memory for the array; this is done in step 2, when we instantiate the array.

For example, this code:

```
double [7][52] dailyTemps;
```

will generate compiler errors.

9.1.2 Instantiating Multidimensional Arrays

Just like instantiating single-dimensional arrays, we instantiate a multidimensional array using the *new* keyword. Here is the syntax for instantiating a two-dimensional array:

```
arrayName = new datatype [exp1][exp2];

  where exp1 and exp2 are expressions that evaluate to integers and specify,
  respectively, the number of rows and the number of columns in the array.
```

This statement allocates memory for the array. The number of elements in a two-dimensional array is equal to the sum of the number of elements in each row. When all the rows have the same number of columns, the number of elements in the array is equal to the number of rows multiplied by the number of columns.

For example, if we instantiate the following *dailyTemps* array with 52 rows and 7 columns, the array will have 52 * 7, or 364, elements:

```
dailyTemps = new double [52][7]; // dailyTemps has 52 rows
                                 // and 7 columns,
                                 // for a total of 364 elements
```

These statements will instantiate the other arrays declared above:

```
int numberOfStudents = 25;
int numberOfQuizzes = 10;
quizzes = new char [numberOfStudents][numberOfQuizzes];
// quizzes has 25 rows and 10 columns
// for a total of 250 elements

cars = new Auto [5][50];
// cars has 5 rows and 50 columns
// cars will store 250 Auto objects

brian = new int [80][20];
// brian has 80 rows and 20 columns
// there are 80 games per season
// brian played baseball for 20 seasons

jon = new int [80][10];
// jon has 80 rows and 10 columns
// jon played baseball for 10 seasons
```

When a multidimensional array is instantiated, the elements are given initial values automatically. Elements of arrays with numeric types are initialized to 0, elements of *char* type are initialized to the Unicode null character, elements of *boolean* type are initialized to *false*, and elements of class types are initialized to *null*.

9.1.3   Combining the Declaration and Instantiation of Multidimensional Arrays

Multidimensional arrays, like single-dimensional arrays, can also be instantiated when they are declared. To combine the declaration and instantiation of a two-dimensional array, use this syntax:

```
datatype [ ][ ] arrayName = new datatype [exp1][exp2];

    where exp1 and exp2 are expressions that evaluate to integers and specify,
    respectively, the number of rows and columns in the array.
```

Thus, this statement:

```
double [ ][ ] dailyTemps = new double [52][7];
```

is equivalent to:

```
double [ ][ ] dailyTemps;
dailyTemps = new double [52][7];
```

Similarly, this statement:

```
char [ ][ ] quizzes = new char [25][10];
```

is equivalent to:

```
char [ ][ ] quizzes;
quizzes = new char [25][10];
```

9.1.4   Assigning Initial Values to Multidimensional Arrays

We can instantiate a two-dimensional array by assigning initial values when the array is declared. To do this, we specify the initial values using comma-separated lists, enclosed in an outer set of curly braces:

```
datatype [ ][ ] arrayName =
     { { value00, value01, ... }, { value10, value11, }, ... };
```

```
  where valueMN is an expression that evaluates to the data type of the array and
  is the value to assign to the element at row M and column N.
```

The list contains a number of sublists, separated by commas. The number of these sublists determines the number of rows in the array. For each row, the number of values in the corresponding sublist determines the number of columns in the row. Thus, Java allows a two-dimensional array to have a different number of columns in each row. For example, in our *Auto* array, each country (row) could have a different number of employees (columns) with company cars.

Indeed, a two-dimensional array is an array of arrays. The first dimension of a two-dimensional array consists of an array of array references, with each reference pointing to a single-dimensional array. Thus, a two-dimensional array is composed of an array of rows, where each row is a single-dimensional array.

For example, this statement declares and instantiates a two-dimensional array of integers:

```
int [ ][ ] numbersList1 = { { 0, 5, 10 },
                            { 0, 3, 6, 9 } };
```

Because two sublists are given, this two-dimensional array has two rows. The first sublist specifies three values, and therefore, the first row will have three columns; the second sublist specifies four values, and therefore, the second row will have four columns.

Figure 9.2 shows the *numbersList1* array after the preceding statement is executed.

An initialization list can be given only when the array is declared. If a two-dimensional array has already been instantiated, attempting to assign values to an array using an initialization list will generate a compiler error. For example, this code:

```
int [ ][ ] grades = new int [2][3];
grades = { { 89, 73, 98 },
           { 88, 65, 92 } };
```

will generate compiler errors.

We can declare and instantiate an array of objects by providing object references in the list:

```
Auto sportsCar = new Auto( "Ferrari", 0, 0.0 );
Auto sedan1 = new Auto( "BMW", 0, 0.0 );
Auto sedan2 = new Auto( "BMW", 100, 15.0 );
Auto sedan3 = new Auto( "Toyota", 0, 0.0 );
Auto rv1 = new Auto( "Jeep", 0, 0.0 );

Auto [ ][ ] cars = { { sportsCar, sedan1 },
                     { rv1, new Auto( ) },
                     { sedan2, sedan3 } };
```

This array of *Auto* objects has three rows with two columns in each row. The elements of the array *cars* are object references to *Auto* objects.

In most situations, the number of columns will be the same for each row. However, there are situations where it is useful to have a different number of columns for each row. For instance, Dr. Smith, a college professor, keeps track of grades using a two-dimensional array. The rows represent the courses she teaches and the columns represent the grades for the students in those sections. Grades are A, B, C, D, or F, so she declares the array with *char* elements. Dr. Smith teaches four

COMMON ERROR TRAP
An initialization list can be given only when the two-dimensional array is declared. Attempting to assign values to an array using an initialization list after the array is instantiated will generate a compiler error.

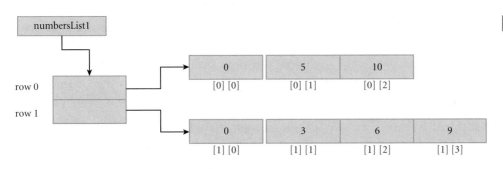

Figure 9.2

The *numbersList1* Array After Instantiation

courses: CS1, CS2, Database Management, and Operating Systems. Thus, she has four rows in the array. But in each course, Dr. Smith has a different number of students: There are 23 students in CS1, 16 in CS2, 12 in Database Management, and 28 in Operating Systems. So the first row will have 23 columns, the second row 16 columns, the third row 12 columns, and the fourth and last row will have 28 columns.

Using an initialization list, it is easy to instantiate a two-dimensional array with a different number of columns for every row. But sometimes the data is retrieved dynamically—read from a file, for example—and it is not possible to use an initialization list.

To instantiate a two-dimensional array with a different number of columns for each row, we can do the following:

- First, instantiate the two-dimensional array.

- Second, instantiate each row as a single-dimensional array.

For the preceding example, we can use the following code:

```
char [ ][ ] grades;          // declare the array
grades = new char [4][ ];    // instantiate the array
                             // grades has 4 null array elements
grades[0] = new char [23];   // instantiate row 0; 23 char elements
grades[1] = new char [16];   // instantiate row 1; 16 char elements
grades[2] = new char [12];   // instantiate row 2; 12 char elements
grades[3] = new char [28];   // instantiate row 3; 28 char elements
```

The second statement:

```
grades = new char [4][ ];
```

instantiates the two-dimensional array *grades* as an array having four rows, none of which has been instantiated yet. Because a two-dimensional array is an array of arrays, each element of the first dimension of the *grades* array is an array reference. Thus, before being instantiated, each element of the first dimension of the *grades* array has the value *null*.

As explained earlier, in a two-dimensional array, each row is a single-dimensional array. The last four statements instantiate each row, *grades[0]*, *grades[1]*, *grades[2]*, and *grades[3]*, each row having a different number of elements, or columns. The elements in these arrays are *chars*, initialized to the Unicode null character.

Later in this chapter, we will define a general pattern for processing two-dimensional array elements so that it applies to all situations: an identical number of columns for each row, or a different number of columns for each row.

9.2   Accessing Multidimensional Array Elements

Elements of a two-dimensional array are accessed using this syntax:

```
arrayName[exp1][exp2]
```
> where *exp1* and *exp2* are expressions that evaluate to integers.

Exp1 is the element's row position, or **row index**, within the two-dimensional array. *Exp2* is the element's column position, or **column index**, within the two-dimensional array. The row index of the first row is always 0; the row index of the last row is always 1 less than the number of rows. The column index of the first column is always 0. The column index of the last column is always 1 fewer than the number of columns in that row.

Because a two-dimensional array is an array of arrays, the length of a two-dimensional array is its number of arrays, or rows. We access the number of rows in a two-dimensional array using the following syntax:

```
arrayName.length
```

Similarly, the length of each row is the number of columns (or elements) in that row's array. To access the number of columns in row *i* of a two-dimensional array named *arrayName*, we use this syntax:

```
arrayName[i].length
```

Table 9.1 summarizes the syntax for accessing elements of a two-dimensional array.

Suppose we want to analyze the monthly cell phone bills for the past three months for a family of four persons. The parents, Joe and Jane, each have a cell phone, and so do the children, Mike and Sarah. We want to calculate the average monthly bill for each person, the total payments for the three months, and determine which family

TABLE 9.1   Accessing Two-Dimensional Array Elements

Array Element	Syntax
Row 0, column *j*	`arrayName[0][j]`
Row *i*, column *j*	`arrayName[i][j]`
Last row, column *j*	`arrayName[arrayName.length - 1][j]`
Last row, last column	`arrayName[arrayName.length - 1]` `    [arrayName[arrayName.length - 1].length - 1]`
Number of rows in the array	`arrayName.length`
Number of columns in row *i*	`arrayName[i].length`

TABLE 9.2   **Visualizing a Two-Dimensional Array**

	Joe	Jane	Mike	Sarah
July	45.24	54.67	32.55	25.61
August	65.29	49.75	32.08	26.11
September	75.24	54.53	34.55	28.16

member had the lowest and highest bills. We could use a two-dimensional array of *doubles* with three rows and four columns. The rows will represent the months and the columns will represent the family members. For example, we could have the following mapping for the row and column indexes:

> row 0 : July
>
> row 1 : August
>
> row 2 : September
>
> column 0 : Joe
>
> column 1 : Jane
>
> column 2 : Mike
>
> column 3 : Sarah

We could visualize our two-dimensional array as the table shown in Table 9.2.

We'll name the array *familyCellBills*. Each element in the array will be referenced as *familyCellBills[i][j]*, where *i* is the index of the row (the month), and *j* is the index of the column (the person). Remember that the first element in a row or column is at index 0, so the first element in the first row is at index [0][0].

In lines 13–15 of Example 9.1, we declare and instantiate the *familyCellBills* array. Because the elements of *familyCellBills* are *doubles*, instantiating the array also initializes each element to 0.0. Lines 18–31 store values into each element of the array. Figure 9.3 shows how the *familyCellBills* array looks after lines 18–31 are executed.

```
1 /* Two-Dimensional Array of Cell Phone Bills
2    Anderson, Franceschi
3 */
4
5 public class FamilyCellBills
```

```java
6 {
7  public static void main( String [ ] args )
8  {
9   // declare constants for the number of rows and columns
10   final int NUMBER_OF_MONTHS = 3;
11   final int NUMBER_OF_PERSONS = 4;
12
13   // declare and instantiate the array
14   double [ ][ ] familyCellBills =
15      new double [NUMBER_OF_MONTHS][NUMBER_OF_PERSONS];
16
17   // assign values to array elements
18   familyCellBills[0][0] = 45.24;  // row 0
19   familyCellBills[0][1] = 54.67;
20   familyCellBills[0][2] = 32.55;
21   familyCellBills[0][3] = 25.61;
22
23   familyCellBills[1][0] = 65.29;  // row 1
24   familyCellBills[1][1] = 49.75;
25   familyCellBills[1][2] = 32.08;
26   familyCellBills[1][3] = 26.11;
27
28   familyCellBills[2][0] = 75.24;  // row 2
29   familyCellBills[2][1] = 54.53;
30   familyCellBills[2][2] = 34.55;
31   familyCellBills[2][3] = 28.16;
32
33   System.out.println( "The first monthly cell bill for the first "
34      + "family member is\n"
35      + familyCellBills[0][0] );
36   System.out.println( "The last monthly cell bill for the last "
37      + "family member is\n"
38      + familyCellBills[NUMBER_OF_MONTHS - 1][NUMBER_OF_PERSONS - 1] );
39
40   int numRows = familyCellBills.length;
41   System.out.println( "\nThe number of rows is " + numRows );
42
43   for ( int i = 0; i < numRows; i++ )
44   {
45    System.out.print( "The number of columns in row " + i + " is " );
46    System.out.println( familyCellBills[i].length );
47   }
48  }
49 }
```

EXAMPLE 9.1 The *familyCellBills* Array

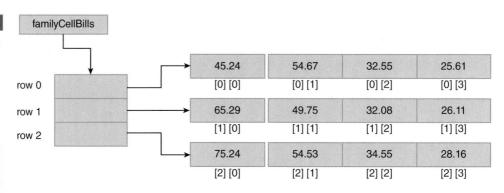

Note that the last element is *familyCellBills[2][3]*, with a row index that is 1 less than *familyCellBills.length*, and a column index that is 1 less than *familyCellBills[2].length*, which is the number of columns in the last row. More generally, for a two-dimensional array named *arr*, the last element is:

```
arr[arr.length - 1][arr[arr.length - 1].length - 1]
```

Lines 33–38 output the first and last element of the array *familyCellBills*.

Line 40 assigns the number of rows in the *familyCellBills* array to the *int* variable *numRows*. The variable *numRows* now has the value 3 and is output at line 41.

At lines 43–47, a *for* loop outputs the number of columns in each row of *familyCellBills*. Figure 9.4 shows the output of this example.

Row indexes of a two-dimensional array *must* be between 0 and *arrayName. length – 1*. Attempting to access an element of an array using a row index less than 0 or greater than *arrayName.length – 1* will compile without errors, but will generate an *ArrayIndexOutOfBoundsException* at run time. By default, this exception halts execution of the program.

For example, all the following expressions are invalid:

```
// invalid row indexes for the familycellBills array!!

familyCellBills[-1][2]
// the lowest valid row index is 0
```

```
The first monthly cell bill for the first family member is 45.24
The last monthly cell bill for the last family member is 28.16

The number of rows is 3
The number of columns in row 0 is 4
The number of columns in row 1 is 4
The number of columns in row 2 is 4
```

```
familyCellBills[cellBills.length][2]
// the highest valid row index is familyCellBills.length - 1
```

Similarly, column indexes of a two-dimensional array *must* be between 0 and *arrayName[i].length – 1*, where *i* is the row index. Attempting to access an element of row *i* in a two-dimensional array using a column index less than 0 or greater than *arrayName[i].length – 1* will compile without errors, but will generate an *ArrayIndexOutOfBoundsException* at run time.

For example, all the following expressions are invalid:

```
// invalid column indexes for the familyCellBills array!!

familyCellBills[1][-1]
// the lowest valid column index is 0

familyCellBills[1][familyCellBills[1].length]
// the highest valid column index of row i is
// familyCellBills[i].length - 1
```

Example 9.2 illustrates how to work with an array of objects. In this example, we use an *Auto* class that has three instance variables; *model*, a *String*; *milesDriven,* an *int*; and *gallonsOfGas*, a *double*. At lines 17–20, we declare and initialize *cars*, a two-dimensional array of *Auto* objects. Before using an element of *cars*, that *Auto* element has to be instantiated; failure to do so could generate a *NullPointerException* at run time.

There are three rows in *cars*: the first row has three columns, and the second and third rows have two columns each. Line 22 retrieves the array element at row 1 and column 0—here *sportsCar*—and assigns it to the *Auto* object reference *retrievedCar*, which is then printed at lines 25–26, where *toString* is called implicitly. Figure 9.5 shows the output of this example.

```
 1 /* Working with a Two-Dimensional Array of Objects
 2    Anderson, Franceschi
 3 */
 4
 5 public class TwoDimAutoArray
 6 {
 7  public static void main( String [ ] args )
 8  {
 9    // instantiate several Auto object references
10    Auto sedan1 = new Auto( "BMW", 0, 0.0 );
11    Auto sedan2 = new Auto( "BMW", 100, 15.0 );
12    Auto sedan3 = new Auto( "Toyota", 0, 0.0 );
13    Auto sportsCar = new Auto( "Ferrari", 0, 0.0 );
14    Auto rv1 = new Auto( "Jeep", 0, 0.0 );
15    Auto rv2 = new Auto( "Ford", 200, 30.0 );
```

```
16
17    // declare and initialize two-dimensional array of Autos
18    Auto [ ][ ] cars = { { sedan1, sedan2, sedan3 },
19                         { sportsCar, new Auto( ) },
20                         { rv1, rv2 } };
21
22    Auto retrievedCar = cars[1][0];
23    // retrievedCar gets the sportsCar object reference
24
25    System.out.println( "cars[1][0]'s description is:\n"
26                        + retrievedCar );
27  }
28 }
```

EXAMPLE 9.2   Two-Dimensional Array of *Auto* Objects

Figure 9.5

Output of
Example 9.2

```
cars[1][0]'s description is:

Model: Ferrari; miles driven; 0; gallons of gas: 0.0
```

Skill Practice
with these end-of-chapter questions

9.10.1   Multiple Choice Exercises

Questions 1, 2, 3, 4, 5, 6, 7, 8

9.10.2   Reading and Understanding Code

Questions 14, 15, 16, 17, 18

9.10.3   Fill In the Code

Questions 33, 34

9.10.4   Identifying Errors in Code

Questions 50, 51, 52, 53

9.10.5   Debugging Area

Question 59

9.10.6   Write a Short Program

Question 65

9.10.8   Technical Writing

Question 97

9.3   Aggregate Two-Dimensional Array Operations

As with single-dimensional arrays, Java does not support aggregate operations on multidimensional arrays. For example, we cannot print the contents of an array using only the array name. Instead, we need to process each element individually.

9.3.1   Processing All the Elements of a Two-Dimensional Array

To process all the elements of a two-dimensional array, we use nested *for* loops that access and process each element individually. Often, the most logical way to process all elements is in row order, and within each row, in column order. We could also process elements one column at a time if that is more logical for the problem at hand.

In our nested *for* loops, the outer *for* loop will process the rows and the inner *for* loop will process the columns within each row. We will use *i* for the row index and *j* for the column index.

For the outer *for* loop, we can use the same header as we use to process single-dimensional arrays:

```java
for ( int i = 0; i < arrayName.length; i++ )
```

Note that the initialization statement of the outer loop:

```java
int i = 0;
```

sets *i* to the index of the first row of the two-dimensional array. Then the outer loop update statement increments *i*, so that we process each row in order.

The outer loop condition:

```java
i < arrayName.length
```

continues execution of the outer loop as long as the row index is less than the *length* of the two-dimensional array, which represents the number of rows. Note that we use the *less than* operator (<) instead of the *less than or equal to* operator (<=). Using the *less than or equal to* operator would cause us to illegally attempt to reference an element with a row index of *arrayName.length*.

The *for* loop header for the inner loop, which processes the columns of the current row, is as follows:

```java
for ( int j = 0; j < arrayName[i].length; j++ )
```

The initialization statement of the inner loop:

```java
int j = 0;
```

sets *j* to the index of the first column of the current row. Then the inner loop update statement increments *j* to the next column index, so that we process each column of the current row in order.

The inner loop condition:

`j < arrayName[i].length`

continues execution of the inner loop as long as the column index is less than the *length* of the current row (row *i*). Given that each row can have a different number of columns, this will ensure that we do not attempt to access an element beyond the last column index of the current row.

Note, again, that we use the *less than* operator (<), not the *less than or equal to* operator (<=), which would cause us to illegally attempt to reference an element with a column index of *arrayName[i].length*.

Inside the inner *for* loop, we refer to the current element being processed as:

`arrayName[i][j]`

Thus, the general pattern for processing the elements of a two-dimensional array called *arrayName* in row-first, column-second order using nested *for* loops is:

```
for ( int i = 0; i < arrayName.length; i++ )
{
   for ( int j = 0; j < arrayName[i].length; j++ )
   {
      // process element arrayName[i][j]
   }
}
```

Example 9.3 illustrates how to print all the elements of the two-dimensional array *familyCellBills* in row order. The array is declared and initialized at lines 10–12. At lines 16–23, the nested *for* loops, using the standard pattern described earlier, print all the elements of the array. Figure 9.6 shows the output of the program.

```
1  /* Processing a Two-Dimensional Array of Cell Phone Bills
2     Anderson, Franceschi
3  */
4
5  public class OutputFamilyCellBills
6  {
7    public static void main( String [ ] args )
8    {
9      // declare and initialize the array
10     double [ ][ ] familyCellBills = { {45.24, 54.67, 32.55, 25.61},
11                                       {65.29, 49.75, 32.08, 26.11},
12                                       {75.24, 54.53, 34.55, 28.16} };
13
14     System.out.println( "\tData for family cell bills" );
15
16     for ( int i = 0; i < familyCellBills.length; i++ )
```

```
17   {
18     System.out.print( "\nrow " + i + ":\t" );
19     for ( int j = 0; j < familyCellBills[i].length; j++ )
20     {
21       System.out.print( familyCellBills[i][j] + "\t" );
22     }
23   }
24   System.out.println( );
25 }
26 }
```

EXAMPLE 9.3   Two-Dimensional Array Processing

```
    Data for family cell bills

  row 0:    45.24    54.67    32.55    25.61

  row 1:    65.29    49.75    32.08    26.11

  row 2:    75.24    54.53    34.55    28.16
```

Figure 9.6

Output of
Example 9.3

9.3.2   Processing a Given Row of a Two-Dimensional Array

What if we want to process just one row of a two-dimensional array? For instance, we could be interested in calculating the sum of the cell bills for the whole family for a particular month, or identifying who had the highest cell bill in a particular month.

The general pattern for processing the elements of row i of a two-dimensional array called *arrayName* uses a single *for* loop:

```
for ( int j = 0; j < arrayName[i].length; j++ )
{
    // process element arrayName[i][j]
}
```

Example 9.4 shows how to sum all the elements of a particular row of the two-dimensional array *familyCellBills*.

```
 1 /* Processing One Row of a Two-Dimensional Array
 2    Anderson, Franceschi
 3 */
 4
 5 import java.util.Scanner;
 6 import java.text.NumberFormat;
 7
 8 public class SumARowFamilyCellBills
 9 {
10   public static void main( String [ ] args )
```

```
11  {
12    // declare and initialize the array
13    double [ ][ ] familyCellBills = { {45.24, 54.67, 32.55, 25.61},
14                                       {65.29, 49.75, 32.08, 26.11},
15                                       {75.24, 54.53, 34.55, 28.16} };
16
17    String [ ] months = { "July", "August", "September" };
18    for ( int i = 0; i < months.length; i++ )
19      System.out.println( "Month " + i + " : " + months[i] );
20
21    Scanner scan = new Scanner( System.in );
22    int currentMonth;
23    do
24    {
25      System.out.print( "Enter a month number between 0 and 2 > " );
26      currentMonth = scan.nextInt( );
27    } while ( currentMonth < 0 || currentMonth > 2 );
28
29    double monthlyFamilyBills = 0.0;
30    for ( int j = 0; j < familyCellBills[currentMonth].length; j++ )
31    {
32      // add current family member bill to total
33      monthlyFamilyBills += familyCellBills[currentMonth][j];
34    }
35
36    NumberFormat priceFormat = NumberFormat.getCurrencyInstance( );
37    System.out.println( "\nThe total family cell bills during "
38                        + months[currentMonth] + " is "
39                        + priceFormat.format( monthlyFamilyBills ) );
40  }
41 }
```

EXAMPLE 9.4   Processing One Row in a Two-Dimensional Array

Since the rows correspond to the months, we declare and initialize at line 17 a single-dimensional *String* array named *months* in order to make our prompt more user-friendly. At lines 18–19, we print a menu for the user, providing month names and the corresponding indexes. At lines 23–27, we use a *do/while* loop to prompt the user for a month index until the user enters a valid value between 0 and 2.

To calculate the total of the family cell bills for the month index that the user inputs, we first initialize the variable *monthlyFamilyBills* to 0.0 at line 29. We then use a single *for* loop at lines 30–34, following the pattern described earlier, to sum all the family member bills for the month chosen by the user. We then format and output the total at lines 36–39. Figure 9.7 shows the output of the program when the user chooses 1 for the month.

```
Month 0 : July
Month 1 : August
Month 2 : September
Enter a month number between 0 and 2 > 1

The total family cell bills during August is $173.23
```

Figure 9.7

Output of
Example 9.4

9.3.3 Processing a Given Column of a Two-Dimensional Array

If we want to determine the highest cell bill for Mike or calculate the average cell bill for Sarah, we will need to process just one column of the two-dimensional array.

The general pattern for processing the elements of column *j* of a two-dimensional array called *arrayName* uses a single *for* loop:

```
for ( int i = 0; i < arrayName.length; i++ )
{
    if ( j < arrayName[i].length )
      // process element arrayName[i][j]
}
```

Because rows may have a different number of columns, a given row *i* may not have a column *j*. Thus, we need to check that the current column number is less than *arrayName[i].length* before we attempt to access *arrayName[i][j]*.

Because our two-dimensional array *familyCellBills* has the same number of columns (4) in every row, no extra precaution is necessary here. It is a good software engineering practice, however, to verify that the column index is valid before attempting to process the array element.

Example 9.5 shows how to find the maximum value of all the elements of a particular column.

SOFTWARE ENGINEERING
Before processing an element in a column, check whether the current row contains an element in that column. Doing so will avoid an *ArrayIndexOut-OfBounds-Exception.*

```
1 /* Processing One Column of a Two-Dimensional Array
2    Anderson, Franceschi
3 */
4
5 import java.util.Scanner;
6 import java.text.NumberFormat;
7
8 public class MaxMemberBill
9 {
10   public static void main( String [ ] args )
11   {
12     // declare and initialize the array
13     double [ ][ ] familyCellBills = { {45.24, 54.67, 32.55, 25.61},
14                                       {65.29, 49.75, 32.08, 26.11},
```

```
15                                              {75.24, 54.53, 34.55, 28.16} };
16
17    String [ ] familyMembers = { "Joe", "Jane", "Mike", "Sarah" };
18    for ( int i = 0; i < familyMembers.length; i++ )
19         System.out.println( "Family member " + i + " : "
20                                  + familyMembers[i] );
21
22    Scanner scan = new Scanner( System.in );
23    int currentMember;
24    do
25    {
26     System.out.print( "Enter a family member between 0 and 3 > " );
27     currentMember = scan.nextInt( );
28    } while ( currentMember < 0 || currentMember > 3 );
29
30    double memberMaxBill = familyCellBills[0][currentMember];
31    for ( int i = 1; i < familyCellBills.length; i++ )
32    {
33     if ( currentMember < familyCellBills[i].length )
34     {
35        // update memberMaxBill if necessary
36        if ( familyCellBills[i][currentMember] > memberMaxBill )
37          memberMaxBill = familyCellBills[i][currentMember];
38     }
39    }
40
41    NumberFormat priceFormat = NumberFormat.getCurrencyInstance( );
42    System.out.println ( "\nThe max cell bill for "
43                             + familyMembers[currentMember] + " is "
44                             + priceFormat.format( memberMaxBill ) );
45  }
46 }
```

EXAMPLE 9.5　Processing a Column in a Two-Dimensional Array

At line 17, we declare and initialize a single-dimensional *String* array named *familyMembers* to make our prompt more user-friendly. At lines 24–28, we again use a *do/while* loop to prompt the user for a valid family member index.

To calculate the maximum value of the family member cell bills, we first initialize the variable *memberMaxBill* to the first element in the column (*familyCellBills[0][currentMember]*) at line 30. We then use a standard *for* loop at lines 31–39, following the pattern described earlier to update the value of *memberMaxBill* as necessary. There is one minor difference; we do not need to start the row at index 0 because we initialized *memberMaxBill* to the value of the element in row 0 of the column *currentMember*. Note that we assume that there is an element at column 0 of each row; that is, each row

```
Family member 0 : Joe
Family member 1 : Jane
Family member 2 : Mike
Family member 3 : Sarah
Enter a family member between 0 and 3 > 2

The max cell bill for Mike is $34.55
```

Figure 9.8

Output of
Example 9.5

has been instantiated. The value of the variable *memberMaxBill* is then formatted and printed at lines 41–44. Figure 9.8 shows the output of the program.

9.3.4 Processing a Two-Dimensional Array One Row at a Time

Earlier, we calculated the sum of the elements of a given row of a two-dimensional array. But what if we are interested in calculating that sum for each row? In this case, we need to initialize our total variable before we process each row and print the results after we process each row.

The general pattern for processing each row of a two-dimensional array called *arrayName* using nested *for* loops is

```
for ( int i = 0; i < arrayName.length; i++ )
{
   // initialize processing variables for row i
   for ( int j = 0; j < arrayName[i].length; j++ )
   {
      // process element arrayName[i][j]
   }
   // finish the processing of row i
}
```

There are two important additions to the general pattern for processing all elements of the array:

- Before processing each row, that is, before the inner loop, we need to initialize the processing variables for the current row. If we are summing elements, we initialize the total variable to 0. If we are calculating a minimum or maximum value, we initialize the current minimum or maximum to the value of the first element of the current row.

- When we reach the end of each row, that is, after each completion of the inner loop, we finish processing the current row. For instance, we may want to print the sum or maximum value for that row.

Example 9.6 shows how to sum the elements of each row of the two-dimensional array *familyCellBills*.

```
1 /* Processing Each Row of a Two-Dimensional Array
2    Anderson, Franceschi
3 */
4
5 import java.util.Scanner;
6 import java.text.NumberFormat;
7
8 public class SumEachRowFamilyCellBills
9 {
10  public static void main( String [ ] args )
11  {
12   // declare and initialize the array
13   double [ ][ ] familyCellBills = { {45.24, 54.67, 32.55, 25.61},
14                                     {65.29, 49.75, 32.08, 26.11},
15                                     {75.24, 54.53, 34.55, 28.16} };
16
17   String [ ] months = { "July", "August", "September" };
18
19   NumberFormat priceFormat = NumberFormat.getCurrencyInstance( );
20   double currentMonthTotal;
21   for ( int i = 0; i < familyCellBills.length; i++ )
22   {
23    currentMonthTotal = 0.0;  // initialize total for row
24    for ( int j = 0; j < familyCellBills[i].length; j++ )
25    {
26     // add current family member bill to current monthly total
27     currentMonthTotal += familyCellBills[i][j];
28    }
29    // print total for row
30    System.out.println( "The total for " + months[i] + " is "
31                        + priceFormat.format( currentMonthTotal ) );
32   }
33  }
34 }
```

EXAMPLE 9.6 **Processing Each Row in a Two-Dimensional Array**

Again, the rows correspond to the months, and we declare and initialize at line 17 a *String* array named *months* in order to make the output user-friendly.

To calculate the total of the family cell bills for each month, we use nested *for* loops at lines 21–32, following the pattern described earlier.

Inside the outer *for* loop, we initialize the *currentMonthTotal* at line 23 before processing each row. Without this statement, the variable *currentMonthTotal* would continue to accumulate, as if we were summing all the elements of the array instead of calculating a separate sum for each row.

```
The total for July is $158.07
The total for August is $173.23
The total for September is $192.48
```

Figure 9.9
Output of
Example 9.6

After the inner loop finishes, we complete the processing of row *i* by printing the value of *currentMonthTotal* at lines 29–31. Figure 9.9 shows the output of the program.

COMMON ERROR TRAP
Failing to initialize the row processing variables before each row is a logic error and will generate incorrect results.

9.3.5 Processing a Two-Dimensional Array One Column at a Time

Processing each column of a two-dimensional array requires a little extra checking. If the number of columns in each row differs, we must be careful not to attempt to access an element with an out-of-bounds column index. Generally, we will need to determine the number of columns in the largest row in the array before coding the outer loop header.

For example, suppose we are keeping track of our test grades in three classes: Intro to Java, Database Management, and English Composition. We have two test grades in Intro to Java, four in Database Management, and three in English Composition. We can use a two-dimensional array to store these test grades as follows:

```
int [ ][ ] grades = { { 89, 75 },
                      { 84, 76, 92, 96 },
                      { 80, 88, 95 } };
```

There are three rows in the array *grades*. The maximum number of columns in any row is four; therefore, in order to process all the columns, our outer loop should loop from column index 0 to column index 3. Our inner loop should check that the current column number exists in the row before attempting to process the element.

Let's assume, at this point, that we stored the maximum number of columns in an *int* variable called *maxNumberOfColumns*. The general pattern for processing elements of a two-dimensional array, *arrayName*, one column at a time is:

```
// maxNumberOfColumns holds the number of columns
// in the largest row of familyCellBills
for ( int j = 0; j < maxNumberOfColumns; j++ )
{
   for ( int i = 0; i < arrayName.length; i++ )
   {
      if ( j < arrayName[i].length )
      {
         // process element arrayName[i][j]
      }
   }
}
```

The outer loop condition:

```
j < maxNumberOfColumns
```

continues execution of the outer loop as long as the column index is less than the maximum number of columns of the two-dimensional array, which has been computed and assigned to the variable *maxNumberOfColumns*.

The inner loop condition:

```
i < arrayName.length
```

continues execution of the inner loop as long as the row index is less than the number of rows.

Again, because each row may have a different number of columns, a given row *i* may not have a column *j*. Thus, using the following *if* condition, we check that an element in column *j* exists—*j* is less than *arrayName[i].length*—before we attempt to access *arrayName[i][j]*:

```
if ( j < arrayName[i].length )
```

Example 9.7 shows how this pattern can be implemented in a program.

```
 1 /* Processing Each Column in a Two-Dimensional Array
 2     Anderson, Franceschi
 3 */
 4
 5 public class GradesProcessing
 6 {
 7   public static void main( String [ ] args )
 8   {
 9     int [ ][ ] grades = { { 89, 75 },
10                           { 84, 76, 92, 96 },
11                           { 80, 88, 95 } };
12
13     // compute the maximum number of columns
14     int maxNumberOfColumns = grades[0].length;
15     for ( int i = 1; i < grades.length; i++ )
16     {
17       if ( grades[i].length > maxNumberOfColumns )
18           maxNumberOfColumns = grades[i].length;
19     }
20     System.out.println( "The maximum number of columns in grades is "
21                         + maxNumberOfColumns );
22
23     for ( int j = 0; j < maxNumberOfColumns; j++ )
24     {
```

```
25    System.out.print( "\nColumn " + j + ": " );
26    for ( int i = 0; i < grades.length; i++ )
27    {
28     if ( j < grades[i].length )
29          System.out.print( grades[i][j] );
30     System.out.print( "\t" );
31    }
32   }
33   System.out.println( );
34  }
35 }
```

EXAMPLE 9.7   Processing a Two-Dimensional Array in Column Order

The array *grades* is declared and initialized at lines 9–11. Lines 13–19 compute the maximum number of columns in a row and store the value in the *int* variable *maxNumberOfColumns*. First, we initialize *maxNumberOfColumns* to the number of columns of row 0 at line 14. At lines 15 to 19, we loop through each remaining row in *grades* and update *maxNumberOfColumns* if we find that the current row has more columns than *maxNumberOfColumns*.

At lines 23–32, we use nested loops to print all the elements of *grades* in column order, following the general pattern described earlier. The output of the program is shown in Figure 9.10.

9.3.6   Displaying Two-Dimensional Array Data as a Bar Chart

Another way to display two-dimensional array data is graphically, by drawing a bar chart. For example, the bar chart in Figure 9.11 displays the data in the *familyCellBills* array.

Each bar is a rectangle. In order to draw a rectangle, we need to provide four arguments to the *fillRect* method of the *GraphicsContext* class: the *x* and *y* coordinate of the upper-left corner of the rectangle and the width and height of the rectangle. We use the variables *xStart* and *yStartBar*, adjusted by the value of the array element, for

```
The maximum number of columns in grades is 4

Column 0: 89     84     80
Column 1: 75     76     88
Column 2:        92     95
Column 3:        96
```

Figure 9.10

The Output of Example 9.7

Figure 9.11

The *familyCellBills* Array as a Bar Chart

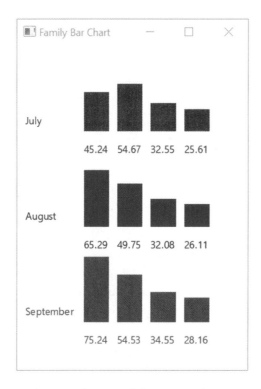

the *x* and *y* coordinates of the rectangle. We use a constant, *BAR_WIDTH*, for the width of each rectangle, and the value of the array element for its height.

So to create a bar chart, we use our standard nested *for* loops, and call the *fillRect* method of the *GraphicsContext* class to draw a rectangle for each element. We use the *fillText* method to display the value of each element. To change colors for each row, we set up an array of *Color* objects, and loop through the array to set the current color for each row iteration. Furthermore, each time we process a row, we must reset the (*x*, *y*) coordinates of the first bar for the next row.

Example 9.8 shows the code that displays the bar chart shown in Figure 9.11.

```
1 /* A two-dimensional bar chart application
2    Anderson, Franceschi
3 */
4
5 import javafx.application.Application;
6 import javafx.stage.Stage;
7 import javafx.scene.canvas.GraphicsContext;
8 import javafx.scene.paint.Color;
9
10 public class FamilyBarChartApplication extends Application
```

```
11  {
12    final int LEFT_MARGIN = 80;          // starting x coordinate
13    final int BASE_Y_BAR   = 100;        // bottom of the bars
14    final int BASE_Y_VALUE = 125;        // bottom of the values
15    final int BAR_WIDTH = 30;            // width of each bar
16    final int SPACE_BETWEEN_BARS = 10;   // pixels between bars
17    final int ROW_HEIGHT = 110;          // pixels between rows
18
19    double [ ][ ] familyCellBills = { {45.24, 54.67, 32.55, 25.61},
20                                      {65.29, 49.75, 32.08, 26.11},
21                                      {75.24, 54.53, 34.55, 28.16} };
22
23    String [ ] months = { "July", "August", "September" };
24    Color [ ] colors = { Color.RED, Color.BLUE, Color.MAGENTA };
25
26    @Override
27    public void start( Stage stage )
28    {
29      // set up window title and size
30      GraphicsContext gc = JIGraphicsUtility.setUpGraphics(
31                   stage, "Family Bar Chart", 275, 375 );
32
33      int xStart = LEFT_MARGIN;    // x value for 1st column (bars)
34      int yStart = BASE_Y_VALUE;   // y value for 1st row (data)
35      int yStartBar = BASE_Y_BAR;  // y value for 1st row (bars)
36
37      for ( int i = 0; i < familyCellBills.length; i++ )
38      {
39        gc.setFill( colors[i] ); // set color for current row
40        gc.fillText( months[i], xStart - LEFT_MARGIN + 10,
41                          yStart - .3 * ROW_HEIGHT );
42
43        for ( int j = 0; j < familyCellBills[i].length; j++ )
44        {
45          gc.fillRect( xStart, yStartBar - familyCellBills[i][j],
46                     BAR_WIDTH, familyCellBills[i][j] );
47
48          gc.fillText( Double.toString( familyCellBills[i][j] ),
49                     xStart, yStart );
50
51          // move to starting x value for next bar
52          xStart += BAR_WIDTH + SPACE_BETWEEN_BARS;
53        }
54
55        // new row: increase yStart and yStartBar
```

```
56        yStart += ROW_HEIGHT;
57        yStartBar += ROW_HEIGHT;
58        xStart = LEFT_MARGIN;
59      }
60    }
61
62    public static void main( String [ ] args )
63    {
64      launch( args );
65    }
66 }
```

EXAMPLE 9.8   **Displaying a Two-Dimensional Array as a Bar Chart**

The *Color* single-dimensional array *colors* that we use to determine the color of each row of bars is declared and initialized at line 24. The first row of bars will be displayed in red, the second row in blue, and the third row in magenta. We use a *String* single-dimensional array, *months*, to label each row. Both arrays have the same number of rows as *familyCellBills*.

In the *start* method, at the beginning of the outer loop and before the inner loop, we set the color for the current row (line 39) by using the row number as an index into the *colors* array. At lines 40–41, we display the month.

In the body of the inner loop (lines 45–52), we draw the rectangle for the element value at row *i* and column *j* of *familyCellBills*, then display a *String* representing the same value. We then increment *xStart* to the location of the next bar to draw.

After the inner loop and before restarting the outer loop, we update the values of *yStart*, *yStartBar*, and *xStart* (lines 55–58) so that they are properly set for processing the next row. Earlier, we said that initializing variable values for the next row is usually done at the beginning of the outer loop body before entering the inner loop, but it also can be done after the inner loop and before re-entering the outer loop, as shown here.

CODE IN ACTION

To see a step-by-step illustration showing how to use two-dimensional arrays, look for the movie within the online resources. Click on the link to this chapter to start the movie.

Skill Practice
with these end-of-chapter questions

9.4   Two-Dimensional Arrays Passed to and Returned from Methods

Writing methods that take two-dimensional arrays as parameters and/or return two-dimensional arrays is similar to working with single-dimensional arrays.

The syntax for a method that accepts a two-dimensional array as a parameter is the following:

```
returnType methodName( arrayType [ ][ ] arrayParameterName )
```

The syntax for a method that returns a two-dimensional array is the following:

```
returnArrayType [ ][ ] methodName( parameterList )
```

The caller of the method passes the argument list and assigns the return value to a reference to a two-dimensional array of the appropriate data type.

Combining both possibilities, the syntax for a method that accepts a two-dimensional array as a parameter and whose return value is a two-dimensional array is the following:

```
returnArrayType [ ][ ] methodName( arrayType [ ][ ] arrayParameterName )
```

The caller of the method simply passes the name of the array without any brackets and assigns the return value to a reference to a two-dimensional array of the appropriate data type.

For example, suppose we want to tally votes in an election. We have four candidates running in six districts. We want to know how many votes each candidate received and how many votes were cast in each district. Thus, we can set up a two-dimensional array with each row representing a district and each column representing a candidate, with the values in each element representing the votes a candidate received in that district. We need to compute the sum of each row to find the number of votes per district and the sum of each column to find the number of votes per candidate.

To do this, we create a class, *Tally*, that has a two-dimensional array instance variable, *voteData*, storing the votes. The *Tally* class also has a method, *arrayTally*, that will compute the sums for each column and row of *voteData*. The sums will be returned from the method as a two-dimensional array with two rows. The first row will hold the totals for each column of *voteData*, and the second row will hold the totals for each row of *voteData*.

Example 9.9 shows the *Tally* class.

```
 1 /** Two-Dimensional Arrays as Method Parameters
 2  *    and Return Values: the Tally class
 3  *    Anderson, Franceschi
 4  */
 5
 6 public class Tally
 7 {
 8   int [ ][ ] voteData;
 9
10   /** constructor
11    * @param     voteData a 2-D array of vote counts
12    */
13   public Tally( int [ ][ ] voteData )
14   {
15     this.voteData = new int [voteData.length][ ];
16     for ( int i = 0; i < voteData.length; i++ )
17         this.voteData[i] = new int [voteData[i].length];
18
19     for ( int i = 0; i < voteData.length; i++ )
20     {
21       for ( int j = 0; j < voteData[i].length; j++ )
22       {
23         this.voteData[i][j] = voteData[i][j];
24       }
25     }
26   }
27
28   /** arrayTally method
29    *    @return a two-dimensional array of votes
30    */
31   public int [ ][ ] arrayTally( )
32   {
```

```
33      // create array of tallies, all elements are 0
34      int [ ][ ] returnTally = new int [2][ ];
35      returnTally[0] = new int [voteData[0].length];
36      returnTally[1] = new int [voteData.length];
37
38      for ( int i = 0; i < voteData.length; i++ )
39      {
40        for ( int j = 0; j < voteData[i].length; j++ )
41        {
42          returnTally[0][j] += voteData[i][j]; // add to column sum
43          returnTally[1][i] += voteData[i][j]; // add to row sum
44        }
45      }
46      return returnTally;
47    }
48 }
```

EXAMPLE 9.9   The *Tally* Class

The constructor, coded at lines 10–26, receives the two-dimensional array argument *voteData*. After instantiating the instance variable *voteData* at line 15, we copy the parameter *voteData* into the instance variable *voteData* one element at a time at lines 19–25.

We coded the *arrayTally* method at lines 28–47. Our first job is to instantiate the *returnArray*, which is the array the method will return to the caller. We know that the array will have two rows, one holding the sums of the columns and one holding the sums of the rows. Because each row in the *returnArray* will have a different number of columns, we instantiate the array with two rows, but do not give a value for the number of columns (line 34). We then instantiate each row with the appropriate number of columns (lines 35–36). Row 0, the sums of the columns, will have the same number of columns as the *voteData* array. In the interest of keeping this example simple, we have assumed that *voteData* has the same number of columns in every row, that is, each candidate was on the ballot in each district. Thus, that number is therefore equal to the number of columns in the first row, *voteData[0].length* (line 35). Row 1, the sum of the rows, will have the same number of columns as the number of rows in the *voteData* array.

In lines 38–45, we loop through the *voteData* array, computing the sums. We add each element's value to the sum for its column (line 42) and the sum for its row (line 43). When we finish, we return the *returnTally* array to the caller (line 46).

Example 9.10 shows a client program that instantiates a *Tally* object reference and calls the *arrayTally* method.

```
 1 /** Tally votes: the VoteTally class
 2 *    Anderson, Franceschi
 3 */
```

```
 4
 5 public class VoteTally
 6 {
 7   public static void main( String [ ] args )
 8   {
 9     // votes are for 4 candidates in 6 districts.
10     int [ ][ ] votes = { { 150, 253, 125, 345 },
11                          { 250, 750, 234, 721 },
12                          { 243, 600, 212, 101 },
13                          { 234, 243, 143, 276 },
14                          { 555, 343, 297, 990 },
15                          { 111, 426, 834, 101 } };
16     // candidate names
17     String [ ] candidates = { "Smith", "Jones",
18                               "Berry", "Chase" };
19
20     // instantiate a Tally object reference
21     Tally tally = new Tally( votes );
22
23     // call arrayTally method to count the votes
24     int [ ][ ] voteCounts = tally.arrayTally( );
25
26     // print totals for candidates
27     System.out.println( "Total votes per candidate" );
28     for ( int i = 0; i < candidates.length; i++ )
29       System.out.print( candidates[i] + "\t" );
30     System.out.println( );
31     for ( int j = 0; j < voteCounts[0].length; j++ )
32       System.out.print( voteCounts[0][j] + "\t" );
33     System.out.println( );
34
35     // print totals for districts
36     System.out.println("\nTotal votes per district" );
37     for ( int i = 0; i < voteCounts[1].length; i++ )
38       System.out.print( ( i + 1 ) + "\t\t" );
39     System.out.println( );
40     for ( int i = 0; i < voteCounts[1].length; i++ )
41       System.out.print( voteCounts[1][i] + "\t" );
42     System.out.println( );
43   }
44 }
```

EXAMPLE 9.10   The *VoteTally* Class

We start by defining our two-dimensional array, *votes*, which holds the votes for each candidate for each district (lines 9–15). Most likely, we would read these values from a file, but for simplicity, we hard-coded the values in the initialization list. We

```
Total votes per candidate
Smith       Jones       Berry       Chase
1543        2615        1845        2534


Total votes per district
1       2       3       4       5       6
873     1955    1156    896     2185    1472
```

Figure 9.12

Output from
Example 9.10

also define a single-dimensional array of *Strings*, *candidates*, which holds the candidates' names (lines 16–18). Each name in the *candidates* array corresponds to the column in the *votes* array that holds that candidate's votes.

On lines 20–21, we instantiate the *Tally* object *tally*, passing the two-dimensional array *votes* to the *Tally* constructor. Notice that for the argument, we use only the array name, *votes*, without brackets.

On line 24, we call the *arrayTally* method, assigning the return value to a two-dimensional array reference named *voteCounts*.

Lines 26–33 print the totals per candidate by printing the elements in row 0 of the returned array, and lines 35–42 print the totals per district by printing the elements in row 1 of the returned array. The output is shown in Figure 9.12.

9.5 Programming Activity 1: Working with Two-Dimensional Arrays

In this activity, you will work with a 4-row, 20-column, two-dimensional array of integers. Specifically, you will write methods to perform the following operations:

1. Fill the array with random numbers between 50 and 80.

2. Print the array.

3. Set every array element of a given row to a specified value. The value is a parameter of a method.

4. Find the minimum value in a given column of the array. The column is a parameter of a method.

5. Count the number of elements of the array having a specified value. The value is a parameter of a method.

The framework for this Programming Activity will animate your algorithm so that you can check the accuracy of your code. For example, Figure 9.13 shows the application counting the elements having the value 61.

At this point, the application has found the value 61 in four array elements.

Figure 9.13

Animation of the Programming Activity

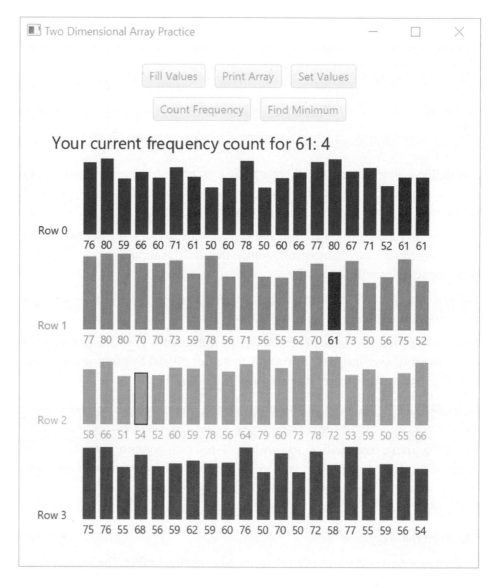

Instructions

In this chapter's Programming Activity 1 folder in the supplied code files, you will find the source files needed to complete this activity. Copy all the files to a folder on your computer. Note that all files should be in the same folder.

Open the *TwoDimArrayPracticeController.java* source file. Searching for five asterisks (*****) in the source code will position you at the sample method and the four other locations where you will add your code. We have provided the sample code for task number 1, which you can use as a model for completing the other tasks. In every task, you will fill in the code for a method that will manipulate an existing array of

4 rows and 20 columns. You should not instantiate the array; we have done that for you. Example 9.11 shows the section of the *TwoDimArrayPracticeController* source code where you will add your code.

Note that for the *countFound* and *findMinimum* methods, we provide a dummy *return* statement: (*return 0;*). We do this so that the source code will compile. In this way, you can write and test each method separately, using step-wise refinement. When you are ready to write the *countFound* and *findMinimum* methods, just replace the dummy *return* statements with the appropriate *return* statement for that method.

```java
// ***** 1.  This method has been coded as an example
/** Fills the array with random numbers between 50 and 80
 *  The instance variable named intArray is the integer array to be
 *  filled with values
 */
public void fillValues( )
{
  Random rand = new Random( );
  for ( int row = 0; row < intArray.length; row++ )
  {
      System.out.print( row + "\t" );
      for ( int column = 0; j < intArray[row].length; column++ )
      {
        intArray[row][column] = rand.nextInt( 31 ) + 50;
        animate( row, column, −1 );  // needed for visual feedback
      }
      System.out.println( );
  }
}   // end of fillValues method


// ***** 2.  Student writes this method
/** Prints array to the console, elements are separated by a space
 *  The instance variable named intArray is the integer array to be
 *  printed
 */
public void printArray( )
{
  // Note:  To animate the algorithm, put this method call as the
  // last statement in your inner for loop
  //             animate( row, column, -1 );
  //      where row is the index of the array's current row
  //   and column is the index of the array's current column
  // Write your code here:

} // end of printArray method


// ***** 3.  Student writes this method
```

```
/** Sets all the elements in the specified row to the specified value
*   The instance variable named intArray is the integer array
*   @param value     the value to assign to the element of the row
*   @param row       the row in which to set the elements to value
*/
public void setValues( int value, int row )
{
   // Note:  To animate the algorithm, put this method call as the
   // last statement in your for loop
   //            animate( row, column, -1);
   //      where row is the index of the array's current row
   //      where column is the index of the array's current column
   // Write your code here:


}   // end of setValues method


// ***** 4.  Student writes this method
/** Finds minimum value in the specified column
*   The instance variable named intArray is the integer array
*   @param column    the column to search
*   @return          the minimum value found in the column
*/
public int findMinimum( int column )
{
   // Note:  To animate the algorithm, put this method call as the
   // last statement in your for loop
   //            animate( row, column, minimum );
   //   where row is the index of the array's current row
   //        column is the index of the array's current column
   //        minimum is the variable storing the current minimum
   // Write your code here:

  return 0; // replace this line with your return statement


}   // end of findMinimumn method


// ***** 5.  Student writes this method
/** Finds the number of times value is found in the array
*   The instance variable named intArray is the integer array
*   @param value    the value to count
*   @return         the number of times value was found
*/
public int countFound( int value )
{
   // Note:  To animate the algorithm, put this method call as the
   // last statement in your inner for loop
   //            animate( row, column, num );
```

```
// where row is the index of the array's current row
//       column is the index of the array's current column
//       num is the local variable storing the current frequency
//         count
// Write your code here:


  return 0;  // replace this line with your return statement


}
// end of countFound method
```

EXAMPLE 9.11   Location of Student Code in *TwoDimArrayPracticeController*

The framework will animate your algorithm so that you can watch your code work. For this to happen, be sure that your single or nested *for* loops call the method *animate*. The arguments that you send to *animate* are not always the same and the location of the call to *animate* will differ depending on the task you are coding. Detailed instructions for each task are included in the code.

To test your code, compile *TwoDimArrayPracticeController.java* and run the *TwoDimArrayPracticeApplication* source code. Figure 9.14 shows the graphics window when the program begins. Because the values of the array are randomly generated, the values will be different each time the program runs. To test any method, click on the appropriate button.

Troubleshooting

If your method implementation does not animate, check these tips:

- Verify that the last statement in your single *for* loop or inner *for* loop is a call to the *animate* method and that you passed the appropriate arguments. For example:

  ```
  animate( row, column );
  ```

- Verify that your exit conditions for your *for* loops are correct. Sometimes the exit condition depends on the length of the array (i.e., the number of rows in the array), and sometimes it depends on the number of columns in the current row of the array.

? DISCUSSION QUESTIONS

1. With a two-dimensional array, for which operations would you use nested *for* loops and for which operations would you use a single *for* loop?

2. When performing an operation on a given row, which index is fixed and which index is used as the looping variable? When performing an operation on a given column, which index is fixed and which index is used as the looping variable?

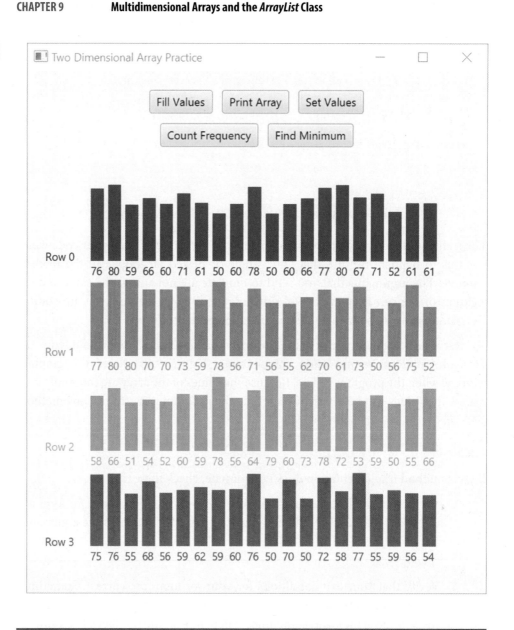

9.6   Other Multidimensional Arrays

Sometimes we might need an array with more than two dimensions. For example, we might be interested in keeping track of sales on a per-year, per-week, and per-day basis. In this case, we would use a three-dimensional array as follows:

1st dimension: year

2nd dimension: week

3rd dimension: day of the week

TABLE 9.3 Structure of an *n*-Dimensional Array

Dimension	Array Element
first	arrayName[i$_1$] is an (n − 1)-dimensional array
second	arrayName[i$_1$][i$_2$] is an (n − 2)-dimensional array
k^{th}	arrayName[i$_1$][i$_2$][i$_3$][..][i$_k$] is an (n − k) multi-dimensional array
$(n-2)^{th}$	arrayName[i$_1$][i$_2$][i$_3$][..][i$_{n-2}$] is a two-dimensional array
$(n-1)^{th}$	arrayName[i$_1$][i$_2$][i$_3$][..][i$_{n-1}$] is a single-dimensional array
n^{th}	arrayName[i$_1$][i$_2$][i$_3$][..][i$_{n-1}$][i$_n$] is an array element

Earlier in this chapter, we explained that a two-dimensional array is an array of single-dimensional arrays. Similarly, a three-dimensional array is an array of two-dimensional arrays. And a four-dimensional array is an array of three-dimensional arrays. More generally, an *n*-dimensional array is an array of (*n* – 1)-dimensional arrays.

Table 9.3 shows how an *n*-dimensional array is structured dimension by dimension; $i_1, i_2, ..., i_n$ are used as generic indexes for the first dimension, second dimension, ..., and n^{th} dimensions.

If we keep track of sales over a period of 10 years, then we would have a 10-by-52-by-7 array. The principles discussed for a two-dimensional array still apply; we just have three dimensions instead of two. The following code sequence illustrates how to declare, instantiate, and access elements of this three-dimensional array:

```
double [ ][ ][ ] Sales;           // declare a four-dimensional array
Sales = new double [10][52][7];   // instantiate the array
Sales[0][0][0] = 638.50;          // access the first element
sales[4][22][3] = 928.30;         // access another element
sales[9][51][6] = 1234.90;        // access the last element
```

To process elements of a single-dimensional array, we use a simple *for* loop; for a two-dimensional array, we use a double *for* loop. For a three-dimensional array, we use a triple *for* loop.

The general pattern for processing elements in a three-dimensional array is

```
for ( int i = 0; i < arrayName.length; i++ )
{
```

```java
   for ( int j = 0; j < arrayName[i].length; j++ )
   {
      for ( int k = 0; k < arrayName[i][j].length; k++ )
      {
         // access and process the element arrayName[i][j][k]
      }
   }
}
```

The following code sequence will print the elements of the three-dimensional array *sales*:

```java
for ( int i = 0; i < sales.length; i++ )
{
   for ( int j = 0; j < sales[i].length; j++ )
   {
      for ( int k = 0; k < sales[i][j].length; k++ )
      {
      // access the element at sales[i][j][k]
      System.out.println( sales[i][j][k] + "\t" );
      }
      // skip a line when second dimension index changes
      System.out.println( );
   }
   // skip a line when first dimension index changes
   System.out.println( );
}
```

If we are interested in keeping track of sales on a state-by-state basis, we can use a four-dimensional array as follows:

1st dimension: state

2nd dimension: year

3rd dimension: week

4th dimension: day of the week

The following code sequence illustrates how to declare, instantiate, and access the elements of such a four-dimensional array:

```java
double [ ][ ][ ][ ] stateSales;            // declare a four-dimensional
                                           // array

stateSales = new double [50][10][52][7];   // instantiate the array

stateSales[0][0][0][0] = 58.50;            // access the first element

sales[34][4][22][3] = 98.30;               // access another element

sales[49][9][51][6] = 137.70;              // access the last element
```

To process elements of a four-dimensional array, we use a quadruple *for* loop. That quadruple *for* loop pattern parallels the ones for the two-dimensional and three-dimensional arrays. For a four-dimensional array called *arrayName*, it is:

```
for ( int i = 0; i < arrayName.length; i++ )
{
    for ( int j = 0; j < arrayName[i].length; j++ )
    {
        for ( int k = 0; k < arrayName[i][j].length; k++ )
        {
            for ( int l = 0; l < arrayName[i][j][k].length; l++ )
            {
                // process element arrayName[i][j][k][l]
            }
        }
    }
}
```

9.7   The *ArrayList* Class

As we have seen, single-dimensional and multidimensional arrays are useful in many situations. However, they have limitations.

Let's say we are designing a search engine for a large website, for example, an online bookstore. The user will type a word in a text field box, our code will access a database, retrieve all the books with titles that contain this word, and return them to the user.

We could store the book information in an array of books. One problem, however, is that we don't know how many books we will have. There could be 3, 32, 500, or 5,000 books, or maybe even more. Without knowing the number of books, we do not know what size to make the array. The safest bet would be to create the array with the maximum possible number of elements, that is, the maximum number of books that we anticipate. If we actually have fewer books than we anticipated, however, we will waste space.

And if we end up with more books than we anticipated, we would need to increase the size of the array. Because the size of an array is fixed when it is instantiated, changing the size of an array is a tedious process. We have to instantiate a new array and copy the elements of the original array to the new array.

The *ArrayList* class, in the *java.util* package, solves these problems. An *ArrayList* object automatically expands its capacity as needed. The *ArrayList* class uses **generics**. Generics are **parameterized types**, meaning that the data type will be defined at the time a client class declares and instantiates an object of the class. Generics allow programmers to design and code classes that use objects without specifying the class—or data type—of the object.

Thus, for example, we could have an *ArrayList* of *Book* objects, an *ArrayList* of *Auto* objects, or an *ArrayList* of *Strings*. The specified type must be a class, not a primitive type. If we want to store primitive data types in an *ArrayList*, then we need to use one of the wrapper classes such as *Integer*, *Double*, or *Character*.

The *ArrayList* class, and more generally a class using generics, can be used for many purposes. This is another facet of object-oriented programming that allows programmers to reuse code.

Because the *ArrayList* class is in the *java.util* package, programs using an *ArrayList* object will need to provide the following *import* statement:

```
import java.util.ArrayList;
```

9.7.1   Declaring and Instantiating *ArrayList* Objects

Here is the syntax for declaring an *ArrayList* of objects:

```
ArrayList<ClassName> arrayListName;
```

Inside the brackets, we declare the class type of the objects that will be stored in the *ArrayList*. A space is optional between the *ArrayList* class name and the opening bracket.

For example, these two statements declare an *ArrayList* of *Strings* and an *ArrayList* of *Auto* objects:

```
ArrayList<String> listOfStrings;
ArrayList<Auto> listOfCars;
```

If we try to declare an *ArrayList* object reference using a primitive data type instead of a class type, as in

```
ArrayList<int> listOfInts;
```

we will get this compiler error:

```
Test.java:7: error: unexpected type
  ArrayList<int> listOfInts;
           ^
required: reference
found:    int
1 error
```

Two constructors of the *ArrayList* class are shown in Table 9.4.

If we know how many elements we will store in the *ArrayList* object, we can use the overloaded constructor to specify the initial capacity; otherwise, we can simply use the default constructor. As we add elements to the *ArrayList* object, its capacity will increase automatically, as needed.

TABLE 9.4   *ArrayList* Constructors

ArrayList Constructors Summary
Constructor name and argument list
`ArrayList<ClassName>( )`   constructs an *ArrayList* object of *ClassName* type with an initial capacity of 10
`ArrayList<ClassName>( int initialCapacity )`   constructs an *ArrayList* object of *ClassName* type with the specified initial capacity

Here is the syntax for instantiating an *ArrayList* using the default constructor:

```
arrayListName = new ArrayList<ClassName>( );
  where ClassName is the class type of the objects that will be stored
  in the ArrayList and arrayListName has been declared previously as an
  ArrayList reference for that class.
```

These statements will instantiate the *ArrayList* objects declared earlier, with an initial capacity of 10:

```
listOfStrings = new ArrayList<String>( );
listOfCars = new ArrayList<Auto>( );
```

If we try to instantiate an *ArrayList* object without specifying the object type, as in

```
listOfCars = new ArrayList( );
```

we get the following warnings from the compiler (using Xlint):

```
Test.java:11: warning: [rawtypes] found raw type: ArrayList
    listOfCars = new ArrayList( );
                  ^
  missing type arguments for generic class ArrayList<E>
  where E is a type-variable:
    E extends Object declared in class ArrayList

Test.java:11: warning: [unchecked] unchecked conversion
    listOfCars = new ArrayList( );
                  ^
  required: ArrayList<Auto>
  found:    ArrayList
2 warnings
```

In *ArrayLists*, there is a distinction between capacity and size. The **capacity** of an *ArrayList* is the number of elements allocated to the list. The **size** is the number of those elements that are filled with objects. Thus, when we instantiate an *ArrayList* using the default constructor, its capacity is 10, but its size is 0. In other words, the *ArrayList* has room for 10 objects, but no objects are currently stored in the list.

These statements will declare, then instantiate, an *ArrayList* of *String* objects with an initial capacity of 5, using the overloaded constructor:

```
ArrayList<String> listOfStrings1;
listOfStrings1 = new ArrayList<String>( 5 );
```

In this case, the capacity of *listOf Strings1* is 5 and its size is 0.

We can also combine the declaration and instantiation of an *ArrayList* object into one statement. Here is the syntax using the default constructor:

```
ArrayList<ClassName> arrayListName = new ArrayList<ClassName>( );
```

These statements will declare and instantiate two *ArrayList* objects of *Integers* and *Strings*, respectively:

```
ArrayList<Integer> listOfInts = new ArrayList<Integer>( );
ArrayList<String> listOfStrings2 = new ArrayList<String>( );
```

9.7.2   Methods of the *ArrayList* Class

Like arrays, the *ArrayList* class uses indexes to refer to elements. Among others, it provides methods that provide the following functions:

- add an item at the end of the list
- replace an item at a given index
- remove an item at a given index
- remove all the items in the list
- search the list for a specific item
- retrieve an item at a given index
- retrieve the index of a given item
- check to see if the list is empty
- return the number of items in the list, that is, its size
- optimize the capacity of the list by setting its capacity to the number of items in the list

Some of the most useful methods are shown in Table 9.5. Note that some of the method headers include *E* as their return type or parameter data type (as opposed to a class name or simply the *Object* class). *E* represents the data type of the *ArrayList*. Thus, for an *ArrayList* of *Integer* objects, *E* is an *Integer*; and the *get* method, for example, returns an *Integer* object. Similarly, for an *ArrayList* of *Auto* objects, *E* is an *Auto* object. In this case, the *get* method returns an *Auto* object.

TABLE 9.5   *ArrayList* Methods

Useful Methods of the *ArrayList* Class	
Return value	**Method name and argument list**
boolean	add(E element)
	appends the specified *element* to the end of the list
E	remove(int index)
	removes and returns the element at the specified *index* position in the list
void	clear( )
	removes all the elements from this list
E	get(int index)
	returns the element at the specified *index* position in the list; the element is not removed from the list
E	set(int index, E element)
	replaces the element at the specified *index* position in this list with the specified *element*
int	size( )
	returns the number of elements in this list
void	trimToSize( )
	sets the capacity to the list's current size

9.7.3   Looping Through an *ArrayList* Using an Enhanced *for* Loop

The general pattern for processing elements of an *ArrayList* of *ClassName* objects called *arrayListName* using a *for* loop is

```
ClassName currentObject;
for ( int i = 0; i < arrayListName.size( ); i++ )
{
     currentObject = arrayListName.get( i );
     // process currentObject
}
```

For instance, to process elements of an *ArrayList* of *String* object references called *listOfStrings* using a standard *for* loop, the general pattern is:

```
String currentString;
for ( int i = 0; i < listOfStrings.size( ); i++ )
```

```
{
     currentString = listOfStrings.get( i );
     // process currentString
}
```

Java provides a simplified way to process the elements of an *ArrayList*, called the **enhanced *for* loop**. The general pattern for processing elements of an *ArrayList* of *ClassName* objects called *arrayListName* using the enhanced *for* loop is:

```
for ( ClassName currentObject : arrayListName )
{
     // process currentObject
}
```

A variable of the class type of the objects stored in the *ArrayList* is declared in the enhanced *for* loop header, followed by a colon and name of the *ArrayList*. The enhanced *for* loop enables looping through the *ArrayList* objects automatically. Your code does not call the *get* method; inside the body of the loop, *currentObject* is directly available for processing.

For example, to process elements of an *ArrayList* of *Strings* called *names* using the enhanced *for* loop, the general pattern is:

```
for ( String currentString : names )
{
     // process currentString
}
```

Example 9.12 shows how to create and use an *ArrayList* of *Integers*. Line 11 declares and instantiates the *ArrayList* object reference *list* using the default constructor. Three elements are added to *list* using the *add* method at lines 12–14. As the arguments to the *add* method, we use *ints*. The autoboxing feature of Java automatically converts an *int* to an *Integer* object when an *int* variable is used where an *Integer* object is expected.

After an *ArrayList* object has been declared and instantiated as being of a certain class type, you cannot add an object of a different class type. For example, you could not add a *Double* value to an *ArrayList* of *Integers*.

At lines 17–18, we print the elements of *list* using a traditional *for* loop, using the *get* method to retrieve the element at the current index. At lines 22–23, we use the enhanced *for* loop to print the elements. At lines 27–28, we also use the enhanced *for* loop to print the elements; but this time, we use an *int* as the looping variable, using the unboxing feature of Java, which converts *Integer* objects to *int* values, as needed. At line 31, we use the *set* method to change the value of the element at index 1 to 100, also using autoboxing. At line 37, we use the *remove* method to delete the element at index 0 and assign it to the variable *removed*, using unboxing again.

```
1 /* A Simple ArrayList of Integers
2    Anderson, Franceschi
3 */
4
5 import java.util.ArrayList;
6
7 public class ArrayListOfIntegers
8 {
9  public static void main( String [ ] args )
10  {
11   ArrayList<Integer> list = new ArrayList<Integer>( );
12   list.add( 34 ); // autoboxing
13   list.add( 89 ); // autoboxing
14   list.add( 65 ); // autoboxing
15
16   System.out.println( "Using the traditional for loop:" );
17   for ( int i = 0; i < list.size( ); i++ )
18     System.out.print( list.get( i ) + "\t" );
19   System.out.println( );
20
21   System.out.println( "\nUsing the enhanced for loop:" );
22   for ( Integer currentInteger : list )
23     System.out.print( currentInteger + "\t" );
24   System.out.println( );
25
26   System.out.println( "\nUsing unboxing and enhanced for loop:" );
27   for ( int currentInt : list ) // unboxing
28     System.out.print( currentInt + "\t" );
29   System.out.println( );
30
31   list.set( 1, 100 );
32   System.out.println( "\nAfter calling set( 1, 100 ):" );
33   for ( int currentInt : list ) // unboxing
34     System.out.print( currentInt + "\t" );
35   System.out.println( );
36
37   int removed = list.remove( 0 );
38   System.out.println( "\nAt index 0, " + removed + " was removed" );
39   System.out.println( "\nAfter removing the element at index 0:" );
40   for ( int currentInt : list ) // unboxing
41     System.out.print( currentInt + "\t" );
42   System.out.println( );
43  }
44 }
```

EXAMPLE 9.12   Using *ArrayList* Methods

The output of this example is shown in Figure 9.15.

Figure 9.15

Output of
Example 9.12

```
Using the traditional for loop:
34        89        65

Using the enhanced for loop:
34        89        65

Using unboxing and enhanced for loop:
34        89        65

After calling set( 1, 100 ):
34        100        65

At index 0, 34 was removed

After removing the element at index 0:
100        65
```

9.7.4   Using the *ArrayList* Class in a Program

Now let's see how we can use the *ArrayList* class in a Java program. Going back to our example of a bookstore and a search engine, we want to design and code a simple program that enables users to search for books.

We will have three classes in this program:

- a *Book* class, encapsulating the concept of a book
- a *BookStore* class, encapsulating the concept of a bookstore
- a *BookSearchEngine* class, including the *main* method, which provides the user interface

In the interest of keeping things simple, our *Book* class will contain only three instance variables: the book title, which is a *String*; the book's author, which is also a *String*; and the book price, which is a *double*.

Example 9.13 shows a simplified *Book* class with constructors, accessor methods, and a *toString* method.

```
1 /* Book class
2    Anderson, Franceschi
3 */
4
5 public class Book
6 {
7  private String title;
```

```
 8    private String author;
 9    private double price;
10
11    /** default constructor
12    */
13    public Book( )
14    {
15      title = "";
16      author = "";
17      price = 0.0;
18    }
19
20    /** overloaded constructor
21    * @param title     the value to assign to title
22    * @param author    the value to assign to author
23    * @param price     the value to assign to price
24    */
25    public Book( String title, String author, double price )
26    {
27      this.title = title;
28      this.author = author;
29      this.price = price;
30    }
31
32    /** getTitle method
33    *    @return the title
34    */
35    public String getTitle( )
36    {
37      return title;
38    }
39
40    /** getAuthor method
41    *    @return the author
42    */
43    public String getAuthor( )
44    {
45      return author;
46    }
47
48    /** getPrice method
49    *    @return the price
50    */
51    public double getPrice( )
52    {
53      return price;
```

```
54    }
55
56    /** toString
57     * @return title, author, and price
58     */
59    @Override
60    public String toString( )
61    {
62      return ( "title: " + title + "\t"
63              + "author: " + author + "\t"
64              + "price: " + price );
65    }
66  }
```

EXAMPLE 9.13   **The *Book* Class**

Our *BookStore* class, shown in Example 9.14, will simply have one instance variable: an *ArrayList* of *Book* objects, representing the collection of books in the bookstore, which we name *library*.

In most cases, when an *ArrayList* is filled with data, that data will come from a database or a file. In the interest of focusing on the *ArrayList* class and its methods, we have hard-coded the objects for the *ArrayList library* in the *BookStore* class, rather than reading them from a database or a file.

In the default constructor (lines 11 to 24), we instantiate the *library* instance variable, then add six *Book* objects to *library* using the *add* method from the *ArrayList* class. At line 23, we call the *trimToSize* method to set the capacity of *library* to its current size, which is 6, in order to minimize the memory resources used.

The *toString* method is coded from lines 26 to 38. It generates and returns a *String* representing all the books in *library*, one book per line. In order to do that, we use an enhanced *for* loop from lines 33 to 36. The header of that loop, at line 33, follows the general pattern of the enhanced *for* loop header by declaring a *Book* variable named *tempBook*, followed by a colon, followed by *library*, the *ArrayList* object to loop through.

The *searchForTitle* method, coded from lines 40 to 54, performs the task of searching for a keyword within the title of each *Book* object stored in *library*. The keyword, a *String*, is the parameter of the method and is named *searchString*. This method returns an *ArrayList* containing the *Book* objects that have the keyword in their title. We create that *ArrayList* of *Books*, which we name *searchResult* at line 46 and loop through *library* using an enhanced *for* loop from lines 47 to 51. Inside the body of the loop, we use the *indexOf* method of the *String* class to test if the current *Book* object contains the keyword *searchString* in its *title*. If it does, we add that *Book* object to *searchResult*. Finally, we call the method *trimToSize* to set the capacity of *searchResult* to the current number of elements, then return the *ArrayList* to the caller.

```java
 1 /*  BookStore class
 2      Anderson, Franceschi
 3 */
 4
 5 import java.util.ArrayList;
 6
 7 public class BookStore
 8 {
 9   private ArrayList<Book> library;
10
11   /** default constructor
12   *    instantiates ArrayList of Books
13   */
14   public BookStore( )
15   {
16     library = new ArrayList<Book>( );
17     library.add( new Book( "Intro to Java", "James", 56.99 ) );
18     library.add( new Book( "Advanced Java", "Green", 65.99 ) );
19     library.add( new Book( "Java Servlets", "Brown", 75.99 ) );
20     library.add( new Book( "Intro to HTML", "James", 29.49 ) );
21     library.add( new Book( "Intro to Flash", "James", 34.99 ) );
22     library.add( new Book( "Advanced HTML", "Green", 56.99 ) );
23     library.trimToSize( );
24   }
25
26   /** toString
27   *   @return  each book in library, one per line
28   */
29   @Override
30   public String toString( )
31   {
32     String result = "";
33     for ( Book tempBook : library )
34     {
35       result += tempBook.toString( ) + "\n";
36     }
37     return result;
38   }
39
40   /** Generates list of books containing searchString
41   * @param searchString      the keyword to search for
```

```
42  * @return         the ArrayList of books containing the keyword
43  */
44  public ArrayList<Book> searchForTitle( String searchString )
45  {
46   ArrayList<Book> searchResult = new ArrayList<Book>( );
47   for ( Book currentBook : library )
48   {
49    if ( currentBook.getTitle( ).indexOf( searchString ) != -1 )
50        searchResult.add( currentBook );
51   }
52   searchResult.trimToSize( );
53   return searchResult;
54  }
55 }
```

EXAMPLE 9.14　　The *BookStore* Class

Our *BookSearchEngine* class, shown in Example 9.15, contains the *main* method: it creates a *BookStore* object, asks the user for a keyword, and searches for partial matches in our *BookStore* object.

A *BookStore* object, *bs*, is declared and instantiated at line 11. At lines 13–15, the user is then prompted for a keyword that will be used to search for books whose title contains that keyword. Lines 16 and 17 simply output the collection of *Books* in the *BookStore* object *bs*; later, when the search results are output, we can compare that output to the original list of *Books* to check our results. At line 19, we call the *searchForTitle* method with *keyword* as its argument; the *ArrayList* of *Book* objects returned is assigned to the variable *results*. At lines 23–24, we loop through *results* and output its contents, again using the enhanced *for* loop. Figure 9.16 shows a run of the program with the user searching for books containing the word "Java."

Figure 9.16

Results of a
Search for the
Keyword "Java"

```
Enter a keyword > Java
Our book collection is:
title: Intro to Java      author: James    price: 56.99
title: Advanced Java      author: Green    price: 65.99
title: Java Servlets      author: Brown    price: 75.99
title: Intro to HTML      author: James    price: 29.49
title: Intro to Flash     author: James    price: 34.99
title: Advanced HTML      author: Green    price: 56.99

The search results for Java are:
title: Intro to Java      author: James    price: 56.99
title: Advanced Java      author: Green    price: 65.99
title: Java Servlets      author: Brown    price: 75.99
```

```
1 /* BookSearchEngine class
2    Anderson, Franceschi
3 */
4
5 import java.util.*;
6
7 public class BookSearchEngine
8 {
9  public static void main( String [ ] args )
10 {
11   BookStore bs = new BookStore( );
12
13   Scanner scan = new Scanner( System.in );
14   System.out.print( "Enter a keyword > " );
15   String keyword = scan.next( );
16   System.out.println( "Our book collection is:" );
17   System.out.println( bs.toString( ) );
18
19   ArrayList<Book> results = bs.searchForTitle( keyword );
20
21   System.out.println( "The search results for " + keyword
22                       + " are:" );
23   for ( Book tempBook : results )
24        System.out.println( tempBook.toString( ) );
25 }
26 }
```

EXAMPLE 9.15   A Search Engine for Books

CODE IN ACTION

To see a step-by-step illustration showing how to use the *ArrayList* class, look for the movie within the online resources. Click on the link to start the movie.

© Hemera Technologies/
Photos.com/Thinkstock

9.8   Programming Activity 2: Working with the *ArrayList* Class

In this activity, you will work with an *ArrayList* object. Specifically, you will write the code to perform the following operations:

1. Fill the *ArrayList* object with *Auto* elements.

2. Print the *Auto* elements contained in the *ArrayList* object.

3. Set the *model* instance variable of every *Auto* element in the *ArrayList* object to a specified model.

4. Find the maximum number of miles of all *Auto* elements contained in the *ArrayList* object.

5. Count the number of *Auto* elements in the *ArrayList* with a specified model.

Table 9.6 provides the API for the *Auto* class.

TABLE 9.6   Constructors and Some Methods of the *Auto* Class

Auto Class Constructor Summary
`Auto( )`
creates an *Auto* object with initial default values of "unknown," 0, and 0.0.
`Auto( String model, int milesDriven, double gallonsOfGas )`
creates an *Auto* object with the initial values of *model, milesDriven,* and *gallonsOfGas.*

Auto Class Method Summary	
Return value	**Method name and argument list**
String	`getModel( )` returns the value of *model*
int	`getMilesDriven( )` returns the value of *milesDriven*
double	`getGallonsOfGas( )` returns the value of *gallonsOfGas*
Auto	`setModel( String model )` mutator for *model*
Auto	`setMilesDriven( int milesDriven )` mutator for *milesDriven*
Auto	`setGallonsOfGas( double gallonsOfGas )` mutator for *gallonsOfGas*
double	`milesPerGallon( )` returns the gas mileage for this *Auto* object
String	`toString( )` returns a *String* representation of this object
boolean	`equals( Object obj )` compares this *Auto* object to another object

The framework for this Programming Activity will animate your algorithm so that you can check the accuracy of your code. For example, Figure 9.17 shows the application counting the number of *Auto* elements in the *ArrayList* object having a *model* value equal to "Ferrari." The application accesses each element in the *ArrayList* in order, checking the *model* for the desired value, "Ferrari." At this point, the current element being accessed is a *BMW* and the application has found two *Auto* elements with the *model* value, "Ferrari."

Instructions

In this chapter's Programming Activity 2 folder in the supplied code files, you will find the source files needed to complete this activity. Copy all the files to a folder on your computer. Note that all files should be in the same folder.

Open the *ArrayListController.java* source file. Searching for five asterisks (*****) will position you at the sample method and the four other locations where you will add your code. We have provided the sample code for task number 1. In every task, you will fill in the code for a method that will manipulate an existing *ArrayList* of *Auto* elements. You should not instantiate the *ArrayList* object; we have done that for you. Example 9.16 shows the section of the *ArrayListController* source code where you will add your code.

Note that for the *countFound* and *findMaximumMilesDriven* methods, we provide a dummy *return* statement (*return 0;*). We do this so that the source code will compile. In this way, you can write and test each method separately, using step-wise refinement. When you are ready to write the *countFound* and *findMaximumMiles-Driven* methods, just replace the dummy *return* statements with the appropriate *return* statement for that method.

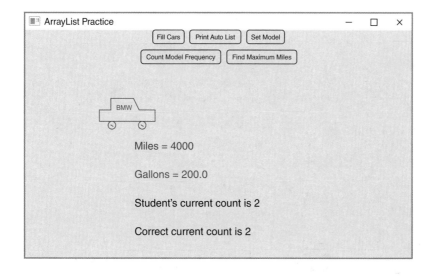

Figure 9.17

Animation of the Programming Activity

```java
// ***** 1.  This method has been coded as an example
/** Fills the carList with hard-coded Auto objects
*     The instance variable carList is the ArrayList
*         to be filled with Auto objects
*/
public void fillWithCars( )
{
  // clear carList before adding cars
  carList.clear( );
  // Reset the number of Autos to 0
  // This is needed so that the animation feedback works correctly
  Auto.clearNumberAutos( );

  Auto car1 = new Auto( "BMW", 0, 0.0 );
  Auto car2 = new Auto( "Ferrari", 100, 500.0 );
  Auto car3 = new Auto( "Jeep", 1000, 90.0 );
  Auto car4 = new Auto( "Ferrari", 10, 3.0 );
  Auto car5 = new Auto( "BMW", 4000, 200.0 );
  Auto car6 = new Auto( "Ferrari", 1000, 50.0 );

  carList.add( car1 );
  animate( car1 );
  carList.add( car2 );
  animate( car2 );
  carList.add( car3 );
  animate( car3 );
  carList.add( car4 );
  animate( car4 );
  carList.add( car5 );
  animate( car5 );
  carList.add( car6 );
  animate( car6 );
}
// end of fillWithCars method

// ***** 2.  Student writes this method
/**  Prints carList to console, elements are separated by a space
*     The instance variable carList is the ArrayList to be printed
*/
public void printAutoList( )
{
 // Note:  To animate the algorithm, put this method call as the
 // last statement in your for loop
 //               animate( car );
 // where car is the variable name for the current Auto object
 // as you loop through the ArrayList object
 // Write your code here:

}
```

```
// end of printAutoList method

// ***** 3.  Student writes this method
/** Sets the model of all the elements in carList to parameter value
 * The instance variable carList is the ArrayList to be modified
 *  @param model the model to assign to all Auto objects in carList
 */
public void setModelValues( String model )
{
 // Note:  To animate the algorithm, put this method call as the
 // last statement in your for loop
 //            animate( car );
 //  where car is the variable name for the current Auto object
 //  as you loop through the ArrayList object
 // Write your code here:

}
// end of setModelValues method

// ***** 4.  Student writes this method
/** Finds maximum number of miles driven
 *    Instance variable carList is the ArrayList to search
 *  @return     the maximum miles driven by all the Auto objects
 */
public int findMaximumMilesDriven( )
{
 // Note:  To animate the algorithm, put this method call as the
 // last statement in your for loop
 //            animate( car, maximum );
 //  where car is the variable name for the current Auto object
 //  and maximum is the int variable storing the current maximum
 //  number of miles for all Auto elements you have already tested
 //  as you loop through the ArrayList object
 // Write your code here:

 return 0; // replace this statement with your return statement

}
// end of findMaximumMilesDriven method

// ***** 5.  Student writes this method
/** Finds number of times parameter model is found in the carList
 *    Instance variable carList is the ArrayList in which we search
 *  @param model      the model to count
 *  @return           the number of times m odel was found
 */
public int countFound( String model )
{
 // Note:  To animate the algorithm, put this method call as the
 // last statement in your for loop
```

```
//              animate( car, num );
//   where car is the variable name for the current Auto object
//   and num is the int variable storing the current number of
//   Auto elements whose model is equal to the method's parameter
//   as you loop through the ArrayList object
// Write your code here:

return 0;// replace this statement with your return statement

}
// end of countFound method
```

EXAMPLE 9.16   **Location of Student Code in *ArrayListController***

The framework will animate your code so that you can watch it work. For this to happen, be sure that your *for* loops call the *animate* method. The arguments that you send to *animate* are not always the same, but the location of the call to *animate* is always the same, that is, the last statement of your *for* loop. Detailed instructions for each task are included in the code.

To test your code, compile *ArrayListController.java and* run the *ArrayListApplication* source code. Figure 9.18 shows the graphics window when the program begins. Because the *Auto* elements of the *ArrayList* object are hard-coded, the values will be the same each time the program runs. Click on the "Fill Cars" button first. To test any method, click on the appropriate button.

Troubleshooting

If your method implementation does not animate, check these tips:

- Verify that the last statement in your *for* loop is a call to the *animate* method and that you passed the loop variable(s) as the argument(s), as in the following:

Figure 9.18

The Graphics Window When the Application Begins

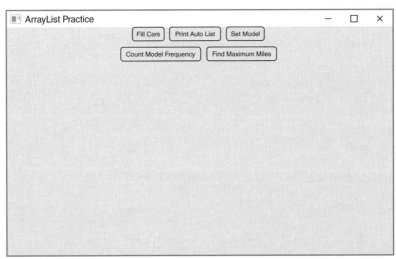

```
animate( car ); // or
animate( car, maximum ); // or
animate( car, num );
```

- Verify that the headers of your *for* loops are correct. They should all be the same.

- Verify that you update the variables *maximum* and *num* correctly.

?   DISCUSSION QUESTIONS

1. Change the code in the *fillWithCars* method so that there are more or fewer *Auto* objects in the *ArrayList*. How does the number of *Auto* objects impact how the other methods are coded? Explain.

2. Explain how looping through an *ArrayList* is different from looping through an array.

Skill Practice
with these end-of-chapter questions

9.10.1   Multiple Choice Exercises

Questions 9, 10, 11, 12, 13

9.10.2   Reading and Understanding Code

Questions 29, 30, 31, 32

9.10.3   Fill In the Code

Questions 46, 47, 48, 49

9.10.4   Identifying Errors in Code

Questions 55, 56, 57, 58

9.10.5   Debugging Area

Questions 63, 64

9.10.6   Write a Short Program

Questions 80, 81, 82

9.10.8   Technical Writing

Question 98

CHAPTER REVIEW

9.9 Chapter Summary

- Arrays can be single-dimensional, two-dimensional, three-dimensional, or more generally, *n*-dimensional.

- In a two-dimensional array, each row is an array.

- Each element in a two-dimensional array is accessed using the array name with a row index and column index that refer to the element's position in the array.

- Concepts such as declaration, instantiation, initial values, indexing, and aggregate operations from single-dimensional arrays also apply to two-dimensional arrays.

- Two-dimensional arrays can be instantiated by assigning initial values in a comma-separated list of comma-separated lists at the declaration.

- Each row in a two-dimensional array can have a different number of columns.

- A two-dimensional array has an instance variable, *length*, which holds the number of rows in the array.

- Each row of a two-dimensional array has an instance variable, *length*, which holds the number of elements in that row.

- The *ArrayList* class implements generics and is part of the *java.util* package.

- An *ArrayList* can be thought of as an expandable single-dimensional array of objects.

- To define an *ArrayList* to hold elements of primitive data types, use the wrapper classes.

- An *ArrayList* object expands automatically as objects are added.

- We access an element of an *ArrayList* via its index.

- We can process each element in an *ArrayList* using the enhanced *for* loop.

9.10 Exercises, Problems, and Projects

9.10.1 Multiple Choice Exercises

1. What is/are the valid way(s) to declare a two-dimensional integer array named *a*? (Check all that apply.)

   ❏ `int [ ][ ] a;`

☐ `int a [ ][ ];`

☐ `array [ ] int a;`

☐ `int array [ ] a;`

2. A two-dimensional array is an array of arrays.

☐ true

☐ false

3. In a two-dimensional array, every row must have the same number of columns.

☐ true

☐ false

4. What is the default value of the elements of a two-dimensional array of *booleans* after declaration and instantiation of the array?

☐ *true*

☐ *false*

☐ undefined

5. How do you access the element of array *a* located at row 2 and column 4?

☐ `a{2}{4}`

☐ `a( 2,4 )`

☐ `a[2][4]`

☐ `a[4][2]`

6. How do you retrieve the number of rows in a two-dimensional array *a*?

☐ `a.rows`

☐ `a.length`

☐ `a.rows( )`

☐ `a.size`

7. How do you retrieve the number of columns in row 2 in a two-dimensional array *a*?

☐ `a.length`

☐ `a[2].length`

☐ `a.size`

☐ `a[2].size`

8. All the elements of a two-dimensional array must be of the same type.

   ❏ true

   ❏ false

9. An *ArrayList* can be returned by a method.

   ❏ true

   ❏ false

10. It is possible to declare and instantiate an *ArrayList* of a user-defined class type.

    ❏ true

    ❏ false

11. As we add objects to an *ArrayList*, how can we be sure it has enough capacity?

    ❏ Use the *setCapacity* method.

    ❏ Use the *trimToSize* method.

    ❏ We don't need to do anything; capacity expands automatically as needed.

12. Where does the *add* method of the *ArrayList* class add an object?

    ❏ at the beginning of the list

    ❏ at the end of the list

13. To what package does the class *ArrayList* belong?

    ❏ *java.io*

    ❏ *java.util*

    ❏ *java.array*

    ❏ *java.list*

9.10.2   Reading and Understanding Code

For Questions 14 to 24, consider the following two-dimensional array declaration and initialization:

```
String [ ][ ] cities = { { "New York", "LA", "San Francisco", "Chicago" },
                         { "Munich", "Stuttgart", "Berlin", "Bonn" },
                         { "Paris", "Ajaccio", "Lyon" },
                         { "Montreal", "Ottawa", "Vancouver" } };
```

14. How many rows are in the array *cities*?

15. What is the value of the expression *cities[2][1]*?

16. What is the index of the last row in the array *cities*?

17. What are the row and column indexes of *Chicago* in the array *cities*?

18. What is the output of this code sequence?

```
System.out.println( cities[3][2] );
```

19. What is the output of this code sequence?

```
for ( int j = 0; j < cities[1].length; j++ )
    System.out.println( cities[1][j] );
```

20. What is the output of this code sequence?

```
for ( int i = 0; i < cities.length; i++ )
    System.out.println( cities[i][1] );
```

21. What is the output of this code sequence?

```
for ( int i = 0; i < cities.length; i++ )
{
    for ( int j = 0; j < cities[i].length; j++ )
        System.out.print( cities[i][j] + "\t" );
    System.out.println( );
}
```

22. What is the output of this code sequence?

```
for ( int i = 0; i < cities.length; i++ )
{
    for ( int j = 0; j < cities[i].length; j++ )
    {
        if ( cities[i][j].length( ) == 6 )
            System.out.println( cities[i][j] );
    }
}
```

23. What is the output of this code sequence?

```
int count = 0;
for ( int i = 0; i < cities.length; i++ )
{
    for ( int j = 0; j < cities[i].length; j++ )
    {
        if ( cities[i][j].length( ) == 7 )
            count++;
    }
}
System.out.println( "count is " + count );
```

24. What is the output of this code sequence?

```java
for ( int i = 0; i < cities.length; i++ )
{
    for ( int j = 0; j < cities[i].length; j++ )
    {
        if ( cities[i][j].charAt( 0 ) == 'S' )
            System.out.println( cities[i][j] );
    }
}
```

25. What does this method do?

```java
public static int foo( double [ ][ ] a )
{
    int b = 0;
    for ( int i = 0; i < a.length; i++ )
    {
        for ( int j = 0; j < a[i].length; j++ )
            b++;
    }
    return b;
}
```

26. What does this method do?

```java
public static boolean foo( char [ ][ ] a )
{
    int b = a[0].length;
    for ( int i = 1; i < a.length; i++ )
    {
        if ( a[i].length != b )
            return false;
    }
    return true;
}
```

27. What does this method do?

```java
public static int foo( String [ ][ ] a )
{
    int b = 0;
    for ( int i = 0; i < a.length; i++ )
        b++;
    return b;
}
```

28. What does this method do?

```
public static int [ ] foo( float [ ][ ] a )
{
    int [ ] temp = new int [a.length];
    for ( int i = 0; i < a.length; i++ )
        temp[i] = a[i].length;
    return temp;
}
```

29. What does this method do?

```
public static int foo( ArrayList<Integer> a )
{
    int b = 0;
    for ( Integer i : a )
        b++;
    return b;
}
```

30. After the following code sequence is executed, what are the contents and index of each element of a?

```
ArrayList<Integer> a = new ArrayList<Integer>( );
a.add( 7 );
a.add( 4 );
a.add( 21 );
```

31. After the following code sequence is executed, what are the contents and index of each element of a?

```
ArrayList<Integer> a = new ArrayList<Integer>( );
a.add( 7 );
a.add( 4 );
a.add( 21 );
a.set( 1, 45 );
```

32. After the following code sequence is executed, what are the contents and index of each element of a?

```
ArrayList<Integer> a = new ArrayList<Integer>( );
a.add( 7 );
a.add( 4 );
a.add( 21 );
a.add( 1, 45 );
```

9.10.3   Fill In the Code

For Questions 33 to 37, consider the following statement:

```
String [ ][ ] geo = { { "MD", "NY", "NJ", "MA", "ME", "CA", "MI", "OR" },
                      { "Detroit", "Newark", "Boston", "Seattle" } };
```

33. This code prints the element at row index 1 and column index 2 of the two-dimensional array *geo*.

```
// your code goes here
```

34. This code prints the element of the array *geo* whose value is "CA."

```
// your code goes here
```

35. This code prints all the states (i.e., the first row) that start with an *M* in the array *geo*.

```
for ( int j = 0; j < geo[0].length; j++ )
{
      // your code goes here
}
```

36. This code prints all the cities (i.e., the second row) in the array *geo*.

```
for ( int j = 0; j < geo[1].length; j++ )
{
      // your code goes here
}
```

37. This code prints all the elements of the array *geo*.

```
for ( int i = 0; i < geo.length; i++ )
{
      // your code goes here
}
```

For Questions 38 to 41, consider the following statement:

```
int [ ][ ] a = { { 9, 6, 8, 10, 5 },
                 { 7, 6, 8, 9, 6 },
                 { 4, 8, 10, 6, 6 } };
```

38. This code calculates and prints the sum of all the elements in the array *a*.

```
int sum = 0;
for ( int i = 0; i < a.length; i++ )
{
      // your code goes here
}
System.out.println( "sum is " + sum );
```

39. This code counts and prints the number of times the value 8 appears in the array *a*.

```java
int count = 0;
for ( int i = 0; i < a.length; i++ )
{
    // your code goes here
}
System.out.println( "# of 8s in a: " + count );
```

40. This code counts and prints the number of times the value 6 appears in the second row (i.e., the row whose index is 1) of array *a*.

```java
int count = 0;

// your code for the for loop header goes here
{
    if ( a[1][j] == 6 )
        count++;

}
System.out.println( "# of 6s in the 2nd row: " + count );
```

41. This code calculates the sum of the elements in the second column (i.e, the column with index 1) of array *a*.

```java
int sum  = 0;
for ( int i = 0; i < a.length; i++ )
{
    // your code goes here


}
System.out.println( "sum is " + sum );
```

42. This method returns *true* if an element in an array of *Strings* is equal to "Java"; otherwise, it returns *false*.

```java
public static boolean foo( String [ ][ ] a )
{
    // your code goes here
}
```

43. This method returns the product of all the elements in an array.

```java
public static int foo( int [ ][ ] a )
{
    // your code goes here
}
```

44. This method returns *true* if there is at least one row in the array that has exactly five columns; otherwise, it returns *false*.

```
public static boolean foo( char [ ][ ] a )
{
    // your code goes here
}
```

45. This method takes an array of *ints* as a parameter and returns a single-dimensional array of *booleans*. The length of the array returned should be equal to the number of rows in the two-dimensional array parameter. The element at index *i* of the returned array will be *true* if there is a 0 in the corresponding row of the parameter array; otherwise, it will be *false*. Assume that every row in *a* has the same number of columns.

```
public static boolean [ ] foo( int [ ][ ] a )
{
    // your code goes here
    // every row has the same number of columns
}
```

For Questions 46 to 49, consider the following statements:

```
ArrayList<String> languages = new ArrayList<String>( );
languages.add( "SQL" );
languages.add( "Java" );
languages.add( "HTML" );
languages.add( "PHP" );
languages.add( "Perl" );
```

46. This code prints the number of elements in *languages*.

```
// your code goes here
```

47. This code retrieves the *String* "HTML" from *languages* (without deleting it) and assigns it to the *String* variable *webLanguage*.

```
// your code goes here
```

48. This code replaces "HTML" *with* "C++" in *languages*.

```
// your code goes here
```

49. This code prints all the elements of *languages* that start with the letter *P*.

```
for ( String s : languages )
{
    // your code goes here
}
```

9.10.4   Identifying Errors in Code

50. Where is the error in this code sequence?

```java
double [ ][ ] a = { 3.3, 26.0, 48.4 };
```

51. Where is the error in this code sequence?

```java
int [ ][ ] a = { { 3, 26, 4 }, { 14, 87 } };
System.out.println( a[1][2] );
```

52. Where is the error in this code sequence?

```java
double [ ][ ] a = new double [ ][10];
```

53. Where is the error in this code sequence?

```java
int [ ][ ] a = { { 1, 2 },
                 { 10.1, 10.2 } };
```

54. Where is the error in this code sequence? (This code compiles and runs, but does not output the array values.)

```java
int [ ][ ] a = { { 3, 26, 48 }, { 5, 2, 9 } };
System.out.println( "The array elements are " + a );
```

55. Where is the error in this code sequence?

```java
ArrayList<double> al;
```

56. Where is the error in this code sequence?

```java
ArrayList<Float> al = new ArrayList( )<Float>;
```

57. Where is the error in this code sequence? (The compiler may ask you to recompile.)

```java
ArrayList<Double> a;
a = new ArrayList<Float>( );
```

58. Where is the error in this code sequence?

```java
// a is an ArrayList of Strings
// a has already been declared and instantiated
a.size( ) = 10;
```

9.10.5   Debugging Area—Using Messages from the Java Compiler and Java JVM

59. You coded the following on line 14 of the *Test.java* class:

```java
int a[2][ ] = { { 2, 7 }, { 9, 2 } }; // line 14
```

When you compile, you get the following message:

```
Test.java:14: error: ']' expected
     int a[2][ ] = { { 2, 7 }, { 9, 2 } }; // line 14
          ^

Test.java:14: error: not a statement
     int a[2][ ] = { { 2, 7 }, { 9, 2 } }; // line 14
              ^

Test.java:14: error: ';' expected
     int a[2][ ] = { { 2, 7 }, { 9, 2 } }; // line 14
                ^

Test.java:14: error: illegal start of expression
     int a[2][ ] = { { 2, 7 }, { 9, 2 } }; // line 14
                   ^

Test.java:14: error: not a statement
     int a[2][ ] = { { 2, 7 }, { 9, 2 } }; // line 14
                    ^

Test.java:14: error: ';' expected
     int a[2][ ] = { { 2, 7 }, { 9, 2 } }; // line 14
                     ^

6 errors
```

Explain what the problem is and how to fix it.

60. You coded the following in the *Test.java* class:

```
int [ ][ ] a = { { 1, 2, 3, 4 },
                 { 10, 20, 30 } };
for ( int i = 0; i < a.length; i++ )
{
     for ( int j = 0; j < a[0].length; j++ )
     {
          System.out.println( a[i][j] ); // line 14
     }
}
```

The code compiles properly but when you run, you get the following output:

```
1
2
3
4
10
20
30
Exception in thread "main" java.lang.ArrayIndexOutOfBoundsException: 3
         at Test.main(Test.java: 14)
```

Explain what the problem is and how to fix it.

61. You coded the following in the *Test.java* class in order to output the smallest
    element in the array *a*:

```
int [ ][ ] a = { { 9, 8, 7, 6 },
                 { 10, 20, 30, 40 } };
int min = a[0][0];
for ( int i = 1; i < a.length; i++ )
{
    for ( int j = 0; j < a[i].length; j++ )
    {
        if ( a[i][j] < min )
            min = a[i][j];
    }
}
System.out.println( "The minimum is " + min );
```

The code compiles properly, but when you run, you get the following output:

```
The minimum is 9
```

You expected the value of *min* to be 6. Explain what the problem is and how to
fix it.

62. You coded the following in file *Test.java*:

```
int [ ][ ] a = { { 9, 8, 7, 6 },
                 { 10, 20, 30, 40 } };
for ( int j = 0; j <= a[1].length; j++ )
{
  if ( a[1][j] == 20 ) // line 14
  {
      System.out.println( "Found 20 at column index " + j
                            + " of second row" );
  }
}
```

The code compiles properly, but when you run, you get the following output:

```
Found 20 at column index 1 of second row
Exception in thread "main" java.lang.ArrayIndexOutOfBoundsException: 4
        at Test.main(Test.java:14)
```

Explain what the problem is and how to fix it.

63. You coded the following in the *Test.java* class:

```
// cars is an ArrayList of Auto objects
// cars has already been declared and instantiated
for ( Auto a ; cars )      // line 12
{
```

```
        System.out.println( a.toString( ) );
    }   // line 15
```

When you compile, you get the following message :

```
Test.java:12: error: ';' expected
    for ( Auto a ; cars ) // line 12
                      ^

1 error
```

Explain what the problems are and how to fix them.

64. You coded the following in the *Test.java* class:

```
ArrayList<String> a = new ArrayList<String>( );
a.add( "Cloudy" );
a.add( "Snowy" );
a.add( "Cloudy" );
System.out.println( "Weather is " + a.get( 3 ) ); // line 14
```

The code compiles properly, but when you run, you get the following output:

```
Exception in thread "main" java.lang.IndexOutOfBoundsException: Index 3 out-of-
bounds for length 3
```

Explain what the problem is and how to fix it.

65. You coded the following in the file *Test.java*:

```
ArrayList<Integer> a = new ArrayList( );
```

When you compile (using Xlint), you get the following warning message:

```
Test.java:10: warning: [rawtypes] found raw type: ArrayList
    ArrayList<Integer> a = new ArrayList( );
                               ^

    missing type arguments for generic class ArrayList<E>
    where E is a type-variable:
    E extends Object declared in class ArrayList

Test.java:10: warning: [unchecked] unchecked conversion
    ArrayList<Integer> a = new ArrayList( );
                               ^

  required: ArrayList<Integer>
  found:    ArrayList
2 warnings
```

Explain what the problem is and how to fix it.

66. You coded the following in the file *Test.java*:

```
ArrayList<Double> a = new ArrayList<Double>( );
a.add( 2.3 );
a.add( 8.4 );
a.add( 5 ); // line 11
```

When you compile, you get the following message:

```
Test.java:11: error: no suitable method found for add(int)
 a.add( 5 ); // line 11
   ^
```

Explain what the problem is and how to fix it.

67. You coded the following in the file *Test.java*:

```
ArrayList<Character> a = new ArrayList<Character>( );
a.add( 'X' );
a.add( 'A' );
a.add( 'V' );
a.add( 'A' );
a.set( 1, 'J' );
for ( Character c : a )
  System.out.print( c + " " );
```

The code compiles properly, but when you run, you get the following output:

```
X J V A
```

when you expected:

```
J A V A
```

Explain what the problem is and how to fix it.

9.10.6   Write a Short Program

68. Write a value-returning method that returns the number of rows in a two-dimensional array of *doubles*. Include code to test your method.

69. Write a value-returning method that returns the number of elements in a two-dimensional array of *floats*. Include code to test your method.

70. Write a value-returning method that returns the number of columns that have two elements in a two-dimensional array of *booleans*. Include code to test your method.

71. Write a value-returning method that returns the number of columns with n elements in a two-dimensional array of *chars*, where n is a parameter of the method. Include code to test your method.

72. Write a value-returning method that returns the sum of all the elements in a two-dimensional array of *floats*. Include code to test your method.

73. Write a method with a *void* return value that sets to 0 all the elements of the even-numbered rows and sets to 1 all the elements of odd-numbered rows of a two-dimensional array of *ints*. Include code to test your method.

74. Write a value-returning method that returns the sum of the elements in the last column of each row in a two-dimensional array of *ints*. Include code to test your method.

75. Write a method with a *void* return value that inverts all the elements of a two-dimensional array of *booleans* (*true* becomes *false* and *false* becomes *true*). Include code to test your method.

76. Write a method that returns the number of elements having the value *true* in a two-dimensional array of *booleans*. Include code to test your method.

77. Write a method that returns the percentage of elements having the value *false* in a two-dimensional array of *booleans*. Include code to test your method.

78. Write a method that returns the average of all elements in a two-dimensional array of *ints*. Include code to test your method.

79. Write a method that returns the *String* "regular" if all the rows of a two-dimensional array of *floats* have the same number of columns; otherwise, it returns "irregular." Include code to test your method.

80. Write a method that returns the concatenation of all elements in a two-dimensional array of *Strings*. Include code to test your method.

81. Write an array-returning method that takes a two-dimensional array of *chars* as a parameter and returns a single-dimensional array of *Strings* as follows: The array returned should have a number of elements equal to the number of rows in the parameter array; every element of the array returned should be the concatenation of all the column elements of the corresponding row in the parameter array. Include code to test your method.

82. Write a method that takes as parameters two *ArrayLists* of *Strings* of the same size. The method returns a *Hashtable* (look up the *Hashtable* class in the Java Class Library) such that the *Hashtable's* keys are the elements of the first *ArrayList*, and the *Hashtable's* values are the elements of the second *ArrayList*.

Test your method in a program using an *ArrayList* of state codes and an *ArrayList* of state names.

83. Write a method that returns the sum of all the elements of an *ArrayList* of *Integer* objects. Include code to test your method.

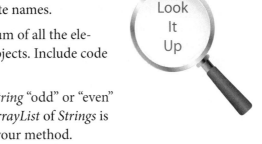

84. Write a method that returns the *String* "odd" or "even" if the number of elements of an *ArrayList* of *Strings* is odd or even. Include code to test your method.

85. Write a method that takes an *ArrayList* of *Integer* objects and returns an *ArrayList* of *Character* objects of the same size. The returned elements of the *ArrayList* are assigned a letter grade corresponding to the integer grade of the same index element of the *ArrayList* parameter (A if 90 or above, ..., F if less than 60). Include code to test your method.

9.10.7   Programming Projects

86. Write a class (and a client class to test it) that encapsulates statistics for summer job salaries for a group of people over several years. Your only instance variable should be a two-dimensional array of values representing salaries. Dimension 1 represents the people and dimension 2 represents the year of the summer job. Your constructor can simply take two integers representing the number of people and the number of years, then randomly generate the salaries and fill the array. You should include the following methods:

❑ a method returning the index of the person having made the most money over the years

❑ a method returning the year when the highest salary was earned

❑ a method returning the total amount of money made by all the people over the years

87. Write a class (and a client class to test it) that encapsulates the evolution of the passwords of three students over four months. Your only instance variable should be a two-dimensional array of values representing the passwords. Dimension 1 represents the student and dimension 2 represents the month. (Since we are concerned about security, we are assuming that people

change their password once a month; we only care about the value of the password at the end of a given month.) Your constructor can simply take a single-dimensional array of words representing the 12 passwords; they can be assigned to the two-dimensional array elements one at a time, starting with the first row. You should include the following methods:

- ❏ a method returning the index of the person who changed his or her password the most times

- ❏ a method returning the longest password

- ❏ a method changing all the passwords to "unlock"

- ❏ a method returning *true* if at least one person had a given word—the method's parameter—as his/her password in at least one month; *false* otherwise

88. Write a class (and a client class to test it) that encapsulates the evolution of the sales tax rates in the 50 U.S. states over the last 10 years. Your only instance variable should be a two-dimensional array of values representing the sales tax rates. Dimension 1 represents the state and dimension 2 represents the year. Your constructor can simply be a default constructor, randomly generating the sales tax rates, which should be between 0 and 0.06. You should include the following methods:

- ❏ a method returning the index of the state that has the biggest average tax rate over the years

- ❏ a method returning an array of indexes of the states that have had at least one year with a tax rate less than 0.001

- ❏ a method returning the highest sales tax rate over the years for a given state (which will be a parameter)

89. Write a class (and a client class to test it) that encapsulates the evolution of the quality ratings of various hotels over the years. Hotel ratings are represented by a number of stars, which can vary from one star (lowest quality) to five stars (highest quality). Your only instance variable should be a two-dimensional array of values representing the quality ratings. Dimension 1 represents the hotel and dimension 2 represents the year. Your constructor can take two parameters representing the number of hotels and the number of years. The ratings can simply be generated randomly. You should include the following methods:

- ❏ a method returning an array of indexes of the hotels that have earned five stars at least once over the years

- ❏ a method returning the average rating of all the hotels over the years

❑ a method printing the indexes of the hotels that have earned five stars every year

❑ a method returning *true* if at least one hotel earned five stars for at least one year; *false* otherwise

90. Write a class (and a client class to test it) that encapsulates the value of the 26 letters of the English alphabet in the game of Scrabble in 10 countries. You should have three instance variables:

❑ a two-dimensional array of integers representing the point values of the letters in the various countries

❑ a single-dimensional array representing the alphabet from a to z

❑ another single-dimensional array representing 10 countries

For the two-dimensional array, dimension 1 represents the letter and dimension 2 represents the country. Your constructor can simply be a default constructor, randomly generating the values between 1 and 10. You should include the following methods:

❑ a method returning an array of letters with their highest point value in any country

❑ a method printing the names of the countries that have at least one letter with a point value of 10

❑ a method taking a *String* as a parameter and printing the score of the word represented by that *String* in every country

91. Write a class (and a client class to test it) that encapsulates the numbers of the various chessboard pieces in a chess game. You should have two instance variables:

❑ a two-dimensional array of integers; each array element represents how many of a particular chess piece of a particular color are on the board. In order to set it up, consider the following:

▪ The first dimension represents the color of the pieces. On a chessboard, there are white and black pieces.

▪ The second dimension represents the pieces themselves. On a chessboard, we have on each side: one king, one queen, two bishops, two knights, two rooks, and eight pawns.

❑ a single-dimensional array describing the pieces (king, queen, etc.)

Your constructor can simply be a default constructor, declaring and instantiating the two arrays to match the preceding information. You should include the following methods:

- ❏ a method with a *void* return value, called *playerATakesPlayerB*, updating the array based on a piece being taken by the opponent. It takes two parameters:

  - ▪ a *boolean* parameter representing whether "white takes black" or "black takes white"

  - ▪ an *int* parameter representing which piece gets taken

- ❏ a method returning how many of a particular piece are on the board (this method takes a parameter representing the piece)

- ❏ a method taking a *boolean* as a parameter, representing a color and returning the value of the board for that particular color. You can consider that a king is worth 0 points, a queen is worth 6 points, a rook is worth 4 points, a knight and a bishop are each worth 3 points, and a pawn is worth 1 point

92. Write a class (and a client class to test it) that encapsulates a deck of cards. A deck of cards is made up of 52 cards. You should have three instance variables:

    - ❏ a two-dimensional array of values representing the cards

    - ❏ a single-dimensional array describing the suit: spades, hearts, diamonds, and clubs

    - ❏ an instance variable representing the trump suit

    For the two-dimensional array, dimension 1 represents the suit and dimension 2 represents the type of card (ace, two, three, ..., jack, queen, king). Your constructor should take one parameter, which will represent the suit of the trump. Based on that, the cards should be given the following values:

    - ❏ Non-trump from 2 to 10: 1 point

    - ❏ Non-trump jack = 2

    - ❏ Non-trump queen = 3

    - ❏ Non-trump king = 4

    - ❏ Non-trump ace = 5

    - ❏ Any trump card = Non-trump value + 1

    You should include the following methods:

    - ❏ a method returning the trump suit, by name

❏ a method printing the whole deck of cards, suit by suit, with the value for each card

❏ a method taking a *String* as a parameter representing a suit, and returning the total value of the cards of that suit

93. Write a class (and a client class to test it) that encapsulates a tic-tac-toe board. A tic-tac-toe board looks like a table of three rows and three columns partially or completely filled with the characters X and O. At any point, a cell of that table could be empty or could contain an X or an O. You should have one instance variable, a two-dimensional array of values representing the tic-tac-toe board.

Your default constructor should instantiate the array so that it represents an empty board.

You should include the following methods:

❏ a method, returning a *boolean*, simulating a play with three parameters as follows: If the first parameter is *true*, then X is playing; otherwise, O is playing. The other two parameters represent what cell on the board is being played. If the play is legal, that is, the cell is a legal cell on the board and is empty, then the method should update the array and return *true*; otherwise, the array should not be updated and the method should return *false*

❏ a method returning how many valid plays have been made so far

❏ a method checking if a player has won based on the contents of the board; this method takes no parameter. It returns X if the "X player" has won, O if the "O player" has won, T if the game was a tie. A player wins if he or she has placed an X (or an O) in all cells in a row, all cells in a column, or all cells in one of the two diagonals

94. Modify the *BookStore* and *BookSearchEngine* classes from the chapter.

You should include the following additional methods and test them:

❏ a method returning the book with the lowest price in the library

❏ a method searching the library for *Books* of a given author and returning an *ArrayList* of such *Books*

❏ a method returning an *ArrayList* of *Books* whose price is less than a given number

95. Write a *Garage* class (and a client class to test it) with one instance variable: an *ArrayList* of *Autos* (you can use the *Auto* class from this chapter).

You should include the following methods:

❑ a method returning the average number of miles of all cars in the garage

❑ a method returning "full" if the garage has 100 cars or more, "below minimum" if the garage has fewer than 25 cars, and "normal load" if the garage has between 25 and 100 cars in it

❑ a method returning the total number of gallons of gas used by all cars in the garage

96. Write a *ComputerPart* class and a *ComputerKit* class (and a client class to test them).

The *ComputerPart* class has two instance variables: a *String* representing an item (for instance, "cpu" or "disk drive"), and a *double* representing the price of that item. The *ComputerKit* class has just one instance variable: an *ArrayList* of *ComputerPart* objects (they make up a computer) representing the list of parts for the computer kit.

You should include the following methods:

❑ a method returning "expensive" if the total of the prices of the *ComputerPart* objects is greater than 1,000, "cheap" if it is less than 250, "normal" if it is between 250 and 1,000

❑ a method returning *true* if a certain item is included in the list of parts; *false* otherwise

❑ a method returning how many times a particular item (for instance, "cpu," or "memory") is found in the list of parts

9.10.8   Technical Writing

97. A two-dimensional array can have a different number of columns in every row. Do you see that as an advantage or a disadvantage? Discuss.

98. Discuss the pros and cons of using an array vs. using an *ArrayList*.

9.10.9   Group Project (for a group of 1, 2, or 3 students)

99. Design and code a program including the following classes, as well as a client class to test all the methods coded:

A *Passenger* class, encapsulating a passenger. A passenger has two attributes: a name, and a class of service, which will be 1 or 2.

A *Train* class, encapsulating a train of passengers. A train of passengers has one attribute: a list of passengers, which must be represented with an *ArrayList*. Your constructor will build the list of passengers by reading data from a file called *passengers.txt*. You can assume that *passengers.txt* has the following format:

<name1> <class1>

<name2> <class2>

...

For instance, the file could contain:

James	1
Ben	2
Suri	1
Sarah	1
Jane	2

...

You should include the following methods in your *Train* class:

- ❑ a method returning the percentage of passengers traveling in first class

- ❑ a method taking two parameters representing the price of traveling in first and second class and returning the total revenue for the train

- ❑ a method checking if a certain person is on the train; if he/she is, the method returns *true*; otherwise, it returns *false*

CHAPTER 10

Object-Oriented Programming, Part 3: Inheritance, Polymorphism, and Interfaces

CHAPTER CONTENTS

Introduction

One of the most common ways to reuse a class is through inheritance. Inheritance helps us to organize related classes into **hierarchies**, or ordered levels of functionality. To set up a hierarchy, we begin by defining a class that contains methods and fields (instance variables and class variables) that are common to all classes in the hierarchy. Then we define new classes at the next lower level of the hierarchy, which inherit the behavior and fields of the original class. In the new classes, we define additional fields and more specific methods. The original class is called the **superclass**, and the new classes that inherit from the superclass are called **subclasses**. Some OOP developers call a superclass the **base class** and call a subclass the **derived class**.

As in life, a superclass (parent) can have multiple subclasses (children), and each subclass can be a superclass (parent) of other subclasses (children) and so on. Thus, a class can be both a subclass (child) and a superclass (parent). In contrast to life, however, Java subclasses inherit directly from only one superclass.

A subclass can add fields and methods, some of which may **override**, or hide, a field or method inherited from a superclass.

Let's look at an example. To represent a hierarchy of vehicle types, we define a *Vehicle* class as a superclass. We then define an *Automobile* class that inherits from *Vehicle*. We also define a *Truck* class, which also inherits from *Vehicle*. We further refine our classes by defining a *Pickup* class and a *TractorTrailer* class, both of which inherit from the *Truck* class. Figure 10.1 depicts our hierarchy using a UML (Unified Modeling Language) diagram. Arrows pointing from a subclass to a superclass indicate that the subclass refers to the superclass for some of its methods and fields. The boxes below the class name are available for specifying instance variables and methods for each class. For simplicity, we leave those boxes blank. Later in the chapter, we will illustrate UML diagrams complete with fields and methods.

The Java Class Library contains many class hierarchies. At the root of all Java class hierarchies is the *Object* class, the superclass for all classes. Thus, all classes inherit from the *Object* class.

The most important advantage to inheritance is that in a hierarchy of classes, we write the common code only once. After the common code has been tested, we can reuse it with confidence by inheriting it into the subclasses. And when that common code needs revision, we need to revise the code in only one place.

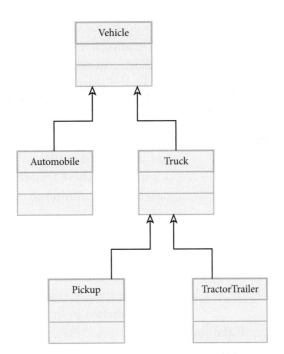

Figure 10.1

Vehicle Class
Hierarchy

10.1   Inheritance

The syntax for defining a subclass class that inherits from another class is to add an *extends* clause in the class header:

```
accessModifier class SubclassName extends SuperclassName
{
    // class definition
}
```

The *extends* keyword specifies that the subclass inherits members of the superclass. That means that the subclass begins with a set of predefined methods and fields inherited from its hierarchy of superclasses.

For example, if we want to code a class named *DrawASprite*, we extend the *Application* class, and we use the following header:

```
public class DrawASprite extends Application
```

This means that the *DrawASprite* class inherits from the *Application* class.

The *DrawASprite* class hierarchy is shown in Figure 10.2. At the top of the hierarchy is the *Object* class. It defines 11 methods. The *Application* class extends

Figure 10.2

The *DrawASprite*
Class Hierarchy

the *Object* class, so it inherits those 11 methods. In turn, the *Application* class defines two fields and 10 additional methods. So when our *DrawASprite* class extends *Application*, the *DrawASprite* class inherits 21 methods and two fields. All along the hierarchy, subclasses inherit methods and fields. True, not every class has a use for all the inherited methods and fields, but they are available if needed, and the benefit is that we don't need to write these methods or define these fields in our classes. Thus, we can build classes with a minimum of effort.

As we can see from Figure 10.2, our *DrawASprite* class has two superclasses. The class that a subclass refers to in the *extends* clause of the class definition is called its **direct superclass**. Thus, *Application* is the direct superclass of *DrawASprite*. Similarly, the class that *extends* the superclass is called the **direct subclass** of the superclass, so *DrawASprite* is a direct subclass of the *Application* class. A class can have multiple direct subclasses, but only one direct superclass.

10.2   Inheritance Design

We say that an "is a" relationship exists between a subclass and a superclass; that is, a subclass object "is a" superclass object. For example, we could define a student class hierarchy with a *Student* superclass and derive a *GraduateStudent* subclass. A graduate student "is a" student, but actually a special type of student. We could also define an employee class hierarchy with an *Employee* superclass and derive *Faculty* and *Staff* subclasses, because faculty and staff are both special types of employees.

SOFTWARE
ENGINEERING
TIP
The superclasses
in a class
hierarchy should
contain fields
and methods
common to
all subclasses.
The subclasses
should add
specialized fields
and methods.

To design classes for inheritance, our superclass should define fields and methods that will be common to all classes in the hierarchy. Each subclass will provide specialization by adding methods and fields. Where appropriate, subclasses can also provide new versions of inherited methods, which is called **overriding methods**.

Let's build a bank account class hierarchy. We start by defining a generic *BankAccount* superclass. The *BankAccount* class will contain the fields and methods that are common to all bank accounts. Then we will define a *CheckingAccount* class that inherits from the *BankAccount* class. The *CheckingAccount* class will add instance variables and methods that specifically support checking accounts. Our class hierarchy is shown in the UML diagram in Figure 10.3. In this diagram, we display the instance variables in the box immediately below the class name and the methods in the next lower box. A "+" preceding a class member indicates that the member is

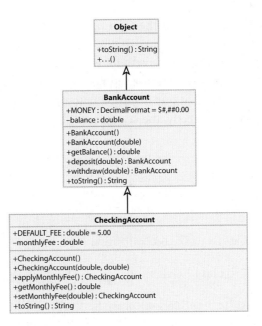

Figure 10.3

The *BankAccount*
Class Hierarchy

public, while a "–" indicates that the member is *private*. Each method's signature is given with each parameter's type within parentheses and the return type following a colon. The *Object* class has more methods than we indicate on the UML diagram. However, the *toString* method is the only method of *Object* that we will deal with in this hierarchy, so we have omitted the other methods of *Object* on the diagram and indicate that other methods exist (+...()).

10.2.1   Inherited Members of a Class

As shown in Example 10.1, our *BankAccount* class has two instance variables, the *balance*, which is a *double* (line 11), and a constant *DecimalFormat* object that we will use for formatting the *balance* as money (lines 9–10). We provide two constructors. The default constructor (lines 13–19) sets the *balance* instance variable to 0.0. The overloaded constructor (lines 21–27) takes a starting balance and passes that parameter to the *deposit* method (lines 37–48), which adds any non-negative amount to the *balance*. Otherwise, it leaves *balance* unchanged.

The *withdraw* method (lines 50–62) validates that the *amount* parameter is not less than 0.0 and is not greater than the *balance*. If *amount* is valid, the *withdraw* method subtracts *amount* from *balance*; otherwise, it leaves *balance* unchanged.

Other methods of the *BankAccount* class include the *balance* accessor (lines 29–35) and the *toString* method (lines 64–71), which uses the *DecimalFormat* object, *MONEY*, to return the balance formatted as money. Note that we write @*Override* before the header of the *toString* method. We are replacing the version of *toString* that is in the *Object* class, that is, we are overriding the *Object* version of the *toString* method. To replace a method, we must write our method header exactly the same as the method we are overriding. By using the *@Override* annotation, we signal to the compiler that our intention is to override the method. If our method header is not coded correctly, the compiler will generate an error. Thus, it is a way to check our work.

```
 1 /**    BankAccount class, version 1
 2 *      Anderson, Franceschi
 3 *      Represents a generic bank account
 4 */
 5 import java.text.DecimalFormat;
 6
 7 public class BankAccount
 8 {
 9   public final DecimalFormat MONEY
10                     = new DecimalFormat( "$#,##0.00" );
11   private double balance;
12
13   /** default constructor
14   *    sets balance to 0.0
15   */
16   public BankAccount( )
17   {
18     balance = 0.0;
19   }
20
21   /** overloaded constructor
22   *    @param balance beginning balance
23   */
24   public BankAccount( double balance )
25   {
26     deposit( balance );
27   }
28
29   /** accessor for balance
30   *    @return  current account balance
31   */
32   public double getBalance( )
33   {
34     return balance;
35   }
36
37   /** deposit amount to account
```

```
38   *    @param amount   amount to deposit;
39   *                    amount must be >= 0.0
40   *    @return  a reference to this object
41   */
42   public BankAccount deposit( double amount )
43   {
44     if ( amount >= 0.0 )
45       balance += amount;
46
47     return this;
48   }
49
50   /** withdraw amount from account
51    *    @param amount   amount to withdraw;
52    *                    amount must be >= 0.0
53    *                    amount must be <= balance
54    *    @return a reference to this object
55    */
56   public BankAccount withdraw( double amount )
57   {
58     if ( amount >= 0.0 && amount <= balance )
59       balance -= amount;
60
61     return this;
62   }
63
64   /** toString
65    * @return  the balance formatted as money
66    */
67   @Override
68   public String toString( )
69   {
70     return "balance is " + MONEY.format( balance );
71   }
72 }
```

EXAMPLE 10.1   *BankAccount* Class, Version 1

Now we can derive our *CheckingAccount* subclass. Example 10.2 shows Version 1 of our *CheckingAccount* class. For this initial version, we simply define the *CheckingAccount* class as extending *BankAccount* (line 5). The body of our class is empty for now, so we can demonstrate the fields and methods that a subclass inherits from its superclass.

```
1 /* CheckingAccount class, Version 1
2    Anderson, Franceschi
```

```
3 */
4
5 public class CheckingAccount extends BankAccount
6 { }
```

EXAMPLE 10.2   *CheckingAccount* Class, Version 1

When a class *extends* a superclass, all the *public* fields and methods of the superclass (excluding constructors) are inherited. That means that the *CheckingAccount* class inherits the *MONEY* instance variable and the *getBalance, deposit, withdraw,* and *toString* methods from the *BankAccount* class. An inherited field is directly accessible from the subclass, and an inherited method can be called by the other methods of the subclass. In addition, *public* inherited methods can be called by a client application using a subclass object reference.

Any fields and methods that are declared *private* are not inherited, and therefore are not directly accessible by the subclass. Nevertheless, the *private* fields are still part of the subclass object. Remember that a *CheckingAccount* object "is a" *BankAccount* object, so a *CheckingAccount* object has a *balance* instance variable. However, the *balance* is declared to be *private* in the *BankAccount* class, so the *CheckingAccount* methods cannot directly access the *balance*. The *CheckingAccount* methods must call the accessor and mutator methods of the *BankAccount* class to access or change the value of *balance*.

Calling methods to retrieve and change values of an instance variable may seem a little tedious, but it enforces encapsulation. Allowing the *CheckingAccount* class to set the value of *balance* directly would complicate the maintenance of the program. The *CheckingAccount* class would need to be responsible for maintaining a valid value for *balance*, which means that the *CheckingAccount* class would need to know all the validation rules for *balance* that the *BankAccount* class enforces. If these rules change, then the *CheckingAccount* class would also need to change. As long as the *BankAccount* class ensures the validity of *balance*, there is no reason for the *CheckingAccount* class to duplicate that code.

Java provides the **protected** access modifier so that fields and methods can be inherited by subclasses (like *public* fields and methods), while still being hidden from client classes (like *private* fields and methods). In addition, any class in the same package as the superclass can directly access a *protected* field, even if that class is not a subclass. Because more than one class can directly access a *protected* field, *protected* access compromises encapsulation and complicates the maintenance of a program. For that reason, we prefer to use *private*, rather than *protected*, for our instance variables. We will discuss the difference between *private* and *protected* in greater detail later in the chapter.

TABLE 10.1   Inheritance Rules

Superclass Members	Inherited by Subclass?	Directly Accessible by Subclass?	Directly Accessible by Client of Subclass?
public fields	yes	yes, by using field name	yes
public methods	yes	yes, by calling method from other subclass methods	yes
protected fields	yes	yes, by using field name	no, must use accessors and mutators
protected methods	yes	yes, by calling method from subclass methods	no
private fields	no	no, must use accessors and mutators	no, must use accessors and mutators
private methods	no	no	no

Table 10.1 summarizes the fields and methods that are inherited by a subclass. We will add to this table as we explain more about inheritance.

Example 10.3 shows a client for the *CheckingAccount* class. In line 9, we instantiate an object of the *CheckingAccount* class. After instantiation, the *c1* object has two fields (*balance* and *MONEY*), and it has inherited four methods (*getBalance*, *deposit*, *withdraw*, and *toString*) from *BankAccount*.

We illustrate this by using the *c1* object reference to call the *deposit* method in line 12 and the *withdraw* method in line 15, and to call the *toString* method implicitly in lines 13 and 16. Figure 10.4 shows the output from this program.

```
1 /* CheckingAccount Client, Version 1
2    Anderson, Franceschi
3 */
4
5 public class CheckingAccountClient
6 {
7  public static void main( String [ ] args )
8  {
9    CheckingAccount c1 = new CheckingAccount( );
10   System.out.println( "New checking account: " + c1 );
11
12   c1.deposit( 350.75 );
13   System.out.println( "\nAfter depositing $350.75: " + c1 );
14
```

```
15    c1.withdraw( 200.25 );
16    System.out.println( "\nAfter withdrawing $200.25: " + c1 );
17  }
18 }
```

EXAMPLE 10.3   *CheckingAccountClient*, Version 1

Figure 10.4

Output from
*CheckingAccount-
Client*, Version 1

```
New checking account: balance is $0.00
After depositing $350.75: balance is $350.75
After withdrawing $200.25: balance is $150.50
```

10.2.2   Subclass Constructors

Although constructors are *public*, they are not inherited by subclasses. However, to initialize the *private* instance variables of the superclass, a subclass constructor can call a superclass constructor either implicitly or explicitly.

When a class extends another class, the default constructor of the subclass automatically calls the default constructor of the superclass. This is called **implicit** invocation. Athough we did not code any constructors in our *CheckingAccount* class in Example 10.2, we were able to instantiate a *CheckingAccount* object (with a 0.0 *balance*) because the Java compiler provided a default constructor for the *CheckingAccount* class, which implicitly called the default constructor of the *Bank-Account* class.

To **explicitly** call the constructor of the direct superclass, the subclass constructor uses the following syntax:

```
super( argument list );
```

**COMMON ERROR
TRAP**
In a constructor,
the call to the
direct superclass
constructor, if
used, must be
the first state-
ment.

Thus, if we want to instantiate a *CheckingAccount* object with a starting balance other than 0.0, we need to provide an overloaded constructor for the *CheckingAccount* class. That constructor will take the starting balance as a parameter and pass that starting balance to the overloaded constructor in the *BankAccount* class.

This call to the direct superclass constructor, if used, must be the first statement in the subclass constructor. Otherwise, the following compiler error is generated:

```
call to super must be first statement in constructor
```

Example 10.4 shows Version 2 of the *BankAccount* class, which, for simplicity and to help us focus on constructors, has only a default and overloaded constructor and the *toString* method. To illustrate the order in which the constructors execute, we print a message in each constructor (lines 21 and 33), indicating that it has been called.

```java
 1 /**   BankAccount class, Version 2
 2 *      Constructors and toString method only
 3 *      Anderson, Franceschi
 4 *      Represents a generic bank account
 5 */
 6
 7 import java.text.DecimalFormat;
 8
 9 public class BankAccount
10 {
11     public final DecimalFormat MONEY
12                     = new DecimalFormat( "$#,##0.00" );
13     private double balance;
14
15     /** default constructor
16     *    sets balance to 0.0
17     */
18     public BankAccount( )
19     {
20       balance = 0.0;
21       System.out.println( "In BankAccount default constructor" );
22     }
23
24     /** overloaded constructor
25     *    @param balance beginning balance
26     */
27     public BankAccount( double balance )
28     {
29       if ( balance >= 0.0 )
30           this.balance = balance;
31       else
32           this.balance = 0.0;
33       System.out.println( "In BankAccount overloaded constructor" );
34     }
35
36     /** toString
37     *    @return the balance formatted as money
38     */
39     @Override
40     public String toString( )
```

```
41    {
42       return "balance is " + MONEY.format( balance );
43    }
44 }
```

EXAMPLE 10.4   *BankAccount* Class, Version 2

Example 10.5 shows Version 2 of the *CheckingAccount* class, which has both a default constructor and an overloaded constructor. Again, we have inserted messages (lines 13–14 and 24–25) to indicate when a constructor is called.

```
 1 /*  CheckingAccount class, Version 2
 2      Anderson, Franceschi
 3 */
 4
 5 public class CheckingAccount extends BankAccount
 6 {
 7    /** default constructor
 8     *   explicitly calls the BankAccount default constructor
 9     */
10    public CheckingAccount( )
11    {
12        super( ); // optional, call BankAccount constructor
13        System.out.println( "In CheckingAccount "
14                            + "default constructor" );
15    }
16
17    /** overloaded constructor
18     *   calls BankAccount overloaded constructor
19     *   @param balance starting balance
20     */
21    public CheckingAccount( double balance )
22    {
23        super( balance ); // call BankAccount constructor
24        System.out.println( "In CheckingAccount "
25                            + "overloaded constructor" );
26    }
27 }
```

EXAMPLE 10.5   *CheckingAccount* Class, Version 2

COMMON ERROR TRAP
An attempt by a subclass to directly access a *private* field or call a *private* method defined in a superclass will generate a compiler error. To set initial values for *private* variables, call the appropriate constructor of the direct superclass.

In the *CheckingAccount* default constructor, we explicitly call the default constructor of the *BankAccount* class (line 12). This statement is optional; without it, the *Bank-Account* default constructor is still called implicitly.

In the *CheckingAccount* overloaded constructor, we pass the *balance* parameter to the *BankAccount* constructor (line 23) to initialize the *balance* instance variable. Because the *balance* instance variable has *private* access in the *BankAccount* class, our *CheckingAccount* class cannot access the *balance* instance variable directly. If we attempted to initialize the *balance* directly using the following statement:

```
this.balance = balance;
```

the compiler would generate the following error:

```
balance has private access in BankAccount
```

We might be tempted to call the *deposit* method instead of *super* to initialize the balance. Although this would work in this case, we don't always know what operations a constructor is performing. Perhaps the constructor also assigns an account number, in which case, calling the *deposit* method would cause us to skip that step. Thus, it is always a good practice to call the constructor of the superclass so that the superclass data will be correctly initialized.

Example 10.6 shows Version 2 of our *CheckingAccount* client. On line 10, we instantiate a *CheckingAccount* object using the default constructor and print the balance by implicitly calling the *toString* method on line 11. Then on line 14, we instantiate a second *CheckingAccount* object with a starting balance of $100.00. Again we verify the result by printing the balance (line 15).

SOFTWARE ENGINEERING TIP
Overloaded constructors in a subclass should explicitly call the direct superclass constructor to initialize the fields in its superclasses.

```
1 /* CheckingAccount Client, Version 2
2    Anderson, Franceschi
3 */
4
5 public class CheckingAccountClient
6 {
7    public static void main( String [ ] args )
8    {
9      // use default constructor
10      CheckingAccount c1 = new CheckingAccount( );
11      System.out.println( "New checking account: " + c1 + "\n" );
12
13      // use overloaded constructor
14      CheckingAccount c2 = new CheckingAccount( 100.00 );
15      System.out.println( "New checking account: " + c2 );
16    }
17 }
```

EXAMPLE 10.6   *CheckingAccountClient*, Version 2

Figure 10.5 shows the output from this program. As we can see, when we construct the *c1* object, the *BankAccount* default constructor runs. When it finishes, the *CheckingAccount* default constructor runs. Similarly, when we construct the *c2* object, the *BankAccount* overloaded constructor runs, then the *CheckingAccount* overloaded constructor runs.

```
In BankAccount default constructor
In CheckingAccount default constructor
New checking account: balance is $0.00

In BankAccount overloaded constructor
In CheckingAccount overloaded constructor
New checking account: balance is $100.00
```

TABLE 10.2   Inheritance Rules for Constructors

Superclass Members	Inherited by Subclass?	Directly Accessible by Subclass?	Directly Accessible by Client of Subclass Using a Subclass Reference?
constructors	no	yes, using `super( arg list )` in a subclass constructor	no

Table 10.2 summarizes the inheritance rules for constructors.

10.2.3   Adding Specialization to the Subclass

At this point, our *CheckingAccount* class provides no more functionality than the *BankAccount* class. But our purpose for defining a *CheckingAccount* class was to provide support for a specialized type of bank account. To add specialization to our *CheckingAccount* subclass, we define new fields and methods. For example, we can define a *monthlyFee* instance variable, as well as an accessor and mutator method for the monthly fee and a method to charge the monthly fee to the account.

Example 10.7 shows Version 3 of the *CheckingAccount* class with the specialization added. This version *extends* the complete *BankAccount* class shown in Example 10.1. We added the *monthlyFee* instance variable on line 8, as well as a constant default value for the monthly fee (line 7). Our default constructor (lines 10–18) still calls the default constructor of the *BankAccount* class to initialize the *balance*, but it also initializes the *monthlyFee* to the default value.

Similarly, the overloaded constructor (lines 20–30) passes the *balance* parameter to the overloaded constructor of the *BankAccount* class and adds a *monthlyFee* parameter to accept an initial value for the *monthlyFee*, which it passes to the *setMonthlyFee* mutator method (lines 50–60).

The *applyMonthlyFee* method (lines 32–40), which charges the monthly fee to the checking account, calls the *withdraw* method inherited from the *BankAccount* class to access the *balance* instance variable, which is declared *private* in the *BankAccount* class.

```
1 /* CheckingAccount class, version 3
2    Anderson, Franceschi
3 */
4
5 public class CheckingAccount extends BankAccount
6 {
7    public final double DEFAULT_FEE = 5.00;
8    private double monthlyFee;
9
10   /** default constructor
11    *    explicitly calls the BankAccount default constructor
12    *    sets monthlyFee to default value
13    */
14   public CheckingAccount( )
15   {
16       super( ); // optional
17       monthlyFee = DEFAULT_FEE;
18   }
19
20   /** overloaded constructor
21    *  calls BankAccount overloaded constructor
22    *  @param  balance  starting balance
23    *  @param  monthlyFee starting monthly fee
24    */
25   public CheckingAccount( double balance,
26                           double monthlyFee )
27   {
28      super( balance ); // call BankAccount constructor
29      setMonthlyFee( monthlyFee );
30   }
31
32   /** applyMonthlyFee method
33    * charges the monthly fee to the account
34    * @return a reference to this object
35    */
36   public CheckingAccount applyMonthlyFee( )
37   {
38     withdraw( monthlyFee );
39     return this;
40   }
41
42   /** accessor method for monthlyFee
43    *  @return  monthlyFee
```

```
44     */
45     public double getMonthlyFee( )
46     {
47       return monthlyFee;
48     }
49
50     /** mutator method for monthlyFee
51      *  @param monthlyFee new value for monthlyFee
52      *  @return a reference to this object
53      */
54     public CheckingAccount setMonthlyFee( double monthlyFee )
55     {
56       if ( monthlyFee >= 0.0 )
57         this.monthlyFee = monthlyFee;
58
59       return this;
60     }
61 }
```

EXAMPLE 10.7   *CheckingAccountClient*, Version 3

Example 10.8 shows Version 3 of our client program, which instantiates a *CheckingAccount* object and charges the monthly fee. The output is shown in Figure 10.6.

```
1 /* CheckingAccount Client, Version 3
2    Anderson, Franceschi
3 */
4
5 public class CheckingAccountClient
6 {
7    public static void main( String [ ] args )
8    {
9      CheckingAccount c3 = new CheckingAccount( 100.00, 7.50 );
10     System.out.println( "New checking account:\n"
11                         + c3.toString( )
12                         + "; monthly fee is "
13                         + c3.getMonthlyFee( ) );
14
15     c3.applyMonthlyFee( ); // charge the fee to the account
16     System.out.println( "\nAfter charging monthly fee:\n"
17                         + c3.toString( )
18                         + "; monthly fee is "
19                         + c3.getMonthlyFee( ) );
20   }
21 }
```

EXAMPLE 10.8   *CheckingAccountClient*, Version 3

```
New checking account:
balance is $100.00; monthly fee is $7.50

After charging monthly fee:
balance is $92.50; monthly fee is $7.50
```

Figure 10.6

Output from *CheckingAccount-Client*, Version 3

10.2.4 Overriding Inherited Methods

When the methods our subclass inherits do not fulfill the functions we need, we can **override** the inherited methods by providing new versions of those methods.

To override an inherited method, we provide a new method with the same header as the inherited method; that is, the new method must have the same name, the same number and type of parameters, and the same return type. Overriding a method makes the inherited version of the method invisible to the client of the subclass. We say that the overridden method is hidden from the client. When the client calls the method using a subclass object reference, the subclass version of the method is invoked.

Methods in a subclass can still access the inherited version of the method by preceding the method call with the *super* object reference as in the following syntax:

```
super.methodName( argument list )
```

In our *CheckingAccount* class, we inherited the *toString* method from the *BankAccount* class. But this method returns only the *balance*. In Example 10.8, we needed to call the *CheckingAccount* method *getMonthlyFee* to print the value of *monthlyFee*. Furthermore, as Figure 10.6 shows, the *balance* value is formatted and the *monthlyFee* value is not. Instead, the *toString* method in the *CheckingAccount* class should return formatted versions of both the *balance* and the *monthlyFee*. We can accomplish this by overriding the inherited *toString* method.

Example 10.9 shows Version 4 of the *CheckingAccount* class with the new *toString* method (lines 62–71). To format the *balance*, we call the *toString* method of the *BankAccount* class (line 69), then add the formatted value of *monthlyFee* to the *String* being returned. Again, we used the *@Override* annotation so that the compiler will alert us if we do not correctly code the header of the method. Notice that we didn't need to instantiate a new *DecimalFormat* object in order to format the *monthlyFee* instance variable. Because the *MONEY* object is declared to be *public* in the *BankAccount* class, we inherited the *MONEY* object, so we can simply call the *format* method using the *MONEY* object reference. An advantage to making the *MONEY* object *public* is that both the balance and the monthly fee will be printed using the same formatting rules. Another advantage is that if we want to change the formatting for printing the data, we need to make only one change: We redefine the value of the *MONEY* constant in the *BankAccount* class.

```java
1   /* CheckingAccount class, version 4
2      Anderson, Franceschi
3   */
4
5   public class CheckingAccount extends BankAccount
6   {
7      public final double DEFAULT_FEE = 5.00;
8      private double monthlyFee;
9
10     /** default constructor
11     *    explicitly calls the BankAccount default constructor
12     *    sets monthlyFee to default value
13     */
14     public CheckingAccount( )
15     {
16         super( ); // call BankAccount constructor
17         monthlyFee = DEFAULT_FEE;
18     }
19
20     /** overloaded constructor
21     *   calls BankAccount overloaded constructor
22     *   @param  balance   starting balance
23     *   @param  monthlyFee starting monthly fee
24     */
25     public CheckingAccount( double balance,
26                             double monthlyFee )
27     {
28         super( balance ); // call BankAccount constructor
29         setMonthlyFee( monthlyFee );
30     }
31
32     /** applyMonthlyFee method
33     * charges the monthly fee to the account
34     * @return a reference to this object
35     */
36     public CheckingAccount applyMonthlyFee( )
37     {
38         withdraw( monthlyFee );
39         return this;
40     }
41
42     /** accessor method for monthlyFee
```

```
43      *   @return   monthlyFee
44      */
45     public double getMonthlyFee( )
46     {
47        return monthlyFee;
48     }
49
50     /** mutator method for monthlyFee
51      *   @param monthlyFee new value for monthlyFee
52      *   @return a reference to this object
53      */
54     public CheckingAccount setMonthlyFee( double monthlyFee )
55     {
56        if ( monthlyFee >= 0.0 )
57           this.monthlyFee = monthlyFee;
58
59        return this;
60     }
61
62     /* toString method
63      *   @return String containing formatted balance and monthlyFee
64      *      invokes superclass toString to format balance
65      */
66     @Override
67     public String toString( )
68     {
69        return super.toString( )
70              + "; monthly fee is " + MONEY.format( monthlyFee );
71     }
72  }
```

EXAMPLE 10.9   *CheckingAccount* Class, Version 4

Example 10.10 shows Version 4 of the *CheckingAccountClient* class. In this class, we again instantiate a *CheckingAccount* object with an initial balance of $100.00 and a monthly fee of $7.50 (line 9), then implicitly invoke the *toString* method to print the data of the object (line 10). This time, we invoke the *toString* method of the *CheckingAccount* class, which returns both the *balance* and *monthlyFee* values, formatted as money, as shown in Figure 10.7.

```
New checking account:
balance is $100.00; monthly fee is $7.50
```

COMMON ERROR TRAP
Do not confuse overriding a method with overloading a method. A subclass overriding a method provides a new version of that method, which hides the superclass version. A class overloading a method adds a version of that method, which varies in the number and/or type of parameters.

Figure 10.7

Output from *CheckingAccountClient*, Version 4

```
1 /* CheckingAccount Client, Version 4
2    Anderson, Franceschi
3 */
4
5 public class CheckingAccountClient
6 {
7    public static void main( String [ ] args )
8    {
9      CheckingAccount c4 = new CheckingAccount( 100.00, 7.50 );
10     System.out.println( "New checking account:\n" + c4 );
11   }
12 }
```

EXAMPLE 10.10   *CheckingAccountClient*, **Version 4**

Table 10.3 summarizes the inheritance rules for inherited methods that have been overridden.

When we override a method, the method signature must be identical to the inherited method. However, wherever the overridden method specifies a class as a parameter or return type, we can substitute a subclass for that parameter or return type.

This is possible because a subclass object is a superclass object, so a subclass object reference can be substituted for any superclass object reference. If two methods of a class have the same name but different signatures (that is, if the number, order, or type of parameters is different), then the method is *overloaded*, not *overridden*.

For example, if we were to write the *toString* method in the *CheckingAccount* class with the following header that specifies an *int* parameter:

```
public String toString( int a )
```

TABLE 10.3   Inheritance Rules for Overridden Methods

Superclass Members	Inherited by Subclass?	Directly Accessible by Subclass?	Directly Accessible by Client of Subclass Using a Subclass Reference?
public or *protected* inherited methods that have been overridden in the subclass	no	yes, using `super.methodName ( arg list )`	no

then our *toString* method would have a different signature from the *toString* method we inherited from the *BankAccount* class, which does not take any parameters. In this case, we are overloading the *toString* method, not overriding it. In other words, we are providing an additional version of the *toString* method. The inherited version is still visible and available to be called.

Table 10.4 illustrates the differences between overriding *public* methods and overloading *public* methods.

SOFTWARE
ENGINEERING
TIP
Methods
that override
inherited
methods should
explicitly call the
direct superclass
method
whenever
appropriate.

TABLE 10.4   Overriding vs. Overloading Methods

	Method Names	Argument Lists	Return Types	Directly Accessible by Subclass Client Using a Subclass Object Reference?
Overriding a *public* Method	identical	identical	identical	only the subclass version can be called
Overloading a *public* Method	identical	different in number or type of parameters	identical	all versions of the overloaded method can be called

Skill Practice
with these end-of-chapter questions

10.10.1   Multiple Choice Exercises

Questions 1, 2, 4, 8, 9

10.10.3   Fill In the Code

Questions 21, 22, 23, 24

10.10.5   Debugging Area

Questions 32, 34, 35

10.10.6   Write a Short Program

Questions 36, 37, 38, 39, 40, 41, 42, 43, 44, 45, 46

10.10.8   Technical Writing

Question 56

10.3   The *protected* Access Modifier

We have seen that the subclass does not inherit constructors or *private* members of the superclass. However, the superclass constructors are still available to be called from the subclass and the *private* fields of the superclass are implemented as fields of the subclass.

Although *private* fields preserve encapsulation, there is additional processing overhead involved with calling methods. Whenever a method is called, the JVM saves the return address and makes copies of the arguments. Then when a value-returning method completes, the JVM makes a copy of the return value available to the caller. The *protected* access modifier was designed to avoid this processing overhead and to facilitate coding by allowing the subclass to access any *protected* field without calling its accessor or mutator method.

Be aware, however, that *protected* fields and methods also can be accessed directly by other classes in the same package, even if the classes are not within the same inheritance hierarchy.

To classes outside the package, a *protected* member of a class has the same restrictions as a *private* member. In other words, a class outside the package in which the *protected* member is declared may not call any *protected* methods and must access any *protected* fields through *public* accessor or mutator methods.

SOFTWARE ENGINEERING TIP
Unless high performance is a critical requirement, avoid using the *protected* access modifier because doing so compromises encapsulation and complicates the maintenance of a program. Where possible, call superclass methods to change the values of *protected* instance variables.

The *protected* access modifier has tradeoffs. As we mentioned, any fields declared as *protected* can be accessed directly by subclasses. Doing so, however, compromises encapsulation because multiple classes can set the value of a *protected* instance variable defined in another class.

Thus, maintaining classes that define or use *protected* members becomes more difficult. For example, we need to verify that any class that has access to the *protected* instance variable either does not set the variable's value, or if the class does change the value, that the new value is valid. Because of this added maintenance complexity, we recommend that *protected* access be used only when high performance is essential.

We also recommend that subclass methods avoid directly setting the value of a *protected* instance variable. Instead, wherever possible, call superclass methods when values of *protected* variables need to be changed.

To illustrate how *protected* access can be used in class hierarchies, let's look closely at our *CheckingAccount* class. We have been calling the *withdraw* method inherited from the *BankAccount* class to apply the monthly fee. However, the *withdraw* method leaves the *balance* unchanged if the withdrawal amount is greater than the balance. Thus, if the account does not have sufficient funds, the monthly fee is not charged. We would like the *CheckingAccount* class to be able to charge the monthly fee to the account and let the balance become negative.

To accomplish this, we declare the *balance* instance variable to be *protected* instead of *private*. This allows us to directly access *balance* inside the *applyMonthlyFee* method of the *CheckingAccount* class, because *balance* is now inherited by *CheckingAccount*.

Example 10.11 shows the *BankAccount* class, Version 3. The only change, compared to Version 1 (Example 10.1), is that the *balance* instance variable is declared as *protected*, rather than *private* (line 11).

```
 1 /**    BankAccount class, version 1
 2 *      Anderson, Franceschi
 3 *      Represents a generic bank account
 4 */
 5 import java.text.DecimalFormat;
 6
 7 public class BankAccount
 8 {
 9   public final DecimalFormat MONEY
10                    = new DecimalFormat( "$#,##0.00" );
11   protected double balance;
12
13   /** default constructor
14   *    sets balance to 0.0
15   */
16   public BankAccount( )
17   {
18     balance = 0.0;
19   }
20
21   /** overloaded constructor
22   *    @param balance  beginning balance
23   */
24   public BankAccount( double balance )
25   {
26     deposit( balance );
27   }
28
29   /** accessor for balance
30   *    @return  current account balance
31   */
32   public double getBalance( )
33   {
34     return balance;
35   }
36
```

```
37   /** deposit amount to account
38    *    @param amount  amount to deposit;
39    *                      amount must be >= 0.0
40    *    @return  a reference to this object
41    */
42   public BankAccount deposit( double amount )
43   {
44     if ( amount >= 0.0 )
45       balance += amount;
46
47     return this;
48   }
49
50   /** withdraw amount from account
51    *    @param amount   amount to withdraw;
52    *                       amount must be >= 0.0
53    *                       amount must be <= balance
54    *    @return a reference to this object
55    */
56   public BankAccount withdraw( double amount )
57   {
58     if ( amount >= 0.0 && amount <= balance )
59       balance -= amount;
60
61     return this;
62   }
63
64   /** toString
65    * @return  the balance formatted as money
66    */
67   @Override
68   public String toString( )
69   {
70     return "balance is " + MONEY.format( balance );
71   }
72 }
```

EXAMPLE 10.11   *BankAccount* **Class, Version 3**

Example 10.12 shows Version 5 of the *CheckingAccount* class, which inherits from the *BankAccount* class in Example 10.11 that declares the *balance* as *protected*. The *CheckingAccount* class now inherits *balance*, and our *CheckingAccount* methods can access the *balance* variable directly. Nevertheless, in the default and overloaded constructors, we still call the superclass constructor to set the value of *balance* (lines 16 and 28). Otherwise, to avoid setting *balance* to an invalid initial value, we would need to know the validation rules for *balance* in *BankAccount* and unnecessarily duplicate that code.

Also, in the *toString* method (lines 63–72), we call the *toString* method of the *BankAccount* class. Again, we do this to be consistent with the superclass functionality, which formats the balance, and to avoid duplicating code.

In the *applyMonthlyFee* method (lines 32–41), however, we access *balance* directly. For this checking account, our bank will charge the monthly fee even if it results in a negative balance for the account, so we subtract *monthlyFee* from *balance*, which allows the balance to be negative. Notice that we change the value of *balance* directly instead of calling the *withdraw* method, which does not allow the balance to become negative.

```
 1 /* CheckingAccount class, version 5
 2    Anderson, Franceschi
 3 */
 4
 5 public class CheckingAccount extends BankAccount
 6 {
 7    public final double DEFAULT_FEE = 5.00;
 8    private double monthlyFee;
 9
10    /** default constructor
11     *    explicitly calls the BankAccount default constructor
12     *    set monthlyFee to default value
13     */
14    public CheckingAccount( )
15    {
16      super( );   // call BankAccount constructor
17      monthlyFee = DEFAULT_FEE;
18    }
19
20    /** overloaded constructor
21     *   calls BankAccount overloaded constructor
22     *   @param balance     starting balance
23     *   @param monthlyFee starting monthly fee
24     */
25    public CheckingAccount( double balance,
26                              double monthlyFee )
27    {
28      super( balance );   // call BankAccount constructor
29      setMonthlyFee( monthlyFee );
30    }
31
32    /** applyMonthlyFee method
33     *    charges the monthly fee to the account
34     *    @return a reference to this object
35     */
36    public CheckingAccount applyMonthlyFee( )
37    {
```

```
38       balance -= monthlyFee;
39
40       return this;
41    }
42
43    /** accessor method for monthlyFee
44     *  @return  monthlyFee
45     */
46    public double getMonthlyFee( )
47    {
48      return monthlyFee;
49    }
50
51    /** mutator method for monthlyFee
52     *  @param monthlyFee new value for monthlyFee
53     *  @return a reference to this object
54     */
55    public CheckingAccount setMonthlyFee( double monthlyFee )
56    {
57      if ( monthlyFee >= 0.0 )
58        this.monthlyFee = monthlyFee;
59
60      return this;
61    }
62
63    /* toString method
64     *  @return String containing formatted balance and monthlyFee
65     *     invokes superclass toString to format balance
66     */
67    @Override
68    public String toString( )
69    {
70      return super.toString( )
71            + "; monthly fee is " + MONEY.format( monthlyFee );
72    }
73 }
```

EXAMPLE 10.12   *CheckingAccount Class, Version 5*

Example 10.13 shows Version 5 of the *CheckingAccountClient* class. In this class, we again instantiate a *CheckingAccount* object with an initial balance of $100.00 and a monthly fee of $7.50 (line 9). We then call *withdraw* (line 12), so that the resulting balance is less than the monthly fee. Next we call the *applyMonthlyFee* method (line 16). We then check whether the balance is negative (line 17). If so, we output a warning message that the account is overdrawn (line 18). In any case, we output the new balance (line 19). The output of Example 10.13 is shown in Figure 10.8.

```
1 /*   CheckingAccount Client, Version 5
2      Anderson, Franceschi
3 */
4
5 public class CheckingAccountClient
6 {
7  public static void main( String [ ] args )
8  {
9     CheckingAccount c5 = new CheckingAccount( 100.00, 7.50 );
10    System.out.println( "New checking account:\n" + c5 );
11
12    c5.withdraw( 95 );
13    System.out.println( "\nAfter withdrawing $95:\n" + c5 );
14
15    System.out.println( "\nApplying the monthly fee:" );
16    c5.applyMonthlyFee( );
17    if ( c5.getBalance( ) < 0.0 )
18        System.out.println( "Warning: account is overdrawn!" );
19    System.out.println( c5 );
20 }
21 }
```

EXAMPLE 10.13   *CheckingAccountClient* **Class, Version 5**

Table 10.5 compiles all the inheritance rules we have discussed.

```
New checking account:
balance is $100.00; monthly fee is $7.50

After withdrawing $95:
balance is $5.00; monthly fee is $7.50

Applying the monthly fee:
Warning: account is overdrawn!
balance is -$2.50; monthly fee is $7.50
```

Figure 10.8

Output from *Checking-AccountClient*, Version 5

TABLE 10.5   Inheritance Rules

Superclass Members	Inherited by Subclass?	Directly Accessible by Subclass?	Directly Accessible by Client of Subclass?
public fields	yes	yes, by using field name	yes
public methods	yes	yes, by calling method from other subclass methods	yes, by calling method using a subclass object reference

(continued)

TABLE 10.5 *(continued)*

Superclass Members	Inherited by Subclass?	Directly Accessible by Subclass?	Directly Accessible by Client of Subclass?
protected fields	yes	yes, by using field name	no, must use accessors and mutators
protected methods	yes	yes, by calling method from subclass methods	no
private fields	no	no, must use accessors and mutators	no, must use accessors and mutators
private methods	no	no	no
constructors	no	yes, using `super( arg list )` in a subclass constructor	no
public or *protected* inherited methods that have been overridden in the subclass	no	yes, using `super.methodName ( arg list )`	no

Skill Practice
with these end-of-chapter questions

10.10.2   Reading and Understanding Code

Questions 12, 13, 14, 15, 16, 17, 18, 19, 20

CODE IN ACTION

Within the online resources, you will find a movie with a step-by-step illustration of the use of inheritance in a program. Click on the link to start the movie.

10.4 Programming Activity 1: Using Inheritance

For this Programming Activity, you will create the *SavingsAccount* class, which inherits directly from the *BankAccount* class. The *SavingsAccount* class is similar to the *CheckingAccount* class in that both classes inherit from *BankAccount*. Figure 10.9 shows the resulting hierarchy.

The *SavingsAccount* class inherits from the version of the *BankAccount* class in which the *balance* is declared to be *private*. The *SavingsAccount* subclass adds an annual *interestRate* instance variable, as well as supporting methods to access, change, and apply the interest rate to the account balance.

Instructions

Copy the source files in the Programming Activity 1 folder for this chapter to a folder on your computer. Load the *SavingsAccount.java* source file and search for five asterisks in a row (*****). This will position you to the six locations in the file where you will add code to complete the *SavingsAccount* class. The *SavingsAccount. java* file is shown in Example 10.14.

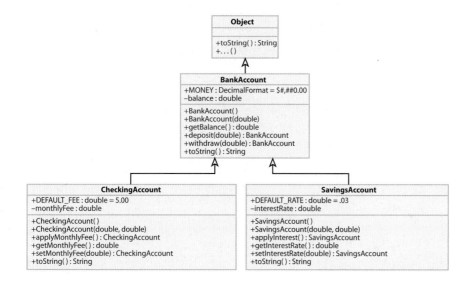

Figure 10.9

Bank Account Hierarchy

```
1 /* SavingsAccount class
2  *  Anderson, Franceschi
3  */
4
5 import java.text.DecimalFormat;
6
```

```
 7 // 1. ***** indicate that SavingsAccount inherits
 8 //          from BankAccount
 9 public class SavingsAccount
10 {
11    public final double DEFAULT_RATE = .03;
12    // 2. ****** define the private interestRate instance variable
13    // interestRate, a double, represents an annual rate
14
15
16    // 3 ***** write the default constructor
17    /** default constructor
18     *   explicitly calls the BankAccount default constructor
19     *   set interestRate to default value DEFAULT_RATE
20     *   print a message to System.out indicating that the
21     *      constructor is called
22     */
23
24
25    // 4 ***** write the overloaded constructor
26    /** overloaded constructor
27     *   explicitly calls BankAccount overloaded constructor
28     *   call setInterestRate method, passing interestRate
29     *   print a message to System.out indicating that
30     *      constructor is called
31     * @param  balance      starting balance
32     * @param  interestRate starting interest rate
33     */
34
35
36    // 5 ****** write this method:
37    /** applyInterest method, no parameters.
38     *   call the deposit method, passing a month's worth of interest
39     *   remember that the interestRate instance variable is annual rate
40     *
41     *   @return a reference to this object
42     */
43
44
45    /** accessor method for interestRate
46     * @return  interestRate
47     */
48    public double getInterestRate( )
49    {
50      return interestRate;
51    }
```

```
52
53    /** mutator method for interestRate
54     *   @param  interestRate new value for interestRate
55     *            interestRate must be >= 0.0
56     *               if not, do not change the value
57     *            stores interestRate as input value / 100
58     *               that is, 3.5 is stored as .035
59     *   @return  a reference to this object
60     */
61    public SavingsAccount setInterestRate( double interestRate )
62    {
63      if ( interestRate >= 0.0 )
64         this.interestRate = interestRate / 100;
65
66      return this;
67    }
68
69    // 6 *****  write this method
70    /* toString method
71     *   @return a String containing formatted balance and interestRate
72     *       invokes superclass toString to format balance
73     *       formats interestRate as percent using a DecimalFormat object
74     *       To create a DecimalFormat object for formatting percentages
75     *       use this pattern in the constructor: "0.00%"
76     */
77
78 }
```

EXAMPLE 10.14   *SavingsAccount.java*

When you have completed the six tasks, load, compile, and run the Teller application (*Teller.java*), which you will use to test your *SavingsAccount* class. When the Teller application begins, you will be prompted with a dialog box for a starting balance. If you press "Enter" or the "OK" button without entering a balance, the Teller application will use the default constructor to instantiate a *SavingsAccount* object. If you enter a starting balance, the Teller application will prompt you for an interest rate and will instantiate a *SavingsAccount* object using the overloaded constructor. Once the *SavingsAccount* object has been instantiated, the Teller application will open the window shown in Figure 10.10, which provides buttons for calling the *SavingsAccount* methods to test your code.

Below the buttons is a ledger that displays the current state of the savings account. As you click on the various buttons, the ledger will display the operation performed and the values of the balance and the interest rate when that operation is complete.

The operations performed by each button are already coded for you and are the following:

- *Change* interest rate—prompts for a new interest rate and calls your *setInterestRate* method

- *Apply interest*—calls your *applyInterest* method

- *Deposit*—prompts for the deposit amount and calls the *deposit* method inherited from *BankAccount*

- *Withdraw*—prompts for the withdrawal amount and calls the *withdraw* method inherited from *BankAccount*

- *Display account information*—calls your *toString* method and displays the result in a dialog box

- *Exit*—exits the program

Figure 10.11 shows the Teller window after several operations have been performed.

Figure 10.10

The Teller
Window

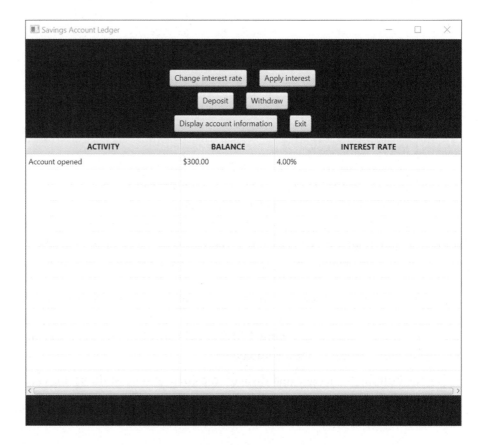

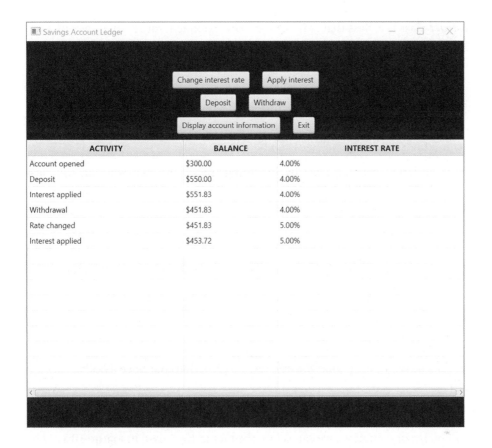

Figure 10.11

Sample Teller
Window After
Performing
Several
Operations

DISCUSSION QUESTIONS

1. **Explain why the Teller application can call the *withdraw* and *deposit* methods using a *SavingsAccount* object reference, even though you did not define these methods in the *SavingsAccount* class.**

2. **Explain why your *applyInterest* method in the *SavingsAccount* class needs to call the *deposit* method of the *BankAccount* class.**

10.5   *Abstract* Classes and Methods

In our Bank Account hierarchy, we could instantiate *BankAccount* objects, *Checking-Account* objects, and *SavingsAccount* objects. In some situations, however, we will design a class hierarchy where one or more classes at the top of the hierarchy are not intended to be instantiated. Rather, they typically specify patterns for methods that subclasses in the hierarchy must implement. Often, the superclasses do not implement these methods. In these situations, we do not intend that these superclasses will be used to instantiate objects, and we define the superclasses as ***abstract***.

An **abstract class** is a class that is intended to be extended, rather than instantiated. Usually, an *abstract* class contains at least one **abstract method**, that is, a method that specifies an API that subclasses should implement, but does not provide an implementation for the method.

An *abstract* class cannot be used to instantiate objects. An *abstract* class can be extended, however, so that its subclasses can complete the implementation of the *abstract* methods and the subclasses can be instantiated.

A class is declared to be *abstract* by including the *abstract* keyword in the class header, as shown in the following syntax:

`accessModifier abstract class ClassName`

An *abstract* method is defined by including the *abstract* keyword in the method header and by using a semicolon to indicate that there is no code for the method, as shown in the following syntax:

`accessModifier abstract returnType methodName( argument list );`

Note that we do not include opening and closing curly braces for the method body—just a semicolon to indicate that the *abstract* method does not have a body.

Java imposes a few restrictions on *abstract* methods: constructors cannot be defined as *abstract*; and an *abstract* method cannot be declared as *private* or *static*.

For example, to draw figures, we can set up the hierarchy shown in Figure 10.12. The root superclass under *Object* is the *abstract Figure* class, and we derive two **concrete**

Figure 10.12

The *Figure*
Hierarchy

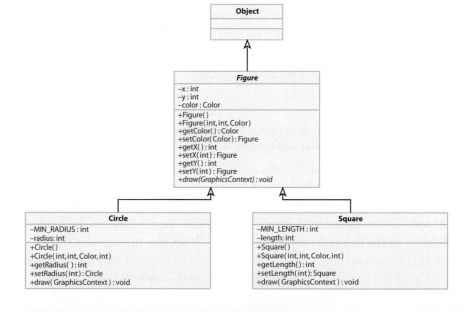

(non-*abstract*) subclasses: *Circle* and *Square*. In the UML diagram, the name of the *Figure* class is set in italics to indicate that it is an *abstract* class.

All figures will have an (*x*, *y*) coordinate and a color, so the *Figure* class defines three fields: two *ints*, *x* and *y*, and a *Color* object named *color*.

We want all classes in the hierarchy to provide a *draw* method to render the figure; however, the *Figure* class has nothing but a point to draw, so its *draw* method has nothing to do. Thus, we do not provide an implementation of the *draw* method in the *Figure* class; instead, we define the *draw* method as an *abstract* method. Like the *abstract* class name, we indicate that the *draw* method is *abstract* by setting it in italics in the UML.

Let's look at the code for the *Figure* hierarchy in detail. Example 10.15 shows the *abstract Figure* class. We define the class as *abstract* in the class header (line 7). The constructors (lines 13–22 and lines 24–34) initialize the *x* and *y* values and instantiate the *Color* object that all figures will have in common. The *Figure* class also provides accessor and mutator methods for its instance variables. The *abstract draw* method (lines 94–97) provides the API for the *draw* method, but no implementation—just a semicolon. The *Circle* and *Square* subclasses of the *Figure* class will provide appropriate implementations of the *draw* method.

```
 1 /** abstract Figure superclass for drawing shapes
 2 *    Anderson, Franceschi
 3 */
 4 import javafx.scene.canvas.GraphicsContext;
 5 import javafx.scene.paint.Color;
 6
 7 public abstract class Figure
 8 {
 9    private int x;
10    private int y;
11    private Color color;
12
13    /** default constructor
14     *    sets x and y to 0
15     *    sets color to black
16     */
17    public Figure( )
18    {
19       x = 0;
20       y = 0;
21       color = Color.BLACK;
22    }
23
```

```
24   /** overloaded constructor
25    *   @param  x      starting x coordinate for figure
26    *   @param  y      starting y coordinate for figure
27    *   @param  color  figure color
28    */
29   public Figure( int x, int y, Color color )
30   {
31     this.x = x;
32     this.y = y;
33     this.color = color;
34   }
35
36   /** accessor method for color
37    *   @return current figure color
38    */
39   public Color getColor( )
40   {
41
42     return color;
43   }
44
45   /** mutator method for color
46    *   @param color  new color for figure
47    *   @return a reference  to this object
48    */
49   public Figure setColor( Color color )
50   {
51     this.color = color;
52
53     return this;
54   }
55
56   /** accessor method for x
57    *   @return current x value
58    */
59   public int getX( )
60   {
61     return x;
62   }
63
64   /** mutator method for x
65    *   @param x  new value for x
66    *   @return a reference to this object
67    */
68   public Figure setX( int x )
69   {
70     this.x = x;
```

```
71
72     return this;
73   }
74
75   /** accessor method for y
76    *   @return current y value
77    */
78   public int getY( )
79   {
80     return y;
81   }
82
83   /** mutator method for y
84    *   @param y new y value
85    *   @return a reference to this object
86    */
87   public Figure setY( int y )
88   {
89     this.y = y;
90
91     return this;
92   }
93
94   /** abstract draw method
95    *   @param gc GraphicsContext for drawing figure
96    */
97   public abstract void draw( GraphicsContext gc );
98 }
```

EXAMPLE 10.15   The *abstract Figure* Class

When a subclass inherits from an *abstract* class, it can provide implementations for any, all, or none of the *abstract* methods. If the subclass does not completely implement all the *abstract* methods of the superclass, then the subclass must also be declared *abstract*. If, however, the subclass implements all the *abstract* methods in the superclass, and the subclass is not declared *abstract*, then the class is not *abstract* and we can instantiate objects of that subclass.

Example 10.16 shows the *Circle* class, which inherits from the *Figure* class and adds a *radius* instance variable, as well as a constant for the minimum radius. In the overloaded constructor, we pass the *x, y,* and *color* parameters to the constructor of the *Figure* class (line 35). On lines 61–71, the *Circle* class implements the *draw* method. We get the (*x, y*) coordinate and the color for the circle by calling the accessor methods of the *Figure* class because the *x, y,* and *color* instance variables are declared *private*.

```
1 /* Circle class
2  *  inherits from abstract Figure class
```

COMMON ERROR TRAP
Do not include opening and closing curly braces in the definition of an *abstract* method. Including them would mean that the method is implemented, but does nothing. Instead, indicate an unimplemented method by using only a semicolon.

COMMON ERROR TRAP
Attempting to instantiate an object of an *abstract* class will generate the following compiler error:
`className is abstract; cannot be instantiated` where *className* is the name of the *abstract* class.

```
 3 *  Anderson, Franceschi
 4 */
 5
 6 import javafx.scene.canvas.GraphicsContext;
 7 import javafx.scene.paint.Color;
 8
 9 public class Circle extends Figure
10 {
11    private final int MIN_RADIUS = 15;
12    private int radius;
13
14    /** default constructor
15     *   calls default constructor of Figure class
16     *   sets radius to minimum value
17     */
18    public Circle( )
19    {
20       super( );
21       radius = MIN_RADIUS;
22    }
23
24    /** overloaded constructor
25     *   sends x, y, color parameters to Figure constructor
26     *   sends radius to setRadius method
27     *   @param x        starting x coordinate
28     *   @param y        starting y coordinate
29     *   @param color  color for circle
30     *   @param radius radius of circle
31     */
32    public Circle( int x, int y, Color color,
33                              int radius )
34    {
35       super( x, y, color );
36       setRadius( radius );
37    }
38
39    /** mutator method for radius
40     *   @param radius  new value for radius
41     *   @return a reference to this object
42     */
43    public Circle setRadius( int radius )
44    {
45       if ( radius > MIN_RADIUS )
46          this.radius = radius;
47       else
48          this.radius = MIN_RADIUS;
49
50       return this;
```

```
51     }
52
53     /** accessor method for radius
54      *   @return radius
55      */
56     public int getRadius( )
57     {
58        return radius;
59     }
60
61     /** draw method
62      *  sets color and draws a circle
63      *  @param gc  GraphicsContext for drawing the circle
64      */
65     @Override
66     public void draw( GraphicsContext gc )
67     {
68        gc.setFill( getColor( ) );
69        gc.fillOval ( getX( ), getY( ),
70                          radius * 2, radius * 2 );
71     }
72 }
```

EXAMPLE 10.16   The *Circle* Class

Similarly, Example 10.17 shows the *Square* class, which also inherits from the *Figure* class. The *Square* class adds a *length* instance variable, as well as a constant for the minimum length, and uses code similar to the *Circle* class to call the constructors of the *Figure* class (lines 20 and 35) and to implement its own version of the *draw* method (lines 61–71).

```
 1 /* Square class
 2 *  inherits from abstract Figure class
 3 *  Anderson, Franceschi
 4 */
 5
 6 import javafx.scene.canvas.GraphicsContext;
 7 import javafx.scene.paint.Color;
 8
 9 public class Square extends Figure
10 {
11     private final int MIN_LENGTH = 10;
12     private int length;
13
14     /** default constructor
15      *    calls default constructor of Figure class
16      *    sets length to minimum value
17      */
```

```
18    public Square( )
19    {
20      super( );
21      length = MIN_LENGTH;
22    }
23
24    /** overloaded constructor
25     *   sends x, y, and color parameters to Figure constructor
26     *   sends length to setLength method
27     *   @param x       starting x coordinate
28     *   @param y       starting y coordinate
29     *   @param color  color for square
30     *   @param length length of square
31     */
32    public Square( int x, int y, Color color,
33                      int length )
34    {
35      super( x, y, color );
36      setLength( length );
37    }
38
39    /** mutator method for length
40     *   @param length  new value for length
41     *   @return a reference to this object
42     */
43    public Square setLength( int length )
44    {
45      if ( length > MIN_LENGTH )
46        this.length = length;
47      else
48        this.length = MIN_LENGTH;
49
50      return this;
51    }
52
53    /** accessor method for length
54     *   @return length
55     */
56    public int getLength( )
57    {
58      return length;
59    }
60
61    /** draw method
62     *   sets color and draws a square
63     *   @param gc  GraphicsContext for drawing the square
64     */
```

```
65    @Override
66    public void draw( GraphicsContext gc )
67    {
68       gc.setFill( getColor( ) );
69       gc.fillRect( getX( ), getY( ),
70                       length, length );
71    }
72 }
```

EXAMPLE 10.17   The *Square* Class

Because we want to instantiate *Circle* and *Square* objects, we do not declare these classes *abstract* and they are forced to implement the *draw* method. Example 10.18 shows a graphical application, *TrafficLight*, which paints a traffic light, shown in Figure 10.13. On lines 13 and 14, we declare two *ArrayLists*, one to hold *Circle* objects and one to hold *Square* objects. In the *start* method, we instantiate both *ArrayLists* and add three *Square* objects to *squaresList* and three *Circle* objects to *circlesList* (lines 26–40). Then, we create the traffic light by calling the *draw* methods for all the *Squares* in the *squaresList* (lines 42–43), then calling the *draw* method for all the *Circles* in the *circlesList* (lines 45–46).

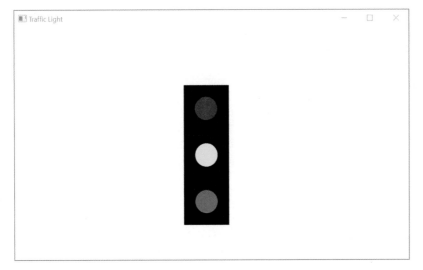

Figure 10.13

The *TrafficLight* Application

```
1 /* Figure Hierarchy Client
2  * Anderson, Franceschi
3  */
4 import javafx.application.Application;
5 import javafx.scene.canvas.GraphicsContext;
6 import javafx.scene.paint.Color;
7 import javafx.stage.Stage;
8
9 import java.util.ArrayList;
10
```

```
11 public class TrafficLight extends Application
12 {
13    private ArrayList<Square> squaresList;
14    private ArrayList<Circle> circlesList;
15
16    @Override
17    public void start( Stage stage )
18    {
19      GraphicsContext gc = JIGraphicsUtility.setUpGraphics(
20                          stage, "Traffic Light", 700, 400 );
21
22      final int SQUARE_SIZE = 80, CIRCLE_RADIUS = 20;
23      final int SQUARE_X = 300, CIRCLE_X = SQUARE_X + 20;
24      final int SQUARE_Y = 100, CIRCLE_Y = SQUARE_Y + 20;
25
26      squaresList = new ArrayList<Square>( );
27      squaresList.add( new Square( SQUARE_X, SQUARE_Y,
28                                Color.BLACK, SQUARE_SIZE ) );
29      squaresList.add( new Square( SQUARE_X, SQUARE_Y + SQUARE_SIZE,
30                                Color.BLACK, SQUARE_SIZE ) );
31      squaresList.add( new Square( SQUARE_X, SQUARE_Y + ( SQUARE_SIZE * 2 ),
32                                Color.BLACK, SQUARE_SIZE ) );
33
34      circlesList = new ArrayList<Circle>( );
35      circlesList.add( new Circle( CIRCLE_X, CIRCLE_Y,
36                                Color.RED, CIRCLE_RADIUS ) );
37      circlesList.add( new Circle( CIRCLE_X, CIRCLE_Y + SQUARE_SIZE,
38                                Color.YELLOW, CIRCLE_RADIUS ) );
39      circlesList.add( new Circle( CIRCLE_X, CIRCLE_Y + ( SQUARE_SIZE * 2 ),
40                                Color.GREEN, CIRCLE_RADIUS ) );
41
42      for ( Square s : squaresList )
43        s.draw( gc );
44
45      for ( Circle c : circlesList )
46        c.draw( gc );
47    }
48
49    public static void main( String [ ] args )
50    {
51      launch( args );
52    }
53 }
```

EXAMPLE 10.18   The *TrafficLight* Application

Java's restrictions on declaring and using *abstract* classes and methods are summarized in Table 10.6.

TABLE 10.6 Restrictions for *abstract* Classes and *abstract* Methods Within Classes

abstract classes	• Classes must be declared *abstract* if the class contains any *abstract* methods.
	• *abstract* classes can be extended.
	• *abstract* classes cannot be used to instantiate objects.
abstract methods within classes	• *abstract* methods cannot be declared within a non-*abstract* class.
	• An *abstract* method must consist of a method header followed by a semicolon.
	• *abstract* methods cannot be declared as *private* or *static*.
	• A constructor cannot be declared *abstract*.

10.6 Polymorphism

An important concept in inheritance is that an object of a class is also an object of any of its superclasses. That concept, "is a", is the basis for an important OOP feature, called **polymorphism**, which simplifies the processing of various objects in the same class hierarchy. The word *polymorphism*, which is derived from the word fragment *poly* and the word *morpho* in the Greek language, literally means "multiple forms."

Polymorphism allows us to use the same method call for any object in the hierarchy. We make the method call using an object reference of the superclass. At run time, the JVM determines to which class in the hierarchy the object actually belongs and calls the version of the method implemented for that class.

To use polymorphism in our application, the following conditions must be true:

- The classes are in the same hierarchy.
- The subclasses override the same method.
- A subclass object reference is assigned to a superclass object reference (that is, a subclass object is referenced by a superclass reference).
- The superclass object reference is used to call the method.

For example, we can take advantage of polymorphism in our traffic light graphical application by calling the *draw* method for either a *Circle* or *Square* object using a *Figure* object reference. Although we cannot instantiate an object from an *abstract* class, Java allows us to define object references of an *abstract* class.

Example 10.19 shows the rewritten traffic light graphical application. Instead of using separate *ArrayLists* for *Circle* and *Square* objects, we can declare and instantiate only one *ArrayList* of *Figure* references (lines 13 and 25). As each *Circle* and

Square object is instantiated, we add its object reference to the *ArrayList* of *Figure* references (lines 27–39).

This greatly simplifies drawing the traffic light because we step through just one *ArrayList*, *figuresList*, calling the *draw* method for each element (lines 41–42). For the method call, it doesn't matter whether the object reference in *figuresList* is a *Circle* or *Square* reference. We just call the *draw* method using that reference. At run time, the JVM determines whether the object is a *Circle* or a *Square* and calls the appropriate *draw* method for the object type. Because the *ArrayList* is composed of *Figure* references, any element can be either a *Circle* or a *Square*—because a *Circle* and a *Square* are both *Figures*. The output of this application is identical to that of Example 10.18, as shown in Figure 10.13.

```
 1 /* Figure hierarchy Client
 2  * Anderson, Franceschi
 3  */
 4 import javafx.application.Application;
 5 import javafx.scene.canvas.GraphicsContext;
 6 import javafx.scene.paint.Color;
 7 import javafx.stage.Stage;
 8
 9 import java.util.ArrayList;
10
11 public class TrafficLightPolymorphism extends Application
12 {
13     private ArrayList<Figure> figuresList;
14
15     @Override
16     public void start( Stage stage )
17     {
18       GraphicsContext gc = JIGraphicsUtility.setUpGraphics(
19                     stage, "Traffic Light", 700, 400 );
20
21       final int SQUARE_SIZE = 80, CIRCLE_RADIUS = 20;
22       final int SQUARE_X = 300, CIRCLE_X = SQUARE_X + 20;
23       final int SQUARE_Y = 100, CIRCLE_Y = SQUARE_Y + 20;
24
25       figuresList = new ArrayList<Figure>( );
26
27       figuresList.add( new Square( SQUARE_X, SQUARE_Y,
28                         Color.BLACK, SQUARE_SIZE ) );
29       figuresList.add( new Square( SQUARE_X, SQUARE_Y + SQUARE_SIZE,
30                         Color.BLACK, SQUARE_SIZE ) );
31       figuresList.add( new Square( SQUARE_X, SQUARE_Y + ( SQUARE_SIZE * 2 ),
32                         Color.BLACK, SQUARE_SIZE ) );
33
34       figuresList.add( new Circle( CIRCLE_X, CIRCLE_Y,
35                         Color.RED, CIRCLE_RADIUS ) );
```

```
36    figuresList.add( new Circle( CIRCLE_X, CIRCLE_Y + SQUARE_SIZE,
37                                 Color.YELLOW, CIRCLE_RADIUS ) );
38    figuresList.add( new Circle( CIRCLE_X, CIRCLE_Y + ( SQUARE_SIZE * 2 ),
39                                 Color.GREEN, CIRCLE_RADIUS ) );
40
41    for ( Figure f : figuresList )
42        f.draw( gc );
43
44    }
45
46    public static void main( String [ ] args )
47    {
48      launch( args );
49    }
50 }
```

EXAMPLE 10.19   Traffic Light Application Using Polymorphism

Skill Practice
with these end-of-chapter questions

10.10.1   Multiple Choice Exercises

Questions 7, 10, 11

10.10.4   Identifying Errors in Code

Question 31

10.10.5   Debugging Area

Questions 33, 34, 35

10.7   Programming Activity 2: Using Polymorphism

In this Programming Activity, you will complete the implementation of the Tortoise and the Hare race. The Tortoise runs a slow and steady race, while the Hare runs in spurts with rests in between. Figure 10.14 shows a sample run of the race. In this figure, we show only one tortoise and one hare; however, using polymorphism we can easily run the race with any number and combination of tortoises and hares.

The class hierarchy for this Programming Activity is shown in Figure 10.15.

The code for the *Racer* class, which is the superclass of the *Tortoise* and *Hare* classes, is shown in Example 10.20. The *Racer* class has three instance variables

Figure 10.14

A Sample Run of the Tortoise and the Hare Race

Figure 10.15

Racer Hierarchy

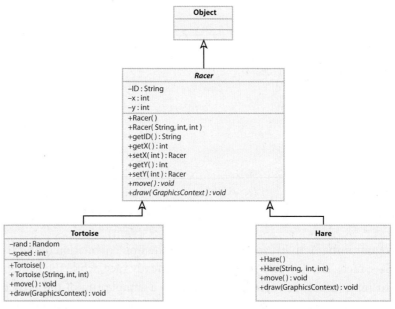

(lines 10–12): a *String ID*, which identifies the type of racer; and *x* and *y* positions, both of which are *ints*. The class has the usual constructors, as well as accessor and mutator methods for the *x* and *y* positions and ID. These instance variables and methods are common to all racers, so we define them in the *Racer* class. Individual racers, however, will differ in the way they move and in the way they are drawn.

Thus, in line 8, we declare the *Racer* class to be *abstract*, and in lines 78–85, we define two *abstract* methods, *move* and *draw*. Classes that inherit from the *Racer* class will need to provide implementations of these two methods (or be declared *abstract* as well).

```java
 1 /**   Racer class
 2  *     Abstract class intended for racer hierarchy
 3  *     Anderson, Franceschi
 4  */
 5
 6 import javafx.scene.canvas.GraphicsContext;
 7
 8 public abstract class Racer
 9 {
10   private String ID;   // racer ID
11   private int x;       // x position
12   private int y;       // y position
13
14   /** default constructor
15    *    Sets ID to blank
16    */
17   public Racer( )
18   {
19     ID = "";
20   }
21
22   /** constructor
23    *    @param ID   racer ID
24    *    @param x    x position
25    *    @param y    y position
26    */
27   public Racer( String ID, int x, int y )
28   {
29     this.ID = ID;
30     this.x = x;
31     this.y = y;
32   }
33
34   /** accessor for ID
35    *    @return   ID
36    */
37   public String getID( )
38   {
39     return ID;
40   }
41
42   /** accessor for x
```

```
43    *    @return   current x value
44    */
45    public int getX( )
46    {
47      return x;
48    }
49
50    /** accessor for y
51    *    @return   current y value
52    */
53    public int getY( )
54    {
55      return y;
56    }
57
58    /** mutator for x
59    *    @param  x new value for x
60    *    @return a reference to this object
61    */
62    public Racer setX( int x )
63    {
64      this.x = x;
65      return this;
66    }
67
68    /** mutator for y
69    *    @param  y new value for y
70    *    @return a reference to this object
71    */
72    public Racer setY( int y )
73    {
74      this.y = y;
75      return this;
76    }
77
78    /** abstract method for Racer's move
79    */
80    public abstract void move( );
81
82    /** abstract method for drawing Racer
83    *    @param   gc    GraphicsContext
84    */
85    public abstract void draw( GraphicsContext gc );
86 }
```

EXAMPLE 10.20   **The *abstract Racer* Class**

The *Tortoise* and *Hare* classes inherit from the *Racer* class. Their only job is to pass constructor arguments to the *Racer* class and implement the *draw* and *move* methods. For this Programming Activity, we have provided the *Tortoise* and *Hare* classes with the *draw* and *move* methods already written.

Your job is to add *Tortoise* and *Hare* objects to an *ArrayList* of *Racer* objects, as specified by the user. Then you will add code to run the race by stepping through the *ArrayList*, calling *move* and *draw* for each *Racer* object.

Instructions

Copy the source files in the Programming Activity folder for this chapter to a folder on your computer. Open the *PolymorphismController.java* file.

1. Write the code to determine which racers will run the race. Search for five asterisks in a row (*****). This will position you inside the *prepareToRace* method.

```
/** prepareToRace method
 *    @param input       racer type entered by the user
 *                       racer types are 't' or 'T' for Tortoise,
 *                                        'h' or 'H' for Hare
 */
private void prepareToRace( char input )
{
   final int START_LINE = 60;     // x position of start of race
   final int RACER_SPACE = 50;    // spacing between racers

   /** 1. ***** Student writes this switch statement
    *  input parameter contains the racer type
    *      entered by the user
    *  If input is 'T' or 't',
    *     add a Tortoise object to the ArrayList named racerList,
    *           which is an instance variable of this class
    *  The API of the Tortoise constructor is:
    *          Tortoise( String ID, int x, int y )
    *    a sample call to the constructor is
    *          new Tortoise( "Tortoise", START_LINE, yPos )
    *          where START_LINE is a constant local variable
    *            representing the starting x position for the race
    *          and yPos is an instance variable representing
    *            the racer's y position
    *
    *  If input is 'H' or 'h',
    *     add a Hare object to the ArrayList named racerList
    *  The API of the Hare constructor is:
```

```
 *           Hare( String ID, int x, int y )
 *        a sample call to the constructor is
 *           new Hare( "Hare", START_LINE, yPos )
 *           where START_LINE is a constant local variable
 *             representing the starting x position for the race
 *           and yPos is an instance variable representing
 *               the racer's y position
 *
 *   After adding a racer to the ArrayList racerList,
 *           increment yPos by the value of
 *           the constant local variable RACER_SPACE
 *
 *   if input is anything other than 'T', 't',
 *           'H' or 'h', do nothing
 */
// write your switch statement here

/** end of student code, part 1 */

} // end prepareToRace
```

2. Next, write the code to display the racers at the starting position. Again, search for five asterisks (*****). This will position you inside the *getReady* method, which is called whenever a new *Racer* is added. The method draws the finish line and displays the racers at the starting position. The code to display the finish line is already written. For this task, you will write code to loop through the *ArrayList* of *Racers*, calling the *draw* method for each racer. The portion of the *getReady* method where you will add your code is shown below.

```
/** getReady method
 *   @param gc   GraphicsContext context
 *   draws the finish line and draws the racers
 */
protected void getReady( GraphicsContext gc )
{
  // draw the finish line
  finishX = (int) canvas.getWidth( ) - 20;
  gc.setStroke( Color.BLUE );
  gc.strokeLine( finishX, 0, finishX, canvas.getHeight( ) );

  // display racers before race begins
  /* 2. ***** student writes this code
   *   loop through instance variable ArrayList racerList,
   *     which contains Racer object references,
   *     calling draw for each element. (Do not call move!)
   *   The API for draw is:
   *       void draw( GraphicsContext gc )
```

```
*          where gc is the graphics context
*          passed to this getReady method
*/
// student code goes here

/** end of student code, part 2 */

} // end getReady
```

3. Finally, write the code to run the race. Again, search for five asterisks (*****); this will position you inside the *runRace* method, which is called when the user presses the "Start Race" button. Task 3 is similar to task 2 in that you will loop through the *ArrayList* of *Racers*. In this task, however, you will call both the *move* and *draw* methods. The portion of the *runRace* method where you will add your code is shown below.

```
/** runRace method
 *  @param gc    GraphicsContext context
 *  moves and draws racers
 */
public void runRace( GraphicsContext gc )
{
  gc.setStroke( Color.BLUE );
  gc.strokeLine( finishX, 0, finishX, canvas.getHeight( ) );

  /* 3. ***** student writes this code
   *      loop through instance variable ArrayList racerList,
   *      which contains Racer object references,
   *      calling move, then draw for each element
   *   The API for move is:
   *          void move( )
   *   The API for draw is:
   *          void draw( GraphicsContext gc )
   *             where gc is the GraphicsContext object
   *             passed to this runRace method
   */
  // student code goes here

  /** end of student code, part 3 */

} // end runRace
```

When you have finished writing the code, compile the source code and run the *PolymorphismApplication* file. Try several runs of the race with a different number of racers and with a different combination of *Tortoises* and *Hares*. Figure 10.16 shows the race with four *Tortoises* and three *Hares*.

Figure 10.16

Another Run of the Race

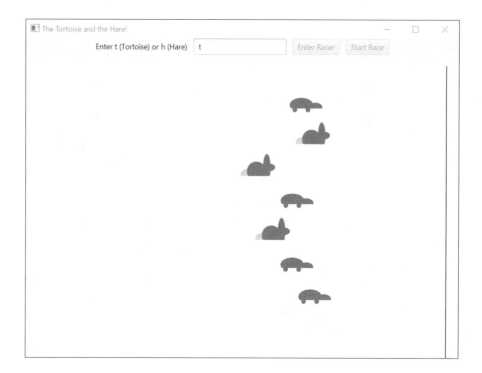

DISCUSSION QUESTIONS **?**

1. **Explain how polymorphism simplifies this application.**

2. **If you wanted to add another racer, for example, an aardvark, explain what code you would need to write and what existing code, if any, you would need to change.**

10.8   Interfaces

In Java, a class can inherit directly from only one class; that is, a class can *extend* only one class. To allow a class to inherit behavior from multiple sources, Java provides the **interface**. Interfaces are often used to provide a specification for performing common tasks. They can also be used to promote code reusability.

An interface typically specifies behavior that a class will *implement*.

Interface members can be any of the following:

- constants
- methods
- classes
- other interfaces

To define an interface, we use the following syntax:

```
accessModifier interface InterfaceName
{
    // body of interface
}
```

Like classes, the Java convention is to name interfaces starting with a capital letter and capitalizing internal words.

All interfaces are *abstract*; thus, they cannot be instantiated. The *abstract* keyword, however, is usually omitted from the interface definition. If the interface's access modifier is *public*, its members are implicitly *public* as well.

Any field defined in a *public* interface is implicitly *public, static,* and *final.* These keywords can be specified, but typically we omit them because they are implicit. When we define a constant in the interface, we must also assign a value to that field. Note that because all fields are *static*, interfaces cannot have instance variables.

We can define various types of methods in interfaces:

- *public abstract* methods
- *public default* methods
- *public* or *private static* methods
- *private* methods

To define an *abstract* method, we provide only the method header followed by a semicolon. We do not provide a body for the method.

For the other method types, we do provide a method body; that is, *default, static,* and *private* methods are not *abstract.*

Private methods, introduced in Java version 9, allow us to define methods that provide a service to another method in the interface. For example, several methods in the interface may contain common code. By putting that common code into a *private* method, we can eliminate duplication of code. Each method can simply call the *private* method to access the needed functionality.

To inherit from an interface, our class declares that it *implements* the interface, using the following syntax:

```
accessModifier class ClassName extends SuperclassName
                        implements Interface1, Interface2, ...
```

The *extends* clause is optional if our class inherits only from the *Object* class. A class can *implement* 0, 1, or more interfaces. If our class *implements* more than one interface, the interfaces are specified in a comma-separated list of interface names.

When our class implements an interface, we inherit any *default* and *public static* methods, but we must provide method bodies for all the *abstract* methods.

Default methods, introduced in Java version 8, are *public* methods with a method body that all classes implementing the interface inherit. *Default* methods solve a problem: how can we add a new method to an existing interface? For example, assume we have defined an interface that specifies three *abstract* methods. Any class that implements our interface must provide method bodies for those three methods. Then suppose we want to add new functionality to the interface that would require adding a fourth method. If we add that fourth method as *abstract*, any existing class that implements the interface will no longer compile. We don't want to break existing code!

So we have two options. The first option is to define a new interface that *extends* our original interface, that is, the new interface would inherit the original three *abstract* methods, and we would add the fourth method to the new interface as an *abstract* method. If existing classes want to take advantage of the new functionality, those classes would need to change their code to implement the new interface and thus add a body for the fourth method. The second simpler option is to add the fourth method to the original interface as a *default* method that provides some basic functionality. In this way, classes that already implement the original interface would automatically inherit the new functionality without needing to change their code. In addition, a class that implements an interface can optionally override any *default* methods. Thus, if the basic functionality is not appropriate, the implementing class can provide their own custom version of the method by overriding the *default* method.

Let's consider the general problem of parsing a string of characters. We could have two applications: determining whether a password contains required characters, and converting a *String* containing hexadecimal digits to a decimal number. In each application, we need to parse (analyze) a *String* character by character. In the second application, we also need to validate the *String*.

Figure 10.17 shows the interfaces and classes used in these two applications. In this figure, we introduce the <<interface>> notation and a new UML symbol, the dotted line, which indicates a class that implements an interface.

Each application needs to process the characters of the *String*, determining whether each character of the *String* is a digit, a letter, or another character (neither a digit nor a letter). But each application handles digits, letters, and other characters differently. We create an interface, *StringHandler*, shown in Example 10.21, that allows the implementing class to define a strategy for processing a *String*, one character at a time. The *StringHandler* interface specifies three *abstract* methods, and a *default parse* method that iterates through the *String* determining the type of each character, and calling the appropriate method. Any class that implements the *StringHandler* interface automatically inherits the *parse* method, and must implement the *processLetter*, *processDigit*, and *processOther* methods.

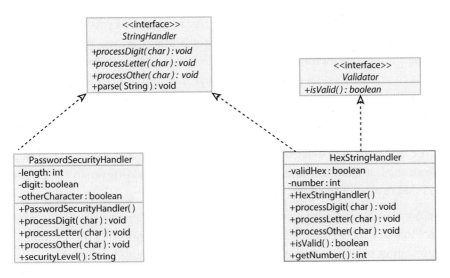

Figure 10.17

UML for String Parsing Interfaces and Classes

```
1  /*   StringHandler interface
2   *   Anderson, Franceschi
3   */
4
5  public interface StringHandler
6  {
7    // abstract methods to implement
8    void processLetter( char c );
9    void processDigit( char c );
10   void processOther( char c );
11
12   /** default parse method
13    * @param s the String to parse
14    */
15   default void parse( String s )
16   {
17     for ( int i = 0; i < s.length( ); i++ )
18     {
19       char c = s.charAt( i );
20       if ( Character.isDigit( c ) )
21         processDigit( c );
22       else if ( Character.isLetter( c ) )
23         processLetter( c );
24       else
25         processOther( c );
26     }
27   }
28 }
```

EXAMPLE 10.21   The *StringHandler* Interface

The *parse* method, at lines 12–27, takes the *String* to parse as a parameter and walks through the *String*, a character at a time, determining the type of character, and calling the appropriate method of the *StringHandler* interface. In order to determine whether a character is a digit or a letter, the *parse* method calls two *static* methods of the *Character* wrapper class, *isDigit* and *isLetter*, shown in Table 10.7. Any class that implements the *StringHandler* interface must provide fully implemented versions of the three *abstract* methods: *processDigit*, *processLetter*, and *processOther*. Additionally, if the implementing class needs to process the *String* in a different order, perhaps from the last letter to the first, that class can write its own version of the *parse* method that overrides the *parse* method in the interface.

We are now ready to design a specialized class that implements the *StringHandler* interface to parse the string with a particular objective in mind. In our example, the first application processes a password to determine its strength. A strong password must contain at least eight characters, at least one digit, and at least one special character. A password containing fewer than six characters is considered weak; otherwise, we consider that the password security level is medium.

The *PasswordSecurityHandler* class, shown in Example 10.22, implements the *StringHandler* interface (line 9); thus, it provides implementations of the *processLetter*, *processDigit*, and *processOther* methods. The *default parse* method meets this application's needs, so we do not override the *default* implementation of the *parse* method.

We define three instance variables (lines 11–13): *length* to hold the number of characters in the password and two flag variables, *digit* and *otherCharacter*, which will indicate whether a digit and a special character were found in the password. The constructor (lines 15–23) initializes *length* to 0 and the flag

TABLE 10.7   Some *Static* Methods of the *Character* Wrapper Class

Useful *Static* Methods of the *Character* Class	
Return value	Method name and argument list
boolean	isDigit(char ch)
	returns *true* if ch represents a digit from '0' to '9'; *false* otherwise.
boolean	isLetter(char ch)
	returns *true* if ch represents a letter from 'a' to 'z' or 'A' to 'Z'; *false* otherwise.
int	getNumericValue(char ch)
	returns the integer value of the specified Unicode character ch.

variables to *false*. The *processLetter* method (lines 25–33) simply increments the *length* variable. The *processDigit* method (lines 35–44) increments *length* and also sets the *digit* flag to *true* to indicate that at least one digit has been found. Similarly, the *processOther* method (lines 46–56) increments *length* and sets the *otherCharacter* flag to *true* to indicate that at least one special character has been found.

The *securityLevel* method (lines 58–73) tests the strength of the password based on its length and the *digit* and *otherCharacter* flags that were set as the password was processed and returns either "weak," "medium," or "strong."

```
 1 /*  PasswordSecurityHandler class
 2  *   Implements methods of the StringHandler interface
 3  *   to parse a String containing a password.
 4  *
 5  *   Anderson, Franceschi
 6 */
 7
 8 public class PasswordSecurityHandler
 9                        implements StringHandler
10 {
11    private int length;
12    private boolean digit;
13    private boolean otherCharacter;
14
15    /** default constructor
16     *  sets length to 0, digit and otherCharacter flags to false
17     */
18    public PasswordSecurityHandler( )
19    {
20      length = 0;
21      digit = false;
22      otherCharacter = false;
23    }
24
25    /** processLetter method
26     * @param c   character to process
27     * adds 1 to length
28     */
29    @Override
30    public void processLetter( char c )
31    {
32      length++;
33    }
```

```
34
35   /** processDigit method
36    * @param c  character to process
37    * adds 1 to length, sets digit flag to true
38    */
39   @Override
40   public void processDigit( char c )
41   {
42     length++;
43     digit = true;
44   }
45
46   /** processOther method
47    * @param c  character to process
48    * adds 1 to length,
49    * sets otherCharacter flag to true
50    */
51   @Override
52   public void processOther( char c )
53   {
54     length++;
55     otherCharacter = true;
56   }
57
58   /** securityLevel method
59    * @return  "weak" if password contains fewer than 6 characters
60    *             "strong" if password has at least 8 characters, at least
61    *                 one digit, and at least one other character
62    *                    that is neither a letter nor a digit
63    *             "medium" otherwise
64    */
65   public String securityLevel( )
66   {
67     if ( length < 6 )
68       return "weak";
69     else if ( length >= 8 && digit && otherCharacter )
70       return "strong";
71     else
72       return "medium";
73   }
74 }
```

EXAMPLE 10.22   The *PasswordSecurityHandler* Class

Example 10.23 shows a client program for parsing a password. We ask the user to enter a password at lines 12–16. At line 18, we instantiate a *PasswordSecurityHandler* object. We then call the *parse* method (line 19), passing the password entered by the user. After the password has been parsed, we call the *securityLevel* method of the *PasswordSecurityHandler* class and output the strength of the password (lines 21–22). Figure 10.18 shows the output of Example 10.23 when the user enters the password *open@jbc*.

```
 1 /* PasswordSecurityHandlerClient
 2 * Anderson, Franceschi
 3 */
 4
 5 import java.util.Scanner;
 6
 7 public class PasswordSecurityHandlerClient
 8 {
 9   public static void main( String [ ] args )
10   {
11     Scanner scan = new Scanner( System.in );
12     System.out.println( "A strong password has at least 8 \n"
13             + "characters and contains at least one digit \n"
14             + "and one special character." );
15     System.out.print( "Enter a password > " );
16     String password = scan.next( );
17
18     PasswordSecurityHandler psh = new PasswordSecurityHandler( );
19     psh.parse( password );
20
21     System.out.println( password + "'s security is "
22                 + psh.securityLevel( ) );
23   }
24 }
```

EXAMPLE 10.23   The *PasswordSecurityHandlerClient* Class

For the second application, where we analyze a *String* representing a hexadecimal number, we reuse the *StringHandler* interface. This application determines whether the *String* contains only valid hexadecimal characters and calculates the decimal equivalent of the hex value represented by the *String*.

As we discussed earlier, a class can implement several interfaces. We now define another interface, *Validator*, shown in Example 10.24, which specifies one *abstract*

Figure 10.18

Output from Example 10.23

```
A strong password has at least 8
characters and contains at least one digit
and one special character.
Enter a password > open@jbc
open@jbc's security is medium.
```

method to implement: *isValid*. We created the *Validator* interface because determining whether a string is valid is a generic operation and not necessarily specific to parsing a hexadecimal number. Thus, other classes can also implement the *Validator* interface.

```
 1 /** Validator interface
 2 *    Anderson, Franceschi
 3 */
 4
 5 @FunctionalInterface
 6 public interface Validator
 7 {
 8   // abstract method to implement
 9   boolean isValid( );
10 }
```

EXAMPLE 10.24   The *Validator* Interface

If the interface has only one *abstract* method to implement, the interface is called a **functional interface** and can be used with **lambda expressions**. We cover lambda expressions later in the text. To ensure that the interface we are defining is, in fact, **a functional interface,** we can precede the definition with the *@FunctionalInterface* annotation. Because *Validator* has only one method to implement and is thus a functional interface, we precede its definition with the above annotation (line 5).

The *HexStringHandler* class, shown in Example 10.25, implements both the *String-Handler* and the *Validator* interfaces (line 11). Again, the *default parse* method meets our needs, so we do not override that method. Our *HexStringHandler* class has two instance variables (lines 13–14): a flag variable, *validHex*, which will indicate whether the string being parsed contains only valid hex characters, and *number*, which will hold the decimal equivalent of the hex value. The default constructor (lines 16–24) initializes these variables to *true* and *0*, respectively. The decimal equivalent of the hex number is calculated as each character of the *String* is parsed in the *processLetter* method (providing that the letter is a valid hex digit) and the *processDigit* method. The *processLetter* and *processDigit* methods use the *static getNumericValue* method of the *Character* wrapper class, also shown in Table 10.7, to retrieve the numeric equivalent of the character being processed. If the *processLetter* method (lines 26–40) finds that the letter is not valid or if the *processOther* method (lines 53–62) is called—indicating that the character is neither a letter nor a digit—the *validHex* flag is set to *false*.

At lines 64–72, the *isValid* method returns *true* if the parsed string represents a valid hexadecimal number, and *false* otherwise. At lines 74–84, the *getNumber* method returns the decimal number if the *String* parsed contains only hexadecimal digits, and *–1* otherwise.

```
 1 /* HexStringHandler class
 2  *  Implements the StringHandler interface
 3  *  to parse a String that contains a hex number
 4  *  into its decimal equivalent
 5  *  Implements the Validator interface to determine
 6  *  validity of String
 7  *  Anderson, Franceschi
 8  */
 9
10 public class HexStringHandler
11                   implements StringHandler, Validator
12 {
13   private boolean validHex;
14   private int number;
15
16   /** default constructor
17    *  initializes number to 0
18    *  and validHex to true
19    */
20   public HexStringHandler( )
21   {
22     validHex = true;
23     number = 0;
24   }
25
26   /** processLetter method
27    * @param c  the character to process
28    * if c is between 10 and 15 (hex A through F),
29    * uses its value to update the decimal value (number)
30    * otherwise, character is invalid letter
31    */
32   @Override
33   public void processLetter( char c )
34   {
35     int n = Character.getNumericValue( c );
36     if ( n >= 10 && n <= 15 ) // valid hex character?
37       number = 16 * number + n; // update number
38     else // invalid hex character
39       validHex = false;
40   }
41
42   /** processDigit method
43    * @param c  the character to process
44    * uses numeric value of c to update the decimal value (number)
45    */
46   @Override
47   public void processDigit( char c )
```

```
48   {
49     int n = Character.getNumericValue( c );
50     number = 16 * number + n; // update number
51   }
52
53   /** processOther method
54    * @param c   the character to process
55    * character is not a valid hex digit
56    */
57   @Override
58   public void processOther( char c )
59   {
60     // c is an invalid hex character
61     validHex = false;
62   }
63
64   /** isValid method
65    * @return true if all characters
66    * in String are valid hex characters,
67    * else returns false
68    */
69   public boolean isValid( )
70   {
71     return validHex;
72   }
73
74   /** getNumber method
75    * @return if valid, returns the calculated decimal value
76    * else, returns -1
77    */
78   public int getNumber( )
79   {
80     if ( isValid( ) )
81       return number;
82     else
83       return -1;
84   }
85 }
```

EXAMPLE 10.25   *HexStringHandler* Class

Example 10.26 shows a similar client program for the hex conversion application. We ask the user to enter a hexadecimal number at lines 12–13. At lines 15–16, we instantiate a *HexStringHandler*. At line 16, we call the *parse* method, passing it the hex *String* entered by the user. After parsing the *String*, we test if the *String* entered by the user is a valid hexadecimal number by calling the *isValid* method of the

HexStringHandler class (line 18). If it is valid, we call the *getNumber* method of the *HexStringHandler* class to output the decimal equivalent of that number (line 19); otherwise, we output a message that the hex number was not valid (line 21). Figure 10.19 shows the output of Example 10.26 when the user enters the valid hex number *A56E.*

```
 1 /*  HexStringHandlerClient class
 2  *    Anderson, Franceschi
 3  */
 4
 5 import java.util.Scanner;
 6
 7 public class HexStringHandlerClient
 8 {
 9   public static void main( String [ ] args )
10   {
11     Scanner scan = new Scanner( System.in );
12     System.out.print( "Enter a hexadecimal number > " );
13     String hex = scan.next( );
14
15     HexStringHandler hsh = new HexStringHandler( );
16     hsh.parse( hex );
17
18     if ( hsh.isValid( ) )
19       System.out.println( hex + " = " + hsh.getNumber( ) );
20     else
21       System.out.println( hex + " is not a valid hex number." );
22   }
23 }
```

EXAMPLE 10.26   The *HexStringHandlerClient* Class

Polymorphism can also be used with interfaces. Although interfaces cannot be instantiated, we can assign an object of a class that implements an interface to an interface reference, and we use that reference to call the methods of the interface.

To illustrate polymorphism with interfaces, let's assume that we are a company that needs to calculate shipping costs for items our customers purchase. We have decided to offer three different pricing strategies based on the weight of the item. With flat-rate shipping, we charge a fixed fee per pound. For standard shipping, we charge a base rate for the first 5 pounds, then a fixed rate for each additional pound. And for express shipping, we add a fixed fee to the standard shipping charge.

Figure 10.19

Output from
Example 10.26

```
Enter a hexadecimal number > A56E
A56E = 42350
```

Note that in each case, we are calculating a price based on weight. To handle this situation, we can create a *ShippingCost* interface and derive three classes that implement the *ShippingCost* interface, each performing its appropriate shipping cost calculation. The UML for this application is shown in Figure 10.20.

The *ShippingCost* interface is shown in Example 10.27. This interface has one *abstract* method, *calculateShipping*, that accepts the weight as a parameter and returns the shipping cost (line 9).

```
 1 /** Shipping Cost
 2 *    Anderson, Franceschi
 3 */
 4
 5 @FunctionalInterface
 6 public interface ShippingCost
 7 {
 9    double calculateShipping( double weight );
10 }
```

EXAMPLE 10.27   The *ShippingCost* Interface

We can now define three classes that implement the *ShippingCost* interface: *FlatRateShipping*, *StandardShipping*, and *ExpressShipping*, with each providing a custom version of the *calculateShipping* method.

Example 10.28 shows the *FlatRateShipping* class. In line 6, we specify that this class implements the *ShippingCost* interface, and in lines 10–14 we provide the *calculateShipping* method, which simply returns the weight multiplied by a constant rate.

Figure 10.20

UML for the
Shipping Strategy

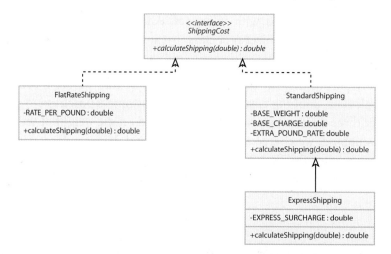

```
1 /** FlatRateShipping
2 *   cost is .50/pound
3 *   Anderson, Franceschi
4 */
5
6 public class FlatRateShipping implements ShippingCost
7 {
8    private final double RATE_PER_POUND = .50;
9
10   @Override
11   public double calculateShipping( double weight )
12   {
13      return RATE_PER_POUND * weight;
14   }
15 }
```

EXAMPLE 10.28   The *FlatRateShipping* Class

Example 10.29 shows the *StandardShipping* class, which also implements the *ShippingCost* interface (line 7). Its *calculateShipping* method (lines 13–21) computes a fixed charge for the first 5 pounds, plus a dollar for each additional pound.

```
1 /** StandardShipping
2 *   cost is $2.50 for the first 5 pounds,
3 *      and $1 for each additonal pound
4 *   Anderson, Franceschi
5 */
6
7 public class StandardShipping implements ShippingCost
8 {
9    private final double BASE_WEIGHT = 5;
10   private final double BASE_CHARGE = 2.5;
11   private final double EXTRA_POUND_RATE = 1.00;
12
13   @Override
14   public double calculateShipping( double weight )
15   {
16      if ( weight > BASE_WEIGHT )
17        return BASE_CHARGE
18            + ( ( weight - BASE_WEIGHT ) * EXTRA_POUND_RATE );
19      else
20        return BASE_CHARGE;
21   }
22 }
```

EXAMPLE 10.29   The *StandardShipping* Class

Because for express shipping we charge the standard rate plus a fixed fee, we want to use the same calculation as the standard shipping and just add the fixed fee. Rather than repeat the code for the standard shipping calculation, we can define the *ExpressShipping* class as extending the *StandardShipping* class. Example 10.30 shows the *ExpressShipping* class. In line 6, we specify that *ExpressShipping* inherits from *StandardShipping*. Note that we don't need to specify that this class implements the *ShippingCost* interface because *StandardShipping* already does that. Any subclass automatically implements any interfaces implemented by the superclass. In lines 10–14, we override the *calculateShipping* method defined in the *StandardShipping* superclass. Inside our method, we call the version of the *calculateShipping* method in the *StandardShipping* class to determine the standard fee (line 13) and add the express fixed fee to the returned value.

```
 1 /** ExpressShipping
 2 *    cost is $10, in addition to standard shipping
 3 *    Anderson, Franceschi
 4 */
 5
 6 public class ExpressShipping extends StandardShipping
 7 {
 8    private final double EXPRESS_SURCHARGE = 10;
 9
10    @Override
11    public double calculateShipping( double weight )
12    {
13       return EXPRESS_SURCHARGE + super.calculateShipping( weight );
14    }
15 }
```

EXAMPLE 10.30   The *ExpressShipping* Class

Putting all this together, Example 10.31 shows a client class, *ShippingCalculator*, that allows a user to select a shipping option and then calculates the shipping cost for an item. In line 14, we define a reference to the *ShippingCost* interface named *shippingCost*, which we initialize to *null*. Remember that we cannot instantiate an interface, but we can define a reference to an interface. In lines 16–24, we prompt the user for the weight of the item and provide a menu from which the user can select a shipping option. Then using a *switch* statement (lines 27–40), we instantiate an object of the appropriate class and assign that object to the *shippingCost* reference (lines 30, 33, and 36). If the user selects a valid option, we call the *calculateShipping* method using the *shippingCost* reference (lines 43–44). As a result, the correct method for the selected pricing strategy is called at runtime. Figure 10.21 shows the output of the program when the user selects express shipping for an item that weighs 6.5 pounds.

This application meets the four requirements for polymorphism. All classes are in the same hierarchy; the subclasses override the same method; we assign subclasses to a superclass/interface reference; and we use the superclass/interface reference to call the method.

```java
 1 /** ShippingCalculator
 2 *    Anderson, Franceschi
 3 */
 4 import java.util.Scanner;
 5 import java.text.NumberFormat;
 6
 7 public class ShippingCalculator
 8 {
 9    public static void main( String [ ] args )
10    {
11       Scanner scan = new Scanner( System.in );
12       NumberFormat money = NumberFormat.getCurrencyInstance( );
13
14       ShippingCost shippingCost = null;
15
16       System.out.print( "What is the weight of the item? " );
17       double weight = scan.nextDouble( );
18
19       System.out.println( "Our shipping options are: "
20                          + "\n\t1 Express shipping: 1-2 business days"
21                          + "\n\t2 Standard shipping: 3-5 business days"
22                          + "\n\t3 Flat Rate: 6-8 business days" );
23       System.out.print( "Select your shipping option > " );
24       int option = scan.nextInt( );
25
26       double cost = 0.0;
27       switch ( option )
28       {
29          case 1:
30             shippingCost = new ExpressShipping( );
31             break;
32          case 2:
33             shippingCost = new StandardShipping( );
34             break;
35          case 3:
36             shippingCost = new FlatRateShipping( );
37             break;
38          default:
39             System.out.println( "Invalid selection." );
40       }
41
42       if ( shippingCost != null )
```

```
43            System.out.println( "Your shipping cost is "
44                 + money.format( shippingCost.calculateShipping( weight ) ) );
45         else
46            System.out.println( "No valid shipping option selected." );
47    }
48 }
```

EXAMPLE 10.31   The *ShippingCalculator* Class

Figure 10.21

Output from
Example 10.31

```
What is the weight of the item? 6.5
Our shipping options are:
   1 Express shipping: 1–2 business days
   2 Standard shipping: 3–5 business days
   3 Flat Rate: 6–8 business days
Select your shipping option > 1
Your shipping cost is $14.00
```

Skill Practice
with these end-of-chapter questions

10.10.1   Multiple Choice Exercises

Questions 3, 5, 6

10.10.3   Fill In the Code

Question 25

10.10.4   Identifying Errors in Code

Questions 26, 27, 28, 29, 30

10.10.8   Technical Writing

Questions 56, 57

CODE IN ACTION

Within the online resources, you will find a movie with a step-by-step illustration of the use of *abstract* classes and interfaces in a program. Click on the link to start the movie.

CHAPTER REVIEW

10.9 Chapter Summary

- Inheritance lets us organize related classes into ordered levels of functionality, called hierarchies. The advantage is that we write the common code only once and reuse it in multiple classes.

- A subclass inherits methods and fields of its superclass. A subclass can have only one direct superclass, but many subclasses can inherit from a common superclass.

- Inheritance implements the "is a" relationship between classes. Any object of a subclass is also an object of the superclass.

- All classes inherit from the *Object* class.

- To specify that a subclass inherits from a superclass, the subclass uses the *extends* keyword in the class definition, as in the following syntax:

  accessModifier class ClassName extends SuperclassName

- A subclass does not inherit constructors or *private* members of the superclass. However, the superclass constructors are still available to be called from the subclass, and the *private* fields of the superclass are implemented as fields of the subclass object.

- To access *private* fields of the superclass, the subclass needs to call the accessor and mutator methods provided by the superclass.

- To call the constructor of the superclass, the subclass constructor uses the following syntax:

  super(argument list);

  If used, this statement must be the first statement in the subclass constructor.

- A subclass can override an inherited method by providing a new version of the method. The new method's API must be identical to the inherited method. To call the inherited version of the method, the subclass uses the *super* object reference using the following syntax:

  super.methodName(argument list)

- Any field declared using the *protected* access modifier is inherited by the subclass. As such, the subclass can directly access the field without calling its accessor or mutator method.

- An *abstract* class can be used to specify APIs for methods that subclasses should implement. An *abstract* class cannot be used to instantiate objects. A class is declared to be *abstract* by including the *abstract* keyword in the class header.

- An *abstract* class typically has one or more *abstract* methods. An *abstract* method specifies the API of the method, but does not provide an implementation. The API of an *abstract* method is followed by a semicolon.

- When a subclass inherits from an *abstract* class, it can provide implementations for any, all, or none of the *abstract* methods. If the subclass does not implement all the *abstract* methods of the superclass, then the subclass must also be declared as *abstract*. If, however, the subclass implements all the *abstract* methods in the superclass and is not declared *abstract*, then the class is not *abstract* and we can instantiate objects of that subclass.

- Polymorphism simplifies the processing of various objects in a hierarchy by allowing us to use the same method call for any object in the hierarchy. We assign an object reference of a subclass to a superclass reference, then make the method call using the superclass object reference. At run time, the JVM determines to which class in the hierarchy the object actually belongs and calls the appropriate version of the method for that class.

- Interfaces allow a class to inherit behavior from multiple sources. Interface members can be classes, constants, *abstract* methods, *default* methods, *private* or *public* non-*abstract static* methods, *private* non-*static* non-*abstract* methods, or other interfaces.

- To define an interface, use the following syntax:

```
accessModifier interface InterfaceName
{
  // body of interface
}
```

- To use an interface, a class header includes the *implements* keyword and the name of the interface, as in the following syntax:

```
accessModifier class ClassName implements InterfaceName
```

- A class that implements an interface must provide full implementations of any *abstract* methods, and can either accept or override any *default* methods.

- To specify that a subclass both inherits from a superclass and uses an interface, a class header includes both the *extends* and the *implements* keywords as in the syntax that follows:

```
accessModifier class ClassName extends SuperclassName
                          implements Interface1, Interface2, ...
```

10.10   Exercises, Problems, and Projects

10.10.1   Multiple Choice Exercises

1. The *extends* keyword applies to
   - ❏ a class inheriting from another class.
   - ❏ a variable.
   - ❏ a method.
   - ❏ an expression.

2. A Java class can inherit from two or more classes.
   - ❏ true
   - ❏ false

3. In Java, multiple inheritance is implemented using the concept of
   - ❏ an interface.
   - ❏ an *abstract* class.
   - ❏ a *private* class.

4. Which of the following is inherited by a subclass?
   - ❏ all instance variables and methods
   - ❏ *public* instance variables and methods only
   - ❏ *protected* instance variables and methods only
   - ❏ *protected* and *public* instance variables and methods

5. What Java keyword is used in a class header when a class is defined as inheriting from an interface?
   - ❏ *inherits*
   - ❏ *includes*
   - ❏ *extends*
   - ❏ *implements*

6. A Java class can implement one or more interfaces.
   - ❏ true
   - ❏ false

7. How do you instantiate an object from an *abstract* class?

   ❑ With any constructor.

   ❑ With the default constructor only.

   ❑ You cannot instantiate an object from an *abstract* class.

8. When a class overrides a method, what object reference is used to call the method inherited from the superclass?

   ❑ *inherited*

   ❑ *super*

   ❑ *class*

   ❑ *methodName*

9. Where should the following statement be located in the body of a subclass constructor?

   ```
   super( );
   ```

   ❑ It should be the last statement.

   ❑ It should be the first statement.

   ❑ It can be anywhere.

10. If a class contains an *abstract* method, then

    ❑ the class must be declared *abstract*.

    ❑ the class is not *abstract*.

    ❑ the class may or may not be *abstract*.

    ❑ all of the above

11. What can you tell about the following method?

    ```
    public void myMethod( )
    {
    }
    ```

    ❑ This method is *abstract*.

    ❑ This method is not *abstract*.

10.10.2   Reading and Understanding Code

For Questions 12 to 20, consider the following three classes:

```java
public class A
{
  private int number;
  protected String name;
  public double price;

  public A( )
  {
   System.out.println( "A( ) called" );
  }

  private void foo1( )
  {
   System.out.println( "A version of foo1( ) called" );
  }

  protected int foo2( )
  {
   System.out.println( "A version of foo2( ) called" );
   return number;
  }

  public String foo3( )
  {
   System.out.println( "A version of foo3( ) called" );
   return "Hi";
  }
}
public class B extends A
{
 private char service;

 public B( )
 {
   super( );
   System.out.println( "B( ) called" );
 }

 public void foo1( )
 {
   System.out.println( "B version of foo1( ) called" );
 }

 protected int foo2( )
 {
   int n = super.foo2( );
   System.out.println( "B version of foo2( ) called" );
   return ( n + 5 );
 }

 public String foo3( )
```

```
{
  String temp = super.foo3( );
  System.out.println( "B version of foo3( )" );
  return ( temp + " foo3" );
  }
}
public class C extends B
{
  public C( )
  {
  super( );
  System.out.println( "C( ) called" );
  }
  public void foo1( )
  {
  System.out.println( "C version of foo1( ) called" );
  }
}
```

12. Draw the UML diagram for the class hierarchy.

13. What fields and methods are inherited by which class?

14. What fields and methods are not inherited?

15. What is the output of the following code sequence?

```
B b1 = new B( );
```

16. What is the output of the following code sequence?

```
B b2 = new B( );
b2.foo1( );
```

17. What is the output of the following code sequence?

```
B b3 = new B( );
int n = b3.foo2( );
```

18. What is the output of the following code sequence?

```
// b4 is a B object reference
System.out.println( b4.foo3( ) );
```

19. What is the output of the following code sequence?

```
C c1 = new C( );
```

20. What is the output of the following code sequence?

```
// c2 is a C object reference
c2.foo1( );
```

10.10.3 Fill In the Code

For Questions 21 to 25, consider the following class *F* and the interface *I*:

```java
public class F
{
  private String first;
  protected String name;

  public F( )
  { }

  public F( String first, String name )
  {
    this.first = first;
    this.name = name;
  }
  public String getFirst( )
  {
   return first;
  }
  public String getName( )
  {
   return name;
  }
  public String toString( )
  {
   return  "first: " + first + "\tname: " + name ;
  }
  public boolean equals( Object f )
  {
   if ( ! ( f instanceof F ) )
      return false;
   else
   {
      F objF = ( F ) f;
      return( first.equals( objF.first ) && name.equals( objF.name ) );
   }
  }
}
public interface I
{
 String TYPE = "human";
 int age( );
}
```

21. The *G* class inherits from the *F* class. Code the class header of the *G* class.

```
// your code goes here
```

22. Inside the *G* class, which inherits from the *F* class, declare a *private* instance variable for the middle initial and code a constructor with three parameters, calling the constructor of the *F* class and assigning the third parameter, a *char*, to the new instance variable.

```
// your code goes here
```

23. Inside the *G* class, which inherits from the *F* class, code the *toString* method, which returns a printable representation of a *G* object reference.

```
// your code goes here
```

24. Inside the *G* class, which inherits from the *F* class, code the *equals* method, which compares two *G* objects and returns *true* if they have identical instance variables; *false* otherwise.

```
// your code goes here
```

25. The *K* class inherits from the *F* class and the *I* interface; code the class header of the *K* class.

```
// your code goes here
```

10.10.4   Identifying Errors in Code

For Questions 26 to 31, consider the following two classes, *C* and *D*, and interface *I*:

```
public abstract class C
{
  private void foo1( )
  {
    System.out.println( "Hello foo1( )" );
  }
  public abstract void foo2( );
  public abstract int foo3( );
}
public class D extends C
{
  public void foo2( )
  {
    System.out.println( "Hello foo2( )" );
  }
  public int foo3( )
```

```
  {
   return 10;
  }
  private void foo4( )
  {
   System.out.println( "Hello foo4( )" );
  }
 }
 public interface I
 {
  double PI = 3.14;
 }
```

26. Where is the error in this code sequence?

```
C c1 = new C( );
```

27. Where is the error in this code sequence?

```
D d1 = new D( );
d1.foo1( );
```

28. Is there an error in this code sequence? Why or why not?

```
C c2;
c2 = new D( );
```

29. Where is the error in this new class?

```
public class E extends D
{
 public void foo4( )
 {
  super.foo4( );
  System.out.println( "Hello E foo4()" );
 }
}
```

30. Where is the error in this class?

```
public class J extends I
{

}
```

31. Where is the error in this class?

```
public class K
{
 public void foo( );
}
```

10.10.5   Debugging Area—Using Messages from the Java Compiler and Java JVM

For questions 32-35, explain what the problem is and how to fix it.

32. You coded the following class:

```java
public class N extends String, Integer
{
}
```

When you compile, you get the following message:

```
N.java:1: error: '{' expected
public class N extends String, Integer
                             ^
1 error
```

Explain what the problem is and how to fix it.

For Exercises 33 to 35, consider the following class:

```java
public abstract class M
{
  private int n;
  protected double p;
  public abstract void foo1( );
}
```

33. You coded the following class:

```java
public class P extends M
{
}
```

When you compile, you get the following message:

```
P.java:1: error: P is not abstract and does not override abstract method foo1()
in M
public class P extends M
       ^
1 error
```

34. You coded the following class:

```java
public class P extends M
{
  public void foo1( )
  {
    System.out.println( "n is: " + n );
  }
}
```

When you compile, you get the following message:

```
P.java:5: error: n has private access in M
  System.out.println( "n is: " + n );
                    ^

1 error
```

35. You coded the following classes:

```java
public class P extends M
{
 public P( double newP )
 {
  p = newP;
 }
 public void foo1( )
 {
 }
}
public class Q extends P
{
 private int z;
 public Q( double newP, int  z )
 {
  this.z = z;
  super( newP ); // line 7
 }
}
```

When you compile, you get the following message:

```
Q.java:5: error: constructor P in class P cannot be applied to given types
   {
   ^
   required: double
   found: no arguments
   reason: actual and formal argument lists differ in length
Q.java:7: call to super must be first statement in constructor
   super( newP ); // line 7
         ^

2 errors
```

10.10.6 Write a Short Program

For Exercises 36 to 40, consider the following class:

```java
public class Game
{
```

```
    private String description;

    public Game( String description )
    {
     setDescription( description );
    }
    public String getDescription( )
    {
     return description;
    }

    public void setDescription( String description )
    {
     this.description = description;
    }

    public String toString( )
    {
     return "description: " + description ;
    }
}
```

36. Write a class encapsulating a PC-based game, which inherits from *Game*. A PC-based game has the following additional attributes: the minimum megabytes of RAM needed to play the game, the number of megabytes needed on the hard drive to install the game, and the minimum GHz performance of the CPU. Code the constructor and the *toString* method of the new class. You also need to include a client class to test your code.

37. Write a class encapsulating a board game, which inherits from *Game*. A board game has the following additional attributes: the number of players and whether the game can end in a tie. Code the constructor and the *toString* method of the new class. You also need to include a client class to test your code.

38. Write a class encapsulating a sports game, which inherits from *Game*. A sports game has the following additional attributes: whether the game is a team or individual game, and whether the game can end in a tie. Code the constructor and the *toString* method of the new class. You also need to include a client class to test your code.

39. Write a class encapsulating a trivia game, which inherits from *Game*. A trivia game has the following additional attributes: the ultimate money prize and the number of questions that must be answered to win the ultimate money. Code the constructor and the *toString* method of the new class. You also need to include a client class to test your code.

40. Write a class encapsulating a board game, which inherits from *Game*. A board game has the following additional attributes: the minimum number of players, the maximum number of players, and whether there is a time limit to finish the game. Code the constructor and the *toString* method of the new class. You also need to include a client class to test your code.

For Exercises 41 to 45, consider the following class:

```java
public class Store
{
  public final double SALES_TAX_RATE = 0.06;
  private String name;

  public Store( String name )
  {
    setName( name );
  }

  public String getName( )
  {
    return name;
  }

  public void setName( String name )
  {
    this.name = name;
  }

  public String toString( )
  {
    return ( "name: " + name );
  }
}
```

41. Write a class encapsulating a web store, which inherits from *Store*. A web store has the following additional attributes: an Internet address and the programming language in which the website was written. Code the constructor and the *toString* method of the new class. You also need to include a client class to test your code.

42. Write a class encapsulating a music store, which inherits from *Store*. A music store has the following additional attributes: the number of titles it offers and its address. Code the constructor and the *toString* method of the new class. You also need to include a client class to test your code.

43. Write a class encapsulating a bike store, which inherits from *Store*. A bike store has the following additional attributes: the number of bicycle brands that it carries and whether it sponsors a bike club. Code the constructor and the

toString method of the new class. You also need to include a client class to test your code.

44. Write a class encapsulating a grocery store, which inherits from *Store*. A grocery store has the following additional attributes: annual revenues and whether it is an independent store or part of a chain. Code the constructor and the *toString* method of the new class; also code a method returning the annual taxes paid by the store. You also need to include a client class to test your code.

45. Write a class encapsulating a restaurant, which inherits from *Store*. A restaurant has the following additional attributes: how many people are served every year and the average price per person. Code the constructor and the *toString* method of the new class; also code a method returning the average taxes per year. You also need to include a client class to test your code.

10.10.7 Programming Projects

46. Write a superclass encapsulating a rectangle. A rectangle has two attributes representing the width and the height of the rectangle. It has methods returning the perimeter and the area of the rectangle. This class has a subclass, encapsulating a parallelepiped, or box. A parallelepiped has a rectangle as its base, and another attribute, its length; it has two methods that calculate and return its area and volume. You also need to include a client class to test these two classes.

47. Write a superclass encapsulating a circle; this class has one attribute representing the radius of the circle. It has methods returning the perimeter and the area of the circle. This class has a subclass, encapsulating a cylinder. A cylinder has a circle as its base, and another attribute, its length; it has two methods, calculating and returning its area and volume. You also need to include a client class to test these two classes.

48. Write an *abstract* superclass encapsulating a shape: A shape has two *abstract* methods: one returning the perimeter of the shape, another returning the area of the shape. It also has a constant field named PI. This class has two non-*abstract* subclasses: one encapsulating a circle, and the other encapsulating a rectangle. A circle has one additional attribute, its radius. A rectangle has two additional attributes, its width and height. You also need to include a client class to test these two classes.

49. Write an *abstract* superclass encapsulating a vehicle: A vehicle has two attributes: its owner's name and its number of wheels. This class has two

non-abstract subclasses: one encapsulating a bicycle, and the other encapsulating a motorized vehicle. A motorized vehicle has the following additional attributes: its engine volume displacement, in liters; and a method computing and returning a measure of horsepower—the number of liters times the number of wheels. You also need to include a client class to test these two classes.

50. Write an *abstract* superclass encapsulating some food; it has two attributes: its description and the number of calories per serving. It also has an *abstract* method taking a number of servings as a parameter and returning the number of calories. This class has two non-*abstract* subclasses: one encapsulating a liquid food (such as a drink, for instance), and the other encapsulating a fruit. A liquid food has an additional attribute: its viscosity. A fruit has an additional attribute: its season. You also need to include a client class to test these two classes.

51. Write an *abstract* superclass encapsulating a college applicant: A college applicant has two attributes: the applicant's name and the college the applicant is applying to. This class has two non-*abstract* subclasses: one encapsulating an applicant for undergraduate school, and the other encapsulating an applicant for graduate school. An applicant for undergraduate school has two additional attributes: an SAT score and a GPA. An applicant for graduate school has one additional attribute: the college of origin. It also has a method that returns "from inside" if the college of origin is the same as the college applied to; otherwise, it returns "from outside." You also need to include a class to test these two classes.

52. Write an *abstract* superclass encapsulating a vacation: A vacation has two attributes: a budget and a destination. It has an *abstract* method returning by how much the vacation is over or under budget. This class has two non-*abstract* subclasses: one encapsulating an all-inclusive vacation, and the other encapsulating a vacation bought piecemeal. An all-inclusive vacation has three additional attributes: a brand (for instance ClubMed®); a rating, expressed as a number of stars; and a price. A piecemeal vacation has two additional attributes: a set of items (hotel, meal, airfare, …), and a set of corresponding costs. You also need to include a class to test these two classes.

53. Write an *abstract* superclass encapsulating a part, with two attributes: the part number, and a budget cost for it. This class has two non-*abstract* subclasses: one encapsulating a self-manufactured part, and the other encapsulating an outsourced part. A self-manufactured part has a cost and a drawing number; it also has a method returning whether it is over budget or under budget. An outsourced part has a set of suppliers, each with a price for the part. It also has a method to retrieve the lowest-cost supplier for a part and the corresponding cost. You also need to include a class to test these two classes.

54. Write an *abstract* superclass encapsulating a number; this class has one *abstract* void method: *square*. This class has two non-*abstract* subclasses: one encapsulating a rational number, and the other encapsulating a complex number. A rational number is represented by two integers, the numerator and the denominator of the rational number. A complex number is represented by two real numbers, the real part and the complex part of the complex number. You also need to include a class to test these two classes.

55. Define an *abstract UtilityCustomer* class that has one instance variable, an account number, and an *abstract* method, *calculateBill*, that returns the bill amount as a *double*. Also define the constructor, accessors, mutators, and a *toString* method that outputs the account number. Define a *GasCustomer* class that inherits from the *UtilityCustomer* class, and adds an instance variable *cubicMetersUsed* and a constant for the price of gas per cubic meter. Also define an *ElectricCustomer* class that also inherits from the *UtilityCustomer* class and adds a *kWattHourUsed* instance variable along with two constants for the price of electricity per kilowatt hour, plus a flat power delivery fee ($30) that is added to every bill. For each subclass, define the constructor, accessor, and mutator for its instance variable, a *toString* method, which calls the *toString* method of the *UtilityCustomer* class, and an implementation for the *calculateBill* method. Create a client that instantiates several *GasCustomer* and *ElectricCustomer* objects, adds them to an *ArrayList* of *UtilityCustomer* objects, and then using polymorphism, steps through the *ArrayList*, calling the *calculateBill* method and outputting the bill amount for each customer.

10.10.8 Technical Writing

56. In a large organization, programmers develop a library of classes as they work on various projects. Discuss, in such an environment, how inheritance can be helpful in reusing code and therefore saving time.

57. Other programming languages allow multiple inheritance; that is, a class can inherit from several classes. In Java, a class can extend only one class, but can implement several interfaces. Discuss potential problems that can arise in other programming languages that allow inheritance from multiple classes.

10.10.9 Group Project (for a group of 1, 2, or 3 students)

58. Design and code a program that allows the user to select a drawing style for a graphics program. The styles should be black and white, grayscale, or inverted color. To do this, define a *DrawingStyle* interface with these methods: *setColor* and

setOutline. Both methods accept a *GraphicsContext* object and a *Color*, convert the color appropriately, and call the *GraphicsContext* methods *setFill* or *setStroke*, respectively, with the new color value.

For each style, define the following classes that implement the *DrawingStyle* interface: *BlackAndWhite*, *Grayscale*, and *InvertColor*.

In the client class, define a *DrawingStyle* instance variable. Prompt the user for the desired style, and assign a reference to an object of the appropriate class that implements the *DrawingStyle* interface. The application should then call *setColor* and *setOutline* to set the fill or stroke color using a reference to the *DrawingStyle* object. Make a drawing of your choice using the selected drawing style.

Hint: Look up the *grayscale* and *invert* methods of the *Color* class. The *BlackAndWhite* class can simply convert any color whose average value for the red, green, and blue components is >= .0.5 to white; otherwise, it converts the color to black.

CHAPTER 11
Exceptions and Input/Output Operations

CHAPTER CONTENTS

Introduction

Programs often use existing data accumulated by an organization, such as a university, a government, or a corporation. Typically, the volume of data is significant, making data entry through the keyboard impractical.

Furthermore, these large amounts of data typically reside in two types of storage:

- disk files
- databases

Working with databases is beyond the scope of this book. In most of this chapter, we concentrate on reading from and writing to files.

But there is a prerequisite to all this: understanding the concept of exceptions, their associated classes, and exception handling.

11.1   Simple Exception Handling

By now we have discovered that sometimes our program doesn't work, even though we didn't get any compiler errors. At run time, logic errors can surface. For example, we might attempt to divide an integer by 0 or try to access the 11th element in a 10-element array. Java is a robust language and does not allow these "illegal" operations to occur unnoticed.

These illegal operations generate **exceptions**. Some exceptions are generated by the Java Virtual Machine, while others are generated by constructors or other methods. For example, a method might generate an exception when it detects an attempted illegal operation or an illegal parameter.

By default, when an exception is generated in an application that does not have a graphical user interface, the program will terminate. In many cases, however, we can attempt to recover from the exception and continue running the program. This is called **handling the exception**. For the programmer to handle an exception, Java provides two tools:

- exception classes
- the *try*, *catch*, and *finally* blocks

The *Exception* class is the superclass of all exception classes, which encapsulate specific exceptions such as integer division by 0, attempting to access an out-of-bounds array index, unsuccessfully converting a *String* to a number, using a *null* object reference to call a method, trying to open a file that does not exist, and others.

Figure 11.1 is an inheritance hierarchy showing only a few of the Java exception classes. The *Exception* class and *RuntimeException* and its subclasses are in the *java.lang* package. The *IOException* class and its subclass, *FileNotFoundException*, are in the *java.io* package.

We want to avoid situations when an exception occurs and abruptly terminates the execution of our program. Java provides *try* and *catch* blocks to allow us to handle exceptions so that our code can continue to run. We put the code that might generate an exception inside the *try* block, and we put the code to recover from the exception inside a *catch* block. If an exception is thrown by the code inside the *try* block, then execution will jump to the *catch* block, where we provide code to handle that exception. If nothing illegal happens in the *try* block, the code in the *catch* block will be skipped.

The minimum syntax for a *try* and *catch* block is as follows:

```
try
{
   // code that might generate an exception
}
catch ( ExceptionClass exceptionObjRef )
{
   // code to recover from the exception
}
```

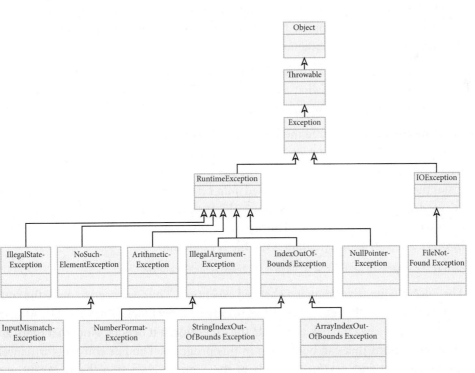

Figure 11.1

Inheritance Hierarchy for Various *Exception* Classes

COMMON ERROR TRAP
Omitting curly braces around the *try* and *catch* blocks will generate a compiler error. A *catch* clause listing several *Exception* classes as parameters will also generate a compiler error. Use multiple *catch* blocks instead.

The curly braces are required for both the *try* body and the *catch* body even if the bodies have only one statement, or even no statements.

Any variable defined within the *try* block is local to that block; that is, the variable cannot be referenced after the *try* block, not even in the *catch* block. Note that the *ExceptionClass* parameter of the *catch* clause specifies one and only one *ExceptionClass*. Listing zero or two or more *ExceptionClasses* in the *catch* clause will generate a compiler error.

Java distinguishes between two types of exceptions:

- unchecked, those that are subclasses of *Error* or *RuntimeException*
- checked, any other exception class

An **unchecked exception**, such as an *ArithmeticException* caused by attempting integer division by 0, a *NumberFormatException*, or a *NullPointerException*, does not have to be handled with a *try* and *catch* block. In other words, if we omit the *try* and *catch* blocks, our code will compile without an error. If one of these unchecked exceptions is generated at run time, however, the JVM will catch it and print output similar to that shown in Figure 11.2.

Code that could generate a **checked exception**, such as an *IOException*, must be coded within a *try* block. Optionally, the method header can acknowledge that the checked exception could occur by using a *throws* clause. This is required; otherwise, the program will not compile. Thus, when we perform I/O on a file, our code must deal with a potential *IOException*.

In the *catch* block, we can use the *Exception* parameter as an object reference to get more information about what caused the exception. Table 11.1 shows three methods inherited by the *Exception* classes.

We demonstrate these three methods, as well as how to use *try* and *catch* blocks to detect and handle an exception if it occurs, in Example 11.1. When we want to read data from a file, we first must open the file for reading. At line 15, we declare and instantiate a *File* object for a file named *data.txt* located in the current folder. At line 16, we declare and instantiate a *Scanner* object so we can read from the input stream represented by that *File* object. The *Scanner* constructor, whose API is shown below, *throws* a *FileNotFoundException* if the file is not found.

```
public Scanner( File source ) throws FileNotFoundException
```

The *FileNotFoundException* is a checked exception. Thus, we need to place the code that can generate that exception (line 16) inside a *try* block (lines 13–23). At lines 24–29, we use a *catch* block to handle the exception if it occurs. Note that there are other exceptions that can be thrown in this program. The *File* constructor, as well the *hasNextInt* and *nextInt* methods of the *Scanner* class, can throw exceptions;

TABLE 11.1   Useful Methods of Exception Classes

Methods of Exception Classes	
Return value	**Method name and argument list**
String	getMessage( )
	returns a message indicating the cause of the exception
String	toString( )
	returns a *String* containing the exception class name and a message indicating the cause of the exception
void	printStackTrace( )
	prints the line number of the code that caused the exception, along with the sequence of method calls leading up to the exception

however, all those exceptions are unchecked exceptions and do not require the use of *try/catch* blocks.

When the program runs, if there is no file named *data.txt* in the current folder, the *try* block stops executing at line 16. Next, the *catch* block is executed, and we print the values from the *getMessage*, *toString*, and *printStackTrace* methods of the *FileNotFoundException* class. Figure 11.2 shows the output of Example 11.1 when there is no file named *data.txt* in the current folder. As we can see, the only difference between the return values from the *getMessage* and *toString* methods is that the *toString* method returns the exception class name, as well as the message. The output of the *printStackTrace* method may look familiar. It is similar to a message that the JVM prints when an *ArithmeticException*, *StringIndexOutOfBoundsException*, or *ArrayIndexOutOfBoundsException* occurs when we do not have *try* and *catch* blocks.

```
 1 /* Reading a Text File
 2    Anderson, Franceschi
 3 */
 4
 5 import java.io.File;
 6 import java.io.FileNotFoundException;
 7 import java.util.Scanner;
 8
 9 public class EchoFileData
10 {
```

```java
11   public static void main( String [ ] args )
12   {
13     try
14     {
15       File inputFile = new File( "data.txt" );
16       Scanner file = new Scanner( inputFile );
17
18       while ( file.hasNextInt( ) )
19       {
20         int number = file.nextInt( );
21         System.out.println( number );
22       }
23     }
24     catch ( FileNotFoundException fnfe )
25     {
26       System.out.println( "Message: " + fnfe.getMessage( ) );
27       System.out.println( "\ntoString( ): " + fnfe + "\n" );
28       fnfe.printStackTrace( );
29     }
30   }
31 }
```

EXAMPLE 11. 1　　Using *try* and *catch* blocks

Figure 11.2

Output of
Example 11.1

```
Message: data.txt (The system cannot find the file specified)

toString( ): java.io.FileNotFoundException: data.txt (The system cannot find
the file specified)

java.io.FileNotFoundException: data.txt (The system cannot find the
file specified)
        at java.base/java.io.FileInputStream.open0(Native Method)
        at java.base/java.io.FileInputStream.open(Unknown Source)
        at java.base/java.io.FileInputStream.<init>(Unknown Source)
        at java.base/java.util.Scanner.<init>(Unknown Source)
        at EchoFileData.main(EchoFileData.java:16)
```

11.2　Catching Multiple Exceptions

If the code in the *try* block might generate multiple types of exceptions, we can provide multiple *catch* blocks, one for each possible exception. When an exception is generated, the JVM searches the *catch* blocks in order. The first *catch* block with a parameter that matches the exception thrown will execute; any remaining *catch* blocks will be skipped.

Remember that subclass objects are also objects of their superclasses, so an exception will match any *catch* block for an exception that names any of its superclasses. For example, a *NumberFormatException* will match a *catch* block with a *Runtime-Exception* parameter, and all exceptions will match a *catch* block with an *Exception* parameter. Therefore, when coding several *catch* blocks, put the *catch* blocks for the specialized exceptions first, followed by more general exceptions.

Furthermore, after a *try* block and its associated *catch* blocks, we may optionally add a *finally* block, which will always be executed, whether an exception occurred or not. In the *finally* block, we can include some clean-up code. We will demonstrate a *finally* block when we read from a file later in this chapter.

Here is the syntax for using a *try* block, several *catch* blocks, and a *finally* block:

```
try
{
   // code that might generate an exception
}
catch ( Exception1Class e1 )
{
   // code to handle an Exception1Class exception
}
...
catch ( ExceptionNClass eN )
{
   // code to handle an ExceptionNClass exception
}
finally
{
   // code to execute regardless of whether an exception occurs
}
```

Again, the curly braces around the various blocks are required, whether these blocks contain zero, one, or more statements.

Having provided several examples of exceptions, we must also consider this: Not every problem needs to be addressed by generating an exception. As a matter of fact, generating and handling exceptions considerably slows down execution of our code due to the processing overhead. Often, for example when using Java's I/O classes, we will have no choice but to use *try* and *catch* blocks. Sometimes, however, we can use a simple *if/else* statement instead of *try* and *catch* blocks. For example, we can test if the value of the divisor is not zero before attempting a division, rather than placing the code in a *try* block and catching an *ArithmeticException*.

How do we know if a constructor or a method *throws* an exception and what type of exception it *throws*? As always, our best source of information is the Java Class Library

SOFTWARE ENGINEERING TIP
Arrange *catch* blocks to handle the more specialized exceptions first, followed by more general exceptions.

SOFTWARE ENGINEERING TIP
Whenever possible, use a simple *if/else* statement to detect an unchecked exception, rather than *try* and *catch* blocks. This will improve the performance of your code.

REFERENCE POINT
Consult the Oracle Java Class Library to see if a constructor or a method *throws* an exception and, if so, what type of exception.

on Oracle's Java website. After we have identified a constructor or a method that we would like to use, we simply look at its description in order to determine whether it *throws* any exceptions, and, if so, which ones.

11.3   Reading Text Files Using *Scanner*

Java supports two file types, text and binary. In text files, data is stored as characters; in binary files, data is stored as raw bytes. Different classes are used for writing and reading each file type. The type of a file is determined when the file is written and depends on which classes were used to write to the file. Thus, to read from an existing file, we must know the file's type in order to select the appropriate classes.

In this section, we concentrate on text files.

As we have seen from Example 11.1, the *Scanner* class can be used to read from a text file. If the file is not found, the *Scanner* constructor throws a *FileNotFoundException*. More exceptions can be thrown by *Scanner* methods while reading the file.

Table 11.2 shows some constructors of the *Scanner* and *File* classes and methods of the *Scanner* class for reading from a file, as well as the exceptions that each method can throw.

TABLE 11.2   Useful Methods of the *Scanner* and *File* Classes for Reading from a File

File Constructor		Exceptions thrown
`File( String pathname )`		`NullPointerException`
constructs a *File* object with the *pathname* file name so that the file name is platform-independent.		
Scanner Constructor and Methods		**Exceptions thrown**
`Scanner( File file )`		`FileNotFoundException`
constructs a *Scanner* object for reading from a file.		
Return value	**Method name and argument list**	**Exceptions thrown**
`boolean`	`hasNext( )`	Both methods throw an `IllegalStateException`
	returns *true* if there is another token in the input stream	

(*continued*)

TABLE 11.2 (*continued*)

Return value	Method name and argument list	Exceptions thrown
boolean	hasNextLine( ) returns *true* if there is another line or line separator in the input stream	
boolean boolean boolean	hasNextInt( ) hasNextDouble( ) hasNextFloat( ) ... returns *true* if there is another token in the input stream of the specified data type	All these methods throw an IllegalStateException
String	next( ) returns the next token in the input stream as a *String*	Both methods throw NoSuchElementException, IllegalStateException
String	nextLine( ) returns the remainder of the line as a *String*. Positions the pointer to the next line.	
int double float	nextInt( ) nextDouble( ) nextFloat( ) ... returns the next token in the input stream as the specified data type	All these methods throw InputMismatchException, NoSuchElementException, IllegalStateException
void	close( ) releases the resources associated with an open input stream	None

In Example 11.2, we read a text file named *movies.txt*, which contains titles of classic movies and the movies' running times in minutes. Each movie occupies two lines in the file: the title on one line and the running time on the following line. Each line in the file, including the last line, is terminated by a *newline* character. In this example, we simply read the movie titles and running times and echo them to the console. However, we could read this file to find the longest or shortest movie, or to instantiate *Movie* objects to be stored in an *ArrayList* or other data structure for further processing.

```
1 /** Classic Movies - Reading from a text file
2  *    Anderson, Franceschi
3  */
4
5 import java.util.Scanner;
6 import java.io.File;
7 import java.util.NoSuchElementException;
8 import java.io.FileNotFoundException;
9
10 public class ClassicMovies
11 {
12   public static void main( String [ ] args )
13   {
14     try ( Scanner file = new Scanner( new File( "movies.txt" ) ) )
15     {
16      while ( file.hasNext( ) ) // test for the end of the file
17      {
18         String movieTitle = file.nextLine( );
19
20         if ( ! file.hasNextInt( ) )
21         {
22           System.out.println( "Invalid file format" );
23           String invalidData = file.nextLine( ); // skip the line
24         }
25         else
26         {
27           int runningTime = file.nextInt( );
28           String newLine = file.nextLine( ); // read newline character
29           System.out.println( movieTitle + ", "
30                             + runningTime + " minutes" );
31         }
32      }
33     }
34
35     catch ( FileNotFoundException fnfe )
36     {
37       System.out.println( "Unable to find movies.txt, exiting" );
38     }
39
40     catch ( NoSuchElementException nsee )
41     {
42       System.out.println( "Attempt to read past the end of the file" );
43     }
44   }
45 }
```

EXAMPLE 11.2   Reading from a Text File

Lines 7–8 import the *NoSuchElementException* and *FileNotFoundException* classes. The *IllegalStateException* class does not need to be imported because it is in the *java.lang* package. Line 14 instantiates a *Scanner* object from a *File* object, passing the name of the file to be read, *movies.txt*, as the argument to the *File* constructor.

The *File* object is used only as the argument of the *Scanner* constructor; it is not used anywhere else in the program. In this case, instead of creating a *File* object reference, many programmers prefer to use an anonymous *File* object as the argument of the *Scanner* constructor. In other words, instead of writing the following two statements:

```
File f = new File( "movies.txt" );
Scanner file = new Scanner( f );
```

we use the following single statement:

```
Scanner file = new Scanner( new File( "movies.txt" ) );
```

It is a matter of preference as to which code we use.

When we associate a file with an input stream or output stream, we are **opening the file**. As we read the data in a file, a **file pointer** keeps track of the next data to read. When we open the file, the file pointer is set to the beginning of the file. When we are finished with a file, we can call the *close* method (shown in Table 11.2) to release the resources associated with the file. Calling the *close* method is optional. When the program finishes executing, all of its resources are released, including the resources of any unclosed files. Nevertheless, it is good practice, in general, to call the *close* method, especially if we will be opening a number of files (or opening the same file multiple times). In contrast, the standard input stream (*System.in*), the standard output stream (*System.out*), and the standard error stream (*System.err*) are open when the program begins. They are intended to stay open and should not be closed.

> **SOFTWARE ENGINEERING TIP**
>
> Either use a *try-with-resources* statement or close files when you have finished processing their data. Do not close the standard input, output, or error devices.

At lines 14–33, we use a **try-with-resources** statement. A **resource** is an object reference, for example a *Scanner*, that should be closed after we no longer need it. A *try*-with-resources is a statement that declares one or more resources. Using a *try*-with-resources statement guarantees that the resource will be automatically closed at the end of the *try* block. If we did not use a *try*-with-resources statement at line 14, we would need to close the *Scanner* in the *finally* block to guarantee that it is closed. Closing the *Scanner* as the last statement of the *try* block would not guarantee that the *Scanner* is closed because if an exception occurs, the *try* block will not finish executing.

Thus, the following code:

```
try ( Scanner file = new Scanner( new File( "movies.txt" ) ) )
{
   . .
}
catch ( .. )
```

```
{
  ..
}
```

is equivalent to:

```
Scanner file;
try
{
  file = new Scanner( new File( "movies.txt" ) );
  ..
}
catch ( .. )
{
  ..
}
finally
{
  file.close( );
}
```

The *Scanner* constructor throws a *FileNotFoundException* if the file does not exist. We catch this exception at lines 35–38. Since the program cannot continue without the file being open, we print a message to the user that we were not able to find the file and that the program is exiting. Thus, instead of facing a *FileNotFoundException* with a stack trace, the user now sees a friendly message explaining the problem.

If no exception is thrown, we begin to read the file. The *while* loop condition, at line 16, uses the *Scanner hasNext* method to test whether the file pointer has reached the end of the file. If not, *hasNext* returns *true*, and we execute the *while* loop body. Since the movie title could contain more than one word, we use the *nextLine* method to read the entire line (line 18).

We then test whether the next token in the file is an *int* (line 20). If not, then the running time is not a whole number. We output a message that the file format is invalid, then skip the line by using the *nextLine* method to read whatever data is on that line into the *String invalidData* (lines 22–23). Another option is to use a *try/catch* block to read the running time. With that option, calling the *nextInt* method to read the invalid data would generate an *InputMismatchException*, which we would need to handle. Given that exception handling results in additional processing overhead, our using the *hasNextInt* method of the *Scanner* class to test whether the file format is valid makes the code more efficient.

If the next token is an *int*, we read the running time using the *nextInt* method (line 27). At this point, it is worthwhile to discuss the difference between the *nextLine* method and the other *Scanner next...* methods (such as *next/nextInt/nextDouble*, etc.). The *nextLine* method reads any part of the line that has not already been read, including leading and trailing white space (spaces, tabs, and the *newline* character) and moves the file pointer to the next line. The *nextLine* method does not include the *newline* character in its returned *String*. In contrast, the *nextInt* method and its *next....* method counterparts skip leading white space, then read the next token on the line, stopping when trailing white space is encountered. That means that after we have read the running time using the *nextInt* method, the *newline* character is still in the input stream. If we then attempt to read the next movie title using the *nextLine* method, the *nextLine* method would instead read just the *newline* character that follows the running time and return an empty *String*. So on line 28, we insert an additional call to the *nextLine* method to remove that *newline* character from the input stream.

On lines 29–30, we echo the title and running time to the console.

We continue looping through the file until there is no more data to read.

An attempt to access a file after it has been closed generates an *IllegalStateException*. Because we use a *try*-with-resources statement, the *Scanner* will be closed after the last *catch* block. Thus, we cannot access the file after it has been closed and do not need to *catch* an *IllegalStateException*. If we attempt to read beyond the end of the file, the *nextLine* or *nextInt* methods will throw a *NoSuchElementException*. We catch this exception on lines 40–43, and output a message explaining the cause of the exception.

Let's assume the file *movies.txt* contains the data shown in Figure 11.3. When the program in Example 11.2 runs, it will produce the output shown in Figure 11.4 if the file is found, and the output in Figure 11.5 if the file is not found.

```
The Matrix
136
Finding Nemo
100
Titanic
194
Casablanca
102
Gone With the Wind
220
```

Figure 11.3

Contents of *movies.txt*

```
The Matrix, 136 minutes
Finding Nemo, 100 minutes
Titanic, 194 minutes
Casablanca, 102 minutes
Gone With the Wind, 220 minutes
```

Figure 11.4

Output of Example 11.2 When File Is Found

```
Unable to find movies.txt, exiting
```

Figure 11.5

Output of Example 11.2 When File Is Not Found

11.4   The *java.io* Package

In addition to the *Scanner* class in the *java.util* package, Java provides a number of classes in the *java.io* package for reading from files and for writing to files. We will use only a few of those classes here. Table 11.3 describes a group of classes designed for data input.

Figure 11.6 shows an inheritance hierarchy for the Java classes described in Table 11.3.

Table 11.4 describes a group of classes designed for data output, and Figure 11.7 shows an inheritance hierarchy for Java output classes in Table 11.4.

Figure 11.6

The Inheritance Hierarchy for Input Classes

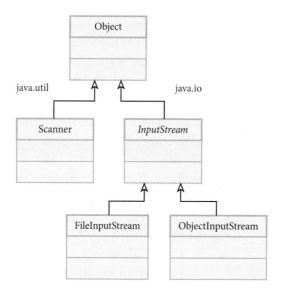

TABLE 11.3   Selected Input Classes

Input Classes	
Class	**Description**
Scanner	Class to read and parse characters in text files
InputStream	*Abstract* superclass representing an input stream of raw bytes
FileInputStream	Input stream to read raw bytes of data from files
ObjectInputStream	Class to read/recover objects from a file written using *ObjectOutputStream*

TABLE 11.4   Selected Output Classes

Output Classes	
Class	**Description**
Writer	*Abstract* superclass for writing characters to output streams
OutputStream	*Abstract* superclass representing an output stream of raw bytes
FileWriter	Convenience class for writing characters to files
PrintWriter	Convenience class to output basic data types, *Strings*, and objects
FileOutputStream	Output stream to write raw bytes of data to files
ObjectOutputStream	Class to write objects to a file

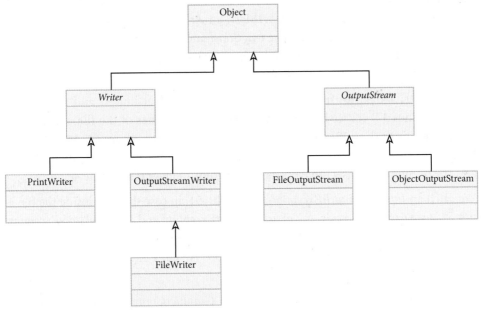

Figure 11.7

The Inheritance Hierarchy for Output Classes

11.5   Recovering from an Exception

In the next example, we read data from a file and use that data to draw a flag. Figure 11.8 shows the contents of the *HungarianFlag.txt* file. We also show how to catch and recover from an exception; that is, how to enable our program to continue to run when an exception occurs. The data is organized in a similar manner, but it is simpler than what is used by the GIF run-length encoding algorithm:

- The first line is an integer storing the width of the flag.

- Each line thereafter contains four numbers. The first number, an integer, stores the number of consecutive pixels (as we go left to right on the flag image) of the same color; the next three numbers store the red, green, and blue coefficients of that color as *doubles* between 0 and 1.

The width of the Hungarian flag represented by our file is 300, it has 15,000 consecutive red pixels (i.e., 15,000 divided by 300, which is equal to 50, red lines), then 15,000 consecutive white pixels (i.e., 50 white lines), and 15,000 consecutive green pixels (i.e., 50 green lines).

Example 11.3 shows the *GIFDecoding* class. Its constructor accepts an already instantiated *Scanner* parameter and reads the data in the associated file into three instance variables: *width*, an *int*; *lengthList*, an *ArrayList* of *Integers*; and *colorList*, an *ArrayList* of *Color* references. The *lengthList* and *colorList* are parallel *ArrayLists*; that is, the color stored at a given index in *colorList* applies to the number of pixels stored in *lengthList* at that same index.

Inside the *try* block, we first read the width of the flag at line 33 and assign it to *width*. At lines 37–46, we loop through the remaining lines of the file, reading the number of pixels (line 39) and their three color components (lines 42–44). With the three color components, we create a *Color* object and add it to *colorList* at line 45; we add the number of consecutive pixels of that color to *lengthList* at line 40.

We catch an *InputMismatchException* at lines 48–51, in case the data inside the file is not what we expect, and exit. A *NoSuchElementException* and an *IllegalStateException* can also be thrown by the *nextInt* and *nextDouble* methods. We catch them both in the generic *Exception catch* block at lines 52–55. We close the *Scanner* in the *finally* block (lines 56–59).

The *drawGIF* method (lines 62–94) accepts a *GraphicsContext* parameter and uses it to draw the GIF. The upper-left coordinates of the GIF are defined by the *x* and

Figure 11.8

The *HungarianFlag.-txt* File

```
300
15000 1.0 0.0 0.0
15000 1.0 1.0 1.0
15000 0.0 1.0 0.0
```

y parameters passed to *drawGIF*. At lines 74–93, we loop through all the lengths stored in *lengthList*. At line 76, we retrieve the corresponding color for the current pixels and set the stroke color of the *GraphicsContext* to that color at line 77. Because the number of consecutive pixels of the same color can be larger than the width of the drawing, several consecutive lines could have the same color. Thus, we draw the GIF one line at a time using a *while* loop (lines 79–86). After the loop, we draw a line with the current color if there are pixels left over (lines 88–89).

```java
 1 /* GIF decoding class
 2    Anderson, Franceschi
 3 */
 4
 5 import java.io.*;
 6 import java.util.*;
 7 import javafx.scene.canvas.GraphicsContext;
 8 import javafx.scene.paint.Color;
 9
10 public class GIFDecoding
11 {
12   private int width; // the width of the GIF
13
14   // ArrayList instance variables:
15   // colorList stores Color references
16   // lengthList stores integers, the length of each run
17   private ArrayList<Color> colorList;
18   private ArrayList<Integer> lengthList;
19
20   /* GIFDecoding constructor
21    * @param file a Scanner, already open for reading a GIF file
22    * initializes width with the first int in file
23    * fills the two ArrayLists with the
24    * ints and colors stored in file
25    */
26   public GIFDecoding( Scanner file )
27   {
28     colorList = new ArrayList<Color>( );
29     lengthList = new ArrayList<Integer>( );
30
31     try
32     {
33       width = file.nextInt( );
34       int length;
35       double red, green, blue;
```

```
36
37      while ( file.hasNext( ) )
38      {
39        length = file.nextInt( );
40        lengthList.add( length );
41
42        red = file.nextDouble( );
43        green = file.nextDouble( );
44        blue = file.nextDouble( );
45        colorList.add( Color.color( red, green, blue ) );
46      }
47    }
48    catch ( InputMismatchException ime )
49    {
50      System.out.println( "Invalid file format; exiting" );
51    }
52    catch ( Exception e )
53    {
54      System.out.println( e.getMessage( ) );
55    }
56    finally
57    {
58      file.close( );
59    }
60  }
61
62  /*
63   * drawGIF method
64   * @param gc a GraphicsContext reference, the graphics context
65   * @param x an int, the drawing's upper left corner x coordinate
66   * @param y an int, the drawing's upper left corner y coordinate
67   */
68  public void drawGIF( GraphicsContext gc, int x, int y  )
69  {
70    // draw the gif
71    Color currentColor;
72    int index = 0;
73    int deltaX = 0;
74    for ( int length : lengthList )
75    {
76      currentColor = colorList.get( index );
77      gc.setStroke( currentColor );
78
79      // draw one or more lines using length pixels with currentColor
```

```
80          while ( length >= width - deltaX )
81          {
82            gc.strokeLine( x + deltaX, y, x + width, y );
83            y++;
84            length = length - ( width - deltaX );
85            deltaX = 0;
86          }
87
88          if ( length > 0 )
89            gc.strokeLine( x + deltaX, y, x + deltaX + length, y );
90
91          deltaX = deltaX + length;
92          index++;
93        }
94    }
95  }
```

EXAMPLE 11.3   The *GIFDecoding* Class

In Example 11.4, we ask the user to input a file name, instantiate a *Scanner* to
read the file, create and instantiate a *GIFDecoding* object, then call the *drawGIF*
method to draw the flag. If there is no file in the current folder with the name
entered by the user or if the user mistypes the file name, a *FileNotFoundException*
is thrown. Instead of terminating the program, we use the *try* and *catch* blocks
to recover from erroneous user input. We use a *do/while* loop at lines 25–40 that
keeps asking the user for a file name as long as no file with that name can be found
in the current folder. At line 23, we declare a *boolean* variable, *fileFound*, initialized to *false*. As long as *fileFound* is *false* (line 40), we keep entering the loop and
asking the user for a file name. If the user enters an invalid file name, our code
instantiating the *Scanner file* (line 33) will throw a *FileNotFoundException*. We
will then skip line 34 and execute the catch block (lines 36–39). Thus, *fileFound*
will remain *false* and our loop condition will remain *true*. When the user enters
a valid file name, *file* will be successfully instantiated and no exception will be
thrown. Line 34 will execute, changing *fileFound* to *true* and we will then exit the
loop.

Notice that we declare and initialize the variables *file* and *filename* at lines 21 and
22 before we enter the *try* block. If we do not initialize them and then try to access
them in the *catch* block or after the *try/catch* blocks, we will receive the following
compiler error (shown for *filename*):

```
variable filename might not have been initialized
```

Figure 11.9

Output of
Example 11.4

At lines 42–46, we create a *GraphicsContext*, instantiate a *GIFDecoding* object using *file* at line 48, and draw the flag at line 49.

When we run and enter *HungarianFlag.txt* at the prompt, the window shown in Figure 11. 9 appears.

COMMON ERROR TRAP
Failing to initialize a variable that is assigned a value in a *try* block, then accessed after the *try* block, will generate a compiler error.

```
1  /* Drawing a GIF
2     Anderson, Franceschi
3  */
4
5  import java.io.*;
6  import java.util.Scanner;
7  import javafx.application.Application;
8  import javafx.scene.canvas.GraphicsContext;
9  import javafx.scene.paint.Color;
10 import javafx.stage.Stage;
11
12 public class DrawAGIF extends Application
13 {
14   final int WIDTH = 500;
15   final int HEIGHT = 300;
16
17   @Override
18   public void start( Stage stage )
19   {
20     Scanner scan = new Scanner( System.in );
21     Scanner file = null;
22     String filename = "";
```

```
23      boolean fileFound = false;
24
25      do
26      {
27        try
28        {
29          System.out.print( "Enter the name of the file > " );
30          filename = scan.next( );
31
32          File inputFile = new File( filename );
33          file = new Scanner( inputFile );
34          fileFound = true;
35        }
36        catch ( FileNotFoundException fnf )
37        {
38          System.out.println( "Unable to find " + filename );
39        }
40      } while ( !fileFound );
41
42      // set up window title and size
43      GraphicsContext gc = JIGraphicsUtility.setUpGraphics(
44             stage, "Draw a flag", WIDTH, HEIGHT );
45      gc.setFill( Color.LIGHTSKYBLUE );
46      gc.fillRect( 0, 0, WIDTH, HEIGHT );
47
48      GIFDecoding flag = new GIFDecoding( file );
49      flag.drawGIF( gc, 50, 50 );
50    }
51
52    public static void main( String [ ] args )
53    {
54      launch( args );
55    }
56 }
```

EXAMPLE 11.4   Reading a File and Drawing the Corresponding GIF

SOFTWARE
ENGINEERING
TIP
Write code
to catch
and handle
exceptions
generated by
invalid user
input. Although
the methods of
the *Exception*
class are good
debugging
tools, they are
not necessarily
appropriate
to use in the
final version of
a program. Try
to write user-
friendly error
messages.

11.6   Writing and Appending to Text Files

In the previous sections, we learned how to read data from a text file. But how did the data get into the file in the first place? It could be that someone put the data into the file using a text editor, such as Notepad in Windows, or TextEdit in MacOS. Typing data into a file is convenient when the amount of data is small. But very often files contain a significant amount of data, typically written to the file by a computer

TABLE 11.5   Writing or Appending to an Existing or New File

Operation	If the file exists ...	If the file does not exist ...
write	the current contents of the file are deleted, and writing starts at the beginning of the file	the file is created and writing starts at the beginning of the file
append	data is added to the end of the file, keeping the existing contents	the file is created and writing starts at the beginning of the file

program. For instance, a web server writes to log files to keep track of the visitors accessing the website, how the visitors got to the website, the time they arrived, etc. If the web server comes under attack from a hacker, these log files can be consulted to determine where the hacker came from, who the hacker was, and other information.

In this section, we will learn how to write to a text file. But before going into the details, we must distinguish among several situations:

- Creating/writing to a new file, that is, the file does not exist.
- Writing to an existing file and replacing the contents of the file with new data.
- Writing to an existing file, but keeping the contents of the file and adding data at the end of the file. This is called **appending** to the file.

Java provides us with the necessary tools to perform all the preceding actions. Table 11.5 summarizes what will happen, depending on the action we perform and whether the file already exists.

11.6.1   Writing to Text Files

The data that we write to files can be primitive data types, such as *ints*, *doubles*, or *booleans*, or even objects, such as *Strings*.

FileWriter, a subclass of the *Writer* class, is designed to write characters to a file. It has several constructors, one of which takes a file name and a mode as its two arguments. The *boolean mode* variable specifies whether we are writing (*false*) or appending (*true*) to the file.

The *PrintWriter* class is designed for converting basic data types to characters and writing them to a text file. The *PrintWriter* class provides *print* and *println* methods for all primitive data types, as well as for *Strings* and objects, that is, it calls the *toString* method of the object's class. The *print* method writes the argument value to the file, whereas the *println* method writes the argument value to the file followed by a *newline* character. The constructors and method APIs are shown in Table 11.6.

TABLE 11.6 Useful Classes, Constructors, and Methods for Writing to a Text File

Classes, Constructors, and Methods for Writing to a Text File		
Class	**Constructors**	**Exceptions thrown**
FileWriter	FileWriter(String filename, boolean mode)	IOException
	constructs a *FileWriter* object from a *String* representing the name of a file; if *mode* is *false*, we will write to the file; if *mode* is *true*, we will append to the file	
PrintWriter	PrintWriter(Writer wr)	None
	constructs a *PrintWriter* object from the *Writer* object *wr*	
	Method APIs	
PrintWriter	void print(int i) void print(double d) void print(char c) void print(boolean b) . . . void println(int i) void println(double d) . . . writes the argument to a text file	None
PrintWriter	void close( )	None
	releases the resources associated with the *PrintWriter* object	

Example 11.5 shows how we can use the *FileWriter* and *PrintWriter* classes to write *Strings* and primitive data types to a text file named *ItalianFlag.txt*. We write data for the Italian flag that can later be read and drawn using the *DrawAGIF* example.

```
 1 /*  Writes a GIF encoding to a file
 2      Anderson, Franceschi
 3 */
 4
 5 import java.io.*;
 6
 7 public class WriteFlagToFile
 8 {
 9   private static final int HEIGHT = 10;
10
```

```
11   public static void main( String [ ] args )
12   {
13     try
14     {
15       FileWriter fw = new FileWriter( "ItalianFlag.txt", false );
16       PrintWriter pw = new PrintWriter( fw );
17       pw.println( 30 ); // width of GIF
18       // write HEIGHT lines of color and pixels data
19       for ( int i = 0; i < HEIGHT; i++ )
20       {
21         pw.print( 10 ); // 10 green pixels
22         pw.print( ' ' ); // white space character
23         pw.print( 0.0 ); // red color component
24         pw.println( " 1.0 0.0" ); // green and blue color components
25
26         pw.println( "10 1.0 1.0 1.0" ); // 10 white pixels
27         pw.println( "10 1.0 0.0 0.0" ); // 10 red pixels
28       }
29
30       pw.close( );
31     }
32
33     catch ( IOException ioe )
34     {
35       System.out.println( ioe.getMessage( ) );
36     }
37   }
38 }
```

EXAMPLE 11.5   Writing *Strings* and Primitive Data Types to a Text File

Line 15 instantiates a *FileWriter* object to write to the file *ItalianFlag.txt*. The *FileWriter* constructor could throw an *IOException*. Our code catches that exception at lines 33–36. This is the only *catch* block because the methods of the *PrintWriter* class do not throw exceptions.

Line 16 instantiates a *PrintWriter* object, which we will use to write to the file. At lines 17–28, using the *PrintWriter* object *pw*, we call the methods *print* and *println*, passing various *String* and primitive data type arguments (*int, char,* and *double*) to be written to the file. When we want a *newline* character appended to the output, we call *println*, rather than *print*.

On line 30, we close the file. Although calling the *close* method is optional when we are reading a file, it is essential to call the *close* method when we are writing to a file. Closing the file flushes any buffered data to the output file. If we omit calling the *close* method, we may find that the file is empty when the program ends.

```
30
10 0.0 1.0 0.0
10 1.0 1.0 1.0
10 1.0 0.0 0.0
10 0.0 1.0 0.0
10 1.0 1.0 1.0
10 1.0 0.0 0.0
10 0.0 1.0 0.0
10 1.0 1.0 1.0
10 1.0 0.0 0.0
10 0.0 1.0 0.0
10 1.0 1.0 1.0
10 1.0 0.0 0.0
10 0.0 1.0 0.0
10 1.0 1.0 1.0
10 1.0 0.0 0.0
10 0.0 1.0 0.0
10 1.0 1.0 1.0
10 1.0 0.0 0.0
10 0.0 1.0 0.0
10 1.0 1.0 1.0
10 1.0 0.0 0.0
10 0.0 1.0 0.0
10 1.0 1.0 1.0
10 1.0 0.0 0.0
10 0.0 1.0 0.0
10 1.0 1.0 1.0
10 1.0 0.0 0.0
10 0.0 1.0 0.0
10 1.0 1.0 1.0
10 1.0 0.0 0.0
```

Figure 11.10

The *ItalianFlag.txt* file after running Example 11.5

After this program is executed, the file *ItalianFlag.txt* will contain the data shown in Figure 11.10. Because we wrote all the output to the file *ItalianFlag.txt*, there is no output to the console.

11.6.2   Appending to Text Files

Appending text to a file is similar to writing text; the only difference is that the second argument of the *FileWriter* constructor is *true*, instead of *false*.

Example 11.6 shows how the *FileWriter* and *PrintWriter* classes can be used in a Java program to append text to our file named *ItalianFlag.txt*.

```
1 /* Appends to a file
2    Anderson, Franceschi
```

```java
 3 */
 4
 5 import java.io.*;
 6 import java.util.*;
 7
 8 public class AppendToFlagFile
 9 {
10   static final int PIXELS = 10;
11
12   public static void main( String [ ] args )
13   {
14     int lines = 0;
15     Scanner scan = new Scanner( System.in );
16     boolean goodInput = false;
17
18     do
19     {
20       try
21       {
22         // prompt for input; expected value is an int
23         System.out.print( "Enter a number of lines (20 to 50) "
24                         + "to append > " );
25         lines = scan.nextInt( );
26         if ( lines >= 20 && lines <= 50 )
27           goodInput = true;
28       }
29
30       catch ( InputMismatchException ime )
31       {
32         // consume invalid data left in input stream
33         String garbage = scan.nextLine( );
34         System.out.print( "You did not enter an integer; "
35                         + "please enter an integer > " );
36       }
37     } while ( !goodInput );
38
39     try
40     {
41       FileWriter fw = new FileWriter( "ItalianFlag.txt", true );
42       PrintWriter pw = new PrintWriter( fw );
43       // append lines of color and pixels data for this flag
44       for ( int i = 0; i < lines; i++ )
45       {
46         pw.println( PIXELS + " 0.0 1.0 0.0" ); // PIXELS green pixels
47         pw.println( PIXELS + " 1.0 1.0 1.0" ); // PIXELS white pixels
48         pw.println( PIXELS + " 1.0 0.0 0.0" ); // PIXELS red pixels
49       }
```

```
50      pw.close( );
51    }
52
53    catch ( IOException ioe )
54    {
55      System.out.println( ioe.getMessage( ) );
56    }
57  }
58 }
```

EXAMPLE 11.6   Appending to a Text File

Example 11.6 is similar to Example 11.5. The major difference is that when we instantiate the *FileWriter* object (line 41), the second argument is *true*, which means that we will append to the file *ItalianFlag.txt*. If the file *ItalianFlag.txt* exists, we will start writing at the end of its current contents, whereas if the file does not exist, it will be created. In this program, we ask the user how many lines he or she wants to append to the file. At lines 18–37, we loop until the user inputs an integer whose value is between 20 and 50, inclusive. We use a *boolean* variable, *goodInput*, to monitor the validity of the value entered by the user. As long as *goodInput* is *false* (line 37), we keep asking the user for a new value. If the user does not enter an integer, we execute the *catch* block and flush the input stream (lines 32–33). If we instead leave the invalid user input in the input stream, we would attempt to read that invalid user input again at line 25 at the next iteration of the loop. If the user enters an integer, we test that the value is between 20 and 50 at line 26. If the input is valid, we change *goodInput* to *true* and exit the loop.

If the *ItalianFlag.txt* file is the one that was created by Example 11.5, we can use two approaches to check if we did append to the file when we ran this program: We can open the file in Notepad and check that it contains the extra lines. We can also run Example 11.4 again, using the newly created file, and we can verify that the drawing is larger than before.

COMMON ERROR TRAP

Opening a file for writing will cause the existing file data to be deleted. If you intend to add new data to a file while maintaining the original contents, open the file for appending.

11.7   Reading Structured Text Files

Sometimes a text file is organized so that each line represents data related to a particular record or object. For instance, an airline company could have data stored in a file where each line represents a flight segment, with the following comma-separated data:

- flight number
- origin airport
- destination airport

- number of passengers
- average ticket price

Such a file could contain the following data:

```
AA123,BWI,SFO,235,239.5
AA200,BOS,JFK,150,89.3
AA900,LAX,CHI,201,201.8

...
```

As we read the file, we should **parse** each line, that is, separate the line into the individual pieces of data (flight number, origin airport, etc.), called **tokens**. In this case, the comma is the **delimiter**; that is, a comma separates one token from the next. We will store the tokens from each line into a corresponding *FlightRecord* object.

11.7.1   Parsing a *String* Using *Scanner*

In addition to accepting input from the console and text files, *Scanner* can also be used to parse *Strings*, that is, to separate *Strings* into tokens.

A constructor of the *Scanner* class, which takes a *String* to parse, is shown in Table 11.7.

Scanner's default delimiters are the white space characters. We can specify different delimiters through the *useDelimiter* method (also shown in Table 11.7), which accepts as its argument a *String* representing a **regular expression**. Regular expressions allow us to specify a pattern against which to match sequences of characters using standard characters as well as **meta-characters**, which have special meanings.

TABLE 11.7   Useful Constructor and Method of the *Scanner* Class for Parsing a *String*

Constructor	Exceptions thrown
Scanner(String source)	None
constructs a *Scanner* object that produces tokens from the specified *String*	

Method API		
Return value	**Method name and argument list**	
Scanner	useDelimiter(String pattern)	None
sets this *Scanner* object's delimiters based on the specified *pattern*		

Further discussion of regular expressions is outside the scope of this book. For our purposes, we can specify a delimiter consisting of a single or multiple specific characters as a simple *String* argument for the *useDelimiter* method. For example, to parse a *String* like *AA123,BWI,SFO,235,239.5*, we call the *useDelimiter* method and pass a comma as its argument.

Example 11.7 shows how the *Scanner* class can be used in a Java program to parse a *String*.

```java
1   /* Demonstrating how to parse a String with the Scanner class
2      Anderson, Franceschi
3   */
4
5   import java.util.Scanner;
6   import java.util.InputMismatchException;
7   import java.util.NoSuchElementException;
8
9   public class UsingScannerToParseAString
10  {
11    public static void main( String [ ] args )
12    {
13      String flightRecord1 = "AA123,BWI,SFO,235,239.5";
14
15      try ( Scanner parse = new Scanner( flightRecord1 ) )
16      {
17        // set the delimiter to a comma
18        parse.useDelimiter( "," );
19
20        System.out.println( parse.next( ) ); // flight number
21        System.out.println( parse.next( ) ); // origin airport
22        System.out.println( parse.next( ) ); // destination airport
23        System.out.println( parse.nextInt( ) ); // number of passengers
24        System.out.println( parse.nextDouble( ) ); // average ticket price
25      }
26
27      catch ( InputMismatchException ime )
28      {
29        System.out.println( "Error in data format" );
30      }
31
32      catch ( NoSuchElementException nse )
33      {
34        System.out.println( "No more tokens" );
35      }
36
37      catch ( IllegalStateException ise )
38      {
```

```
39          ise.printStackTrace ( );
40      }
41    }
42  }
```

EXAMPLE 11.7   Demonstrating How to Parse a *String* with the *Scanner* Class

At line 15, the *Scanner* object *parse* is instantiated using the constructor with a *String* argument, *flightRecord1*, the *String* that we want to tokenize (See line 13). At lines 17–18, we call the *useDelimiter* method to set the delimiter to a comma.

At lines 20–24, we call the *next, nextInt,* and *nextDouble* methods to retrieve the five tokens of *flightRecord1* and process them, echoing them to the console. Since we know the format of the *String flightRecord1*, we can call the appropriate method based on the data type we expect to find at that position in the *String*. Although these methods throw exceptions, these exceptions are unchecked exceptions and thus the *try* and *catch* blocks are not mandatory. The *nextInt, nextDouble,* ... methods will throw an *InputMismatchException* if the token retrieved cannot be converted to the expected data type. They will throw a *NoSuchElementException* if there are no more tokens to retrieve. Finally, they will throw an *IllegalStateException* if the *Scanner* object has been closed. We *catch* all these exceptions at lines 27–40, from the most specific to the most general and in the order in which they are most likely to be thrown.

REFERENCE POINT
You can read more about the *Scanner* class at www.oracle.com /technetwork /java.

When the program in Example 11.7 runs, it will produce the output shown in Figure 11.11.

If we want to process all the tokens as *Strings* with a loop construct, we can call the *hasNext* method to check if there are more tokens to process as in the following:

```
while ( parse.hasNext( ) )
  System.out.println( parse.next( ) );
```

Eventually, when all tokens have been retrieved, the *hasNext* method returns *false*, which causes us to exit the *while* loop.

11.7.2   Reading Structured Data Using *Scanner*

Let's say that we have a file named *flights.txt* containing many flight records, and we want to read the data into variables. Suppose that each line in the file is in the same format as the *flightRecord1 String* in Section 11.7.1; that is, the file looks like the following:

```
AA123,BWI,SFO,235,239.5
AA200,BOS,JFK,150,89.3
AA900,LAX,CHI,201,201.8
...
```

```
AA123
BWI
SFO
235
239.5
```

Figure 11.11

Output from
Example 11.7

where each line represents a flight segment with the following comma-separated data: flight number, origin airport, destination airport, number of passengers, and average ticket price.

First, we build a class called *FlightRecord*, encapsulating a flight record as reflected by the data in the file. Each line read from the file will be parsed and used to instantiate a *FlightRecord* object. Since we do not know how many lines (i.e., how many flight records) are in the file, we place all the flight records into an *ArrayList* object as opposed to a fixed-length array.

Our simplified *FlightRecord* class is shown in Example 11.8. It has only a constructor (lines 17–35) and the *toString* method (lines 37–49).

```java
 1 /* The FlightRecord class
 2    Anderson, Franceschi
 3 */
 4
 5 import java.text.DecimalFormat;
 6
 7 public class FlightRecord
 8 {
 9    public static final DecimalFormat MONEY
10                        = new DecimalFormat( "$###.00" );
11    private String flightNumber;      // ex. = AA123
12    private String origin;            // origin airport; ex. = BWI
13    private String destination;       // destination airport; ex. = SFO
14    private int numPassengers;        // number of passengers
15    private double avgTicketPrice;    // average ticket price
16
17    /** Constructor
18    *  @param  flightNumber    flight number
19    *  @param  origin          origin airport
20    *  @param  destination     destination airport
21    *  @param  numPassengers   number of passengers
22    *  @param  avgTicketPrice average ticket price
23    */
24    public FlightRecord( String flightNumber,
25                         String origin,
26                         String destination,
27                         int numPassengers,
28                         double avgTicketPrice )
```

```
29    {
30      this.flightNumber = flightNumber;
31      this.origin = origin;
32      this.destination = destination;
33      this.numPassengers = numPassengers;
34      this.avgTicketPrice = avgTicketPrice;
35    }
36
37    /** toString
38    * @return flight number, origin, destination,
39    *          number of passengers, and average ticket price
40    */
41    @Override
42    public String toString( )
43    {
44      return "Flight " + flightNumber
45            + ": from " + origin
46            + " to " + destination
47            + "\n\t" + numPassengers + " passengers"
48            + "; average ticket price: "
49            + MONEY.format( avgTicketPrice );
50    }
51    // accessors, mutators, and other methods ...
52 }
```

EXAMPLE 11.8   The *FlightRecord* Class

Example 11.9 shows our client class, which reads the file *flights.txt*, parses each line using *Scanner*, then instantiates a *FlightRecord* object and adds it to the *ArrayList* named *listFlightRecords*.

```
1 /* Reading structured data from a text file
2     Anderson, Franceschi
3 */
4
5 import java.io.File;
6 import java.io.FileNotFoundException;
7 import java.util.Scanner;
8 import java.util.InputMismatchException;
9 import java.util.ArrayList;
10
11 public class ReadFlights
12 {
13    public static void main( String [ ] args )
14    {
15      // instantiate ArrayList to hold FlightRecord objects
```

```
16       ArrayList<FlightRecord> listFlightRecords =
17                            new ArrayList<FlightRecord>( );
18
19       try
20       {
21         Scanner file = new Scanner( new File( "flights.txt" ) );
22
23         while ( file.hasNext( ) ) // test for the end of the file
24         {
25             // read a line
26             String stringRead = file.nextLine( );
27
28             // process the line read
29             Scanner parse = new Scanner( stringRead );
30             parse.useDelimiter( "," );
31             String flightNumber = parse.next( );
32             String origin = parse.next( );
33             String destination = parse.next( );
34
35             try
36             {
37                 int numPassengers = parse.nextInt( );
38                 double avgTicketPrice = parse.nextDouble( );
39
40                 FlightRecord frTemp = new FlightRecord(
41                             flightNumber, origin, destination,
42                             numPassengers, avgTicketPrice );
43
44                 // add FlightRecord obj to listFlightRecords
45                 listFlightRecords.add( frTemp );
46             }
47
48             catch ( InputMismatchException ime )
49             {
50                 System.out.println( "Error in flight record: "
51                         + stringRead + "; record ignored" );
52             }
53         }
54
55         // release resources associated with flights.txt
56         file.close( );
57       }
58
59       catch ( FileNotFoundException fnfe )
60       {
61         System.out.println( "Unable to find flights.txt" );
62       }
```

```
63
64      catch ( Exception ioe )
65      {
66         ioe.printStackTrace( );
67      }
68
69      // print the FlightRecords read
70      for ( FlightRecord flight : listFlightRecords )
71          System.out.println( flight );
72   }
73 }
```

EXAMPLE 11.9   Demonstrating How to Read Structured Data from a File

Lines 5–9 import the classes needed for input, parsing, and exception handling, as well as *ArrayList*. The *FlightRecord* class is also used in this program, but is assumed to be in the same folder as the *ReadFlights* class.

In this example, we instantiate two *Scanner* objects: one to read the lines from the file into a *String* and a second *Scanner* object to parse the *String*.

With the first *Scanner* object (instantiated on line 21), we use the *nextLine* method to read one line at a time (line 26). We provide *catch* blocks for both *FileNotFoundException* (lines 59–62) and *Exception* (lines 64–67). The *Scanner* constructor can throw a *FileNotFoundException* and the *File* constructor can throw a *NullPointerException*. Both *FileNotFoundException* and *NullPointerException* are subclasses of *Exception*. Remember that when an exception occurs, the *catch* blocks are scanned, in order, for a match between the *catch* block parameter and the type of exception that occurred. Because the *FileNotFoundException* is a subclass of *Exception*, a *FileNotFoundException* will also match a *catch* block for an *Exception*. Therefore, we need to put the *catch* block for the *FileNotFoundException* before the *catch* block for *Exception*. This way, if the file does not exist, the exception will match the first *catch* block, which handles the *FileNotFoundException*, and we will be able to output a meaningful message for the user. If the *File* constructor throws a *NullPointerException*, which we don't expect to happen, that will match the *catch* block for *Exception* and we print the stack trace.

As we read each line from the file, we instantiate a second *Scanner* object (line 29) and pass the data we extract as our arguments to the *FlightRecord* constructor to instantiate a *FlightRecord* object (lines 40–42).

The *FlightRecord* object is then added to the *ArrayList listFlightRecords* at lines 44–45. The *ArrayList listFlightRecords* is declared and instantiated at lines 15–17, before the *try* block so that *listFlightRecords* is available for printing the *FlightRecord* objects at lines 69–71, after we finish reading the file. If the *flights.txt* file contains the data shown in Figure 11.12, the program will produce the output shown in Figure 11.13.

```
AA123,BWI,SFO,235,239.5
AA200,BOS,JFK,150,89.3
AA900,LAX,CHI,201,201.8
```

Figure 11.12

Contents of
flights.txt

```
Flight AA123: from BWI to SFO
        235 passengers; average ticket price: $239.50
Flight AA200: from BOS to JFK
        150 passengers; average ticket price: $89.30
Flight AA900: from LAX to CHI
        201 passengers; average ticket price: $201.80
```

Figure 11.13

Output from
ReadFlights.java

CODE IN ACTION

Within the online resources, you will find a movie with a step-by-step illustration of reading from and writing to a text file. Click on the link to start the movie.

© Hemera Technologies/
Photos.com/Thinkstock

Skill Practice
with these end-of-chapter questions

11.15.1   Multiple Choice Exercises

Questions 1, 2, 4, 5, 6, 7, 8, 9

11.15.2   Reading and Understanding Code

Questions 12, 13, 14, 15, 17, 18, 19, 20, 21, 22, 23

11.15.3   Fill In the Code

Questions 24, 25, 26, 28, 29, 30, 31, 32, 33

11.15.4   Identifying Errors in Code

Questions 34, 35, 36

11.15.5   Debugging Area

Questions 37, 38, 39, 40, 41, 42

11.15.6   Write a Short Program

Questions 43, 44, 45, 46, 47, 48, 50, 51

11.8   Programming Activity 1: Reading from a Structured Text File

In this activity, you will read from a text file using an end-of-file controlled *while* loop performing this activity:

> Read a text file containing transaction items for a bank account. Loop through all the transaction items and calculate the new balance of the bank account. Assume that we do not know the number of transaction items (i.e., lines) in the file.

The framework will display the current transaction and current balance so that you can check the correctness of your code as the program executes.

For example, Figure 11.14 demonstrates the animation: We are currently scanning a check for the amount of $200.00. The original balance was $0.00 and the new balance is −$200.00. Ideally, this is not your bank account.

Instructions

In this chapter's folder in the supplied code, you will find the Programming Activity 1 folder. Copy the contents of the folder onto a folder on your disk.

- Open the file *transactions.txt* with a text editor. You will see that each line contains a transaction name and transaction amount separated by a colon, as shown in Figure 11.15.

- Note that the transaction amounts are positive or negative. For instance:

  - A check or a withdrawal has a negative amount.

  - A deposit has a positive amount.

  - An unknown transaction has either a positive or negative amount.

Figure 11.14

Animation
Showing a $200
Check and the
New Balance

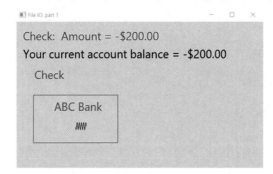

```
Check # 13 :-200.00
Check # 14 :-100.00
Withdrawal June 12 :-200.00
Withdrawal June 17 :-400.00
Withdrawal June 23 :-100.00
Deposit :4000.00
Deposit :100.00
Something else :-1000.00
Check # 16 :-500.00
Check # 15 :-100.00
```

Figure 11.15

Contents of the
transactions.txt
File

- Now open the *AccountingDrawing.java* file. Search for five asterisks (*****)
  to find the *balanceCheckBook* method where you will add your code. The
  method header has already been coded for you. Write the code to read all
  the transactions from the file *transactions.txt*, process each transaction
  against the account, and calculate the balance after all the transactions in
  that file have been processed.

  The code for the *balanceCheckBook* method is shown in Example 11.10.

```java
public void balanceCheckBook( )
{
  // ***** Write the body of this method *****
  //
  // Using a while loop, read the file transactions.txt
  // The file transactions.txt contains money
  // transactions between you and your bank
  //
  // You will need to call the method animate inside
  // the body of the loop reading the file contents
  //
  // The animate method takes 3 arguments:
  //    a String, representing the type of transaction
  //    a double, representing the transaction money amount
  //    a double, representing the new checkbook balance
  // So if these 3 variables are:
  //    transactionName, currentAmount, and balance,
  // then the call to animate will be:
  //
  //  animate( transactionName, currentAmount, balance );
  //
  // You should make that call in the body of your while
  // loop, after you have updated the checkbook balance
  //
```

```
//
// end of student code
//
}
```

EXAMPLE 11.10   The *balanceCheckBook* Method in *Accounting Drawing.java*

- Begin with a checkbook balance of 0.00.

- To process the transactions, you will need to read one line at a time from the *transactions.txt* file and parse the *String* that you retrieve. You can use the *Scanner* class for this. The delimiter will be a colon. Then process the transaction; you do not need to check the type of transaction. Just add the amount of the transaction to the checkbook balance. Adding a negative transaction amount will decrease the balance, as expected. Be sure to use *try/catch* blocks where appropriate.

- After you have processed each transaction, call the *animate* method. This method belongs to the *AccountingDrawing* class, so you will call *animate* without using an object reference. The API of the *animate* method is the following:

```
public void animate( String currentTransaction,
                     double currentAmount,
                     double currentBalance )
```

As you can see, the *animate* method takes three arguments: *currentTransaction* is the transaction name ("Deposit," for example), *currentAmount* is the amount of the transaction (*-45.00*, for example), and *currentBalance* is the current balance of the checkbook. Assuming that you have a *String* variable called *transactionName*, a *double* variable called *amount*, and another *double* called *balance*, a call to *animate* will look like the following:

```
animate( transactionName, amount, balance );
```

- When you call *animate*, the window will display the current transaction graphically. It will also display the transaction amount (red if negative, blue if positive), and the current checkbook balance (in black). By adding the previous checkbook balance to the current transaction amount, you will be able to determine if your program is working correctly.

- When you reach the end of the file, print the final balance and write it to a file named *balance.txt*.

To test your code, compile and run the *AccountingApplication.java* application file.

If you have time ...

- Modify the file *transactions.txt* by deleting or adding transactions manually with a text editor. Run the program again and check that your code still gives the correct result.

- Using a text editor, modify the file *transactions.txt* by entering a positive amount to all transactions. Change your *balanceCheckBook* method so that it determines which transactions are positive and which are negative. Run the program again and check that your code still gives the correct result.

Troubleshooting

If your method implementation does not animate or animates incorrectly, check these items:

- Verify that you coded the call to *animate* at the proper time.

- Verify that you coded the condition for exiting the loop correctly.

- Verify that you coded the body of the loop correctly.

? DISCUSSION QUESTIONS

1.   **What exceptions can occur during this program?**

2.   **Explain why we use the *Scanner* class.**

11. 9   Streams

Streams were introduced with Java 8 to support aggregate sequential and parallel operations on a collection of elements. The *Stream* interface (*java.util.stream* package) specifies functionality to perform those operations on a collection of objects. It uses generics, so we need to specify the type of object that a *Stream* will be working on. The *java.util* .*stream* package includes more specialized stream interfaces such as *IntStream*, *DoubleStream*, or *LongStream*. *Streams* cannot directly access individual elements and thus are designed for performing computations on all or a subset of their elements.

A *Stream* computation goes through a **stream pipeline**. A stream pipeline includes a source of elements that is first converted into a *Stream*; then zero or more operations are performed on those elements, for example filtering or selecting, resulting in another *Stream*. A final operation, for example counting or summing, is then performed, producing a result. Table 11.8 lists some of the methods of the *Stream* interface.

Let's take a closer look at how we can use these methods, for example the *filter* method. If we want to process only the data in the *Stream* that meets some condition, we can use the *Predicate* interface in the *java.util.function* package. The *Predicate* interface uses generics and allows us to test if the data meets a condition. The *filter* method accepts a parameter of type *Predicate<? super T>*. That means the data type of the *Stream* being tested can be of class *T* or a superclass of *T*. Thus, if *cityPredicate* tests if a *String* meets some condition and *cityStream* is an existing *Stream* of type *String*, we can call the *filter* method as follows:

```
cityStream = cityStream.filter( cityPredicate );
```

TABLE 11.8   Selected Methods of the *Stream* Interface

Return value	Method and description
long	count( )
	returns the number of elements in this *Stream*
Stream	filter(Predicate<? super T> predicate)
	returns a *Stream* made of the elements of this *Stream* that satisfy *predicate*
Optional	min(Comparator<? super T> comparator)
	returns the minimum element of this *Stream* using the comparator
Optional	max(Comparator<? super T> comparator)
	returns the maximum element of this *Stream* using the comparator
DoubleStream	mapToDouble(ToDoubleFunction <? super T > mapper)
	returns a *DoubleStream* made up of the elements resulting from applying *mapper* to the *Stream* elements; *mapToInt* and *mapToLong* are similar methods

TABLE 11.9   Methods of the *Predicate, DoublePredicate, Comparator,* and *ToDoubleFunction* Interfaces

Interface	Abstract method
Predicate	boolean test(T t)
	tests *t* and returns *true* or *false*.
DoublePredicate	boolean test(double d)
	tests *d* and returns *true* or *false*.
Comparator	int compare(T t1, T t2)
	compares *t1* and *t2* for order.
ToDoubleFunction	double applyAsDouble(T t)
	converts *t* to a *double* and returns that value.

The *Predicate* interface has only one *abstract* method, *test*. Table 11.9 shows the *test* method as well as the *abstract* methods of the *DoublePredicate, Comparator,* and *ToDoubleFunction* functional interfaces. Note that except for *DoublePredicate*, all these functional interfaces use generics. If we want *cityPredicate* to filter *Strings* that start with the letter *B*, we can implement the *test* method of the *Predicate* interface as shown in Example 11.11.

```
 1 /*  Predicate testing whether a String starts with B
 2      Anderson, Franceschi
 3 */
 4 import java.util.function.*;
 5
 6 public class StartWithBPredicate<T> implements Predicate<T>
 7 {
 8   public boolean test( T t )
 9   {
10     if ( !( t instanceof String ) )
11       return false;
12     else
13     {
14       String s = ( String ) t;
15       return s.charAt( 0 ) == 'B';
16     }
17   }
18 }
```

EXAMPLE 11.11   Implementing the *Predicate* Interface

Below is how we can use the *StartWithBPredicate* test method to filter our *Stream*:

```
StartWithBPredicate<String> cityPredicate
  = new StartWithBPredicate<String>( );
cityStream = cityStream.filter( cityPredicate );
```

Because the *Predicate* interface contains only one *abstract* method that must be implemented, it is a **functional interface**. Thus, we can use a **lambda expression** to replace the code above, as well as the code in Example 11.11, in a single statement as follows:

```
cityStream = cityStream.filter( city -> city.charAt( 0 ) == 'B' );
```

Lambda expressions, introduced in Java version 8, can be used only with functional interfaces, which are interfaces that have only one *abstract* method to implement. A lambda expression contains the following elements:

- A comma-separated list of parameters enclosed in parentheses
- The data types of the parameters may be omitted. The parentheses may also be omitted if there is only one parameter (in the above example, *city* is the parameter).

- The arrow token, ->

- A method body, which can be a single expression or a block enclosed in curly braces

- If the body of the method consists of a single expression, the JVM evaluates the expression and returns its value (in the above example, the JVM returns the value of the expression `city.charAt( 0 ) == 'B')`. As an alternative, we can use a *return* statement, but that requires curly braces.

After we have filtered the *Stream*, we may want to perform a final operation, such as counting. In this example, we count how many cities in the *cities.txt* file start with the letter *B*. After filtering the *Stream*, we call the *count* method, which returns a result, as follows:

```
long count = cityStream.count( );
```

Because the *filter* method returns a *Stream* reference, we can chain the method calls as follows:

```
long count = cityStream.filter( city -> city.charAt( 0 ) == 'B' )
                       .count( );
```

Before processing a *Stream*, we need to create one. Table 11.10 shows some classes and methods that can be used for that purpose. The *stream* method of the *ArrayList* class, inherited from the *Collection* interface, returns a *Stream* consisting of the elements in the *ArrayList*. To create a *Stream* from the contents of a file, we can call the *static lines* method of the *Files* class and pass a *Path* argument for that file. The *Path* interface and the *Paths* and *Files* classes are all in the *java.nio.file* package. A *Path* can be obtained for a file by calling the *static get* method of the *Paths* class. As shown, the *get* method accepts a variable number of arguments for specifying folders in the path to the filename; if the file is located in the current folder, we just pass the name of the file. We can combine the two method calls in one statement as follows:

COMMON ERROR TRAP
Do not confuse the *Path* interface with the *Paths* class. They work together but are different.

```
Stream<String> cityStream = Files.lines( Paths.get( "cities.txt" ) );
```

Example 11.12 shows how we can use *Streams* to perform some aggregate operations on the contents of two files, *cities.txt* and *expenses.txt*, shown in Figures 11.16 and 11.17.

We count the number of cities that begin with *B* in *cities.txt* and calculate the total of the values that are greater than 0.0 in *expenses.txt*.

At lines 19–21, we build a *Stream* using the contents of the *cities.txt* file. At lines 22–24, we compute how many cities start with the letter *B*. We output that count at line 25.

TABLE 11.10 Useful Classes and Methods for Creating a *Stream*

Class	Method	Exceptions thrown
Paths	static Path get(String first, String… more) returns a *Path* constructed with the *String* parameters.	InvalidPathException
Files	static Stream<String> lines(Path p) reads all the lines from *p* and returns them as a *Stream*.	IOException, SecurityException
ArrayList	Stream stream( ) returns a *Stream* consisting of the elements in this *ArrayList*.	

At lines 27–29, we build a *Stream* using the contents of the *expenses.txt* file. At lines 30–34, we select the positive *doubles* from that *Stream* and calculate a sum. We output that total using a currency format at line 35. At line 32, we call the *mapToDouble* method in order to convert the *Stream* of *Strings* to a *DoubleStream*. Since *ToDoubleFunction* is a functional interface, we use the lambda expression

```
data -> Double.parseDouble( data )
```

as the argument of *mapToDouble*. We then call the *filter* method of the *DoubleStream* interface at line 33, which accepts a *DoublePredicate* parameter. Our predicate test determines whether the cost is greater than 0.0. Since *DoublePredicate* is also a functional interface, we use the lambda expression

```
cost -> cost > 0.0
```

as the argument of *filter*. At line 34, we call the *sum* method with the filtered *DoubleStream* in order to sum all its elements. Both the *filter* and *sum* methods are shown in Table 11.11.

```
 1 /*  Reading file data into a Stream and processing it
 2  *   Anderson, Franceschi
 3  */
 4
 5 import java.io.IOException;
 6 import java.nio.file.*;
 7 import java.text.NumberFormat;
 8 import java.util.stream.Stream;
 9
10 public class FilterAndProcessStream
11 {
```

```
12   public static void main( String [ ] args  )
13   {
14    NumberFormat money = NumberFormat.getCurrencyInstance( );
15    String cityFile = "cities.txt";
16    String expenseFile = "expenses.txt";
17    try
18    {
19      // build a Stream using cities.txt
20      Stream<String> cityStream =
21        Files.lines( Paths.get( cityFile ) );
22      // select cities starting with a B and count them
23      long count = cityStream.filter( city -> city.charAt( 0 ) == 'B' )
24                             .count( );
25      System.out.println( "Number of cities starting with B: " + count );
26
27      // build a Stream using expenses.txt
28      Stream<String> numberStream =
29        Files.lines( Paths.get( expenseFile ) );
30      // select positive costs and add them up
31      double sum =
32        numberStream.mapToDouble( data -> Double.parseDouble( data ) )
33                    .filter( cost -> cost > 0.0 )
34                    .sum( );
35      System.out.println( "\nTotal expenses are " + money.format( sum ) );
36    }
37
38    catch ( InvalidPathException ipe )
39    {
40      System.out.println( ipe.getMessage( ) );
41    }
42
43    catch ( IOException ioe )
44    {
45      System.out.println( "Could not find file: " + ioe.getMessage( ) );
46    }
47
48    catch ( SecurityException se )
49    {
50      System.out.println( se.getMessage( ) );
51    }
52  }
53 }
```

EXAMPLE 11.12   Processing *Streams*

Figure 11.18 shows the output of Example 11.12.

```
Paris
Baltimore
Seattle
San Francisco
Boston
Los Angeles
Madrid
Barcelona
Buenos Aires
```

Figure 11.16

The *cities.txt* File

```
1100.50
-100.48
200.39
150.00
```

Figure 11.17

The *expenses.txt* File

TABLE 11.11   The *filter* and *sum* Methods of the *DoubleStream* Interface

Return value	Method and description
DoubleStream	filter(DoublePredicate predicate)
	returns a *DoubleStream* made of the elements of this *DoubleStream* that satisfy *predicate*.
double	sum( )
	returns the sum of the elements in this *DoubleStream*.

```
There are 4 cities starting with B
Total expenses are $1,450.89
```

Figure 11.18

Output of Example 11.12

11.10   Reading Formatted Open Data from a Remote Location

More and more organizations open their data to the general public, and to programmers in particular. In this section, we show how to access data located on a remote server, parse the data, convert the data to a *Stream*, and process the *Stream*.

11.10.1   Accessing Remote Data

The city of Baltimore, Maryland, opens a lot of its data to the public. For this example, we have chosen to retrieve and process data on polling places. The data is located at the following Uniform Record Locator (URL):

```
https://data.baltimorecity.gov/api/views/u7bw-gha5/rows.json?accessType=DOWNLOAD
```

In order to access the data, we use the *URL* and *Scanner* classes. Some of their constructors and methods are listed in Table 11.12. The code sequence below shows how we can access and read the data. The *String resource* stores the name of the *URL* where the data source we want to process is located. We first create and instantiate a *URL* object using the URL of the resource that we want to access. If the resource's URL does not have proper syntax, the *URL* constructor throws a *URLMalformedException*. With the *URL* reference, we then call the *openStream* method, which returns an *InputStream* reference and will throw an *IOException* if there is no resource at that URL. We catch both exceptions. We now can read data from the remote resource with the *Scanner* named *dataSource*.

```
String resource = "https://data.baltimorecity.gov/api/views/"
                 + "u7bw-gha5/rows.json?accessType=DOWNLOAD";
try
{
  URL url = new URL( resource );
  InputStream is = url.openStream( );
  Scanner dataSource = new Scanner( is );

  . .
}
catch ( MalformedURLException murle )
{

  . .
}
catch ( IOException ioe )
{

  . .
}
```

TABLE 11.12   Useful Classes, Constructors, and Methods for Accessing Remote Data

Class	Constructor or method	Exceptions thrown
URL	URL(String url) constructs a URL object.	MalformedURLException will be thrown if *url* is not a properly formed URL.
URL	InputStream openStream( ) creates and returns an *InputStream* for this URL	IOException
Scanner	Scanner(InputStream is) constructs a *Scanner* object that can read from the *InputStream is*.	

11.10.2   JSON Formatting and Parsing

Many open data files are formatted in **XML** or **JSON**. XML stands for eXtended Markup Language. It is similar to HTML except that tags are user-defined instead of predefined. JSON stands for JavaScript Object Notation and is based on JavaScript syntax. JavaScript is an interpreted language that typically runs inside a browser. The JSON format is often the format of choice for transferring data over the Internet between a client and a server. The file that we access in Example 11.13 is a JSON-formatted file. A JSON string includes two data structures:

- A JSON array
- A JSON object, representing a mapping of key/value pairs

Those two data structures can be nested. A JSON array is a list of comma-separated values enclosed in square brackets. A JSON object is enclosed in curly braces and includes a comma-separated list of key/value pairs. A colon separates a key from its associated value. Keys are strings enclosed in quotes. Values can be strings, numbers, true, false, null, an object, or an array.

Here are some examples of valid JSON strings:

```
{ "email":"jane45@gmail.com", "age": 21 }
{ "states": { "MD":"Maryland", "NY":"New York", "CA":"California" } }
[ "New York", "London", "Buenos Aires"]
{ "countries": ["USA", "China", "Brazil"] }
```

The first JSON string is a JSON object that contains two key/value pairs.

The second JSON string is a JSON object that contains one key/value pair. The key states maps to a value that is a JSON object itself, containing three key/value pairs.

The third JSON string is a JSON array that contains three values.

The fourth JSON string is a JSON object that contains one key/value pair. The key countries maps to a JSON array that contains three values.

In order to parse a *JSON* string, we can use the *JSONObject* and *JSONArray* classes of the *org.json* package. Some of their constructors and methods are listed in Table 11.13. The *org.json* package does not come as part of the standard JDK distribution and needs to be downloaded. After you download the *org.json* package, either place it in the folder where the example is located, or, preferably, update the CLASS-PATH environment variable to include the folder where the package is located.

Figure 11.19 shows sample contents of the data at the above URL. The JSON string contains the keys *meta* and *data*. The *meta* values describe the data and contain some aggregated values. We will use the value mapped to the key *data*, which is a JSON array that itself contains 291 JSON arrays (shown in red). The zip codes of the polling places, located at index 11 of those arrays, are shown in green. Assuming that we have read the entire data set into a *String* named *json*, we can use the following code sequence to retrieve the zip code of the polling place at index *i* within the array of polling places:

```
// json is a String that contains the data in Figure 11.19
JSONObject jsonObject = new JSONObject( json );
JSONArray dataJsonArray = jsonObject.getJSONArray( "data" );
// get the JSONArray at index i
JSONArray pollPlaceJsonArray = dataJsonArray.getJSONArray( i );
// retrieve the zip code of the current polling place
String currentZipCode = pollPlaceJsonArray.getString( 11 );
```

First, we create and instantiate a *JSONObject* using the *String json*. With it, we call the *getJSONArray* method, passing the key *data*. The resulting *JSONArray*, *dataJsonArray*, is a *JSONArray* of 291 *JSONArrays*. We retrieve the *JSONArray* at index *i* by calling the *getJSONArray* method and passing *i*. The resulting *JSONArray*, *pollPlaceJsonArray*, contains the data for that polling place. The zip code for that

TABLE 11.13   Useful Classes, Constructors, and Methods for Parsing a JSON *String*

Class	Constructor or method	Exceptions thrown
JSONObject	JSONObject(String json) constructs a URL	JSONException will be thrown if *json* cannot be parsed into a *JSONObject*.
JSONArray	JSONArray getJSONArray(String key) gets and returns the *JSONArray* for *key*	JSONException will be thrown if the mapping for *key* does not exist or does not result in a *JSONArray*.
	int length( ) returns the number of values in this *JSONArray*	
	JSONArray getJSONArray(int index) returns the *JSONArray* at *index*	JSONException will be thrown if *index* is invalid or there is no *JSONArray* at that *index*.
	dataType getDataType(int index) returns the value at that *index*. The data type can be a primitive data type or *String*.	JSONException will be thrown if *index* is invalid or the value at *index* is not compatible with the expected return value.

```
{
  "meta" : {
    ...
  },
  "data" : [ [ 1, "6F093AEC-7C4C-4E6C-BCB1-56982E1DACA2", 1,
1323860520, "393202", 1323860520, "393202", "{\n}", "Hampstead
Hill Academy", "School No. 47", "1", "21224", "46", "3",
"8", "6", "1", "1", "Primary", [ "{\"address\":\"500 Linwood
Avenue\",\"city\":\"Baltimore\",\"state\":\"MD\",\"zip\":\"\"}",
"39.28596538", "-76.5758974", null, false ] ]
, [ 2, "697EBA1A-E68F-47B0-9A84-1005F2F89204", 2, 1323860520,
"393202", 1323860520, "393202", "{\n}", "Engine House No.
5", "Engine House No. 5", "2", "21231", "46", "3", "8",
"6", "1", "1", "Primary", [ "{\"address\":\"2120 Eastern
Avenue\",\"city\":\"Baltimore\",\"state\":\"MD\",\"zip\":\"\"}",
"39.28596212", "-76.58637911", null, false ] ]

...
, [ 291, "BC775625-F29F-4B7C-8453-9DB0F53057FC", 291, 1323860520,
"393202", 1323860520, "393202", "{\n}", "St. Leo's Church
Hall", "St. Leo's Church Hall", "3", "21202", "46", "3",
"8", "6", "1", "1", "Primary", [ "{\"address\":\"225 Exeter
Street\",\"city\":\"Baltimore\",\"state\":\"MD\",\"zip\":\"\"}",
"39.2873401", "-76.60104623", null, false ] ]
  ]
}
```

Figure 11.19

Sample JSON Content Listing Polling Places for Baltimore

polling place is located at index *11* and is stored as a *String*. We call the *getString* method, passing *11* to retrieve the zip code.

11.10.3 Reading, Parsing, Streaming, and Processing Remote Data

Example 11.13 shows how we can read remote data, then parse it and process it. At lines 11–12, we declare a *String* storing the URL resource that we want to access. At lines 16–18, we create a *URL* for that *String*, an *InputStream* for the *URL*, and a *Scanner* ready to read from that *InputStream*. At lines 21–25, we read all the lines from the data source and accumulate them into a *String* named *json*. At lines 27–28, we convert *json* to a *JSONObject* and retrieve the value mapped to the key *data*, which is a *JSONArray* containing 291 *JSONArrays*. Because one *JSONArray* is used to describe each polling place in Baltimore, calling the *length* method of the *JSONArray* class at line 29 gives us the number of polling places in Baltimore.

At lines 32–43, we loop through the *JSONArray dataJsonArray* collecting the zip code into the *zipCodes ArrayList* of *Strings*, which we declare and instantiate at line 33.

At line 36, we retrieve the *JSONArray* for the current polling place. At line 38, we retrieve its zip code, which is located at index 11 in the *JSONArray*. Sometimes open data contains erroneous or invalid data, and we want to process only valid data. Thus, we test if the zip code is invalid (not five characters) at line 39 and add it to the *ArrayList* at line 42 only if it is valid. This is called **cleaning the data**.

At lines 45–51, we convert the *ArrayList* to a *Stream* and compute the lowest and highest zip codes using the *compareTo* method of the *String* class, assigning those values to *minZip* and *maxZip*.

The *min* and *max* methods of the *Stream* interface (previously shown in Table 11.8) accept a parameter of a class that implements the *Comparator* interface. As shown in Table 11.9, the only *abstract* method of *Comparator*, which uses generics, is:

```
int compare( T t1, T t2 )
```

Inside the *compare* method, we specify how two elements are compared. The *min* and *max* methods use that specification to compute the minimum and the maximum of a list of elements. We retrieve the zip codes as *Strings*, so we want to specify that the *min* and *max* methods should use the *compareTo* method of the *String* class to compare the zip codes.

Comparator is a functional interface, so we can use the following lambda expression as the argument of *min* and *max*:

```
( t1, t2 ) -> ( ( String ) t1 ).compareTo( ( String ) t2 )
```

The *min* and *max* methods return an *Optional* reference. *Optional* is a class that uses generics. An *Optional* object may or may not contain a non-null value. We can use the *isPresent* method to test if there is a non-null value and the *get* method to retrieve the value if it exists; both methods are shown in Table 11.14. Using the above lambda expression, we could retrieve the maximum zip code as follows:

```
Optional maxZipOptional = zipCodes.stream( ).max(
  ( t1, t2 ) -> ( ( String ) t1 ).compareTo( ( String ) t2 ) );
String maxZip = ( String ) maxZipOptional.get( );
```

TABLE 11.14   Useful Methods of the *Optional* Class

```
boolean isPresent( )
```
   returns *true* if there is a value present, *false* otherwise.
```
T get( )
```
   returns the value in this *Optional*; if there is no value, throws a *NoSuchElementException*.

Note that in order to keep this example simple, we do not call the *isPresent* method before we call the *get* method. Calling *isPresent* would make the code more robust, however.

When we want to implement the *Comparator* interface and specify the method of another class, we can use the following double colon notation in place of a lambda expression:

```
ClassName::methodName
```

Because we want to use the *compareTo* method of the *String* class, we write:

```
String::compareTo
```

Thus, in order to retrieve the highest zip code, we write the following statement at lines 49–51:

```
String maxZip = zipCodes.stream( )
                    .max( String::compareTo )
                    .get( );
```

After we have collected the zip codes, we ask the user to enter a zip code that is between the lowest and highest zip codes at lines 53–57. At lines 59–64, we compute and output the number of polling places in that zip code.

```
 1 import java.io.*;
 2 import java.net.*;
 3 import java.util.*;
 4 import org.json.*;
 5
 6 public class PollingPlaces
 7 {
 8   public static void main( String [ ] args  )
 9   {
10     final int ZIP_CODE_DIGITS = 5;
11     String resource = "https://data.baltimorecity.gov/api/views/"
12                     + "u7bw-gha5/rows.json?accessType=DOWNLOAD";
13
14     try
15     {
16       URL url = new URL( resource ) ;
17       InputStream is = url.openStream( );
18       Scanner dataSource = new Scanner( is );
19       String json = "";
20       String s = null;
21       while ( dataSource.hasNext( ) )
22       {
```

```
23          s = dataSource.nextLine( );
24          json += s;
25        }
26
27        JSONObject jsonObject = new JSONObject( json );
28        JSONArray dataJsonArray = jsonObject.getJSONArray( "data" );
29        System.out.println( "There are " + dataJsonArray.length( )
30                          + " polling places in Baltimore" );
31
32        // Build ArrayList of zip codes
33        ArrayList<String> zipCodes = new ArrayList<String>( );
34        for ( int i = 0; i < dataJsonArray.length( ); i++ )
35        {
36          JSONArray pollPlaceJsonArray = dataJsonArray.getJSONArray( i );
37          // Clean up data, discard bad zip codes
38          String currentZip = pollPlaceJsonArray.getString( 11 );
39          if ( currentZip.length( ) != ZIP_CODE_DIGITS )
40            System.out.println( "Discarding invalid code " + currentZip );
41          else
42            zipCodes.add( currentZip );
43        }
44
45        // Retrieve min and max zip codes
46        String minZip = zipCodes.stream( )
47                               .min( String::compareTo )
48                               .get( );
49        String maxZip = zipCodes.stream( )
50                               .max( String::compareTo )
51                               .get( );
52
53        // Ask user to enter a valid zip code
54        Scanner scan = new Scanner( System.in );
55        System.out.print( "\nPlease enter a zip code between "
56                         + minZip + " and " + maxZip + " > " );
57        String zip = scan.next( );
58
59        // Retrieve number of polling places in that zip code
60        long count = zipCodes.stream( )
61                            .filter( zipCode -> zipCode.equals( zip ) )
62                            .count( );
63        System.out.println( "There are " + count
64              + " polling places in the " + zip + " zip code" );
65      }
66
67    catch ( MalformedURLException murle )
68      {
```

```
69        System.out.println( murle.getMessage( ) );
70     }
71
72     catch ( IOException ioe )
73     {
74       System.out.println( ioe.getMessage( ) );
75     }
76
77     catch ( JSONException e )
78     {
79       System.out.println( e.getMessage( ) );
80     }
81   }
82 }
```

EXAMPLE 11.13   Reading, Parsing, and Processing Remote Data

Figure 11.20 shows the output of Example 11.13 when the user enters the zip code 21218.

```
There are 291 polling places in Baltimore
Discarding invalid code
Discarding invalid code
Discarding invalid code
Discarding invalid code
Discarding invalid code
Discarding invalid code
Discarding invalid code


Please enter a zip code between 21201 and 21239 > 21218
There are 28 polling places in the 21218 zip code
```

Figure 11.20

Output of
Example 11.13

11.11   Reading and Writing Objects to a File

Throughout this text, we have emphasized the benefits of object-oriented programming. Just as we can write text and primitive data types to a file and subsequently read them from the file, we can also write objects to a file and subsequently read them as objects. This is convenient for two reasons:

- We can write these objects directly to a file without having to convert the objects to primitive data types or *Strings*.

- We can read the objects directly from a file, without having to read *Strings* and convert these *Strings* to primitive data types in order to instantiate objects.

To read objects from a file, the contents of the file must have been written as objects. So our first order of business should be to learn how to write objects to a file.

11.11.1 Writing Objects to Files

The *ObjectOutputStream* class, coupled with the *FileOutputStream* class, provides the functionality to write objects to a file. The *FileOutputStream* class, a subclass of *OutputStream,* is used to write raw data, rather than characters, to a file.

The *ObjectOutputStream* class, also a subclass of *OutputStream*, provides a convenient way to write objects to a file. Its *writeObject* method takes one argument—the object to be written.

The classes, constructors, and methods we will use are shown in Table 11.15.

We will use the *FlightRecord* class developed earlier in the chapter. However, in order for an object to be written to a file (and later to be read using the *ObjectInputStream*

TABLE 11.15   **Useful Classes, Constructors, and Methods for Writing Objects to a File**

Classes, Constructors, and Methods for Writing Objects to a File		
Class	**Constructor**	**Exceptions thrown**
FileOutputStream	FileOutputStream(String filename, boolean mode)	FileNotFoundException
	constructs a *FileOutputStream* object from a *String* representing the name of a file; if *mode* is *false*, we will write to the file; if *mode* is *true*, we will append to the file	
ObjectOutputStream	ObjectOutputStream(OutputStream out)	IOException
	creates an *ObjectOutputStream* that writes to the *OutputStream out*	
	Method API	
ObjectOutputStream	void writeObject(Object o)	IOException, NotSerializableException, InvalidClassException
	writes the object argument to a file. That object must be an instance of a class that implements the *Serializable* interface. Otherwise, a run-time exception will be generated	

class), that object must implement the *Serializable* interface. When an object implements the *Serializable* interface, its state can be converted to a byte stream to be written to a file, such that this byte stream can be converted back into a copy of the object when read from the file. Therefore, our modified *FlightRecord2* class will implement *Serializable*, which is in the *java.io* package.

The *Serializable* interface has no methods to implement. As a result, the only things we have to worry about when writing a class implementing *Serializable* are the following:

- the *import* statement
- the class header showing the class *implements Serializable*

Example 11.14 shows the *FlightRecord2* class. This class is identical to the *FlightRecord* class except that it *imports Serializable* (line 5), *implements* the *Serializable* interface (line 8), and includes accessors for the *origin* and *numPassengers* instance variables (we use these accessors when we read objects from the file and process the results).

```
 1 /* The FlightRecord2 class
 2    Anderson, Franceschi
 3 */
 4
 5 import java.io.Serializable;
 6 import java.text.DecimalFormat;
 7
 8 public class FlightRecord2 implements Serializable
 9 {
10    public static final DecimalFormat MONEY
11                        = new DecimalFormat( "$###.00" );
12    private String flightNumber;    // ex. = AA123
13    private String origin;          // origin airport; ex. = BWI
14    private String destination;     // destination airport; ex. = SFO
15    private int numPassengers;      // number of passengers
16    private double avgTicketPrice;  // average ticket price
17
18    /** Constructor
19     * @param flightNumber    flight number
20     * @param origin          origin airport
21     * @param destination     destination airport
22     * @param numPassengers   number of passengers
23     * @param avgTicketPrice  average ticket price
24     */
25    public FlightRecord2( String flightNumber,
26                          String origin,
27                          String destination,
28                          int numPassengers,
29                          double avgTicketPrice )
```

```
30  {
31    this.flightNumber = flightNumber;
32    this.origin = origin;
33    this.destination = destination;
34    this.numPassengers = numPassengers;
35    this.avgTicketPrice = avgTicketPrice;
36  }
37
38  /** toString
39   * @return flight number, origin, destination,
40   *          number of passengers, and average ticket price
41   */
42  @Override
43  public String toString( )
44  {
45    return "Flight " + flightNumber
46            + ": from " + origin
47            + " to " + destination
48            + "\n\t" + numPassengers + " passengers"
49            + "; average ticket price: "
50            + MONEY.format( avgTicketPrice );
51  }
52
53  /** getOrigin method
54   * @return origin
55   */
56  public String getOrigin( )
57  {
58    return origin;
59  }
60
61  /** getNumPassengers method
62   * @return numPassengers
63   */
64  public int getNumPassengers( )
65  {
66    return numPassengers;
67  }
68
69  // other accessors, mutators, and other methods …
70 }
```

EXAMPLE 11.14   The *FlightRecord2* Class

Example 11.15 shows how the *FileOutputStream* and *ObjectOutputStream* classes can be used in a Java program to write *FlightRecord2* objects to a file named *objects*.

```
1  /* Demonstrating how to write objects to a file
2     Anderson, Franceschi
3  */
4
5  import java.io.FileOutputStream;
6  import java.io.ObjectOutputStream;
7  import java.io.FileNotFoundException;
8  import java.io.IOException;
9
10 public class WritingObjects
11 {
12   public static void main( String [ ] args )
13   {
14    // instantiate the objects
15    FlightRecord2 fr1 = new FlightRecord2( "AA31", "BWI", "SFO",
16                                   200, 235.9 );
17    FlightRecord2 fr2 = new FlightRecord2( "CO25", "LAX", "JFK",
18                                   225, 419.9 );
19    FlightRecord2 fr3 = new FlightRecord2( "US57", "IAD", "DEN",
20                                   175, 179.5 );
21
22    try
23    {
24     FileOutputStream fos = new FileOutputStream
25                                    ( "objects", false );
26             // false means we will write to objects
27
28     ObjectOutputStream oos = new ObjectOutputStream( fos );
29
30     // write the objects to the file
31     oos.writeObject( fr1 );
32     oos.writeObject( fr2 );
33     oos.writeObject( fr3 );
34
35     // release resources associated with the objects file
36     oos.close( );
37    }
38
39    catch ( FileNotFoundException fnfe )
40    {
41      System.out.println( "Unable to write to objects" );
42    }
43
44    catch ( IOException ioe )
45    {
46      ioe.printStackTrace( );
47    }
```

```
48  }
49  }
```

EXAMPLE 11.15   Writing Objects to a File

Lines 14–20 declare and instantiate three *FlightRecord2* objects that we will write to the *objects* file.

Lines 24 and 25 instantiate a *FileOutputStream* object for writing to the *objects* file, then line 28 instantiates an *ObjectOutputStream* object, which we will use to write the *FlightRecord2* objects to the file.

At lines 30–33, using the *ObjectOutputStream* object *oos*, we call the *writeObject* method, passing the three *FlightRecord2* objects we instantiated. The *writeObject* method takes a *Serializable* object as its parameter, here a *FlightRecord2* object, and writes it to the file in such a way that the stream of bytes can be read using the *readObject* method from the *ObjectInputStream* class. Both the *ObjectOutputStream* constructor and the *writeObject* method can throw an *IOException*, which will be caught at line 44.

After this program is executed, the *objects* file will contain a representation of the three *FlightRecord2* objects.

One more note about writing objects to files: A file containing objects can be quite large. Not only does the object data get written to the file, but also the name of the class, a description of each data field, and other information needed to reconstruct the objects when the file is subsequently read.

The *writeObject* method, however, does not write any *static* class variables to the file. Thus, we may consider declaring any constants as *static*, if appropriate. For example, the object file we create in Example 11.15 by writing three *FlightRecord* objects is 240 bytes long. If we had not declared the constant *DecimalFormat* object *MONEY* as *static* in the *FlightRecord2* class, the size of the object file would be 2,137 bytes!

Similarly, the *writeObject* method does not write to the file any instance variable that is declared to be *transient*. Thus, we can also save space in the file by declaring an instance variable as *transient*. An instance variable is a good candidate to be declared *transient* if we can easily reproduce its value, or if the variable has a value of 0 at the time the file is created. For example, suppose our *FlightRecord* had an additional instance variable named *totalRevenue*, which stored a value we calculated by multiplying *avgTicketPrice* by *numPassengers*. Because we can easily recalculate the value for *totalRevenue*, we can declare it as *transient*; then, that instance variable will not be written to the object file.

We declare an instance variable as *transient* by inserting the keyword *transient* between the access modifier and the data type of the instance variable, as in the following syntax:

```
accessModifier transient dataType instanceVariableName
```

Thus, the following declaration would declare the *totalRevenue* instance variable as *transient*:

```
private transient double totalRevenue;
```

11.11.2   Reading Objects from Files

Reading objects from a file somewhat parallels writing objects to a file.

The class *ObjectInputStream*, a subclass of *InputStream*, coupled with *FileInputStream*, provides the functionality we need. The *FileInputStream* class is used to read streams of binary data from a file.

ObjectInputStream is designed to read objects from a file. The *readObject* method, which does not take any arguments, reads the next object from the file and returns it. Because the *readObject* method returns a generic *Object*, we must type cast the returned object to the appropriate class. When the end of the file is reached, the *readObject* method throws an *EOFException*. This is in contrast to the *Scanner* class, which provides the *hasNext* method to test whether the end of the file has been reached.

The classes, constructors, and methods discussed previously are shown in Table 11.16.

> **SOFTWARE ENGINEERING TIP**
> To save disk space when writing to an object file, declare the class data as *static* or *transient* where appropriate.

TABLE 11.16   Useful Classes, Constructors, and Methods for Reading Objects from a File

Classes, Constructors, and Methods for Reading Objects from a File		
Class	**Constructors**	**Exceptions thrown**
FileInputStream	FileInputStream(String filename)	FileNotFoundException
	constructs a *FileInputStream* object from a *String* representing the name of a file	
ObjectInputStream	ObjectInputStream(InputStream in)	IOException
	constructs an *ObjectInputStream* from the *InputStream in*	
	Method API	
ObjectInputStream	Object readObject( )	IOException, ClassNotFoundException, EOFException
	reads the next object and returns it. The object must be an instance of a class that implements the *Serializable* interface. When the end of the file is reached, an *EOFException* is thrown	

Example 11.16 shows how these *FileInputStream* and *ObjectInputStream* classes can be used in a Java program to read objects from a file. We assume that the file *objects* contains *FlightRecord2* objects, as written in the previous section.

```
 1 /* Demonstrating how to read objects from a file
 2    Anderson, Franceschi
 3 */
 4
 5 import java.io.*;
 6 import java.util.ArrayList;
 7
 8 public class ReadingObjectsIntoStream
 9 {
10   public static void main( String [ ] args )
11   {
12     ArrayList<FlightRecord2> flights = new ArrayList<FlightRecord2>( );
13     try
14     {
15       FileInputStream fis = new FileInputStream ( "objects" );
16       ObjectInputStream ois = new ObjectInputStream ( fis );
17
18       try
19       {
20         while ( true )
21         {
22           // read object, type cast returned object to FlightRecord2
23           FlightRecord2 temp = ( FlightRecord2 ) ois.readObject( );
24
25           // add the FlightRecord2 object read to flights
26           flights.add( temp );
27         }
28       } // end inner try block
29
30       catch ( EOFException eofe )
31       {
32         System.out.println( "End of the file reached" );
33       }
34
35       catch ( ClassNotFoundException cnfe )
36       {
37         System.out.println( cnfe.getMessage( ) );
38       }
39
40       finally
41       {
42         System.out.println( "Closing file" );
43         ois.close( );
```

```
44       }
45     } // end outer try block
46
47     catch ( FileNotFoundException fnfe )
48     {
49       System.out.println( "Unable to find objects" );
50     }
51
52     catch ( IOException ioe )
53     {
54       ioe.printStackTrace( );
55     }
56
57     // calculate number of flights originating from BWI
58     long count =
59       flights.stream( )
60               .filter( flight -> flight.getOrigin( ).equals( "BWI" ) )
61               .count( );
62     System.out.println( "There are " + count + " flights from BWI" );
63
64     // calculate average number of passengers on all flights
65     double avgNumPassengers =
66       flights.stream( )
67               .mapToInt( FlightRecord2::getNumPassengers )
68               .average( )
69               .getAsDouble( );
70     System.out.println( "Average number of passengers: "
71                         + avgNumPassengers );
72   }
73 }
```

EXAMPLE 11.16   Reading, Filtering, and Processing Objects

Lines 5–6 import the needed classes from the *java.io* and *java.util* package. The *ClassNotFoundException* class is part of the *java.lang* package and does not need to be imported.

Line 15 associates a *FileInputStream* object with the *objects* file, and line 16 instantiates an *ObjectInputStream* object for reading the objects from the file.

The *while* loop, from lines 20 to 27, reads and adds each object in the file to the *ArrayList flights*, declared and instantiated at line 12. We continue reading until the *readObject* method throws an *EOFException*, which transfers control to the *catch* block (lines 30–33). Thus, our condition for the *while* loop is

```
while ( true )
```

In that *catch* block, we print a message that the end of the file was detected. Given this *while* loop construction, we do not need a priming read. Inside the *while* loop, we read an object, then print it. When the end of the file is detected, the statement adding the current object to *flights* (line 26) will not be executed.

On line 23, we read an object from the file and assign it to the *FlightRecord2* object reference *temp*. Because the *readObject* method returns an *Object*, we need to type cast the return value to a *FlightRecord2* object. The *readObject* method can also throw a *ClassNotFoundException* or an *IOException*, which will be caught at lines 35 or 52, respectively.

Because an *EOFException* will occur when the end of the file is reached, the *EOFException catch* block will always execute in a normal program run. Thus, any code following the *while* loop in the *try* block will not execute. To close the *objects* file, we use nested *try/catch* blocks. The inner *try* block (lines 18–28) encloses the *while* loop; its associated *catch* blocks handle the *EOFException* and *ClassNotFoundException*. The outer *try* block (lines 13–45) encloses the instantiations of the *FileInputStream* and *ObjectInputStream* objects, the inner *try* block, and the *finally* block where we close the file (line 43). We can close the file in the *finally* block because the *ois* object reference, declared in the outer *try* block, is visible (that is, in scope) inside the *finally* block.

The *catch* blocks following the outer *try* block handle any *FileNotFoundException* and any other *IOExceptions* that occur in the inner or outer *try* blocks.

It is important to place the *catch* clause with the *EOFException* ahead of the *catch* clause with the *IOException*; otherwise, the *EOFException catch* block will never be reached because *EOFException* is a subclass of *IOException*, and therefore will match an *IOException catch* block.

Figure 11.21 shows the console output when this program is executed. Note that after we read the last object in the file and we try to read another object, the code executes the *catch* block for the *EOFException*, then the *finally* block.

At lines 57–62, we chain several method calls to compute and output the number of flights originating from *BWI*. After creating a *Stream* from *flights* at line 59, we filter the *Stream* and keep only the objects whose origin airport is *BWI*. The call to the *filter* method at line 60 is similar to the ones in Example 11.12. Again, we can use a lambda expression because *Predicate*, the parameter of the *filter* method, is a functional interface. This time, each element of the *Stream* is a *FlightRecord2* reference rather than a *String*. With the *flight* reference, we call the *getOrigin* method and compare the returned value to *BWI* as our filtering criteria. At line 61, we call the

Figure 11.21	
| Output of Example 11.16 | ```
End of the file reached
Closing file
There are 2 flights from BWI
Average number of passengers: 200.0
``` |
```

count method to retrieve the number of elements in the *Stream* resulting from the filtering operation.

At lines 64–71, we again chain several method calls to compute and output the average number of passengers for all flights. The call to the *mapToInt* method at line 67 is similar to the call to *mapToDouble* in Example 11.12. We define each element in the resulting *Stream* as the result of the call to the *getNumPassengers*, using the same syntax as in Example 11.13 when we call the *min* and *max* methods. We then calculate the average of that resulting *Stream* at line 68 and retrieve the result as a *double* at line 69.

Skill Practice
with these end-of-chapter questions

11.15.1   Multiple Choice Exercises

Questions 10, 11

11.15.2   Reading and Understanding Code

Question 16

11.15.3   Fill In the Code

Question 27

11.15.6   Write a Short Program

Questions 49

11.15.8   Technical Writing

Question 63

11.12   Programming Activity 2: Reading Objects from a File

In this activity, you will read objects from a file and perform this activity:

Read an object file containing bank account transaction objects. Loop through all the objects and calculate the new balance of the bank account. Assume that we do not know the number of transaction items, that is, objects, in the file.

Notice that this activity is identical to Programming Activity 1, except that the transactions you will read are stored in the file as objects.

The framework will display the current transaction and current balance so that you can check the correctness of your code as the program executes.

Figure 11.22

Animation of a
$500 Check and
the New Balance

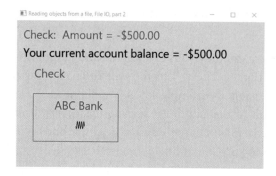

Check: Amount = -$500.00
Your current account balance = -$500.00
Check

ABC Bank

For example, Figure 11.22 demonstrates the animation: We are currently scanning a check transaction for the amount of $500.00. The original balance was $0.00 and the new balance is now –$500.00.

Task Instructions: Reading from the transactions.obj File

In this chapter's folder in the supplied code, you will find a Programming Activity 2 folder. Copy the contents of the folder onto a folder on your computer.

- Open the *AccountingDrawing.java* file. Search for five asterisks (*****) to find the *balanceCheckBook* method where you will add your code. The method header has been coded for you. Write the code to read the transactions from the *transactions.obj* file, and calculate the balance after all the transactions in that file have been executed. This program first writes *Transaction* objects to the file *transactions.obj*; that code is provided. You need to code the body of the *balanceCheckBook* method in order to read that file. Example 11.17 shows the student code section of the *AccountingDrawing.java* file.

```java
public void balanceCheckBook( )
{
//
// ***** Student writes the body of this method *****
//
// Using a while loop, read the file transactions.obj
// The file transactions.obj contains transaction objects
//
// You will need to call the animate method inside
// the body of the loop that reads the objects
//
// The animate method takes 2 arguments:
//    a Transaction object, representing the transaction
//    a double, representing the new checkbook balance
```

```
// So if these two variables are transaction and balance,
// then the call to animate will be:
//
// animate( transaction, balance );
//
// You should make that call in the body of your while
// loop, after you have updated the checkbook balance
//
//
//
//
// end of student code
//
}
```

EXAMPLE 11.17   The *balanceCheckBook* Method

- Begin with a checkbook balance of 0.00.

- To process the transactions, you will need to read one *Transaction* object at a time from the *transactions.obj* file; you will retrieve the transaction amount using the *getAmount* method of the *Transaction* class. The API for that method is:

  ```
  public double getAmount( )
  ```

- Then process the transaction; you do not need to check the type of transaction. Just add the amount to the checkbook balance.

- After you have processed each transaction, call the *animate* method. This method belongs to the *Accounting* class, so you will call *animate* without using an object reference. The API of the *animate* method is the following:

  ```
  public void animate( Transaction currentTransaction,
                       double currentBalance )
  ```

  As you can see, the *animate* method takes two arguments:

  - *currentTransaction* is the current *Transaction* object
  - *currentBalance* is the current balance of the checkbook

  Assuming that you have a *Transaction* object reference called *transactionObject* and a *double* called *balance*, a call to *animate* will look like the following:

  ```
  animate( transactionObject, balance );
  ```

- When you call *animate*, the window will display the current transaction graphically. It will also display the transaction amount (red if negative, blue if positive) and the current checkbook balance (in black). By adding the previous checkbook balance to the current transaction amount, you will be able to compute the current checkbook balance and check that your program is correct.

- Stop reading from the file when you reach the end of the file. You will need to set up a *catch* block to handle the *EOFException* that occurs when the end of the file is reached.

To test your code, compile and run the *AccountingApplication.java* application file.

If you have time . . .

- Modify the *initialize* method of the *AccountingController* class, adding another transaction. Run the program again and verify that your code still yields the correct result. To add another transaction, you could, for instance, write this code:

```
Withdrawal w2 = new Withdrawal( -200.00 );
transactionList.add( w2 );
```

You can add a transaction of type *Check, Withdrawal, Deposit,* or *UnknownTransaction* (all of which are subclasses of the *abstract* class *Transaction*).

Troubleshooting

If your method implementation does not animate or animates incorrectly, check these items:

- Verify that you have coded the call to *animate* at the proper time.
- Verify that you have coded the condition for exiting the loop correctly.
- Verify that you have coded the body of the loop correctly.

DISCUSSION QUESTIONS   **?**

1. **Explain why we cannot simply read the *transactions.obj* file as a text file.**

2. **Explain why we need to type cast each object that we read from the file.**

11.13   User-Defined Exceptions

There will be times when we want to design our own exception class because the predefined Java exception classes do not fit our needs.

Suppose we are interested in designing a class encapsulating email addresses. We will call that class *EmailAddress*. To keep things simple, we will say that a legal email address is a *String* containing the @ character. In order to prevent instantiation of objects with illegal email addresses, we will design our *EmailAddress* constructor so that it throws an exception if its argument, a *String*, does not contain the @ character.

To do that, we first design an exception class that encapsulates an illegal email exception. We call our class *IllegalEmailException* and we will *throw* an exception when the argument to the *EmailAddress* constructor does not contain the @ character. Oracle recommends that user-defined exceptions be checked exceptions.

More generally, when a user-defined exception class is defined as a subclass of an existing Java exception class, such as *Exception*, *IOException*, or *FileNotFoundException*, our class inherits the functionality of the existing exception class, which simplifies coding the new class. We extend the *Exception* class so that our exception is checked and we can associate a specific error message with the exception. We need to code only the constructor, and the constructor's job is to pass our message to the constructor of the superclass.

Thus, the general pattern of a user-defined exception class is:

```
public class ExceptionName extends ExistingExceptionClassName
{
  public ExceptionName( String message )
  {
    super( message );
  }
}
```

Example 11.18 shows our *IllegalEmailException* class.

```
 1 /* The IllegalEmailException class
 2    Anderson, Franceschi
 3 */
 4
 5 public class IllegalEmailException extends Exception
 6 {
 7   public IllegalEmailException( String message )
 8   {
 9     super( message );
10   }
11 }
```

EXAMPLE 11.18 **The *IllegalEmailException* Class**

The constructor for the class is coded at lines 7 to 10; it takes a *String* parameter and simply passes it to the superclass constructor.

The pattern for a method that *throws* a user-defined exception is:

```
accessModifier dataType methodName( parameter list )
                        throws ExceptionName
{
  if ( parameter list is legal )
      // process the parameter list
  else
      throw new ExceptionName( "Some message here" );
}
```

The message we pass to the *ExceptionName* constructor will identify the type of error we detected. When a client program catches the exception, the client can call the *getMessage* method of the exception class in order to retrieve that message.

Example 11.19 shows our *EmailAddress* class.

```
 1 /* The EmailAddress class
 2     Anderson, Franceschi
 3 */
 4
 5 public class EmailAddress
 6 {
 7    public static final char AT_SIGN = '@';
 8    private String email;
 9
10    public EmailAddress( String email )
11                        throws IllegalEmailException
12    {
13      if ( email.indexOf( AT_SIGN ) != - 1 )
14            this.email = email;
15      else
16            throw new IllegalEmailException
17                ( "Email address does not contain " + AT_SIGN );
18    }
19
20    public String getHost( )
21    {
22      int index = email.indexOf( AT_SIGN );
23      return email.substring( index + 1, email.length( ) );
24    }
25 }
```

EXAMPLE 11.19   The *EmailAddress* Class

We coded the constructor at lines 10–18. We test if the constructor's parameter, *email*, contains the character *AT_SIGN* (a constant equal to the @ character) at line 13. If it does, we proceed normally and initialize the instance variable *email* at line 14. If it does not, we throw an *IllegalEmailException* with the appropriate message at lines 16–17. In addition to the constructor, we coded the *getHost* method at lines 20–24. The *getHost* method returns the substring comprising the characters of *email* after *AT_SIGN*. Thus, for an email address of *myEmailAddress@yahoo.com*, the *getHost* method will return *yahoo.com*.

Now that we have built our own exception class and a class including a method that *throws* that exception, we are ready to use them in a client program. This is identical to using a predefined Java exception. Example 11.20 shows our *EmailChecker* class.

```
1 /* The EmailChecker class
2    Anderson, Franceschi
3 */
4
5 import java.util.Scanner;
6
7 public class EmailChecker
8 {
9   public static void main( String [ ] args )
10   {
11     Scanner scan = new Scanner( System.in );
12     System.out.print( "Enter your email address > " );
13     String myEmail = scan.next( );
14     try
15     {
16       EmailAddress address = new EmailAddress( myEmail );
17       System.out.println( "Your host is " + address.getHost( ) );
18     }
19     catch ( IllegalEmailException iee )
20     {
21       System.out.println( iee.getMessage( ) );
22     }
23   }
24 }
```

EXAMPLE 11.20 The *EmailChecker* Class

We ask the user to input an email address, *myEmail*, at lines 12–13. We then try to instantiate the *EmailAddress* object *address* at line 16, passing *myEmail* to the constructor. If *myEmail* does not contain the @ character, our *EmailAddress* constructor *throws* an *IllegalEmailException*, which we *catch* at line 19. In this *catch* block, we print the message the *EmailAddress* constructor sent to the *IllegalEmailException* constructor. If *myEmail* contains the @ character, we continue executing inside the *try* block. Figure 11.23 shows two runs of this example; the first generates the exception, the second completes without generating an exception.

Figure 11.23

Two Sample Runs
of Example 11.20

```
Enter your email address > mary.jb.com
Email address does not contain @
```

```
Enter your email address > john@jb.com
Your host is jb.com
```

CODE IN ACTION

Within the online resources, you will find a movie with a step-by-step illustration of *try* and *catch* blocks. Click on the link to start the movie.

Skill Practice
with these end-of-chapter questions

11.15.1   Multiple Choice Exercises

              Question 3

11.15.8   Technical Writing

              Question 62

CHAPTER REVIEW

11.14   Chapter Summary

- Java provides exception classes so that unexpected, illegal operations at run time can be trapped and handled. This provides the programmer with a tool to keep the program running instead of terminating.

- When calling a constructor or method that *throws* a checked exception, we must use *try* and *catch* blocks; otherwise, the code will not compile.

- For calls to a constructor or method that *throws* an unchecked exception *try* and *catch* blocks are optional. If *try* and *catch* blocks are not used, the exception will be caught at run time by the Java Virtual Machine.

- When a *try* block assigns a value to a variable and that variable is used after the *try/catch* block, the variable must be initialized before the *try* block is entered.

- A variable defined inside a *try* block is local to that block.

- The *java.io* package contains classes for input and output operations.

- In order to read from a file, that file must exist; otherwise, a *FileNotFound-Exception* will be thrown.

- When we open a file for writing, the file is created if it does not exist. If the file already exists, the contents of the file are deleted.

- When we open a file for appending, the file is created if it does not exist. If the file already exists, we start writing at the end of the file.

- The *Scanner* class in the *java.util* package is helpful in parsing a *String* consisting of fields separated by one or more delimiters.

- The *FileWriter* and *PrintWriter* classes provide functionality to write primitive data types to a text file.

- The *Stream* interface includes functionality to perform aggregate sequential and parallel operations on a collection of elements.

- We can use the *Path* and *Files* classes to convert file contents to a *Stream*. An *ArrayList* can also be converted to a *Stream*.

- Many methods of the *Stream* interface accept one parameter whose type is from a functional interface. In this case, we can use a lambda expression when calling such a method.

- We can use the *URL*, *InputStream*, and *Scanner* classes in order to read data from a remote resource.

- Data in remote sites are often formatted using XML or JSON. The *org.json* package includes classes, such as *JSONObject* and *JSONArray*, that provide the functionality to parse a JSON string.

- Objects can be written to a file; they must be instantiated from a class that *implements* the *Serializable* interface.

- The *Serializable* interface has no methods; therefore, no additional methods need to be implemented in a class that *implements* the *Serializable* interface.

- The *FileOutputStream* and *ObjectOutputStream* classes provide functionality to write objects to a file.

- To avoid writing class data to a file of objects, declare the data as *static* or *transient*, where appropriate.

- The *FileInputStream* and *ObjectInputStream* classes provide the functionality to read objects from a file.

- The *readObject* method returns the object read as an *Object* class reference. That object reference must be type cast to the appropriate class.

- To define our own exception, we create a class that extends an existing exception class. This class will consist of a constructor that accepts a message and passes the message to the superclass constructor.

- The method that will generate the exception includes the *throws* clause in the method header. If the invalid condition is detected, the method *throws* a new object of the user-defined exception.

11.15 Exercises, Problems, and Projects

11.15.1 Multiple Choice Exercises

1. Why are *try/catch* blocks useful?

   ❑ They can replace selection statements, thus saving CPU time.

   ❑ *try/catch* blocks enable programmers to attempt to recover from illegal situations and continue running the program.

2. Some methods that *throw* an exception require *try* and *catch* blocks, while some do not.

   ❑ true

   ❑ false

3. What keyword is found in the header of a method that could detect an error and generate an appropriate exception?

   ❑ *throw*

   ❑ *throws*

   ❑ *exception*

   ❑ *exceptions*

4. When coding a *try* and *catch* block, it is mandatory to code a *finally* block.

   ❑ true

   ❑ false

5. Most input- and output-related classes can be found in the package

   ❑ *java.file*

   ❑ *java.inputoutput*

   ❑ *java.io*

   ❑ *java.readwrite*

6. If we open a file for reading and the file does not exist,

   ❑ there is a compiler error.

   ❑ an exception is thrown.

   ❑ the file will be created automatically.

7. When we open a file for writing,

   ❑ we will be adding data at the end of the file.

   ❑ the contents of the file, if any, will be deleted.

   ❑ there is a run-time error if the file does not exist.

8. When we open a file for appending,

   ❑ we will be adding data at the end of the file.

   ❑ the contents of the file, if any, will be deleted.

   ❑ there is a run-time error if the file does not exist.

9. In the following code located inside a *try* block:

```
Scanner file = new Scanner(
                new File( "data.txt" ) );
```

   ❑ the code will not compile.

   ❑ the argument to the *Scanner* constructor is an anonymous object.

   ❑ there will be a run-time error, even if the file *data.txt* exists.

10. What method can we use to convert an *ArrayList* to a *Stream*?

   ❑ *convert*

   ❑ *stream*

   ❑ *toStream*

11. Which interface must be implemented by a class whose objects will be written to a file directly?

   ❑ none

   ❑ *Serializable*

   ❑ *IO*

   ❑ *Object*

11.15.2   Reading and Understanding Code

12. Assuming the file *words.txt* holds the following data:

   CS1 Java Illuminated

   what is the output of this code sequence:

   a. if the file is found?

   b. if the file is not found?

```
try
{
  Scanner file = new Scanner( new File( "words.txt" ) );

  String result = "";

  while ( file.hasNext( ) )
  {
    String s = file.next( );

    result += s;
    result += " AND ";
```

```
    }
    System.out.println( "result is " + result );
    file.close( );


}
catch ( FileNotFoundException fnfe )
{
    System.out.println( "Unable to find words.txt" );
}
catch ( IOException ioe )
{
    ioe.printStackTrace( );
}
```

13. What is the output of this code sequence?

```
Scanner parse = new Scanner( "A B C D" );
while ( parse.hasNext( ) )
    System.out.print( parse.next( ) );
```

14. What is the output of this code sequence?

```
Scanner parse = new Scanner( "AA:BB:CC" );
parse.useDelimiter( ":" );
while ( parse.hasNext( ) )
    System.out.println( parse.next( ) );
```

15. What is the output of this code sequence?

```
Scanner parse = new Scanner( "oneANDtwoANDthreeANDfour" );
parse.useDelimiter( "AND" );
while ( parse.hasNext( ) )
    System.out.println( parse.next( ) );
```

For Questions 16, 17, 18, and 19, you should assume that the file *data.txt* contains
the following text:

```
A
B
C
A
B
A
```

16. What is the output of this code sequence?

```
try
{
    Stream<String> dataStream = Files.lines( Paths.get( "data.txt" ) );
    long count = dataStream.filter( letter -> letter.charAt( 0 ) == 'A' )
                           .count( );
```

```
    System.out.println( "count = " + count );
  }

  catch ( InvalidPathException ipe )
  {
    System.out.println( ipe.getMessage( ) );
  }

  catch ( IOException ioe )
  {
    System.out.println( ioe.getMessage( ) );
  }

  catch ( SecurityException se )
  {
    System.out.println( se.getMessage( ) );
  }
```

17. What is the output of this code sequence?

```
try
{
  Scanner file = new Scanner( new File( "data.txt" ) );

  int n = 0;
  while ( file.hasNext( ) )
  {
    String s = file.nextLine( );

    if ( s.equals( "A" ) )
        n++;
  }

  System.out.println( "The value of n is " + n );
  file.close( );
}
catch ( IOException ioe )
{
  ioe.printStackTrace( );
}
```

18. What is the output of this code sequence?

```
try
{
  Scanner file = new Scanner( new File( "data.txt" ) );

  while ( file.hasNext( ) )
  {
```

```
        String s = file.nextLine( );
        if ( s.equals( "A" ) )
            System.out.println( "Excellent" );
        else if ( s.equals( "B" ) )
            System.out.println( "Good" );
        else
            System.out.println( "Try to do better" );
    }
    file.close( );
}
catch ( IOException ioe )
{
    ioe.printStackTrace( );
}
```

19. What is the output of this code sequence?

```
try
{
  Scanner file = new Scanner( new File( "data.txt" ) );

  String s = "";
  while ( file.hasNext( ) )
  {
    s = file.nextLine( );
  }

  if ( s.equals( "A" ) )
    System.out.println( "Nice finish" );

  file.close( );
}
catch ( IOException ioe )
{
  ioe.printStackTrace( );
}
```

20. The file *data.txt* contains the following text:

CS1

What does the file *data.txt* contain after this code sequence is executed?

```
try
{
  FileWriter fw = new FileWriter( "data.txt", true );
  PrintWriter pw = new PrintWriter( fw );

  pw.println( "Java Illuminated" );
```

```
    pw.close( );
  }
  catch ( IOException ioe )
  {
    ioe.printStackTrace( );
  }
```

21. The file *data.txt* contains the following text:

    CS1

    What does the file *data.txt* contain after this code sequenced is executed?

    ```
    try
    {
      FileWriter fw = new FileWriter( "data.txt", false );
      PrintWriter pw = new PrintWriter( fw );

      String s = "ABCDEFGH";

      for ( int i = 0; i < s.length( ); i++ )
      {
        if ( i % 2 == 0 )
          pw.print( s.charAt( i ) );
      }
      pw.println( );
      pw.close( );
    }
    catch ( IOException ioe )
    {
      ioe.printStackTrace( );
    }
    ```

22. The file *data.txt* contains the following text:

    CS1

    What does the file contain after the following code sequence is executed?

    ```
    try
    {
      FileWriter fw = new FileWriter( "data.txt", true );
      PrintWriter pw = new PrintWriter( fw );

      for ( int i = 0; i < 5; i++ )
        pw.println( i );
      pw.close( );
    }
    catch ( IOException ioe )
    {
    ```

```
    ioe.printStackTrace( );
}
```

23. What does the file *data.txt* contain after the following code sequence is executed?

```
try
{
    FileWriter fw  = new FileWriter( "data.txt", false );
    PrintWriter pw = new PrintWriter( fw );

    int s = 0;
    for ( int i = 0; i < 5; i++ )
    {
        s += i;
    }
    pw.print( "The result is " );
    pw.print( s );
    pw.close( );
}
catch ( IOException ioe )
{
    ioe.printStackTrace( );
}
```

11.15.3   Fill In the Code

24. This code segment reads a file named *data.txt* that contains one data item per line, and outputs only the data items that are integers. Hint: You may need to use nested *try* and *catch* blocks.

```
String s = "";
int n = 0;
try
{
    Scanner file = new Scanner( new File( "data.txt" ) );
    while ( file.hasNext( ) )
    {
        s = file.nextLine( );
        // your code goes here
    }
}
catch ( IOException ioe )
{
    ioe.printStackTrace( );
}
```

25. This code retrieves the "*C*" in the string "*A-B-C-D*" using *Scanner* and outputs it:

```
Scanner parse = new Scanner( "A-B-C-D" );
parse.useDelimiter( "-" );
String s = "";
// your code goes here

System.out.println( s );
```

For Questions 26–29, you should assume that the file *data.txt* contains the following:

```
Java
Illuminated:
Programming
Is Not A
Spectator
Sport
```

26. This code sequence reads the first two lines of the file *data.txt* and outputs them to the console.

```
try
{
  Scanner file = new Scanner( new File( "data.txt" ) );
  // your code goes here
```

27. This code sequence reads the file *data.txt* and outputs the lowest *String* in lexicographic order to the console. Assume that *data.txt* contains one word per line.

```
try
{
  Stream<String> dataStream = Files.lines( Paths.get( "data.txt" ) );
  // your code goes here

}
catch ( InvalidPathException ipe )
{
  System.out.println( ipe.getMessage( ) );
}
catch ( IOException ioe )
{
  System.out.println( ioe.getMessage( ) );
}
catch ( SecurityException se )
{
  System.out.println( se.getMessage( ) );
}
```

28. This code sequence reads the file *data.txt*, concatenates all the lines with a space between them, and outputs them as:

```
Java Illuminated: Programming Is Not A Spectator Sport
try
{
  Scanner file = new Scanner( new File( "data.txt" ) );

  String result = "";
  // your code goes here


}
catch ( IOException ioe )
{
  ioe.printStackTrace( );
}
```

29. This code sequence reads the file *data.txt* and outputs only the lines that start with the *String "Sp"*. Assume that we do not know the contents of the file before reading it.

    For the current example, the output will be:

```
Spectator
Sport
try
{
  Scanner file = new Scanner( new File( "data.txt" ) );

  String result = "";
  // your code goes here


}
catch ( IOException ioe )
{
  ioe.printStackTrace( );
}
```

30. This code sequence loops through the array *grades* and writes all its elements to the file *data.txt*, one per line:

```
int [ ] grades = { 98, 76, 82, 90, 100, 75 };
try
{
  FileWriter fw = new FileWriter( "data.txt", false );
  // your code goes here


}
// and your code continues here
```

31. This code sequence loops through the array *grades*, calculates the average, and writes the average to the file *data.txt*:

```java
int [ ] grades = { 98, 76, 82, 90, 100, 75 };
double average = 0.0;
for ( int i = 0; i < grades.length; i++ )
{
   // some of your code goes here

}
// and more code goes here
try
{
   FileWriter  fw = new  FileWriter( "data.txt", false );
   PrintWriter pw = new PrintWriter( fw );
   // and more code goes here

}
catch ( IOException ioe )
{
   ioe.printStackTrace( );
}
```

32. This code sequence writes the values of the variables *i* and *d* to the file *data.txt*, one line at a time.

```java
int i = 45;
double d = 6.7;
try
{
   FileWriter  fw = new  FileWriter( "data.txt", false );
   PrintWriter pw = new PrintWriter( fw );
   // your code goes here

}
catch ( IOException ioe )
{
   ioe.printStackTrace( );
}
```

33. This code sequence appends the value of the variable *f* to the file *data.txt*:

```java
float f = 13.5f;
try
{
   // your code goes here
```

11.15.4   Identifying Errors in Code

34. Where is the error in this code sequence?

```
Scanner parse = new Scanner( "1 2 3" );
int i = parse.next( );
```

35. Where is the error in this code sequence?

```
try
{
  Scanner file = new Scanner( new File( "data.txt" ) );
  String s = file.nextLine( );
}
catch ( ArithmeticException ae )
{
  System.out.println( ae.getMessage( ) );
}
```

36. Where is the error in this code sequence?

```
try
{
  Scanner file = new Scanner( new File( "data.txt" ) );
  file.write( "Hello" );
}
catch ( IOException ioe )
{
  ioe.printStackTrace( );
}
```

11.15.5   Debugging Area—Using Messages from the Java Compiler and Java JVM

37. You coded the following in the class *Test.java*:

```
import java.io.IOException;
import java.io.File;
import java.util.Scanner;
public class Test
{
  public static void main( String [ ] args )
  {
      try // line 9
      {
              Scanner file = new Scanner( new File( "data.txt" ) );

              String stringRead = file.nextLine( );
              System.out.println( stringRead );
      }
  }
}
```

At compile time, you get the following error:

```
Test.java:9: error: 'try' without 'catch', 'finally' or resource
declarations
   try     // line 9
   ^
1 error
```

Explain what the problem is and how to fix it.

38. You coded the following in the class *Test.java*:

```java
import java.io.IOException;
import java.io.File;
import java.util.Scanner;

public class Test
{
  public static void main( String [ ] args )
  {
      try
      {
       Scanner file = new Scanner( new File( "data.txt" ) );

       String stringRead = file.nextLine( );
      }
      catch ( IOException ioe )
      {
       ioe.printStackTrace( );
      }
      System.out.println( "string read: " + stringRead );
      // line above is 19
    }
}
```

At compile time, you get the following error:

```
Test.java:19: error: cannot find symbol
   System.out.println( "string read: " + stringRead );
                                          ^
symbol:   variable stringRead
location: class Test
1 error
```

Explain what the problem is and how to fix it.

39. You coded the following in the class *Test.java*:

```java
import java.io.IOException;
import java.io.File;
import java.util.Scanner;
```

```java
public class Test
{
  public static void main( String [ ] args )
  {
      String stringRead;
      try
      {
          Scanner file = new Scanner( new File( "data.txt" ) );

          stringRead = file.nextLine( );
      }
      catch ( IOException ioe )
      {
          ioe.printStackTrace( );
      }
      System.out.println( "string read: " + stringRead );
      // line above is line 21
  }
}
```

At compile time, you get the following error:

```
Test.java:21: error: variable stringRead might not have been
initialized
System.out.println( "string read: " + stringRead );
                                      ^
1 error
```

Explain what the problem is and how to fix it.

40. You coded the following in the class *Test.java*:

```java
Scanner parse = new Scanner( "1 3.5 6" );
try
{
  while ( parse.hasNext( ) )
  {
   int number = parse.nextInt( );
   System.out.println( number );
  }
}
catch ( InputMismatchException e )
{
  System.out.println( "In catch block" );
}
```

The code compiles and runs, but the result is:

```
1
In catch block
```

Explain why the *catch* block executes and change the data so that all the numbers are processed.

41. In order to read from the file *data.txt*, you coded the following in the *Test.java* class:

```
try
{
  Scanner file = new Scanner( new File( "datatxt" ) );

  String s = file.nextLine( );
  System.out.println( "Line read is " + s );
}
catch ( IOException ioe )
{
  System.out.println( ioe.getMessage( ) );
}
```

The code compiles and runs, but here is the output:

```
datatxt (The system cannot find the file specified)
```

Explain what the problem is and how to fix it.

42. You coded the following in the class *Test.java*:

```
import java.io.*;

public class Test
{
 public static void main( String [ ] args )
 {
    FileWriter fw = new FileWriter( "data.txt", false );
    PrintWriter pw = new PrintWriter( fw );

    pw.println( "hi" );
    pw.close( );
 }
}
```

At compile time, you get the following error:

```
Test.java:7: error: unreported exception IOException; must be
caught or declared to be thrown
    FileWriter  fw = new  FileWriter ( "data.txt", false);
                 ^

1 error
```

Explain what the problem is and how to fix it.

11.15.6   Write a Short Program

43. Write a program that reads a file and writes a copy of the file to another file with line numbers inserted.

44. In Internet programming, programmers receive parameters via a query string, which looks like a *String* with fields separated by the "&" character. Each field typically has a metadata part that identifies the data followed by an equals sign and then the data. An example of a query string is:

```
first=Mike&last=Jones&id=mike1&password=hello
```

Using *Scanner* at least once, parse a query string and output each field on a different line after replacing the equal sign with a colon followed by a space. For example, for the preceding sample query string, the output should be:

```
first: Mike
last: Jones
id: mike1
password: hello
```

45. Write a program that reads a file that contains only one line; output all the characters, one character per line.

46. Write a program that reads a file and counts how many lines it contains.

47. Write a program that reads a text file that contains a grade (for instance, 87) on each line. Calculate and print the average of the grades.

48. Write a program that reads a text file and writes to a file every line of the file separated by a blank line.

49. Modify Example 11.13 and output to the console the number of polling places that are in schools. We can assume that we will find that information in the *String* that is located two indexes before the zip code in the same array as the zip code. If that *String* has the word School in it, then we will assume that the polling place is in a school.

50. Often websites display the visitor count ("You are visitor number 5246"). Write a program that reads a file that holds the visitor count, outputs it, and updates the file, incrementing the visitor count by 1.

51. Often on websites, the beginning of an article is displayed followed by the word more and several dots (as in *more…*). Write a graphical application that reads the first two lines of a file, and displays them inside a window, adding the word *more* in blue followed by three dots.

11.15.7   Programming Projects

52. Design a class that checks if a *String* is made of tokens of the same data type (for this, you may only consider four data types: *boolean, int, double,* or *char*). This class has two instance variables: the *String* of data and its delimiter. Other than the constructor, you should include a method, *checkTokens,* that takes

one parameter, representing the data type expected (for example, 0 could represent *boolean*, 1 could represent *int*, 2 could represent *double*, and 3 could represent *char*). The method returns *true* if all the tokens in the *String* are of the specified data type; otherwise, it returns *false*.

53. We are interested in checking the number of times a given word (for example, the word *secret*) appears in a file. You should assume that lines do not wrap, that is, a line does not continue on the next line. Warning: You could have letters arranged like *secsecret*. Design a class that encapsulates that idea. Test it with a client program.

54. Design a class that checks if the contents of two text files are identical and, if not, determines how many lines are different. Lines are different if they differ in one or more characters. Test your class with a client program.

55. Design a class that encapsulates the contents of a text file. Include the following methods in your class: *numberOfLinesInFile*, *longestLineInFile* (the line number of the line containing the maximum number of characters), *shortestLineInFile*, and *averageNumberOfCharactersPerLine*. Test your class with a client program.

56. Alter Example 11.7 so that *Scanner* will use a comma and semicolon as delimiters. Hint: you will need to use a *Pattern*.

Look It Up

57. A file contains web addresses, one on each line. Design a class that encapsulates the concept of counting the number of college addresses (contains *.edu*), government addresses (contains *.gov*), business addresses (contains *.com*), organization addresses (contains *.org*), or other addresses. Test your class with a client program.

58. In cryptograms, each character is encoded into another. If the text is long enough, one can, as a strategy, use the frequency of occurrence of each character. The most frequently occurring character will likely be the code for an *e*, because *e* is the most frequently used letter of the English alphabet. Design a class that attempts to determine the relative frequency of each letter by reading a file and keeping track of the number of times each of the 26 English alphabet characters appears. Also provide methods, such as *highestFrequencyCharacter* and *lowestFrequencyCharacter*. Test your class with a client program.

59. Design a class that calculates statistics on data in a file. We expect the file to contain grades represented by integer values, one per line. If you encounter a value that is not an integer, you should throw an exception, print a message to the console, skip that value, and continue processing. Store the grades that you read in an *ArrayList* so that all the grades are available for retrieval. You should also have, as a minimum, methods that return the grade average, the highest

grade, the lowest grade, and ones that return all the grades as an array of letter grades. Test your class with a client class.

60. Write a class encapsulating the concept of a home, assuming that it has the following attributes: the number of rooms, the square footage, and whether it has a basement. Write a client program that creates five *Home* objects, writes them to a file as objects, then reads them from the file as objects, outputs a description of each object using the *toString* method (which the *Home* class should override), and outputs the number of *Home* objects. When reading the objects, you should assume that you do not know the number of objects in the file.

61. Using *Streams*, output the number of the following in a Java file: constructors, *public* variables or methods, *private* variables or methods, *static* variables or methods. Assume that the words *public*, *private*, and *static* can appear at most once per line. Also output if the number of opening curly braces is equal to the number of closing curly braces. Also assume that there can be only one open-ing or closing curly brace per line at the most.

11.15.8 Technical Writing

62. Are exceptions a good thing or a bad thing? Argue both sides.

63. With respect to writing objects to and reading objects from a file, discuss the importance of documenting your code well.

11.15.9 Group Project (for groups of 2, 3, or more students)

64. A friend of yours owns two houses at Football City, the site of the next Super Bowl. Your friend wants to rent those two houses for the Friday, Saturday, and Sunday of the Super Bowl weekend. House #1 has 3BR (3 bedrooms), 3BA (3 baths), and house #2 has 1BR, 1BA.

For this project, concurrency is not an issue; you should assume that two cus-tomers will never access your system at exactly the same time. You should also assume that the management-side software and the customer-side software will never run at the same time. We can assume that we run the management-side software first, then the customer-side software.

This friend has asked you to build a file-based reservation system enabling the following:

A. Management-side software:

Your friend controls the rental price and may change it every day. He/she sends you a change file every day; this file may be empty, in which case there are no pricing changes. If the file is not empty, pricing has changed (for one or more houses, or for one or more days). You are in charge of this project, and therefore, you are in charge of specifying the file format; however, this must be a simple text file because your friend is not a computer person.

You do not have to simulate the act of sending the file by your friend; you should assume that the file is a text file in your directory and that you only need to read the data.

Your management-side software needs to read this file and update a different file, with which you control the reservation system. You can create your own design for the structure of that file. Of course, prices for existing reservations cannot be changed.

Finally, your management-side software should write to a file the status of the reservations; that is, which house is rented to whom, when, and for what price.

B. Customer-side software:

The customer-side software allows a customer to make a reservation. You should prompt the customer for a possible reservation, offering whatever house is available, when, and at what price. Do not offer a customer a house that is already rented.

In this simple version, a customer makes and pays for the reservation at the same time. Also, a reservation cannot be cancelled. When a reservation is made, the customer-side software automatically updates the file controlling the reservations.

CHAPTER 12
Graphical User Interfaces Using *JavaFX*

CHAPTER CONTENTS

Introduction

Many applications we use every day have a Graphical User Interface, or GUI (pronounced Goo-ey). These GUIs allow the user to communicate to the application by entering text into boxes; pressing buttons; or selecting items from a list, a set of radio buttons, or checkboxes.

GUIs allow the user to drive the application by selecting the next function to be performed, entering the needed data, or setting program preferences, such as colors or fonts. Applications with GUIs are usually easier to learn and use because the interface is familiar to the user.

One way to create a GUI is to use the Swing components. Recently, Oracle introduced JavaFX, a new approach to making GUIs. All the classes needed to create a JavaFX application are automatically included with Java SE; nothing more needs to be downloaded. In this chapter, we present some of the many JavaFX classes, along with the main concepts associated with developing a JavaFX application.

12.1   The Structure of a *JavaFX* Application

The top-level structure in a JavaFX application is the **stage**, which corresponds to a window. A stage can have one or more **scenes**, which are top-level containers for **nodes** that make up the window contents. A node can be a user interface control, such as a button or a drop-down list; a layout; an image or other media; a graphical shape; a web browser; a chart; or a group. In this chapter, we concentrate on user interface controls, layouts, charts, and images.

To create a JavaFX GUI, we add nodes to a scene. These nodes are arranged in a hierarchy, called a **scene graph**, in which some nodes are children of other nodes. The top node is called the **root**.

JavaFX applications can be built in several ways. If we know which controls our interface needs and how they should be arranged, we can use **FXML**, a scripting language based on **XML (Extensible Markup Language)**. In this case, we create an FXML file where we specify the layout container and nodes and their properties. For dynamic GUIs where the number or types of controls are determined at runtime, we can define the number, type, properties, and positioning of controls programmatically (that is, through Java code).

In this chapter, we start by using FXML and use Java code later. By defining our GUI using FXML, we separate the GUI from the logic of the code. Also, FXML allows nonprogrammers to contribute to a team by defining the GUI without knowledge of programming.

Examples 12.1 and 12.2 show the basic structure of a JavaFX application that uses FXML.

REFERENCE POINT
You can get more information about the JavaFX classes at Oracle's Java website: *www.oracle.com /technetwork /java.*

```
1  /*  JavaFX Shell Application
2      Anderson, Franceschi
3  */
4
5  import java.net.URL;
6  import javafx.application.Application;
7  import javafx.fxml.FXMLLoader;
8  import javafx.scene.layout.HBox;
9  import javafx.scene.Scene;
10 import javafx.stage.Stage;
11
12 public class FXShellApplication extends Application
13 {
14   @Override
15   // start is main entry point for the application.
16   // It receives a Stage object – the main window for the
17   // GUI application
18   public void start( Stage stage ) // throws Exception
19   {
20     try
21     {
22       // Locate the FXML resource
23       URL url
24         = getClass( ).getResource( "fxml_shell.fxml" );
25
26       // Load the FXML resource, instantiate root Node;
27       // use appropriate layout class for root Node;
28       // here we use HBox
29       HBox root = FXMLLoader.load( url );
30
31       // create a scene associated with the root
32       // and set its width and height
33       Scene scene = new Scene( root, 300, 275 );
34
35       // assign the scene to the stage object
36       stage.setScene( scene );
37
38       // set title of stage (optional)
39       stage.setTitle( "JavaFX Shell" );
40
41       // make the stage visible
42       stage.show( );
43     }
```

```
44      // The FXMLLoader load method throws an exception if
45      // the FXML file is invalid or the URL was not found
46      catch ( Exception e )
47      {
48        e.printStackTrace( );
49      }
50   }
51
52   public static void main( String [ ] args )
53   {
54     launch( args );
55   }
56 }
```

EXAMPLE 12.1   A JavaFX Shell Application

Lines 5 through 10 import the classes we need in most applications. Notice that the JavaFX classes are stored in packages having the prefix of *javafx*.

At line 12, we define our class as inheriting from the *abstract Application* class, which is the entry point for all JavaFX applications. When a JavaFX application is launched, the runtime first calls the *init* method, and then *start*. When the application closes its last window or if it calls the *Platform.exit* method, the runtime calls the *stop* method. The *Application* class provides concrete implementations of the *init* and *stop* methods, so overriding *init* and *stop* is optional. The *Application* class defines the *start* method as *abstract*, however, so we must override the *start* method. Table 12.1 shows some methods of the *Application* class.

Lines 14 through 50 define the *start* method. In line 14, we use the *@Override* annotation. It is good practice to use this annotation whenever we intend to override an inherited method. Using the annotation causes the compiler to alert us if our method header does not correctly override the method in the superclass.

A lot is happening in lines 22 through 29. The FXML file contains the definitions for our GUI components. In order to associate the FXML file with the application, we need to create a URL object containing the file's location; then we load the file as an application resource. We inherit the *getClass* method from the *Object* class. It returns the *Class* object associated with our application. We then use that object reference to call the *getResource* method in the *Class* class, shown in Table 12.2.

Once we have a URL for the FXML file, we call the *static load* method of the *FXML-Loader* class, shown in Table 12.3, to instantiate the layout and components that we

SOFTWARE ENGINEERING TIP

Using the *@Override* annotation whenever you intend to override an inherited method reduces errors because the compiler alerts you if your method header is not correct.

TABLE 12.1 Some Methods of the *Application* Class

Package	javafx.application
Return value	**Method name and argument list**
void	init( )
	called by the JavaFX runtime when the application is launched. Overriding this method is optional.
void	launch(String ... args)
	static method that launches the application. Passes any command-line arguments to the application.
Application.Parameters	getParameters( )
	returns any command-line arguments as an *Application.Parameters* object.
void	start(Stage primaryStage)
	the main entry point for JavaFX applications. The application places its scene onto the *primaryStage*. This *abstract* method needs to be implemented.
void	stop( )
	called when the application signals that it is ready to end. Overriding this method is optional.

TABLE 12.2 The *getResource* Method of the *Class<T>* Class

Package	java.lang
Return value	**Method name and argument list**
URL	getResource(String resource)
	returns a URL object representing the location of the *resource,* or *null* if the *resource* is not found

TABLE 12.3 The *load* Method of the *FXMLLoader* Class

Package	javafx.fxml
Return value	**Method name and argument list**
<T> T	load(URL location)
	static method that instantiates the nodes defined in the FXML file specified by *location* and returns a reference to the root node

defined in our FXML file. This method throws an *IOException* if the format of the FXML file is invalid. In this example, the top-level node is an *HBox* layout object, which arranges its child nodes horizontally across the window. The root and its children make up the scene graph. The return value from the *load* method is a reference to the top-level, or root, node in the FXML file.

After we have the resources loaded, we instantiate a *Scene* object (line 33), which is the container for our GUI content. Table 12.4 shows a constructor of the *Scene* class. Some of the other *Scene* constructors do not require width and height parameters. With those constructors, the scene is sized to fit its contents. For this scene, we specify the layout node returned from the *load* method as the root, and we size the scene to be 300 pixels wide and 275 pixels high.

Now we are ready to set the stage, literally. Notice that the *start* method receives a *Stage* object as a parameter (line 18). This corresponds to the top-level window. At line 36, we allocate our newly created scene to the *stage* object. At line 39, we set the text to appear in the title bar, and at line 42, we make the window visible. Table 12.5 shows some useful methods of the *Stage* class.

TABLE 12.4   A Constructor of the *Scene* Class

Package	javafx.scene
Scene(Parent root, double width, double height)	
instantiates the *Scene* with a top-level node of *root* and sets the width and height to the pixel values specified	

TABLE 12.5   Useful Methods of the *Stage* Class

Package	javafx.stage
Return value	Method name and argument list
void	setScene(Scene scene)
	specifies the scene to be hosted by the *Stage*.
void	setTitle(String title)
	sets the text to appear in the window title bar.
void	show( )
	makes the window visible. By default, windows are not visible.

We placed most of the code in the *start* method into a *try* block because several exceptions can occur. If the *getResource* method of the *Class* class does not find the FXML file, it returns *null*. This causes a *NullPointerException* when the *FXML-Loader load* method tries to access the file. The *load* method also throws an *IOException* if the FXML file format is invalid. To simplify the examples in this chapter, we use one *catch* block (lines 44–49) that specifies *Exception*, which is a superclass of both *IOException* and *NullPointerException*. In the *catch* block, we print the stack trace to help with debugging errors in our applications. It is good software engineering practice, however, in the final application to catch each exception separately and output a meaningful message to the user.

At lines 52 through 55, we include the *main* method. Its only job is to start the application by calling the *launch* method of the *Application* class, passing any parameters that have been sent to the application. An application may access these parameters using the *getParameters* method.

In Example 12.2, we show a shell FXML file. In this file, we use FXML to define the layouts and controls that make up the GUI.

```
1 <?xml version="1.0" encoding="UTF-8"?>
2
3 <!-- import classes -->
4 <?import javafx.scene.layout.HBox ?>
5
6 <!-- use appropriate layout manager -->
7 <HBox xmlns:fx="http://javafx.com/fxml" >
8     <!-- define GUI components here -->
9 </HBox>
```

EXAMPLE 12.2   Shell FXML file: *fxml_shell.fxml*

Line 1 is the header. Like other lines that do not specify XML elements, it begins with <? and ends with ?>. It defines the XML version as 1.0 and the encoding to be UTF-8, which is essentially Unicode, except that the first 128 characters are stored as 8 bits. Lines 3, 6, and 8 are comments, which use the same syntax as an HTML comment; that is, they begin with <!-- and end with -->. These comments can span more than one line.

At line 4 we import the *HBox* class because it is the root element defined in this sample file. Similarly, we need to import any classes referenced in the FXML file.

At line 7, we have chosen the *HBox* layout class as an example. In other applications, we put the appropriate top-level layout class here, which becomes the root node for our layout. Lines 7 through 9 illustrate the syntax of an **element**, which we use to define the components of the GUI.

COMMON ERROR TRAP
Windows are hidden by default. Be sure to call the *show* method at the end of the *start* method. Otherwise, the window will not appear.

SOFTWARE ENGINEERING TIP
Catch each possible exception separately. If recovering from the exception is not possible, output a meaningful message to the user.

REFERENCE POINT
You can get more information about FXML at *http://docs .oracle.com /javafx/2 /get_started /jfxpub-get _started .htm*. For more information about XML, visit *http://www .w3.org/XML*

COMMON ERROR TRAP

Be sure to include an *import* statement for any controls or layout containers referenced in the FXML file. Omitting an *import* statement will generate an exception when the FXML Loader loads the file.

Elements begin with a **start tag** with the element's name enclosed in angle brackets (< >). Some elements, such as the *HBox* definition here, have **closing tags**, which are simply the element's name preceded by a forward slash (/), also enclosed in angle brackets (line 9). Some tags, illustrated later in this chapter, have an empty closing tag and end with />.

Elements can have **attributes**, which further define the element or set properties of the element. Attribute definitions are inserted between the element's name and its closing tag.

The syntax for a JavaFX attribute is

```
attributeName = "value"
```

or

```
attributeName = 'value'
```

COMMON ERROR TRAP

Be sure to enclose attribute values in single or double quotes. Omitting one or both quotes will generate an exception when the FXML Loader loads the file.

At line 7, we define an attribute for the root layout:

```
xmlns:fx="http://javafx.com/fxml"
```

This attribute defines the **namespace** for FXML elements. A namespace prevents duplication of variable names, called *name collisions*, by defining a scope for variable names.

Figure 12.1 shows the window created when we run *FXShellApplication.java*. Note that the text in the title bar is "JavaFX Shell" as set in Example 12.1, line 39. The window is empty because we have not added any controls. We add some content to a window in the next section.

Figure 12.1

The Window Created by *FXShellApplication*

12.2 GUI Controls

JavaFX provides an extensive set of classes that can be used to add a GUI to our applications. A GUI control performs at least one of these functions:

- Displays information
- Collects data from the user
- Allows the user to initiate program functions

Table 12.6 lists some JavaFX classes that encapsulate GUI controls. All classes listed in Table 12.6 belong to the package *javafx.scene.control*.

Figure 12.2 shows the hierarchy of some JavaFX controls. Recall that because of the "is a" relationship in inheritance, a subclass object is also an object of each of its superclasses. Thus, all the controls are a *Node* (an element of the scene), a *Parent* (a *Node* that can have children controls), a *Region* (a resizable container that can be styled), and a *Control* (a GUI component). Along the hierarchy, each control has gained methods and properties from its superclasses.

In our applications, we place the controls into the scene by using layout containers, which organize the controls according to each layout's rules. Some of these layout containers are shown in Table 12.7. These classes are in the *javafx.scene.layout* package.

TABLE 12.6   Selected GUI Controls and Their JavaFX Classes

Package	javafx.scene.control
JavaFX Class	**Purpose**
Label	Displays an image or read-only text. Labels are often used to identify the contents of *TextFields*.
TextField	A single-line text box for accepting user input.
Button	Command button that the user clicks to signal that an operation should be performed.
RadioButton	Toggle button that the user clicks to select one option in a group.
CheckBox	Toggle button that the user clicks to select or deselect 0, 1, or more options in a group.
ComboBox	List of options from which the user selects one item.
Slider	Displays a set of continuous values along a horizontal or vertical line. The user can select a value by moving the knob, or thumb.

Figure 12.2

The Hierarchy
of Some JavaFX
Controls

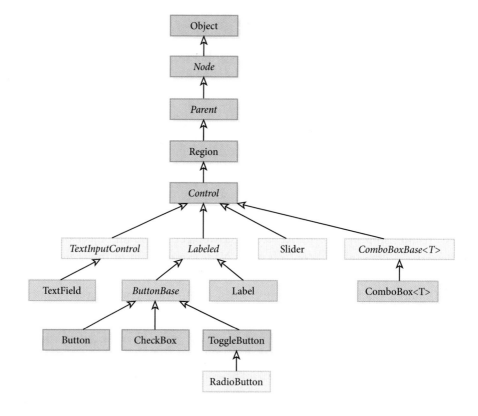

TABLE 12.7   Commonly Used JavaFX Layout Classes

Package	javafx.scene.layout
Layout Container	**Lays out its children nodes . . .**
HBox	In a single horizontal row.
VBox	In a single vertical column.
BorderPane	With at most one child in its top, left, right, bottom, and center positions.
GridPane	In a grid of rows and columns. A child can span more than one row or column.
StackPane	In a front-to-back stack.

The hierarchy of the layout classes is shown in Figure 12.3. Like the controls, the layout classes also inherit from *Node, Parent,* and *Region.* Instead of inheriting from *Control,* however, these classes inherit from *Pane,* which provides a method for accessing all the children in the scene graph. We use that method later in this chapter.

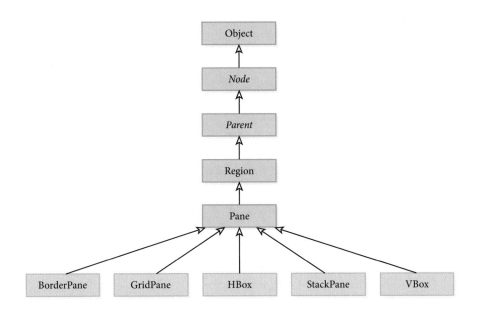

Figure 12.3

The Layout
Classes Hierarchy

In the examples in this chapter, we set the root node of our scenes to be one of these layouts and add controls, images, and even other layouts as child nodes. We show how to nest layouts in later examples in this chapter.

12.3   A Simple Control: *Label*

Starting with our shell JavaFX application, let's add a simple control to the window, a *Label*, and an image, which we display through an *ImageView* node. Example 12.3 shows the application code. Notice that the code is almost identical to Example 12.1, except for the name of the FXML file (line 22), the title bar text (line 32), and that the *root* node is a *VBox* layout (line 24).

```
 1 /*  Displaying a Label and image
 2     Anderson, Franceschi
 3 */
 4
 5 import java.net.URL;
 6 import javafx.application.Application;
 7 import javafx.fxml.FXMLLoader;
 8 import javafx.scene.layout.VBox;
 9 import javafx.scene.Scene;
10 import javafx.stage.Stage;
11
12 public class Dinner extends Application
```

```
13 {
14
15    @Override
16    public void start( Stage stage )
17    {
18      try
19      {
20        // find the XML resource
21        URL url
22          = getClass( ).getResource( "fxml_dinner.fxml" );
23        // load the XML resource and instantiate the root node
24        VBox root = FXMLLoader.load( url );
25
26        // create a scene
27        Scene scene = new Scene( root, 350, 275 );
28
29        // set the scene
30        stage.setScene( scene );
31        // set title of stage
32        stage.setTitle( "What's for dinner?" );
33        // show the stage
34        stage.show( );
35      }
36      catch ( Exception e )
37      {
38        e.printStackTrace( );
39      }
40    }
41
42    public static void main( String [ ] args )
43    {
44      launch( args );
45    }
46 }
```

EXAMPLE 12.3   *Dinner.java*

Again, we have an accompanying FXML file, shown in Example 12.4. We begin this file like the shell FXML file, with the definition of the FXML version and encoding scheme (line 1); then we import all the classes we reference (lines 3–5). In this file, we define the layout to be a *VBox* (lines 7–12). We use attributes to assign values to properties of the *VBox* layout (line 7); we set the *alignment* property to center the child nodes in the window and the *spacing* property to insert 25 pixels between the nodes in the layout.

```
1 <?xml version="1.0" encoding="UTF-8"?>
2
3 <?import javafx.scene.control.*?>
4 <?import javafx.scene.image.*?>
5 <?import javafx.scene.layout.*?>
6
7 <VBox id="root" alignment="CENTER" spacing="25" >
8   <Label text="Sushi tonight?" textFill="BLUE" />
9   <ImageView>
10      <Image url="@sushi.jpg" />
11   </ImageView>
12 </VBox>
```

EXAMPLE 12.4   The *fxml_dinner.fxml* File

At line 8, we define a *Label* control and use attributes to set its text to "Sushi tonight?" and its text color (*textFill*) to blue. All attribute values must be plain text, enclosed in double quotes. If an object or primitive value is needed, the FXML Loader performs any necessary conversion. Thus for the text color, we specify the attribute value as "BLUE," and the FXML Loader converts the text to the object *Color.BLUE*.

At lines 9 through 11, we define a second child node as an *ImageView* element. We set the *Image* property of the *ImageView* to the file "sushi.jpg" (line 10). We preface the filename with "@" to indicate that we are specifying the filename relative to the current folder. Thus, the file *sushi.jpg* is stored in the same folder as the *.java* file. When this application runs, we see the window shown in Figure 12.4.

REFERENCE POINT
To find the properties that can be set for any layout or control, see the JavaFX class documentation. Remember also that controls inherit properties from their superclasses.

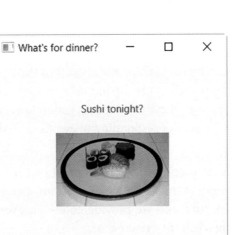

Figure 12.4

The Window Produced by Examples 12.3 and 12.4

Skill Practice
with these end-of-chapter questions

12.4   Event Handling: Managing User Interactions

Now we know how to open a window in an application, and we know how to display a label and an image. The user, however, cannot yet interact with our application. We need to add some interesting GUI controls, such as text entry fields and a button. By interacting with those controls, the user can enter data and initiate operations in our programs.

GUI programming uses an **event-driven model**, as opposed to the procedural model of programming that we have used thus far. By event-driven, we mean that by using a GUI, we put the user in control of what happens next. For example, we might display some text entry fields, some buttons, and a selectable list of items. Then our program "sits back" and waits for the user to interact with the controls. When the user presses a button or selects an item from the list, our application responds by performing the operation the user requested. Then the application sits back again and waits for the user to press another button or select another item from the list. These user actions generate **events**. Thus, the processing of our application consists of responding to events caused by the user interacting with our GUI controls.

When the user interacts with a GUI control, the control **fires an event.** To handle that event, we register our application's interest in being notified when a particular event occurs, and we provide code—an **event handler**, also called a **listener**—to execute when the event occurs.

JavaFX supports and encourages the **Model-View-Controller** architecture for writing GUI applications. In this architecture,

- The **Model** manages the data of the application and its state.

- The **View** presents the user interface.

- The **Controller** handles events generated by the user and communicates those changes to the Model, which updates its state accordingly and communicates any changes back to the Controller. The Controller then updates the View to reflect those changes.

These three components can be placed in the same or in different files.

12.5   Text Fields and Command Buttons

Let's illustrate event handling and the Model-View-Controller architecture with an example that allows a user to square or cube a number. We provide a *TextField* for entering the number; two *Buttons*, one for squaring the number and the other for cubing the number; and *Labels* for displaying a prompt and for displaying the squared or cubed result.

The interface we want to create is shown in Figure 12.5A. Figure 12.5B shows the window after the user entered "3" into the *TextField* and clicked the "Cube" button.

For this application, our Model, shown in Example 12.5, is minimal. It provides two *static* methods, *square* (lines 7–14) and *cube* (lines 16–23), to perform the calculations.

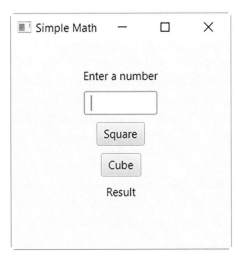
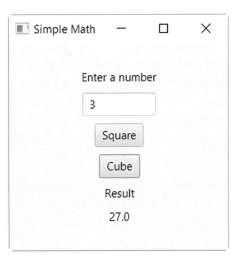

Figure 12.5

(A) The Initial Window (B) The Window After User Interaction

```
 1 /*  Simple Math Class
 2     Anderson, Franceschi
 3 */
 4
 5 public class SimpleMath
 6 {
 7   /** square method
 8    *  @param operand  number to square
 9    *  @return the square of operand
10   */
11   public static double square( double operand )
12   {
13     return operand * operand;
14   }
15
16   /** cube method
17    *  @param operand  number to cube
18    *  @return the cube of operand
19   */
20   public static double cube( double operand )
21   {
22     return operand * operand * operand;
23   }
24 }
```

EXAMPLE 12.5   The Model, *SimpleMath.java*

The controls and their layout are defined in the FXML file, shown in Example 12.6, which acts as our View. Because we want to respond to the user clicking either button, we define a controller at line 6 using the *fx:controller* attribute of the layout container with its value set to the class name of the Java file that contains our controller. Thus, in this case, the controller is *SimpleMathController.java*.

The two buttons are defined at lines 12 through 15. The *text* attribute specifies the wording to appear on the button. The *onAction* attribute specifies a method in the controller that should be executed when the user clicks the button. Thus, our controller must define a method named *calculate*. Usually, we code the method as accepting an *ActionEvent* object, as shown below, although this is not required.

```
void calculate( ActionEvent event )
```

The *ActionEvent* object is automatically created when the user clicks a button, selects an item from a list or a menu, or presses the *Enter* key in a *TextField*. The *ActionEvent* object contains data we can query, such as which control fired the event.

The *calculate* method is our event handler or listener, and by setting the *onAction* attribute for a control, we **register** the event handler on our control: our buttons, in this example. Thus, when the user clicks on either of the buttons, the *calculate* method executes.

We have also used the *fx:id* attribute to define a name for all the controls that the controller needs to access. Assigning an *fx:id* to a control puts the control in the *fx* namespace, making the control accessible outside the file in which the control is defined. This allows the Controller to access controls using their *fx:id* value.

```
 1 <?xml version="1.0" encoding="UTF-8"?>
 2
 3 <?import javafx.scene.control.*?>
 4 <?import javafx.scene.layout.*?>
 5
 6 <VBox fx:controller="SimpleMathController"
 7        xmlns:fx="http://javafx.com/fxml"
 8        alignment="center" spacing="10" >
 9
10    <Label text="Enter a number" />
11    <TextField fx:id="operand" maxWidth="100" />
12    <Button fx:id="square" text="Square"
13            onAction="#calculate" />
14    <Button fx:id="cube" text="Cube"
15            onAction="#calculate" />
16    <Label text="Result" />
17    <Label fx:id="result" />
18
19 </VBox>
```

EXAMPLE 12.6   The View, *fxml_simple_math.fxml*

Our controller is shown in Example 12.7. It defines as instance variables all the controls it needs to access using their *fx:id* names that we defined in the FXML file (lines 7–10). We use the *@FXML* annotation in front of the instance variable definitions to indicate that these controls, although defined as *private*, are also accessible to FXML.

The *calculate* method is defined at lines 12–27. We also precede the method header with the *@FXML* annotation, again to give FXML access to this *protected* method. The *calculate* method takes as a parameter an *ActionEvent* object. As mentioned, this object is created when the user clicks on the button and contains information about the event that occurred.

At line 16, we use the *getText* method to extract the text that the user typed into the *operand TextField*. The *getText* method is shown along with its companion *setText* method in Table 12.8. Because the *getText* method returns a *String,* we call the *static parseDouble* method of the *Double* wrapper class to convert the *String* to a *double*.

TABLE 12.8   Useful Methods of the *TextField* Class

Package	javafx.scene.control
Return value	**Method name and argument list**
String	getText( )
	returns the text typed into the *TextField*
void	setText(String newText)
	sets the text in the *TextField* to *newText*

TABLE 12.9   The *getSource* Method of the *ActionEvent* Class

Package	javafx.event
Return value	**Method name and argument list**
Object	getSource( )
	returns the object on which the event was triggered

We enclose this operation in a *try/catch* block (lines 14–26) because the *parseDouble* method throws a *NumberFormatException* if the text the user entered cannot be converted to a *double*.

If the conversion goes well, we then determine which button the user pressed. The *ActionEvent* class provides a useful method, *getSource*, shown in Table 12.9, which we can use to determine which button the user actually clicked. At line 17, we test whether the user clicked the *square* button. If so, we call the *static square* method in our *SimpleMath* Model, passing the converted number and setting the *result Label* to the return value. Because the *setText* method requires a *String* argument, we call the *static valueOf* method of the *String* class to convert the return value to a *String*.

Similarly, at lines 19 and 20, we test whether the user clicked the *cube Button*; if so, we call the *static cube* method of the *SimpleMath* class and set the *result Label* to the return value.

```
1 import javafx.event.ActionEvent;
2 import javafx.fxml.FXML;
3 import javafx.scene.control.*;
4
5 public class SimpleMathController
6 {
7   @FXML private TextField operand;
8   @FXML private Label result;
```

```
 9   @FXML private Button square;
10   @FXML private Button cube;
11
12   @FXML protected void calculate( ActionEvent event )
13   {
14     try
15     {
16       double op = Double.parseDouble( operand.getText( ) );
17       if ( event.getSource( ) == square )
18         result.setText( String.valueOf( SimpleMath.square( op ) ) );
19       else if ( event.getSource( ) == cube )
20         result.setText( String.valueOf( SimpleMath.cube( op ) ) );
21     }
22     catch ( NumberFormatException nfe )
23     {
24       operand.setText( "" );
25       result.setText( "???" );
26     }
27   }
28 }
```

EXAMPLE 12.7   The Controller, *SimpleMathController.java*

Finally, *SimpleMathPractice*, the launch class, shown in Example 12.8, performs the usual operations of loading the *fxml_simple_math.fxml* file, setting the scene and stage parameters, and displaying the prepared window.

```
 1 /*  Simple Math Operations Using Buttons
 2     Anderson, Franceschi
 3 */
 4
 5 import java.net.URL;
 6 import javafx.application.Application;
 7 import javafx.fxml.FXMLLoader;
 8 import javafx.scene.layout.VBox;
 9 import javafx.scene.Scene;
10 import javafx.stage.Stage;
11
12 public class SimpleMathPractice extends Application
13 {
14   @Override
15   public void start( Stage stage ) // throws Exception
16   {
17     try
18     {
19       URL url =
20         getClass( ).getResource( "fxml_simple_math.fxml" );
21       VBox root = FXMLLoader.load( url );
```

```
22          Scene scene = new Scene( root, 300, 275 );
23          stage.setTitle( "Simple Math" );
24          stage.setScene( scene );
25          stage.show( );
26       }
27       catch ( Exception e )
28       {
29          e.printStackTrace( );
30       }
31    }
32
33    public static void main( String [ ] args )
34    {
35       launch( args );
36    }
37 }
```

EXAMPLE 12.8   *SimpleMathPractice.java*

12.6   Radio Buttons and Checkboxes

If you have ever completed a survey on the web, you are probably familiar with radio buttons and checkboxes.

Radio buttons prompt the user to select one of several mutually exclusive options. Clicking on any radio button deselects any previously selected radio button. Thus, in a group of radio buttons, a user can select only one option at a time.

Checkboxes are often associated with the instruction "check all that apply"; that is, the user is asked to select 0, 1, or more options. A checkbox is a toggle button in that if the option is not currently selected, clicking on a checkbox selects the option; if the option is currently selected, clicking on the checkbox deselects the option.

We present two similar examples to illustrate how to use the *RadioButton* and *CheckBox* classes and how they differ. Both examples allow the user to select the background color for a label. We display three color options: red, green, and blue. Using radio buttons, only one color can be selected at a time. Thus, by clicking on a radio button, the user causes the background of the label to be displayed in one of three colors. Using checkboxes, the user can select any combination of the three color options, so the label color can be set to any of eight possible combinations.

We start with the example using radio buttons. The window when the application starts running is shown in Figure 12.6.

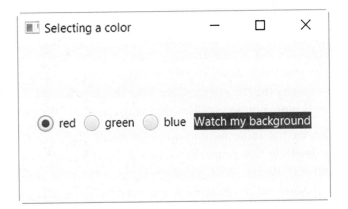

Figure 12.6

The GUI for the
ChangingColors
Application

We begin with the Model, *ColorSelector.java*, shown in Example 12.9. Again, this model is minimal, having only one *static* method, *colorToHexString* (lines 11–25). For convenience in passing parameters, we define three *public static* constants at lines 7 through 9. The controller uses these constants as arguments for the *colorTo-HexString* method.

```
 1 /*  ColorSelector class
 2     Anderson, Franceschi
 3 */
 4
 5 public class ColorSelector
 6 {
 7   public static final int RED = 0;
 8   public static final int GREEN = 1;
 9   public static final int BLUE = 2;
10
11   /** colorToHexString method
12    *  @param selection   the selected color
13    *  @return the hex representation of the selected color
14    */
15   public static String colorToHexString( int selection )
16   {
17     String result = "#";
18     if ( selection == RED )
19       result += "FF0000";
20     else if ( selection == GREEN )
21       result += "00FF00";
22     else if ( selection == BLUE )
23       result += "0000FF";
24     return result;
25   }
26 }
```

EXAMPLE 12.9   The Model, *ColorSelector.java*

Next, we look at the View, the FXML file that defines the layout and the controls for the GUI, which is shown in Example 12.10. For this application, we use an *HBox* layout (lines 6–28), which arranges controls horizontally. We set attributes (line 8) to specify that the controls should be centered with 10 pixels between each control. We also specify the class of the Controller that handles the events caused by the user selecting a radio button, as *ChangingColorsController* (line 6).

In order for the radio buttons to be mutually exclusive (i.e., selecting one radio button deselects any previously selected radio button), we define a *ToggleGroup* (lines 10–12). We use the *<fx:define>* element to create objects, such as this *Toggle-Group*, that are not in the scene graph but need to be referenced by a control. In the definition of each radio button (lines 14–22), we add the radio button to the group by setting its *toggleGroup* property to the id of the *ToggleGroup*. We preface the id with "$" to indicate that *colorGroup* is a variable, rather than a predefined property value.

For each radio button, we also use the *onAction* property to specify that the *color-Chosen* method in the *ChangingColorsController* should be executed when the user clicks the radio button.

REFERENCE POINT
To learn more about using CSS for styling controls, read the JavaFX CSS Reference Guide at https://docs .oracle.com /javafx/2/api /javafx/scene /doc-files/cssref .html

At line 14, we set the red radio button's *selected* property to *true*. This automatically sets the radio button as selected when the program starts.

Finally, we define the label whose background we color as the user clicks on the radio buttons (lines 24–26). Here we introduce *style* definitions. If you are familiar with Cascading Style Sheets (CSS) used with HTML pages, this should look familiar to you. We explain how to use CSS at the end of this chapter. The *background-color* property sets the background color of a control. Its value can be either a CSS named constant (such as *red*) or the RGB hexadecimal value of the color preceded by a "#" (such as *#FF0000*).

We set the label's background to the color red (*#FF0000*) to be consistent with the *red* radio button being selected when the application starts.

```
 1  <?xml version="1.0" encoding="UTF-8"?>
 2
 3  <?import javafx.scene.control.*?>
 4  <?import javafx.scene.layout.*?>
 5
 6  <HBox fx:controller="ChangingColorsController"
 7        xmlns:fx="http://javafx.com/fxml"
 8        alignment="center" spacing="10" >
 9
10    <fx:define>
11      <ToggleGroup fx:id="colorGroup" />
```

```
12  </fx:define>
13
14  <RadioButton fx:id="red" text="red" selected="true"
15               toggleGroup="$colorGroup"
16               onAction="#colorChosen" />
17  <RadioButton fx:id="green" text="green"
18               toggleGroup="$colorGroup"
19               onAction="#colorChosen" />
20  <RadioButton fx:id="blue" text="blue"
21               toggleGroup="$colorGroup"
22               onAction="#colorChosen" />
23
24  <Label fx:id="label" text="Watch my background"
25         textFill="WHITE"
26         style="-fx-background-color:#FF0000" />
27
28  </HBox>
```

EXAMPLE 12.10 *fxml_changing_colors.fxml*

Table 12.10 summarizes the special FXML language elements that we have used.

TABLE 12.10   FXML Language Elements and Their Meaning

FXML Element	Meaning
fx:define	Used to create objects not in the scene graph that need to be referenced later
FXML Attributes	**Meaning**
fx:id	Defines a name that can be referenced across the FXML application
fx:controller	Defines a class that contains event handling code for one or more controls
onAction	Defines a method name (preceded by "#") in the controller that should be executed when the user interacts with the control
FXML Annotation	**Meaning**
@FXML	Allows FXML to access a *private* or *protected* class, method, or data
FXML Prefixes	**Meaning**
-fx-	Used to distinguish a JavaFX style attribute from a CSS attribute
$	Used as a prefix to a variable name when the variable is used as a property value
@	Used as a prefix for a URI to specify that the path of the URI starts with the current folder

The Controller, *ChangingColorsController.java*, is shown in Example 12.11. At lines 11 through 14, we define instance variables for all the controls, using the *fx:id* values we defined in the FXML file. The *colorChosen* event handler method, defined at lines 16 through 31, takes as a parameter the *ActionEvent* that is generated when the user clicks on a radio button. We want to set the background color of the label to correspond with the radio button that was clicked. Thus, we set the *style* property of the label. We start by setting a *String* to characters that are common for any color selected (line 18). We then use the *getSource* method of the *ActionEvent* to determine which radio button was clicked and call the *colorToHexString* method in our Model, passing as a parameter one of the *public static* constants (*RED*, *GREEN*, or *BLUE*) defined in the Model. We then append the returned hexadecimal *String* to *style*. At line 30, we call the *setStyle* method of the *Label* class, passing it the completed *String*. Note that for any property that can be set using attributes in the FXML file, JavaFX usually also provides accessor and mutator methods in the GUI control's class for setting or getting the property programmatically.

```
 1 /*  ChangingColorsController class
 2      Anderson, Franceschi
 3 */
 4
 5 import javafx.event.ActionEvent;
 6 import javafx.fxml.FXML;
 7 import javafx.scene.control.*;
 8
 9 public class ChangingColorsController
10 {
11   @FXML private RadioButton red;
12   @FXML private RadioButton green;
13   @FXML private RadioButton blue;
14   @FXML private Label label;
15
16   @FXML protected void colorChosen( ActionEvent event )
17   {
18     String style = "-fx-background-color: ";
19
20     if ( event.getSource( ) == red )
21       style +=
22        ColorSelector.colorToHexString( ColorSelector.RED );
23     else if ( event.getSource( ) == green )
24       style +=
25        ColorSelector.colorToHexString( ColorSelector.GREEN );
26     else if ( event.getSource( ) == blue )
27       style +=
28        ColorSelector.colorToHexString( ColorSelector.BLUE );
29
```

SOFTWARE
ENGINEERING
TIP
Ensure that the
initial state of
the GUI controls
represents the
state of the
Model.

```
30      label.setStyle( style );
31    }
32 }
```

EXAMPLE 12.11 The Controller, *ChangingColorsController.java*

The last part of the application is *ChangingColors*, the launching class, shown in Example 12.12. It follows the format of the previous application launching classes.

```
 1 /*  Select a Color Using RadioButtons
 2      Anderson, Franceschi
 3 */
 4
 5 import java.net.URL;
 6 import javafx.application.Application;
 7 import javafx.fxml.FXMLLoader;
 8 import javafx.scene.layout.HBox;
 9 import javafx.scene.Scene;
10 import javafx.stage.Stage;
11
12 public class ChangingColors extends Application
13 {
14   @Override
15   public void start( Stage stage )
16   {
17     try
18     {
19       URL url =
20        getClass( ).getResource( "fxml_changing_colors.fxml" );
21       HBox root = FXMLLoader.load( url );
22       Scene scene = new Scene( root, 400, 200 );
23       stage.setTitle( "Selecting a color" );
24       stage.setScene( scene );
25       stage.show( );
26     }
27     catch ( Exception e )
28     {
29       e.printStackTrace( );
30     }
31   }
32
33   public static void main( String [ ] args )
34   {
35     launch( args );
36   }
37 }
```

EXAMPLE 12.12 The Application Launcher: *ChangingColors.java*

Figure 12.7

The GUI for the
MixingColors
Application

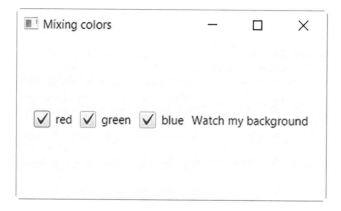

We now demonstrate a similar application using *CheckBoxes*. For this example, we create the interface shown in Figure 12.7.

Example 12.13 shows the Model, *ColorMixer.java.* The Model's job is to manage the color mixing based on which colors are selected or deselected. As in our *RadioButton* example, the *ColorMixer* also provides *public static* constants (lines 7–9) for the controller's convenience in passing parameters. To manage which colors are selected, the *ColorMixer* defines an array of three *boolean* values (line 11), with each element representing whether the corresponding color is selected *(true)* or deselected *(false).*

The constructor (lines 13–23) instantiates the array and sets all elements to *true,* representing the color white (all colors selected). The *RED, GREEN,* and *BLUE* constants also come in handy here as logical names for the array indexes.

The *toggleColor* method (lines 25–32) alternates the state of a color between *true* and *false.* This is consistent with the behavior of *CheckBoxes,* where each click of the *CheckBox* changes its state between selected and deselected.

Finally, the *hexStringColor* method (lines 34–47) composes a *String* containing the hexadecimal equivalent of the current color. Using the conditional operator, we set each color's contribution to the *String* as either *"FF"* (full color) if selected or *"00"* (no color) if deselected.

```
1 /*  ColorMixer class
2      Anderson, Franceschi
3 */
4
5 public class ColorMixer
6 {
7   public static final int RED = 0;
8   public static final int GREEN = 1;
9   public static final int BLUE = 2;
```

```
10
11    private boolean [ ] rgb;
12
13    /** default constructor
14    *    sets all elements in the rgb array to true
15    *    to represent the color white
16    */
17    public ColorMixer( )
18    {
19      rgb = new boolean[3];
20      rgb[RED]   = true;
21      rgb[GREEN] = true;
22      rgb[BLUE]  = true;
23    }
24
25    /** toggleColor method
26    *    toggles the color on/off
27    *    @param color  the color to be toggled
28    */
29    public void toggleColor( int color )
30    {
31      rgb[color] = !rgb[color];
32    }
33
34    /** hexStringColor
35    *    @return the hexadecimal representation
36    *            of the color mix
37    */
38    public String hexStringColor( )
39    {
40      String result = "#";
41
42      result += ( rgb[RED]   ? "FF" : "00" );
43      result += ( rgb[GREEN] ? "FF" : "00" );
44      result += ( rgb[BLUE]  ? "FF" : "00" );
45
46      return result;
47    }
48 }
```

EXAMPLE 12.13   The Model, *ColorMixer.java*

Next, the FXML file, *fxml_mixing_colors.fxml,* shown in Example 12.14, defines the GUI. At lines 11 through 16, we define the three *CheckBoxes* to represent the red, green, and blue color components. We also preselect each *CheckBox* and set the *Label* background to white (line 19) to be consistent with the original state of the Model.

Our controller for this application, *MixingColorsController*, is named at line 6, and we specify that the *mix* method in the controller is the handler for a user selecting or deselecting any of the *CheckBoxes* (lines 12, 14, and 16).

```
 1 <?xml version="1.0" encoding="UTF-8"?>
 2
 3 <?import javafx.scene.control.*?>
 4 <?import javafx.scene.layout.*?>
 5
 6 <HBox fx:controller="MixingColorsController"
 7      xmlns:fx="http://javafx.com/fxml"
 8      alignment="center" spacing="10"
 9      style="-fx-background-color:#CCCCCC" >
10
11   <CheckBox fx:id="red" selected="true"
12            text="red" onAction="#mix" />
13   <CheckBox fx:id="green" selected="true"
14            text="green" onAction="#mix" />
15   <CheckBox fx:id="blue" selected="true"
16            text="blue" onAction="#mix" />
17
18   <Label fx:id="label" text="Watch my background"
19          style="-fx-background-color:#FFFFFF" />
20
21 </HBox>
```

EXAMPLE 12.14   *fxml_mixing_colors.fxml*

The controller, *MixingColorsController.java,* is shown in Example 12.15. The methods in this Model are not *static*, so we define an instance variable, *mixer*, representing the Model (line 11) and the controller instantiates the Model in the constructor (lines 18–21). The *mix* event handler method (lines 23–35) calls the *getSource* method of the *ActionEvent* object to determine which *CheckBox* was clicked. It calls the *toggleColor* method in the Model to invert the state of the color in the *rgb* array. In this way, we do not need to check whether the *CheckBox* was just selected or deselected. Once the clicked color component is updated, we compose the new color *String* by calling the *hexStringColor* method of the model (line 33); then we use that *String* to set the *label*'s background color.

```
 1 /*  MixingColorsController class
 2      Anderson, Franceschi
 3 */
 4
 5 import javafx.event.ActionEvent;
```

```
 6 import javafx.fxml.FXML;
 7 import javafx.scene.control.*;
 8
 9 public class MixingColorsController
10 {
11   private ColorMixer mixer;
12
13   @FXML private CheckBox red;
14   @FXML private CheckBox green;
15   @FXML private CheckBox blue;
16   @FXML private Label label;
17
18   public MixingColorsController( )
19   {
20     mixer = new ColorMixer( );
21   }
22
23   @FXML protected void mix( ActionEvent event )
24   {
25     if ( event.getSource( ) == red )
26       mixer.toggleColor( ColorMixer.RED );
27     else if ( event.getSource( ) == green )
28       mixer.toggleColor( ColorMixer.GREEN );
29     else if ( event.getSource( ) == blue )
30       mixer.toggleColor( ColorMixer.BLUE );
31
32     String style = "-fx-background-color: ";
33     style += mixer.hexStringColor( );
34     label.setStyle( style );
35   }
36 }
```

EXAMPLE 12.15   The Controller, *MixingColorsController.java*

The final piece to this application is the standard launch class, shown in Example 12.16.

```
1 /*  Mixing Colors Using CheckBoxes
2     Anderson, Franceschi
3 */
4
5 import java.net.URL;
6 import javafx.application.Application;
7 import javafx.fxml.FXMLLoader;
8 import javafx.scene.layout.HBox;
9 import javafx.scene.Scene;
```

```
10 import javafx.stage.Stage;
11
12 public class MixingColors extends Application
13 {
14   @Override
15   public void start( Stage stage )
16   {
17     try
18     {
19       URL url =
20         getClass( ).getResource( "fxml_mixing_colors.fxml" );
21       HBox root = FXMLLoader.load( url );
22       Scene scene = new Scene( root, 400, 200 );
23       stage.setTitle( "Mixing colors" );
24       stage.setScene( scene );
25       stage.show( );
26     }
27     catch ( Exception e )
28     {
29       e.printStackTrace( );
30     }
31   }
32
33   public static void main( String [ ] args )
34   {
35     launch( args );
36   }
37 }
```

EXAMPLE 12.16   The Launch Class, *MixingColors.java*

12.7   Programming Activity 1: Working with Buttons

In this activity, you will work with two *Buttons* that control a simulated electrical switch. Specifically, you will write the code to perform the following operations:

1. If the user clicks on the "OPEN" button, open the switch.

2. If the user clicks on the "CLOSE" button, close the switch.

The framework for this Programming Activity will animate your code so that you can check its accuracy. Figures 12.8 and 12.9 show the application after the user has clicked the button labeled "OPEN" and the button labeled "CLOSE," respectively.

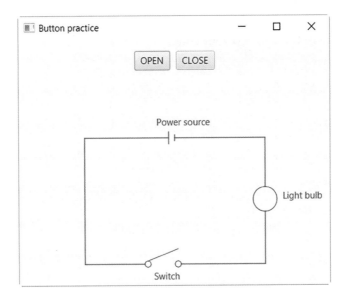

Figure 12.8

User Clicked
"OPEN"

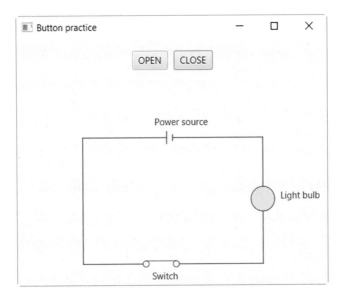

Figure 12.9

User Clicked
"CLOSE"

Instructions

Copy the source files in the Programming Activity 1 folder for this chapter to a folder on your computer. Note that all files should be in the same folder.

Open the *fxml_button_practice.fxml* file. Searching for five asterisks (*****) in the source code will position you to the first code section and then to the second location where you will add your code. In task 1, you will specify the name of the controller as *ButtonPracticeController*. In task 2, you will define an *HBox* layout with the two buttons. Example 12.17 shows the section of the *fxml_button_practice.fxml* file where you will add your code.

```
 1 <?xml version="1.0" encoding="UTF-8"?>
 2
 3 <?import javafx.scene.*?>
 4 <?import javafx.scene.control.*?>
 5 <?import javafx.scene.layout.*?>
 6
 7 <!-- ***** 1. Student code starts here -->
 8 <!-- add the code to this element definition to specify
 9     the controller as ButtonPracticeController -->
10 <BorderPane fx:id="bp"
11              xmlns:fx="http://javafx.com/fxml" >
12
13   <top>
14     <!-- ***** 2. Student code restarts here -->
15     <!-- add code to define an HBox layout that is centered
16          with an id of hBox and 10 pixels between controls.
17          Inside the HBox, add 2 Buttons, with text OPEN and
18          CLOSE, and ids of open and close. Clicking on either
19          button triggers a call to the event handler flip
20          method -->
21
22
23
24   </top>
25
26 </BorderPane>
```

EXAMPLE 12.17   Location of Student Code in *fxml_button_practice.fxml*

Note that we define an *HBox* layout container inside a *BorderPane* layout container, illustrating that layouts can be nested. We demonstrate nested layouts again later in the chapter.

Next, open *ButtonPracticeController.java* and search for five asterisks (*****). This will position you at the third and final task for this Programming Activity, writing the event handler for the buttons. Example 12.18 shows the section of the source code where you will add your code.

```
48    // ***** 3. Student code restarts here
49    // Code the flip method.
50    // To open the switch, call the open method
51    //   with circuit, the object reference of the
52    //   Circuit object.
53    //   The open method does not take any parameters.
```

```
54    // To close the switch, call the close method
55    //    with circuit.
56    //     The close method does not take any parameters.
57    // The last statement of the method should be
58    //     animate( );
```

EXAMPLE 12.18   Location of Student Code in *ButtonPracticeController.java*

Our framework will animate your code so that you can watch your code work. For this to happen, be sure that you call the *animate* method as the last statement in the *flip* method.

Troubleshooting

If your *flip* method does not animate, check these tips:

- Verify that the last statement in your *flip* method is:

  animate( );

- Verify that your listener is registered on the buttons (*onAction*).

- Verify that you have correctly identified the button that fired the event using the *getSource* method.

? DISCUSSION QUESTIONS

1. **Explain why the *getSource* method is useful here.**

2. **Could you implement this application with *RadioButtons* instead of *Buttons*? What definition would you need to add to the *FXML* file? How would the *flip* method change, if at all?**

3. **Which class is the Model?**

12.8   Combo Boxes

A *ComboBox* implements a drop-down list. When the combo box appears, either no item or one item is displayed, along with a down arrow icon. When the user presses on the down arrow, the combo box "drops" open and displays a list of items, with a scroll bar for viewing more items. The user can select one item from the list. When the user selects an item, the list closes and only the selected item is displayed.

In this example, we allow the user to select a country from a combo box, and in response, we display an image of a typical food from the selected country. Figure 12.10 shows the window when our application begins.

Figure 12.10

The Food
Sampling
Application

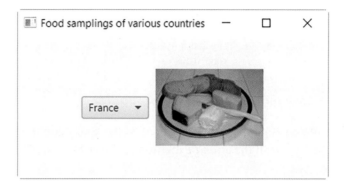

We begin as usual with the Model, *FoodSampler.java*, shown in Example 12.19. Lines 9 through 16 define two arrays. The *countryList* array contains the country names to be displayed in the *ComboBox,* and the *foods* array contains the corresponding images of food stored in the same order as the country names. The instance variable *selectedIndex,* defined at line 17, holds the index of the selected country. We use this index to retrieve the appropriate food image to display. With *selectedIndex* set to 0, the Model's initial state is that the country name "France" is selected and *cheese.jpg* is the corresponding image.

The remainder of the Model consists of accessor methods for the *countryList* array (lines 19–25) and *selectedIndex* (lines 27–33), a mutator method for *selectedIndex* (lines 35–41), and an accessor for the image corresponding to *selectedIndex* (lines 43–50).

```
 1 /*  FoodSampler class
 2     Anderson, Franceschi
 3 */
 4
 5 import javafx.scene.image.Image;
 6
 7 public class FoodSampler
 8 {
 9   private String [ ] countryList =
10       { "France", "Greece", "Italy", "Japan", "USA" };
11   private Image [ ] foods =
12       { new Image( "cheese.jpg" ),
13         new Image( "fetasalad.jpg" ),
14         new Image( "pizza.jpg" ),
15         new Image( "sushi.jpg" ),
16         new Image( "hamburger.jpg" ) };
17   private int selectedIndex = 0;
18
```

```
19   /** getCountryList method
20    *  @return a reference to the countryList array
21    */
22   public String [ ] getCountryList( )
23   {
24     return countryList;
25   }
26
27   /** the accessor for selectedIndex
28    *  @return the index selected
29    */
30   public int getSelectedIndex( )
31   {
32     return selectedIndex;
33   }
34
35   /** the mutator for selectedIndex
36    * @param selection the new value for selectedIndex
37    */
38   public void updateSelection( int selection )
39   {
40     selectedIndex = selection;
41   }
42
43   /** the accessor for the image to display
44    *  @return the image from the Image array
45    *          using the index selectedIndex
46    */
47   public Image getImageSelected( )
48   {
49     return foods[selectedIndex];
50   }
51 }
```

EXAMPLE 12.19   The Model, *FoodSampler.java*

Next we look at the FXML file, *fxml_food_samplings.fxml*, shown in Example 12.20. At line 7, we identify the Controller as *FoodSamplingsController.java*. Lines 11 through 13 define our *ComboBox* control and that the *itemSelected* method in the Controller class will handle the event fired by a user selecting an item from the *ComboBox* drop-down list. We also set the *visibleRowCount* property to 3, specifying that when the user opens the *ComboBox*, three items should be displayed along with a scrollbar for viewing the other hidden items. The default value for the *visibleRowCount* property is 10. If the list contains fewer items than specified in the *visibleRowCount* property, the *ComboBox* displays all the items in the list.

At lines 15 and 16 we also define an *ImageView* control to display the appropriate food image. We do not specify the initial image here; we let the Controller get the appropriate image from the Model.

```
1 <?xml version="1.0" encoding="UTF-8"?>
2
3 <?import javafx.scene.control.*?>
4 <?import javafx.scene.image.*?>
5 <?import javafx.scene.layout.*?>
6
7 <HBox fx:controller="FoodSamplingsController"
8       xmlns:fx="http://javafx.com/fxml"
9       alignment="center" spacing="10" >
10
11    <ComboBox fx:id="countries" visibleRowCount="3"
12              onAction="#itemSelected" >
13    </ComboBox>
14
15    <ImageView fx:id="foodImage">
16    </ImageView>
17
18 </HBox>
```

EXAMPLE 12.20   **The** *fxml_food_samplings.fxml File*

We turn now to the Controller, *FoodSamplingsController.java*, shown in Example 12.21. New to this Controller is the *initialize* method, which is called after the scene graph has been created, and can be used to add items to the scene graph that could not be fully defined in the FXML file. Because the Model stores the list of countries and corresponding images, we cannot specify the items for *ComboBox* in the FXML file. However, this approach also has some advantages: By adding the items to the *ComboBox* at runtime, we can easily handle changes in the list without needing to change our Controller or FXML code, and we can use this application with another Model that has a different set of items and images.

A *ComboBox* control is a generic class, so when the Controller defines the *Combo-Box* (line 14), we need to specify the class type of the items to be displayed; in this example, we are displaying *Strings*.

A *ComboBox*, like other controls that allow users to select items, uses a *Selection-Model* to handle the user's interactions with the control. The *ComboBox* uses the *SingleSelectionModel*, which is a subclass of *SelectionModel*, to restrict the user to a choice of only one item from the list. The *SingleSelectionModel* class is also a generic class; thus, we specify the class type to be *String* in line 16. Table 12.11 shows some useful methods of the *SingleSelectionModel* class for setting and getting the user's selection.

In order for our Controller event handler method, *itemSelected,* to be notified when the user selects an item, we need to put our items into an *ObservableList* object. Table 12.12 shows the *getItems* method of the *ComboBox*, which returns an *Observable-List.* The *addAll* method of the *ObservableList* class, shown in Table 12.13, can be used to insert items into the list. The *addAll* method uses the *varargs* syntax to accept a variable number of arguments.

Putting this all together, in the *initialize* method, we instantiate the Model (line 20), and then call the *getItems* method, which returns an empty *ObservableList.* Next, we call the *addAll* method of the *ObservableList* class to insert into the *ComboBox* the array of country names returned by the Model's *getCountryList* method (lines 22–23).

TABLE 12.11   Useful Methods of the *SingleSelectionModel* Class

Package	javafx.scene.control
Return value	**Method name and argument list**
int	getSelectedIndex( )
	returns the index of the currently selected item.
T	getSelectedItem( )
	returns the currently selected item.
void	select(int index)
	selects the item at *index*. Any previously selected item is deselected.

TABLE 12.12   A Useful Method of the *ComboBox<T>* Class

Package	javafx.scene.control
Return value	**Method name and argument list**
ObservableList	getItems( )
	returns the values of the items in the *ComboBox* as an *ObservableList*

TABLE 12.13   A Useful Method of the *ObservableList<E>* Interface

Package	javafx.collections
Return value	**Method name and argument list**
boolean	addAll(E... elements)
	adds the elements to the list

At line 26, we get a reference to the *SingleSelectionModel*; we then use that reference to select the item using the index returned from the Model's *getSelectedIndex* method (line 29). At this point, the value returned will be 0, because in the Model, we initialize the *selectedIndex* instance variable to 0. We then set the image for our *foodImage ImageView* to the filename returned by the Model's *getImageSelected* method (line 30). Thus, when the window first appears, the country *France* is selected and we display the *cheese.jpg* image.

The *itemSelected* event handler, which executes whenever the user selects a new item from the *ComboBox* (lines 33–41), retrieves the index of the selected item by calling the *getSelectedIndex* method, using the *selectionModel* reference. Using that index, we notify the model that the user has changed the selection. Then we determine which new image to display by calling the Model's *getImageSelected* method.

```
1 /* FoodSamplingsController class
2    Anderson, Franceschi
3 */
4
5 import javafx.event.ActionEvent;
6 import javafx.fxml.FXML;
7 import javafx.scene.control.*;
8 import javafx.scene.image.*;
9
10 public class FoodSamplingsController
11 {
12   private FoodSampler sampler;
13
14   @FXML private ComboBox<String> countries;
15   @FXML private ImageView foodImage;
16   private SingleSelectionModel<String> selectionModel;
17
18   public void initialize( )
19   {
20     sampler = new FoodSampler( );
21
22     // populate combobox with data from the Model
23     countries.getItems( ).addAll( sampler.getCountryList( ) );
24
25     // get a reference to the SingleSelectionModel
26     selectionModel = countries.getSelectionModel( );
27
28     // initialize View with initial data from Model
29     selectionModel.select( sampler.getSelectedIndex( ) );
30     foodImage.setImage( sampler.getImageSelected( ) );
31   }
32
```

```
33   @FXML protected void itemSelected( ActionEvent event )
34   {
35     // retrieve index of country selected
36     int index = selectionModel.getSelectedIndex( );
37     // update the Model
38     sampler.updateSelection( index );
39     // update the View with Image from the Model
40     foodImage.setImage( sampler.getImageSelected( ) );
41   }
42 }
```

EXAMPLE 12.21   The Controller, *FoodSamplingsController.java*

The last piece of the application is the launch class, shown in Example 12.22.

```
 1 /*  Using ComboBox to show a sampling of international foods
 2     Anderson, Franceschi
 3 */
 4
 5 import java.net.URL;
 6 import javafx.application.Application;
 7 import javafx.fxml.FXMLLoader;
 8 import javafx.scene.layout.HBox;
 9 import javafx.scene.Scene;
10 import javafx.scene.Stage;
11
12 public class FoodSamplings extends Application
13 {
14   @Override
15   public void start( Stage stage )
16   {
17     try
18     {
19       URL url =
20         getClass( ).getResource( "fxml_food_samplings.fxml" );
21       HBox root = FXMLLoader.load( url );
22       Scene scene = new Scene( root, 450, 200 );
23       stage.setTitle( "Food samplings of various countries" );
24       stage.setScene( scene );
25       stage.show( );
26     }
27     catch ( Exception e )
28     {
29       e.printStackTrace( );
30     }
31   }
32
33   public static void main( String [ ] args )
```

```
34  {
35    launch( args );
36  }
37 }
```

EXAMPLE 12.22   *FoodSamplings.java*

CODE IN ACTION

Within the online resources, you will find a movie with a step-by-step illustration of working with GUI components. Click on the link to start the movie.

12.9 Sliders

The *Slider* control is capable of displaying a set of continuous values along a horizontal or vertical line, called a **track**. The user "slides" the knob, called the **thumb**, along the track to select a value from the set. To illustrate the *Slider* control, we create an application that allows the user to control the level of gray in a photo. A gray color is created when the red, green, and blue components have the same value. Each color component's value can range from 0.0 to 1.0.

Figure 12.11 shows the GUI when the application begins. The top photo is the original version of the image; this may look familiar as the *sushi.jpg* photo from the *ComboBox* example in the last section. The lower photo has been converted to a middle level of gray. As the user slides the knob left, we darken the photo; as the user slides the knob to the right, we lighten the photo. The vertical lines and numbers shown under the slider are **tick marks** and **tick values.** The values represent a multiplier we use to convert the red, green, and blue color values of the photo to a new level of gray.

We define the *Slider* control in the FXML file, shown in Example 12.23. At lines 20 through 23, we specify the minimum multiplier value as 0, the maximum as .33, and the initial value in the middle of that range as .165. We set properties to show the tick marks and tick labels and to display the tick marks at intervals of .055 units.

Figure 12.11

The Photo Graying GUI

In line 10, we add a *style* property to define padding values for the *VBox*. We add 10 pixels of padding on the left and right sides of the *VBox,* but no padding on the top and bottom.

The *Label* control defined at line 18 aids the user by showing that moving the thumb to the left will darken the image and moving the thumb to the right will lighten the image. Because angle brackets have syntactic meaning in FXML, we use the special character encoding sequences *<* and *>* to represent the left and right angle brackets, respectively. Table 12.14 shows the encoding sequences for the XML and FXML special characters. The five XML encoding sequences start with an ampersand and end with a semicolon. In addition, FXML adds three special characters; the encoding sequences for these FXML special characters consist simply of a leading backslash followed by the special character. These encoding sequences are useful whenever a control's text value contains any of these special characters as data.

SOFTWARE ENGINEERING TIP
Labels can help guide the user through the interface.

TABLE 12.14   XML and FXML Special Characters

Character	XML Encoding Sequence
<	<
>	>
&	&
"	"
'	'
Character	**FXML Encoding Sequence**
@	\@
$	\$
%	\%

```
 1  <?xml version="1.0" encoding="UTF-8"?>
 2
 3  <?import javafx.scene.control.*?>
 4  <?import javafx.scene.image.*?>
 5  <?import javafx.scene.layout.*?>
 6
 7  <VBox fx:controller="PhotoGrayerController"
 8      xmlns:fx="http://javafx.com/fxml"
 9      alignment="center" spacing="10"
10      style="-fx-padding:0 10 0 10;" >
11
12    <ImageView fx:id="originalImageView" >
13      <Image url = "Sushi.jpg" />
```

COMMON ERROR TRAP
Be sure to use the XML and FXML encoding sequences when specifying text values that contain characters having syntactic meaning in XML and FXML. Otherwise, the FXML Loader will generate an error.

```
14    </ImageView>
15
16    <ImageView fx:id="grayImageView" />
17
18    <Label text="&lt;-darker      lighter -&gt;" />
19
20    <Slider fx:id="slider" min="0" max=".33"
21            value=".165" showTickMarks="true"
22            showTickLabels="true" majorTickUnit="0.055" />
23
24 </VBox>
```

EXAMPLE 12.23   The View, _fxml_photo_grayer.fxml_

By looking at the Model (Example 12.24), we can see how the _Slider's_ multiplier values are used to adjust the image's color. The Model, _PhotoGrayer.java,_ extends the _Image_ class, which is used to load graphical images (GIF, BMP, JPG, and PNG) from a URL. In our constructor (lines 13–21), we pass the image filename to the constructor of the _Image_ superclass, shown in Table 12.15.

The purpose of the _gray_ method (lines 23–50) is to create an image composed of varying levels of gray. The gray level of each pixel in the new image is computed by multiplying the red, green, and blue components of the corresponding pixel in the orginal image by the parameter _coeff._

Let's look at the _gray_ method in detail. To get the size of the image, we call the _getWidth_ and _getHeight_ methods, shown in Table 12.15, which we have inherited

TABLE 12.15   A Constructor and Useful Methods of the _Image_ Class

Package	javafx.scene.image	
Constructor		
Image(String URL)		
constructs an _Image_ from the file named in _URL_		
Return value	**Method name and argument list**	
PixelReader	getPixelReader( )	
	returns a _PixelReader_ object for accessing the pixels in the _Image_	
double	getHeight( )	
	returns the height of the image in pixels	
double	getWidth( )	
	returns the width of the image in pixels	

from the *Image* class. Using this information, we create an empty *WritableImage* object of the same size. A *WritableImage* object can be used to create an image from pixels. Table 12.16 shows the constructor and useful methods of the *WritableImage* class, which also inherits from the *Image* class.

We then use the *getPixelWriter* factory method (line 34) to obtain a *PixelWriter* object to write pixel data into the *WritableImage*.

At line 35, we call the *getPixelReader* factory method to get a *PixelReader* object to read pixel data from the original image. A *PixelReader* object provides access to each pixel in the original image (see Table 12.17), while a *PixelWriter* object allows us to set the color of each pixel in the *WritableImage* (see Table 12.18).

TABLE 12.16 A Constructor and a Useful Method of the *WritableImage* Class

Package	javafx.scene.image
Constructor	
`WritableImage( int width, int height )`	
constructs an empty WritableImage of the specified width and height	
Return value	**Method name and argument list**
`PixelWriter`	`getPixelWriter( )`
	returns a *PixelWriter* object for writing the pixels in the *Image*

TABLE 12.17 A Method of the *PixelReader* Interface

Package	javafx.scene.image
Return value	**Method name and argument list**
`Color`	`getColor( int x, int y )`
	returns the *Color* of the pixel at coordinate (*x*, *y*) in the image

TABLE 12.18 A Method of the *PixelWriter* Interface

Package	javafx.scene.image
Return value	**Method name and argument list**
`void`	`setColor( int x, int y, Color c )`
	sets the pixel at coordinate (*x*, *y*) to the color *c*

TABLE 12.19   **Useful Methods of the *Color* Class**

Package	javafx.scene.paint
Return value	**Method name and argument list**
double	getRed( )
	returns the red component of the color in the range 0.0–1.0
double	getGreen( )
	returns the green component of the color in the range 0.0–1.0
double	getBlue( )
	returns the blue component of the color in the range 0.0–1.0
Color	gray(double value)
	returns a *Color* object where the red, green, and blue components are set to *value*, which can range from 0.0 to 1.0

Using a nested *for* loop (lines 37–48), we use that *PixelReader* reference to move through each pixel in the original image. We first retrieve the color of each pixel by calling the *getColor* method of the *PixelReader*, passing it the current *x* and *y* values (lines 40–41).

Using the current color of the original image, we then multiply the sum of the red, green, and blue components by the *coeff* parameter (lines 42–44) and pass the resulting value to the *gray* method of the *Color* class (line 45); this returns a *Color* object where the red, green, and blue components have the *grayValue* parameter's value. The methods of the *Color* class that we use in this example are shown in Table 12.19. Finally, we use the *PixelWriter* to set the color of the corresponding pixel within the *WritableImage* (line 46) to the newly computed gray color.

We return the new image at line 49.

```
 1 /*  Adjusts the gray value of an image
 2     Anderson, Franceschi
 3 */
 4
 5 import javafx.scene.image.Image;
 6 import javafx.scene.image.PixelReader;
 7 import javafx.scene.image.PixelWriter;
 8 import javafx.scene.image.WritableImage;
 9 import javafx.scene.paint.Color;
10
11 public class PhotoGrayer extends Image
12 {
```

```
13   /** constructor
14    * @param file  filename of the image
15    *     passes the filename to the Image class
16    *     constructor
17    */
18   public PhotoGrayer( String file )
19   {
20     super( file );
21   }
22
23   /** gray method
24    *  @param coeff the multipler to determine the
25    *         color for each pixel
26    *  @return a WritableImage
27    */
28   public WritableImage gray( double coeff )
29   {
30     int width = ( int ) getWidth( );
31     int height = ( int ) getHeight( );
32     WritableImage grayImage
33         = new WritableImage( width, height );
34     PixelWriter pw = grayImage.getPixelWriter( );
35     PixelReader pr = getPixelReader( );
36
37     for ( int x = 0; x < width; x++ )
38     {
39       for ( int y = 0; y < height; y++ )
40       {
41         Color currentColor = pr.getColor( x, y );
42         double grayValue =  coeff *
43           ( currentColor.getRed( ) + currentColor.getGreen( )
44             + currentColor.getBlue( ) );
45         currentColor = Color.gray( grayValue );
46         pw.setColor( x, y, currentColor );
47       }
48     }
49     return grayImage;
50   }
51 }
```

EXAMPLE 12.24   The Model, *PhotoGrayer.java*

The Controller, *PhotoGrayerController.java,* shown in Example 12.25, handles any changes to the *Slider's* value made by the user dragging the thumb in either direction. In the *initialize* method (lines 14–25), we instantiate the Model (line 16), sending the filename of the photo to the constructor.

```
1  import javafx.beans.value.*;
2  import javafx.event.*;
3  import javafx.fxml.FXML;
4  import javafx.scene.control.*;
5  import javafx.scene.image.*;
6
7  public class PhotoGrayerController
8  {
9    private PhotoGrayer photoGrayer;
10
11   @FXML private ImageView grayImageView;
12   @FXML private Slider slider;
13
14   public void initialize( )
15   {
16     photoGrayer = new PhotoGrayer( "sushi.jpg" );
17
18     // initialize grayImageView
19     Image grayImage = photoGrayer.gray( slider.getValue( ) );
20     grayImageView.setImage( grayImage );
21
22     // set up event handling for slider
23     SliderHandler sh = new SliderHandler( );
24     slider.valueProperty( ).addListener( sh );
25   }
26
27   private class SliderHandler
28                  implements ChangeListener<Number>
29   {
30     @Override
31     public void changed( ObservableValue<? extends Number> o,
32                          Number oldValue, Number newValue )
33     {
34       // update grayImageView
35       grayImageView.setImage(
36             photoGrayer.gray( newValue.doubleValue( ) ) );
37     }
38   }
39 }
```

EXAMPLE 12.25   The Controller, *PhotoGrayerController.java*

At lines 18 through 20, we initialize the second photo by calling the *gray* method in the Model, sending it the current slider value by calling the *getValue* method of the *Slider* class, as shown in Table 12.20.

The final initialization task is to register the event handler for the *Slider* control. Before we cover that, let's look at lines 27 through 38, where we define the event handler as a *private* **inner class** named *SliderHandler*. A *private* inner class is defined inside a *public* class and has access to all the members of the *public* class. Thus, declaring our event handler as a *private* inner class simplifies our code by giving the event handler direct access to our application's GUI components.

Similar to the *ComboBox*, for which we set up an *ObservableList*, the slider value is an *ObservableValue*, meaning that we can register an event handler that will be notified when the value changes. The *SliderHandler* class implements the *ChangeListener* interface, which has one method that we must override, shown in Table 12.21 and here:

```
void changed( ObservableValue<? extends T> observable,
                 T oldValue, T newValue )
```

The syntax *<? extends T>* means that the observable value can be of any type that is a subclass of the generic type *T* or the type *T* itself. At lines 30 through 37, where we

TABLE 12.20 Some Useful Methods of the *Slider* Class

Package	javafx.scene.control
Return value	Method name and argument list
double	getValue( )
	returns the current value of the *Slider* as a *double*
DoubleProperty	valueProperty( )
	returns the current value of the *Slider* as a *DoubleProperty*, which is a *Property* wrapper class for a *double*, and implements the *ObservableValue<Number>* interface

TABLE 12.21 The Method of the *ChangeListener<T>* Interface

Package	javafx.beans.value
Return value	Method name and argument list
void	changed(ObservableValue<? extends T> observable, T oldValue, T newValue)
	The *ChangeListener* must implement this method to handle changes to the *ObservableValue*

override the method above, we specify the *T* parameter to be *Number* (in *java.lang*), which is an *abstract* superclass extended by Java's numeric wrapper classes: *Byte*, *Short*, *Integer*, *Long*, *Float*, and *Double*. This works because our observable value is a *Double*.

Inside the method, we set the new color for the *ImageView grayImageView* by calling the *gray* method of the Model and sending it the new value of the *Slider*, obtained by calling the *doubleValue* method of the *Double* class, shown in Table 12.22.

Now we're ready to look at lines 23 and 24. At line 23, we instantiate an object of the *SliderHandler* inner class. At line 24, we call the *valueProperty* method of the *Slider* class (shown in Table 12.20), which returns the value of the *Slider* as a *DoubleProperty* object. Because the *DoubleProperty* class implements the *ObservableValue* interface, we can call the *addListener* method of that class to register our event handler. The *ObservableValue* interface, shown in Table 12.23, is also generic. The syntax

TABLE 12.22   A Useful Method of the *Double* Class

Package	java.lang
Return value	**Method name and argument list**
double	doubleValue( )
	abstract method in the *Number* class overridden by the *Double* class; it returns the value of a *Double* object as a *double*.

TABLE 12.23   The Methods of the *ObservableValue*<T> Interface

Package	javafx.beans.value
Return value	**Method name and argument list**
void	addListener(ChangeListener<? super T> listener)
	adds a *ChangeListener* whose code will execute whenever the value of the *ObservableValue* changes
T	getValue( )
	returns the current value of the *ObservableValue* object
void	removeListener(ChangeListener<? super T> listener)
	removes the listener so that it is no longer notified of changes to the value of the *ObservableValue*

<? super T> means that the observable value can be of any type that is a superclass of the generic type *T* or the type *T* itself.

The last piece of the application is the launch class, shown in Example 12.26.

```
1 /*  Slider demo
2     Anderson, Franceschi
3 */
4
5 import java.net.URL;
6 import javafx.application.Application;
7 import javafx.fxml.FXMLLoader;
8 import javafx.scene.layout.VBox;
9 import javafx.scene.Scene;
10 import javafx.stage.Stage;
11
12 public class PhotoGraying extends Application
13 {
14   @Override
15   public void start( Stage stage )
16   {
17     try
18     {
19       URL url =
20         getClass( ).getResource( "fxml_photo_grayer.fxml" );
21       VBox root = FXMLLoader.load( url );
22       Scene scene = new Scene( root, 350, 320 );
23       stage.setTitle( "Graying a photo" );
24       stage.setScene( scene );
25       stage.show( );
26     }
27     catch ( Exception e )
28     {
29       e.printStackTrace( );
30     }
31   }
32
33   public static void main( String [ ] args )
34   {
35     launch( args );
36   }
37 }
```

EXAMPLE 12.26 *PhotoGraying.java*

Skill Practice
with these end-of-chapter questions

12.20.1 Multiple Choice Exercises

Questions 6, 7, 8, 9

12.20.2 Reading and Understanding Code

Questions 21, 22, 23, 24, 25, 26, 27, 28, 29

12.20.3 Fill In the Code

Questions 33, 34, 35

12.20.4 Identifying Errors in Code

Question 52

12.20.5 Debugging Area—Using Messages from the Java Compiler and Java JVM

Question 61

12.20.6 Write a Short Program

Questions 64, 65, 66, 68, 69, 70, 71, 72, 75

12.10   Building a GUI Programmatically

We have been defining GUIs using FXML, which works well when we know the number and type of controls in our GUI. Sometimes, however, the GUI is dynamic and because we may not know how many buttons or other controls we need until runtime, we must define the GUI, that is, instantiate the controls and set their properties, programmatically. For example, the GUI may include buttons that represent URL links stored in a file or on a web server. In that case, the number of buttons can vary each time we run our application. In other applications, it may be more convenient to build the GUI by code rather than with FXML. For example, if the GUI represents a tic-tac-toe game or a chessboard, it is convenient to represent the GUI as a two-dimensional array of buttons, which we define and instantiate programmatically.

We illustrate this approach with an example where we build a chessboard and reveal the position of a square as its column letter and row number when the user clicks on it. Figure 12.12 shows the application running after the user has clicked on several buttons.

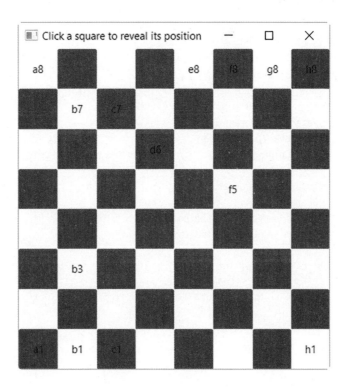

Figure 12.12

Running the
Chessboard
Example

Before defining the View and the Controller, we define our Model, the *BoardGame*
class, shown in Example 12.27. We define a board with an array of *chars* representing the column letters and an array of *ints* representing the row numbers. We declare
two instance variables for these arrays at lines 12 and 13. We include an array of
colors (line 14) so that clients of this class can use custom colors for the board. The
getSquareText method (lines 29–37) returns a *String* representation of a square on
the board as the concatenation of the letter and digit at the row and column indexes
requested by the two parameters.

The *getSquareColor* method (lines 39–49) returns a hexadecimal representation of
the color of the square on the board given its row and column numbers, which are
sent as parameters to the method. This method can be used to color the board with
alternating colors retrieved from the array *colors*.

We provide accessors for the number of rows and the number of columns (lines
81–87 and 89–95).

```
1 /*  BoardGame class
2      Anderson, Franceschi
3 */
4
5 import javafx.scene.paint.Color;
```

```
 6
 7  public class BoardGame
 8  {
 9    private static char [ ] hexDigits =
10          { '0', '1', '2', '3', '4', '5', '6', '7', '8', '9',
11            'A', 'B', 'C', 'D', 'E', 'F' };
12    private int [ ] rows;
13    private char [ ] columns;
14    private Color [ ] colors; // to color the rows and columns
15
16    /** Overloaded Constructor
17     *  @param newRows      the row numbers
18     *  @param newColumns   the column letters
19     *  @param newColors    the colors
20     */
21    public BoardGame( int [ ] newRows, char [ ] newColumns,
22                      Color [ ] newColors )
23    {
24      rows = newRows;
25      columns = newColumns;
26      colors = newColors;
27    }
28
29    /** getSquareText method
30     *  @param row      the row index
31     *  @param column   the column index
32     *  @return a String, a concatenation of columns[column] and rows[row]
33     */
34    public String getSquareText( int row, int column )
35    {
36      return String.valueOf( columns[column] ) + rows[row];
37    }
38
39    /** getSquareColor method
40     *  @param row      the row index
41     *  @param column   the column index
42     *  @return a String, a hex representation of
43     *                    colors[(row + col) % colors.length]
44     */
45    public String getSquareColor( int row, int col )
46    {
47      Color squareColor = colors[(row + col) % colors.length];
48      return toHexString( squareColor );
49    }
50
51    /** toHex utility method
52     *  @param colorIntensity    a double between 0 and 1 inclusive
```

```
53    *  @return a String, the hex representation of colorIntensity times 255
54    */
55    public String toHex( double colorIntensity )
56    {
57      int colorIntensityAsInt = ( int ) ( colorIntensity * 255 );
58      if ( colorIntensityAsInt > 255 )
59        colorIntensityAsInt = 255;
60      else if ( colorIntensityAsInt < 0 )
61        colorIntensityAsInt = 0;
62
63      int firstDigit = colorIntensityAsInt / 16;
64      int secondDigit = colorIntensityAsInt % 16;
65
66      return String.valueOf( hexDigits[firstDigit] ) + hexDigits[secondDigit];
67    }
68
69    /** toHexString method
70     *  @param color  a Color
71     *  @return a String, a hex representation of color
72     */
73    public String toHexString( Color color )
74    {
75      String colorText = "#" + toHex( color.getRed( ) )
76                             + toHex( color.getGreen( ) )
77                             + toHex( color.getBlue( ) );
78      return colorText;
79    }
80
81    /** getNumberOfRows method
82     *  @return the number of rows
83     */
84    public int getNumberOfRows( )
85    {
86      return rows.length;
87    }
88
89    /** getNumberOfColumns method
90     *  @return the number of columns
91     */
92    public int getNumberOfColumns( )
93    {
94      return columns.length;
95    }
96  }
```

EXAMPLE 12.27   The *BoardGame* Class

Even though we are defining the GUI by code, it is possible to separate the View class from the Controller class, as in the previous examples. However, in order to keep this example simple, we put the View and the Controller in the same class.

Regardless of the layout container used, the constructor of our application needs to perform the following operations:

- Instantiate components
- Add components to the layout container

For this example, we use a *GridPane* layout container that allows us to arrange components in a grid. We can visualize a *GridPane* as a table made up of cells in rows and columns. Each cell can contain one component. These cells can have different sizes. In this application, as in many, however, each cell has the same size. Components are placed on the grid at a specified column and row using one of the *add* methods of the *GridPane* class, such as the one shown in Table 12.24. Note that the column parameter is given before the row parameter.

By default, the rows and columns in the grid are sized to their preferred size, which is based on the content of each cell and independent of the size of the *GridPane*. A *GridPane* maintains lists of row and column constraints that it uses to size each cell in the grid. There are no row or column constraints when a *GridPane* is first instantiated, so these two lists are originally empty. If we want to control the height of each row in the grid, we add as many row constraints as there are rows in the grid; similarly, if we want to control the width of each column in the grid, we add as many column constraints as there are columns in the grid. In this example, we want all the rows to have the same height and all the columns to have the same width. We also want all the cells to fill the space in the *GridPane*.

The *getRowConstraints* and *getColumnConstraints* methods of the *GridPane* class, shown in Table 12.24, retrieve the list of row and column constraints, respectively.

We use the *add* method of the *ObservableList* interface, inherited from the *List* interface, to add a row or a column constraint to the appropriate list. When we add a constraint to the list of row or column constraints, it is automatically added to the list of constraints in the *GridPane*. This method is shown in Table 12.25.

The *RowConstraints* and *ColumnConstraints* classes can be used to define the height of a row and width of a column in a *GridPane*, respectively. Often, we want to set the dimensions of a row or column as a percentage of the available space within the *GridPane*. We do this with the *setPercentHeight* and *setPercentWidth* methods of the *RowConstraints* and *ColumnConstraints* classes. These methods are shown in Tables 12.26 and 12.27.

TABLE 12.24   Useful Methods of the *GridPane* Class

Package	javafx.scene.layout
Return value	**Method name and argument list**
void	add(Node child, int columnIndex, int rowIndex)
	adds *child* to this *GridPane* at row *rowIndex* and column *columnIndex*
ObservableList<RowConstraints>	getRowConstraints( )
	returns a list of row constraints for this *GridPane*
ObservableList<ColumnConstraints>	getColumnConstraints( )
	returns a list of column constraints for this *GridPane*

TABLE 12.25   The *add* and *clear* Methods of the *List* Interface

Package	java.util
Return value	**Method name and argument list**
boolean	add(E e)
	appends *e* to the end of the list
void	clear( )
	removes all the elements from the list

TABLE 12.26   The *setPercentHeight* Method of the *RowConstraints*

Package	javafx.scene.layout
Return value	**Method name and argument list**
void	setPercentHeight(double value)
	sets the height of a row as a percentage of the total height of the *GridPane*

TABLE 12.27   The *setPercentWidth* Method of the *ColumnConstraints* Class

Package	javafx.scene.layout
Return value	**Method name and argument list**
void	setPercentWidth(double value)
	sets the width of a column as a percentage of the total width of the *GridPane*

Example 12.28 shows how to define a GUI by code using a *GridPane* to display a chessboard. Each position on a chessboard is identified by a letter (a – h) and a number (1–8). From the standpoint of the white player, the lower left square is a1, and from the standpoint of the black player, the lower left square is h8. When the user clicks on a square on the chessboard, our application displays its position.

The *BoardView* class, shown in Example 12.28, extends *GridPane*. In this way, we can set a *BoardView* object as the root of the scene that we place on the stage.

A two-dimensional array of *Buttons*, named *squares* (line 13), makes up the chessboard. We declare an instance variable of type *BoardGame*, our Model, at line 12. The constructor (lines 15–57) defines the GUI and sets up event handling. We call the constructor of *GridPane* at line 17 and retrieve the number of rows and columns from the Model at lines 20 through 22. At lines 23 through 30, we define and add row and column constraints. After instantiating a *RowConstraints* object at line 23, we set its percentage height to 100%, divided by the number of rows. We then add that row constraint to the list of row constraints as many times as there are rows (lines 27–28). In this way, each row has the same height. We define the column constraints similarly, so that each column has the same width.

At line 33, we declare and instantiate the listener *bh*, a *ButtonHandler* object reference. Because we are interested in events related to buttons, our *ButtonHandler private* inner class implements the *EventHandler* interface and overrides the *handle* method. At line 32, we instantiate the two-dimensional array *squares*. We have a two-dimensional array of *Buttons*, so we use nested *for* loops at lines 35 through 56 to instantiate the *Buttons*, add them to the *GridPane*, and register the listener on all the buttons. Using FXML, to include a *Button* in a layout container, we define a *Button* element and specify attributes for that *Button* element in an *.fxml* file. To create and define a *Button* programmatically, we instantiate the *Button* using a constructor and call various methods to set its properties. These setter methods typically accept a parameter that represents the new value for the *Button* property. Some of these methods are shown in Table 12.28. Remember from Figure 12.2 that the *Button* class is a subclass of *ButtonBase, Labeled, Control, Region, Parent, Node*, and *Object*, and inherits some properties from its superclasses.

At lines 42 through 44, we color the squares according to the coloring pattern and colors set in the Model. In order to do this, we call the *setStyle* method of the *Button* class, inherited from *Node*, and also shown in Table 12.28. The *setStyle* method accepts a CSS-like *String* parameter composed of a semicolon-separated list of attribute-value pairs, with each attribute and value separated by a colon (:). The format of the CSS-style *String* parameter is as follows:

```
"styleAttribute1:value1;styleAttribute2:value2;styleAttribute3:value3; ..."
```

For example, if we want to set the background color to blue and the text's font size to 25, we could use the following *String* as the parameter to the *setStyle* method:

```
"-fx-background-color:blue;-fx-font-size:25"
```

At lines 49 through 51, we ensure that each *Button* will fill the available space within the *GridPane* by setting its maximum width and height to the maximum possible value by calling the *setMaxWidth* and *setMaxHeight* methods (see Table 12.28), using the *static* constant of the *Double* wrapper class (*Double.MAX_VALUE*) that represents the maximum value that a *double* data type can hold. If we remove these statements, the *Buttons* will be sized to their default size, which is based on their contents: in this case, the button's text and the font size of that text. At lines 53 and 54, we call the *setOnAction* method (see Table 12.28) to register the *ButtonHandler bh* on each *Button*.

In the *handle* method, we use nested *for* loops at lines 65 through 75 to identify the source of the event, that is, which button the user clicked. We then set the text of that button to its board position (line 71), retrieving the corresponding value from

REFERENCE POINT
For a complete listing of JavaFX style attributes, see https://docs .oracle.com /javafx/2/api /javafx/scene /doc-files/cssref .html

TABLE 12.28   Selected Methods of and Inherited by the *Button* Class

Package	javafx.scene.control
Constructor	
`Button( )`	
creates an empty Button	

Return value	Method name and argument list
void	`setStyle( String style )`
	sets the value of the *style* property of this *Button* to *style*, which is expected to be a CSS-like *String*. This method is inherited from *Node*.
void	`setMaxWidth( double value )`
	sets the value of the *maxWidth* property of this *Button* to *value*. This method is inherited from *Region*.
void	`setMaxHeight( double value )`
	sets the value of the *maxHeight* property of this *Button* to *value*. This method is inherited from *Region*.
void	`setOnAction( EventHandler<ActionEvent> handler )`
	registers *handler* as the event handler for this *Button*. When the button is clicked, the *handle* method of handler's class will be called automatically. This method is inherited from *ButtonBase*.

the Model. Having found the source of the event, we then exit the event handler via the *return* statement (line 72) to interrupt the *for* loops and thus avoid unnecessary processing.

```
 1 /*  Using GridPane to organize our window
 2      Anderson, Franceschi
 3 */
 4
 5 import javafx.event.ActionEvent;
 6 import javafx.event.EventHandler;
 7 import javafx.scene.control.Button;
 8 import javafx.scene.layout.*;
 9
10 public class BoardView extends GridPane
11 {
12   private BoardGame game;
13   private Button [ ][ ] squares;
14
15   public BoardView( BoardGame newGame )
16   {
17     super( );
18     game = newGame;
19
20     // set up grid according to Model
21     int rows = game.getNumberOfRows( );
22     int columns = game.getNumberOfColumns( );
23     RowConstraints row = new RowConstraints( );
24     row.setPercentHeight( 100.0 / rows );
25     ColumnConstraints col = new ColumnConstraints( );
26     col.setPercentWidth( 100.0 / columns );
27     for ( int i = 0; i < rows; i++ )
28       getRowConstraints( ).add( row );
29     for ( int j = 0; j < columns; j++ )
30       getColumnConstraints( ).add( col );
31
32     squares = new Button[rows][columns];
33     ButtonHandler bh = new ButtonHandler( );
34
35     for ( int i = 0; i < rows; i++ )
36     {
37       for ( int j = 0; j < columns; j++ )
38       {
39         // instantiate the button with no text
40         squares[i][j] = new Button( );
41
```

```
42          // color the button
43          squares[i][j].setStyle( "-fx-background-color:"
44            + game.getSquareColor( i, j ) );
45
46          // add the button
47          add( squares[i][j], j, i );
48
49          // make button fill up available width and height
50          squares[i][j].setMaxWidth( Double.MAX_VALUE );
51          squares[i][j].setMaxHeight( Double.MAX_VALUE );
52
53          // register listener on button
54          squares[i][j].setOnAction( bh );
55        }
56      }
57    }
58
59    // private inner class event handler
60    private class ButtonHandler implements EventHandler<ActionEvent>
61    {
62      @Override
63      public void handle( ActionEvent event )
64      {
65        for ( int i = 0; i < squares.length; i++ )
66        {
67          for ( int j = 0; j < squares[i].length; j++ )
68          {
69            if ( event.getSource( ) == squares[i][j] )
70            {
71              squares[i][j].setText( game.getSquareText( i, j ) );
72              return;
73            }
74          }
75        }
76      }
77    }
78 }
```

EXAMPLE 12.28   The *BoardView* Class

Finally, the *ChessBoard* class, shown in Example 12.29, includes the *main* and *start* methods to create a *BoardView* showing a *BoardGame* game. The *letters*, *digits*, and *boardColors* arrays (lines 14–16) define the board. Try changing either the *letters*, *digits*, or *boardColors* array and running the application again. The grid will be resized correctly and with new colors, showing the reusability of our classes.

```
 1 /*  ChessBoard class
 2      Anderson, Franceschi
 3 */
 4
 5 import javafx.application.Application;
 6 import javafx.scene.paint.Color;
 7 import javafx.scene.Scene;
 8 import javafx.stage.Stage;
 9
10 public class ChessBoard extends Application
11 {
12   public void start( Stage stage )
13   {
14     char [ ] letters = { 'a', 'b', 'c', 'd', 'e', 'f', 'g', 'h' };
15     int [ ] digits = { 8, 7, 6, 5, 4, 3, 2, 1 };
16     Color [ ] boardColors = { Color.WHITE, Color.RED };
17
18     BoardGame game = new BoardGame( digits, letters, boardColors );
19     BoardView view = new BoardView( game );
20
21     Scene scene = new Scene( view, 450, 450 );
22     stage.setScene( scene );
23     stage.setTitle( "Click a square to reveal its position" );
24     stage.show( );
25   }
26
27   public static void main( String [ ] args )
28   {
29     launch( args );
30   }
31 }
```

EXAMPLE 12.29   The *ChessBoard* Class

Figure 12.13 shows the application if we eliminate the row and column constraints by commenting out lines 23 through 30 of Example 12.28. Similarly, we will have the same result if we comment out lines 49 through 51, because the buttons will have their computed preferred size, which is based on their content. As we see, the cells do not fill up the width and height of the *GridPane*; the buttons have their default minimum size because they are empty. When we click on a button, it expands in width to display its new text, and the width of the whole column increases accordingly.

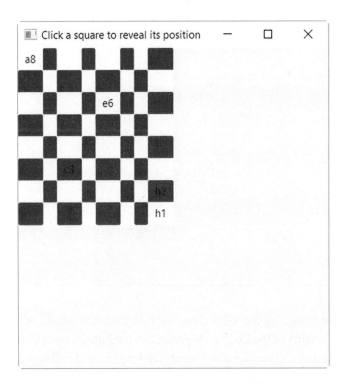

Figure 12.13

Running the
Chessboard
Example Without
Row and Column
Constraints

12.11 Layout Containers: Dynamically Setting Up the GUI Using *GridPane*

Layout managers can be set dynamically, based on user input. For example, the user could enter the number of rows or columns of the grid. Based on user input, we can also rearrange the components using another layout container, such as *HBox*. The user could also instruct us to remove components and add others. Our next example, the Tile Puzzle game, will illustrate some of these capabilities.

In the Tile Puzzle game, eight tiles displaying the digits 1 through 8 are scrambled on a 3-by-3 grid, leaving one cell empty. Any tile adjacent to the empty cell can be moved to the empty cell by clicking on the numbered tile. The goal is to rearrange the tiles so that the numbers are in the correct order, as shown in Figure 12.14.

The Tile Puzzle game can also be played on a 4-by-4, 5-by-5, and more generally, *n*-by-*n* grid. In this example, we set up a 3-by-3 grid for the first game and then randomly select a 3-by-3, 4-by-4, 5-by-5, or 6-by-6 grid for subsequent games. Later, we can modify this example to allow the user to specify the size of the grid.

Figure 12.14

The Winning
Position of a
3-by-3 Tile Puzzle
Game

Before designing the GUI class, we first code the Model, a class to encapsulate the functionality of the tile puzzle game; the *TilePuzzle* class (Example 12.30) handles the creation of a game of a given size, enables play, and enforces the rules of the game.

The instance variable *tiles* (line 7), a two-dimensional array of *Strings*, stores the state of the puzzle. Each element of *tiles* represents a cell in the puzzle grid. The instance variable *side*, declared at line 8, holds the size of the grid. The instance variables *emptyRow* and *emptyCol*, declared at lines 9 and 10, identify the empty cell in the puzzle grid.

The constructor (lines 12–18) calls the *setUpGame* method (lines 20–44), passing the size of the grid (*newSide*) as an argument. The controller also calls the *setUpGame* method before starting each new game.

Inside the *setUpGame* method, we assign *newSide* to *side*. Rather than randomly generating each tile label, which would complicate this example, we assign the labels to the tiles in descending order using nested *for* loops (lines 33–41). We set the empty cell to the last cell in the grid (lines 42 and 43).

The *tryToPlay* method (lines 71–89) first checks if the play is legal by calling the *possibleToPlay* method (line 77). The play is legal if the tile the user clicked is next to the empty tile. If the *possibleToPlay* method returns *true*, we proceed with the play and return *true*; otherwise, we return *false*. Playing means swapping the values of the empty cell (*emptyRow*, *emptyCol*) and the cell that was just played, represented by the two parameters of the *tryToPlay* method, *row* and *col*.

The *possibleToPlay* method is coded at lines 91 through 101. If the play is legal—that is, if the tile played is within one cell of the empty cell—the method returns *true*; otherwise, the method returns *false*.

The *won* method (lines 103–119) checks if the tiles are in order. If so, the *won* method returns *true*; otherwise, the method returns *false*.

```
 1 /** TilePuzzle class
 2 *    Anderson, Franceschi
 3 */
 4
 5 public class TilePuzzle
 6 {
 7   private String [ ][ ] tiles;
 8   private int side; // grid size
 9   private int emptyRow;
10   private int emptyCol;
11
12   /** constructor
13    * @param newSide grid size
14    */
15   public TilePuzzle( int newSide )
16   {
17     setUpGame( newSide );
18   }
19
20   /** setUpGame
21    * @param newSide grid size
22    */
23   public void setUpGame( int newSide )
24   {
25     if ( newSide < 3 )
26       side = 3;
27     else
28       side = newSide;
29     emptyRow = side - 1;
30     emptyCol = side - 1;
31     tiles = new String[side][side];
32
33     // initialize tiles
34     for ( int i = 0; i < side; i++ )
35     {
36       for ( int j = 0; j < side; j++ )
37       {
38         tiles[i][j] = String.valueOf( ( side * side )
39                                     - ( side * i + j + 1 ) );
40       }
41     }
42     // set empty cell label to blank
43     tiles[side - 1][side - 1] = "";
44   }
```

```
45
46   /** getSide
47    * @return side
48    */
49   public int getSide( )
50   {
51     return side;
52   }
53
54   /** getTiles
55    * @return a copy of tiles
56    */
57   public String[ ][ ] getTiles( )
58   {
59    String[ ][ ] copyOfTiles = new String[side][side];
60
61     for ( int i = 0; i < side; i++ )
62     {
63      for ( int j = 0; j < side; j++ )
64      {
65        copyOfTiles[i][j] = tiles[i][j];
66      }
67     }
68     return copyOfTiles;
69   }
70
71   /** tryToPlay
72    * enable play if play is legal
73    * @return true if the play is legal, false otherwise
74    */
75   public boolean tryToPlay( int row, int col )
76   {
77    if ( possibleToPlay( row, col ) )
78    {
79     // play: switch empty String and tile label at row, col
80     tiles[emptyRow][emptyCol] = tiles[row][col];
81     tiles[row][col] = "";
82     // update emptyRow and emptyCol
83     emptyRow = row;
84     emptyCol = col;
85      return true;
86    }
87    else
88      return false;
89   }
90
91   /** possibleToPlay
```

```
 92   * @return true if the play is legal, false otherwise
 93   */
 94   public boolean possibleToPlay( int row, int col )
 95   {
 96    if ( ( col == emptyCol && Math.abs( row - emptyRow ) == 1 )
 97            || ( row == emptyRow && Math.abs( col - emptyCol ) == 1 ) )
 98      return true;
 99    else
100      return false;
101   }
102
103   /** won
104   * @return true if correct tile order, false otherwise
105   */
106   public boolean won( )
107   {
108    for ( int i = 0; i < side ; i++ )
109    {
110     for ( int j = 0; j < side; j++ )
111     {
112      if ( !( tiles[i][j].equals(
113             String.valueOf( i * side + j + 1 ) ) )
114        && ( i != side - 1 || j != side - 1 ) )
115        return false;
116     }
117    }
118    return true;
119   }
120   }
```

EXAMPLE 12.30   The *TilePuzzle* Class

As in the chessboard example, when the user clicks on a button, we need to identify the row and the column of that button. In order to avoid looping through all the buttons, we create a class that *extends* the *Button* class and we add two instance variables for the row and column indexes. In this way, when a button belonging to a two-dimensional array of buttons is clicked, we can access its *row* and *column* instance variables in order to identify which button was clicked.

Example 12.31 shows the *GridButton* class, which extends the *Button* class and adds two instance variables, *row* and *column* (lines 9–10). The constructor at lines 12 through 22 allows the client to create a *GridButton* object with a specified text, row, and column. Note that this class is not specific to the tile puzzle application and can be reused for other applications involving an array of buttons placed on a grid.

```
1 /** GridButton class
2 *    Anderson, Franceschi
3 */
4
5 import javafx.scene.control.Button;
6
7 public class GridButton extends Button
8 {
9   private int row;
10  private int column;
11
12  /** Constructor
13   * @param title text for button
14   * @param newRow row
15   * @param newColumn column
16   */
17  public GridButton( String title, int newRow, int newColumn )
18  {
19    super( title );
20    setRow( newRow );
21    setColumn( newColumn );
22  }
23
24  /** getRow method, accessor for row
25   * @return row
26   */
27  public int getRow( )
28  {
29     return row;
30  }
31
32  /** getColumn method, accessor for column
33   * @return column
34   */
35  public int getColumn( )
36  {
37     return column;
38  }
39
40  /** setRow method, mutator for row
41   * @param row, new value for row
42   */
43  public void setRow( int row )
44  {
45    if ( row >= 0 )
46       this.row = row;
47  }
```

```
48
49  /** setColumn method
50   * @param column, new value for column
51   */
52  public void setColumn( int column )
53  {
54    if ( column >= 0 )
55      this.column = column;
56  }
57  }
```

EXAMPLE 12.31   The *GridButton* Class

Figure 12.15 shows the UML diagram for the *TilePuzzle* and *TilePuzzleViewController* classes.

Example 12.32 shows the *TilePuzzleViewController* class; as in the *BoardView* class in the previous example, it is a subclass of *GridPane* (line 12) and combines the View and the Controller.

Each tile in the game is a *GridButton*. The instance variable *squares* (line 14) holds a two-dimensional array of *GridButtons* so that each element of *squares* is a cell in the game grid. The *TilePuzzle* instance variable *game*, declared at line 15, represents the

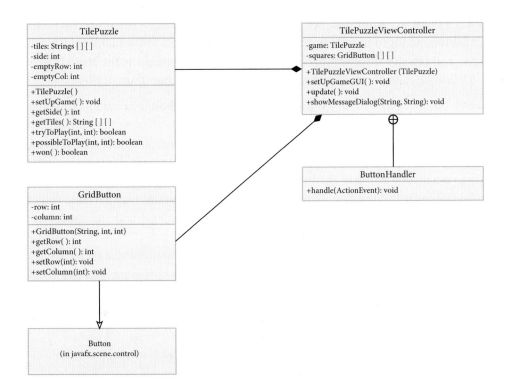

Figure 12.15

The UML Diagram for *TilePuzzle* and *TilePuzzleViewController*

Model. When the user plays, we call the various methods of the *TilePuzzle* class to enforce the rules of the game.

The constructor (lines 17–22) calls the constructor of *GridPane*, instantiates *game,* and calls the *setUpGameGUI* method. The constructor and the *setUpGameGUI* method define the View. The *private* inner class *ButtonHandler* (lines 90–100) and the *update* method (lines 63–78) make up the Controller.

The *setUpGameGUI* method (lines 24–61) displays the game in its starting position. We first remove all the components and the row and column constraints from this *GridPane* (lines 26–29). In order to access the children of this *GridPane*, we call the *getChildren* method inherited from *Pane* and shown in Table 12.29. It returns an *ObservableList* of *Nodes* that are the children of this *GridPane*. With it, we call the *clear* method that *ObservableList* inherits from the *List* interface. That removes all the *Buttons* from this *GridPane*. Because the next game may be 3-by-3, 4-by-4, or 5-by-5 grids, we also need to remove the current row and column constraints of this *GridPane*. We access them using the *getRowConstraints* and *getColumn-Constraints* methods of the *GridPane* class, shown earlier in Table 12.24. They also return a list of *Observable* objects, *RowConstraints,* and *ColumnConstraints*, respectively. We remove these constraints by calling the *clear* method, shown in Table 12.25. We then reset the row and column constraints of this *GridPane* layout container at lines 31 through 39. We instantiate the *squares* array and our event handler at lines 41 and 42. After that, we use nested *for* loops (lines 44–60) to instantiate each button, add it to the container, force the button to fill the available width and height, and register the event handler. The *squares* array parallels the *tiles* array of the *TilePuzzle* class; the *squares* buttons are labeled with the values of *tiles*.

When a button is clicked, our *ButtonHandler handle* method is executed. To determine which button was clicked, we call the *getSource* method using the *ActionEvent* event object that was sent to the method (line 96). Because the *getSource* method returns an *Object*, we need to type cast the return value to a *GridButton*. We then need to determine whether the button clicked was a legal play. To do this, we call the *tryToPlay* method at line 97 with the *row* and *column* instance variable values of the button. If that method returns *true*, the play was legal and the model has

TABLE 12.29   The *getChildren* Method of the *GridPane* Class Inherited from the *Pane* Class

Package	javafx.scene.layout
Return value	Method name and argument list
ObservableList<Node>	getChildren( )
	returns the children of this pane as an *ObservableList* of *Nodes*

changed (i.e., a tile has been moved). We then call the *update* method to make the view (i.e., the buttons) reflect the model (line 98).

The *update* method first updates the *squares* button array (lines 65–67). We then test if the current move solved the puzzle by calling the *won* method (line 69) of the *TilePuzzle* class. If the *won* method returns *true*, we congratulate the user by popping up a dialog box at lines 71 and 72.

The *Alert* class, part of the *javafx.scene.control* package, enables us to display one of many predefined dialog boxes. A constructor and several methods are shown in Table 12.30. Most methods of *Alert* are inherited from its superclass, *Dialog*. The constructor accepts an *Alert.AlertType* parameter that defines the type of dialog box that we want to display. *Alert.AlertType*, a *static* inner class of *Alert*, is an *enum* that defines several constants that can be used to configure the icon and style of the dialog box. The INFORMATION type is used to configure the dialog box so that it just informs the user of something. Other types are CONFIRMATION, ERROR, WARNING, and NONE. At line 82 of the *showMessageDialog* method (lines 80–87), we instantiate a dialog box using the INFORMATION type. We then set the contents of the dialog box at lines 83–85. Note that if we did not set the header text of the dialog box to an empty *String* at line 84, the dialog box would be

TABLE 12.30   Constructor and Useful Methods of the *Alert* Class

Package	javafx.scene.control
Constructor	
Alert(Alert.AlertType type)	
constructs an *Alert* of type *type*.	

Return value	Method name and argument list
void	setTitle(String title)
	sets the title of this dialog box.
void	setHeaderText(String message)
	sets the text to display in the header of this dialog box. If *message* is the empty *String*, no space is allocated for the header and the dialog box will be smaller.
void	setContentText(String message)
	sets the text to display inside dialog box.
Optional<R>	showAndWait( )
	shows this dialog box and waits for the user's response.

bigger and look a bit awkward. Finally, we display the dialog box at line 86 by calling the *showAndWait* method.

We then randomly generate a grid size between three and six (lines 73–74) for the next game and call the *setUpGame* method (line 75) and the *setUpGameGUI* method (line 76) to begin a new game with the new grid size.

```java
1  /* Using GridPane dynamically
2     Anderson, Franceschi
3  */
4
5  import java.util.Random;
6  import javafx.event.ActionEvent;
7  import javafx.event.EventHandler;
8  import javafx.scene.control.Alert.AlertType;
9  import javafx.scene.control.*;
10 import javafx.scene.layout.*;
11
12 public class TilePuzzleViewController extends GridPane
13 {
14   private GridButton [ ][ ] squares;
15   private TilePuzzle game; // the tile puzzle game
16
17   public TilePuzzleViewController( TilePuzzle newGame )
18   {
19     super( );
20     game = newGame;
21     setUpGameGUI( );
22   }
23
24   public void setUpGameGUI( )
25   {
26     // remove all components and constraints
27     getChildren( ).clear( );
28     getRowConstraints( ).clear( );
29     getColumnConstraints( ).clear( );
30
31     // set up grid constraints
32     RowConstraints row = new RowConstraints( );
33     row.setPercentHeight( 100.0 / game.getSide( ) );
34     ColumnConstraints col = new ColumnConstraints( );
35     col.setPercentWidth( 100.0 / game.getSide( ) );
36     for ( int i = 0; i < game.getSide( ); i++ )
37       getRowConstraints( ).add( row );
38     for ( int j = 0; j < game.getSide( ); j++ )
39       getColumnConstraints( ).addAll( col );
40
```

```
41      squares = new GridButton [game.getSide( )][game.getSide( )];
42      ButtonHandler bh = new ButtonHandler( );
43
44      for ( int i = 0; i < game.getSide( ); i++ )
45      {
46        for ( int j = 0; j < game.getSide( ); j++ )
47        {
48          squares[i][j] = new GridButton( game.getTiles( )[i][j], i, j );
49
50          // add the button
51          add( squares[i][j], j, i );
52
53          // make button fill up available width and height
54          squares[i][j].setMaxWidth( Double.MAX_VALUE );
55          squares[i][j].setMaxHeight( Double.MAX_VALUE );
56
57          // register listener on button
58          squares[i][j].setOnAction( bh );
59        }
60      }
61    }
62
63    public void update( )
64    {
65      for ( int i = 0; i < game.getSide( ); i++ )
66        for ( int j = 0; j < game.getSide( ); j++ )
67          squares[i][j].setText( game.getTiles( )[i][j] );
68
69      if ( game.won( ) )
70      {
71        showMessageDialog( "Congratulations",
72                          "You won\nSetting up a new game" );
73        Random random = new Random( );
74        int sideOfPuzzle = 3 + random.nextInt( 4 );
75        game.setUpGame( sideOfPuzzle );
76        setUpGameGUI( );
77      }
78    }
79
80    public void showMessageDialog( String title, String message )
81    {
82      Alert alert = new Alert( AlertType.INFORMATION );
83      alert.setTitle( title );
84      alert.setHeaderText( "" );
85      alert.setContentText( message );
86      alert.showAndWait( );
87    }
```

```
 88
 89   // private inner class event handler
 90   private class ButtonHandler implements EventHandler<ActionEvent>
 91   {
 92     @Override
 93     public void handle( ActionEvent event )
 94     {
 95       GridButton button = ( GridButton ) event.getSource( );
 96       if ( game.tryToPlay( button.getRow( ), button.getColumn( ) ) )
 97         update( );
 98     }
 99   }
100 }
```

EXAMPLE 12.32   The *TilePuzzleViewController* **Class**

Finally, the *PlayTilePuzzle* class, shown in Example 12.33, includes the *main* and *start* methods to create a *TilePuzzleViewController* application showing a *TilePuzzle* game. Figure 12.16 shows a run of this game after the user has moved some tiles.

Figure 12.16

The Tile Puzzle
Game in Progress

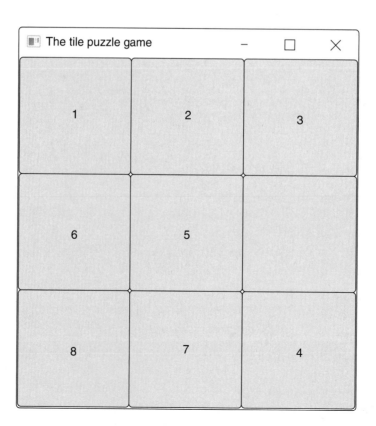

```
 1 /* PlayTilePuzzle class
 2    Anderson, Franceschi
 3 */
 4
 5 import javafx.application.Application;
 6 import javafx.scene.Scene;
 7 import javafx.stage.Stage;
 8
 9 public class PlayTilePuzzle extends Application
10 {
11
12   @Override
13   public void start( Stage stage )
14   {
15     TilePuzzle puzzle= new TilePuzzle( 3 );
16     TilePuzzleViewController root
17       = new TilePuzzleViewController( puzzle );
18
19     Scene scene = new Scene( root, 350, 350 );
20     stage.setTitle( "The tile puzzle game" );
21     stage.setScene( scene );
22     stage.show( );
23   }
24
25   public static void main( String [ ] args )
26   {
27     launch( args );
28   }
29 }
```

EXAMPLE 12.33 The *PlayTilePuzzle* Class

12.12 *BorderPane* Layout, Animations, Sounds, and Lambda Expressions

We have a lot to talk about in this section. We introduce a new layout class, *Border-Pane*. We demonstrate animating nodes with some accompanying sound. And we explain using lambda expressions for event handlers.

A *BorderPane* layout container organizes its nodes into five positions: *top*, *bottom*, *left*, *right*, and *center*, with each position holding, at most, one node. The size of each position expands or contracts depending on the size of the node in that position, the sizes of the nodes in the other positions, and whether the other positions contain a node. The *center* position expands to fill any remaining space; if not enough space is allocated, some positions may overlap other positions. Thus, for each position, we can add zero or one node. In contrast to the previously discussed layout containers,

Figure 12.17

The Five Positions
of the *BorderPane*
Layout

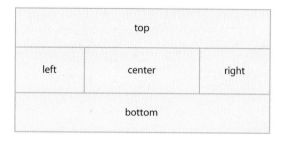

we can define the positions and nodes for a *BorderPane* in any order. Figure 12.17 shows the five possible positions in a *BorderPane* layout.

To illustrate the *BorderPane* layout, we will write an application that animates a Sprite defined in Example 12.34. We've made some changes to the *Sprite* class. Because we want to animate the Sprite, we define the class as extending the *Canvas* class. The default constructor (lines 15–22) calls the constructor of the *Canvas* class, setting the width and height of the canvas to be the width and height of the Sprite. The overloaded constructor is similar (lines 24–35), except that it sets the canvas size to the Sprite's width and height multiplied by the validated *scale*. Figure 12.18 shows the window when the *AnimationSampler* application begins, and Example 12.35 shows the FXML file we use to define the layout and nodes.

Figure 12.18

The *Animation
Sampler*
Window

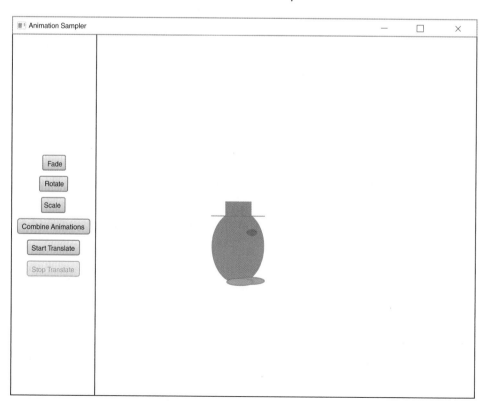

```
1  /* Sprite class
2     Anderson, Franceschi
3  */
4  import javafx.scene.canvas.*;
5  import javafx.scene.paint.*;
6
7  public class Sprite extends Canvas
8  {
9
10   private static final int WIDTH = 95, HEIGHT = 138;
11   private int sX;
12   private int sY;
13   private double scale;
14
15   /** default constructor
16    *  sX = sY = 0; scale is set to 1
17    */
18   public Sprite( )
19   {
20     super( WIDTH, HEIGHT );
21     scale = 1;
22   }
23
24   /* overloaded constructor
25    *  accepts values for starting x and y coordinates
26    *  and scale
27    */
28   public Sprite( int sX, int sY, double scale )
29   {
30     super( );
31     setCoordinates( sX, sY );
32     this.scale = ( scale > 0.0 ? scale : 1 );
33     setWidth( this.scale * WIDTH );
34     setHeight( this.scale * HEIGHT );
35   }
36
37   /* setCoordinates
38    * accepts new values for starting x and y;
39    * returns a reference to this object
40    */
41   public Sprite setCoordinates( int sX, int sY )
42   {
43     this.sX = sX;
44     this.sY = sY;
45     return this;
46   }
47
48   /* mutator for scale
49    *  returns a reference to this object
50    */
51   public Sprite setScale( double scale )
52   {
```

```
53      this.scale = ( scale > 0.0 ? scale : this.scale );
54      return this;
55   }
56
57   /* draw method
58    *  draws Sprite at current sX and sY
59    *  multiplying lengths by scale
60    *  accepts the GraphicsContext of the canvas
61    */
62   public void draw( GraphicsContext gc )
63   {
64     gc.setFill( Color.CORAL ); // body
65     gc.fillOval( sX, sY + 15 * scale, 90 * scale, 120 * scale );
66     gc.setFill( Color.DARKGOLDENROD ); // hat
67     gc.fillRect( sX + 23 * scale, sY, 45 * scale, 22 * scale );
68     gc.setStroke( Color.DARKGOLDENROD ); // hat brim
69     gc.setLineWidth( 3 );
70     gc.strokeLine( sX, sY + 23 * scale,
71                    sX + 90 * scale, sY + 23 * scale );
72     gc.setFill( Color.CHOCOLATE ); // eye
73     gc.fillOval( sX + 60 * scale, sY + 45 * scale,
74                  18 * scale, 12 * scale );
75     gc.setFill( Color.DARKSALMON ); // feet
76     gc.setLineWidth( 1 );
77     gc.fillOval( sX + 45 * scale, sY + 125 * scale,
78                  45 * scale, 12 * scale );
79     gc.strokeOval( sX + 45 * scale, sY + 125 * scale,
80                    45 * scale, 12 * scale );
81     gc.fillOval( sX + 27 * scale, sY + 127 * scale,
82                  45 * scale, 12 * scale );
83     gc.strokeOval( sX + 27 * scale, sY + 127 * scale,
84                    45 * scale, 12 * scale );
85   }
86 }
```

EXAMPLE 12.34   The *Sprite.java* File

```
1 <?xml version="1.0" encoding="UTF-8"?>
2 <?import javafx.scene.control.*?>
3 <?import javafx.scene.layout.*?>
4
5 <BorderPane xmlns:fx="http://javafx.com/fxml"
6         fx:controller="AnimationController">
7   <center>
8    <VBox fx:id="canvasContainer" alignment="center"
9       style="-fx-border-color:navy;-fx-border-width:1"/>
10   </center>
11   <left>
12    <VBox spacing="10" alignment="center"
13       style="-fx-border-color:navy;-fx-border-width:1;-fx-padding:8">
14
```

```
15      <Button text="Fade" fx:id="fadeButton" />
16      <Button text="Rotate" fx:id="rotateButton" />
17      <Button text="Scale" fx:id="scaleButton" />
18      <Button text="Combine Animations" fx:id="combineButton" />
19      <Button text="Start Translate" fx:id="startTranslateButton" />
20      <Button text="Stop Translate" fx:id="stopTranslateButton" />
21    </VBox>
22   </left>
23 </BorderPane>
```

EXAMPLE 12.35 The *fxml_animation.fxml* File

In Example 12.35, we define the top-level layout as a *BorderPane* (lines 5–6 and 23). We specify the *BorderPane* positions using FXML elements. In the *center* position, we place an empty *VBox* (lines 7–10). In the controller's *initialize* method, we will add the Sprite to this *VBox* and draw it. In the *left* position, we place the *VBox* containing the buttons (lines 11–22). Because at most one node can be placed into each position, we place multiple nodes into the *VBox* layout and place the *VBox* layout as the single node in the *left* position. We do not define any nodes for the *top*, *right*, or *bottom* positions. Thus, the *left* position is sized to fit the buttons, and the *center* position expands to fill the window. We define navy borders around the *VBoxes* (lines 9 and 13) so we can see their relative sizes and placement.

JavaFX supports two kinds of animations: transitions and timeline animations. Animations vary the properties of nodes, such as the opacity, position, or size, over a specified time period. In timeline animations, we can define custom variations of properties over time. In this chapter, we concentrate on predefined transitions.

Transitions use a technique called **tweening**, which gives the illusion of a property varying "between" two states by creating and displaying a series of intermediate frames over time. We can define individual transitions or combine multiple transitions to be played sequentially or in parallel.

JavaFX's *abstract Transition* class inherits from the *abstract Animation* class. Each type of transition is a concrete subclass of the *Transition* class. All these classes are in the *javafx.animation* package.

To create an animation, we instantiate an object of the appropriate *Transition* subclass, tie the animation to a node, and specify the beginning and ending states of a property and the time period over which to vary the property. When ready, we play the transition. JavaFX automatically handles the variation of the property over time by creating intermediate frames. By default, the property varies from the start state to the end state at a constant rate.

In our *AnimationSampler* application, we demonstrate several kinds of transitions:

- *FadeTransition*, which varies the opacity of a node so that it fades in or out
- *RotateTransition*, which rotates a node a specified number of degrees
- *ScaleTransition*, which varies the size of a node
- *TranslateTransition*, which moves a node by varying its *x* or *y* coordinate, or both
- *SequentialTransition*, which plays a series of transitions one after the other
- *ParallelTransition*, which plays multiple transitions simultaneously

Some methods that all transitions inherit from the *Animation* class are shown in Table 12.31. The *setCycleCount* method allows us to specify how many times to run the animation. If we set the *autoReverse* property to *true*, the animation will play in reverse every other cycle. When we call the *play* method, the JavaFX platform manages the playing of the transition. We cannot alter the properties of the transition while it is playing. The only method that affects a running animation is *stop*. The *setOnFinished* method allows us to define an event handler to execute when the animation finishes. In addition, each transition has properties and methods specific to its animation.

TABLE 12.31   Some Methods Common to *Animation* **Subclasses**

Package	javafx.animation
Common Methods of *Animation* **Subclasses**	
Return value	**Method name and argument list**
void	play( )
	plays the animation from its current position
void	setAutoReverse(boolean value)
	if *value* is true, animation reverses on alternate cycles; if false, animation repeats from start position on each cycle
void	setCycleCount(int value)
	sets the animation to execute *value* times; if set to Animation.INDEFINITE, animation will run until stopped
void	setOnFinished(EventHandler<ActionEvent> handler)
	registers event handler's code to run when the animation finishes
void	stop( )
	stops the animation, if playing

We manage all the animations for our application in the controller, shown in Example 12.36. In the *initialize* method, we create our Sprite, which is a *Canvas*, and add it to the *VBox* we placed in the *center* position of the *BorderPane* (lines 34–37).

```
1  /*  Animation Controller
2      Anderson, Franceschi
3  */
4  import java.net.URL;
5
6  import javafx.animation.*;
7  import javafx.event.*;
8  import javafx.fxml.*;
9  import javafx.scene.canvas.*;
10 import javafx.scene.control.*;
11 import javafx.scene.layout.*;
12 import javafx.scene.media.AudioClip;
13 import javafx.util.Duration;
14
15 public class AnimationController
16 {
17   @FXML private Button fadeButton, rotateButton,
18                        scaleButton, combineButton,
19                        startTranslateButton, stopTranslateButton;
20   @FXML private VBox canvasContainer;
21
22   private FadeTransition ftFade;
23   private RotateTransition rtHalf, rtFull;
24   private TranslateTransition ttStraight, ttDiagonal;
25   private ScaleTransition stLarger, stSmaller, stSqueeze;
26   private SequentialTransition sequential;
27   private ParallelTransition parallel;
28
29   private AudioClip sound;
30
31   @FXML public void initialize( )
32   {
33     // Sprite extends Canvas
34     Sprite sprite = new Sprite( 0, 0, 1 );
35     GraphicsContext gc = sprite.getGraphicsContext2D( );
36     sprite.draw( gc );
37     canvasContainer.getChildren( ).add( sprite );
38
39     // fade for 3 seconds, then reverse
40     ftFade = new FadeTransition( Duration.seconds( 3 ), sprite );
41     ftFade.setFromValue( 1.0 );
42     ftFade.setToValue( 0.1 );
43     ftFade.setCycleCount( 2 );
```

```
44        ftFade.setAutoReverse( true );
45        fadeButton.setOnAction( event -> runTransition( ftFade ) );
46
47        // sound effect
48        URL resource = getClass( ).getResource( "whoosh.m4a" );
49        sound = new AudioClip( resource.toString( ) );
50        sound.setCycleCount( 2 );
51
52        // rotate 180 degrees and back
53        rtHalf = new RotateTransition( Duration.millis( 3000 ), sprite );
54        rtHalf.setFromAngle( 0 );
55        rtHalf.setToAngle( 180 );
56        rtHalf.setCycleCount( 2 );
57        rtHalf.setAutoReverse( true );
58        rotateButton.setOnAction( event ->
59                                    {
60                                        runTransition( rtHalf );
61                                        sound.play( );
62                                    }
63                                  );
64
65        // reduce size to 1/2, return to start size
66        stSmaller = new ScaleTransition( Duration.millis( 1500 ), sprite );
67        stSmaller.setToX( 0.5f );
68        stSmaller.setToY( 0.5f );
69        stSmaller.setCycleCount( 2 );
70        stSmaller.setAutoReverse( true );
71
72        // reduce x size to 1/2, return to start size
73        stSqueeze = new ScaleTransition( Duration.millis( 1500 ), sprite );
74        stSqueeze.setToX( 0.5f );
75        stSqueeze.setCycleCount( 2 );
76        stSqueeze.setAutoReverse( true );
77
78        sequential = new SequentialTransition( stSmaller, stSqueeze );
79        scaleButton.setOnAction( event -> runTransition( sequential ) );
80
81        // move right 80 pixels, then return to start
82        ttStraight = new TranslateTransition( Duration.seconds( 3 ), sprite );
83        ttStraight.setFromX( 0 );
84        ttStraight.setToX( 80 );
85        ttStraight.setCycleCount( 2 );
86        ttStraight.setAutoReverse( true );
87
88        // rotate 360 degrees
89        rtFull = new RotateTransition( Duration.millis( 3000 ), sprite );
90        rtFull.setByAngle( 360 );
```

```
 91
 92     // increase size by half, return to start size
 93     stLarger = new ScaleTransition( Duration.millis( 1500 ), sprite );
 94     stLarger.setToX( 1.5f );
 95     stLarger.setToY( 1.5f );
 96     stLarger.setCycleCount( 2 );
 97     stLarger.setAutoReverse( true );
 98
 99     parallel = new ParallelTransition( ttStraight, rtFull, stLarger );
100     combineButton.setOnAction( event -> runTransition( parallel ) );
101
102     // move diagonally up 100 pixels, then return to start
103     ttDiagonal = new TranslateTransition( Duration.millis( 1500 ), sprite );
104     ttDiagonal.setFromX( 0 );
105     ttDiagonal.setToX( 100 );
106     ttDiagonal.setFromY( 0 );
107     ttDiagonal.setToY( -100 );
108     ttDiagonal.setCycleCount( Animation.INDEFINITE );
109     ttDiagonal.setAutoReverse( true );
110     stopTranslateButton.setDisable( true );
111     startTranslateButton.setOnAction( event ->
112                 {
113                     stopTranslateButton.setDisable( false );
114                     runTransition( ttDiagonal );
115                 } );
116
117     stopTranslateButton.setOnAction( event ->
118                 {
119                     stopTranslateButton.setDisable( true );
120                     ttDiagonal.stop( );
121                     disableButtons( false );
122                 } );
123   }
124
125   /**
126    *   runTransition
127    *   @param t, the transition to run
128    *   disables buttons, sets animation finished event handler
129    *   plays the animation
130    */
131   public void runTransition( Transition t )
132   {
133     disableButtons( true );
134     t.setOnFinished( event -> disableButtons( false ) );
135     t.play( );
136   }
137
```

```
138   /** disableButtons
139    *   @param mode   true to disable, false to enable
140    */
141   public void disableButtons( boolean mode )
142   {
143      fadeButton.setDisable( mode );
144      startTranslateButton.setDisable( mode );
145      rotateButton.setDisable( mode );
146      scaleButton.setDisable( mode );
147      combineButton.setDisable( mode );
148   }
149 }
```

EXAMPLE 12.36 *AnimationController.java*

In the *initialize* method, we define the animations, but we play them only in response to the user pressing a button. Our first transition is a *FadeTransition* that will fade the Sprite out, then in. A constructor for this transition and several useful methods are shown in Table 12.32.

At line 40, we instantiate our *FadeTransition* object. The first argument to the constructor is the length of time the animation should run, specified as a *Duration* object. The *Duration* class (in the *java.util* package) supplies several *static* factory methods to create *Duration* objects in units of milliseconds, seconds, minutes, or hours. These methods are shown in Table 12.33. Here we use the *static* factory method *seconds* to specify the length of the animation to be 3 seconds. The second argument of the constructor is the node we are animating, which is the Sprite we created.

TABLE 12.32   A Constructor and Method of the *FadeTransition* Class

Package	javafx.animation	
A *FadeTransition* Constructor		
`FadeTransition( Duration time, Node node )`		
creates a *FadeTransition* that will animate *node* for a duration of *time*		
Selected Methods of the *FadeTransition* Class		
Return value	Method name and argument list	
void	`setFromValue( double opacity )`	
	sets the beginning opacity of the animation; the *opacity* can range from 1.0 (fully opaque) to 0.0 (fully transparent)	
void	`setToValue( double opacity )`	
	sets the ending opacity of the animation; the *opacity* can range from 1.0 (fully opaque) to 0.0 (fully transparent)	

TABLE 12.33   Several *static* Factory Methods of the *Duration* Class

Package	java.util
	Selected *static* Factory Methods of the *Duration* Class
Return value	Method name and argument list
Duration	millis(double ms)
	creates a *Duration* object for *ms* milliseconds
Duration	seconds(double secs)
	creates a *Duration* object for *secs* seconds
Duration	minutes(double mins)
	creates a *Duration* object for *mins* minutes
Duration	hours(double hrs)
	creates a *Duration* object for *hrs* hours

At lines 41–44, we define the properties of the transition. We set the opacity to vary from fully opaque (1.0) to almost transparent (0.1). We then set the cycle count to 2 so that the animation will repeat once. And we set *autoReverse* to *true* so that on the repeat cycle, the animation will reverse and the opacity will vary from almost transparent to fully visible. The result is that when this transition plays, the Sprite will appear to fade out for 3 seconds, then fade in for 3 seconds.

For running all our animations, we define a method, *runTransition* (lines 125–136), that accepts as a parameter the transition to play. This method calls the *disableButtons* method defined on lines 138–148 so that the user cannot attempt to start another transition while the current transition is running. The method then registers an *onFinished* event handler that re-enables the buttons when the transition ends, and then plays the transition.

Line 134 registers the *onFinished* event handler using a **lambda expression**.

In the examples in this chapter so far, we have defined event handlers in two ways: as *protected* methods that are referenced in the FXML file as the *onAction* property for a node, and as *private* inner classes in the controller. When an event handler is dedicated to only one control, a third option is to define the event handler as an **anonymous class**, that is, a class that we define inline without giving the class a name. Using this option, we can define and register the event handler at the same time. Let's explore this option with the event handler for the *onFinished* event handler. The only action for our event handler is to call the *disableButtons* method to enable the buttons when the animation finishes.

We can register our event handler using the *setOnFinished* method of the *Transition* class (inherited from the *Animation* class). To do this, we define a class that

TABLE 12.34   The *handle* Method of the *EventHandler<T extends Event>* Interface

Package	javafx.event
Return value	Method name and argument list
void	handle(T event)
	provides code to run when *event* occurs on a registered control

implements the *EventHandler<ActionEvent>* interface. To implement this class, we need to define one method, *handle*, shown in Table 12.34.

In the *runTransition* method, we could register and define our event handler as an anonymous class that implements the *EventHandler* interface using this code:

```
t.setOnFinished( new EventHandler<ActionEvent>( )
               {
                   @Override
                   public void handle( ActionEvent event )
                   {
                       disableButtons( false );
                   }
               }
           );
```

Thus, the argument we send to the *setOnFinished* method is an object reference of the class that implements the *EventHandler<ActionEvent>* interface. We instantiate the object using *new* and define the class by providing the body of the *handle* method inline. Although this code is compact, misplacing a curly brace, parenthesis, or semicolon can generate errors that are difficult to debug. To write this code in a more readable form, we can use lambda expressions, introduced in Java Version 8.

Lambda expressions can be used only with **functional interfaces**, which are interfaces that have only one *abstract* method that the class implementing that interface must define. Thus, the *EventHandler* interface is a functional interface.

A lambda expression contains the following elements:

- A comma-separated list of parameters enclosed in parentheses. The data types of the parameters may be omitted. The parentheses may also be omitted if there is only one parameter.

- The arrow token, ->

- A method body, which can be a single expression or a block enclosed in curly braces

  - If the body of the method consists of a single expression, then the JVM evaluates the expression and returns its value. As an alternative, we can use a *return* statement, but that requires curly braces.

Given this syntax for lambda expressions, we can replace the code above with this single statement:

```
t.setOnFinished( event -> disableButtons( false ) );
```

In fact, this is line 134 in Example 12.36. When the animation finishes, we execute the *disableButtons* method to re-enable the buttons.

We have another opportunity to use lambda expressions in our button handlers. For example, we want the *FadeTransition* to play when the user presses the "Fade" button. This is the only action we want to register for the "Fade" button, and the *setOnAction* method takes an *EventHandler* object, so we are also able to set up an event handler for the button using a lambda expression. Following the syntax explained above, creating and registering the event handler for the "Fade" button is accomplished on line 45. The event handler calls the *runTransition* method passing the name of our *FadeTransition (ftFade)* as an argument.

We gain several advantages by using lambda expressions. The code is even more compact than defining an anonymous class; the code is more readable; and, by defining a separate event handler for each button, we avoid calling the *getSource* method from the event handler to determine which button the user clicked.

Our next animation is a *RotateTransition* that rotates the Sprite 180 degrees clockwise, then reverses to its original orientation while playing a sound effect.

The *AudioClip* class, in the *javafx.scene.media* package, is useful for playing short sounds, such as sound effects. When an *AudioClip* object is instantiated, the sound file is loaded entirely into memory. Thus, this class is intended for playing relatively short sounds. For longer sounds, we would use the *Media* class. You can read more about the *Media* class on Oracle's Java website.

Table 12.35 shows the constructor and the *play* and *stop* methods of the *Audio-Clip* class. The constructor accepts a *String* representing a URL for the sound. In this case, we use a locally stored sound, although we could load a sound from the Internet.

In addition to the methods shown in Table 12.35, the *AudioClip* class also provides methods for setting the rate and volume at which the sound is played and other properties. Like animations, we need to set all the properties of the sound before calling the *play* method. Once a sound is playing, the only method that affects it is *stop*.

At line 48, we instantiate a *URL* object for our sound file, *whoosh.m4a*. On line 49, we instantiate the *AudioClip* object. Because the *AudioClip* constructor accepts a *String* argument, we need to call the *toString* method on the *URL* object. We set the cycle count to 2 at line 50 so that the sound will play twice.

TABLE 12.35   A Constructor and Selected Methods of the *AudioClip* Class

Package	javafx.scene.media

AudioClip Constructor
AudioClip(String source)
loads an audio clip from the URL represented by *source*

Selected Methods of the *AudioClip* Class	
Return value	Method name and argument list
void	setCycleCount(int count)
	count is the number of times to play the sound
void	play( )
	plays the sound
void	stop( )
	stops the sound, if playing

Now we're ready to set up the rotation animation. A constructor for the *RotateTransition* class and several useful methods are shown in Table 12.36. When calling those methods, we specify angle values in degrees.

On lines 52–57, we instantiate the transition and set the rotation for 180 degrees, to repeat in reverse.

When the user presses the *Rotate* button, we want both to start the animation and to play the sound. That means that our event handler (lines 58–63) consists of more than one statement, so, using a lambda expression, we need to place the two statements inside curly braces. Otherwise, the syntax is the same as for the fade animation.

Our next animation is actually two animations that we play sequentially. Using *ScaleTransitions*, we decrease, then "squeeze" the size of the Sprite. A constructor for the *ScaleTransition* class and several useful methods are shown in Table 12.37. When calling those methods, we specify relative, not absolute, values.

At lines 65–70, we instantiate a *ScaleTransition* and decrease the size of the Sprite by setting its *x* and *y* scales to 50%. The *x* scale determines how large the node is horizontally, and the *y* scale determines how large the node is vertically. At lines 72–76, we create another *ScaleTransition* that decreases only the *x* scale by 50%. Because we are not changing the *y* scale, when this animation plays, the Sprite appears to be squeezed horizontally.

We want to play these two animations one after the other, so we create a *SequentialTransition* and add both animations as children (line 78). The *SequentialTransition* constructor shown in Table 12.38 accepts children as a *varargs* argument, so we can add as many animations as desired. When the user presses the "Scale" button, we start the *SequentialTransition* (line 79), which plays the *stSmaller* animation to completion, then automatically plays the *stSqueeze* animation.

Another way to combine animations is to define a *ParallelTransition*, which plays multiple animations simultaneously. For this, we create three animations: moving the Sprite horizontally, rotating the Sprite, and changing its scale.

TABLE 12.36   **A Constructor and Methods of the *RotateTransition* Class**

Package	javafx.animation
A *RotateTransition* Constructor	
RotateTransition(Duration time, Node node)	
creates a *RotateTransition* that will animate *node* for a duration of *time*	
Selected Methods of the *RotateTransition* Class	
Return value	Method name and argument list
void	setFromAngle(double startAngle)
	sets the angle from which to begin the rotation
void	setToAngle(double endAngle)
	sets the angle at which to end the rotation
void	setByAngle(double angle)
	sets the angle relative to the start at which to stop

TABLE 12.37   **A Constructor and Method of the *ScaleTransition* Class**

Package	javafx.animation
A *ScaleTransition* Constructor	
ScaleTransition(Duration time, Node node)	
creates a *ScaleTransition* that will animate *node* for a duration of *time*	
Selected Methods of the *ScaleTransition* Class	
Return value	Method name and argument list
void	setToX(double value)
	sets the x scale at which to stop
void	setToY(double value)
	sets the y scale at which to stop

To move the Sprite horizontally, we define a *TranslateTransition*, which allows us to change the *x* or *y* coordinate of a node. A constructor for the *TranslateTransition* class and several useful methods are shown in Table 12.39.

We define the *TranslateTransition* at lines 81–86. We move the Sprite right by increasing the *x* coordinate by 80 pixels. Then, because we have two cycles and we have set *autoReverse* to *true*, the Sprite returns to its starting position.

We define the second animation in our set to rotate the Sprite 360 degrees (lines 88–90). We do not set a cycle count or *autoReverse*, so these properties default to one cycle and no *autoReverse*. As a result, the animation will run once.

Our final animation in this set scales the Sprite to 1.5 times and then back to the original size (lines 92–97).

TABLE 12.38   A Constructor of the *SequentialTransition* **Class**

Package	javafx.animation
SequentialTransition(Animation… children)	
creates a *SequentialTransition* that will play all *children* animations in sequence	

TABLE 12.39   A Constructor and Method of the *TranslateTransition* **Class**

Package	javafx.animation
A *TranslateTransition* Constructor	
TranslateTransition(Duration time, Node node)	
creates a *TranslateTransition* that will animate *node* for a duration of *time*	
Selected Methods of the *TranslateTransition* Class	
Return value	Method name and argument list
void	setFromX(double value)
	sets the starting x value
void	setToX(double value)
	sets the ending x value
void	setFromY(double value)
	sets the starting y value
void	setToY(double value)
	sets the ending y value

TABLE 12.40   A Constructor of the *ParallelTransition* Class

Package	javafx.animation

`ParallelTransition( Animation… children )`

creates a *ParallelTransition* that will play all *children* animations simultaneously

Using the constructor in Table 12.40, we now create a *ParallelTransition*, adding our three animations (line 99). When the user presses the "Combine Animations" button, we set the listener to play the parallel animation (line 100), which starts all three animations simultaneously. Notice that not all animations in the set need to have the same duration. For the first 1.5 seconds, the Sprite rotates 180 degrees, moves right 40 pixels, and scales to 1.5 times its size. For the next 1.5 seconds, the Sprite completes its move right, rotates the remaining 180 degrees, and scales back to its original size. For the last 3 seconds, the Sprite moves left to its starting position.

For the final animation, we define a *TranslateTransition* that alters both the *x* and *y* values so that the Sprite moves diagonally up to the right (lines 104–111). Note that we set a cycle count of *Animation.INDEFINITE*, which specifies that the animation should keep running until the *stop* method is called. When the user presses the "Start Translate" button, we start the animation, and when the user presses the "Stop Translate" button, we stop the animation. Because the "Stop Translate" button should be enabled only while the animation is running, we set its initial state as disabled (line 110). In the event handler for the "Start Translate" button, we enable the "Stop Translate" button, then start the animation (lines 111–115). In the event handler for the "Stop Translate" button, we disable the "Stop Translate" button, call the *stop* method, then re-enable the rest of the buttons (lines 117–122).

As an animation plays, a **play head** keeps track of the current frame. When we call the *stop* method, the animation stops playing, and its play head is reset to the beginning of the animation. The node, however, remains in the state at which it was stopped. When we again press the "Start Translate" button, we see that because the play head has been reset, the Sprite returns to the start position before beginning the animation.

Example 12.37 shows the *AnimationSampler* code that launches the application.

```
1 /*  Animation Sampler
2       demonstrates various animations
3       Anderson, Franceschi
4 */
5
```

```
 6 import java.net.URL;
 7 import javafx.application.*;
 8 import javafx.fxml.*;
 9 import javafx.scene.layout.*;
10 import javafx.scene.*;
11 import javafx.stage.*;
12
13 public class AnimationSampler extends Application
14 {
15   @Override
16   public void start( Stage stage ) // throws Exception
17   {
18     try
19     {
20       URL url =
21         getClass( ).getResource( "fxml_animation.fxml" );
22       BorderPane root = FXMLLoader.load( url );
23       Scene scene = new Scene( root, 800, 600 );
24       stage.setTitle( "Animation Sampler" );
25       stage.setScene( scene );
26       stage.show( );
27     }
28     catch ( Exception e )
29     {
30       e.printStackTrace( );
31     }
32   }
33
34   public static void main( String [ ] args )
35   {
36     launch( args );
37   }
38 }
```

EXAMPLE 12.37   *AnimationSampler.java*

© Hemera Technologies/
Photos.com/Thinkstock

CODE IN ACTION

Within the online resources, you will find a movie with a step-by-step illustration of working with layout containers and animation. Click on the link to start the movie.

12.13   Nesting Components

Components can be nested. Indeed, because the layout containers are subclasses of *Parent*, itself a subclass of *Node*, layout containers are both containers and components. As such, they can contain other layout containers, which in turn can contain components. We can use this feature to achieve more precise layouts.

When nesting components, we usually place several components into a layout container and place that layout container into another layout container. Each layout container can be different so that components can be arranged in many ways. We can even have multiple levels of nesting, as needed.

We illustrate nesting of components in an example where, using three colors (red, green, and blue), we randomly generate an 8-by-8 grid of colors. The user tries to guess the most frequently occurring color by clicking on one of the buttons.

Figure 12.19A shows our window when the application begins, and Figure 12.19B shows the underlying layout of the window. We use a *BorderPane* overall, with a *VBox* containing the three buttons on the left side of the *BorderPane*, and a *GridPane*

(A)

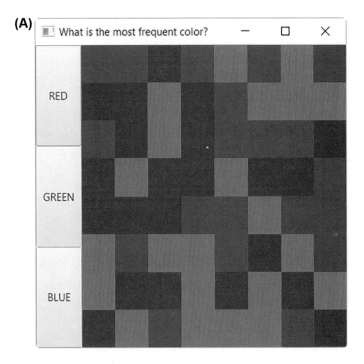

Figure 12.19

(A) The Color Frequency Game (B) The Underlying Nested Layout

(B)

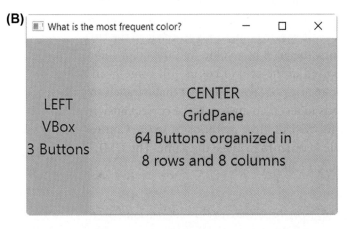

with eight rows and eight columns containing the 64 colored labels in the center position of the *BorderPane*; thus, the two positions we are using, left and center, adjust to fill the space.

Again, we use the MVC architecture and design our classes for reusability. This time, we also code the Controller so that it is reusable under certain conditions. Inside the *Controller* class, instead of using a class for the Model, we use an interface. Thus, the Controller is now reusable, along with the same View, with any Model that implements that interface. Note that we could also make the View an interface, but in order to keep this example relatively simple, we do not. To achieve reusability for the Controller, we use the following pattern for the *Controller* class:

```
public class Controller
{
  private ModelInterface model; // ModelInterface is an interface
  private View view;

  ...
}
```

The *ModelInterface* specifies several methods to be implemented that the Controller will call to manage the game. The *Model* class uses this pattern:

```
public class Model implements ModelInterface
{
  // Implements ModelInterface methods

  ...
}
```

We want the *Controller* class to be reusable with any class whose functionality is based on the user clicking buttons on the left panel with a grid of labels in the center position. We could use this class in an application where the user tries to guess the most frequent color, or the least frequent color, or with a different color system (e.g., HSL—Hue, Saturation and Lightness).

Thus, we design an interface to support this type of application that has buttons on the left and a grid of labels in the center. Example 12.38 shows the *ColorGridGame* interface. It specifies methods to retrieve the title for the grid, its size, its number of colors, the label of a color, and the color index of a label. (It is implied that the colors used in the grid of colors will come from an array of colors, and that there will be an array of *Strings* [labels] that parallels that array of colors.) It also specifies methods to test if an answer is the correct answer, as well as to access each color in the grid. We call these methods from the Controller class with the Model instance variable in order to manage the game. The UML diagram for this example is shown in Figure 12.20.

```
1 /* ColorGridGame interface
2 *  Anderson, Franceschi
3 */
4
5 import javafx.scene.paint.Color;
6
7 public interface ColorGridGame
8 {
9    public String getTitle( );
10   public int getSize( );
11   public int getNumberOfColors( );
12   public String getLabel( int index );
13   public int getIndex( String label );
14   public boolean isCorrect( int index );
15   public String getGridHexColor( int row, int col );
16 }
```

EXAMPLE 12.38   The *ColorGridGame* Interface

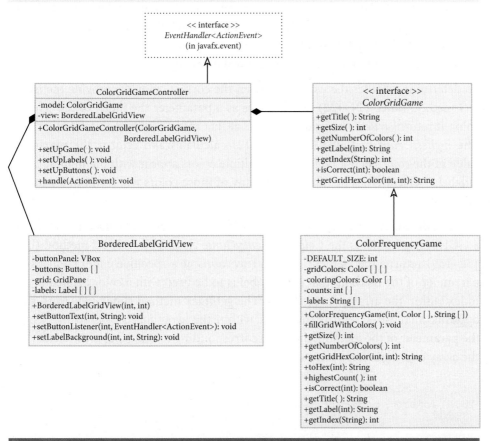

Figure 12.20

The UML Diagram for the Color Frequency Game Application

We now code our Model for the color frequency game. In this application, we generate colors for our grid of labels. Example 12.39 shows the *ColorFrequencyGame* class, which *implements ColorGridGame* (line 8). At lines 10 through 12, we declare a *char* array storing hexadecimal digits. We use this array to convert an integer to its hexadecimal equivalent *String*. Its *gridColors* instance variable (line 15) stores a two-dimensional array, or grid, of colors. The *coloringColors* and *counts* arrays (lines 16–17) are parallel arrays: *coloringColors* stores the colors used for coloring the grid, and *counts* stores the frequency of each color. The instance variable *labels* (line 19) is an array of *Strings* that is meant to be labels for the buttons. The *labels* array also parallels the *coloringColors* array.

The constructor (lines 21–36) instantiates all three arrays and calls the *fillGridWithColors* method at line 34. The *fillGridWithColors* method (lines 38–53) fills the *colorGrid array* with colors randomly generated from the *coloringColors* array and keeps track of their respective frequency in the *counts* array (line 50).

The *getGridHexColor* method (lines 71–83) returns a hexadecimal representation of the color stored at a specified row and column within the array *gridColors*. It uses the utility method *toHex* (lines 85–98), which converts an integer whose value is between 0 and 255 to its hexadecimal equivalent *String*.

To determine whether the user has chosen the correct color, we provide the *isCorrect* method (lines 114–122), which takes as a parameter the index of the selected color. It returns *true* if the value in *counts* at that index is maximal, *false* otherwise. The *highestCount* method (lines 100–112) calculates and returns the maximum value in the *counts* array. Note that if multiple colors appear with the highest count of labels—essentially a tie, then picking any of those colors will result in a winning selection.

The *getTitle* method (lines 124–130) returns a *String* that can be used as the title of a GUI whose Model is the *ColorFrequencyGame* class. The *getLabel* method (lines 132–139) returns the element of the array *labels* at a specified index, sent as the parameter of the method; that is, the label is to be used with a color located at that index within the array *coloringColors*. The *getIndex* method (lines 141–153) is the opposite method: It returns the index within the array *labels* of a *String*, sent as the parameter of the method; the color corresponding to that label is the element in the array *coloringColors* at that index.

```
1 /** ColorFrequencyGame class
2      Anderson, Franceschi
3 */
4
5 import java.util.Random;
6 import javafx.scene.paint.Color;
```

```
 7
 8 public class ColorFrequencyGame implements ColorGridGame
 9 {
10  private static char [ ] hexDigits =
11      { '0', '1', '2', '3', '4', '5', '6', '7', '8', '9',
12        'A', 'B', 'C', 'D', 'E', 'F' };
13
14  private final int DEFAULT_SIZE = 8;
15  private Color [ ][ ] gridColors;
16  private Color [ ] coloringColors;
17  private int [ ] counts; // color frequencies in gridColors
18
19  private String [ ] labels;
20
21  /** Constructor
22   * @param size number of rows and columns in gridColors
23   * @param colors array of colors
24   * @param labels the starting labels
25   */
26  public ColorFrequencyGame( int size, Color [ ] colors,
27                              String [ ] labels )
28  {
29   if ( size <= 0 )
30    size = DEFAULT_SIZE;
31   gridColors = new Color[size][size];
32   coloringColors = colors;
33   counts = new int[coloringColors.length];
34   fillGridWithColors( );
35   this.labels = labels;
36  }
37
38  /** fillGridWithColors method
39   * randomly fills gridColors with colors from coloringColors
40   */
41  public void fillGridWithColors( )
42  {
43   Random random = new Random( );
44   for ( int i = 0; i < gridColors.length; i++ )
45   {
46    for ( int j = 0; j < gridColors[i].length; j++ )
47    {
48     int colorIndex = random.nextInt( coloringColors.length );
49     gridColors[i][j] = coloringColors[colorIndex];
50     counts[colorIndex] += 1;
51    }
52   }
```

```
53  }
54
55  /** getSize method
56  * @return length of gridColors
57  */
58  public int getSize( )
59  {
60    return gridColors.length;
61  }
62
63  /** getNumberOfColors method
64  * @return length of coloringColors
65  */
66  public int getNumberOfColors( )
67  {
68    return coloringColors.length;
69  }
70
71  /** getGridHexColor method
72  * @param row, an int, the row index
73  * @param col, an int, the column index
74  * @return a String, the hex equivalent of gridColor[row][col]
75  */
76  public String getGridHexColor( int row, int col )
77  {
78    String colorText = "#"
79      + toHex( ( int ) ( 255 * gridColors[row][col].getRed( ) ) )
80      + toHex( ( int ) ( 255 * gridColors[row][col].getGreen( ) ) )
81      + toHex( ( int ) ( 255 * gridColors[row][col].getBlue( ) ) );
82    return colorText;
83  }
84
85  /** toHex method
86  * @return a String, the Hex equivalent of colorIntensity
87  */
88  public String toHex( int colorIntensity )
89  {
90    if ( colorIntensity > 255 )
91      colorIntensity = 255;
92    else if ( colorIntensity < 0 )
93      colorIntensity = 0;
94
95    int firstDigit = colorIntensity / 16;
96    int secondDigit = colorIntensity % 16;
97    return String.valueOf( hexDigits[firstDigit]) + hexDigits[secondDigit];
```

```
 98  }
 99
100  /** highestCount method
101   * @return the highest color frequency in the grid
102   */
103  public int highestCount( )
104  {
105   int max = counts[0];
106   for ( int i = 1; i < counts.length; i++ )
107   {
108    if ( counts[i] > max )
109     max = counts[i];
110   }
111   return max;
112  }
113
114  /** isCorrect method
115   * @param index, the index in the coloringColors array to check
116   * @return true if the frequency of the color for index
117   * is the highest, false otherwise
118   */
119  public boolean isCorrect( int index )
120  {
121   return counts[index] == highestCount( );
122  }
123
124  /** getTitle method
125   * @return a String representing a title for this object
126   */
127  public String getTitle( )
128  {
129   return "What is the most frequent color?";
130  }
131
132  /** getLabel method
133   * @param index, the index of the Color name
134   * @return the color name
135   */
136  public String getLabel( int index )
137  {
138   return labels[index];
139  }
140
141  /** getIndex method
142   * @param label, a color name in the labels array
```

```
143    * @return index of the color name in the labels array
144    */
145    public int getIndex( String label )
146    {
147      for ( int i = 0; i < labels.length; i++ )
148      {
149        if ( labels[i].equals( label ) )
150          return i;
151      }
152      return -1;
153    }
154 }
```

EXAMPLE 12.39   The *ColorFrequencyGame* Class

Example 12.40 shows the *BorderedLabelGridView* class. It is a layout container class that *extends BorderPane* (line 16). At its left position, it contains an array of buttons arranged vertically. At its center position, it contains a grid of labels.

Thus, our instance variables are a *VBox* (line 18), which contains an array of *Buttons* (line 19), and a *GridPane* (line 20), which contains a two-dimensional array of *Labels* (line 21). We place the *VBox* in the left position and the *GridPane* in the center position. The other positions within the *BorderPane* are not used.

The constructor (lines 23–67) defines a GUI consisting of an array of buttons on the left, arranged vertically, and a grid of labels in the center, assumed to be a square. Its two parameters represent the number of buttons and the size of the grid. For simplicity, we are not validating these parameters, but both parameters must be greater than 0. The grid of labels is defined at lines 27 through 50 inside the *GridPane*. The array of buttons is defined at lines 52 through 63 inside the *VBox*. At lines 65 and 66, we add the *VBox* and the *GridPane* to this *BorderPane* in the left and center positions, respectively. The *BorderPane* class provides similar methods (*setCenter, setLeft, setRight, setTop,* and *setBottom*) for adding a component to each of its five positions.

We instantiate *grid*, the *GridPane* instance variable, at line 27. At lines 29 through 37, we define row and column constraints so that all the rows in the grid have the same height, all the columns have the same width, and the rows and columns take all the available space in the grid. At lines 39 through 50, we instantiate the labels and add them to the grid, making sure that each label fills the available width and height (lines 45–47).

We instantiate *buttonPanel*, the *VBox* instance variable, at line 52. At lines 54 through 63, we instantiate the buttons and add them to *buttonPanel*, also making sure that each label fills the available width and height (lines 58–61). It is important to set

TABLE 12.41   The *setVgrow* Method of the *VBox* Class

Package	javafx.scene.layout
Return value	Method name and argument list
void	setVgrow(Node child, Priority value) *static* method that sets the vertical grow priority of *child*, assuming that *child* is contained in a *VBox*. If set, the *VBox* will allocate additional space for *child* if space is available.

not only the maximum height of the buttons to a high value (line 60), but also their maximum width (line 59). If we do not, the buttons will have uneven width because their text contents are different. It is also important to call the *setVgrow* method (line 61), shown in Table 12.41, so that the buttons are expanded vertically in order to fill the available space within the *VBox* to which they belong. The *setVgrow* method sets the priority level for expanding the height of a node that is contained in the *VBox* container. The *setVgrow* method is *static*, so there is no reference to a specific *VBox* when we call this method; thus, it is assumed that the node is or will be contained in a *VBox*. If we do not call *setVgrow*, the heights of the buttons are not expanded. *Priority* is an *enum* with three possible values: *ALWAYS*, *NEVER*, and *SOMETIMES*. The *ALWAYS* value ensures that the node grows in order to fill the available space in the *VBox* container. We specify the same priority level for all of the buttons so that they grow equally.

Finally, we provide methods so that the text of each button and the background color of each label can be set from outside the class (lines 69–72 and 79–82). We also provide a method (lines 74–77) to set an *EventHandler* for each button in the array *buttons*. By calling these methods, the Controller can set up event handling and update this View.

```
 1 /** BorderedLabelGridView class
 2 * Reusable generic layout using a BorderPane's
 3 * left and center positions.
 4 * The left VBox is made up of a vertical array of buttons.
 5 * The center position is made up of a grid of labels.
 6 * Accessors are provided so that a Controller can access
 7 * the array of buttons and the 2-dim array (grid) of labels.
 8 * Anderson, Franceschi
 9 */
10
```

```java
11 import javafx.event.*;
12 import javafx.scene.control.*;
13 import javafx.scene.layout.*;
14 import javafx.scene.paint.Color;
15
16 public class BorderedLabelGridView extends BorderPane
17 {
18  private VBox buttonPanel; // left, holds array of buttons
19  private Button [ ] buttons;
20  private GridPane grid; // center, holds grid of labels
21  private Label [ ][ ] labels; // grid of labels
22
23  // numberOfButtons and gridSize must be greater than 0
24  public BorderedLabelGridView( int numberOfButtons, int gridSize )
25  {
26   super( );
27   grid = new GridPane( );
28
29   // set up grid as gridSize by gridSize
30   RowConstraints row = new RowConstraints( );
31   row.setPercentHeight( 100.0 / gridSize );
32   ColumnConstraints col = new ColumnConstraints( );
33   col.setPercentWidth( 100.0 / gridSize );
34   for ( int i = 0; i < gridSize; i++ )
35    grid.getRowConstraints( ).add( row );
36   for ( int j = 0; j < gridSize; j++ )
37    grid.getColumnConstraints( ).addAll( col );
38
39   labels = new Label[gridSize][gridSize];
40   for ( int i = 0; i < labels.length; i++ )
41   {
42    for ( int j = 0; j < labels[i].length; j++ )
43    {
44     labels[i][j] = new Label( );
45     // make label fill up available width and height
46     labels[i][j].setMaxWidth( Double.MAX_VALUE );
47     labels[i][j].setMaxHeight( Double.MAX_VALUE );
48     grid.add( labels[i][j], j, i );
49    }
50   }
51
52   buttonPanel = new VBox( );
53
54   buttons = new Button[numberOfButtons];
55   for ( int i = 0; i < buttons.length; i++ )
```

```
56   {
57     buttons[i] = new Button( );
58     // make button fill up available width and height
59     buttons[i].setMaxWidth( Double.MAX_VALUE );
60     buttons[i].setMaxHeight( Double.MAX_VALUE );
61     VBox.setVgrow( buttons[i], Priority.ALWAYS );
62     buttonPanel.getChildren( ).add( buttons[i] );
63   }
64
65   setLeft( buttonPanel );
66   setCenter( grid );
67   }
68
69   public void setButtonText( int row, String text )
70   {
71     buttons[row].setText( text );
72   }
73
74   public void setButtonListener( int row, EventHandler<ActionEvent> eh )
75   {
76     buttons[row].setOnAction( eh );
77   }
78
79   public void setLabelBackground( int row, int col, String hexColor )
80   {
81     labels[row][col].setStyle( "-fx-background-color: " + hexColor );
82   }
83 }
```

EXAMPLE 12.40   The *BorderedLabelGridView* Class

Example 12.41 shows the *ColorGridGameController* class. At lines 13 and 14, we declare our two instance variables: (1) *model*, a *ColorGridGame*; and (2) *view*, a *BorderedLabelGridView*. These instance variables enable us to get user input from the View, call the appropriate methods of the Model, and update the View accordingly.

The constructor (lines 16–22) accepts two parameters that it assigns to *model* and *view*, and it calls the *setUpGame* method at line 21. The *setUpGame* method (lines 24–28) calls the *setUpLabels* and *setUpButtons* methods.

The *setUpLabels* method (lines 30–35) uses a nested loop to color the grid of labels in the View based on the grid of colors in the Model. At line 34, we set the background color of the current label by calling the View's *setLabelBackground* method, passing the row index, column index, and background color that we retrieve from the Model by calling the *getGridHexColor* method.

The *setUpButtons* method (lines 37–44) places a label on each button in the View based on the label data in the Model and sets up event handling using a single loop. At line 41, we set the text for the current button, passing its index and the label that we retrieve from the Model by calling the *getLabel* method. At line 42, we register *this* object (i.e., this controller, which implements *EventHandler*) on the current button.

We handle the events for the buttons in the *handle* method at lines 46 through 56. We first retrieve the button that originated the event by calling *getSource* at line 48. The *getSource* method returns an *Object*, so we need to type cast the return value to a *Button*. We then retrieve the index of that button's corresponding label by calling the Model's *getIndex* method, passing the text of the button. Next, we check whether the user won or lost by calling the Model's *isCorrect* method, passing that index. Depending on the result, we pop up a dialog box indicating whether the user has won or lost (lines 51–54). The *showMessageDialog* method (lines 58–65) is identical to the one in the puzzle game. After the game is won or lost, we should disable the buttons. This is left as an exercise.

```
 1 /** ColorGridGameController class
 2 *    Anderson, Franceschi
 3 */
 4
 5 import javafx.event.*;
 6 import javafx.scene.control.Alert.AlertType;
 7 import javafx.scene.control.*;
 8 import javafx.scene.layout.*;
 9 import javafx.scene.paint.Color;
10
11 public class ColorGridGameController implements EventHandler<ActionEvent>
12 {
13   private ColorGridGame model;
14   private BorderedLabelGridView view;
15
16   public ColorGridGameController( ColorGridGame model,
17                                   BorderedLabelGridView view )
18   {
19     this.model = model;
20     this.view = view;
21     setUpGame( );
22   }
23
24   public void setUpGame( )
```

```
25  {
26   setUpLabels( );
27   setUpButtons( );
28  }
29
30  public void setUpLabels( )
31  {
32   for ( int i = 0; i < model.getSize( ); i++ )
33    for ( int j = 0; j < model.getSize( ); j++ )
34     view.setLabelBackground( i, j, model.getGridHexColor( i, j ) );
35  }
36
37  public void setUpButtons( )
38  {
39   for ( int i = 0; i < model.getNumberOfColors( ); i++ )
40   {
41    view.setButtonText( i, model.getLabel( i ) );
42    view.setButtonListener( i, this );
43   }
44  }
45
46  public void handle( ActionEvent event )
47  {
48   Button button = ( Button ) event.getSource( );
49   int index = model.getIndex( button.getText( ) );
50
51   if ( model.isCorrect( index ) )
52       showMessageDialog( "Congratulations", "You won" );
53   else
54       showMessageDialog( "Sorry", "You lost" );
55   // disable buttons here
56  }
57
58  public void showMessageDialog( String title, String message )
59  {
60    Alert alert = new Alert (AlertType.INFORMATION );
61    alert.setTitle( title );
62    alert.setHeaderText( "" );
63    alert.setHeaderText( message );
64    alert.showAndWait( );
65  }
66 }
```

EXAMPLE 12.41   The *ColorGridGameController* Class

Finally, the *PlayColorCount* class, shown in Example 12.42, includes the *main* and *start* methods to create a color count application. We declare an array of three *Colors* at line 16 and a parallel array of *Strings* at line 17, and pass these arrays to the constructor of the *ColorFrequencyGame* at lines 19 through 20. We then create the *BorderedLabelGridView* object *root* at lines 22 and 23. Using *game* and *root*, we create a *ColorGridGameController* at lines 25 and 26. At line 29, we retrieve and set the title of the window. Note that *game* "is a" *ColorGridGame* object because *ColorFrequencyGame* inherits from *ColorGridGame*. Figure 12.21 shows a run of this example after the user has clicked on the button "GREEN." To play the game with more colors, we could simply add more colors and labels to the *colors* and *labels* array.

```
 1 /** PlayColorCount class
 2  *    Anderson, Franceschi
 3  */
 4
 5 import javafx.application.Application;
 6 import javafx.scene.paint.Color;
 7 import javafx.scene.Scene;
 8 import javafx.stage.Stage;
 9
10 public class PlayColorCount extends Application
11 {
12
13   @Override
14   public void start( Stage stage )
15   {
16     Color [ ] colors = { Color.RED, Color.GREEN, Color.BLUE };
17     String [ ] labels = { "RED", "GREEN", "BLUE" };
18
19     ColorFrequencyGame game
20       = new ColorFrequencyGame( 8, colors, labels );
21
22     BorderedLabelGridView root
23       = new BorderedLabelGridView( colors.length, game.getSize( ) );
24
25     ColorGridGameController controller
26       = new ColorGridGameController( game, root );
27
28     Scene scene = new Scene( root, 450, 425 );
29     stage.setTitle( game.getTitle( ) );
30     stage.setScene( scene );
31     stage.show( );
```

```
32 }
33
34 public static void main( String [ ] args )
35 {
36   launch( args );
37 }
38 }
```

EXAMPLE 12.42 The *PlayColorCount* Class

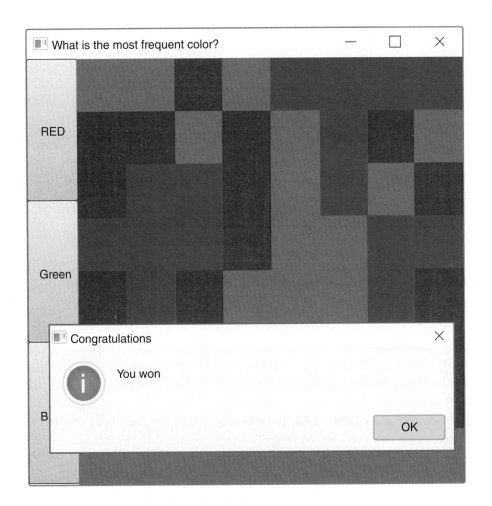

Figure 12.21

The User Clicked on the Button GREEN

Skill Practice
with these end-of-chapter questions

12.20.1 Multiple Choice Exercises

Questions 10, 11, 12, 13, 14, 15, 16, 17, 18

12.20.2 Reading and Understanding Code

Questions 30, 31, 32

12.20.3 Fill In the Code

Questions 36, 37, 38, 39, 40, 41, 42, 43, 44, 45, 46, 47, 48, 49

12.20.4 Identifying Errors in Code

Questions 54, 55, 56

12.20.5 Debugging Area—Using Messages from the Java Compiler and Java JVM

Question 63

12.20.6 Write a Short Program

Questions 67, 73, 74, 76, 78, 79, 80

12.14 Mouse and Touch Events

A truly interactive application allows the user to point and click using the mouse or to touch the screen. Any mouse activity (clicking, moving, or dragging) by the user generates a *MouseEvent*. Any touch activity by the user generates a *TouchEvent*. When any mouse or touch activity occurs, we will be interested in determining where it happened on the window. To determine the (x, y) coordinate of a mouse event, we can call two methods of the *MouseEvent* class, *getSceneX* and *getSceneY*, which are described in Table 12.42. To determine the (x, y) coordinate of a touch event, we can first call the *getTouchPoint* method of the *TouchEvent* class, which returns a *TouchPoint*, and then call the *getSceneX* and *getSceneY* methods of the *TouchPoint* class. These methods are also shown in Table 12.42.

Our application will implement the *EventHandler* interface. The *EventHandler* interface uses generics. We specify the event type that it uses depending on the type of event that we want to handle. It includes only one method, *handle*, described in Table 12.43. Thus, the *EventHandler* interface is a functional interface, and we can use lambda expressions when implementing it.

TABLE 12.42   Useful Classes and Methods for Mouse and Touch Events

Package	javafx.scene.input
Methods of the *MouseEvent* Class	
Return value	**Method name and argument list**
double	getSceneX( )
	returns the *x* coordinate of this *MouseEvent* in the *Scene* where it occurs
double	getSceneY( )
	returns the *y* coordinate of this *MouseEvent* in the *Scene* where it occurs
double	getX( )
	returns the x coordinate of the *MouseEvent* relative to the node on which the mouse listener is registered
double	getY( )
	returns the y coordinate of the *MouseEvent* relative to the node on which the mouse listener is registered
Method of the *TouchEvent* Class	
Return value	**Method name and argument list**
TouchPoint	getTouchPoint( )
	returns the touch point for this *TouchEvent*
Methods of the *TouchPoint* Class	
Return value	**Method name and argument list**
double	getSceneX( )
	returns the *x* coordinate of this *TouchPoint* in the *Scene* in which it occurs
double	getSceneY( )
	returns the *y* coordinate of this *TouchPoint* in the *Scene* in which it occurs
double	getX( )
	returns the x coordinate of the *TouchPoint* relative to the node on which the touch listener is registered
double	getY( )
	returns the y coordinate of the *TouchPoint* relative to the node on which the touch listener is registered

The *Node* class includes many methods to set up event handling for mouse and touch events, as well as key events. Some of these methods are shown in Table 12.44. All the layout container classes, like *VBox* for example, inherit these methods from *Node*. The mouse-related methods accept a parameter of type *EventHandler <? super MouseEvent>*. *EventHandler* is an interface that uses generics. The syntax *<? super MouseEvent>* means that the type of event should be a *MouseEvent* or a superclass of the *MouseEvent* class. Similarly, the event handler for touch events accepts an event that is a *TouchEvent* or a superclass of *TouchEvent*.

To illustrate mouse and touch events, we will build a simple submarine hunt game. A submarine is hidden somewhere in the window, and the user will try to sink the submarine by clicking the mouse or touching the screen at various locations in the window, simulating the dropping of a depth charge. Each time the user clicks the mouse or touches the screen, we will indicate how close that location is to the submarine. If the user's click or touch is too far from the submarine, we will display "In the water" in the title bar and draw a blue circle at the corresponding location. If the user's click or touch is close to the submarine, we will display "Close …" in

TABLE 12.43   **The *handle* Method of the *EventHandler<T extends Event>* Interface**

`void handle( T event )`
This method is called when an event occurs for which this handler is registered.

TABLE 12.44   **Useful Methods of the *Node* Class for Mouse and Touch Events**

Methods of the *Node* Class	
Return value	**Method name and argument list**
void	`setOnMousePressed( EventHandler<? super MouseEvent> handler )`
	registers *handler* as the listener to execute when the user presses the mouse. A parameter of *null* removes any previously registered handler.
void	`setOnMouseMoved( EventHandler<? super MouseEvent> handler )`
	registers *handler* as the listener to execute when the user moves the mouse. A parameter of *null* removes any previously registered handler.
void	`setOnTouchPressed( EventHandler<? super TouchEvent> handler )`
	registers *handler* as the listener to execute when the user touches the screen. A parameter of *null* removes any previously registered handler.
void	`setOnTouchMoved( EventHandler<? super TouchEvent> handler )`
	registers *handler* as the listener to execute when the user moves the touch point on the screen. A parameter of *null* removes any previously registered handler.

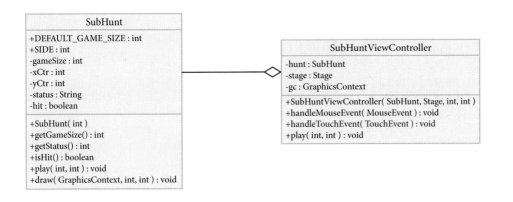

Figure 12.22

UML Diagram
for the Sub Hunt
Game

the title bar. Finally, if the submarine is hit, we will change the title bar to "Sunk!", display the submarine, and remove the listeners so the game ends.

Figure 12.22 shows the UML diagram for this application. We first code our Model, the *SubHunt* class (Example 12.43). It encapsulates the submarine hunt game and enables us to create a game of a given size, enable play, and enforce the rules of the game.

```
 1 /* SubHunt class
 2 *   Anderson, Franceschi
 3 */
 4
 5 import javafx.scene.canvas.GraphicsContext;
 6 import javafx.scene.paint.Color;
 7 import java.util.Random;
 8
 9 public class SubHunt
10 {
11   public static int DEFAULT_GAME_SIZE = 300;
12   public static int SIDE = 36; // size of submarine
13
14   private int gameSize;
15   private int xCtr; // x coordinate of center of submarine
16   private int yCtr; // y coordinate of center of submarine
17   private String status = "";
18   private boolean hit;
19
20   /** Constructor
21   * @param gameSize the game size
22   */
23   public SubHunt( int gameSize )
24   {
25     if ( gameSize > SIDE )
26       this.gameSize = gameSize;
27     else
```

```
28          this.gameSize = DEFAULT_GAME_SIZE;
29       // generate submarine center
30       Random random = new Random( );
31       xCtr = SIDE / 2 + random.nextInt( this.gameSize - SIDE );
32       yCtr = SIDE / 2 + random.nextInt( this.gameSize - SIDE );
33       hit = false;
34    }
35
36    /** getStatus Accessor
37    * @return status
38    */
39    public String getStatus( )
40    {
41       return status;
42    }
43
44    /** getGameSize Accessor
45    * @return gameSize
46    */
47    public int getGameSize( )
48    {
49       return gameSize;
50    }
51
52    /** isHit method
53    * @return hit, which indicates whether the sub has been hit
54    */
55    public boolean isHit( )
56    {
57       return hit;
58    }
59
60    /** play method
61    * @param x the x coordinate of the play
62    * @param y the y coordinate of the play
63    */
64    public void play( int x, int y )
65    {
66       // is click within the submarine?
67       if ( Math.abs( x - xCtr ) < SIDE / 2
68            && Math.abs( y - yCtr ) < SIDE / 2 )
69       {
70          status = "Sunk!";
71          hit = true;
72       }
73       // is click close?
74       else if ( Math.abs( x - xCtr ) < 2 * SIDE
```

```
75                     && Math.abs( y - yCtr ) < 2 * SIDE )
76         status = "Close ...";
77       // click is too far from submarine
78       else
79         status = "In the water";
80     }
81
82    /** draw method
83     * @param gc a GraphicsContext object
84     * @param x the x coordinate of the play
85     * @param y the y coordinate of the play
86     */
87    public void draw( GraphicsContext gc, int x, int y )
88    {
89      if ( status.equals( "Sunk!" ) )
90      {
91        // draw sunken submarine
92        gc.setFill( Color.BLACK );
93        gc.fillRoundRect( xCtr - SIDE/2, yCtr - SIDE/2,
94                          SIDE/2, SIDE, SIDE/2, SIDE/2 );
95
96        gc.fillRoundRect( xCtr - SIDE/4, yCtr - SIDE/3,
97                          SIDE/2, SIDE/2, SIDE/4, SIDE/4 );
98
99        gc.strokeLine( xCtr + SIDE/4, yCtr - SIDE/9,
100                       xCtr + SIDE/2, yCtr - SIDE/9 );
101
102       // draw red depth charge
103       gc.setFill( Color.RED );
104       gc.fillOval( x - SIDE/2, y - SIDE/2, SIDE, SIDE );
105     }
106     else if ( status.equals( "In the water" ) ) // draw blue circle
107     {
108       gc.setFill( Color.BLUE );
109       gc.fillOval( x - SIDE/2, y - SIDE/2, SIDE, SIDE );
110     }
111     // else Close ... , do not draw
112   }
113 }
```

EXAMPLE 12.43   The _SubHunt_ Class

Example 12.44 shows the _SubHuntViewController_ class, which extends _VBox_ (line 11). It combines the View and the Controller. At lines 13–15, we declare our instance variables. The _SubHunt_ instance variable _sub_ (line 13) represents the Model, the submarine hunt game that we display inside the window. At line 14, we include the instance variable _stage_, a reference to the _Stage_. We use _stage_ to call the _setTitle_ method (line

64) to update the title of the window each time the user plays. In the next example, we will show how to retrieve a reference to the *Stage* from the Controller class.

The constructor receives *SubHunt* and *Stage* references as parameters, which we store in the *sub* and *stage* instance variables at lines 26–27. When the user plays, we use the *sub* reference to call the various methods of the *SubHunt* class to enable play and enforce the rules of the game. When the user interacts with the View by clicking on the window, the Controller captures that information, calls the appropriate method of the *SubHunt* class, and updates the View accordingly. The constructor (lines 17–34) defines and displays the original View. It sets up event handling at lines 32–33 for mouse clicks and touch presses. At line 32, we use a lambda expression to define the listener for mouse events, which will execute the *handleMouseEvent* method.

The *handleMouseEvent* method (lines 36–44) retrieves the *x* and *y* coordinates of the mouse event (lines 41–42) and calls the *play* method (line 43) to enable play. On line 33, we again use a lambda expression to define the listener for touch events, which will execute the *handleTouchEvent* method (lines 46–54), which performs equivalent operations for a touch event.

Inside the *play* method (lines 56–70), we call the *play* method of the *SubHunt* model (line 62) to process the user's action, passing its location. Next, we update the View by drawing the current play (line 63). Then we update the title of the window by getting the updated status, and we display that status in the window title bar by calling the *setTitle* method (line 64). Finally, if the game is over (line 65), we disable event handling (lines 67–68) by passing a *null* argument to the *setOnMouseClicked* and *setOnTouchPressed* methods.

```
 1 /* SubHuntViewController class
 2  *  Anderson, Franceschi
 3  */
 4
 5 import javafx.scene.layout.*;
 6 import javafx.scene.input.*;
 7 import javafx.scene.canvas.Canvas;
 8 import javafx.scene.canvas.GraphicsContext;
 9 import javafx.stage.Stage;
10
11 public class SubHuntViewController extends VBox
12 {
13   private SubHunt sub; // submarine
14   private Stage stage;
15   private GraphicsContext gc;
16
17   /** Constructor
18    * @param sub the Model reference for this game
19    * @param stage the Stage for this game
```

```
20     * @param width the width of the Canvas rendering the game
21     * @param height the height of the Canvas rendering the game
22     */
23    public SubHuntViewController( SubHunt sub,
24                                   Stage stage, int width, int height )
25    {
26      this.sub = sub;
27      this.stage = stage;
28      Canvas canvas = new Canvas( width, height );
29      getChildren( ).add( canvas );
30      gc = canvas.getGraphicsContext2D( );
31
32      this.setOnMouseClicked( event -> handleMouseEvent( event ) );
33      this.setOnTouchPressed( event -> handleTouchEvent( event ) );
34    }
35
36    /** handleMouseEvent method
37     * @param event the MouseEvent generated by the user
38     */
39    public void handleMouseEvent( MouseEvent event )
40    {
41      int x = ( int ) event.getSceneX( );
42      int y = ( int ) event.getSceneY( );
43      play( x, y );
44    }
45
46    /** handleTouchEvent method
47     * @param event the TouchEvent generated by the user
48     */
49    public void handleTouchEvent( TouchEvent event )
50    {
51      int x = ( int ) event.getTouchPoint( ).getSceneX( );
52      int y = ( int ) event.getTouchPoint( ).getSceneY( );
53      play( x, y );
54    }
55
56    /** play method
57     * @param x the x coordinate of the play
58     * @param y the y coordinate of the play
59     */
60    public void play( int x, int y )
61    {
62      sub.play( x, y );
63      sub.draw( gc, x, y );
64      stage.setTitle( sub.getStatus( ) );
65      if ( sub.isHit( ) )
66      {
```

```
67          this.setOnMouseClicked( null );
68          this.setOnTouchPressed( null );
69      }
70   }
71 }
```

EXAMPLE 12.44   The *SubHuntViewController* Class

The *PlaySubHunt* class, shown in Example 12.45, instantiates a *SubHunt* object (line 16). It then instantiates a *SubHuntViewController* passing the *SubHunt* object we just instantiated as an argument, along with the stage and the game size. The controller extends *VBox*, so we set the controller as the *root* node for our *Scene*. Figure 12.23 shows a run of this game. At this point, the user has sunk the submarine.

```
1 /* PlaySubHunt class
2    Anderson, Franceschi
3 */
4
5 import javafx.application. Application;
6 import javafx.scene.Scene;
7 import javafx.stage.Stage;
8
9 public class PlaySubHunt extends Application
10 {
11   private final int GAME_SIZE = 500;
12
13   @Override
14   public void start( Stage stage )
15   {
16     SubHunt sub = new SubHunt( GAME_SIZE );
17     SubHuntViewController root =
18       new SubHuntViewController( sub, stage, GAME_SIZE, GAME_SIZE );
19
20     Scene scene = new Scene( root, 500, 500 );
21     stage.setTitle( "Play !!" );
22     stage.setScene( scene );
23     stage.show( );
24   }
25
26   public static void main( String [ ] args )
27   {
28     launch( args );
29   }
30 }
```

EXAMPLE 12.45   The *PlaySubHunt* Class

In the sub hunt game, we handled mouse click and touches. But we didn't handle mouse movements or touch movements. To illustrate how to handle mouse and

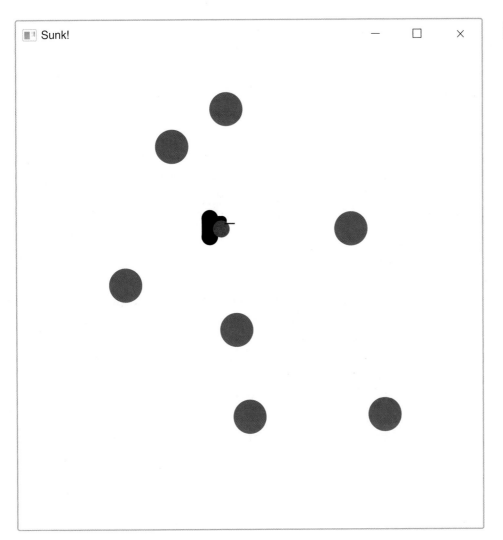

Figure 12.23
A Run of the
SubHunt Game

touch movements, we build a simple treasure hunt game that is similar to the submarine hunt game. A treasure is hidden somewhere in the window, and the user will try to find it by moving either the mouse or his or her finger inside the window. Depending on how close the mouse or touch is to the treasure, we display a message at the mouse or touch location so the user can eventually find the treasure and win the game. Figure 12.24 shows the UML diagram for the treasure hunt game.

Again, we first code the Model, a class that encapsulates the functionality of our treasure hunt game (Example 12.46). It enables us to create a game of a given size, handle plays, determine when the game is over, and display the status of the game.

The *status* (line 18) instance variable, a *String*, stores the state of the player's position compared to the location of the treasure. We also define a *boolean* flag variable,

Figure 12.24

UML Diagram for
the Treasure Hunt
Game

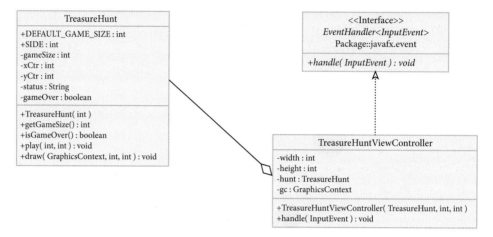

gameOver, which is initially *false* (line 19); when the user finds the treasure, we will change its value to *true*.

In the constructor, we randomly generate the (*x*, *y*) coordinate for the center of the treasure and store the generated values in the *xCtr* and *yCtr* instance variables (lines 30–33). The *play* method (lines 52–79) sets the value of *status*. If the player is far from the treasure, we set the value of *status* to "Cold." As the user moves closer and closer to the treasure, the value becomes "Lukewarm," then "Warm," and then "Hot," and finally "Found" when the player finds the treasure. If the treasure is found, we set the value of *gameOver* to *true* (line 62).

Like the sub hunt game, the *draw* method (lines 81–101) draws what is happening in the game. We first test if the value of *status* is "Found" (line 91). If it is, the treasure has been found and we reveal its location by drawing it (lines 93–97). If the treasure has not been found, we display *status* at the current mouse or touch location (line 100), determined by the parameters *x* and *y* sent to the *draw* method.

```
 1 /* TreasureHunt class
 2 *  Anderson, Franceschi
 3 */
 4
 5 import java.util.Random;
 6 import javafx.scene.canvas.GraphicsContext;
 7 import javafx.scene.paint.Color;
 8 import javafx.scene.text.Font;
 9
10 public class TreasureHunt
11 {
12   public static int DEFAULT_GAME_SIZE = 300; // side of window
13   public static int SIDE = 40; // side of treasure
14
15   private int gameSize;
```

```
16   private int xCtr; // x coordinate of center of treasure
17   private int yCtr; // y coordinate of center of treasure
18   private String status = ""; // message
19   private boolean gameOver = false;
20
21   /** Constructor
22   * @param gameSize the size of the game
23   */
24   public TreasureHunt( int gameSize )
25   {
26     if ( gameSize > SIDE )
27       this.gameSize = gameSize;
28     else
29       this.gameSize = DEFAULT_GAME_SIZE;
30     // generate treasure center
31     Random random = new Random( );
32     xCtr = SIDE / 2 + random.nextInt( this.gameSize - SIDE );
33     yCtr = SIDE / 2 + random.nextInt( this.gameSize - SIDE );
34   }
35
36   /** getGameSize accessor
37   * @return gameSize
38   */
39   public int getGameSize( )
40   {
41     return gameSize;
42   }
43
44   /** isGameOver method
45   * @return gameOver
46   */
47   public boolean isGameOver( )
48   {
49     return gameOver;
50   }
51
52   /** play method
53   * @param x the x coordinate of the play
54   * @param y the y coordinate of the play
55   */
56   public void play( int x, int y )
57   {
58     // is mouse within treasure?
59     if ( Math.abs( x - xCtr ) < SIDE / 2
60         && Math.abs( y - yCtr ) < SIDE / 2 )
61     {
62       gameOver = true;
```

```
63       status = "Found";
64    }
65    // is mouse within half-length of the treasure?
66    else if ( Math.abs( x - xCtr ) < ( 1.5 * SIDE )
67                && Math.abs( y - yCtr ) < ( 1.5 * SIDE ) )
68       status = "Hot";
69    // is mouse within 1 length of the treasure?
70    else if ( Math.abs( x - xCtr ) < ( 2 * SIDE )
71                && Math.abs( y - yCtr ) < ( 2 * SIDE ) )
72       status = "Warm";
73    // is mouse within 2 lengths of the treasure?
74    else if ( Math.abs( x - xCtr ) < ( 3 * SIDE )
75                && Math.abs( y - yCtr ) < ( 3 * SIDE ) )
76       status = "Lukewarm";
77    else // mouse is not near treasure
78       status = "Cold";
79  }
80
81  /** draw method
82   * @param gc a GraphicsContext reference
83   * @param x the x coordinate of the play
84   * @param y the y coordinate of the play
85   */
86  public void draw( GraphicsContext gc, int x, int y )
87  {
88    gc.setFill( Color.BLUE );
89    gc.setFont( new Font( 24 ) );
90    gc.clearRect( 0, 0, gameSize, gameSize );
91    if ( status.equals( "Found" ) ) // if found, draw treasure
92    {
93      gc.setFont( new Font( 16 ) );
94      gc.setFill( Color.RED );
95      gc.fillRect( xCtr - SIDE / 2, yCtr - SIDE / 2, SIDE, SIDE );
96      gc.setFill( Color.GREEN );
97      gc.fillText( "$$$", xCtr - SIDE / 3, yCtr + SIDE / 6 );
98    }
99    else
100     gc.fillText( status, x, y ); // display current status
101 }
102 }
```

EXAMPLE 12.46   The *TreasureHunt* **Class**

Example 12.47 shows the *TreasureHuntViewController* class. Like the sub hunt example, it combines the View and the Controller. The constructor (lines 19–35) defines and displays the View in a *Canvas* (lines 29–30). The Model is represented by the instance variable *hunt* (line 16), which stores the *TreasureHunt* object sent to the constructor from the *start* method (line 26). In this application, instead of coding the event handler as a *private* inner class, we define our application class as implementing the *EventHandler* interface. As a result, our application is a listener, and we register the listener on itself. Thus, in our class definition, we include the clause *implements EventHandler<InputEvent>* (line 13). We choose the *InputEvent* class because it is a superclass of both *MouseEvent* and *TouchEvent*, and thus we can register both mouse and touch events on our *TreasureHuntViewController*. At lines 33–34, we register this *TreasureHuntViewController* object on itself as an *EventHandler* for both mouse and touch movements.

In this game, the events we want to handle are the user moving the mouse or his or her finger on the screen. Because *TreasureHuntViewController* implements the *EventHandler* interface, we must provide a *handle* method, which we do at lines 37–66. Because the ways we retrieve the *x* and *y* coordinates of a mouse event and a touch event are different, we first test if the event is a mouse event (line 43) or a touch event (line 49) by calling the *getEventType* method, inherited from the *Event* class. We compare the return value to the appropriate constant of either the *MouseEvent* class or the *TouchEvent* class. Both constants are shown in Table 12.45. We type cast the event to the appropriate event at lines 45 and 51, then retrieve the *x* and *y* coordinates of the mouse or touch movement.

Then we call the *play* method of the *TreasureHunt* model (line 56) to process the play. Next, we display the result of the current move (line 58) by calling the *draw* method of *TreasureHunt*, passing the *GraphicsContext* reference *gc* and the mouse or touch location. If the game is over (i.e., the treasure has been found), we remove this object, the current *TreasureHuntViewController*, as a listener (lines 61–62) for both mouse and touch moving events.

At lines 63–64, we update the title of the window to reflect the fact that the user has found the treasure and the game is over. In order to do that, we need a reference to the *Stage* of this *VBox*, so we can call the *setTitle* method. The *getScene*

TABLE 12.45   Useful *EventType* Constants of the *MouseEvent* and *TouchEvent* Classes

Class	Constant
MouseEvent	MOUSE_MOVED
	constant identifying a mouse move event
TouchEvent	TOUCH_MOVED
	constant identifying a touch move event

TABLE 12.46   Useful Classes and Methods to Retrieve the Stage

Class	Method
Node	Scene getScene( )
	returns the *Scene* containing this *Node*
Scene	Window getWindow( )
	returns the window for this *Scene*

method, inherited by *VBox* from the *Node* class, returns the *Scene* containing this *Node*, the *TreasureHuntViewController*. With it, we call the *getWindow* method in order to get a reference to the window, which represents the stage. *Stage* is a subclass of *Window*, so we cast the return value of *getWindow* to a *Stage* in order to get a reference to the stage. Table 12.46 shows the *getScene* and *getWindow* methods.

```
 1 /* TreasureHuntViewController class
 2 *  Anderson, Franceschi
 3 */
 4
 5 import javafx.event.*;
 6 import javafx.scene.layout.*;
 7 import javafx.scene.input.*;
 8 import javafx.scene.canvas.Canvas;
 9 import javafx.scene.canvas.GraphicsContext;
10 import javafx.stage.Stage;
11
12 public class TreasureHuntViewController extends VBox
13        implements EventHandler<InputEvent>
14 {
15   private int width, height;
16   private TreasureHunt hunt;
17   private GraphicsContext gc;
18
19   /** Constructor
20   * @param hunt the model reference
21   * @param width the width of the Canvas rendering the game
22   * @param height the height of the Canvas rendering the game
23   */
24   public TreasureHuntViewController( TreasureHunt hunt, int width, int height )
25   {
26     this.hunt = hunt;
27     this.width = width;
28     this.height = height;
```

```
29    Canvas canvas = new Canvas( width, height );
30    getChildren( ).add( canvas );
31    gc = canvas.getGraphicsContext2D( );
32
33    this.setOnMouseMoved( this );
34    this.setOnTouchMoved( this );
35  }
36
37  /** handle method
38   * @param event the InputEvent generated by the user
39   */
40  public void handle( InputEvent event )
41  {
42    int x = -100, y = -100;
43    if ( event.getEventType( ) == MouseEvent.MOUSE_MOVED )
44    {
45      MouseEvent mEvent = ( MouseEvent ) event ;
46      x = ( int ) mEvent.getSceneX( );
47      y = ( int ) mEvent.getSceneY( );
48    }
49    else if ( event.getEventType( ) == TouchEvent.TOUCH_MOVED )
50    {
51      TouchEvent tEvent = ( TouchEvent ) event ;
52      x = ( int ) tEvent.getTouchPoint( ).getSceneX( );
53      y = ( int ) tEvent.getTouchPoint( ).getSceneY( );
54    }
55
56    hunt.play( x, y );
57
58    hunt.draw( gc, x , y );
59    if ( hunt.isGameOver( ) )
60    {
61      this.setOnMouseMoved( null );
62      this.setOnTouchMoved( null );
63      Stage stage = ( Stage ) getScene( ).getWindow( );
64      stage.setTitle( "Thank you for playing" );
65    }
66  }
67 }
```

EXAMPLE 12.47   The *TreasureHuntViewController* Class

Finally, the *PlayTreasureHunt* class, shown in Example 12.48, includes the *main* method to create a *TreasureHuntViewController* application showing a *Treasure-Hunt* game. Figures 12.25 and 12.26 show the program running. In Figure 12.25, the user is getting close to the treasure, and in Figure 12.26, the user has found the treasure.

Figure 12.25

The User Is
Getting Close to
the Treasure

```
1  /* PlayTreasureHunt class
2     Anderson, Franceschi
3  */
4
5  import javafx.application.Application;
6  import javafx.scene.Scene;
7  import javafx.stage.Stage;
8
9  public class PlayTreasureHunt extends Application
10 {
11   private final int GAME_SIZE = 500;
12
13   @Override
14   public void start( Stage stage )
15   {
16     TreasureHunt th = new TreasureHunt( GAME_SIZE );
17     TreasureHuntViewController root =
18       new TreasureHuntViewController( th, GAME_SIZE, GAME_SIZE );
```

```
19
20    Scene scene = new Scene( root, GAME_SIZE, GAME_SIZE );
21    stage.setTitle( "Play !!" );
22    stage.setScene( scene );
23    stage.show( );
24  }
25
26  public static void main( String [ ] args )
27  {
28    launch( args );
29  }
30 }
```

EXAMPLE 12.48   The *PlayTreasureHunt* Class

In both the sub hunt and treasure hunt examples, the Model is reusable in another application. However, the View and the Controller are combined in the same class and are not reusable. Later in the chapter, we will make the View reusable too.

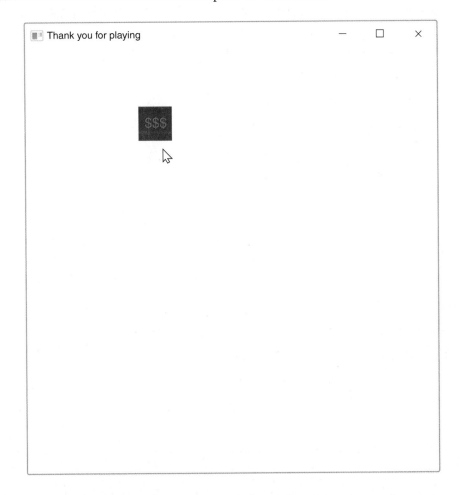

Figure 12.26

The User Has Found the Treasure

12.15   Using a List to Display a Pie Chart

JavaFX includes classes that make it easy to display various types of charts, including line charts, pie charts, and bar charts. To display a chart, we first create a list that stores the data we want to display. We then assign that data to the appropriate chart object. After we include the chart object in a scene, the chart draws itself automatically. The *ObservableList* interface, from the *javafx.collections* package, is a list that can be linked to a GUI component, such as a *ComboBox*. Whenever the values in the list change, the associated GUI component is automatically updated to reflect those changes. Several chart classes, such as *PieChart* and *BarChart*, can be constructed by linking their data to an *ObservableList*.

In this example, we use the *PieChart* class to display a pie chart, a filled circle composed of colored slices, where each slice represents a percentage of the whole pie. The *PieChart* constructor, listed in Table 12.47, accepts an *ObservableList* of *PieChart.Data* as its only parameter. *PieChart.Data* is an inner class of *PieChart* and each object represents one slice of the pie chart. A slice is defined by its label and its value. The *PieChart.Data* constructor shown in Table 12.47 accepts a *String* parameter for the label and a *double* parameter for the value.

To display a pie chart, we do the following:

- Create a list of *PieChart.Data* objects.
- Convert that list to an *ObservableList*.
- Create a *PieChart* associated with that *ObservableList*.
- Create a *Scene* with that *PieChart*.

Example 12.49 creates a pie chart displaying the various parts of a monthly budget so we can visualize the percentage of the total for each category. At lines 11–14, we declare two arrays, *categories* and *expenses*, which hold the labels and the corresponding values for the pie chart slices. At lines 19–22, we create and fill *list*, an *ArrayList* of *PieChart.Data*. Each *PieChart.Data* is defined with a label from the *categories* array

TABLE 12.47   *PieChart.Data* and *PieChart* Constructors

Package	javafx.scene.chart
***PieChart.Data* and *PieChart* Constructors**	
`PieChart.Data( String name, double value )`	
creates a *PieChart.Data*, a slice of a *PieChart*; the slice value is *value* and its label is *name*	
`PieChart( ObservableList<PieChart.Data> data )`	
creates a *PieChart* using *data* as its data for all its slices	

and a value from the *expenses* array (line 22). At lines 23–24, we call the *observableList* method of the *FXCollections* class, shown in Table 12.48, to construct the *Observable-List pieChartData* from that *ArrayList*. The *ArrayList* class *implements* the *List* interface, and thus an *ArrayList* can be used as an argument of the *observableList* method.

At lines 26–28, we construct the *PieChart* chart with *pieChartData* and set its title. At lines 30–34, we construct a *Scene* with the *PieChart* (line 31) and set the *Stage* with that *Scene*. The *PieChart* class inherits from the *Parent* class, and thus a *Pie-Chart* can be used to construct a scene. Figure 12.27 shows the pie chart.

TABLE 12.48   The *observableList* Method of the *FXCollections* Class

The *observableList static* Method of the *FXCollections* Class	
Return value	**Method name and argument list**
ObservableList<E>	observableList(List<E> list) constructs and returns an *ObservableList* composed of elements of type E from *list*. Changes to that *ObservableList* will be reflected in components that are registered on that *ObservableList*.

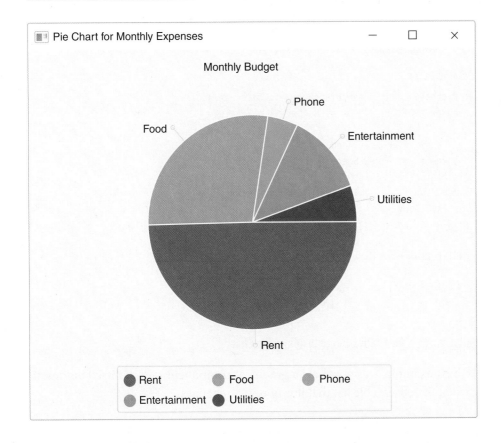

Figure 12.27

Displaying a Pie Chart for a Monthly Budget

```
1 import java.util.ArrayList;
2 import javafx.application.Application;
3 import javafx.collections.FXCollections;
4 import javafx.collections.ObservableList;
5 import javafx.scene.chart.*;
6 import javafx.scene.Scene;
7 import javafx.stage.Stage;
8
9 public class MonthlyBudgetPieChart extends Application
10 {
11   private String [ ] categories
12     = { "Rent", "Food", "Phone", "Entertainment", "Utilities" };
13   private double [ ] expenses
14     = { 800, 450, 72.50, 200, 90 };
15
16   @Override
17   public void start( Stage stage )
18   {
19     // Create a PieChart.Data of monthly expenses
20     ArrayList<PieChart.Data> list = new ArrayList<PieChart.Data>( );
21     for ( int i = 0; i < expenses.length; i++ )
22       list.add( new PieChart.Data( categories[i], expenses[i] ) );
23     ObservableList<PieChart.Data> pieChartData
24       = FXCollections.observableList( list );
25
26     // Create a PieChart with pieChartData
27     PieChart chart = new PieChart( pieChartData );
28     chart.setTitle( "Monthly Budget" );
29
30     // Define the scene and stage
31     Scene scene = new Scene( chart, 500, 400 );
32     stage.setScene( scene );
33     stage.setTitle( "Pie Chart for Monthly Expenses" );
34     stage.show( );
35   }
36
37   public static void main( String [ ] args )
38   {
39     launch( args );
40   }
41 }
```

EXAMPLE 12.49 **An Application to Display a Pie Chart**

In the next example, we show how a graphical component redraws itself automatically when the observable list that it is bound to changes.

12.16   Using a List to Display a Dynamic Bar Chart

In this example, we display a bar chart that displays projected values of stocks and bonds over 4 years for an initial investment of $100. The *BarChart* class can be used to create a two-dimensional bar chart. A *BarChart* is defined using a horizontal axis, a vertical axis, and a list consisting of one or two *series* of data, each series representing a single-dimensional list of data. Thus, if we use only one series in that list, we can define a one-dimensional bar chart as a special case of a two-dimensional bar chart. Our example uses two series of data, one for stocks and one for bonds. The projected values of the bonds are fixed, but the projected values of the stocks toggle between two sets of values, depending on what growth rate we use. The user can toggle between the two sets of values by clicking on a button. The *BarChart* is bound to an *ObservableList*. When the user clicks on the button, we change the data inside the *ObservableList* to the alternate set of values. Because the *BarChart* is bound to the *ObservableList*, it is automatically updated. Figures 12.28 and 12.29 show both states of the *BarChart*.

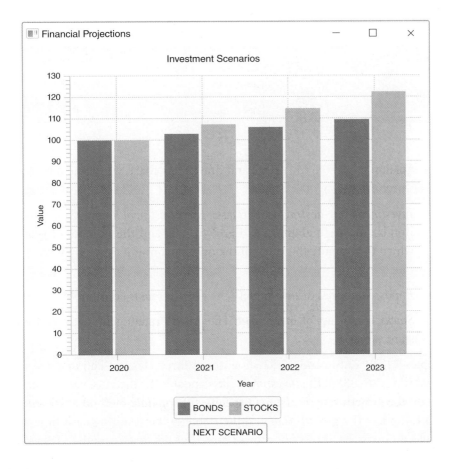

Figure 12.28

The Stocks and Bonds Using the First Set of Values for Stocks

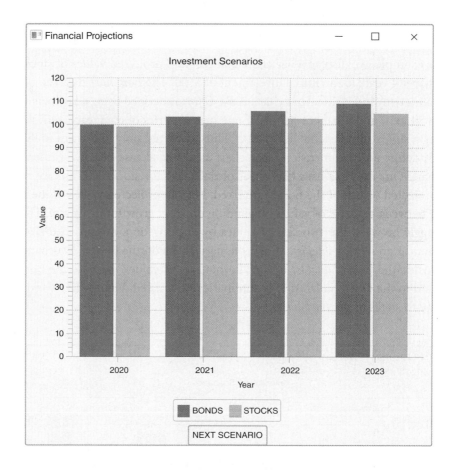

Before explaining how we can create and draw a bar chart, we define our Model. It includes three classes:

- *Investment*, an *abstract* superclass: An *Investment* has a type (Stocks or Bonds), an original amount, a growth rate, and the number of years over which to compute the value of the original amount as we apply the growth rate.

- *Bonds*, a subclass of *Investment*: The growth rate is constant.

- *Stocks*, a subclass of *Investment*: The growth rate toggles between two constant values.

Examples 12.50, 12.51, and 12.52 show these three classes. The *updateAmounts* method (lines 76–83) of the *Investment* class updates the instance variable *amounts* based on the growth rate. *Investment* specifies the *update* method as *abstract*. It is meant to update the growth rate and then update the resulting cash flow. In this example, a *Bonds* has a constant growth rate; thus, its *update* method (lines 19–25 of Example 12.51) does nothing, that is, it leaves the growth rate unchanged. The *update* method of the *Stocks* class (lines 20–31 of Example 12.52) makes the growth rate of a *Stocks* investment toggle between two constant values (lines 7–8).

```java
 1 /** abstract Investment class
 2 *    Anderson, Franceschi
 3 */
 4
 5 public abstract class Investment
 6 {
 7   public static final int DEFAULT_YEARS = 4;
 8   public static final double BEGIN_INVEST_AMOUNT = 100;
 9   private double [ ] amounts;
10   private int years;
11   private double growthRate;
12   private String type;
13
14   /* Constructor
15    * @param years, an int, the new value of years
16    * @param type, a String, the new value for the investment type
17    */
18   public Investment( int years, String type )
19   {
20     if ( years < 1 )
21       this.years = DEFAULT_YEARS;
22     else
23       this.years = years;
24
25     amounts = new double[this.years];
26     amounts[0] = BEGIN_INVEST_AMOUNT;
27
28     this.type = type;
29   }
30
31   /* getAmounts method
32    * @return a copy of amounts, a double [ ]
33    */
34   public double [ ] getAmounts( )
35   {
36     double [ ] temp = new double[amounts.length];
37     for ( int i = 0; i < amounts.length; i++ )
38         temp[i] = amounts[i];
39     return temp;
40   }
41
42   /* Accessor method for years
```

```
43    * @return number of years
44    */
45    public int getYears( )
46    {
47      return years;
48    }
49
50    /* Accessor method for type
51    * @return investment type
52    */
53    public String getType( )
54    {
55      return type;
56    }
57
58    /* Accessor method for growthRate
59    * @return growthRate
60    */
61    public double getGrowthRate( )
62    {
63      return growthRate;
64    }
65
66    /* Mutator method for growthRate
67    * @param growthRate, the new value for growthRate
68    * @return a reference to this object
69    */
70    public Investment setGrowthRate( double growthRate )
71    {
72      this.growthRate = growthRate;
73      return this;
74    }
75
76    /* updateAmounts method
77    * updates amounts based on growthRate
78    */
79    public void updateAmounts( )
80    {
81      for ( int i = 1; i < amounts.length; i++ )
82        amounts[i] = amounts[i-1] * ( 1 + growthRate );
83    }
84
85    /* update abstract method
86    */
87    public abstract void update( );
88 }
```

EXAMPLE 12.50   The *Investment* **Class**

```
 1 /** Bonds class
 2  *    Anderson, Franceschi
 3  */
 4
 5 public class Bonds extends Investment
 6 {
 7   private final double BOND_GROWTH_RATE = .03;
 8
 9   /* Constructor
10    * @param years the new number of years
11    */
12   public Bonds( int years )
13   {
14     super( years, "Bonds" );
15     setGrowthRate( BOND_GROWTH_RATE );
16     updateAmounts( );
17   }
18
19   /* update method
20    * do nothing method: Leaves the growth rate unchanged
21    */
22   public void update( )
23   {
24     // growth rate does not change
25   }
26 }
```

EXAMPLE 12.51   The *Bonds* Class

```
 1 /** Stocks class
 2  *    Anderson, Franceschi
 3  */
 4
 5 public class Stocks extends Investment
 6 {
 7   private static final double SLOW_GROWTH_RATE = .02;
 8   private static final double FAST_GROWTH_RATE = .07;
 9
10   /* Constructor
11    * @param years the new number of years
12    */
13   public Stocks( int years )
14   {
15     super( years, "Stocks" );
16     setGrowthRate( SLOW_GROWTH_RATE );
17     updateAmounts( );
18   }
```

```
19
20    /* update method
21     *  toggles the growth rate and updates amounts accordingly
22     */
23    public void update( )
24    {
25      if ( Math.abs( getGrowthRate( ) - SLOW_GROWTH_RATE ) < 0.0001 )
26        setGrowthRate( FAST_GROWTH_RATE );
27      else
28        setGrowthRate( SLOW_GROWTH_RATE );
29
30      updateAmounts( );
31    }
32 }
```

EXAMPLE 12.52   The *Stocks* Class

The *XYChart* class, which uses generics, is the base class for charts involving two axes. *XYChart* is the direct superclass of *BarChart*. The *XYChart* class provides the functionality to draw the two axes and the contents of the chart. It contains two inner classes:

- *XYChart.Data*, which encapsulates a single data item to be used in two-axis charts

- *XYChart.Series*, a series, or list, of *XYChart.Data* items

XYChart, *BarChart*, *XYChart.Data*, and *XYChart.Series* all use two types of objects; the first object serves as a label for the second. Thus, often, the first type is *String* and the second type is *Number*. The *Number* class is the superclass for all numeric wrapper classes (*Integer, Double, ..*) and thus can be used with all primitive integer data types since Java supports both autoboxing (automatic conversion from a primitive type to a wrapper type) and unboxing (automatic conversion from a wrapper type to a primitive type).

Typically, the observable list bound to a bar chart is a list of lists, that is, it is a two-dimensional data structure. In our example, the observable list contains a list of *XYChart.Series* items. Each *XYChart.Series* is a list of *XYChart.Data* items. Each *XYChart.Data* item contains two elements: the year, which is a *String*; and the value, which is a *double*. The *String* serves as a label for the value. For example, our initial two *XYChart.Series* contain the following data:

Bonds series: "2020",100.0 "2021",103.0 "2022",106.09 "2023",109.2727
Stocks series: "2020",100.0 "2021",107.0 "2022",114.49 "2023",122.5043

The first series is the bonds series, which contains four data items; each data item includes a year and a value. The second series is the stocks series and also contains four data items. Both series are parallel to each other; not only do the two series contain the same number of items, four, but the value of the year for two corresponding data items is the same. In this way, the bar chart not only displays the values, but also enables a quick visual comparison between the two series.

Example 12.53 shows our *BarChartView* class. It extends *BorderPane* and contains a *BarChart* in its center and a button at the bottom. The *BarChart bc* and the *ArrayList series* are defined at lines 20 and 22. The *addBarChart* method (lines 40–71), called by the constructor at line 37, creates the bar chart and places it in the center position of the *BorderPane*. Inside the *addBarChart* method, we do the following:

1. Instantiate an empty *BarChart* with an *x* axis and a *y* axis (lines 42–48).

2. Create an *ArrayList* of *XYChart.Series* objects (lines 50–67).

3. Access the data of the *BarChart* and add the *ArrayList* to it (lines 68–69).

4. Place the *BarChart* at the center of the *BorderPane* (line 70).

Table 12.49 lists one of the *BarChart* constructors. Since the constructor accepts two *Axis* parameters, we first need to create two axes for our bar chart. The *CategoryAxis* and *NumberAxis* classes are subclasses of the *abstract Axis class*:

- *CategoryAxis* encapsulates an axis that displays categories where each value represents a unique category (tick mark) along the axis. In this example, we use a *CategoryAxis* to show the years.

- *NumberAxis* encapsulates an axis that plots a range of numbers with major tick marks every "tickUnit". We can use any *Number* type with this axis, *Integer, Double*, etc … In this example, we use a *NumberAxis* for the values.

At lines 42–44, we create the two axes and the *BarChart*. We set the title of the bar chart at line 46 and the labels of the axis at lines 47–48.

Next, we instantiate *series* (line 51), an *ArrayList* of *XYChart.Series<String, Number>*. For each *Investment* reference in *investments*, we create an *XYChart.Series* and add

TABLE 12.49   A Constructor of the *BarChart* Class

Package	javafx.scene.chart
`BarChart( Axis<X> xAxis, Axis<Y> yAxis )`	
creates a *BarChart* with the two axes. One of the axes should be a *CategoryAxis*, the other one a *ValueAxis*. Their order determines if the bar chart is horizontal or vertical.	

it to *series*. Table 12.50 shows an *XYChart.Series* constructor, as well as an *XYChart. Data* constructor. There are only two elements in *investments* in this example, one *Bonds* object and one *Stocks* object. At lines 55–56, we instantiate an *XYChart. Series<String, Number>* named *currentInvestmentSeries*. At line 57, we set the name that will be displayed for this *currentInvestmentSeries* to the type of investment of the current *Investment* element. To do this, we call the *setName* method shown in Table 12.51. Next, we set the values in *currentInvestmentSeries* to the values in the current *Investment* element. After we retrieve the array of values for the current *Investment* element and assign it to the array *currentAmounts*, we loop through *currentAmounts* at lines 60–65 and create an *XYChart.Data* item for each value in *currentAmounts* (lines 63–64). We set the label of each *XYChart.Data* item to the current year and its value to the current amount. We compute the current year by adding the counting index of the loop, *j*, to *startingYear*. After the loop, we add *currentInvestmentSeries* to the *series ArrayList* at line 66. At line 69, we call *getData* to retrieve the *ObservableList* associated with *bc*. At this point, the observable list is empty, so we call the *addAll* method to set the observable list to *series*. When we add *bc* to the center of the *BorderPane* at line 70, the bar chart is displayed.

TABLE 12.50   *XYChart.Series* and *XYChart.Data* **Constructors**

Package	javafx.scene.chart
`XYChart.Series( )`	
creates an *XYChart.Series* that will contain *XYChart.Data* items	
`XYChart.Data( X xValue, Y yValue )`	
creates data for the two axes of the chart; the X and Y types should match the X and Y types for the *x* and *y* axes	

TABLE 12.51   The *getData* and *setName* **Methods of the *XYChart.Series* Class**

Return value	Method name and argument list
`ObservableList<XYChart.` `Data<X,Y>>`	`getData( )`
	returns the *ObservableList* of data items that make up this series
`void`	`setName( String value )`
	sets the name to be displayed for this series

The *update* method (lines 73–99) is called by the controller when the view needs to be updated because the user updated the data in the model. The *update* method updates the data inside the *ArrayList series* based on the state of the model. Since the *BarChart bc* is bound to *series*, the bar chart will be updated automatically. Since bond values do not change, we only update the data for investments that are not bonds (line 79) when we loop through *investments* at lines 76–98. We first retrieve the current *XYChart.Series* at lines 81–83 and assign it to the reference *currentInvestmentSeries*. Because we add new *XYChart.Data* items storing the updated data to *currentInvestmentSeries* (lines 90–92), we first need to empty *currentInvestmentSeries* by calling the *clear* method (line 86). If we do not, we would be adding new *XYChart.Data* items to the existing ones. At lines 95–96, we update the current element of *series*.

The *setButtonListener* method (lines 101–104), meant to be called by the controller, sets up event handling for the button.

```
 1 /** BarChartView class
 2  * Layout using a BorderPane's
 3  * bottom and center positions.
 4  * The bottom HBox is made up of one button.
 5  * The center position is made up of a BarChart.
 6  * Anderson, Franceschi
 7  */
 8
 9 import java.util.ArrayList;
10 import javafx.event.*;
11 import javafx.geometry.Pos;
12 import javafx.scene.control.*;
13 import javafx.scene.layout.*;
14 import javafx.scene.chart.*;
15
16 public class BarChartView extends BorderPane
17 {
18   private HBox buttonPanel; // bottom, holds button
19   private Button button;
20   private BarChart<String, Number> bc; // center, holds chart
21
22   ArrayList<XYChart.Series<String, Number>> series;
23   private int startingYear;
24
25   public BarChartView( int startingYear, Investment [ ] investments )
26   {
27     super( );
```

```
28      this.startingYear = startingYear;
29
30      buttonPanel = new HBox( );
31      button = new Button( );
32      button.setText( "NEXT SCENARIO" );
33      buttonPanel.setAlignment( Pos.CENTER );
34      buttonPanel.getChildren( ).add( button );
35      setBottom( buttonPanel );
36
37      addBarChart( investments );
38   }
39
40   public void addBarChart( Investment [ ] investments )
41   {
42     // Create a BarChart for investment
43     CategoryAxis xAxis = new CategoryAxis( );
44     NumberAxis yAxis = new NumberAxis( );
45     bc = new BarChart<String, Number>( xAxis, yAxis );
46     bc.setTitle( "Investment Scenarios" );
47     xAxis.setLabel( "Year" );
48     yAxis.setLabel( "Value" );
49
50     // Create an ArrayList of XYChart.Series using investments data
51     series = new ArrayList<XYChart.Series<String, Number>>( );
52
53     for ( int i = 0; i < investments.length; i++ )
54     {
55       XYChart.Series<String, Number> currentInvestmentSeries
56         = new XYChart.Series<String, Number>( );
57       currentInvestmentSeries.setName( investments[i].getType( ) );
58
59       double [ ] currentAmounts = investments[i].getAmounts( );
60       for ( int j = 0; j < currentAmounts.length; j++ )
61       {
62         currentInvestmentSeries.getData( ).add(
63            new XYChart.Data<String, Number>(
64              String.valueOf( startingYear + j ), currentAmounts[j] ) );
65       }
66       series.add( currentInvestmentSeries );
67     }
68     // Fill BarChart with XYChart.Series array
69     bc.getData( ).addAll( series );
70     setCenter( bc );
71   }
72
73   public void update( Investment [ ] investments )
```

```
74   {
75      // update investments
76      for ( int i = 0; i < investments.length; i++ )
77      {
78         // do not update bonds series
79         if ( ! investments[i].getType( ).equals( "Bonds" ) )
80         {
81            // retrieve series
82            XYChart.Series<String, Number> currentInvestmentSeries
83               = series.get( i );
84
85            // change data of series
86            currentInvestmentSeries.getData( ).clear( );
87            double [ ] currentAmounts = investments[i].getAmounts( );
88            for ( int j = 0; j < currentAmounts.length; j++ )
89            {
90               currentInvestmentSeries.getData( ).add(
91                  new XYChart.Data<String, Number>( ""
92                     + ( startingYear + j ), currentAmounts[j] ) );
93            }
94
95            // update series
96            series.set( i, currentInvestmentSeries );
97         }
98      }
99   }
100
101   public void setButtonListener( EventHandler<ActionEvent> eh )
102   {
103      button.setOnAction( eh );
104   }
105 }
```

EXAMPLE 12.53   A View Class Displaying a Bar Chart

Example 12.54 shows the *BarChartViewController* class, the controller for our bar chart application. It includes the instance variables *investments* and *view* (lines 10–11), which represent the View and the Model for the application, respectively. The *BarChartViewController* class implements *EventHandler* and is its own event handler. We set up event handling at line 18 and handle the event in the *handle* method (lines 21–28) by first updating the Model (lines 23–25) and then updating the View (lines 26–27).

```
1 /** BarChartViewController class
2 *    Anderson, Franceschi
3 */
4
```

```
 5 import javafx.event.*;
 6 import javafx.scene.control.*;
 7
 8 public class BarChartViewController implements EventHandler<ActionEvent>
 9 {
10   private BarChartView view;
11   private Investment [ ] investments;
12
13   public BarChartViewController( BarChartView view,
14                                  Investment [ ] investments )
15   {
16     this.investments = investments;
17     this.view = view;
18     ( this.view ).setButtonListener( this );
19   }
20
21   public void handle( ActionEvent event )
22   {
23     // update the model
24     for ( int i = 0; i < investments.length; i++ )
25       investments[i].update( );
26     // update the view
27     view.update( investments );
28   }
29 }
```

EXAMPLE 12.54   **The Controller for the Bar Chart Application**

Example 12.55 shows the *InvestmentApplication* class. We create an array of two *Investment* objects at lines 14–18, create the View for the app at line 19, and create the Controller for the application at lines 27–28. We specify that *2020* is the starting year for our data (line 19).

```
 1 /** InvestmentApplication class
 2 *    Anderson, Franceschi
 3 */
 4
 5 import javafx.application.Application;
 6 import javafx.scene.Scene;
 7 import javafx.stage.Stage;
 8
 9 public class InvestmentApplication extends Application
10 {
11   @Override
12   public void start( Stage stage )
13   {
14     int years = 4;
15     Stocks stocks = new Stocks( years );
```

```
16      Bonds bonds = new Bonds( years );
17      Investment [ ] investments = { bonds, stocks };
18
19      BarChartView root = new BarChartView( 2020, investments );
20
21      Scene scene = new Scene( root, 540, 510 );
22      stage.setTitle( "Financial Projections" );
23      stage.setScene( scene );
24      stage.show( );
25
26      BarChartViewController controller
27         = new BarChartViewController( root, investments );
28    }
29
30    public static void main( String [ ] args )
31    {
32      launch( args );
33    }
34 }
```

EXAMPLE 12.55   The *InvestmentApplication.java* File

12.17   Using a Style Sheet to Style the View

GUI components come with a default style. For example, the background color is white and the text is black. Labels have a rectangular shape, and buttons have a rectangular shape with rounded corners. We can create our own style and customize the look and feel of our application. It is typical to define a style in a separate file, thus separating the contents of the GUI from its style. In this way, it is easier to edit and separately maintain the contents of the GUI and its style; we can modify the style file, also called a **style sheet**, and the new style is automatically applied to the app.

Earlier in the chapter we introduced CSS. JavaFX supports **Cascading Style Sheets** (**CSS**), a language that describes how a document should be styled. CSS is often used with web pages, and the JavaFX version of CSS is similar to the CSS used with web pages.

The general syntax to style a GUI component in a style sheet is:

```
selector
{
  attribute1: value1;
  attribute2: value2;

  ...

}
```

The *selector* can be a GUI component, such as a *Label*, but it can also be something identifying a group of components or a specific component. Attributes are prefixed with *–fx-*.

To illustrate this, we add styles to our Simple Math application, shown previously in Examples 12.5 through 12.8. Example 12.56 shows a style sheet for the Simple Math application. At lines 6–10, we style all the labels so their background color is deepskyblue and their foreground color is blue. If we want to give a specific style to a single component, we can give it an id in the FXML file and style that id in the style sheet. In Example 12.6, we gave the id result to the bottom label, which displays the result of the Math operation. To style that label differently from the other labels, we define a style for its id. A selector for an id starts with the # sign followed by the id. At lines 12–16, we style the component with id result so that its background color is aqua (line 14) and its text is bold (line 15). Note that the background color of the bottom label is styled twice: once at line 8 where all the labels are styled, and another time at line 14 where the id result is styled. The id's style prevails over the component's general style. Thus, the background color of the bottom label is aqua. However, because the id's style does not redefine the foreground color, the foreground color defined for all the labels at line 9 applies to the bottom label.

Finally, at lines 18–21, we define the background color of the buttons when the mouse hovers over them as green.

```
 1 VBox
 2 {
 3   -fx-background-color: skyblue;
 4 }
 5
 6 Label
 7 {
 8   -fx-background-color: deepskyblue;
 9   -fx-text-fill: blue;
10 }
11
12 #result
13 {
14   -fx-background-color: aqua;
15   -fx-font-weight: bold;
16 }
17
18 Button:hover
19 {
20   -fx-background-color: #00FF00;
21 }
```

EXAMPLE 12.56   A JavaFX Style Sheet for the Simple Math Application

To apply our style sheet to our application, we link the style sheet to the scene. Example 12.57 shows the modified *SimpleMathPractice* class. We link the style sheet at line 23 by calling the *getStylesheets* method of the *Scene* class. If we have more than one style sheet, we can add as many as desired using this method.

```
 1 /*  Simple Math Operations Using Buttons
 2      Anderson, Franceschi
 3 */
 4
 5 import java.net.URL;
 6 import javafx.application.Application;
 7 import javafx.fxml.FXMLLoader;
 8 import javafx.scene.layout.VBox;
 9 import javafx.scene.Scene;
10 import javafx.stage.Stage;
11
12 public class SimpleMathPractice extends Application
13 {
14   @Override
15   public void start( Stage stage ) // throws Exception
16   {
17     try
18     {
19       URL url =
20           getClass( ).getResource( "fxml_simple_math.fxml" );
21       VBox root = FXMLLoader.load( url );
22       Scene scene = new Scene( root, 300, 275 );
23       scene.getStylesheets( ).add( "simple_math.css" );
24       stage.setTitle( "Simple Math" );
25       stage.setScene( scene );
26       stage.show( );
27     }
28     catch ( Exception e )
29     {
30       e.printStackTrace( );
31     }
32   }
33
34   public static void main( String [ ] args )
35   {
36     launch( args );
37   }
38 }
```

EXAMPLE 12.57   Importing a Style Sheet

Figures 12.30 and 12.31 show the application running as the user first hovers over the "Cube" button and then clicks on it.

The "Cube" Button
Changes Color as
the Mouse Hovers
Over It

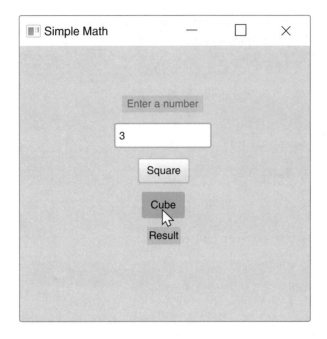

The User entered
3 and Clicked on
"Cube"

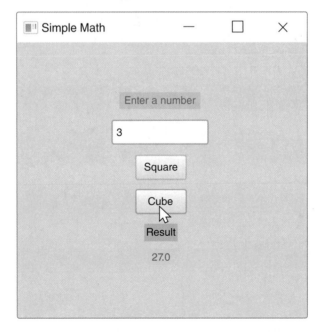

12.18   Programming Activity 2: Working with Layout Containers

In this Programming Activity, you will complete the implementation of a version of the Tile Puzzle game using a more complex GUI. As it stands now, the application compiles and runs, but it is missing a lot of code. Figure 12.32 shows the window that will open when you run the application without adding your code. Once you have completed the five tasks of this Programming Activity, you should see the window in Figure 12.33 when you run your program and click on the "3-by-3" button. When you click on one of the buttons labeled "3-by-3," "4-by-4," or "5-by-5," the tile puzzle will reset to a grid of that size.

Figure 12.32

The Starting Window When Running the Prewritten Code

Figure 12.33

The Starting Window When the Activity Is Completed

In addition to the *TilePuzzle* class, we provide you with a prewritten *GameView* class, which encapsulates a View for the Tile Puzzle game. We have implemented the *GameView* class as a *GridPane* container, so you can add it to another layout container, such as a *BorderPane*. It has two important methods, shown in Table 12.52. Thus, your job in this Programming Activity is not to write the game code, but to organize components in a window.

You need to edit the *NestedLayoutPractice* class, which *extends BorderPane*. Your job is to:

1. Declare an HBox named *top* and three *Buttons* that will be added to the *top* position of the *BorderPane*.

2. Set the layout containers for the *center* and *top* positions.

3. Add the *top* and the *gameView* layout containers to the *BorderPane*.

4. Code an appropriate *private* listener class.

5. Instantiate the listener and register it on the appropriate components.

Instructions

Copy the source files in the Programming Activity 2 folder for this chapter to a folder on your computer.

1. Write the code to declare the needed instance variables. Load the *NestedLayout-Practice.java* source file and search for five asterisks in a row (*****). This will position you at the instance variables declaration.

```
// ***** Task 1: declare an HBox named top
// also declare three Button instance variables
// that will be added to the HBox top.
// These buttons will determine the grid size of the game:
// 3-by-3, 4-by-4, or 5-by-5

// task 1 ends here
```

TABLE 12.52   **The *GameView* Class API**

Constructor		
GameView(int nSides)		
instantiates a tile puzzle View having an *nSides*-by-*nSides* grid		
Return value	**Method Name and Argument List**	
void	setUpGame(int nSides)	
resets the grid as an *nSides*-by-*nSides* grid		

2. Next, write the code to set the layout manager of the window and add the component *gameView* in the center position of the window. In the *NestedLayoutPractice.java* source file, search again for five asterisks in a row (*****). This will position you inside the constructor.

```
// ***** Task 2: student code starts here
// instantiate the GameView object

// add gameView to the center of this BorderPane

// task 2 ends here
```

3. Next, write the code to instantiate the *HBox* top component, instantiate the buttons from task 1, add them to *top*, and finally add *top* at the top position of our *BorderPane*. In the *NestedLayoutPractice.java* source file, search again for five asterisks in a row (*****). This will position you inside the constructor.

```
// ***** Task 3: Student code restarts here
// instantiate the HBox component named top
// instantiate the Buttons that determine the grid size

// add the buttons to HBox top
// make them take all the available space

// add HBox top to this BorderPane as its top component

// task 3 ends here
```

4. Next, write the code for the *private* inner class that implements the appropriate listener. In the *NestedLayoutPractice.java* source file, search again for five asterisks in a row (*****). This will position you between the constructor and the end of the class.

```
// ***** Task 4: Student code restarts here
// create a private inner class that implements EventHandler
// your method should identify which of the 3 buttons
//    was the source of the event
// depending on which button was pressed,
//    call the setUpGame method of the GameView class
//    with arguments 3, 4, or 5
// the API of that method is:
//    public void setUpGame( int nSides )

// task 4 ends here
```

5. Next, write the code to declare and instantiate a listener, and register it on the appropriate components. In the *NestedLayoutPractice.java* source file, search again for five asterisks in a row (*****). This will position you inside the constructor.

```
// ***** Task 5: Student code restarts here
// Note: search for and complete Task 4 before performing this task
// declare and instantiate an EventHandler


// register the handler on the 3 buttons
// that you declared in Task 1


// task 5 ends here
```

After completing each task, compile your code.

When you have finished writing all of the code, compile the source code and run *NestedLayoutPracticeApplication*. Try clicking on the three buttons that you added.

DISCUSSION QUESTIONS   **?**

1. **Identify the various layout containers you used and the screen positions they occupy.**

2. **Explain why the left and right positions are not shown on the window.**

CHAPTER REVIEW

12.19   Chapter Summary

- A Graphical User Interface (GUI) allows the user to enter data and initiate actions for an application by entering text into boxes; pressing buttons; moving the thumb of a slider; or selecting items from a list, a set of radio buttons, or checkboxes.

- Applications with GUIs are usually easier to learn and use because the interface is familiar to the user.

- JavaFX is a set of classes included with Java SE for creating GUIs.

- The top-level structure in a JavaFX application is the stage, which corresponds to a window. A stage can have one or more scenes, which are top-level containers for nodes that make up the window contents. A node can be a user interface control, such as a button or drop-down list; a layout container; an image or other media; a graphical shape; a web browser; a chart; or a group.

- JavaFX applications can be built in several ways. If we know which controls our interface needs and how they should be arranged, we can specify the layout, controls, and their properties using FXML, a scripting language based on XML. For more complicated GUIs or for dynamic GUIs where the number or type of control is determined at runtime, we can control the number, type, properties, and positioning of controls programmatically.

- A JavaFX application extends the *Application* class and, at minimum, implements the *start* method.

- Some JavaFX GUI controls are *Label*, *TextField*, *Button*, *RadioButton*, *CheckBox*, *ComboBox*, and *Slider*. These controls inherit from the *Node* class.

- Controls can be arranged in a window using layout containers, such as *HBox*, *VBox*, *BorderPane*, *GridPane*, or *StackPane*. Layout containers can be nested.

- GUI applications use an event-driven model, where the user determines which functions are performed by interacting with the application controls, consequently firing events. To handle an event, we register our interest in being notified of the event and provide code: an event handler or listener, to be executed when the event occurs.

- JavaFX supports and encourages the Model-View-Controller architecture in GUI applications. The Model manages the data of the application and its state. The View presents the user interface. The Controller handles events generated by the user and communicates those changes to the Model, which updates its state accordingly and communicates any changes back to the Controller. The Controller then updates the View to reflect those changes.

- FXML can be used to define not only the application's layout containers, GUI controls, and their properties, but also the controller class and the method to be executed when an event fires.

- An *ActionEvent* object is created when the user clicks a button, selects an item from a list or a menu, or presses the *Enter* key in a *TextField*. The *getSource* method of the *ActionEvent* object returns a reference to the control that fired the event.

- To make *RadioButtons* mutually exclusive, we define a *ToggleGroup* and then set each *RadioButton*'s *toggleGroup* property accordingly.

- A Controller can have an *initialize* method, which is called after the scene graph has been created. The *initialize* method can be used to add nodes and set properties that could not be fully defined in the FXML file. In the *initialize* method, we also can retrieve initial values from the Model and update the View accordingly so that the View reflects the initial state of the Model when the application starts.

- We put *ComboBox* items into an *ObservableList* and use the *SingleSectionModel* to manage the selection of items.

- The *Slider* control is capable of displaying a set of continuous values along a horizontal or vertical line called a track. The user "slides" the knob, called the thumb, along the track to select a value. We can set properties of a *Slider* to display tick marks and tick values.

- An event handler for a *Slider* control needs to implement the *ChangeListener<T>* interface.

- Defining our application's GUI components, properties, and event handlers programmatically is useful for dynamic GUIs where the number or type of controls is not known until run time, or when we have an array of controls that are handled similarly.

- A *VBox* is a layout container that arranges its components vertically.

- An *HBox* is a layout container that arranges its components horizontally.

- A *GridPane* can be visualized as a table made up of cells in rows and columns. Each cell can contain one component. These cells can have different sizes, which we specify using row and column constraints.

- The *Alert* class enables us to construct and display dialog boxes.

- A *BorderPane* layout container organizes its nodes into five positions—*top*, *bottom*, *left*, *right*, and *center*—with each position holding one node at most.

- Lambda expressions can be used to simplify the definition of an event handler as an anonymous class that *implements* a functional interface, that is, an interface that requires only one method to be implemented.

- A lambda expression contains (1) a comma-separated list of parameters enclosed in parentheses—the data types of the parameters may be omitted, and the parentheses can also be omitted if there is only one parameter; (2) the arrow token, ->; and (3) a method body, which can be a single expression or a block enclosed in curly braces. If the body of the method consists of a single expression, then the JVM evaluates the expression and returns its value. We can also use a return statement, but that requires curly braces.

- JavaFX includes many classes that allow us to animate a node on a scene. *FadeTransition*, *RotateTransition*, *TranslateTransition*, and *ScaleTransition* are examples of such classes.

- Each transition class typically provides methods to play the animation, set the number of types it repeats, play the animation in reverse, and execute some code after it finishes.

- A mouse activity generates a *MouseEvent*. A touch activity generates a *TouchEvent*.

- To handle a mouse or touch event, we implement the *EventHandler* interface and implement its *handle* method.

- The *getScene* method from the *Node* class allows us to get a reference to the *Scene* that a *Node* is in. The *getWindow* method from the *Scene* class allows us to get a reference to the *Stage* that the scene is in.

- JavaFX includes classes that make it easy to display various types of charts, including line charts, pie charts, and bar charts.

- The *ObservableList* interface is a list that can be linked to a GUI component that displays a list of values. Whenever the values in the list change, the GUI component is automatically updated to reflect those changes.

- *PieChart* and *BarChart* are examples of classes that can be bound to an *ObservableList*.

12.20 Exercises, Problems, and Projects

12.20.1 Multiple Choice Exercises

1. An example of a GUI component class is

   ❏ *FXML*

   ❏ *controller*

   ❏ *TextField*

   ❏ *Stage*

2. What are the primary uses of GUI components? (Check all that apply.)

   ❏ Display information

   ❏ Facilitate the coding of methods

   ❏ Let the user control the program

   ❏ Collect information from the user

3. In what package do you find the *Button*, *TextField*, and *ComboBox* classes?

   ❏ *javafx.scene*

   ❏ *javafx.scene.control*

   ❏ *java.scene*

   ❏ *java.awt*

   ❏ *java.io*

4. V*Box* is a

   ❏ Label

   ❏ Layout container that arranges components vertically

   ❏ Layout container that arranges components horizontally

   ❏ Scene

5. The property of a *Label* element that specifies the text inside the label is

   ❏ *Label*

   ❏ *Word*

   ❏ *Phrase*

   ❏ *text*

6. The property that specifies the name of the Controller class for the View defined in the FXML document is

   ❏ *control*

   ❏ *fx:control*

   ❏ *controller*

   ❏ *fx:controller*

7. The property of a *Button* element that specifies the method called when the user clicks the button is

   ❏ *action*

   ❏ *press*

   ❏ *onAction*

   ❏ *onPress*

8. What attribute and annotation do we use with an instance variable of the Controller to reference a GUI component defined in an FXML document?

   ❏ *id* and *FXML*

   ❏ *id* and *@FXML*

   ❏ *fx:id* and *FXML*

   ❏ *fx:id* and *@FXML*

9. Assume that we have correctly defined the FXML attribute of a *Button* element that specifies the method to call when the user clicks on that button. What is the return type of that method?

   ❏ *Button*

   ❏ *void*

   ❏ *boolean*

   ❏ *onAction*

10. With JavaFX, a user interface must be defined using FXML; it cannot be defined programmatically.

   ❏ True

   ❏ False

11. We want to set up event handling programmatically when the user clicks on a button. What should the programmer do? (Check all that apply.)

   ❏ Code a class that implements the *EventHandler<ActionEvent>* interface.

   ❏ Declare and instantiate an object reference (a listener) of the class above.

   ❏ Call the *handle* method.

   ❏ Register the listener on the button.

12. Assuming everything has been coded correctly in the previous question, what happens when the user clicks a button?

   ❏ The *handle* method executes.

   ❏ The *Button* constructor executes.

   ❏ The *start* method executes.

13. We want to build a class that implements an interface that listens to key events. What interface should we implement?

   ❏ *EventHandler<ActionEvent>*

   ❏ *EventHandler<KeyEvent>*

   ❏ *EventHandler<MouseEvent>*

   ❏ *KeyHandler<Event>*

   Look
   It
   Up

14. We are designing a GUI programmatically with three buttons; a different action will be taken depending on which button the user clicks. We want to code only one *private* class implementing the *EventHandler<ActionEvent>* interface. Inside the *handle* method, which method do we call to determine which button was clicked?

   ❏ *getButton*

   ❏ *getSource*

   ❏ *getOrigin*

15. *NewLayout* is a layout container.

   ❏ True

   ❏ False

16. What is the maximum number of top-level controls that *a BorderPane* can manage?

    ❑ 2

    ❑ 3

    ❑ 4

    ❑ 5

    ❑ 6

17. FXML elements can be nested.

    ❑ True

    ❑ False

18. Which one is not a transition class?

    ❑ *FadeTransition*

    ❑ *SequentialTransition*

    ❑ *ParallelTransition*

    ❑ *Scale*

19. What class encapsulates a touch event?

    ❑ *Touch*

    ❑ *TouchEvent*

    ❑ *EventTouch*

20. What does the *getData* method of *XYChart.Series* return?

    ❑ An *XYChart.Data* items

    ❑ An *ObservableList* of *XYChart.Data* items

    ❑ A *double*

    ❑ A *Series*

12.20.2   Reading and Understanding Code

For Questions 21 to 25, consider the following FXML file representing the View for the application:

```
<?xml version="1.0" encoding="UTF-8"?>
<?import javafx.scene.control.*?>
<?import javafx.scene.layout.*?>
<HBox fx:controller="MyController"
```

```
        xmlns:fx="http://javafx.com/fxml"
        alignment="center" spacing="10" >
    <Button fx:id="button1" text="Button 1"
            onAction="#go" />
    <Button fx:id="button2" text="Button 2"
            onAction="#go" />
    <Label fx:id="result" />
    <Button fx:id="button3" text="Button 3"
            onAction="#go" />
    <Button fx:id="button4" text="Button 4"
            onAction="#go" />
</HBox>
```

21. How many buttons will be displayed in the window?

22. How are the buttons and the label organized in the window?

23. What class should we code in order to process clicks on the buttons by the user?

24. What method will execute when the user clicks on one of the buttons?

25. What is the return type of that method?

For Questions 26 through 29, consider the following code (and assume that the FXML file defines the text for cb1, cb2, and cb3 as "Choice 1," "Choice 2," and "Choice 3"):

```
/*  Controller class
 *    Anderson, Franceschi
 */
import javafx.event.ActionEvent;
import javafx.fxml.FXML;
import javafx.scene.control.*;

public class Controller
{
  @FXML private CheckBox cb1;
  @FXML private CheckBox cb2;
  @FXML private CheckBox cb3;
  @FXML private Label label;
  private int read, write, execute;
  @FXML protected void mix( ActionEvent event )
  {
    CheckBox cb = ( CheckBox ) event.getSource( );
    if ( cb == cb1 )
      read = ( cb.isSelected( ) ? 4 : 0 );
    else if ( cb == cb2 )
      write = ( cb.isSelected( ) ? 2 : 0 );
    else if ( cb == cb3 )
```

```
      execute = ( cb.isSelected( ) ? 1 : 0 );
    int mode = read + write + execute;
    label.setText( "mode: " + mode );
  }
}
```

26. What happens when the user checks "Choice 1" only?

27. What happens when the user checks "Choice 1" and then checks "Choice 2"?

28. What happens when the user checks "Choice 1," then "Choice 2," and then "Choice 3"?

29. What happens when the user checks "Choice 3," then "Choice 2," and then "Choice 2" again?

For Questions 30 through 32, consider the following code (and assume that the class extending *Application* exists and is correctly coded):

```
import javafx.event.*;
import javafx.scene.control.Button;
import javafx.scene.layout.*;
public class BoardView extends GridPane
{
  private Button [ ][ ] buttons;

  public BoardView( )
  {
    super( );

    ColumnConstraints col = new ColumnConstraints( );
    col.setPercentWidth( 25 );
    RowConstraints row = new RowConstraints( );
    row.setPercentHeight( 20 );

    for ( int i = 0; i < 5; i++ )
      getRowConstraints( ).add( row );
    for ( int j = 0; j < 4; j++ )
      getColumnConstraints( ).add( col );
    buttons = new Button[5][4];
    ButtonHandler bh = new ButtonHandler( );
    for ( int i = 0; i < 5; i++ )
    {
      for ( int j = 0; j < 4; j++ )
      {
        // instantiate the buttons
        buttons[i][j] = new Button( );
        buttons[i][j].setMaxWidth( Double.MAX_VALUE );
        buttons[i][j].setMaxHeight( Double.MAX_VALUE );
```

```
          add( buttons[i][j], j, i );
          buttons[i][j].setOnAction( bh );
        }
      }
    }
    private class ButtonHandler implements EventHandler<ActionEvent>
    {
      public void handle(  ActionEvent event )
      {
        for ( int i = 0; i < buttons.length; i++ )
          for ( int j = 0; j < buttons[i].length; j++ )
            if ( event.getSource( ) == buttons[i][j] )
              buttons[i][j].setText( "" + String.valueOf ( i + j ) );
      }
    }
}
```

30. How many rows and columns are in the grid?

31. What happens when the user clicks on the *Button* located at the top left of the grid?

32. What happens when the user clicks on the *Button* located at the bottom right of the grid?

12.20.3   Fill In the Code

For Questions 33 through 35, consider the following FXML document representing a GUI:

```xml
<?xml version="1.0" encoding="UTF-8"?>

<?import javafx.scene.control.*?>
<?import javafx.scene.layout.*?>

<BorderPane fx:controller="MyController"
            xmlns:fx="http://javafx.com/fxml"  >
  <top>
    <HBox alignment="center">
      <Button fx:id="button1" text="INSERT" />
    </HBox>
  </top>

  <left>
    <HBox alignment="center">
      <Button fx:id="button2" text="UPDATE" onAction="#go"/>
    </HBox>
```

```
    </left>

    <!-- answer to questions 33 to 35 go here -->




    </BorderPane>
```

33. Add a *VBox* element that contains a button at the *right* position within the *BorderPane*. The text of the button should say DELETE; when the user clicks on it, the *test* method of the *MyController* class should execute. The id of the button should be *button3*.

34. Add an *HBox* element that contains a label at the *center* position of the *BorderPane*. The text of the label should be SELECT. The id of the label should be *label1*.

35. Add a *VBox* element that contains a button at the bottom position within the *BorderPane*. The text of the button should be CREATE; when the user clicks on it, the *table* method of the *MyController* class should execute. The id of the button should be *button4*.

For Questions 36 through 40, consider the following class:

```
import javafx.event.*;
import javafx.scene.control.*;
import javafx.scene.layout.*;

public class A extends HBox
{
    private Button b;
    private Label l;

}
```

36. Inside the constructor, this code instantiates the button *b* with the text "Button."

```
// your code goes here
```

37. Inside the constructor, this code instantiates the label *l* with the text "Hello."

```
// your code goes here
```

38. Inside the constructor, this code adds *b* and *l* to this *HBox* so that *b* is on the right and *l* is on the left:

```
// your code goes here
```

39. Inside the constructor, this code registers the listener *mh* on the button *b*:

```
// the MyHandler class is a private class implementing EventHandler
MyHandler mh = new MyHandler( );
// your code goes here
```

40. Inside the *handle* method of a *private* inner class implementing the *EventHandler* interface, this code changes the text of *l* to "Button clicked" if the button *b* was clicked:

```
public void handle( ActionEvent ae )
{
  // your code goes here
}
```

For Questions 41 through 46, consider the following class:

```
import javafx.scene.control.*;
import javafx.scene.layout.*;

public class B extends BorderPane
{
  private VBox left;
  private HBox top;
  private Button [ ] buttons; // length 4
  private TextField [ ] textfields; // length 3
  private Label label1;
  private Label label2;

}
```

Also, assume that none of the instance variables have been instantiated and you are coding inside the constructor.

41. This code instantiates *top* and *left*.

```
// your code goes here
```

42. This code instantiates the text fields with text *TF0*, *TF1*, and *TF2*, and it places them in that order inside *top*. They should fill the whole available width of *top*.

```
// your code goes here
```

43. This code instantiates the buttons with text *Button 0, Button 1, Button 2*, and *Button 3*, and it places them in that order inside *left*. They should fill the whole available height of *left*.

```
// your code goes here
```

44. This code adds *left* and *top* at the left and top positions of the *BorderPane*, respectively.

```
// your code goes here
```

45. This code instantiates *label1* and *label2* with the text *CENTER* and *BOTTOM*, respectively.

```
// your code goes here
```

46. This code adds *label1* and *label2* at the center and bottom positions within the *BorderPane*, respectively.

```
// your code goes here
```

47. Replace the anonymous class definition for a *Button* event handler with a lambda expression.

```
quit.setOnAction( new EventHandler<ActionEvent>( )
                {
                  @Override
                  public void handle( ActionEvent event )
                  {
                    System.exit( 0 );
                  }
                }
);
```

48. We have a reference named *myCanvas* to a *Canvas*. Define a rotation animation that will take place on *myCanvas* as follows: it should last 2.5 seconds, repeat five times, and go from a 45-degree angle to a 135-degree angle.

49. A sound file named *music.wav* is located in the current folder. Write code to play the sound three times in a row.

50. We have a reference named *myEvent* to a touch event that just happened. Retrieve and output the *x* and *y* coordinates of where the touch event happened.

51. We have already defined an *ArrayList* of *PieChart.Data* named *myList*. Create an *ObservableList* with it, and create a *PieChart* using that *ObservableList*.

12.20.4 Identifying Errors in Code

52. Where is the error in this code sequence?

```
<?xml version="1.0" encoding="UTF-8"?>
<HBox xmlns:fx="http://javafx.com/fxml"
      alignment="center" spacing="10" >
  <Button text="Button 1" />
</HBox>
```

53. Where is the error in this code sequence?

```
<?xml version="1.0" encoding="UTF-8"?>
<?import javafx.scene.control.*?>
<?import javafx.scene.layout.*?>
<HBox>
```

```
    <Label text=result />
  </HBox>
```

54. Where is the error in this code sequence?

```java
import java.scene.layout.*;
public class MyGame extends GridPane
{

}
```

55. Where is the error in this code sequence?

```java
import javafx.event.*;
import javafx.scene.control.Button;
import javafx.scene.layout.*;
public class MyGame extends GridPane
{
  // some code here
  private class MyHandler extends EventHandler<ActionEvent>
  {
    public void handle( ActionEvent ae )
    { }
  }
}
```

56. Where is the error in this code sequence?

```java
import javafx.event.*;
import javafx.scene.control.Button;
import javafx.scene.layout.*;
public class MyGame extends GridPane
{
  // some code here
  private class MyHandler implements EventHandler
  {
    public void handle( ActionEvent ae )
    { }
  }
}
```

57. Where is the error in this code sequence?

```java
XYChart.Series<String, Number> series
  = new XYChart.Series<String, Number>( );
series.add( new XYChart.Data<String, Number>( "HI", 2.0 ) );
```

58. Where is the error in this code sequence?

```java
// bc is a BarChart and has been instantiated
ArrayList<XYChart.Series<String, Number>> series
  = new ArrayList<XYChart.Series<String, Number>>( );
// fill in series here
bc.addAll( series );
```

12.20.5   Debugging Area—Using Messages from the Java Compiler and Java JVM

59. You coded the following class:

```java
import java.net.URL;
import javafx.application.Application;
import javafx.fxml.FXMLLoader;
import javafx.scene.layout.VBox;
import javafx.scene.Scene;
import javafx.stage.Stage;

public class Test59 extends Application
{
  @Override
  public void start( Stage stage )
  {
    try
    {
      URL url = getClass( ).getResource( "fxml_ex1.fxml" );
      VBox root = FXMLLoader.load( url );
      Scene scene = new Scene ( root, 300, 275 );
      stage.setTitle( "Test" );
      stage.setScene( scene );
      stage.show( );
    }
    catch ( Exception e )
    {
      System.out.println( e.getMessage( ) );
    }
  }

  public static void main( String [ ] args )
  {
    launch( args );
  }
}
```

The code compiles; when you run, the window does not open and you get the
following message:

```
Location is required
```

What do think the problem is?

60. You coded the following FXML file, whose name is *fxml_ex60.fxml*:

```
<?xml version="1.0" encoding="UTF-8"?>
<?import javafx.scene.control.*?>
<?import javafx.scene.layout.*?>
<VBox xmlns:fx="http://javafx.com/fxml"
```

```
        alignment="center" spacing="20" >
    <Label text=Welcome />
    <Label text="FXML Test" />
</VBox>
```

Assume that the *Application* class is correctly coded. When you run, the window does not open and you get a LoadException with this message:

```
fxml_ex60.fxml:6
```

Explain what the problem is and how to fix it.

61. You coded the following FXML file *(fxml_ex61.fx*ml*)* and *Controller61* class:

```
<?xml version="1.0" encoding="UTF-8"?>

<?import javafx.scene.control.*?>
<?import javafx.scene.layout.*?>

<VBox fx:controller="Controller61"
      xmlns:fx="http://javafx.com/fxml"
      alignment="center" spacing="10" >
  <Button fx:id="button" text="GO"
          onAction="#go" />
</VBox>
```

```
import javafx.event.ActionEvent;
import javafx.fxml.FXML;
import javafx.scene.control.*;

public class Controller61
{
  protected void go( ActionEvent event )
  {
    System.out.println( "Inside go" );
  }
}
```

Assume that the *Application* class is correctly coded. The code compiles but when you run, the window does not open and you get a message starting with:

```
javafx.fxml.LoadException: Error resolving onAction='#go', either the event
handler is not in the Namespace or there is an error in the script
```

Explain what the problem is and how to fix it.

62. You coded the following in the file *Test62.java*:

```
import javafx.application.Application;
import javafx.scene.Scene;
import javafx.stage.Stage;
public class Test62 extends Application
```

```
{
  public void start( Stage stage )
  {
    Ex62 root = new Ex62( );
    Scene scene = new Scene( root, 300, 275 );
    stage.setTitle( "Test" );
    stage.setScene( scene );
  }
  public static void main( String [ ] args )
  {
    launch( args );
  }
}
```

Assume that the *Ex62* class is correctly coded. The code compiles and runs, but the window does not show. Explain what the problem is and how to fix it.

63. You coded the following in the *Ex63.java* file:

```
import javafx.scene.control.*;
import javafx.scene.layout.*;
import javafx.event.*;
public class Ex63 extends VBox
{
  private Button button;
  private Label label;

  public Ex63( )
  {
    super( );
    label = new Label( "HI" );
    button = new Button( "GO" );
    getChildren( ).add( label );
    getChildren( ).add( button );
  }
  private class ButtonHandler implements EventHandler<ActionEvent>
  {
    public void handle( ActionEvent ae )
    {
      label.setText( "Hello" );
    }
  }
}
```

Assume that the *Application* class has been correctly coded. The code compiles and runs. However, when you click the button, the text in the label does not change. Explain what the problem is and how to fix it.

12.20.6 Write a Short Program

64. Write a program that displays a text field and two buttons labeled "upper-case" and "lowercase." When the user clicks on the uppercase button, the text changes to uppercase; when the user clicks on the lowercase button, the text changes to lowercase. Use FXML for the GUI and to set up event handling; include a Model. Be sure that the initial state of the View matches the initial state of the Model.

65. Write a program with two radio buttons and a text field. When the user clicks on one radio button, the text changes to lowercase; when the user clicks on the other radio button, the text changes to uppercase. Use FXML for the GUI and to set up event handling; include a Model. Be sure that the initial state of the View matches the initial state of the Model.

66. Same as 65, except create the GUI programmatically, not using FXML.

67. Write a program with three checkboxes that allows a user to select toppings for a pizza order: extra cheese, sausage, and anchovies. As the user selects/deselects each checkbox, display the current order in a label.

68. Write a program that simulates a multiple choice question of your choice; the question should be a "check all that apply" type of question. There should be at least four possible answers, each using a checkbox. When the user selects any checkbox, your program should process the user's answer and show whether the answer is true (all checkbox selections are correct) or false (at least one checkbox selection is incorrect) in a label. Use FXML for the GUI and to set up event handling; include a Model.

69. Same as 68, but include a button to process the answer; do not process the answer when the user selects checkboxes.

70. Write a program that simulates a guessing game in a GUI program. Ask the user for a number between 1 and 6 in a text field, and then roll a die randomly and indicate whether or not the user won. Write the program in such a way that any invalid user input (i.e., not an integer between 1 and 6) is rejected and the user is asked again for input. Use FXML for the lay-out but generate and handle the checkboxes programmatically; include a Model. Be sure that the initial state of the View matches the initial state of the Model.

71. Write a program that simulates a guessing game in a GUI program. Generate a secret random number between 1 and 100; that number is hidden from the user. Ask the user to guess a number between 1 and 100 in a text field, and then tell the user whether the number is too high, too low, or is the correct

number. Let the user continue to guess until the correct number is guessed. Use FXML for the GUI and to set up event handling; include a Model. Be sure that the initial state of the View matches the initial state of the Model.

72. Modify the *ComboBox* example in this chapter to use *ListView* instead.

73. Write a program that displays a 4-by-6 grid of buttons, each with some unique text. One button is the "winning" button, which your model determines randomly. When the user clicks on the winning button, change its text to "Won." If the user clicks on any other button, change its text to "No." Use code for the GUI and to set up event handling; include a Model.

74. Same as Exercise 73 with the following additions: Keep track of how many times the user clicks on buttons. If the user has not won after five clicks, the text on the last button clicked should be changed to "Lost." Once the user has lost or won, you should disable the game; that is, the buttons should no longer respond to clicks from the user.

75. Write a program that displays a combo box and a label. The combo box displays five U.S. states using two letters for each state (e.g., CA, MD). When the user selects a state from the combo box, the label is populated with the full name of the state (e.g., if the user selects MD, the label is populated with Maryland). Use FXML for the GUI and to set up event handling; include a Model. Be sure that the initial state of the View matches the initial state of the Model.

76. Same as 75, except use code for the GUI instead of FXML.

77. Write a program that counts and displays how many times the user touches the screen and plays a short sound every time the user touches the screen. The count should be displayed and incremented each time the user touches the screen.

78. Write a program that plays the same greeting in three languages. Provide a button for each language. When the user presses a button, play the greeting in that language. Use code for the GUI and use lambda expressions to define the listener for each button.

79. Write a program that shows a ball bouncing on the ground. When the user touches the screen, the ball drops and bounces on the ground. The touch event should be disabled after that. The ball bounces down and up five times; each time it bounces up, it travels half the previous distance.

80. Write a program that shows a ball at the center of a *BorderPane*. Include a button at the bottom of the *BorderPane*. When the user clicks on the button,

animate the ball so that it travels in a square. Disable the button while the animation is running and enable the button when the animation stops.

12.20.7   Programming Projects

81. Write a GUI-based tic-tac-toe game for two players. Use code for the GUI and to set up event handling; include a Model.

82. Write a GUI-based program that analyzes a word. The user will type the word in a text field. Provide buttons for the following:

   ❑ One button, when clicked, displays the length of the word.

   ❑ Another button, when clicked, displays the number of vowels in the word.

   ❑ Another button, when clicked, displays the number of uppercase letters in the word.

   Use FXML for the GUI and to set up event handling; include a Model. Be sure that the initial state of the View matches the initial state of the Model.

83. Write a GUI-based program that analyzes a soccer game. The user will type the names of two teams and the score of the game in four text fields. You should add appropriate labels and create buttons for the following:

   ❑ One button, when clicked, displays which team won the game.

   ❑ Another button, when clicked, displays the game score.

   ❑ Another button, when clicked, displays by how many goals the winning team won.

   Use FXML for the GUI and to set up event handling; include a Model. Be sure that the initial state of the View matches the initial state of the Model.

84. Same as 83, except use code for the GUI, not FXML.

85. Write a GUI-based program that analyzes a round of golf. You will retrieve the data for 18 holes from a text file. Each line in the file will include the par for that hole (3, 4, or 5) and your score for that hole. Your program should read the file and display a combo box listing the 18 holes. When the user selects a hole, the score for that hole should be displayed in a label. Provide buttons for the following:

   ❑ One button, when clicked, displays whether your overall score was over par, under par, or par.

   ❑ Another button, when clicked, displays the number of holes for which you made par.

❑ Another button, when clicked, displays how many birdies you scored. (A birdie on a hole is 1 under par.)

Use FXML for the GUI and to set up event handling; include a Model. Be sure that the initial state of the View matches the initial state of the Model.

86. Same as 85, except use code for the GUI, not FXML.

87. Write a GUI-based program that analyzes statistics for tennis players. You will retrieve the data from a text file. Each line in the file will list the name of a player, the player's number of wins for the year, and the player's number of losses for the year. Your program should read the file and display the list of players. When the user selects a player, the winning percentage of the player should be displayed in a label. Provide buttons for the scenarios that follow:

❑ One button, when clicked, displays which player had the most wins for the year.

❑ Another button, when clicked, displays which player had the highest winning percentage for the year.

❑ Another button, when clicked, displays how many players had a winning record for the year.

Use FXML for the GUI and to set up event handling; include a Model. Be sure that the initial state of the View matches the initial state of the Model.

88. Write a GUI-based program that simulates the selection of a basketball team. You will retrieve the data from a text file containing 10 lines. Each line will list the name of a player. Your program needs to read the file and display 10 checkboxes representing the 10 players. A text area will display the team, made up of the players being selected. A basketball team has five players. Your program should not allow the user to change his or her selection after the team has five players. Every time the user checks or unchecks a checkbox, the team in the text area should be updated accordingly. Provide buttons for the following:

❑ One button, when clicked, displays how many players are currently on the team.

❑ Another button, when clicked, displays how many players remain unselected.

Use code for the GUI and to set up event handling; include a Model. Be sure that the initial state of the View matches the initial state of the Model.

89. Write a GUI-based program that enables the user to choose a file containing an image. Your application then displays that image in a label. Your GUI should include a button and a label. When the user clicks on the button, open a file-choosing dialog box to enable the user to select a file. (Hint: look up the

FileChooser class in the Java Class Library.) The dialog box should show the files in the current directory with an extension of either *jpg* or *gif*.

Look It Up

Use FXML for the GUI and to set up event handling; include a Model.

90. Write a GUI-based program that displays a team on a soccer field. You will retrieve data from a text file containing 11 lines. Each line will contain the name of a player. Your program should read the file and display the following window when it starts. (You can assume that the players in the file are not in any particular order.) Each cell is a button; when the user clicks on a button, the button replaces its text with the name of the player.

Left wing (11)		Striker (9)			Right wing (7)
Left midfielder (6)		Midfielder (10)			Right midfielder (8)
Left defender (3)	Stopper (4)	Sweeper (5)			Right defender (2)
		Goalie (1)			

Use FXML for the GUI and to set up event handling; include a Model.

91. Write a program that displays a color on canvas and allows the user to change the color by changing its red, green, and blue components. Provide three sliders, with each slider representing a coefficient between 0 and 1 for the red, green, and blue amount, respectively. As the user manipulates each slider, change the color displayed on the canvas. Hint: use the *fillRect* method to create a rectangle the same size as the canvas.

Use FXML for the GUI and to set up event handling; include a Model. Be sure that the initial state of the View matches the initial state of the Model.

92. Same as 91, but create the GUI programmatically instead.

93. Write a GUI-based program that includes three sliders and a label. The sliders are used to define the red, green, and blue components of a color that you should use for the background color of the label. Each slider represents a coefficient between 0 and 255 for the red, green, and blue amount, respectively. As the user moves a slider, the background color of the label changes.

Use FXML for the GUI and to set up event handling; include a Model. Be sure that the initial state of the View matches the initial state of the Model.

94. Same as 93, but create the GUI programmatically instead.

95. Write a GUI-based program that generates a UNIX permission command; the UNIX permission command format is:

```
chmod xyz filename
```

where *x*, *y*, and *z* have values between 0 and 7

Provide the following:

- ❏ Three combo boxes for the permission level for all, the group, and the owner of a file. In each combo box, the user can choose the permission level, a number between 0 and 7

- ❏ One text field, where the user enters the name of a file.

- ❏ A label that displays the permission command for that file based on the values of the three combo boxes. Every time the user interacts with one of the combo boxes, the label should be updated.

Use FXML for the GUI and to set up event handling; include a Model. Be sure that the initial state of the View matches the initial state of the Model.

96. Same as 95, except that you should update the label every time the user updates the name of the file.

97. Same as 95, but create the GUI programmatically instead of with FXML.

98. Write a GUI-based program that simulates entering the destination in a car's GPS system. The user can enter a destination by typing it in a text field or by choosing a destination from a drop-down list of previous destinations. The list of previous destinations is sorted as follows: the most recent destination is at the top and the least recent is at the bottom of the list. If the user enters a destination in a text field, the user needs to click a button to validate it. A label displays the destination selected. When a destination is either entered or selected by the user, the list of previous destinations should be updated; the current destination goes to the top of the list. There should not be any duplicate destinations in the list. In this version, the list is empty when we start the program. Data are not persistent: Every time we start the program, the list of previous destinations is empty.

Use FXML for the GUI and to set up event handling; include a Model. Be sure that the initial state of the View matches the initial state of the Model.

99. Same as 98, but the list of previous destinations should be persistent. It can be stored in a file and the drop-down list can be populated by the contents of the file.

100. Write a program that manages and displays a list of your friends' names and phone numbers. The list of names and phone numbers is displayed in a *ListView* component. Your program should allow the user to add and delete names and phone numbers one at a time. Furthermore, the data should be persistent and stored in a file. When the program starts, the contents of the file are displayed in the *ListView*.

Every time a name and phone number are added or deleted, the file should be updated.

101. Write a drawing program. A *BorderPane* divides the screen into two parts: on the right, the drawing takes place. On the left are four buttons that enable the user to change the drawing color to any of three colors and to clear the drawing on the right side of the screen. The user draws by touching and moving his or her finger on the screen. The drawing is made with the selected color.

102. Write a program that displays a pie chart on the left and its equivalent bar chart on the right. Both charts are dynamic and reflect four values that are input by the user at the bottom of the screen. You can use default values when the program starts.

12.20.8   Technical Writing

103. You are part of a team writing a complex program that includes a GUI. Our team is made up of programmers, as well as one artist and one HTML/XML developer who do not know programming but could learn some basic things quickly. We know that the GUI uses many different components and does not lend itself to using simple data structures like arrays. We know that the GUI is well defined and that the initial data in all its components are always the same. Would you define the GUI with FXML or programmatically? Discuss the pros and cons.

12.20.9   Group Project (for a group of 1, 2, or 3 students)

104. Design and code a program that simulates an auction. You should consider the following:

A file contains a list of items to be auctioned. You can decide on the format of this file and its contents. For example, the file could look like this:

```
Oldsmobile,oldsmobile.gif,100
World Cup soccer ticket,soccerTickets.gif,50
Trip for 2 to Rome,trip.gif,100
```

In the preceding file sample, each line represents an item as follows: The first field is the item's description, the second field is the name of a file containing an image of the item, and the third field is the minimum bid. You can assume that each item's description is unique.

Items are offered via an online-like auction. (You do not need to include any network programming; your program is a single-computer program.) Users of the program can choose which item to bid on from a list or combo box. Along with displaying the description of the item, your program should show a picture of the item and the current highest bid. (At the beginning, the current highest bid is the minimum bid.) Users bid on an item by selecting the item, typing a name (you can assume a different name), and entering a price for the item. Each time a bid is made, the item's highest bid, displayed on the screen, should be updated if necessary.

Use FXML for the GUI and to set up event handling; include a Model. Be sure that the initial state of the View matches the initial state of the Model.

CHAPTER 13
Recursion

CHAPTER CONTENTS

Introduction

Small problems are easier to solve than big ones, with or without the help of a computer. For example, it is easy to see that 14 is a multiple of 7, but determining if 12,348 is a multiple of 7 requires some thinking . . . or a well-programmed computer.

If we knew that 12,341 is a multiple of 7, then it would be easy to determine that 12,348 is also a multiple of 7, because 12,348 is simply 12,341 + 7. But then, it is not that easy to determine that 12,341 is a multiple of 7. But again, if we knew that 12,334 is a multiple of 7, then it would be easy to determine that 12,341 is also a multiple of 7, because 12,341 is simply 12,334 + 7. Well, if we keep subtracting 7 from the current number, eventually, either we will arrive at 0, which means that 12,348 is a multiple of 7, or we will arrive at a number less than 7 but not 0, which means that 12,348 is not a multiple of 7. Thus, we have reduced a large problem to a small problem that is easy to solve.

The idea of **recursion** is to reduce the size of a problem at each step so that we eventually arrive at a very small, easy-to-solve problem. That easy-to-solve problem is called the **base case**. The formula that reduces the size of the problem is called the **general case**. The general case takes us from solving a bigger problem to solving a smaller problem.

A method that uses recursion calls itself. In other words, in the body of a **recursive method**, there is a call to the method itself. The arguments passed are smaller in value (that is, they get us closer to the base case) than the original arguments. The recursive method will keep calling itself with arguments that are smaller and smaller in value, until eventually we reach the base case.

Any problem that can be solved recursively can also be solved using a loop, or iteration. Often, however, a recursive solution to a problem provides simpler, more elegant, and more compact code than its iterative counterpart.

13.1   Simple Recursion: Identifying the General and Base Cases

When designing a recursive solution for a problem, we need to do two things:

- define the base case
- define the rule for the general case

For example, if we want to print "Hello World" 100 times, we can do the following:

- print "Hello World" once
- print "Hello World" 99 times

Note that we do two things: First, we print "Hello World" once, which is easy to do. Then we reduce the size of the remaining problem to printing "Hello World" 99 times. In order to print "Hello World" 99 times, we print "Hello World" once, then we print "Hello World" 98 times. Continuing the same approach, to print "Hello World" 98 times, we print "Hello World" once, then we print "Hello World" 97 times, and so on. Eventually, we will reach a point where we print "Hello World" once, then print "Hello World" 0 times. Printing "Hello World" 0 times is an easy-to-solve problem; we simply do nothing. That is our base case for this problem.

Thus, our general approach to printing "Hello World" *n* times (where *n* is greater than 0) is to print "Hello World" once, and then print "Hello World" *n* − 1 times. As we reduce the number of times we print "Hello World," we will eventually reach 0, the base case. This condition is easy to detect. Thus, we can solve the large problem by reducing the problem to smaller and smaller problems until we find a problem that we know how to solve.

The following pseudocode illustrates the approach for our recursive method.

```
void printHelloWorldNTimes( int n )
{
   if ( n is greater than 0 )
   {
      print "Hello World"
      printHelloWorldNTimes( n - 1 )
   }
   // else do nothing
}
```

When *n* is greater than 0, we will execute the body of the *if* statement, printing "Hello World" once, then printing it *n* − 1 times. This is the general case for this problem. We can see that we are going from a problem of size *n* (print "Hello World" *n* times) to a problem of size (*n* − 1) (print "Hello World" *n* − 1 times).

When *n* is 0 (or less), we do nothing; that is, the call to *printHelloWorldNTimes* with an argument of 0 does not generate any action. This is the base case, and this is when the recursive calls will end.

Example 13.1 shows this method.

```
1  /* Printing Hello World n times using recursion
2     Anderson, Franceschi
3  */
4
5  public class RecursiveHelloWorld
6  {
7     public static void main( String [ ] args )
```

```
8    {
9        // print "Hello World" 5 times using our recursive method
10       printHelloWorldNTimes( 5 );
11   }
12
13   // the recursive method
14   public static void printHelloWorldNTimes( int n )
15   {
16     if ( n > 0 )
17     {
18       // print "Hello World" once
19       System.out.println( "Hello World" );
20
21       // now print "Hello World" ( n - 1 ) times
22       printHelloWorldNTimes( n - 1 );
23     }
24     // if n is 0 or less, do nothing
25   }
26 }
```

EXAMPLE 13.1   Recursively Printing "Hello World" *n* Times

We coded the *printHelloWorldNTimes* method from line 13 to line 25. That method prints "Hello World" *n* times, where *n* is an *int*, the only parameter of the method. We test at line 16 for the general case: *n* is greater than 0. There is no *else* clause: if *n* is 0 or less, we have reached the base case and the method does nothing.

The code for the general case is executed at lines 18–22. At line 19, we print "Hello World" once. At line 22, we make a recursive call to the *printHelloWorldNTimes* method in order to print "Hello World" $(n - 1)$ times. The method calls itself, but with an argument that is 1 less than its argument *n*.

On line 10, we call the *printHelloWorldNTimes* method, passing the argument 5. Because *main* is *static*, it can call only *static* methods; therefore, we need to define our *printHelloWorldNTimes* method as *static*. In general, recursive methods can be defined as *static* or *nonstatic*.

Figure 13.1 shows the output of Example 13.1. As we can see, "Hello World" is indeed printed five times. Figure 13.2 illustrates how the recursive calls are executed and the output resulting from the calls.

SOFTWARE ENGINEERING TIP
If the method does nothing in the base case, it is important to document that fact to show when the recursive calls will end.

Figure 13.1

Output of Example 13.1

```
Hello World
Hello World
Hello World
Hello World
Hello World
```

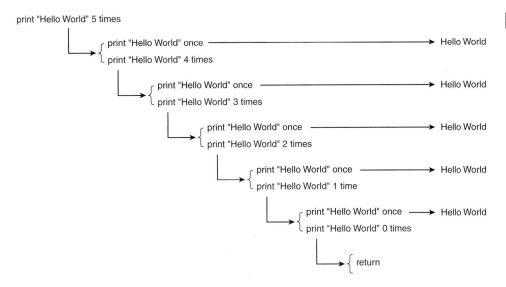

Figure 13.2

Recursive Method Calls

Skill Practice
with these end-of-chapter questions

13.2   Recursion with a Return Value

In the preceding example, we coded a very simple method. Now let's look at some examples that are a little more complex, with recursive methods that return a value.

In a value-returning method, the *return* statement can include a call to another value-returning method, as in:

```java
public static int multiplyAbsoluteValueBy3( int n )
{
   return ( 3 * Math.abs( n ) );
}
```

In this case, the *multiplyAbsoluteValueBy3* method cannot return its value until the *abs* method returns a value, allowing the expression in the *return* statement to be fully evaluated.

The same principle applies to a value-returning method that is recursive. The return value of the recursive method often consists of an expression that includes a call to the method itself.

Thus, in the general case of the method, we could see code like:

```
return ( expression including a recursive call to the method );
```

Each execution of the recursive method must wait to return its value until its recursive call to the method returns a value. When the base case is reached, the method simply returns a value without making another recursive call. At that point, the method that invoked the method with the base case argument receives its return value, which allows that method to return a value to its caller, and so on, until the method is able to return a value to the initial caller. In this way, the return values unravel up to the initial caller.

To see how this works, let's look at an example of a recursive method that returns a value.

13.2.1   Computing the Factorial of a Number

We will define a recursive method to compute and return the factorial of a positive integer.

The factorial of a positive number is defined as follows:

$$\text{factorial}(n) = n\,! = n * (n - 1) * (n - 2) * (n - 3) * \ldots * 2 * 1$$

The factorial of a negative number is not defined. The factorial of 0, by convention is 1.

$$\text{factorial}(0) = 0\,! = 1$$

Let's define the base case and the general case for computing the factorial of a number.

In order to define the rule for the general case, we need to find a relationship between the problem at hand (computing the factorial of a number n), and a smaller, similar problem, involving, for example, $(n - 1)$, $(n - 2)$, or other smaller values of n. So, here we will try to establish a relationship between factorial(n) and factorial($n - 1$), factorial($n - 2$), and so on.

Let's first examine what the value of factorial($n - 1$) is. Applying the preceding formula, we get:

$$\text{factorial}(n - 1) = (n - 1)\,! = (n - 1) * (n - 2) * (n - 3) * \ldots * 2 * 1$$

As we can see from the preceding formulas, there is a very simple relationship between factorial(n) and factorial($n - 1$):

factorial(n) = n * factorial($n - 1$)

This is the relationship we will use for the formulation of the general case.

Using this formula, at each step we reduce the size of the problem (measured by the value of the input n) from n to ($n - 1$). In order to compute factorial(n), we will call the factorial method with the argument ($n - 1$) and multiply the returned value by n. The call to the factorial method with the argument ($n - 1$) will generate a recursive call to the factorial method with argument ($n - 2$), until eventually we generate a recursive call to the factorial method with the argument 0. We know how to compute factorial (0): by convention, it is 1. That is our base case and we have reached it. We will return 1, which will allow the unraveling of the recursive method calls until we solve the original problem, factorial(n).

Example 13.2 shows the code for calculating a factorial recursively. In order to keep things simple, we will also return 1 if the argument sent to the method is negative. However, we are careful in documenting our method to emphasize that the argument should be greater than or equal to 0. If we do not want to return anything when a negative argument is passed to the method, we would need to throw an exception, because the method is a value-returning method.

Here is how our *factorial(int n)* method will work:

- Base case: if n is negative or 0, the method returns 1
- General case: if n is greater than 0, the method returns n * *factorial(n – 1)*

```
1 /* Computing the factorial of a number using recursion
2    Anderson, Franceschi
3 */
4
5 public class RecursiveFactorial
6 {
7   public static void main( String [ ] args )
8   {
9     // compute factorial of 5 and output it
10    System.out.println( "Factorial( 5 ) is "
11                        + factorial( 5 ) );
12  }
13
14  /** recursive factorial method
15   *   @param    n  a positive integer
16   *   @return      the factorial of n
17   */
```

```
18   public static int factorial( int n )
19   {
20     if ( n <= 0 ) // base case
21       return 1;
22     else              // general case
23       return ( n * factorial( n - 1 ) );
24   }
25 }
```

EXAMPLE 13.2   Computing a Factorial Using Recursion

At lines 10–11, we make the initial call to the *factorial* method and print the result. We simply compute the factorial of 5. We can modify the example to prompt the user for another value.

We coded the *factorial* method at lines 14–24. The *factorial* method takes an *int* parameter named *n*, and returns the factorial of *n* as an *int*. At line 20, we test if *n* is less than or equal to 0. If that is true, we have reached the base case, and the *factorial* method returns 1. If *n* is greater than 0, the code skips to line 23, where we have coded the general case. We make a recursive call to the *factorial* method with an argument of $(n - 1)$. The value returned by that recursive call is then multiplied by *n* and the result is returned.

Figure 13.3 shows the output of Example 13.2.

We can verify that factorial(5) is 120. Indeed,

$$5! = 5 * 4 * 3 * 2 * 1 = 120$$

To illustrate how recursive method calls are processed and their values are returned, let's modify Example 13.2 to include some output statements inside the *factorial* method. In this way, we can trace the recursive calls.

The JVM manages method calls using a **stack**. When a method is called, the JVM places the method's arguments and the caller's return address in a **frame** on the stack in a last-in, first-out order. Each method invocation adds another frame to the top of the stack. When a method completes and returns to the caller, its frame is removed from the top of the stack and is discarded. To help us trace the processing of recursive calls, we will use the *StackWalker* class, introduced in Java 9, which allows us to display the current contents of the stack at each invocation of the recursive method.

Example 13.3 is similar to Example 13.2 except that we have added statements to trace these features.

- each call to the factorial method and its argument
- the detection of the base case and the value returned at that point

```
Factorial( 5 ) is 120
```

Figure 13.3

Output of
Example 13.2

- the expression that evaluates to the return value

- the current stack at each method invocation

The *factorial* method is coded at lines 17–57.

When the method begins executing, we capture the current state of the stack into a *List* of *StackWalker.StackFrame* elements at lines 23–24. We get the current stack by calling the *getInstance* method of the *StackWalker* class. We then call the *walk* method, also in the *StackWalker* class, which creates a **stream** of stack frames. Streams, introduced in Java 8, are sequences of elements to which aggregate functions can be applied. The *walk* method, using a lambda expression, then traverses the stream, calling the *Stream collect* method, which calls on the *Collectors' static toList* method to accumulate the stack frames into a list. We skip the first frame, *(skip(1))*, because the first frame represents the method call to create the list.

The *StackWalker* class is in *java.lang*, so we do not need an *import* statement. On lines 5–6, we import the *List* interface and the *Collectors* class from *java.util* and *java.util.stream*, respectively.

At line 26, we output a message indicating that the *factorial* method has been called, along with the parameter value. When the base case is detected, we output a message indicating that the method has reached the base case and report its return value (lines 34–36). For the general case, we output the expression that will be returned by the method (lines 48–49). At each of these places, we also output the current state of the stack, displaying for each stack frame the line number from which the method was called and the name of the method. On lines 27–30 we output the stack when the *factorial* method starts executing. On lines 37–40 we output the stack when the method has detected the base case and is returning a known value (1), and on lines 50–53 we output the stack after the method makes a recursive call in the general case.

Figure 13.4 shows the output of Example 13.3. We can see the recursive calls to the *factorial* method with the value of the argument being reduced by 1 until the base case, 0, is reached. At that point, each recursively called method, in turn, returns a value to its caller until the initial invocation of the method returns the value 120. We also see that each time we detect the general case, another invocation of the *factorial* method is added to the stack. Once the base case is reached, the *factorial* methods on the stack start returning their value, and as they complete, the frame for their method invocation is removed from the stack.

```
1  /* Tracing the calculation of the factorial
2     of a number using recursion
3     Anderson, Franceschi
4  */
5  import java.util.List;
6  import java.util.stream.Collectors;
7
8  public class RecursiveFactorialWithStackTrace
9  {
10    public static void main( String [ ] args )
11    {
12      // compute factorial of 5 and output it
13      System.out.println( "\nFactorial( 5 ) is "
14                          + factorial( 5 ) );
15    }
16
17    /** recursive factorial method
18     *   @param   n  a positive integer
19     *   @return   the factorial of n
20     */
21    public static int factorial( int n )
22    {
23      List<StackWalker.StackFrame> stack = StackWalker.getInstance( )
24               .walk( s -> s.skip(1).collect( Collectors.toList( ) ) );
25
26      System.out.println( "factorial( " + n + " ) called" );
27      System.out.println( "\tCurrent Stack" );
28      for ( StackWalker.StackFrame f : stack )
29        System.out.println( "\t\t" + f.getLineNumber( ) + " "
30                            + f.getMethodName( ) );
31
32      if ( n == 0 )  // base case
33      {
34        System.out.println( "\nBase case detected\n" );
35
36        System.out.println( "factorial( " + n + " ) returning 1" );
37        System.out.println( "\tCurrent Stack"  );
38        for ( StackWalker.StackFrame f : stack )
39          System.out.println( "\t\t" + f.getLineNumber( ) + " "
40                              + f.getMethodName( ) );
41
42        return 1;
43      }
44      else         // general case
45      {
46        int factorialNMinus1 = factorial( n - 1 );
47
```

```
48        System.out.println( "factorial( " + n + " ) returning "
49                               + n + " * " + factorialNMinus1 );
50        System.out.println( "\tCurrent Stack"  );
51        for ( StackWalker.StackFrame f : stack )
52          System.out.println( "\t\t" + f.getLineNumber( ) + " "
53                                 + f.getMethodName( ) );
54
55        return ( n * factorialNMinus1 );
56    }
57  }
58 }
```

EXAMPLE 13.3   Tracing Recursive Calls of the *factorial* Method

```
factorial( 5 ) called
   Current Stack
      14 main
factorial( 4 ) called
   Current Stack
      52 factorial
      14 main
factorial( 3 ) called
   Current Stack
      52 factorial
      52 factorial
      14 main
factorial( 2 ) called
   Current Stack
      52 factorial
      52 factorial
      52 factorial
      14 main
factorial( 1 ) called
   Current Stack
      52 factorial
      52 factorial
      52 factorial
      52 factorial
      14 main
factorial( 0 ) called
   Current Stack
      52 factorial
      52 factorial
      52 factorial
      52 factorial
```

Figure 13.4

The Trace of the
factorial Method

(continued)

Figure 13.4

(continued)

```
          52 factorial
          14 main

Base case detected

factorial( 0 ) returning 1
   Current Stack
          52 factorial
          52 factorial
          52 factorial
          52 factorial
          52 factorial
          14 main
factorial( 1 ) returning 1 * 1
   Current Stack
          52 factorial
          52 factorial
          52 factorial
          52 factorial
          14 main
factorial( 2 ) returning 2 * 1
   Current Stack
          52 factorial
          52 factorial
          52 factorial
          14 main
factorial( 3 ) returning 3 * 2
   Current Stack
          52 factorial
          52 factorial
          14 main
factorial( 4 ) returning 4 * 6
   Current Stack
          52 factorial
          14 main
factorial( 5 ) returning 5 * 24
   Current Stack
          14 main

Factorial( 5 ) is 120
```

COMMON ERROR TRAP
Failure to code the base case will result in a run-time error.

Identifying the base case is critical. If a recursive method never reaches a base case, the method continues calling itself indefinitely, causing the JVM to continue placing frames on the stack until memory for the stack is full. At this time, the JVM generates a *StackOverflowError*, which terminates the program.

```
Exception in thread "main" java.lang.StackOverflowError
    at RecursiveFactorial.factorial(RecursiveFactorial.java:23)
    at RecursiveFactorial.factorial(RecursiveFactorial.java:23)
    at RecursiveFactorial.factorial(RecursiveFactorial.java:23)
    at RecursiveFactorial.factorial(RecursiveFactorial.java:23)
```

Figure 13.5

The First Few
Lines of a Run of
Example 13.2 if
the Base Case Is
Not Coded

For example, if we did not code the base case in our *factorial* method, the method would look like the following:

```
public static int factorial( int n )
{
    // n must be a positive integer
    return ( n * factorial ( n - 1 ) );
}
```

When the method is called, the recursive calls keep being made because the base case is never reached. This eventually generates a *StackOverflowError*. Figure 13.5 shows the first few lines of output from a run of Example 13.2 (the *RecursiveFactorial* class) with lines 20 to 22 commented out.

CODE IN ACTION

Within the online resources, you will find a movie with a step-by-step illustration of computing a factorial using recursion. Click on the link to start the movie.

© Hemera Technologies/Photos
.com/Thinkstock

13.2.2   Computing the Greatest Common Divisor

A common algebra problem is to calculate the greatest common divisor, or **gcd**, of two positive integers. The gcd is the greatest positive integer that divides evenly into both numbers.

For example, consider 50 and 20. We can figure in our head that 5 divides evenly into both numbers, but so does 10. Since we can't find a number greater than 10 that divides evenly into both numbers, 10 is the gcd of 50 and 20.

It is easy to guess the gcd of two small numbers, but it is more difficult to guess the gcd of two large numbers, such as 474 and 162. The following Euclidian algorithm finds the gcd of two positive integers a and b. This algorithm derives from the fact that the gcd of two integers a and b (with $a > b$) is the same as the gcd of b and the remainder of a / b.

```
Step 1:
  r0 = a % b
  if ( r0 is equal to 0 )
      gcd ( a, b ) = b
      stop
  else
      go to step 2

Step 2:
  repeat step 1 with b and r0, instead of a and b.
```

Let's run the algorithm on our first example, 50 and 20. We substitute 50 for *a* and 20 for *b*.

```
Step 1:
  r0 = 50 % 20 = 10
  is 10 equal to 0 ? no, go to Step 2.

Step 2:
  r0 = 20 / 10 = 0
  is 0 equal to 0 ?
      yes. gcd( 50, 20 ) = 10
      stop
```

Therefore, the gcd of 50 and 20 is 10.

Let's now run the algorithm on our second example, 474 and 162.

The remainder of 474 divided by 162 is 150

    150 is not equal to 0

        so we take the remainder of 162 divided by 150, which is 12

            12 is not equal to 0

                so we take the remainder of 150 divided by 12, which is 6

                    6 is not equal to 0

                        so we take the remainder of 12 divided by 6, which is 0

                            0 is equal to 0

                              so the gcd of 474 and 162 is 6

Let's go back to our algorithm and look at Step 1 as a method taking two parameters, *a* and *b*. Step 2 is a method call to Step 1 with two different parameters, *b* and *r0*. It is very simple to calculate *r0*, since *r0* is the remainder of the division of *a* by *b*. Using the modulus operator, *r0* is *a % b*. Therefore, this algorithm can easily be coded as a recursive method.

Let's call the two parameters of the method, *dividend* and *divisor*, in that order.

When the remainder of the division of *dividend* by *divisor* is 0, we have reached the base case and the method returns *divisor*. The general case is when the remainder of the division of *dividend* by *divisor* is not 0. The method then calls itself with *divisor* and the remainder of the division of *dividend* by *divisor*.

Example 13.4 shows the code for the recursive implementation of the greatest common divisor solution.

```
1  /* Computing the greatest common divisor using recursion
2     Anderson, Franceschi
3  */
4
5  public class RecursiveGCD
6  {
7    public static void main( String [ ] args )
8    {
9      // compute and output gcd of 474 and 162
10     System.out.println( "The GCD of " + 474 + " and "
11                         + 162 + " is " + gcd( 474, 162 ) );
12   }
13
14   /** recursive gcd method
15    *   @param    dividend  the first strictly positive integer
16    *   @param    divisor   the second strictly positive integer
17    *   @return             the gcd of dividend and divisor
18    */
19   public static int gcd( int dividend, int divisor )
20   {
21     if ( dividend % divisor == 0 )      // base case
22       return divisor;
23     else                               // general case
24       return ( gcd ( divisor, dividend % divisor ) );
25   }
26 }
```

EXAMPLE 13.4 Computing the GCD of Two Integers Using Recursion

We make the call to the *gcd* method at lines 10–11 with arguments 474 and 162 and output the result.

The *gcd* method is coded from lines 14–25. The method header shows that the *gcd* method takes two *int* parameters named *dividend* and *divisor*, and returns an *int*, the greatest common divisor of *dividend* and *divisor*. At line 21, we check for the base case by testing if the remainder of the integer division of *dividend* by *divisor* is 0. If so, the *gcd* method returns *divisor* without making another recursive call.

Figure 13.6

Output of
Example 13.4

> The GCD of 474 and 162 is 6

If the remainder is not 0, we are in the general case, so we make a recursive call at line 24 with the arguments *divisor* and the remainder of the division (*dividend % divisor*). We return the value returned by that call.

Figure 13.6 shows the output of Example 13.4.

As we did with the recursive *factorial* method, let's modify Example 13.4 to include some output statements inside the *gcd* method in order to trace the recursive calls.

The *gcd* method in Example 13.5 (lines 16–60) is the same as the *gcd* method in Example 13.4, except that each time the method is called, we print the parameter values and result of the modulus operation (lines 27–29) to verify that the method is correctly detecting the general and base cases. We also print a message when the base case is reached (lines 37–38). At lines 49–51, we output the value returned by the method in the general case. As in Example 13.3, at each of these places, we also output the current state of the stack (lines 30–33, 39–42, and 53–56), displaying for each stack frame the line number from which the method was called and the name of the method.

Figure 13.7 shows the output of Example 13.5. We can see the recursive calls all the way to the base case, and the return value from each recursive call. We also see that each time we detect the general case, we call the *gcd* method recursively, and the current method is added to the stack because the current method cannot complete until the invoked method returns. Once the base case is reached, the *gcd* methods on the stack start returning their value. One by one each method completes and its stack frame is removed from the stack. Note that the return value stays the same throughout the process. Such a recursive method is called **tail recursive** because the method does no further processing when the recursive call returns.

```
 1 /* Computing the greatest common divisor using recursion
 2    Anderson, Franceschi
 3 */
 4 import java.util.List;
 5 import java.util.stream.Collectors;
 6
 7 public class RecursiveGCDWithStackTrace
 8 {
 9   public static void main( String [ ] args )
10   {
11     // compute gcd of 123450 and 60378 and output it
12     System.out.println( "\nThe GCD of " + 474 + " and "
13                         + 162 + " is " + gcd( 474, 162 ) );
14   }
15
16   /** recursive gcd method with trace
```

```
17   *     @param     dividend    the first strictly positive integer
18   *     @param     divisor     the second strictly positive integer
19   *     @return                the gcd of dividend and divisor
20   */
21   public static int gcd( int dividend, int divisor )
22   {
23     List<StackWalker.StackFrame> stack = StackWalker.getInstance( )
24            .walk( s -> s.skip(1).collect( Collectors.toList( ) ) );
25
26
27     System.out.print( "gcd( " + dividend + ", " + divisor + " )" );
28     System.out.println( "    " + dividend + " % " + divisor + " = "
29                            + ( dividend % divisor ) );
30     System.out.println( "\tCurrent stack" );
31     for ( StackWalker.StackFrame f : stack )
32       System.out.println( "\t\t" + f.getLineNumber( )
33                              + " " + f.getMethodName( ) );
34
35     if ( dividend % divisor == 0 )   // base case
36     {
37       System.out.println( "\nbase case reached, returning "
38                            + divisor );
39       System.out.println( "\tCurrent stack" );
40       for ( StackWalker.StackFrame f : stack )
41         System.out.println( "\t\t" + f.getLineNumber( )
42                                + " " + f.getMethodName( ) );
43
44       return divisor;
45     }
46     else                            // general case
47     {
48       int temp = gcd( divisor, dividend % divisor );
49       System.out.println( "gcd( " + divisor + ", "
50                              + ( dividend % divisor )
51                              + " ) returning " + temp );
52
53       System.out.println( "\tCurrent stack" );
54       for ( StackWalker.StackFrame f : stack )
55         System.out.println( "\t\t" + f.getLineNumber( )
56                                + " " + f.getMethodName( ) );
57
58       return temp;
59     }
60   }
61 }
```

EXAMPLE 13.5   Tracing the Recursive Calls of the *gcd* Method

Figure 13.7

The Trace of the
gcd Method

```
gcd( 474, 162 )    474 % 162 = 150
    Current stack
        13 main
gcd( 162, 150 )    162 % 150 = 12
    Current stack
        48 gcd
        13 main
gcd( 150, 12 )    150 % 12 = 6
    Current stack
        48 gcd
        48 gcd
        13 main
gcd( 12, 6 )    12 % 6 = 0
    Current stack
        48 gcd
        48 gcd
        48 gcd
        13 main

base case reached, returning 6
    Current stack
        48 gcd
        48 gcd
        48 gcd
        13 main
gcd( 12,6 } returning 6
    Current stack
        48 gcd
        48 gcd
        13 main
gcd( 150,12 } returning 6
    Current stack
        48 gcd
        13 main
gcd( 162,150 } returning 6
    Current stack
        13 main

The GCD of 474 and 162 is 6
```

© Hemera Technologies/
Photos.com/Thinkstock

CODE IN ACTION

Within the online resources, you will find a movie with a step-by-step illustration of
computing a GCD and various other recursive methods. Click on the link to start the movie.

13.3   Recursion with Two Base Cases

Recursive formulations can be more complex than the examples we have discussed. The general case can involve more than one recursive call, with different arguments. This, in turn, means that we can have more than one base case.

Suppose we are playing a networked video game online. There are n players who would like to play. Unfortunately, that game can be played with only p players. We will make the assumption that p is an integer between 0 and n (for instance, n could be 100 and p could be 8). Otherwise, we simply cannot play the game.

Our problem is to determine how many different ways we can choose p players from among n players. We will call that number *Combinations(n, p)*.

The math formula for *Combinations(n, p)* is:

$$Combinations(n, p) = n! / ((n - p)! * p!)$$

Our goal here is to come up with a recursive solution to the problem and thus to code *Combinations(n, p)* recursively.

There are some obvious cases to consider. If we have the same number of players as the number who can play the game, then p equals n, and we pick all the players. There is only one way to do that, so *Combinations(n, n)* = 1.

If the game requires no players, then p equals 0, and we do not pick any players. Again, there is only one way to do that, so *Combinations(n, 0)* = 1.

But what is the answer in the general case where the value of *Combinations(n, p)* may not be so obvious?

One way to look at that problem is as follows:

Among these n potential players, let's focus on one player in particular. We will call that player Louis. We can either pick Louis or not pick Louis. Therefore, the total number of possibilities of picking p players among n potential players is equal to the sum of the following two numbers:

- the number of possibilites of picking p players, including picking Louis, among n

- the number of possibilities of picking p players, without picking Louis, among n

If we pick Louis, then we will have to choose $(p - 1)$ more players. But we cannot pick Louis again, so there are only $(n - 1)$ potential players left. The number of such possibilities is *Combinations(n – 1, p – 1)*.

If we do not pick Louis, then we still have to choose p players. But since we are not picking Louis, there are only $(n - 1)$ potential players left. The number of such possibilities is *Combinations(n – 1, p)*.

Therefore, we can write the following recursive formula:

```
Combinations( n, p ) = Combinations( n − 1, p − 1 )
                     + Combinations( n − 1, p )
```

If we look at the two terms on the right side of the preceding formula, we can see that:

- In the first term, both parameters, n and p, have been decreased by 1.

- In the second term, one parameter, n, has been decreased by 1, while p is unchanged.

Therefore, solving the problem of computing *Combinations(n, p)* using this formula translates into solving two similar, but smaller, problems. That is our general case.

Our next concern is to decide what the base case or cases are. In other words, as we apply the preceding formula repeatedly, when will we reach an easy-to-solve problem? Since we have two recursive terms on the right side of the formula, we will have two base cases.

Let's look at the first term, *Combinations(n – 1, p – 1)*. We can see that both n and p decrease by 1 at the same time. When we start, p is greater than or equal to 0 and less than or equal to n. Therefore, as we keep applying the formula and concentrate on the first term, we can see that p will eventually reach 0, and that p will reach 0 before n does. As discussed earlier, *Combinations(n, 0)* = 1, because there is only one way to pick 0 players from a set of n players—do not pick any. This is one base case.

Let's now look at the second term, *Combinations(n − 1, p)*. We can see that n decreases by 1 while p is unchanged. We know that p must be less than or equal to n (we cannot pick more than n players among n players). As n decreases and p does not, n will eventually reach p. As discussed earlier, *Combinations(n, n)* = 1, because there is only one way to pick n players among n players—pick them all. This is our other base case.

Example 13.6 shows the code for this example.

```
1 /* Computing the number of combinations
2    of picking p objects among n, using recursion
3    Anderson, Franceschi
4 */
5
6 public class RecursiveCombinations
7 {
8   public static void main( String [ ] args )
```

```
 9   {
10     // compute and output number of combinations
11     System.out.println( "C( 5, 2 ) = "
12                         + combinations( 5, 2 ) );
13   }
14
15   /** recursive combinations method
16    *    @param    n a positive number
17    *    @param    p a positive number, less than or equal to n
18    *    @return   the number of combinations of choosing p among n
19    */
20   public static int combinations( int n, int p )
21   {
22     if ( p == 0 )            // base case # 1
23       return 1;
24     else if ( n == p )      // base case # 2
25       return 1;
26     else                    // general case
27       return ( combinations( n - 1, p - 1 )
28               + combinations( n - 1, p ) );
29   }
30 }
```

EXAMPLE 13.6   Computing Combinations Recursively

In this example, we use the *combinations* method to compute the number of ways of picking 2 players from among 5.

We call the *combinations* method with arguments, 5 and 2, and output the returned value at lines 11–12.

The *combinations* method is coded at lines 15–29. The method header, at line 20, shows that the *combinations* method takes two *int* parameters, the number of players (n) and the number of players to select (p). The return value, an *int*, is the number of combinations of picking p players among n.

At line 22, we test for the first base case ($p == 0$). If true, we return 1. If p is not equal to 0, we test for the second base case (n is equal to p). If that is *true*, we return 1. If p is not equal to 0 and n is not equal to p, then we are in the general case and the code skips to lines 27–28. We make two recursive calls to the *combinations* method. The first recursive call is with arguments $n - 1$ and $p - 1$. The second recursive call is with arguments $n - 1$ and p. We add the values returned by these two recursive calls and return the result.

The output of Example 13.6 is shown in Figure 13.8.

```
C( 5, 2 ) = 10
```

Figure 13.8

Output of
Example 13.6

We can verify that our algorithm is correct. As discussed earlier,

Combinations(n, p) = n! / ((n – p)! * p!)

Thus,

Combinations(5, 2) = 5! / (3! * 2!) = 10

Those of us with a mathematics background can verify that

```
Combinations( n, p ) = Combinations( n – 1, p – 1 ) +
                       Combinations( n – 1, p )
```

COMMON ERROR TRAP
There can be more than one base case. Failing to take into account all base cases can result in a *StackOverflowError* at run time.

that is,

```
n! / ( ( n – p )! * p! ) = ( n – 1 )! / ( ( n – p )! * ( p – 1 )! )
                         + ( n – 1 )! / ( ( n – 1 – p )! * p! )
```

What happens if we code for only one base case when there are two or more base cases?

When the method is called, the recursive calls will continue to be made, because the missing base cases will never be detected. This will eventually generate a *StackOverflowError*.

13.4   Programming Activity 1: Checking for a Palindrome

In this activity, you will work with recursion to perform this function:

Code a recursive method to determine if a *String* is a palindrome.

A palindrome is a word, phrase, or sentence that is symmetrical; that is, it is spelled the same forward and backward. Examples are "otto," "mom," "madam," and "able was I ere I saw elba."

How can we determine, using recursion, whether a *String* is a palindrome?

If the *String* has two or more characters, we can check if the first and last characters are identical. If they are not identical, then the *String* is not a palindrome. That is a base case.

If the first and last characters are identical, then we need to check if the substring comprised of all the characters between the first and last characters is a palindrome. That is the general case.

If the *String* is a palindrome, each recursive call will reduce the size of the argument—that is, the number of characters in the argument *String*—by 2. Eventually, the recursive calls will result in a *String* argument consisting of 0 or 1 character. Both are trivial palindromes. That is our second base case. Note that we will reach this base case only if the *String* is a palindrome. Indeed, if the *String* is not a palindrome, the recursive calls will detect the first base case as soon as the first and last characters of the *String* argument are different, and the recursive method will return *false*.

For example, to check if "madam" is a palindrome, we take the following steps.

Here is the original *String*:

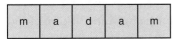

We compare the first and last characters.

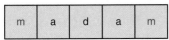

They are equal, so we now check the substring comprised of the characters between the first and last characters. Again, we compare the first and last characters of this substring.

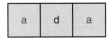

They are equal, so we now check the substring comprised of the characters between the first and last characters.

There is only one character in this substring, so we have reached our second base case. The *String* "madam" is a palindrome.

Let's now check if "modem" is a palindrome.

Here is the original *String*:

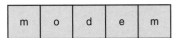

We compare the first and last characters.

They are equal, so we now check the substring comprised of the characters between the first and last characters. Again, we check the first and last characters.

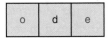

They are not equal, so we have reached the first base case. The *String* "modem" is not a palindrome.

Instructions

In this chapter's Programming Activity 1 folder, you will find the source files needed to complete this activity. Copy all of the files to a folder on your computer. Note that all files should be in the same folder.

Open the *PalindromeDrawing.java* source file. Searching for five asterisks (*****) in the source code will position you to the location where you will add your code. In this task, you will fill in the code inside the *recursivePalindrome* method to determine if a *String* representing a word or a sentence is a palindrome. The method returns *true* if the *String* is a palindrome, *false* if the *String* is not a palindrome. Example 13.7 shows the section of the *PalindromeDrawing* source code where you will add your code.

```java
public boolean recursivePalindrome( String pal )
{
    // ***** Student writes the body of this method *****

    // Using recursion, determine if a String representing
    // a word or a sentence is a palindrome
    // If it is, return true, otherwise return false

    // We call the animate method inside the body of this method
    // The call to animate is already coded below

    animate( pal );

    //
    // Student code starts here
    //

    return true; // replace this dummy return statement

    //
    // End of student code - PA 1
    //
}
```

EXAMPLE 13.7   Location of Student Code in *PalindromeDrawing*

The framework will animate your code so that you get some feedback on the correctness of your code. It will display the argument *String* passed to the recursive method at each recursive call of that method. Your result will be displayed in red and the correct result will be displayed in green.

To test your code, compile *PalindromeDrawing.java* and run *PalindromeApplication*. When the program begins, you will see a text box in which to enter a word or a sentence, as shown in Figure 13.9.

Click "check" to animate your code.

If you enter an empty *String* or a *String* with more than 26 characters, the text box will display "enter 1–26 characters". This part is already coded for you.

Figure 13.9

Opening Window

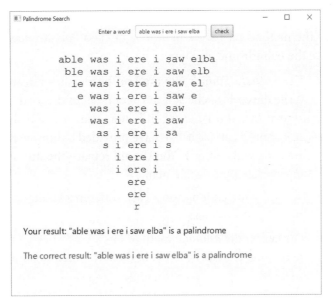

Figure 13.10

Sample Final Screen for Programming Activity 1 When a Palindrome Is Found

Figure 13.10 shows the output if you enter "able was I ere I saw elba." We can see the argument *String* of our recursive method shrinking by two characters at each recursive call until we reach a base case.

If you insert an extra "h" into the preceding phrase, and enter "able was I here I saw elba," which is not a palindrome, the final result of your animation is shown in Figure 13.11. When the argument *String* of our recursive method becomes "here," the recursive calls stop and the method returns *false*.

Figure 13.11

Sample Final
Screen for
Programming
Activity 1 When a
Palindrome Is Not
Found

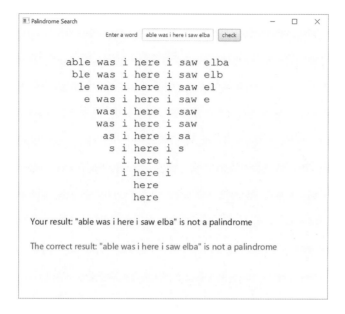

Inside the method *recursivePalindrome* of class *PalindromeDrawing* write the code to solve the palindrome problem:

- The *recursivePalindrome* method header has already been coded for you. Write the code to check if the parameter of the method, *pal*, is a palindrome. Return *true* if it is, *false* if it is not. Your method should be recursive; that is, it should call itself. We have provided a dummy *return* statement so that the code will compile. You should replace the dummy statement with your appropriate *return* statement.

- Be sure your code ignores case differences; that is, Otto and Racecar are indeed palindromes.

- The call to the *animate* method has already been written for you. It should be the first statement in the body of the method and is simply:

  ```
  animate( pal );
  ```

If your method implementation does not animate or animates incorrectly, check these items:

- Check the feedback on the output to see if your code gives the correct result.
- Verify that you coded the base cases correctly.
- Verify that you coded the general case and its corresponding recursive call correctly.

1. **What are the base cases for this method?**

2. **Is this method tail recursive?**

3. **What happens if you do not code one of the base cases?**

13.5   Binary Search: A Recursive Solution

We can use a binary search algorithm to search a sorted array for a given value.

Let's look at how we can define a recursive solution to this problem. We will assume that the array is sorted in ascending order.

Again, we need to define the base cases and the general case, and the general case must reduce the size of the problem.

When searching for a value in an array, we have two possible outcomes:

- We find the value and return its array index.

- We do not find the value and return -1.

Overall, our strategy is this. First, we will look at the middle element of the array. If the value of the middle element is the value we are looking for, we will return its index. That is our first base case.

If the value of the middle element is greater than the value we are looking for, then the value we are looking for cannot be found in elements with array indexes higher than the index of the middle element. Therefore, we will continue our search in the lower half of the array only. We will do that by making a recursive call to our search method, specifying the lower half of the original array as the subarray to search.

Similarly, if the value of the middle element is lower than the value we are looking for, then the value we are looking for cannot be found in elements with array indexes lower than the index of the middle element. Therefore, we will continue our search in the upper half of the array only. We will do that by making a recursive call to our search method, specifying the upper half of the original array as the subarray to search. That is our formulation for the general case.

As we continue searching, the size of the subarray that we search will shrink with every recursive call. Indeed, every recursive call cuts the size of the subarray we search in half. In this recursive algorithm, not only does the size of the problem decrease with each recursive call, but it also decreases by a large amount.

If the value we are looking for is not in the array, the part of the array that we are searching will continue shrinking until it is empty. At that point, we know that we will not find our value in the array. We have reached our other base case, and we return -1.

Example 13.8 shows the code for a recursive binary search.

```
1  /* Searching a sorted array using recursion
2     Anderson, Franceschi
3  */
4
5  import java.util.Scanner;
6
7  public class RecursiveBinarySearch
8  {
9    public static void main( String [ ] args )
10   {
11     // define an array sorted in ascending order
12     int [ ] numbers = { 3, 6, 7, 8, 12, 15, 22, 36, 45,
13                         48, 51, 53, 64, 69, 72, 89, 95 };
14
15     Scanner scan = new Scanner( System.in );
16     System.out.print( "Enter a value to search for > " );
17     int value = scan.nextInt( );
18
19     int index = recursiveBinarySearch
20                 ( numbers, value, 0, numbers.length - 1 );
21     if ( index != -1 )
22       System.out.println( value + " found at index " + index );
23     else
24       System.out.println( value + " not found" );
25   }
26
27   /** recursiveBinarySearch method
28    *   @param    arr   the array sorted in ascending order
29    *   @param    key   the value to search for in the subarray
30    *   @param    start the subarray's first index
31    *   @param    end   the subarray's last index
32    *   @return   the array index at which key was found,
33    *             or -1 if key was not found
34    */
35   public static int recursiveBinarySearch
36              ( int [ ] arr, int key, int start, int end )
37   {
38     if ( start <= end )
39     {
40       // look at the middle element of the subarray
41       int middle = ( start + end ) / 2;
42
43       if ( arr[middle] == key )       // found key, base case
44         return middle;
45       else if ( arr[middle] > key )  // look lower
```

```
46              return recursiveBinarySearch( arr, key, start, middle - 1 );
47          else                                // look higher
48              return recursiveBinarySearch( arr, key, middle + 1, end );
49      }
50      else                                    // key not found, base case
51          return -1;
52  }
53 }
```

EXAMPLE 13.8   Searching an Array Sorted in Ascending Order

We coded the *recursiveBinarySearch* method at lines 27–52. That method takes four parameters: *arr*, the array we are searching; *key*, the value we are searching for; and *start* and *end*, which represent, respectively, the first and last index of the subarray of *arr* that we should search.

At line 38, we test if the subarray we are searching contains at least one element. If it does not, we have reached a base case and we know that we will not find *key*. Thus, we return −1 in the *else* clause at line 51. If the subarray has at least one element, we assign the index of the middle element of the subarray to *middle* at line 41. We then compare the array element at index *middle* to *key* at line 43. If they are equal, we have reached the other base case (we have found *key*) so we return *middle* at line 44.

If the array element at index *middle* is greater than *key*, we call the *recursiveBinary-Search* method with the subarray consisting of all elements with values lower than *middle* (from *start* to *middle* − 1) at line 46. If the array element at index *middle* is smaller than *key*, then we call the *recursiveBinarySearch* method with the subarray consisting of all elements with values higher than *middle* (from *middle* + 1 to *end*) at line 48. In both cases, whatever is returned by the recursive call is returned by the method.

In *main*, we begin by instantiating our array to search. Note that the values are in ascending order (lines 12–13). We then prompt the user for the search key and make the call to the recursive binary search method, passing the entire array as the subarray to search (lines 19–20). We output the result of our search at lines 21–24.

Figure 13.12 shows the output from Example 13.8 when the key value is found, and when the key value is not found.

```
Enter a value to search for > 7
7 found at index 2
```

```
Enter a value to search for > 34
34 not found
```

Figure 13.12

Two Runs of
Example 13.8

Let's run the preceding example on the value 7 in order to illustrate the various recursive calls and the case where the value is found.

Here is the array *numbers*, sorted in ascending order:

Value	3	6	7	8	12	15	22	36	45	48	51	53	64	69	72	89	95
Index	0	1	2	3	4	5	6	7	8	9	10	11	12	13	14	15	16

We calculate the index *middle* by adding the indexes *start* and *end*, then dividing by 2. Thus, when the *recursiveBinarySearch* method is first called, *middle* is 8.

The element at index 8 (45) is greater than 7, so we call the *recursiveBinarySearch* method, searching the left subarray, highlighted here.

Value	3	6	7	8	12	15	22	36	45	48	51	53	64	69	72	89	95
Index	0	1	2	3	4	5	6	7	8	9	10	11	12	13	14	15	16

The index *middle* is now calculated to be 3 ((0 + 7)/2).

The element at index 3 (8) is greater than 7, so we call the *recursiveBinarySearch* method, searching the left subarray, highlighted here.

Value	3	6	7	8	12	15	22	36	45	48	51	53	64	69	72	89	95
Index	0	1	2	3	4	5	6	7	8	9	10	11	12	13	14	15	16

The index *middle* is now calculated to be 1 ((0 + 2)/2).

The element at index 1 (6) is smaller than 7, so we call the *recursiveBinarySearch* method, searching the right subarray, highlighted here.

Value	3	6	7	8	12	15	22	36	45	48	51	53	64	69	72	89	95
Index	0	1	2	3	4	5	6	7	8	9	10	11	12	13	14	15	16

The index *middle* is now calculated to be 2 ((2 + 2)/2).

The element at index 2 (7), is equal to 7. We have found the value and return its index, 2.

Let's now run the preceding example on the value 34 in order to illustrate the various recursive calls and the base case when the value is not found.

Here is the array *numbers* again:

Value	3	6	7	8	12	15	22	36	45	48	51	53	64	69	72	89	95
Index	0	1	2	3	4	5	6	7	8	9	10	11	12	13	14	15	16

The index *middle* when the *recursiveBinarySearch* method is first called is 8 ((0 + 16)/2).

The element at index 8 (45) is greater than 34, so we call the *recursiveBinarySearch* method, searching the left subarray highlighted here.

Value	3	6	7	8	12	15	22	36	45	48	51	53	64	69	72	89	95
Index	0	1	2	3	4	5	6	7	8	9	10	11	12	13	14	15	16

The index *middle* is now calculated to be 3 ((0 + 7)/2).

The element at index 3 (8) is smaller than 34, so we call the *recursiveBinarySearch* method, searching the right subarray, highlighted here.

Value	3	6	7	8	12	15	22	36	45	48	51	53	64	69	72	89	95
Index	0	1	2	3	4	5	6	7	8	9	10	11	12	13	14	15	16

The index *middle* is now calculated to be 5 ((4 + 7)/2).

The element at index 5 (15) is smaller than 34, so we call the *recursiveBinarySearch* method, searching the right subarray, highlighted here.

Value	3	6	7	8	12	15	22	36	45	48	51	53	64	69	72	89	95
Index	0	1	2	3	4	5	6	7	8	9	10	11	12	13	14	15	16

The index *middle* is now calculated to be 6 ((6 + 7)/2).

The element at index 6 (22) is smaller than 34, so we call the *recursiveBinarySearch* method, searching the right subarray, highlighted here.

Value	3	6	7	8	12	15	22	36	45	48	51	53	64	69	72	89	95
Index	0	1	2	3	4	5	6	7	8	9	10	11	12	13	14	15	16

The index *middle* is now calculated to be 7 ((7 + 7)/2).

The element at index 7 (36) is larger than 34, so we call the *recursiveBinarySearch* method, searching the left subarray. However, that left subarray is empty. We have not found 34, so we return −1.

Skill Practice
with these end-of-chapter questions

13.9.1 Multiple Choice Exercises

Questions 2, 6, 7, 8

13.9.2 Reading and Understanding Code

Questions 9, 10, 11, 12, 13, 14, 15, 20, 21, 22, 23

13.9.3 Fill In the Code

Questions 24, 25, 26, 27, 28

13.9.4 Identifying Errors in Code

Questions 29, 30, 31, 32

13.9.5 Debugging Area

Questions 33, 34, 35, 36, 37, 38

13.9.6 Write a Short Program

Questions 42, 43, 45, 46, 47

13.9.8 Technical Writing

Question 63

13.6   Programming Activity 2: The Towers of Hanoi

A well-known problem that lends itself to an elegant recursive formulation is the Towers of Hanoi. Here it is:

- There are three towers, which we can represent as the source tower, the temporary tower, and the destination tower.

- We have a stack of n disks piled on the source tower; all the disks have a different diameter. The largest disk is at the bottom and the smallest disk is at the top.

- The goal is to transfer all the disks, one at a time, to the destination tower using all three towers for help. No larger disk can be placed on top of a smaller one.

The recursive solution to the problem for the general case ($n >= 1$) is as follows:

1. Transfer the top ($n - 1$) disks from the source tower to the temporary tower.

2. Transfer the one remaining disk (the largest) from the source tower to the destination tower.

3. Transfer the ($n - 1$) disks from the the temporary tower to the destination tower.

The base case, when $n = 0$ (there are 0 disks to transfer), is to do nothing.

The first and third operations are simply recursive calls using a smaller number of disks $(n - 1)$ than the original problem.

In the case of $n = 5$, Figures 13.13–13.16 illustrate the recursive solution and formulation. In the figures, the left, middle, and right towers represent the source, temporary, and destination towers, respectively.

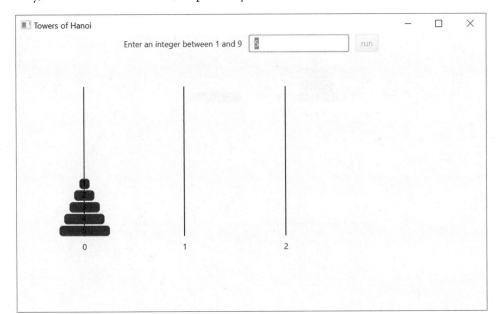

Figure 13.13

Starting Position with Five Disks

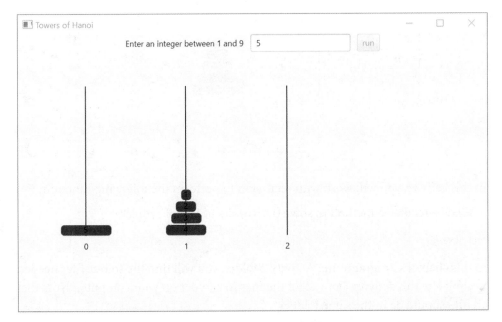

Figure 13.14

Position After Step 1

Figure 13.15

Position After
Step 2

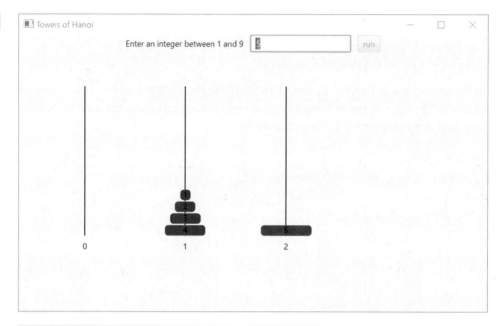

Figure 13.16

Position After
Step 3

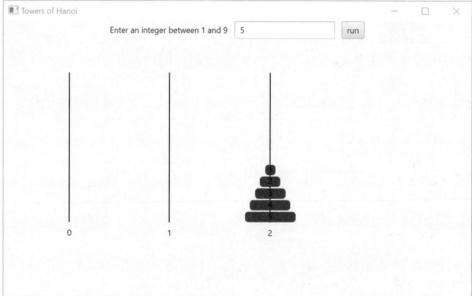

In this activity, you will work with recursion to perform the following function:

Code a recursive method to solve the Towers of Hanoi problem

Instructions

In this chapter's Programming Activity 2 folder, you will find the source files needed to complete this activity. Copy all of the files to a folder on your computer. Note that all files should be in the same folder.

Open the *HanoiDrawing.java* source file. Searching for five asterisks (*****) in the source code will position you to the code section where you will add your code. In this task, you will fill in the code inside the *recursiveTOfH* method to solve the Towers of Hanoi problem. Example 13.9 shows the section of the *HanoiDrawing* source code where you will add your code.

```java
public void recursiveTOfH( int numDisks, int fromTower,
                           int toTower, int useTower )
{
   // ***** Student writes the body of this method *****
   //
   // Using recursion, transfer numDisks disks from the tower
   // fromTower to the tower toTower using the tower
   // useTower

   // The disks are numbered as follows: if we started with n disks,
   //    the disk at the top is disk # 1
   //    and the disk at the bottom is disk # n

   // We call the moveDisk method inside the body of this method

   // The moveDisk method moves one disk and takes 3 arguments:
   //    an int, representing the disk number to be moved
   //    an int, representing the tower to move the disk from
   //    an int, representing the tower to move the disk to

   // So if these three variables are:
   //    diskNumber, fromTower, and toTower
   //    then the call to moveDisks will be:

   //    moveDisk( diskNumber, fromTower, toTower );

   if ( numDisks > 0 )
   {
   // Student code starts here
   // 1. Move ( numDisks - 1 ) disks from fromTower
   //    to useTower using toTower
   // 2. Move one disk from fromTower to toTower
   //    Print a message to the screen, then
   //    call moveDisk in order to animate.

   // 3. Move ( numDisks - 1 ) disks from useTower to toTower
   //    using fromTower

   }

   // Base case: 0 disks to move ==> do nothing
```

```
//
// end of student code
//
}
```

EXAMPLE 13.9   Location of Student Code in *HanoiDrawing*

The framework will animate your code so that you get some feedback on the correctness of your code. It will display the disks being moved from one tower to another until the whole set of disks has been moved from the left tower to the right tower. Code to enforce the rules has already been written.

To test your code, compile *HanoiDrawing.java* and run *HanoiApplication*; when the program begins, a text box will allow you to enter the number of disks as shown in Figure 13.17.

Click "run" to animate your code.

If you enter an integer less than 1 or greater than 9, the program will use a default value of 4. If you enter 5, as shown in Figure 13.17, the first screen will be as shown in Figure 13.13.

Task Instructions

- In the file *HanoiDrawing.java* the *recursiveTOfH* method header is:

```
public void recursiveTOfH( int numDisks, int fromTower,
                           int toTower, int useTower )
```

Figure 13.17

Opening Window

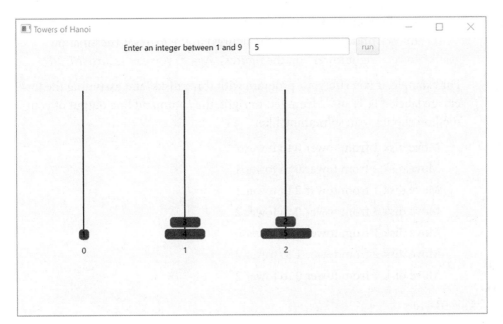

Figure 13.18

An Intermediate
Position in the
Animation

- This method takes four parameters: *numDisks*, representing the number of disks to be moved, and 3 *ints* representing the tower to move the disks from, the tower to move the disks to, and the tower to use to accomplish that task of moving *numDisks* disks from tower *fromTower* to tower *toTower*. For instance, with five disks, our method call in the *main* method is:

```
recursiveTOfH( 5, 0, 2, 1 );
```

- The preceding method call is interpreted as: move 5 disks from tower 0 to tower 2, using tower 1 as a temporary holding tower.

- Your code goes in three places, all of them inside the *if* statement.

  1. First, you need to move all the disks except the bottom one from the *fromTower* (source tower, "left tower" on the figures) to the *useTower* (temporary tower, "middle tower" on the figures) using the *toTower* ("destination tower, right tower" on the figures). You do this by calling *recursiveTOfH* with the appropriate arguments.

  2. Then, you need to move the bottom disk from the *fromTower* (source tower, "left tower" on the figures) to the *toTower* (destination tower, "right tower" on the figures). To track your progress, output the move to the command line ("Move disk *x* from tower *y* to tower *z*"). You also need to call the *moveDisk* method so that the code animates. The API of *moveDisk* is explained in Example 13.9.

3. Finally, you need to move all the disks from the *useTower* (temporary tower, "middle tower" on the figures) to the *toTower* (destination tower, "right tower" on the figures). Again, you call *recursiveTOfH.*

For example, if you run your program with three disks, and assuming the towers are labeled 0, 1, and 2 from left to right, the command line output of your method should read something like:

Move disk 1 from tower 0 to tower 2

Move disk 2 from tower 0 to tower 1

Move disk 1 from tower 2 to tower 1

Move disk 3 from tower 0 to tower 2

Move disk 1 from tower 1 to tower 0

Move disk 2 from tower 1 to tower 2

Move disk 1 from tower 0 to tower 2

Troubleshooting

If your method implementation does not animate or animates incorrectly, check these items:

- Check the feedback on the output to see if your code violates the rules.
- Verify that you coded the first recursive call correctly.
- Verify that you coded the second recursive call correctly.

DISCUSSION QUESTIONS   ?

1. **What is the base case for the method?**

2. **As the number of disks increases, what happens to the time it takes for the method to run?**

13.7   Recursion Versus Iteration

Recursion and iteration are different approaches to solving a problem.

- A recursive function is implemented using decision constructs (e.g., *if/else* statements) and repeatedly calls itself.

- An iterative function is implemented with looping constructs (e.g., *while* or *for* statements) and repeatedly executes the loop.

Most programmers would not use recursion to print "Hello World" *n* times; they would simply use the following *for* loop:

```
for ( int i = 0; i < n; i++ )
    System.out.println( "Hello World" );
```

Similarly, a factorial method can easily be coded using iteration.

However, other problems, such as the Towers of Hanoi and the binary search, are more easily coded using recursion rather than iteration.

Often, the recursive solution to a problem is more elegant and easier to understand than an equivalent iterative solution. The main difficulty in coding a recursive method is the problem-solving part. The implementation, using Java or any other programming language, is easier than the equivalent code that uses iteration.

Another consideration when deciding to use recursion or iteration is the efficiency of the method at execution time. This is called the running time of the method, and is often measured in order of magnitude as a function of the size of the input.

For instance, for the Hello World example, the input is *n*. Using iteration, we will execute the loop *n* times, and the test condition of the *for* statement will be executed $(n + 1)$ times. When the running time of a method can be expressed as *n* multiplied by a constant value $(n \times c)$, we say that the order of magnitude of its running time is *n*; we say it is "big-Oh" of *n* or $O(n)$.

Using recursion, and considering Example 13.1, the *printHelloWorldNTimes* method will call itself *n* times before reaching the base case $(n = 0)$, for which the method does nothing. At each recursive call, the method performs a small and finite number of operations: it tests for *n* being greater than 0, and then prints "Hello World" once before calling itself; so it performs two operations before calling itself. Since it calls itself *n* times overall, the approximate running time of the method is $2 * n$, and therefore the order of magnitude of its running time is also $O(n)$ (orders of magnitude ignore constant factors).

So in this case, the running times of iteration and recursion are of the same order of magnitude. However, the overhead associated with all the recursive method calls will add to the running time. That will make recursion slower than iteration, which is often the case.

SOFTWARE ENGINEERING TIP

Readability and maintenance are important considerations when coding a method. If running times are equivalent and a recursive implementation is easier to understand than the equivalent iterative implementation, choose recursion over iteration; otherwise, iteration is generally preferred.

CHAPTER REVIEW

13.8   Chapter Summary

- The idea of recursion is to convert or reduce a bigger problem to a smaller, similar problem. The relationship between the bigger problem and the smaller problem is called the general case.

- By reducing the size of a problem to a smaller problem recursively, we eventually arrive at a small problem that is easy to solve. That small problem is called the base case.

- Solving a problem using recursion typically involves coding a recursive method.

- A recursive method

  - can be a *static* method or an instance method,

  - can take 0, 1, or more parameters, and

  - can be a *void* or a value-returning method.

- A recursive method calls itself.

- Problem solving using recursion involves two steps: generating a recursive formulation of the problem for the general case, and solving the base case(s).

- There can be one or more base cases.

- Most base cases are simple, but some can be more complex.

- Most general cases are simple, but some can be more complex.

- A recursive method calls itself repeatedly until a base case is reached.

- A recursive method typically includes an *if/else* statement that tests for the base case.

- If the recursive method does not test for the base case, calling the method will typically result in a stack overflow run-time error.

- Recursion is typically an alternative to iteration. The coding of a recursive method is typically compact and elegant. However, a recursive method may not be as efficient as its iterative equivalent.

13.9 Exercises, Problems, and Projects

13.9.1 Multiple Choice Exercises

1. A recursive method
   - ❏ is always a *static* method.
   - ❏ is never a *static* method.
   - ❏ may or may not be *static*.

2. A recursive method
   - ❏ is always a method with a *void* return value.
   - ❏ is always a value-returning method.
   - ❏ can be either of the above.

3. When formulating a recursive solution, what should we consider?
   - ❏ base cases and general case
   - ❏ base cases only
   - ❏ general case only

4. A recursive method
   - ❏ is a method containing a loop.
   - ❏ calls itself.
   - ❏ is part of the *java.recursion* package.

5. When coding a class that includes a recursive method, we need to import the *java.recursion* package.
   - ❏ true
   - ❏ false

6. If the base case of a recursive method is not taken into account when coding the method, the likely outcome is
   - ❏ a compiler error.
   - ❏ a run-time error.
   - ❏ no error.

7. If there are several base cases in a recursive method, omitting the code for one of them will result in

   ❏ a compiler error.

   ❏ a run-time error.

   ❏ no error.

8. If a recursive method makes a recursive call with the same argument that it was passed, the likely outcome is

   ❏ a compiler error.

   ❏ a run-time error.

   ❏ no error.

13.9.2   Reading and Understanding Code

For Questions 9 to 11, consider the following method:

```
public static int foo1( int n )
{
  if ( n == 0 )
    return 0;
  else if ( n > 0 )
    return foo1( n - 1 );
  else
    return foo1( n + 1 );
}
```

9. What is the value of *i* after the following code is executed?

```
int i = foo1( 0 );
```

10. What is the value of *i* after the following code is executed?

```
int i = foo1( 4 );
```

11. What does the *foo1* method do?

For Questions 12 to 15, consider the following method:

```
public static int foo2( int n )
{
  // n is guaranteed to be >= 0
  if ( n < 10 )
    return n;
```

```
    else
        return foo2( n - 10 );
}
```

12. What is the value of *i* after the following code is executed?

```
int i = foo2( 7 );
```

13. What is the value of *i* after the following code is executed?

```
int i = foo2( 13 );
```

14. What is the value of *i* after the following code is executed?

```
int i = foo2( 65 );
```

15. What does the *foo2* method return when the argument is a positive integer?

For Questions 16 to 19, consider the following method:

```
public static void foo3( String s )
{
    if ( s.length( ) > 0 )
    {
        System.out.print( s.charAt( s.length( ) - 1 ) );
        foo3( s.substring( 0, s.length( ) - 1 ) );
    }
}
```

16. What is the output of the following code?

```
foo3( "" );
```

17. What is the output of the following code?

```
foo3( "Hi" );
```

18. What is the output of the following code?

```
foo3( "Hello" );
```

19. What does the *foo3* method do?

For Questions 20 to 23, consider the following method:

```
public static int foo4( int n, int p )
{
    // p is guaranteed to be >= 0
    if ( p == 0 )
        return 1;
    else
        return ( n * foo4( n, p - 1 ) );
}
```

20. What is the value of *i* after the following code is executed?

```
int i = foo4( 6, 0 );
```

21. What is the value of *i* after the following code is executed?

```
int i = foo4( 5, 1 );
```

22. What is the value of *i* after the following code is executed?

```
int i = foo4( 4, 3 );
```

23. What does the *foo4* method return as a function of its two parameters, *n* and *p*?

13.9.3   Fill In the Code

24. This recursive method returns the number of times a given character is found in a *String*.

```
public static int foo( String s, char c )
{
  if ( s.length( ) == 0 )
    return 0;
  else
  {
    // your code goes here

  }
}
```

25. This recursive method returns "even" if the length of a given *String* is even, and "odd" if the length of the *String* is odd.

```
public static String foo( String s )
{
  if ( s.length( ) == 0 )
      return "even";
  else if ( s.length( ) == 1 )
      return "odd";
  else
      // your code goes here
}
```

26. This recursive method returns the sum of all the integers from 0 to a given number.

```
public static int foo( int n )
{
  // n is guaranteed to be >= 0
  if ( n == 0 )
      return 0;
```

```
    else
    {
        // your code goes here

    }
}
```

27. This recursive method returns *true* if its *String* parameter contains the charac-
    ters *A* and *B* in consecutive locations; otherwise, it returns *false*.

```
public static boolean foo( String s )
{
    if (        )              // base case # 1

    else if (      )      // base case # 2

    else                       // general case
        return foo( s.substring( 1, s.length( ) ) );
}
```

28. This recursive method squares a number until the result is greater than or equal
    to 1000, then returns the result. For instance, *foo(10)* returns 10000, *foo(6)*
    returns 1296, and *foo(1233)* returns 1233.

```
public static int foo( int n )
{
    // n is guaranteed to be greater than 1
    if ( n >= 1000 )              // base case

    else                          // general case

}
```

13.9.4   Identifying Errors in Code

29. You coded the following in the file *Test.java*. Where is the error?

```
int p = foo( 4 );
// more code here

public static int foo( int n )
{
    int p = foo( n - 1 );
    if ( n == 0 )
        return 1;
    else
        return ( n * p );
}
```

30. You coded the following method. Where is the error?

```java
public static double foo( int n )
{
  if ( n == 0 )
    return 1.0;
  else if ( n < 0 )
    return foo( n - 1 );
  else
    return foo( n + 1 );
}
```

31. You coded the following method. Where is the error?

```java
public static boolean foo( int n )
{
  // n is guaranteed to be >= 0
  if ( n == 0 )
    return true;
  else
    foo( n - 1 );
}
```

32. You coded the following method. Where is the error?

```java
public static boolean foo( int n )
{
  // n is guaranteed to be >= 0
  if ( n == 0 )
    return true;
  else
    return foo( n );
}
```

13.9.5 Debugging Area—Using Messages from the Java Compiler and Java JVM

33. You coded the following in the file *Test.java*:

```java
// inside main
System.out.println( foo( 5 ) );
// more code here

public static int foo( int n )
{
  return ( n * foo( n - 1 ) );  // line 15
}
```

The code compiles, but when it runs, you get the following output:

```
Exception in thread "main" java.lang.StackOverflowError
at Test.foo(Test.java:15)
at Test.foo(Test.java:15)
at Test.foo(Test.java:15)
....
```

Explain what the problem is and how to fix it.

34. You coded the following in the file *Test.java*:

```
// inside main
System.out.println( foo( 5 ) );
// more code here

public static int foo( int n )
{
  if ( n == 0 )
    return foo( 0 );  // line 15
  else
    return ( n * foo( n - 1 ) );
}
```

The code compiles, but when it runs, you get the following output:

```
Exception in thread "main" java.lang.StackOverflowError
at Test.foo(Test.java:15)
at Test.foo(Test.java:15)
at Test.foo(Test.java:15)
....
```

Explain what the problem is and how to fix it.

35. You coded the following in the file *Test.java*:

```
// inside main
System.out.println( foo( 5 ) );
// more code here

public static int foo( int n ) // line 9
{
  if ( n == 0 )
    return 1;
  else
    System.out.println( n * foo( n - 1 ) );
}          // line 15
```

At compile time, you get the following error:

```
Test.java:15: error: missing return statement
}          // line 15
^

1 error
```

Explain what the problem is and how to fix it.

36. You coded the following in the file *Test.java*:

```
// inside main
System.out.println( foo( 5 ) );
// more code here

public static int foo( int n )
{
  if ( n == 0 )
    return 1;
  else
    return ( foo( n ) * ( n - 1 ) );
}
```

The code compiles, but when it runs, you get the following message, repeated many times, before finally stopping:

```
Exception in thread "main" java.lang.StackOverflowError
    at Test.foo(Test.java:15)
    at Test.foo(Test.java:15)
    at Test.foo(Test.java:15)
```

Explain what the problem is and how to fix it.

37. You coded the following in the file *Test.java*:

```
// inside main
System.out.println( foo( "Hello" ) ); // line 6
// more code here

public static int foo( String s )        // line 9
{
  if ( s.length( ) == 0 )
    return 0;
  else
    return ( 1 +
        foo( s.substring( 0, s.length( ) - 2 ) ) ); // line 15
}
```

The code compiles, but when it runs, you get the following output:

```
Exception in thread "main" java.lang.StringIndexOutOfBoundsException: begin 0,
end -1, length 1
    at java.base/java.lang.String.checkBoundsBeginEnd(Unknown source)
    at java.base/java.lang.String.substring(Unknown source)
    at Test.foo(Test.java:15)
    at Test.foo(Test.java:15)
    at Test.foo(Test.java:15)
    at Test.main(Test.java:6)
```

Explain what the problem is and how it happens.

38. You coded the following in the file *Test.java*:

```
// inside main
System.out.println( foo( "Hello" ) ); // line 6
// more code here

public static int foo( String s ) // line 9
{
  if ( s.length( ) == 0 ) // line 11
    return 0;
  else
  {
    String temp = null;
    if ( s.length( ) > 1 )
        temp = s.substring( 0, s.length( ) - 1 );
    return ( 1 + foo( temp ) ); // line 18
  }
}
```

The code compiles, but when it runs, you get the following output:

```
Exception in thread "main" java.lang.NullPointerException
        at Test.foo(Test.java:11)
        at Test.foo(Test.java:18)
        at Test.foo(Test.java:18)
        at Test.foo(Test.java:18)
        at Test.foo(Test.java:18)
        at Test.foo(Test.java:18)
        at Test.main(Test.java:6)
```

Explain what the problem is and how to fix it.

13.9.6   Write a Short Program

39. Using recursion, write a program that takes a word as an input and outputs that word backward.

40. Using recursion, write a program that keeps prompting the user for a word containing a $ character. As soon as the user inputs a word containing the $ character, you should output that word and your program will terminate.

41. Using recursion, write a program that takes a word as an input and outputs that word with all characters separated by a space.

42. Using recursion, write a program that takes a word as an input and outputs the number of times the letter *a* is found in that word.

43. Using recursion, write a program that takes an integer value as an input and outputs the Fibonacci value for that number. The Fibonacci value of a number is defined as follows:

```
Fib( 1 ) = 1
Fib( 2 ) = 1
Fib( n ) = Fib ( n - 1 ) + Fib( n - 2 ) for n >= 3
```

44. Using recursion, write a program that takes a positive number as an input and keeps dividing that number by 3 until the result is less than 1, at which time output that result.

45. Using recursion, write a program that takes 10 numbers as inputs and outputs the minimum of these numbers.

46. Using recursion, write a program that takes 10 words representing Internet addresses as inputs and outputs the number of words containing .edu.

47. Rewrite Example 13.8, *RecursiveBinarySearch*, using an array sorted in descending order.

13.9.7   Programming Projects

48. Write a class with just one instance variable, a *String* representing a binary number. Write a recursive method taking only one parameter that converts that binary number to its decimal equivalent. Your program should include a client class to test your class.

49. Write a class with just one instance variable, an *int*. Your constructor should take an *int* as its only parameter. Write a recursive method that checks if that *int* is a multiple of 5. Your program should include a client class to test your class.

50. Write a class with just one instance variable, a *String* representing some HTML code. Your constructor should take a file name as its only parameter (you will need to make up some sample HTML files to test your program). Write a recursive method returning the number of occurrences of a specified character in the HTML *String*. Your program should include a client class to test your class. In particular, call the recursive method to check whether the sample files contain an equal number of < and > characters.

51. Write a class with just one instance variable, a *String* representing a password. Write a recursive method to check if the password contains at least one character that is a digit (0 to 9). Your program should include a client class to test your class.

52. Write a class with two instance variables, representing the same password. Write a recursive method that checks if both passwords are equal. Your program should include a client class to test your class.

53. Write a class with two instance variables, representing an old password and a new password. Write a recursive method that returns the number of places where the two passwords have different characters. The passwords can have different lengths. Write another, nonrecursive method returning whether the two passwords are sufficiently different. The method takes an *int* parameter indicating the minimum number of differences that qualify the passwords as being sufficiently different. Your program should include a client class to test your class.

54. Write a class with just one instance variable, an integer array. Your constructor should take an integer array as its only parameter. Write a recursive method that returns the sum of all elements in the array. Your program should include a client class to test your class.

55. Write a class with just one instance variable, an integer array. Your constructor should take an integer array as its only parameter. Write a recursive method that returns the maximum value of all the elements in the array. Your program should include a client class to test your class.

56. Write a class with the functionality of checking a list of names to determine whether the same name is present in two consecutive locations; you can assume that the list contains fewer than 100 names. The method solving that problem should be recursive. Your program should include a client class to test your class.

57. A professor has a policy to give at least one A in his or her class. Write a class that encapsulates that idea, including a recursive method checking for at least one A in a set of grades. You can assume that there are 30 students. Your program should include a client class to test your class.

58. Write a class with just one instance variable, an array representing grades between 0 and 100. You can assume that there are 15 grades. Your constructor should take an array as its only parameter. Write a recursive method that returns the average of all grades. Your program should include a client class to test your class.

59. Write a class with just one instance variable, an *int*. Your constructor should take an *int* as its only parameter. Write a recursive method that converts that *int* to a *String* representing that number in binary. Your program should include a client class to test your class.

60. Write a class potentially representing a *String* of binary digits (0s and 1s). Your constructor should take a *String* as its only parameter (that *String* may contain only 0s and 1s, or it may not). Write a recursive method that checks whether that *String* contains 0s and 1s only. Write another recursive method that converts that *String* to its decimal equivalent. Your method should be different from the one in Exercise 48: it should take two parameters, the *String* representing the binary number, and an *int* representing an exponent. Your program should include a client class to test your class.

61. Write a class with an *int* array as its only instance variable. Write a recursive method that uses the following recursive strategy in order to sort the array:

   ❑ Sort the left half of the array (this is a recursive call).

   ❑ Sort the right half of the array (this is another recursive call).

   ❑ Merge the two sorted halves of the array so that the array is sorted (there is no recursive call here).

62. Write a class that includes a recursive method that converts a prefix arithmetic expression to an infix arithmetic expression. You should assume that a prefix arithmetic expression uses this syntax:

   operator integerl integer2 integer3 …

   The corresponding infix arithmetic expression is:

   integer1 operator integer2 operator integer3 …

   The operator can be +, −, *, or /.

   For example, with this prefix arithmetic expression:

   − 6 123 45

your method should return the following infix arithmetic expression:

6 − 123 − 45

And for this prefix arithmetic expression:

+ 76543 12 4 5 6 7

Your method should return the following infix arithmetic expression:

76543 + 12 + 4 + 5 + 6 + 7

For simplicity, assume that there is just one space between the operator and the first integer and between the integers. Look up the documentation for the *Matcher* and *Pattern* classes and regular expressions. Your program should include a client class to test your program.

13.9.8 Technical Writing

63. Think of an example of a problem, different from the chapter problems, which can be solved by an iterative formulation and a recursive formulation. Discuss which one you would prefer to code and why.

13.9.9 Group Projects (for a group of 1, 2, or 3 students)

64. Consider a rectangular grid of integers. We are interested in computing recursively the largest sum of any path from a top position to a bottom position. A valid path is defined as follows:

❏ It should start at a number in the top row and end at a number in the bottom row.

❏ It should include a number in every row.

❏ From row i to row $(i + 1)$, a valid path can be created:

  ▪ down vertically (in the same column)

  ▪ down diagonally one column to the left (if possible)
  ▪ down diagonally one column to the right (if possible)

For instance, let's assume we have the following rectangle of numbers:

2	5	17	12	3
15	8	4	11	10
9	18	6	20	16
14	13	12	1	7

Note: Your program should accept any positive number at any spot within the rectangle.

Examples of valid paths are:

$2 \rightarrow 8 \rightarrow 18 \rightarrow 14$
$17 \rightarrow 4 \rightarrow 18 \rightarrow 14$
$5 \rightarrow 4 \rightarrow 20 \rightarrow 12$
In this example, the path generating the largest sum is:

$17 \rightarrow 11 \rightarrow 20 \rightarrow 12$ for a total of $17 + 11 + 20 + 12 = 60$

Your program should accept from the user a rectangle of integers; to keep it simple, you can limit the size of the rectangle to a maximum of 10 columns by 20 rows. Your program should, recursively, compute and output the path that generates the largest sum.

65. Write a class with an *int* array as its only instance variable. Write a recursive method that uses the following Merge Sort algorithm in order to sort the array.

   ❑ If the array has only 1 element, then the array is already sorted and there is nothing to do; otherwise:

   ▪ Sort the left half of the array by calling the method (this is a recursive call).

   ▪ Sort the right half of the array by calling the method (this is another recursive call).

   ▪ Merge the two sorted half arrays into one so that the resulting array is sorted.

Because of the recursive nature of this method, you need to think about what parameters that method should have, in addition to the array itself. In fact, at each recursive call, the method sorts a subarray of the original array; so your parameters should define a subarray within the original array.

To merge the two sorted half arrays into one resulting sorted array, you can loop through both half arrays and compare each pair of elements, and place the smaller of the two in the resulting array. The following is an example of what an array would look like before and after the various steps of the algorithm.

The unsorted array, before applying the algorithm:

Value	78	12	37	25	24	20	55	9
Index	0	1	2	3	4	5	6	7

The array, after the first recursive call. The left half array, from index 0 to index 3, is sorted.

Value	12	25	37	78	24	20	55	9
Index	0	1	2	3	4	5	6	7

The array, after the second recursive call and before the merging step. The left half array, from index 0 to index 3, and the right half array, from index 4 to index 7, are sorted.

Value	12	25	37	78	9	20	24	55
Index	0	1	2	3	4	5	6	7

The array after the merge step. The array is now sorted.

Value	9	12	20	24	25	37	55	78
Index	0	1	2	3	4	5	6	7

Here is an example of what the array and resulting array would look like during the merge step: The elements 9, 12, and 20 have been processed and placed at their correct place in the resulting array. We are now processing 25 from the left half array and 24 from the right half array. Note that during the merge step, we need a separate array to store the sorted elements.

The array:

Value	12	25	37	78	9	20	24	55
Index	0	1	2	3	4	5	6	7

The resulting array:

Value	9	12	20					
Index	0	1	2	3	4	5	6	7

For tracing purposes, add a statement as you enter the method to out-put that the method is called; include the starting and ending indexes delimiting the subarray on which the method is called. Also, add a counter to track how many times the method is called as the recursive calls unfold. In your client program, use arrays with 4, 8, 16, 32, and 64 elements. How many recursive calls are made in each case? More generally, if the array contains 2^n elements, how many recursive calls are made?

CHAPTER 14
An Introduction to Data Structures

CHAPTER CONTENTS

Introduction

As our programs execute, we often need a means to organize data in memory. Arrays are a convenient method to store multiple variables of the same data type. *ArrayLists* improve on arrays by dynamically expanding, as needed.

In fact, arrays and *ArrayLists* are just two examples of **data structures**, which are methodologies a program uses to store its data in memory.

An *ArrayList* dynamically adjusts its size by increasing its capacity whenever it runs out of space. In fact, in many cases, the capacity exceeds the space needed to hold our elements. Then memory is allocated but not used. Obviously, this is not an efficient use of memory space.

However, *ArrayLists* are useful in some situations, such as reading data from a file, where we don't know in advance how many items we will need to store in memory. Once the data is read, we know that the size of the *ArrayList* will not change further, so we can trim the capacity of the *ArrayList* to its current size using the *trimToSize* method, thus releasing the unused memory.

In other situations, however, the number of data items may dynamically increase or decrease as the program executes. For these cases, we need a data structure that efficiently grows and shrinks as items are added and removed.

A new data structure that we will illustrate in this chapter is the **linked list**, which can expand (or shrink) one object at a time, keeping the size of the list to a minimum at all times. An advantage, then, of linked lists is that they do not consume unnecessary memory.

14.1   Linked Lists

14.1.1   Linked-List Concepts and Structure

A **linked list** can be thought of as a chain of linked nodes.

A **node** is an object with two attributes:

- data—The data can be a primitive data type (for example, an *int*), or it can be a reference to an object of a specified class.

- the location of the next node in the chain—We say that a node "**points to**" or "**refers to**" the next node.

Figure 14.1 shows how we can visualize a node containing the integer value 5. The arrow points to the next node in the list.

In the last node of the list, the location of the next node contains the value *null*, to indicate that there are no more nodes in the list.

Figure 14.2 illustrates a linked list of four video game players. The object data stored at each node has the following attributes: the player's ID, the player's name, and the name of the player's favorite game.

From the standpoint of program design, this linked list can be implemented using three classes:

- a *Player* class, encapsulating a player
- a *PlayerNode* class, encapsulating a node
- a *PlayerLinkedList* class, encapsulating the linked list

In the *Player* class, we will have three instance variables:

- an *int* storing the user ID of the player
- a *String* storing the name of the player
- a *String* storing the name of the player's favorite game

Often, a node class is designed in a general manner to store a generic *Object*. Implementing a list of generic *Objects* has the advantage of reusability; indeed, we could instantiate the list with any type of *Object* we want. In this chapter, we will first implement a linked list of the primitive type, *int*, then a linked list of *Player* objects, and then a linked list of generic *Objects*.

In the *IntegerNode* class, we have two instance variables:

- an *int*
- an *IntegerNode* object reference, representing the next node

Thus, the *IntegerNode* class is defined using an object reference of its own type. Indeed, one of its instance variables is an *IntegerNode* object reference.

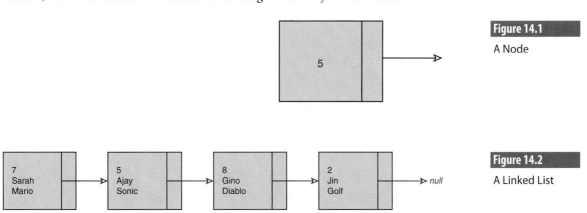

Figure 14.1

A Node

Figure 14.2

A Linked List

We define our two instance variables using the following statements:

```
private int data;
private IntegerNode next;
```

Based on this definition of the *IntegerNode* class, we need only one instance variable in the linked-list class, a reference to the first node, which we call the **head** of the linked list. Indeed, the first node will give us access to the second node, which in turn will give us access to the third node, and so on, until we reach the last node. We will know when we have reached the end of the linked list, because the reference to the next *IntegerNode* will have the value *null*.

Often, linked-list classes have another instance variable that holds the number of items in the linked list. Although the number of items can be calculated by looping through and counting all the nodes in the linked list, it is convenient to store the number of items as an instance variable. So our *IntegerLinkedList* class, encapsulating the linked list, will have two instance variables:

SOFTWARE ENGINEERING TIP
Include an instance variable in the linked-list class to store the number of items in the list for quick and direct access to that information as needed.

- an *IntegerNode* object reference, named *head*, representing the first node of the linked list

- an *int*, named *numberOfItems*, representing the number of items in the linked list

14.1.2   Linked-List Basics

Example 14.1 shows our *IntegerNode* class:

```
 1  /* The IntegerNode class
 2      Anderson, Franceschi
 3  */
 4
 5  public class IntegerNode
 6  {
 7    private int data;
 8    private IntegerNode next;
 9
10    /** default constructor
11     *    sets data to 0, and next to null
12     */
13    public IntegerNode( )
14    {
15      data = 0;
16      next = null;
17    }
18
19    /** overloaded constructor
```

```
20    *    @param data data value
21    */
22    public IntegerNode( int data )
23    {
24      setData ( data );
25      next = null;
26    }
27
28    /** accessor for data
29     *    @return    the value of the node
30     */
31    public int getData( )
32    {
33      return data;
34    }
35
36    /** accessor for next
37     *    @return    the reference to the next node
38     */
39    public IntegerNode getNext( )
40    {
41      return next;
42    }
43
44    /** mutator for data
45     *    @param    data   the new value for the node
46     *    @return  a reference to this object
47     */
48    public IntegerNode setData( int data )
49    {
50      this.data = data;
51      return this;
52    }
53
54    /** mutator for next
55     *    @param next the new value for next
56     *    @return a reference to this object
57     */
58    public IntegerNode setNext( IntegerNode next )
59    {
60      this.next = next;
61      return this;
62    }
63 }
```

EXAMPLE 14.1   The *IntegerNode* Class

The code for this class is straightforward. We code two constructors at lines 10 to 26. Both of these constructors set the value of *next* to *null*. This will be the desired action when a node is created. However, to allow a client (which will be the linked-list class) to reset the value of *next* as the list expands and shrinks, we provide the *setNext* method.

14.1.3   Methods of a Linked List

For our class encapsulating a linked list, we need to consider the following issues:

- We do not want client programs to change the head node of our list. Thus, we will not provide an accessor or a mutator for the head node.

- Client programs should not be able to change the number of items in the list. Only the methods of the class should update the number of items as we insert or delete items in the list. Thus, we will provide an accessor for the number of items in the list so that the client can view the number of items, but no mutator.

With a linked list, there is some basic functionality that we need to provide, such as

- insert an item,

- delete an item, and

- list, in order, all the items in the list, and return that list as a *String*.

Table 14.1 shows the APIs of the *insert*, *delete*, and *toString* methods.

In our linked list of *ints*, we do not store the *ints* in any predetermined order. Thus, there are only two logical places to insert a node: at the beginning and at the end of the list. Inserting at the end will consume CPU time, since we will have to loop through all nodes in the list to find the end. So we have decided to insert at the beginning of the linked list

TABLE 14.1   *IntegerLinkedList* **Methods**

Methods of the *IntegerLinkedList* Class	
Return value	**Method name and argument list**
void	insert(int value)
	inserts *value* at the beginning of the list.
boolean	delete(int value)
	removes the first item on the list that is equal to *value* and returns *true*. If there is no such item on the list, the method returns *false*.
String	toString( )
	returns a *String* representation of the list.

because it is easier and faster. Unless we run out of memory, it will always be possible to insert a new node at the beginning of a list, so our *insert* method has a *void* return value.

Other options for implementing a linked list include providing methods to insert at the end of the list, or at a specified position in the list, or at a position before or after a node containing a specified value or object.

When inserting a new *int*, our *insert* method performs the following steps:

1. Instantiate a new node containing the *int* to be inserted.

2. Attach that node at the beginning of the list; that is, make that node point to the previous head node. If the list originally was empty, that is, *head* has the value *null*, then the *next* field of the new node is given the value *null*.

3. Indicate that the new node is now the head of the list; that is, make *head* point to the new node.

4. Increase the number of items in the list by 1.

Figures 14.3a to 14.3d illustrate the first three steps.

There are many alternatives for deleting an item from a linked list. We can delete the first element or the last item, or delete an item based on specified criteria. Such a criterion can be the value of the item, or it can be the position of an item in the list. We will implement one *delete* method only: one that deletes an item based on its value.

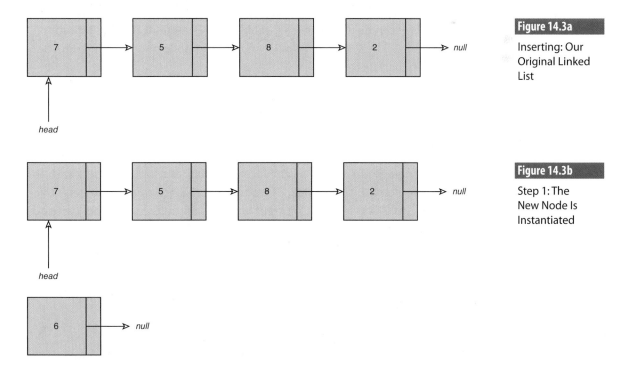

Figure 14.3a

Inserting: Our Original Linked List

Figure 14.3b

Step 1: The New Node Is Instantiated

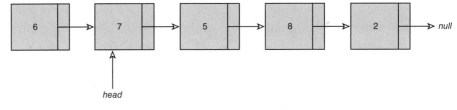

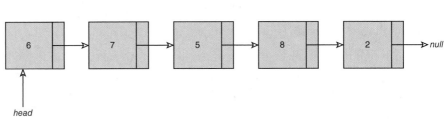

In order to delete an item, we will traverse the list searching for an item whose value matches a specified value passed as the argument of the *delete* method. **Traversing** a list means looping through the nodes in the list, one after the other, starting at the first node. If we find such an item, we will remove it from the list and return *true*. If we do not find the item, we will return *false*.

There are three possible outcomes when searching for such an item:

1. Such an item can be found and is located somewhere after the head node.

2. Such an item can be found and is located at the head node. Special care must be taken here. There will be a change in the head node of the list and our code will need to handle that.

3. Such an item cannot be found. In this case, no deletion can take place, and we will return *false*.

In the first case, when the node to delete is located after the first node in the list, we need to connect the node before the deleted node (the "previous" node) to the node after the deleted node. To do this, we replace the previous node's *next* field with the *next* field of the deleted node. Thus, as we traverse the list, we need to keep track of the previous node, as well as the current node. To do this, we maintain two node references, *previous* and *current*.

Once we have located the node to delete and it is not the first node of the list, we perform the following steps:

1. Set the *next* field in the *previous* node to the *next* field in the node to be deleted (*current*).

2. Decrease the number of items in the list by 1.

The *current* node becomes unreachable and is therefore a candidate for garbage collection.

Figures 14.4a and 14.4b illustrate deleting a node with the value 8, which is located somewhere in the middle of the list.

When the node to delete is the head node, we need to make the node pointed to by the deleted node the new *head* of the list. Thus, we perform the following steps:

1. Assign the *next* field of the *current* node to *head*.

2. Decrease the number of items in the list by 1.

Figures 14.5a and 14.5b illustrate deleting the first node in the list.

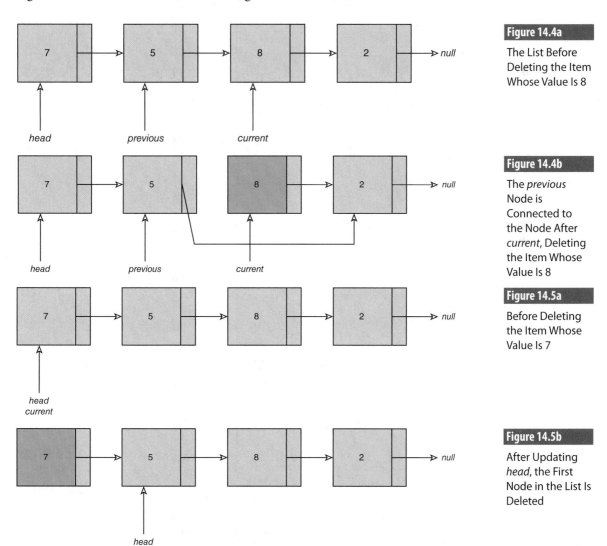

Figure 14.4a

The List Before Deleting the Item Whose Value Is 8

Figure 14.4b

The *previous* Node is Connected to the Node After *current*, Deleting the Item Whose Value Is 8

Figure 14.5a

Before Deleting the Item Whose Value Is 7

Figure 14.5b

After Updating *head*, the First Node in the List Is Deleted

Example 14.2 shows our *IntegerLinkedList* class.

```
1  /* The IntegerLinkedList class
2     Anderson, Franceschi
3  */
4
5  public class IntegerLinkedList
6  {
7    private IntegerNode head;
8    private int numberOfItems;
9
10   /** default constructor
11   *    constructs an empty list
12   */
13   public IntegerLinkedList( )
14   {
15     head = null;
16     numberOfItems = 0;
17   }
18
19   /** accessor for numberOfItems
20   *    @return   numberOfItems
21   */
22   public int getNumberOfItems( )
23   {
24     return numberOfItems;
25   }
26
27   /** insert method
28   *    @param  value    data to insert
29   *      inserts node at head
30   */
31   public void insert( int value )
32   {
33     IntegerNode nd = new IntegerNode( value );
34     nd.setNext( head );
35     head = nd;
36     numberOfItems++;
37   }
38
39   /** delete method
40   *    @param    value    the value to delete
41   *    @return   true if value was deleted from the list, false otherwise
42   */
43   public boolean delete( int value )
44   {
45     IntegerNode current = head;
```

```
46       IntegerNode previous = null;
47       while ( current != null
48              && current.getData( ) != value )
49       {
50         previous = current;
51         current = current.getNext( );
52       }
53
54       if ( current == null ) // not found
55           return false;
56       else
57       {
58         if ( current == head )
59           head = head.getNext( ); // delete head
60         else
61           previous.setNext( current.getNext( ) );
62
63         numberOfItems--;
64         return true;
65       }
66     }
67
68     /** toString
69      *   @return    values in list separated by a space
70      */
71     @Override
72     public String toString( )
73     {
74       String listString = "";
75       IntegerNode current = head;
76       for ( int i = 0; i < numberOfItems; i++ )
77       {
78         listString += current.getData( ) + " ";
79         current = current.getNext( );
80       }
81       return listString;
82     }
83 }
```

EXAMPLE 14.2   The *IntegerLinkedList* Class

The default constructor (lines 10–17) initializes the *head* and *numberOfItems* instance variables to *null* and 0, respectively. The *insert* method, coded from lines 27 to 37, inserts a node containing its parameter *value* at the beginning of the list. At line 33, we create a new node, *nd*, with the data *value*. At line 34, we connect *nd* to the first node in the list by setting its *next* field to the current head of the list. At line 35, we assign the new node, *nd*, to *head*, making it the first node in the linked list.

Figures 14.3a to 14.3d illustrate the impact on the list of lines 33–35. At line 36, we increment *numberOfItems* to reflect the addition of a node to the list.

The *delete* method, coded from lines 39 to 66, returns *true* if the deletion is successful and *false* if the deletion is not successful.

Using a *while* loop at lines 47–52, we walk through, or traverse, the list searching for a node containing *value*, our *delete* method's parameter. At lines 45 and 46, we declare and initialize two *IntegerNode* references, which we will use to track the current and previous nodes as we traverse the list. Because each node points only to the next node in the list, we can traverse the list in a forward direction only. Once we have reached a node, we do not have a way to backtrack to the previous node. Thus, as we traverse the list, we must remember the previous node because we will need to change the value of its next node. We update *previous* and *current* at lines 50–51 by assigning *current* to *previous*, then moving *current* to the next node in the list by calling the *getNext* method.

Once we find *value*, we will connect *previous* to the *IntegerNode* after *current*. If we have reached the end of the list—that is, *current* is *null* (line 47)—or if we have found *value* (line 48), we are ready to either return *false* or delete the node by updating the links in our list. At that point, we exit the *while* loop and skip to line 54.

Note that the order of the expressions in the *while* loop condition is critical. Expressions in a compound condition are evaluated left to right, so (*current != null*) is evaluated first. If this expression is *false* (that is, *current* is *null*), then the whole *while* loop condition cannot evaluate to *true*, so the second expression is not evaluated. This is important because the second expression uses *current* to call the *getData* method. If *current* is *null*, the evaluation of the second expression would generate a *NullPointerException*. In this way, we are taking advantage of Java's short-circuit evaluation of logical AND operations.

Thus, if we reversed the order of the expressions in the *while* loop condition, as shown here,

```
// incorrect ordering of expressions!
while ( current.getData( ) != value
        && current != null )
```

reaching the end of the list would always generate a *NullPointerException*.

At line 54, we test whether *current* is *null*, because a *null* value indicates that we exited the *while* loop because the list is empty or we reached the end of the list without finding *value*. Either way, the deletion is unsuccessful and we return *false* at line 55.

If *current* is not *null*, we have found *value*. We update the list and return *true* at lines 58–64. If *current* is the head node, we found *value* at the beginning of the list, so we need to update the *head* instance variable. In this case, we assign the node after *head* to *head* at line 59. Note that if there was only one element in the list before the deletion, *head* becomes *null* (at this point the list will be empty). Figures 14.5a and 14.5b show the impact of executing line 59 on the list (before and after).

If *current* is not the head node, we skip to line 61 where we set the node pointed to by *previous* to be the node after *current*. At this point, *current* is no longer part of the linked list.

At line 63, we decrement *numberOfItems*, to reflect that we now have one fewer item in the list. Finally, at line 64, we return *true*. Figures 14.4a and 14.4b show the impact of executing line 61 on the list (before and after).

Our last method, *toString*, is at lines 68–82. Our *toString* method traverses the list and returns a *String* containing the data from each item in the list. A *toString* method traversing the list is especially useful at the debugging stage, when we want to verify that we have properly added or deleted an element. We can test our code by calling *toString* before and after such operations.

14.1.4   Testing a Linked-List Class

Like any class that we design, we want to test the class before using it in a program. In particular, we should test two important methods: *insert* and *delete*. Furthermore, we want to test all possible scenarios.

Considering our *insert* method, which always inserts at the head of the list, we want to test a minimum of two situations:

- inserting into an empty list
- inserting into a nonempty list

As we will see later in the chapter, there are other types of linked lists and their *insert* methods may require more test cases than the ones previously mentioned.

After each insertion, we can use the *toString* method to verify that the items were inserted correctly.

For the *delete* method, we should test the following scenarios:

- attempting to delete from an empty list
- deleting an item in the middle of the list
- deleting an item stored in the head node

SOFTWARE ENGINEERING TIP
There are many ways to code the deletion of a node in the list. Try to write code that is easy to read and maintain.

- deleting an item stored in the last node in the list

- attempting to delete an item not in the list

After each deletion, we can use the *toString* method to check that the items were deleted correctly.

Example 14.3 shows a client program that tests the *IntegerLinkedList* class.

```java
1 /* The IntegerLinkedListTest class
2    Anderson, Franceschi
3 */
4
5 public class IntegerLinkedListTest
6 {
7   public static void main( String [ ] args )
8   {
9     // construct empty IntegerLinkedList
10    IntegerLinkedList numbers = new IntegerLinkedList( );
11    System.out.println( "Number of items in the list: "
12     + numbers.getNumberOfItems( ) + "\n" + numbers.toString( ) );
13
14    numbers.insert( 7 ); // insert in empty list
15    System.out.println ( "Number of items in the list: "
16     + numbers.getNumberOfItems( ) + "\n" + numbers.toString( ) );
17
18    numbers.insert( 2 ); // insert in list with one item
19    System.out.println( "Number of items in the list: "
20     + numbers.getNumberOfItems ( ) + "\n" + numbers.toString( ) );
21
22    numbers.insert( 5 ); // insert in list with two items
23    System.out.println( "Number of items in the list: "
24     + numbers.getNumberOfItems( ) + "\n" + numbers.toString( ) );
25
26    if ( ! numbers.delete( 8 ) )      // unsuccessful - not in list
27       System.out.println( "8 could not be deleted:" );
28
29    if ( numbers.delete( 2 ) )        // successful
30       System.out.println( "2 was successfully deleted:" );
31    System.out.println( "Number of items in the list: "
32     + numbers.getNumberOfItems( ) + "\n" + numbers.toString( ) );
33
34    if ( numbers.delete( 7 ) )        // successful
35       System.out.println( "7 was successfully deleted:" );
36    System.out.println( "Number of items in the list: "
37     + numbers.getNumberOfItems( ) + "\n" + numbers.toString( ) );
38
39    if ( numbers.delete( 5 ) )        // successful
```

```
40          System.out.println( "5 was successfully deleted:" );
41       System.out.println( "Number of items in the list: "
42          + numbers.getNumberOfItems( ) + "\n" + numbers.toString ( ) );
43
44       if ( ! numbers.delete( 8 ) )     // unsuccessful - empty list
45          System.out.println( "8 could not be deleted:" );
46       System.out.println( "Number of items in the list: "
47          + numbers.getNumberOfItems( ) + "\n" + numbers.toString ( ) );
48    }
49 }
```

EXAMPLE 14.3   The *IntegerLinkedListTest* Class

In this example, we instantiate the *IntegerLinkedList numbers* object at line 10, then traverse the empty list at lines 11–12.

We successively insert 7, 2, and 5 and traverse *numbers* after each insertion at lines 14–24.

After that, we test our *delete* method. At line 26, we attempt to delete the value 8; we know this will fail, as the output in Figure 14.6 shows.

We then delete in the middle of the list at line 29, at the end of the list at line 34, and at the beginning of the list (actually the only item left at that point) at line 39. Another attempt to delete is made at line 44, but at that time the list is empty, which causes us to execute line 45, as shown in Figure 14.6.

SOFTWARE ENGINEERING TIP
Testing all the methods in a linked list is critical to avoid errors at run time. Try to test all possible scenarios of all methods.

```
Number of items in the list: 0

Number of items in the list: 1
7
Number of items in the list: 2
2 7
Number of items in the list: 3
5 2 7
8 could not be deleted:
2 was successfully deleted:
Number of items in the list: 2
5 7
7 was successfully deleted:
Number of items in the list: 1
5
5 was successfully deleted:
Number of items in the list: 0

8 could not be deleted:
Number of items in the list: 0
```

Figure 14.6

Output of Example 14.3

CODE IN ACTION

Within the online resources, you will find a movie with a step-by-step illustration of linked-list methods. Click on the link to start the movie.

14.2   Linked Lists of Objects

Our next step is to design and code a linked list of objects, for example, *Player* objects, described earlier in the chapter.

Since each node in our list will store a *Player* reference, we start by defining our *Player* class, shown in Example 14.4.

```
 1 /* The Player Class
 2    Anderson, Franceschi
 3 */
 4
 5 public class Player
 6 {
 7   private int id;
 8   private String name;
 9   private String game;
10
11   /** constructor
12    * @param id     player's id
13    * @param name   player's name
14    * @param game   player's game
15    */
16   public Player( int id, String name, String game )
17   {
18      setID( id );
19      setName( name );
20      setGame( game );
21   }
22
23   /** accessor for id
24    * @return    id
25    */
26   public int getID( )
27   {
28      return id;
29   }
30
31   /** accessor for name
```

```
32    * @return name
33    */
34   public String getName( )
35   {
36      return name;
37   }
38
39   /** accessor for game
40    * @return game
41    */
42   public String getGame( )
43   {
44      return game;
45   }
46
47   /** mutator for Id
48    * @param id   new value for id
49    * @return     a reference to this object
50    */
51   public Player setID( int id )
52   {
53      this.id = id;
54      return this;
55   }
56
57   /** mutator for name
58    * @param name   new value for name
59    * @return       a reference to this object
60    */
61   public Player setName( String name )
62   {
63      this.name = name;
64      return this;
65   }
66
67   /** mutator for game
68    * @param game   new value for game
69    * @return       a reference to this object
70    */
71   public Player setGame( String game )
72   {
73      this.game = game;
74      return this;
75   }
76
77   /** equals method
78    *  @param o reference to object to compare to this object
```

```
79    *    @return   true if o is a Player object
80    *     and id, name, and game are equal in both objects; false otherwise
81    */
82   @Override
83   public boolean equals( Object o )
84   {
85     if (  ! ( o instanceof  Player ) )
86        return false;
87     else
88     {
89        Player  objPlayer = ( Player ) o;
90        return ( id == objPlayer.id && name.equals( objPlayer.name )
91               && game.equals( objPlayer.game ) );
92     }
93   }
94
95   /** toString method
96    *  @return  String representation of Player object
97    */
98   @Override
99   public String toString( )
100  {
101     return ( "id: " + id + "\tname: "
102             + name + "\tgame: " + game );
103  }
104 }
```

EXAMPLE 14.4 **The *Player* Class**

The code for this class is straightforward. We declared the three instance variables, along with a constructor, accessors and mutators, and the standard *equals* and *toString* methods.

Example 14.5 shows our *PlayerNode* class:

```
1 /* The PlayerNode class
2    Anderson, Franceschi
3 */
4
5 public class PlayerNode
6 {
7   private Player player;
8   private PlayerNode next;
9   /** default constructor
10   * initializes player and next references to null
11   */
12  public PlayerNode( )
13  {
```

```
14      player = null;
15      next = null;
16    }
17
18    /** overloaded constructor
19    * @param  player
20    * initializes player reference to player reference to Player object
21    */
22    public PlayerNode( Player player )
23    {
24      setPlayer( player );
25      next = null;
26    }
27
28    /** accessor for player
29    * @return player
30    */
31    public Player getPlayer( )
32    {
33      return player;
34    }
35
36    /** accessor for next
37    * @return next
38    */
39    public PlayerNode getNext( )
40    {
41      return next;
42    }
43
44    /**  mutator for player
45    *  @param player  new Player reference
46    *  @return        a reference to this object
47    */
48    public PlayerNode setPlayer( Player player )
49    {
50      this.player = player;
51      return this;
52    }
53
54    /**  mutator for next
55    *  @param next  new reference to next PlayerNode
56    *  @return        a reference to this object
57    */
58    public PlayerNode setNext( PlayerNode next )
59    {
60      this.next = next;
```

```
61     return this;
62   }
63 }
```

EXAMPLE 14.5   The *PlayerNode* Class

The code for this class is similar to the code of the *IntegerNode* class. The overloaded constructor allows the client to set the *Player* object, while the default constructor sets the reference for the *Player* object to *null*.

14.2.1   A Linked-List Shell

For our class encapsulating a linked list of *Player* objects, we need to consider the following issues:

- We anticipate having many linked-list classes. Therefore, it makes sense to set up a linked-list superclass from which our more specialized linked-list classes will inherit.

- We provide some basic utility methods, but we omit methods to insert or delete nodes in the list, because those methods will have different names and implementations, depending on the functionality of a given subclass.

- We do not intend to instantiate objects from our superclass; thus, we declare our superclass *abstract*.

Example 14.6 shows our *abstract ShellLinkedList* class. This class defines methods that will be common to all subclasses. For example, in addition to the default constructor and the accessor for the number of items in the list, we provide a method to determine whether the list is empty and a *toString* method that can be used to print each node in the list. We declare both instance variables as *protected* so that our linked-list subclasses inherit the head and number of items in the list.

Table 14.2 shows the APIs of *ShellLinkedList* constructor and methods.

SOFTWARE ENGINEERING TIP

Do not include a mutator method for the number of items. Only the linked-list class should alter the number of items as items are inserted or deleted. Including a mutator method for the number of items could allow the client to corrupt its value.

```
1 /* The ShellLinkedList class
2    Anderson, Franceschi
3 */
4
5 public abstract class ShellLinkedList
6 {
7   protected PlayerNode head;
8   protected int numberOfItems;
9
10  /** constructor
11   * sets head to null and numberOfItems to 0
```

```
12   */
13   public ShellLinkedList( )
14   {
15     head = null;
16     numberOfItems = 0;
17   }
18
19   /** accessor for numberOfItems
20    *  @return    numberOfItems
21    */
22   public int getNumberOfItems( )
23   {
24     return numberOfItems;
25   }
26
27   /** isEmpty method
28    * @return   true if no items in list; false otherwise
29    */
30   public boolean isEmpty( )
31   {
32     return ( numberOfItems == 0 );
33   }
34
35   /** toString method
36    * @return the contents of the list
37    */
38   @Override
39   public String toString( )
40   {
41     String listString = "";
42     PlayerNode current = head;
43     while ( current != null )
44     {
45       listString += current.getPlayer( ).toString( ) + "\n";
46       current = current.getNext( );
47     }
48     return listString;
49   }
50 }
```

EXAMPLE 14.6   The *ShellLinkedList* Class

We coded the method *isEmpty* at lines 27 to 33. It returns *true* if the list is empty, *false* otherwise.

The *toString* method, at lines 35–49, traverses the linked list until it reaches the end of the list, where *current* will be *null*.

SOFTWARE ENGINEERING TIP
Do not provide an accessor or mutator for the head node instance variable of the linked list. This will protect the head node from being accessed or changed outside the class.

SOFTWARE ENGINEERING TIP
Choose names for instance variables and methods that illustrate their function within the data structure. Your class will be easier for others and yourself to understand at maintenance time.

SOFTWARE ENGINEERING TIP
Provide a *toString* method that traverses the list. This is helpful in testing the other methods of the class. In particular, traversing the list after calling the insert or delete methods can verify that an item was correctly added or removed.

TABLE 14.2 *ShellLinkedList* **Constructor and Methods**

Constructor and Methods of the *abstract ShellLinkedList* Class	
Class	**Constructor and argument list**
ShellLinkedList	ShellLinkedList( ) constructs an empty list
Return value	**Method name and argument list**
int	getNumberOfItems( ) returns the number of items in the list
boolean	isEmpty( ) returns *true* if the list contains 0 items, *false* otherwise
String	toString( ) returns the contents of every node in the list

14.2.2 Generating an Exception

Now that we have a shell class for a linked list, we want to add some methods to perform operations on the linked list, such as inserting or deleting elements.

An issue may arise with the return value of the *delete* method. When deleting a node, we want to return the item that we are deleting. Indeed, we want to be able to delete a node based on the value of one or more of the fields of the object stored at that node, that is, the value of one or more of the instance variables of the *Player* class. For example, if the client wants to delete the first *Player* on the list with an ID of 5, we would then return that *Player* object to the client. If the list is empty or we cannot find a *Player* with ID 5, we do not want to return *null* because the client likely will attempt to use the returned object reference, which would generate a *NullPointerException*. A solution to this problem is to *throw* an exception when we are unable to delete the requested node. To do this, we create our own exception class, *DataStructureException*, which we use throughout this chapter.

It is good practice to define our own exception class as a subclass of another exception class. This way, our class inherits the existing functionality of the exception class, which simplifies coding the new class: we need to code only the constructor.

Example 14.7 shows our *DataStructureException* class, which *extends* the *NoSuchElementException* class, which is in the *java.util* package.

```
1  /* The DataStructureException Class
2     Anderson, Franceschi
3  */
4  import java.util.NoSuchElementException;
5
6  public class DataStructureException extends NoSuchElementException
7  {
8     /** constructor
9      * @param s error message
10     */
11    public DataStructureException( String s )
12    {
13       super( s );
14    }
15 }
```

EXAMPLE 14.7   The *DataStructureException* Class

The constructor for the class is coded at lines 8 to 14; it simply takes a *String* parameter and passes it to the superclass constructor. When one of our methods detects an error situation, such as an attempt to delete from an empty list, we will *throw* the exception using a statement like the following:

```
throw new DataStructureException( "Some error message here" );
```

The message we pass to the constructor will identify the type of error we detected.

The header of any method that *throws* the *DataStructureException* will add a *throws* clause, as in the following template:

```
accessModifier dataType methodName( parameter list )
                   throws DataStructureException
```

The *NoSuchElementException* class inherits from *RuntimeException*, and thus is not a checked exception. This means that the client does not need to use *try/catch* blocks when invoking any method that could throw a *DataStructureException*. Nevertheless, we will always use *try/catch* blocks so that when a *DataStructureException* occurs, the client will see our custom message and can better understand the source of the problem.

Now we are ready to expand our shell linked-list class with more meaningful methods.

14.2.3 Other Methods of a Linked List

In addition to our *insert* and *delete* methods, we also provide the functionality to retrieve, or **peek** at, the contents of a node, without deleting it.

Table 14.3 shows the APIs of the *insert*, *delete*, and *peek* methods.

Again, we will insert at the beginning of the list and our *insert* method has a *void* return value; our insert method works in the same manner as the insert method for a list of *ints*.

Our *delete* method will also delete a node based on specific criteria. With our list of *ints*, the criterion was simply the value of an item; here, the criterion can be the value of one (or several) instance variables of an item. We will implement one *delete* method only: one that deletes an item based on a specified value of its *id* field. The implementation of a *delete* method that deletes an item based on a specified value of its *name* or *game* field is similar.

If we find such an item, we will remove it from the list and return a reference to that item. When deleting from a list of *ints*, it made sense to return a *boolean* value rather than the value of the item, because we already knew the value of the item since it was passed as a parameter to the method. Here, we delete a node based on the value of the *id* field of an object, so we do not know the values of the other fields of that object. Thus, it makes sense to return an object reference rather than just *true* or *false*. If the item cannot be found, we will *throw* a *DataStructureException*.

TABLE 14.3 *PlayerLinkedList* Methods

Methods of the *PlayerLinkedList* Class	
Return value	**Method name and argument list**
void	insert(Player p)
	inserts *Player p* at the beginning of the list.
Player	delete(int searchID)
	returns and removes the first *Player* in the list with an ID equal to *searchID*. If there is no such *Player* in the list, the method throws a *DataStructureException*.
Player	peek(int searchID)
	returns the first *Player* on the list whose ID is equal to *searchID*. If there is no such *Player* in the list, the method throws a *DataStructureException*.

Otherwise, the mechanics of deleting a node within the list, whether that node is the *head* node or is in the middle of the list, are exactly the same as with our linked list of *ints*.

Example 14.8 shows our *PlayerLinkedList* class. This class *extends* and inherits the functionality of our *ShellLinkedList* class; thus *head* and *numberOfItems* are inherited instance variables.

```
1  /* The PlayerLinkedList class
2      Anderson, Franceschi
3  */
4
5  public class PlayerLinkedList extends ShellLinkedList
6  {
7
8    /** default constructor
9     *   calls constructor of ShellLinkedList class
10    */
11   public PlayerLinkedList( )
12   {
13     super( );
14   }
15
16   /** insert method
17    *    @param      p    Player object to insert
18    */
19   public void insert( Player p )
20   {
21     // insert as head
22     PlayerNode pn = new PlayerNode( p );
23     pn.setNext( head );
24     head = pn;
25     numberOfItems++;
26   }
27
28   /** delete method
29    *    @param        searchID     id of Player to delete
30    *    @return       the Player deleted
31    */
32   public Player delete( int searchID )
33                              throws DataStructureException
34   {
35     PlayerNode current = head;
36     PlayerNode previous = null;
37     while ( current != null
38              && current.getPlayer( ).getID( ) != searchID )
```

```
39    {
40       previous = current;
41       current = current.getNext( );
42    }
43
44    if ( current == null ) // not found
45        throw new DataStructureException( searchID
46                    + " not found: cannot be deleted" );
47    else
48    {
49      if ( current == head )
50        head = head.getNext( ); // delete head
51      else
52        previous.setNext( current.getNext( ) );
53
54      numberOfItems--;
55      return current.getPlayer( );
56    }
57  }
58
59  /** peek method
60   *   @param      searchID    id of Player to search for
61   *   @return     the Player found
62   */
63  public Player peek( int searchID )
64                throws DataStructureException
65  {
66    PlayerNode current = head;
67    while ( current != null
68            && current.getPlayer( ).getID( ) != searchID )
69    {
70      current = current.getNext( );
71    }
72
73    if ( current == null ) // not found
74      throw new DataStructureException( searchID
75                  + " not found: cannot be deleted" );
76    else
77    {
78      return current.getPlayer( );
79    }
80  }
81 }
```

EXAMPLE 14.8   The *PlayerLinkedList* Class

The default constructor (lines 8–14) calls the constructor of the superclass to initialize the *head* and *numberOfItems* instance variables. The *insert* method, coded from lines 16 to 26, is similar to our insert method for a linked list of *ints*, except that it inserts a *Player* object instead of an *int*.

The *delete* method, coded from lines 28 to 57, returns the *Player* deleted if the deletion was successful and *throws* a *DataStructureException* if the deletion was not successful.

The *while* loop at lines 37–42 is very similar to the *delete* method for our linked list of *ints*. We first traverse the list searching for a node containing a *Player* object whose *id* has the same value as *searchID*, our *delete* method's parameter.

Once we find a *Player* whose *id* field matches *searchID*, we will connect *previous* to the *PlayerNode* after *current*. If we have reached the end of the list, that is, *current* is *null* (line 37), or if we have found a *Player* whose *id* value is *searchID* (line 38), we are ready to either *throw* an exception or delete the node by updating the links in our list. At that point, we exit the *while* loop and skip to line 44.

At line 44, we test whether *current* is *null*, because a *null* value indicates that we exited the *while* loop because the list is empty or we reached the end of the list (without finding a *Player* whose id is *searchID*). If the deletion is unsuccessful, we *throw* a *DataStructureException* with an appropriate message at lines 45–46.

If *current* is not *null*, that means that we have found a *Player* whose *id* is *searchID*. We update the list and return the deleted *Player* at lines 49–55.

The *peek* method is coded at lines 59–80. We traverse the list in the same way as the *delete* method, except that because we will not delete a node, we do not need to mark the node before *current*.

If we do not find a node containing a *Player* whose id is *searchID*, we *throw* an exception at lines 74–75. If we find one, we return that *Player* object. In this way, the client can directly update the objects in the list.

14.2.4 Testing a Linked-List Class

Again, we want to test the class before using it in a program, and we want to test all possible scenarios, similarly to what we did with our linked list of *ints*.

After each insertion and deletion, we use the *toString* method to verify that the items were inserted and deleted correctly.

Example 14.9 shows a client program that tests the *PlayerLinkedList* class.

```
1 /* The PlayerLinkedListTest class
2    Anderson, Franceschi
3 */
4
5 public class PlayerLinkedListTest
6 {
7   public static void main( String [ ] args )
8   {
9     Player p1 = new Player( 7,"Sarah","Mario" );
10    Player p2 = new Player( 2,"Jin","Golf" );
11    Player p3 = new Player( 5,"Ajay","Sonic" );
12
13    // construct empty PlayerLinkedList
14    PlayerLinkedList players = new PlayerLinkedList( );
15    System.out.println( "Number of items in the list: "
16      + players.getNumberOfItems( ) + "\n" + players.toString( ) );
17
18    players.insert( p1 );  // insert in empty list
19    System.out.println( "Number of items in the list: "
20      + players.getNumberOfItems( ) + "\n" + players.toString( ) );
21
22    players.insert( p2 );  // insert in list of one item
23    System.out.println( "Number of items in the list: "
24      + players.getNumberOfItems( ) + "\n" + players.toString ( ) );
25
26    players.insert( p3 );  // insert in list of two items
27    System.out.println( "Number of items in the list: "
28      + players.getNumberOfItems( ) + "\n" + players.toString( ) );
29
30    Player temp;    // will be assigned the deleted item
31
32    try
33    {
34     temp = players.delete( 8 );            // unsuccessful
35     System.out.println( "Player deleted: " + temp );
36    }
37    catch ( DataStructureException dse1 )
38    {
39     System.out.println( dse1.getMessage( ) + "\n" );
40    }
41
42    try
43    {
44     temp = players.peek( 2 );               // test peek
```

```
45       System.out.println( "Player retrieved: " + temp );
46       System.out.println( "Number of items in the list: "
47         + players.getNumberOfItems( ) + "\n" + players.toString( ) );
48
49       temp = players.delete( 2 );            // delete in the middle
50       System.out.println( "Player deleted: " + temp );
51       System.out.println( "Number of items in the list: "
52         + players.getNumberOfItems( ) + "\n" + players.toString( ) );
53
54       temp = players.delete( 7 );            // delete the last item
55       System.out.println( "Player deleted: " + temp );
56       System.out.println( "Number of items in the list: "
57         + players.getNumberOfItems( ) + "\n" + players.toString( ) );
58
59       temp = players.delete( 5 );          // delete the first item
60       System.out.println( "Player deleted: " + temp );
61       System.out.println( "Number of items in the list: "
62         + players.getNumberOfItems( ) + "\n" + players.toString( ) );
63
64       temp = players.delete( 7 );          // delete from empty list
65       System.out.println( "Player deleted: " + temp );
66       System.out.println( "Number of items in the list: "
67         + players.getNumberOfItems( ) + "\n" + players.toString( ) );
68     }
69     catch ( DataStructureException dse2 )
70     {
71       System.out.println( dse2.getMessage( ) );
72     }
73   }
74 }
```

EXAMPLE 14.9   The *PlayerLinkedListTest* Class

In this example, we instantiate three *Player* object references *p1*, *p2*, and *p3* at lines 9, 10, and 11. We instantiate the *PlayerLinkedList* players object reference at line 14, then traverse the empty list *players* at lines 15–16.

We successfully insert *p1*, *p2*, and *p3* and traverse *players* after each insertion at lines 18–28.

After that, we test our *delete* method. Because our *delete* method *throws* a *Data-StructureException*, we use *try* and *catch* blocks when calling that method.

At line 34, we attempt to delete an item in the list whose *id* is 8; we know this will fail, and as the output shows in Figure 14.7, we execute the *catch* block at lines 37–40.

In the next *try* block, at line 44, we call the *peek* method to see if there is a *Player* whose *id* is 2. We traverse the list at lines 46–47 and can verify that the list has not been modified by the call to *peek*.

We then delete in the middle of the list at line 49, at the end of the list at line 54, and at the beginning of the list (actually the only item left at that point) at line 59. Another attempt to delete is made at line 64, but at that time the list is empty. This causes us to execute the second *catch* block at lines 69–72, as shown in Figure 14.7.

Figure 14.7

Output of
Example 14.9

```
Number of items in the list: 0

Number of items in the list: 1
id: 7    name: Sarah      game: Mario

Number of items in the list: 2
id: 2    name: Jin        game: Golf
id: 7    name: Sarah      game: Mario

Number of items in the list: 3
id: 5    name: Ajay       game: Sonic
id: 2    name: Jin        game: Golf
id: 7    name: Sarah      game: Mario

8 not found: cannot be deleted

Player retrieved: id: 2 name: Jin        game: Golf
Number of items in the list: 3
id: 5    name: Ajay       game: Sonic
id: 2    name: Jin        game: Golf
id: 7    name: Sarah      game: Mario

Player deleted: id: 2 name: Jin        game: Golf
Number of items in the list: 2
id: 5    name: Ajay       game: Sonic
id: 7    name: Sarah      game: Mario

Player deleted: id: 7    name: Sarah      game: Mario
Number of items in the list: 1
id: 5    name: Ajay       game: Sonic

Player deleted: id: 5    name: Ajay       game: Sonic
Number of items in the list: 0

7 not found: cannot be deleted
```

Skill Practice
with these end-of-chapter questions

14.14.2   Reading and Understanding Code

> Questions 14, 15, 16, 17, 18, 19, 20, 21

14.14.3   Fill In the Code

> Questions 22, 23, 24, 25, 26, 27, 28, 29, 30, 31, 32

14.14.4   Identifying Errors in Code

> Questions 33, 34

14.14.5   Debugging Area—Using Messages from the Java Compiler and Java JVM

> Questions 39, 40, 41, 42

14.14.6   Write a Short Program

> Questions 43, 44, 45, 46, 48, 50

14.14.8   Technical Writing

> Question 72

14.3 Implementing a Stack Using a Linked List

Imagine a group of college students on a spring break, sharing an apartment. After they eat, they typically pile up the dirty dishes in the kitchen sink. Another meal is consumed, and more dirty dishes are piled on top of the existing ones. At the top of the pile is the dirty dish that was placed there last. Soon the students run out of clean dishes, and somebody will have to start cleaning them. He or she will start by cleaning the dish at the top of the pile, that is, the last dish placed on the pile. That approach is called **last in, first out**, or **LIFO**.

A **stack** is a linear data structure that organizes items in a last in, first out manner. Figure 14.8 shows a stack of trays. The tray at the top of the stack was put on the stack last, but will be taken off the stack first.

A stack can be represented by a linked list. In a linked list representing a stack:

- we insert, or **push**, at the beginning of the list
- we delete, or **pop**, the item at the beginning of the list

Since we insert and delete at the beginning of the list, the item deleted is the last one that was inserted, reflecting the LIFO pattern.

Table 14.4 shows the APIs of the *push*, *pop*, and *peek* methods.

The *push* method is identical to the *insert* method of the *PlayerLinkedList* class discussed earlier, and is illustrated in Figures 14.3a to 14.3d.

The *pop* method is different from the *delete* method we coded earlier in our *PlayerLinkedList* class. In a stack, we always delete the first item in the list. Therefore, in a linked list implementing a stack, we do not delete an item based on the value of one of its instance variables. The *pop* method for our stack returns a *Player* object, the one stored at the head of the linked list. If our stack is empty, our *pop* method will *throw* a *DataStructureException* in order to avoid returning a *null* object reference.

The steps required to pop the first item are identical to the steps for deleting the first node in the *PlayerLinkedList*. That is illustrated in Figures 14.5a and 14.5b.

Figure 14.8

A Stack of Trays

top of the stack

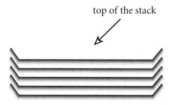

TABLE 14.4   *PlayerStackLinkedList* **Methods**

Methods of the *PlayerStackLinkedList* Class	
Return value	**Method name and argument list**
void	push(Player p)
	inserts *Player p* at the top of the stack.
Player	pop( )
	returns and removes the first *Player* of the list. If the list is empty, the method throws a *DataStructureException*.
Player	peek( )
	returns the first *Player* on the list without deleting it. If the list is empty, the method throws a *DataStructureException*.

Example 14.10 shows our *PlayerStackLinkedList* class. This class also *extends* and inherits the functionality of our *ShellLinkedList* class.

```
1  /* The PlayerStackLinkedList class
2     Anderson, Franceschi
3  */
4
5  public class PlayerStackLinkedList extends ShellLinkedList
6  {
7    // head and numberOfItems are inherited instance variables
8
9    public PlayerStackLinkedList( )
10   {
11     super( );
12   }
13
14   /** push method
15    *   @param p Player object to insert
16    */
17   public void push( Player p )
18   {
19     PlayerNode pn = new PlayerNode( p );
20     pn.setNext( head );
21     head = pn;
22     numberOfItems++;
23   }
24
25   /** pop method
26    *   @return    the Player object deleted
27    */
28   public Player pop( ) throws DataStructureException
29   {
30     if ( isEmpty( ) )
31       throw new DataStructureException
32                   ( "empty stack: cannot be popped" );
33     else
34     {
35       Player deleted = head.getPlayer( );
36       head = head.getNext( );
37       numberOfItems--;
38       return deleted;
39     }
40   }
41
42   /** peek method
43    *   @return    the Player object retrieved
```

```
44    */
45    public Player peek( ) throws DataStructureException
46    {
47      if ( isEmpty( ) )
48          throw new DataStructureException
49                  ( "empty stack: cannot peek" );
50      else
51      {
52          return head.getPlayer( );
53      }
54    }
55 }
```

EXAMPLE 14.10   The *PlayerStackLinkedList* Class

The *push* method, coded from lines 14 to 23, is identical to the *insert* method in the *PlayerLinkedList* class (Example 14.8).

In the *pop* method (lines 25–40), we first test if the stack is empty at line 30. If it is empty, we *throw* a *DataStructureException* with the appropriate argument at lines 31–32. If the stack is not empty, we delete the first item in the stack and return it. We call the *getPlayer* method from the *PlayerNode* class to get the *Player* stored at the head of the stack, and assign it to the *Player* reference *deleted* (line 35). The *deleted* reference is then returned at line 38. At lines 36 and 37, we perform the bookkeeping on the stack to reflect the deletion. We update *head* at line 36 and decrement *numberOfItems* at line 37.

COMMON ERROR TRAP
Before popping an item from a linked list representing a stack, always check if the linked list is empty. Not doing so results in a *NullPointer-Exception* at run time.

The *peek* method is coded at lines 42–54. If the list is empty, we *throw* an exception at lines 48–49. If the list is not empty, we return the *Player* at the head of the list at line 52.

Like our previous linked-list implementation, it is very important to test if the stack is empty before trying to delete a node; failure to do so will generate a *NullPointerException* at run time.

A similar program to Example 14.9 can be coded to test all possible scenarios when using the methods of the *PlayerStackLinkedList* class. This is proposed in the short program section of the exercises.

14.4 Implementing a Queue Using a Linked List

Imagine a line of people at an automated teller machine, or ATM, waiting to withdraw cash. The person at the front of the line is using the ATM. When a new customer arrives, the customer goes to the back of the line. As customers use the ATM, they exit the line, and the next customer moves to the front of the line. Thus, customers use the ATM in the order of their arrival times. We call this pattern "**first in, first out**," or **FIFO**.

A **queue** is a linear data structure that organizes items in a first in, first out manner.

Figure 14.9 shows a queue of people at an ATM. The person at the front of the queue arrived first and will use the ATM first. The person at the back arrived last and will use the ATM last. The next person to arrive will stand after the person currently at the back of the queue. That newly arrived person will become the new back of the line.

A queue can be represented by a linked list by providing the following operations:

- we insert, or **enqueue**, an item at the end of the list
- we delete, or **dequeue**, the item at the beginning of the list
- we *peek* at the item at the beginning of the list

Table 14.5 shows the APIs of the *enqueue*, *dequeue*, and *peek* methods.

back   front

Figure 14.9

A Queue of People Waiting at the ATM

TABLE 14.5   *PlayerQueueLinkedList* Methods

Methods of the *PlayerQueueLinkedList* Class	
Return value	**Method name and argument list**
void	enqueue(Player p)
	inserts *Player p* at the end of the list.
Player	dequeue( )
	returns and removes the first *Player* from the list. If the list is empty, the method throws a *DataStructureException*.
Player	peek( )
	returns the first *Player* on the list, but does not delete the *Player*. If the list is empty, the method throws a *DataStructureException*.

We can implement a queue using a linked list; however, we will make an important change. Because a queue inserts items at the end of the list, we will add an instance variable that represents the last node of the linked list. We call this the **tail reference**.

This way we will have direct access to the last node, without having to traverse the list. We will call that instance variable representing the last node in the list *tail*.

When inserting a new *Player*, our *enqueue* method will perform the following operations:

1. Instantiate a new node containing the *Player* to be inserted.

2. Attach that new node at the end of the list, i.e., make the last node in the list, *tail*, point to that new node.

3. Mark the new node so that it is the last node of the list, i.e., assign that node to *tail*.

4. Increase the number of items by 1.

Figure 14.10a to Figure 14.10d illustrate the *enqueue* operation.

Figure 14.10a

Enqueueing: Our Original Queue

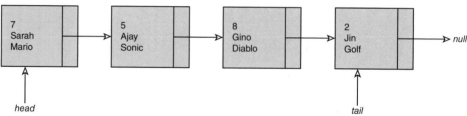

Figure 14.10b

Enqueueing: Our Queue and the New Node

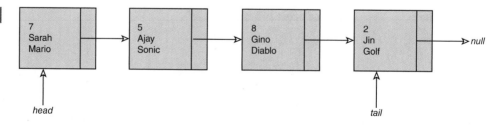

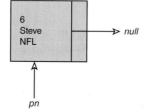

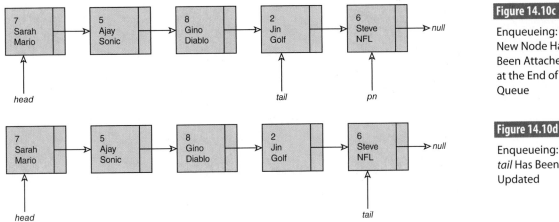

Figure 14.10c

Enqueueing: The New Node Has Been Attached at the End of the Queue

Figure 14.10d

Enqueueing: *tail* Has Been Updated

Example 14.11 shows our *PlayerQueueLinkedList* class. This class also extends and inherits the functionality of our *ShellLinkedList* class.

```
1  /* The PlayerQueueLinkedList class
2       Anderson, Franceschi
3  */
4
5  public class PlayerQueueLinkedList extends ShellLinkedList
6  {
7      // head and numberOfItems are inherited instance variables
8      private PlayerNode tail; // last node
9
10     public PlayerQueueLinkedList( )
11     {
12         super( );
13         tail = null;
14     }
15
16     /** enqueue method
17      * @param p Player object to insert
18      */
19     public void enqueue( Player p )
20     {
21         // insert as tail
22         PlayerNode pn = new PlayerNode( p );
23         if ( isEmpty( ) )
24         {
25             tail = pn;
26             head = pn;
27         }
28         else
```

```
29        {
30          tail.setNext( pn );
31          tail = pn;
32        }
33        numberOfItems++;
34    }
35
36    /** dequeue method
37     *   @return    a reference to the Player object deleted
38     */
39    public Player dequeue( ) throws DataStructureException
40    {
41      if ( isEmpty( ) )
42         throw new DataStructureException
43            ( "empty queue: cannot dequeue" );
44      else
45      {
46        Player deleted = head.getPlayer( );
47        head = head.getNext( );
48        if ( --numberOfItems == 0 )
49            tail = null;
50        return deleted;
51      }
52    }
53
54    /** peek method
55     *   @return    a reference to the Player object retrieved
56     */
57    public Player peek( ) throws DataStructureException
58    {
59      if ( isEmpty( ) )
60         throw new DataStructureException
61            ( "empty queue: cannot peek" );
62      else
63      {
64        return head.getPlayer( );
65      }
66    }
67 }
```

EXAMPLE 14.11   The *PlayerQueueLinkedList* Class

The constructor, from lines 10 to 14, calls the constructor of the superclass, and because it constructs an empty list, sets *tail* to *null*. The *peek* method is identical to the *peek* method of our *PlayerStackLinkedList* class, except for the message passed to the *DataStructureException* constructor.

The *enqueue* method, which we coded at lines 16–34, inserts an item at the end of the list. We first instantiate a *PlayerNode* object reference named *pn* at line 22, using the parameter *Player p* of the *enqueue* method.

Because we insert at the end of the list, we must properly handle the case when the queue is empty, in which case *tail* is *null*. We test if the queue is empty at line 23. If it is, we assign *pn* to *head* and *tail* at lines 25 and 26. After we execute these two lines, the queue contains one element, and that element is both the first and last item in the queue.

If the list is not empty, control skips to line 30, where we attach *pn* at the end of the list by setting the *next* instance variable of *tail* to *pn*. We then assign *pn* to *tail* in order to reflect that *pn* is now the last node of the list. Finally, and in all cases (empty list or not), we increment *numberOfItems* by 1 at line 33.

Figures 14.10a to 14.10d show the impact on the list of executing lines 22, 30, and 31 step by step.

It is important to test if a queue is empty when coding the *enqueue* method. Indeed, if the queue is empty, then both *head* and *tail* are *null*. The code

```
tail.setNext( pn )
```

at line 30 would, in this case, generate a *NullPointerException*.

The *dequeue* method, lines 36–52, is identical to the *pop* method of a linked list implementing a stack, except for lines 48 and 49. After decrementing *numberOfItems*, we check whether the list is empty. If so, we set *tail* to *null*.

A similar program to Example 14.9 can be coded to test all possible scenarios when using the methods of the *PlayerQueueLinkedList* class. This is proposed in the short program section of the exercises.

COMMON ERROR TRAP
Before inserting or deleting an item in a linked list representing a queue, always check if the linked list is empty. Not doing so results in a *NullPointer-Exception* at run time.

Skill Practice
with these end-of-chapter questions

14.14.1 Multiple Choice Exercises

Questions 2, 3, 4, 5, 6, 7

14.14.6 Write a Short Program

Questions 52, 53

14.14.8 Technical Writing

Question 73

14.5 Array Representation of Stacks

Earlier in this chapter, we discussed how a stack can be represented by a linked list. Since a stack is a last in, first out data structure, we coded the *push* (insert) and *pop* (delete) methods of the linked list to insert or delete at the beginning of the list. Linked lists offer the advantage of being expandable one object at a time, so we do not have to worry about running out of capacity.

However, if we know in advance that the number of objects on a stack will always be less than some maximum number, we can represent the stack using an array, which is easier to implement.

Table 14.6 shows the APIs of the *push*, *pop*, and *peek* methods for a stack implemented using an array.

To match the LIFO functionality of a stack, we instantiate the array with the maximum number of elements. We add items to the stack starting at index 0, storing the items in adjacent locations in the array. To keep track of the array index of the last element inserted, we maintain an index **top**, short for "top of the stack." We always remove (*pop*) the item at the top of the stack.

To push an item onto the stack, we increment the value of *top* by 1 and store the element at the new *top* index. To pop an item from the stack, we return the item at index *top* and decrement the value of *top* by 1.

Figure 14.11a shows how we can visualize a stack of *Players*. Figure 14.11b and 14.11c show the stack after pushing a *Player* (6, *Steve*, *NFL*) and then popping one

TABLE 14.6 *ArrayStack* Methods

Methods of the *ArrayStack* Class	
Return value	**Method name and argument list**
boolean	push(Player p)
	inserts *Player p* at the top of the stack, if the stack is not full. Returns *true* if the insertion was successful; *false* otherwise.
Player	pop( )
	removes and returns the *Player* at the top of the stack, if the stack is not empty. If the stack is empty, the method throws a *DataStructureException*.
Player	peek( )
	returns the *Player* at the top of the stack if the stack is not empty. If the stack is empty, the method throws a *DataStructureException*.

element. Figure 14.11c shows that the array element at index 3 is still *Player* (6, *Steve*, *NFL*), but that is irrelevant. Since *top* has the value 2, the element at index 3 is not on the stack. When the next item is pushed onto the stack, we will reuse that element.

One disadvantage of implementing a stack with an array is that the array has a fixed size, and it is possible that the array can be filled completely with elements of the stack. Thus, our *push* method needs to test if the array is full before pushing an

	index	*Player* object
top	2	(8, Gino, Diablo)
	1	(7, Sarah, Mario)
	0	(2, Jin, Golf)

Figure 14.11a

Our Original Stack

	index	*Player* object
top	3	(6, Steve, NFL)
	2	(8, Gino, Diablo)
	1	(7, Sarah, Mario)
	0	(2, Jin, Golf)

Figure 14.11b

Our Stack After Pushing Player (6, Steve, NFL)

	index	*Player* object
	3	(6, Steve, NFL)
top	2	(8, Gino, Diablo)
	1	(7, Sarah, Mario)
	0	(2, Jin, Golf)

Figure 14.11c

Our Stack After Popping Once

element onto the stack. Similarly, our *pop* method needs to test if the array is empty before popping an element from the stack.

Example 14.12 shows our *ArrayStack* class.

```
1  /* The ArrayStack class
2     Anderson, Franceschi
3  */
4
5  public class ArrayStack
6  {
7    private static final int STACK_SIZE = 100; // maximum array size
8    private Player [ ] stack;              // array of Player objects
9    private int top;                 // last used index; top of the stack
10
11   public ArrayStack( )
12   {
13     stack = new Player[STACK_SIZE];
14     top = -1; // stack is empty
15   }
16
17   /** push method
18    * @param p Player object to insert
19    * @return    true if insertion was successful false otherwise
20    */
21   public boolean push( Player p )
22   {
23     if ( !isFull( ) ) // is there room to insert?
24     {
25       stack[++top] = p;
26       return true;
27     }
28     else
29       return false;
30   }
31
32   /** pop method
33    *   @return    the Player deleted
34    */
35   public Player pop( ) throws DataStructureException
36   {
37     if ( !isEmpty( ) ) // is there an item to delete?
38       return stack[top--];
39     else
40       throw new DataStructureException
41                    ( "Stack empty: cannot pop" );
42   }
43
```

```
44    /** peek method
45     *    @return    the Player at the top of the stack
46     */
47    public Player peek( ) throws DataStructureException
48    {
49      if ( !isEmpty( ) ) // stack is not empty
50        return stack[top];
51      else
52        throw new DataStructureException
53                    ( "Stack empty: cannot peek");
54    }
55
56    /** isEmpty method
57     *    @return    true if stack is empty, false otherwise
58     */
59    public boolean isEmpty( )
60    {
61      return ( top == -1 );
62    }
63
64    /** isFull method
65     *    @return    true if stack is full, false otherwise
66     */
67    public boolean isFull( )
68    {
69        return ( top == ( STACK_SIZE - 1 ) );
70    }
71
72    /** toString method
73     *    @return the stack elements starting at top
74     */
75    @Override
76    public String toString( )
77    {
78      String stackString = "";
79      for ( int i = top; i >= 0; i-- )
80        stackString += ( i + ": " + stack[i] + "\n" );
81      return stackString;
82    }
83 }
```

EXAMPLE 14.12 The *ArrayStack* Class

We declare *STACK_SIZE*, *stack*, and *top*, our three fields at lines 7–9.

Stack is an array of *Players*. *STACK_SIZE* is the size of the array *stack*. *Top* represents the index of the element of the array *stack* that is at the top of the stack. The value of *top* will vary from *–1* (when the stack is empty) to *STACK_SIZE – 1* (when the stack is full).

In the default constructor, coded at lines 11–15, we instantiate *stack* and then set *top* to −1, which indicates that the stack is empty. When a client program pushes the first *Player* onto the stack, *top* will be incremented, so that the top of the stack will be the array element at index 0.

We coded the *push* method at lines 17–30. The *push* method returns *true* (line 26) if the stack is not full before we insert, and *false* (line 29) if it is, in which case we cannot insert. We test if the stack is not full at line 23. If it is not full, we use the prefix auto-increment operator to combine two operations at line 25: first increment *top* by 1, then assign *p*, the *Player* parameter of the *push* method, to the element at index *top*.

We coded the *pop* method at lines 32–42. The *pop* method attempts to delete and return a *Player* object from the top of the stack. The method *throws* a *DataStructure-Exception* at lines 40–41 if the stack is empty, in which case we cannot pop. If it is not empty, we use the postfix auto-decrement operator to combine two operations at line 38: first return the *Player* stored at index *top* in the array *stack*, then decrement *top* by 1.

COMMON ERROR TRAP
Do not confuse the top of the stack with the last index in the array. Array elements with an index higher than *top* are not on the stack.

We have also coded a few other methods in this class. The *peek* method (lines 44–54) is similar to *pop*, except that it does not delete from the stack and it returns the element at the top of the stack. Again, this enables the client to directly update that object in the stack. The *isEmpty* and *isFull* methods are coded at lines 56–62 and 64–70, respectively. And the *toString* method, coded at lines 72–82, returns a *String* representation of the contents of the stack. Note that in that method, we loop from *top* to 0, not from *STACK_SIZE – 1* to 0.

As before, a program similar to Example 14.9 can be coded to test all possible scenarios on the methods of the *ArrayStack* class. This is proposed in the short program section of the exercises.

14.6 Programming Activity 1: Writing Methods for a Stack Class

In this activity, you will work with a stack represented by an array, performing this activity:

> Code the *push* and *pop* methods to insert onto and delete from a stack represented by an array of *ints*.

The framework will animate your code to give you feedback on the correctness of your code. It will display the state of the stack at all times. The result of your operation will be displayed, reflecting the value returned by your *push* or *pop* method. The items in the stack will be displayed in black while the array elements that are not part of the stack will be displayed in red.

Instructions

Copy the contents of the Programming Activity 1 folder for this chapter from the companion website for this text onto a folder on your computer. Open the

StackArray.java source file. Searching for five asterisks (*****) in the source code will position you to the code section where you will add your code.

In this task, you will fill in the code inside the methods *push* and *pop* to insert onto and delete from a stack. Example 14.13 shows the section of the *StackArray* source code where you will add your code. This example is different from the one in the chapter. The stack is an array of *ints*, not *Players*. The *isFull* and *isEmpty* methods have not been provided; you can code them or not, depending on how you want to implement the *push* and *pop* methods.

```java
/** push method
*     @param    value   value to be pushed onto the stack
*     @return   true if successful, false if unsuccessful
*/
public boolean push( int value )
{
 // ***** 1. Student code starts here *****
 // stack is an int array instance variable representing
 // the array that stores our stack

 // top is an instance variable representing
 // the index of the top of the stack

 // CAPACITY is a static constant representing
 // the size of the array stack

 // The push method adds the argument value
 // to the top of the stack, if it is possible
 // code the push method here
 // end of student code, part 1
}

/** pop method
*     @return   the value of the top element of the stack, if
*                successful
*/
public int pop( ) throws DataStructureException
{
 // ***** 2. Student code restarts here *****
 // stack is an int array instance variable representing
 // the array that stores our stack

 // top is an instance variable representing
 // the index of the top of the stack

 // CAPACITY is a static constant representing
 // the size of the array stack
```

```
// The pop method deletes the element
// at the top of the stack, if it is possible
// code the pop method here

 // end of student code, part 2
}
```

EXAMPLE 14.13   Location of Student Code in *StackArray* Class

To test your code, compile *StackArray.java* and run the *StackPracticeApplication* class, which contains the *main* method. When the program begins, a window will display the state of the stack, along with two buttons labeled "push" and "pop," as shown in Figure 14.12.

Enter a value into the text box, then click on the "push" button to insert onto the stack. Click on the "pop" button to delete from the stack. Close the window to exit the program.

If you successfully push 34, 56, 12, and 98 onto the stack, then pop once, the window will look like the one shown in Figure 14.13.

Troubleshooting

If your method implementation does not animate or animates incorrectly, check these items:

- Check the feedback in the window to see if your code gives the correct result.

- Verify that you updated the value of *top* correctly.

- Verify that you correctly coded the cases where the stack is full (*push* method) and the stack is empty (*pop* method).

Figure 14.12

Opening Window

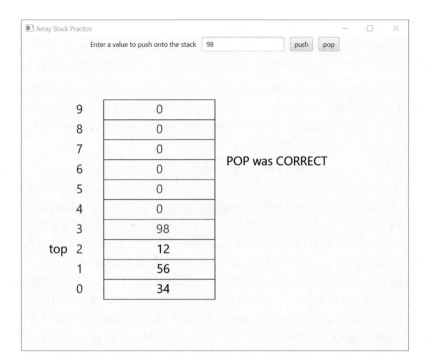

Figure 14.13

Sample Window
After Performing
Some Stack
Operations

1. **Explain how the array elements above the index *top* can have assigned values, but are still irrelevant.**

2. **Explain what happens if you do not test whether the stack is empty in the *pop* method or full in the *push* method.**

14.7 Array Representation of Queues

Earlier in this chapter, we also saw how a queue can be represented by a linked list. Again, if we know in advance that the number of objects in a queue will always be less than some maximum number, we can also use an array to represent the queue.

To match the FIFO functionality of a queue, we will need to keep track of two things:

1. the location of the back of the queue. This is the index of the last element enqueued or added to the queue. We will call the index of that element *back*.

2. the location of the front of the queue. That is the index of the element that will be dequeued or retrieved next. We will call the index of that element *front*.

The queue will be comprised of the elements whose indexes are between *back* and *front*, inclusive.

To dequeue, or delete from the queue, we will return the item at index *front* and increase the value of *front* by one. To enqueue, or insert an element in the queue, we will increment the value of *back* by one, and insert the element at the array index *back*.

There is one important problem in representing a queue with a standard array: the number of available elements for the queue in the array will shrink over time as we enqueue and dequeue, since enqueueing and dequeueing both advance their indexes toward the end of the array.

To illustrate this point, let's consider a queue represented by an array of eight elements. We start by enqueueing five players in this order: (5, *Ajay, Sonic*), (2, *Jin, Golf*), (7, *Sarah, Mario*), (8, *Gino, Diablo*), and (6, *Steve, NFL*). Since (5, *Ajay, Sonic*) was the first to be inserted in the queue, that *Player* is now at the front of the queue. (6, *Steve, NFL*), inserted last, is at the back of the queue. Thus, (5, *Ajay, Sonic*) will be stored at index 0 and (6, *Steve, NFL*) will be stored at index 4, as shown in Figure 14.14a. Suppose now that we dequeue once. *Front* now has the value 1, as shown in Figure 14.14b. The array element at index 0 is no longer in the queue and its value is irrelevant. Since we insert at the back, the array element at index 0 can no longer be used for the queue. If we dequeue again, *front* will have the value 2, and we will no longer be able to use the array element at index 1. As we keep enqueueing and dequeueing, the values of *back* and *front* keep increasing and we have less and less usable space in the array. Indeed, when *back* reaches 7, we will no longer be able to enqueue at all.

SOFTWARE ENGINEERING TIP
When implementing a queue as an array, think of it as a circular array.

There is a solution to this problem: deal with the array as if it were circular. After *back* reaches the last index of the array, we start enqueueing again at index 0. Thus, in a circular array, the next index after the last array index is 0. Let's say that at one point the *back* marker reaches 7 and the *front* marker is at 5. When we enqueue a new object, we will store that object at index 0, which is the "next" index after 7 if we imagine that the array is circular. In this way, our useful array capacity never shrinks and is always 8.

How do we know that we have reached the last array index and that the next index should be 0? We simply add 1 to the value of *back*, and then take that number modulo the size of the array, which we call QUEUE_SIZE.

Table 14.7 shows the APIs of the *enqueue* and *dequeue* methods.

Figure 14.15 illustrates a sequence of insertions and deletions in a queue of *Players* implemented as a circular array. When we begin, the queue is empty. The value of *front* is 0 and the value of *back* is *QUEUE_SIZE – 1*. When we enqueue the first item, that element is placed at index

```
( back + 1 ) % QUEUE_SIZE
```

which is now 0, and *back* will be given the value 0. If we enqueue again, the new element will be placed at index 1 and *back* will be given the value 1. If we enqueue two more items, they will be placed at indexes 2 and 3, respectively, and back will be

	index	*Player* object
	7	
	6	
	5	
back	4	(6, Steve, NFL)
	3	(8, Gino, Diablo)
	2	(7, Sarah, Mario)
	1	(2, Jin, Golf)
front	0	(5, Ajay, Sonic)

Figure 14.14a

Our Queue After Enqueueing the First Five Elements

	index	*Player* object
	7	
	6	
	5	
back	4	(6, Steve, NFL)
	3	(8, Gino, Diablo)
	2	(7, Sarah, Mario)
front	1	(2, Jin, Golf)
	0	(5, Ajay, Sonic)

Figure 14.14b

Our Queue After Dequeueing Once

TABLE 14.7   *ArrayQueue* Methods

Methods of the *ArrayQueue* Class	
Return value	**Method name and argument list**
boolean	enqueue(Player p)
	inserts *Player p* at the back of the queue if the queue is not full. Returns *true* if the insertion was successful, *false* otherwise.
Player	dequeue( )
	returns and removes the *Player* at the front of the queue. If the queue is empty, the method throws a *DataStructureException*.
Player	peek( )
	returns the *Player* at the front of the queue. If the queue is empty, the method throws a *DataStructureException*.

Figure 14.15

Starting with an
Empty Queue,
Four Successive
Enqueues
Followed by Two
Dequeues

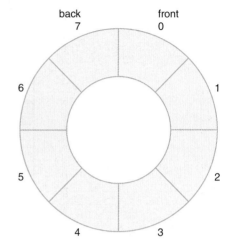

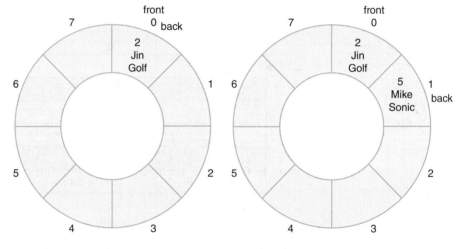

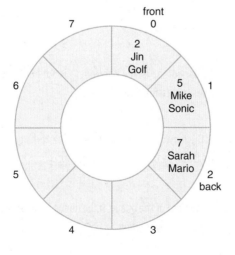

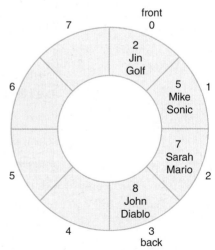

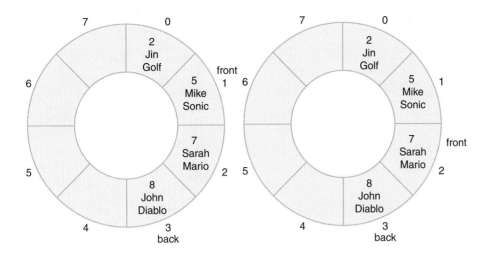

Figure 14.15

(continued)

given the value 3. If we then dequeue, we will return the item at index 0, and *front* will become 1. If we dequeue again, we will return the item at index 1, and *front* will become 2.

When we enqueue, we first need to check if the queue is full. When the queue is full, the relationship between *back* and *front* is:

```
( back + 1 - front ) % QUEUE_SIZE == 0
```

For example, in a full queue with 8 elements, the values of *front* and *back* could be 0 and 7, respectively, or they could be 5 and 4 or any other pair of values for which the expression above is *true*.

When we dequeue, we first need to check if the queue is empty. When the queue is empty, the relationship between *front* and *back* is the same as when the queue is full:

```
( back + 1 - front ) % QUEUE_SIZE == 0
```

Indeed, when there is only one item in the queue, *back* and *front* have the same index value. When we dequeue that last item from the queue, *front* will increase by 1 modulo *QUEUE_SIZE*, resulting in the preceding relationship between *front* and *back*. Figure 14.16 shows an example of an empty queue and a full queue.

So, how do we know if the queue is full or empty? In order to distinguish a full queue from an empty queue, we must add another instance variable to our class. We will keep track of the number of elements in the queue: if the number of elements is 0, then the queue is empty; if the number of elements is equal to the size of the array, then the queue is full.

COMMON ERROR TRAP
Do not confuse array indexes 0 and *QUEUE_SIZE − 1* with *front* and *back*. In a queue represented by a circular array, the indexes 0 and *QUEUE_SIZE − 1* are irrelevant.

Figure 14.16

An Empty Queue
and a Full Queue

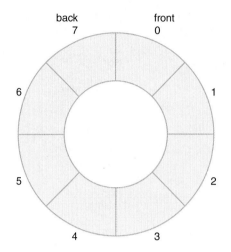
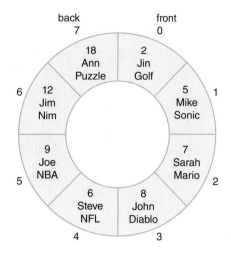

Example 14.14 shows our *ArrayQueue* class.

```
1  /* The ArrayQueue class
2     Anderson, Franceschi
3  */
4
5  public class ArrayQueue
6  {
7      private static final int QUEUE_SIZE = 8;
8      private Player [ ] queue;
9      private int front;
10     private int back;
11     private int numberOfItems;
12
13     public ArrayQueue( )
14     {
15       queue = new Player[ QUEUE_SIZE ];
16       front = 0;
17       back = QUEUE_SIZE - 1;
18       numberOfItems = 0;
19     }
20
21     public boolean isFull( )
22     {
23       return ( numberOfItems == QUEUE_SIZE );
24     }
25
26     public boolean isEmpty( )
27     {
28       return ( numberOfItems == 0 );
29     }
30
```

```
31    /** enqueue method
32     *   @param    p    the Player to insert
33     *   @return   true if list is not full, false otherwise
34     */
35    public boolean enqueue( Player p )
36    {
37      if ( !isFull( ) )
38      {
39        queue[( back + 1 ) % QUEUE_SIZE] = p;
40        back = ( back + 1 ) % QUEUE_SIZE;
41        numberOfItems++;
42        return true;
43      }
44      else
45        return false;
46    }
47
48    /** dequeue method
49     *   @return    the Player deleted
50     */
51    public Player dequeue( ) throws DataStructureException
52    {
53      if ( !isEmpty( ) )
54      {
55        front = ( front + 1 ) % QUEUE_SIZE;
56        numberOfItems--;
57        return queue[( QUEUE_SIZE + front - 1 ) % QUEUE_SIZE];
58      }
59      else
60        throw new DataStructureException
61                  ( "Queue empty: cannot dequeue" );
62    }
63
64    /** toString method
65     * @return a front-to-back String representation of the queue
66     */
67    @Override
68    public String toString( )
69    {
70      String queueString = "";
71      for ( int i = front; i < front + numberOfItems; i++ )
72        queueString += queue[i % QUEUE_SIZE].toString( ) + "\n";
73      return queueString;
74    }
75 }
```

EXAMPLE 14.14   The *ArrayQueue* **Class**

In the constructor, coded at lines 13–19, we instantiate the array *queue*, set *front* to 0, *back* to *QUEUE_SIZE – 1*, and *numberOfItems* to 0. When the first element is inserted in the queue, *back* will be increased by 1 modulo *QUEUE_SIZE* and its value will become 0.

The *isFull* and *isEmpty* methods, coded at lines 21–24 and 26–29, enable a client program to check if the queue is full or empty before enqueueing or dequeueing a *Player*. Our *enqueue*, *dequeue*, and *toString* methods also call these methods.

In the *enqueue* method, coded at lines 31–46, we attempt to insert a *Player* into the queue. The *enqueue* method returns *false* if the queue is full (line 45) to indicate that we cannot insert. If the queue is not full, we place the *Player* at the back of the queue, update *back* accordingly, increment the number of items, and return *true* (lines 39–42).

In the *dequeue* method, coded at lines 48–62, we attempt to delete and return a *Player* from the front of the queue. The method *throws* a *Data StructureException* at lines 60–61 if the queue is empty, in which case there are no *Players* to delete. If the queue is not empty, we update *front*, decrement the number of items, and return the *Player* that was at the front of the queue (lines 55–57). Note that we add *QUEUE_SIZE* to the expression *front + 1* to guarantee that it will be nonnegative.

We could also code a *peek* method. It would be similar to the *peek* method we coded for the *StackArray* class, except that *top* would be replaced by *front*. Coding the *peek* method is included as an exercise at the end of the chapter.

The *toString* method, coded at lines 64–74, is slightly different from the *toString* methods we have written so far. Since we know that there are *numberOfItems* items in the queue and that the first item is at index *front*, we can simply start at *front* and loop *numberOfItems* times to build our *String* representation of the queue. Depending on how many items are in the queue and the value of *front*, the looping variable could get larger than *QUEUE_SIZE – 1*, so we use the modulus operator (line 72) to make sure we have a valid index.

As before, a very similar program to Example 14.9 can be coded to test all possible scenarios on the methods of the *ArrayQueue* class. This is proposed in the short program section of the exercises.

As we have demonstrated, a stack or queue can be implemented using either an array or a linked list. Each implementation has advantages and disadvantages. Arrays are easier to code and every item in the stack or queue can be accessed directly through its index. Linked lists are easily expanded one item at a time. To expand an array, we would need to instantiate a new, larger array and copy the elements of the existing stack or queue to the new array, which is quite tedious.

Table 14.8 summarizes these trade-offs.

TABLE 14.8 Array Versus Linked-List Implementation of a Stack or a Queue

	Array	Linked List
Easily expanded	No	Yes
Direct access to every item	Yes	No
Easy to code	Yes	No

14.8 Sorted Linked Lists

Let's go back to our linked list of video game players. If we want to display that list on a website so that all the players can see it, we might want to display the list in ascending (or descending) order by *id* number, or in alphabetical order by name or game. If we store the items in the list in sorted order, we can display the list by simply calling the *toString* method.

The items can be sorted based on the values of one of their instance variables. Often, but not always, a class is designed so that one of the instance variables uniquely identifies an object: that instance variable is called a key. For the *Player* class, it is reasonable to assign a different *id* value to every *Player* object, and designate the *id* instance variable as the key. If items do not include an instance variable as a natural key, we should provide a method that enables us to compare two items.

A linked list that stores its nodes in ascending order (or descending order) according to a criterion is called a **sorted linked list**. Without loss of generality, we will consider a linked list sorted in ascending order.

Table 14.9 shows the APIs of the *insert* and *delete* methods for a sorted linked list. The only difference in this API from that of our unsorted list is that the location for inserting an element is dependent on the key value, rather than always inserting at the beginning of the list.

By default, an empty list is sorted, so a newly instantiated list is sorted. As we add elements, we need to maintain the sorted order of the list. Thus, the *insert* method must locate the proper position for inserting each element so that the inserted element's *id* is greater than the *id* of the previous element (if any) and less than or equal to the *id* of the next element (if any). We will find that proper place by traversing the list, comparing the value of the *id* of the new *Player* with the values of the *ids* of the *Players* stored at the various nodes in the list.

If the value of the item to insert will place it at the beginning of the list, then we will insert it in the same manner as we did in our earlier examples.

TABLE 14.9 *PlayerSortedLinkedList* Methods

Methods of the *PlayerSortedLinkedList* Class	
Return value	**Method name and argument list**
void	insert(Player p)
	inserts *Player p* in a location that keeps the list sorted in ascending order.
Player	delete(int searchID)
	returns and removes the first *Player* of the list with an *id* equal to *searchID*. If there is no such *Player* on the list, the method throws a *DataStructureException*.

When inserting a new *Player* in the middle or at the end of the list, our *insert* method will do the following:

1. Instantiate a new node containing the *Player* to be inserted.

2. Traverse the list to identify the location to insert the new node. We will call the node before the insertion point *previous*, and the node after the insertion point *current*.

3. Attach the new node to *current*; that is, make the new node point to *current*.

4. Attach *previous* to the new node; that is, make *previous* point to the new node.

5. Increase the number of items in the list by 1.

Figures 14.17a to 14.17d illustrate inserting a node somewhere in the middle of the sorted list.

The insertion code corresponding to Figures 14.17c and 14.17d is shown in Example 14.15 at lines 38–39.

Keeping the list in sorted order also impacts our *delete* method. If the item we are looking for is not in the list, we may be able to determine that fact without traversing the entire list. As soon as we visit an item with a value greater than the key value, we know that the item we are looking for is not in the list. Because the list is sorted in ascending order, all the *Players* stored after that node must have an *id* value greater than the key. Thus, we will be able to exit our *delete* method at this point, saving processing time.

Example 14.15 shows our *PlayerSortedLinkedList* class. This class also extends and inherits the functionality of our *ShellLinkedList* class. The list is sorted in ascending order according to the value of each *Player's id*.

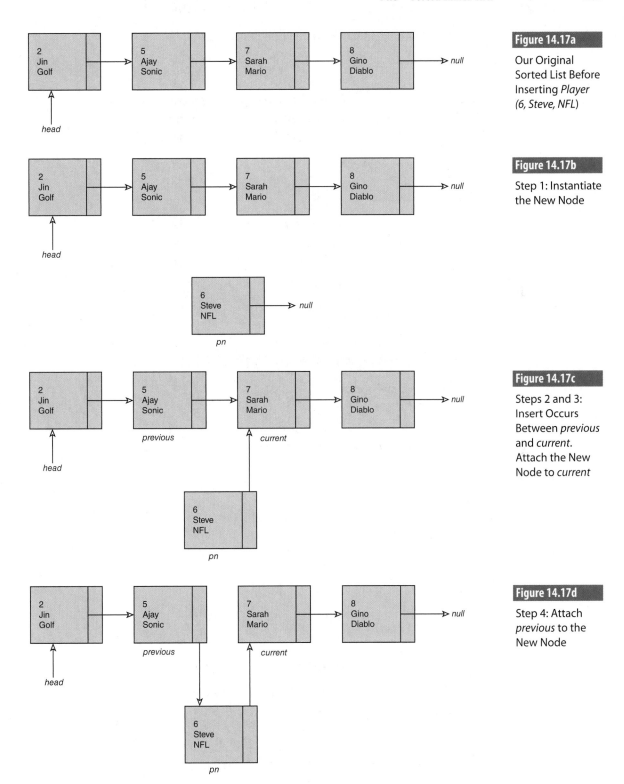

Figure 14.17a

Our Original Sorted List Before Inserting *Player (6, Steve, NFL)*

Figure 14.17b

Step 1: Instantiate the New Node

Figure 14.17c

Steps 2 and 3: Insert Occurs Between *previous* and *current*. Attach the New Node to *current*

Figure 14.17d

Step 4: Attach *previous* to the New Node

```
1  /* The PlayerSortedLinkedList class
2     Anderson, Franceschi
3  */
4
5  public class PlayerSortedLinkedList extends ShellLinkedList
6  {
7    // head and numberOfItems are inherited instance variables
8
9    public PlayerSortedLinkedList( )
10   {
11     super( );
12   }
13
14   /** insert method
15   *   @param    p    Player object to insert
16   */
17   public void insert( Player p )
18   {
19     PlayerNode pn = new PlayerNode( p );
20
21     // we will insert after previous and before current
22     PlayerNode current = head;
23     PlayerNode previous = null;
24     while ( current != null
25          && current.getPlayer( ).getID( ) < p.getID( ) )
26     {
27       previous = current;
28       current = current.getNext( );
29     }
30
31     if ( previous == null ) // insert as head
32     {
33       pn.setNext ( head );
34       head = pn;
35     }
36     else
37     {
38       pn.setNext ( current );
39       previous.setNext ( pn );
40     }
41     numberOfItems++;
42   }
43
44   /** delete method
45   *   @param    searchID    id of Player to delete
46   *   @return the Player deleted
47   */
```

```
48    public Player delete( int searchID )
49                        throws DataStructureException
50    {
51      PlayerNode current = head;
52      PlayerNode previous = null;
53      while ( current != null
54              && current.getPlayer( ).getID( ) != searchID )
55      {
56        if ( current.getPlayer( ).getID( ) > searchID )
57            throw new DataStructureException
58                ( searchID + " not found: cannot be deleted" );
59        previous = current;
60        current = current.getNext( );
61      }
62
63      if ( current == null ) // not found
64            throw new DataStructureException
65                ( searchID + " not found: cannot be deleted" );
66      else        // searchID found at Player at node current
67      {
68        if ( current == head )
69            head = head.getNext( ); // delete head
70        else
71            previous.setNext ( current.getNext ( ) );
72
73        numberOfItems--;
74        return current.getPlayer( );
75      }
76    }
77  }
```

EXAMPLE 14.15 The *PlayerSortedLinkedList* Class

The *insert* method, which we coded at lines 14 to 42, inserts a node containing its *Player* parameter *p*. Line 19 declares and instantiates a *PlayerNode* object, called *pn*, which we will insert in the linked list. To get ready to search for the insertion point for the new *Player*, we declare two *PlayerNode* object references, *current* and *previous*, at lines 22–23, and assign them *head* and *null*. We use *current* to traverse the list, going just past the point of insertion, and we use *previous* to track the node just before *current*. We will insert *pn* between *previous* and *current*. From lines 24 to 29, we use a *while* loop to traverse the list. We construct our *while* loop condition so that we will exit the loop if the list is empty or if we have reached the end of the list (we test if current is *null* at line 24), or if we are visiting a node containing a *Player* whose *id* is larger than or equal to the *id* value of *p*, the *Player* parameter of the *insert* method (line 25).

As mentioned earlier, there are two different cases for insertion: either we insert at the beginning of the list, or we insert in the middle or at the end of the list. At line 31 we test if *previous* is *null*, in which case we never entered the *while* loop because the list is empty or because the head node contains a *Player* whose *id* value is greater than *p's id*. Either way, we insert at the beginning of the list at lines 33 and 34.

If *previous* is not *null*, we will insert in the middle of the list or at the end of the list. To insert the node *pn* between *previous* and *current*, we connect *pn* to *current* at line 38, and *previous* to *pn* at line 39. Figures 14.17a to 14.17d show the step-by-step impact of lines 19, 38, and 39 on the sorted linked list.

The *delete* method (lines 44–76) is very similar to the *delete* method of the *Player-LinkedList* class. The only difference is at lines 56–58. We first test at line 56 if the *id* of the *Player* at *current* is greater than *searchID*. If that is *true*, we have no chance of finding a *Player* object with an *id* of *searchID* since the list is sorted in ascending order. Therefore, we *throw* a *DataStructureException* with an appropriate message, and we exit the method.

Let's test our *PlayerSortedLinkedList* class. In order to keep things simple, we will test the *insert* method only, because the *delete* method is, as discussed, almost identical to the *delete* method of the *PlayerLinkedList* class.

We want to test the following cases:

- insert in an empty list
- insert at the beginning of the list
- insert in the middle of the list
- insert at the end of the list

We traverse the list after each insertion to check that the *Player* was inserted at the correct location in the sorted linked list.

Example 14.16 shows how to use the *PlayerSortedLinkedListTest* class and how to test its methods.

```
1   /* The PlayerSortedLinkedListTest class
2      Anderson, Franceschi
3   */
4
5   public class PlayerSortedLinkedListTest
6   {
7     public static void main( String [ ] args )
8     {
```

```
9       Player p1 = new Player( 7, "Sarah","Mario" );
10      Player p2 = new Player( 2, "Jin","Golf" );
11      Player p3 = new Player( 5, "Ajay","Sonic" );
12      Player p4 = new Player( 8, "Gino","Diablo" );
13
14      // construct empty PlayerSortedLinkedList
15      PlayerSortedLinkedList players =
16                      new PlayerSortedLinkedList( );
17
18      System.out.println( "Number of items in the list: "
19         + players.getNumberOfItems( ) + "\n" + players.toString( ) );
20
21      System.out.println( "inserting " + p1 );
22      players.insert( p1 ); // insert in empty list
23      System.out.println( "Number of items in the list: "
24         + players.getNumberOfItems( ) + "\n" + players.toString( ) );
25
26      System.out.println( "inserting " + p2 );
27      players.insert( p2 );    // insert at the beginning of the list
28      System.out.println( "Number of items in the list: "
29         + players.getNumberOfItems( ) + "\n" + players.toString( ) );
30
31      System.out.println( "inserting " + p3 );
32      players.insert( p3 ); // insert in the middle of the list
33      System.out.println( "Number of items in the list: "
34         + players.getNumberOfItems( ) + "\n" + players.toString( ) );
35
36      System.out.println( "inserting " + p4 );
37      players.insert( p4 ); // insert at the end of the list
38      System.out.println( "Number of items in the list: "
39         + players.getNumberOfItems( ) + "\n" + players.toString( ) );
40   }
41 }
```

EXAMPLE 14.16   The *PlayerSortedLinkedListTest* Class

In Example 14.16, we instantiate our usual four *Player* objects *p1*, *p2*, *p3*, and *p4* at lines 9–12. We choose the *id* values so that our four test cases will be covered when we successively insert the *Player* objects. We instantiate the *PlayerSortedLinkedList players* object at lines 14–16.

We first traverse the empty list at lines 18–19. Then, we successively insert *p1*, *p2*, *p3*, and *p4*, traversing the list after each insertion (lines 21–39). Figure 14.18 shows the output of Example 14.16. As we can see, *players* remains sorted in ascending order after each insertion.

Figure 14.18

Output of
Example 14.16

```
Number of items in the list: 0

inserting id: 7          name: Sarah          game: Mario
Number of items in the list: 1
id: 7    name: Sarah    game: Mario

inserting id: 2          name: Jin            game: Golf
Number of items in the list: 2
id: 2    name: Jin       game: Golf
id: 7    name: Sarah     game: Mario

inserting id: 5          name: Ajay           game: Sonic
Number of items in the list: 3
id: 2    name: Jin       game: Golf
id: 5    name: Ajay      game: Sonic
id: 7    name: Sarah     game: Mario

inserting id: 8          name: Gino           game: Diablo
Number of items in the list: 4
id: 2    name: Jin       game: Golf
id: 5    name: Ajay      game: Sonic
id: 7    name: Sarah     game: Mario
id: 8    name: Gino      game: Diablo
```

© Hemera Technologies/
Photos.com/Thinkstock

CODE IN ACTION

Within the online resources, you will find a movie with a step-by-step illustration of sorted linked-list methods. Click on the link to start the movie.

14.9 Programming Activity 2: Writing *Insert* and *Delete* Methods for a Sorted Linked List

In this activity, you will work with a sorted linked list of integers, performing the following activity:

Code the *insert* and *delete* methods to insert and delete nodes in a sorted linked list of *ints*.

The framework will animate your code to give you feedback on the correctness of your code. It will display the state of the sorted linked list at all times.

Instructions

Copy the contents of the Programming Activity 2 folder for this chapter from the companion website for this text onto a folder on your computer. Open the *LinkedList.java* source file. Searching for five asterisks (*****) in the source code will position you to the code section where you will add your code.

In this task, you will fill in the code inside the *insert* and *delete* methods for a sorted linked list of integers. Example 14.17 shows the section of the *LinkedList* source code where you will add your code. This example is different from the one presented earlier in the chapter. The nodes of the linked list contain *ints*, not *Players*. The *delete* method returns a *boolean* value to indicate whether the deletion was successful. Because the client has already provided the *int* value to delete, there is no reason to return the value to the client.

You can first code the *insert* method and run the application. Once the *insert* method works properly, you can code the *delete* method and run the application again. We have provided a dummy *return* statement in the *delete* method so that the *LinkedList.java* file will compile if only the *insert* method is coded. When you write the *delete* method, modify the dummy *return* statement to return the appropriate value.

```java
public void insert( int value )
{
    // ***** Student writes the body of this method *****
    // code the insert method of a linked list of ints
    // the int to insert in the linked list is value

    //
    // Student code starts here
    //



    //
    // End of student code, part 1
    //
}
public boolean delete( int value )
{
    // ***** Student writes the body of this method *****

    // code the delete method of a linked list of ints
    // the int to delete in the linked list is value
    // if deletion is successful, return true
    // otherwise, return false

    //
```

```
// Student code starts here
//

    return true; // replace this return statement
//
// End of student code, part 2
//
}
```

EXAMPLE 14.17   Location of Student Code in *LinkedList*

When coding the *insert* and *delete* methods, you will need to use constructors and methods of the *Node* class. The API of the *Node* class is shown in Table 14.10.

To test your code, compile and run the *LinkedListPractice.java* file, which contains the *main* method. When the program begins, a window will display the state

TABLE 14.10   API of the *Node* Class

Constructors and Methods of the *Node* Class

Constructors

Class	**Constructor and argument list**
Node	Node(int data)
	constructs a new *Node* object whose *data* instance variable is *data*. The pointer to the next node is set to the value *null*.
Node	Node(int data, Node nextNode)
	constructs a new *Node* object whose *data* instance variable is *data*. The *Node* points to *nextNode*.

Methods

Return value	**Method name and argument list**
Node	setNext(Node nextNode)
	sets the *Node* object reference pointed to by this *Node* to *nextNode*.
Node	setData(int data)
	sets the *data* instance variable to data
Node	getNext( )
	returns an object reference to the *Node* pointed to by this *Node*.
int	getData( )
	returns the *data* stored in this *Node*.

of the linked list (the list is empty when we start), along with various buttons labeled "insert," "delete," "toString," "count," and "clear," as shown in Figure 14.19.

To insert or delete a value, type the integer into the text field labeled "Node Data," then click on the "insert" or "delete" button. The application only accepts integers greater than or equal to 0 and less than or equal to 9999; it will not let you enter characters that are not digits. The main panel will visually represent the sorted linked list. The text area at the bottom will give you feedback on your operations. Close the window to exit the program.

Figure 14.20 shows the application after successively inserting 45, 67, and 78, traversing the list, then deleting 67.

Figure 14.19

Opening Window

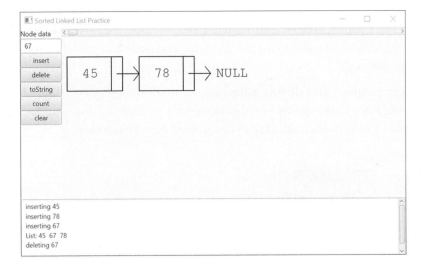

Figure 14.20

Sample Window After Performing Some Operations

Troubleshooting

If your method implementation does not animate or animates incorrectly, check these items:

- Check the feedback in the window to see if your code gives the correct result.

- Verify that you correctly coded both cases of the *insert* method: insert at the beginning and insert in the middle of the list.

- Verify that you correctly coded all the cases of the *delete* method: fail to delete, delete at the beginning, and delete in the middle or at the end of the list.

DISCUSSION QUESTIONS ?

1. **Explain why it is important to update *head* when inserting at the beginning of a list.**

2. **Explain the difference between deleting in a nonsorted list and deleting in a sorted list.**

14.10   Doubly Linked Lists

So far, when traversing a linked list and looking for a node containing a particular value, we have used two nodes, which we called *previous* and *current*. We kept track of the *previous* node because we had no way to go backward in the list from the *current* node.

This problem can be solved by using a **doubly linked list**, which provides two links between nodes, one forward and one backward. Using the backward link, we can now backtrack from *current* if needed. The backward link is also represented by a node object reference.

Figure 14.21 shows how we can visualize such a node. The data in the node is *5*, *Ajay*, and *Sonic*. The right arrow points to the next node and the left arrow points to the previous node.

In order to implement a doubly linked list, we need to modify our *Player Node* class by adding a *previous* instance variable along with its accessor and mutator methods. Example 14.18 shows a summary of our revised *PlayerNode* class.

Figure 14.21

A Node with Two Links

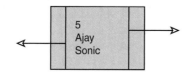

```
1  /* The PlayerNode class
2     Anderson, Franceschi
3  */
4
5  public class PlayerNode
6  {
7    private Player player;          // the player at that node
8    private PlayerNode next;        // the next PlayerNode
9    private PlayerNode previous;    // the previous PlayerNode
10
11   // constructors
12   // accessors are getPlayer, getNext, getPrevious
13   // mutators are setPlayer, setNext, setPrevious
14 }
```

EXAMPLE 14.18   Summary of the *PlayerNode* Class for a Doubly Linked List

When inserting a node, we need to reset both forward and backward links, i.e., the *next* and *previous* instance variables. Suppose, for example, that we insert a node containing *Player p* before a node named *current*. We will illustrate only the general case, when *current* is in the middle or at the end of the doubly linked list; that is, *current* is neither *head* nor *null*.

The steps we need to perform are the following:

1. Instantiate the new node.

2. Attach the new node to *current* by setting its *next* field to *current*.

3. Attach the node before *current* to the new node by setting its *next* field to the new node.

4. Set *previous* in the new node to point to the node before *current*.

5. Set *previous* in *current* to point to the new node.

6. Add 1 to the number of items in the list.

Steps 2 and 3 set the forward links, and Steps 4 and 5 set the backward links.

Figures 14.22a to 14.22f provide a step-by-step illustration for inserting a node in the middle of a doubly linked list. Note that we no longer need to keep a *previous* object reference, because we can get the location of the previous node from the *current* node.

Figure 14.22a

Our Original Doubly Linked List

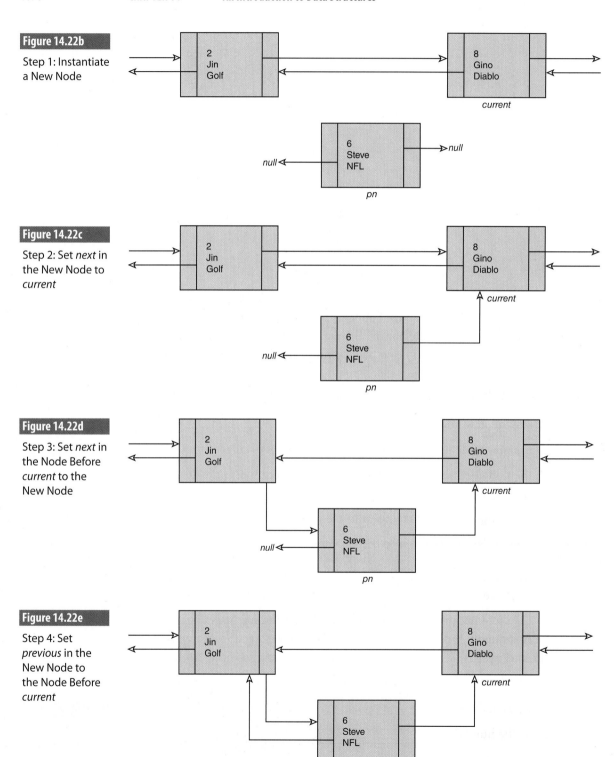

Figure 14.22b

Step 1: Instantiate a New Node

Figure 14.22c

Step 2: Set *next* in the New Node to *current*

Figure 14.22d

Step 3: Set *next* in the Node Before *current* to the New Node

Figure 14.22e

Step 4: Set *previous* in the New Node to the Node Before *current*

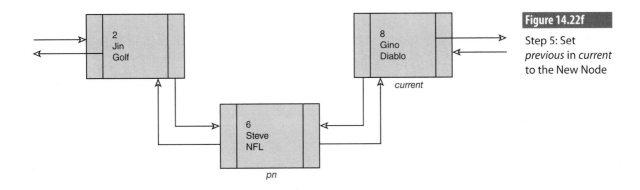

Figure 14.22f

Step 5: Set
previous in *current*
to the New Node

Our code updating the links inside the *insert* method of the doubly linked list class will be the following:

```
PlayerNode pn = new PlayerNode( p );              // Step 1
pn.setNext( current );                            // Step 2
current.getPrevious( ).setNext( pn );             // Step 3
pn.setPrevious( current.getPrevious( ) );         // Step 4
current.setPrevious( pn );                        // Step 5
numberOfItems++;                                  // Step 6
```

The order in which these statements are executed is important. Indeed, if Step 5 were executed immediately after Step 1, we would overwrite the reference to the previous node. Then we could not access the node before *current*, and we would be unable to properly reset the links between the nodes.

Note that if *current* is either *head* (insert at the beginning) or *null* (insert at the end), the preceding code needs to be modified; that is proposed in the group project.

When deleting a node, we also need to reset all the appropriate forward and backward links. Suppose, for example, that we delete a node named *current*. We will illustrate only the general case, when *current* is in the middle of the doubly linked list. In this case, *current* is neither the *head* nor the last node in the list (since we are deleting *current*, we are assuming that *current* is not *null*); that is, there is a node after *current* in the list.

To delete a node, *current*, from the middle of a doubly linked list, we need to perform the following steps.

1. Set *next* in the node before *current* to the node after *current*.

2. Set *previous* in the node after *current* to the node before *current*.

3. Decrease the number of items by 1.

Figures 14.23a to 14.23c give a step-by-step illustration of deleting a node.

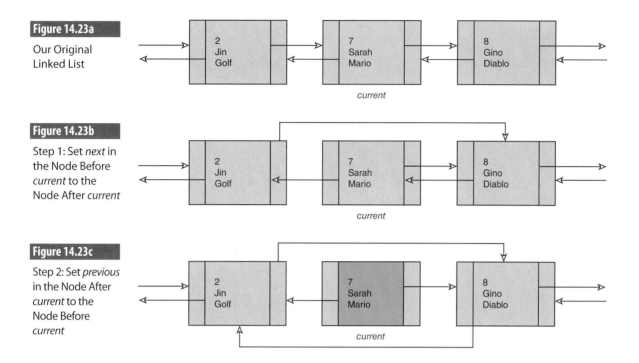

Figure 14.23a

Our Original Linked List

Figure 14.23b

Step 1: Set *next* in the Node Before *current* to the Node After *current*

Figure 14.23c

Step 2: Set *previous* in the Node After *current* to the Node Before *current*

Our code updating the links inside the *delete* method of the doubly linked list class is:

```
current.getPrevious( ).setNext( current.getNext( ) );          // Step 1
current.getNext( ).setPrevious( current.getPrevious( ) );      // Step 2
numberOfItems--;                                               // Step 3
```

Again, note that if *current* is either *head* or the last node in the list, the previous code would need to be modified; that is also proposed in the group project at the end of the chapter, which builds a sorted, doubly linked list.

14.11 Linked Lists Using Generic Types

Many classes in the Java Class Library, such as the *ArrayList* class, implement generics, meaning that the data type for the data of the class can be specified by the client. User-defined classes can also implement generic types. In this section, we will build a linked list class that implements generic types, so that the client can specify the class type of the data stored in our linked list. In a linked list, the data of the item is stored in the node; thus, the data in our *Node class* will be a generic object.

The basic syntax for the header of a class that implements generics is:

```
accessModifier class ClassName<IdentifierForGenericClass>
```

For the identifier for our generic class, we will use the uppercase letter *T*. Thus, for our *Node* class, the header will be:

```
public class Node<T>
```

Inside the class, we can then use that identifier, here *T*, as we would use an existing or user-defined class. For example, to declare an instance variable named *data* of class *T*, we write:

```
private T data;
```

In order to use an object reference of a class implementing generics, we use the following syntax:

```
ClassName<IdentifierForGenericClass>
```

Thus, in order to declare an object reference of the *Node* class as a return type or a parameter for a method, we use the notation *Node<T>*.

Example 14.19 shows our *Node<T>* class.

```
 1 /** The Node class
 2  *    Anderson, Franceschi
 3  */
 4
 5 public class Node<T>
 6 {
 7   private T data;
 8   private Node<T> next;
 9
10   /** default constructor
11    *   sets data and next to null
12    */
13   public Node( )
14   {
15     data = null;
16     next = null;
17   }
18
19   /** constructor
20    *   @param data reference to data
21    *   sets next to null
22    */
23   public Node( T data )
24   {
25     setData( data );
26     next = null;
27   }
28
29   /** accessor for data
```

```
30     *    @return reference to data item
31     */
32     public T getData( )
33     {
34       return data;
35     }
36
37     /** accessor for next
38     *    @return next
39     */
40     public Node<T> getNext( )
41     {
42       return next;
43     }
44
45     /**  mutator for data
46     *     @param data reference to new data item
47     *     @return reference to this object
48     */
49     public Node setData( T data )
50     {
51       this.data = data;
52       return next;
53     }
54
55     /**  mutator for next
56     *     @param reference to next Node
57     *     @return reference to this object
58     */
59     public Node setNext( Node<T> next )
60     {
61       this.next = next;
62       return this;
63     }
64 }
```

EXAMPLE 14.19   The *Node* Class Using Generics

Example 14.20 shows our *ShellLinkedList< T >* class.

```
1 /* The ShellLinkedList class
2      Anderson, Franceschi
3 */
4
5 public abstract class ShellLinkedList<T>
6 {
7   protected Node<T> head;
8   protected int numberOfItems;
```

```
 9
10    /**   constructor
11     *       sets head to null and numberOfItems to 0
12     */
13    public ShellLinkedList( )
14    {
15       head = null;
16       numberOfItems = 0;
17    }
18
19    /**   accessor for numberOfItems
20     *    @return numberOfItems
21     */
22    public int getNumberOfItems( )
23    {
24       return numberOfItems;
25    }
26
27    /** isEmpty method
28     *  @return true if no items in list; false otherwise
29     */
30    public boolean isEmpty( )
31    {
32       return ( numberOfItems == 0 );
33    }
34
35    /**   toString method
36     *    @return all items in the list
37     */
38    @Override
39    public String toString( )
40    {
41       String listString = "";
42       Node<T> current = head;
43       for ( int i = 0; i < numberOfItems; i++ )
44       {
45          listString += current.getData( ).toString ( ) + "\n";
46          current = current.getNext( );
47       }
48       return listString;
49    }
50 }
```

EXAMPLE 14.20   The *ShellLinkedList* Class Using Generics

Our *GenericLinkedList* class, shown in Example 14.21, implements the same methods as our *PlayerLinkedList* from earlier in the chapter. The only differences in the code are the class header and the declaration and instantiation of *Node* variables.

```
1  /* The GenericLinkedList class
2     Anderson, Franceschi
3  */
4
5  public class GenericLinkedList<T> extends ShellLinkedList<T>
6  {
7    // head and numberOfItems are inherited instance variables
8
9    /** constructor
10   *   calls constructor of ShellLinkedList
11   */
12   public GenericLinkedList( )
13   {
14     super( );
15   }
16
17   /** insert method
18   *   @param    item   T object to insert
19   */
20   public void insert( T item )
21   {
22     // insert as head
23     Node<T> nd = new Node<T>( item );
24     nd.setNext( head );
25     head = nd;
26     numberOfItems++;
27   }
28
29   /** delete method
30   *   @param    item   T object to delete
31   *   @return   true if the deletion was successful, false otherwise
32   */
33   public boolean delete( T item )
34   {
35     Node<T> current = head;
36     Node<T> previous = null;
37     while ( current != null
38            && ! ( item.equals ( current.getData( ) ) ) )
39     {
40       previous = current;
41       current = current.getNext( );
42     }
43
44     if ( current == null ) // not found
45         return false;
46     else
47     {
```

```
48      if ( current == head )
49        head = head.getNext( ); // delete head
50      else
51        previous.setNext ( current.getNext( ) );
52
53      numberOfItems--;
54      return true;
55    }
56  }
57 }
```

EXAMPLE 14.21 The *GenericLinkedList* Class with Generics

Our *GenericLinkedList* class, shown in Example 14.21, implements the same methods as our *PlayerLinkedList*

The *insert* method, coded at lines 17–27, is very similar to the *insert* method of the *PlayerLinkedList* class. Instead of a *Player* reference, its parameter *item* is a *T* reference, where *T* is a generic class. It also inserts *item* at the beginning of the list. At line 23, we declare and instantiate a *Node<T>* object reference, which is then connected to the list. The rest of the *insert* method is identical to the code in our *insert* method of a nongeneric linked-list class.

Because we do not know in advance what type of object our class will be instantiated with, we implemented our *delete* method differently. We cannot delete an item based on the value of one of its fields because we do not know what the fields of that item are, since that item is a generic object. Thus, the parameter of our *delete* method is a generic object of the same type as the items in the list. There is no need to return an item if we find it and can delete it because we already have that item as the parameter of the method. For that reason, our *delete* method returns a *boolean* value: *true* if we were able to delete the parameter item, *false* otherwise. In order to compare *item* with the items in the list, we call the *equals* method at line 38, inherited by any class from the *Object* class, and which will need to be overwritten in the class the client specifies as the type for the linked list.

Now that we have defined and implemented our linked list class storing generic objects, how do we use it in a client class? We use the same syntax as we would using an existing Java class implementing generics. In fact, in the *GenericLinkedList* class, we used the *Node* class, which implements generics.

Example 14.22 shows a client class using the *GenericLinkedList* class.

```
1 /* The LinkedListTest class
2    Anderson, Franceschi
3 */
4
```

```
5  public class LinkedListTest
6  {
7    public static void main( String [ ] args )
8    {
9      Player p1 = new Player( 7,"Sarah","Mario" );
10     Player p2 = new Player( 2,"Jin","Golf" );
11     Player p3 = new Player( 5,"Ajay","Sonic" );
12
13     // construct empty LinkedList of Player objects
14     GenericLinkedList<Player>players = new GenericLinkedList<Player>( );
15     System.out.println( "Number of items in the list: "
16       + players.getNumberOfItems( ) + "\n" + players.toString( ) );
17
18     players.insert( p1 ); // insert in empty list
19     System.out.println( "Number of items in the list: "
20       + players.getNumberOfItems( ) + "\n" + players.toString( ) );
21
22     players.insert( p2 ); // insert in list of one item
23     System.out.println( "Number of items in the list: "
24       + players.getNumberOfItems( ) + "\n" + players.toString( ) );
25
26     players.insert( p3 ); // insert in list of two items
27     System.out.println( "Number of items in the list: "
28       + players.getNumberOfItems( ) + "\n" + players.toString( ) );
29
30     if ( players.delete( p2 ) ) // delete in the middle
31         System.out.println( "Player successfully deleted: " );
32     System.out.println( "Number of items in the list: "
33       + players.getNumberOfItems( ) + "\n" + players.toString( ) );
34
35     if ( players.delete( p3 ) ) // delete at the beginning
36         System.out.println( "player successfully deleted: " );
37     System.out.println( "Number of items in the list: "
38       + players.getNumberOfItems( ) + "\n" + players.toString( ) );
39   }
40 }
```

EXAMPLE 14.22   The *LinkedListTest* Class

The only statement that is specific to the generic character of the *GenericLinkedList* is at line 14 when we declare and instantiate an object reference of *GenericLinkedList*. If we wanted to declare and instantiate a list containing *Integer* objects, we would have written:

```
GenericLinkedList<Integer> numbers = new GenericLinkedList<Integer>( );
```

Figure 14.24 shows the output of Example 14.22.

```
Number of items in the list: 0

Number of items in the list: 1
id: 7    name: Sarah    game: Mario

Number of items in the list: 2
id: 2    name: Jin      game: Golf
id: 7    name: Sarah    game: Mario

Number of items in the list: 3
id: 5    name: Ajay     game: Sonic
id: 2    name: Jin      game: Golf
id: 7    name: Sarah    game: Mario

Player successfully deleted:
Number of items in the list: 2
id: 5    name: Ajay     game: Sonic
id: 7    name: Sarah    game: Mario

Player successfully deleted:
Number of items in the list: 1
id: 7    name: Sarah    game: Mario
```

Figure 14.24

Output of
Example 14.22

14.12 Recursively Defined Linked Lists

A linked list can be defined recursively. A recursively defined linked list is made up of two items:

- *first*, an item, which is the first item in the linked list
- *rest*, a linked list, which consists of the rest of the linked list

Figure 14.25 shows a representation of a recursively defined linked list.

In our recursively defined linked list, we have two instance variables: the item *first* and the linked list *rest*. Because we can access the rest of the list through the *rest* instance variable, we do not need a node class.

In designing our class encapsulating a recursive linked list of generic objects, we will limit ourselves to an unsorted linked list. We will insert at the beginning of the list. When we delete, we will attempt to delete and return an object that matches a parameter object. When we cannot delete, we will return *false*.

Table 14.11 shows the APIs of the *insert* and *delete* methods.

first (an item)	rest (a linked list)

Figure 14.25

A Recursively
Defined Linked List

TABLE 14.11 *RecursiveLinkedList* **Methods**

Methods of the *RecursiveLinkedList* Class	
Return value	**Method name and argument list**
void	insert(T item)
	inserts *item* at the beginning of the list.
boolean	delete(T item)
	removes the first object of the list that matches *item* and returns *true*. If there is no such object in the list, the method returns *false*.

After we insert, *first* will hold the item inserted, and *rest* will hold the original list. Figures 14.26a and 14.26b show a recursively defined linked list before and after inserting a *Player* named *p*. In the figures, *p1* represents the current first item, and *r1* represents the rest of the list before the insertion. The *insert* method is not recursive.

The *delete* method is recursive. We have three base cases:

- The list is empty.

- The element to delete is the first item of the list.

- The element to delete is not the first item of the list and the rest of the list is empty.

In the general case, we try to delete the element from the rest of the list.

If the list is empty (the first base case), we will return *false*. If the list is not empty, we will look at *first* and check to see if it matches the parameter *item*. If it does (the second base case), we will delete *first*, and *rest* will become our list. If it does not, then we will attempt to delete inside *rest*. If rest is *null*, we cannot delete (the third base case) and we will return *false*. If rest is not *null*, we will make a recursive call to the *delete* method with *rest* (the general case).

More generally, we want to do the following:

- If the list is empty (base case #1), the method returns.

- Process *first*, that is, the first element in the list (base case #2); the method may or may not return at that point.

- If *rest* is *null*—that is, the list has only 1 item (base case #3)—the method returns.

- If *rest* is not *null*, make a recursive call on *rest*.

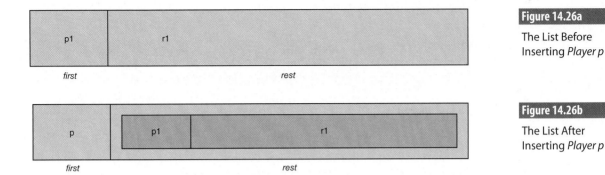

Figure 14.26a

The List Before
Inserting *Player p*

Figure 14.26b

The List After
Inserting *Player p*

Example 14.23 shows our *RecursiveLinkedList* class. Because of its recursive design, the *RecursiveLinkedList* class does not extend the *ShellLinkedList* class.

```
1  /* The RecursiveLinkedList class
2     Anderson, Franceschi
3  */
4
5  public class RecursiveLinkedList<T>
6  {
7    private T first;
8    private RecursiveLinkedList<T> rest;
9
10   public RecursiveLinkedList( )
11   {
12     first = null;
13     rest = null;
14   }
15
16   /** insert method
17    *   @param    item object to insert at beginning of list
18    */
19   public void insert( T item )
20   {
21     if ( isEmpty ( ) ) // is list empty?
22       first = item;
23     else
24     {
25       RecursiveLinkedList<T> tempList =
26                 new RecursiveLinkedList<T>( );
27       tempList.first = first;
28       tempList.rest = rest;
29       first = item;
30       rest = tempList;
31     }
```

```
32   }
33
34   /** delete method
35   *   @param     item    the T object to delete
36   *   @return    true if item is deleted, false otherwise
37   */
38   public boolean delete( T item )
39   {
40     if ( isEmpty( ) )                    // is list empty?
41       return false;
42     else if ( first.equals( item ) )   // found it
43     {
44       T temp = first;
45       if ( rest == null )
46           first = null;
47       else       // rest not null
48       {
49           first = rest.first;
50           rest = rest.rest;
51       }
52       return true;
53     }
54     else if ( rest == null )
55         return false;
56     else                           // try to delete in rest
57         return rest.delete( item );
58   }
59
60   /** isEmpty  method
61   *   @return    true if the list has no elements;
62   *              false, otherwise
63   */
64   public boolean isEmpty( )
65   {
66     return ( first == null );
67   }
68
69   /** toString method
70   *  @return a String listing the elements in the list
71   */
72   @Override
73   public String toString( )
74   {
75     String listString = "";
76     if ( first != null )
77     {
```

```
78          listString = first.toString( ) + "\n";
79          if ( rest != null )
80             listString += rest.toString( );
81       }
82       return listString;
83    }
84 }
```

EXAMPLE 14.23   The *RecursiveLinkedList* Class

We declare the two instance variables at lines 7–8: *first* represents the first *T* object in the list, and *rest* represents the rest of the list, which is a *RecursiveLinkedList* object reference itself. We coded the default constructor, which constructs an empty list, at lines 10–14.

We coded the *insert* method at lines 16–32. After insertion, *first* will be the method's *T* parameter *item*, and *rest* will be the list before we inserted *item*. We begin by testing if the list is empty by calling the *isEmpty* method (defined at lines 60 to 67), which returns *true* if *first* is *null*. If the list is empty, we assign *item* to *first* at line 22. If *first* is not *null*, we copy the current list into a new list at lines 25–28. We instantiate a temporary list, *tempList*. We then assign *first* to the *first* instance variable of *tempList* and *rest* to the *rest* instance variable of *tempList*. At that point, we have copied the current list into *tempList*. Now we can insert the new item into the first position (line 29) and make *tempList* the rest of the list (line 30).

The recursive *delete* method (lines 34–58) takes the *T* parameter *item*. If the list is empty (line 40), we return *false*. If the list is not empty, then *first* is not *null*, and we can call the *equals* method on *first*. More generally, when processing a recursively designed list, not testing for all the base case conditions could result in a *NullPointerException*.

If the list is not empty and *first* is equal to *item* (line 42), we do the necessary bookkeeping on the list to delete the first element at lines 44–51 before returning *true* at line 52. In order to delete the first element of the list, we need to update *first* and *rest*. *First* will be assigned the first element of *rest*. However, *rest* could be *null*, in which case *rest* does not have a first element. Thus, we test if *rest* is *null* at line 45. If it is, the list is now empty, so we assign *null* to *first* at line 46. If *rest* is not *null*, we assign the first element of *rest* to *first* at line 49, and we assign the *rest* of *rest* to *rest* at line 50.

Figures 14.27a to 14.27c show the list before deleting *Player p*, after line 49 is executed, and after line 50 is executed, when *Player p* has been deleted from the list.

Finally, if the list is not *null* and the *first* is not equal to *item*, we skip to line 54, where we test if *rest* is *null*. If it is, we cannot delete and return *false*. If *rest* is not *null*, we make the recursive call to try to delete from *rest* at line 57.

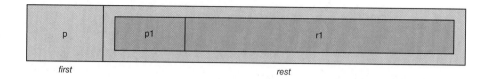

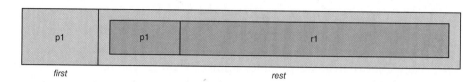

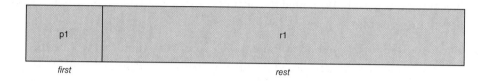

We coded our *toString* method at lines 69–83. This method is also recursive. If the list is empty, it returns the empty *String*. If the list is not empty, we assign the contents of *first* to the temporary variable *listString* at line 78. Note that the class the client specifies as the type of the *RecursiveLinkedList* will need to provide an overriding *toString* method. We then need to traverse *rest* in order to add its contents to *listString*. But *rest* could be *null*, in which case we are finished traversing the list. So if *rest* is not *null* (line 79), we traverse *rest* at line 80 by making the recursive call:

```
rest.toString( )
```

That recursive call returns a *String* representing the contents of *rest*; we concatenate that *String* to *listString* at line 80 before returning *listString* at line 82.

Example 14.24 shows how to use our *RecursiveLinkedList* class in a client program.

```
 1 /* The RecursiveLinkedListTest class
 2    Anderson, Franceschi
 3 */
 4
 5 public class RecursiveLinkedListTest
 6 {
 7   public static void main( String [ ] args )
 8   {
 9     Player p1 = new Player( 7,"Sarah","Mario" );
10     Player p2 = new Player( 2,"Jin","Golf" );
11     Player p3 = new Player( 5,"Ajay","Sonic" );
12
13     RecursiveLinkedList<Player> players =
```

```
14              new RecursiveLinkedList<Player>( );
15       System.out.println( "The list is\n"
16           + ( players.isEmpty( ) ? "empty\n" : players.toString( ) ) );
17
18       players.insert( p1 );
19       System.out.println( "Inserting " + p1 );
20       System.out.println( "The list is\n"
21           + ( players.isEmpty( ) ? "empty\n" : players.toString( ) ) );
22
23       players.insert( p2 );
24       System.out.println( "Inserting " + p2 );
25       System.out.println( "The list is\n"
26           + ( players.isEmpty( ) ? "empty\n" : players.toString( ) ) );
27
28       players.insert( p3 );
29       System.out.println( "Inserting " + p3 );
30       System.out.println( "The list is\n"
31           + ( players.isEmpty( ) ? "empty\n" : players.toString( ) ) );
32
33       if ( players.delete( p2 ) )  // delete in middle of list
34         System.out.println( "Player deleted: " + p2 );
35       System.out.println( "The list is\n"
36           + ( players.isEmpty( ) ? "empty\n" : players.toString( ) ) );
37
38       if ( players.delete( p1 ) )  // delete at end of the list
39         System.out.println( "Player deleted: " + p1 );
40       System.out.println( "The list is\n"
41           + ( players.isEmpty( ) ? "empty\n" : players.toString( ) ) );
42
43       if ( players.delete( p1 ) )  // attempt to delete will fail
44         System.out.println( "The list deleted: " + p1 );
45       System.out.println( "The list is\n"
46           + ( players.isEmpty( ) ? "empty\n" : players.toString( ) ) );
47
48       if ( players.delete( p3 ) )  // delete only Player in list
49         System.out.println( "Player deleted: " + p3 );
50       System.out.println( "The list is\n"
51           + ( players.isEmpty( ) ? "empty\n" : players.toString( ) ) );
52
53       if ( players.delete( p3 ) )  // try to delete from empty list
54         System.out.println( "Player deleted: " + p3 );
55       System.out.println( "The list is\n"
56           + ( players.isEmpty( ) ? "empty\n" : players.toString( ) ) );
57  }
58 }
```

EXAMPLE 14.24   The *RecursiveLinkedListTest* Class

COMMON ERROR TRAP
When processing a recursively defined list, not testing for all the base case conditions can eventually result in a *NullPointerException* at run time.

SOFTWARE
ENGINEERING
TIP
When a class
is defined
recursively,
think in terms of
implementing
recursive
methods.

In Example 14.24, we again instantiate our usual three *Player* object references *p1*, *p2*, and *p3* at lines 9–11. We instantiate the *RecursiveLinkedList players* at lines 13–14. This example tests the following operations:

- inserting in an empty list (line 18)

- inserting in a list of one element (line 23)

- inserting in a list of two elements (line 28)

- deleting an element in the middle of the list (line 33)

- deleting an element at the end of the list (line 38)

- failing to delete from a non-empty list (line 43)

- deleting the only element in the list (line 48)

- failing to delete from an empty list (line 53)

Figure 14.28 shows the output of Example 14.24.

Figure 14.28

Output of
Example 14.24

```
The list is
empty

Inserting id: 7        name: Sarah   game: Mario
The list is
id: 7    name: Sarah      game: Mario

Inserting id: 2        name: Jin  game: Golf
The list is
id: 2    name: Jin        game: Golf
id: 7    name: Sarah      game: Mario

Inserting id: 5        name: Ajay  game: Sonic
The list is
id: 5    name: Ajay       game: Sonic
id: 2    name: Jin        game: Golf
id: 7    name: Sarah      game: Mario

Player deleted: id: 2   name: Jin  game: Golf
The list is
id: 5    name: Ajay       game: Sonic
id: 7    name: Sarah      game: Mario

Player deleted: id: 7   name: Sarah  game: Mario
The list is
id: 5    name: Ajay       game: Sonic
```

Figure 14.28

(continued)

```
The list is
id: 5   name: Ajay        game: Sonic

Player deleted: id: 5      name: Ajay   game: Sonic
The list is
empty

The list is
empty
```

Skill Practice
with these end-of-chapter questions

14.14.1   Multiple Choice Exercises

   Questions 1, 8, 9, 10, 11, 12, 13

14.14.4   Identifying Errors in Code

   Questions 35, 36, 37, 38

14.14.6   Write a Short Program

   Questions 47, 49, 51, 54, 55, 56, 57, 58

14.14.8   Technical Writing

   Question 72

14.13 Chapter Summary

- A data structure is a mechanism for organizing the data a program stores in memory.

- A linked list is a data structure consisting of nodes linked together like a chain.

- Typical instance variables for a node are an object reference to the data stored at the node, and a node reference, which points to the next node in the list.

- Because each node has a reference to the next node as an instance variable, a linked list needs only one instance variable, its first node, which is usually called *head*. Often, for convenience, we also include an instance variable representing the number of items in the list.

- A linked list can be expanded one node at a time, therefore optimizing memory use.

- A stack is a data structure organized as last in, first out.

- A queue is a data structure organized as first in, first out.

- A linked list can be used to represent a stack. In that case, we push onto the stack by inserting an item at the beginning of the list. We pop by deleting the first item of the list.

- A linked list can also be used to represent a queue. In that case, we enqueue by inserting at the end of the list. We dequeue by deleting the first item of the list. Because we insert at the end of the list, it is useful to have an instance variable representing the last node in the list, often called *tail*.

- A stack can also be represented by an array, if we know in advance the maximum number of items that will be stored on the stack at one time. An instance variable called *top* represents the index of the last array element pushed onto the stack. We pop, or delete, that element, unless the stack is empty. We push, or insert, onto the stack a new element at index (*top + 1*), unless the stack is full.

- A queue can also be represented by an array, if we know in advance the maximum number of items that will be stored in the queue at one time. A circular array is usually implemented for the queue. Two instance variables called *front* and *back* represent the indexes of the first and last element inserted in the queue. We dequeue, or delete, the element at index *front* unless the queue is empty. We enqueue, or insert, a new element at index (*back* + 1% *QUEUE_SIZE*), unless the queue is full.

- In a class encapsulating a data structure, a method returning an object can *throw* an exception if we cannot return or cannot find the object. Indeed, when the object we are looking for is not found, it is preferable to *throw* an exception rather than to return *null*.

- A linked list can be sorted in ascending or descending order. One of the instance variables of the list objects is used as the key to sort the list elements. The *insert* method finds the appropriate location to insert an item so that the list remains sorted.

- A variation of the linked list includes a doubly linked list. In this case, each node contains three instance variables: an object representing the data, a node reference representing the next node, and another node reference representing the previous node. The latter enables us to backtrack in the list, if we need to, whereas in a singly linked list, we can traverse the list in a forward direction only. However, implementing such a list is more difficult; each method, in particular *insert* and *delete*, involves more operations to maintain these double links between nodes.

- Linked lists can implement generic types; when such a linked list is instantiated, the client specifies the class of the items for the list.

- Linked lists can also be recursively defined. A recursively defined linked list is made up of two elements: *first*, which is the first item in the linked list, and *rest*, a linked list that consists of the rest of the linked list.

14.14 Exercises, Problems, and Projects

14.14.1 Multiple Choice Exercises

1. What is an advantage of linked lists over arrays?

    ❑ Linked lists are easily expanded.

    ❑ Linked lists are limited in size.

    ❑ Linked lists can store objects, whereas arrays are limited to primitive data types.

2. How is a stack organized?

❑ FIFO

❑ LIFO

❑ Items are sorted in ascending order.

❑ Items are sorted in descending order.

3. How is a queue organized?

❑ FIFO

❑ LIFO

❑ Items are sorted in ascending order.

❑ Items are sorted in descending order.

4. The following linked list represents a stack. If we pop once from the stack, what item is popped?

(*7, Ajay, NFL*) → (*3, Sarah, Mario*) → (*9, Jin, Golf*)

head

→ (*5, Joe, Sonic*) → *null*

❑ (*7, Ajay, NFL*)

❑ (*3, Sarah, Mario*)

❑ (*9, Jin, Golf*)

❑ (*5, Joe, Sonic*)

5. The linked list that follows represents a stack. After we push the player (*5, Joe, Sonic*) onto the stack, what are the first and last items on the stack?

(*7, Ajay, NFL*) → (*3, Sarah, Mario*) → (*9, Jin, Golf*) → *null*

head

❑ (*7, Ajay, NFL*) and (*9, Jin, Golf*)

❑ (*5, Joe, Sonic*) and (*9, Jin, Golf*)

❑ (*3, Sarah, Mario*) and (*5, Joe, Sonic*)

❑ (*7, Ajay, NFL*) and (*5, Joe, Sonic*)

6. The linked list that follows represents a queue. If we dequeue once, what item is dequeued?

(*7, Ajay, NFL*) → (*3, Sarah, Mario*) → (*9, Jin, Golf*) →

head

(5, Joe, Sonic) → *null*

   tail

❑ (7, Ajay, NFL)

❑ (3, Sarah, Mario)

❑ (9, Jin, Golf)

❑ (5, Joe, Sonic)

7. The linked list that follows represents a queue. After we enqueue the player (5, Joe, Sonic), what are now the first and last items on the queue?

(7, Ajay, NFL) → (3, Sarah, Mario) → (9, Jin, Golf) → *null*

   head   *tail*

❑ (7, Ajay, NFL) and (9, Jin, Golf)

❑ (5, Joe, Sonic) and (9, Jin, Golf)

❑ (3, Sarah, Mario) and (5, Joe, Sonic)

❑ (7, Ajay, NFL) and (5, Joe, Sonic)

8. The diagram that follows shows the current state of a stack represented by an array of 50 integers. After pushing 36 and 62 onto the stack and then popping once, what will be the value of *top*, and what element will be stored at index *top*?

Index	Item stored
47 (top)	28
46	98
...	...
3	17
2	12
1	20
0	45

❑ *top* is 47 and the element at index *top* is 28

❑ *top* is 49 and the element at index *top* is 62

❑ *top* is 48 and the element at index *top* is 36

❑ *top* is 49 and the element at index *top* is 20

9. The diagram that follows shows the current state of a stack represented by an array of 50 integers. After pushing 36, 88, and 62 onto the stack and popping three times from the stack, what will be the value of *top* and what element will be stored at index *top*?

Index	Item stored
47 (top)	28
46	98
...	...
3	17
2	12
1	20
0	45

❏ *top* is 49 and the element at index *top* is 62

❏ *top* is 47 and the element at index *top* is 28

❏ *top* is 46 and the element at index *top* is 98

❏ *top* is 50 and the element at index *top* is 17

10. The diagram that follows shows the current state of a queue represented by a circular array of 8 integers. After enqueuing 36 and 62, and dequeuing once, what are the values of *front* and *back*, and what elements are stored at indexes *front* and *back*?

Index	Item stored
7	
6 (back)	28
5	97
4	25
3	54
2 (front)	12
1	
0	

❑ *front* = 0, stores 62; *back* = 5, stores 97

❑ *front* = 3, stores 54; *back* = 0, stores 62

❑ *front* = 3, stores 54; *back* = 8, stores 62

❑ *front* = 1, stores 36; *back* = 6, stores 28

11. The diagram that follows shows the current state of a queue represented by a circular array of 8 integers. After enqueuing 36, 100, 83, 77, and 62, what are the values of *front* and *back*, and what elements are stored at indexes *front* and *back*?

Index	Item stored
7	
6 (back)	28
5	97
4	25
3	54
2 (front)	12
1	
0	

❑ *front* = 2, stores 12; *back* = 11, stores 62

❑ *front* = 2, stores 12; *back* = 3, stores 62

❑ *front* = 3, stores 62; *back* = 6, stores 28

❑ *front* = 2, stores 12; *back* = 1, stores 83

12. The diagram that follows shows the current state of a queue represented by a circular array of 8 integers. After dequeuing 5 times, what are the values of *front* and *back*, and what elements are stored at indexes *front* and *back*?

Index	Item stored
6 (back)	28
5	97
4	25
3	54
2 (front)	12

Index	Item stored
1	
0	

- ❑ *front* = 7; *back* = 6; the queue is empty
- ❑ *front* = 2; *back* = 1; the queue is empty
- ❑ *front* = 2; *back* = 6; the queue is empty

13. The diagram that follows shows the current state of a queue represented by a circular array of 8 integers. After dequeuing 8 times, what are the values of *front* and *back*, and what elements are stored at indexes *front* and *back*?

Index	Item stored
7	
6 (back)	28
5	97
4	25
3	54
2 (front)	12
1	
0	

- ❑ *front* = 7; *back* = 6; the queue is empty
- ❑ *front* = 2; *back* = 1; the queue is empty
- ❑ *front* = 2; *back* = 6; the queue is empty
- ❑ *front* = 6; *back* = 2; the queue is empty

14.14.2 Reading and Understanding Code

For Questions 14 to 21, consider the following classes from this chapter: *Player*, *PlayerNode*, and *PlayerLinkedList*.

14. What does this method of the *PlayerLinkedList* class do?

```
public void foo1( Player p, Player q )
{
  insert( p );
  insert( q );
}
```

15. What does this method of the *PlayerLinkedList* class do?

```java
public int foo2( )
{
 PlayerNode nd = head;
 int i = 0;
 while ( nd != null )
 {
   i++;
   nd = nd.getNext( );
 }
 return i;
}
```

16. What does this method of the *PlayerLinkedList* class do?

```java
public boolean foo3( )
{
 if ( numberOfItems > 0 )
 {
   head = null;
   numberOfItems = 0;
   return true;
 }
 else
    return false;
}
```

17. What does this method of the *PlayerLinkedList* class do?

```java
public int foo4( )
{
 PlayerNode nd = head;
 int i = 0;
 while ( nd != null )
 {
   if ( nd.getPlayer( ).getGame( ).equals( "Sonic" ) )
       i++;
   nd = nd.getNext( );
 }
 return i;
}
```

18. What does this method of the *PlayerLinkedList* class do?

```java
public boolean foo5( int i )
{
 PlayerNode nd = head;
 while ( nd != null )
```

```
{
 if ( nd.getPlayer( ).getID( ) == i )
    return true;
 nd = nd.getNext( );
 }
 return false;
 }
```

19. What does this method of the *PlayerLinkedList* class do?

```
public void foo6( )
{
 PlayerNode nd = head;
 while ( nd != null )
 {
   if ( nd.getPlayer( ).getGame( ).equals( "Diablo" ) )
     System.out.println( nd.getPlayer( ).toString( ) );
   nd = nd.getNext( );
 }
}
```

20. What does this method of the *PlayerLinkedList* class do?

```
public void foo7( Player p )
{
   if ( numberOfItems == 0 )
     System.out.println( "Do nothing" );
   else
   {
     PlayerNode pn = new PlayerNode( p );
     pn.setNext( head.getNext( ) );
     head.setNext( pn );
     numberOfItems++;
   }
}
```

21. What does this method of the *PlayerLinkedList* class do?

```
public boolean foo8( )
{
 if ( numberOfItems <= 2 )
   return false;
 else
 {
   head.setNext( ( head.getNext( ) ).getNext( ) );
   numberOfItems--;
   return true;
 }
}
```

14.14.3 Fill In the Code

22. Consider the following state of a linked list of *Player* items.

$\rightarrow$ (*7, Ajay, NFL*) $\rightarrow$ (*3, Sarah, Mario*) $\rightarrow$ (*9, Jin, Golf*) $\rightarrow$ (*5, Joe, Sonic*)

   previous

As indicated, *previous* is the *PlayerNode* whose player is (*7, Ajay, NFL*).

Write the code to modify the list so that (*9, Jin, Golf*) has been deleted.

$\rightarrow$ (*7, Ajay, NFL*) $\rightarrow$ (*3, Sarah, Mario*) $\rightarrow$ (*5, Joe, Sonic*) $\rightarrow$

// your code goes here

23. Consider the following state of a linked list of *Player* items.

$\rightarrow$ (*7, Ajay, NFL*) $\rightarrow$ (*3, Sarah, Mario*) $\rightarrow$ (*9, Jin, Golf*) $\rightarrow$ (*5, Joe, Sonic*)

   previous

As indicated, *previous* is the *PlayerNode* whose player is (*7, Ajay, NFL*).

Write the code to modify the list so that the two items in the middle have been deleted.

$\rightarrow$ (*7, Ajay, NFL*) $\rightarrow$ (*5, Joe, Sonic*) $\rightarrow$

// your code goes here

24. Consider the following state of a linked list of Player items.

$\rightarrow$ (*7, Ajay, NFL*) $\rightarrow$ (*3, Sarah, Mario*) $\rightarrow$ (*9, Jin, Golf*) $\rightarrow$ (*5, Joe, Sonic*)

   previous   *current*

As indicated, *previous* is the *PlayerNode* whose player is (*7, Ajay, NFL*) and *current* is the *PlayerNode* whose player is (*3, Sarah, Mario*). Write the code to modify the list so that the two nodes in the middle have been swapped as shown here. (You need to swap the actual nodes, rather than modify their respective data.)

$\rightarrow$ (*7, Ajay, NFL*) $\rightarrow$ (*9, Jin, Golf*) $\rightarrow$ (*3, Sarah, Mario*) $\rightarrow$ (*5, Joe, Sonic*)

// your code goes here

For Questions 25 to 28, consider the *LLNode* class that follows, representing a node with a *char* instance variable, representing a grade (A, B, C, D, or F):

```
public class LLNode
{
 private char grade;
 private LLNode next;
     // constructors and methods here
}
```

25. Code the overloaded constructor with one parameter, a *char*.

```
// your code goes here
```

26. Code the overloaded constructor with two parameters.

```
// your code goes here
```

27. Code the accessors for the class.

```
// your code goes here
```

28. Code the mutators for the class.

```
// your code goes here
```

For Questions 29 to 31, consider the following *DifferentLinkedList* class, using the *LLNode* class from Questions 25 to 28 (assume that the *LLNode* class has all appropriate accessors, mutators, and other methods).

```
public class DifferentLinkedList
{
 private LLNode head;
 // there is no instance variable for
 // the number of items in the list

 // constructors and methods here
}
```

29. Code a method that returns *true* if the list is empty; *false* otherwise.

```
// your code goes here
```

30. Code a method that returns *true* if the list contains at least one item; *false* otherwise.

```
// your code goes here
```

31. Code a method that returns the number of items in the list.

```
// your code goes here
```

32. Consider a method of class *PlayerLinkedList* with the following header:

```
public Player retrieveMe( int index )
```

Write a few statements showing how you would call that method from a client program.

```
// your code goes here
```

14.14.4   Identifying Errors in Code

33. What would happen if you execute the following code just before traversing a linked list?

```
head.setNext( head );
```

34. Suppose we have coded the following method in the *PlayerLinkedList* class. Where is the error?

```
public int getHeadID( )
{
  return head.getID( );
}
```

35. Suppose we modify the code of the *push* method in the *StackArray* class as follows (that is, without incrementing *top*). What type of problem could that method create?

```
public boolean push( Player p )
{
  if ( !isFull( ) ) // is there room to insert?
  {
    stack[ top ] = p;
    return true;
  }
  else
    return false;
}
```

36. Suppose we modify the code of the *pop* method in the *StackArray* class as follows (that is, without decrementing *top*). What type of problem could that method create?

```
public Player pop( ) throws DataStructureException
{
  if ( !isEmpty( ) ) // is there an item to delete?
  return ( stack[top] );
  else
   throw new DataStructureException
          ( "Stack empty: cannot pop" );
}
```

37. Suppose we modify the code of the *enqueue* method in the *QueueArray* class as follows (that is, without incrementing the number of items). What type of problem could that method create?

```java
public boolean enqueue( Player p )
{
  if ( !isFull( ) )
  {
    queue[( back + 1 ) % QUEUE_SIZE] = p;
    back = ( back + 1 ) % QUEUE_SIZE;
    return true;
  }
  else
    return false;
}
```

38. Suppose we modify the code of the *dequeue* method in the *QueueArray* class as follows (that is, with a change in the expression computing the index in the *return* statement). Where is the error?

```java
public Player dequeue( ) throws DataStructureException
{
  if ( !isEmpty( ) )
  {
    front = ( front + 1 ) % QUEUE_SIZE;
    numberOfItems--;
    return queue[( front - 1 ) % QUEUE_SIZE];
  }
  else
    throw new DataStructureException
                ( "Queue empty: cannot dequeue" );
}
```

14.14.5 Debugging Area—Using Messages from the Java Compiler and Java JVM

39. You coded the following inside the *main* method of the *Test* class, using the *Player* and *PlayerNode* classes.

```java
PlayerNode pn = new PlayerNode( );
Player p = pn.getPlayer( );
p.setID( 10 );              // line 10
```

The code compiles, but at run time you get a *NullPointerException* at line 10.

```
Exception in thread "main" java.lang.NullPointerException
    at Test.main(Test.java:10)
```

Explain what the problem is and how to fix it.

40. You coded the following in the *main* method of the *Test* class, using the *Player* and *PlayerLinkedList* classes.

```
Player p = new Player( 5,"Ajay","Mario" );
PlayerLinkedList pll = new PlayerLinkedList( );
pll.insert( p );
PlayerNode temp = pll.getHead( );              // line 10
System.out.println( "head is " + temp.toString( ) );
```

At compile time, you get the following error:

```
Test.java:10: error: cannot find symbol
    PlayerNode temp = pll.getHead( ); // line 10
                        ^
    symbol  : method getHead ()
    location: variable pll of type PlayerLinkedList
1 error
```

Explain what the problem is and how to fix it.

41. You coded the following in the *main* method of the *Test class*, using the *Player* and *PlayerLinkedList* classes.

```
Player p = new Player( 5,"Ajay","Mario" );
PlayerLinkedList pll = new PlayerLinkedList( );
pll.insert( p );
if ( pll.delete( 5 ) )      // line 10
      System.out.println( "Successful deletion" );
```

At compile time, you get the following error:

```
Test.java:10: error: incompatible types: Player cannot be
converted to boolean
   if ( pll.delete( 5 ) )    // line 10
                 ^
1 error
```

Explain what the problem is and how to fix it.

42. You coded the following inside the *foo* method of the *PlayerLinkedList* class.

```
PlayerNode current = head;    // line 9
while ( current.getPlayer( ).getID( ) != 99 )
      current = current.getNext( );
// more code here but no problem
```

The code compiles, but when you call *foo* inside *main*, you get a *NullPointer-Exception* at run time at line 10.

```
Exception in thread "main" java.lang.NullPointerException
```

```
at PlayerLinkedList.foo(PlayerLinkedList.java:10)
at Test.main(Test.java:24)
```

What would be a possible scenario that may have caused this error? Explain how to fix this problem.

14.14.6   Write a Short Program

43. Modify the *PlayerLinkedList* class to include one more method: that method inserts a new player in the third position of the list, *head* being the first position. If the list is empty, the method will insert the new player as the head of the list. Be sure to test your method with the appropriate client code.

44. Modify the *PlayerLinkedList* class to include one more method: that method inserts a new player in the next-to-last position of the list. If the list is empty, the method will insert the new player as the head of the list. Be sure to test your method with the appropriate client code.

45. Modify the *PlayerLinkedList* class to include one more method: that method inserts a new player in the last position of the list. For this, you cannot use the *tail* instance variable. Be sure to test your method with the appropriate client code.

46. Modify the *PlayerLinkedList* class to include one more method: that method deletes the second node of the list, if there is one. Be sure to test your method with the appropriate client code.

47. Modify the *GenericLinkedList* class to include one more method: that method inserts a new item at a given position (a parameter of the method). If the list is empty, the method will insert the new item as the head of the list. If the value of the parameter is greater than the number of items in the list, then the method inserts at the end of the list. You should consider that *head* is at position 1 in the list. Be sure to test your method with the appropriate client code.

48. Modify the *GenericLinkedList* class to include one more method: that method deletes an item at a given position (a parameter of the method). If the value of the parameter is greater than the number of elements in the list, then no item is deleted and an exception is thrown. Your method should return the item deleted, if any. You should consider that the first node is at position 1 in the list. Be sure to test your method with the appropriate client code.

49. Modify the *PlayerLinkedList* class to include one more method: that method takes a parameter that represents a game. The method inserts a new player at a position just after the first *Player* of the list with a *game* instance variable equal to that game. If there is no such node, then your method should insert at the end of the list. Be sure to test your method with the appropriate client code.

50. Modify the *PlayerLinkedList* class to include one more method: a traversal that outputs the players in the list until we reach a player with a given *id*; that player's data should not be output. Be sure to test your method with the appropriate client code.

51. Modify the *GenericLinkedList* class to include one more method: a method that returns the *n*th item on the list (*n* is a parameter of the method). If there is no *n*th item on the list, the method should *throw* an exception. Test your method with a client that traverses the list by requesting each item in position order.

52. Modify the *PlayerStackLinkedList* class to include one more method: a method that returns the ID of the last player on the stack. Be sure to test your method with the appropriate client code.

53. Modify the *PlayerQueueLinkedList* class to include one more method: a method that outputs every other player in the queue; that is, it outputs the first player, skips the second, outputs the third player, skips the fourth, and so on. Be sure to test your method with the appropriate client code.

54. Modify the *RecursiveLinkedList* class to include one more method: one that inserts at the end of the list. Be sure to test your method with the appropriate client code.

55. Modify the *RecursiveLinkedList* class to include one more method: one that deletes at the end of the list. Be sure to test your method with the appropriate client code.

56. Modify the *RecursiveLinkedList* class to include one more method: one that deletes at the beginning of the list. Be sure to test your method with the appropriate client code.

57. Code a class encapsulating a stack of *doubles* using an array of 10 elements. Be sure to test your methods with the appropriate client code.

58. Code a class encapsulating a queue of *chars* using a circular array of 10 elements. Be sure to test your methods with the appropriate client code.

14.14.7   Programming Projects

59. Modify the *PlayerLinkedList* to include two more methods: one that returns the *Player* with the minimum *id*, and one that returns all the games played by players with a given *id*. You also need to include the appropriate client code to test your classes.

60. Modify the *PlayerLinkedList* to include two more methods: one that returns the *Player* with the first name in alphabetical order, and one that returns all of

the *ids* of the players playing a given game. You also need to include the appropriate client code to test your classes.

61. Code a class encapsulating a singly linked list of website objects. A website has two attributes: a URL address (a *String*, you do not need to use the existing URL Java class) and 10 or fewer keywords describing the topic of the website. In addition to *insert*, *delete*, *peek*, and *toString*, add one more method: a method that, based on a keyword, returns all URL addresses in the list containing that keyword. Your *delete* method should delete an item based on the value of its URL. You also need to include the appropriate client code to test your classes.

62. Code a class encapsulating a singly linked list of football teams. A football team has three attributes: its nickname, its number of wins, and its number of losses (assume there are no tied games). In addition to *insert*, *delete*, *peek*, and *toString*, add two more methods: a method that returns the nicknames of the teams with the most wins, and another method that returns the five best teams based on winning percentages (if multiple teams have the same winning percentage, you can return the first five such teams in the list). You also need to include the appropriate client code to test your classes.

63. Code a class encapsulating a singly linked list of HTML tags. We will define a valid HTML tag as a string of characters starting with < and ending with >. In addition to *insert*, *delete*, *peek*, and *toString*, add two more methods: a method that returns *true* or *false*, checking if the list contains valid HTML tags only (as previously defined), and another that counts how many items in the list contain the slash (/) character in them. You also need to include the appropriate client code to test your classes.

64. Code a class encapsulating a singly linked list of stocks. A stock is defined by the following attributes: its ticker symbol (a short word, for instance AMD), its price (for example 54.35), and the company's earnings per share (for example 3.25). In addition to *insert*, *delete*, *peek*, and *toString*, add two more methods: a method that returns the list of all the tickers for the penny stocks (a penny stock is a stock whose price is $1.00 or less), and another method that, given a number representing a price earnings ratio (the price earnings ratio of a stock, also known as P/E ratio, is the price of the stock divided by the earnings per share), returns all the tickers with a price earnings ratio less than or equal to that number. You also need to include the appropriate client code to test your classes.

65. Code a class encapsulating a singly linked list of books. A book is defined by the following attributes: its title, its author, its price, and how many are in

stock. In addition to *insert, delete, peek,* and *toString,* add two more methods: a method that, based on a word, returns all the book titles in the list containing that word, and another returning the list of book titles that are out of stock (i.e., there are quantity 0 in stock). You also need to include the appropriate client code to test your classes.

66. Code a class encapsulating a stack of clothes using an array. A clothing item has the following attributes: its name, its color, and whether it can be washed at high temperature. We will limit our stack to 100 clothing items. In addition to *push, pop, peek,* and *toString,* add two more methods: a method that returns all the clothing items of a given color, and another method that returns how many clothing items in the stack can be washed at high temperature. You also need to include the appropriate client code to test your classes.

67. Code a class encapsulating a queue of foods using a circular array. A food has the following attributes: its name, the number of calories per serving, and the number of servings per container. We will limit our queue to 100 foods. In addition to *enqueue, dequeue, peek,* and *toString,* add two more methods: a method that returns the average calories per serving of all the foods in the queue, and another method that returns the food item with the highest "total calories" (i.e., calories per serving times number of servings). You also need to include the appropriate client code to test your classes.

68. Code a class encapsulating a sorted linked list of foods; a *Food* class is defined in question 67. Your list should be sorted in ascending order using the name of the food as the key. In addition to *insert, delete, peek,* and *toString,* add two more methods: a method that returns all the *Food* objects in the list that have a number of calories per serving lower than a given value, and another method that returns all the *Food* objects in the list that are located after a given food name. You also need to include the appropriate client code to test your classes.

69. Look at the documentation of the *LinkedList* class in the *java.util* package. Create a class of your choice and code a client class to test the *LinkedList* class; in particular use the *addFirst, add,* and *addLast* methods to build a linked list. Also test the *set* and *get* methods. Do you have access to a *toString* method that returns a *String* representation of the linked list? In this implementation, what is the index of the first element in the list? Do the *get* and *element* methods return a copy of an element of the list or a reference to it?

Look
It
Up

70. Code a stack class using a generic type; the stack should be represented by an array. You should include *push, pop,* and *toString* methods. You also need to

include the appropriate client code to test your class. In the client class, you should declare and instantiate stacks using at least two different class types.

71. Code a queue class using generics; the queue should be represented by a circular array. You should include *enqueue*, *dequeue*, and *toString* methods. You also need to include the appropriate client code to test your class. In the client class, you should declare and instantiate queues using at least two different class types.

14.14.8   Technical Writing

72. In this chapter, we coded a linked-list class with just two instance variables: the head node and the number of items in the list. We also said that we did not really need the number of items in the list. Explain how we can traverse the whole list if the class has only one instance variable, *head*.

73. Consider the *PlayerQueueLinkedList* class presented in this chapter, which includes an instance variable called *tail*, in addition to *head*. We want to make the list circular; that is, *tail* "points to" *head*. If you made the method call *tail.getNext( )*, it would return *head*. Describe why and how you would need to modify the *toString* method of the class (assume you do not know the number of items in the list).

14.14.9   Group Project (for a group of 1, 2, or 3 students)

74. Code a doubly linked, sorted list (in ascending order). Each item of the list will just store an *int*.

You need to code three classes: *Node*, *SortedList*, and *GroupProject*.

The Node class has three instance variables, all *private*:

❑ an *int*, representing the value stored inside the *Node*

❑ a *Node* (*next*)

❑ another *Node* (*previous*)

The methods to code are: constructor (at least one), accessors, mutators.

The *SortedList* class is a doubly linked list, sorted in ascending order.

It has two instance variables, both private:

❑ an *int*, representing the number of items in the list

❑ a *Node*, representing the head node in the list

The methods to code are:

❏ *insert*: this method takes one parameter, an *int*; it has a *void* return value.

❏ *delete*: this method takes one parameter, an *int*; it returns a *boolean* value. If we were successful in deleting the item (i.e., the value of the parameter was found in the list), then we return *true*; if we were not successful, then we want to output a message that the value was not found, and therefore, not deleted, and return *false*.

❏ *toString*: this method takes no parameters and returns a *String* representation of the list.

❏ constructor (at least one), and accessors and mutators as appropriate.

All methods should keep the list sorted in ascending order.

The *GroupProject* class contains the *main* method; it should do the following:

❏ create a *SortedList* object reference

❏ insert successively the values 25, 17, 12, 21, 78, and 47 in the sorted list

❏ output the contents of the sorted list using the *toString* method

❏ delete from the sorted list the value 30, using the *delete* method (obviously, 30 will not be found)

❏ output the contents of the sorted list using the *toString* method

❏ delete from the sorted list the value 21, using the *delete* method

❏ output the contents of the sorted list using the *toString* method

Your *insert* and *delete* methods should work properly in all possible scenarios: inserting in an empty list, inserting at the beginning of a list, inserting in the middle of a list, inserting at the end of a list, deleting from an empty list (cannot delete), deleting an item not in the list (cannot delete), deleting the first item in a list, deleting in the middle of a list, deleting the last item in a list.

CHAPTER 15
Running Time Analysis

CHAPTER CONTENTS

Introduction

Today's Internet websites have millions of users. The databases storing data on the web servers have grown in size dramatically to accommodate both the growing number of users and the growing volume of data that is posted by these users.

Scientific applications have also experienced a data explosion. Sensors used in these scientific applications, such as meteorology or fluid mechanics, are becoming more precise while at the same time they are getting cheaper. More and more sensors are being used, and application programs have to manage more and more data.

Programs that handle and manipulate this ever-increasing amount of Big Data need to use algorithms that are well-designed and efficient so that they minimize waiting time for users. Two programs that solve the same problem using different algorithms can result in completely different levels of performance—everything else, in particular the hardware platform, being equal. For example, two search engines performing the same search could run at different speeds: one could return its results in tenths of a second while the other could take several seconds to return results.

Many programmers tend to disregard speed and space (memory utilization) issues when writing code. They rely on increasing hardware performance to solve speed problems and the decreasing cost of memory to solve space problems. However, with the Big Data explosion and the resulting data processing issues that we are experiencing today across many industries, designing efficient algorithms has become more and more important. In this chapter, we will focus on algorithms' speed performance.

When we measure the performance of an algorithm, we use the expression **running time**. We cannot predict a single, precise running time for many algorithms, because the amount of processing depends in large part on the number of inputs and the values of those inputs. So we express the running time of an algorithm as a mathematical function of its inputs. This allows us to compare the relative performance of multiple algorithms. For example, the running time for computing the factorial of an integer varies according to the integer value. Factorials of larger numbers require more processing to compute than factorials of smaller numbers. If we can express the running time of multiple algorithms that compute a factorial as a function of their input, then we can compare the relative efficiency of each algorithm. In other cases, such as sorting an array of integers, the running time depends on the number of array elements. Similarly, if we express the running time as a function of the number of elements in the array, we can compare the relative efficiency of multiple sorting algorithms.

The input value or number of inputs for an algorithm represents the size of the problem for which we are trying to compute the running time. We will call that number n. We are interested in relative time, independent of the hardware platform, not absolute time. Furthermore, we are typically interested in the order of magnitude of the algorithm, rather than a precise mathematical expression as a function of n. Indeed, if n is very large (for example, 1 million or more), performance does not vary noticeably if the algorithm takes n steps or $n + 17$ steps to complete.

However, if an algorithm has a running time expressed as n^2, then the number of inputs has a big impact on performance. For example, we can predict that 10 inputs will require the execution of 100 statements and 1,000 inputs will require the execution of 1 million statements.

The objectives of this chapter are:

- To be able to evaluate the running time of a given algorithm through various methodologies

- To understand that how we code an algorithm directly impacts its running time

15.1 Orders of Magnitude and Big-Oh Notation

Table 15.1 shows examples of various orders of magnitude for an algorithm as a function of the number of inputs n, along with the corresponding number of statement executions for different values of n.

Let's look at an example to see how we can use these values. As we will demonstrate later in the chapter, Sequential Search has a running time of n, and Binary Search has a running time of $log\ n$. Thus, if we are searching an array of 1 million users for a

TABLE 15.1 Comparisons of Various Functions Representing Running Times

Order of Magnitude	Number of Statements Executed			
	$n = 10$	$n = 20$	$n = 1,000$	$n = 1$ million
$log\ n$	2.23	3.23	Approx. 10	Approx. 20
n	10	20	1,000	10^6
$n\ log\ n$	22.3	64.6	Approx. 10,000	Approx. $20*10^6$
n^2	100	400	10^6	10^{12}
n^3	1,000	8,000	10^9	10^{18}
2^n	1,024	Approx. 10^6	Approx. 10^{300}	Approx. 10^{300000}

particular user name, a Sequential Search will take, on average, the execution of an order of 1 million statements, while a Binary Search will require the execution of only 20 statements. Remember, however, that for a Binary Search to work, the array must already be sorted. Later in this chapter, we will discuss how to compute these running times.

As we can see from the table, algorithms that have a running time where n is the exponent of the function, such as 2^n, take a very large number of statement executions and are very slow; they should be used only if no better algorithm can be found.

Running times of algorithms are often represented using the **Big-Oh** or the **Big-Theta** notation, as in $O(n)$ or $\Theta(n^2)$, for example. The mathematical definition of Big-Theta is as follows:

A function $f(n)$ is Big-Theta of another function $g(n)$, or $\Theta(g(n))$, if and only if:

1. $f(n)$ is **Big-Omega** of $g(n)$, or $\Omega(g(n))$, i.e., there exist two positive constants, $n1$ and $c1$, such that for any $n >= n1$, $f(n) >= c1 * g(n)$.

    In other words, for n sufficiently big, $g(n)$ is a lower bound of $f(n)$; that is, $g(n)$ is smaller than $f(n)$, if we ignore the constants.

and

2. $f(n)$ is Big-Oh of $g(n)$, or $O(g(n))$, i.e., there exist two positive constants, $n2$ and $c2$, such that for any $n >= n2$, $f(n) <= c2 * g(n)$.

    In other words, for n sufficiently big, $g(n)$ is an upper bound of $f(n)$; that is, $g(n)$ is bigger than $f(n)$, if we ignore the constants.

It has become common in the industry to say Big-Oh instead of Big-Theta. Indeed, we are really interested in an upper bound running time (Big-Oh), and as tight an upper bound as possible (Big-Theta).

Although the preceding definition may sound a bit complex, when trying to estimate the Big-Oh of a particular function representing a running time, the following rules can be used:

- Keep only the dominant term, i.e., the term that grows the fastest as n grows.
- Ignore the coefficient of the dominant term.

Table 15.2 shows a few examples illustrating these rules.

As an example, we will show that the function $f(n) = 3 * n^2 + 6 * n + 12$ is $\Theta(n^2)$.

First we show that $f(n)$ is $\Omega(n^2)$:

For $n >= 0$,

$f(n) = 3 * n^2 + 6 * n + 12 >= 3 * n^2$

TABLE 15.2   Examples of Functions Representing Running Times and Their Respective Big-Oh

$f(n)$	Dominant Term	Big-Oh
$2*n+19$	$2*n$	$O(n)$
$3*n^2+6*n+12$	$3*n^2$	$O(n^2)$
$n^3+9*n^2+5*n+2$	n^3	$O(n^3)$
$3*2^n+5*n^3+3*n+7$	$3*2^n$	$O(2^n)$
$n+7*\log n$	n	$O(n)$
$2*n*\log n+8*n+\log n+8$	$2*n*\log n$	$O(n*\log n)$
$3*\log n+35$	$3*\log n$	$O(\log n)$

So if we choose $n1 = 0$ and $c1 = 3$, we just proved by definition that $f(n)$ is $\Omega(n^2)$.

Now we show that the same function $f(n)$ is $O(n^2)$.

For $n >= 1$, we can rewrite $f(n)$ as

$$f(n) = n^2 * (3 + 6 / n + 12 / n^2)$$

For $n >= 6$, we have

$$6 / n <= 1 \text{ and } 12 / n^2 < 1$$

therefore,

$$f(n) <= n^2 * (3 + 1 + 1) = 5 * n^2$$

So if we choose $n2 = 6$ and $c2 = 5$, we just proved by definition that $f(n)$ is $O(n^2)$.

Since $f(n)$ is both Big-Omega(n^2) and Big-Oh(n^2), then $f(n)$ is Big-Theta(n^2).

To show that a polynomial function is Big-Oh of its most dominant term, we simply factor by the most dominant term as follows:

For $n > 0$,

$$f(n) = a_p n^p + a_{p-1} n^{p-1} + \ldots + a_2 n^2 + a_1 n + a_0, \text{ where } a_p \text{ is strictly positive}$$

$$f(n) = a_p n^p (1 + (a_{p-1} / a_p) 1 / n + \ldots + (a_2 / a_p) 1 / n^{p-2} + (a_1 / a_p) 1 / n^{p-1} + (a_p / a_0) 1 / n^p)$$

$$f(n) <= a_p n^p (1 + |(a_{p-1} / a_p)| 1 / n + \ldots + |(a_2 / a_p)| 1 / n^{p-2} + |(a_1 / a_p)| 1 / n^{p-1} + |(a_p / a_0)| 1 / n^p)$$

All a_i's are constants; let M be the maximum of all $|(a_i / a_p)|$.

Thus,

$$f(n) <= a_p \, n^p \, (1 + M \, 1 \, / \, n + \ldots + M \, 1 \, / \, n^{p-2} + M \, 1 \, / \, n^{p-1} + M \, 1 \, / \, n^p)$$

$$f(n) <= a_p \, n^p \, (1 + M \, (1 \, / \, n + \ldots + 1 \, / \, n^{p-2} + 1 \, / \, n^{p-1} + 1 \, / \, n^p))$$

$$f(n) <= a_p \, n^p \, (1 + M \, (-1 + 1 + 1 \, / \, n + \ldots + 1 \, / \, n^{p-2} + 1 \, / \, n^{p-1} + 1 \, / \, n^p))$$

since we know mathematically that

$1 + a + a^2 + \ldots + a^p = \Sigma \, a^i$ from $i = 0$ to p is equal to $(1 - a^{p+1}) \, / \, (1 - a)$ for a different from 1.

Using $a = 1/n$ and $n >= 2$, we get

$$f(n) <= a_p \, n^p \, (1 + M \, (-1 + (1 - 1 \, / \, n^{p+1}) \, / \, (1 - 1 \, / \, n)))$$

$$f(n) <= a_p \, n^p \, (1 + M \, (-1 + (1 - 1 \, / \, n^{p+1}) * (n \, / \, (n - 1))))$$

Thus,

$$f(n) <= a_p \, n^p \, (1 + M \, (-1 + (n \, / \, (n - 1))))$$

$$f(n) <= a_p \, n^p \, (1 + M \, ((-n + 1 + n) \, / \, (n - 1)))$$

$$f(n) <= a_p \, n^p \, (1 + M \, (1 \, / \, (n - 1)))$$

Thus,

$$f(n) <= a_p \, n^p \, (1 + M) \text{ for } n >= 2$$

choosing $n_0 = 2$ and $c_0 = a_p \, (1 + M)$.

For $n >= n_0$, we have

$$f(n) <= c_0 \, n^p$$

and therefore,

$f(n)$ is $O(n^p)$, i.e., $f(n)$ is Big-Oh of its most dominant term.

15.2   Running Time Analysis of Algorithms: Counting Statements

One simple method to analyze the running time of a code sequence or a method is simply to count the number of times each statement is executed and to calculate a total count of statement executions.

Example 15.1 is a method that calculates the total value of all the elements of an array of size n and returns the sum.

```
public static int addElements( int [ ] arr )
{
    int sum = 0;                    // ( 1 )
    int i = 0;                      // ( 2 )
```

```
while ( i < arr.length )      // ( 3 )
{
    sum += arr[i];            // ( 4 )
    i++;                      // ( 5 )
}
return sum;                   // ( 6 )
}
```

EXAMPLE 15.1   A Single Loop

Let's count how many times each statement is executed.

Assuming the array has n elements, we can develop the following analysis:

Statement	# Times Executed
(1)	1
(2)	1
(3)	$n + 1$
(4)	n
(5)	n
(6)	1

Note that the loop condition, $i < arr.length$, is executed one more time than each statement of the loop body: when i is equal to $arr.length$, we evaluate the loop condition, but we exit the loop and thus do not execute the two statements in the loop body. Thus, the total number of statements executed, $T(n)$, is equal to:

$$T(n) = 1 + 1 + (n + 1) + n + n + 1$$
$$= 3n + 4$$
$$= O(n)$$

So we can say that the running time of the *addElements* method is $O(n)$. Note that in the end, we do not need an exact count of the statements executed, since we are really interested in the Big-Oh running time of the function.

Example 15.2 is a method that determines the maximum value in a two-dimensional array of *ints*.

```
public static int calculateMaximum( int [ ][ ] arr )
{
    int maximum  = arr[0][0];                    // ( 1 )
    for ( int i = 0; i < arr.length; i++ )       // ( 2 )
    {
        for ( int j = 0; j < arr[i].length; j++ )  // ( 3 )
        {
```

```
   if ( maximum < arr[i][j] )                    // ( 4 )
         maximum = arr[i][j];                    // ( 5 )
   }
 }
 return maximum;                                 // ( 6 )
}
```

EXAMPLE 15.2   A Double Loop

Let's count how many times each statement is executed. In order to keep things simple, we assume that the array has n rows and each row has n columns. We can then develop the following analysis:

Statement	# Times Executed
(1)	1
(2)	$1 + (n + 1) + n = 2 * n + 2$
(3)	$n * (1 + (n + 1) + n) = 2 * n^2 + 2 * n$
(4)	$n * n = n^2$
(5)	between 0 and $n * n$
(6)	1

Statement (2) actually contains three statements: *int i = 0* is executed 1 time, *i < arr. length* is executed $(n + 1)$ times as i goes from 0 to n, and *i++* is executed n times as i is incremented n times.

In evaluating the number of times statements (3), (4), and (5) will be executed, we first note that we will enter the outer loop n times. Statement (3) also contains three statements: *int j = 0* is executed each time we enter the outer loop, or n times; *j < arr. length*[i] is executed $(n + 1)$ times each time we enter the outer loop, or $n * (n + 1)$ times, as j goes from 0 to n; and *j++* is executed n times each time we enter the outer loop, or $n * n$ times.

Since we enter the outer loop n times and for each outer loop iteration, we enter the inner loop n times, statement (4) will be executed $n * n$ times. As for statement (5), it will be executed once each time the Boolean expression *maximum < arr*[i][j] evaluates to *true*. We cannot tell how many times that will happen, but we can tell that it will happen no more than $n * n$ times. We will call this unknown value x.

Thus, the total number of statements executed, $T(n)$, is equal to:

$$T(n) = 1 + (2 * n + 2) + (2 * n^2 + 2 * n) + (n^2) + x + 1$$
$$= 3 * n^2 + 4 * n + 4 + x$$

with $x <= n * n$

Furthermore, since the value of x is between 0 and n^2,

$$3 * n^2 + 4 * n + 4 <= T(n) <= 3 * n^2 + 4 * n + 4 + n^2$$
$$3 * n^2 + 4 * n + 4 <= T(n) <= 4 * n^2 + 4 * n + 4$$

since $T(n)$ has both lower and upper bounds that are $O(n^2)$, $T(n)$ is $O(n^2)$.

For our third example, let's compute the running time of a Sequential Search, implemented by the code shown in Example 15.3.

```java
public static int sequentialSearch( int [ ] array, int key )
{
    for ( int i = 0; i < array.length; i++ )     // ( 1 )
        if ( array[ i ] == key )                  // ( 2 )
            return i;                             // ( 3 )
    return -1;                                    // ( 4 )
}
```

EXAMPLE 15.3   Sequential Search Algorithm

Let's count how many times each statement is executed. Assuming the array has n elements, we can develop the following analysis:

Statement	# Times Executed
(1)	1 + (between 1 and (n + 1)) + (between 0 and n)
(2)	between 1 and n
(3)	0 or 1
(4)	1 or 0

Thus, if $T(n)$ represents the total number of statements executed, we can say that

$$1 + (1) + (0) + 1 + 1 \ <= \ T(n) \ <= \ 1 + (n + 1) + n + n + 1$$
$$4 \ <= \ T(n) \ <= \ 3n + 3$$

$T(n) <= 3n + 3$ shows that $T(n)$ is $O(n)$.

However, we cannot really tell, from the coding of the function, how many statements will be executed as a function of n. In these situations, it is interesting to consider three running times:

- the worst-case running time
- the best-case running time
- the average-case running time

In the worst case, where the search key is not found in the array or it is found in the last element, $T(n) = 3n + 3$, and therefore $T(n)$ is $O(n)$, as mentioned earlier.

In the best case, the element we are looking for is at index 0 of the array, and only four statements will be executed, independently of the value of n. Thus, the best-case running time is $O(1)$ since we do not take the multiplying constant into consideration when we compute a Big-Oh.

In the average case, we find the element we are looking for in the middle of the array, and the value of $T(n)$ will be

$$T(n) = 1 + (n + 1)/2 + n/2 + n/2 + 1$$
$$= 3n/2 + 2 \tfrac{1}{2}$$
$$= O(n)$$

15.3   Running Time Analysis of Algorithms and Impact of Coding: Evaluating Recursive Methods

In this section, we will learn how to compute the running time of a recursive method. We will also look at how coding a method has a direct impact on its running time.

Consider coding a recursive method that takes one parameter, n, and returns 2^n. There are several ways to code that method, and we will consider two of them here so that we can assess which algorithm is more efficient.

Our first method, *powerOf2A*, is designed using this approach:

- when $n = 0$, $2^0 = 1$. This is our base case.

- For our general case, we use this calculation: $2^n = 2 * 2^{n-1}$

This first problem formulation results in the method shown in Example 15.4.

```java
public static int powerOf2A( int n ) // n >= 0
{
    if ( n == 0 )
        return 1;
    else
        return 2 * powerOf2A( n - 1 );
}
```

EXAMPLE 15.4   First Recursive Formulation of 2^n

Our second method, *powerOf2B*, is designed using this approach:

- when $n = 0$, $2^0 = 1$. This is our base case.

- For our general case, we use this calculation: $2^n = 2^{n-1} + 2^{n-1}$

This second problem formulation results in the method shown in Example 15.5.

```java
public static int powerOf2B( int n ) // n >= 0
{
   if ( n == 0 )
      return 1;
   else
      return powerOf2B( n - 1 ) + powerOf2B( n - 1 );
}
```

EXAMPLE 15.5   Second Recursive Formulation of 2^n

Let's compute the running time of *powerOf2A* as a function of the input *n*; we will call it $T1(n)$.

In the base case (*n* is equal to 0), *powerOf2A* makes only one comparison and returns 1. Thus,

$$T1(0) = 1$$

Generally, since it takes $T1(n)$ to compute and return *powerOf2A(n)*, then it takes $T1(n - 1)$ to compute and return *powerOf2A(n – 1)*.

Thus, in the general case, the comparison in the *if* statement will cost us 1 instruction; computing and returning *powerOf2A(n – 1)* will cost us $T1(n - 1)$; and multiplying that result by 2 will cost us 1 instruction. Thus, the total time $T1(n)$ can be expressed as follows:

$$T1(n) = 1 + T1(n - 1) + 1$$
$$= T1(n - 1) + 2 \quad \text{// Equation 15.1}$$

The preceding equation, which we will call Equation 15.1, is called a recurrence relation between $T1(n)$ and $T1(n - 1)$ because $T1(n)$ is expressed as a function of $T1(n - 1)$.

From there, we can use a number of techniques to compute the value of $T1(n)$ as a function of *n*.

Handwaving Method

This method is called handwaving because it is more an estimation method, rather than a method based on strict mathematics.

From the preceding recurrence relation, we can say that it costs us two instructions to go down one step (from *n* to *n – 1*). Therefore, to go down *n* steps will cost us $2 * n$ instructions. We then add one instruction for $T(0)$, and get

$$T1(n) = 2 * n + 1$$

Iterative Method

This method involves iterating several times, starting with the recurrence relation until we can identify a pattern. In general, we can say that

$$T1(x) = T1(x - 1) + 2, \text{ where } x \text{ is some integer} \quad \text{// Equation 15.2}$$

We call this Equation 15.2, which is the same as Equation 15.1, except that x has been substituted for n.

We now want to express $T(n)$ as a function of $T(n - 2)$; thus, we want to replace $T(n - 1)$ in Equation 15.1 by an expression using $T(n - 2)$.

Substituting $n - 1$ for x in Equation 15.2, we get

$$T1(n - 1) = T1(n - 2) + 2$$

Plugging the value of $T1(n - 1)$ into Equation 15.1, we get

$$T1(n) = T1(n - 2) + 2 + 2$$
$$= T1(n - 2) + 2 * 2 \quad \text{// Equation 15.3}$$

SOFTWARE ENGINEERING TIP

When trying to develop and identify a pattern using iteration, do not precisely compute all the terms. Instead, leave them as patterns.

Note that in Equation 15.3, we do not simplify 2 * 2. In this way, we are trying to let a pattern develop so we can easily identify it.

Using $x = n - 2$ in Equation 15.2, we get

$$T1(n - 2) = T1(n - 3) + 2$$

Plugging the value of $T1(n - 2)$ into Equation 15.3, we get

$$T1(n) = T1(n - 3) + 2 + 2 * 2$$
$$= T1(n - 3) + 2 * 3 \quad \text{// Equation 15.4}$$

Using $x = n - 3$ in Equation 15.2, we get

$$T1(n - 3) = T1(n - 4) + 2$$

Plugging the value of $T1(n - 3)$ into Equation 15.4, we get

$$T1(n) = T1(n - 4) + 2 + 2 * 3$$
$$= T1(n - 4) + 2 * 4$$

Now we can see the pattern as follows:

$$T1(n) = T1(n - k) + 2 * k, \text{ where } k \text{ is an integer between 1 and } n$$
$$\text{// Equation 15.5}$$

Plugging $k = n$ in Equation 15.5 in order to reach the base case of $T1(0)$, we get

$$T1(n) = T1(0) + 2 * n = 1 + 2 * n = 2 * n + 1$$

Proof by Induction Method

If we can guess the value of $T1(n)$ as a function of n, then we can use a proof by induction in order to prove that our guess is correct. We can use the preceding iteration method to come up with a guess for $T1(n)$.

Generally, a proof by induction works as follows:

- Verify that our statement (equation in this case) is true for a base case.

- Assume that out statement is true up to n.

- Prove that it is true for $n + 1$.

Let's go through the induction steps with our guess that $T1(n) = 2 * n + 1$, which we may have generated from our iterative or handwaving method.

Step 1: Verify that the value that our guess gives to $T1(0)$ is correct.

$$T1(0) = 2 * 0 + 1$$
$$= 1$$

Thus, our guess is correct for $T1(0)$.

Step 2: Assume that $T1(n) = 2 * n + 1$.

Step 3: Prove that $T1(n + 1) = 2 * (n + 1) + 1$.

Plugging $x = n + 1$ in Equation 15.2, we get
$$T1(n + 1) = T1(n) + 2$$

Then, using our assumption and replacing $T1(n)$ by $2 * n + 1$, we get

$$T1(n + 1) = 2 * n + 1 + 2$$
$$= 2 * n + 2 + 1$$
$$= 2 * (n + 1) + 1$$

Thus, we just proved, by induction, that our guess $T1(n) = 2 * n + 1$ is correct.

Other Methods

When applicable, another method is to use the Master Theorem, but that is beyond the scope of this text.

So the running time of $powerOf2A(n)$ is $2 * n + 1$, or $O(n)$.

Let's now compute the running time of $powerOf2B$ as a function of the input n. We will call it $T2(n)$.

In the base case (n is equal to 0), $powerOf2B$ takes only one comparison to return 1. Thus,

$$T2(0) = 1$$

Generally, since it takes $T2(n)$ to compute and return *powerOf2B(n)*, then it takes $T2(n - 1)$ to compute and return *powerOf2B(n - 1)*. Thus, in the general case, the comparison in the *if* statement will cost us one instruction; computing and returning *powerOf2B(n - 1)* will cost us $T2(n - 1)$; doing it a second time will cost us another $T2(n - 1)$; and adding the two and returning the sum as the result will cost us one instruction. Thus, the total time $T2(n)$ can be expressed as follows:

$$T2(n) = 1 + T2(n - 1) + T2(n - 1) + 1$$
$$= 2 * T2(n - 1) + 2 \quad \text{// Equation 15.6}$$

From there, we will use the iteration method in order to compute the value of $T2(n)$ as a function of n.

Substituting x for n, we can rewrite Equation 15.6 as follows:

$$T2(x) = 2 * T2(x - 1) + 2 \quad \text{// Equation 15.7}$$

Using $x = n - 1$ in Equation 15.7, we get

$$T2(n - 1) = 2 * T2(n - 2) + 2$$

Plugging the value of $T2(n - 1)$ into Equation 15.6, we get

$$T2(n) = 2 * (2 * T2(n - 2) + 2) + 2$$
$$= 2^2 * T2(n - 2) + 2^2 + 2 \quad \text{// Equation 15.8}$$

Again, we leave $2^2 + 2$ as an expression to try to let a pattern develop.

Using $x = n - 2$ in Equation 15.7, we get

$$T2(n - 2) = 2 * T2(n - 3) + 2$$

Plugging the value of $T2(n - 2)$ into Equation 15.8, we get

$$T2(n) = 2^2 * (2 * T2(n - 3) + 2) + 2^2 + 2$$
$$= 2^3 * T2(n - 3) + 2^3 + 2^2 + 2 \quad \text{// Equation 15.9}$$

Using $x = n - 3$ in Equation 15.7, we get

$$T2(n - 3) = 2 * T2(n - 4) + 2$$

Plugging the value of $T2(n - 3)$ into Equation 15.9, we get

$$T2(n) = 2^3 * (2 * T2(n - 4) + 2) + 2^3 + 2^2 + 2$$
$$= 2^4 * T2(n - 4) + 2^4 + 2^3 + 2^2 + 2 \quad \text{// Equation 15.10}$$

Now we can see the pattern as follows:

$$T2(n) = 2^k * T2(n - k) + 2^k + 2^{k-1} + \ldots + 2^2 + 2, \text{ where } k \text{ is an integer between}$$
1 and n // Equation 15.11

Noting that

$$2^k + 2^{k-1} + \ldots + 2^2 + 2 = -1 + 2^k + 2^{k-1} + \ldots + 2^2 + 2 + 1$$
$$= -1 + (2^{k+1} - 1) / (2 - 1)$$
$$= 2^{k+1} - 2$$

Equation 15.11 becomes

$T2(n) = 2^k * T2(n - k) + 2^{k+1} - 2$, where k is an integer between 1 and n
// Equation 15.12

Plugging $k = n$ in Equation 15.12 in order to reach the base case of $T2(0)$, we get

$$T2(n) = 2^n * T2(0) + 2^{n+1} - 2$$
$$= 2^n * 1 + 2^{n+1} - 2$$
$$= 2^n + 2^{n+1} - 2$$
$$= 2^n (1 + 2) - 2$$
$$= 3 * 2^n - 2$$
$$= O(2^n)$$

Thus, *powerOf2A* runs in $O(n)$ while *powerOf2B* runs in $O(2^n)$, although they perform the same function.

As a result, computing 2^{20} using *powerOf2A* will cost 20 statement executions, while computing 2^{20} using *powerOf2B* will cost 1 million statement executions.

This simple example shows that how we code a method can have a significant impact on its running time.

15.4 Programming Activity: Tracking How Many Statements Are Executed by a Method

In this activity, you will work with a variable-size integer array. Specifically, you will perform the following operations:

1. Write code to keep track of the number of statement executions during a selection sort.

2. Run a simulation to compute the number of statements executed as a function of the number of elements in the array.

3. Estimate the running time of Selection Sort as a function of n, the number of elements in the array being sorted.

The framework for this Programming Activity will animate your algorithm so that you can perform a simulation on the number of statement executions inside the *selectionSort* method compared to the number of elements in the array that is

Figure 15.1

Animation of the
Programming
Activity

sorted. For example, Figure 15.1 shows the current number of statement executions for an array of 15 elements.

At this point, the application has executed 47 statements.

Instructions

In this chapter's Programming Activity folder, you will find the source files needed to complete this activity. Copy all the files to a folder on your computer. Note that all files should be in the same folder.

Open the *RunningTimePracticeController.java* source file. Searching for five asterisks (*****) in the source code will position you at the sample method where you will add your code. In this task, you will fill in the code for the *selectionSort* method in order to keep track of the number of statement executions needed to sort an array using the Selection Sort algorithm. You should not instantiate the array; we have done that for you. Example 15.6 shows the section of the *RunningTimePracticeController* source code where you will add your code.

Note that we provide a dummy *return* statement (*return 0;*). We do this so that the source code will compile. Just replace the dummy *return* statement with the appropriate *return* statement for the method.

```
// 1. *****  student writes this method
/** Sorts arr in ascending order using the selection sort algorithm
*    Adds a counter to count the number of statement executions
*/
public int selectionSort( )
```

```
{
    // Note:  To count the number of statement executions, use a counter
    // The variable counter has been declared and initialized for you
    // at the beginning of this method
    // Inside the body of the inner loop, increment the counter
    // Replace the return statement so that this method returns the value of
    // the counter. To slow down or accelerate the animation, modify the
    // argument of Pause.wait in the handle method of the ArrayAnimationTimer inner class
    int counter = 0;
    int temp, indexOfMax;
    for ( int i = 0; i < arr.length - 1; i++ )
    {
        // find index of largest value in the subarray
        indexOfMax = 0;
        animate( i,  0,  0,  counter );
        for ( int j = 1; j < arr.length - i; j++ )
        {
          if ( arr[j] > arr[indexOfMax] )
             indexOfMax = j;
          animate( i, j, indexOfMax, counter );
        }
        // swap arr[indexOfMax] and arr[arr.length - i - 1]
        temp = arr[indexOfMax];
        arr[indexOfMax] = arr[arr.length - i - 1];
        arr[arr.length - i - 1] = temp;
    }
    animate( arr.length  -  1,  0,  0,  counter );
    return 0;
} // end of selectionSort
```

EXAMPLE 15.6   Location of Student Code in *RunningTimePracticeController*

Our framework will animate your algorithm so that you can watch your code work. If you want to accelerate or slow down the animation, modify the argument of *Pause.wait* in the *handle* method of the *ArrayAnimationTimer* inner class.

To test your code, compile *RunningTimeController.java* and run the *RunningTime-PracticeApplication*. When the program begins, you will see a text box. Enter the number of elements for the array, and press the "Show Array" button to populate the array. Then press the "Selection Sort" button to execute your selection sort code. Because the values of the array are randomly generated, the values will be different each time the program runs.

Troubleshooting

If the animation is incorrect, and you think your method does return a correct value for the counter, verify that you correctly incremented the counter inside the inner loop.

In order to derive a closed-end expression for the number of statement executions as a function of the size of the array, follow these tips:

- If n is the size of the array, compare n, n^2, n^3, n^4, ..., 2^n, to the value of the counter.

- When doing the preceding, divide n, n^2, n^3, n^4, ..., 2^n by the number of statements executed.

DISCUSSION QUESTIONS   ?

1. What is the value of the counter with the following array sizes: 5, 10, 15, 20, 25?

2. In relation to n, the size of the array, what is the value of the counter?

3. What is the running time of Selection Sort in Big-Oh notation?

4. If the array is already sorted in either the correct or opposite order, does that make a difference in the number of statement executions? What can you say about the worst-case and best-case running times?

15.5   Running Time Analysis of Searching and Sorting Algorithms

In studying the running time of various searching and sorting algorithms, we will look at the following scenarios:

- best case
- worst case
- average case

Some methods have a very efficient running time. We mentioned earlier that the running time of Binary Search was log n. Thus, searching a sorted array of 1 billion items using Binary Search will take only 30 statement executions since log (1 billion) is approximately 30.

Example 15.7 shows the code for a recursive binary search.

```
public static int recursiveBinarySearch
                ( int [ ] arr, int key, int start, int end )
{
  if ( start <= end )
  {
  // look at the middle element of the subarray
  int middle = ( start + end ) / 2;
  if ( arr[middle] == key )      // found key, base case
    return middle;
  else if ( arr[middle] > key )  // look lower
    return recursiveBinarySearch( arr, key, start, middle - 1 );
```

```
    else                           // look higher
        return recursiveBinarySearch( arr, key, middle + 1, end );
    }
    else                           // key not found, base case
        return -1;
}
```

EXAMPLE 15.7   Recursive Binary Search

In the best-case scenario, we will find the search value exactly in the middle of the array, at the array index we check first. Thus, the best-case running time of Binary Search is $O(1)$. In the worst-case scenario, we will not find the search value in the array. Let's compute the running time of the worst-case scenario.

In the general case, the comparison of the first *if* statement will cost us one instruction; the assignment statement will cost us two instructions; the comparison in the second *if* statement will cost us one instruction; the comparison in the *else/if* statement will also cost us one instruction; computing and returning *recursiveBinarySearch(arr, key, start, middle − 1)* or *recursiveBinarySearch(arr, key, middle + 1, end)* will cost us $T(n/2 - 1)$ or $T(n/2)$ instructions. Note that only one recursive call will be made. Thus, the total time $T(n)$ can be expressed as follows:

$$T(n) = 1 + 2 + 1 + 1 + T(n / 2)$$
$$= T(n / 2) + 5 \quad \text{// Equation 15.13}$$

In the base case (*n* is equal to 1), *recursiveBinarySearch* makes only the first comparison, one addition, one division, the second comparison, and then returns the index of the found element or −1. Thus,

$$T(1) = 5.$$

From there, we will use the iteration method in order to compute the value of $T2(n)$ as a function of *n*.

Substituting *x* for *n*, we can rewrite Equation 15.13 as follows:

$$T(x) = T(x / 2) + 5 \quad \text{// Equation 15.14}$$

Using $x = n / 2$ in Equation 15.14, we get

$$T(n / 2) = T((n / 2) / 2) + 5$$
$$= T(n / 2^2) + 5$$

Plugging the value of $T(n / 2)$ into Equation 15.13, we get

$$T(n) = (T(n / 2^2) + 5) + 5$$
$$= T(n / 2^2) + 5 * 2 \quad \text{// Equation 15.15}$$

Using $x = n / 2^2$ in Equation 15.14, we get

$$T(n\ /\ 2^2) = T((n\ /\ 2^2)\ /\ 2) + 5$$
$$= T(n\ /\ 2^3) + 5$$

Plugging the value of $T(n\ /\ 2^2)$ into Equation 15.15, we get

$$T(n) = (T(n\ /\ 2^3) + 5) + 5 * 2$$
$$= T(n\ /\ 2^3) + 5 * 3 \quad \text{// Equation 15.16}$$

Using $x = n\ /\ 2^3$ in Equation 15.14, we get

$$T(n\ /\ 2^3) = T((n\ /\ 2^3)\ /\ 2) + 5$$
$$= T(n\ /\ 2^4) + 5$$

Plugging the value of $T(n\ /\ 2^3)$ into Equation 15.16, we get

$$T(n) = (T(n\ /\ 2^4) + 5) + 5 * 3$$
$$= T(n\ /\ 2^4) + 5 * 4 \quad \text{// Equation 15.17}$$

Now we can see the pattern as follows:

$$T(n) = T(n\ /\ 2^k) + 5 * k,$$

$$\text{where } k \text{ is an integer between 1 and } n \quad \text{// Equation 15.18}$$

We now want to choose k such that $n\ /\ 2^k$ is equal to 1 in order to reach our base case. If $n\ /\ 2^k = 1$, then $n = 2^k$, and taking the log of each side:

$$\log n = \log 2^k$$
$$= k \log 2$$
$$= k * 1$$
$$= k$$

Plugging $k = \log n$ in Equation 15.18, we get

$$T(n) = T(1) + 5 * \log n$$
$$= 2 + 5 * \log n$$
$$= O(\log n)$$

Thus, Binary Search is $O(\log n)$ in the worst case. Note that the value of the original constant, here 5, does not impact the order of magnitude of the running time.

In the average case, we will find the search value after performing half the number of comparisons as in the worst-case scenario. Thus, the average running time of binary search is also $O(\log n)$.

Now, let's calculate the running time of Insertion Sort as a function of n, the number of elements in the array. The code for an Insertion Sort is shown in Example 15.8.

```
/** Performs an Insertion Sort on an integer array
 *     @param array   array to sort
```

```
*/
public static void insertionSort( int [ ] array )
{
   int j, temp;
   for ( int i = 1; i < array.length; i++ )
   {
      j = i;
      temp = array[i];
      while ( j != 0 && array[j - 1] > temp )
      {
         array[j] = array[j - 1];
         j--;
      }
      array[j] = temp;
   }
}
```

EXAMPLE 15.8   Insertion Sort

The *for* loop header will execute *n* times. We will execute the body of the *for* loop *n* – 1 times.

In the best case, the array is already sorted. In this case, the *while* loop condition will always evaluate to *false*, and we will never execute the *while* loop body. So inside the *for* loop, the three statements and the loop condition will each execute once for each iteration of the *for* loop, thus executing a total of 4 * (*n* – 1) times. Therefore, the best-case running time is $O(n)$.

In the worst case, the array is sorted in the opposite order. In this case, the *while* loop condition will always be *true* for its first evaluation, and we will enter the *while* loop every time we iterate the *for* loop. Thus, the two statements inside the *while* loop will each execute (1 + 2 + 3 + 4 + ... + (*n* – 1)) times. Since (1 + 2 + 3 + 4 + ... + (*n* – 1)) = *n* * (*n* – 1) / 2, the worst-case running time of insertion sort is $O(n^2)$.

In the average case, we will enter the *while* loop half the times we try. The average case is still $O(n^2)$.

Bubble Sort, like Insertion Sort, is implemented with a double loop and also is $O(n^2)$.

Merge Sort and Quick Sort are two sorting algorithms implemented recursively.

The pseudocode for Merge Sort is as follows:

- If the array has only one element, it is already sorted, thus do nothing; otherwise:

  - Merge sort the left half of the array.

- Merge sort the right half of the array.
- Merge the two sorted half arrays into one so that the resulting array is sorted.

The last operation involves looping through all the elements of the two half-arrays; it takes $O(n)$; thus, we can derive the following recursive formulation for its running time of Merge Sort:

$$T(n) = T(n / 2) + T(n / 2) + n$$
$$= 2\ T(n / 2) + n$$

Using derivation, we get

$$T(n) = 2\ T(n / 2) + n$$
$$= 2\ (2\ T(n / 2^2) + n / 2) + n$$
$$= 2^2\ T(n / 2^2) + 2n$$

Continuing to iterate,

$$T(n) = 2^2\ T(n / 2^2) + 2n$$
$$= 2^2\ (2\ T(n / 2^3) + n / 2^2) + 2n$$
$$= 2^3\ T(n / 2^3) + 3n$$

$$T(n) = 2^3\ T(n / 2^3) + 3n$$
$$= 2^3\ (2\ T(n / 2^3) + n / 2^3) + 3n$$
$$= 2^4\ T(n / 2^4) + 4n$$

Thus, we identify the general pattern

$$T(n) = 2^k\ T(n / 2^k) + kn$$

Choosing k so that $n / 2^k = 1$ in order to reach the base case, i.e., $n = 2^k$, $k = \log n$, we get

$$T(n) = n\ T(1) + n \log n$$
$$= O(n \log n)$$

So Merge Sort is $O(n \log n)$, which is better than Insertion Sort, Bubble Sort, and Selection Sort. It is the same for best-case, worst-case, and average-case scenarios.

The analysis of the running time of Quick Sort is the subject of the Group Project for this chapter.

CODE IN ACTION

Within the online resources, you will find a movie with a step-by-step illustration of how to compute running times for various methods. Click on the link to start the movie.

Skill Practice
with these end-of-chapter questions

15.7.1   Multiple Choice Exercises

       Questions 1, 2, 3, 4, 5, 6, 7, 8, 9, 10

15.7.2   Compute the Running Time of a Method

       Questions 11, 12, 13, 14, 15, 16, 17, 18

15.7.4   Technical Writing

       Question 27

CHAPTER REVIEW

15.6   Chapter Summary

- The running time of an algorithm is expressed as a function of its inputs or its number of inputs.

- Orders of magnitude are, in increasing order of execution time: constant, log, polynomial, and exponential. Exponential running times are undesirable.

- Big-Oh notation is the industry standard notation for running times.

- Considering a mathematical function that represents a running time of an algorithm, that function is Big-Oh of its most dominant term, and we ignore the coefficient of that term..

- The coding of a method directly impacts its running time.

15.7   Exercises, Problems, and Projects

15.7.1   Multiple Choice Exercises

1. What is the Big-Oh of this function:

   T(n) = n² - 2 n + 99

   ❑ $O(n^2)$

   ❑ $O(99)$

   ❑ $O(n)$

   ❑ $O(1)$

2. What is the Big-Oh of this function:

   T(n) = n³ + 10 n² + 20 n + 30

   ❑ $O(n^3)$

   ❑ $O(n^2)$

   ❑ $O(n)$

   ❑ $O(1)$

3. What is the Big-Oh of this function:

   T(n) = n² + n * log n + 12 n + 5

   ❑ $O(n * \log n)$

   ❑ $O(n^2)$

❑ OO(*n*)

❑ O(1)

4. We have the following recurrence relation representing the running time of a function; what is the running time of that function?

```
T(n) = T(n - 1) + 1
```

❑ $O(2^n)$

❑ $O(n * \log n)$

❑ $O(n^2)$

❑ $O(n)$

5. Which of these running times is the worst?

❑ $O(n^5)$

❑ $O(2^n)$

❑ $O(n * \log n)$

❑ $O(n)$

6. Look at the following method:

```java
public static int foo1( int n )
{
  if ( n > 1 )
    return ( 2 * foo1( n / 4 ) );
  else
    return 1;
}
```

What recurrence formulation best illustrates the running time of the preceding method?

❑ $T(n) = T(n * 4) + 3$

❑ $T(n) = T(n / 4) + 3$

❑ $T(n) = T(n - 4) + 3$

❑ $T(n) = T(n + 4) + 3$

7. What is $\Sigma\, i$ for $i = 1$ to n equal to?

❑ n^2

❑ $n * (n + 1) / 2$

❑ $2n$

❑ n

8. What is Σ 1 for $i = 1$ to n equal to?

   ❑ n^2

   ❑ n

   ❑ $n * (n + 1) / 2$

   ❑ i

9. What is the running time of the *foo2* method?

```java
public static void foo2( int n )
{
    for ( int i = n; i > 0; i-- )
    {
        for ( int j = 0; j < n; j++ )
            System.out.println( "Hello" );
    }
}
```

   ❑ $O(n^4)$

   ❑ $O(n^3)$

   ❑ $O(n^2)$

   ❑ $O(n)$

10. What is the running time of the *foo3* method?

```java
public static void foo3( int n )
{
    for ( int i = 0; i < n; i++ )
    {
        for ( int j = 0; j < i; j++ )
            System.out.println( "Hello" );
    }
}
```

   ❑ $O(n^4)$

   ❑ $O(n^3)$

   ❑ $O(n^2)$

   ❑ $O(n)$

15.7.2   Compute the Running Time of a Method

11. What is the running time of the *foo4* method (assume that the parameter *arr* is a two-dimensional array of *n* rows and *n* columns)?

```java
public static void foo4( int [ ][ ] arr )
{
```

```
for ( int i = 0; i < arr.length; i++ )
{
  for ( int j = arr[i].length - 1; j >= 0; j-- )
    System.out.println( "Hello world" );
}
}
```

12. What is the running time of the *foo5* method (assume that the parameter *arr* is a three-dimensional array where each dimension has exactly *n* elements)?

```
public static void foo5( int [ ][ ][ ] arr )
{
  for ( int i = 0; i < arr.length; i++ )
  {
    for ( int j = 0; j < arr[i].length; j++ )
    {
      for ( int k = 0; k < arr[i][j].length; k++ )
        System.out.println( "Hello world" );
    }
  }
}
```

13. What is the running time of the *foo6* method?

```
public static void foo6( int n )
{
  if ( n <= 0 )
    System.out.println( "Hello world" );
  else
    foo6( n - 1 );
}
```

14. What is the running time of the *foo7* method?

```
public static int foo7( int n )
{
  // n is guaranteed to be >= 0
  if ( n == 0 )
    return 0;
  else
    return ( n + foo7( n - 1 ) );
}
```

15. What is the running time of the *foo8* method?

```
public static int foo8( int n )
{
  // n is guaranteed to be >= 1
  if ( n == 1 || n == 2 )
```

```
        return 1;
    else
        return ( foo8( n - 1 ) + foo8( n - 2 ) );
}
```

Hint: Note that $T(n - 2) <= T(n - 1)$.

16. What is the running time of the *foo9* method?

```
public static void foo9( int n )
{
    // n is guaranteed to be >= 0
    if ( n == 0 )
        System.out.println( "done" );
    else
        foo9( n / 2 );
}
```

17. What is the running time of the *foo10* method as a function of *n* and *p*?

```
public static void foo10( int n, int p )
{
    // n and p are guaranteed to be >= 1
    if ( p >= n )
        System.out.println( "done" );
    else
        foo10( n, 2 * p );
}
```

18. What is the running time of the *foo11* method?

```
public static void foo11( int n )
{
    // n is guaranteed to be >= 0
    if ( n == 0 )
        return 0;
    else
        return ( 5 + 2 * foo11( n - 1 ) );
}
```

15.7.3 Programming Projects

19. Write a program that includes a method taking a single-dimensional array of *ints* as its only parameter, and returning the average of all the elements of the array. Add the necessary code to count how many statements are executed in the innermost loop. Run several simulations depending on the number of elements in the parameter integer array. What is the running time of that method as a function of the number of elements of the parameter array?

20. Write a program that includes a method converting a two-dimensional array of *ints* to a two-dimensional array of *boolean* values. If the integer value is greater than or equal to 0, then the corresponding *boolean* value is *true*; otherwise it is *false*. Add the necessary code to count how many statements are executed in the innermost loop. Run several simulations depending on the number of rows and columns in the argument integer array. What is the running time of that method as a function of the number of rows and columns of the parameter array? (You should assume that each row has the same number of columns.)

21. Write a program that includes a method computing the largest element of a given column (represented by a parameter of the method) of a two-dimensional array of *ints*. Add the necessary code to count how many statements are executed in the innermost loop. Run several simulations depending on the number of rows and columns in the parameter integer array, as well as the index of the column for which the method calculates the largest element. Does the running time of the method depend on the column index? the number of rows? the number of columns? What is the running time of that method as a function of the number of rows and columns of the parameter array and the column index? (You should assume that each row has the same number of columns.)

22. Write a program that includes a method taking a two-dimensional array of *ints* as its only parameter, and returning a single dimensional array of *ints* such that each element of the returned array is the sum of the corresponding row in the parameter array. Add the necessary code to count how many statements are executed in the innermost loop. Run several simulations depending on the number of rows and columns in the parameter integer array. What is the running time of that method as a function of the number of rows and columns of the parameter array? (You should assume that each row has the same number of columns.)

23. Write a program that implements a recursive Binary Search, and add the necessary code to count how many times *binarySearchRecursive* is being called. Run several simulations on arrays of 32, 64, and 128 elements. How many times is the method called in the best-case scenario and worst-case scenario? Does that match our analysis in the chapter?

24. Write a program that implements a recursive method to compute the factorial of a number and add the necessary code to count how many times the method is being called. Run several simulations depending on the value of n. How many times is the method called? What is the running time of this method?

25. Write a program that includes a method converting a *String* of 0s and 1s to its equivalent decimal number and add the necessary code to count how many times the method is being called. Run several simulations depending on the length of the input *String*. How many times is the method called? What is the running time of that method?

26. Write a program that implements Counting Sort to sort an array of integers. Research how Counting Sort works before you implement it. What is the main difference between Counting Sort and other sorting algorithms such as Selection Sort, Bubble Sort, and Insertion Sort? In what situations would Counting Sort be efficient or inefficient to sort an array of integers?

15.7.4   Technical Writing

27. Explain why it is important to consider running time when coding algorithms. Use an example to illustrate your point. Your example, web-based or not, should deal with a lot of data.

15.7.5   Group Project (for a group of 1, 2, or 3 students)

28. Write a class with an *int* array as its only instance variable. Write a recursive method that uses the Quick Sort algorithm in order to sort the array. (Quick Sort is explained below.) You will then add the appropriate code and perform the appropriate simulations to evaluate the running time of the method as a function of the number of elements in the array.

Here is how Quick Sort works:

❏ Partition the array so that all the elements to the left of a certain index are smaller than the element at that index and all the elements to the right of that index are greater than or equal to the element at that index. You should code a separate method to partition the array. (See explanation that follows.)

❏ Sort the left part of the array using Quick Sort (this is a recursive call).

❏ Sort the right part of the array using Quick Sort (this is another recursive call).

To partition the array elements in the manner previously explained, you should code another method (this one nonrecursive) as explained in the following:

❏ Choose an element of the array (for example, the first element). We call this element the **pivot**.

❑ This method partitions the array elements so that all the elements left of the pivot are less than the pivot, and all the element right of the pivot are greater than or equal to the pivot.

❑ This method returns an *int* representing the array index of the pivot (after the elements have been partitioned in the order described previously).

❑ In order to rearrange the array elements as previously described, implement the following pseudocode.

The following is pseudocode to partition a subarray whose lower index is *low* and higher index is *high*:

```
Assign element at index low to the pivot
Initialize j to low
Loop from (low + 1) to high with variable i
    If (array element at index i is smaller than pivot)
        Increase j by 1
        Swap array elements at indexes i and j
Swap array elements at index low and j
Return j
```

Using a counter, keep track of the number of statement executions performed when using Quick Sort to sort an array of *n* elements. In particular, you should run simulation runs on these two situations:

❑ The array is not sorted

❑ The array is presorted in the correct order

You should perform a mathematical analysis of the running time of Quick Sort in the average case based on its recursive formulation (using iteration, as we did in the chapter examples).

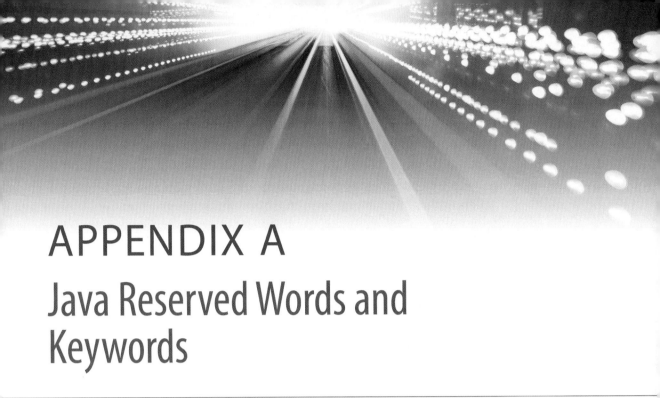

APPENDIX A
Java Reserved Words and Keywords

These words have contextual meaning for the Java language and cannot be used as identifiers.

abstract	default	goto	package	synchronized
assert	do	if	private	this
boolean	double	implements	protected	throw
break	else	import	public	throws
byte	enum	instanceof	return	transient
case	extends	int	short	true
catch	false	interface	static	try
char	final	long	strictfp	void
class	finally	native	super	volatile
const	float	new	switch	while
continue	for	null	_	

The words *true*, *false*, and *null* are literals. The remainder of the words are Java keywords, although *const* and *goto* are not currently used in the Java language.

APPENDIX B
Operator Precedence

These rules of operator precedence are followed when expressions are evaluated. Operators in a higher level in the hierarchy—defined by their row position in the table—are evaluated before operators in a lower level. Thus, an expression in parentheses is evaluated before a shortcut postincrement is performed, and so on with the operators in each level. When two or more operators on the same level appear in an expression, the evaluation of the expression follows the corresponding rule for same-statement evaluation shown in the second column.

Operators	Order of Same-Statement Evaluation	Operation
( )	left to right	parentheses for explicit grouping
++ --	right to left	shortcut postincrement and postdecrement
++ --!	right to left	shortcut preincrement and predecrement, logical unary NOT
* / %	left to right	multiplication, division, modulus
+ -	left to right	addition or *String* concatenation, subtraction
< <= > >= instanceof	left to right	relational operators: less than, less than or equal to, greater than, greater than or equal to; instanceof
== !=	left to right	equality operators: equal to and not equal to
&&	left to right	logical AND
||	left to right	logical OR
?:	left to right	conditional operator
= += -= *= /= %=	right to left	assignment operator and shortcut assignment operators

APPENDIX C
The Unicode Character Set

Java characters are encoded using the Unicode Character Set, which is designed to support international alphabets, punctuation, and mathematical and technical symbols. Each character is stored as 16 bits, so as many as 65,536 characters are supported.

The American Standard Code for Information Interchange (ASCII) character set is supported by the first 128 Unicode characters from 0000 to 007F, which are called the controls and Basic Latin characters, as shown on the next page.

Any character from the Unicode set can be specified as a *char* literal in a Java program by using the following syntax: '\uNNNN' where NNNN are the four hexadecimal digits that specify the Unicode encoding for the character.

For more information on the Unicode character set, visit the Unicode Consortium's website: *www.unicode.org*.

Controls and Basic Latin Characters

	000	001	002	003	004	005	006	007
0	NUL 0000	DLE 0010	SP 0020	0 0030	@ 0040	P 0050	` 0060	p 0070
1	SOH 0001	DC1 0011	! 0021	1 0031	A 0041	Q 0051	a 0061	q 0071
2	STX 0002	DC2 0012	" 0022	2 0032	B 0042	R 0052	b 0062	r 0072
3	ETX 0003	DC3 0013	# 0023	3 0033	C 0043	S 0053	c 0063	s 0073
4	EOT 0004	DC4 0014	$ 0024	4 0034	D 0044	T 0054	d 0064	t 0074
5	ENQ 0005	NAK 0015	% 0025	5 0035	E 0045	U 0055	e 0065	u 0075
6	ACK 0006	SYN 0016	& 0026	6 0036	F 0046	V 0056	f 0066	v 0076
7	BEL 0007	ETB 0017	' 0027	7 0037	G 0047	W 0057	g 0067	w 0077
8	BS 0008	CAN 0018	(0028	8 0038	H 0048	X 0058	h 0068	x 0078
9	HT 0009	EM 0019	) 0029	9 0039	I 0049	Y 0059	i 0069	y 0079
A	LF 000A	SUB 001A	* 002A	: 003A	J 004A	Z 005A	j 006A	z 007A
B	VT 000B	ESC 001B	+ 002B	; 003B	K 004B	[005B	k 006B	{ 007B
C	FF 000C	FS 001C	, 002C	< 003C	L 004C	\ 005C	l 006C	| 007C
D	CR 000D	GS 001D	- 002D	= 003D	M 004D	] 005D	m 006D	} 007D
E	SO 000E	RS 001E	. 002E	> 003E	N 004E	^ 005E	n 006E	~ 007E
F	SI 000F	US 001F	/ 002F	? 003F	O 004F	_ 005F	o 006F	DEL 007F

APPENDIX D
Representing Negative Integers

The industry standard method for representing negative integers is called **two's complement**. Here is how it works:

For an integer represented using 16 bits, the leftmost bit is reserved for the sign bit. If the sign bit is 0, then the integer is positive; if the sign bit is 1, then the integer is negative.

For example, let's consider two numbers, one positive and one negative.

0000 0101 0111 1001 is a positive integer, which we call a.
1111 1111 1101 1010 is a negative integer, which we will call b.

Using the methodology presented in Chapter 1 for converting a binary number to a decimal number, we can convert the binary number, a, to its decimal equivalent. Hence, the value of a is calculated as follows:

$$a = 2^{10} + 2^8 + 2^6 + 2^5 + 2^4 + 2^3 + 2^0$$
$$= 1{,}024 + 256 + 64 + 32 + 16 + 8 + 1$$
$$= 1{,}401$$

In contrast, b, the negative number, is represented in binary using the two's complement method. The leftmost bit, which is the sign bit, is a 1, indicating that b is negative. To calculate the value of a negative number, we first calculate its two's complement. The two's complement of any binary number is another binary number, which, when added to the original number, will yield a sum consisting of all 0s and a carry bit of 1 at the end.

To calculate the two's complement of a binary number, n, subtract n from 2^d, where d is the number of binary digits in n. The following formula summarizes that rule:

```
Two's complement of n = 2d - n
```

Knowing that $2^d - 1$ is always a binary number containing all 1s, we can simplify our calculations by first subtracting 1 from 2^d, then adding a 1 at the end.

```
Two's complement of n = 2d - 1 - n + 1
```

So to calculate the two's complement of b, which has 16 digits, we subtract b from a binary number consisting of 16 1s, then add 1, as shown here.

```
            2d - 1   1111 1111 1111 1111
               - b   1111 1111 1101 1010
                     0000 0000 0010 0101
               + 1                      1
two's complement of b   0000 0000 0010 0110
```

Thus, the two's complement of b, which we will call c, is 0000 0000 0010 0110.

Another, simpler, way to calculate a two's complement is to invert each bit, then add 1. Inverting bits means to change all 0s to 1s and to change all 1s to 0s. Using this method, we get

```
        b   1111 1111 1101 1010

b inverted  0000 0000 0010 0101
      + 1                      1
        c   0000 0000 0010 0110
```

We can verify that the two's complement of b is correct by calculating the sum of b and c.

```
    b     1111 1111 1101 1010
    c     0000 0000 0010 0110
b + c   1 0000 0000 0000 0000
```

Converting c to decimal will give us the value of our original number b, which, as we remember, is negative. We have

```
b =  - (   2^5 +  2^2 +  2^1  )
  =  - (  32 +   4  + 2  )
  =   -38
```

Because a leftmost bit of 0 indicates that the number is positive, using 16 bits, the largest positive number (we will call it *max*) that we can represent is

```
0111 1111 1111 1111
```

$max = (2^{14} + 2^{13} + 2^{12} + 2^{11} + 2^{10} + 2^9 + 2^8 + 2^7 + 2^6 + 2^5 + 2^4 + 2^3 + 2^2 + 2^1 + 2^0)$

This is equivalent to $2^{15} - 1$, which is 32,768 − 1, or 32,767.

Using 16 bits, then, the smallest negative number (we will call it *min*) that we can represent is

1000 0000 0000 0000

The two's complement of *min* is *min* itself. If we invert the bits and add 1, we get the same value we started with:

```
           min            1000 0000 0000 0000

    min inverted    0111 1111 1111 1111
             + 1    _____1
two's complement    1000 0000 0000 0000
```

and therefore *min* is -2^{15} or $-32,768$.

Thus, using 16 bits, we can represent integers between $-32,768$ and $32,767$.

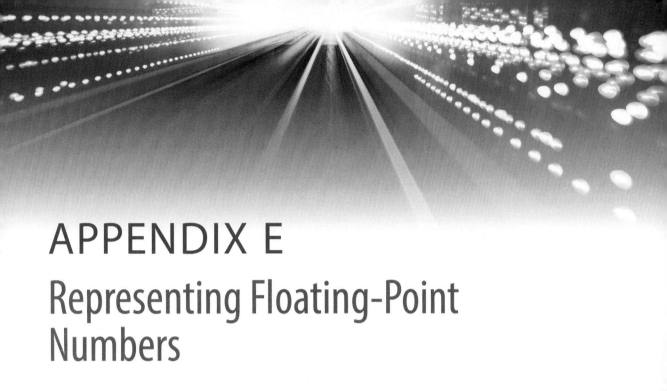

APPENDIX E
Representing Floating-Point Numbers

IEEE 754, a specification accepted worldwide and used by the Java language, defines how to represent floating-point numbers in binary numbers. Single-precision floating-point numbers use 32 bits of memory, and double-precision floating-point numbers use 64 bits.

Here is how single- and double-precision floating-point numbers are represented:

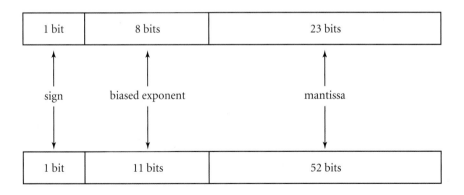

The leftmost bit stores the sign of the floating-point number; a 0 indicates a positive number, while a 1 indicates a negative number.

To represent the exponent of the number, which can be positive or negative, each representation stores a positive, biased exponent, calculated by adding a fixed bias, or scaling factor, to the real exponent of the number. The purpose of the bias is to be able to represent both extremely large and extremely small numbers. The bias is equal to

$$2^{(\text{\# of bits of the biased exponent} - 1)} - 1$$

Thus, for single precision, the bias is

$$2^{(8-1)} - 1 = 2^7 - 1 = 127$$

In single-precision, the 8-bit biased exponent can store 256 positive values (0 to 255). Thus, with a bias of 127, we can represent floating-point numbers with real exponents from -127 to 128, as shown here:

Real exponent	-127	-126	...	0	...	127	128
+ Bias	127	127	...	127	...	127	127
Biased exponent	0	1	...	127	...	254	255

Conversely, to find the real exponent from the biased exponent, we subtract the bias. For example, if the biased exponent is 150, then the real exponent is $150 - 127$, which is 23. Similarly, if the biased exponent is 3, the actual exponent is $3 - 127$, which is -124.

For double precision, the bias is

$$2^{(11-1)} - 1 = 2^{10} - 1 = 1023$$

A floating-point number is considered to be in the form

$$(-1)^{\text{sign}} * (1 + \text{significand}) * 2^{(\text{biased exponent} - \text{bias})}$$

By definition, the significand is of the form 0 followed by a dot followed by a string of 0s and 1s, for example, 0.1101. That string of 0s and 1s is known as the mantissa.

For example, if the significand is 0.1101, then the mantissa is 110100...0

As an example, let's convert a single-precision binary number to a decimal floating-point number. We will convert the following single-precision IEEE 754 floating-point number:

0	10000111	11010000...0

The leftmost digit, 0, tells us that the number is positive. The biased exponent is 10000111, which converted to decimal, is

$$= 2^7 + 2^2 + 2^1 + 2^0$$
$$= 128 + 4 + 2 + 1$$
$$= 135$$

The bias for single-precision floating-point numbers is 127, so the number is

$$= (-1)^0 * (1 + .1101) * 2^{(135 - 127)}$$
$$= 1.1101 * 2^8$$
$$= 1\ 1101\ 0000$$

In decimal, the number is

$$= 2^8 + 2^7 + 2^6 + 2^4$$
$$= 256 + 128 + 64 + 16$$
$$= 464$$

Given that .1 is $\frac{1}{2}1$ or $\frac{1}{2}$ in decimal, and .01 is $\frac{1}{2}2$ or $\frac{1}{4}$, and .0001 is $\frac{1}{2}4$ or $\frac{1}{16}$ in decimal, we also could have calculated the number using this method:

$$= 1.1101 * 2^8$$
$$= (1 + 1 * \frac{1}{2}1 + 1 * \frac{1}{2}2 + 0 * \frac{1}{2}3 + 1 * \frac{1}{2}4) * 2^8$$
$$= (1 + \frac{1}{2} + \frac{1}{4} + \frac{1}{16}) * 2^8$$
$$= (1 + \frac{1}{2} + \frac{1}{4} + \frac{1}{16}) * 256$$
$$= 464$$

Now, let's convert a decimal floating-point number into single-precision, binary format. Here, we will convert the number 25.375, which we'll call y. First we convert the whole number portion (5) to binary, getting 101:

$$5 = 101$$

Then we convert the fractional part to binary:

$$.375 = .25 + .125$$
$$= \frac{1}{4} + \frac{1}{8}$$
$$= \frac{1}{2}2 + \frac{1}{2}3$$
$$= 0 * \frac{1}{2}1 + 1 * \frac{1}{2}2 + 1 * \frac{1}{2}3$$

Thus, .375 as represented in binary is .011.

Therefore, y can be represented in binary as

$$y = -101.011$$
$$= -1.01011 * 2^2$$

We now can deduce the sign, the biased exponent, and the mantissa. The sign is 1 because the number is negative. The significand is 1.01011, and therefore the mantissa is 01011000 ... 00. The exponent is 2, so the biased exponent is 129 (2 plus the bias for single-precision numbers, which is 127):

$$\text{Biased exponent} = 2 + 127$$
$$= 129$$

Converting 129 to binary, we get

$$129 = 1000\ 0001$$

Therefore, the IEEE 754 single-precision value of the number y is

1	10000001	010110000...0

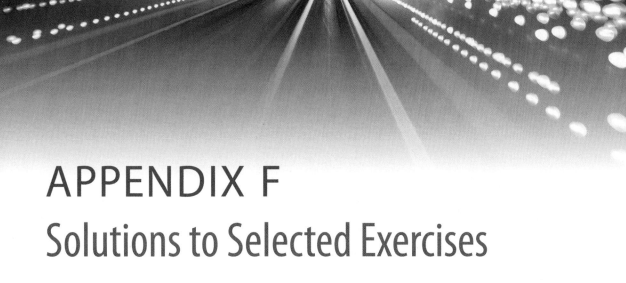

APPENDIX F
Solutions to Selected Exercises

1.7 Exercises, Problems, and Projects

1.7.1 Multiple Choice Exercises:

1. Java
4. servers.
7. is a multiple of 4.
10. C
13. *javac Hello.java*

1.7.2 Converting Numbers

16. 0110 0001 1100
19. 0x15

1.7.3 General Questions

22. 2.5 billion
25. red = 51; green = 171; blue = 18
28. *javac*

2.6 Exercises, Problems, and Projects

2.6.1 Multiple Choice Exercises

1. `int a;`

2.6.2 Reading and Understanding Code

4. 12.5
7. 2.0
10. 4
13. 5
16. 2.4
19. 5
22. 0

2.6.3 Fill In the Code

25. ```
boolean a;
a = false;
```

28. ```
double avg = (double) ( a + b ) / 2;
System.out.println( "The average is " + avg );
```

31. ```
a *= 3;
```

### 2.6.4 Identifying Errors in Code

34. Cannot assign a *double* to a *float* variable (possible loss of precision).
37. There should not be a space between – and =.

### 2.6.5 Debugging Area—Using Messages from the Java Compiler and Java JVM

40. Cannot assign a *double* to an *int* variable (possible loss of precision). Change to:
```
int a = 26;
```

43. =+ is different from += (shortcut operator). Here, *a* is assigned the value + 3. To add 3 to *a*, change the second statement to:
```
a += 3;
```

## 3.18 Exercises, Problems, and Projects

### 3.18.1 Multiple Choice Exercises

1. ```import```
4. ```new```
7. It is a class method.
10. ```double```
13. ```Math.E;```
```

3.18.2   Reading and Understanding Code

16. hello
19. 3.141592653589793
22. 8

3.18.3   Fill In the Code

25. ```
System.out.println(s.length( ));
```

28. ```
System.out.print( "Welcome " );
System.out.print( "to " );
System.out.print( "Java " );
System.out.print( "Illuminated\n" );
```

31. ```
// code below assumes we have imported Scanner
Scanner scan = new Scanner(System.in);
System.out.print("Enter two integers > ");
int i = scan.nextInt( );
int j = scan.nextInt( );
int min = Math.min(i, j);
System.out.println("min of " + i + " and " + j + " is " + min);
```

34. ```
// code below assumes we have imported Scanner
Scanner scan = new Scanner( System.in );
System.out.print( "Enter a double > " );
double number = scan.nextDouble( );
double square = Math.pow( number, 2 );
System.out.println( number + " squared = " + square );
```

3.18.4   Identifying Errors in Code

37. The *System* class begins with a capital S. It should be *System*, not system.
40. The *round* method of the *Math* class returns a *long*; a *long* cannot be assigned to a *short* variable due to a potential loss of precision.
43. The char *'H'* cannot be assigned to the *String s*. The two data types are not compatible.

3.18.5   Debugging Area—Using Messages from the Java Compiler and Java JVM

46. Java is case sensitive. The *Math* class needs to be spelled with an uppercase M.
49. In the output statement, we are just printing the value of *grade* without any formatting. To format *grade* as a percentage, the output statement should be:
```
System.out.println( "Your grade is " + percent.format( grade ) );
```

4.7   Exercises, Problems, and Projects

4.7.1   Multiple Choice Exercises

1. *javafx.scene.canvas*
4. true
7. the *(x, y)* coordinate of the upper-left corner of the rectangle we are drawing
10. 256

4.7.2   Reading and Understanding Code

13. 250 pixels

4.7.3   Fill In the Code

16. ```
    gc.setFill( Color.RED );
    gc.setStroke( Color.GREEN );
    ```
19. ```
    gc.fillRect( 50, 30, 50, 270 );
    ```

4.7.4   Identifying Errors in Code

22. There should be double quotes around the literal *Find a bug*, not single quotes. Single quotes are used for a *char*, not a *String*.
25. There is no *public color* instance variable in the *GraphicsContext* class. The *setFill* or *setStroke* method should be used to set the current color.

4.7.5   Debugging Area—Using Messages from the Java Compiler and Java JVM

28. The rectangle is being drawn outside the bounds of the window. The largest visible x coordinate is 699.

5.14   Exercises, Problems, and Projects

5.14.1   Multiple Choice Exercises

1.

❏	a < b	true
❏	a != b	true
❏	a == 4	false
❏	(b - a) <= 1	false
❏	Math.abs(a - b) >= 2	true
❏	(b % 2 == 1)	true
❏	b <= 5	true

4. yes

7.

❑   `a < b || b < 10`   no

❑   `a != b && b < 10`   yes

❑   `a == 4 || b < 10`   yes

❑   `a > b && b < 10`   no

5.14.2   Reading and Understanding Code

10. *true*

13. 27 is divisible by 3
    End of sequence

16. Hello 3
    Hello 4
    Done

19. Number 3
    Number 4
    Other number

5.14.3   Fill In the Code

22.
```
if ( a )
    a = false;
else
    a = true;
```

25.
```
if ( b % c == 0 )
    a = true;
else
    a = false;
```

28.
```
if ( a && b > 10 )
    c++;
```

5.14.4   Identifying Errors in Code

31. The && operator cannot be applied to two *int* operands (*a1* and *a2*).

34. We need a set of parentheses around *b1*.

37. There is no syntax error.

5.14.5   Debugging Area—Using Messages from the Java Compiler and Java JVM

40. The expression `a = 31` evaluates to an *int*, 31. The *if* condition requires a *boolean* expression. To fix the problem, replace `a = 31` with `a == 31`.

6.14   Exercises, Problems, and Projects

6.14.1   Multiple Choice Exercises

1. The code runs forever.
4. true

6.14.2   Reading and Understanding Code

7. Enter an int > 3
   Enter an int > 5
   Hello
   Enter an int > –1
   Hello
10. *i* is 8 and *product* is 42
13. 3
16. *i* is 40 and *sum* is 60
19. 3
    3
    3
    3
    4

6.14.3   Fill In the Code

22.
```java
System.out.print( "Enter an integer > " );
int value = scan.nextInt( );
while ( value != 20 )
{
  if ( value >= start )
    System.out.println( value );
  System.out.print( "Enter an integer > " );
  value = scan.nextInt( );
}
```

25.
```java
Scanner scan = new Scanner( System.in );
System.out.print( "Enter a word > " );
word = scan.next( );
while ( ! word.equals( "end" ) )
{
  sentence += word + " ";
  System.out.print( "Enter a word > " );
  word = scan.next( );
}
```

28.
```java
Scanner scan = new Scanner( System.in );
int sum = 0;
```

```
System.out.println( "Enter an integer > " );
int value = scan.nextInt( );
while ( value != 0 && value != 100 )
{
  sum += value;
  System.out.println( "Enter an integer > " );
  value = scan.nextInt( );
}
System.out.println( "sum is " + sum );
```

6.14.4   Identifying Errors in Code

31. The variable *num* needs to be initialized after it is declared, and a priming read is needed.
34. The loop is infinite; *number* is always different from 5 or different from 7. The logical OR (||) should be changed to a logical AND (&&).

6.14.5   Debugging Area—Using Messages from the Java Compiler and Java JVM

37. It is an infinite loop; *i* should be incremented, not decremented, inside the body of the *while* loop so that the loop eventually terminates.
40. In the *for* loop header, the loop initialization statement, the loop condition, and the loop update statement should be separated by semicolons (;), not commas(,).

7.18   Exercises, Problems, and Projects

7.18.1   Multiple Choice Exercises

1. The convention is to start with an uppercase letter.
4. true
7. can be basic data types, existing Java types, or user-defined types (from user-defined classes).
10. one parameter, of the same type as the corresponding field.
13. these fields do not need to be passed as parameters to the methods because the class methods have direct access to them.
16. All of the above.

7.18.2   Reading and Understanding Code

19. *double*
22. an instance method (keyword *static* not used)
25. `public static void foo3( double d )`

7.18.3   Fill In the Code

28.
```
private int grade;
private char letterGrade;
```

31.
```
public TelevisionChannel( String newName, int newNumber,
                          boolean newCable )
{
  name = newName;
  number = newNumber;
  cable = newCable;
}
```

34.
```
public String toString( )
{
  return ( "name: " + name + "\tnumber: "
          + number + "\tcable: " + cable );
}
```

37.
```
public String typeOfChannel( )
{
  if ( cable )
    return "cable";
  else
    return "network";
}
```

7.18.4   Identifying Errors in Code

40. The *toString* method needs to return a *String*, not output data.
43. The method header is incorrect; it should be
```
public double calcTax( )
```
46. There are two errors: The assignment operator = should not be used when declaring an *enum* set. And the *enum* constant objects should not be *String* literals but identifiers. The statement should be:
```
enum Months { January, February, March };
```

7.18.5   Debugging Area—Using Messages from the Java Compiler and Java JVM

49. The compiler understands that *Grade* is a method since its header says it returns a *char*. It looks as if it is intended to be a constructor so the keyword *char* should be deleted from the constructor header.
52. The constructor assigns the parameter *numberGrade* to itself, therefore not changing the value of the instance variable *numberGrade*, which by default is 0. The constructor could be recoded as follows:
```
public Grade( int newGrade )
{
  numberGrade = newGrade;
}
```

8.11   Exercises, Problems, and Projects

8.11.1   Multiple Choice Exercises:

1. `int [ ] a;` and `int a[ ];`
4. 0
7. `a.length`
10. false

8.11.2   Reading and Understanding Code

13. 48.3
16. 12
    48
    65
19. 14
22. It counts and returns how many elements in the argument array have the value 5.
25. It returns an array of *Strings* identical to the argument array except that the *Strings* are all in lowercase.

8.11.3   Fill In the Code

28. ```
if (a[i] > 20)
   System.out.println(a[i]);
```

31. ```
System.out.println( "a[" + i + "] = " + a[i] );
```

34. ```
if (a.length < 2)
   return false;
else if (a[0].equals(a[1]))
   return true;
else
   return false;
```

### 8.11.4    Identifying Errors in Code

37. Index −1 is out of bounds; the statement `System.out.println( a[-1] );` will generate an *ArrayIndexOutOfBoundsException* at run time.
40. When declaring an array, the square brackets should be empty. Replace `a[3]` with `a[ ]`.
43. Although the code compiles, it outputs the hash code of the array a. To output the elements of the array, we need to loop through the array elements and output them one by one.
```

8.11.5   Debugging Area—Using Messages from the Java Compiler and Java JVM

46. Index `a.length` is out of bounds; when i is equal to `a.length`, the expression `a[i]` will generate a run-time exception. Replace `<=` with `<` in the loop condition.

9.10   Exercises, Problems, and Projects

9.10.1   Multiple Choice Exercises

1. `int[ ][ ] a;` and `int a[ ][ ];`
4. false
7. `a[2].length`
10. true
13. *java.util*

9.10.2   Reading and Understanding Code

16. 3
19. Munich
    Stuttgart
    Berlin
    Bonn
22. Munich
    Berlin
    Ottawa
25. It counts and returns the number of elements in the parameter array *a*.
28. It returns an *int* array of the same length as the length of the parameter array *a*. Each element of the returned array stores the number of columns of the corresponding row in *a*.
31. 7 (at index 0) 45 (at index 1) 21 (at index 2)

9.10.3   Fill In the Code

34. `System.out.println( geo[0][5] );`
37.
```
for ( int i = 0; i < geo.length; i++ )
{
    for ( int j = 0; j < geo[i].length; j++ )
        System.out.println( geo[i][j] );
}
```
40.
```
int count = 0;
for ( int j = 0; j < a[1].length; j++ )
{
    if ( a[1][j] == 6 )
        count++;
```

```
    }
    System.out.println( "# of 6s in the 2nd row: " + count );
```

43. This method returns the product of all the elements in an array.

```
public static int foo( int [ ][ ] a )
{
  int product = 1;
  for ( int i = 0; i < a.length; i++ )
  {
    for ( int j = 0; j < a[i].length; j++ )
    {
      product *= a[i][j];
    }
  }
  return product;
}
```

46. `System.out.println( languages.size( ) );`

49.
```
for ( String s : languages )
{
  if ( s.charAt( 0 ) == 'P' )
    System.out.println( s );
}
```

9.10.4   Identifying Errors in Code

52. Array dimension missing in `new double [ ][10]`
    Example of correct code: `double [ ][ ] a = new double [4][10];`

55. Cannot declare an *ArrayList* of a primitive data type; the type needs to be a class (for example: *Double*)

58. Correct syntax is `variable = expression`. Because `a.size( )` is not a variable, we cannot assign a value to it.

9.10.5   Debugging Area—Using Messages from the Java Compiler and Java JVM

61. Other than `a[0][0]`, the first row is not taken into account because *i* is initialized to 1 in the outer loop. It should be `int i = 0;` not `int i = 1`.

64. Index 3 is out of bounds. There are only 3 elements in *a*; the last index is 2.

67. Because *ArrayList* elements begin at index 0, the statement
    `a.set( 1, 'J' );`
    sets the value of the second element of the *ArrayList*. To set the value of the first element, use this statement:
    `a.set( 0, 'J' );`

10.10　Exercises, Problems, and Projects

10.10.1　Multiple Choice Exercises

1. a class inheriting from another class.
4. *protected* and *public* instance variables and methods
7. You cannot instantiate an object from an *abstract* class.
10. the class must be declared *abstract*.

10.10.2　Reading and Understanding Code

13. *B* inherits from *A: name, price (foo2* and *foo3* are overridden)
    C inherits from *B: name, price, foo2,* and *foo3 (foo1* is overridden)

16. ```
    A( ) called
    B( ) called
    B version of foo1( ) called
    ```

19. ```
    A( ) called
    B( ) called
    C( ) called
    ```

10.10.3　Fill In the Code

22. ```
    private char middle;
    public G( String f, String n, char middle )
    {
      super( f, n );
      this.middle = middle;
    }
    ```

25. ```
    public class K extends F implements I
    ```

10.10.4　Identifying Errors in Code

28. There is no error. `new D( )` returns a *D* object reference. *D* inherits from *C*; therefore a *D* object reference "is a" *C* object reference. Thus, it can be assigned to *c2*. Although a *C* object cannot be instantiated, a subclass object reference can be assigned to a superclass reference.

31. The *foo* method does not have a method body; it must be declared *abstract*. The *K* class must be declared *abstract* as well.

10.10.5　Debugging Area—Using Messages from the Java Compiler and Java JVM

34. The instance variable *n* of class *M* is private, and is not inherited by *P*. Therefore, *n* is not visible inside class *P*.

11.15   Exercises, Problems, and Projects

11.15.1   Multiple Choice Exercises

1. *try/catch* blocks enable programmers to attempt to recover from illegal situations and continue running the program.

4. false

7. the contents of the file, if any, will be deleted.

10. the *stream* method

11.15.2   Reading and Understanding Code

13. ABCD

16. count = 3

19. Nice finish

22. CS1

    0

    1

    2

    3

    4

11.15.3   Fill In the Code

25.
```
while ( parse.hasNext( ) )
{
  s = parse.next( );
  if ( s.equals( "C" ) )
    break;
}
```

28.
```
while ( file.hasNext( ) )
{
  result += file.nextLine( ) + " ";
}
file.close( );
System.out.println( result );
```

31.
```
average += grades[i];
...
average /= grades.length;
...
pw.println( average );
pw.close( );
```

11.15.4   Identifying Errors in Code

34. The *next* method returns a *String*; the return value cannot be assigned to an *int* variable. Use *nextInt* instead.

11.15.5   Debugging Area—Using Messages from the Java Compiler and Java JVM

37. The *catch* block is missing; you need to add it after the *try* block as follows:
```
catch ( IOException ioe )
{
    ioe.printStackTrace( );
}
```

40. When we try to read 3.5 as an *int*, the method generates an *InputMismatchException* and we execute the *catch* block. To fix the problem, replace 3.5 with 3, for example, or use the *nextDouble* method and change *number* to a *double*.

12.20   Exercises, Problems, and Projects

12.20.1   Multiple Choice Exercises

1. *TextField*.
4. Layout container that arranges components vertically
7. *onAction*
10. false
13. *EventHandler<KeyEvent>*
16. 5
19. *TouchEvent*

12.20.2   Reading and Understanding Code

22. In a horizontal line left to right
25. *void*
28. The label displays "mode: 7"
31. That button's text is set to 0

12.20.3   Fill in the Code

34.
```
<center>
    <Label fx:id="label1" text="SELECT" />
</center>
```
37. `l = new Label( "Hello" );`
40. `l.setText( "Button clicked" ); // listener is registered only on`
    `                               // the button, so getSource is`
    `                               // not needed`

43.
```
buttons = new Button[4];
for ( int i = 0; i < buttons.length; i++ )
{
    buttons[i] = new Button( "Button " + i );
    VBox.setVgrow( buttons[i], Priority.ALWAYS );
    buttons[i].setMaxHeight( Double.MAX_VALUE );
    left.getChildren( ).add( buttons[i] );
}
```
46.
```
setCenter( label1 );
setBottom( label2 );
```
49.
```
URL resource = getClass( ).getResource( "music.wav" );
AudioClip music = new AudioClip( resource.toString( ) );
music.setCycleCount( 5 );
music.play( );
```
51.
```
ObservableList<PieChart.Data> pieChartData
                   = FXCollections.observableList( myList );
PieChart chart = new PieChart( pieChartData );
```

12.20.4 Identifying Errors in Code

54. The *import* statement should be `import javafx.scene.layout.*;`
57. We need to get the series data before adding a new set of data:
```
series.getData( ).add( new XYChart.Data<...
```

12.20.5 Debugging Area – Using Messages from the Java Compiler and Java JVM

60. On line 6, *Welcome* needs to be enclosed in quotes:
```
<Label text="Welcome" />
```

63. The *ButtonHandler* event handler is not registered on the button. In the constructor, we need to instantiate an instance of *ButtonHandler* and set that object as the listener for the button:
```
ButtonHandler bh = new ButtonHandler( );
button.setOnAction( bh );
```

13.9   Exercises, Problems, and Projects

13.9.1 Multiple Choice Exercises

1. may or may not be *static*.
4. calls itself.
7. a run-time error.

13.9.2   Reading and Understanding Code

10. 0
13. 3
16. There is no output
19. *foo3* outputs the parameter *String* in reverse
22. 64

13.9.3   Fill In the Code

25. `return foo( s.substring( 2, s.length( ) ) );`
28. `if ( n >= 1000 )     // base case`
    `   return n;`
    `else                  // general case`
    `   return foo( n * n );`

13.9.4   Identifying Errors in Code

31. In the *else* clause, the *return* keyword is missing.

13.9.5   Debugging Area—Using Messages from the Java Compiler and Java JVM

34. The base case is not coded properly; it needs to return a value, not make another recursive call. Instead of *return foo(0)*, you can code *return 1*.
37. In the general case, the method makes the recursive call with the original *String* less the last two characters as the argument. Therefore, there should be two base cases: when the *String* has 0 characters (that is, an empty *String*) and when the *String* has one character. Assuming this method counts the number of characters in the *String* argument, we can add the following code after the first base case:

     `else if ( s.length( ) == 1 )`
     `        return 1;`

14.14   Exercises, Problems, and Projects

14.14.1   Multiple Choice Exercises

1. Linked lists are easily expanded.
4. (7, *Ajay*, *NFL*)
7. (7, *Ajay*, *NFL*) and (5, *Joe*, *Sonic*)
10. *front* = 3, stores 54; *back* = 0, stores 62
13. *front* = 7; *back* = 6; the list is empty

14.14.2   Reading and Understanding Code

16. If the list is not empty, it resets it to empty and returns *true*. Otherwise, it returns *false*.

19. It outputs all the *Player* objects in the list whose *game* field is *Diablo*.

14.14.3   Fill In the Code

22.
```
previous.getNext( ).setNext(
                     previous.getNext( ).getNext( ).getNext( ) );
```

25.
```
public LLNode( char newGrade )
{
  grade = newGrade;
  next = null;
}
```

28.
```
public LLNode setGrade( char grade )
{
  this.grade = grade;
  return this;
}
public LLNode setNext( LLNode next )
{
  this.next = next;
  return this;
}
```

31.
```
public int numberOfItems( )
{
  int count = 0;
  LLNode current = head;
  while ( current != null )
  {
    count++;
    current = current.getNext( );
  }
  return count;
}
```

14.14.4   Identifying Errors in Code

34. The *getID* method belongs to the *Player* class and cannot be called using *head*, a *PlayerNode* object reference. The code should be
```
return head.getPlayer( ).getID( );
```

37. The number of items in the queue would never increase and we would always be able to insert into that queue, eventually overwriting items that are in the

queue. This is a logic error. Furthermore, the queue would always be considered empty since the number of items always has the value 0. We would never be able to delete an item from the queue.

14.14.5   Debugging Area—Using Messages from the Java Compiler and Java JVM

40. There is no *getHead* method in the *PlayerLinkedList* class. In order to get a copy of the *Player* object stored at the first node of the list, we can code a method returning the *Player*.

15.7   Exercises, Problems, and Projects

15.7.1   Multiple Choice Exercises

1. $O(n^2)$
4. $O(n)$
7. $n * (n + 1) / 2$
10. $O(n^2)$

15.7.2   Compute the Running Time of a Method

13. $O(n)$
16. $O(\log n)$

Index

Note: Page numbers followed by *f* or *t* indicate material in figures or tables respectively.